Fodor's Ninetee[n]

Eastern and Central Europe

The complete guide, thoroughly up-to-date

Packed with details that will make your trip

The must-see sights, off and on the beaten path

What to see, what to skip

Mix-and-match vacation itineraries

City strolls, countryside adventures

Smart lodging and dining options

Essential local do's and taboos

Transportation tips, distances and directions

Key contacts, savvy travel tips

When to go, what to pack

Clear, accurate, easy-to-use maps

Helpful vocabulary

Fodor's Eastern and Central Europe

EDITORS: Bonnie Bills, Matt Lombardi, Julie Tomasz

Editorial Contributors: John Babb, Eleanore Boyse, Joyce Dalton, Jane Foster, Ky Krauthamer, Martha Lagace, Jay Lee, Betsy Maury, Paul Olchváry, Tatiana Repková, Robert Rigney, Kristin Rimington, Helayne Schiff, Julie Tomasz, Annie Ward, Scott Young
Editorial Production: Ira-Neil Dittersdorf
Maps: David Lindroth, *cartographer*; Rebecca Baer and Robert Blake, *map editors*
Design: Fabrizio La Rocca, *creative director*; Guido Caroti, *art director*; Jolie Novak, *senior picture editor*
Cover Design: Pentagram
Production/Manufacturing: Robert B. Shields
Cover Photograph: David Hanson/Stone

Copyright

Nineteenth Edition

ISBN 0-679-00668-0

ISSN 1074-1216

Important Tip

Although all prices, opening times, and other details in this book are based on information supplied to us at press time, changes occur all the time in the travel world, and Fodor's cannot accept responsibility for facts that become outdated or for inadvertent errors or omissions. So **always confirm information when it matters,** especially if you're making a detour to visit a specific place.

Special Sales

Fodor's Travel Publications are available at special discounts for bulk purchases for sales promotions or premiums. Special editions, including personalized covers, excerpts of existing guides, and corporate imprints, can be created in large quantities for special needs. For more information, contact your local bookseller or write to Special Markets, Fodor's Travel Publications, 280 Park Avenue, New York, NY 10017. Inquiries from Canada should be directed to your local Canadian bookseller or sent to Random House of Canada, Ltd., Marketing Department, 2775 Matheson Boulevard East, Mississauga, Ontario L4W 4P7. Inquiries from the United Kingdom should be sent to Fodor's Travel Publications, 20 Vauxhall Bridge Road, London SW1V 2SA, England.

PRINTED IN THE UNITED STATES OF AMERICA

10 9 8 7 6 5 4 3 2 1

CONTENTS

Maps and Charts

ON THE ROAD WITH FODOR'S

EVERY TRIP is a significant trip. Acutely aware of that fact, we've pulled out all stops in preparing *Fodor's Eastern and Central Europe*. To guide you in putting together your vacation, we've created multiday itineraries and neighborhood walks. And to direct you to the places that are truly worth your time and money, we've rallied the team of endearingly picky know-it-alls we're pleased to call our writers. Having seen all corners of the regions they cover for us, they're real experts. If you knew them, you'd poll them for tips yourself.

John Babb, an updater on our Poland chapter, began life on the tiny Caribbean island of St. Vincent and the Grenadines before being whisked off to Canada. He lived there for nearly 30 years, five of which were spent as a reporter and producer in Toronto at the Canadian Broadcasting Corporation. His next stop was Warsaw, Poland, where for the last two years he has been the editor of a daily news digest documenting the rapid pace of economic change for the *Warsaw Business Journal*. Drawn again by the call of island life, John is now pursuing new challenges in Dublin, Ireland. He has also contributed to the Fodor's Europe guide.

Romania updater **Joyce Dalton,** a New Jersey–based travel writer and photographer, contributes to numerous trade and consumer publications. She fell under the spell of Romaniaís mountains and traditional villages in 1988, and although her travels have taken her to some 150 countries on six continents, itís Romania that draws her back again and again. She recently purchased land in the traditional Maramureş region and hopes to construct a house, complete with hand-carved Maramureş gate.

Jane Foster, who put together this edition's new Slovenia chapter, is a freelance writer from the Yorkshire Dales, UK. She studied for a degree in architecture before moving to Rome in 1990, where travel, art, and culture became her main interests. In 1996 she made a brief visit to Croatia and was immediately captivated by the countries of the former Yugoslavia. She now lives in Split, Dalmatia, and has traveled extensively through Slovenia, Croatia, and Bosnia-Herzegovina, rating the Adriatic coast, "where the mountains reach the sea," as the most stunningly beautiful region in Europe. She writes for a number of American and European travel publications, focusing primarily on Slovenia, Croatia, and Italy.

Minnesota-born **Ky Krauthamer,** who updated the Czech chapter, came to Prague in 1992 and settled in as a journalist and freelance writer specializing in travel and culture. He has contributed to several Fodor's guides, including the two previous editions of *Fodor's Eastern and Central Europe.*

Jay Lee, our Bulgaria updater, is a public relations and campaign consultant working primarily on conservation, national parks development, and wildlife issues. After earning an anthropology degree from the University of North Carolina, he spent the early stages of his career in the political hothouse of Washington, DC. In 1998 he transplanted to Sofia, where he currently lives with his wife and son.

Betsy Maury, a former senior editor with the U.S. publisher Bantam Doubleday Dell, spent four years in Slovenia before settling in Budapest, where she now lives with her husband and works as a freelance writer. She updated the Budapest dining and lodging reviews for our guide.

Upon receiving an MA in writing in 1990, **Paul Olchváry,** a western New York native, moved to the land of his ancestors, Hungary, expecting to stay a year or so. He stayed for ten. Initially a university composition instructor, he went on to hold a fellowship at the U.S. Embassy in Budapest before becoming founding editor of an English-language digest of Hungarian news. From the mid-1990s on, he focused on his own writing, literary translation, and copyediting. In addition to updating our Hungary chapter, he has published numerous stories and essays, many in Hungarian translation, and written three novels, two of them set in present-day Hungary. He has also rendered seven books and numerous shorter works from Hungarian to English.

Eastern and Central Europe

RUSSIA
LITHUANIA
Minsk
Białystok
BELARUS
Varsaw
Lublin
Kiev
Rzeszów
L'vov
UKRAINE
Przemyśl
MOLDOVA
Suceava
ROMANIA
Piatra-Neamț
Iași
Chișinău
Odessa
Oradea
Târgu Mureș
Cluj-Napoca
Bacău
Bîrlad
Alba Iulia
Brașov
Sibiu
Galați
Buzău
Brăila
Turnu Severin
Pitești
Ploiești
Urziceni
Hîrșova
Bucharest
Craiova
Constanța
Black Sea
Giurgiu
Ruse
Belogradčik
Pleven
Šumen
Varna
Veliko Tărnovo
Kazanlăk
KEY
Rail Lines
Sofia
BULGARIA
Jambol
Burgas
Plovdiv
Rila
Pazardžik
Bačkovo
0
180 miles
0
270 km
TURKEY
Istanbul

Slovakia chapter updater **Tatiana Repková** was born and raised in Slovakia; she earned her degree from the Bratislava School of Economics. After the fall of communism, she became the cofounder, publisher, and editor of the independent Slovak business weekly *Trend* and later the publisher and editor of the daily *Narodna Obroda*. She is now a European director of the World Free Press Institute, based in Bratislava. She has been working on a manual for publishing and editing newspapers in emerging democracies, which will be published in eight languages, including English.

Poland updater **Scott Alexander Young,** who currently divides his time between Budapest and Prague, spent over a year living in Kraków, writing about the city and struggling along in Kiwi (New Zealand) accented Polish. Though originally he took the attitude that writing assignments in Central and Eastern Europe would lead to "better things," he now finds it difficult to imagine life back west. He is currently at work on an account of the larger-than-life expat characters he has encountered in the region. Although the final work will be a toned-down version of reality, he's convinced he will be forced to label these memoirs fiction.

We would like to thank Malév Hungarian Airlines for its help with realizing the Hungary chapter.

Don't Forget to Write

Keeping a travel guide fresh and up-to-date is a big job. So we love your feedback—positive and negative—and follow up on all suggestions. Contact the Eastern and Central Europe editor at editors@fodors.com or c/o Fodor's, 280 Park Avenue, New York, NY 10017. And have a wonderful trip!

Karen Cure
Editorial Director

SMART TRAVEL TIPS A TO Z

Basic Information on Traveling in Eastern and Central Europe, Savvy Tips to Make Your Trip a Breeze, and Companies and Organizations to Contact

AIR TRAVEL

BOOKING

When you book **look for nonstop flights** and **remember that "direct" flights stop at least once.** Try to avoid connecting flights, which require a change of plane.

CARRIERS

In most cases, flights from the United States on major U.S. airlines have a European co-carrier that provides a connecting flight from a gateway in Europe. Some European national airlines offer nonstop service from the United States to their own countries as well as connecting flights; others only provide connections within Europe.

➤ MAJOR AIRLINES: **Continental** (☎ 800/231–0856). **Delta** (☎ 800/241–4141). **Northwest** (☎ 800/447–4747). **United** (☎ 800/538–2929).

➤ FROM THE U.K.: **British Airways** (✉ 156 Regent St., London W1R 5TA, ☎ 0207/434–4700; 0845/722–2111 outside London). **Czech Airlines** (☎ 0207/255–1898 in London).

➤ NATIONAL AIRLINES WITH SERVICE FROM U.S.: Bulgaria: **Balkan Air** (☎ 212/573–5530, ☎ 02/684-148 in Sofia). The Czech Republic: **Czech Airlines** (CSA; ☎ 212/765–6022, ☎ 02/2010–4310 in Prague). Hungary: **Malév Hungarian Airlines** (☎ 212/757–6446, in Budapest, ☎ 1/235–3535; 06/40–212–121 toll free; 1/235–3804 [ticketing]). Poland: **LOT Polish Airlines** (☎ 212/869–1074, ☎ 22/953; 22/952 in Warsaw). Romania: **Tarom Romanian Airlines** (☎ 212/687–6240, ☎ 01/659–4125; 01/337–2037 in Romania).

➤ NATIONAL AIRLINES WITH INTERNATIONAL SERVICE WITHIN EUROPE: Slovenia: **Adria Airways** (☎ 01/252–2700). Slovakia: **Slovak Airlines** (☎ 07/48575170).

CHECK-IN & BOARDING

Assuming that not everyone with a ticket will show up, airlines routinely overbook planes. When everyone does, airlines ask for volunteers to give up their seats. In return, these volunteers usually get a certificate for a free flight and are rebooked on the next flight out. If there are not enough volunteers, the airline must choose who will be denied boarding. The first to get bumped are passengers who checked in late and those flying on discounted tickets, so **get to the gate and check in as early as possible,** especially during peak periods.

Always **bring a government-issued photo I.D. to the airport.** You may be asked to show it before you are allowed to check in.

CUTTING COSTS

The least expensive airfares to Central and Eastern Europe must usually be purchased in advance and are non-refundable. —the same fare may not be available the next day. Always **check different routings** and look into using different airports. Travel agents, especially low-fare specialists (☞ Discounts & Deals, *below*), are helpful.

Consolidators are another good source. They buy tickets for scheduled international flights at reduced rates from the airlines, then sell them at prices that beat the best fare available directly from the airlines, usually without restrictions. Sometimes you can even get your money back if you need to return the ticket. Carefully read the fine print detailing penalties for changes and cancellations, and **confirm your consolidator reservation with the airline.**

➤ CONSOLIDATORS: **Cheap Tickets** (☎ 800/377–1000). **Discount Airline Ticket Service** (☎ 800/576–1600). **Unitravel** (☎ 800/325–2222). **Up &**

Away Travel (☎ 212/889–2345). World Travel Network (☎ 800/409–6753).

ENJOYING THE FLIGHT

For more legroom, **request an emergency-aisle seat.** Don't sit in the row in front of the emergency aisle or in front of a bulkhead, where seats may not recline. If you have dietary concerns, **ask for special meals when booking.** These can be vegetarian, low-cholesterol, or kosher, for example. On long flights, try to maintain a normal routine, to help fight jet lag. At night, **get some sleep.** By day, **eat light meals, drink water** (not alcohol), and **move around the cabin** to stretch your legs.

HOW TO COMPLAIN

If your baggage goes astray or your flight goes awry, complain right away. Most carriers require that you **file a claim immediately.**

➤ AIRLINE COMPLAINTS: U.S. Department of Transportation **Aviation Consumer Protection Division** (✉ C-75, Room 4107, Washington, DC 20590, ☎ 202/366–2220, airconsumer@ost.dot.gov, www.dot.gov/airconsumer). **Federal Aviation Administration Consumer Hotline** (☎ 800/322–7873).

AIRPORTS

For more in-depth airport information, and for the best way to get between the airport and your destination, *see* Arriving and Departing in the A to Z section at the end of each country chapter, or in the A to Z section of the city you are flying into.

➤ BULGARIA: **Sofia Airport** (☎ 02/722–414 for domestic flight information; 02/720–672; 02/876–612 for international flight information).

➤ CZECH REPUBLIC: Prague: **Ruzyně Airport** (☎ 02/2011–1111).

➤ HUNGARY: Budapest: **Ferihegy Repülőtér** (Ferihegy Airport) (☎ 1/296–9696 or for same-day flight information; 1/296–8000 for arrivals, 1/296–7000 for departures; 1/296–8108 for lost & found).

➤ POLAND: **Warszawa Okęcie** (☎ 022/650–30–00); **Gdańsk-Rębiechowo** (☎ 058/341-52-51); **Kraków-Balice** (☎ 012/411–19–55); **Poznań-Ławica** (☎ 061/868-15-11); **Szczecin-Goleniów** (☎ 091/418-27-08); **Wrocław-Strachowice** (☎ 071/358-12-03); **Rzeszów-Jasionka** (017/853-27-21).

➤ ROMANIA: Bucharest: **Otopeni Airport** (☎ 01/230–0022); **Baneasa Airport** (☎ 01/232–0020).

➤ SLOVAKIA: **M. R. Štefánik Airport** (☎ 07/48573353); **Košice Airport** (☎ 0956/221093).

➤ SLOVENIA: **Brnik Airport** (☎ 04/202–2700); **Maribor Airport** (☎ 02/629–1175); **Portorož Airport** (☎ O5/672–2525).

BIKE TRAVEL

The prevalence of bicycles varies greatly from country to country within Eastern and Central Europe. While, for instance, bike touring and mountain biking are gaining popularity in the Czech Republic, in Romania recreational cycling is uncommon and on some roads can be dangerous. Most major cities have some sort of bike rental available, and in less populated areas it's sometimes possible to arrange rentals through informal sources; your hotel is often a good resource for finding rentals. For more information, *see* the Pleasures and Pastimes and Outdoor Activities and Sports sections *in* individual country chapters.

BIKES IN FLIGHT

Most airlines accommodate bikes as luggage, provided they are dismantled and boxed. For bike boxes, often free at bike shops, you'll pay about $5 from airlines (at least $100 for bike bags). International travelers can sometimes substitute a bike for a piece of checked luggage at no charge; otherwise, the cost is about $100. Domestic and Canadian airlines charge $25–$50.

BOAT & FERRY TRAVEL

Ferries offer a pleasant and cheap mode of transportation to Eastern and Central Europe, although you have to be fairly close to your destination already to hop a Europe-bound ferry or hydrofoil. Flying into the appropriate hub, however, is an option. Water bookings connect Copenhagen, Denmark, to Świnoujście and Gdańsk, Poland. A hydrofoil shuttles visitors from Vienna to Bratislava, Slovakia, or Budapest, Hungary. For further country-specific information, *see* Arriving and Departing in the A to Z section in Budapest (Chapter 4); Gdańsk and the Northeast (Chapter 6), and the Poland A to Z section; the Black Sea Golden Coast (Chapter 7), and the Bulgaria A to Z section; and the Black Sea Coast and Danube Delta (Chapter 8).

In Hungary, ferries operate on the Danube River and on Lake Balaton. In Poland, you can take ferries or hydrofoils between various points on the Baltic coast, two of the more popular routes being Szczecin to Świnoujście, near the German border on the coast, and Sopot to Hel, farther east near Gdańsk. Ferries also travel daily from Gdańsk to Helsinki and to Oxelösund, Sweden.

➤ FERRY LINES: Bulgaria: **Balkantourist,** (✉ 1, bul. Vitosha, Sofia, ☎ 02/43–331) for information. Hungary: **MAHART Tours** (✉ V, Belgrád rakpart, Budapest, ☎ 1/484–4025; 1/484–4010 for information). Poland: **Orbis** in the Hotel Hevelius (✉ Ul. Heweliusa 22 Gdańsk, ☎ 058/301–45–44); **Polish Baltic Shipping Co** (✉ Ul. Przemysłowa 1, Gdańsk, ☎ 058/830–09–30); **Polske Linie Oceaniczne** (Polish Ocean Lines, ☎ 022/830–14–12); **Stena Line** (☎ 058/665–14–14). Slovakia:**Slovenská plavba dunajská** (☎ 07/52963522 or 07/52932226 for reservations) in Bratislava. Slovenia: **Kompas Turizem** (✉ Obala 41, Portorož, ☎ 05/617–8000 for information).

BUS TRAVEL

Bus travel is generally more costly than travel by train, although this varies by country. In some instances, especially where trains are largely local (and stop seemingly every 100 feet), buses are actually speedier than rail travel. Comfort is minimal, though; roads tend to be bumpy and seats lumpy. Buses are generally tidier; train bathrooms are notoriously rank. It's a bit of a gamble; seats on buses are a rarity during prime traveling hours, and drivers don't always stop where they should, although most leave punctually (especially when you're still waiting in line for a ticket). Comfort and fares vary drastically by nation. *See* Arriving and Departing by Bus *in* the A to Z section at the end of each country chapter.

FROM THE U.K.

Unless you latch onto a real deal on airfare, a bus ticket from London's Victoria Terminal (☎ 0171/730–0202) is probably the cheapest transit from the United Kingdom to Eastern and Central Europe, although it may take a little research, as regularly scheduled routes to all cities except Warsaw and Prague are practically nonexistent. Check newspaper ads for eastbound passage.

BUSINESS HOURS

For country-specific opening and closing times and business hours, *see* Opening and Closing Times in the A to Z section at the end of each country chapter.

CAMERAS & PHOTOGRAPHY

With picturesque villages, mountain scenery and intriguing medieval sites, **Romania** is a great place for photographers. In general, people are pleased to be photographed, but ask first. Never photograph Gypsies, however colorful their attire, without explicit permission and payment clearly agreed upon. Photographing anything military, assuming you'd want to, is prohibited.

➤ PHOTO HELP: **Kodak Information Center** (☎ 800/242–2424). ***Kodak Guide to Shooting Great Travel Pictures,*** available in bookstores or from Fodor's Travel Publications (☎ 800/533–6478; $18 plus $5.50 shipping).

EQUIPMENT PRECAUTIONS

Always **keep your film and tape out of the sun.** Carry an extra supply of batteries, and **be prepared to turn on your camera or camcorder** to prove to security personnel that the device is real. Always **ask for hand inspection of film,** which becomes clouded after repeated exposure to airport X-ray machines, and **keep videotapes away from metal detectors.**

FILM & DEVELOPING

Major brands of film are available throughout the region, and 24-hour developing is the rule rather than the exception in large and medium-size cities. The variable is cost—prices fluctuate widely from place to place.

VIDEOS

Due to differing television systems, VHS tapes bought in Europe will run about 30% shorter than the time indicated on the box when operated with U.S. equipment. Also note that tapes may be hard to find outside of major urban areas.

CAR RENTAL

Major rental agencies are represented throughout the region, but **don't overlook local firms;** they can offer bargains, but watch for hidden insurance conditions. Rates and regulations vary widely from country to country. For more information, *see* the A to Z sections *in* individual country chapters.

➤ MAJOR AGENCIES: **Alamo** (☎ 800/522–9696; 020/8759–6200 in the U.K.). **Avis** (☎ 800/331–1084; 800/331–1084 in Canada; 02/9353–9000 in Australia; 09/525–1982 in New Zealand). **Budget** (☎ 800/527–0700;0870/607–5000 in the U.K., through affiliate Europcar). **Dollar** (☎ 800/800–6000; 0124/622–0111 in the U.K., through affiliate Sixt Kenning; 02/9223–1444 in Australia). **Hertz** (☎ 800/654–3001; 800/263–0600 in Canada; 020/8897–2072 in the U.K.; 02/9669–2444 in Australia; 09/256–8690 in New Zealand). **National Car Rental** (☎ 800/227–7368; 020/8680–4800 in the U.K., where it is known as National Europe).

CUTTING COSTS

To get the best deal, **book through a travel agent who will shop around.** Do **look into wholesalers,** companies that do not own fleets but rent in bulk from those that do and often offer better rates than traditional car-rental operations. Payment must be made before you leave home.

➤ WHOLESALERS: **Auto Europe** (☎ 207/842–2000 or 800/223–5555, FAX 800/235–6321, www.autoeurope.com). **DER Travel Services** (✉ 9501 W. Devon Ave., Rosemont, IL 60018, ☎ 800/782–2424, FAX 800/282–7474 for information; 800/860–9944 for brochures, www.dertravel.com). **Kemwel Holiday Autos** (☎ 800/678–0678, FAX 914/825–3160, www.kemwel.com).

INSURANCE

When driving a rented car you are generally responsible for any damage to or loss of the vehicle. Before you rent see what coverage your personal auto-insurance policy and credit cards already provide.

Before you buy collision coverage, check your existing policies—you may already be covered. However, collision policies that car-rental companies sell for European rentals usually do not include stolen-vehicle coverage.

REQUIREMENTS & RESTRICTIONS

In most Eastern and Central European countries, visitors need an International Driver's Permit; U.S. and Canadian citizens can obtain one from the American or Canadian Automobile Association, respectively. In some countries, such as Hungary, many car rental agencies will accept an international license, but the formal permit is technically required. If you intend to drive across a border, ask about **restrictions on driving into other countries.** The minimum age required for renting is usually 21 or older, and some companies also have maximum ages; be sure to inquire when making your arrangements.

SURCHARGES

Before you pick up a car in one city and leave it in another, **ask about drop-off charges or one-way service fees,** which can be substantial. Note, too, that some rental agencies charge extra if you return the car before the time specified in your contract. To avoid a hefty refueling fee, **fill the tank just before you turn in the car,** but be aware that gas stations near the rental outlet may overcharge.

CAR TRAVEL

The plus side of driving is an itinerary free from the constraints of bus and train schedules and lots of trunk room for extra baggage. The negatives are many, however (☞ Car Rental, *above*), not the least of which are shabbily maintained secondary roads, the risk of theft and vandalism, and difficulty finding gas. Crowded roads and fast and/or careless drivers add to the danger element, particularly in Poland. However, car travel does make it much easier to get to out-of-the-way monasteries and other sights not easily accessible by public transportation. Good road maps are usually available.

A word of caution: If you have any alcohol whatsoever in your body, do not drive. Penalties are fierce, and the blood-alcohol limit is practically zero. (In Hungary, it *is* zero.)

AUTO CLUBS

➤ IN EASTERN AND CENTRAL EUROPE: Czech Republic: **Autoturist** (✉ Prague 4, Na Strži 9, ☎ 02/6110–4333). Hungary: **Hungarian Automobile Club** (✉ Budapest II, Rómer Flóris u. 4/A, ☎ 212–0300). Poland: **Polish Motoring Association** (PZMot; ☎ 022/629–83–36). Romania: **Touring ACR** (Romanian Auto Club; ✉ Şos. Colentina 1, Bucharest, ☎ FAX 01/252–7923). Slovakia: **Auto-Moto-Klub** (✉ Račianska 71, Bratislava, ☎ 0820/140123). Slovenia: **Automobile Association of Slovenia** (✉ Dunajska 128, Ljubljana, ☎ 01/534–1341).

➤ IN AUSTRALIA: **Australian Automobile Association** (☎ 02/6247–7311).

➤ IN CANADA: **Canadian Automobile Association** (CAA, ☎ 613/247–0117).

➤ IN NEW ZEALAND: **New Zealand Automobile Association** (☎ 09/377–4660).

➤ IN THE U.K.: **Automobile Association** (AA, ☎ 0990/500–600). **Royal Automobile Club** (RAC, ☎ 0990/722–722 for membership; 0345/121–345 for insurance).

➤ IN THE U.S.: **American Automobile Association** (☎ 800/564–6222).

EMERGENCY SERVICES

In case of a breakdown, your best friend is the telephone. Try contacting your **rental agency** or the appropriate national breakdown service.

➤ CONTACTS: **Bulgaria:** ☎ 146. **Czech Republic:** ABA (☎ 124, or 0124 in rural areas) or ÚAMK (☎ 123, or 0123 in rural areas). **Hungary:** Hungarian Automobile Club (☎ 188). **Poland:** ☎ 9637. **Romania:** ACR (Romanian Auto Club, in Bucharest: ☎ 01/252–7923). **Slovakia:** ☎ 154. **Slovenia:** AMZS (Automobile Association of Slovenia, ☎ 987.

FROM THE U.K.

Theoretically it's possible to travel by car from the United Kingdom to Eastern and Central Europe, although it's really not recommended due to lack of parts and mechanical know-how. However, if you do choose to drive your own vehicle, don't leave home without the car registration, third-party insurance, driver's license, and (if you're not the car's owner) a notarized letter of permission from the owner. The vehicle must bear a country ID sticker.

The best ferry ports for Eastern and Central Europe are Rotterdam, Holland, or Ostende, Belgium, from which you drive to Cologne (Köln), Germany, and then through either Dresden or Frankfurt and on to Prague.

GASOLINE

Gas stations are easy to come by on major thoroughfares and near large cities. Many are open around the clock, particularly in the Czech Republic and Hungary. At least two grades of gasoline are sold in Eastern and Central European countries, usually 90–93 octane (regular) and 94–98 octane (super). Lead-free gasoline is now available in most gas stations.

For additional country-specific information relating to roads, gasoline, and insurance, *see* Getting Around by Car in the A to Z section at the end of each country chapter.

ROAD CONDITIONS

Eastern and Central Europe's main roads are built to a fairly high standard. There are now quite substantial stretches of highway on main routes, and a lot of rebuilding is being done.

ROAD MAPS

In Sofia, **Bulgaria,** maps are plentiful at street kiosks, and you can also find them at the **Ministry of Trade and Tourism National Advertising Center** across from the Sheraton (✉ 1, ul. Sveta Sofia, ☎ 02/981–9965). Outside the capital, the many Shell gas stations along the highway usually offer a good selection of road maps. In the **Czech Republic,** the ubiquitous 24-hour gas stations often sell road maps, or try a bookstore. In Prague, the downstairs level of the **Jan Kanzelsberger bookshop** on Wenceslas Square (✉ Václavské nám. 42, ☎ 02/2421–7335) has a good selection of hiking maps and auto atlases. In **Hungary,** good maps are sold at most large gas stations. In Budapest, the **Globe Térképbolt** (Globe Map Store; ✉ VI, Bajcsy-Zsilinszky út 37, ☎ 1/312–6001) has an excellent supply of domestic and foreign maps. In **Poland,** check at large bookshops for driving maps; major hotels will also supply them, and all the modern gas stations have them. Esso driving maps are available at Esso gas stations and sometimes elsewhere. For maps of **Romania** check bookstores, travel agencies, and sidewalk vendors. They may also be obtained from the Romanian Tourism Promotion Office in your home country (☞ Visitor Information, below). In **Slovakia,** road maps are available at most gas stations. In Bratislava, the most convenient place selling road maps is **Academia Bookstore** (✉ Štúrova 9, ☎ 07/52968772). In **Slovenia** road maps are available from larger bookshops and gas stations throughout the country. The Slovenian Tourist Board (☞ Visitor Information, below) offer a comprehensive tourist map, free of charge.

RULES OF THE ROAD

Throughout Eastern and Central Europe, driving is on the right and the same basic rules of the road practiced in the the United States and the rest of Europe apply. For further information *see* Getting Around by Car in the A to Z section at the end of each country chapter.

CHILDREN IN EASTERN AND CENTRAL EUROPE

Be sure to plan ahead and **involve your youngsters** as you outline your trip. When packing, include things to keep them busy en route. On sightseeing days try to schedule activities of special interest to your children. If you are renting a car, don't forget to **arrange for a car seat** when you reserve.

FLYING

If your children are two or older, **ask about children's airfares.** As a general rule, infants under two not occupying a seat fly at greatly reduced fares or even for free. When booking, **confirm carry-on allowances** if you're traveling with infants. In general, for babies charged 10% of the adult fare you are allowed one carry-on bag and a collapsible stroller; if the flight is full, the stroller may have to be checked or you may be limited to less.

Experts agree that it's a good idea to use safety seats aloft for children weighing less than 40 pounds. Airlines set their own policies: U.S. carriers usually require that the child be ticketed, even if he or she is young enough to ride free, since the seats must be strapped into regular seats. Do **check your airline's policy about using safety seats during takeoff and landing.** And since safety seats are not allowed just everywhere in the plane, get your seat assignments early.

When reserving, **request children's meals or a freestanding bassinet** if you need them. But note that bulkhead seats, where you must sit to use the bassinet, may lack an overhead bin or storage space on the floor.

LODGING

Most hotels in Eastern and Central Europe allow children under a certain age to stay in their parents' room at no extra charge, but others charge for them as extra adults; be sure to **find out the cutoff age for children's discounts.** Some spa hotels don't allow children under 12.

The **Novotel** chain, which has hotels in Budapest, Warsaw, and five other Polish cities, allows up to two children under 12 to stay free in their parents' room. The same policy theoretically holds for Novotel branches in Sofia and Plovdiv in Bulgaria, but you will have to ask or even bargain. For Novotel branches in Poland, the cutoff age is 16. The **Budapest Hilton** has an unusual policy allowing children of any age—even middle-aged adults—to stay for free in their parents' room. In Bratislava, Slovakia, there are a few hotels with discounts; the Danube Hotel allows kids under 3 to stay free in their parents' room, and gives a 50% discount for children between 3 and 10. The Perugia Hotel will add a children's bed in the parents' room, charging an additional $30 for the entire stay.

Young visitors to the Czech Republic will enjoy staying at one of Prague's picturesque floating "botels." For further information contact the Czech Tourist Authority (☞ Visitor Information, *below*). Prague's luxurious Palace and Savoy hotels, managed by Vienna International, allow children under 12 to stay free in their parents' room.

➤ BEST CHOICES: **Novotel** (☎ 800/221–4542). **Budapest Hilton** (☎ 1/214–3000 in Budapest).

SIGHTS & ATTRACTIONS

Places that are especially appealing to children are indicated by a rubber duckie icon in the margins throughout the book.

SUGGESTED READING

The Adventures of Mickey, Taggy, Pupo, and Cica and How They Discover Budapest, by Kati Rekai (Canadian Stage Arts Publications, Toronto), is an animal fantasy story set in Budapest, written by a Hungarian-born author. ***The Trumpeter of Krakow*** by Eric P. Kelly is a delightful, Newbery medal–winning book set in Kraków in the early Renaissance; though first published in 1928, it was reprinted in 1992. Intricate illustrations of Prague fill Czech-American Peter Sis's ***The Three Golden Keys*** (Doubleday); aimed at young readers, it evokes the city of the author's childhood.

SUPPLIES & EQUIPMENT

In Eastern and Central Europe, disposable diapers and formula are generally available in larger grocery stores and (with less frequency in some areas) pharmacies. For crayons and craft supplies, try a stationer's.

TRANSPORTATION

In the Czech Republic and Slovakia, car passengers under 12 years of age, or less than 150 cm (5 ft) in height, must ride in the back seat.

On Romanian trains, children of school age and under travel at a discount; there is no charge for infants, although it is expected the baby will sit on a parent's lap unless there is an unoccupied seat. Bassinets and children's meals are not available. Car seats are not required or easily available.

COMPUTERS ON THE ROAD

Bring an adapter for your laptop plug. Adapters are inexpenseive, and some models have several plugs suitable for different systems throughout the world. Some hotels lend adapters to guests for use during their stay.

At the airport, **be prepared to turn on your laptop** to prove to security personnel that the device is real. Security X-ray machines are damaging to a laptop, but **keep computer disks away form metal detectors.**

CONSUMER PROTECTION

Whenever buying travel services for a trip to Eastern and Central Europe, **pay with a major credit card** so you can cancel payment or get reimbursed if there's a problem. This is also a good philosophy when making purchases during your trip, but be aware that credit cards are not as widely accepted in the region as they are in western Europe and the United States—many hotels and restaurants operate on a cash-only basis. If you're doing business with a travel-services company for the first time, **contact your local Better Business Bureau and the attorney general's offices** in your own state and the company's home state, as well. Have any complaints been filed? Finally, if you're buying a package or tour, always **consider**

travel insurance that includes default coverage (☞ Insurance, *below*).

➤ BBBs: **Council of Better Business Bureaus** (✉ 4200 Wilson Blvd., Suite 800, Arlington, VA 22203, ☎ 703/276–0100, FAX 703/525–8277 www.bbb.org).

CUSTOMS & DUTIES

When shopping, **keep receipts** for all purchases. Upon reentering the country, **be ready to show customs officials what you've bought.** If you feel a duty is incorrect or object to the way your clearance was handled, note the inspector's badge number and ask to see a supervisor. If the problem isn't resolved, write to the appropriate authorities, beginning with the port director at your point of entry.

IN AUSTRALIA

Australian residents who are 18 or older may bring home $A400 worth of souvenirs and gifts (including jewelry), 250 cigarettes or 250 grams of tobacco, and 1,125 ml of alcohol (including wine, beer, and spirits). Residents under 18 may bring back $A200 worth of goods. Prohibited items include meat products. Seeds, plants, and fruits need to be declared upon arrival.

➤ INFORMATION: **Australian Customs Service** (Regional Director, ✉ Box 8, Sydney, NSW 2001, Australia, ☎ 02/9213–2000, FAX 02/9213–4000, www.customs.gov.au).

IN CANADA

Canadian residents who have been out of Canada for at least 7 days may bring home C$500 worth of goods duty-free. If you've been away less than 7 days but more than 48 hours, the duty-free allowance drops to C$200; if your trip lasts 24–48 hours, the allowance is C$50. You may not pool allowances with family members. Goods claimed under the C$500 exemption may follow you by mail; those claimed under the lesser exemptions must accompany you. Alcohol and tobacco products may be included in the 7-day and 48-hour exemptions but not in the 24-hour exemption. If you meet the age requirements of the province or territory through which you reenter Canada, you may bring in, duty-free, 1.14 liters (40 imperial ounces) of wine or liquor *or* 24 12-ounce cans or bottles of beer or ale. If you are 16 or older you may bring in, duty-free, 200 cigarettes and 50 cigars. Check ahead of time with Revenue Canada or the Department of Agriculture for policies regarding meat products, seeds, plants, and fruits.

You may send an unlimited number of gifts worth up to C$60 each duty-free to Canada. Label the package UNSOLICITED GIFT—VALUE UNDER $60. Alcohol and tobacco are excluded.

➤ INFORMATION: **Revenue Canada** (✉ 2265 St. Laurent Blvd. S, Ottawa, Ontario K1G 4K3, Canada, ☎ 613/993–0534; 800/461–9999 in Canada, FAX 613/991–4126, www.ccra-adrc.gc.ca).

IN EASTERN AND CENTRAL EUROPE

You may import duty-free into Slovakia, Hungary, Poland, or Bulgaria 250 cigarettes or the equivalent in tobacco, 1 liter of spirits, and 2 liters of wine (in Poland, 1 liter of spirits and 2 liters of wine). In addition to the above, you are permitted to import into Hungary gifts valued up to 30,500 Ft; into Poland, gifts valued at up to 70 euro; into Slovakia, gifts valued at up to 1,000 Sk (approximately $30). You may import duty-free into the Czech Republic tobacco products equivalent to 200 cigarettes, 100 cigarillos, 250 grams of tobacco, or 50 cigars; 1 liter of spirits, 2 liters of wine, and personal medicines, as well as gifts and personal items valued at up to 6,000 Kč (3,000 Kč for visitors under 15) (about $170/$85). On arrival in Romania, you may bring in a personal computer and printer, two cameras, 10 rolls of film, one small video camera and VCR, 10 videocassette tapes, one typewriter, binoculars, one radio/tape recorder, one small television set, one bicycle, one child's stroller, 200 cigarettes, 2 liters of liquor, and 4 liters of wine or beer. Gifts are permitted, though you may be charged duty on some electronic goods. Cash in excess of $10,000 should be declared on arrival. Arriving in Slovenia, personal items are not subject to any toll, but duty-free restrictions are 200 cigarettes or 50 cigars, 1 liter of wine, and 0.75 liter of spirits.

If you are bringing into any of these countries any valuables or foreign-made equipment from home, such as cameras, it's wise to carry the original receipts with you or register the items with U.S. Customs before you leave (Form 4457). Otherwise you could end up paying duty upon your return. When traveling to Bulgaria, you should declare video cameras, personal computers, and expensive jewelry upon arrival. Be aware that leaving the country without expensive items declared upon entering can present a huge hassle with airport police.

IN NEW ZEALAND

Homeward-bound residents 17 or older may bring back $700 worth of souvenirs and gifts. Your duty-free allowance also includes 4.5 liters of wine or beer; one 1,125-ml bottle of spirits; and either 200 cigarettes, 250 grams of tobacco, 50 cigars, or a combination of the three up to 250 grams. Prohibited items include meat products, seeds, plants, and fruits.

➤ INFORMATION: **New Zealand Customs** (Custom House, ✉ 50 Anzac Ave., Box 29, Auckland, New Zealand, ☎ 09/300–5399, FAX 09/359–6730), www.customs.govt.nz.

IN THE U.K.

From countries outside the EU, including Eastern and Central Europe, you may bring home, duty-free, 200 cigarettes or 50 cigars; 1 liter of spirits or 2 liters of fortified or sparkling wine or liqueurs; 2 liters of still table wine; 60 ml of perfume; 250 ml of toilet water; plus £136 worth of other goods, including gifts and souvenirs. If returning from outside the EU, prohibited items include meat products, seeds, plants, and fruits.

➤ INFORMATION: **HM Customs and Excise** (✉ Dorset House, Stamford St., Bromley, Kent BR1 1XX, U.K., ☎ 020/7202–4227, www.hmce.gov.uk).

IN THE U.S.

U.S. residents who have been out of the country for at least 48 hours (and who have not used the $400 allowance or any part of it in the past 30 days) may bring home $400 worth of foreign goods duty-free.

U.S. residents 21 and older may bring back 1 liter of alcohol duty-free. In addition, regardless of your age, you are allowed 200 cigarettes and 100 non-Cuban cigars. Antiques, which the U.S. Customs Service defines as objects more than 100 years old, enter duty-free, as do original works of art done entirely by hand, including paintings, drawings, and sculptures.

You may also mail or ship packages home duty-free: up to $200 worth of goods for personal use, with a limit of one parcel per addressee per day (except alcohol or tobacco products or perfume worth more than $5); label the package PERSONAL USE and attach a list of its contents and their retail value. Do not label the package UNSOLICITED GIFT or your duty-free exemption will drop to $100. Mailed items do not affect your duty-free allowance on your return.

➤ INFORMATION: **U.S. Customs Service** (✉ 1300 Pennsylvania Ave. NW, Washington, DC 20229, www.customs.gov; inquiries ☎ 202/354–1000; complaints c/o ✉ 1300 Pennsylvania Ave. NW, Room 5.4D, Washington, DC 20229; registration of equipment c/o ✉ Resource Management, ☎ 202/354–1000).

DINING

For country-specific dining information, *see* Dining *in* Pleasures and Pastimes at the beginning of each country chapter. Additional city-specific dining information may also be found at the start of a city's dining listings. The restaurants we list are the cream of the crop in each price category. Unless otherwise noted, the restaurants listed are open daily for lunch and dinner.

RESERVATIONS & DRESS

Reservations are always a good idea: we mention them only when they're essential or not accepted. Book as far ahead as you can, and reconfirm as soon as you arrive. We mention dress only when men are required to wear a jacket or a jacket and tie.

DISABILITIES & ACCESSIBILITY

Provisions for travelers with disabilities in Eastern and Central Europe are extremely limited; probably the best solution is to travel with a nondisabled companion. While many hotels, especially large American or international chains, offer some wheelchair-accessible rooms, special facilities at museums and restaurants and on public transportation are difficult to find. In Poland wheelchairs are available at all airports, and most trains have special seats designated for people with disabilities, but it is wise to notify ahead. In Slovenia a law was passed in 1997 requiring all public buildings and infrastructure, including hotels, to be made fully accessible to people with disabilities.

➤ LOCAL RESOURCES: Bulgaria: **Center for Independent Living** (✉ Buzludja 43, Sofia 1463, ☎ 02/954–9892, cil@aster.net). Czech Republic: **Sdružení zdravotně postižených** (Association of Disabled Persons; ✉ Karlínské nám. 12, Prague 8, ☎ 02/2481–5914, www.czechia.com/szdp). Hungary: **Mozgáskorlátozottak Egyesületeinek Országos Szövetsége** (National Association of People with Mobility Impairments, or MEOSZ; ✉ 1032 Budapest, San Marco u. 76, ☎ 1/388–5529). Slovakia: **Slovenský zväz telesne postihnutých** (Slovak Association of People with Mobility Impairments; ✉ Bratislava, Jakubovo nám. 12, ☎ 07/52963284; must arrange for an English-language interpreter in advance). Slovenia: **Slovenian Union of People with Mobility Impairments** (✉ Stihova 14, Ljubljana, ☎ 01/432–7138).

LODGING

Most hotels take few or no measures to accommodate travelers with disabilities. Your best bets the best are newer hotels and international chains.

RESERVATIONS

When discussing accessibility with an operator or reservations agent, **ask hard questions.** Are there any stairs, inside *or* out? Are there grab bars next to the toilet *and* in the shower/tub? How wide is the doorway to the room? To the bathroom?

SIGHTS & ATTRACTIONS

Most tourist attractions in the region pose significant problems. Many are historic structures without ramps or other means to improve accessibility. Streets are often cobblestone, and potholes are common.

TRANSPORTATION

A few Czech trains are equipped with carriages for travelers using wheelchairs. Some stations on the Prague metro have elevators, and there are two lines of accessible buses, but the system is light-years from being barrier-free. For information on Prague public transport, call ☎ 02/2264–6055. Elsewhere in the region, public transportation is difficult, if not impossible, for many travelers with disabilities.

➤ COMPLAINTS: **Disability Rights Section** (✉ U.S. Department of Justice, Civil Rights Division, Box 66738, Washington, DC 20035-6738, ☎ 202/514–0301 or 800/514–0301; 202/514–0383 TTY; 800/514–0383 TTY, FAX 202/307–1198, www.usdoj.gov/crt/ada/adahom1.htm) for general complaints. **Aviation Consumer Protection Division** (☞ Air Travel, *above*) for airline-related problems. **Civil Rights Office** (✉ U.S. Department of Transportation, Departmental Office of Civil Rights, S-30, 400 7th St. SW, Room 10215, Washington, DC 20590, ☎ 202/366–4648, FAX 202/366–9371) for problems with surface transportation.

TRAVEL AGENCIES

In the United States, the Americans with Disabilities Act requires that travel firms serve the needs of all travelers. Some agencies specialize in working with people with disabilities.

➤ TRAVELERS WITH MOBILITY PROBLEMS: **Access Adventures** (✉ 206 Chestnut Ridge Rd., Scottsville, NY 14624, ☎ 716/889–9096, dltravel@prodigy.net), run by a former physical-rehabilitation counselor. **Flying Wheels Travel** (✉ 143 W. Bridge St., Box 382, Owatonna, MN 55060, ☎ 507/451–5005 or 800/535–6790, FAX 507/451–1685, thq@ll.net, www.flyingwheels.com). **Hinsdale Travel Service** (✉ 201 E. Ogden Ave., Suite 100, Hinsdale, IL 60521, ☎ 630/

325–1335, FAX 630/325–1342, hinsdaletravel@hinsdaletravel.com).

DISCOUNTS & DEALS

Be a smart shopper and **compare all your options** before making decisions. A plane ticket bought with a promotional coupon from travel clubs, coupon books, and direct-mail offers may not be cheaper than the least expensive fare from a discount ticket agency. And always keep in mind that what you get is just as important as what you save.

In Budapest, the **Budapest Card** entitles holders to unlimited travel on public transportation; free admission to many museums and sights; and discounts on various services from participating businesses. The cost (at press time) is 2,800 Ft. for two days, 3,400 Ft. for three days; one card is valid for an adult plus one child under 14. It is available at many tourist offices along with a similar pass called the **Hungary Card,** which gives discounts to museums, sights, and service in the entire country.

DISCOUNT RESERVATIONS

To save money, **look into discount reservations services** with toll-free numbers, which use their buying power to get a better price on hotels, airline tickets, even car rentals. When booking a room, always **call the hotel's local toll-free number** (if one is available) rather than the central reservations number—you'll often get a better price. Always ask about special packages or corporate rates.

When shopping for the best deal on hotels and car rentals, **look for guaranteed exchange rates,** which protect you against a falling dollar. With your rate locked in, you won't pay more, even if the price goes up in the local currency.

➤ AIRLINE TICKETS: ☎ **800/FLY–ASAP.**

➤ HOTEL ROOMS: **International Marketing & Travel Concepts** (☎ 800/790–4682, imtc@mindspring.com). **Steigenberger Reservation Service** (☎ 800/223–5652, www.srs-worldhotels.com). **Travel Interlink** (☎ 800/888–5898, www.travelinterlink.com).

PACKAGE DEALS

Don't confuse packages and guided tours. When you buy a package, you travel on your own, just as though you had planned the trip yourself. Fly/drive packages, which combine airfare and car rental, are often a good deal. If you buy a rail/drive pass, you may save on train tickets and car rentals. All Eurail- and Europass holders get a discount on Eurostar fares through the Channel Tunnel.

ECOTOURISM

In the Czech Republic, the most active organization promoting ecotourism is **Greenways** (www.pragueviennagreenways.org). Ecotourism—often just another word for rural B&Bs—is slowly gathering pace in mountainous such as the south Bohemian Šumava, and in the flatter, bike-friendly country of south Moravia.

In Poland there are plenty of eco- and agrotourist destinations, which are increasingly popular spots for Dutch and German tourists. For more information on contact **Polska Federacja Wiejskiej,** ✉ ul. Jasna 15, Warsaw, ☎ 022/827–51–56.

Romania offers wonderful opportunities for hiking through the beautiful countryside and in the forested mountains. Animals such as bears, chamois, and boar still inhabit the forests, but as yet, there is no organized program for ecotourism.

ELECTRICITY

To use your U.S.-purchased electric-powered equipment, **bring a converter and adapter.** The electrical current in Eastern and Central Europe is 220 volts, 50 cycles alternating current (AC); wall outlets generally take plugs with two round prongs.

If your appliances are dual-voltage, you'll need only an adapter. Don't use 110-volt outlets marked FOR SHAVERS ONLY for high-wattage appliances such as blow-dryers. Most laptops operate equally well on 110 and 220 volts and so require only an adapter.

EMBASSIES

For Australian, Canadian, U.S., and U.K. embassy and consulate contact information, *see* the A to Z section for the first-listed city in each country chapter. There are no New Zealand embassies or consulates in the region.

EMERGENCIES

For country-specific emergency numbers, *see* Emergencies in the A to Z section at the end of each country chapter. For medical emergency contacts, *see also* Health, *below.*

ENGLISH-LANGUAGE MEDIA

The largest cities in the region have English-language weekly newspapers that cover current events and culture. Prague in particular is remarkably rich in English-language publishing of all kinds, from general-interest newspapers to poetry chapbooks, reflecting the city's large, relatively stable community of English-speaking expatriates.

In the broadcast media, BBC World Service and CNN are widely available.

GAY & LESBIAN TRAVEL

Throughout Eastern and Central Europe, gay and lesbian resources are thin on the ground, if not underground. While the level of tolerance varies, the region is generally conservative; strongly Catholic countries are the most intolerant.

Though gays and lesbians are gaining acceptance in **Bulgaria,** they do not have any national organizations. Social steps towards acceptance are quite new; the first openly gay disco opened in Sofia in 1997. In general, attitudes towards homosexuality throughout the Bulgarian interior are hostile, while at the more cosmopolitan Black Sea coast resorts people tend to be more open-minded.

The **Czech Republic** is one of the most liberal countries. Prague fosters a growing gay and lesbian scene, but up-to-date information is not easy to find. You could try visiting one of the gathering places that attract both gays and straights, such as the **Radost FX club** (☞ Prague Nightlife).

Hungary is relatively open-minded, though even in Budapest, the gay population keeps a fairly low profile. Some of Budapest's thermal baths are popular meeting places (*see* Exploring Budapest in the Budapest section of the country chapter), as are the city's several gay bars and clubs, which you can find listed in English-language newspapers and the monthly magazine *Mások*.

Gay and lesbian organization is a relatively new thing in **Poland,** and clubs and meeting points change addresses frequently. One of the longest-standing gay organizations is **Lambda** (✉ Ul. Śniadeckich 1/15, Warsaw, ☎ 022/628–52–22).

Until fairly recently, homosexuality was illegal in **Romania**. Though greater acceptance exists today, especially among the young and better educated, it remains basically a closed topic.

In **Slovakia** resources are limited; the **Ganymedes hotline** (☎ 0905/618291) operates on Tuesdays and Thursdays from 6 to 8 PM.

In **Slovenia** homosexuality is widely tolerated. Gays and lesbians are united in several associations and clubs, with the main center at the student-run nightclub **K4** (✉ Kersnikova 4, Ljubljana, ☎ 01/131–7010). K4 run a gay night every Sunday 10 PM–4 AM.

➤ GAY- & LESBIAN-FRIENDLY TRAVEL AGENCIES: **Different Roads Travel** (✉ 8383 Wilshire Blvd., Suite 902, Beverly Hills, CA 90211, ☎ 323/651–5557 or 800/429–8747, FAX 323/651–3678, leigh@west.tzell.com). **Kennedy Travel** (✉ 314 Jericho Turnpike, Floral Park, NY 11001, ☎ 516/352–4888 or 800/237–7433, FAX 516/354–8849, kennedytravel1@yahoo.com, www.kennedytravel.com). **Now Voyager** (✉ 4406 18th St., San Francisco, CA 94114, ☎ 415/626–1169 or 800/255–6951, FAX 415/626–8626, www.nowvoyager.com). **Skylink Travel and Tour** (✉ 1006 Mendocino Ave., Santa Rosa, CA 95401, ☎ 707/546–9888 or 800/225–5759, FAX 707/546–9891, skylinktvl@aol.com, www.skylinktravel.com), serving lesbian travelers.

HEALTH

You may gain weight, but there are few other serious health hazards for the traveler in Eastern and Central Europe. Tap water may taste bad but is generally drinkable (though see the precautions below); when it runs rusty out of the tap or the aroma of chlorine is overpowering, it might help to have some iodine tablets or bottled water handy. Tap water isn't considered safe in Romania's Danube Delta. Throughout the country, bottled water is inexpensive and widely available; it might be a better choice, especially for children, as there is a history of tap water with heavy lead content. In Bulgaria and Poland, faulty plumbing, especially in cities, ruins the water quality. Buy bottled water, particularly if staying in an older home or a hotel.

Vegetarians and those on special diets may have a problem with the heavy local cuisine, which is based largely on pork and beef. To prevent your vitamin intake from dropping to danger levels, buy fresh fruits and vegetables at seasonal street markets—regular grocery stores often don't sell them. In Romania, unrefrigerated milk sold in outdoor markets or in villages may not be pasteurized and can make Westerners sick. In Bulgaria, mayonnaise-based fillings are very common in "sandvitchee"—the ubiquitous toasted sandwiches sold at many street kiosks; avoid them.

No vaccinations are required for entry into any of the Eastern and Central European countries covered in this book, but selective vaccinations are recommended. Those traveling in forested areas of most Eastern and Central European countries should consider vaccinating themselves against Central European, or tick-borne, encephalitis. Tick-borne Lyme disease is also a risk in the Czech Republic. If you plan to travel for an extended period of time in rural Bulgaria, it is a good idea to consider a vaccination for hepatitis spread through food and water. Schedule vaccinations well in advance of departure because some require several doses, and others may cause uncomfortable side effects.

To avoid problems clearing customs, diabetic travelers carrying needles and syringes should have on hand a letter from their physician confirming their need for insulin injections.

OVER-THE-COUNTER REMEDIES

Pharmacies throughout the region carry a variety of nonprescription as well as prescription drugs. For recommended pharmacies, *see* the A to Z sections in each country chapter.

HOLIDAYS

For country-specific holidays, *see* National Holidays in the A to Z section at the end of each country chapter.

INSURANCE

The most useful travel-insurance plan is a comprehensive policy that includes coverage for trip cancellation and interruption, default, trip delay, and medical expenses (with a waiver for pre-existing conditions).

Without insurance you will lose all or most of your money if you cancel your trip, regardless of the reason. Default insurance covers you if your tour operator, airline, or cruise line goes out of business. Trip-delay covers expenses that arise because of bad weather or mechanical delays. Study the fine print when comparing policies.

When you're traveling internationally, a key component of travel insurance is coverage for medical bills incurred if you get sick on the road. Such expenses are not generally covered by Medicare or private policies. U.K. residents can buy a travel-insurance policy valid for most vacations taken during the year in which it's purchased (but check pre-existing-condition coverage). British and Australian citizens need extra medical coverage when traveling overseas.

Always **buy travel policies directly from the insurance company**; if you buy them from a cruise line, airline, or tour operator that goes out of business you probably will not be covered for the agency or operator's default, a major risk. Before making any purchase, **review your existing health and home-owner's policies** to find what they cover away from home.

➤ TRAVEL INSURERS: In the U.S.: Access America (✉ 6600 W. Broad St., Richmond, VA 23230, ☎ 804/285–3300 or 800/284–8300, FAX 804/

673–1586, www.previewtravel.com), **Travel Guard International** (✉ 1145 Clark St., Stevens Point, WI 54481, ☎ 715/345–0505 or 800/826–1300, FAX 800/955–8785, www.noelgroup.com).

➤ INSURANCE INFORMATION: In the U.K.: **Association of British Insurers** (✉ 51–55 Gresham St., London EC2V 7HQ, U.K., ☎ 020/7600–3333, FAX 020/7696–8999, info@abi.org.uk, www.abi.org.uk). In Canada: **Voyager Insurance** (✉ 44 Peel Center Dr., Brampton, Ontario L6T 4M8, Canada, ☎ 905/791–8700, 800/668–4342 in Canada). In Australia: **Insurance Council of Australia** (☎ 03/9614–1077, FAX 03/9614–7924). In New Zealand: **Insurance Council of New Zealand** (✉ Box 474, Wellington, New Zealand, ☎ 04/472–5230, FAX 04/473–3011, www.icnz.org.nz).

LANGUAGE

For country-specific information about language issues, *see* Language in the A to Z section at the end of each country chapter.

LODGING

If your experience of Eastern and Central European hotels is limited to capital cities such as Prague and Budapest, you may be pleasantly surprised. There are baroque mansions turned guest houses and elegant high-rise resorts, not to mention bed-and-breakfast inns presided over by matronly babushkas. Many facilities throughout the region are being upgraded.

Outside major cities, hotels and inns are more rustic than elegant. Standards of service generally do not suffer, but in most rural areas the definition of "luxury" includes little more than a television and a private bathroom. In some instances, you may have no choice but to stay in one of the cement high-rise hotels that scar skylines from Poland to the Czech Republic. Huge, impersonal, concrete hotels are part of the Communist legacy, and it may take a few more years to exorcise or "beautify" these ubiquitous monsters. However, even in Bulgaria, where changes are very slow, new, luxurious hotels can be found in most regions of the country, if you're willing to pay Western prices.

In rural Eastern and Central Europe, you may have difficulty parting with more than $25–$30 per night for lodgings. Reservations are vital if you plan to visit Prague, Budapest, Warsaw, or most other major cities during the summer season. Reservations are a good idea but aren't imperative if you plan to strike out into the countryside.

For country-specific lodging information, *see* Lodging *in* Pleasures and Pastimes at the beginning of each country chapter. Additional city-specific lodging information may also be found at the start of a city's lodging listings. The lodgings we list are the cream of the crop in each price category. We always list the facilities that are available—but we don't specify whether they cost extra: when pricing accommodations, always ask what's included and what costs extra.

APARTMENT & VILLA RENTALS

If you want a home base that's roomy enough for a family and comes with cooking facilities, **consider a furnished rental.** These can save you money, especially if you're traveling with a group. Home-exchange directories sometimes list rentals as well as exchanges.

Rental apartments are common in Hungary. In Budapest, the best bet is to go through an agency; and in the rest of the country, either check with a local tourist information office or, especially in smaller cities, simply walk around until you see a sign outside a house reading *apartman*.

If you are looking for a private room in Warsaw, try **Syrena.** In Poland outside Warsaw look to the local tourist information for assistance.

➤ INTERNATIONAL AGENTS: **Hometours International** (✉ Box 11503, Knoxville, TN 37939, ☎ 865/690–8484 or 800/367–4668, hometours@aol.com, http://thor.he.net/àhometour/). **Interhome** (✉ 1990 N.E. 163rd St., Suite 110, N. Miami Beach, FL 33162, ☎ 305/940–2299 or 800/882–6864, FAX 305/940–2911, interhomeu@aol.com, www.interhome.com).

➤ LOCAL AGENTS: Hungary: In Budapest, **Amadeus Apartments** (✉ IX, Üllői út 197, H-1091, ☎ 06/309–422–893); **TRIBUS Welcome Hotel Service** (✉ V, Apáczai Csere János u. 1, ☎ 1/318–5776); **Cooptourist** (✉ XI, Bartók Béla út 4, ☎ 1/466–5349). Poland: In Warsaw, **Syrena** (✉ ul. Krucza 17, ☎ 022/628-75-40).

B&BS

Although B&Bs of the traditional English variety aren't prevalent in the region, there are numerous variations on the concept available, including comfortable and elaborately decorated facilities in Hungary and agrotourism (essentially rural home stays) in Romania. For further information, *see* B&B Reservation Agencies *in* the A to Z sections of the individual country chapters.

CAMPING

For information on camping in the **Czech Republic,** contact the Czech Tourist Authority (☞ Visitor Information, *below*). The Prague Information Service can supply a map of the dozen or so campgrounds in and around Prague.

For **Hungary,** campground information, reservations, and an informative map listing all campgrounds can be obtained from travel agencies and Tourinform (☞ Visitor Information in the Hungary A to Z section of chapter 4). You may also contact the **Hungarian Camping and Caravanning Club** (✉ VIII, Mária u. 34, Budapest, ☎ 1/267–5255 or 1/267–5256).

There are over 500 official campsites in **Poland.** Check *Campingi w Polsce,* which is available in major bookstores, for details.

More than 100 campsites exist in **Romania;** conditions vary. Many are in mountain, seaside and spa areas.

For information on camping facilities in **Slovakia,** contact Satur or Tatratour travel agencies (☞ Visitor Information, Bratislava A to Z, *in* Chapter 3).

HOME EXCHANGES

If you would like to exchange your home for someone else's, **join a home-exchange organization,** which will send you its updated listings of available exchanges for a year and will include your own listing in at least one of them. It's up to you to make specific arrangements.

➤ EXCHANGE CLUBS: **Intervac U.S.** (✉ Box 590504, San Francisco, CA 94159, ☎ 800/756–4663, FAX 415/435–7440, intervacus@aol.com, www.intervacus.com; $93 per year includes two catalogues).

HOSTELS

No matter what your age you can **save on lodging costs by staying at hostels.** In some 5,000 locations in more than 70 countries around the world, Hostelling International (HI), the umbrella group for a number of national youth-hostel associations, offers single-sex, dorm-style beds and, at many hostels, couples rooms and family accommodations. Membership in any HI national hostel association, open to travelers of all ages, allows you to stay in HI-affiliated hostels at member rates (one-year membership is about $25 for adults; hostels run about $10–$25 per night). Members also have priority if the hostel is full; they're eligible for discounts around the world, even on rail and bus travel in some countries.

In Hungary, most hostels are geared toward the college crowd. Among several good ones in Budapest are the friendly, Internet-equipped **Back Pack Guesthouse** (✉ XI, Takács Menyhért u. 33, ☎ 1/385–8946), where rates range from 1,300 Ft. (8-10 bed rooms) to 1,900 Ft. (2-bed rooms), and the **Sirály Youth Hostel** (✉ XIII, Margit-sziget (Margaret Island), ☎ 1/329–3952), situated in the relative peace, quiet, and clean air of an island-park on the Danube, where the per-person rate in 12-bed rooms is 1,400 Ft. For further information, consult the free annual accommodations directory published by **Tourinform** (☞ Visitor Information in the Hungary A to Z section of Chapter 4) or the listings in **Budapest In Your Pocket,** available at newsstands.

All but one or two Czech hostels are located in two towns: Prague and Český Krumlov. They tend to be either backpacker-happy, party-all-night places, or affiliated with sports clubs or colleges. Most accommodation services in Prague book hostel rooms. The Prague representative of Hostelling International is **KMC Travel Service**, Karolíny Světlé 30, ☎ 02/2222–1328. A relatively well-run Prague hostel, with six local sites and affiliates in Český Krumlov, Budapest, and Berlin, is **Travellers' Hostel** (main location: Dlouhá 33, ☎ 02/231–1318).

Hostels in Slovakia are only run in university dormitories during summer vacation, July to September. For general orientation, contact **Satur** or **Bratislavská Informačná Služba** (☞ Visitor Information, Bratislava A to Z, *in* Chapter 3).

➤ ORGANIZATIONS: **Hostelling International—American Youth Hostels** (✉ 733 15th St. NW, Suite 840, Washington, DC 20005, ☎ 202/783–6161, FAX 202/783–6171, hiayhserv@hiayh.org, www.hiayh.org). **Hostelling International—Canada** (✉ 400–205 Catherine St., Ottawa, Ontario K2P 1C3, Canada, ☎ 613/237–7884, FAX 613/237–7868, info@hostellingintl.ca, www.hostellingintl.ca). **Youth Hostel Association of England and Wales** (✉ Trevelyan House, 8 St. Stephen's Hill, St. Albans, Hertfordshire AL1 2DY, U.K., ☎ 0870/8708808, FAX 01727/844126, customerservices@yha.org.uk, www.yha.org.uk). **Australian Youth Hostel Association** (✉ 10 Mallett St., Camperdown, NSW 2050, Australia, ☎ 02/9565–1699, FAX 02/9565–1325, www.yha.com.au). **Youth Hostels Association of New Zealand** (✉ Box 436, Christchurch, New Zealand, ☎ 03/379–9970, FAX 03/365–4476, info@yha.org.nz, www.yha.org.nz).

HOTELS

Throughout the past decade the quality of hotels in Eastern and Central Europe improved notably. Many formerly state-run hotels were privatized, much to their benefit—a transition process that is still on-going in some countries. International hotel chains have established a strong presence in the region; while they may not be strong on local character, they do provide a reliably high standard of quality.

Hotels listed throughout the book have private bath unless otherwise noted.

➤ TOLL-FREE NUMBERS: **Best Western** (☎ 800/528–1234, www.bestwestern.com). **Choice** (☎ 800/221–2222, www.hotelchoice.com). **Hilton** (☎ 800/445–8667, www.hilton.com). **Holiday Inn** (☎ 800/465–4329, www.basshotels.com). **Hungarian Hotels** (☎ 800/448–4321). **Hyatt Hotels & Resorts** (☎ 800/233–1234, www.hyatt.com). **Inter-Continental** (☎ 800/327–0200, www.interconti.com). **Marriott** (☎ 800/228–9290, www.marriott.com). **Radisson** (☎ 800/333–3333, www.radisson.com). **Renaissance Hotels & Resorts** (☎ 800/468–3571, www.renaissancehotels.com/).

MAIL & SHIPPING

For country-specific mail information, *see* Mail in the A to Z section at the end of each country chapter.

MONEY MATTERS

For country-specific money information, *see* Money and Expenses in the A to Z section at the end of each country chapter.

Prices throughout this guide are given for adults. Substantially reduced fees are almost always available for children, students, and senior citizens. For information on taxes, *see* Taxes, *below*.

ATMS

The rule of thumb throughout the region is: ATMs are common in large and mid-size cities and more often than not are part of the Cirrus and Plus networks; outside of urban areas, machines are scarce and you should plan to carry enough cash to meet your needs.

CREDIT CARDS

Credit cards are accepted in places that cater regularly to foreign tourists and business travelers: hotels, restaurants, and shops, particularly in major urban centers. When you leave the beaten path, be prepared to pay cash. Always inquire about credit card policies when booking hotel rooms. Visa and EuroCard/Master-

Card are the most commonly accepted credit cards in the region.

It's smart to **write down (and keep separate) the number of each credit card you're carrying** along with the international service phone number that usually appears on the back of the card.

Throughout this guide, the following abbreviations are used: AE, American Express; D, Discover; DC, Diners Club; MC, Master Card; and V, Visa.

CURRENCY EXCHANGE

In many Eastern and Central European countries, you should **change money at banks** for the most favorable exchange rate. Although fees charged for ATM transactions may be higher abroad than at home, Cirrus and Plus exchange rates are excellent, because they are based on wholesale rates offered only by major banks. You often won't do as well at exchange booths in airports or rail and bus stations, in hotels, in restaurants, or in stores, although you may find their hours more convenient. Romania is an exception; exchange bureaus have the best rates, especially in Bucharest and other large cities. To avoid lines at airport exchange booths, **get a bit of local currency before you leave home.**

➤ EXCHANGE SERVICES: **International Currency Express** (☎ 888/278–6628 for orders, www.foreignmoney.com). **Thomas Cook Currency Services** (☎ 800/287–7362 for telephone orders and retail locations, www.us.thomascook.com).

TRAVELER'S CHECKS

Do you need traveler's checks? It depends on where you're headed. If you're going to rural areas and small towns, go with cash; traveler's checks are best used in cities. However, traveler's checks are virtually useless in Bulgaria, and in Romania are accepted only at large hotels, banks and selected exchange offices. Lost or stolen checks can usually be replaced within 24 hours. To ensure a speedy refund, buy your own traveler's checks—don't let someone else pay for them: irregularities like this can cause delays. The person who bought the checks should make the call to request a refund.

PACKING

Don't worry about packing lots of formal clothing. Fashion was all but nonexistent under 40 years of Communist rule, although residents of Budapest, Prague, and even Bucharest and Sofia—catching up with their counterparts in other European capitals—are considerably more fashionably dressed than even a few years ago. Still, Western dress of virtually any kind is considered stylish: A sports jacket for men and a dress or pants for women are appropriate for an evening out. Everywhere else, you'll feel comfortable in casual pants or jeans.

Eastern and Central Europe enjoy all the extremes of an inland climate, so plan accordingly. In the higher elevations winter can last until April, and even in summer the evenings will be on the cool side.

Many areas are best seen on foot, so take a pair of sturdy walking shoes and be prepared to use them. High heels will present considerable problems on the cobblestone streets of Prague, Sofia, Warsaw, and towns in Hungary, or the potholed streets in Romania. If you plan to visit the mountains, make sure your shoes have good traction and ankle support, as some trails can be quite challenging.

Some items that you take for granted at home are occasionally unavailable or of questionable quality in Eastern and Central Europe, though the situation has been steadily improving. Toiletries and personal-hygiene products have become relatively easy to find, but it's always a good idea to bring necessities when traveling in rural areas. If you're heading to Bulgaria, make sure you have a flashlight with you at all times. Streetlights are rare, even in city centers, and often interior hallways are unlit.

In your carry-on luggage, **pack an extra pair of eyeglasses or contact lenses** and **enough of any medication you take** to last the entire trip. You may also ask your doctor to write a spare prescription using the drug's generic name, since brand names may vary from country to country. In luggage to be checked, **never pack prescription drugs or valuables.** To avoid customs delays, carry medications in their original packaging. And don't forget to carry with you the addresses of offices that handle refunds of lost traveler's checks.

CHECKING LUGGAGE

How many carry-on bags you can bring with you is up to the airline. Most allow two, but not always, so make sure that everything you carry aboard will fit under your seat or in the overhead bin, and get to the gate early. Note that if you have a seat at the back of the plane, you'll probably board first, while the overhead bins are still empty.

When flying internationally, note that baggage allowances may be determined not by piece but by weight—generally 88 pounds (40 kilograms) in first class, 66 pounds (30 kilograms) in business class, and 44 pounds (20 kilograms) in economy.

Airline liability for baggage is limited to $1,250 per person on flights within the United States. On international flights it amounts to $9.07 per pound or $20 per kilogram for checked baggage (roughly $640 per 70-pound bag) and $400 per passenger for unchecked baggage. You can buy additional coverage at check-in for about $10 per $1,000 of coverage, but it excludes a rather extensive list of items, shown on your airline ticket.

Before departure, **itemize your bags' contents** and their worth, and label the bags with your name, address, and phone number. (If you use your home address, cover it so potential thieves can't see it readily.) Inside each bag, **pack a copy of your itinerary.** At check-in, **make sure that each bag is correctly tagged** with the destination airport's three-letter code. If your bags arrive damaged or fail to arrive at all, file a written report with the airline before leaving the airport.

PASSPORTS & VISAS

When traveling internationally, **carry your passport** even if you don't need one (it's always the best form of I.D.) and **make two photocopies of the data page** (one for someone at home and another for you, carried separately from your passport). If you lose your passport, promptly call the nearest embassy or consulate and the local police.

ENTERING EASTERN AND CENTRAL EUROPE

See the A to Z section at the end of each country chapter for specific entrance requirements.

PASSPORT OFFICES

The best time to apply for a passport or to renew is in fall and winter. Before any trip, check your passport's expiration date, and, if necessary, renew it as soon as possible.

➤ AUSTRALIAN CITIZENS: **Australian Passport Office** (☎ 131–232, www.dfat.gov.au/passports).

➤ CANADIAN CITIZENS: **Passport Office** (☎ 819/994–3500; 800/567–6868 in Canada, www.dfait-maeci.gc.ca/passport).

➤ NEW ZEALAND CITIZENS: **New Zealand Passport Office** (☎ 04/494–0700, www.passports.govt.nz).

➤ U.K. CITIZENS: **London Passport Office** (☎ 0870/521–0410, www.ukpa.gov.uk) for fees and documentation requirements and to request an emergency passport.

➤ U.S. CITIZENS: **National Passport Information Center** (☎ 900/225–5674; calls are 35¢ per minute for automated service, $1.05 per minute for operator service; www.travel.state.gov/npicinfo.html).

REST ROOMS

Public rest rooms are more common, and cleaner, than they used to be in the **Czech Republic.** You nearly always have to pay 2 Kč–10 Kč to the attendant. Restaurant and bar toilets are generally for customers only, but, as prices are low, this isn't a significant burden.

While the rest rooms at Budapest's Ferihegy Airport may sparkle and smell of soap, don't expect the same of those at **Hungarian** train and bus stations—which, by the way, usually have attendants on hand who collect a fee of about 40 Ft. Especially outside Budapest, public restrooms are often run-down and sometimes rank. Pay the attendant on the way in; you will receive toilet tissue in exchange. Since public rest rooms are generally few and far between, you will sometimes find yourself entering cafés, bars, or restaurants primarily to use their toilets; when doing so, unless it happens to be a bustling fast-food place, you should probably order a little something.

In **Poland,** public washrooms generally have an attendant who will charge zł 1 for use. This usually ensures that the facilities are clean. There are plenty of hotels, pubs, and fast food restaurants with restrooms that can be used.

Public rest rooms are clean in major hotels and restaurants in **Romania.** Another safe bet is MacDonald's. Otherwise, cleanliness and the supply of toilet paper and paper towels are hit and miss. Toilets in trains and train stations are only for the most desperate.

In **Slovakia,** toilets in restaurants and bars are generally well kept. Other public rest rooms are rare.

SAFETY

Crime rates are still relatively low in Eastern and Central Europe, but travelers should beware of pickpockets in crowded areas, especially on public transportation, at railway stations, and in big hotels. In general, always keep your valuables with you—in open bars and restaurants, purses hung on or placed next to chairs are easy targets. Make sure your wallet is safe in a buttoned pocket, or watch your handbag.

Keep a sharp eye out for pickpockets in **Bulgaria** and be very careful with your passport. (The black market price for an American or Canadian passport is around $1,000, which is almost the average yearly salary.) Ironically, you are required by Bulgarian law to carry your passport on your person at all times. In urban areas, you should also watch out for packs of stray dogs. In the **Czech Republic,** except for widely scattered attacks against people of color, violent crime against tourists is extremely rare. Pickpocketing and bill-padding are the most common complaints.

In **Hungary,** pickpocketing and car theft are the main concerns. While a typical rental car is less likely to be stolen, expensive German makes such as Audi, BMW, and Mercedes are hot targets for car thieves. Crime rates have been rising in major cities in **Poland;** besides watching out for the omnipresent pickpockets, you should observe the usual urban rules of caution: be extra attentive and stick to well-lit, well-trafficked areas at night.

In **Romania,** the streets are generally safe, but pickpocketing and scams are on the rise in cities, especially on trains and buses and in stations. In **Slovakia,** car theft and pickpocketing at crowded areas and stores are the main concern. **Slovenia** claims to have one of the lowest crime rates in Europe.

LOCAL SCAMS

To avoid potential trouble in the Czech Republic: Ask taxi drivers what the approximate fare will be before getting in, and ask for a receipt (*paragon*); carefully look over restaurant bills; be extremely wary of handing your passport to anyone who accosts you with a demand for I.D.; and never exchange money on the street.

A notorious scam in some **Romanian** cities involves men flashing fake police badges and accusing you of exchanging currency illegally. Do not hand over your passport or money; instead, offer to accompany them (on foot) to your hotel or a police station. If you spot a uniformed policeman, summon him. On trains and buses, groups sometimes cause distractions, then make off with your valuables.

In **Slovakia,** ask taxi drivers about the expected fare before getting in. Asking for a receipt (*potvrdenka*) might also discourage a driver from charging you enormous fare, or it could be used when complaining about a fare to a taxi dispatcher.

WOMEN IN EASTERN AND CENTRAL EUROPE

Women generally move about the region with no more problems than they'd encounter in any western European country. The same general precautions apply: It isn't wise for a woman to go alone to a bar or nightclub or to wander the streets late at night. When traveling by train at night, seek out compartments that are well populated.

SENIOR-CITIZEN TRAVEL

To qualify for age-related discounts, **mention your senior-citizen status up front** when booking hotel reservations (not when checking out) and before you're seated in restaurants (not when paying the bill). When renting a car, ask about promotional car-rental discounts, which can be cheaper than senior-citizen rates.

➤ EDUCATIONAL PROGRAMS: **Elderhostel** (✉ 75 Federal St., 3rd floor, Boston, MA 02110, ☎ 877/426–8056, FAX 877/426–2166, www.elderhostel.org). **Interhostel** (✉ University of New Hampshire, 6 Garrison Ave., Durham, NH 03824, ☎ 603/862–1147 or 800/733–9753, FAX 603/862–1113, learn.dce@unh.edu, www.learn.unh.edu).

STUDENTS IN EASTERN AND CENTRAL EUROPE

For country-specific student and youth travel information, *see* Student and Youth Travel in the A to Z section at the end of each country chapter.

➤ I.D.S & SERVICES: **Council Travel** (CIEE; ✉ 205 E. 42nd St., 14th floor, New York, NY 10017, ☎ 212/822–2700 or 888/268–6245, FAX 212/822–2699, info@councilexchanges.org, www.councilexchanges.org) for mail orders only, in the U.S. **Travel Cuts** (✉ 187 College St., Toronto, Ontario M5T 1P7, Canada, ☎ 416/979–2406 or 800/667–2887 in Canada, www.travelcuts.com).

TAXES

Most Eastern and Central European countries have some form of value-added tax (VAT); rebate rules vary by country, and seem to be in an ongoing state of evolution. Check with tourism offices (☞ *See* Visitor Information, *below*) for current regulations. One thing you can depend on, you'll need to present your receipts on departure.

TELEPHONES

For additional country-specific telephone information, *see* Telephones in the A to Z section at the end of each country chapter.

AREA & COUNTRY CODES

Country and select city codes are as follows: Bulgaria (359), Sofia (2); Czech Republic (420), Prague (2); Hungary (36), Budapest (1); Poland (48), Warsaw (22); Romania (40), Bucharest (1); Slovakia (421), Bratislava (7); Slovenia (386), Ljubljana (1).

When dialing an Eastern or Central European number from abroad, drop the initial 0 from the local area code. The country code for the United States is 1 for the United States and Canada, 61 for Australia, 64 for New Zealand, and 44 for the U.K.

LONG-DISTANCE SERVICES

AT&T, MCI, and Sprint access codes make calling long distance relatively convenient, but you may find the local access number blocked in many hotel rooms. First ask the hotel operator to connect you. If the hotel operator balks, ask for an international operator, or dial the international operator yourself. One way to improve your odds of getting connected to your long-distance carrier is to travel with more than one company's calling card (a hotel may block Sprint, for example, but not MCI). If all else fails, call from a pay phone.

➤ ACCESS CODES: **AT&T Direct** (☎ 008000010 in Bulgaria; 0042000101 in the Czech Republic; 0042100101 in Slovakia; 0080001111 in Hungary; 008001111111 in Poland; 01/800–4288 in Romania; 800/435–0812 for other areas). **MCI WorldPhone** (☎ 008000001 in Bulgaria; 0042000112 in the Czech Republic; 0680001411 in Hungary; 008001112122 in Poland; 01/800–1800 in Romania; 0018814220042 in Slovakia; 080–8808 in Slovenia). **Sprint International Access** (☎ 008001010 in Bulgaria; 0042087187 in the Czech Republic; 0680001877 in Hungary; 008001113115 in Poland; 01/800–0877 in Romania; 0018818249242 in Slovakia; 800/877–4646 for other areas).

TIME

The Czech Republic, Hungary, Poland, Slovakia, and Slovenia are on Central European Time (CET), one hour ahead of Greenwich Mean Time and six hours ahead of the eastern time zone of the United States. Bulgaria and Romania are two hours ahead of Greenwich Mean Time.

TOURS & PACKAGES

Because everything is prearranged on a prepackaged tour or independent vacation, you'll spend less time planning—and often get it all at a good price.

BOOKING WITH AN AGENT

Travel agents are excellent resources. But it's a good idea to collect brochures from several agencies as some agents' suggestions may be influenced by relationships with tour and package firms that reward them for volume sales. If you have a special interest, **find an agent with expertise in that area**; the American Society of Travel Agents (ASTA; ☞ Travel Agencies, *below*) has a database of specialists worldwide.

Make sure your travel agent knows the accommodations and other services of the place they're recommending. Ask about the hotel's location, room size, beds, and whether it has a pool, room service, or programs for children, if you care about these. Has your agent been there in person or sent others whom you can contact?

Do some homework on your own, too: local tourism boards can provide information about lesser-known and small-niche operators, some of which may sell only direct.

BUYER BEWARE

Each year consumers are stranded or lose their money when tour operators—even large ones with excellent reputations—go out of business. So **check out the operator.** Ask several travel agents about its reputation, and try to **book with a company that has a consumer-protection program.** (Look for information in the company's brochure.) In the United States, members of the National Tour Association and the United States Tour Operators Association are required to set aside funds to cover your payments and travel arrangements in the event that the company defaults. It's also a good idea to choose a company that participates in the American Society of Travel Agents' Tour Operator Program (TOP); ASTA will act as mediator in any disputes between you and your tour operator.

Remember that the more your package or tour includes the better you can predict the ultimate cost of your vacation. Make sure you know exactly what is covered, and **beware of hidden costs.** Are taxes, tips, and transfers included? Entertainment and excursions? These can add up.

➤ TOUR-OPERATOR RECOMMENDATIONS: **American Society of Travel Agents** (☞ Travel Agencies, *below*). **National Tour Association** (NTA; ✉ 546 E. Main St., Lexington, KY 40508, ☎ 859/226–4444 or 800/682–8886, www.ntaonline.com). **United States Tour Operators Association** (USTOA; ✉ 342 Madison Ave., Suite 1522, New York, NY 10173, ☎ 212/599–6599 or 800/468–7862, FAX 212/599–6744, ustoa@aol.com, www.ustoa.com).

GROUP TOURS

Among companies that sell tours to Eastern and Central Europe, the following are nationally known, have a proven reputation, and offer plenty of options. The classifications used below represent different price categories, and you'll probably encounter these terms when talking to a travel agent or tour operator. The key difference is usually in accommodations, which run from budget to better, and better-yet to best.

➤ SUPER-DELUXE: **Abercrombie & Kent** (✉ 1520 Kensington Rd., Oak Brook, IL 60521-2141, ☎ 630/954–2944 or 800/323–7308, FAX 630/954–3324). **Travcoa** (✉ Box 2630, 2350 S.E. Bristol St., Newport Beach, CA 92660, ☎ 714/476–2800 or 800/992–2003, FAX 714/476–2538).

➤ DELUXE: **Globus** (✉ 5301 S. Federal Circle, Littleton, CO 80123-2980, ☎ 303/797–2800 or 800/221–0090, FAX 303/347–2080). **Maupintour** (✉ 1515 St. Andrews Dr.,

Lawrence, KS 66047, ☎ 785/843–1211 or 800/255–4266, FAX 785/843–8351). **Tauck Tours** (✉ Box 5027, 276 Post Rd. W, Westport, CT 06881-5027, ☎ 203/226–6911 or 800/468–2825, FAX 203/221–6866).

➤ FIRST-CLASS: **Brendan Tours** (✉ 15137 Califa St., Van Nuys, CA 91411, ☎ 818/785–9696 or 800/421–8446, FAX 818/902–9876). **Caravan Tours** (✉ 401 N. Michigan Ave., Chicago, IL 60611, ☎ 312/321–9800 or 800/227–2826, FAX 312/321–9845). **Čedok Travel** (✉ 10 E. 40th St., #3604, New York, NY 10016, ☎ 212/725–0948 or 800/800–8891). **Collette Tours** (✉ 162 Middle St., Pawtucket, RI 02860, ☎ 401/728–3805 or 800/340–5158, FAX 401/728–4745). **DER Travel Services** (✉ 9501 W. Devon Ave., Rosemont, IL 60018, ☎ 800/937–1235, FAX 847/692–4141; 800/282–7474; 800/860–9944 for brochures). **General Tours** (✉ 53 Summer St., Keene, NH 03431, ☎ 603/357–5033 or 800/221–2216, FAX 603/357–4548). **Insight International Tours** (✉ 745 Atlantic Ave., #720, Boston, MA 02111, ☎ 617/482–2000 or 800/582–8380, FAX 617/482–2884 or 800/622–5015). **Trafalgar Tours** (✉ 11 E. 26th St., New York, NY 10010, ☎ 212/689–8977 or 800/854–0103, FAX 800/457–6644).

➤ BUDGET: **Cosmos** (☞ Globus, *above*). **Trafalgar Tours** (☞ *above*).

PACKAGES

Like group tours, independent vacation packages are available from major tour operators and airlines. The companies listed below offer vacation packages in a broad price range.

➤ AIR/HOTEL: **Continental Vacations** (☎ 800/634–5555). **DER Travel Services** (☞ Group Tours, *above*). **General Tours** (☞ Group Tours, *above*). THEME TRIPS

➤ BALLOONING: **Buddy Bombard European Balloon Adventures** (✉ 333 Pershing Way, West Palm Beach, FL 33401, ☎ 561/837–6610 or 800/862–8537, FAX 561/837–6623).

➤ BARGE/RIVER CRUISES: **KD River Cruises of Europe** (✉ 2500 Westchester Ave., Purchase, NY 10577, ☎ 914/696–3600 or 800/346–6525, FAX 914/696–0833).

➤ BEER/WINE: **MIR Corporation** (✉ 85 S. Washington St., #210, Seattle, WA 98104, ☎ 206/624–7289 or 800/424–7289, FAX 206/624–7360).

➤ BICYCLING: **Backroads** (✉ 801 Cedar St., Berkeley, CA 94710-1800, ☎ 510/527–1555 or 800/462–2848, FAX 510-527–1444). **Butterfield & Robinson** (✉ 70 Bond St., Toronto, Ontario, Canada M5B 1X3, ☎ 416/864–1354 or 800/678–1147, FAX 416/864–0541). **Euro-Bike Tours** (✉ Box 990, De Kalb, IL 60115, ☎ 800/321–6060, FAX 815/758–8851). **Uniquely Europe** (✉ 1940 116th Ave. NE, Bellevue, WA 98004, ☎ 425/455–4445 or 800/927–3876, FAX 425/455–2111).

➤ CRUISING: **EuroCruises** (✉ 303 W. 13th St., New York, NY 10014-1207, ☎ 800/688–3876, FAX 212/366–4747).

➤ HISTORY & ART: **IST Cultural Tours** (✉ 225 W. 34th St., New York, NY 10122-0913, ☎ 212/563–1202 or 800/833–2111, FAX 212/594–6953). **Smithsonian Study Tours and Seminars** (✉ 1100 Jefferson Dr. SW, Room 3045, 20560, Washington, DC 20560, ☎ 202/357–4700, FAX 202/633–9250).

➤ NATURAL HISTORY: **Earthwatch** (✉ Box 9104, 680 Mount Auburn St., Watertown, MA 02272, ☎ 617/926–8200 or 800/776–0188, FAX 617/926–8532) for research expeditions. **Questers** (✉ 381 Park Ave. S, New York, NY 10016, ☎ 212/251–0444 or 800/468–8668, FAX 212/251–0890). **Victor Emanuel Nature Tours** (✉ Box 33008, Austin, TX 78764, ☎ 512/328–5221 or 800/328–8368, FAX 512/328–2919).

➤ PERFORMING ARTS: **Dailey-Thorp Travel** (✉ 330 W. 58th St., #610, New York, NY 10019-1817, ☎ 212/307–1555 or 800/998–4677, FAX 212/974–1420).

➤ SINGLES AND YOUNG ADULTS: **Club Europa** (✉ 802 W. Oregon St., Urbana, IL 61801, ☎ 217/344–5863 or 800/331–1882, FAX 217/344–4072). **Contiki Holidays** (✉ 300 Plaza Alicante, #900, Garden Grove, CA

92640, ☎ 714/740–0808 or 800/266–8454, FAX 714/740–0818).

➤ SPAS: **Great Spas of the World** (✉ 55 John St., New York, NY 10038, ☎ 212/267–5500 or 800/772–8463, FAX 212/571–0510). **Spa-Finders** (✉ 91 5th Ave., #301, New York, NY 10003-3039, ☎ 212/924–6800 or 800/255–7727).

➤ TRAIN TOURS: **Abercrombie & Kent** (☞ Group Tours, *above*).

➤ WALKING/HIKING: **Backroads** (☞ Bicycling, *above*). **Himalayan Travel** (✉ 110 Prospect St., Stamford, CT 06901, ☎ 203/359–3711 or 800/225–2380, FAX 203/359–3669). **Mountain Travel-Sobek** (✉ 6420 Fairmount Ave., El Cerrito, CA 94530, ☎ 510/527–8100 or 800/227–2384, FAX 510/525–7710). **Uniquely Europe** (☞ Bicycling, *above*).

TRAIN TRAVEL

Although standards have improved, on the whole they are far short of what is acceptable in the West. Trains are very busy, and it is rare to find one running less than full or almost so. All seven countries operate their own dining, buffet, and refreshment services. Always crowded, they tend to open and close at the whim of the staff. In Bulgaria and Hungary, couchette cars are second class only and can be little more than a hard bunk without springs and adequate bed linen. In Romania, there are first class couchettes (though they are comparable to second or third class compartments in more Westernized countries); these have room for two people and are relatively safe and clean. First class couchettes are also available on Czech and Slovak trains, and there are two types of second class couchettes. The cheaper have six hard beds per compartment; the slightly more expensive have three beds and a sink and are sex-segregated. Some of the most comfortable trains are the express trains in the Czech Republic, Hungary, Poland, Slovakia, and Slovenia—they're normally less crowded and more comfortable. (You should make a reservation.)

Although trains in Eastern and Central Europe can mean hours of sitting on a hard seat in a smoky car, traveling by rail is very inexpensive. Rail networks in all the Eastern and Central European countries are very extensive, though trains can be infuriatingly slow. You'll invariably enjoy interesting and friendly traveling company, however; most Eastern and Central Europeans are eager to hear about the West and to discuss the enormous changes in their own countries.

For information about fares and schedules and other country-specific train information, *see* Arriving and Departing and Getting Around in the A to Z section at the end of each country chapter.

CUTTING COSTS

To save money, **look into rail passes.** But be aware that if you don't plan to cover many miles you may come out ahead by buying individual tickets.

You can use the **European East Pass** on the national rail networks of Austria, the Czech Republic, Hungary, Poland, and Slovakia. The pass covers five days of unlimited first-class travel within a one-month period for $199. Additional travel days may be purchased.

You can also combine the East Pass with a national rail pass. The Bulgarian Flexipass costs $70 for three days of unlimited first-class travel within a one-month period. A pass for the Czech Republic costs $69 for five days of train travel within a 15-day period—far more than you'd spend on individual tickets. The Hungarian Flexipass costs $64 for five days of unlimited first-class train travel within a 15-day period or $80 for 10 days within a one-month period.

The **Balkan Flexipass** covers first-class train travel through Bulgaria and Romania, as well as Greece, Macedonia, Turkey, and Yugoslavia; there are passes for 5, 10, or 15 travel days in a one-month period for $152, $264, and $317, respectively.

Hungary is one of 17 countries in which you can **use Eurailpasses,** which provide unlimited first-class rail travel, in all of the participating countries, for the duration of the pass. If you plan to rack up the miles, get a standard pass. These are available for 15 days ($554), 21 days ($718), one month ($890), two months ($1,260), and three months ($1,558).

In addition to standard Eurailpasses, **ask about special rail-pass plans.** Among these are the Eurail Youthpass (for those under age 26), the Eurail Saverpass (which gives a discount for two or more people traveling together), a Eurail Flexipass (which allows a certain number of travel days within a set period), the Euraildrive Pass and the Europass Drive (which combines travel by train and rental car). Whichever pass you choose, remember that you must **purchase your pass before you leave** for Europe.

Many travelers assume that rail passes guarantee them seats on the trains they wish to ride. Not so. You need to **book seats ahead even if you are using a rail pass**; seat reservations are required on some European trains, particularly high-speed trains, and are a good idea on trains that may be crowded—particularly in summer on popular routes. You will also need a reservation if you purchase sleeping accommodations.

➤ INFORMATION AND PASSES: **Rail Europe** (✉ 500 Mamaroneck Ave., Harrison, NY 10528, ☎ 914/682–5172 or 800/438–7245, FAX 800/432–1329; ✉ 2087 Dundas E, Suite 106, Mississauga, Ontario L4X 1M2, ☎ 800/361–7245, FAX 905/602–4198). **DER Travel Services** (✉ 9501 W. Devon Ave., Rosemont, IL 60018, ☎ 800/782–2424, FAX 800/282–7474 for information; 800/860–9944 for brochures). **CIT Tours Corp.** (✉ 15 West 44th Street, 10th Floor, New York, NY 10036, ☎ 212/730–2400; 800/248–7245 in the U.S.; 800/387–0711; 800/361–7799 in Canada).

FROM THE U.K.

There are no direct trains from London. You can take a direct train from Paris to Warsaw or via Frankfurt to Prague (daily) or from Berlin to Warsaw or via Dresden to Prague (5 times a day). Vienna is a good starting point for Prague, Brno, or Bratislava. There are three trains a day to Prague from Vienna's Südbahnhof (South Station) via Brno (5 hours). Bratislava can be reached from Vienna by a 67-minute shuttle service, which runs every two hours during the day. You should check out times and routes before leaving. Sofia has service to Bucharest, Budapest and Vienna, but for travelers without the necessary visas, it can be a long, out-of-the-way journey to skirt Serbia.

TRAVEL AGENCIES

A good travel agent puts your needs first. Look for an agency that has been in business at least five years, emphasizes customer service, and has someone on staff who specializes in your destination. In addition, **make sure the agency belongs to a professional trade organization.** The American Society of Travel Agents (ASTA), with 27,000 agents in some 170 countries, is the largest and most influential in the field. Operating under the motto "Integrity in Travel," it maintains and enforces a strict code of ethics and will step in to help mediate any agent-client disputes if necessary. ASTA also maintains a Web site that includes a directory of agents. (If a travel agency is also acting as your tour operator, *see* Buyer Beware *in* Tours & Packages, *above.*)

➤ LOCAL AGENT REFERRALS: **American Society of Travel Agents** (ASTA; ☎ 800/965–2782 24-hr hot line, FAX 703/684–8319, www.astanet.com). **Association of British Travel Agents** (✉ 68–71 Newman St., London W1P 4AH, U.K., ☎ 020/7637–2444, FAX 020/7637–0713, information@abta.co.uk, www.abtanet.com). **Association of Canadian Travel Agents** (✉ 1729 Bank St., Suite 201, Ottawa, Ontario K1V 7Z5, Canada, ☎ 613/237–3657, FAX 613/521–0805, acta.ntl@sympatico.ca). **Australian Federation of Travel Agents** (✉ Level 3, 309 Pitt St., Sydney 2000, Australia, ☎ 02/9264–3299, FAX 02/9264–1085, www.afta.com.au). **Travel Agents' Association of New Zealand** (✉ Box 1888, Wellington 10033, New Zealand, ☎ 04/499–0104, FAX 04/499–0827, taanz@tiasnet.co.nz).

VISITOR INFORMATION

➤ BULGARIA: **Balkan USA/Affordable Europe Vacations** (✉ 20 E. 46th St., New York, NY 10017, ☎ 212/338–6838, FAX 212/338–6830); in the U.K. **Balkan Tourist** (✉ Osbourne Hills, 111 Bartholomew Rd., London NW5 2BJ, ☎ 0171/485–5280, FAX 0171/485–5864).

➤ CZECH REPUBLIC: **Czech Tourist Authority** (in the U.S.: ✉ 1109–1111 Madison Ave., New York, NY 10028, ☎ 212/288–0830, FAX 212/288–0971, www.czechcenter.com; in Canada: ✉ Czech Airlines office, Simpson Tower, 401 Bay St., Suite 1510, Toronto, Ontario M5H 2YA, ☎ 416/363–3174, FAX 416/363–0239; in the U.K.: ✉ 95 Great Portland St., London W1N 5RA, ☎ 0171/291–9925, FAX 0171/436–8300).

➤ HUNGARY: In the United States and Canada: **Hungarian National Tourist Office** (✉ 150 E. 58th St., New York, NY 10155, ☎ 212/355–0240, FAX 212/207–4103). In Canada: **Hungarian Consulate General Office** (✉ 121 Bloor St. E, Suite 1115, Toronto M4W3M5, Ontario, ☎ 416/923–8981, FAX 416/923–2732). In the United Kingdom: **Hungarian National Tourist Board** (✉ c/o Embassy of the Republic of Hungary, Commercial Section, 46 Eaton Pl., London, SW1X 8AL, ☎ 0171/823–1032 or 0171/823–1055, FAX 0171/823–1459).

➤ POLAND: **Polish National Tourist Office** (in the U.S. and Canada: ✉ 275 Madison Ave., Suite 1711, New York, NY 10016, ☎ 212/338–9412, FAX 212/338–9283; in the U.K.: ✉ Remo House, 1st floor, 310–312 Regent St., London W1R 5AJ, ☎ 0171/580–8811, FAX 0171/580–8866).

➤ ROMANIA: **Romanian Tourism Promotion Office** (in the U.S. and Canada: ✉ 14 East 38th St., 12th floor, New York, NY 10016, ☎ 212/545–8484, FAX 212/251–0429, www.rezq.com/ronto; in the U.K.: ✉ 83A Marylebone High St., London W1M 3DE, ☎ 0171/224–3692, FAX 0171/935–6435).

➤ SLOVAKIA: In the U.S.: **The Slovak Information Center** (✉ 406 E. 67th St., New York, NY 10021, ☎ 212/737–3971, FAX 212/737–3454). In Canada: **Slovak Culture and Information Center** (✉ 12 Birch Ave., Toronto, Ontario M4V 1C8, ☎ 416/925–0008, FAX 416/925–0009). In the U.K.: **Embassy of the Slovak Republic** (✉ Information Dept., 25 Kensington Palace Gardens, London W8 4QY, ☎ 0171/243–0803, FAX 0171/727–5824).

➤ SLOVENIA: In the U.S.: **Slovenian Tourist Office** (✉ 345 East 12th St., New York, NY 10003, ☎ 212/358–9686, FAX 212/358–9025). In the U.K.: **Slovenian Tourist Office** (✉ 49 Conduit St., London W1R 9FB, ☎ 0207/287–7133, FAX 0207/287–5476).

➤ U.S. GOVERNMENT ADVISORIES: **U.S. Department of State** (✉ Overseas Citizens Services Office, Room 4811 N.S., 2201 C St. NW, Washington, DC 20520, ☎ 202/647–5225 for interactive hot line, 301/946–4400 for computer bulletin board, FAX 202/647–3000 for interactive hot line); enclose with inquiries a self-addressed, stamped, business-size envelope.

WEB SITES

Do check out the World Wide Web when you're planning. You'll find everything from current weather forecasts to virtual tours of famous cities. Fodor's Web site, www.fodors.com, is a great place to start your online travels. When you see a 🖱 in this book, go to www.fodors.com/urls for an up-to-date link to that destination's site.

➤ SUGGESTED WEB SITES

Bulgaria: **Ministry of Trade and Tourism** (www.mtt.govrn.bg/tourinfo/). Czech Republic: **Czech Tourist Authority** (www.visitczech.cz). Hungary: **Live Budapest** (www.livebudapest.com). Poland: **Poland National Tourist Office** (www.polandtour.org). Romania: **Romania Tourist Promotion Office** (www.rezq.com/ronto). Slovakia: **Interactive Slovakia** (nic.savba.sk/logos/interactive/list.html). Slovenia: **Slovenia Tourism Board** (www.slovenia-tourism.si/).

WHEN TO GO

The tourist season generally runs from April or May through October; spring and fall combine good weather with a more bearable level of tourism. The ski season lasts from mid-December through March. Outside the mountain resorts you will encounter few other visitors; you'll have the opportunity to see the region covered in snow, but many of the sights are closed, and it can get very, very cold. If you're not a skier, try visiting the Giant Mountain of Bohemia, the High Tatras in Slovakia and Poland, and the Romanian Carpathians in late spring or fall; the colors are dazzling, and you'll have the hotels and restaurants pretty much to yourself. Bear in mind that many attractions are closed November through March.

Prague and Budapest are beautiful year-round, but avoid midsummer (especially July and August) and the Christmas and Easter holidays, when the two cities are choked with visitors. Warsaw, too, suffers a heavy influx of tourists during the summer season, though not on quite the same grand scale. Lake Balaton in Hungary becomes a mob scene in July and August. In Slovenia, the Adriatic coast is terribly busy through midsummer: Better to visit in June or September, or head for the mountain lakes of Triglav National Park instead. In Bulgaria, the best summer destinations are the gorgeous Black Sea fishing villages, or the medieval mountain towns in the interior, where cool breezes and sports opportunities make for a refreshing, if rugged, summer holiday. At the opposite end of the spectrum, Bucharest and Sofia are rarely crowded, even at the height of summer. In July and August, however, the weather in these capitals sometimes borders on stifling.

For additional country-specific information, *see* When to Tour following the Great Itineraries at the beginning of each country chapter.

CLIMATE

The following are the average daily maximum and minimum temperatures for major cities in the region.

Forecasts: WEATHER CHANNEL CONNECTION (☎ 900/932–8437), 95¢ PER MINUTE FROM A TOUCH-TONE PHONE.

BRATISLAVA

Jan.	36F	2C	May	70F	21C	Sept.	72F	22C
	27	– 3		52	11		54	12
Feb.	39F	4C	June	75F	24C	Oct.	59F	15C
	28	– 2		57	14		45	7
Mar.	48F	9C	July	79F	26C	Nov.	46F	8C
	34	1		61	16		37	3
Apr.	61F	16C	Aug.	79F	26C	Dec.	39F	4C
	43	6		61	16		32	0

BUCHAREST

Jan.	34F	1C	May	74F	23C	Sept.	78F	25C
	19	– 7		51	10		52	11
Feb.	38F	4C	June	81F	27C	Oct.	65F	18C
	23	– 5		57	14		43	6
Mar.	50F	10C	July	86F	30C	Nov.	49F	10C
	30	– 1		60	16		35	2
Apr.	64F	18C	Aug.	85F	30C	Dec.	39F	4C
	41	5		59	15		26	– 3

BUDAPEST

Jan.	34F	1C	May	72F	22C	Sept.	73F	23C
	25	– 4		52	11		54	12
Feb.	39F	4C	June	79F	26C	Oct.	61F	16C
	28	– 2		59	15		45	7
Mar.	50F	10C	July	82F	28C	Nov.	46F	8C
	36	2		61	16		37	3
Apr.	63F	17C	Aug.	81F	27C	Dec.	39F	4C
	25	– 4		61	16		30	– 1

LJUBLJANA

Jan.	36F	2C	May	68F	20C	Sept.	71F	22C
	25	– 4		48	9		51	11
Feb.	41F	5C	June	75F	24C	Oct.	59F	15C
	25	– 4		54	12		43	6
Mar.	50F	10C	July	80F	27C	Nov.	47F	8C
	32	0		57	14		36	2
Apr.	60F	15C	Aug.	78F	26C	Dec.	39F	4C
	40	4		57	14		30	– 1

PRAGUE

Jan.	36F	2C	May	66F	19C	Sept.	68F	20C
	25	– 4		46	8		50	10
Feb.	37F	3C	June	72F	22C	Oct.	55F	13C
	27	– 3		52	11		41	5
Mar.	46F	8C	July	75F	24C	Nov.	46F	8C
	32	0		55	13		36	2
Apr.	58F	14C	Aug.	73F	23C	Dec.	37F	3C
	39	4		55	13		28	– 2

SOFIA

Jan.	35F	2C	May	69F	21C	Sept.	70F	22C
	25	– 4		50	10		52	11
Feb.	39F	4C	June	76F	24C	Oct.	63F	17C
	27	– 3		56	14		46	8
Mar.	50F	10C	July	81F	27C	Nov.	48F	9C
	33	1		60	16		37	3
Apr.	60F	16C	Aug.	79F	26C	Dec.	38F	4C
	42	5		59	15		28	– 2

WARSAW

Jan.	32F	0C	May	68F	20C	Sept.	66F	19C
	21	– 6		48	9		50	10
Feb.	32F	0C	June	73F	23C	Oct.	55F	13C
	21	– 6		54	12		41	5
Mar.	43F	6C	July	75F	24C	Nov.	43F	6C
	28	– 2		59	15		34	1
Apr.	54F	12C	Aug.	73F	23C	Dec.	36F	2C
	37	3		57	14		27	– 3

1 DESTINATION: EASTERN AND CENTRAL EUROPE

WHAT A DIFFERENCE A DECADE MAKES

DIVERSITY HAND IN HAND with unity—today, as for centuries past, this paradox underlies the special character of Eastern and Central Europe. The region is so diverse that it might seem to have no unifying features at all. From the Baltic to the Black Sea, from the European heartland to the Asian frontier, it presents a historical and ethnic crazy quilt that can both attract and confound you.

But what a difference a decade makes! Not very long ago, most outsiders would have lumped all the region's countries into a single pile of unlikely compatriots under the Soviet umbrella. The Soviet empire, however, was only the last in a string of imperial overlords that have molded this part of Europe for two millennia. Rome, Byzantium, Ottoman Turkey, Austria-Hungary, and Nazi Germany all left their indelible marks. In the short span of time since the epochal year of 1989, the states of the region have each been free, as hardly ever before in their long histories, to find their own paths. The results have been successful in some cases, as with Poland, Hungary, and the Czech Republic, new NATO members who are knocking on the European Union's door. Elsewhere, long-suppressed tensions in Bosnia and Kosovo exploded into Europe's worst conflict since World War II.

Where countries have chosen the road of peaceful development, travel today is far more comfortable than it used to be. Surly service and grim, cell-like accommodations are becoming little more than bad memories, at least in the more prosperous western half of the region. Here, trains and buses are far more comfortable, the phones work, and ATMs have sprung up everywhere. You'll still find a sense of exoticism further east, in the lands shaped by Ottoman Muslim and Orthodox Christian influences. Change here is happening with dizzying speed, largely because of launching from a much lower platform. Data from Bulgaria, for example, indicate that the Internet there reached fewer than 1,000 people in 1995. By 2000 the soaring figure had already passed 300,000.

In every country of the region, local peoples have forged their own cultures while drawing freely on the contributions of other groups sharing the same territory. Ancient Greeks, Romans, Thracians, and Dacians left their footprints in Bulgaria and Romania. In Central Europe, from Bohemia to Transylvania, from Poland to Slovenia, the touch of German and Austrian culture is found everywhere, in Gothic churches, in Baroque manors, in institutions and customs. Jewish communities maintain a tenuous hold, though one that in many places may not survive the current generation. Another group, stateless as the Jews once were, still ekes a living in every country of the region: the much-reviled Roma, or Gypsies, who are only just beginning to nurture a sense of themselves as a distinct people.

In the 1930s, also a period of great social change in these lands, the Austrian novelist Joseph Roth wrote his masterly elegy for Austria-Hungary, *The Radetzky March*. In Central Europe before the First World War, Roth mused, "Anything that grew took its time growing, and anything that perished took a long time to be forgotten. But everything that had once existed left its traces."

Three empires may have fallen since the period Roth was recalling, but today, throughout this fascinating land, the traces are still there to find and follow.

— Ky Krauthamer

WHAT'S WHERE

Bulgaria

The southernmost frontier of Eastern and Central Europe, Bulgaria borders Greece and Turkey to the south and the Black Sea to the east; to the west are the territories of the former Yugoslavia. Covering approximately 111,000 square km (43,000 square mi), Bulgaria has a population of about 9 million. **Sofia,** the bustling, cosmopolitan capital, sits on the Sofia Plain in western Bulgaria and is surrounded by rugged mountain ranges. The wooded and mountainous interior is sprinkled with attractive "museum" villages and ancient towns. In the **Balkan Range** in the north is the old Bulgarian capital of **Veliko Târnovo.** South of there, in the foothills of the Balkan Range, you'll find the verdant Valley of Roses, and beyond that **Plovdiv,** the country's second-largest city and reputed intellectual center. South of Plovdiv are the **Rhodope Mountains,** whose villages and monasteries keep alive many of Bulgaria's folk traditions. South of Sofia are the **Pirin** and **Rila** mountains, the highest range of mountains between the Alps and the Caucasus, and home to two national parks and well-established ski resorts. The sunny, sandy beaches of Bulgaria's **Black Sea coast** attract visitors from all over Europe; the historic port city of **Varna** makes a good base for exploring the region.

Czech Republic

Planted firmly in the heart of Central Europe—Prague is some 320 km (200 mi) north*west* of Vienna—the Czech Republic is culturally and historically more closely linked to Western, particularly Germanic, culture than any of its former East-bloc brethren. Encompassing some 79,000 square km (30,500 square mi), the Czech Republic is made up of the regions of Bohemia in the west (sharing long borders with Germany and Austria) and Moravia in the east. Moravia's White Carpathian Mountains (Bílé Karpaty) form the border with the young Slovak Republic, which broke its 74-year-old union with the Czechs in 1993 to establish itself as an independent nation. With a population of over 10 million, the Czech Republic is one of the most densely populated countries of Eastern and Central Europe.

The capital city of **Prague** sits on the Vltava (Moldau) River, roughly in the middle of Bohemian territory. A stunning city of human dimensions, Prague offers the traveler a lesson in almost all the chief architectural styles of Western European history; relatively unscathed by major wars, most of Prague's buildings are remarkably well preserved. **Southern Bohemia** is dotted with stunning medieval towns, several of which played important roles in the Hussite religious wars of the 15th century. The two most notable towns are Tábor and Český Krumlov. **Western Bohemia,** especially the far western hills near the German border, remains justly famous for its mineral springs and spa towns, in particular Karlovy Vary, Mariánské Lázně, and Františkovy Lázně. **Northern Bohemia,** with its rolling hills and the not-so-giant **Krkonoše** (Giant Mountains), is a hiker's and camper's delight. The wine country in the south of **Moravia,** dotted with attractive towns such as Znojmo, rises gently toward the extensive forested hills in the north and east, where bear and, some say, wolves roam. The country's second city, **Brno,** offers its own array of historical and cultural attractions.

Hungary

Sandwiched between Slovakia and Romania, Hungary was the Austro-Hungarian Empire's eastern frontier. Measuring approximately 93,000 square km (36,000 square mi), with a population of more than 10 million, it is the geographical link between the Slavic regions of Central Europe and the Black Sea region's amalgam of Orthodox and Islamic cultures. The heart of the nation is **Budapest,** in the northwest on the Danube, just 1½ hours from Bratislava in Slovakia and under three hours from Vienna. Just north of Budapest, the Danube River forms a gentle, heart-shape curve along which lie the romantic and historic towns of the region called the **Danube Bend.** Southwest of Budapest are the vineyards, quaint villages, and popular, developed summer resorts around **Lake Balaton,** the largest lake in Central Europe. The more rural and gently mountainous stretch of **northern Hungary** also includes the handsome, vibrant town of Eger and the famous wine village of Tokaj; the contrastingly flat and dry expanses of the Great Plain, in the east, are known for traditions of horsemanship and agriculture and anchored by the interesting and lively cities of Kecskemét and Debrecen. The verdant, rolling countryside of **Transdanubia** stretches west of the Danube to the borders of Austria, Slovenia, and Croatia; in the northern hills nestle the beautifully restored towns of Sopron and Kőszeg and, in the south, the dynamic, beautiful city of Pécs.

Poland

The northernmost country in Central Europe, Poland has a long coastline on the Baltic Sea. A vast nation of 312,677 square km (119,755 square mi), Poland is made up primarily of a great plain in the north and central region and a small but dramatic stretch of mountainous territory to the south (on its border with Slovakia and the Czech Republic). **Warsaw,** just to the east of the country's center, has rebuilt itself several times over the course of its tumultuous history and since the end of communism has been changing faster than any other city or region in Poland.

Travelers interested in art and architecture shouldn't miss **Kraków** in the south and the historic small towns of the surrounding region known as Little Poland. Outdoor enthusiasts will want to move on to the west and south, to the **Podhale** region and the **Tatra Mountains.** Many of the natural wonders and recreational areas of these two regions are within two hours' drive of downtown Kraków.

Gdańsk and the north offer wide-open vistas, long stretches of coast, great lakes dotting large stretches of forest, and historic cities and castles rising up from the plain. This is a great area for enjoying water sports, hiking, and camping. **Lublin** and the east offer a trip back into the traditional way of life of rural Central Europe: small towns, whose great age was in the Renaissance but which have slept since, vast palaces of the nobility, and gently varied countryside where the tractor has not yet replaced the horse.

Apart from the far southwest and a few park areas around **Poznań** and **Wrocław,** the countryside of western Poland is flat and somewhat monotonous—lots of dairy farms and hay fields. Poznań and Wrocław have fine historic centers and a thriving cultural life.

Romania

Although Romania continues to struggle economically, it is one of the most beautiful countries on the continent. Bordered by Bulgaria, the Black Sea, the Republic of Moldova, Ukraine, Hungary, and Serbia, its 238,000 sq km (92,000 sq mi) encompass cities with intact medieval districts and villages where traditional culture thrives. From **Bucharest,** the capital, you can explore the province of **Transylvania,** where cities such as Braşov, Sighişoara, and Sibiu have preserved their historic core. In the northwest, **Maramureş** county transports you back to the past with hand-carved wooden gates, tiny wooden churches, and villagers in traditional dress.

Bucovina, in the province of Moldavia to the northeast, has five 15th and 16th century monasteries whose exterior walls are covered, ground to eaves, with glorious frescoes. UNESCO has conferred World Heritage Monument status on them. Bucovina also claims lovely villages where colorful traditional houses are common and festivals keep old customs alive.

In the east, the **Black Sea** coast claims a string of hotels where sea and sand offer a respite from sightseeing. Roman ruins, wineries, and the port city of **Constanța** all merit a look. The prime attraction is the **Danube Delta,** Europe's largest wetland and home to 300-plus bird species.

Slovakia

Having declared its independence from the Czech Republic in 1993, the smaller and more agrarian Slovak Republic has been struggling to revive its economic life and adjust to new post–Cold War realities. The 49,000 square km (19,000 square mi) of Slovak territory are both less urbanized and less industrialized than that of the country's Moravian and Bohemian neighbors to the west. **Bratislava,** the capital, lies on the Danube in the southwestern corner of the country, just a few miles away from both the Austrian and Hungarian borders. Its small Old Town is charming and contains several buildings and churches of note (especially to those interested in the history of the Austro-Hungarian Empire), but Slovakia's real assets lie to the north and east. **Central Slovakia,** a hilly region crossed by hiking trails, is rich in folklore and medieval history. The **High Tatra Mountains** attract skiers, campers, and mountaineers from all across Europe; they are a meeting ground for tourists from east and west. And relatively undiscovered **eastern Slovakia** lures travelers with its country lanes—watch out for herds of sheep and gaggles of geese—fairy-tale-like villages, castles, and wooden churches.

Slovenia

Geographically, politically, and culturally, Slovenia lies in a fascinating corner of Europe: Here the former Yugoslavia meets the former Soviet bloc meets the gradually expanding European Union.

Covering a territory of just 20,300 square km (7,900 square mi), Slovenia has a population of 2 million, 90% of whom are Slovene; the remaining 10% is made up primarily of Italians, Hungarians, and natives of the other former Yugoslav republics.

The refined yet progressive capital, **Ljubljana,** lies in the center of the country. In less than three hours you can reach the border with Italy to the west, Austria to the north, Hungary to the northeast, Croatia to the southeast, and the Adriatic coast to the southwest.

The greatest draw for tourists, and the pride of Slovenes, lies northeast of Ljubljana. The beautiful **Triglav National Park** and the **Soča Valley** offer a dramatic alpine landscape, perfect for skiing in winter, and hiking, biking, and water sports in summer. In contrast, the **Adriatic Coast and Karst region,** southeast of the capital, provide sea and sunshine, plus intriguing underground caves.

East of Ljubljana the River Krka forms the **Krka Valley,** winding its way through gently undulating farmland dotted with lonely monasteries and medieval castles. Northeast of the capital lies the country's second largest city, Maribor. The region of **Maribor, Ptuj, and the Haloze Hills** produces some of the finest Slovenian wines.

NEW AND NOTEWORTHY

Bulgaria

The pace of change is evident every day in Bulgaria—newspapers tout (or lament) the advent of new economic policies, the opening of new shops and restaurants, and the laborious efforts by the government to privatize state holdings and court EU membership. Suddenly the old coins are obsolete, the price of bread has quadrupled, and neon signs glow with the names of foreign companies. For citizens of this small Balkan country recovering from a *peaceful* revolution in 1997, recent times have been hard and chaotic, though from a historical perspective, undoubtedly interesting.

Despite the hardships facing local people in an economy where the average monthly salary is stalled at about US$300, the **tourism industry is developing rapidly**—especially since tourism is the most immediate hope for incoming revenue. Most cities now have privately owned luxury hotels, and restaurants, bars, and discos mirror the standards of the West. Prices remain low, so Bulgaria is a great destination for bargain hunters.

The pace of change is fastest in Sofia, where new businesses (and Western franchises) have established a beachhead. A **new telephone system** is being installed in Sofia and its suburbs; many numbers are changing with the adoption of digital lines. The **Sofia subway,** once slated for a 1996 grand opening, is still a muddy eyesore. Elsewhere, many parts of Bulgaria seem to exist outside of time, oblivious to the rapid political and social changes going on around them.

Czech Republic

At the turn of the millennium signs abound that the country is pulling itself out of a three-year slump. "What slump?" visitors who see only Prague might ask, dazzled by the booming capital. The truth is that large parts of the Czech Republic, particularly along the northern industrial belt, remain in deep decline. Promising indicators are that inflation and joblessness seem to be in check.

Industrial reform continues to gain momentum, and the country is on track to **join the European Union.** The Czech Republic, along with Hungary and Poland, became **NATO member states** in 1999, thus accomplishing a major goal for all three nations, but at the price of alienating Russia, their former "socialist brother." **President Václav Havel** ends his final term in 2003, and as yet there is no clear successor in sight.

Although visitor-swamped Prague hardly needed any more publicity, its role as one of nine European Cities of Culture in 2000 encouraged modest extra funding for the arts from public and private donors. A new **museum of Central European modern art** was set to open on Kampa Island by year's end.

Outside the capital, tourism also keeps growing, although more slowly than regional planners would like. UNESCO spotlighted the country's inexhaustible legacy of architectural splendor by giving

World Heritage Site status to the Litomyšl Château in 1999. There are now nine Czech towns, buildings, and cultural landscapes on the prestigious list. In Bohemia's far north, a scenic stretch of sandstone labyrinths and gorges now bears the name **Bohemian Switzerland National Park.** The picturesque region borders Germany's Saxon Switzerland National Park.

The number of **hotels and restaurants** keeps pace with the growing number of visitors. This is even true of Prague, now firmly established among Europe's leading tourist destinations. The arrival of visitors and long-term residents from all over the world has brought forth new restaurants offering Cajun, Indian, vegetarian, and other exotic fare alongside the traditional ones serving pork and dumplings.

Prague remains the hub of tourism and cultural life. As ever, the city is a dream for classical-music lovers and opera fans. The annual Prague Spring music festival, which even before the collapse ofthe Communist government was one of the great events on the European calendar, is attracting record numbers of music lovers. Meanwhile, the Karlovy Vary International Film Festival grows ever more popular with the public—many of whom sleep on park benches during festival week every July.

Hungary

Two years into **NATO membership** and expected to join the European Union by around mid-decade (the pundits differ on the probable timing), Hungary continues to strengthen both its international position and its internal assets. The triple excitement of the year 2000—which coincided with the **Magyar Millennium,** the 1,000th anniversary of Hungary's founding as a state, and marked a decade as a multi-party democracy—is still in the air. Much important restoration work was completed in the year 2000, and more is underway.

Grand old **Budapest** is seeing more and more development, from private restoration of crumbling buildings to city-funded projects, such as the increase in pedestrian-only zones. Political tensions between the governments of capital and country may have stalled construction of a new National Theater and a fourth metro line, but Hungary's overall stability and continued attraction of foreign investment have fostered ongoing revitalization. Indeed, theater and café culture seems no worse for politics. While many Hungarians can hardly afford to go out to eat, an emerging middle class has gradually instilled Budapest with confidence unseen since the heady days of the Austro-Hungarian empire a century ago.

Slowly but surely, Hungary continues to **improve its infrastructure,** helping it fill its increasingly important role as a link between Eastern and Western Europe. Over the next several years, major highways will continue to be upgraded and extended, and the airport in Budapest has seen major expansion in the past few years. Last but not least, the once-antiquated telephone system is being overhauled. While progress is apparent, travelers should note that in Hungary, silence at the other end of the line is still assumed to be a broken connection rather than a crank call.

As the **May 2002 elections** approach, the main parties at Hungary's helm—the center-right FIDESZ (Alliance of Young Democrats–Hungarian Civic Party) and the junior governing partner, the more right-wing Smallholders—are preparing to face off against the MSZP (Hungarian Socialist Party), which they barely managed to oust from power in the 1998 elections. What with its vast resources and nostalgia in many voters for the "certainties" of the past, the MSZP, whose leadership includes mostly former Communists, remains a formidable force.

At press time, Hungary's annual inflation rate had dropped under 10% from the 25% of five years earlier, and with continued significant devaluation of the forint, exchange rates keep improving for visitors from North America and Great Britain. Yet, while Hungary remains a bargain compared to Western Europe, strictly rock-bottom prices are a thing of the past.

Poland

Poland's political and economic profile is becoming increasingly attractive to foreigners. Along with the Czech Republic and Hungary, the country became a member of **NATO** in 1999. It is also currently in negotiations with the **European Union** and in the process of harmonizing its laws to EU standards. Poland is aiming to become a member of the EU by 2003.

Transportation both to and within Poland has been on a steady upswing. **New terminals** have opened at most major airports, and public transportation has been expanded by a network of express buses that serve the bigger cities. Major highways are being widenedand improved, albeit slowly; gasoline is readily available; and major car-rental companies are competing to offer better prices.

The financial services and banking sectors have been slower to change, but **credit cards** are now accepted in almost all tourist-class hotels, restaurants, and large stores. In major cities it is also becoming much easier to cash **traveler's checks** and to use cash cards (such as American Express or Eurocheque) in the growing network of ATMs. In 1999 Poland introduced a value-added tax (VAT) refund for visitors. Refund services are available at all border crossings as well as Warsaw and Kraków airports.

Romania

If you visited Romania years ago, expect a pleasant surprise. While the countryside remains as lovely as ever, most tourist services and facilities have improved immeasurably. As a result, tourism figures from North America tripled in the last decade and have climbed 10% annually in the past five years.

Improvements begin at your likely arrival point, **Otopeni Airport.** Avio-bridges now eliminate the need for busing between terminals and aircraft, and customs procedures are speedier. **Tarom,** the Romanian national carrier, has upgraded its domestic and international fleets. The airline now serves Montréal as well as New York and Chicago.

Bucharest's main train station, **Gara de Nord,** has been spiffed up with well-posted train information, a McDonald's, and a significant decrease in the number of vagrants. Newer trains, designated **Intercity,** provide a more comfortable trip. Pollution controls are now in effect for trucks, making road travel more pleasant though road maintenance needs improvement.

Many **hotels** have changed ownership, resulting in major renovations. Although the need still exists for good lodging outside the main cities, small hotels are opening in once-remote places such as Maramureş. New **restaurants** and upscale **bars** proliferate in principal cities; elsewhere, dining choices continue to be limited.

Slovakia

Under the leadership of a new pro-democratic government, Slovakia has been readmitted to the group of 14 Eastern and Central European countries negotiating for membership in the European Union. **Hotels and restaurants** have been privatized, and as a result many have seen improvements in the quality of service and ambience. Almost all cities now have pensions, often housed in beautifully renovated historic buildings. Eastern Slovakia, known for its natural beauty and unusual architecture, remains largely uncharted territory but can now offer accommodations that are up to Western standards.

Slovenia

Economically, Slovenia has a **high standard of living** compared to other Eastern and Central European countries, and looks set to become a member of the European Union, possibly as early as 2002.

Since gaining independence in 1991, low inflation, the stability of the Slovenian tolar, and international credibility have led to **increased prosperity,** and the new generation of multilingual, highly skilled Slovenes seems to have everything going for it.

Despite an image problem, caused by the conflicts that have plagued the sister republics that once made up Yugoslavia, the **tourist industry is thriving.** Many hotels have been modernized, though care has been taken to conserve buildings of historic value. Dining out, if you don't mind paying for it, can be a joy, especially in the capital. Several museums have installed audiovisual presentations that transcend language barriers. As of 2001, Telekom Slovenia will have introduced a **new telephone number system** compatible with EU standards: There will be six regional codes, and each number will have seven digits.

FODOR'S CHOICE

Dining

Bulgaria

★ **Nad Aleyata, Zad Shkafut, Sofia.** You can dine among diplomats in this old brick house; the menu shares the clientele's international bent. $$$$

★ **La Rotisserie du Tzar Ivan Assen II, Sofia.** Come here for a fine meal and old-fashioned elegance, all at pleasantly affordable prices. The Bulgarian and Continental menu emphasizes seasonal specialities. $$$

Czech Republic

★ **V Zátiší, Prague.** In one of the city's oldest and calmest squares—the restaurant's name means "still life"—this refined dining room offers tantalizing international specialties and wonderful service. $$$$

★ **Lobkovická, Prague.** This atmospheric, 17th-century restaurant has an imaginative menu and an enticing roster of Moravian wines. $$$

★ **Kavárna Slavia, Prague.** To lap up some of the artistic scene, come to this Art Deco café; the views of the Prague Castle and the National Theater aren't too shabby either. $

Hungary

★ **Gundel, Budapest.** Established at the turn of the 20th century, Budapest's most famous restaurant continues its legacy of Old World grandeur and elegant cuisine. $$$$

★ **Művészinas, Budapest.** The chef at this romantic, bustling bistro in downtown Pest has a flair for taking typical Hungarian dishes to new heights. $$$

★ **Aranysárkány, Szentendre.** Its small size and turbulent open kitchen give this restaurant a decidedly convivial atmosphere. $$

★ **Hortobágyi Csárda, Hortobágy.** A favorite of wayfarers since it opened in 1699, the Great Plain's legendary old inn consistently serves excellent traditional fare. $

Poland

★ **Belvedere, Warsaw.** It doesn't get much more romantic than this: exquisitely prepared Polish cuisine in an elegant candlelit orangerie in Warsaw's serene Łazienki Park. $$$$

★ **Wierzynek, Kraków.** Poland's most famous restaurant, in a room glittering with chandeliers and silver, has been charming diners since the 14th century. $$$$

★ **Pod Łososiem, Gdańsk.** This historic Old Town inn is named for its strong suit: fish (though there's also fowl on the menu). $$$

Romania

★ **Club Contele Dracula, Bucharest.** Tasty Romanian dishes are served amid a decor that's faithful to the Dracula novel and its inspiration, Prince Vlad Ţepeş. $$$

★ **Coliba Haiducilor, Poina Braşov.** This updated version of a traditional Romanian hunting lodge, specializing in bear, venison, and chicken served flaming on a stake, will make you feel like you've just returned from a wild-boar hunt. $$–$$$

Slovakia

★ **Kláštorná vináreň, Bratislava.** Sample the best of the happy—and spicy—merger of Hungarian and Slovak cuisines at this dark and intimate monastery wine cellar not far from the banks of the Danube. $$$

★ **Restaurant Koliba, Starý Smokovec.** This charming, rustic spot on the slopes of the Tatra Mountains serves up grilled specialties to the accompaniment of Gypsy folk music. $$

★ **Slovenská reštauracia, Poprad.** The very best of eastern Slovakian comfort food is served in a cheery village-style atmosphere. $

Slovenia

★ **AS, Ljubljana.** This excellent fish restaurant has old-fashioned ambience but takes a modern approach to good food and wine. $$$

★ **Gostilna Lectar, Radovljica.** One of Slovenia's best-known restaurants, Gostlina Lectar serves local dishes by candlelight, not far from the sublime Lake Bled. $$$

★ **Ribič, Portorož.** A perfect place for a summer evening—take a table in the garden and indulge in locally caught fresh fish. $$

★ **Spajza, Ljubljana.** Informal and bohemian in appearance, Spajza offers a creative menu featuring the season's best fresh ingredients. $$

Lodging

Bulgaria

★ **Grand Hotel Varna, Sveti Konstantin.** The best hotel on Bulgaria's Black Sea coast, the Varna offers its guests spa services in addition to lodging. *$$$$*

★ **Sheraton Sofia Hotel Balkan, Sofia.** It's hard to beat the central location of this first-class hotel. *$$$$*

Czech Republic

★ **Grandhotel Pupp, Karlovy Vary.** Expansive and redolent of a more refined era, the Pupp is the undoubted queen of this gracious spa town. *$$$–$$$$*

★ **Dům U Červeného lva, Prague.** Spare decor sets off beautiful antiques and painted-beam ceilings in this polished Baroque building. *$$$*

★ **Růže, Český Krumlov.** Some rooms in this refurbished monastery on a hill facing Krumlov Castle afford stunning views of the loveliest of Bohemian towns. *$$$*

★ **Pension 189 Karel Bican, Tábor.** This lovely family-run guest house dates from the 14th century but has all the modern conveniences you've come to expect in the 21st. *$$*

Hungary

★ **Danubius Hotel Gellért, Budapest.** This grand 1918 Art Nouveau hotel on the Danube at the foot of Gellért Hill is the pride of Budapest. Housing an extensive, elegant complex of marble bathing facilities fed by ancient curative springs, it is also one of Europe's most famous Old World spas. *$$$$*

★ **Epona Rider Village, Máta.** You don't have to rough it to spend a night out on the wide open spaces of Hungary's Great Plain; this luxurious modern complex offers sparkling facilities and world-class equestrian entertainment. *$$$$*

★ **Hotel Palota, Miskolc-Lillafüred.** This turreted castle in a magical setting in the forested hills of northern Hungary provides comfortable lodging and a perfect base for walking and fishing. *$$$*

★ **Kulturinov, Budapest.** Set on one of historic Castle Hill's most famous cobblestone squares, this neo-Baroque castle provides budget accommodations in a priceless location. *$*

Poland

★ **Bristol, Warsaw.** Warsaw's only truly legendary hotel, the Bristol has emerged from a decade of extensive refurbishing and is once again pampering guests with luxurious service. *$$$$*

★ **Sheraton, Warsaw.** This American-run hotel has much to recommend it: outstanding service, the best health club in the city, and a great location near parks and downtown Warsaw. *$$$$*

★ **Grand Hotel, Sopot.** This legendary late-19th-century luxury hotel fronts directly onto Sopot Beach and stands in its own gorgeous gardens. *$$$*

★ **Pod Różą, Kraków.** One of Kraków's oldest hotels, this property has bright, modern guest rooms and a prime location. *$$$*

Romania

★ **Athenée Palace Hilton, Bucharest.** This Bucharest landmark, dating to 1914, retains its shine with attractive rooms and a grand lobby. *$$$$*

★ **Holiday Inn Resort, Sinaia.** Spectacular mountain views and a wide range of sports and health facilities make this an appealing choice. *$$$$*

★ **Hotel Tirol, Poiana Brașov.** Opened in 1999, this small hotel offers attractive rooms, each furnished differently; a fireplace in the lobby; and a mountain-view restaurant. *$$$$*

Slovakia

★ **Danube, Bratislava.** This gleaming French-run hotel on the banks of the Danube has all the comforts of a modern, international chain. *$$$$*

★ **Grandhotel Praha, Tatranská Lomnica.** This multiturreted mansion in the foothills of the Tatras has retained the elegance and gentility of an earlier age. *$$$*

★ **Arkada Hotel, Levoča.** The bright and comfortable rooms in this boutique hotel belie the building's 13th-century origins. *$$*

Slovenia

★ **Vila Bled, Bled.** Tito's former hunting lodge has been converted into a top-flight hotel, with views over the exquisite Lake Bled. *$$$$*

★ **Hotel Tartini, Piran.** Take a front room overlooking the delightful oval-shape piazza, Trg Tartini: You couldn't hope to wake up in a nicer place. $$$

★ **Kendov Dvorec, Spodnje Idrija.** This beautifully restored 14th-century manor house has antique furniture and traditional cuisine to match. $$$

★ **Hotel Hvala, Kobarid.** The management of this family-run hotel treats its guests like old friends and feeds them like royalty. $$

Castles and Churches

Bulgaria

★ **Hram-pametnik Alexander Nevski (Alexander Nevski Memorial Cathedral), Sofia.** A modern, neo-Byzantine structure with glittering interlocking domes, this memorial to Bulgaria's Russian neighbor-liberators can hold some 5,000 worshipers; the Crypt Museum has an outstanding collection of icons and religious artifacts.

Czech Republic

★ **Chrám svaté Barbory (St. Barbara's Cathedral), Kutná Hora.** Arguably the best example of the Gothic impulse in Bohemia, St. Barbara's Cathedral lifts the spirit and gives the town of Kutná Hora its unmistakable skyline.

★ **Chrám svatého Víta (St. Vitus's Cathedral), Prague.** Soaring above the castle walls and dominating the city at its feet, St. Vitus's is among the most memorable churches in Europe. Its stained-glass windows are particularly brilliant.

★ **Španělská synagóga (Spanish Synagogue), Prague.** The interior of this florid 19th-century Moorish temple has been restored to its original splendor.

★ **Church of the Virgin Mary Before Týn, Old Town Square, Prague.** The exterior of this soaring church, with its twin gold-tip, jet-black spires, is a sterling example of Prague Gothic.

★ **Vranov Castle, Vranov, Moravia.** You'll admire or wince at this multicolor mix of Gothic, Renaissance, and Baroque styles; the eclectic effect always sparks an opinion.

Hungary

★ **Bazilika (Cathedral), Esztergom.** The imposing neoclassical dome of Hungary's largest church looming over the village and river below is one of the Danube Bend's best sights.

★ **Eszterházy Palace, Fertőd.** Known as the Hungarian Versailles, this yellow, 18th-century Baroque palace near Sopron in northern Transdanubia was a residence of the noble Eszterházy family.

★ **Fellegvár (Citadel), Visegrád.** This 13th-century hilltop fortress was once the seat of Hungarian kings. The hike up will reward you with gorgeous, panoramic views of the Danube Bend.

★ **Festetics Kastély (Festetics Palace), Keszthely.** A tremendous library, lush park, and distinctive tower make this one of the finest Baroque complexes in Hungary.

★ **Mátyás Templom (Matthias Church), Budapest.** Castle Hill's soaring Gothic church is colorfully ornate inside with lavishly frescoed Byzantine pillars.

★ **Nagy Zsinagóga (Great Synagogue), Budapest.** This giant Byzantine-Moorish beauty (Europe's largest synagogue) underwent a massive restoration four decades after being ravaged by Hungarian and German Nazis during World War II.

★ **Pécs Bazilika (Pécs Basilica), Pécs.** This four-spire cathedral is one of Europe's most magnificent, its breathtaking interior resplendent with shimmering frescoes and ornate statuary.

★ **Szent István Bazilika (St. Stephen's Basilica), Budapest.** Inside this massive neo-Renaissance beauty, the capital's biggest church, is a rich collection of mosaics and statuary, as well as the mummified right hand of Hungary's first king and patron saint, St. Stephen.

Poland

★ **Kaplica Trójcy świętego (Chapel of the Holy Trinity), Lublin.** This stunning 14th-century chapel recently reopened after decades of restoration; it's filled with Byzantine-style murals.

★ **Klasztor Paulinów (Pauline Monastery), Częstochowa.** The 14th-century church in this monastic complex holds Poland's holiest religious image, the famous Black Madonna of Częstochowa, a destination for pilgrims from around the world.

★ **Kościół Mariacki (Church of Our Lady), Kraków.** This church on Kraków's central marketplace has a magnificent wooden altarpiece with more than 200 carved figures, works of the 15th-century master Wit Stwosz.

★ **Kościół Najświętszej Marii Panny (St. Mary's Church), Gdańsk.** Climbing up the tower of the largest church in Poland results in breathtaking views.

★ **Łańcut Palace, Łańcut.** This aristocratic residence is truly grandiose; there are extensive gardens, an impressive art collection, and even a small, private theater.

★ **Pałac Wilanów (Wilanów Palace), Warsaw.** A Baroque gem on the outskirts of the capital, this palace was home to several Polish kings and queens; when you get tired of royal portraits and gilt, explore the Romantic gardens with their pagodas, summerhouses, and bridges overlooking a lake.

★ **Zamek Królewski (Royal Castle), Kraków.** Stroll the courtyards and chambers of Kraków's 14th-century Royal Castle to get a compact lesson in the trials and tribulations of Polish history and to view fine collections of artwork, arms and armor, and tapestries.

★ **Zamek w Malborku (Malbork Castle).** This huge, redbrick castle was one of the most powerful strongholds in medieval Europe, serving as the residence for the Grand Master of the Teutonic Order. The museum contains beautiful examples of amber.

Romania

★ **Biserica Stavropoleos (Stavropoleos Church), Bucharest.** Inside this Orthodox church are superb examples of Romanian folk-style carvings and a richly ornate iconostasis.

★ **Peleş Castle, Sinaia.** This 19th century castle, summer home of Romania's former royalty, is ornately decorated and features the heavy carved wood furnishings typical of German Renaissance style.

★ **Voroneţ Monastery, Bucovina.** The most famous of Bucovina's "painted monasteries," Voroneţ's exterior walls are covered with vivid frescoes depicting scenes from the Bible. The unusually penetrating shade of blue that predominates is known to art historians and artists as "Voroneţ blue."

Slovakia

★ **Dóm svätej Alžbety (Cathedral of St. Elizabeth), Košice.** Inside this 15th-century Gothic cathedral—the largest in Slovakia—stands a monumental piece of wood carving, the 35-ft Altar of the Holy Elizabeth.

★ **Kostol svätého Jakuba (St. Jacob's Church), Levoča.** This is the most impressive memorial to Gothic art in Eastern Europe; front and center on the main altar is wood-carver Pavol of Levoča's breathtaking masterpiece, *The Last Supper.*

★ **Krásna Hôrka, Krásnohorské Podhradie.** Visible from miles around, this fairy-tale castle on a hill is one of Slovakia's best-preserved medieval fortifications.

★ **Wooden churches of eastern Slovakia.** Even the nails are made of wood in these handsome structures that combine elements of Byzantine and Baroque styles; religious paintings and icons line the interior walls of many.

Slovenia

★ **Cerkev sveti Trojice (Church of the Holy Trinity), Hrastovlje.** Up on a hill above the Adriatic, the interior walls of this tiny church are decorated with an intriguing cycle of 15th-century frescoes.

★ **Pleterje Samostan (Pleterje Monastery), Šentjernej.** You can't go inside the monastery, but you can visit the beautiful Gothic church and watch an enlightening audio-visual presentation about the way the monks live.

Museums

Bulgaria

★ **Natzionale Archeologicheski Musei (National Archaeological Museum), Sofia.** Housed in the former Great Mosque, this collection is devoted to the various peoples who have inhabited Bulgarian territory over the centuries.

★ **Natzionalen Istoricheski Musei (National History Museum), Sofia.** Considered the city's most important museum, it houses priceless Thracian treasures, Roman mosaics, and enameled jewelry from the First Bulgarian Kingdom.

Czech Republic

★ **Malá Pevnost (Small Fortress), Terezín.** The grounds and buildings of the most notorious Nazi concentration camp on Czech territory have been preserved as a testament to the horrific legacy of the Holocaust.

★ **Národní galerie (National Gallery), Prague.** Spread among a half dozen branches around the city, the National Gallery's collections span most major periods of European art, from medieval and Baroque masters to a vast constructivist gallery of modern and contemporary works.

★ **Židovské muzeum v Praze (Prague Jewish Museum), Prague.** Actually a collection of several must-see sights and exhibits, the Jewish Museum includes the Old Jewish Cemetery, crowded with tombstones, and several historic synagogues.

Hungary

★ **Néprajzi Múzeum (Museum of Ethnography), Budapest.** A majestic 1890s structure across from the Parliament building—the lavish marble entrance hall alone is worth a visit—houses an impressive exhibit on Hungary's folk traditions.

★ **Szépművészeti Múzeum (Museum of Fine Arts), Budapest.** Hungary's best collection of fine art includes esteemed works by Dutch and Spanish old masters, as well as exhibits on major Hungarian artists.

★ **Zsolnay Múzeum (Zsolnay Museum), Pécs.** Pécs's oldest surviving building houses an extensive collection of the world-famous Zsolnay family's exquisite porcelain art.

Poland

★ **Czartoryski Collection, Kraków.** Part of the National Museum's holdings, housed in Municipal Arsenal, this is one of the best art collections in Poland; among its highlights are works by Leonardo, Raphael, and Rembrandt.

★ **Muzeum Narodowe (National Museum), Warsaw.** This is a remarkable collection of contemporary Polish and European paintings and ceramics, as well as Gothic icons and works from antiquity.

★ **Oświęcim (Auschwitz-Birkenau), near Kraków.** A million Jews, Gypsies, and others were killed by the Nazis at this concentration camp, which more than any other has come to be seen as the epicenter of the moral collapse of the West; it has been preserved as a museum.

Romania

★ **Muzeul Satului (Village Museum), Bucharest.** This fascinating open-air museum exhibits some 300 village homes and other structures from around the country.

★ **Muzeul Ţăranului Român (Peasant Museum), Bucharest.** You can catch an evocative glimpse of Romanian peasantry through these beautifully displayed costumes, icons, carpets, and other items of rural life.

Slovakia

★ **Múzeum židovskej kultúry (Museum of Jewish Culture in Slovakia), Bratislava.** Housed in a mid-17th-century Renaissance mansion, this exhibition covers the history of Jews in Slovakia from the time of the Great Moravian Empire to the present.

★ **Šariš (Icon Museum), Bardejov.** The myth of St. George and the dragon is one of the favorite themes in this captivating collection of Russian Orthodox artwork from the region's churches.

★ **Múzeum moderného umenia rodiny Warholovcov (Warhol Family Museum of Modern Art), Medzilaborce.** In this tiny town, view original Andy Warhol silk screens, including two from the famous Campbell's Soup series, as well as portraits of Lenin and singer Billie Holiday.

Slovenia

★ **Kobariški muzej (Kobarid Museum), Kobarid.** This award-winning museum records the tragic battles fought in the Soča Valley during World War I, which were immortalized by Ernest Hemingway in *A Farewell to Arms.*

★ **Muzej Novejše Zgodovine (Museum of Modern History), Ljubljana.** A recent installation, "Slovenes in the 20th century," gives an even-handed account of political events since the fall of the Austro-Hungarian Empire in 1918.

★ **Vinska Klet (Ptuj Wine Cellars), Ptuj.** At the home of Slovenia's oldest vintage wines, a tour of the underground cellars is followed by a wine-tasting session.

Towns and Villages

Bulgaria

★ **Koprivshtitsa (Inland Bulgaria).** Situated among mountain pastures and pine forests in the Sredna Gora Range, Koprivshtitsa is a showcase of the Bulgarian Renaissance style, where buildings are covered in brightly painted designs and ornate carvings.

Czech Republic

★ **Český Krumlov, Bohemia.** The repainted Renaissance facades and the new shops and pensions that now crowd the lanes have banished much of Krumlov's charming old decay, but the hard-earned dignity of the houses and the sweet melancholy of the streetscapes abide in this lovely southern Bohemian town.

★ **Mariánské Lázně, Bohemia.** In this genteel spa town, you can take the waters while strolling under gracious colonnades.

★ **Telč, Moravia.** The perfectly preserved town square, clustered with superb examples of Gothic, Renaissance, and Baroque architecture, is almost preternaturally perfect.

Hungary

★ **Pécs, Transdanubia.** This vibrant, cultured city's numerous museums—among the best in the country—glorious basilica, and picturesque location in the Mecsek Hills make it one of Hungary's lesser-known gems.

★ **Szentendre, the Danube Bend.** A tremendously popular day-trip destination from Budapest, this quaint town offers cobblestone streets for strolling and numerous art galleries for browsing and buying.

★ **Szigliget, Lake Balaton.** A tranquil, attractive little village on the lakeshore, Szigliget is a collection of traditional thatch-roof houses clustered together on narrow streets at the base of a hill crowned by a 13th-century fortress; the views of the lake from the ruins are exceptional.

Poland

★ **Kazimierz Dolny, eastern Poland.** Perched on a steep, hilly bank above the Vistula River, Kazimierz Dolny is a cluster of whitewashed facades and red-tile roofs; known in an earlier incarnation as the "Pearl of the Polish Renaissance," the town is something of an artists' colony.

★ **Toruń, western Poland.** One of the few cities to come through World War II unscathed, Toruń is a lovely blend of medieval, Baroque, Gothic, and Renaissance buildings.

★ **Zamość, eastern Poland.** The main square of this fortified town is a graceful, arcaded plaza punctuated by a Baroque town hall.

Romania

★ **Sighișoara, Transylvania.** The birthplace of Vlad Ţepeş, the real-life inspiration for Dracula, Sighişaora's cobble streets, clock tower, and medieval citadel are among the best preserved in Europe.

Slovakia

★ **Levoča, eastern Slovakia.** The medieval capital of the Spiš region seems frozen in time; between the 14th and 17th centuries it flourished as an important center of trade, crafts, and art.

Slovenia

★ **Piran.** An architect's dream, the Old Town of Piran has at its center an oval piazza, Trg Tartini, which opens onto the harbor. The surrounding facades are pure Venice, and the scene is presided over by a hilltop cathedral.

FESTIVALS AND SEASONAL EVENTS

BULGARIA

For exact dates of annual events or other information, check with any local tourist agency or contact **Balkan Holidays International** (✉ 5, ul. Triaditsa, Sofia, ☎ 02/86–861) or **Balkantourist** (✉ 1, bul. Vitosha, ☎ 02/43–331). These agencies generally have an English-speaking staff member on hand who will have the most up-to-date information.

DECEMBER–JANUARY➢ **Sofia International New Year's Music Festival** is a winter version of the summer Music Days (☞ *below*). Parties on New Year's Eve turn almost every *mehana* (folk restaurant) in the mountain towns of Bansko, Pamporovo, and Borovets into must-see Bulgarian folk spectacles.

MAY–JUNE➢ **SOFIA MUSIC DAYS,** focusing on classical and contemporary orchestral repertoire, attract internationally recognized musicians, conductors, orchestras, and choruses. Concerts are held at the Bulgaria Concert Hall and the National Palace of Culture. The **Albena Chess Festival and International Masters' Tournament** is held annually at the Black Sea resort of Albena. The **Rose Festival** in the Valley of the Roses is held in the town of Kazanlak. Dancers and singers perform after the predawn gathering of rosebuds by "rose maidens." In Stara Zagora, in May, you can spend a week learning to appreciate Bulgarian stagecraft during the **Festival of Opera and Ballet,** or in the first weekend of June, check out the newly instituted **Festival of Folk Arts.** At the end of June Plovdiv hosts the **International Chamber Music Festival,** when many intimate concerts are held in the small churches of the Old Town.

JUNE–JULY➢ **Varna Summer International Music Festival** is held in Varna and Golden Sands. It also incorporates the **International Ballet Festival,** held in July. A variant of **Sofia Music Days,** focusing on modern and international music, continues through the end of July in the capital. On June 16, the border town of Rousse holds a folk festival called **Golden Rebec,** featuring singing, crafts, and feasts with a slight Romanian influence.

JUNE–AUGUST➢ The **International Windsurfing Regatta** takes place at the Black Sea resorts of Golden Sands, Sunny Beach, and Sozopol.

AUGUST➢ **Rozhen Sings National Fair,** held in Rozhen near the Pamporovo mountain resort, features Bulgarian folk singers, dancers, and revelers outfitted in traditional costumes. A similar gathering can be found at the end of the month on the Black Sea in the city of Burgas. Plovdiv also has a **Folk Festival** held on the last weekend in August. The most popular August event is the **Golden Orpheus,** an international festival of Bulgarian pop music. It has been drawing crowds to Sunny Beach, or Slanchev Bryag, from August 28 to September 3, for the last 30 years. The historic village of **Koprivshtitsa** also hosts a folk music festival over an early August weekend.

SEPTEMBER➢ Probably the most famous and popular festival in all of Bulgaria, the **Apollonia Festival of the Arts** is held in Sozopol, including art exhibitions, theater, poetry readings, and street events. At the end of the month, the cosmopolitan crowds move to Varna for the **Golden Rose International Film Festival.** Though the event has taken place annually for more than 40 years, it has only recently begun to feature some of the best and brightest filmmakers in Eastern Europe and farther abroad.

OCTOBER➢ Rousse attracts jazz lovers to its **International Jazz Forum,** with concerts in the larger performance venues as well as a tight schedule of back-to-back jazz in bars and clubs.

NOVEMBER➢ **Kinomania,** roughly translated as Film Fever, turns Sofia's National Palace of Culture into a giant film complex for three weeks. With the newest and best Bulgarian and international films of the year playing all day long in all 15 theaters, it is a movie lover's extravaganza.

CZECH REPUBLIC

DECEMBER➢ **Christmas Fairs and Programs** take place in most towns and cities; among those particularly worth catching are **Christmas in Valašsko,** in Rožnov pod Radhoštěm, and the **Arrival of Lady Winter Festival,** in Prachatice.

JANUARY➢ Prague hosts the **FebioFest International Film, Television and Video Festival.**

MARCH➢ The Czech Republic's **Alpine Skiing Championships** take place in Špindlerův Mlýn; Prague holds **St. Matthew's Fair,** an annual children's fair at the Výstaviště exhibition grounds. Prague is also the site of **Days of European Film.**

APRIL➢ Eastertime brings two festivals of sacred music to Prague, **Musica Ecumenica** and **Musica Sacra Praga.** Brno puts on an **Easter Spiritual Music Festival.** English-language and world authors appear at the **Prague Writers' Festival.**

MAY➢ There are events both athletic and artistic in Prague; there's the **Prague Spring International Music Festival** as well as the **Prague Marathon.** An **International Children's Film Festival** is held in Zlín, while the **Janáček's May Music Festival** begins in Ostrava. For music in a Bohemian spa town, head to the **Karlovy Vary International Jazz Festival.**

JUNE➢ The international dance festival **Tanec Praha** hits the capital. There's an **International Folklore Festival** in the Moravian town Strážnice, and world-record attempts and other weirdness grace the **Town of Records Festival** in Pelhřimov. The long-running **Smetana's Litomyšl** festival brings opera lovers to the composer's birthplace; and the equally venerable **Kmoch's Kolín** lures brass-band enthusiasts to central Bohemia.

JULY➢ Karlovy Vary has its own **International Film Festival. Chrudim Puppeteering** is a puppet theater festival; Jindřichův Hradec puts on a folk music festival, **Folk Rose.** The **Dvořák's Nelahozeves** concert series gets started in that composer's home village.

AUGUST➢ This is a great month for music of all kinds. Prague's **Verdi Festival** is staged at the State Opera, while Český Krumlov has an **International Music Festival** and Strakonice hosts the **International Bagpipe Festival.** For something more musically ornate, visit the **Baroque Opera Festival** in Valtice.

SEPTEMBER➢ You'll need to book a hotel room well in advance for Brno's **International Engineering Fair.** Prague holds several arts festivals, preeminently the **Prague Autumn International Music Festival.** It's also the season for wine festivals, such as the **Pálava Vintage Celebrations** in Mikulov and the **Mělník Vintage Celebrations.**

OCTOBER➢ The capital continues its run of cultural events, including an **International Jazz Festival** and the **Dance Theater Festival.** Out in eastern Bohemia, the **Velká Pardubická Steeplechase** is considered one of Europe's toughest racing events, and Hradec Králové holds its **Jazz Goes to Town Festival.**

NOVEMBER➢ Prague stokes the cultural fires against the approach of winter with the **Czech Press Photo Exhibition** and **Musica Iudaica,** a festival of Jewish music.

HUNGARY

For contact information about most of these festivals, *see* the city or town's Nightlife and the Arts section or inquire at the Budapest Tourinform office or the local visitor information center.

MID-MARCH–EARLY APRIL➢ The season's first and biggest arts festival, the **Budapest Spring Festival,** showcases Hungary's best opera, music, theater, fine arts, and dance, as well as visiting foreign artists. Other towns—including Kecskemét, Szentendre, and Pécs—also participate. This includes, for example, the **Debrecen Jazz Festival,** which features local and international ensembles.

MAY➢ THE **Balaton Festival** in Keszthely features high-caliber classical concerts and other festivities held in venues around town and outdoors on Kossuth Lajos utca.

JUNE➢ Kőszeg's biggest cultural event, held early in the month, is the annual **East West Folk Festival**—a weekend of open-air international folk music and dance performances. Szombathely's gala **Savaria International Dance Competition** (one day in early June) features a full day of elegant ballroom dancing by competing pairs from around the world. The monthlong **Sopron Festival Weeks,** beginning in mid-June, brings music, dance, and theater performances and art exhibits to churches and venues around town.

LATE JUNE–EARLY JULY➢ The **World Music Festival** in Budapest, held in early July, has several days of world music concerts by local and international artists. The **International Puppet Festival** draws puppeteers from Hungary and abroad to Sárospatak from July 1–4 every two years, next in 2002.

JULY➢ The **Szentendre Summer Days** festival, which begins in late June and goes right through August 20, offers open-air theater performances and jazz and classical concerts.

The **Visegrád International Palace Games** includes medieval jousting tournaments and festivities. Late in the month, Balatonfüred's **Anna Ball** is a traditional ball and beauty contest. In Vác the last weekend in July, the **Váci Világi Vígalom** (Vác World Jamboree) festival is held, with folk dancing, music, crafts fairs, and other festivities.

Every two years in early or mid-July (the next scheduled for 2002), Kecskemét hosts a giant children's festival, **Európa Jövője Gyermektalálkozó** (Future of Europe Children's Convention), during which children's groups from some 25 countries put on colorful folk-dance and singing performances. Debrecen's biannual **Béla Bartók International Choral Festival,** scheduled for early July 2002, is an international choir competition.

JULY–AUGUST➢ Equestrian fans will not want to miss the **Hortobágy International Horse Show,** held in Máta annually for three or four days between early July and mid-August. Established in the 1930s, the annual **Szegedi Szabadtéri Napok** (Open-Air Days) offers a gala series of dramas, operas, operettas, classical concerts, and folk-dance performances by Hungarian and international artists. Tickets are always a hot commodity; plan far ahead. From around the last week in July and the first in August, the **Festival Weeks in Baroque Eger** presents classical concerts, dance, and other arts programs.

AUGUST➢ Toward mid-month, Budapest hosts a **Formula 1** car race, while the weeklong **BudaFest** opera and ballet festival takes place mid-month at the opera house after the opera season ends. **St. Stephen's Day** (August 20) is a major national holiday. Two highlights are the fireworks in Budapest and Debrecen's **Flower Carnival,** which features a festive parade of flower-covered floats and carriages. Held annually around August 20, **Hortobágy Bridge Fair** brings horse shows, a folk-art fair, ox roasts, and festive crowds to the plot beneath the famous Nine-Arch Bridge. The weeklong **Jewish Summer Festival,** held in late August and early September, features cantors, classical concerts, a kosher cabaret, films, and theater and dance performances, in Budapest and sometimes elsewhere.

Every two years Esztergom hosts the **Nemzetközi Gitár Fesztivál** (International Guitar Festival), during which renowned classical guitarists from around the world hold master classes and workshops for participants. The festival runs for two weeks early in the month; the next one will be held in 2001.

SEPTEMBER➢ The **Eger Harvest Festival** early in the month celebrates the grape harvest with a traditional parade and wine tastings.

EARLY OCTOBER➢ Tokaj's annual **Szüreti Hét** (Harvest Week) celebrates the autumn grape harvest with a parade, street ball, folk-art markets, and a plethora of wine-tasting opportunities from the local vintners' stands set up on and around the main square.

POLAND

DECEMBER➢ **St. Nicholas Day** (December 6) is prevalent in the south; children receive gifts and dress as mummers. Kraków's **Christmas Crèche Competition** displays handmade nativity crèches.

JANUARY➢ Warsaw holds a Polish theater festival, **Warsawskie Spotkania Teatralne.**

MAY➢ Spring starts off with plenty of music; there's a **Chamber Music Festival** in Łańcut, an **International Jazz Festival "Jazz on the Oder"** in Wrocław, and the **International Festival of Music** in Częstochowa. The **Warsaw International Book Fair** is Central and Eastern Europe's largest fair of books, magazines, and manuscripts.

MAY–JUNE➢ The **International Festival of Short Feature Films** (Kraków) presents hundreds of short, video, documentary, animated, and experimental films.

JUNE➢ Kraków has a **Festival of Jewish Culture.** The **International Oratorios and Cantata Festival "Wratislavia Cantans"** is staged in Wrocław. Warsaw's **Midsummer Ceremonies** (June 23) include throwing candlelit wreaths into the Vistula; the capital also has Sunday morning and afternoon **Open-air Chopin Concerts** at the Chopin Memorial in Łazienki Park and **Chopin Concerts** at Żelazowa Wola (these run until October) and the **Warsaw Summer Jazz Days Festival.** For **Folk Music and Dance,** head to the festival in Kazimierz Dolny.

JUNE–JULY➢ Warsaw offers a **Mozart Festival.** There are two **International Festivals of Organ, Choir, and Chamber Music,** one in Gdańsk–Oliwa, the other in Kamien Pomorski, near Szczecin. Poznań's **International Theater Festival** offers performances in various outdoor venues.

JULY➢ The **Music of Karol Szymanowski** is celebrated in Zakopane, the village where the Polish composer lived during the 1920s.

AUGUST➢ Artisans, folk dancers, and musicians take over the streets of Gdańsk for the **Dominican Fair and Festival,** the annual commemoration of St. Dominic. The **International Festival of Highland Folklore** in Zakopane celebrates highland cultures with folk-art and costume exhibits, poetry competitions, and musical concerts. The **International Country Music Festival** in Mrągowo features local and foreign performers. Other August festivals include the **International Song Festival** (Sopot), **International Festival of Choir Songs** (Międzyzdroje), **International Chopin Festival** (Duszniki Zdrój), and **Knights and Crossbow Tournament for the Sword of Jan III Sobieski** (Gniew).

SEPTEMBER➢ **Wratislavia Cantans** in Wrocław features oratorio and cantata music. The **"Warsaw Autumn" Festival of Contemporary Music** showcases symphony and chamber concerts, opera, ballet, and electronic-music performances. Krynica presents the **Jan Kiepura Festival of Opera Songs,** and during the last week of September, the archaeological site of **Biskupin** has a festival, including historic reenactments.

OCTOBER➢ **Warsaw's Jazz Jamboree** is the oldest jazz festival in Europe. Kraków hosts its own **Jazz Festival.**

NOVEMBER➢ Thousands of candles are placed on graves in cemeteries on **All Saints' Day** (November 1).

ROMANIA

JULY➢ In times past, young men chose brides at **Târgu de Fete** (Maidens' Fair). Now, folk songs, dances, and traditional dress characterize this event atop Mount Găina.

AUGUST➢ **Hora la Prislop,** staged at the Prislop Pass between Maramureş and Moldavia, attracts costume-clad participants from several counties for traditional dance, music, and food.

DECEMBER ➢ In Sighetu Marmaţiei, the **Festivalul Datinilor de Iarnă** (Winter Festival) recreates old Christmas–New Year's customs with a multitude of traditionally garbed villagers, masked demons, folk dance, and music.

SLOVAKIA

In addition to hosting the events noted below, many villages also have annual folklore festivals, usually on a weekend in late summer or early fall, which are often filled with singing, dancing, and drinking. For more information, look for the English-language annual events calendar put out by the Slovak Ministry of Economy, available in travel agencies and tourist information centers, or check the weekly *Slovak Spectator,* available at newsstands.

DECEMBER➢ **Christmas at the Castle** is in Bojnice. Visiting children are presented with Christmas gifts by local historical characters.

MARCH➢ Bardejov has a **Musical Spring** performance series; Liptovský Mikuláš has a **Folk Song Festival.**

APRIL➢ The **International Festival of Ghosts and Phantoms** is held every year at the end of April in the striking castle in Bojnice.

MAY➢ **Košice Musical Spring** takes place in May.

JUNE➢ An **International Folklore Festival** is held in Košice.

JULY➢ **Folklore Festival Východná** takes place in Eastern Slovakia.

SEPTEMBER➢ A **Vintage Festival** takes place in Pezinok, near Bratislava.

OCTOBER➢ The **Bratislava Music Festival** attracts

national and international musicians to venues throughout the capital late in the month. The capital also hosts the **Jazz Days Festival.**

SLOVENIA

For exact dates and further information about the following events and festivals, contact the Slovenian Tourist Board.

FEBRUARY➢ **Kurentovanje** in Ptuj is the largest and most spectacular of numerous Carnival celebrations throughout the country.

MARCH➢ The **World Cup Ski-jump Championship** is held at Planica, Kranjska Gora.

JUNE➢ **Lent Festival** in Maribor, featuring music and dance events through June and July, opens with the traditional *Rafters' Baptism* on the River Drava. **Druga Godba,** a one-week festival of alternative and world music, takes place in Ljubljana.

JULY AND AUGUST➢ The **International Jazz Festival** is held in Ljubljana in July, followed by the **International Summer Festival,** running through July and August, incorporating a range of events from classical music recitals to street theater. The **Primorski Summer Festival** of open-air theater and dance is staged in the coastal towns of Piran, Koper, Portorož, and Izola. **Piran Musical Evenings** are held in the cloisters of the Minorite Monastery in Piran, every Friday through July and August. The **Lace-making Festival** is held in Idrija in August, lasting one week.

SEPTEMBER➢ The **Kravji Bal** (Cow Ball) in Bohinj marks the end of summer and the return of herdsmen and their cows from the mountain pastures to the valleys. The **Maritime Baptism** celebrates the initiation of new students to the Portorož Maritime Academy.

OCTOBER➢ The **Ceremonial Grape Harvest** on October 1 marks the gathering of grapes from Slovenia's oldest vineyard, in Maribor.

NOVEMBER➢ **St. Martin's Day,** on November 11, sees festivities throughout the country, culminating with the traditional blessing of the season's young wine.

2 THE CZECH REPUBLIC

In the decade since the fall of the Communist regime, the Czech Republic has developed into a thriving democracy that offers visitors some of Central Europe's most alluring attractions. The "hundred-spired" capital city of Prague—one of the world's best-preserved architectural cityscapes—offers world-class cultural performances and increasingly distinctive dining and shopping. In the countryside beyond, medieval castles perch quietly near lost-in-time Baroque and Renaissance villages. Pine forests and gentle green mountains beckon outdoor enthusiasts with a multitude of pleasures.

By Mark Baker

Updated by Ky Krauthamer

A **VICTIM OF ENFORCED OBSCURITY** throughout much of the 20th century, the Czech Republic, encompassing the provinces of Bohemia and Moravia, is once again in the spotlight. In 1989, in a world where revolution was synonymous with violence, and in a country where truth was quashed by the tanks of Eastern-bloc socialism, Václav Havel's sonorous voice proclaimed the victory of the "Velvet Revolution" to enthusiastic crowds on Wenceslas Square and preached the value of "living in truth." Recording the dramatic events of the time, television cameras panned across Prague's glorious skyline and fired the world's imagination with the image of political renewal superimposed on somber Gothic and voluptuous Baroque.

Travelers have rediscovered the country, and Bohemians and Moravians have rediscovered the world. The stagnant "normalization" of the last two decades under Communist rule gave way in the 1990s to a new dynamism and international outlook. Visitors now encounter enthusiasm, and such conveniences as English-language newspapers and attentive service. Not that the Czech Republic has joined the ranks of "Western" countries. It remains the poor relation compared with its Central European neighbors Germany and Austria, with the average Czech worker's wage standing at around $350 a month. This makes the signs of modernity even more remarkable. Nowadays there are cybercafés and cell phones to help visitors stay in touch with the outer world. It's all happening fastest in Prague, but the pace of change is accelerating everywhere. In the small towns and villages where so many Czechs still live, however, you may struggle with a creeping sensation of melancholy and neglect—or, putting a positive spin on it, you may enjoy the slower, more relaxed tempo.

The drab remnants of socialist reality are still omnipresent on the back roads of Bohemia and Moravia. But many of the changes made by the Communists were superficial—adding ugliness but leaving the society's core more or less intact. The colors are less jarring, not designed to attract the moneyed eye; the fittings are as they always were, not adapted to the needs of a new world.

The experience of visiting the Czech Republic still involves stepping back in time. Even in Prague, now deluged by tourists two-thirds of the year, the sense of history—stretching back through centuries of wars, empires, and monuments to everyday life—remains uncluttered by the trappings of modernity. The peculiar melancholy of Central Europe still lurks in narrow streets and forgotten corners. Crumbling facades, dilapidated palaces, and treacherous cobbled streets both shock and enchant the visitor used to a world where what remains of history has been spruced up for tourist eyes.

The arrival of designer boutiques, chain restaurants, and shopping malls does mean that the country has lost some of the "feel" it had just a few years ago. Although the dark side of freedom—rising unemployment and corruption—began to hit home in the late 1990s, the Czechs continued to move toward harmonization with Western ways. The country joined the NATO alliance in 1999 and will become a European Union member state, perhaps as early as 2003. Yet the process goes slowly. Economic and social integration into the "common European home," which in the postrevolutionary euphoria seemed possible within a few years, must now be measured in decades.

The strange, old-world, and at times frustratingly bureaucratic, atmosphere of the Czech Republic is not all a product of the Communist era. Many of the everyday rituals are actually remnants of the Haps-

Czech Republic (Česká Republika)

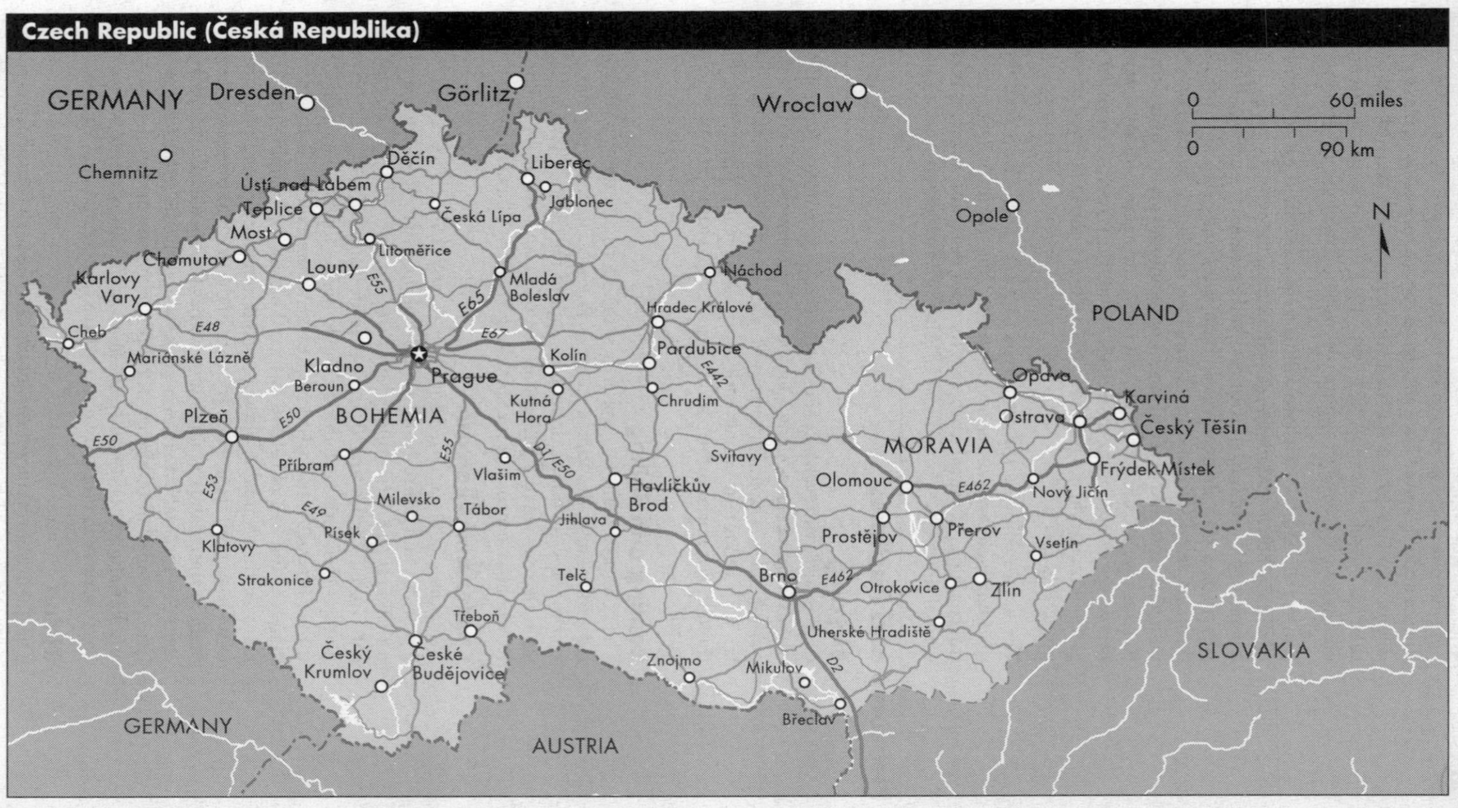

burg Empire and are also to be found, perhaps to a lesser degree, in Vienna and Budapest. The *šatna* (coat room), for example, plays a vivid role in any visit to a restaurant or theater at any time of year other than summer. Coats must be given with a few coins to the attendant, usually an old lady with a sharp eye for ignorant or disobedient tourists.

Outside the capital, for those willing to put up with the inconveniences of shabby hotels and mediocre restaurants, the sense of rediscovering a neglected world is even stronger. And the range is startling, from imperial spas, with their graceful colonnades and dilapidated villas, to the many arcaded town squares, modestly displaying the passing of time with each splendid layer of once-contemporary style. Gothic towers, Renaissance facades, Baroque interiors, and aging modern supermarkets merge. Between the man-made sights, the visitor is rewarded with glorious mountain ranges and fertile rolling countryside laced with carp ponds and forests.

The key to enjoying the country is to relax. There is no point in demanding high levels of service or quality. And for the budget-conscious traveler, this is Central Europe at its most beautiful, at prices that are several times lower than those of Austria and Germany.

Pleasures and Pastimes

Bicycling

Czechs are avid cyclists. The flatter areas of southern Bohemia and Moravia are ideal for biking. Outside the larger towns, quiet roads stretch out for miles. The hillier terrain of northern Bohemia makes it popular with mountain-biking enthusiasts. Not many places rent bikes, though. For rental information, inquire at a visitor bureau or at your hotel.

Boating and Sailing

The country's main boating area is the enormous series of dams and reservoirs along the Vltava south of Prague. The most popular reservoir is Slapy, an hour's drive due south of the capital, where it is possible to rent small paddleboats or relax and swim on a hot day. Rowboats are available for rent along Prague's Vltava in summertime.

Castles and Châteaus

More than 2,000 castles, manor houses, and châteaus collectively form a precious and not-to-be-missed part of the country's cultural and historical heritage. Grim ruins glower from craggy hilltops, and fantastical Gothic castles guard ancient trade routes. Hundreds of noble houses—Renaissance, Baroque, and Empire—dot the countryside. Their former bourgeois and aristocratic owners were expelled in the anti-German reaction of 1945–1946 or forced out by the Communists. Today, many of their valuable old seats stand in near ruin, and just as many more have been returned to the care of the original owners. Others remain in state hands as museums, homes for the elderly, or conference centers. More sights than ever are now open to the public. Picture galleries, rooms full of historic furniture, exquisite medieval stonework, and Baroque chapels—all speak of a vanished way of life whose remnants survive in every town and village of Bohemia and Moravia.

Dining

The quality of restaurant cuisine and service in the Czech Republic remains uneven. The exception is found in the capital, where dozens of restaurants compete for an increasingly discriminating clientele. The traditional dishes—roast pork or duck with dumplings, or broiled meat with sauce—can be light and tasty when well prepared. Grilled pond trout appears on most menus and is often the tastiest item available. An annoying "cover charge" (20 Kč–50 Kč in expensive places) usually makes its way onto restaurant bills, seemingly to subsidize the salt and pepper shakers. You should discreetly check the bill, since a few unscrupulous proprietors still overcharge foreigners.

Restaurants generally fall into three categories. A *pivnice* or *hospoda* (beer hall) usually offers a simple, inexpensive menu of goulash or pork with dumplings. The atmosphere tends to be friendly and casual, and you can expect to share a table. More attractive, and more expensive, are the *vinárna* (wine cellar) and the *restaurace* (restaurant), which serve a full range of dishes. Wine cellars, some occupying Romanesque basements, can be a real treat.

Ignoring the familiar fast-food outlets that are now a common sight, the quickest and cheapest dining option is the *lahůdky* (snack bar or deli). In larger towns, the *kavárna* (café) and *čajovna* (tea house) are ever more popular—and welcome—additions to the dining scene.

Lunch, usually eaten between noon and 2, is the main meal for Czechs and the best deal. Many restaurants put out a special luncheon menu (*denní lístek*), with more appetizing selections at better prices. If you don't see it, ask your waiter. Dinner is usually served from 5 until 9 or 10, but don't wait too long to eat. Most Czechs eat only a light meal in the evening. Also, restaurant cooks frequently knock off early on slow nights, and the later you arrive, the more likely it is that the kitchen will be closed. In general, dinner menus do not differ substantially from lunch offerings, except the prices are higher.

CATEGORY	PRAGUE*	OTHER AREAS*
$$$$	over $40	over $30
$$$	$20–$40	$15–$30
$$	$10–$20	$7–$15
$	under $10	under $7

**per person for a three-course meal, excluding wine and tip*

Hiking

The Czech Republic is a hiker's paradise, with 40,000 km (25,000 mi) of well-kept, -marked, and -signposted trails both in the mountainous regions and leading through beautiful countryside from town to town. The most scenic areas are the Beskydy range in northern Moravia and the Krkonoše range (Giant Mountains) in northern Bohemia. The rolling Šumava hills of southern Bohemia are also excellent hiking territory, and the environment there is the purest in the country. You'll find colored markings denoting trails on trees, fences, walls, rocks, and elsewhere. The main paths are marked in red, others in blue and green, while the least important trails are marked in yellow. Hiking maps can be found in almost any bookstore; look for the large-scale *Soubor turistických* maps.

Lodging

The number of hotels and pensions has increased dramatically throughout the Czech Republic, in step with the influx of tourists. Finding a suitable room should pose no problem, although it is highly recommended that you book ahead during the peak tourist season (nationwide, July and August; in Prague, April through October and the Christmas, New Year, and Easter holidays). Hotel prices, in general, remain high. This is especially true in Prague and in the spa towns of western Bohemia. Some Prague hotels reduce rates slightly in July and August, when many European travelers prefer to head for the beaches. Better value can often be found at private pensions and with individual home-owners offering rooms to let. In the outlying towns, the best strategy is to inquire at the local tourist information office or simply fan out around the town and look for room-for-rent signs on houses (usually in German: ZIMMER FREI or PRIVATZIMMER).

Most of the old-fashioned hotels away from the major tourist centers, invariably situated on a town's main square, have been modernized and now provide private bathrooms in most or all rooms and a higher comfort level throughout. Newer hotels, often impersonal concrete boxes, tend to be found on the outskirts of towns; charming, older buildings in the center of town, newly transformed into hotels and pensions, are often the best choice. Bare-bones hostels are a popular means of circumventing Prague's summer lodging crunch; many now stay open all year. In the mountains you can often find little *chaty* (chalets), where pleasant surroundings compensate for a lack of basic amenities. *Autokempink* parks (campsites) generally have a few bungalows.

Czech hotels set their own star ratings, which more or less match the international star system. Often you can book rooms—both at hotels and in private homes—through visitor bureaus. Otherwise, try calling or writing the hotel directly. Keep in mind that in many hotels, except at the deluxe level, a "double" bed means two singles that can be pushed together. (Single-mattress double beds are generally not available.)

At certain times, such as Easter and during festivals, prices can jump 15%–25%. As a rule, always ask the price before taking a room. Your best bet for lodging in the $ price range will usually be a private room. Unless otherwise noted, breakfast is included in the rate.

As for camping, there are hundreds of sites for tents and trailers throughout the country, but most are open only in summer (May to mid-September), although a number of campsites in and around Prague have year-round operation. You can get a map from the Prague Information Service of all the sites, with addresses, opening times, and facilities. Camping outside official sites is prohibited. Campgrounds generally have hot water and toilets.

CATEGORY	PRAGUE*	OTHER AREAS*
$$$$	over $200	over $100
$$$	$100–$200	$50–$100
$$	$50–$100	$25–$50
$	under $50	under $25

**All prices are for a standard double room during peak season, including breakfast.*

🔗 following the text of a review is your signal that the property has a Web site, where you will find details and, usually, images; for a link, visit www.fodors.com/urls.

Shopping

In Prague, Karlovy Vary, and elsewhere in Bohemia, look for elegant and unusual crystal and porcelain. Bohemia is also renowned for the quality and deep-red color of its garnets; keep an eye out for beautiful garnet rings and brooches. You can also find excellent ceramics, especially in Moravia, as well as other folk artifacts, such as printed textiles, lace, hand-knit sweaters, and painted eggs. There are attractive crafts stores throughout the Czech Republic. Karlovy Vary is blessed with a variety of unique items to buy, including the strange pipelike drinking mugs used in the spas; vases left to petrify in the mineral-laden water; and Becherovka, a tasty herbal aperitif that makes a nice gift to take home.

Skiing

The two main skiing areas in the Czech Republic are the Giant Mountains in northern Bohemia and, for cross-country skiing especially, the

Šumava hills of southern Bohemia. Lifts operate from January through March. In both areas you'll find a number of organizations renting skis—although supplies may be limited and lines may be long.

Wine and Beer

Czechs are reputed to drink more beer per capita than any people on earth; small wonder, as many connoisseurs rank Bohemian lager-style beer as the best in the world. This cool, crisp brew was invented in Plzeň in 1842, although Czech beer had already been brewed for centuries prior to that time. Aside from the world-famous Plzeňský Prazdroj (Pilsner Urquell) and milder Budvar (the original Budweiser) brands, some typical beers are the slightly bitter Krušovice; fruity Radegast; and the sweeter, Prague-brewed Staropramen. *Světlé pivo,* or golden beer, is most common, although many pubs also serve *černé* (dark), which is often slightly sweeter than the light variety.

Czechs also produce quite drinkable wines: peppy, fruity whites and mild, versatile reds. Southern Moravia, with comparatively warm summers and rich soil, grows the bulk of the wine harvest. Look for the Mikulov and Znojmo regional designations. Favorite white varietals are *Müller-Thurgau,* with a fine muscat bouquet and light flavor, and *Neuburské,* yellow-green in color and with a dry, smoky bouquet. *Rulandské bílé,* a semidry Burgundy-like white, has a flowery bouquet and full-bodied flavor. Belying the notion that northerly climes are more auspicious for white than red grapes, northern Bohemia's scant few hundred acres of vineyards produce reliable reds and the occasional jewel. *Frankovka* is fiery red and slightly acidic, while the cherry-red *Rulandské červené* is an excellent, drier choice. *Vavřinecké* is dark and slightly sweet.

Exploring the Czech Republic

The stunning silhouette of Prague is undeniably one of the country's strongest magnets, but there are plenty of beautiful vistas, spired castles, and peaceful town squares beyond the capital. Bohemia, for centuries its own kingdom, spreads around Prague to the borders of Germany, Austria, and Poland. This region is rich with spa towns in the west, walled towns and castles to the south, and moving reminders of World War II in the north. Moravia, the area east of Prague, is anchored by Brno. This relatively modern city is surrounded by smaller, traditional towns, some tied to the wine trade. To the north a stretch of rural hills leads into Slovakia's more rugged ranges.

Great Itineraries

Numbers in the text correspond to numbers in the margin and on the Prague, Prague Castle (Pražský hrad), and Bohemia maps.

IF YOU HAVE 3 DAYS

Make **Prague** ①–㊿ your base. This will allow you plenty of time to explore the beauties and wonders of the Old Town and Hradčany and to make a day trip to one of the country's fascinating smaller cities, the splendid spa town of **Karlovy Vary** ㊵, nestled in the hills of western Bohemia.

IF YOU HAVE 5 DAYS

Plan to spend three full days exploring Prague. You could easily spend a day each in the Old Town, the Lesser Quarter, and the castle and the other two days visiting the well-preserved medieval mining town of **Kutná Hora** (59) and the unforgettable concentration camp **Terezín** (76). Or you could spend a day amid the Renaissance charm of **Český Krumlov** (65).

When to Tour

Prague is beautiful year-round, but in summer and during the Christmas and Easter holidays the city is overrun with tourists. Spring and fall generally combine good weather with a more bearable level of tourism. In winter you'll encounter fewer other visitors and have the opportunity to see Prague breathtakingly covered in snow, but it can get very cold. In much of the rest of Bohemia and Moravia, even in midsummer, the number of visitors is far smaller than in Prague. The Giant Mountains of Bohemia come into their own in winter. January and February generally bring the best skiing—and great difficulty in finding a room. If you're not a skier, try visiting the mountains in late spring (May or June) or fall, when the colors are dazzling and you'll have the hotels and restaurants nearly to yourself. The "off" season keeps shrinking as visitors discover the pleasures of touring the country in every season. Castles and museums now frequently stay open 9, 10, or even 12 months of the year. In midwinter, however, you may well come across this disappointing notice tacked to the door of a museum or even a hotel: CLOSED FOR TECHNICAL REASONS—which, for those in the proper frame of mind, merely adds to the charm of winter travel.

PRAGUE

In the years since November 17, 1989, when Prague's students took to the streets to help bring down the 40-year-old Communist regime, the city has enjoyed an exhilarating cultural renaissance. Amid Prague's cobblestone streets and gold-tip spires, new galleries, cafés, and clubs teem with young Czechs (the middle-aged are generally too busy trying to make a living) and members of the city's colony of "expatriates." New shops and, perhaps most noticeably, scads of new restaurants have opened, expanding the city's culinary reach far beyond the traditional roast pork and dumplings. Many have something to learn in the way of presentation and service, but Praguers still marvel at a variety that was unthinkable not so many years ago.

The arts and theater are also thriving in the "new" Prague. Young playwrights, some writing in English, regularly stage their own works. Weekly poetry readings are standing room only. Classical music maintains its famous standards, while rock, jazz, and dance clubs are jammed nightly. The arts of the new era—nonverbal theater, "installation" art, world music—are as trendy in Prague as in any European capital, but possess a distinctive Czech flavor.

All of this frenetic activity plays well against a stunning backdrop of towering churches and centuries-old bridges and alleyways. Prague achieved much of its present glory in the 14th century, during the long reign of Charles IV, king of Bohemia and Moravia and Holy Roman Emperor. It was Charles who established a university in the city and laid out the New Town, charting Prague's growth.

During the 15th century, the city's development was hampered by the Hussite Wars, a series of crusades launched by the Holy Roman Empire to subdue the fiercely independent Czech noblemen. The Czechs were eventually defeated in 1620 at the Battle of White Mountain (Bílá Hora) near Prague and were ruled by the Hapsburg family for the next 300 years. Under the Hapsburgs, Prague became a German-speaking city and an important administrative center, but it was forced to play second fiddle to the monarchy's capital, Vienna. Much of the Lesser Quarter, on the left bank of the Vltava, was built up at this time, becoming home to Austrian nobility and its Baroque tastes.

Prague regained its status as a national capital in 1918, with the creation of the modern Czechoslovak state, and quickly asserted itself in the interwar period as a vital cultural center. Although the city escaped World War II essentially intact, Czechoslovakia fell under the political and cultural domination of the Soviet Union until the 1989 popular uprisings. The election of dissident playwright Václav Havel to the post of national president set the stage for the city's renaissance, which has since proceeded at a dizzying, quite Bohemian rate.

Exploring Prague

The spine of the city is the River Vltava (also known by its German name, Moldau), which runs through the city from south to north with a single sharp curve to the east. Prague originally comprised five independent towns, represented today by its main historic districts: Hradčany (Castle Area), Malá Strana (Lesser Quarter), Staré Město (Old Town), Nové Město (New Town), and Josefov (the Jewish Quarter).

Hradčany, the seat of Czech royalty for hundreds of years, has as its center the Pražský hrad (Prague Castle), which overlooks the city from its hilltop west of the Vltava. Steps lead down from Hradčany to the Lesser Quarter, an area dense with ornate mansions built by 17th- and 18th-century nobility.

Karlův most (Charles Bridge) connects the Lesser Quarter with the Old Town. Just a few blocks east of the bridge is the district's focal point, Staroměstské náměstí (Old Town Square). The Old Town is bounded by the curving Vltava and three large commercial avenues: Revoluční to the east, Na Příkopě to the southeast, and Národní třída to the south. North of Old Town Square, the diminutive Jewish Quarter fans out around the wide avenue called Pařížská.

Beyond the Old Town to the south is the New Town, a highly commercial area that includes the city's largest square, Karlovo náměstí (Charles Square). Roughly 1 km (½ mi) farther south is Vyšehrad, an ancient castle high above the river.

On a promontory to the east of Václavské náměstí (Wenceslas Square) stretches Vinohrady, once the favored neighborhood of well-to-do Czechs. Bordering Vinohrady are the crumbling neighborhoods of Žižkov to the north and Nusle to the south. On the west bank of the Vltava lie many older residential neighborhoods and several sprawling parks. About 3 km (2 mi) from the center in every direction, Communist-era housing projects begin their unsightly sprawl.

Numbers in the text correspond to numbers in the margin and on the Prague map.

Staré Město (Old Town)

A GOOD WALK

Ever-hopping Wenceslas Square (☞ Nové Město [New Town] and Vyšehrad, *below*), convenient to hotels and transportation, is an excellent place to begin a tour of the Old Town, although it actually lies within the New Town. To begin the approach to the Old Town proper, start at the lower end of the square, walk past the tall, Art Deco Koruna complex, and turn right onto the handsome pedestrian zone of **Na Příkopě.** Turn left onto Havířská ulice and follow this small alley to the glittering green-and-cream splendor of the 18th-century theater called the **Stavovské divadlo** ①.

Return to Na Příkopě, turn left, and continue to the end of the street. On weekdays between 8 AM and 5 PM, it's well worth taking a peek at

Prague

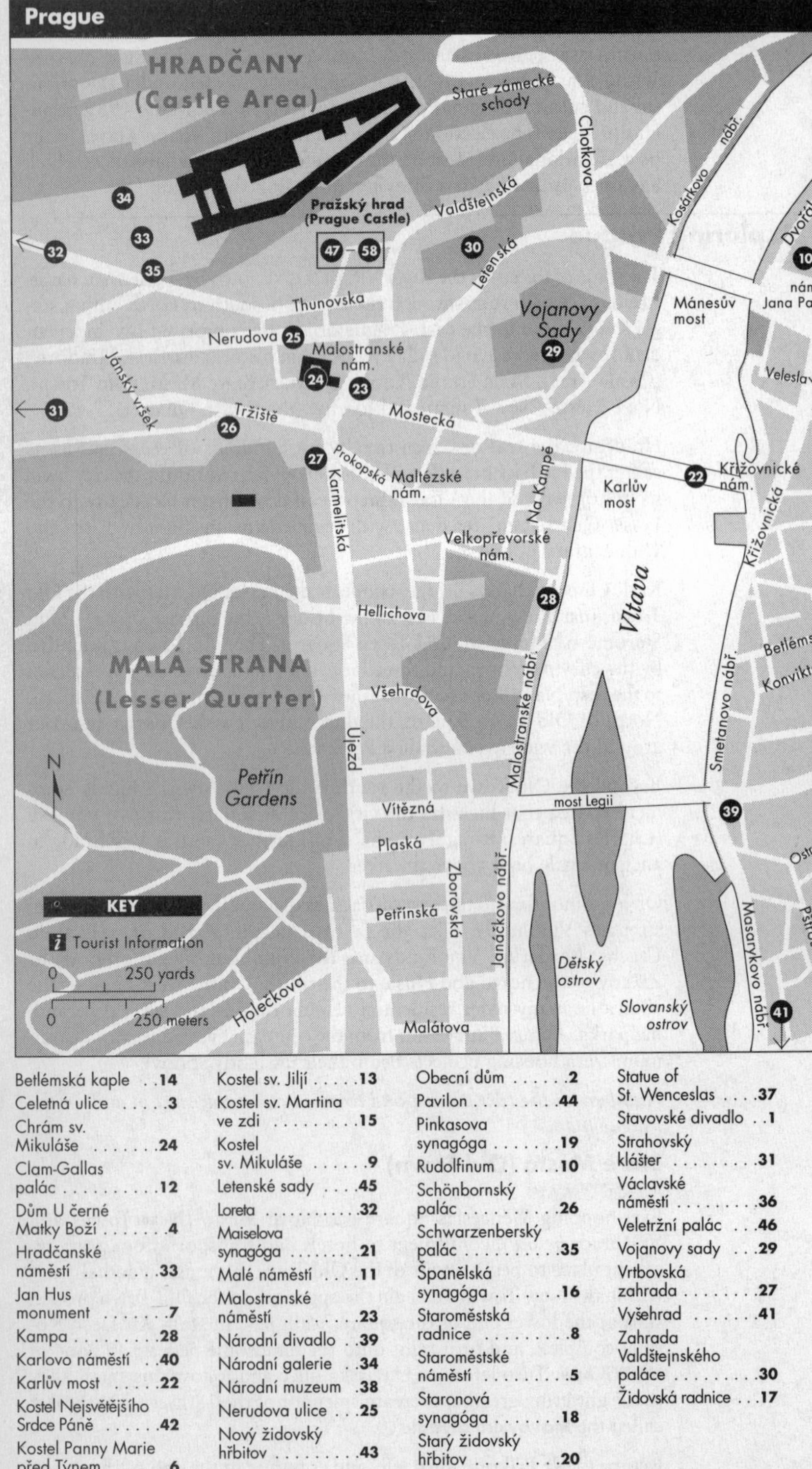

Betlémská kaple . . **14**
Celetná ulice **3**
Chrám sv. Mikuláše **24**
Clam-Gallas palác **12**
Dům U černé Matky Boží **4**
Hradčanské náměstí **33**
Jan Hus monument **7**
Kampa **28**
Karlovo náměstí . . **40**
Karlův most **22**
Kostel Nejsvětějšího Srdce Páně **42**
Kostel Panny Marie před Týnem **6**
Kostel sv. Jiljí **13**
Kostel sv. Martina ve zdi **15**
Kostel sv. Mikuláše **9**
Letenské sady **45**
Loreta **32**
Maiselova synagóga **21**
Malé náměstí **11**
Malostranské náměstí **23**
Národní divadlo . . **39**
Národní galerie . . **34**
Národní muzeum . **38**
Nerudova ulice . . . **25**
Nový židovský hřbitov **43**
Obecní dům **2**
Pavilon **44**
Pinkasova synagóga **19**
Rudolfinum **10**
Schönbornský palác **26**
Schwarzenberský palác **35**
Španělská synagóga **16**
Staroměstská radnice **8**
Staroměstské náměstí **5**
Staronová synagóga **18**
Starý židovský hřbitov **20**
Statue of St. Wenceslas **37**
Stavovské divadlo . . **1**
Strahovský klášter **31**
Václavské náměstí **36**
Veletržní palác . . . **46**
Vojanovy sady . . . **29**
Vrtbovská zahrada **27**
Vyšehrad **41**
Zahrada Valdštejnského paláce **30**
Židovská radnice . . . **17**

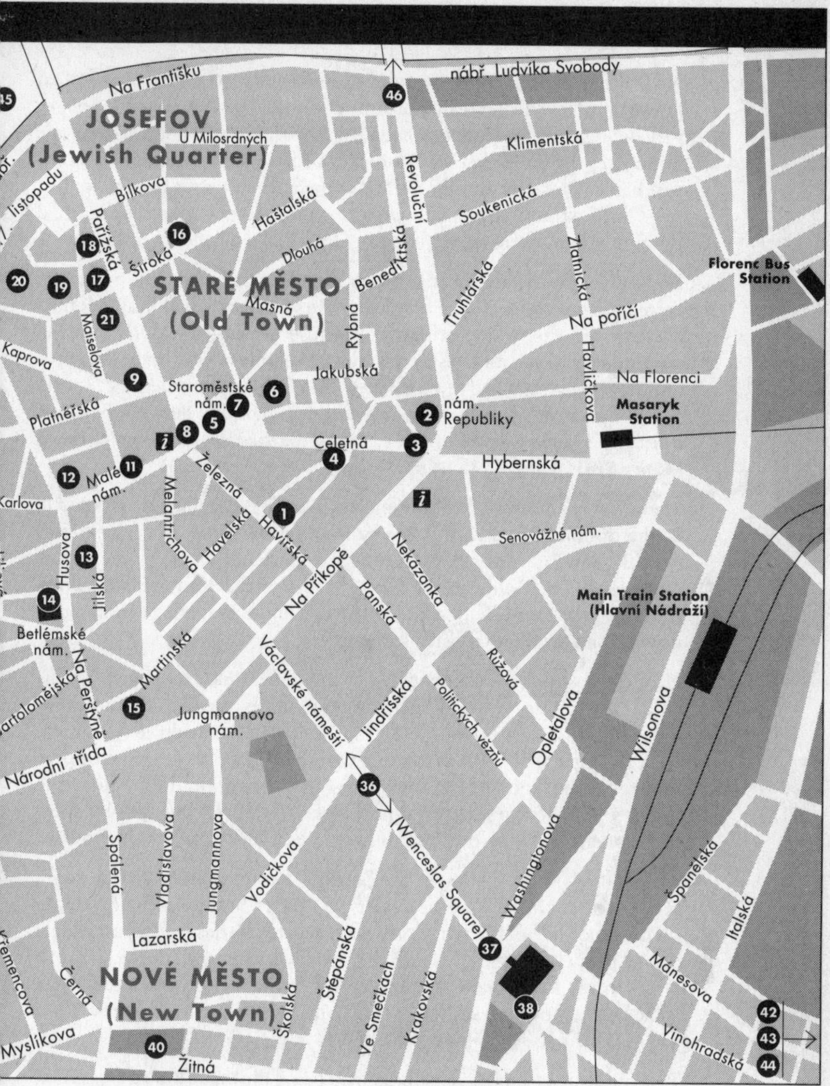

nábř. Ludvíka Svobody
Na Františku
JOSEFOV
(Jewish Quarter)
U Milosrdných
Klimentská
Revoluční
listopadu
Bílkova
Haštalská
Soukenická
Pařížská
Široká
Dlouhá
Benediktská
Zlatnická
Florenc Bus Station
STARÉ MĚSTO
(Old Town)
Masná
Truhlářská
Na poříčí
Maiselova
Rybná
Havlíčkova
Kaprova
Jakubská
Na Florenci
Staroměstské nám.
Masaryk Station
Platnéřská
nám. Republiky
Celetná
Hybernská
Malé nám.
Karlova
Železná
Melantrichova
Havířská
Senovážné nám.
Husova
Havelská
Nekázanka
Na Příkopě
Panská
Main Train Station (Hlavní Nádraží)
Jilská
Betlémské nám.
Martinská
Václavské náměstí
Růžová
Na Perštýně
Jindřišská
Politických vězňů
Jungmannovo nám.
Opletalova
Wilsonova
Národní třída
(Wenceslas Square)
Spálená
Vladislavova
Jungmannova
Vodičkova
Washingtonova
Španělská
Italská
Lazarská
Štěpánská
Ve Smečkách
Krakovská
Mánesova
Černá
NOVÉ MĚSTO
(New Town)
Školská
Vinohradská
Myslíkova
Žitná

the stunning interior of the Živnostenská banka (Merchant's Bank), at No. 20.

Na Příkopě ends abruptly at náměstí Republiky (Republic Square), an important New Town transportation hub (with a metro stop). The severe depression-era facade of the Česká Národní banka (at Na Příkopě 30) makes the building look more like a fortress than the nation's central bank. Close by stands a stately tower, the **Prašná brána,** its festive Gothic spires looming above the square. Adjacent to this dignified building, the **Obecní dům** ② concert hall looks decidedly decadent.

Walk through the arch at the base of the Prašná brána and down the formal **Celetná ulice** ③, the first leg of the so-called Royal Way. Monarchs favored this route primarily because the houses along Celetná were among the city's finest, providing a suitable backdrop to the coronation procession. The pink U Sixtu (Sixt House), at Celetná 2, sports one of the street's handsomest, if restrained, Baroque facades. Baroque influence is even visible in the Cubist department store **Dům U černé Matky Boží** ④, now a museum.

Staroměstské náměstí ⑤, at the end of Celetná, is dazzling, thanks partly to the double-spired **Kostel Panny Marie před Týnem** ⑥, which rises over the square from behind a row of patrician houses. To the immediate left of this church, at No. 13, is Dům U Kamenného zvonu (House at the Stone Bell), a Baroque town house that has been stripped down to its original Gothic elements.

Next door stands the gorgeous pink-and-ocher **Palác Kinských.** At this end of the square, you can't help noticing the expressive **Jan Hus monument** ⑦. Just beyond is the Gothic **Staroměstská radnice** ⑧, which, with its impressive 200-ft tower, gives the square its sense of importance. As the hour approaches, join the crowds milling below the tower's 15th-century astronomical clock for a brief but spooky spectacle taken straight from the Middle Ages, every hour on the hour.

The square's second church, the Baroque **Kostel svatého Mikuláše** ⑨, is not to be confused with the Lesser Quarter's Chrám svatého Mikuláše on the other side of the river (☞ Karlův most [Charles Bridge] and Malá Strana [Lesser Quarter], *below*). For a small detour, head down Kaprova street to the **Rudolfinum** ⑩ concert hall and gallery; across the street is the Uměleckoprůmyslové muzeum (Museum of Decorative Arts). Both are notable neo-Renaissance buildings.

Returning to Staroměstské náměstí, you'll find the **Franz Kafka Exposition** adjoining Kostel svatého Mikuláše on náměstí Franze Kafky, a little square that used to be part of U Radnice street. Continue along U Radnice proper just a few yards until you come to **Malé náměstí** ⑪, a mini-square with arcades on one side. Look for tiny Karlova ulice, which begins in the southwest corner of the square, and take another quick right to stay on it (watch the signs—this medieval street seems designed to confound the visitor). At the České muzeum výtvarných umění (Czech Museum of Fine Arts), pause and inspect the exotic **Clam-Gallas palác** ⑫, behind you at Husova 20. You'll recognize it easily: look for the Titans in the doorway holding up what must be a very heavy Baroque facade. Head the other way down Husova for a glimpse of ecstatic Baroque stuffed inside somber Gothic at the **Kostel svatého Jiljí** ⑬, at No. 8.

Continue walking along Husova to Na Perštýně and turn right at tiny Betlémská ulice. The alley opens up onto a quiet square, Betlémské náměstí, and upon the most revered of all Hussite churches in Prague, the **Betlémská kaple** ⑭.

Return to Na Perštýně and continue walking to the right. As you near the back of the buildings of the busy Národní třída (National Boulevard), turn left at Martinská ulice. At the end of the street, the forlorn but majestic church **Kostel svatého Martina ve zdi** ⑮ stands like a postwar ruin. Walk around the church to the left and through a little archway of apartments onto the bustling Národní třída. To the left, a five-minute walk away, lies Wenceslas Square and the starting point of the walk.

TIMING

Wenceslas Square and Old Town Square are busy with activity around-the-clock almost all year round. If you're in search of a little peace and quiet, you will find the streets at their most subdued on early weekend mornings or right after a sudden downpour. The streets in this walking tour are reasonably close together and can be covered in half a day. Remember to be in the Old Town Square just before the hour if you want to see the astronomical clock in action.

SIGHTS TO SEE

14 **Betlémská kaple** (Bethlehem Chapel). The church's elegant simplicity is in stark contrast to the diverting Gothic and Baroque of the rest of the city. The original structure dates from the end of the 14th century, and the Czech religious reformer Jan Hus was a regular preacher here from 1402 until his exile in 1412. After the Thirty Years' War the church fell into the hands of the Jesuits and was finally demolished in 1786. Excavations carried out after World War I uncovered the original portal and three windows, and the entire church was reconstructed during the 1950s. Although little remains of the first church, some remnants of Hus's teachings can still be read on the inside walls. ⊠ *Betlémské nám. 5.* 🎫 *30 Kč.* ⏲ *Daily 10–5.*

3 **Celetná ulice.** Most of this street's facades indicate the buildings are from the 17th or 18th century, but appearances are deceiving: many of the houses in fact have foundations dating from the 12th century. U Sixtu (Sixt House), at Celetná 2, dates from the 12th century—its Romanesque vaults are still visible in the cellar. The house is being converted into a luxury hotel, due to open in 2001.

12 **Clam-Gallas palác** (Clam-Gallas Palace). The beige-and-brown palace dates from 1713–1729 and is the work of Johann Bernhard Fischer von Erlach, the famed Viennese architectural virtuoso of the day. Enter the building for a glimpse of the finely carved staircase, the work of the master himself, and of the Italian frescoes featuring Apollo that surround it. The building now houses the municipal archives and is rarely open to visitors (so walk in as if you have business there). ⊠ *Husova 20.*

4 **Dům U černé Matky Boží** (House of the Black Madonna). In the second decade of the 20th century, young Czech architects boldly applied Cubism's radical reworking of visual space to structures. Adding a decided jolt to the architectural styles along Celetná, this Cubist building, designed by Josef Gočár, is unflinchingly modern yet topped with an almost Baroque tile roof. It now houses a permanent exhibit of Czech Cubist design and hosts temporary art shows. ⊠ *Celetná 34,* ☎ *02/2421–1732.* 🎫 *35 Kč.* ⏲ *Tues.–Sun. 10–6.*

Franz Kafka Exposition. Kafka came into the world on July 3, 1883, in a house next to the Kostel svatého Mikuláše (Church of St. Nicholas). For years the writer was only grudgingly acknowledged by the Communist cultural bureaucrats, reflecting the traditionally ambiguous attitude of the Czech government toward his work. The Communists were always too uncomfortable with Kafka's themes of bureaucracy and alienation to sing his praises loudly, if at all. As a German and a Jew, moreover, Kafka could easily be dismissed as standing outside the mainstream of Czech literature. Following the 1989 revolution, however, Kafka's popularity soared, and his works are now widely available in Czech. Only the portal of the original house remains; inside the building is a fascinating little exhibit (mostly photographs) on Kafka's life, with commentary in English. ✉ *Nám. Franze Kafky 3 (formerly U Radnice 5).* 🎫 *50 Kč.* ⏲ *Tues.–Fri. 10–6, Sat. 10–5.*

7 **Jan Hus monument.** Few memorials have elicited as much controversy as this one, which was dedicated in July 1915, exactly 500 years after Hus was burned at the stake in Constance, Germany. Some maintain that the monument's Secessionist style (the inscription seems to come right from turn-of-the-20th-century Vienna) clashes with the Gothic and Baroque of the square. Others dispute the romantic depiction of Hus, who appears here in flowing garb as tall and bearded. The real Hus, historians maintain, was short and had a baby face. Still, no one can take issue with the influence of this fiery preacher, whose ability to transform doctrinal disputes, both literally and metaphorically, into the language of the common man made him into a religious and national symbol for the Czechs. ✉ *Staroměstské nám.*

Klášter svaté Anežky České (St. Agnes's Convent). Situated near the river between Pařížská and Revoluční streets, this peaceful complex has Prague's first buildings in the Gothic style, built from the 1230s to the 1280s. The convent is to be home to the National Gallery's marvelous collection of Czech Gothic art, which was scheduled to be moved here from the Klášter svatého Jiří in Prague Castle (☞ *below*) at the end of 2000. Check the status of this maneuver at a visitor bureau or any gallery branch. ✉ *U Milosrdných 17,* ☎ *02/2481–0628.* 🎫 *90 Kč.* ⏲ *Tues.–Sun. 10–6.*

★ 6 **Kostel Panny Marie před Týnem** (Church of the Virgin Mary Before Týn). The exterior of the church is one of the best examples of Prague Gothic and is in part the work of Peter Parler, architect of the Charles Bridge and Chrám svatého Víta (St. Vitus's Cathedral). Construction of its twin black-spire towers was begun later, by King Jiří of Poděbrad in 1461, during the heyday of the Hussites. Jiří had a gilded chalice, the symbol of the Hussites, proudly displayed on the front gable between the two towers. Following the defeat of the Czech Protestants by the Catholic Hapsburgs, the chalice was removed and eventually replaced by a Madonna. As a final blow, the chalice was melted down and made into the Madonna's glimmering halo (you still can see it by walking into the center of the square and looking up between the spires). The entrance to the church is through the arcades on Old Town Square, under the house at No. 604.

Much of the interior, including the tall nave, was rebuilt in the Baroque style in the 17th century. Some Gothic pieces remain, however: look to the left of the main altar for a beautifully preserved set of early Gothic carvings. The main altar itself was painted by Karel Škréta, a luminary of the Czech Baroque. Before leaving the church, look for the grave marker (tucked away to the right of the main altar) of the great Danish astronomer Tycho Brahe, who came to Prague as "Imperial Mathematicus" in 1599 under Rudolf II. As a scientist, Tycho had a place in history that is assured: Johannes Kepler (another resident of the Prague court) used Tycho's observations to formulate his laws of planetary motion. But it is myth that has endeared Tycho to the hearts of Prague residents. The robust Dane, who was apparently fond of duels, lost part of his nose in one (take a closer look at the marker). He quickly had a wax nose fashioned for everyday use but preferred to parade around on holidays and festive occasions sporting a bright silver one. ⊠ *Staroměstské nám., between Celetná and Týnská.* ⊙ *Hours vary.*

13 **Kostel svatého Jiljí** (Church of St. Giles). This was another important outpost of Czech Protestantism in the 16th century. The exterior is a powerful example of Gothic architecture, including the buttresses and a characteristic portal. The interior, as in many important Czech churches, is Baroque, with a design by Johann Bernhard Fischer von Erlach and sweeping frescoes by Václav Reiner. The interior can be viewed during the day from the vestibule or at the evening concerts held several times a week. ⊠ *Husova 8.*

15 **Kostel svatého Martina ve zdi** (Church of St. Martin-in-the-Wall). It was here in 1414 that Holy Communion was first given to the Bohemian laity in the form of both bread and wine, in defiance of the Catholic custom of the time, which dictated that only bread was to be offered to the masses, with wine reserved for the priests and clergy. From then on, the chalice came to symbolize the Hussite movement. The church is open for evening concerts, held several times each week. ⊠ *Martinská ul.*

9 **Kostel svatého Mikuláše** (Church of St. Nicholas). Designed in the 18th century by Prague's own master of late Baroque, Kilian Ignaz Dientzenhofer, this church is probably less successful in capturing the style's lyric exuberance than its namesake across town, the Chrám svatého Mikuláše. Still, Dientzenhofer utilized the limited space to create a well-balanced structure. The interior is compact, with a beautiful but small chandelier and an enormous black organ that seems to overwhelm the rear of the church. The church hosts almost continuous afternoon and evening tourist concerts. ⊠ *Staroměstské nám. Apr.–Oct., Mon. noon–4, Tues.–Sat. 10–4, Sun. noon–3; Nov.–Mar., Tues.–Fri. and Sun. 10–noon (Wed. until 4).*

11 **Malé náměstí** (Small Square). Note the iron fountain dating from around 1560 in the center of the square. The colorfully painted house at No. 3, originally a hardware store, is not as old as it looks, but here and there you can find authentic Gothic portals and Renaissance sgraffiti that betray the square's true age.

Na Příkopě. The name means "At the Moat" and harks back to the time when the street was indeed a moat separating the Old Town from the New Town. Today the pedestrian zone Na Příkopě is prime shopping territory. At No. 19 an oversize new building, one of the worst excesses of the 1990s in Prague, houses a Marks & Spencer store. Have a look at the chic, hard-edged black-and-white Černá Růže (Black Rose) arcade at No. 12.

2 **Obecní dům** (Municipal House). The city's Art Nouveau showpiece still fills the role it had when it was completed in 1911: it's a center for concerts, rotating art exhibits, and café society. The mature Art Nouveau style recalls the lengths the Czech middle classes went to at the turn of the 20th century to imitate Paris, then the epitome of style and glamour. Much of the interior bears the work of Art Nouveau master Alfons Mucha, Max Švabinský, and other leading Czech artists. Mucha decorated the Hall of the Lord Mayor upstairs with impressive, magical frescoes depicting Czech history; unfortunately it's not open to the public. The beautiful **Smetanova síň** (Smetana Hall), which hosts concerts by the Prague Symphony Orchestra as well as international guests, is on the second floor. The ground-floor café is touristy, but a lovely sight with its glimmering chandeliers and exquisite woodwork. There's also a beer hall in the cellar with passable beer and mediocre food and superbly executed ceramic murals on the walls. ⊠ *Nám. Republiky 5,* ☎ *02/2200–2100.* ⊙ *Information center and box office daily 10–6.*

NEED A BREAK? If you prefer subtle elegance, head around the corner to the café at the **Hotel Paříž** (✉ U Obecního domu 1, ☎ 02/2422–2151), a Jugendstil jewel tucked away on a relatively quiet street.

Palác Kinských (Kinský Palace). This exuberant building, built in 1765 from Kilian Ignaz Dientzenhofer's design, is considered one of Prague's finest late-Baroque structures. With its exaggerated pink overlay and numerous statues, the facade looks extreme when contrasted with the more staid Baroque elements of other nearby buildings. (The interior, however, was "modernized" under Communism.) The palace once housed a German school—where Franz Kafka was a student for nine misery-laden years—and presently contains the National Gallery's graphics collection. At press time exhibitions were scheduled to reopen by the end of 2000 following reconstruction of the interior. It was from this building that Communist leader Klement Gottwald, flanked by his Slovak comrade Vladimír Clementis, first addressed the crowds after seizing power in February 1948—an event recounted in the first chapter of Milan Kundera's novel *The Book of Laughter and Forgetting.* ✉ *Staroměstské nám. 12.*

Prašná brána (Powder Tower). Construction of the tower, which replaced one of the city's 13 original gates, was begun by King Vladislav II of Jagiello in 1475. At the time, the kings of Bohemia maintained their royal residence next door, on the site of the current Obecní dům (☞ *above*), and the tower was intended to be the grandest gate of all. But Vladislav was Polish and thus heartily disliked by the rebellious Czech citizens of Prague. Nine years after he assumed power, fearing for his life, he moved the royal court across the river to Prague Castle. Work on the tower was abandoned, and the half-finished structure was used for storing gunpowder—hence its odd name—until the end of the 17th century. The oldest part of the tower is the base. The golden spires were not added until the end of the 19th century. Climb to the top for a striking view of the Old Town and Prague Castle in the distance. ✉ *Nám. Republiky.* 🎫 *20 Kč.* ⏲ *Apr.–Oct., daily 9–6.*

10 **Rudolfinum.** Thanks to a thorough makeover and exterior sandblasting, this neo-Renaissance monument designed by Josef Zítek and Josef Schulz presents the cleanest, brightest stonework in the city. Completed in 1884 and named for then–Hapsburg Crown Prince Rudolf, the rather low-slung sandstone building was meant to be a combination concert hall and exhibition gallery. After 1918 it was converted into the parliament of the newly independent Czechoslovakia until German invaders reinstated the concert hall in 1939. Czech writer Jiří Weil's novel *Mendelssohn Is on the Roof* tells of the cruel farce that ensued when officials ordered the removal of the Jewish composer's statue from the roof balustrade. Now the Czech Philharmonic has its home base here. The 1,200-seat **Dvořákova síň** (Dvořák Hall) has superb acoustics (the box office faces 17. listopadu). ✉ *Nám. Jana Palacha,* ☎ *02/2489–3111.*

Behind Dvořák Hall is a set of large exhibition rooms, the **Galerie Rudolfinum**, an innovative, state-supported gallery for rotating shows of contemporary art. Four or five large shows are mounted here annually, showcasing excellent Czech work along with international artists such as photographer Cindy Sherman. ✉ *Alšovo nábř. 12,* ☎ *02/2489–3205.* 🎫 *40 Kč.* ⏲ *Tues.–Sun. 10–6.*

★ 8 **Staroměstská radnice** (Old Town Hall). This is one of Prague's magnets: hundreds of people gravitate to it to see the hour struck by the mechanical figures of the **astronomical clock**. Just before the hour, look to the upper part of the clock, where a skeleton begins by tolling a death knell and turning an hourglass upside down. The Twelve Apostles parade momentarily, and then a cockerel flaps its wings and crows, piercing the air as the hour finally strikes. To the right of the skeleton, the dreaded Turk nods his head, seemingly hinting at another invasion like those of the 16th and 17th centuries. This small spectacle doesn't clue viewers in to the way this 15th-century marvel indicates the time—by the season, the zodiac sign, and the positions of the sun and moon. The calendar under the clock dates from the mid 19th century.

The Old Town Hall served as the center of administration for the Old Town beginning in 1338, when King John of Luxembourg first granted the city council the right to a permanent location. The impressive 200 ft **Town Hall Tower**, where the clock is mounted, was first built in the 14th century and given its current late-Gothic appearance around 1500 by the master Matyáš Rejsek. For a rare view of the Old Town and its maze of crooked streets and alleyways, climb the ramp or ride the elevator to the top of the tower.

If you walk around the hall to the left, you'll see it's actually a series of houses jutting into the square; they were purchased over the years and successively added to the complex. On the other side, jagged stonework reveals where a large, neo-Gothic wing once adjoined the tower until it was destroyed during fighting between townspeople and Nazi troops in May 1945.

Guided tours (most guides speak English, and English texts are on hand) of the Old Town Hall depart from the main desk inside. However, the only notable features are the fine Renaissance ceilings, the Gothic Council Room, and the Gothic chapel, where you can see the clock's apostles up close. ✉ *Staroměstské nám.* 🎫 *Tower 30 Kč, tours 30 Kč each.* ⏲ *Tues.–Sun. 9–6, Mon. 11–6 (until 5, Oct.–Apr.).*

★ ❺ **Staroměstské náměstí** (Old Town Square). There are places that, on first glimpse, stop you dead in your tracks in sheer wonder. Old Town Square is one such place. Long the heart of the Old Town, the square grew to its present proportions when the city's original marketplace was moved away from the river in the 12th century. Its shape and appearance have changed little over the years. During the day the square has a festive atmosphere as musicians vie for the favor of onlookers and artists display renditions of Prague street scenes. At night, the gaudily lit towers of the Church of the Virgin Mary Before Týn rise ominously over the glowing Baroque facades. The crowds thin out, and the ghosts of the square's stormy past return.

During the 15th century the square was the focal point of conflict between Czech Hussites and German Catholics. In 1422 the radical Hussite preacher Jan Želivský was executed here for his part in storming the New Town's town hall three years earlier (☞ Karlovo náměstí *in* Nové Město [New Town] and Vyšehrad, *below*). In the 1419 uprising, three Catholic consuls and seven German citizens were thrown out the window—the first of Prague's many famous defenestrations. Within a few years, the Hussites had taken over the town, expelled the Germans, and set up their own administration.

Twenty-seven white crosses set flat in the paving stones in the square, at the Old Town Hall's base, mark the spot where 27 Bohemian noblemen were killed by the Hapsburgs in 1621 during the dark days following the defeat of the Czechs at the Battle of White Mountain. The grotesque spectacle, designed to quash any further national or religious opposition, took some five hours to complete, as the men were put to the sword or hanged one by one.

One of the square's most interesting houses, at No. 3, juts out into the small extension leading into Malé náměstí. This is the house called U

Minuty, with its 16th-century Renaissance sgraffiti of biblical and classical motifs. The young Franz Kafka lived here in the 1890s.

❶ **Stavovské divadlo** (Estates Theater). Built in the 1780s in the classical style, this handsome theater was for many years a beacon of Czech-language culture in a city long dominated by the German variety. It is probably best known as the site of the world premiere of Mozart's opera *Don Giovanni* in October 1787, with the composer himself conducting. Prague audiences were quick to acknowledge Mozart's genius: the opera was an instant hit here, though it flopped nearly everywhere else in Europe. Mozart wrote most of the opera's second act in Prague at the Villa Bertramka (☞ Karlův most [Charles Bridge] and Malá Strana [Lesser Quarter], *below*), where he was a frequent guest. ✉ *Ovocný trh 1,* ☎ *02/2421–5001 (box office).*

Josefov (Jewish Quarter)

Prague's Jews survived centuries of discrimination, but two unrelated events of modern times have left their historic ghetto little more than a collection of museums. Around 1900, city officials decided for hygienic purposes to raze the minuscule neighborhood—it had ceased to be a true ghetto with the political reforms of 1848–49, and by this time the majority of its residents were poor Gentiles—and pave over its crooked streets. Only some of the synagogues, the town hall, and the cemetery survived this early attempt at urban renewal. The second event was the Holocaust. Under Nazi occupation, a staggering percentage of the city's Jews were deported or murdered in concentration camps. Of the 35,000 Jews living in Prague before World War II, only about 1,200 returned to resettle the city after the war. The community is still tiny. Only a scant few Jews, mostly elderly, live in the "ghetto" today.

Treasures and artifacts of the ghetto are now the property of the **Židovské muzeum v Praze** (Prague Jewish Museum; ☎ 02/231–7191), which includes the Old Jewish Cemetery and collections installed in four surviving synagogues and the Ceremony Hall. (The Staronová synagóga, or Old-New Synagogue, a functioning house of worship, technically does not belong to the museum, but the Prague Jewish Community oversees both.) The museum was founded in 1906, but traces the vast majority of its holdings to the Nazis' destruction of 150 Jewish communities in Bohemia and Moravia. Dedicated museum workers, nearly all of whom were to die at Nazi hands, gathered and cataloged the stolen artifacts under German supervision. Exhibitions were even held during the war. A ticket good for all museum sites may be purchased at any of the synagogues but the Old-New Synagogue; single-site tickets apply only at the Old-New Synagogue and during occasional exhibits at the Spanish Synagogue. All museum sites are closed Saturday and Jewish holidays.

A GOOD WALK

To reach the Jewish Quarter, leave Old Town Square via handsome Pařížská ulice, centerpiece of the urban renewal effort, and head north toward the river. The festive atmosphere changes suddenly as you enter the area of the ghetto. The buildings are lower here; the mood is hushed. Take a right on Široká and stroll two blocks down to the recently restored **Španělská synagóga** ⑯. Head back the other way, past Pařížská, turn right on Maiselova, and you'll come to the **Židovská radnice** ⑰, home to the Jewish Community Center. Adjoining it on Červená is the 16th-century High Synagogue. Across the street, at Červená 2, you see the **Staronová synagóga** ⑱, the oldest surviving synagogue in Prague.

Go west on the little street U starého hřbitova. The main museum ticket office is at the **Klausová synagóga** at No. 3A. Next door, separated from the synagogue by the exit gate of the Old Jewish Cemetery, is the former building of the Jewish Burial Society, **Obřadní síň,** which exhibits traditional Jewish funeral objects.

Return to Maiselova and follow it to Široká. Turn right to find the **Pinkasova synagóga** ⑲, a handsome Gothic structure. Here also is the entrance to the Jewish ghetto's most astonishing sight, the **Starý židovský hřbitov** ⑳.

Return to Maiselova once more and turn right in the direction of the Old Town. Look in at the displays of Czech Jewish history in the **Maiselova synagóga** ㉑.

TIMING

The Jewish Quarter is one of the most popular visitor destinations in Prague, especially in the height of summer, when its tiny streets are jammed to bursting with tourists almost all the time. The best time for a quieter visit is early morning when the museums and cemetery first open. The area itself is very compact, and a fairly thorough tour should only take half a day.

SIGHTS TO SEE

Klausová synagóga (Klausen Synagogue). This Baroque former synagogue was built at the end of the 17th century in the place of three small buildings (a synagogue, school, and ritual bath) that were destroyed in a fire that devastated the ghetto in 1689. Inside, displays of Czech Jewish traditions emphasize celebrations and daily life. ✉ *U starého hřbitova 3A.* 🎫 *Combined ticket to museum sites and Old-New Synagogue, 480 Kč; museum sites only, 280 Kč.* ⏲ *Apr.–Oct., Sun.–Fri. 9–6; Nov.–Mar., Sun.–Fri. 9–4:30.*

21 **Maiselova synagóga** (Maisel Synagogue). Here, the history of Czech Jews from the 10th to the 18th century is illustrated with the aid of some of the Prague Jewish Museum's most precious objects, including silver Torah shields and pointers, spice boxes, and candelabra; historic tombstones; and fine ceremonial textiles, including some donated by Mordechai Maisel to the synagogue he founded. The richest items come from the late 16th and early 17th century—a prosperous era for Prague's Jews. ✉ *Maiselova 10.* 🎫 *Combined ticket to museum sites and Old-New Synagogue, 480 Kč; museum sites only, 280 Kč.* ⏲ *Apr.–Oct., Sun.–Fri. 9–6; Nov.–Mar., Sun.–Fri. 9–4:30.*

Obřadní síň (Ceremony Hall). In this neo-Romanesque building, the focus is on rather grim subjects: Jewish funeral paraphernalia, old gravestones, and medical instruments. Special attention is paid to the activities of the Jewish Burial Society through many fine objects and paintings. ✉ *U starého hřbitova 3A.* 🎫 *Combined ticket to museum sites and Old-New Synagogue, 480 Kč; museum sites only, 280 Kč.* ⏲ *Apr.–Oct., Sun.–Fri. 9–6; Nov.–Mar., Sun.–Fri. 9–4:30.*

19 **Pinkasova synagóga** (Pinkas Synagogue). This synagogue has two particularly moving testimonies to the appalling crimes perpetrated against the Jews during World War II. One tribute astounds by sheer numbers: The inside walls are covered with nearly 80,000 names of Bohemian and Moravian Jews murdered by the Nazis. Among them are the names of the paternal grandparents of U.S. Secretary of State Madeleine Albright, who learned of their fate only in 1997. There is also an exhibition of drawings made by children at the Nazi concentration camp Terezín [☞ Northern Bohemia, *below*]. The Nazis used the camp for propaganda purposes to demonstrate their "humanity" toward the Jews, and prisoners were given relative freedom to lead "normal" lives. However, transports to death camps in Poland began in earnest in 1944, and

many thousands of Terezín prisoners, including many of these children, eventually perished. ✉ *Enter from Široká 3.* 🎫 *Combined ticket to museum sites and Old-New Synagogue, 480 Kč; museum sites only, 280 Kč.* ⏲ *Apr.–Oct., Sun.–Fri. 9–6; Nov.–Mar., Sun.–Fri. 9–4:30.*

★ 16 **Španělská synagóga** (Spanish Synagogue). A domed Moorish-style synagogue was built in 1868 on the site of the Altschul, the city's oldest synagogue. Here, the historical exposition that begins in the Maisel Synagogue (☞ *above)* continues, taking the story up to the post–World War II period. The displays are not that compelling, but the building's painstakingly restored interior definitely is. ✉ *Vězeňská 1.* 🎫 *Combined ticket to museum sites and Old-New Synagogue, 480 Kč; museum sites only, 280 Kč.* ⏲ *Apr.–Oct., Sun.–Fri. 9–6; Nov.–Mar., Sun.–Fri. 9–4:30.*

★ 18 **Staronová synagóga** (Old-New Synagogue, or Altneuschul). Dating from the mid 13th century, this is one of the most important works of early Gothic in Prague. The odd name recalls the legend that the synagogue was built on the site of an ancient Jewish temple and that stones from the temple were used to build the present structure. The oldest part of the synagogue is the entrance, with its vault supported by two pillars. The synagogue has not only survived fires and the razing of the ghetto at the end of the last century but also emerged from the Nazi occupation intact; it is still in active use. As the oldest synagogue in Europe that still serves its original function, it is a living storehouse of Bohemian Jewish life. Note that men are required to cover their heads inside and that during services men and women sit apart. ✉ *Červená 2.* 🎫 *Combined ticket to Old-New Synagogue and museum sites, 480 Kč; Old-New Synagogue only, 200 Kč.* ⏲ *Apr.–Oct., Sun.–Thurs. 9–6; Nov.–Mar., Sun.–Thurs. 9–4:30; closes 2–3 hrs early on Fri.*

★ 20 **Starý židovský hřbitov** (Old Jewish Cemetery). This unforgettably melancholy sight not far from the busy city was, from the 15th century to 1787, the final resting place for all Jews living in Prague. The confined space forced graves to be piled one on top of the other. Tilted at crazy angles, the 12,000 visible tombstones are but a fraction of countless thousands more buried below. Walk the path amid the gravestones; the relief symbols you see represent the names and professions of the deceased. The oldest marked grave belongs to the poet Avigdor Kara, who died in 1439; the grave is not accessible from the pathway, but the original tombstone can be seen in the Maisel Synagogue. The best-known marker is that of Jehuda ben Bezalel, the famed Rabbi Loew (died 1609), a chief rabbi of Prague and profound scholar who is credited with creating the mythical Golem. Even today, small scraps of paper bearing wishes are stuffed into the cracks of the rabbi's tomb in the hope he will grant them. Loew's grave lies near the exit. ✉ *Široká 3.,* 🎫 *Combined ticket to museum sites and Old-New Synagogue, 480 Kč; museum sites only, 280 Kč.* ⏲ *Apr.–Oct., Sun.–Fri. 9–6; Nov.–Mar., Sun.–Fri. 9–4:30.*

17 **Židovská radnice** (Jewish Town Hall). The hall was the creation of Mordechai Maisel, an influential Jewish leader at the end of the 16th century. It was restored in the 18th century and given its clock and bell tower at that time. A second clock, with Hebrew numbers, keeps time counterclockwise. Now home to the Jewish Community Center, the building also houses a kosher restaurant, Shalom. ✉ *Maiselova 18.*

Karlův most (Charles Bridge) and Malá Strana (Lesser Quarter)

One of Prague's most exquisite neighborhoods, the Lesser Quarter (or Little Town) was established in 1257 and for years was home to the merchants and craftsmen who served the royal court. The Lesser Quarter is not for the methodical traveler. Its charm lies in the tiny lanes, the sudden blasts of bombastic architecture, and the soul-stirring views that emerge for a second before disappearing behind the sloping roofs.

A GOOD WALK

Begin your tour on the Old Town side of **Karlův most** ㉒, which you can reach by foot in about 10 minutes from the Old Town Square. Rising above it is the majestic **Staroměstská mostecká věž.** The climb of 138 steps is worth the effort for the view you get of the Old Town and, across the river, of the Lesser Quarter and Prague Castle.

It's worth pausing to take a closer look at some of the statues as you walk across Karlův most toward the Lesser Quarter. You'll see Kampa Island below you, separated from the mainland by an arm of the Vltava known as Čertovka (Devil's Stream).

By now you are almost at the end of the bridge. In front of you is the striking conjunction of the two Malá Strana bridge towers, one Gothic, the other Romanesque. Together they frame the Baroque flamboyance of Chrám svatého Mikuláše in the distance. At night this is an absolutely wondrous sight.

Walk under the gateway of the towers into the little uphill street called Mostecká. You have now entered the Lesser Quarter. Follow Mostecká up to the rectangular **Malostranské náměstí** ㉓, now the district's traffic hub rather than its heart. In the middle of the square stands **Chrám svatého Mikuláše** ㉔.

Nerudova ulice ㉕ runs up from the square toward Prague Castle. Lined with gorgeous houses (and in recent years an ever-larger number of places to spend money), it's sometimes burdened with the moniker "Prague's most beautiful street." A tiny passageway at No. 13, on the left-hand side as you go up, leads to Tržiště ulice and the **Schönbornský palác** ㉖, once Franz Kafka's home, now the embassy of the United States. Tržiště winds down to the quarter's traffic-plagued main street, Karmelitská, where the famous Infant Jesus of Prague resides in the **Kostel Panny Marie vítězné.** A few doors away, closer to Tržiště, is a quiet oasis, the **Vrtbovská zahrada** ㉗. Tiny Prokopská ulice leads off of Karmelitská, past the former Church of St. Procopius (now converted, oddly, into an apartment block), and into Maltézské náměstí (Maltese Square), a characteristically noble compound. The square next door, **Velkopřevorské náměstí,** boasts even grander palaces.

A tiny bridge at the cramped square's lower end takes you across the creeklike Čertovka to the island of **Kampa** ㉘ and its broad lawns, cafés, and river views. Winding your way underneath Karlův most and along the street U lužického semináře brings you to a quiet walled garden, **Vojanovy sady** ㉙. To the northwest, hiding off busy Letenská ulice near the Malostranská metro station, is **Zahrada Valdštejnského paláce** ㉚, a more formal garden with an unbeatable view of Prague Castle looming above.

TIMING

The area is at its best in the evening, when the softer light hides the crumbling facades and brings you into a world of glimmering beauty. The basic walk described here could take as little as half a day—longer if you'd like to explore the area's lovely nooks and crannies.

SIGHTS TO SEE

★ ㉔ **Chrám svatého Mikuláše** (Church of St. Nicholas). With its dynamic curves, this church is one of the purest and most ambitious examples of high Baroque. The celebrated architect Christoph Dientzenhofer began the Jesuit church in 1704 on the site of one of the more active Hussite churches of 15th-century Prague. Work on the building was taken over by his son Kilian Ignaz Dientzenhofer, who built the dome and presbytery. Anselmo Lurago completed the whole in 1755 by adding the bell tower. The juxtaposition of the broad, full-bodied dome with the slender bell tower is one of the many striking architectural contrasts that mark the Prague skyline. Inside, the vast pink-and-green space is impossible to take in with a single glance. Every corner bristles with movement, guiding the eye first to the dramatic statues, then to the hectic frescoes, and on to the shining faux-marble pillars. Many of the statues are the work of Ignaz Platzer, and in fact they constitute his last blaze of success. Platzer's workshop was forced to declare bankruptcy when the centralizing and secularizing reforms of Joseph II toward the end of the 18th century brought an end to the flamboyant Baroque era. ✉ *Malostranské nám.* 🎫 *30 Kč.* ⏲ *Daily 9–4.*

28 **Kampa.** Prague's largest island is cut off from the "mainland" by the narrow Čertovka streamlet. The name Čertovka, or Devil's Stream, reputedly refers to a cranky old lady who once lived on Maltese Square (given the river's present filthy state, the name is certainly appropriate). The unusually well-kept lawns of the **Kampa Gardens** that occupy much of the island are one of the few places in Prague where sitting on the grass is openly tolerated. If it's a warm day, spread out a blanket and bask for a while in the sunshine. The row of benches that lines the river is also a popular spot from which to contemplate the city. At night this stretch along the river is especially romantic.

★ 22 **Karlův most** (Charles Bridge). The view from the foot of the bridge on the Old Town side is nothing short of breathtaking, encompassing the towers and domes of the Lesser Quarter and the soaring spires of St. Vitus's Cathedral to the northwest. This heavenly vision changes subtly in perspective as you walk across the bridge, attended by the host of Baroque saints that decorate the bridge's peaceful Gothic stones. At night its drama is spellbinding: St. Vitus's Cathedral lit in a ghostly green, the castle in monumental yellow, and the Church of St. Nicholas in a voluptuous pink, all viewed through the menacing silhouettes of the bowed statues and the Gothic towers. If you do nothing else in Prague, you must visit the Charles Bridge at night. During the day the pedestrian bridge buzzes with activity. Street musicians vie with artisans hawking jewelry, paintings, and glass for the hearts and wallets of the passing multitude. At night the crowds thin out a little, the musicians multiply, and the bridge becomes a long block party—nearly everyone brings a bottle.

When the Přemyslid princes set up residence in Prague in the 10th century, there was a ford across the Vltava at this point—a vital link along one of Europe's major trading routes. After several wooden bridges and the first stone bridge had washed away in floods, Charles IV appointed the 27-year-old German Peter Parler, the architect of St. Vitus's Cathedral, to build a new structure in 1357. After 1620, following the defeat of Czech Protestants by Catholic Hapsburgs at the Battle of White Mountain, the bridge became a symbol of the Counter-Reformation's vigorous re-Catholicization efforts. The many Baroque statues that began to appear in the late 17th century, commissioned by Catholics, eventually came to symbolize the totality of the Austrian (hence Catholic) triumph. The Czech writer Milan Kundera sees the statues from this perspective: "The thousands of saints looking out from all sides, threatening you, following you, hypnotizing you, are the raging hordes of occupiers who invaded Bohemia 350 years ago to tear the people's faith and language from their hearts."

The religious conflict is less obvious nowadays, leaving only the artistic tension between Baroque and Gothic that gives the bridge its allure. It's worth pausing to take a closer look at some of the statues as you walk toward the Lesser Quarter. The third on the right, a bronze crucifix from the mid 17th century, is the oldest of all. It is mounted on the location of a wooden cross destroyed in a battle with the Swedes (the golden Hebrew inscription was reputedly financed by a Jew accused of defiling the cross). Eighth on the right, the statue of St. John of Nepomuk, designed by Johann Brokoff in 1683, begins the Baroque lineup of saints. On the left-hand side, sticking out from the bridge between the 9th and 10th statues (the latter has a wonderfully expressive vanquished Satan), stands a Roland (Bruncvík) statue. This knightly figure, bearing the coat of arms of the Old Town, was once a reminder that this part of the bridge belonged to the Old Town before Prague became a unified city in 1784.

In the eyes of most art historians, the most valuable statue is the 12th on the left, near the Lesser Quarter end. Mathias Braun's statue of St. Luitgarde depicts the blind saint kissing Christ's wounds. The most compelling grouping, however, is the second from the end on the left, a work of Ferdinand Maxmilian Brokoff (son of Johann) from 1714. Here the saints are incidental; the main attraction is the Turk, his face expressing extreme boredom at guarding the Christians imprisoned in the cage at his side. When the statue was erected, just 31 years after the second Turkish siege of Vienna, it scandalized the Prague public, who smeared it with mud. A half-dozen of the 30 bridge sculptures are 19th-century replacements for originals damaged in wars or sunk in a 1784 flood. All but a couple of the bridge's surviving Baroque statues, including St. Luitgarde and the Turk, have been replaced by modern copies. The 17th- and 18th-century originals are in safer quarters, protected from Prague's acidic air. Several, including St. Luitgarde, can be viewed in the Lapidarium museum at the Výstaviště exhibition grounds in Prague 7; a few more occupy a man-made cavern at Vyšehrad (☞ Nové Město [New Town] and Vyšehrad, *below*).

Kostel Panny Marie vítězné (Church of Our Lady Victorious). This comfortably ramshackle church on the Lesser Quarter's main street is the unlikely home of one of Prague's best-known religious artifacts, the *Pražské Jezulátko* (Infant Jesus of Prague). Originally brought to Prague from Spain in the 16th century, this tiny porcelain doll (now bathed in neon lighting) is renowned worldwide for showering miracles on anyone willing to kneel before it and pray. Nuns from a nearby convent arrive at dawn each day to change the infant's clothes; pieces of the doll's extensive wardrobe have been sent by believers from around the world. ✉ *Karmelitská 9A.* 🎫 *Free.* ⏲ *Mon.–Sat. 10–5:30, Sun. 1–5.*

Ledeburská zahrada (Ledeburg Garden). Rows of steeply banked Baroque gardens rise behind the palaces of Valdštejnská ulice. This one makes a pleasant spot for a rest amid shady arbors and niches. The garden, with its frescoes and statuary, was restored with support from a fund headed by Czech president Václav Havel and Charles, Prince of Wales. ✉ *Entrance at Valdštejnské nám. 3; also from the south gardens of Prague Castle in summer.* 🎫 *25 Kč.* ⏲ *Daily 10–6.*

23 **Malostranské náměstí** (Lesser Quarter Square). The arcaded houses on the east and south sides of the square, dating from the 16th and 17th centuries, exhibit a mix of Baroque and Renaissance elements. The Czech Parliament resides partly in the gaudy yellow-and-green palace on the square's north side, partly in the street behind the palace, Sněmovní. The huge bulk of the Church of St. Nicholas divides the lower, busier

section—buzzing with restaurants, street vendors, clubs, and shops—from the quieter upper part.

25 **Nerudova ulice.** This steep little street used to be the last leg of the Royal Way walked by the king before his coronation, and it is still the best way to get to Prague Castle. It was named for the 19th-century Czech journalist and poet Jan Neruda (after whom Chilean poet Pablo Neruda renamed himself). Until Joseph II's administrative reforms in the late 18th century, house numbering was unknown in Prague. Each house bore a name, depicted on the facade, and these are particularly prominent on Nerudova ulice. House No. 6, **U červeného orla** (At the Red Eagle), proudly displays a faded painting of a red eagle. No. 12 is known as **U tří housliček** (At the Three Fiddles). In the early 18th century, three generations of the Edlinger violin-making family lived here. Joseph II's scheme numbered each house according to its position in its "town" (here the Lesser Quarter) rather than its sequence on the street. The red plates record the original house numbers; the blue ones are the numbers used in addresses today. To confuse the tourist, many architectural guides refer to the old, red-number plates.

Two palaces break the unity of the burghers' houses on Nerudova ulice. Both were designed by the adventurous Baroque architect Giovanni Santini, one of the Italian builders most in demand by wealthy nobles of the early 18th century. The **Morzin Palace,** on the left at No. 5, is now the Romanian Embassy. The fascinating facade, with an allegory of night and day, was created in 1713 and is the work of Ferdinand Brokoff of Charles Bridge statue fame. Across the street at No. 20 is the **Thun-Hohenstein Palace,** now the Italian Embassy. The gateway with two enormous eagles (the emblem of the Kolovrat family, who owned the building at the time) is the work of the other great Charles Bridge statue sculptor, Mathias Braun. Santini himself lived at No. 14, the **Valkoun House.**

The archway at Nerudova 13 hides one of the many winding passageways that give the Lesser Quarter its enchantingly ghostly character at night. Higher up the street at No. 33 is the **Bretfeld Palace,** a rococo house on the corner of Jánský vršek. The relief of St. Nicholas on the facade is the work of Ignaz Platzer, a sculptor known for his classic and rococo work, but the building is valued more for its historical associations than for its architecture: this is where Mozart, his lyricist partner Lorenzo da Ponte, and the aging but still infamous philanderer and music lover Casanova stayed at the time of the world premiere of *Don Giovanni* in 1787.

NEED A BREAK? Nerudova ulice is filled with little restaurants and snack bars and offers something for everyone. **U zeleného čaje** (✉ Nerudova 19) is a fragrant little tearoom offering herbal and fruit teas as well as light salads and sweets. **U Kocoura** (✉ Nerudova 2) is a traditional pub that hasn't caved in to touristic niceties.

26 **Schönbornský palác** (Schönborn Palace). Franz Kafka had an apartment in this massive Baroque building at the top of Tržiště ulice in mid-1917, after moving from Zlatá ulička, or Golden Lane (☞ Pražský hrad [Prague Castle], *below*). The U.S. Embassy now occupies this prime location. If you look through the gates, you can see the beautiful formal gardens rising up to the Petřín hill. They are unfortunately not open to the public, but can be glimpsed from the neighboring garden, Vrtbovská zahrada (☞ *below*). ✉ *Tržiště at Vlašská.*

Staroměstská mostecká věž (Old Town Bridge Tower). This was where Peter Parler, the architect of St. Vitus's Cathedral and eventually the Charles

Bridge, began his bridge building. The carved facades he designed for the sides of the tower were destroyed by Swedish soldiers in 1648, at the end of the Thirty Years' War. The sculptures facing the Old Town, however, are still intact (although some are recent copies); they depict an old and gout-ridden Charles IV with his son, who later became Wenceslas IV. Above them are two of Bohemia's patron saints, Adalbert of Prague and Sigismund. Inside the tower is a small exhibit of antique musical instruments. *20 Kč. Daily 10–5 (until 7 in summer).*

Velkopřevorské náměstí (Grand Priory Square). This square lies just south of the Charles Bridge, next to the Čertovka. The Grand Prior's Palace fronting the square is considered one of the finest Baroque buildings in the Lesser Quarter, though it is now part of the Embassy of the Knights of Malta and no longer open to the public. Opposite is the flamboyant orange-and-white stucco facade of the Buquoy Palace, built in 1719 by Giovanni Santini and the present home of the French Embassy. The so-called **John Lennon Peace Wall,** leading to a bridge over the Čertovka, was once a kind of monument to youthful rebellion, emblazoned with a large painted head of the former Beatle, lyrics from his songs, and other messages of peace. It has lost much social significance, not to mention attractiveness, since the years around the 1989 revolution when graffiti actually meant something in Prague.

29 **Vojanovy sady** (Vojan Park). Once the gardens of the Monastery of the Discalced Carmelites, later taken over by the Order of the English Virgins, and now part of the Ministry of Finance, this walled garden, with its weeping willows, fruit trees, and benches, makes another peaceful haven in summer. Exhibitions of modern sculptures are often held here, contrasting sharply with the two Baroque chapels and the graceful Ignaz Platzer statue of John of Nepomuk standing on a fish at the entrance. The park is surrounded by the high walls of the old monastery and new Ministry of Finance buildings, with only an occasional glimpse of a tower or spire to remind you that you're in Prague. ✉ *U lužického semináře, between Letenská ul. and Míšeňská ul. Nov.–Mar., daily 8–5; Apr.–Oct., daily 8–7.*

★ 27 **Vrtbovská zahrada** (Vrtba Garden). An unobtrusive door on noisy Karmelitská hides the entranceway to a fascinating oasis that also has one of the best views over the Lesser Quarter. The street door opens onto the intimate courtyard of the Vrtbovský palác (Vrtba Palace), which is now private housing. Two Renaissance wings flank the courtyard; the left one was built in 1575, the right one in 1591. The owner of the latter house was one of the 27 Bohemian nobles executed by the Hapsburgs in 1621 before the Old Town Hall. The house was given as confiscated property to Count Sezima of Vrtba, who bought the neighboring property and turned the buildings into a late-Renaissance palace. The Vrtba Garden, created a century later, reopened in summer 1998 after an excruciatingly long renovation. This is the most elegant of the Lesser Quarter's public gardens, built in five levels rising behind the courtyard in a wave of statuary-bedecked staircases and formal terraces to reach a seashell-decorated pavilion at the top. (The fenced-off garden immediately behind and above belongs to the U.S. Embassy.) The powerful stone figure of Atlas that caps the entranceway in the courtyard and most of the other classically derived statues are from the workshop of Mathias Braun, perhaps the best of the Czech Baroque sculptors. ✉ *Karmelitská 25. 20 Kč. Apr.–Oct., daily 10–6.*

OFF THE BEATEN PATH

VILLA BERTRAMKA – Mozart fans won't want to pass up a visit to this villa, where the great composer lived during a couple of his visits to Prague. The small, well-organized W. A. Mozart Museum is packed with memorabilia, including a flyer for a performance of *Don Giovanni* in 1788, only months after the opera's world premiere at the Estates Theater. Also on hand is one of the master's pianos. Take Tram No. 12 from Karmelitská south (or ride Metro Line B) to the Anděl metro station, then transfer to Tram No. 4, 7, 9, or 10 and ride to the first stop (Bertramka). A 10-minute walk, following the signs, brings you to the villa. ✉ *Mozartova ul. 169, Prague 5 (Smíchov),* ☎ *02/540–012.* 🎫 *90 Kč.* ⏲ *Apr.–Oct., daily 9:30–6; Nov.–Mar., daily 9:30–5.*

★ ㉚ **Zahrada Valdštejnského paláce** (Wallenstein Palace Gardens). Albrecht von Wallenstein, onetime owner of the house and gardens, began a meteoric military career in 1622 when the Austrian emperor Ferdinand II retained him to save the empire from the Swedes and Protestants during the Thirty Years' War. Wallenstein, wealthy by marriage, offered to raise 20,000 men at his own cost and lead them personally. Ferdinand II accepted and showered Wallenstein with confiscated land and titles. Wallenstein's first acquisition was this enormous area. Having knocked down 23 houses, a brick factory, and three gardens, in 1623 he began to build his magnificent palace with its idiosyncratic high-walled gardens and superb, vaulted Renaissance *sala terrena* (room opening onto a garden). Walking around the formal paths, you'll come across numerous statues, an unusual fountain with a woman spouting water from her breasts, and a lava-stone grotto along the wall. Most of the palace itself now serves the Czech Senate as meeting chamber and offices. The palace's cavernous former *Jízdárna,* or riding school, now hosts occasional art exhibitions. ✉ *Garden entrance: Letenská 10.* 🎫 *Garden free.* ⏲ *Garden May–Sept., daily 9–7; Mar. 21–Apr. 30, and Oct., daily 10–6.*

Hradčany (Castle Area)

To the west of Prague Castle is the residential Hradčany (Castle Area), the town that during the early 14th century emerged out of a collection of monasteries and churches. The concentration of history packed into Prague Castle and Hradčany challenges visitors not versed in the ups and downs of Bohemian kings, religious uprisings, wars, and oppression. The picturesque area surrounding Prague Castle, with its breathtaking vistas of the Old Town and the Lesser Quarter, is ideal for just wandering. But the castle itself, with its convoluted history and architecture, is difficult to appreciate fully without investing a little more time.

A GOOD WALK

Begin on Nerudova ulice (☞ Karlův most [Charles Bridge] and Malá Strana [Lesser Quarter], *above*), which runs east–west a few hundred yards south of Prague Castle. At the western (upper) end of the street, look for a flight of stone steps guarded by two saintly statues. Take the stairs up to Loretánská ulice, and take in panoramic views of the Church of St. Nicholas and the Lesser Quarter. At the top of the steps, turn left and walk a couple hundred yards until you come to a dusty elongated square named Pohořelec (Scene of Fire), which suffered tragic fires in 1420, 1541, and 1741. Go through the inconspicuous gateway at No. 8 and up the steps, and you'll find yourself in the courtyard of one of the city's richest monasteries, the **Strahovský klášter** ㉛.

Retrace your steps to Loretánské náměstí, the square at the head of Loretánská ulice that is flanked by the feminine curves of the Baroque church **Loreta** ㉜. Across the road, the 29 half pillars of the Černínský palác (Černín Palace) now mask the Czech Ministry of Foreign Affairs. At the bottom of Loretánské náměstí, a little lane trails to the left into the area known as **Nový Svět**; the name means "New World," though the district is as old-world as they come. Turn right onto the street Nový

Svět. Around the corner you get a tantalizing view of the cathedral through the trees. Walk down the winding Kanovnická ulice past the Austrian Embassy and the dignified but melancholy Kostel svatého Jana Nepomuckého (Church of St. John of Nepomuk). At the top of the street on the left, the rounded, Renaissance corner house, Martinický palác, catches the eye with its detailed sgraffiti decorations. Martinický palác opens onto **Hradčanské náměstí** ㉝ with its grandiose gathering of Renaissance and Baroque palaces. To the left of the bright yellow Arcibiskupský palác (Archbishop's Palace) on the square is an alleyway leading down to the **Národní galerie** ㉞ and its collections of European art. Across the square, the handsome sgraffito sweep of **Schwarzenberský palác** ㉟ beckons; this is the building you saw from the back side at the beginning of the tour.

TIMING

To do justice to the subtle charms of Hradčany, allow at least an hour just for ambling and admiring the passing buildings and views of the city. The Strahovský klášter halls need about a half hour to take in, more if you tour the small picture gallery there, and the Loreta and its treasures need at least that length of time. The Národní galerie in the Šternberský palác deserves at least a couple of hours. Keep in mind that several places are not open on Monday.

SIGHTS TO SEE

33 **Hradčanské náměstí** (Hradčany Square). With its fabulous mixture of Baroque and Renaissance housing, topped by the castle itself, the square had a prominent role (disguised, ironically, as Vienna) in the film *Amadeus,* directed by the then-exiled Czech director Miloš Forman. The house at No. 7 was the set for Mozart's residence, where the composer was haunted by the masked figure he thought was his father. Forman used the flamboyant rococo **Arcibiskupský palác** (Archbishop's Palace), on the left as you face the castle, as the Viennese archbishop's palace. The plush interior, shown off in the film, is open to the public only on Maundy Thursday. No. 11 was home for a brief time after World War II to a little girl named Marie Jana Korbelová, who would grow up to be U.S. Secretary of State Madeleine Albright.

32 **Loreta** (Loreto Church). The church's seductive lines were a conscious move on the part of Counter-Reformation Jesuits in the 17th century who wanted to build up the cult of Mary and attract the largely Protestant Bohemians back to the church. According to legend, angels had carried Mary's house from Nazareth and dropped it in a patch of laurel trees in Ancona, Italy. Known as *Loreto* (from the Latin for laurel), it immediately became a center of pilgrimage. The Prague Loreto was one of many symbolic reenactments of this scene across Europe, and it worked: pilgrims came in droves. The graceful facade, with its voluptuous tower, was built in 1720 by Kilian Ignaz Dientzenhofer, the architect of the two St. Nicholas churches in Prague. Most spectacular of all is a small exhibition upstairs displaying the religious treasures presented to Mary in thanks for various services, including a monstrance studded with 6,500 diamonds. ✉ *Loretánské nám. 7,* 🎫 *80 Kč (priests, monks, and nuns admitted free).* ⏲ *Tues.–Sun. 9–12:15 and 1–4:30.*

★ 34 **Národní galerie** (National Gallery). Housed in the 18th-century **Šternberský palác** (Sternberg Palace), this collection, though impressive, is limited compared to German and Austrian holdings. During the time when Berlin, Dresden, and Vienna were building up superlative old-master galleries, Prague languished, neglected by her Viennese rulers—one reason why the city's museums lag behind. On the first floor there's an exhibition of icons, Italian religious art from the 3rd to 14th century, and early Dutch Renaissance masters. Up a second flight of steps is an assortment of paintings by Cranach, Holbein, Dürer, Van Dyck, El Greco, Rembrandt, and Rubens. Other branches of the National Gallery are scattered around town. ⊠ *Hradčanské nám. 15,* ☎ *02/2051–4634.* 🎫 *90 Kč.* ⊙ *Tues.–Sun. 10–6.* ♿

Nový Svět. This picturesque, winding little alley, with facades from the 17th and 18th centuries, once housed Prague's poorest residents; now many of the homes are used as artists' studios. The last house on the street, No. 1, was the home of the Danish-born astronomer Tycho Brahe. Living so close to the Loreto, so the story goes, Tycho was constantly disturbed during his nightly stargazing by the church bells. He ended up complaining to his patron, Emperor Rudolf II, who instructed the Capuchin monks to finish their services before the first star appeared in the sky.

35 **Schwarzenberský palác** (Schwarzenberg Palace). This boxy palace with its extravagant sgraffito facade contains the **Vojenské historické muzeum** (Military History Museum), one of the largest of its kind in Europe. A dim, old-fashioned collection, it concentrates on pre-20th-century Czech military history. Of more general interest are the jousting tournaments held in the courtyard in summer. ⊠ *Hradčanské nám. 2.* 🎫 *20 Kč.* ⊙ *Apr.–Oct., Tues.–Sun. 10–6.*

★ 31 **Strahovský klášter** (Strahov Monastery). Founded by the Premonstratensian order in 1140, the monastery remained in its hands until 1952, when the Communists suppressed all religious orders and turned the entire complex into the **Památník národního písemnictví** (Museum of National Literature). The major building of interest is the **Strahov Library,** with its collection of early Czech manuscripts, the 10th-century Strahov New Testament, and the collected works of famed Danish astronomer Tycho Brahe. Also of note is the late-18th-century **Philosophical Hall.** Engulfing its ceilings is a startling sky blue fresco that depicts an unusual cast of characters, including Socrates' nagging wife Xanthippe, Greek astronomer Thales with his trusty telescope, and a collection of Greek philosophers mingling with Descartes, Diderot, and Voltaire. Also on the premises is the order's small art gallery, highlighted by late-Gothic altars and paintings from Rudolf II's time. You can arrange for a tour in English with several days' advance notice. ⊠ *Strahovské nádvoří 1/132,* ☎ *02/2051–6671 (tour arrangements).* 🎫 *Gallery 25 Kč, library tour 20 Kč.* ⊙ *Gallery Tues.–Sun. 9–noon and 12:30–5. Library daily 9–noon and 1–5.* ♿

OFF THE BEATEN PATH

PETŘÍN – For a superb view of the city—from a mostly undiscovered, tourist-free perch—stroll over from the Strahov Monastery along the paths toward Prague's own miniature version of the Eiffel Tower. You'll find yourself in a hilltop park, laced with footpaths, with several buildings clustered together near the tower—just keep going gradually upward until you reach the tower's base. The tower and its breathtaking view, the mirror maze (*bludiště*) in a small structure near the tower's base, and the seemingly abandoned svatý Vavřinec (St. Lawrence) church are beautifully peaceful and well worth an afternoon's wandering. You can also walk up from Karmelitská ulice or Újezd down in the Lesser Quarter or ride the funicular railway from U lanové dráhy ulice, off Újezd. Regular public-transportation tickets are valid. For the descent, take the funicular or meander on foot down through the stations of the cross on the pathways leading back to the Lesser Quarter.

Pražský Hrad (Prague Castle)

Numbers in the text correspond to numbers in the margin and on the Prague Castle (Pražský hrad) map.

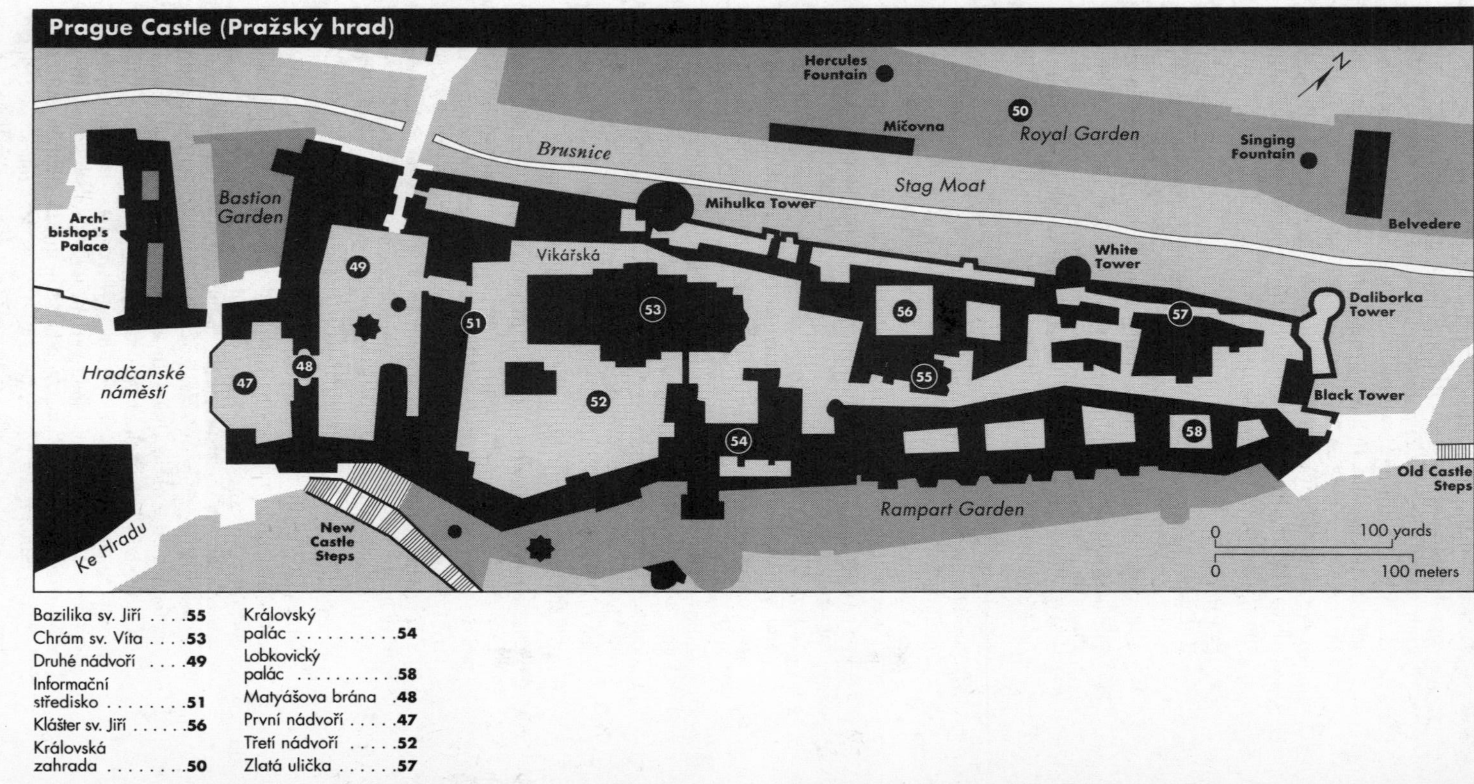

Bazilika sv. Jiří 55
Chrám sv. Víta 53
Druhé nádvoří 49
Informační středisko 51
Klášter sv. Jiří 56
Královská zahrada 50
Královský palác 54
Lobkovický palác 58
Matyášova brána .48
První nádvoří 47
Třetí nádvoří 52
Zlatá ulička 57

Despite its monolithic presence, the Prague Castle is a collection of buildings dating from the 10th to the 20th century, all linked by internal courtyards. The most important structures are **Chrám svatého Víta** (53), clearly visible soaring above the castle walls, and the **Královský palác** (54), the official residence of kings and presidents and still the center of political power in the Czech Republic. The castle is compact and easy to navigate. Be forewarned: in summer, Chrám svatého Víta and Zlatá ulička take the brunt of the heavy sightseeing traffic, although all of the castle is hugely popular.

TIMING

The castle is at its mysterious best in early morning and late evening, and it is incomparable when it snows. The cathedral deserves an hour, as does the Královský palác, while you can easily spend an entire day taking in the museums, the views of the city, and the hidden nooks of the castle. Remember that some sights, such as the Lobkovický palác and the National Gallery branch at Klášter svatého Jiří, are not open on Monday.

SIGHTS TO SEE

55 **Bazilika svatého Jiří** (St. George's Basilica). This church was originally built in the 10th century by Prince Vratislav I, the father of Prince (and St.) Wenceslas. It was dedicated to St. George (of dragon fame), who it was believed would be more agreeable to the still largely pagan people. The outside was remodeled during early Baroque times, although the striking rusty red color is in keeping with the look of the Romanesque edifice. The interior looks more or less as it did in the 12th century and is the best-preserved Romanesque relic in the country. The effect is at once barnlike and peaceful, the warm golden yellow of the stone walls and the small arched windows exuding a sense of enduring harmony. The house-shape painted tomb at the front of the church holds the remains of the founder, Vratislav I. Up the steps, in a chapel to the right, is the tomb Peter Parler designed for St. Ludmila, the grandmother of St. Wenceslas. *Nám. U sv. Jiří.* *For admission information, see Informační středisko, below.* *Apr.–Oct., daily 9–5; Nov.–Mar., daily 9–4.*

★ 53 **Chrám svatého Víta** (St. Vitus's Cathedral). With its graceful, soaring towers, this Gothic cathedral—among the most beautiful in Europe—is the spiritual heart not only of Prague Castle, but of the entire country. It has a long and complicated history, beginning in the 10th century and continuing to its completion in 1929. If you want to hear its history in depth, English-speaking guided tours of the cathedral and the Královský palác (☞ *below*) can be arranged at the information office across from the cathedral entrance.

Once you enter the cathedral, pause to take in the vast but delicate beauty of the Gothic and neo-Gothic interior glowing in the colorful light that filters through the startlingly brilliant stained-glass windows. This western third of the structure, including the facade and the two towers you can see from outside, was not completed until 1929, following the initiative of the Union for the Completion of the Cathedral, set up in the last days of the 19th century. Don't let the neo-Gothic illusion keep you from examining this new section. The six stained-glass windows to your left and right and the large rose window behind are modern masterpieces. Take a good look at the third window up on the left. The familiar Art Nouveau flamboyance, depicting the blessing of Sts. Cyril and Methodius (9th-century missionaries to the Slavs and creators of the Cyrillic alphabet), is the work of the Czech father of the style, Alfons Mucha. He achieved the subtle coloring by painting rather than staining the glass.

If you walk halfway up the right-hand aisle, you will find the **Svatováclavská kaple** (Chapel of St. Wenceslas). With a tomb holding the saint's remains, walls covered in semi-precious stones, and paintings depicting the life of Wenceslas, this square chapel is the ancient heart of the cathedral. Stylistically, it represents a high point of the dense, richly decorated though rather gloomy Gothic favored by Charles IV and his successors. Wenceslas (the "good king" of Christmas-carol fame) was a determined Christian in an era of widespread paganism. Around 925, as prince of Bohemia, he founded a rotunda church dedicated to St. Vitus on this site. But the prince's brother, Boleslav, was impatient to take power, and he ambushed Wenceslas in 929 (or 935 according to some experts) near a church at Stará Boleslav, northeast of Prague. Wenceslas was originally buried in that church, but his grave produced so many miracles that he rapidly became a symbol of piety for the common people, something that greatly irritated the new Prince Boleslav. Boleslav was finally forced to honor his brother by reburying the body in the St. Vitus Rotunda. Shortly afterward, Wenceslas was canonized.

The rotunda was replaced by a Romanesque basilica in the late 11th century. Work was begun on the existing building in 1344. For the first few years the chief architect was the Frenchman Mathias d'Arras, but after his death in 1352 the work was continued by the 22-year-old German architect Peter Parler, who went on to build the Charles Bridge and many other Prague treasures.

The small door in the back of the chapel leads to the **Korunní komora** (Crown Chamber), the repository of the Bohemian crown jewels. It remains locked with seven keys held by seven different people and is definitely not open to the public.

A little beyond the Chapel of St. Wenceslas on the same side, stairs lead down to the underground **royal crypt,** interesting primarily for the information it provides about the cathedral's history. As you descend the stairs, you'll see parts of the old Romanesque basilica and portions of the foundations of the rotunda. Moving around into the second room, you'll find a rather eclectic group of royal remains ensconced in new sarcophagi dating from the 1930s. In the center is Charles IV, who died in 1378. Rudolf II, patron of Renaissance Prague, is entombed at the rear in the original tin coffin. To his right is Maria Amalia, the only child of Empress Maria Theresa to reside in Prague. Ascending the wooden steps back into the cathedral, you'll come to the white-marble **Kralovské mausoleum** (Royal Mausoleum), atop which lie stone statues of the first two Hapsburg kings to rule in Bohemia, Ferdinand I and Maximilian II, and of Ferdinand's consort, Anne Jagiello.

The cathedral's **Kralovské oratorium** (Royal Oratory) was used by the kings and their families when attending mass. Built in 1493, the work is a perfect example of late Gothic, laced on the outside with a stone network of gnarled branches very similar in pattern to the ceiling vaulting in the Královský palác (☞ *below*). The oratory is connected to the palace by an elevated covered walkway, which you can see from outside.

A few more steps toward the east end, you can't fail to catch sight of the ornate silver **sarcophagus of St. John of Nepomuk.** According to legend, when Nepomuk's body was exhumed in 1721 to be reinterred, the tongue was found to be still intact and pumping with blood. This strange tale served a highly political purpose. The Catholic Church and the Hapsburgs were seeking a new folk hero to replace the Protestant forerunner Jan Hus, whom they despised. The 14th-century priest Nepomuk, killed during a power struggle with King Václav IV, was sainted and reburied a few years later with great ceremony in the 3,700-pound silver tomb, replete with angels and cherubim; the tongue was enshrined in its own reliquary.

The eight chapels around the back of the cathedral are the work of the original architect, Mathias d'Arras. A number of old tombstones, including some badly worn grave markers of medieval royalty, can be seen within, amid furnishings from later periods. Opposite the wooden relief, depicting the looting of the cathedral by Protestants in 1619, is the **Valdštejnská kaple** (Wallenstein Chapel). Since the last century, the chapel has housed the Gothic tombstones of its two architects, d'Arras and Peter Parler, who died in 1352 and 1399, respectively. If you look up to the balcony, you can just make out the busts of these two men, designed by Parler's workshop. The other busts around the triforium depict royalty and other VIPs of the time.

The Hussite wars in the 15th century put an end to the first phase of the cathedral's construction. During the short era of illusory peace before the Thirty Years' War, the massive south tower was completed, but lack of money quashed any idea of finishing the building, and the cathedral was closed by a wall built across from the Chapel of St. Wenceslas. Not until the 20th century was the western side of the cathedral, with its two towers, completed in the spirit of Parler's conception.

A key element of the cathedral's teeming, rich exterior decoration is the **Last Judgment mosaic** above the ceremonial entrance, called the Golden Portal, on the south side. The use of mosaic is quite rare in countries north of the Alps; this work, dating from the 1370s, is made of 1 million glass and stone chunks. It's currently undergoing an extensive, desperately needed restoration led by the Getty Conservation Institute. The central field shows Christ in glory, adored by Charles IV and his consort, Elizabeth of Pomerania, as well as several saints; the risen dead and attendant angels are on the left; and on the right the flames of Hell lick around the figure of Satan. ✉ *St. Vitus's Cathedral.* 🎫 *Western section free; chapels, crypt, and tower accessible with castle-wide ticket (see Informační středisko, below).* ⏲ *Apr.–Oct., daily 9–5; Nov.–Mar., daily 9–4.*

49 **Druhé nádvoří** (Second Courtyard). Empress Maria Theresa's court architect, Nicolò Pacassi, received the imperial approval to remake the castle in the 1760s, as it was badly damaged by Prussian shelling during the Seven Years' War in 1757. The Second Courtyard was the main victim of Pacassi's attempts at imparting classical grandeur to what had been a picturesque collection of Gothic and Renaissance styles. Except for the view of the spires of St. Vitus's Cathedral, the exterior courtyard offers little for the eye to feast upon. This courtyard also houses the rather gaudy **Kaple svatého Kříže** (Chapel of the Holy Cross), with decorations from the 18th and 19th centuries.

Built in the late 16th and early 17th century, the Second Courtyard was originally part of a reconstruction program commissioned by Rudolf II, under whom Prague enjoyed a period of unparalleled cultural development. Once the Prague court was established, the emperor gathered around him some of the world's best craftsmen, artists, and scientists, including the brilliant astronomers Johannes Kepler and Tycho Brahe.

Rudolf also amassed a large and famed collection of fine and decorative art, scientific instruments, philosophic and alchemical books, natural wonders, coins, and everything else under the sun. The bulk of the collection was looted by the Swedes during the Thirty Years' War, removed to Vienna when the imperial capital returned there after

Rudolf's death, or auctioned off during the 18th century. Artworks that survived the turmoil, for the most part acquired after Rudolf's time, are displayed in the **Obrazárna** (Picture Gallery), on the left side of the courtyard as you face St. Vitus's. In rooms elegantly redecorated by the official castle architect, Bořek Šípek, there are good Renaissance, Mannerist, and Baroque paintings that hint at the luxurious tastes of Rudolf's court. Across the passageway by the gallery entrance is the **Císařská konírna** (Imperial Stable), where temporary exhibitions are held. The passageway forms the northern entrance to the castle and leads out over a luxurious ravine known as the **Jelení příkop** (Stag Moat), which can be entered (from April through October) either here or at the lower end via the metal catwalk off Chotkova ulice. ✉ *Obrazárna: Second Courtyard.* 🎟 *100 Kč.* ⏲ *Daily 10–6.*

51 **Informační středisko** (Castle Information Office). This is the place to come for entrance tickets, guided tours, headphones for listening to recorded tours in English, tickets to cultural events held at the castle, and money changing. Tickets are valid for three consecutive days and allow admission to the older parts of St. Vitus's Cathedral, Královský palác, St. George's Basilica (but not the adjacent National Gallery exhibition), and a medieval bastion called Mihulka with an exhibition on alchemy. These sights may be visited only with the three-day ticket; the 20th-century section of the cathedral is free. Buy tickets to other castle sights at the door. If you just want to walk through the castle grounds, note that the gates close at midnight from April through October and at 11 PM the rest of the year, while the gardens are open from April through October only. ✉ *Třetí nádvoří, across from the entrance to St. Vitus's Cathedral,* ☎ *02/2437–3368.* 🎟 *3-day tickets 120 Kč; English-language guided tours 300 Kč for up to 5 people, 60 Kč per additional person (advance booking recommended); grounds and gardens free.* ⏲ *Apr.–Oct., daily 9–5; Nov.–Mar., daily 9–4.*

56 **Klášter svatého Jiří** (St. George's Convent). The first convent in Bohemia was founded here in 973 next to the even older St. George's Basilica (☞ *above*). The National Gallery collections of Czech Mannerist and Baroque art are housed here. The highlights include the voluptuous work of Rudolf II's court painters, the giant Baroque religious statuary, and some fine paintings by Karel Škréta and Petr Brandl. At press time the National Gallery's medieval Czech art collection was set to move from here to another monastery, the Klášter svaté Anežky České in the Old Town (☞ *above*), in November 2000. It's worth seeking out, for this fascinating trove contains some of the most memorable artworks made in northern Europe during the high- and late-Gothic periods, by influential Bohemian painters such as Master Theodoric and the Master of the Třeboň Altar. ✉ *Nám. U sv. Jiří,* ☎ *02/5732–0536.* 🎟 *90 Kč.* ⏲ *Tues.–Sun. 10–6.*

50 **Královská zahrada** (Royal Garden). This peaceful swath of greenery affords an unusually lovely view of St. Vitus's Cathedral and the castle's walls and bastions. Originally laid out in the 16th century, it endured devastation in war, neglect in times of peace, and many redesigns, reaching its present parklike form early this century. Luckily, its Renaissance treasures survive. One of these is the long, narrow **Míčovna** (Ball Game Hall), built by Bonifaz Wohlmut in 1568, its garden front completely covered by a dense tangle of allegorical sgraffiti.

The **Královský letohrádek** (Royal Summer Palace, also known as the Belvedere), at the garden's eastern end, deserves its usual description as one of the most beautiful Renaissance structures north of the Alps. Italian architects began it; Wohlmut finished it off in the 1560s with a copper roof like an upturned boat's keel riding above the graceful arcades of the ground floor. During the 18th and 19th centuries, military engineers tested artillery in the interior, which had already lost its rich furnishings to Swedish soldiers during their siege of the city in 1648. The Renaissance-style *giardinetto* (little garden) adjoining the summer palace centers on another masterwork, the Italian-designed, Czech-cast Singing Fountain, which resonates to the sound of falling water. ⊠ *Garden entrances from U Prašného mostu ul. and Mariánské hradby ul. near Chotkovy Park.* 🎫 *Free.* 🕘 *Apr.–Oct., daily 10–5:45.*

54 **Královský palác** (Royal Palace). The palace is an accumulation of the styles and add-ons of many centuries. The best way to grasp its size is from within the **Vladislavský sál** (Vladislav Hall), the largest secular Gothic interior space in Central Europe. The enormous hall was completed in 1493 by Benedikt Ried, who was to late-Bohemian Gothic what Peter Parler was to the earlier version. The room imparts a sense of space and light, softened by the sensuous lines of the vaulted ceilings and brought to a dignified close by the simple oblong form of the early Renaissance windows. In its heyday, the hall was the site of jousting tournaments, festive markets, banquets, and coronations. In more recent times, it has been used to inaugurate presidents, from the Communist Klement Gottwald in 1948 to Václav Havel in 1989, 1993, and 1998.

From the front of the hall, turn right into the rooms of the **Česká kancelář** (Bohemian Chancellery). This wing was built by the same Benedikt Ried only 10 years after the hall was completed, but it shows a much stronger Renaissance influence. Pass through the Renaissance portal into the last chamber of the chancellery. This room was the site of the second defenestration of Prague, in 1618, an event that marked the beginning of the Bohemian rebellion and, ultimately, the Thirty Years' War. This peculiarly Bohemian method of expressing protest (throwing someone out a window) had first been used in 1419 in the New Town Hall, during the lead-up to the Hussite wars. Two hundred years later the same conflict was reexpressed in terms of Hapsburg-backed Catholics versus Bohemian Protestants. Rudolf II had reached an uneasy agreement with the Bohemian nobles, allowing them religious freedom in exchange for financial support. But his next-but-one successor, Ferdinand II, was a rabid opponent of Protestantism and disregarded Rudolf's tolerant "Letter of Majesty." Enraged, the Protestant nobles stormed the castle and chancellery and threw two Catholic officials and their secretary, for good measure, out the window. Legend has it they landed on a mound of horse dung and escaped unharmed, an event the Jesuits interpreted as a miracle. The square window in question is on the left as you enter the room.

At the back of the Vladislav Hall, a staircase leads up to a gallery of the **Kaple všech svatých** (All Saints' Chapel). Little remains of Peter Parler's original work, but the church contains some fine works of art. The large room to the left of the staircase is the **Stará sněmovna** (council chamber), where the Bohemian nobles met with the king in a kind of prototype parliament. The descent from Vladislav Hall toward what remains of the **Romanský palác** (Romanesque Palace) is by way of a wide, shallow set of steps. This **Jezdecké schody** (Riders' Staircase) was the entranceway for knights who came for the jousting tournaments. ⊠ *Royal Palace, Třetí nádvoří.* 🎫 *For admission information, see Informační středisko, above.* 🕘 *Apr.–Oct., daily 9–5; Nov.–Mar., daily 9–4.*

58 **Lobkovický palác** (Lobkowicz Palace). From the beginning of the 17th century until the 1940s, this building was the residence of the powerful Catholic Lobkowicz family. It was supposedly to this house that

the two defenestrated officials escaped after landing on the dung hill in 1618. During the 1970s the building was restored to its early Baroque appearance and now houses the National Museum's permanent exhibition on Czech history. If you want to get a chronological understanding of Czech history from the beginnings of the Great Moravian Empire in the 9th century to the Czech national uprising in 1848, this is the place. Copies of the crown jewels are on display here, but it is the rich collection of illuminated Bibles, old musical instruments, coins, weapons, royal decrees, paintings, and statues that makes the museum well worth visiting. Detailed information on the exhibits is available in English. ✉ *Jiřská ul.* 🎟 *40 Kč.* ⏲ *Tues.–Sun. 9–5.*

48 **Matyášova brána** (Matthias Gate). Built in 1614, the stone gate once stood alone in front of the moats and bridges that surrounded the castle. Under the Hapsburgs, the gate survived by being grafted as a relief onto the palace building. As you go through it, notice the ceremonial white-marble entrance halls on either side that lead up to President Václav Havel's reception rooms (which are only rarely open to the public).

47 **První nádvoří** (First Courtyard). The main entrance to Prague Castle from Hradčanské náměstí is a little disappointing. Going through the wrought-iron gate, guarded at ground level by Czech soldiers and from above by the ferocious *Battling Titans* (a copy of Ignaz Platzer's original 18th-century work), you'll enter this courtyard, built on the site of old moats and gates that once separated the castle from the surrounding buildings and thus protected the vulnerable western flank. The courtyard is one of the more recent additions to the castle, designed by Maria Theresa's court architect, Nicolò Pacassi, in the 1760s. Today it forms part of the presidential office complex. Pacassi's reconstruction was intended to unify the eclectic collection of buildings that made up the castle, but the effect of his work is somewhat flat.

52 **Třetí nádvoří** (Third Courtyard). The contrast between the cool, dark interior of St. Vitus's Cathedral (☞ *above*) and the brightly colored Pacassi facades of the Third Courtyard just outside is startling. The courtyard's clean lines are the work of Slovenian architect Jože Plečnik in the 1930s, but the modern look is a deception. Plečnik's paving was intended to cover an underground world of house foundations, streets, and walls dating from the 9th through 12th centuries and rediscovered when the cathedral was completed. (You can see a few archways through a grating in a wall of the cathedral.) Plečnik added a few eclectic features to catch the eye: a granite obelisk to commemorate the fallen of the First World War, a black-marble pedestal for the Gothic statue of St. George (a copy of the National Gallery's original statue), the inconspicuous entrance to his Bull Staircase leading down to the south garden, and the peculiar golden ball topping the eagle fountain near the eastern end of the courtyard.

57 **Zlatá ulička** (Golden Lane). An enchanting collection of tiny, ancient, brightly colored houses crouches under the fortification wall, looking remarkably like a set for *Snow White and the Seven Dwarfs*. Legend has it that these were the lodgings of the international group of alchemists whom Rudolf II brought to the court to produce gold. The truth is a little less romantic: the houses were built during the 16th century for the castle guards, who supplemented their income by practicing various crafts outside the jurisdiction of the powerful guilds. By the early 20th century, Golden Lane had become the home of poor artists and writers. Franz Kafka, who lived at No. 22 in 1916 and 1917, described the house on first sight as "so small, so dirty, impossible to live in and lacking everything necessary." But he soon came to love the place. As he wrote to his fiancée: "Life here is something special . . . to close out

the world not just by shutting the door to a room or apartment but to the whole house, to step out into the snow of the silent lane." The lane now houses tiny stores selling books, music, and crafts.

Within the walls above Golden Lane, there is a timber-roof **corridor** lined with replica suits of armor and weapons (some of it for sale), mock torture chambers, and the like. At the far end of the lane is the private **Muzeum hraček** (Toy Museum). The building once belonged to a high royal official called the Supreme Burgrave. ✉ *Corridor: enter between No. 23 and No. 24. Toy Museum: enter from Jiřská ul.* *Corridor free, Toy Museum 40 Kč.* ⏲ *Corridor Tues.–Sun. 10–6, Mon. 1–6; Toy Museum daily 9:30–5:30.*

Nové Město (New Town) and Vyšehrad

To this day, Charles IV's building projects are tightly woven into the daily lives of Praguers. His most extensive scheme, the New Town, is still such a lively, vibrant area you may hardly realize that its streets, Gothic churches, and squares were planned as far back as 1348. With Prague fast outstripping its Old Town parameters, Charles IV extended the city's fortifications. A high wall surrounded the newly developed 2½ square km (1½ square mi) area south and east of the Old Town, tripling the walled territory on the Vltava's right bank. The wall extended south to link with the fortifications of the citadel called Vyšehrad. In the mid 19th century, new building in the New Town boomed in a welter of Romantic and neo-Renaissance styles, particularly on Wenceslas Square and avenues such as Vodičkova, Na Poříčí, and Spálená. One of the most important structures was the Národní divadlo (National Theater), meant to symbolize in stone the revival of the Czechs' history, language, and sense of national pride. Both preceding and following Czechoslovak independence in 1918, modernist architecture entered the mix, particularly on the outer fringes of the Old Town and in the New Town. One of modernism's most unexpected products was Cubist architecture, a form unique to Prague, which produced four notable examples at the foot of ancient Vyšehrad.

A GOOD WALK

Václavské náměstí ㊱, marked by the **Statue of St. Wenceslas** ㊲, is a long, gently sloping boulevard rather than a square in the usual sense. It is bounded at the top (the southern end) by the **Národní muzeum** ㊳ and at the bottom by the pedestrian shopping areas of Národní třída and Na Příkopě. Today Václavské náměstí has Prague's liveliest street scene. Don't miss the dense maze of arcades tucked away from the street in buildings that line both sides. You'll find an odd assortment of cafés, shops, ice cream parlors, and movie houses, all seemingly unfazed by the passage of time. One eye-catching building on the square is the Hotel Europa, at No. 25, a riot of Art Nouveau that recalls the glamorous world of turn-of-the-20th-century Prague. Work by the Czech artist whose name is synonymous with Art Nouveau is on show just a block off the square, via Jindřišská, at the **Mucha Museum.**

From the foot of square, head down 28. října to Jungmannovo náměstí, a small square named for the linguist and patriot Josef Jungmann (1773–1847). In the courtyard off the square at No. 18, have a look at the Kostel Panny Marie Sněžné (Church of the Virgin Mary of the Snows). Building ceased during the Hussite wars, leaving a very high, foreshortened church that never grew into the monumental structure planned by Charles IV. Beyond it lies a quiet sanctuary: the walled Františkánská zahrada (Franciscan Gardens). A busy shopping street, Národní třída, extends from Jungmannovo náměstí about ¾ km (½ mi) to the river and the **Národní divadlo** ㊴. From the theater, follow the embankment, Masarykovo nábřeží, south toward Vyšehrad. Note the

Art Nouveau architecture of No. 32, the amazingly eclectic design by Kamil Hilbert at No. 26, and the tile-decorated Hlahol building at No. 16. Opposite, on a narrow island, is a 19th century, yellow-and-white ballroom-restaurant, Žofín.

Straddling an arm of the river at Myslíkova ulice are the modern Galerie Mánes (1928–1930) and its attendant 15th-century water tower, where, from a lookout on the sixth floor, Communist-era secret police used to observe Václav Havel's apartment at Rašínovo nábřeží 78. This building, still part-owned by the president, and the adjoining **Tančící dům** are on the far side of a square named Jiráskovo náměstí after the historical novelist Alois Jirásek. From this square, Resslova ulice leads uphill four blocks to a much larger, parklike square, **Karlovo náměstí** ㊵.

If you have the energy to continue on toward Vyšehrad, a convenient place to rejoin the riverfront is Palackého náměstí via Na Moráni street at the southern end of Karlovo náměstí. The square has a (melo)dramatic monument to the 19th-century historian František Palacký, "awakener of the nation," and the view from here of the Benedictine Klášter Emauzy is lovely. The houses grow less attractive south of here, so you may wish to hop a tram (No. 3, 16, or 17 at the stop on Rašínovo nábřeží) and ride one stop to Výtoň, at the base of the **Vyšehrad** ㊶ citadel. Walk under the railroad bridge on Rašínovo nábřeží to find the closest of four nearby **Cubist buildings.** Another lies just a minute's walk farther along the embankment; two more are on Neklanova, a couple of minutes' walk "inland" on Vnislavova. To get up to the fortress, make a hard left onto Vratislavova (the street right before Neklanova), an ancient road that runs tortuously up into the heart of Vyšehrad.

It's about 2¼ km (1½ mi) between Národní divadlo and Vyšehrad. Note that Tram No. 17 travels the length of the embankment, if you'd like to make a quicker trip between the two points.

TIMING

You might want to divide the walk into two parts, first taking in the busy New Town between Václavské náměstí and Karlovo náměstí, then doing Vyšehrad and the Cubist houses as a side trip. A leisurely stroll from the Národní divadlo to Vyšehrad may easily absorb two hours, as may an exploration of Karlovo náměstí and the Klášter Emauzy. Vyšehrad is open every day, year-round, and the views are stunning on a clear day or evening, but keep in mind that there is little shade along the river walk on hot afternoons.

SIGHTS TO SEE

Cubist buildings. Born of zealous modernism, Prague's Cubist architecture followed a great Czech tradition in that it fully embraced new ideas while adapting them to existing artistic and social contexts. Between 1912 and 1914, Josef Chochol (1880–1956) designed several of the city's dozen or so Cubist projects. His apartment house **Neklanova 30**, on the corner of Neklanova and Přemyslova, is a masterpiece in dingy concrete. The pyramidal, kaleidoscopic window mouldings and roof cornices are completely novel while making an expressive link to Baroque forms; the faceted corner balcony column elegantly alludes to Gothic forerunners. On the same street, at **Neklanova 2**, is another apartment house attributed to Chochol; like the building at Neklanova 30, it uses pyramidal shapes and the suggestion of Gothic columns.

Chochol's **villa,** on the embankment at Libušina 3, has an undulating effect created by smoothly articulated forms. The wall and gate around the back of the house use triangular moldings and metal grating to create an effect of controlled energy. The **three-family house,** about 100 yards away from the villa at Rašínovo nábřeží 6–10, was completed slightly earlier, when Chochol's Cubist style was still developing. Here, the design is touched with Baroque and neoclassical influence, with a mansard roof and end gables.

40 **Karlovo náměstí** (Charles Square). This square began life as a cattle market, a function chosen by Charles IV when he established the New Town in 1348. The horse market (now Wenceslas Square) quickly overtook it as a livestock-trading center, and an untidy collection of shacks accumulated here until the mid-1800s, when it became a green park named for its patron.

Novoměstská radnice (New Town Hall), at the northern edge of the square, has a late-Gothic tower similar to that of the Old Town Hall and three tall Renaissance gables. The first defenestration of Prague occurred here on July 30, 1419, when a mob of townspeople, followers of the martyred religious reformer Jan Hus, hurled Catholic town councillors out the windows. Historical exhibitions and contemporary art shows are held here regularly (admission prices vary), and you can climb the tower for a view of the New Town. ⊠ *Karlovo nám. at Vodičkova, Prague 2.* 🎟 *Tower 20 Kč.* ⊙ *Tower June–Sept., Tues.–Sun. 10–6.*

Just south of the square lies another of Charles IV's gifts to the city, the Benedictine **Klášter Emauzy** (Emmaus Monastery). It is often called Na Slovanech, literally "At the Slavs'," in reference to its purpose when established in 1347: the emperor invited Croatian monks here to celebrate mass in Old Slavonic and thus cultivate religion among the Slavs in a city largely controlled by Germans. A faded but substantially complete cycle of biblical scenes by Charles's court artists lines the four cloister walls. The frescoes, and especially the abbey church, suffered heavy damage from a February 14, 1945, raid by Allied bombers that may have mistaken Prague for Dresden, 121 km (75 mi) away. The church lost its spires, and the interior remains a blackened shell. Some years after the war, two curving concrete "spires" were set atop the church. ⊠ *Vyšehradská 49 (cloister entrance on the left at the rear of the church).* 🎟 *10 Kč.* ⊙ *Weekdays 8–6 or earlier depending on daylight.*

Mucha Museum. For decades it was almost impossible to find an Alfons Mucha original in the homeland of this famous Czech artist, until, in 1998, this private museum opened with nearly 100 works from his long career. What you'd expect to see is here—the theater posters of actress Sarah Bernhardt; the magazine covers; the luscious, sinuous Art Nouveau designs—and there are also paintings, photographs taken in Mucha's studio (one shows Paul Gauguin playing the piano in his underwear), and even Czechoslovak banknotes designed by the artist. ⊠ *Panská 7 (1 block off Wenceslas Square, across from the Palace Hotel),* ☎ *02/628–4162.* 🎟 *120 Kč.* ⊙ *Daily 10–6.*

39 **Národní divadlo** (National Theater). The idea for a Czech national theater began during the revolutionary decade of the 1840s. In a telling display of national pride, donations to fund the plan poured in from all over the country, from people of every socioeconomic stratum. The cornerstone was laid in 1868, and the "National Theater generation" who built the neo-Renaissance structure became the architectural and artistic establishment for decades to come. Its designer, Josef Zítek (1832–1909), was the leading neo-Renaissance architect in Bohemia. The nearly finished interior was gutted by a fire in 1881, and Zítek's onetime student Josef Schulz (1840–1917) saw the reconstruction through to completion two years later. Statues representing Drama and Opera rise above the riverfront side entrances; two gigantic chariots flank figures of Apollo

and the nine Muses above the main facade. The performance space itself is filled with gilding, voluptuous plaster figures and plush upholstery. Next door is the modern (1970s–1980s) Nová scéna (New Stage), where the popular Magic Lantern black-light shows are staged. The Národní divadlo is one of the best places to see a performance; ticket prices start as low as 30 Kč. ✉ *Národní třída 2,* ☎ *02/2490–1448.*

38 **Národní muzeum** (National Museum). This imposing structure, designed by Prague architect Josef Schulz and built between 1885 and 1890, does not come into its own until it is bathed in nighttime lighting. By day the grandiose edifice seems an inappropriate venue for a musty collection of stones and bones, minerals, and coins. This museum is only for dedicated fans of the genre. ✉ *Václavské nám. 68,* ☎ *02/2449–7111.* 🎟 *70 Kč.* ⏲ *May–Sept., daily 10–6; Oct.–Apr., daily 9–5; closed 1st Tues. of month.*

37 **Statue of St. Wenceslas.** Josef Václav Myslbek's huge equestrian grouping of St. Wenceslas with other Czech patron saints around him is a traditional meeting place at times of great national peril or rejoicing. In 1939, Praguers gathered to oppose Hitler's takeover of Bohemia and Moravia. It was here also, in 1969, that the student Jan Palach set himself on fire to protest the bloody invasion of his country by the Soviet Union and other Warsaw Pact countries in August of the previous year. The invasion ended the "Prague Spring," a cultural and political movement emphasizing free expression, which was supported by Alexander Dubček, the popular leader at the time. Although Dubček never intended to dismantle Communist authority completely, his political and economic reforms proved too daring for fellow comrades in the rest of Eastern Europe. In the months following the invasion, conservatives loyal to the Soviet Union were installed in all influential positions. The subsequent two decades were a period of cultural stagnation. Hundreds of thousands of Czechs and Slovaks left the country, a few became dissidents, and many more resigned themselves to lives of minimal expectations and small pleasures. ✉ *Václavské náměstí.*

Tančící dům (Dancing House). This whimsical building was partnered into life in 1996 by architect Frank Gehry (of Guggenheim Museum in Bilbao fame) and his Croatian-Czech collaborator Vlado Milunic. A wasp-waisted glass-and-steel tower sways into the main structure as though they were a couple on the dance floor—a "Fred and Ginger" effect that gave the wacky, yet somehow appropriate, building its nickname. A French restaurant occupies the top floors (☞ La Perle de Prague *in* Dining, *below*), and there is a café at street level. ✉ *Rašínovo nábř. 80.*

36 **Václavské náměstí** (Wenceslas Square). You may recognize this spot from your television set, for it was here that some 500,000 students and citizens gathered in the heady days of November 1989 to protest the policies of the former Communist regime. The government capitulated after a week of demonstrations, without a shot fired or the loss of a single life, bringing to power the first democratic government in 40 years (under playwright-president Václav Havel). Today this peaceful transfer of power is half-ironically referred to as the "Velvet" or "Gentle" Revolution (*něžná revoluce*). It was only fitting that the 1989 revolution should take place on Wenceslas Square: throughout much of Czech history, the square has served as the focal point for popular discontent. The long "square" was first laid out by Charles IV in 1348 as a horse market at the center of the New Town.

At No. 25, the **Hotel Europa** is an Art Nouveau gem, with elegant stained glass and mosaics in the café and restaurant. The terrace is an excellent spot for people-watching.

41 **Vyšehrad.** Bedřich Smetana's symphonic poem *Vyšehrad* opens with four bardic harp chords that seem to echo the legends surrounding this ancient fortress. Today, the flat-top bluff standing over the right bank of the Vltava is a green, tree-dotted expanse showing few signs that splendid medieval monuments once made it a landmark to rival Prague Castle. With its neo-Gothic spires, **Kapitulní kostel svatých Petra a Pavla** (Chapter Church of Sts. Peter and Paul) dominates the plateau as it has since the 11th century. Next to the church lies the burial ground of the nation's revered cultural figures. Most of the buildings still standing are from the 19th century, but scattered among them are a few older structures and some foundation stones of the medieval palaces. Surrounding the ruins are gargantuan, excellently preserved brick fortifications built from the 17th to the mid 19th century; their broad tops allow strollers to take in sweeping vistas up- and downriver.

The historical father of Vyšehrad, the "High Castle," is Vratislav II (ruled 1061–1092), a Přemyslid duke who became first king of Bohemia. He made the fortified hilltop his capital, but, under subsequent rulers, it fell into disuse until the 14th century, when Charles IV transformed the site into an ensemble of palaces, the Gothicized main church, battlements, and a massive gatehouse called *Špička,* whose scant remains are on V pevnosti ulice. By the 17th century, royalty had long since departed, and most of the structures they built were crumbling. Vyšehrad was turned into a fortress.

Vyšehrad's place in the modern Czech imagination is largely thanks to the National Revivalists of the 19th century, particularly writer Alois Jirásek (1851–1930), who mined medieval chronicles for legends and facts to glorify the early Czechs. In his rendition, Vyšehrad was the court of the prophetess-ruler Libuše, who had a vision of her husband-to-be, the ploughman Přemysl—father of the Přemyslid line—and of "a city whose glory shall reach the heavens" called Praha. (In truth, the Czechs first came to Vyšehrad around the beginning of the 900s, slightly later than the building of Prague Castle.)

A concrete result of the National Revival was the establishment of the **Hřbitov** (cemetery) in the 1860s—it peopled the fortress with the remains of luminaries from the arts and sciences. The grave of Smetana faces the Slavín, a mausoleum for more than 50 honored men and women including Alfons Mucha, sculptor Jan Štursa, inventor František Křižík, and the opera diva Ema Destinnová. All are guarded by a winged genius who hovers above the inscription AČ ZEMŘELI, JEŠTĚ MLUVÍ ("Although they have died, they yet speak"). Antonín Dvořák (1841–1904) rests in the arcade along the north wall of the cemetery. Among the many writers buried here are Jan Neruda, Božena Němcová, Karel Čapek, and the Romantic poet Karel Hynek Mácha, whose grave was visited by students on their momentous November 17, 1989, protest march.

Traces of the citadel's distant past do remain. A heavily restored **Romanesque rotunda,** built by Vratislav II, stands on the east side of the compound. Foundations and a few embossed floor tiles from the late-10th-century **Basilika svatého Vavřince** (St. Lawrence Basilica) are in a structure on Soběslavova street (if it is locked, you can ask for the key at the refreshment stand just to the left of the basilica entrance; admission is 5 Kč). Part of the medieval fortifications stand next to the surprisingly confined foundation mounds of a medieval palace overlooking a ruined watchtower called Libuše's Bath. A nearby plot of grass hosts a statue of Libuše and her consort Přemysl, one of four large sculpted images of couples from Czech legend by J. V. Myslbek (1848–1922), the sculptor of the St. Wenceslas monument.

The military history of the fortress and the city is covered in a small exposition inside the **Cihelná brána** (Brick Gate). The gate is also the entrance to the casemates—a long, dark passageway within the walls that ends at a dank hall used to store several original, pollution-scarred Charles Bridge sculptures. A guided tour into the casemates and the statue storage room starts at the military history exhibit. ✉ *Entrances on Vratislavova ul. and V pevnosti ul. Information center: V pevnosti.* *Casemates tour 20 Kč, military exhibit 10 Kč.* ⏲ *Grounds daily. Casemates, military history exhibit, St. Lawrence Basilica Apr.–Oct., daily 9:30–5:30; Nov.–Mar., daily 9:30–4:30. Cemetery Apr.–Oct., daily 8–6; Nov.–Mar., daily 8–4. Metro: Vyšehrad.*

Vinohrady

From Riegrovy Park and its sweeping view of the city from above the National Museum, the eclectic apartment houses and villas of the elegant residential neighborhood called Vinohrady extend eastward and southward. The pastel-tint ranks of turn-of-the-20th-century apartment houses—many crumbling after years of neglect—are slowly but unstoppably being transformed into upscale flats, slick offices, eternally packed new restaurants, and a range of shops unthinkable only a half decade ago. Much of the development lies on or near Vinohradská, the main street, which extends from the top of Wenceslas Square to a belt of enormous cemeteries about 3 km (2 mi) eastward. Yet the flavor of daily life persists: smoky old pubs still ply their trade on the quiet side streets; the stately theater, Divadlo na Vinohradech, keeps putting on excellent shows as it has for decades; and on the squares and in the parks nearly everyone still practices Prague's favorite form of outdoor exercise—walking the dog.

42 **Kostel Nejsvětějšího Srdce Páně** (Church of the Most Sacred Heart). If you've had your fill of Romanesque, Gothic, and Baroque, take the metro to the Jiřího z Poděbrad station (Line A) for a look at a startling Art Deco edifice. Designed in 1927 by Slovenian architect Jože Plečnik (the same architect commissioned to update Prague Castle), the church resembles a luxury ocean liner more than a place of worship. The effect was conscious: during the 1920s and 1930s, the avant-garde imitated mammoth objects of modern technology. Plečnik used many modern elements on the inside. Notice the hanging speakers, seemingly designed to bring the word of God directly to the ears of each worshiper. You may be able to find someone at the back entrance of the church who will let you walk up the long ramp into the fascinating glass clock tower. ✉ *Nám. Jiřího z Poděbrad.* ⏲ *Daily 10–5.*

43 **Nový židovský hřbitov** (New Jewish Cemetery). Tens of thousands of Czechs find eternal rest in Vinohrady's cemeteries. In this, the newest of the city's half-dozen Jewish burial grounds, you'll find the modest **tombstone of Franz Kafka,** which seems grossly inadequate to Kafka's stature but oddly in proportion to his own modest ambitions. The cemetery is usually open, although guards sometimes inexplicably seal off the grounds. Men may be required to wear a yarmulke (you can buy one here). Turn right at the main cemetery gate and follow the wall for about 100 yards. Kafka's thin, white tombstone lies at the front of section 21. City maps may label the cemetery *Židovské hřbitovy.* ✉ *Vinohradská at Jana Želivského.* *Free.* ⏲ *June–Aug., Sun.–Thurs. 9–5, Fri. 9–1; Sept.–May, Sun.–Thurs. 9–4, Fri. 9–1. Metro: Vyšehrad.*

44 **Pavilon.** This gorgeous, turn-of-the-20th-century, neo-Renaissance, three-story market hall is one of the most attractive sites in Vinohrady. It used to be a major old-style market, a vast space filled with stalls selling all manner of foodstuffs plus the requisite grimy pub. After being spiffed up several years ago, it mutated into an upscale shopping mall. Off the

tourist track, Pavilon is a good place to watch Praguers—those who can afford its shops' gleaming designer pens and Italian shoes—ostentatiously drinking in *la dolce vita*, cell phones in hand. ✉ *Vinohradská 50,* ☎ *02/2209–7111.* ⏲ *Mon.–Sat. 8:30* AM*–9* PM*, Sun. noon–6.*

NEED A BREAK? A symbol of this bucolic neighborhood's intellectual leanings, the literary café **Literární kavárna G + G** (✉ Čerchovská 4, ☎ 02/627–3332) serves coffees and light desserts in a well-lit and welcoming shop brimming with books, newspapers, and magazines (most in Czech). It's a block east of Riegrovy Park, or two blocks off Vinohradská via U Kanálky. Several nights a week, the café hosts readings as well as intimate concerts of folk, jazz, or Romany (Gypsy) music.

Letná and Holešovice

From above the Vltava's left bank, the large, grassy plateau called Letná gives you one of the classic views of the Old Town and the many bridges crossing the river. (To get to Letná from the Old Town, take Pařížská street north, cross the Čechův Bridge, and climb the stairs.) Beer gardens, tennis, and Frisbee attract people of all ages, while amateur soccer players emulate the professionals of Prague's top team, Sparta, which plays in the stadium just across the road. A 10-minute walk from Letná, down into the residential neighborhood of Holešovice, brings you to a massive, gray-blue building whose cool exterior gives no hint of the treasures of Czech and French modern art that line its corridors. Just north along Dukelských hrdinů street is Stromovka—a royal hunting preserve turned gracious park.

Numbers in the margin correspond to numbers on the Exploring Prague map.

45 **Letenské sady** (Letna Park). Come to this large, shady park for an unforgettable view of Prague's bridges. From the enormous cement pedestal at the center of the park, the largest statue of Stalin in Eastern Europe once beckoned to citizens on the Old Town Square far below. The statue was ripped down in the 1960s, when Stalinism was finally discredited. On sunny Sundays expatriates often meet up here to play ultimate Frisbee.

46 **Veletržní palác** (Trade Fair Palace). The National Gallery's **Sbírka moderního a soucasného umění** (Collection of Modern and Contemporary Art) has become a keystone in the city's visual-arts scene since its opening in 1995, despite unclear leadership. Touring the vast spaces of this 1920s Constructivist exposition hall and its comprehensive collection of 20th-century Czech art is the best way to see how Czechs surfed the forefront of the avant-garde wave until the cultural freeze following the Communist takeover in 1948, which threw the visual arts into gloom and introspection. (Most of the collections languished in storage for decades, either because some cultural commissar forbade their public display or because there was no exhibition space.) Also on display are works by Western European, mostly French, artists from Delacroix to the present. Especially noteworthy are the early Cubist paintings by Picasso and Braque. The 19th-century Czech art collection of the National Gallery was installed in the palace in the summer of 2000. Watch the papers and posters for information on traveling shows and temporary exhibits by young Czech artists. ✉ *Dukelských hrdinů 47,* ☎ *02/2430–1111.* 🎫 *90 Kč.* ⏲ *Tues.–Sun. 10–6 (Thurs. until 9).*

Dining

Dining choices in Prague have increased greatly in the past decade as hundreds of new places have opened to meet the soaring demand from tourists and locals alike. These days, out-and-out rip-offs have almost disappeared, but before paying up at the end of a meal it's a good idea to take a close look at the added cover charge on your bill. Also keep an eye out for a large fee tacked on to a credit card bill. In pubs and neighborhood restaurants, ask if there is a *denní lístek* (daily menu) of cheaper and often fresher selections, but note that many places provide daily menus for the midday meal only. Special local dishes worth making a beeline for include *cibulačka* (onion soup), *kulajda* (potato soup with sour cream), *svíčková* (beef sirloin in cream sauce), and *ovocné knedlíky* (fruit dumplings, often listed under "meatless dishes").

The crush of visitors has placed tremendous strain on the more popular restaurants. The upshot: reservations are an excellent idea, especially for dinner during peak tourist periods. If you don't have reservations, try arriving a little before standard meal times: 11:30 AM for lunch or 5:30 PM for dinner.

For a cheaper and quicker alternative to the sit-down establishments listed below, try a light meal at one of the city's growing number of street stands or fast-food places. Look for stands offering *párky* (hot dogs) or the fattier *klobásy* (grilled sausages served with bread and mustard). For more exotic fare, try the very good vegetarian cooking at **Country Life** (⊠ Melantrichova 15, in the Old Town, ☎ 02/2421–3366). Chic new cafés and bakeries spring up all the time. **Vzpomínky na Afriku** (⊠ Rybná at Jakubská, near the Kotva department store) has the widest selection of gourmet coffees in town, served at the single table or to go.

Staré Město (Old Town)

$$$$ ✕ **Bellevue.** The first choice for visiting dignitaries and businesspeople blessed with expense accounts, Bellevue has creative, freshly prepared cuisine, more nouvelle than Bohemian—and the elegant setting not far from Charles Bridge doesn't hurt. Look for the lamb carpaccio with fresh rosemary, garlic, and extra-virgin olive oil, or the wild berries marinated in port and cognac, served with vanilla-and-walnut ice cream. Window seats have stunning views of Prague Castle. The Sunday jazz brunch is a winner, too. ⊠ *Smetanovo nábř. 18,* ☎ *02/2222–1449. AE, MC, V.*

$$$$ ✕ **Jewel of India.** Although generally Asian cooking of any stripe is not Prague's forte, here is a sumptuous spot well worth seeking out for northern Indian tandooris and other moderately spiced specialties, including some delicious vegetarian dishes. ⊠ *Pařížská 20,* ☎ *02/2481–1010. AE, MC, V. Metro: Staroměstská.*

$$$$ ★ ✕ **V Zátiší.** White walls and casual grace accentuate the subtle flavors of smoked salmon, plaice, beef Wellington, and other non-Czech specialties. Here, as at most of the city's better establishments, the wine list has expanded in recent years and now includes most of the great wine-producing regions, though good Moravian vintages are still kept on hand. In behavior unusual for the city, the benign waiters fairly fall over each other to serve diners. ⊠ *Liliová 1 at Betlémské nám.,* ☎ *02/2222–2025. AE, MC, V.*

$$$ ✕ **Barock.** Call it chic or call it pretentious, Barock exemplifies the revolution in Prague's dining and social life since those uncool Communists decamped. Thai and Japanese dishes predominate, and there are other Asian choices and international standards. Although eating isn't the main point here—being seen is—the fish dishes and sushi won't let you down. ⊠ *Pařížská 24,* ☎ *02/232–9221. AE, DC, MC, V.*

$$ ✕ **Chez Marcel.** At this authentic French bistro on a quiet street, you can get a little taste of that *other* riverside capital. French owned and operated, Chez Marcel has a smallish but reliable menu listing pâtés,

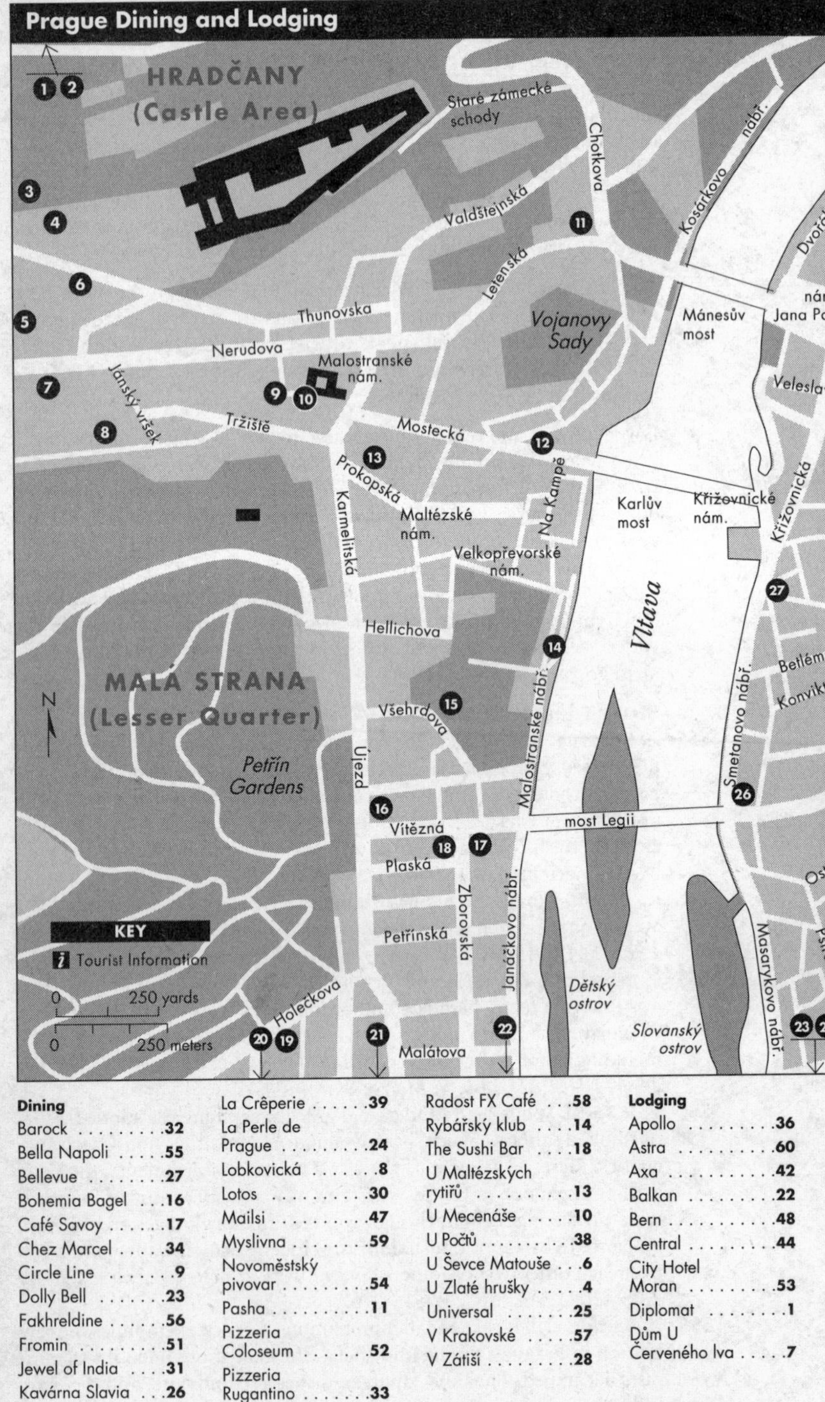

Dining
Barock 32
Bella Napoli 55
Bellevue 27
Bohemia Bagel . . .16
Café Savoy 17
Chez Marcel 34
Circle Line 9
Dolly Bell 23
Fakhreldine 56
Fromin 51
Jewel of India 31
Kavárna Slavia . . .26
La Crêperie 39
La Perle de Prague 24
Lobkovická 8
Lotos 30
Mailsi 47
Myslivna 59
Novoměstský pivovar 54
Pasha 11
Pizzeria Coloseum 52
Pizzeria Rugantino 33
Radost FX Café . . .58
Rybářský klub 14
The Sushi Bar 18
U Maltézských rytířů 13
U Mecenáše 10
U Počtů 38
U Ševce Matouše . . .6
U Zlaté hrušky 4
Universal 25
V Krakovské 57
V Zátiší 28

Lodging
Apollo 36
Astra 60
Axa 42
Balkan 22
Bern 48
Central 44
City Hotel Moran 53
Diplomat 1
Dům U Červeného lva 7

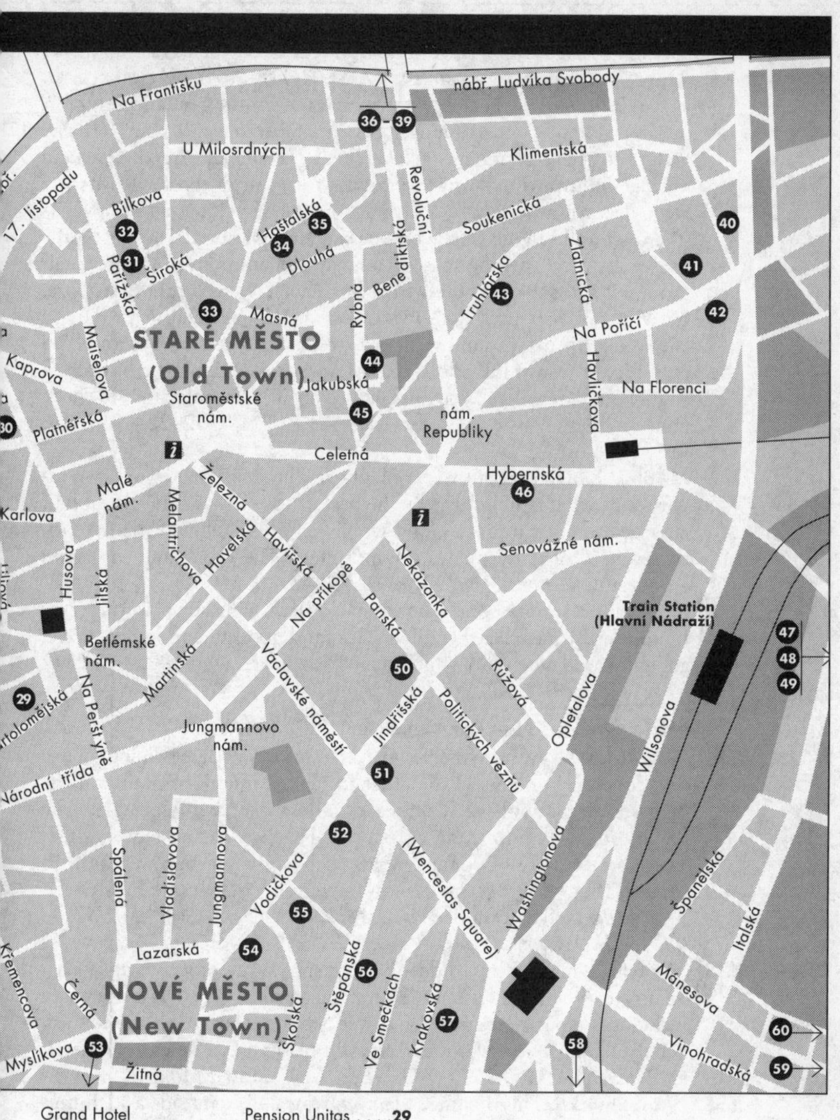

Grand Hotel Bohemia 45
Harmony 41
Kampa 15
Kinsky Garden . . .19
Maximilian 35
Mepro 21
Meteor Plaza 46
Olšanka 49
Opera 40
Palace 50
Pension Louda 37
Pension Unitas 29
Penzion Sprint 2
Petr 20
Romantik Hotel U Raka 3
Salvator 43
Savoy 5
U Tří Pštrosů 12

salads, rabbit and chicken, and some of the best steaks in Prague. The specials board usually has some tempting choices, such as salmon, beef daube, or foie gras. ✉ *Haštalská 12,* ☎ *02/231–5676. No credit cards.*

$ ★ ✕ **Kavárna Slavia.** This legendary hangout for the best and brightest in Czech arts—from composer Bedřich Smetana and poet Jaroslav Seifert to then-dissident Václav Havel—reopened after being held hostage in absurd real-estate wrangles for most of the 1990s. Its Art Deco decor is a perfect backdrop for people watching, and the vistas (the river and Prague Castle on one side, the National Theater on the other) are a compelling reason to linger for hours over a coffee—although it's not the best brew in town. The Slavia is a café to its core, but you can also get a light meal, such as a small salad with Balkan cheese, an open-face sandwich, or breakfast in the form of scrambled eggs (don't even think about toast). And despite what the old-guard coat-check lady will tell you on your way in, it is not obligatory to check your coat with her. ✉ *Smetanovo nábř. 1012/2,* ☎ *02/2422–0957. AE, MC, V.*

$ ✕ **Lotos.** Banana ragout with polenta and broccoli strudel are two favorites at what is undoubtedly the best of the city's scant selection of all-vegetarian restaurants. Blond-wood tables and billowing tie-dye fabric set an informal yet elegant atmosphere. The salads and soups are wonderful. ✉ *Platnéřská 13,* ☎ *02/232–2390. MC, V.*

$ ✕ **Pizzeria Rugantino.** Bright and spacious, this buzzing pizzeria serves up thin-crust pies; big, healthy salads; and good Italian bread. It can get quite loud when full, which is most nights. ✉ *Dušní 4,* ☎ *02/231–8172. No credit cards. No lunch Sun.*

Malá Strana (Lesser Quarter)

$$$$ ✕ **Circle Line.** Now moved out of the cellar into two elegant dining rooms, one done up in blue and the other in pink, Circle Line maintains its high standards with such dishes as fallow deer with spaetzle, pike perch, and yellowfin tuna carpaccio. The service can't be faulted. There are creative seasonal specials such as the warm foie gras with cherries, but be sure to save room for the chocolate plate for dessert. Brunch is served daily until 6 PM. ✉ *Malostranské nám. 12,* ☎ *02/5753–0022. AE, MC, V.*

$$$$ ✕ **Pasha.** This inviting Middle Eastern spot at the foot of Prague Castle hits just the right notes of luxury and easiness. The à la carte menu includes luscious *adana kebab* (skewer of minced lamb), pilaf, and shish kebab. Baklava served with fresh mint tea makes a splendid dessert. ✉ *Letenská 1,* ☎ *02/549–773. AE, MC, V. Closed Mon.*

$$$ ★ ✕ **Lobkovická.** This dignified *vinárna* (wine hall) set inside a 17th-century town palace serves innovative, imaginative dishes by Prague standards. Chicken breast with crabmeat and curry sauce is an excellent main dish and typical of the kitchen's approach to sauces and spices. Deep red carpeting sets the perfect mood for enjoying bottles of Moravian wine. ✉ *Vlašská 17,* ☎ *02/530–185 or 02/5753–2511. AE, MC, V.*

$$$ ✕ **The Sushi Bar.** This chic little joint with the wacky whale sculpture floating overhead could have been transported straight from San Francisco. Given Prague's distance from the sea, the selection of sushi and sashimi is excellent. For the same reason, call ahead to check when the fresh seafood is due (it's delivered twice a week), or stick to the broiled salmon or tempura dishes. ✉ *Zborovská 49,* ☎ *0603/244–882. DC, MC, V.*

$$$ ✕ **U Maltézských rytířů.** The tongue-twisting name means "At the Knights of Malta," a reference to the Catholic order whose embassy is nearby. The upstairs dining room and bar are cozy, but ask for a table in the deep cellar—then ask the proprietress to regale you with yarns about this ancient house. They've dropped some old favorites from the

menu, but still offer good steaks, game, and fish. ✉ *Prokopská 10,* ☎ *02/5753–3666. AE, MC, V.*

$$$ ✕ **U Mecenáše.** A fetching Renaissance inn from the 17th century, with dark, high-back benches in the front room and cozy, elegant sofas and chairs in back, this is a place to splurge. From the aperitifs to the specialty steaks or beef Wellington and the cognac (swirled lovingly in oversize glasses), the presentation is seamless. ✉ *Malostranské nám. 10,* ☎ *02/5753–1631. AE, MC, V.*

$$ ★ ✕ **Rybářský klub.** The "Fishing Club" restaurant shares its building with a real fishing club's headquarters, and it's a great place to try a wide variety of freshwater fish. The friendly staff serves perch, eel, barbel, and the esteemed pike perch at picnic-style tables or by the water in summer. ✉ *U Sovových mlýnů 1, Kampa Island,* ☎ *02/530–223. MC, V.*

$ ✕ **Bohemia Bagel.** It's not New York, but the friendly, North American–owned Bohemia Bagel still serves up a plentiful assortment of fresh bagels, from raisin-walnut to "supreme," with all kinds of toppings. Their thick soups are among the best in Prague for the price, and the bottomless cups of coffee are a further draw. ✉ *Újezd 16,* ☎ *02/531–002. No credit cards.*

$ ✕ **Café Savoy.** Opened in 1887 as a grand café, the Savoy lasted only a few years before the long, airy room was divided up to be made into shops. In 1992 the café was reborn, and best of all, the painted and stuccoed ceiling that had long been covered over was restored. It's best for coffee, a drink, or a fine apple strudel; typical meat dishes such as pork steak with horseradish are also available. ✉ *Vítězná 5,* ☎ *no phone. AE, DC, MC, V.*

Hradčany

$$$$ ✕ **U Zlaté hrušky.** At this fetching little rococo house perched on one of Prague's prettiest cobblestone streets, slide into one of the cozy dark-wood booths and let the cheerful staff advise on wines and specials. Among the regular offerings are a superb leg of venison with pears and millet gnocchi and an excellent appetizer of duck liver in wine sauce. After dinner, stroll to the castle for an unforgettable panorama. ✉ *Nový Svět 3,* ☎ *02/2051–4778. AE, MC, V.*

$$ ✕ **U Ševce Matouše.** Steaks are the raison d'être at this former shoemaker's shop, where a gold shoe still hangs from the ceiling of the arcade outside to guide patrons into the vaulted dining room. Appetizers are hit-and-miss; stick with the dozen or so tenderloins and filet mignons. ✉ *Loretánské nám. 4,* ☎ *02/2051–4536. MC, V.*

Nové Město (New Town) and Vyšehrad

$$$$ ✕ **La Perle de Prague.** Delicious Parisian cooking awaits at the top of the curvaceous "Fred and Ginger" building. The interior of the main room is washed with soft tones of lilac and sea green. This room also has smallish windows—typical of architect Frank Gehry's designs—and rather cheesy nude photographs, but the semiprivate dining room at the very top has a riveting view over the river. Try the red snapper Provençal, freshwater *candát* (pike perch), or tournedos of beef Béarnaise. Make reservations as early as you can. This is also a good reason to unpack your tie. ✉ *Rašínovo nábř. 80,* ☎ *02/2198–4160. AE, DC, MC, V. Closed Sun. No lunch Mon.*

$$$ ✕ **Fakhreldine.** This elegant Lebanese restaurant, now at a more central location, offers an excellent range of authentic dishes, such as *kibbey bisayniyeh* (lamb and ground pine-nut patty), *warakinab* (stuffed grape leaves), and three kinds of baklava. For a moderately priced meal, try several *meze* (appetizers)—hummus and garlic yogurt, perhaps—instead of a main course. ✉ *Štěpánská 32,* ☎ *02/2223–2617. AE, DC, MC, V. Closed Sun.*

$$ ★ ✕ **Bella Napoli.** The decor may be a little much, but the food is genuine and the price-to-quality ratio hard to beat. Close your eyes to the alabaster Venus de Milos astride shopping-mall fountains and head straight for the antipasto bar, which will distract you with fresh olives, eggplant, squid, and mozzarella. For your main course, go with any of a dozen superb pasta dishes or splurge with shrimp or chicken parmigiana. ✉ *V Jámě 8,* ☎ *02/2223–2933. No credit cards.*

$$ ✕ **Dolly Bell.** This restaurant's whimsical design, with upside-down tables hanging from the ceiling, provides a clever counterpoint to the extensive selection of well-prepared Yugoslav dishes. There's an emphasis on meat and seafood—try the corn bread (polenta) with Balkan cheese, *čevapčiči* (pork sausage), and *tufahija* (baked apple with a smooth nut filling). ✉ *Neklanova 20,* ☎ *02/298–815. DC, MC, V.*

$$ ✕ **Fromin.** Come dressed to the teeth—flourishing your mobile phone, preferably—for dinner at this cavernous, postmodern loft high above Wenceslas Square. The food is better than average, with entrées unusual for hereabouts, such as turkey steak with rosemary, lamb cutlets, and fresh tuna steaks. The upstairs café is quiet in the mornings; at 10 PM it becomes a disco whose doorman will turn away unstylishly dressed guests. ✉ *Václavské nám. 21,* ☎ *02/2423–2319. AE, MC, V.*

$ ✕ **Novoměstský pivovar.** It's easy to lose your way in this crowded microbrewery-restaurant with its maze of rooms, some painted in mock-medieval style, others covered with murals of Prague street scenes. *Vepřové koleno* (pork knuckle) is a favorite dish. The beer is the cloudy, fruity "fermented" style. ✉ *Vodičkova 20,* ☎ *02/2223–1662. AE, MC, V.*

$ ✕ **Pizzeria Coloseum.** An early entry in the burgeoning pizza-and-pasta trade, this one has kept its popularity due largely to its position right off Wenceslas Square. Location doesn't have everything to do with it, though; the pizzas have a wonderfully thin, crisp crust, and the pasta with Gorgonzola sauce will have you blessing Italian cows. Long picnic tables make this an ideal spot for an informal lunch or dinner. There's a salad bar, too. ✉ *Vodičkova 32,* ☎ *02/2421–4914. AE, MC, V.*

$ ✕ **Radost FX Café.** Colorful and campy in design, this lively café is a street-level adjunct to the popular Radost dance club. It's a vegetarian heaven for both Czechs and expatriates: the creative specials of a Mexican or Italian persuasion are tasty, and filling enough to satisfy carnivores. If you suddenly find yourself craving a brownie, this is the place to get a fudge fix. Another plus: it's open until around 3 AM. ✉ *Bělehradská 120,* ☎ *02/2425–4776. No credit cards.*

$ ✕ **Universal.** A pioneer in the neighborhood behind the National Theater that's fast becoming a trendy dining ghetto, Universal serves up satisfying French- and Indian-influenced main courses, giant side orders of scalloped potatoes, and luscious lemon tarts or chocolate mousse—all at ridiculously low prices. ✉ *V Jirchářích 6,* ☎ *02/2491–8182. No credit cards.*

$ ✕ **V Krakovské.** At this clean, proper pub close to the major tourist sights, the food is traditional and hearty. This is the place to try *svíčková na smetaně* (thinly sliced sirloin beef in cream sauce) paired with an effervescent pilsner beer. ✉ *Krakovská 20,* ☎ *02/2221–0204. No credit cards.*

Vinohrady

$$ ✕ **Myslivna.** The name means "Hunting Lodge," and the cooks at this neighborhood eatery certainly know their way around venison, quail, and boar. Attentive staff can advise on wines: try Vavřinecké, a hearty red that holds its own with any beast. The stuffed quail and the leg of venison with walnuts get high marks. A cab from the city center to Myslivna should cost under 200 Kč. ✉ *Jagellonská 21,* ☎ *02/627–0209. AE, MC, V.*

Letná and Holešovice

$ ✕ **La Crêperie.** Run by a Czech-French couple, this creperie near the Veletržní palác (Trade Fair Palace) serves all manner of crepes, both sweet and savory. (It may take at least three or four to satisfy a hearty appetite.) Make sure to leave room for the dessert crepe with cinnamon-apple purée layered with lemon cream. The wine list offers both French and Hungarian vintages. ✉ *Janovského 4, Holešovice,* ☏ *02/878–040. No credit cards.*

$ ✕ **U Počtů.** This is a charmingly old-fashioned neighborhood eatery with comparatively skilled service. Garlic soup and chicken livers in wine sauce are flawlessly rendered, and the grilled trout is delicious. ✉ *Milady Horákové 47, Letná,* ☏ *02/3337–1419. AE, MC, V.*

Žižkov

$ ★ ✕ **Mailsi.** Funky paintings of Arabian Nights–type scenes in a low-ceiling cellar make for a casual, cheerful setting at this Pakistani restaurant. Chicken is done especially well here—the *murgh vindaloo* may well be the spiciest dish in Prague, and the thin-sliced marinated chicken (*murgh tikka*) appetizer is a favorite. Take Tram 5, 9, or 26 to the Lipanská stop, then walk one block uphill. ✉ *Lipanská 1,* ☏ *02/9005–9706 or 0603/466–626. No credit cards.*

Lodging

A slow rise in lodging standards continues, but at all but the most expensive hotels standards lag behind those of Germany and Austria—as do prices. In most of the $$$$ and $$$ hotels, you can expect to find a restaurant and an exchange bureau on or near the premises. During the peak season reservations are absolutely imperative; for the remainder of the year they are highly recommended. Many hotels in Prague go by a three-season system: the lowest rates are charged from December through February, excluding Christmas (at some hotels) and New Year's (at all hotels), when high-season rates are charged; the middle season includes March, November, and often July and August; and spring and fall bring the highest rates. Easter sees higher-than-high-season rates, and some hotels up the price for other holidays and trade fairs. It always pays to ask first.

A private room or apartment can be a cheaper and more interesting alternative to a hotel. You'll find agencies offering such accommodations all over Prague, including at the main train station (Hlavní nádraží), Holešovice station (Nádraží Holešovice), and at Ruzyně Airport. These bureaus normally are staffed with people who can speak some English, and most can book rooms in hotels and pensions as well as private accommodations. Rates for private rooms start at around $15 per person per night and can go much higher for better-quality rooms. In general, there is no fee, but you may need to try several bureaus to find the accommodation you want. Ask to see a photo of the room before accepting it, and be sure to pinpoint its location on a map—you don't want to wind up in an inconveniently distant location. You may be approached by (usually) men in the stations hawking rooms, and while these deals aren't always rip-offs, you should be wary of them. **Prague Information Service** (☞ Visitor Information *in* Prague A to Z, *below*) arranges lodging from all of its central offices, including the branch in the main train station, which is in the booth marked TURISTICKÉ INFORMACE on the left side of the main hall as you exit the station.

The bluntly named **Accommodation Service** (✉ Haštalská 7, ☏ 02/231–0202 or 0602/210–515, FAX 02/231–6640) is a small but efficient agency that specializes in Old Town apartments at about 2,000 Kč for either one or two people and also arranges less costly rooms farther from the center. It's open daily between April and October from 9 to 7 and from November to March 9 to 1 and 2 to 6 (Sunday 9 to 1). Another helpful agency is **Hello Ltd.** (✉ Senovážné nám. 3, ☎ FAX 02/2421–2647 or 02/2421–4212), open daily 9 AM–9 PM (weekdays 8–7 in the off-season); it's a 10-minute walk from the main train station. Both these agencies provide car or minivan transfers from the airport and train stations.

Staré Město (Old Town)

$$$$ **Grand Hotel Bohemia.** This beautifully refurbished Art Nouveau town palace sits across the street from Obecní dům (Municipal House), near the Prašná brána (Powder Tower). During the Communist era it was a nameless, secure hideaway for ranking foreign party members. Once restored to private hands, the Austrian owners opted for a muted, modern decor in the rooms but left the sumptuous Boccaccio ballroom in its faux-rococo glory. In the rooms, sweeping, long drapes frame spectacular views of the Old Town. Each room's amenities include a fax, trouser press, and answering machine. ✉ *Králodvorská 4, 110 00 Prague 1,* ☎ *02/2480–4111,* FAX *02/232–9545. 73 rooms, 5 suites. Restaurant, bar, café, in-room safes, minibars, no-smoking floor, meeting rooms. AE, DC, MC, V.*

$$$ **Maximilian.** Oversize beds, classic French cherry-wood furniture, and thick drapes make for a relaxing stay in this luxurious hotel. A relatively new property (opened in 1995), it's located on a peaceful square, well away from traffic, noise, and crowds, yet within easy walking distance to Old Town Square and Pařížská street. There are fax machines and satellite TVs in every room. ✉ *Haštalská 14, 110 00 Prague 1,* ☎ *02/2180–6111,* FAX *02/2180–6110. 72 rooms. Breakfast room, in-room safes, minibars, meeting rooms, no-smoking rooms, parking (fee). AE, DC, MC, V.*

$$ **Central.** This hotel lives up to its name, with a site on a relatively quiet side street near Celetná ulice and náměstí Republiky (Republic Square). Recent "improvements" raised prices more than the quality level, leaving the hallways as drab and the rooms as sparely furnished as ever (most lack TVs), but it remains perhaps the least expensive full-service hotel in the Old Town. ✉ *Rybná 8, 110 00 Prague 1,* ☎ *02/2481–2041,* FAX *02/232–8404. 62 rooms, 4 suites. Restaurant. AE, DC, MC, V.*

$ **Pension Unitas.** Now operated by the Christian charity Unitas, the spartan rooms of this former convent used to serve as interrogation cells for the Communist secret police. (Václav Havel was once a "guest.") Today conditions are much more comfortable, though the ambience is more that of a hostel than a pension. There's a common (but clean) bathroom on each floor. You'll need to reserve well in advance, even in the off-season. No smoking is allowed. Note that there is an adjacent three-star hotel, Cloister Inn, using the same location and phone number; when calling, specify the pension. ✉ *Bartolomějská 9, 110 00 Prague 1,* ☎ *02/232–7700,* FAX *02/232–7709. 40 rooms, none with bath. Restaurant. No credit cards.*

Malá Strana (Lesser Quarter)

$$$ ★ **Dům U Červeného lva.** On the Lesser Quarter's main, historic thoroughfare, a five-minute walk from Prague Castle's front gates, the "Baroque House at the Red Lion" is an intimate, immaculately kept hotel. Guest rooms have parquet floors, 17th-century painted-beam ceilings, superb antiques, and all-white bathrooms with brass fixtures. The two top-floor rooms can double as a suite. Note that there is no elevator, and the stairs are steep. ✉ *Nerudova 41, 118 00 Prague 1.* ☎ *02/5753–3832 or 02/5753–3833,* FAX *02/5753–2746. 5 rooms, 3 suites. 2 restaurants, bar, in-room safes, minibars. AE, DC, MC, V.*

$$$ ★ **Kampa.** This early Baroque armory turned hotel is tucked away on an abundantly picturesque street at the southern end of the Lesser Quarter, just off Kampa Island. The bucolic setting and comparatively low rates make the hotel one of the city's better bargains. Note the late-Gothic vaulting in the massive dining room. ✉ *Všehrdova 16, 118 00 Prague 1,* ☎ *02/5732–0508 or 02/5732–0404,* FAX *02/5732–0262. 85 rooms. Restaurant, minibars. AE, MC, V.*

$$$ **U Tří Pštrosů.** The location could not be better: a romantic corner just a stone's throw from the river and within arms' reach of the Charles Bridge. The airy rooms of the centuries-old building still have their original oak-beam ceilings and antique furniture, and many have views over the river. Massive walls keep out the noise of the crowds on the bridge. An excellent in-house restaurant serves traditional Czech dishes to guests and nonguests alike. Rates drop slightly in July and August—probably because there's no air-conditioning, though the building's thick walls help keep it cool. ✉ *Dražického nám. 12, 118 00 Prague 1,* ☎ *02/5753–2410,* FAX *02/5753–3217. 14 rooms, 4 suites. Restaurant. AE, DC, MC, V.*

Hradčany

$$$$ ★ **Savoy.** A restrained yellow Jugendstil facade conceals one of the city's most luxurious small hotels. The former budget hotel was gutted and lavishly refurbished in the mid-1990s. A harmonious maroon-and-mahogany color scheme carries through the public spaces and the rooms, some of which are furnished in purely modern style while others have a rococo look. The Restaurant Hradčany is one of the city's best hotel dining rooms. The only drawback: although Prague Castle is just up the road, none of the rooms have a view of it. ✉ *Keplerova 6, 118 00 Prague 6,* ☎ *02/2430–2430,* FAX *02/2430–2128. 55 rooms, 6 suites. Restaurant, café, in-room safes, minibars, sauna, exercise room, meeting rooms. AE, DC, MC, V.*

$$$ ★ **Romantik Hotel U Raka.** This private guest house, since 1997 a member of the Romantik Hotels & Restaurants organization, has a quiet location on the ancient, winding streets of Nový Svět, just behind the Loreto Church and a 10-minute walk from Prague Castle. One side of the 18th-century building presents a rare example of half-timbering, and the rooms sustain the country feel with heavy furniture reminiscent of a Czech farmhouse. There are only six rooms, but if you can get a reservation (try at least a month in advance), you will have a wonderful base for exploring Prague. ✉ *Černínská 10/93, 118 00 Prague 1,* ☎ *02/2051–1100,* FAX *02/2051–0511. 5 rooms, 1 suite. Breakfast room. AE, MC, V.*

Nové Město (New Town)

$$$$ ★ **Palace.** For the well-heeled, this is Prague's most coveted address—a muted, pistachio green Art Nouveau building perched on a busy corner only a block from Wenceslas Square. The hotel's spacious, well-appointed rooms, each with a white-marble bathroom, are dressed in velvety pinks and greens cribbed straight from an Alfons Mucha print. The hotel's restaurant is pure Continental, from the classic garnishes to the creamy sauces. Two rooms are set aside for travelers with disabilities. Children 12 and under stay for free. ✉ *Panská 12, 111 21 Prague 1,* ☎ *02/2409–3111,* FAX *02/2422–1240. 114 rooms, 10 suites. 2 restaurants, in-room safes, minibars, 2 no-smoking floors, sauna. AE, DC, MC, V.*

$$$ **Axa.** Funky and functional, this 1932 high-rise was once a mainstay of the budget-hotel crowd. Over the years, the rooms have certainly improved; however, the lobby and public areas are still decidedly tacky, with plastic flowers, lots of mirrors, and glaring lights. There are scores of free weights in Axa's gym, making it one of the best in Prague. ✉ *Na Poříčí 40, 113 03 Prague 1,* ☎ *02/2481–2580,* FAX *02/*

232–2172. 126 rooms, 6 suites. Restaurant, bar, pool, sauna, health club. AE, DC, MC, V.

$$$ **City Hotel Moran.** This renovated 19th-century town house has a bright, inviting lobby and equally bright and clean rooms that are modern, if slightly bland. Some upper-floor rooms have good views of Prague Castle. ✉ *Na Moráni 15, 120 00 Prague 2,* ☎ *02/2491–5208,* FAX *02/2492–0625. 57 rooms. Restaurant. AE, DC, MC, V.*

$$$ **Meteor Plaza.** This Best Western hotel combines modern conveniences with historical ambience (Empress Maria Theresa's son, Joseph II, stayed here when he was passing through in the 18th century). The setting is ideal: a Baroque building that is only five minutes on foot from downtown. To get a sense of the hotel's age, visit the original 14th-century wine cellar. Rates drop markedly in midsummer and even more in winter. ✉ *Hybernská 6, 110 00 Prague 1,* ☎ *02/2419–2111,* FAX *02/2421–3005. 90 rooms, 6 suites. Restaurant, exercise room, parking (fee). AE, DC, MC, V.*

$$$ **Opera.** Once the lodging of choice for divas performing at the nearby Státní opera (State Theater), the Opera greatly declined under the Communists. The mid-1990s saw the grand fin-de-siècle facade rejuvenated with a perky pink-and-white exterior paint job. This exuberance is strictly on the outside, though, and the room decor is modern and easy on the eyes. In the off-season a double room can be had for around 2,500 Kč. ✉ *Těšnov 13, 110 00 Prague 1,* ☎ *02/231–5609,* FAX *02/231–1477. 64 rooms. Restaurant, bar, minibars. AE, DC, MC, V.*

$$ **Harmony.** This is one of the renovated, formerly state-owned standbys. A stern 1930s facade clashes with the bright, 1990s interior, but cheerful receptionists, comfortably casual rooms, and an easy 10-minute walk to the Old Town compensate for the aesthetic flaws. Ask for a room away from the bustle of one of Prague's busiest streets. ✉ *Na Poříčí 31, 110 00 Prague 1,* ☎ *02/232–0016,* FAX *02/231–0009. 60 rooms. 2 restaurants. AE, DC, MC, V.*

$$ **Salvator.** An efficiently run establishment just outside the Old Town, this pension offers more comforts than most in its class, including satellite TV and minibars in most rooms, and a combination breakfast room and bar with a billiard table. Rooms are pristine if plain, with the standard narrow beds; those without private bath also lack TVs but are a good value nonetheless. ✉ *Truhlářská 10, 110 00 Prague 1,* ☎ *02/231–2234,* FAX *02/231–6355. 28 rooms, 16 with bath, 7 suites. Breakfast room, parking (fee). AE (5% fee). Metro: Náměstí Republiky.*

Smíchov

$$$ **Kinsky Garden.** You could walk the mile or so from this hotel to Prague Castle entirely on the tree-lined paths of Petřín, the hilly park that starts across the street. Opened in 1997, the hotel takes its name from a garden established by Count Rudolf Kinsky in 1825 on the southern side of Petřín. The public spaces and some rooms are not spacious, but everything is tasteful and comfortable. Try to get a room on one of the upper floors for a view of the park. The management and restaurant are Italian. ✉ *Holečkova 7, 150 00 Prague 5,* ☎ *02/5731–1173,* FAX *02/5731–1184. 60 rooms. Restaurant, bar, meeting room. AE, DC, MC, V.*

$$ **Mepro.** Standard rooms and service and a reasonably central location make this small hotel worth considering. The Smíchov neighborhood offers a good range of restaurants (including the U Mikuláše Dačického wine tavern, across the street from the hotel) and nice strolls along the river or up the Petřín hill. ✉ *Viktora Huga 3, 150 00 Prague 5,* ☎ *02/548–549,* FAX *02/571–2380. 26 rooms. Snack bar. AE, MC, V.*

$$ **Petr.** Set in a quiet part of Smíchov, just a few minutes' stroll from the Lesser Quarter, this is an excellent value. As a "garni" hotel, it does not have a full-service restaurant, but it does serve breakfast (included in the price). The rooms are simply but adequately furnished. It's a 10-minute walk from metro Anděl (Line B). ✉ *Drtinova 17, 150 00 Prague 5,* ☎ *02/5731–4068,* FAX *02/5731–4072. 37 rooms, 2 suites. AE, MC, V.*

$ **Balkan.** Still holding its own as the city center's lone bare-bones budget hotel, the spartan Balkan is on a busy street not far from the Lesser Quarter and the Národní divadlo (National Theater). Breakfast is served for 85 Kč. ✉ *Svornosti 28, 150 00 Prague 5,* ☎ FAX *02/5732–7180, 02/5732–2150, or 02/5732–5583. 24 rooms. Restaurant. AE (5% fee).*

Žižkov

$$ **Bern.** The cream-color Bern is a comfortable alternative to staying in the city center. Although rather far out, it is situated on several city bus routes into the New and Old Towns; buses run frequently even on evenings and weekends, and the trip takes 10–15 minutes. ✉ *Koněvova 28, 130 00 Prague 3,* ☎ FAX *02/697–5807 or 02/697–4420. 26 rooms with shower. Restaurant, bar, air-conditioning, minibars. AE, DC, MC, V.*

$$ **Olšanka.** The main calling card of this boxy modern hotel is its outstanding 50-meter swimming pool and modern sports center, which includes a pair of tennis courts and aerobics classes. Rooms are clean and, though basic, have the most important hotel amenities. There's also a relaxing sauna with certain nights reserved for men, women, or both. (Note that the sports facilities may be closed in August.) The neighborhood is nondescript, but the Old Town is only 10 minutes away by direct tram. ✉ *Táboritská 23, 130 87 Prague 3,* ☎ *02/6709–2202,* FAX *02/2271–3315. 200 rooms. Restaurant, bar, pool, health club, meeting rooms. AE, MC, V.*

Eastern Suburbs

$$ **Astra.** The location best serves drivers coming into town from the east, although the nearby metro station makes this modern hotel easy to reach from the center. The neighborhood is quiet, if ordinary, and the rooms are more comfortable than most in this price range. ✉ *Mukařovská 1740/18, 100 00 Prague 10,* ☎ *02/781–3595,* FAX *02/781–0765. 43 rooms, 10 suites. Restaurant, nightclub. AE, DC, MC, V. Metro: Skalka (Line A), then walk south on Na padesátém about 5 mins to Mukařovská.*

$ **Apollo.** This is a standard, no-frills, square-box hotel where clean rooms come at a fair price. Its primary flaw is its location: roughly 20 minutes away by metro and tram from the city center. ✉ *Kubišova 23, 182 00 Prague 8,* ☎ *02/688–0628,* FAX *02/688–4570. 35 rooms. MC, V. Metro: Nádraží Holešovice (Line C), then Tram 5, 14, or 17 to the Hercovka stop.*

$ ★ **Pension Louda.** The friendly owners of this family-run guest house go out of their way to make you feel welcome. The large, spotless rooms are an exceptional bargain, and although the place is in the suburbs, the hilltop site offers a stunning view of greater Prague from the south-facing rooms. ✉ *Kubišova 10, 182 00 Prague 8,* ☎ *02/688–1491,* FAX *02/688–1488. 9 rooms. Sauna, exercise room. No credit cards. Metro: Nádraží Holešovice (Line C), then Tram 5, 14, or 17 to the Hercovka stop.*

Western Suburbs

$$$$ **Diplomat.** This sprawling complex opened in 1990 and remains popular with business travelers thanks to its location between the airport and downtown. From the hotel, you can easily reach the city center by metro. The modern rooms may not exude much character, but they are tastefully furnished and quite comfortable. You can drive a miniature racing car at the indoor track next door. ✉ *Evropská 15, 160 00*

Prague 6, ☎ 02/2439–4111, FAX 02/2439–4215. 369 rooms, 13 suites. 2 restaurants, bar, café, 2 no-smoking floors, sauna, exercise room, nightclub, meeting room, parking (fee). AE, DC, MC, V. Metro: Dejvická (Line A).

$ **Penzion Sprint.** Straightforward rooms, most of which have their own bathroom (however tiny), make the Sprint a fine choice. This pension is located on a quiet residential street, next to a large track and soccer field, in the outskirts of Prague about 20 minutes from the airport. Tram 18 rumbles directly to the Old Town from the Batérie stop just two blocks away. ✉ *Cukrovárnická 62, 160 00 Prague 6, ☎ 02/312–3338, FAX 02/312–1797. 21 rooms, 6 with bath. AE, MC, V.*

Nightlife and the Arts

The fraternal twins of the performing arts and nightlife continue to enjoy an exhilarating growth spurt in Prague, and the number of concerts, plays, musicals, and clubs keeps rising. Some venues in the city center pitch themselves to tourists, but there are dozens of places where you can join the local crowds for music, dancing, or the rituals of beer and conversation. For details of cultural and nightlife events, look for the English-language newspaper the *Prague Post* or one of the multilingual monthly guides available at hotels, tourist offices, and newsstands.

Nightlife

CABARET

For adult stage entertainment (with some nudity) try the **Varieté Praga** (✉ Vodičkova 30, ☎ 02/2421–5945).

DISCOS

Dance clubs come and go regularly. The longtime favorite is **Radost FX** (✉ Bělehradská 120, ☎ 02/2251–3144), with imported and homegrown DJs playing the latest house, hip-hop, and dance music. **Karlovy Lázně** (✉ Novotného lávka), near the Charles Bridge, is a four-story dance palace with everything from Czech oldies to ambient chill-out sounds. **La Habana** (✉ Míšeňská 12, ☎ 02/5731–5104), is the place to show off your moves to recorded salsa and merengue music.

JAZZ CLUBS

Jazz gained notoriety under the Communists as a subtle form of protest, and the city still has some great jazz clubs, featuring everything from swing to blues and modern. The listed clubs have a cover charge. **Reduta** (✉ Národní 20, ☎ 02/2491–2246) features a full program of local and international musicians. **AghaRTA** (✉ Krakovská 5, ☎ 02/2221–1275) offers a variety of jazz acts in an intimate space. Music starts around 9 PM, but come earlier to get a seat. **Jazz Club Železná** (✉ Železná 16, ☎ 02/2421–2541) mixes its jazz acts with world music. **Jazz Club U staré paní** (✉ Michalská 9, ☎ 02/264–920) has a rotating list of tried-and-true Czech bands.

PUBS, BARS, AND LOUNGES

Bars and lounges are not traditional Prague fixtures, but bars catering to a young crowd have elbowed their way in over the past few years. Still, most social life of the drinking variety takes place in pubs (*pivnice* or *hospody*), which are liberally sprinkled throughout the city's neighborhoods. Tourists are welcome to join in the evening ritual of sitting around large tables and talking, smoking, and drinking beer. Before venturing in, however, it's best to familiarize yourself with a few points of pub etiquette: Always ask if a chair is free before sitting down (*Je tu volno?*). To order a beer (*pivo*), do not wave the waiter down or shout across the room; he will usually assume you want beer—most pubs serve one brand—and bring it over to you without asking. He will also bring subsequent rounds to the table without asking. To refuse, just shake your head or say no thanks (*ne, děkuju*). At the end of the evening, usually around 10:30 or 11, the waiter will come to tally the bill. There are plenty of popular pubs in the city center, all of which can get impossibly crowded. **U Medvídků** (✉ Na Perštýně 7, ☎ 02/2421–1916) was a brewery at least as long ago as the 15th century. Beer is no longer made on the premises; rather, they serve draft Budvar shipped from České Budějovice. **U svatého Tomáše** (✉ Letenská 12, ☎ 02/5732–0101) brewed beer for Augustinian monks starting in 1358. Now they serve commercially produced beer in a tourist-friendly mock-medieval hall in the Lesser Quarter. **U Zlatého Tygra** (✉ Husova 17, ☎ 02/2222–1111) is famed as one of the three best Prague pubs for Pilsner Urquell, the original and perhaps the greatest of the pilsners. It also used to be a hangout for such raffish types as the writer Bohumil Hrabal, who died in 1997.

One of the oddest phenomena of Prague's post-1989 renaissance is the sight of travelers and tour groups from the United States, Britain, Australia, and even Japan descending on this city to experience the life of—American expatriates. There are a handful of bars guaranteed to ooze Yanks and other native English speakers. The **James Joyce Pub** (✉ Liliová 10, ☎ 02/2424–8793) is authentically Irish (it has Irish owners), with Guinness on tap and excellent food of the fish-and-chips persuasion. **U Malého Glena** (✉ Karmelitská 23, ☎ 02/535–8115) offers a popular bar and a stage for local and expat jazz, blues, and folk.

ROCK CLUBS

Prague's rock, alternative, and world-music scene is thriving. The cavernous **Palác Akropolis** (✉ Kubelíkova 27, ☎ 02/2271–2287), in the Žižkov neighborhood, has top Czech acts and major international world-music performers; as the name suggests, the space has an Acropolis theme. Hard-rock enthusiasts should check out the **Rock Café** (✉ Národní 20, ☎ 02/2491–4416). You can also slouch into the **Lucerna Music Bar** (✉ Vodičkova 36, ☎ 02/2421–7108) to catch popular Czech rock and funk bands and visiting acts. For dance tracks, hip locals congregate at **Roxy** (✉ Dlouhá 33, ☎ 02/2481–0951). **Malostranská Beseda** (✉ Malostranské nám. 21, ☎ 02/539–024) is a dependable bet for sometimes bizarre but always good musical acts from around the country.

The Arts

Prague's cultural flair is legendary, and performances are sometimes booked far in advance by all sorts of Praguers. The concierge at your hotel may be able to reserve tickets for you. Otherwise, for the cheapest tickets go directly to the theater box office a few days in advance or immediately before a performance. Ticket agencies may charge higher prices than box offices do. **Ticketpro** (main branch: ✉ Salvátorská 10, ☎ 02/2481–4020 or 02/1051), with outlets all over town, accepts major credit cards. Another big agency is **Bohemia Ticket International** (✉ Na Příkopě 16, ☎ 02/2421–5031, or Malé nám. 13, ☎ 02/2422–7832). You can also purchase tickets at **American Express** (☞ Travel Agencies *in* Prague A to Z, *below*).

FILM

If a film was made in the United States or Britain, the chances are good that it will be shown with Czech subtitles rather than dubbed. (Film titles, however, are usually translated into Czech, so your only clue to the movie's country of origin may be the poster used in advertisements.) Movies in the original language are normally indicated with the note *českými titulky* (with Czech subtitles). Many downtown cinemas cluster near Wenceslas Square. One of the largest is **Blaník** (✉ Václavské nám. 56, ☎ 02/2221–0110). **Lucerna** (✉ Vodičkova 36, ☎ 02/2421–6972) is a classic picture palace in the shopping arcade of the same name. **Praha** (✉ Václavské nám. 17, ☎ 02/262–035) shows first-run features in the main hall and second-run films in a smaller screening room. Another central cinema with multiple screens is **Světozor** (✉ Vodičkova 39, ☎ 02/2494–7566). Prague's English-language publications carry film reviews and full timetables.

MUSIC

Classical concerts are held all over the city throughout the year. One of the best orchestral venues is the resplendent Art Nouveau **Smetana Hall** (✉ Obecní dům, nám. Republiky 5, ☎ 02/2200–2100), home of the excellent Prague Symphony Orchestra and major venue for the annual Prague Spring music festival. **Dvořák Hall** (✉ Rudolfinum, nám. Jana Palacha, ☎ 02/2489–3111) is home to one of Central Europe's best orchestras, the Czech Philharmonic, led since 1998 by the Russian pianist-conductor Vladimir Ashkenazy. Frequent guest conductor Sir Charles Mackerras is a leading proponent of modern Czech music.

Performances also are held regularly at many of the city's **palaces and churches,** including the Garden on the Ramparts below Prague Castle (where the music comes with a view); both Churches of St. Nicholas; the Church of Sts. Simon and Jude on Dušní in the Old Town; the Church of St. James on Malá Štupartská, near Old Town Square; the Zrcadlová kaple (Mirror Chapel) in the Klementinum on Mariánské náměstí in the Old Town; and the Lobkowicz Palace at Prague Castle. If you're an organ-music buff, you'll most likely have your pick of recitals held in Prague's historic halls and churches. Popular programs are offered at the Church of St. Nicholas in the Lesser Quarter and the Church of St. James, where the organ plays amid a complement of Baroque statuary. Classical ensembles are the most common finds, and the standard of performance ranges from adequate to superb, though the programs tend to take few risks. Serious fans of Baroque music may have the opportunity to hear works of little-known Bohemian composers at these concerts. Some of the best chamber ensembles are the Talich Chamber Orchestra, the Prague Chamber Philharmonic (also known as the Prague Philharmonia), the Wihan Quartet, the Czech Trio, and the Agon contemporary music group.

Concerts at the **Villa Bertramka** (✉ Mozartova 169, in Smíchov, ☎ 02/540–012) emphasize the music of Mozart and his contemporaries.

OPERA AND BALLET

The Czech Republic has a strong operatic tradition. A great venue for a night at the opera is the plush **Národní divadlo** (National Theater; ✉ Národní třída 2, ☎ 02/2490–1448). Performances at the **Statní Opera Praha** (State Opera House; ✉ Wilsonova 4, ☎ 02/265–353), near the top of Wenceslas Square, can also be excellent. Unlike during the Communist period, operas are almost always sung in their original tongue, and the repertoire offers plenty of Italian favorites as well as the Czech national composers Janaček, Dvořák, and Smetana. (Czech operas are supertitled in English.) These two theaters also often stage ballets. The historic **Stavovské divadlo** (Estates Theater; ✉ Ovocný trh 1, ☎ 02/2421–5001), where *Don Giovanni* premiered in the 18th century, plays host to a mix of operas and dramatic works. Appropriate attire is recommended for all venues; the National and Estates theaters instituted a "no jeans" rule in 1998. Ticket prices have risen, but are still quite reasonable at 300 Kč–500 Kč (slightly more at the Estates Theater).

PUPPET SHOWS

This traditional form of Czech popular entertainment has been given new life thanks to the productions mounted at the **Národní divadlo marionet** (National Marionette Theater; ✉ Žatecká 1, ☎ 02/232–2536; in season, shows are also performed at Celetná 13). Children and adults alike can enjoy the hilarity and pathos of famous operas adapted for non-human "singers." The company's bread and butter is a production of Mozart's *Don Giovanni.*

THEATER

A dozen or so professional theater companies play in Prague to ever-packed houses. Visiting the theater is a vital activity in Czech society, and the language barrier can't obscure the players' artistry. Nonverbal theater also abounds: not only tourist-friendly mime and "Black Light Theater"—a melding of live acting, mime, video, and stage trickery—but also serious (or incomprehensible) productions by top local and foreign troupes. The famous **Laterna Magika** (Magic Lantern) puts on a multimedia extravaganza in the National Theater's ugly modern hall (✉ Národní třída 4, ☎ 02/2491–4129). The popular **Archa Theater** (✉ Na Poríčí 26, ☎ 02/232–8800) offers avant-garde and experimental theater, music, and dance and has hosted world-class visiting ensembles such as the Royal Shakespeare Company. Several English-language theater groups operate sporadically. For complete listings, pick up a copy of the *Prague Post.*

Outdoor Activities and Sports

Boats

Rowboats and paddle boats can be rented on Slovanský ostrov, the island in the Vltava just south of the National Theater.

Fitness Clubs

Some luxury hotels have well-equipped fitness centers with swimming pools. The **Corinthia Towers** (✉ Kongresova 1, Prague 4, ☎ 02/6119–1111) is south of the center, near the Vyšehrad metro station. The more centrally located **Hilton** (✉ Pobřežní 1, Prague 8, ☎ 02/2484–1111, Metro: Florenc) has full fitness facilities and tennis courts. Excellent and much less costly facilities can be found at the **Hotel Axa** (✉ Na Poříčí 40, ☎ 02/2481–2580).

Golf

Prague's only course is a nine-holer located in the western suburbs at the **Hotel Golf** (✉ Plzeňská 215, ☎ 02/5721–5185). Take a taxi to the hotel or Tram 4, 7, or 9 from metro station Anděl to the Hotel Golf stop. **Praha Karlštejn Golf Club** offers a more challenging course with a view of the famous Karlštejn Castle. It's 30 km (18 mi) southwest of Prague, just across the Berounka River from the castle.

Jogging

The best place for jogging is **Stromovka,** a large, flat park adjacent to the Výstaviště fairgrounds in Prague 7 (take Tram 5, 12, or 17 to the Výstaviště stop). Closer to the center, another popular park is **Letenské sady** (Letna Park), the park east of the Royal Garden at Prague Castle, across Chotkova street (☞ Letná and Holešovice *in* Exploring Prague, *above*). For safety's sake, unaccompanied women should avoid the more remote corners of this park.

Spectator Sports

Prague plays host to a wide variety of spectator sports, including world-class ice hockey, soccer, and tennis. The best place to find out what's going on (and where) is the weekly sports page of the *Prague Post,* or you can inquire at your hotel.

SOCCER

National and international matches are played regularly at the home of Prague's Sparta team, Sparta Stadium in Letná, behind Letna Park. To reach the stadium, take Tram 1, 25, or 26 to the Sparta stop.

Swimming

The best public swimming pool in Prague is at the **Podolí Swimming Stadium** in Podolí, which you can get to from the city center in 15 minutes or less by taking Tram 3 or 17 to the Kublov stop. The indoor pool is 50 meters long, and the complex also includes two open-air pools, a sauna, a steam bath, and a wild-ride water slide. (A word of warning: Podolí, for all its attractions, is notorious as a local hot spot of petty thievery. Don't entrust any valuables to the lockers—it's best either to check them in the safe with the *vrátnice* [superintendent], or better yet, don't bring them at all.) The pools at the **Hilton** and **Hotel Axa** (☞ Fitness Clubs, *above*) are smaller but more conveniently located.

Tennis

There are public tennis courts at the **Strahov Stadium** in Břevnov. Take Bus 176 from Karlovo náměstí in the New Town, or Bus 143 from the Dejvická metro station (Line A), to the Stadion Strahov stop. The **Hilton** (☞ Fitness Clubs, *above*) has two public indoor courts.

Shopping

Despite the relative shortage of quality clothes—Prague has a long way to go before it can match shopping meccas Paris and Rome—the capital is a great place to pick up gifts and souvenirs. Bohemian crystal and porcelain deservedly enjoy a worldwide reputation for quality, and plenty of shops offer excellent bargains. The local market for antiques and art is still relatively undeveloped, although dozens of antiquarian bookstores harbor some excellent finds, particularly German and Czech books and graphics.

Shopping Districts

The major shopping areas are **Na Příkopě,** which runs from the foot of Wenceslas Square to náměstí Republiky (Republic Square), and the area around **Old Town Square.** The Old Town streets **Pařížská ulice** and **Karlova ulice** are dotted with boutiques and antiques shops. In the Lesser Quarter, try **Nerudova ulice,** the street that runs up to Hradčany.

Department Stores

Prague's department stores are not always well stocked and often have everything except the one item you're looking for, but a stroll through one may yield some interesting finds and bargains. **Bílá Labuť** (✉ Na Poříčí 23, ☏ 02/2481–1364) has a decent selection, but the overall shabbiness harkens back to socialist times. **Kotva** (✉ Nám. Republiky 8, ☏ 02/2480–1111) is comparatively upscale, with a nice stationery shop and a basement supermarket with wine and cheese aisles. The centrally located **Tesco** (✉ Národní třída 26, ☏ 02/2200–3111) is generally the best place for one-stop shopping. It has same-day film developing, a newsstand that stocks English-language newspapers and magazines, American-brand toiletries, a supermarket with Western groceries (if you're dying for corn chips, you'll find them here), and a multilingual staff.

Street Markets

For fruits and vegetables, the best street market in central Prague is on **Havelská ulice** in the Old Town. You'll need to arrive early in the day if you want something a bit more exotic than tomatoes and cucumbers. The biggest market for nonfood items is the flea market in

Holešovice, north of the city center, although there isn't really much of interest here outside of cheap tobacco and electronics products. Take the metro (Line C) to the Vltavská station and then catch any tram heading east (running to the left as you exit the metro station). Exit at the first stop and follow the crowds.

Specialty Stores

ANTIQUES

For antiques connoisseurs, Prague can be a bit of a letdown. Even in comparison with other former Communist capitals such as Budapest, the choice of antiques in Prague can seem depressingly slim, as the city lacks large stores with a diverse selection of goods. The typical Prague *starožitnosti* (antiques shop) tends to be a small, one-room jumble of old glass and bric-a-brac. The good ones distinguish themselves by focusing on one particular specialty.

On the pricey end of the scale is the Prague affiliate of the Austrian **Dorotheum** auction house (✉ Ovocný trh 2, ☎ 02/2422–2001) in the Old Town. It is an elegant pawnshop that specializes in small things: jewelry, porcelain knickknacks, and standing clocks, as well as the odd military sword. The small **JHB Starožitnosti** (✉ Panská 1, ☎ 02/261–425) in the New Town is the place for old clocks: everything from rococo to Empire standing clocks and Bavarian cuckoo clocks. The shop also has a wide array of antique pocket watches. **Nostalgie Antique** (✉ Jánský Vršek 8, ☎ 02/5753–0049) specializes in old textiles and jewelry. Most of the textiles are pre–World War II and include clothing, table linens, curtains, hats, and laces. **Papillio** (✉ Týn 1, ☎ 02/2489–5454), in the elaborately refurbished medieval courtyard behind the Church of the Virgin Mary Before Týn, is probably one of the best antiques shops in Prague, offering furniture, paintings, and especially museum-quality antique glass. Here you can find colorful Biedermeier goblets by Moser and wonderful Loetz vases. **Zlatnictví Vomáčka** (✉ Náprstkova 9, ☎ 02/2222–2017) is a cluttered shop that redeems itself with its selection of old jewelry in a broad price range, including rare Art Nouveau rings and antique garnet brooches. In the shop's affiliate next door, jewelry is repaired, cleaned, and made to order.

ART GALLERIES

The best galleries in Prague are quirky and eclectic affairs, places to sift through artworks rather than browse at arms' length. Many galleries are also slightly off the beaten track and away from the main tourist thoroughfares. Prague's as-yet-untouristed Nový Svět neighborhood is something of a miniature artist's quarter and home to two of Prague's more interesting galleries. One is **Galerie Gambra** (✉ Černínska 5, ☎ 02/2051–4527), owned by the surrealist animator Jan Švankmajer. The space was originally Švankmajer's kitchen, where dissident surrealists used to gather and trade ideas; now the gallery displays Švankmajer's bizarre collages as well as his wife's anthropomorphic ceramics. Books and magazines focusing on Czech surrealist art are also for sale. **Galerie Nový Svět** (✉ Nový Svět 5, ☎ 02/2051–4611) displays interesting paintings and drawings by somewhat obscure Czech artists, as well as ceramics, glass, and art books. At the higher end is **Galerie Peithner-Lichtenfels** (✉ Michalská 12, ☎ 02/2422–7680) in the Old Town, which specializes in modern Czech art. Paintings, prints, and drawings crowd the walls and are propped against glass cases and window sills. Comb through works by Czech Cubists, currently fetching high prices at international auctions.

Galerie Litera (✉ Karlinske nám. 13, Prague 8, ☎ 02/231–7195) is in Karlín, a neighborhood rarely set foot in by tourists—it's not rough but pretty seedy. (It's northeast of the city center; get off the metro at

Florenc and walk five minutes up Sokolovská.) Most of the gallery space is given over to temporary shows of unique, high-quality graphics. There are also some lovely ceramics as well as a refined selection of antiquarian art books.

BOOKS AND PRINTS

Like its antiques shops, Prague's rare book shops, or *antikvariáts,* were once part of a massive state-owned consortium that, since privatization, has split up and diversified. Now most shops tend to cultivate their own specialties. Some have a small English-language section with a motley blend of potboilers, academic texts, classics, and tattered paperbacks. Books in German, on the other hand, are abundant.

Antikvariát Karel Křenek (✉ Celetná 31, ☎ 02/231–4734), near the Prašná brána (Powder Tower) in the Old Town, specializes in books with a humanist slant. It has a good selection of modern graphics and prides itself on its avant-garde periodicals and journals from the 1920s and 1930s. It also has a small collection of English books. **Antikvariát Makovský & Gregor** (✉ Kaprova 9, ☎ 02/232–8335) is a great all-around bookstore as attested by the constant traffic of liberal-arts students from nearby Charles University. It's particularly fun to hunt around in the art section, where you could turn up the *Memoirs of Casanova* with illustrations by Aubrey Beardsley or a book on Leni Riefenstahl's mountaineering movies. If you'd just like a good read, be sure to check out the **Globe Bookstore and Coffeehouse** (✉ Pštrossova 6, ☎ 02/2491–7230), a longtime magnet for the local English-speaking community, in its new, more central site.

U Karlova Mostu (✉ Karlova 2, ☎ 02/2222–0286) is the preeminent Prague bookstore. In a suitably bookish location opposite the Klementinum, it's the place to go if you are looking for that elusive 15th-century manuscript. In addition to housing ancient books too precious to be leafed through, the store has a good selection of books on local subjects, a small foreign-language section, and a host of prints, maps, drawings, and paintings. For new books in English, try **Anagram Books** (✉ Týn 4, ☎ 02/2489–5737). There's also a great selection around the corner at **Big Ben Bookshop** (✉ Malá Štupartská 5, ☎ 02/2482–6565).

FOOD & WINE

Specialty food and beverage stores are slowly catching on in Prague. **Fruits de France** (✉ Jindřišská 9 and Bělehradská 94, ☎ 02/9000–0339) charges Western prices for Prague's freshest fruits and vegetables, imported directly from France. **Cellarius** (✉ Lucerna Passage [Wenceslas Square between Vodičkova and Štěpánská streets], ☎ 02/2421–0979) has a wide choice of Moravian and Bohemian wines and spirits, as well as products from more recognized wine-making lands.

FUN THINGS FOR CHILDREN

Nearly every stationery store has beautiful watercolor and colored-chalk sets available at rock-bottom prices. The Czechs are also master illustrators, and the books they've made for young "pre-readers" are some of the world's loveliest. For delightful Czech-made wooden toys and wind-up trains, cars, and animals, look in at **Hračky** (✉ Pohořelec 24, ☎ 0604/757–214). For the child with a theatrical bent, a marionette—they range from finger-size to nearly child-size—can be a wonder (☞ Marionettes, *below*). For older children and teens, it's worth considering a Czech or Eastern European watch, telescope, or set of binoculars. The quality–price ratio is unbeatable.

GLASS

Glass has traditionally been Bohemia's biggest export, and it was one of the few products manufactured during Communist times that managed to retain an artistically innovative spirit. Today Prague has plenty of shops selling Bohemian glass, much of it tourist kitsch. A good spot is the stylish **Galerie A** (✉ Na Perštýně 10, ☎ 02/261–334), which stocks Art Nouveau, Biedermeier, and medieval replica glass in Art Deco vitrines from the 1920s. Much more contemporary and decidedly less practical are the art-glass offerings at **Galerie 'Z'** (✉ U lužického semináře 7, ☎ 02/9005–5188), which sells limited-edition mold-melted and blown glass, and its sister shop, **Galerie Mozart** (✉ Uhelný trh 11, ☎ 02/2421–1127), off Národní třída, which also has glass sculptures and some colorful vases and bowls. **Moser** (✉ Na Příkopě 12, ☎ 02/2421–1293), the opulent flagship store of the world-famous Karlovy Vary glassmaker, offers the widest selection of traditional glass. Even if you're not in the market to buy, stop by the store simply to look at the elegant wood-paneled salesrooms on the second floor. The staff will gladly pack goods for traveling.

HOME DESIGN

Czech design is wonderfully rich both in quality and imagination, emphasizing old-fashioned craftsmanship while often taking an offbeat, even humorous approach. Strained relations between Czech designers and producers have reined in the potential selection, but there are nevertheless a handful of places showcasing Czech work. **Fast** (✉ Sázavská 32, Vinohrady, ☎ 02/2425–0538) is a little bit off the beaten track but worth the trek. Besides ultramodern furniture, there are ingenious (and more portable) pens, binders, and other office and home accoutrements. **Arzenal** (✉ Valentinská 11, ☎ 02/2481–4099) is a design shop that offers Japanese and Thai food in addition to vases and chairs; it exclusively sells work by Bořek Šípek, President Havel's official designer. **Galerie Bydlení** (✉ Truhlářská 20, ☎ 02/231–7743) is a father-and-son operation focusing exclusively on Czech-made furniture.

JEWELRY

Alfons Mucha is perhaps most famous for his whiplash Art Nouveau posters, but he also designed furniture, lamps, clothing, and jewelry. **Art Décoratif** (✉ U Obecního domu, ☎ 02/2200–2350), right next door to the Art Nouveau Obecní Dům, sells Mucha-inspired designs—the jewelry is especially remarkable. The Old Town's **Granát** (✉ Dlouhá 30, ☎ 02/231–5612) has a comprehensive selection of garnet jewelry, plus contemporary and traditional pieces set in gold and silver. **Halada** (✉ Karlova 25, ☎ 02/2421–8643) offers sleek, Czech-designed silver jewelry; an affiliate shop at Na Příkopě 16 specializes in gold, diamonds, and pearls.

MARIONETTES

Marionettes have a long tradition in Bohemia, going back to the times when traveling troupes used to entertain children with morality plays on town squares. Now, although the art form survives, it has become yet another tourist lure, and you'll continually stumble across stalls selling almost identical marionettes. The marionettes at **Manhartský Dům** (✉ Celetná 17, ☎ 02/2480–9156) are the real thing. These puppets—knights, princesses, and cloven-hoofed devils—are made by the same artists who supply professional puppeteers. Prices may be higher than for the usual stuff on the street, but the craftsmanship is well worth it. Secondhand and antique marionettes are surprisingly hard to find. One place to look is **Antikva Ing. Bürger** (✉ Betlémské nám. 8, in the courtyard, ☎ 02/269–9148).

MUSICAL INSTRUMENTS

Hudební nástroje Kliment (✉ Jungmannova nám. 17, ☎ 02/2421–3966) carries a complete range of quality musical instruments at reasonable prices. **Capriccio** (✉ Újezd 15, ☎ 02/532507) has sheet music of all kinds.

SPORTS EQUIPMENT

Kotva (☞ Department Stores, *above*) has a good selection of sports gear and clothing. For quality hiking and camping equipment, try **Hudy Sport** (✉ Na Perštýně 14, ☎ 02/2421–8600).

Prague A to Z

Arriving and Departing

BY BUS

The Czech complex of regional bus lines known collectively as **ČSAD** operates its dense network from the sprawling Florenc station on Křižíkova (Metro: Florenc, Line B or C). For information about routes and schedules call ☎ 02/1034, consult the confusingly displayed timetables posted at the station, or visit the information window in the lower level lobby, open daily from 6 AM to 9 PM. One of several Web sites with bus and train information in English can be found at idos.datis.cdrail.cz.

BY CAR

Prague is well served by major roads and highways from anywhere in the country. On arriving in the city, simply follow the signs to CENTRUM (city center). During the day, traffic can be stop-and-go. Pay particular attention to the trams, which have the right-of-way in every situation. Avoid, when possible, driving in the congested and labyrinthine Old Town.

BY PLANE

Ruzyně Airport, 20 km (12 mi) northwest of the downtown area, is small but easily negotiated. Construction of a new terminal contiguous with the existing one has eased traffic flow.

ČSA (the Czech national carrier) offers direct flights all over the world from Ruzyně. Major airlines with offices in Prague are **Air Canada** (☎ 02/2489–2730); **Air France** (☎ 02/2422–7164); **Alitalia** (☎ 02/2419–4150); **American Airlines** (☎ 02/9623–6673); **British Airways** (☎ 02/2211–4444); **British Midland** (☎ 02/2481–0180); **ČSA** (☎ 02/2010–4310); **Delta** (☎ 02/2494–7332); **KLM** (☎ 02/2422–8678); **Lufthansa** (☎ 02/2481–1007); **SAS** (☎ 02/2481–1007); and **Swissair** (☎ 02/2481–2111).

Between the Airport and Downtown: The **Cedaz** minibus shuttle links the airport with náměstí Republiky (Republic Square, just off the Old Town). It runs hourly, more often at peak periods, between 6 AM and 9:30 PM daily and makes an intermediate stop at the Dejvická metro station. The one-way fare is 90 Kč. The minibus also serves many hotels for 360 Kč, which is less than the taxi fare in most cases. Regular municipal bus service (Bus 119) connects the airport and the Dejvická station; the fare is 12 Kč (15 Kč if purchased from the driver), and the ticket is transferable to trams or the metro. đFrom Dejvická you can take the metro to the city center. To reach Wenceslas Square, get off at the Můstek station.

Taxis offer the easiest and most convenient way of getting downtown. The trip is a straight shot down Evropská Boulevard and takes approximately 20 minutes. The road is not usually busy, but anticipate an additional 20 minutes during rush hour (7 AM–9 AM and 3 PM–6 PM). The ride should cost 500 Kč–700 Kč.

BY TRAIN

International trains arrive at and depart from either of two stations: The main station, **Hlavní nádraží** (✉ Wilsonova ulice) is about 500 yards east of Wenceslas Square on Opletalova or Washingtonova street. Then there's the suburban **Nádraží Holešovice** (✉ about 2 km [1 mi] north of the city center). This is an unending source of confusion—always make certain you know which station your train is using. Note also that trains arriving from the west usually stop at Smíchov station, on the west bank of the Vltava, before continuing to the main station. Prague's other central train station, **Masarykovo nádraží** (✉ Hybernská 13), serves mostly local trains but has an international ticket window that is often much less crowded than those at the main station. For train times, consult timetables in a station or get in line at the **information office** (☎ 02/2422–4200) upstairs at the main station (for domestic trains; open daily 3 AM–11:45 PM) or downstairs near the exits under the ČD Centrum sign (open daily 6 AM–7:30 PM). The main Čedok office (☞ Visitor Information, *below*) also provides train information and issues tickets.

Wenceslas Square is a convenient five-minute walk from the main station (best not undertaken late at night), or you can take the subway (Line C) one stop in the Háje direction to Muzeum. A taxi ride from the main station to the center should cost about 100 Kč, but the station cabbies are known for overcharging. To reach the city center from Nádraží Holešovice, take the metro (Line C) four stops to Muzeum; a taxi ride should cost roughly 200 Kč–250 Kč.

Getting Around

To see Prague properly, there is no alternative to walking. And the walking couldn't be more pleasant—most of it along the beautiful bridges and cobblestone streets of the city's historic core. Before venturing out, however, be sure you have a good map. The city is divided into 10 administrative districts; Prague 1 and part of Prague 2 lie entirely within the historic center, and the castle area is bordered by Prague 6 and Prague 7.

BY BUS AND TRAM

Prague's extensive bus and streetcar network allows for fast, efficient travel throughout the city. Tickets are the same as those used for the metro, although you validate them at machines inside the bus or tram. Tickets (*jízdenky*) can be bought at hotels, some newsstands, and from dispensing machines in the metro stations. The basic, transferable ticket costs 12 Kč. It permits one hour's travel throughout the metro, tram, and bus network between 5 AM and 8 PM on weekdays, or 90 minutes' travel at other times. Single-ride tickets cost 8 Kč and allow one 15-minute ride on a tram or bus, without transfer, or a metro journey of up to four stations lasting less than 30 minutes (transfer between lines is allowed). You can also buy a one-day pass allowing unlimited use of the system for 70 Kč, a three-day pass for 180 Kč, a seven-day pass for 250 Kč, or a 15-day pass for 280 Kč. The passes can be purchased at the main metro stations, from ticket machines, and at some newsstands in the center. A pass is not valid until stamped in the orange machines in metro stations or aboard trams *and* the required information is entered on the back (there are instructions in English). A refurbished old tram, No. 91, travels through the Old Town and Lesser Quarter on summer weekends. The metro shuts down at midnight, but Trams 50–59 and Buses 500 and above run all night. Night trams run at 40-minute intervals, and all routes intersect at the corner of Lazarská and Spálená streets in the New Town near the Národní třída metro station.

BY CAR

Parking is permitted in the center of town on a growing number of streets with parking meters or in the few small lots within walking distance of the historic center—but parking spaces are scarce. A meter with a green stripe lets you park up to six hours; an orange-stripe meter gives you two. (Use change in the meters.) A sign with a blue circle outlined in red with a diagonal red slash indicates a no-parking zone. Avoid the blue-marked spaces, which are reserved for local residents. Violaters may find a "boot" immobilizing their vehicle.

There's an underground lot at náměstí Jana Palacha, near Old Town Square. There are also park-and-ride (P+R) lots at some suburban metro stations, including Skalka (Line A), Zličín and Černý Most (Line B), and Nádraží Holešovice and Opatov (Line C).

BY SUBWAY

Prague's subway system, the metro, is clean and reliable; the stations are marked with an inconspicuous M sign. Trains run daily from 5 AM to midnight. Validate your ticket at an orange machine before descending the escalator. Trains are patrolled often; the fine for riding without a valid ticket is 200 Kč. Beware of pickpockets, who often operate in large groups on crowded trams and metro cars.

BY TAXI

Dishonest taxi drivers are the shame of the nation. Luckily you probably won't need to rely on taxis for trips within the city center (it's usually easier to walk or take the subway). Typical scams include drivers doctoring the meter or simply failing to turn the meter on and then demanding an exorbitant sum at the end of the ride. In an honest cab, the meter starts at 25 Kč and increases by 17 Kč per km (½ mi) or 4 Kč per minute at rest. (The Airport Cars taxis operating from, but not to, the airport have a monopoly and charge slightly higher rates.) Most rides within town should cost no more than 80 Kč–150 Kč. To minimize the chances of getting ripped off, avoid taxi stands in Wenceslas Square, Old Town Square, and other heavily touristed areas. The best alternative is to phone for a taxi in advance. Two reputable firms are **AAA Taxi** (☎ 02/1080) and **Profitaxi** (☎ 02/1035). Many firms have English-speaking operators.

Contacts and Resources

CAR RENTALS

The following rental agencies are based in Prague:

Alamo (✉ Hilton Hotel, ☎ 02/2484–2407, or Ruzyně Airport, ☎ 02/2011–3676). **Avis** (✉ Klimentská 46 and Ruzyně Airport, ☎ 02/2185–1225). **Budget** (✉ Hotel Inter-Continental, nám. Curieových 5, ☎ 02/231–9595, or Ruzyně Airport, ☎ 02/2011–3253). **Hertz** (✉ Karlovo nám. 28, ☎ 02/2223–1010, or Ruzyně Airport, ☎ 02/312–0717). **Thrifty** (✉ Washingtonova 9, ☎ 02/2421–1587, or Ruzyně Airport, ☎ 02/2011–4370).

EMBASSIES

U.S. Embassy (✉ Tržiště 15, Lesser Quarter, ☎ 02/5753–0663). **U.K. Embassy** (✉ Thunovská 14, Lesser Quarter, ☎ 02/5753–0278). **Canadian Embassy** (✉ Mickiewiczova 6, Hradčany, ☎ 02/7210–1800). There are no Australian or New Zealand embassies.

EMERGENCIES

Federal Police (☎ 158). **Prague city police** (156). **Ambulance** (☎ 155). **Medical emergencies: Lékařská služba první pomoci** (district first-aid clinic; ✉ Downtown: Palackého 5, ☎ 02/2494–9181); **Na Homolce Hospital** (✉ Roentgenova 2, Prague 5, ☎ 02/5727–2146 weekdays [foreigners' department]; 02/5721–1111; 02/5727–2191); **First Medical Clinic of Prague** (✉ Tylovo nám. 3/15, Prague 2, ☎ 02/2425–1319); **American Medical Center** (✉ Janovského 48, Prague 7, ☎ 02/807–756 for 24-hr service). Be prepared to pay in cash for medical treatment, whether you are insured or not. **Dentist** (✉ Palackého 5, ☎ 02/2494–6981 for 24-hr emergency service).

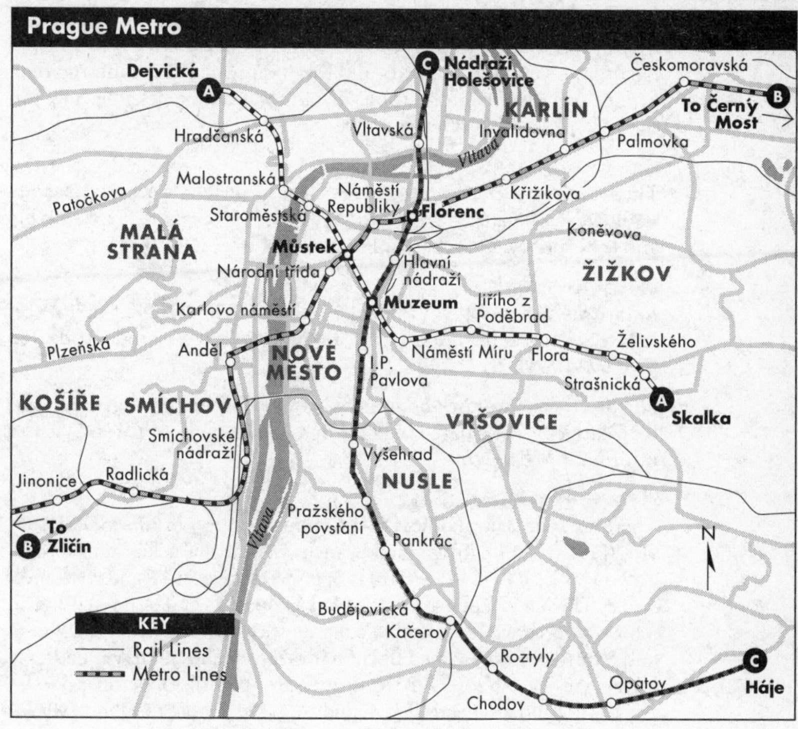

Lost credit cards: American Express (☏ 02/2421–9978); **Diners Club** (☏ 02/6731–4485); **Visa** (☏ 02/2412–5353); **MasterCard** (☏ 02/2424–8110).

ENGLISH-LANGUAGE BOOKSTORES

In the city center nearly every bookstore (☞ Shopping, *above*) carries a few guidebooks and paperbacks. Street vendors on Wenceslas Square and Na Příkopě carry leading foreign newspapers and periodicals. For hiking maps and auto atlases, try the downstairs level of the **Jan Kanzelsberger bookshop** (✉ Václavské nám. 42, ☏ 02/2421–7335) on Wenceslas Square.

GUIDED TOURS

Čedok (☞ Visitor Information, *below*) offers a three-and-a-half-hour "Grand City Tour," a combination bus and walking venture that covers all the major sights with commentary in English. It departs daily at 9:30 AM year-round, and also at 2 PM from April through October, from opposite the Prašná brána (Powder Tower) on Republic Square, near the main Čedok office. The price is about 750 Kč. "Historic Prague on Foot" is a slower-paced, three-hour walking tour for 400 Kč. From April through October, it departs Republic Square on Wednesday, Friday, and Sunday at 9:30 AM; in the off-season, it departs Friday at 9:30 AM. More tours are offered, especially in summer, and the schedules may well vary according to demand. You can also contact Čedok's main office to arrange a personalized walking tour. Times and itineraries are negotiable; prices start at around 500 Kč per hour.

Very similar tours by other operators also depart daily from Republic Square, Národní třída near Jungmannovo náměstí, and Wenceslas Square. Prices are generally a couple hundred crowns less than for Čedok's tours. Themed walking tours are very popular as well. You can choose medieval architecture, "Velvet Revolution walks," visits to

Communist monuments, and any number of pub crawls. Each year, four or five small operators do these tours, which generally last a couple of hours and cost 200 Kč–300 Kč. Inquire at Prague Information Service (☞ Visitor Information, *below*) or a major ticket agency for the current season's offerings.

LATE-NIGHT PHARMACIES

There are two 24-hour pharmacies close to the city's center: **Lékárna U Anděla** (⊠ Štefánikova 6, Prague 5, ☎ 02/537–039 or 02/5732–0918); and **Lékárna** (⊠ Belgická 37, Prague 2, ☎ 02/2251–9731).

TRAVEL AGENCIES

American Express (⊠ Václavské nám. 56, ☎ 02/2421–9992, or Mostecká 12, ☎ 02/5731–3636). **Thomas Cook** (⊠ Národní třída 28, ☎ 02/2110–5276).

For bus tickets to just about anywhere in Europe, try **Bohemia Tour** (⊠ Zlatnická 7, ☎ 02/231–3925) or Čedok's main office (☞ Visitor Information, *below*).

VISITOR INFORMATION

There are four central offices of the municipal **Prague Information Service** (PIS). The **Old Town Hall branch** (⊠ Staroměstská radnice [Old Town Hall], ☎ 02/2448–2018) is open weekdays 9 to 6 and weekends 9 to 5. The **Na Příkopě office** (⊠ Na Příkopě 20, ☎ 02/264–020), just a few doors down from Čedok's main office, is open weekdays 9 to 6 and Saturday 9 to 3. The **Hlavní nádraží branch** (⊠ Hlavní nádraží, lower hall, ☎ 02/2423–9258) is open from April to October, weekdays 9 to 7 and weekends 9 to 4, and from November to March, weekdays 9 to 6 and Saturday 9 to 3. The **Charles Bridge tower office** (⊠ Malostranská mostecká věž, ☎ 02/536–010), in the tower on the Lesser Quarter end of Charles Bridge, is open April through October only. PIS locates lodging, offers city maps and general tourist information, sells tickets to cultural events, and arranges group and individual tours.

Čedok (⊠ Main office: Na Příkopě 18, ☎ 02/2419–7111, FAX 02/232–1656), the ubiquitous travel agency, provides general tourist information and city maps. Čedok will also exchange money, book accommodations, arrange guided tours, and book passage on airlines, buses, and trains. You can pay for Čedok services, including booking rail tickets, with any major credit card. Note limited weekend hours. The main office is open weekdays from 8:30 to 6 and Saturday 9–1.

The **Czech Tourist Authority** (⊠ Staroměstské nám. 6, ☎ FAX 02/2481–0411) on Old Town Square can provide information on tourism outside Prague but does not sell tickets or book accommodations.

To find out what's on and to get the latest tips for shopping, dining, and entertainment, consult Prague's weekly English-language newspaper, the ***Prague Post.*** It prints comprehensive entertainment listings and can be bought at most downtown newsstands as well as in major North American and European cities. The monthly ***Culture in Prague,*** available at newsstands and tourist offices for 40 Kč, provides a good overview of major cultural events.

SOUTHERN BOHEMIA

With Prague at its heart and Germany and the former Austro-Hungarian Empire on its mountainous borders, the kingdom of Bohemia was for centuries buffeted by religious and national conflicts, invasions, and wars. But its position also meant that Bohemia benefited from the cultural wealth and diversity of Central Europe. The result is a glorious array of history-laden castles, walled cities, and spa towns set in a gentle, rolling landscape.

Southern Bohemia (separate sections on the northern and western areas follow) is particularly famous for its involvement in the Hussite religious wars of the 15th century, which revolved around the town of Tábor. But the area also has more than its fair share of well-preserved and stunning walled towns, built up by generations of noble families, who left behind layers of Gothic, Renaissance, and Baroque architecture (particularly notable in Český Krumlov). Farther north and an easy drive east of Prague is the old silver-mining town of Kutná Hora, once a rival to Prague for the royal residence.

Český Krumlov (along with the spas of western Bohemia; ☞ *below*) offers some of the best accommodations in the Czech Republic outside the capital.

Numbers in the margin correspond to numbers on the Bohemia map.

Kutná Hora

59 *70 km (44 mi) east of Prague.*

The approach to Kutná Hora looks much as it has for centuries. The long economic decline of this town, once Prague's chief rival in Bohemia for wealth and beauty, spared it the postwar construction that has blighted the outskirts of so many other Czech cities. Though it is undeniably beautiful, with an intact Gothic and Baroque townscape, Kutná Hora feels a bit melancholy. The town owes its illustrious past to silver, discovered here during the 12th century. For some 400 years the mines were worked with consummate efficiency, the wealth going to support grand projects to rival those of Prague and the nearby Cistercian monastery of Sedlec. As the silver began to run out during the 16th and 17th centuries, however, Kutná Hora's importance faded. In the past decade the town has beautified itself to a degree, but despite a significant tourist industry, modern Kutná Hora is dwarfed by the splendors of the Middle Ages.

★ Forget the town center for a moment and walk to the **Chrám svaté Barbory** (St. Barbara's Cathedral), a 10-minute stroll from the main Palackého náměstí along Barborská ulice. The approach to the church, overlooking the river, is magnificent. Baroque statues line the road in front of a vast former Jesuit college as you near St. Barbara's, which is really just a parish church that is commonly granted the grander title. From a distance, the three-peaked roof of the church gives the impression of a large, magnificent tent more than a religious center. St. Barbara's is undoubtedly Kutná Hora's masterpiece and a high point of the Gothic style in Bohemia. Begun in the 1380s, it drew on the talents of the Peter Parler workshop as well as two luminaries of the late-Gothic flowering a century later, Matyáš Rejsek and Benedikt Ried. The soaring roof was added as late as 1558, replaced in the 18th century, and finally restored, by Josef Mocker, late in the 1800s; the western facade also dates from the end of the 19th century.

St. Barbara is the patron saint of miners, and silver-mining themes dominate the interior. Gothic frescoes depict angels carrying shields with mining symbols. The town's other major occupation, minting, can be seen in frescoes in the **Mintner's Chapel.** A statue of a miner, donning the characteristic smock, that dates from 1700 stands proudly in the nave. But the main attraction of the interior is the vaulting itself—attributed to Ried—which carries the eye effortlessly upward.

Bohemia

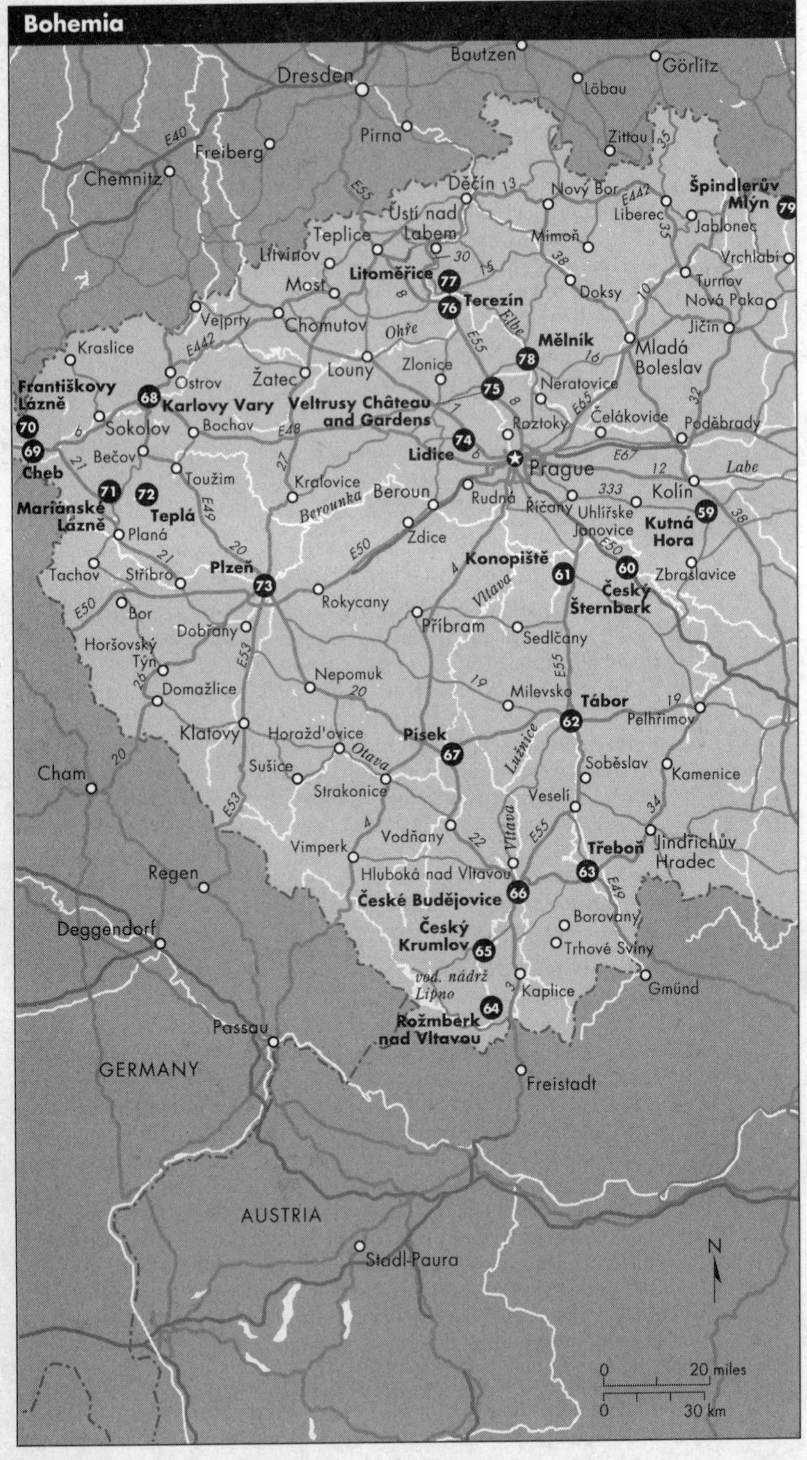

Dresden
Bautzen
Görlitz
Löbau
Zittau
Pirna
Freiberg
Chemnitz
Děčín
Nový Bor
Liberec
Špindlerův Mlýn
Jablonec
Ústí nad Labem
Teplice
Litvínov
Mimoň
Vrchlabí
Most
Litoměřice
Turnov
Doksy
Terezín
Nová Paka
Vejprty
Chomutov
Ohře
Jičín
Mělník
Mladá Boleslav
Kraslice
Louny
Zlonice
Františkovy Lázně
Ostrov
Žatec
Neratovice
Karlovy Vary
Veltrusy Château and Gardens
Sokolov
Bochov
Roztoky
Čelákovice
Poděbrady
Cheb
Bečov
Lidice
Prague
Labe
Toužim
Kralovice
Beroun
Rudná
Kolín
Mariánské Lázně
Teplá
Berounka
Říčany
Uhlířske Janovice
Kutná Hora
Planá
Zdice
Tachov
Stříbro
Plzeň
Konopiště
Český Šternberk
Zbraslavice
Bor
Rokycany
Vltava
Dobřany
Příbram
Sedlčany
Horšovský Týn
Nepomuk
Domažlice
Milevsko
Tábor
Pelhřimov
Klatovy
Horažd'ovice
Písek
Otava
Lužnice
Cham
Sušice
Strakonice
Soběslav
Kamenice
Veselí
Vodňany
Třeboň
Jindřichův Hradec
Vimperk
Hluboká nad Vltavou
Regen
České Budějovice
Borovany
Deggendorf
Český Krumlov
Trhové Sviny
vod. nádrž Lipno
Kaplice
Gmünd
Rožmberk nad Vltavou
Passau
GERMANY
Freistadt
AUSTRIA
Stadl-Paura
N
0
20 miles
0
30 km

✉ *Barborská ul.* 🎫 *30 Kč.* ⏲ *May–Sept., Tues.–Sun. 9–5:30; Oct. and Apr., Tues.–Sun. 9–11:30 and 1–4; Nov.–Mar., Tues.–Sun. 9–11:30 and 2–3:30.*

The romantic view over the town from the cathedral area, marked by the visibly tilting 260-ft tower of St. James's Church (☞ *below*), is impressive, and few modern buildings intrude. As you descend into town along Barborská ulice, you'll pass the **Hrádek** (Little Castle), which was once part of the town's fortifications and now houses a museum of mining and coin production and a claustrophobic medieval mine tunnel. ✉ *Barborská ul.* 🎫 *100 Kč.* ⏲ *Apr. and Oct., Tues.–Sun. 9–5; May, June, and Sept., Tues.–Sun. 9–6; July–Aug., Tues.–Sun. 10–6.*

You'll easily find the **Vlašský dvůr** (Italian Court), the old mint, by following the signs through town. Coins were first minted here in 1300, struck by Italian artisans brought in from Florence—hence the mint's odd name. It was here that the Prague groschen, one of the most widely circulated coins of the Middle Ages, was minted until 1726 and here, too, that the Bohemian kings stayed on their frequent visits. There's a **coin museum,** where you can see the small, silvery groschen being struck and buy replicas. ✉ *Havlíčkovo nám.* 🎫 *30 Kč.* ⏲ *Apr.–Sept., daily 9–6; Oct. and Mar., daily 10–5; Nov.–Feb., daily 10–4.*

If the door to the **Chrám svatého Jakuba** (St. James's Church) next door is open, peek inside. Originally a Gothic church dating from the 1300s, the structure was almost entirely transformed into Baroque during the 17th and 18th centuries. The characteristic onion dome on the tower was added in 1737. The paintings on the wall include works of the best Baroque Czech masters; the *Pietà* is by the 17th-century painter Karel Škréta. ✉ *Havlíčkovo nám.*

Before leaving the city, stop in the nearby suburb of Sedlec for a bone-chilling sight: a chapel decorated with the bones of some 40,000 people. The Kaple všech svatých (All Saints' Chapel), commonly known as the **kostnice** (ossuary) or "Bone Church," just up the road from the former Sedlec Monastery, came into being in the 16th century, when development forced the clearing of a nearby graveyard. Monks of the Cistercian order came up with the bright idea of using the bones for decoration; the most recent creations date from the end of the 19th century. The Sedlec Monastery is now a cigarette factory. Its run-down **Church of the Assumption of the Virgin** exemplifies the work of Giovanni Santini (1667–1723). A master of expressive line and delicate proportion, this one-of-a-kind architect fathered a bravura hybrid of Gothic and Baroque. 🎫 *30 Kč.* ⏲ *Ossuary Apr.–Oct., daily 8–noon and 1–6 (until 5 in Oct.); Nov.–Mar., daily 9–noon and 1–4. Church closed Sun. and Mon.*

Lodging

$$ **Medínek.** The location, on the main square, puts you an easy stroll from the sights, and the ground-floor restaurant offers decent Czech cooking in an atmosphere more pleasant than that found in the local beer halls. Unfortunately, the 1960s architecture blights the surrounding square. ✉ *Palackého nám. 316, 284 01,* ☎ *0327/512–741,* FAX *0327/512–743. 90 rooms, 43 with bath. Restaurant, café. AE, MC, V.*

$$ **U Hrnčíře.** This is a quaint little inn situated next to a potter's shop near the town center. The rooms are very plain and the stairs very steep, but the friendly staff gives the hotel a decidedly homey feel. The restaurant in the back garden has a beautiful view overlooking St. James's Church. ✉ *Barborská 24, 284 01,* ☎ *0327/512–113. 5 rooms. Restaurant. MC, V.*

Český Šternberk

60 *35 km (21 mi) southwest of Kutná Hora, 24 km (15 mi) from Benešov.*

At night this 13th-century castle looks positively forbidding, occupying a forested knoll over the Sázava River. In daylight, the structure, last renovated in the 18th century, is less haunting but still impressive. You can tour some of the rooms fitted out with period furniture (mostly rococo); little of the early Gothic has survived the many renovations. The Šternberk (Sternberg) family has owned the place since the 13th century, except during the Communist era. ⊠ *Český Šternberk,* ☎ *0303/855–166.* 🎫 *110 Kč.* 🕘 *Apr. and Sept.–Oct., Tues.–Sun. 9–5; May–Aug., Tues.–Sun. 9–6; Nov.–Mar., Mon.–Thurs. and weekends 9–4.*

Konopiště

61 *25 km (15 mi) west of Český Šternberk, 45 km (27 mi) southeast of Prague.*

Given its remote location, Český Šternberk is ill equipped for a meal or an overnight stay. Instead, continue on to the superior facilities of Konopiště (via the industrial town of Benešov). The town is best known for its 14th-century castle, which served six centuries later as the residence of the heir to the Austrian crown, Franz Ferdinand. Scorned by the Austrian nobility for marrying a commoner, Franz Ferdinand wanted an impressive summer residence to win back the envy of his peers, and he spared no expense in restoring the castle to its original Gothic form, filling its 82 rooms with outlandish paintings, statues, and curiosities. His dream came to a fateful end in 1914 when he was assassinated at Sarajevo, an event that precipitated World War I. The Austrian defeat in the war ultimately led to the fall of the Hapsburgs. Ironically, the destiny of the Austrian Empire had been sealed at the castle a month before the assassination, when Austrian emperor Franz Joseph I met with German kaiser Wilhelm II and agreed to join forces with him in the event of war.

To visit **Zámek Konopiště** (Konopiště Castle), start from the Konopiště Motel, about 1 km (½ mi) off Highway E55, and walk straight for about 2 km (1 mi) along the trail through the woods. Before long, the rounded, neo-Gothic towers appear through the trees, and you reach the formal garden with its almost mystical circle of classical statues. Built by the wealthy Beneschau family, the castle dates from around 1300 and for centuries served as a bastion of the nobility in their struggle for power with the king. At the end of the 14th century, Catholic nobles actually captured the weak King Wenceslas (Václav) IV in Prague and held him prisoner in the smaller of the two rounded towers. To this day the tower is known affectionately as the Václavka. Several of the rooms, reflecting Archduke Franz Ferdinand's extravagant taste and lifestyle, are open to the public during the high season. A valuable collection of weapons from the 16th through 18th centuries can be seen in the Weapons Hall on the third floor. Less easy to miss are the hundreds of stuffed animals, rather macabre monuments to the archduke's obsession with hunting. The interior is only open to tours; the guides may not speak English, but there are English texts available. ⊠ *Zámek Konopiště, Benešov (about 3 km [2 mi] west of Benešov's train and bus stations on red- or yellow-marked paths).* 🎫 *Each tour 110 Kč, all three tours 240 Kč.* 🕘 *Apr. and Oct., Tues.–Sun. 9–3; May–Aug., Tues.–Sun. 9–5; Sept., Tues.–Sun. 9–4.*

Dining and Lodging

$$$ ✕🏨 **Konopiště Motel.** Long a favorite with Prague-based diplomats, who come for the fresh air and outdoor sports, the motel is about 2 km (1 mi) from Konopiště Castle, on a small road about 1 km (½ mi)

from the main Prague-Tábor highway (E55). Rooms are small but well appointed (ask for one away from the main road). Its lodgelike restaurant, Stodola (open for dinner only), boasts a fine reputation for Bohemian-style grilled meats, chicken, and fish dishes. The live folk music in the evening is romantic rather than obtrusive; the wines and service are excellent. ✉ *256 01 Benešov,* ☎ *0301/22732,* FAX *0301/22053. 40 rooms. 2 restaurants, pool, miniature golf, tennis court, free parking. DC, MC, V.*

Tábor

★ 62 *45 km (27 mi) south of Konopiště on Hwy. E55.*

It's hard to believe this dusty Czech town was built to receive Christ on his return to Earth in the Second Coming. But that's what the Hussites intended when they flocked here by the thousands in 1420 to construct a society modeled on the communities of the early Christians. Tábor's fascinating history is unique among Czech towns—it started out as a combination utopia and fortress.

Following the execution of Jan Hus, a vociferous religious reformer who railed against the Catholic Church and the nobility, reform priests drawing on the support of poor workers and peasants took to the hills of southern Bohemia. These hilltop congregations soon grew into permanent settlements, wholly outside the feudal order. The most important settlement, on the Lužnice River, became known in 1420 as Tábor. Tábor quickly evolved into the symbolic and spiritual center of the Hussites (now called Taborites) and, together with Prague, served as the bulwark of the reform movement.

The early 1420s in Tábor were heady days for religious reformers. Private property was denounced, and the many poor who made the pilgrimage to Tábor were required to leave their possessions at the town gates. Some sects rejected the doctrine of transubstantiation (the belief that the Eucharist becomes the body and blood of Christ), turning Holy Communion into a bawdy, secular feast of bread and wine. Other reformers considered themselves superior to Christ—who by dying had shown himself to be merely mortal. Few, however, felt obliged to work for a living, and the Taborites had to rely increasingly on raids of neighboring villages for survival.

War fever in Tábor at the time ran high, and the town became one of the focal points of the Hussite wars (1419–1434), which pitted reformers against an array of foreign crusaders, Catholics, and noblemen. Under the brilliant military leadership of Jan Žižka, the Taborites enjoyed early successes, but the forces of the established church and the moderate Hussite nobility proved too mighty in the end. Žižka died in 1424, and the Hussite uprising ended at the rout of Lipany 10 years later. Still, many of the town's citizens resisted recatholicization. Fittingly, following the Battle of White Mountain in 1620 (the final defeat for the Czech Protestants), Tábor was the last city to succumb to the conquering Hapsburgs.

Begin exploring the town at **Žižkovo náměstí** (Žižka Square), dominated by a large 19th-century bronze statue of the gifted Hussite military leader. The stone tables in front of the Gothic town hall and the house at No. 6 date from the 15th century and were used by the Hussites to give daily communion to the faithful. Walk, if you dare, the tiny streets around the square, as they curve around, branch off, and then stop; few lead back to the main square. The confusing street plan was purposely laid during the 15th century to thwart incoming invasions.

The **Husitské muzeum** (Hussite Museum), just behind the town hall, documents the history of the reformers. You can visit an elaborate network of tunnels below the Old Town, carved by the Hussites for protection in case of attack. ✉ *Žižkovo nám..* 🎫 *Museum and tunnel tours 40 Kč each.* ⏲ *Apr.–Oct., daily 8:30–5; Nov.–Mar., weekdays.*

Pražská ulice, a main route to the newer part of town, is lined with beautiful Renaissance facades. If you turn right at Divadelní and head to the Lužnice River, you'll see the remaining walls and fortifications of the 15th century, irrefutable evidence of the town's vital function as a stronghold. **Hrad Kotnov** (Kotnov Castle), rising above the river in the distance, dates from the 13th century and was part of the earliest fortifications. The large pond to the northeast of the Old Town was created as a reservoir in 1492; since it was used for baptism, the fervent Taborites named the lake Jordán.

Lodging

$$ **Kapital.** A good bargain, this small hotel on the main street leading from the train and bus stations to the Old Town boasts of its "in door toilets," but in truth offers more than most in its price range, such as a TV (and a bathroom) in every room and covered parking. ✉ *Tř. 9 května 617, 390 01,* ☎ *0361/256–096,* FAX *0361/252–411. 24 rooms. Restaurant, bar, parking (fee). AE, DC, MC, V.*

$$ ★ **Pension 189 Karel Bican.** At this lovely family-run pension, the service couldn't be nicer, nor could the soothing view of the river from some rooms. The premises date from the 14th century, and the Bicans will gladly show you the house's own catacombs, which once linked up to the medieval tunnel network. The chilly basement lounge is a godsend on sweltering summer days. Some rooms have cooking facilities. The level of comfort exceeds that found in many a Czech "luxury" hotel. ✉ *Hradební 189, 390 01,* ☎ FAX *0361/252–109. 6 rooms. Kitchenettes (some), sauna. AE, MC, V.*

Třeboň

63 *48 km (28 mi) south of Tábor.*

Amid a plethora of ponds rests a jewel of a town with a far different historical heritage than Tábor's. Třeboň was settled during the 12th century by the Wittkowitzes (later called the Rožmberks, or Rosenbergs), once Bohemia's noblest family. From the 14th to the end of the 16th century, the dynasty dominated southern Bohemia; they amassed their wealth through silver, real estate, and fish farming. You can see their emblem, a five-petaled rose, on castles, doorways, and coats of arms all over the region. Their official residence was 40 km (25 mi) to the southwest, in Český Krumlov (☞ *below*), but Třeboň was an important second residence and repository of the family archives, which still reside in the town château. Thanks to the Rosenberg family, this unlikely landlocked town has become the center of the Czech Republic's fishing industry. During the 15th and 16th centuries, the Rosenbergs peppered the countryside with 6,000 enormous ponds, partly to drain the land and partly to breed fish. Carp breeding is still big business, and if you are in the area in the late autumn, you may be lucky enough to witness the great carp harvests, when tens of thousands of the glittering fish are netted. The closest pond, **Rybník Svět** (Svět Pond), is on the southern edge of town; try to fit in a stroll along its banks.

Třeboň is an access point in the Czech Greenways network. Greenways is a Czech-American organization that is gradually establishing a chain of hiking, biking, and riding routes from Prague to Vienna, working with local authorities and property owners to develop "ecotourism" along the way. Around Třeboň, hiking and horseback trails snake through the area's ponds and peat bogs. For specific information, contact the tourist office (☞ Visitor Information *in* Southern Bohemia A to Z, *below*).

The partially intact town defenses, made up of walls, 16th-century gates, and three bastions, are among the best in the Czech Republic. Near the **Svinenská Gate,** there's an 18th-century brewery, still producing outstanding beer. First brewed in 1379, as the redbrick tower proudly boasts, beer enjoys nearly as long a tradition here as in Plzeň or České Budějovice. The main square, Masarykovo náměstí (Masaryk Square), has a typical collection of arcaded Renaissance and Baroque houses. Look for the **Bílý Koníček** (Little White Horse), the best-preserved Renaissance house on the square, dating from 1544.

NEED A BREAK? Sample some of the excellent local beer at the **Bílý Koníček** (☎ 0333/721–213), now a modest hotel and restaurant on Masaryk Square.

The entrance to **Zámek Třeboň** (Třeboň Château) lies at the southwest corner of the square. đFrom the outside it looks plain and sober, with its stark white walls, but the walls of the inner courtyard are covered with sgraffito. Tours of the interior feature sumptuous re-creations of the Renaissance lifestyle enjoyed by the Rosenbergs and apartments furnished in late-19th-century splendor. The last of the Rosenbergs died in 1611, and the castle eventually became the property of the Schwarzenberg family, who built their family tomb in a grand park on the other side of Svět Pond. It is now a monumental neo-Gothic destination for Sunday-afternoon picnickers. ✉ *Masarykovo nám.,* ☎ *0333/721–193.* *Each tour 50 Kč.* *Apr. and Oct., weekends 9–4; May and Sept., Tues.–Sun. 9–4; June–Aug., Tues.–Sun. 9–5.*

The **Kostel svatého Jiljí** (Church of St. Giles), adjoining the former Augustine monastery just north of the main square, was home to a set of altar paintings by the Master of the Wittingau Altar (Wittingau is the German name for Třeboň) that dates from the late 14th century. The paintings themselves, the most famous example of Bohemian Gothic art, are now in the Národní galerie (National Gallery) in Prague. The church, with its row of slender columns dividing a double nave, exemplifies the Gothic style of southern Bohemia.

Lodging

$$$ **Zlatá Hvězda.** Less striking than the budget Bílý Koníček Hotel at the other end of the square, the "Golden Star" is a more comfortable alternative. Renovation in the late 1990s left the rooms still exuding a pre-capitalist spareness, while adding such conveniences as relatively spacious bathrooms and satellite TVs. ✉ *Masarykovo nám. 107, 379 01,* ☎ *0333/757–200,* FAX *0333/757–300. 42 rooms. Restaurant, pub. AE, DC, MC, V.*

Outdoor Activities and Sports

You can swim in most of the larger carp ponds around town. The Svět Pond has pleasant little sandy beaches, but it can get crowded in summer.

Rožmberk nad Vltavou

64 *70 km (42 mi) southwest of Třeboň.*

This little village, just a few miles from the former Iron Curtain, was forgotten in the postwar years. It seems like a ghost town, especially at night with the darkened **Hrad Rožmberk** (Rosenberg Castle) keeping lonely vigil atop the hill overlooking the Vltava River. The slender upper tower, the Jakobínka, dates from the 13th century, when the Rosenberg family built the original structure. Most of the exterior, however, is 19th-century neo-Gothic. In summer you can tour some of the rooms and admire the weapons and Bohemian paintings. ✉ *Rožmberk nad Vltavou,* ☎ *0337/749–838.* 🎫 *100 Kč.* ⏲ *Apr. and Oct., weekends 9–3; May–Sept., Tues.–Sun. 9–4.*

Český Krumlov

★ 65 *22 km (13 mi) north of Rožmberk nad Vltavou.*

Český Krumlov, the official residence of the Rosenbergs for some 300 years, is an eye-opener. None of the surrounding towns or villages, with their open squares and mixtures of old and new buildings, will prepare you for the beauty of the Old Town. Here the Vltava works its wonders as nowhere else but in Prague itself, swirling in a nearly complete circle around the town. Across the river stands the proud castle, rivaling any in the country in size and splendor.

For the moment, Český Krumlov's beauty is still intact, even though the dilapidated buildings that lend the town its unique atmosphere are slowly metamorphosing into boutiques and pensions. Visitor facilities are improving but can become overburdened during peak months. Overlook any minor inconveniences, however, and enjoy a rare, unspoiled trip in time back to the Bohemian Renaissance. Greenways trails lead to and from the town; for details, contact the tourist office (☞ Visitor Information *in* Southern Bohemia A to Z, *below*).

The town's main square, **náměstí Svornosti** (Unity Square), may not seem impressive at first sight, diminutive as it is. The **town hall,** at No. 1, built in 1580, is memorable for its Renaissance friezes and Gothic arcades. Tiny alleys fan out from the square in all directions.

Just opposite the empty Hotel Krumlov, a street called Horní ulice leads off toward the **Městské muzeum** (City Museum). A quick visit will get you acquainted with the rise and fall of the Rosenberg dynasty. ✉ *Horní 152,* ☎ *0337/711–674.* 🎫 *30 Kč.* ⏲ *May–June and Sept., daily 10–5; July–Aug., daily 10–6; Oct.–Apr., Tues.–Fri. 9–4, weekends and holidays 1–4.*

Just opposite the City Museum, at No. 154, are the Renaissance facades, complete with lively sgraffiti, of the former **Jesuitská škola** (Jesuit school)—now the semiluxurious Růže hotel (☞ Dining and Lodging, *below*). Like many of Krumlov's most lordly edifices, it owes its abundance of Renaissance detailing to the town's location on the main trading routes to Italy and Bavaria—a perfect site for absorbing incoming fashions. The view over the Old Town and castle is most spectacular from the hotel parking lot.

The tower of the Gothic **Kostel svatého Víta** (St. Vitus's Church), built in the early 1400s, rises from its position on Kostelní ulice to offset the larger, older tower of the castle across the river. Within the church, a marble-column baldachin shelters an elaborate baptismal font. At one time, it covered the tomb of Vilém of Rosenberg (1535–1592), who was one of his line's most august heads and a great patron of the town.

To get to **Hrad Krumlov** (Krumlov Castle), cross the peaceful Vltava via the main street, Radniční, and enter via the staircase leading up from Latrán street, or continue to the massive main gateway. The oldest and most striking part of the castle is the round 13th-century **tower,** renovated in the 16th century to look something like a minaret, with its delicately arcaded Renaissance balcony. The tower is part of the old border fortifications, guarding the Bohemian frontiers from Austrian incursion. Now repainted in something like its Renaissance finery, from various perspectives it appears pompous, absurd, astonishingly lovely—or all of these at once. From dungeon to bells, its inner secrets can be seen from the interior staircase.

Vilém of Rosenberg oversaw a major refurbishment of the castle, adding buildings, heightening the tower, and adding rich decorations—generally making the place suitable for one of the grandest Bohemians of the day. The castle passed out of the Rosenbergs' hands, however, when Vilém's brother and last of the line, the dissolute Petr Vok, sold castle and town to Rudolf II in 1602 to pay off his debts. Under the succeeding Eggenberg and Schwarzenberg dynasties, the castle's transformation into an opulent palace continued. The Eggenbergs' prime addition was a **theater** built in the 1680s and completed in 1766 by Josef Adam of Schwarzenberg. Much of the theater and its accoutrements—sets, props, costumes, stage machinery—survives intact as an extremely rare working display of period stagecraft. After a 30-year closure, the theater reopened for tours in 1997.

As you enter the castle area, look into the old moats, where two playful brown bears now reside—unlikely to be of much help in protecting the castle from attack. In season, the castle rooms are open to the public. Be sure to ask at the ticket office about newly accessible areas of this enormous monument. One sightseeing tour focuses on the Renaissance, Baroque, and rococo rooms, taking in the delightful **Maškarní Sál** (Masquerade Hall), with its richly detailed 18th-century frescoes. A second tour highlights the seigneurial apartments of the Schwarzenbergs, who owned the castle until the Gestapo seized it in 1940. (The castle became state property in 1947.)

The courtyards and passageways of the castle are open to the public all year round. After proceeding through the Renaissance-era third and fourth courtyards, you'll come to a wonderfully romantic elevated passageway with spectacular views of the huddled houses of the Old Town. The Austrian Expressionist painter Egon Schiele often stayed in Český Krumlov in the early 1900s and liked to paint this particular view over the river; he titled his now-famous Krumlov series *Dead City.* From the river down below, the elevated passageway is revealed as the middle level of **most Na plášti** (Cloaked Bridge), a massive construction spanning a deep ravine. Below the passageway are three levels of high arches, looking like a particularly elaborate Roman viaduct. On top runs a narrow three-story block of enclosed passages dressed in light blue and white. At the end of the passageway you'll come to the theater, then to the luxuriously appointed **castle garden**, formal at the near end, leafy and contemplative on the other. In the middle is an 18th-century summer house with a modern, revolving open-air stage in front. Performances are held here in the summer. ⊠ *Hrad Krumlov,* ☎ *0337/711–687.* 🎫 *Garden free, tours 130 Kč, tower 25 Kč, theater 150 Kč.* ⏲ *Garden Apr.–Oct., daily. Interiors Apr. and Oct., Tues.–Sun. 9–3; May and Sept., Tues.–Sun. 9–4; June–Aug., Tues.–Sun. 9–5. Tower Apr. and Oct., daily 9:30–5; May–Sept., daily 9–6. Theater May–Oct., Tues.–Sun. (inquire at the ticket office for tour times).*

The **Egon Schiele Center** exhibits the work of Schiele and other 20th-century and contemporary Austrian, German, and Czech artists in a rambling Renaissance building near the river. ⊠ *Široká 70–72.* ☎ *0337/704–011.* 🎫 *100 Kč.* ⏲ *Daily 10–6 (inquire locally about winter closures).*

Dining and Lodging

Český Krumlov is crammed with pensions and private rooms for rent, many priced around $20 per person per night. The best place to look is along the tiny Parkán ulice, which parallels the river just off the main street. A safe bet is the house at **Parkán No. 107** (☎ 0337/716–396), blessed with several nice rooms and friendly management.

$$ ★ **Na louži.** Lovingly preserved wood furniture and paneling lends a traditional touch to this warm, inviting, family-run pub. The food is unfussy and satisfying; look for the *pstruh* (Vltava trout) with potatoes. The country-style rooms upstairs are small but comfortable. ✉ *Kájovská 66, 381 01,* ☎ FAX *0337/711–280. 5 rooms. Restaurant. No credit cards.*

$$$$ ★ **Růže.** This Renaissance monastery has been transformed into an excellent hotel, only a two-minute walk from the main square. The decor is Ye-Olde-Bohemian, but tastefully done, even extending to the bathroom "thrones." The rooms are spacious, and a few have drop-dead views of the castle, so ask to see several before choosing. Note that some double rooms have two narrow single beds, while some singles have beds large enough for two. The restaurant, too, is top-rate, and the elegant dining room is formal but not stuffy. ✉ *Horní 154, 381 01,* ☎ *0337/772–100,* FAX *0337/713–146. 71 rooms. 2 restaurants, outdoor café, health club, meeting room. AE, MC, V.*

$$$ **Dvořák.** Eminently comfortable, this relatively new small hotel has three other things going for it: location, location, and location. It's situated smack in the center of the historic district, right by the old Barber's Bridge. ✉ *Radniční 101, 381 01,* ☎ *0337/711–020,* FAX *0337/711–024. 17 rooms, 3 suites. Restaurant, bar, in-room safes, sauna. AE, DC, MC, V.*

Nightlife and the Arts

Český Krumlov hosts numerous summertime cultural events, including Renaissance fairs, a chamber-music festival (in June and July), organ and piano festivals (July), and the top-notch International Music Festival, held at the castle every August, with performances by leading Czech and foreign classical ensembles.

České Budějovice

66 *22 km (13 mi) north of Český Krumlov.*

After the glories of Český Krumlov, any other town is a letdown—and České Budějovice, famous primarily for its beer, is no exception. That said, this industrial city of 100,000 has a much livelier scene than its more picturesque neighbors and a large Old Town with several worthwhile sights, notably the well-preserved Gothic Dominican monastery and Church of the Virgin on Piaristické náměstí. The major attraction is the enormously proportioned main square—a rarity, it actually *is* square—named after King Přemysl Otakar II, lined with arcaded houses and worth an hour or two of wandering. For a bite to eat and a sampling of locally brewed Budvar beer in an atmospheric setting, stop by Masné Krámy on Krajinská 13, two blocks north of the square. The delicious local beer is known to Germans as Budweiser (they call the town Budweis)—but this is not the stuff made in St. Louis.

To get a good view over the city, climb the 360 steps up to the Renaissance gallery of the **Černá věž** (Black Tower), at the northeast corner of the square next to St. Nicholas's Cathedral. *10 Kč. Apr.–June and Sept.–Oct., Tues.–Sun. 10–6; July and Aug., daily 10–6.*

Lodging

$$$ **Zvon.** Old-fashioned, well kept, and comfortable, the historic Zvon has an ideal location right on the main square. A room with a view, however, costs about $35 extra, but these rooms are considerably larger and brighter and come with large period bathtubs. ✉ *Nám. Přemysla*

Otakara II 28, 307 01, ☎ 038/731–1384, FAX 038/731–1385. 75 rooms. 2 restaurants, café, pub, meeting room. AE, DC, MC, V.

Hluboká nad Vltavou

★ *9 km (5½ mi) north of České Budějovice.*

This is one of the Czech Republic's most curious châteaus. Although the structure dates from the 13th century, what you see is pure 19th-century excess, perpetrated by the wealthy Schwarzenberg family as proof of their "good taste." If you think you've seen it somewhere before, you're probably thinking of Windsor Castle, near London, on which it was carefully modeled. Take a tour; the rather pompous interior reflects the no-holds-barred tastes of the time, but many individual pieces are interesting. The wooden Renaissance ceiling in the large dining room was removed by the Schwarzenbergs from the castle at Český Krumlov and brought here. Also look for the beautiful late-Baroque bookshelves in the library. If your interest in Czech painting wasn't satisfied in Prague, have a look at the **Galerie Mikolaše Aleše** (Aleš Art Gallery) in the Riding Hall, featuring a major collection of Gothic art and a new exhibition of modern Czech works. ✉ *Rtes. 105 and 146,* ☎ *Château 038/796–7045; gallery 038/796–7041.* 🎫 *Château 130 Kč; gallery 60 Kč.* ⏲ *Château Apr.–June and Sept.–Oct., Tues.–Sun. 9–4:30; July–Aug., daily 9–5. Gallery May–Sept., daily 9–5; Oct.–Apr., daily 9–3:30.*

If you're in the mood for a brisk walk, follow the yellow trail signs 2 km (1 mi) to the **Lovecká chata Ohrada** (Ohrada hunting lodge), which houses a museum of hunting and fishing and also has a small zoo for children. ⏲ *Usually same opening hours as the château.*

Písek

67 *60 km (37 mi) northwest of České Budějovice.*

If it weren't for Písek's 700-year-old **Gothic bridge,** peopled with Baroque statues, you could easily bypass the town and continue on to Prague. After the splendors of Český Krumlov or even Třeboň, Písek's main square, Velké náměstí, is plain, despite its many handsome Renaissance and Baroque houses. The bridge, a five-minute walk from the main square along Karlova ulice, was commissioned in the 1260s—making it the oldest bridge in the land, surpassing by 90 years Prague's Charles Bridge—by Přemysl Otakar II, who sought a secure crossing over the difficult Otava River for his salt shipments from nearby Prachatice. As early as the 9th century, Písek stood at the center of one of the most important trade routes to the west, linking Prague to Passau and the rest of Bavaria, and in the 15th century it became one of five major Hussite strongholds. The statues of saints weren't added to the bridge until the 18th century.

Just off the main square, look for the 240 ft tower of the early-Gothic **Mariánský chrám** (Church of Mary). Construction was started at about the time the bridge was built. The lone surviving tower was completed in 1487. On the inside, look for the *Madonna of Písek,* a 14th-century Gothic altar painting. On a middle pillar is a rare series of early Gothic wall paintings dating from the end of the 13th century. ✉ *Bakaláře at Leoše Janáčka.*

OFF THE BEATEN PATH

ZVÍKOV – If you've got room for still another castle, head for Zvíkov Castle, about 18 km (11 mi) north of town along Route 138. The castle, at the confluence of the Otava and Vltava rivers, is impressive for its authenticity. Unlike many other castles in Bohemia, Zvíkov survived the 18th and 19th centuries unrenovated and still looks just as it did 500 *years ago. 30 Kč. Apr. and Oct., weekends and holidays 9:30–3:30; May and Sept., Tues.–Sun. 9:30–4; June–Aug., Tues.–Sun. 9–5.*

Southern Bohemia A to Z

Arriving and Departing

Prague is the main gateway to southern Bohemia (☞ Arriving and Departing *in* Prague A to Z, *above*). Several Prague-bound trains from Salzburg and Linz call at České Budějovice and Tábor. Most Vienna–Prague trains travel through Moravia, but a few stop at Třeboň and Tábor (with a change at Gmünd). To drive from Vienna, take the E49 toward Gmünd.

Getting Around

BY BUS

All the major sights are reachable from Prague and České Budějovice on the ČSAD bus network (☞ Getting Around by Bus *in* Prague A to Z, *above*).

BY CAR

Car travel affords the greatest ease and flexibility in this region. The main artery through the region, the two-lane E55 from Prague south to Tábor and České Budějovice, though often crowded, is in relatively good shape.

BY TRAIN

Benešov (Konopiště), Tábor, and České Budějovice all lie along the major southern line in the direction of Linz, and train service to these cities from Prague is frequent and comfortable.

Contacts and Resources

EMERGENCIES

Police (☎ 158). **Ambulance** (☎ 155). **Breakdowns** (☎ 1054; Yellow Angels ☎ 1230; Autoklub Bohemia Assistance [ABA] ☎ 1240).

GUIDED TOURS

Čedok (☎ 02/2419–7111) offers several specialized tours that include visits to České Budějovice, Hluboká Castle, Český Krumlov, Kutná Hora, and Konopiště. The main Prague departure point is náměstí Republiky (Republic Square) in central Prague, opposite the Prašná brána (Powder Tower). Most tours need to be booked a day in advance.

VISITOR INFORMATION

České Budějovice (✉ Municipal Information Center, nám. Přemysla Otakára II 1, ☎ 038/635–9480). **Český Krumlov** (✉ Infocentrum, nám. Svornosti 1, ☎ 0337/711–183). **Kutná Hora** (✉ Kulturní a Informační Centrum, Palackého nám. 377, ☎ 0327/512–378). **Písek** (✉ Infocentrum, Fügnerovo nám. 42, ☎ 0362/213–592). **Tábor** (✉ Infocentrum, Žižkovo nám. 2, ☎ 0361/486–230). **Třeboň** (✉ Informační středisko, Masarykovo nám. 103, ☎ 0333/721–169).

WESTERN BOHEMIA

Until World War II, western Bohemia was the playground of Central Europe's rich and famous. Its three well-known spas, Karlovy Vary, Mariánské Lázně, and Františkovy Lázně (better known by their German names, Karlsbad, Marienbad, and Franzensbad, respectively), were the annual haunts of everybody who was anybody: Johann Wolfgang von Goethe, Ludwig van Beethoven, Karl Marx, and England's King Edward VII, to name but a few. Although strictly "proletarianized" in the Communist era, the spas still exude a nostalgic aura of a more elegant past and, unlike most of Bohemia, offer a basic tourist infrastructure that makes dining and lodging a pleasure.

Karlovy Vary

★ 68 *132 km (79 mi) due west of Prague on Rte. 6 (E48).*

Karlovy Vary, better known outside the Czech Republic by its German name, Karlsbad, is the most famous Bohemian spa. It is named for Emperor Charles IV, who allegedly happened upon the springs in 1358 while on a hunting expedition. As the story goes, the emperor's hound—chasing a harried stag—fell into a boiling spring and was scalded. Charles had the water tested and, familiar with spas in Italy, ordered baths to be established in the village of Vary. The spa reached its heyday in the 19th century, when royalty came here from all over Europe for treatment. The long list of those who "took the cure" includes Peter the Great, Goethe (no fewer than 13 times, according to a plaque on one house by the main spring), Schiller, Beethoven, and Chopin. Even Karl Marx, when he wasn't decrying wealth and privilege, spent time at the resort; he wrote some of *Das Kapital* here between 1874 and 1876.

After decades of neglect under the Communists that left many buildings crumbling behind their beautiful facades, the town leaders today face the daunting task of carving out a new role for Karlovy Vary, since few Czechs can afford to set aside weeks or months at a time for a leisurely cure. To raise some quick cash, many sanatoriums have turned to offering short-term accommodations to foreign visitors (at rather expensive rates). By the week or by the hour, "classical" spa procedures, laser treatments, plastic surgery, and even acupuncture are purveyed to German clients or to large numbers of Russians who have bought property in town in the last few years. For most visitors, though, it's enough simply to stroll the streets and parks and allow the eyes to feast awhile on the splendors of the past.

Whether you're arriving by bus, train, or car, your first view of the town on the approach from Prague will be of the ugly new section on the banks of the Ohře River. Don't despair: continue along the main road—following the signs to the Grandhotel Pupp—until you reach the lovely main street of the older spa area, situated gently astride the banks of the little Teplá ("Warm") River. (Drivers, note that driving through or parking in the main spa area is allowed only with a permit obtainable from your hotel.) The walk from the new town to the spa area is about 20 minutes. The **Historická čtvrt** (Historic District) is still largely intact. Tall 19th-century houses, boasting decorative and often eccentric facades, line the spa's proud riverside streets. Throughout you'll see colonnades full of people sipping the spa's hot sulfuric water from odd pipe-shape drinking cups. At night the streets fill with steam escaping from cracks in the earth, giving the town a slightly macabre feel.

Karlovy Vary's jarringly modern **Vřídelní kolonáda** (Vřídlo Colonnade) is built around the spring of the same name, the town's hottest and most dramatic gusher. The Vřídlo is indeed unique, shooting its scalding water to a height of some 40 ft. Walk inside the arcade to watch the hundreds of patients here take the famed Karlsbad drinking cure. They promenade somnambulistically up and down, eyes glazed, clutching drinking glasses filled periodically at one of the five "sources." The waters are said to be especially effective against diseases of the digestive and urinary tracts. They're also good for gout (which probably explains the spa's former popularity with royals!). If you want to join the crowds and take a sip, you can buy your own spouted cup from vendors within the colonnade.

To the right of the Vřídlo Colonnade are steps up to the white **Kostel Maří Magdaleny** (Church of Mary Magdalene). Designed by Kilian Ignaz Dientzenhofer (architect of the two Churches of St. Nicholas in Prague), this church is the best of the few Baroque buildings still standing in Karlovy Vary. ✉ *Moravská ul.,* ☎ *no phone.* ⏲ *Daily 9–6.*

The spa's centerpiece is just a couple minutes' walk along the river, back in the direction of the new town. The neo-Renaissance pillared hall **Mlýnská kolonáda** (Mill Colonnade), built from 1871 to 1881, has four springs: Rusalka, Libussa, Prince Wenceslas, and Millpond.

If you continue down the valley, you'll soon arrive at the very elegant **Sadová kolonáda** (Park Colonnade), a white, wrought iron construction. It was built in 1882 by the Viennese architectural duo of Fellner and Helmer, who sprinkled the Austro-Hungarian Empire with many such edifices during the late 19th century and who also designed the town's theater, the quaint wooden Tržní kolonáda (Market Colonnade) next to the Vřídlo Colonnade, and one of the old bathhouses.

The 20th century emerges at its most disturbing a little farther along the valley across the river, in the form of the huge, bunkerlike **Thermal Hotel,** built in the late 1960s. Although the building is a monstrosity, the view of Karlovy Vary from the rooftop pool is nothing short of spectacular. (The pool is open from 8 AM to 8 PM.) Even if you don't feel like a swim, it's worth taking the winding road up to the baths for the view. ✉ *I.P. Pavlova.*

From the Market Colonnade, a steep street called **Zámecký vrch** leads up to some other sights. A five-minute walk brings you to the redbrick Victorian **Kostel svatého Lukáše** (St. Luke's Church), at the intersection of Zámecký vrch and Petra Velikého, once used by the local English community. A few blocks farther along Petra Velikého street, you'll come to the splendid Russian Orthodox church **Kostel svatých Petra a Pavla** (Church of Sts. Peter and Paul). Return to the Victorian church and take a sharp right uphill on the redbrick road. Then turn left onto a footpath through the woods, following the signs to **Jelení skok** (Stag's Leap). After a while you'll see steps leading up to a bronze statue of a deer looking over the cliffs, the symbol of Karlovy Vary. From here a winding path leads up to **Altán Jelení skok**, a little red gazebo opening onto a fabulous panorama.

NEED A BREAK? Reward yourself for making the climb to Stag's Leap with a light meal at the nearby restaurant **Jelení skok.** You may have to pay an entrance fee if there is a live band (but you'll also get the opportunity to polka). If you don't want to walk up, you can drive up a signposted road from the Victorian church.

It's not necessary to walk for one of the best views of the town. Above Stag's Leap is an observation tower, **rozhledna Diana,** accessible by funicular from behind the Grandhotel Pupp (☞ Dining and Lodging, *below*). There's an elevator to the top of the tower.

The town's most exclusive shopping clusters around the Grandhotel Pupp and back toward town along the river on Stará louka. Here too is the **Elefant** one of the last of a dying breed of sophisticated coffeehouses. This kind of elegant café is now a rarity, but happily the café as an institution is making a real comeback in the Czech Republic. ✉ *Stará louka 30.*

Dining and Lodging

$$$ ✕ **Embassy.** This cozy, sophisticated wine restaurant, conveniently located near the Grandhotel Pupp, serves an innovative menu by local standards. Tagliatelle with smoked salmon in cream sauce makes an excellent main course, as does roast duck with cabbage and dumplings. The wine list features Czech varieties like the dry whites Rulandské bílé and Ryzlink Rýnský (the latter being the domestic version of the Riesling grape) and some pricey imports. ✉ *Nová louka 21,* ☎ *017/322–1161. AE, DC, MC, V.*

$$ ✕ **Karel IV.** Its location atop an old castle tower not far from the Market Colonnade gives diners the best view in town. Good renditions of traditional Czech standbys—*bramborák* (potato pancake) and chicken breast with peaches—are served in small, secluded dining areas that are particularly intimate after sunset. ✉ *Zámecký vrch 2,* ☎ *017/322–7255. AE, MC, V.*

$$$$ ★ **Dvořák.** Consider a splurge here if you're longing for Western standards of service and convenience. Opened in late 1990, this Austrian-owned hotel occupies three renovated town houses that are just a five-minute walk from the main spas. If possible, request a room with a bay-window view of the town. Spa treatments here run to about $750 per person per week in the high season. ✉ *Nová louka 11, 360 21,* ☎ *017/322–4145,* FAX *017/322–2814. 76 rooms, 3 suites. Restaurant, café, pool, beauty salon, massage, sauna, exercise room, casino. AE, DC, MC, V.*

$$$–$$$$ ★ **Grandhotel Pupp.** This enormous hotel with a 215-year history is one of Karlovy Vary's landmarks—it's also one of Central Europe's most famous resorts. Standards and service slipped under the Communists (when the hotel was known as the Moskva), but the highly professional management has more than made up for the decades of neglect. Some guest rooms are furnished in 18th-century period style. The vast public rooms exude the very best taste, circa 1913, when the present building was completed. Every July, the Pupp becomes a temporary home base for international movie stars who come to the Karlovy Vary International Film Festival. (The adjacent Parkhotel Pupp, under the same management, is an affordable alternative to the Grandhotel.) Breakfast costs 375 Kč extra. ✉ *Mírové nám. 2, 360 91,* ☎ *017/310–9111,* FAX *017/310–9620 or 017/322–4032. Grandhotel: 75 rooms, 34 suites. Parkhotel: 108 rooms, 6 suites. 4 restaurants, lounge, sauna, exercise room, casino, 2 nightclubs, parking (fee). AE, DC, MC, V.*

$$$ **Elwa.** Renovations have successfully integrated modern comforts into this older, elegant spa resort located midway between the old and new towns. Modern features include clean, comfortable rooms with contemporary furnishings such as overstuffed chairs. There's also an on-site fitness center. The spa specializes in digestive diseases. ✉ *Zahradní 29, 360 01,* ☎ *017/322–8472,* FAX *017/322–8473. 10 rooms, 7 suites. Restaurant, bar, beauty salon, health club. AE, MC, V.*

$$$ **Růže.** More than adequately comfortable and well-priced given its location smack in the center of the spa district, this is a good choice for travelers who prefer a hotel to a pension or private room. ✉ *I.P. Pavlova 1, 360 01,* ☎ FAX *017/322–1846 or 017/322–1853. 20 rooms. Restaurant. AE, V.*

Nightlife and the Arts

In Karlovy Vary, the upscale action centers on the two nightclubs and the casino of the **Grandhotel Pupp** (☞ Dining and Lodging, *above*). **Club Propaganda** (✉ Jaltská 7, ☎ 017/323–3792) is Karlovy Vary's best venue for live rock and new music. The Karlovy Vary Symphony Orchestra plays regularly at **Lázně III** (✉ Mlýnské nábř. 5, ☎ 017/322–5641).

Outdoor Activities and Sports

Karlovy Vary's warm open-air public pool on top of the **Thermal Hotel** (✉ I.P. Pavlova) offers the unique experience of swimming comfortably even in the coolest weather; the view over the town is outstanding. Marked **hiking trails** snake across the beech-and-pine-covered hills that surround the town on three sides. The **Karlovy Vary Golf Club** is just out of town on the road to Prague.

Shopping

In western Bohemia, Karlovy Vary is best known to glass enthusiasts as the home of **Moser** (✉ Tržiště 7, ☎ 017/323–5303), one of the world's leading producers of crystal and decorative glassware. A number of outlets for lesser-known, although also high-quality, makers of glass and porcelain can be found along Stará louka. For excellent buys in porcelain, try **Karlovarský porcelán** (✉ Tržiště 27, ☎ 017/322–5660).

A cheaper but nonetheless unique gift from Karlovy Vary would be a bottle of the ubiquitous bittersweet (and potent) **Becherovka,** a liqueur produced by the town's own Jan Becher distillery. Another neat gift would be one of the pipe-shape ceramic drinking cups used to take the drinking cure at spas; you can find them at the colonnades. You can also buy boxes of tasty *oplatky* (wafers), sometimes covered with chocolate, at shops in all of the spa towns.

Cheb

69 *42 km (26 mi) southwest of Karlovy Vary.*

Known for centuries by its German name of Eger, the old town of Cheb lies on the border with Germany in the far west of the Czech Republic. The town has been a fixture of Bohemia since 1322 (when it was handed over to King Jan, or Johann, as thanks for his support of a Bavarian prince), but as you walk around the beautiful medieval square, it's difficult not to think you're in Germany. The tall merchants' houses surrounding the main square, with their long, red-tile, sloping roofs dotted with windows like droopy eyelids, are more Germanic in style than anything else in Bohemia. You'll also hear a lot of German on the streets—more from the many German visitors than from the town's residents.

Germany took full possession of the town in 1938 under the terms of the notorious Munich Pact. But following World War II, virtually the entire German population was expelled, and the Czech name of Cheb was officially adopted. A more notorious German connection emerged in the years following the 1989 revolution: Cheb, like other border towns, became an unofficial center of prostitution. Don't be startled to see young women, provocatively dressed, lining the highways and roads into town.

The **statue** in the middle of the central square, náměstí Krále Jiřího z Poděbrad, similar to the Roland statues you see throughout Bohemia and attesting to the town's royal privileges, represents the town hero, Wastel of Eger. Look carefully at his right foot, and you'll see a small man holding a sword and a head—this shows the town had its own judge and executioner.

On the lower part of náměstí Krýle Jiřího z Poděbrad are two rickety groups of timbered medieval buildings, 11 houses in all, divided by a narrow alley. The houses, forming the area known as **Špalíček,** date from the 13th century and were home to many Jewish merchants. Židovská ulice (Jews' Street), running uphill to the left of the Špalíček, served as the actual center of the ghetto. Note the small alley running off to the left of Židovská. This calm street, with the seemingly inappropriate name ulička Zavražděných (Lane of the Murdered), was the scene of an outrageous act of violence in 1350: Pressures had been building for some time between Jews and Christians. Incited by an anti-Semitic bishop, the townspeople finally chased the Jews into the street, closed off both ends, and massacred them. Now only the name attests to the slaughter.

NEED A BREAK? Cheb's main square abounds with cafés and little restaurants, all offering a fairly uniform menu of schnitzel and sauerbraten aimed at visiting Germans. The **Kavárna Špalíček,** nestled in the Špalíček buildings, is one of the better choices and has the added advantage of a unique architectural setting.

History buffs, particularly those interested in the Hapsburgs, will want to visit the **Chebské muzeum** (Cheb Museum) in the Pachelbel House on the main square. It was in this house that the great general of the Thirty Years' War, Albrecht von Wallenstein, was murdered in 1634 on the orders of his own emperor, the Hapsburg Ferdinand II, who was provoked by Wallenstein's increasing power and rumors of treason. According to legend, Wallenstein was on his way to the Saxon border to enlist support to fight the Swedes when his own officers barged into his room and stabbed him through the heart with a stave. In his memory, the stark bedroom with its four-poster bed and dark red velvet curtains has been left as it was. (The story also inspired playwright Friedrich Schiller to write the *Wallenstein* trilogy; he planned the work while living at the top of the square at No. 2.) The museum is interesting in its own right: It has a selection from the Wallenstein family picture gallery, a section on the history of Cheb, and a collection of minerals (including one discovered by Goethe). ✉ *Nám. Krále Jiřího z Poděbrad 3,* ☎ *0166/422–246.* 🎫 *40 Kč.* ⏲ *Mar.–Dec., Tues.–Sun. 9–noon and 1–5.*

The **art gallery** in the bright yellow Baroque house near the top of the square offers a well-chosen sampling of 20th-century Czech art. One of the country's best-known galleries of photography, **Gallery 4,** is just off the square at Kamenná 2.

The plain but imposing **Kostel svatého Mikuláše** (Church of St. Nicholas) was begun in 1230, when the church belonged to the Order of the Teutonic Knights. You can still see Romanesque windows on the towers; renovations throughout the centuries added an impressive Gothic portal and a Baroque interior. Just inside the Gothic entrance is a wonderfully faded plaque commemorating the diamond jubilee of Hapsburg emperor Franz Joseph in 1908. ✉ *Kostelní nám.,* ☎ *no phone.*

Follow Křižovnická, behind the Church of St. Nicholas, up to **Chebský hrad** (Cheb Castle), which stands on a cliff overlooking the Ohře River. The castle—now a ruin—was built in the late 12th century for Holy Roman Emperor Frederick Barbarossa. The square black tower was built with blocks of lava taken from the nearby Komorní Hůrka volcano; the redbrick walls are 17th-century additions. Inside the castle grounds is the carefully restored double-decker Romanesque chapel, notable for the many lovely columns with heads carved into their capitals. The rather dark ground floor was used by commoners. The bright, ornate top floor was reserved for the emperor and his family, who entered via a wooden bridge leading to the royal palace. ✉ *Hradní ul.,* ☎ *0166/422–942.* 🎫 *20 Kč.* ⏲ *Apr. and Oct., Tues.–Sun. 9–4; May and Sept., Tues.–Sun. 9–5; June–Aug., Tues.–Sun. 9–6.*

Dining and Lodging

$$ ✕ **Eva.** Of the many restaurants opened on and around the main square since the tourism boom began in the early 1990s, Eva is certainly one of the best. A decent array of mostly Czech and German dishes is served by a troop of attentive waiters. ✉ *Jateční 4,* ☎ *0166/422–498. No credit cards.*

Cheb's hotels have failed to keep pace with the times. For a short stay, a room in a **private home** is a better bet. The city tourist information center (☞ Visitor Information *in* Western Bohemia A to Z, *below*) can arrange accommodations. Several houses along Přemysla Otakara street north of the city have rooms available, and the hotels in Františkovy Lázně (☞ *below*) are just a few minutes' drive or train ride away.

Františkovy Lázně

70 *6 km (4 mi) from Cheb.*

This little spa town couldn't be a more distinct contrast to nearby Cheb's slightly seedy, hustling air and medieval streetscapes. You might like to ease the transition by walking the path, indicated with red markers, from Cheb's main square westward along the river and then north past **Komorní Hůrka.** The extinct volcano is now a tree-covered hill, but excavations on one side have laid bare the rock, and one tunnel is still open. Goethe instigated and took part in the excavations, and you can still—though barely—make out a relief of the poet carved into the rock face.

Františkovy Lázně, or Franzensbad, the smallest of the three main Bohemian spas, isn't really in the same league as the other two (Karlovy Vary and Mariánské Lázně). Built on a more modest scale at the start of the 19th century, the town's ubiquitous kaiser-yellow buildings have been spruced up after their neglect under the previous regime and now present cheerful facades, almost too bright for the few strollers. The poorly kept parks and the formal yet human-scale neoclassical architecture retain much of their former charm. Overall, a pleasing torpor reigns in Františkovy Lázně. There is no town to speak of, just **Národní ulice,** the main street, which leads down into the spa park. The waters, whose healing properties were already known in the 16th century, are used primarily for treating heart problems—and infertility, hence the large number of young women wandering the grounds.

The most interesting sight in town may be the small **Lázeňský muzeum** (Spa Museum), just off Národní ulice. There is a wonderful collection of spa-related antiques, including copper bathtubs and a turn-of-the-20th-century exercise bike called a Velotrab. The guest books provide an insight into the cosmopolitan world of pre–World War I Central Europe. The book for 1812 contains the entry "Ludwig van Beethoven, composer from Vienna." ✉ *Ul. Doktora Pohoreckého 8,* ☎ *0166/542–344.* 💵 *20 Kč.* ⏲ *Tues.–Fri. 10–5, weekends 10–4 (usually closed mid-Dec.–mid-Jan.).*

The main spring, **Františkův pramen,** is under a little gazebo filled with brass pipes. The colonnade to the left was decorated with a bust of Lenin that was replaced in 1990 by a memorial to the American liberation of the town in April 1945. The oval neo-Classical temple just beyond the spring (amazingly, *not* painted yellow and white) is the **Glauberova dvorana** (Glauber Pavilion), where several springs bubble up into glass cases. ✉ *Národní ul.*

NEED A BREAK?

Only insipid pop music (the scourge of eating and drinking places everywhere in the country) interrupts the cheerful atmosphere of the little café of the **Slovan** (☞ Dining and Lodging, *below*) on Národní. The tiny gallery and lively frescoes make it a great spot for cake, coffee, or drinks.

Dining and Lodging

Most of the establishments in town do a big trade in spa patients, who generally stay for several weeks. Spa treatments usually require a medical check and cost substantially more than the normal room charge.

Walk-in treatment can be arranged at some hotels or at the information center (☞ Visitor Information *in* Western Bohemia A to Z, *below*). Signs around town advertise massage therapy and other treatments for casual visitors.

$$ ★ ✕🏨 **Slovan.** This gracious place is the perfect complement to this relaxed little town. The eccentricity of the original turn-of-the-20th-century design survived a thorough renovation during the 1970s. The airy rooms are clean and comfortable, and some have a balcony overlooking the main street. The main-floor restaurant serves above-average Czech dishes such as tasty *svíčková* (beef sirloin in a citrusy cream sauce) and roast duck. ✉ *Národní 5, 351 01,* ☎ *0166/542–841,* FAX *0166/542–843. 25 rooms, 19 with bath. Restaurant, bar, café. AE, MC, V.*

$$$ 🏨 **Tři Lilie.** Reopened in 1995 after an expensive refitting, the "Three Lilies," which once accommodated the likes of Goethe and Metternich, immediately reestablished itself as the most comfortable spa hotel in town. It is thoroughly elegant, from guest rooms to brasserie. ✉ *Národní 3,* ☎ FAX *0166/542–415. 31 rooms. Restaurant, brasserie, café. AE, MC, V.*

$$ 🏨 **Centrum.** Rooms in this barnlike building are well appointed if a bit sterile. Still, it is among the best-run hotels in town and only a short walk from the main park and central spas. ✉ *Anglická 392, 351 01,* ☎ *0166/543–156,* FAX *0166/543–157. 30 rooms. Restaurant, bar. AE, MC, V.*

Mariánské Lázně

★ 71 *30 km (18 mi) southeast of Cheb, 47 km (29 mi) south of Karlovy Vary.*

Your expectations of what a spa resort should be may come nearest to fulfillment here. It's far larger and more active than Františkovy Lázně and greener and quieter than Karlovy Vary (☞ *above*). This was the spa favored by Britain's Edward VII. Goethe and Chopin also repaired here frequently. Mark Twain, on a visit to the spa in 1892, labeled the town a "health factory" and couldn't get over how new everything looked. Indeed, at that time everything was new. The sanatoriums, most built during the 19th century in a confident, outrageous mixture of "neo" styles, fan out impressively around a finely groomed oblong park. Cure takers and curiosity seekers alike parade through the Empire-style Cross Spring pavilion and the long colonnade near the top of the park. Buy a spouted drinking cup (available at the colonnades) and join the rest of the sippers taking the drinking cure. Be forewarned, though: the waters from the Rudolph, Ambrose, and Caroline springs, though harmless, all have a noticeable diuretic effect. For this reason they're used extensively in treating disorders of the kidney and bladder. For information on spa treatments, inquire at the main **spa offices** (✉ Masarykova 22, ☎ 0165/623–061). Walk-in treatment can be arranged at the **Nové Lázně** (New Spa; ✉ Reitenbergerova 53, ☎ 0165/644–111).

A stay in Mariánské Lázně can be healthful even without special treatment. Special walking trails of all difficulty levels surround the resort in all directions. The best advice is simply to put on comfortable shoes, buy a hiking map, and head out. One of the country's few golf courses lies about 3 km (2 mi) to the east of town. Hotels can also help to arrange special activities, such as tennis and horseback riding. For the less intrepid, a simple stroll around the gardens, with a few deep breaths of the town's famous air, is enough to restore a healthy sense of perspective.

Dining and Lodging

The best place to look for private lodgings is along Paleckého ulice and Hlavní třída, south of the main spa area. Private accommodations can also be found in the neighboring villages of Zádub and Závišín in the woods to the east of town.

$$ ✕ **Filip.** This bustling wine bar is where locals come to find relief from the sometimes large horde of tourists. There's a tasty selection of traditional Czech dishes—mainly pork, grilled meats, and steaks. ✉ *Poštovní 96, ☎ 0165/626–161. No credit cards.*

$$ ★ ✕ **Koliba.** This combination hunting lodge and wine tavern, set in the woods roughly 10 minutes on foot from the spas, is an excellent alternative to the hotel restaurants in town. Grilled meats and shish kebabs, plus tankards of Moravian wine (try the dry, cherry red Rulandské červené), are served with traditional gusto while fiddlers play rousing Moravian tunes. ✉ *Dusíkova 592, in the direction of Karlovy Vary, ☎ 0165/625–169. V.*

$$$$ **Excelsior.** This lovely older hotel is on the main street and is convenient to the spas and colonnade. Rooms have traditional cherry-wood furniture and marble bathrooms, and the views over the town are enchanting. The staff is friendly and multilingual. While the food in the restaurant is only average, the romantic setting provides adequate compensation. ✉ *Hlavní třída 121, 353 01, ☎ 0165/622–705, FAX 0165/625–346. 64 rooms. Restaurant, café, massage, sauna. AE, DC, MC, V.*

$$$ ★ **Bohemia.** At this gracious, century-old hotel, beautiful crystal chandeliers in the main hall set the stage for a comfortable and elegant stay. The crisp beige-and-white rooms let you spread out and *really* unpack; they're spacious and high ceilinged. (If you want to indulge, request one of the enormous suites overlooking the park). The helpful staff can arrange spa treatments and horseback riding. ✉ *Hlavní třída 100, 353 01, ☎ 0165/623–251, FAX 0165/622–943. 73 rooms, 4 suites. Restaurant, café, lounge. AE, MC, V.*

$$$ **Hotel Golf.** Book in advance to secure a room at this stately villa situated 3½ km (2 mi) out of town on the road to Karlovy Vary. The large, open rooms are cheery and modern. The restaurant on the main floor is excellent, but the big draw is the 18-hole golf course on the premises, one of the few in the Czech Republic. The course was opened in 1905 by King Edward VII. ✉ *Zádub 55, 353 01, ☎ 0165/622–651 or 0165/622–652, FAX 0165/622–655. 25 rooms. Restaurant, pool, 18-hole golf course, tennis court, nightclub. AE, DC, MC, V.*

Nightlife and the Arts

The West Bohemian Symphony Orchestra performs regularly in the New Spa (Nové Lázně, ☞ *above*). The town's annual Chopin festival each August brings in pianists from around Europe to perform the Polish composer's works.

Casino Lil (✉ Anglická 336, ☎ 0165/623–293) is open daily 2 PM–7 AM. For late-night drinks, try the **Hotel Golf** (☞ Dining and Lodging, *above*), which has a good nightclub with dancing in season.

Teplá

72 *15 km (9 mi) from Mariánské Lázně.*

It is worth making a detour to the little town of Teplá and its 800-year-old **Klášter premonstrátů Teplá** (Abbey of the Premonstrates), which once played an important role in Christianizing pagan Central Europe. Inquire at the town information office about special bus trips (☞ Visitor Information *in* Western Bohemia A to Z, *below*). The sprawling monastery, founded by the Premonstratensian order of France in 1193 (the same order that established Prague's Strahov Monastery), once controlled the farms and forests in these parts for miles around. The order even owned the spa facilities at Mariánské Lázně and until 1942 used the proceeds from the spas to cover operating expenses. The complex you see before you today, however, betrays none of this earlier prosperity. Over the centuries, the monastery was plundered dozens of times during wars and upheavals, but history reserved its severest blow for the night of April 13, 1950, when security forces employed by the Communists raided the grounds and imprisoned the brothers. The monastery's property was given over to the Czech army, and for the next 28 years the buildings were used as barracks to house soldiers. In 1991 the government returned the monastery buildings and immediate grounds (but not the original land holdings) to the order, and the brothers began the arduous task of picking up the pieces—physically and spiritually.

The most important building on the grounds from an architectural point of view is the Romanesque **abbey church** (1190–1232), with its triple nave, first of its kind in Bohemia. The rest of the monastery complex was originally Romanesque, but it was rebuilt in 1720 by Baroque architect Kilian Ignaz Dientzenhofer. There are several wall and ceiling paintings of interest here, as well as some good sculpture. The most valuable collection is in the **Nová knihovna** (New Library), where you will find illuminated hymnals and rare Czech and foreign manuscripts, including a German translation of the New Testament that predates Luther's by some 100 years. Tours of the church and library are given on the hour (English notes are available); if you'd like an English-speaking guide, try to call in advance. The monastery also offers short-term accommodations (inquire directly at the monastery offices on the grounds). ✉ *Klášter, 364 61,* ☎ *0169/392–264 or 0169/392–691.* 🎫 *Monastery and library 90 Kč.* ⏲ *Feb.–Apr. and Nov.–Dec., Tues.–Sun. 9–3; May–Oct., Tues.–Sun. 9–4:30.*

Plzeň

73 *92 km (55 mi) west of Prague.*

The sprawling industrial city of Plzeň is hardly a tourist mecca, but it's worth stopping off for an hour or two on the way back to Prague. Two sights here are of particular interest to beer fanatics. The first is the **Pilsner Urquell Brewery,** to the east of the city near the railway station. The beer was created in 1842 using the excellent Plzeň water, a special malt fermented on the premises, and hops grown in the region around Žatec. On a group tour of the 19th-century redbrick building you can taste the valuable brew, exported around the world. Tours in English and German are offered weekdays at 12:30 PM (sometimes also at 2 PM in the summer). You can only visit via the tour. ✉ *U Prazdroje 7,* ☎ *019/706–1111.* 🎫 *70 Kč.*

NEED A BREAK? You can continue drinking and find some cheap traditional grub at the large **Na Spilce** beer hall just inside the brewery gates. The pub is open daily from 10 AM to 10 PM.

The second stop on the beer tour is the **Pivovarské muzeum** (Brewery Museum), in a late-Gothic malt house one block northeast of náměstí Republiky (☞ *below*). All kinds of paraphernalia trace the region's brewing history, including the horse-drawn carts used to haul the kegs. ✉ *Veleslavinova 6,* ☎ *019/723–5574.* 🎫 *40 Kč.* ⏲ *Daily 10–6.*

The city's architectural attractions center on the main **náměstí Republiky** (Republic Square). The square is dominated by the enormous Gothic **Chrám svatého Bartoloměje** (Church of St. Bartholomew). Both the square and the church towers hold size records: the former is the largest in Bohemia and the latter, at 335 ft, the tallest in the Czech Republic. Around the square, mixed in with its good selection of stores, are a variety of other architectural jewels, including the town hall, adorned with sgraffiti and built in the Renaissance style by Italian architects during the town's heyday in the 16th century. The Moorish **synagogue,** one of the largest in Europe, is four blocks west of the square, just outside the green strip that circles the old town.

Dining and Lodging

$$$ ✕🏨 **Continental.** Just five minutes on foot from the main square, the fin-de-siècle Continental remains a good choice, even though the hotel is slightly run down and the rooms, though large, are exceedingly plain. The restaurant, however, serves dependably satisfying traditional Czech dishes such as *cibulka* (onion soup) and *svíčková* (beef sirloin in a citrusy cream sauce). ✉ *Zbojnická 8, 305 31,* ☎ *019/723–6477,* FAX *019/722–1746. 46 rooms, 23 with bath or shower. Restaurant, café. AE, DC, MC, V.*

$$$ 🏨 **Central.** This angular 1960s structure is recommendable for its sunny rooms, friendly staff, and great location, right on the main square. Indeed, even such worthies as Czar Alexander of Russia stayed here in the days when the hotel was a charming inn known as the Golden Eagle. ✉ *Nám. Republiky 33, 305 31,* ☎ *019/722–6757,* FAX *019/722–6064. 77 rooms. Restaurant, bar, café. AE, DC, MC, V.*

Western Bohemia A to Z

Arriving and Departing

Prague is the main gateway to western Bohemia (☞ Arriving and Departing *in* Prague A to Z, *above*). Major trains from Nuremberg stop at Cheb and usually at Mariánské Lázně; Munich trains cross the border at Česká Kubice. All long-distance trains in the region stop at Plzeň. It is also an easy drive across the border from Bavaria on the E48 to Cheb and from there to any of the spas.

Getting Around

Good, if slow, train service links all the major towns west of Prague. The best stretches are from Františkovy Lázně to Plzeň and from Plzeň to Prague. The Prague–Karlovy Vary run takes far longer than it should—more than three hours by the shortest route. Frequent bus service between Prague and Karlovy Vary, by contrast, makes the journey in only about two hours each way. If you're driving, you can take the E48 directly from Prague to Karlovy Vary. Roads in the area tend to be in good condition, though they can sometimes be quite narrow.

Contacts and Resources

EMERGENCIES

Police (☎ 158). **Ambulance** (☎ 155). **Breakdowns** (☎ 1054; Yellow Angels ☎ 1230; Autoklub Bohemia Assistance [ABA] ☎ 1240).

GUIDED TOURS

Most of Prague's tour operators offer excursions to Karlovy Vary; inquire at the Prague Information Service or American Express. **Čedok** (☎ 02/2419–7111) offers one-day and longer tours covering western Bohemia's major sights, as well as curative vacations at many Czech spas.

TRAVEL AGENCIES

Karlovy Vary (✉ American Express representative, Vřídelní 51, ☎ 017/323–0368).

VISITOR INFORMATION

Cheb (✉ Nám. Krále Jiřího z Poděbrad 33, ☎ 0166/434–385 or 422–705). **Františkovy Lázně** (✉ Tři Lilie Travel Agency, Národní 3, ☎ 0166/542–430). **Karlovy Vary** (✉ Kur-Info, Vřídelní kolonáda [Vřídlo

Colonnade], ☎ 017/322–4097, or Nám. Dr. M. Horákové 18 [near the bus station], ☎ 017/322–2833). **Mariánské Lázně** (✉ Cultural and Information Center, Hlavní 47, ☎ 0165/625–892 or 0165/622–474). **Plzeň** (✉ Nám. Republiky 41, ☎ 019/703–2750).

NORTHERN BOHEMIA

Northern Bohemia is a paradox: much of it was despoiled by 40 years of rampant postwar industrialization, but here and there you can still find areas of great natural beauty. Along the Labe River, rolling hills, perfect for walking, guard the country's northern frontiers with Germany and Poland. Hikers and campers head for the Krkonoše range on the Polish border. As you move toward the west, the interest is more historical, in an area where the influence of Germany was felt in less pleasant ways than in the spas. You don't have to drive too far to reach the Sudetenland, the German-speaking border area that was handed over to Hitler by the British and French in 1938. The landscape here is riddled with the tragic remains of the Nazi occupation of Czech lands from 1939 to 1945. Most drastically affected was Terezín, better known as the infamous concentration camp, Theresienstadt.

As tourist amenities keep improving, reasonably priced, adequately comfortable small-to-middling hotels are now not too difficult to find. Dining options still generally are standard Czech and German cooking, although Asian restaurants are now a less-than-amazing sight in the area's larger towns, thanks to the presence of sizable Chinese and Vietnamese communities in border areas. Pizzerias, which range from ghastly to quite congenial, are now ubiquitous.

Lidice

74 *18 km (11 mi) from Prague on Rte. 7 (the road to Ruzyně Airport). Head in the direction of Slaný. Turn off at the Lidice exit and follow the country road for 3 km (2 mi).*

The **Lidice museum and monument** are unforgettable sights. The empty field to the right, with a large cross at the bottom, is where the town of Lidice stood until 1942, when it was viciously razed by the Nazis in retribution for the assassination of the German overlord of the Czech lands, Reinhard Heydrich.

The Lidice story really begins with the notorious Munich Pact of 1938, under which the leaders of Great Britain and France permitted Hitler to occupy the largely German-speaking border regions of Czechoslovakia (the so-called Sudetenland). Less than a year later, in March 1939, Hitler used his forward position to occupy the whole of Bohemia and Moravia, making the area into a protectorate of the German Reich. To guard his new possessions, Hitler appointed ruthless Nazi Reinhard Heydrich as Reichsprotektor. Heydrich immediately implemented a campaign of terror against Jews and intellectuals while currying favor with average Czechs by raising rations and wages. As a result, the Czech army-in-exile, based in Great Britain, soon began planning Heydrich's assassination. In the winter of 1941–42 a small band of parachutists was flown in to carry out the task.

The attack took place in the north part of Prague on May 27, 1942, and Heydrich died from his injuries on June 4. Hitler immediately ordered the little mining town of Lidice, west of Prague, "removed from the face of the earth," since it was alleged (although later found untrue) that some of the assassins had been sheltered by villagers there. On the night of June 9, a Gestapo unit entered Lidice, shot the entire adult male population (192 men), and sent the 196 women to the Ravensbrück concentration camp. A handful of the 103 children in the village were sent to Germany to be "Aryanized"; the others perished in death camps. On June 10, the entire village was razed. The assassins and their accomplices were found a week later in the Orthodox Church of Sts. Cyril and Methodius in Prague's New Town. There, the men committed suicide after a shoot-out with Nazi militia.

The monument to these events is a sober place. The arcades are graphic in their depiction of the deportation and slaughter of the inhabitants. The museum itself is dedicated to those killed, with photographs of each person and a short description of his or her fate. You'll also find reproductions of the German documents ordering the village's destruction, including the Gestapo's chillingly bureaucratic reports on how the massacre was carried out and the peculiar problems encountered in Aryanizing the deported children. The exhibits highlighting the international response (a suburb of Chicago was even renamed for the town) are heartwarming. An absorbing 18-minute film in Czech (worthwhile even for non-Czech speakers) tells the Lidice story. ✉ *Museum: ul. 10. června 1942.* 🎫 *60 Kč.* ⏲ *Apr.–Oct., daily 8–5; Nov.–Mar., daily 9–3.*

Lidice was rebuilt after the war on the initiative of a group of miners from Birmingham, England, who called their committee "Lidice Must Live." The wooden cross in the field, starkly decorated with barbed wire, marks the place in Old Lidice where the men were executed. Remains of brick walls are visible here, left over from the Gestapo's dynamite and bulldozer exercise. Still, Lidice is a sad town, not a place to linger.

Veltrusy Château and Gardens

75 *25 km (15 mi) north of Prague.*

The aristocratic retreat of Veltrusy contrasts vividly with the ordinariness of nearby Kralupy, an industrial town better left unexplored. The mansion's late-Baroque splendor lies hidden in a carefully laid out English park full of old and rare trees and scattered with 18th-century architectural follies. Until the end of World War II the château belonged to the Chotek family, whose most famous scion was Sophie Chotek, wife of Archduke Franz Ferdinand. Today the palace is given over to a museum showcasing the cosmopolitan lifestyle of the imperial aristocracy, displaying Japanese and Chinese porcelain, English chandeliers, and 16th-century tapestries from Brussels. ✉ *Off Rte. E55.* 🎫 *Tours 60 Kč each.* ⏲ *Château Mar.–Apr. and Oct.–Dec., weekends and holidays 9–4; May–Sept., Tues.–Sun. 8–5. Park open all year.*

Nelahozeves

25 km (15 mi) north of Prague, or 2½ km (1½ mi) on foot by marked paths from Veltrusy Château. By car: turn right out of Veltrusy onto Rte. 101 and over the Vltava river, then make a sharp left back along the river to Nelahozeves.

Nelahozeves was the birthplace of Antonín Dvořák (1841–1904), the Czech Republic's greatest composer, who was known for weaving folk influences into Romantic music. The pretty corner house on the main road (No. 12), with its tidy windows and arches, has a small **memorial museum.** In Dvořák's time, the house was an inn run by his parents, and it was here that he learned to play the violin. ✉ *Across from the station.* 🎫 *30 Kč.* ⏲ *Tues.–Thurs. and weekends 9–noon and 2–5, Fri. 9–noon.*

Squatting above the village, the brooding Renaissance **château,** with its black-and-white sgraffito, is an increasingly popular attraction.

The owners, a branch of the wealthy Lobkowicz family, lost the property to the Communist state in the 1950s, then regained it, along with their fabulous art collection, in the 1990s. The collection, one of the finest in private hands in Central Europe, includes such masterpieces as one of the paintings from Pieter Brueghel the Elder's six-canvas series depicting the seasons. This painting alone is worth the short, scenic train journey from Prague's Masarykovo station (change in Kralupy nad Vltavou and get off at the next stop, Nelahozeves-zastávka, or walk the 3 km [2 mi] from Kralupy along the peaceful Vltava bank). The one-hour main tour also shows visitors paintings by Rubens and Velázquez, as well as a wonderful pair of London views by Canaletto. There is also valuable memorabilia of the family's musical patronage, including original manuscripts by Beethoven and a score of Handel's *Messiah* annotated by Mozart. ☏ *0205/709–111.* 🎫 *Main tour 250 Kč, both tours 295 Kč.* ⏲ *Tues.–Sun. 9–noon, 1–5.*

Terezín

76 *36 km (22 mi) northwest of Nelahozeves on Rte. 8.*

★ The old garrison town of Terezín gained notoriety under the Nazis as the nefarious concentration camp **Theresienstadt,** though the enormity of Theresienstadt's role in history is difficult to grasp at first. The Czechs have put up few signs to tell you what to see. You could easily pass through it and never learn any of the town's dark secrets.

The **Malá Pevnost** (Small Fortress), the actual prison and death camp, is 2 km (1 mi) south of Terezín. In the strange redbrick complex you'll see the prison more or less as it was when the Nazis left it in 1945. About 32,000 inmates came through the fortress, mostly POWs or political prisoners; those that did not die here were shipped off to other concentration camps. Above the entrance to the main courtyard stands the cynical motto ARBEIT MACHT FREI (Work Brings Freedom). Take a walk around the rooms, still housing a sad collection of rusty bed frames, sinks, and shower units. At the far end of the fortress, opposite the main entrance, is the special wing built by the Nazis when space became tight. The windowless cells are horrific; try going into one and closing the door—and then imagine being crammed in with 14 other people. In the center of the fortress is a museum and a room where films are shown. ☏ *0416/782–225.* 🎫 *Fortress or museum 130 Kč, fortress and museum 150 Kč.* ⏲ *May–Oct., daily 8–6; Nov.–Apr., daily 8–4:30.*

During World War II, the town of Terezín served as a detention center for thousands of Jews and was used by the Nazis as an elaborate prop in a nefarious propaganda ploy. The large barracks buildings around town, once used in the 18th and 19th centuries to house Austrian soldiers, became living quarters for thousands of interred Jews. But in 1942, to placate international public opinion, the Nazis cynically decided to transform the town into a showcase camp—to prove to the world their "benevolent" intentions toward the Jews. To give the place the image of a spa town, the streets were given new names such as Lake Street, Bath Street, and Park Street. Numerous elderly Jews from Germany were taken in by the deception and paid large sums of money to come to the new "retirement village." Just before the International Red Cross inspected the town in early 1944, Nazi authorities began a beautification campaign: they painted the buildings, set up stores, laid out a park with benches in front of the town hall, and arranged for concerts and sports. The map just off the main square shows the town's street plan as the locations of various buildings between 1941 and 1945. The Jews here were able, with great difficulty, to establish a cultural life of their own under the limited self-government that was set up in the camp. The inmates created a library and a theater, and lectures and musical performances were given on a regular basis.

Once it was clear that the war was lost, however, the Nazis dropped any pretense and quickly stepped up transport of Jews to the Auschwitz death camp in Poland. Transports were not new to the ghetto; to keep the population at around 30,000, a train was sent off every few months or so "to the east" to make room for incoming groups. In the fall of 1944, these transports were increased to one every few days. In all, some 87,000 Jews from Terezín were murdered in this way, and another 35,000 died from starvation or disease. The conductor Karel Ančerl, who died in 1973, and the novelist Ivan Klíma are among the few thousand who survived imprisonment at Terezín. The town's horrific story is told in words and pictures at the **Museum of the Terezín Ghetto,** just off the central park in town. The Magdeburg Barracks three blocks away, where the Jewish Council of Elders met, and the Jewish cemetery and crematorium just outside the town walls are among the few structures presently open to the public. ✉ *Museum: Komenského ul.,* ☎ *0416/782–577.* 🎫 *130 Kč.* ⏲ *Apr.–Oct., daily 9–6; Nov.–Mar., daily 9–4:30.*

For all its history, Terezín is no place for an extended stay. Locals have chosen not to highlight the town's role during the Nazi era, and hence little provision has been made for visitors.

Litoměřice

77 *4 km (2½ mi) from Terezín, 70 km (42 mi) north of Prague.*

The decrepit state of the houses and streets belies this riverside town's medieval status as one of Bohemia's leading towns and a rival to Prague. Even today, although there are several factories in the surrounding area, much of central Litoměřice is like a living museum.

The best way to get a feel for Litoměřice is to start at the excellent **Městské muzeum** (City Museum), on the corner of the main square and Dlouhá ulice in the Old Town Hall building. The building itself deserves notice as one of the first examples of the Renaissance style in Bohemia, dating from 1537–39. Unfortunately, the museum's exhibits are described in Czech (with written commentary in German available from the ticket seller); but even if you don't understand the language, you'll find this museum fascinating. Despite its position near the old border with Germany, Litoměřice was a Czech and Hussite stronghold, and one of the museum's treasures is the brightly colored, illuminated gradual, or hymn book, depicting Hus's burning at the stake in Constance. Also take a look at the nearby golden chalice, the old symbol of the Hussites. Farther on you come to an exquisite Renaissance pulpit and altar decorated with painted stone reliefs. On the second floor the most interesting exhibit is from the Nazi era, when Litoměřice became a part of Sudeten Germany and a border town of the German Reich, providing soldiers for nearby Theresienstadt. There's a German commemorative dish marked with the words *Wir sind frei* (We Are Free), celebrating the Nazi annexation of the Sudetenland, and a yellow Star of David patch from Terezín. ✉ *Mírové nám.* 🎫 *10 Kč.* ⏲ *Tues.–Sun. 10–5.*

Mírové náměstí, the central square, has architectural styles from Renaissance arcades to Baroque gables and a Gothic bell tower. The town's trademark is the chalice-shape tower at No. 7, the **Chalice House,** built in the 1560s for an Utraquist patrician. The Utraquists were moderate Hussites who believed that laymen should receive wine as well as bread in the sacrament of Holy Communion. On the left-hand corner of the Old Town Hall on a tall stone pedestal is a replica of a small and unusual Roland statue (the original is in the museum). Statues like this one are found throughout Bohemia and signify that the town is a "royal free town," due all the usual privileges of such a distinction. This particular statue is unique, because instead of showing the usual handsome knight, it depicts a hairy caveman wielding a club. Even in the 16th century, it seems, Czechs had a sense of humor.

A colorful, two-story Baroque house with a facade by the 18th-century Italian master builder Octavio Broggio houses the **Galerie výtvarného umění** (Gallery of Fine Arts). It's one of the country's best provincial art museums, with Czech art from the Gothic to the Baroque. The extensive collection of naive painting and wood sculpture across the courtyard is also worth a gander. ✉ *Michalská 7.* 🎫 *16 Kč.* ⏲ *Mar.–Oct., Tues.–Sun. 10–6; Nov.–Apr., Tues.–Sun. 10–5.*

More of Broggio's work can be seen in the facade and interior of the **Kostel všechní svaté** (All Saints' Church), just off the main square on Kostelní náměstí. The church's high tower keeps its 16th-century appearance. Broggio also remade the monastery **Church of St. Jacob,** across the square from All Saints' and one short block down ulice Velká Dominikánská, though its exterior sorely needs restoration. His most beautiful work is the small **Kostel svatého Václava** (Church of St. Wenceslas), now an Orthodox church, squeezed into an unwieldy square to the north of town on the cathedral hill. Built in 1714–16, it's in ripe Baroque style, filled with lush, curving forms.

Dóm svatého Štěpána (St. Stephen's Cathedral) is monumental but uninspired. Its one real treasure is a Lucas Cranach painting of St. Anthony—but unfortunately the cathedral door is often locked owing to a spate of thefts. Try ringing the bell at the bishop's residence around the corner; someone should let you in.

Lodging

$$ 🏨 **Roosevelt.** The Secessionist-style town bathhouse was converted into a small hotel in 1994, adding to this area's limited supply of decent accommodations. Rooms have modern, no-surprises, wood furniture. It's on a 19th-century residential street, a couple minutes' walk from the town center. ✉ *Rooseveltova 18, 412 01,* ☎ *0416/733–596,* FAX *0416/733–593. 30 rooms. Restaurant. AE, DC, MC, V.*

OFF THE BEATEN PATH

STŘEKOV CASTLE – The Vltava River north of Litoměřice flows through a long, unspoiled, winding valley, packed in by surrounding hills. As you near heavily industrialized Ústí nad Labem, your eyes are suddenly assaulted by the towering mass of Střekov Castle, perched precariously on huge cliffs and rising abruptly above the right bank. The fortress was built in 1319 by King John of Luxembourg to control the rebellious nobles of northern Bohemia. During the 16th century it became the residence of Wenceslas of Lobkowicz, who rebuilt the castle in the Renaissance style. The lonely ruins have inspired many German artists and poets, including Richard Wagner, who came here on a moonlit night in the summer of 1842 and was inspired to write his romantic opera *Tannhäuser.* But if you arrive on a dark night, about the only classic that comes to mind is Mary Shelley's *Frankenstein.* Inside is a small historical exhibit about the Lobkowicz family and wine making.
✉ *400 03 Ústí nad Labem,* ☎ *047/553–0682.* 🎫 *30 Kč.*
⏲ *Apr.–Oct., Tues.–Sun. 9–5; for winter hours inquire locally.*

Mělník

78 *65 km (40 mi) southeast of Střekov Castle, about 40 km (23 mi) north of Prague.*

Mělník is a lively town, known best perhaps for its autumn wine festival and the special Ludmila wine made from local grapes. If coming by car, park on the small streets just off the pretty but hard-to-find main square (head in the direction of the towers to find it). The town's **zámek,** a smallish castle a few blocks from the main square, majestically guards the confluence of the Labe (Elbe) River and two arms of the Vltava. The view here is stunning, and the sunny hillsides are covered with vineyards. As the locals tell it, Emperor Charles IV was responsible for bringing wine production to the area. Having a good eye for favorable growing conditions, he encouraged vintners from Burgundy to come here and plant their vines.

The courtyard's three dominant architectural styles, reflecting alterations to the castle over the years, fairly jump out at you. On the north side, note the typical arcaded Renaissance balconies, decorated with sgraffiti. To the west, a Gothic tract is still easy to make out. The southern wing is clearly Baroque (although also decorated with arcades). Inside the castle at the back, you'll find a *vinárna* with mediocre food but excellent views overlooking the rivers. On the other side is a **museum** of paintings, furniture, and porcelain belonging to the Lobkowicz family—an old aristocratic clan that has recovered quite a few castles and estates from the state. You can also tour the wine cellars under the castle. ☎ 0206/622-121 *Cellar tour 20 Kč, museum 60 Kč.* ⏲ *Daily 10–4:30.*

Lodging

$$ **Ludmila.** Though the hotel is an inconvenient 4 km (2½ mi) outside town, the pleasant English-speaking staff keeps the plain rooms impeccably clean, and the restaurant is better than many you will find in Mělník itself. Breakfast is included. ✉ *Pražská 2639, 276 01 Mělník,* ☎ *0206/622–423,* FAX *0206/623–390. 79 rooms with bath or shower. Restaurant. AE, MC, V.*

Špindlerův Mlýn and the Krkonoše Range

79 *About 150 km (90 mi) northeast of Prague.*

If you're not planning to go to the Tatras in Slovakia but nevertheless want a few days in the mountains, head for the **Krkonoše range**—the so-called Giant Mountains—near the Polish frontier. Here you'll find the most spectacular scenery in Bohemia, although it's something of an exaggeration to call these rolling hills "giant" (the highest point is 5,256 ft). Not only is the scenery beautiful, but the local architecture is refreshingly rural after all the towns and cities. The steep-roof timber houses, painted in warm colors, look just right pitched against sunlit pinewoods or snowy pastures. **Špindlerův Mlýn** is attractively placed astride the rippling Labe (Elbe) River, here in its formative stages; it's a good town to use as a hiking base.

Dining and Lodging

$$$ ★ **Savoy.** This Tudor-style chalet, over a century old, has a comfortable, fresh-air feeling—its cozy reception area is more typical of a family inn than a large hotel. The rooms, although on the smallish side and sparsely furnished, are immaculately clean. The restaurant serves fine traditional Czech dishes in a mellow setting. ✉ *543 51 Špindlerův Mlýn,* ☎ *0438/493–221,* FAX *0438/493–241. 50 rooms, most with bath or shower. Restaurant, bar. AE, MC, V.*

$$$ **Montana.** This "modern" 1970s hotel doesn't fit in with the rustic setting, and the rooms are quite spartan (though they have TVs). But the service is attentive, and the staff can offer good advice for planning walks around this popular resort town. ✉ *543 51 Špindlerův Mlýn,* ☎ *0438/493–251,* FAX *0438/493–156. 70 rooms. Restaurant, bar, café. MC, V.*

$$$ **Nechanický.** This 1920s lodge near the bridge in the center of town was restored to its original owners following the Velvet Revolution, and they have been working to brighten up its somewhat timeworn face. Rooms are cheery, clean, and well proportioned. Front-facing rooms enjoy an excellent view overlooking the town. ✉ *543 51 Špindlerův Mlýn,* ☎ *0438/493–163,* FAX *0438/493–134. 16 rooms. Restaurant. MC, V.*

Outdoor Activities and Sports

Janské Lázně (another spa), Pec pod Sněžkou, and Špindlerův Mlýn are the principal resorts of the area, the last the most sophisticated in its accommodations and facilities. To get out and experience the mountains, take a bus from Špindlerův Mlýn via Janské Lázně to Pec pod Sněžkou—a deceptively long journey of around 50 km (31 mi). From there, embark on a two-stage chairlift to the top of **Sněžka** (the area's highest peak), then walk along the ridge overlooking the Polish countryside; you'll eventually drop into deep, silent pinewoods and return to Špindlerův Mlýn. This hike is just 11 km (7 mi)—three to four hours in good weather. The path actually takes you into Poland at one point; you won't need a visa, but take your passport along just in case. The weather can turn quickly in this high, treeless country, so carry rain gear and wear sturdy shoes.

The Labe's source is on the boggy heights near the Polish border. From the town of Harrachov, you can reach it on foot by a marked trail that heads eastward up the mountain. The distance is about 10 km (6 mi). From Špindlerův Mlýn, a beautiful but sometimes steep trail follows the Labe Valley northwest up 2,000 vertical ft to the source near Labská Bouda. Allow at least half a day for this walk and take good shoes and a map.

Northern Bohemia A to Z

Arriving and Departing

Prague is the gateway to northern Bohemia (☞ Arriving and Departing *in* Prague A to Z, *above*). There are direct buses from the capital to Terezín, Litoměřice, Mělník, Špindlerův Mlýn, and Pec pod Sněžkou. If you are driving, the E55 leads directly into the Czech Republic from Dresden and winds down to Prague via the old spa town of Teplice. The main road from Prague in the direction of the Krkonoše range is the E65, which is a four-lane highway for most of the distance.

Getting Around

Motorists driving through northern Bohemia are rewarded with a particularly picturesque drive on Route 261 along the Labe (Elbe) River on the way to Střekov Castle near Ústí nad Labem (☞ *above*). Train connections in the north are spotty at best; bus is the preferred means of travel. Regular express trains connect Prague with Ústí nad Labem, but to reach other towns you'll have to take slower local trains or the bus.

Contacts and Resources

EMERGENCIES

Police (☎ 158). **Ambulance** (☎ 155). **Breakdowns** (☎ 1054; Yellow Angels ☎ 1230; Autoklub Bohemia Assistance [ABA] ☎ 1240).

GUIDED TOURS

Several private companies offer trips to Lidice, Mělník, Nelahozeves, Terezín, and Veltrusy Château. For a Terezín tour, try **Wittmann Tours** (☎ 02/2225–2472). Their buses leave Prague from the Inter-Continental Hotel, on Pařížská near the Staronová synagóga (Old-New Synagogue), daily from mid-March to December at 10 AM, returning around 5 PM, for a fare of 1,100 Kč.

VISITOR INFORMATION

Litoměřice (✉ Mírové nám., ☎ 0416/732–440). **Mělník** (✉ Nám. Míru 30, ☎ 0206/627–503). **Špindlerův Mlýn** (✉ Svatopetrská 173, ☎ 0438/93656). **Ústí nad Labem** (✉ Hrnčířská 1/10, ☎ 047/522–0421).

SOUTHERN MORAVIA

Lacking the turbulent history of Bohemia to the west or the stark natural beauty of Slovakia farther east, Moravia, the easternmost province of the Czech Republic, is frequently overlooked as a travel destination. Still, although Moravia's cities do not match Prague for beauty and its gentle mountains hardly compare with Slovakia's strikingly rugged Tatras, Moravia's colorful villages and rolling hills certainly do merit a few days of exploration. Come here for the good wine, the folk music, the friendly faces, and the languid pace.

Moravia has a bit of both Bohemia and Slovakia. It is closer culturally to Bohemia: the two were bound together as one kingdom for some 1,000 years, following the fall of the Great Moravian Empire (Moravia's last stab at Slavonic statehood) at the end of the 10th century. All the historical and cultural movements that swept through Bohemia, including the religious turbulence and long period of Austrian Hapsburg rule, were felt strongly here as well. But, oddly, in many ways Moravia resembles Slovakia more than its cousin to the west. The colors come alive here in a way that is seldom seen in Bohemia. The subdued earthen pinks and yellows in towns such as Telč and Mikulov suddenly erupt into the fiery reds, greens, and purples of the traditional folk costumes farther to the east. Folk music, all but gone in Bohemia, is still very much alive in Moravia.

Southern Moravia's highlands define the "border" with Bohemia. Here, towns such as Jihlava and Telč are virtually indistinguishable from their Bohemian counterparts. The handsome squares, with their long arcades, bear witness to the prosperity enjoyed by this part of Europe during the 16th and early 17th century, until the Hapsburg crackdown on the Czech lands at the outset of the Thirty Years' War. In the south along the frontier with Austria—until recently a heavily fortified expanse of the Iron Curtain—the towns and people on both sides of the border seek to reestablish ties going back centuries. One of their common traditions is wine making. Znojmo, Mikulov, and Valtice are to the Czech Republic what the small towns of the *Weinviertel* on the other side of the border are to Austria.

Don't expect gastronomic delights in Moravia. The choices—especially outside Brno—are usually limited to roast pork with sauerkraut and dumplings, ho-hum chicken dishes, and the ever-reliable trout. Hotels are getting better, and the shabby, dim, bathroom-down-the-hall places are practically a thing of the past. In mountainous areas inquire locally about the possibility of staying in a *chata* (cabin). These are abundant and often a pleasant alternative to the faceless modern hotels. Many lack modern amenities, though, so be prepared to rough it.

Numbers in the margin correspond to numbers on the Moravia map.

Jihlava

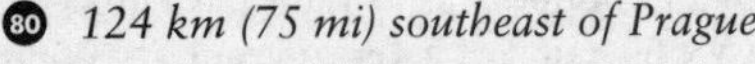

80 *124 km (75 mi) southeast of Prague.*

On the Moravian side of the rolling highlands that mark the border between Bohemia and Moravia, just off the main highway from Prague to Brno, lies the old mining town of Jihlava, a good place to begin an exploration of Moravia. If the silver mines here had held out just a few

Moravia

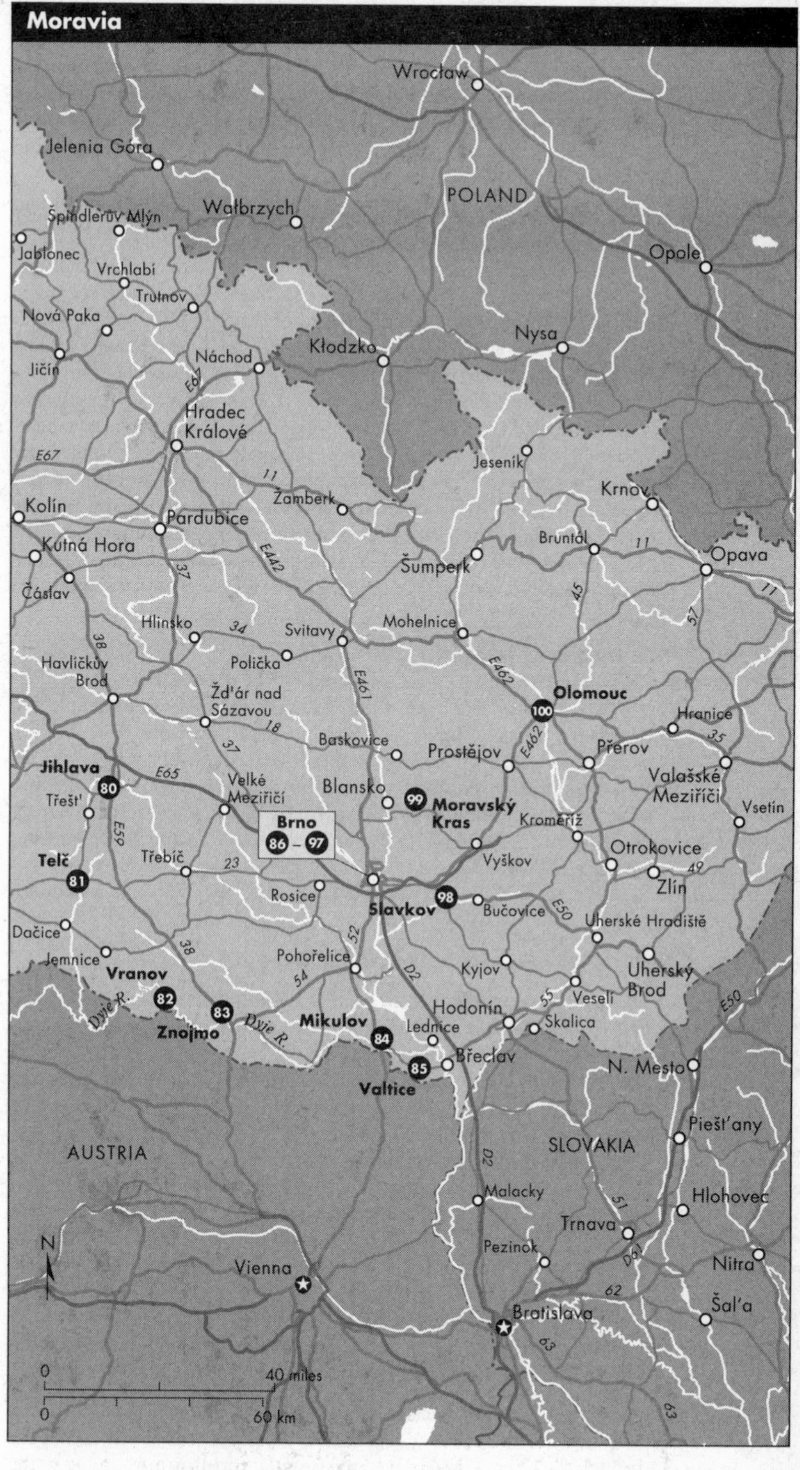

Wrocław
Jelenia Góra
Wałbrzych
POLAND
Opole
Špindlerův Mlýn
Jablonec
Vrchlabí
Trutnov
Nová Paka
Jičín
Náchod
Kłodzko
Nysa
Hradec Králové
E67
Jeseník
Krnov
11
Žamberk
Kolín
Pardubice
Kutná Hora
E442
Bruntál
Opava
Šumperk
Čáslav
37
45
57
Hlinsko
34
Svitavy
Mohelnice
38
Havlíčkův Brod
Polička
E461
E462
Olomouc
100
Žd'ár nad Sázavou
18
Hranice
35
Baskovice
Prostějov
Přerov
Jihlava
80
E65
37
Velké Meziříčí
Blansko
99
Moravský Kras
Valašské Meziříčí
Třešť
Vsetín
Brno
86 – 97
Kroměříž
E59
Telč
81
Třebíč
23
Vyškov
Otrokovice
49
Zlín
Rosice
Slavkov
98
Bučovice
E50
Uherské Hradiště
Dačice
Jemnice
38
52
Pohořelice
Kyjov
Uherský Brod
Vranov
82
54
D2
Veselí
Dyje R.
83
Znojmo
Mikulov
84
Lednice
Hodonín
55
Skalica
E50
85
Valtice
Břeclav
N. Mesto
AUSTRIA
Piešťany
SLOVAKIA
D2
Malacky
Hlohovec
51
Trnava
N
Pezinok
D61
Nitra
Vienna
62
Šal'a
Bratislava
63
0
40 miles
0
60 km
63

more years, the townspeople claim, Jihlava could have become a great European city. Indeed, during the 13th century, the town's enormous main square, **náměstí Míru** (Square of Peace), was one of the largest in Europe, rivaled in size only by those in Cologne and Kraków. But history can be cruel: the mines went bust during the 17th century, and the square today bears witness only to the town's once oversize ambitions.

There are several interesting churches clustered on or around náměstí Míru. The **Kostel svatého Ignáce** (St. Ignace Church) in the northwest corner of the square is relatively young for Jihlava, built at the end of the 17th century, but look inside to see a rare Gothic crucifix, created during the 13th century for the early Bohemian king Přemysl Otakar II. The town's most striking structure is the Gothic **Kostel svatého Jakuba** (St. James Church) to the east of the main square, down the Farní ulice. The church's exterior, with its uneven towers, is Gothic; the interior is Baroque; and the font is a masterpiece of the Renaissance style, dating from 1599. Note also the Baroque Chapel of the Holy Virgin, sandwiched between two late-Gothic chapels, with its oversize 14th-century pietà. Two other Gothic churches worth a look are the **Kostel svatého Kříže** (Church of the Holy Cross), north of the main square, and the **Minoritský kostel** (Minorite Church), to the west of the square. Just next to the latter is the last remaining of the original five medieval town gates.

Dining and Lodging

$$ ✕☐ **Zlatá Hvězda.** Centrally located on the main square, this reconstructed old hotel in a beautiful Renaissance house is comfortable and surprisingly elegant. In keeping with the building, rooms are modestly harmonious, with wood ceilings and down comforters. You're a short walk from Jihlava's restaurants and shops, though the on-site café and wine bar are among the best in town. ✉ *Nám. Míru 32, 586 01,* ☎ *066/730–9421,* FAX *066/730–9496. 17 rooms, 1 apartment. Restaurant, bar, café. AE, MC, V.*

Telč

★ 81 *30 km (19 mi) south of Jihlava, via Rte. 406.*

The little town of Telč has an even more impressive main square than that of Jihlava—but what strikes the eye most here is not its size but the unified style of the buildings. On the lowest levels are beautifully vaulted Gothic halls, just above are Renaissance floors and facades, and all of it is crowned with rich Renaissance and Baroque gables. The square is so perfect you feel like you've entered a film set, not a living town. The town allegedly owes its architectural unity to Zacharias of Neuhaus, and the main square is named after him: **náměstí Zachariáše z Hradce.** During the 16th century, so the story goes, the wealthy Zacharias had the castle—originally a small fort—rebuilt into a Renaissance château. But the contrast between the new castle and the town's rather ordinary buildings was so great that Zacharias had the square rebuilt to match the castle's splendor. Luckily for architecture fans, the Neuhaus dynasty died out shortly thereafter, and succeeding nobles had little interest in refashioning the town according to the vogue of the day.

It's best to approach Telč's main square on foot. If you've come by car, park outside the main walls on the side south of town and walk through the **Great Gate,** part of the original fortifications dating to the 13th century. As you approach on Palackého ulice, the square unfolds nobly in front of you, with the château at the northern end and beautiful houses, bathed in pastel reds and golds, gracing both sides. If you're a fan of Renaissance reliefs, note the black-and-white sgraffito corner house at No. 15, which dates from the middle of the 16th century. The house at No. 61, across from the Černý Orel Hotel, is also noteworthy for its fine detail.

The **château** forms a complex with the former **Jesuit college** and **Kostel svatého Jakuba** (Church of St. James). The château, originally Gothic, was built during the 14th century, perhaps by King John of Luxembourg, the father of Charles IV. It was given its current Renaissance appearance by Italian masters between 1553 and 1568. In season, you can tour the castle and admire the rich Renaissance interiors. Given the reputation of nobles for lively, lengthy banquets, the sgraffito relief in the dining room depicting gluttony (in addition to the six other deadly sins) seems odd indeed. Other interesting rooms with sgraffiti include the Treasury, the Armory, and the Blue and Gold chambers. A curious counterpoint to all this Renaissance splendor is the castle's permanent exhibit of paintings by leading Czech modernist Jan Zrzavý. ☎ *066/724–3943.* 🎫 *80 Kč.* ⏲ *Apr. and Oct., Tues.–Sun. 9–4; May–Sept., Tues.–Sun. 9–5.*

NEED A BREAK? If you're looking for sweets, you can get good homemade cakes at a little private café, **Cukrárna u Matěje,** at Na baště 2, on the street leading past the château to a small lake.

The tiny Palackého ulice leading off the main square takes you to the 160 ft Romanesque tower of the **Kostel svatého Ducha** (Church of the Holy Spirit). This is the oldest standing structure in Telč, dating from the first quarter of the 13th century. The interior, however, is a stylistic hodgepodge, as it was given a late-Gothic makeover and then, due to fire damage, refashioned through the 17th century.

Dining and Lodging

$$ ★ ✕🏨 **Černý Orel.** Here you'll get a very rare treat: an older, refined hotel that puts modern amenities in a traditional setting. The public areas mix architectural details such as vaulted ceilings with plush, contemporary armchairs, and the basic but inviting rooms are well balanced and comfortably furnished. Ask for a room overlooking the square, as the Baroque facade provides a perfect backdrop from which to view it. Even if you don't stay here, take a meal at the excellent hotel restaurant, a great spot for straightforward beef or pork dishes. ✉ *Nám. Zachariáše z Hradce 7, 588 56,* ☎ FAX *066/724–3221. 30 rooms, 25 with bath. Restaurant, bar. AE, MC, V.*

$$ 🏨 **Telč.** This is a slightly upscale alternative to the Černý Orel, even though the bright, polished appearance of the reception area doesn't quite carry over to the functional but pleasant rooms. (Some rooms open onto a courtyard.) The location, in a corner of the main square, is ideal. ✉ *Na Můstku 37, 588 56,* ☎ *066/724–3109,* FAX *066/722–3887. 10 rooms. Restaurant. AE, DC, MC, V.*

Vranov

82 *55 km (34 mi) southeast of Telč.*

As a swimming and boating center for southern Moravia, Vranov would be a good place to stop in its own right. But what makes the ★ town truly noteworthy is the enormous and colorful **Vranovský Hrad** (Vranov Castle), rising 200 ft from a rocky promontory. For nearly 1,000 years, this was the border between Bohemia and Austria, and thus it required a fortress of these dimensions. You'll either love or hate this proud mongrel of a building as its multicolor Gothic, Renaissance, and Baroque elements vie for your attention. In the foreground, the solemn

Renaissance tower rises over some Gothic fortifications. On its left is a golden Baroque church, and there's a beautiful pink-and-white Baroque dome to the back. Each unit is spectacular, but the overall effect of so many styles mixed together is jarring.

Take your eyes off the castle's motley exterior and tour its mostly Baroque (and more harmonious) interior. The most impressive room is certainly the 43-ft-high elliptical **Hall of Ancestors,** the work of the Viennese master Johann Bernhard Fischer von Erlach (builder of the Clam-Gallas Palace in Prague and the Hofburg in Vienna). Look inside the **castle church** as well. The rotunda, altar, and organ were designed by Fischer von Erlach at the end of the 17th century. ☎ *0624/296–215.* *55 Kč.* ⏲ *Apr. and Oct., weekends 9–4; May–Aug., Tues.–Sun. 9–6; Sept., Tues.–Sun. 9–4.*

Znojmo

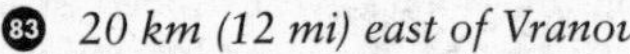

83 *20 km (12 mi) east of Vranov.*

Znojmo enjoys a long history as an important frontier town between Austria and Bohemia and is the cultural center of southern Moravia. The Přemyslid prince Břetislav I had already built a fortress here in the 11th century, and in 1226 Znojmo became the first Moravian town (ahead of Brno) to receive town rights from the king. But modern Znojmo, with its many factories and high-rises, isn't really a place for lingering. Plan on spending no more than a few hours walking through the Old Town and visiting the remaining fortifications and churches that stand between the New Town and the river.

Znojmo's tumbledown **main square,** now usually filled with peddlers selling everything from butter to cheap souvenirs, isn't what it used to be when it was crowned by Moravia's most beautiful **town hall**. Unfortunately, the 14th-century building was destroyed in 1945, just before the end of the war, and all that remains of the original structure is the 250-ft Gothic tower you see at the top of the square—looking admittedly forlorn astride the modern department store that now occupies the space.

Follow the run-down Zelinářská ulice, which trails from behind the town hall's tower to the southwest in the direction of the Old Town and the river. The grand, Gothic **Kostel svatého Mikuláše** (Church of St. Nicholas) dates from 1338, but its neo-Gothic tower was not added until the 19th century. If you can get into the church (it's often locked), look for the impressive sacraments house, which was built around 1500 in late-Gothic style. Just behind it is the curious, two-layer **Kostel svatého Václava** (Church of St. Wenceslas), built at the end of the 15th century. The upper level of this tiny white church is dedicated to St. Anne, the lower level to St. Martin. Along the medieval ramparts that separate the town from the river stands the original 11th-century **Rotunda svaté Kateřiny** (St. Catherine's Rotunda), still in remarkably good condition. Step inside to see a rare cycle of restored frescoes from 1134 depicting various members of the early Přemyslid dynasty.

Dining and Lodging

Znojmo's other claims to fame have endeared the town to the hearts (and palates) of Czechs everywhere. The first is the Znojmo gherkin, first cultivated in the 16th century. You'll find this tasty accompaniment to meals at restaurants all over the country. Just look for the *Znojmo* prefix—as in *Znojemský guláš,* a tasty stew spiced with pickles. Znojmo's other treat is wine. As the center of the Moravian wine industry, this is an excellent place to pick up a few bottles of your favorite grape. The best designations to look for, in addition to Znojmo, are Mikulov and Valtice. Some of the best varieties of grapes are Rulandské and Vavřinecké (for red) and Ryzlink and Müller Thurgau (for white).

$ ★ **Pension Havelka.** Though it is tiny, the charms of this family-run pension's tastefully folksy furnishings and ideal location in the center of Old Town can only be topped by its friendly, obliging management. They'll gladly set you up at one of the family's two other pensions if this one happens to be full. ✉ *Nám. Mikulášské 3, 669 02, ☎ FAX 0624/220–138. 2 rooms with shared bath. Restaurant, café. No credit cards.*

Mikulov

84 *54 km (34 mi) east of Znojmo.*

In many ways, Mikulov is the quintessential Moravian town. The soft pastel pinks and yellows of its buildings look almost mystical in the afternoon sunshine against the greens of the surrounding hills. But aside from the busy wine industry, not much goes on here, even though this is the main border crossing on the Vienna–Brno highway. It's as though the waning of the town's Jewish community left a breach that has never been filled. The striking **château** dominates the tiny main square and surrounding area. The château started out as the Gothic residence of the noble Liechtenstein family in the 13th century and was given its current Baroque appearance some 400 years later. The most famous resident was Napoléon, who stayed here in 1805 while negotiating peace terms with the Austrians after winning the battle of Austerlitz (Slavkov, near Brno). Sixty-one years later, Bismarck used the castle to sign a peace treaty with Austria. The castle's darkest days came at the end of World War II, when retreating Nazi SS units set fire to it. In season, take a walk from the main square up around the side of the castle into the **Regionální muzeum** (Regional Museum). The most remarkable exhibit is a wine cask made in 1643, with a capacity of more than 22,000 gallons. This was used for collecting the vintner's obligatory tithe. *Museum 30 Kč. ⏲ Museum Apr., weekends 9–4; May–Sept., Tues.–Sun. 8–5.*

During the 19th century, Jews constituted nearly half the population of Mikulov. The town was the seat of the chief rabbi of Moravia from the 17th to the 19th century and a center of Jewish learning. Great Talmudic scholars, such as Rabbis Jehuda Loew and David Oppenheimer, lived and taught here. Today, precious little is left of this heritage, but the **Jewish cemetery** remains as a potent evocation of the past. It is tended with care, and some of the most imposing tombstones on the "Rabbis' Hill" are being restored. The cemetery sits above the castle, off Brněnská street. The gate is usually locked, but the key may be borrowed from the Částek family at Brněnská 28 (ring the buzzer).

The Jewish quarter once spread along the western side of the castle hill. Of the many synagogues, baths, schools, and other structures that served the community, one of the few intact survivors is the 16th-century **Altschul** (Old Synagogue), which has been restored and now houses a small exposition and gallery. ✉ *Husova 11.* *6 Kč.* ⏲ *May–Sept., Tues.–Sun. 1–5.*

If you happen to arrive at grape-harvesting time in October, head for one of the many private *sklípeks* (wine cellars) built into the hills surrounding the town. The tradition in these parts is simply to knock on the door; more often than not, you'll be invited in by the owner to taste a recent vintage. If you visit in early September, try to hit Mikulov's renowned wine-harvest festival, which is celebrated with traditional music, folk dancing, and much quaffing of local Riesling.

OFF THE BEATEN PATH

DOLNÍ VĚSTONICE – A tiny town perched alongside the giant Nové Mlýny artificial lake a short drive or bus ride north of Mikulov, Dolní Věstonice is a sleepy fishing resort today. Some 20,000–30,000 years ago, however, the area was home to a thriving prehistoric settlement of mammoth hunters, judging from ivory and graves found here by archaeologists from 1924 onward. Some of the world's earliest ceramics have also been discovered here, among them a curvaceous figurine of ash and clay that has become known as the Venus of Věstonice. The original is kept in Brno's Moravian Museum, but you can see replicas, real mammoth bones, and much else of archaeological interest at the excellent **museum** in the center of town along the main road. It's open from April to October on weekends from 9 to 5; May to September, Tuesday through Sunday 8–5. Admission is 10 Kč. Just a mile or so down the road, the little hill town of Pavlov has several wine cellars built into the hills and makes for a good refreshment stop. At U Venuše (☒ Česká 27), be sure to sample some of the owner's wine, which comes from his private sklípek across the lake in Strachotín.

Dining and Lodging

$$ ★ ✕🏨 **Rohatý Krokodýl.** This is a prim, nicely renovated hotel in the old chief rabbi's house, under the castle. The doubles are on the small side, but the suites, which cost just a little more, are quite roomy. The facilities are the best in Mikulov, particularly the ground-floor restaurant, which serves a typical but delicately prepared selection of traditional Czech dishes. The owners plan to build an extension that will double capacity. ☒ *Husova 8, 692 01,* ☎ *0625/510–692,* FAX *0625/511–695. 13 rooms. Restaurant, pub. AE, MC, V.*

Outdoor Activities and Sports

For walking enthusiasts, the white limestone **Pavlovské vrchy** (Pavlov Hills), where the Stone Age remains in Dolní Věstonice (☞ *above*) were found, are a challenging climb with views of a couple of castle ruins. From **Děvín Peak** (1,800 ft), just south of Dolní Věstonice, a series of clearly marked paths follows the ridges the 10 km (6 mi) to Mikulov.

Shopping

The secret of Moravian wine is only now beginning to extend beyond the country's borders. A vintage bottle from one of the smaller but excellent vineyards in Bzenec, Velké Pavlovice, or Hodonín would be appreciated by any wine connoisseur.

Valtice

85 *13 km (8 mi) east of Mikulov along Hwy. 414.*

This small town would be wholly nondescript except for the fascinating **château,** just off the main street, built for the Liechtenstein family by a group of leading Baroque architects, among them Fischer von Erlach. Next to the town's dusty streets, with their dilapidated postwar storefronts, the castle looks positively grand, a glorious if slightly overexuberant holdover from a long-lost era. There are some 365 windows, painted ceilings, and much ornate woodwork. But best of all is the lure of spending the night—a rare practice in the Czech Republic. The left wing of the castle has been converted into the Hubertus hotel (☞ Dining and Lodging, *below*). You can also tour more than a dozen rooms, the chapel, and a picture gallery. The Valtice winery is behind and to the right of the castle, but it is not open to the public. ☎ *0627/352–423.* 🎫 *40 Kč, 80 Kč for a guided tour in German (occasionally in English).* ⏲ *Apr., Sept., and Oct., Tues.–Sun. 9–4; May–Aug., Tues.–Sun. 8–5.*

OFF THE BEATEN PATH

HLOHOVEC – An abandoned summer palace lies just to the north of Valtice, not far from the tiny town of Hlohovec. In winter you can walk or skate across the adjoining Hlohovec Pond to the golden yellow building; otherwise follow the tiny lane to Hlohovec, just off Route 422 outside Valtice. Emblazoned across the front of the palace is the German slogan ZWISCHEN ÖSTERREICH UND MÄHREN (Between Austria and Moravia), another reminder of the proximity of the border and the long history that these areas share. Consult Greenways maps for scenic horseback and bike tours of the area.

Dining and Lodging

$$ ★ ✕🏨 **Hubertus.** This comfortable hotel is not hard to find. Just look for the only palace in town; the hotel is on the left-hand side. Though the rooms are neither palatial nor furnished in period style, they are nevertheless inviting, with high ceilings and fresh flowers. The restaurant, with garden terrace, has an ample selection of fish, including carp, trout, and pike. Book ahead in summer, as the hotel is popular with Austrians who like to slip across the border for an impromptu holiday. ✉ *Zámek, 691 42,* ☎ *0627/352–537,* FAX *0627/352–538. 29 rooms, 22 with bath. Restaurant, bar. AE, MC, V.*

Lednice

7 km (4½ mi) from Valtice.

As a display of their wealth and taste, the Liechtenstein family sprinkled neoclassical temples and eclectic follies across a huge swath of parkland around Valtice and Lednice throughout the 18th and 19th centuries. The extravagantly neo-Gothic **château** at Lednice, though obviously in disrepair, has a sumptuous interior; particularly resplendent are the blue-and-green silk wall coverings embossed with the Moravian eagle in the formal dining room and bay-window drawing room. The grounds, now a pleasant park open to the public, have a 200-ft-tall minaret and a massive greenhouse filled with exotic flora. ☎ *0627/340–128.* *60 Kč, 110 Kč with guide.* *Apr. and Oct., Tues.–Sun. 9–3; May–Sept., Tues.–Sun. 9–5.*

Southern Moravia A to Z

Arriving and Departing

BY BUS AND TRAIN

Brno, a regional transport hub, is the best base from which to head off into southern Moravia. There are also frequent direct bus connections from Prague to Jihlava (two hours); the bus journey to the other towns on the tour will take three to five hours from Prague.

BY CAR

Southern Moravia is within easy driving distance of Prague and Bratislava. Jihlava is 124 km (75 mi) southeast of Prague along the excellent D1/E65 freeway. From here, it's easy to continue to Brno, or to take the E59, which goes down to Vranov and Znojmo. Southern Moravia is also easily reached by car from Austria; there are major border crossings at Hátě (below Znojmo) and Mikulov.

Getting Around

In general, buses run sporadically, especially on weekends. A local rail line from Znojmo links with international express trains at Břeclav, with stops at Mikulov and Valtice. If you're planning a day trip or two, Mikulov may be the best base, as there is regular bus service to Lednice, Valtice, and Brno. There are also bike paths to Lednice and

Valtice; you can get detailed maps and bike rental information at a tourist information center (☞ Visitor Information, *below*).

Contacts and Resources

EMERGENCIES

Police (☎ 158). **Ambulance** (☎ 155). **Breakdowns** (☎ 1054; Yellow Angels ☎ 1230; Autoklub Bohemia Assistance [ABA] ☎ 1240).

VISITOR INFORMATION

Jihlava (✉ Tourist Information Center, Masarykovo nám. 19, ☎ 066/731–1926). **Mikulov** (✉ Regional Tourist Information Center, Náměstí 30, ☎ 0625/512–200). **Telč** (✉ Information Center, nám. Zachariáše z Hradce 10, ☎ 066/724–3145). **Valtice** (✉ Tourist Information Center, nám. Svobody 4, ☎ 0627/352–977).

BRNO

Moravia's cultural and geographic center, Brno (pronounced *burr*-no) grew rich in the 19th century and has a different feel from any other Czech or Slovak city. Beginning with a textile industry imported from Germany, Holland, and Belgium, Brno became the industrial heartland of the Austro-Hungarian Empire during the 18th and 19th centuries—hence its nickname Manchester of Moravia. You'll search in vain for an extensive old town; you'll also find few of the traditional arcaded storefronts that typify other historic Czech towns. Instead you'll see fine examples of the Empire and neo-Renaissance styles, their formal, geometric facades more in keeping with the conservative tastes of the 19th-century middle class.

In the early 20th century, the city became home to the best young architects working in the cubist and constructivist styles. Experimentation wasn't restricted to architecture. Leoš Janáček, an important composer of the early modern period, lived and worked in Brno, as did Austrian novelist Robert Musil. The modern tradition continues even today, and the city is considered to have the best theater and performing arts in Moravia, as well as a small but thriving café scene.

It's best to avoid Brno at trade-fair time (the biggest are in early spring and early autumn), when hotel and restaurant facilities are strained. If the hotels are booked, the accommodation services at the town hall or main station will help you find a room.

Numbers in the text correspond to numbers in the margin and on the Brno map.

Exploring Brno

A Good Walk

Begin the walking tour at the triangular **náměstí Svobody** ⑧⑥ in the heart of the commercial district. Then walk up Masarykova ulice toward the train station and make a right through the little arcade at No. 6 to see the animated Gothic portal of the **Stará radnice** ⑧⑦. Leave through the portal and turn right into the old **Zelný trh** ⑧⑧. On the far side of the market, dominating the square, stands the severe Renaissance **Dietrichsteinský palác** ⑧⑨ at No. 8. Go through an archway into the palace garden, from where stairs lead down to the Baroque **Kostel Nalezení svatého Kříže** ⑨⓪.

Towering above the church and market is the **Chrám svatých Petra a Pavla** ⑨①, Brno's main church and a fixture of the skyline. The best way to get to it is to return to Zelný trh (via the little street off Kapucínské náměstí), make a left, and walk up narrow Petrská ulice, which begins

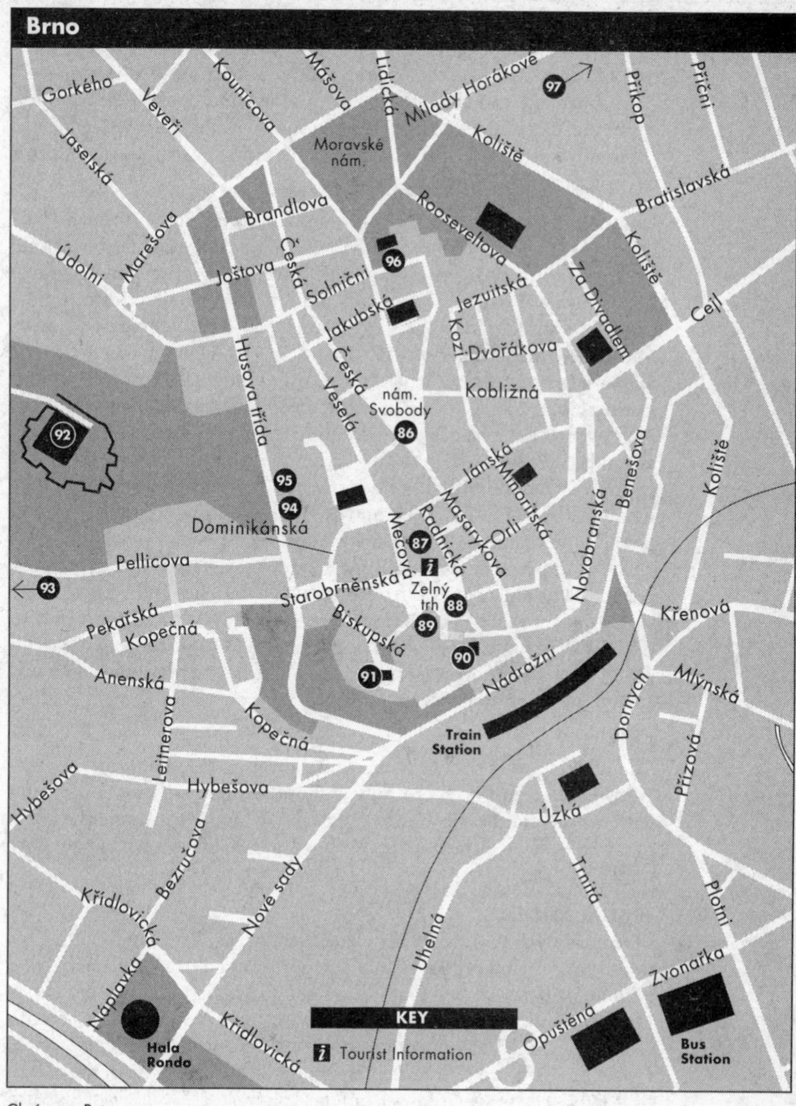

Chrám sv. Petra a Pavla **91**
Dietrichsteinský palác **89**
Kostel Nalezení sv. Kříže **90**
Místodržitelský palác **96**
Náměstí Svobody **86**
Pražákův palác . . . **95**
Špilberk hrad **92**
Stará radnice **87**
Uměleckoprůmyslové muzeum **94**
Villa Tugendhat . . . **97**
Výstaviště **93**
Zelný trh **88**

just to the right of the Dietrichsteinský palác. Before leaving the church area, stroll around the pretty park and grounds. Return to the juncture of Petrská and Biskupská and follow Biskupská to Starobrněnská ulice. Turn left and cross the busy Husova třída onto Pekařská ulice. At the end of the street you'll come to a square named for Gregor Mendel (Mendlovo náměstí) and a medieval monastery with a large Gothic church, Starobrněnský klášter.

Continue the tour along the busy and somewhat downtrodden Úvoz ulice. Take the first right and climb the stairs to the calmer residential street of Pellicova. If there's a unique beauty to Brno, it's in neighborhoods such as this one, with its attractive houses, each in a different architectural style. Many houses incorporate cubist and geometric elements of the early modern period (1920s and 1930s). Begin the ascent to the **Špilberk hrad** (92). There is no direct path to the castle; just follow your instincts (or a detailed map) upward, and you'll get there. From the top, look over to the west at the gleaming Art Deco pavilions of Brno's fairgrounds, **Výstaviště** (93), in the distance. The grounds are now the site of annual trade fairs. After taking in the view, stroll back down one of the windy paths to Husova třída and have a look in two of the Czech Republic's finest museums: the **Uměleckoprůmyslové muzeum** (94) and, just a block further down Husova, Brno's modern art museum, the **Pražákův palác** (95). For old art culled from Moravian churches and estates, make sure to pay a visit to the **Místodržitelský palác** (96). It's also worth it to find a way to Ludwig Mies van der Rohe's **Villa Tugendhat** (97), the city's most famous work of architecture. The house is a bit off the beaten track, so you will need to travel there by car, taxi, or tram.

TIMING

The walking tour should take two to three hours at a leisurely pace. Allow a couple of hours to fully explore the Špilberk castle. Museum enthusiasts could easily spend a half day or more browsing the city's many collections. Brno is relatively busy on weekdays, surprisingly slow on weekends.

Sights to See

91 **Chrám svatých Petra a Pavla** (Cathedral of Sts. Peter and Paul). This is one church that probably looks better from a distance. The interior, a blend of Baroque and Gothic, is light and tasteful but hardly mind-blowing. Still, the slim neo-Gothic twin spires, added in this century to give the cathedral more of its original Gothic dignity, are a nice touch. Don't be surprised if you hear the noon bells ringing from the cathedral at 11. The practice dates from the Thirty Years' War, when Swedish troops were massing for an attack outside the town walls. Brno's resistance had been fierce, and the Swedish commander decreed that he would give up the fight if the town could not be taken by noon the following day. The bell ringer caught wind of the decision and the next morning, just as the Swedes were preparing a final assault, rang the noon bells—an hour early. The ruse worked, and the Swedes decamped. Ever since, the midday bells have been rung an hour early as a show of gratitude. Although the city escaped, the cathedral caught a Swedish cannon shot and suffered severe damage in the resulting fire. ✉ *Petrov at Petrská.* *Free.* *Daylight hrs; closed during services.*

89 **Dietrichsteinský palác** (Dietrichstein Palace). The building was once home to Cardinal Count Franz von Dietrichstein, who led the Catholic Counter-Reformation in Moravia following the Battle of White Mountain in 1620. Today the palace and the adjoining **Biskupský dvůr** (Bishop's Court) house the **Moravské zemské muzeum** (Moravian Museum), with its mundane exhibits of local history, artifacts, and wildlife. To enter the Bishop's Court, walk through the little gate to the left of

the Dietrichstein Palace and then through the lovely Renaissance garden. Note the arcades, the work of 16th-century Italian craftsmen. ✉ *Zelný trh 8,* ☎ *05/4232–1205.* 🎫 *Bishop's Court 30 Kč, palace 36 Kč.* ⌚ *Tues.–Sat. 9–5.*

90 **Kostel Nalezení svatého Kříže** (Church of the Holy Cross). Formerly part of the Capuchin Monastery, this church combines a Baroque silhouette with a rather stark facade. If you've ever wondered what a mummy looks like without its bandages, then enter the door to the monastery's *krypta* (crypt). In the basement are the mummified remains of some 200 nobles and monks from the late 17th and 18th century, ingeniously preserved by a natural system of air circulating through vents and chimneys. The best-known mummy is Colonel František Trenck, commander of the brutal Pandour regiment of the Austrian army, who, at least in legend, spent several years in the dungeons of Špilberk castle before finding his final rest here in 1749. Experts have concluded that his head is real, contrary to stories of its removal by a thief. A note of caution about the crypt: the graphic displays may frighten small children, so ask at the admission desk for the small brochure (20 Kč) with pictures that preview what's to follow. ✉ *Kapucínské nám.* 🎫 *40 Kč.* ⌚ *Tues.–Sat. 9–11:45 and 2–4:30, Sun. 11–11:45 and 2–4:30.*

96 **Místodržitelský palác** (Governor's Palace). Moravia had much stronger artistic ties to Austria than Bohemia did, as can be seen in the impressive collection of Gothic, Baroque, and 19th-century painting and sculpture found in this splendid Baroque palace. Particularly fetching are Austrian painter Franz Anton Maulbertsch's ethereal rococo pageants. ✉ *Moravské nám. 1A,* ☎ *05/4232–1100.* 🎫 *50 Kč.* ⌚ *Apr.–Sept., Wed.–Sun. 10–6, Thurs. until 7; Oct.–Mar., Wed.–Sun. 10–5, Thurs. until 6.*

86 **Náměstí Svobody** (Freedom Square). The square itself is architecturally undistinguished, but here and along the adjoining streets you'll find the city's best stores and shopping opportunities. Anyone who has been to Vienna might experience a feeling of déjà vu here, as many of the buildings were built by 19th-century Austrian architects. Especially noteworthy is the stolid Klein Palace at No. 15, built by Theophil Hansen and Ludwig Foerster, both prominent for their work on Vienna's Ringstrasse.

95 **Pražákův palác** (Pražák Palace). This handsome, 19th-century neo-Renaissance building houses the largest collection of modern and contemporary Czech art outside Prague. While works by many of the same artists represented in Prague's major galleries can be seen here, the emphasis is on Moravian artists, who tended to prefer rural themes—their avant-garde concoctions have a certain folksy flavor. ✉ *Husova 18,* ☎ *05/4221–5758.* 🎫 *50 Kč.* ⌚ *Apr.–Sept., Wed.–Sun. 10–6, Thurs. until 7; Oct.–Mar., Wed.–Sun. 10–5, Thurs. until 6.*

92 **Špilberk hrad** (Spielberg Castle). Once among the most feared places in the Hapsburg Empire, this fortress-cum-prison still broods over the town from behind its menacing walls. The castle's advantageous location was no secret to the early lords of the city, who moved here during the 13th century from neighboring Petrov Hill. Successive rulers gradually converted the old castle into a virtually impregnable fortress. Indeed, it successfully withstood the onslaughts of Hussites, Swedes, and Prussians over the centuries; only Napoléon, in 1809, succeeded in occupying the fortress. But the castle is best known for its gruesome history as a prison for enemies of the Austro-Hungarian monarchy and, later, of the Nazis in World War II. Although tales of torture during the Austrian period are probably untrue (judicial torture had been prohibited prior to the first prisoners' arrival in 1784), conditions for the

hardest offenders were hellish: they were shackled day and night in dark, dank catacombs and fed only bread and water. The most brutal corrections ended with the death of the harsh, rationalist ruler Joseph II in 1790. The casemates (passages within the walls of the castle) have been turned into an exhibition of the late-18th-century prison and their Nazi-era use as an air-raid shelter. Parents should note that young children can easily become lost in the spooky, dim casemates. More dangerous, the low parapets atop the castle walls near the restaurant provide little security for over-curious climbers.

Aboveground, a recently opened museum in the fortress starts off with more displays on the prison era, installed in a row of cells on the ground floor, with detailed English texts. Above that is a new exhibition on the history of Brno, including several panoramic paintings showing the city in the 17th century, and photos showing then-and-now views of 19th- and 20th-century redevelopment in the Old Town. The third floor houses an attractive collection of paintings made by local artists or commissioned by local patrons over a four-century span; visitors who were intrigued by the modern art in the Pražákův palác (☞ *above*) will be interested to find more paintings by the prolific modernist Antonín Procházka here. There is also an exhibit on architecture and design in the 1920s and 1930s, with a turgid English explanation of this fertile period in the city's cultural development. ☎ *05/4221–4145.* 🎫 *Casemates 30 Kč, museum 50 Kč, combined ticket 60 Kč.* ⏲ *Casemates May–Sept., Tues.–Sun. 9–6 (daily in July and Aug.); Oct.–Apr., Tues.–Sun. 10–5. Museum Apr.–Sept., Tues.–Sun. 9–6; Oct.–Mar., Wed.–Sun. 10–5.*

NEED A BREAK? After a long walk and a good climb, what could be better than one of the best beers you'll ever have? The **Stopkova pivnice,** at Česká 5, will set you up with one, or a soft drink. If you're hungry, try the house goulash, a tangy mixture of sausage, beef, rice, egg, and dumpling. For something more substantial, head for the restaurant on the second floor.

87 **Stará radnice** (Old Town Hall). The oldest secular building in Brno has an important Gothic portal. The door is the work of Anton Pilgram, architect of Vienna's St. Stephen's Cathedral. It was completed in 1510, but the building itself is about 200 years older. Look above the door to see a badly bent pinnacle that looks as if it wilted in the afternoon sun. This isn't the work of vandals but was apparently done by Pilgram himself out of revenge against the town. According to legend, Pilgram had been promised an excellent commission for his portal, but when he finished, the mayor and city councillors reneged on their offer. Pilgram was so angry at the duplicity that he purposely bent the pinnacle and left it poised, fittingly, over the statue of justice.

Just inside the door are the remains of two other famous Brno legends, the **Brno Dragon** and the **wagon wheel.** The dragon—a female alligator, to be anatomically correct—apparently turned up at the town walls one day in the 17th century and began eating children and livestock. A gatekeeper came up with the novel idea of filling a sack with limestone and placing it inside a freshly slaughtered goat. The dragon devoured the goat, swallowing the limestone as well, and went to quench its thirst at a nearby river. The water mixed with the limestone, bursting the dragon's stomach (the scars on the preserved dragon's stomach are still clearly visible). The story of the wagon wheel, on the other hand, concerns a bet placed some 400 years ago that a young wheelwright, Jiří Birk, couldn't chop down a tree, fashion the wood into a wheel, and roll it from his home at Lednice (33 mi [53 km] away) to the town walls of Brno—all between sunup and sundown. The wheel stands as a lasting tribute to his achievement. (The townspeople, however, became convinced that Jiří had enlisted the help of the devil to win the bet, so they stopped frequenting his workshop; poor Jiří died penniless.)

No longer the seat of the town government, the Old Town Hall holds exhibitions and performances. To find out what's on, ask in the information center just inside Pilgram's portal. The view from the top of the tower is one of the best in Brno, but the climb (five flights) is strenuous. What catches the eye is not so much any single building—although the cathedral does look spectacular—but the combination of old and new that defines modern Brno. In the distance, next to the crooked roofs and Baroque onion domes, a power plant looks startlingly out of place. ⊠ *Radnická 8.* *Tower 10 Kč.* *Apr.–Sept., daily 9–5.*

94 **Uměleckoprůmyslové muzeum** (Museum of Decorative Arts). Set to reopen in June 2001, following a major reconstruction, this is doubtless the best arts-and-crafts museum in the Czech Republic. It has an assemblage of artifacts far more extensive than the truncated collection in Prague's museum of the same name—at least until the promised expansion of that institution in 2000. The collection includes Gothic work, Art Nouveau and Secessionist pieces, and an excellent, comprehensive overview of Bohemian and Moravian glass. Keep an eye out for the elegant furniture from Josef Hoffmann's Wiener Werkstätte (Vienna Workshop). A jagged, candy-color table by Milan Knížák is a striking example of contemporary work. ⊠ *Husova 14,* ☎ *05/4221–6104.*

97 **Villa Tugendhat.** Designed by Ludwig Mies van der Rohe and completed in 1930, this austere, white Bauhaus villa counts among the most important works of the modern period. The emphasis here is on function and the use of geometric forms, but you be the judge as to whether the house fits the neighborhood. The Tugendhat family fled before the Nazis, and their original furnishings vanished during the war or the house's subsequent heavy-handed remodeling. Replicas of Mies's cool, functional designs have been installed in the downstairs living area. Some of the original exotic wood paneling and an eye-stopping onyx screen remain in place. The best way to get there is to take a taxi or Tram 3, 5, or 11 to the Dětská nemocnice stop and then walk up unmarked Černopolní ulice for 10 minutes or so. ⊠ *Černopolní 45,* ☎ *05/4521–2118.* *80 Kč.* *Wed.–Sun. 10–6.*

93 **Výstaviště** (exhibition grounds). The earliest buildings were completed in 1928, in time to hold the first cultural exhibition to celebrate the 10th anniversary of the Czech state. The Brno-born modern architect Adolf Loos designed the interior of the 19th-century mansion on the grounds; his cool functionality blends with luxurious marble-clad walls and friezes. Bohuslav Fuchs—another modernist linked to Brno—created the City of Brno Pavilion, an airy network of vaulted glass halls. The enormous, circular Pavilion Z dates from 1959. The grounds are now the site of annual trade fairs and may be closed between fairs. From the main train station, take Tram 1 west to the Výstaviště stop. ⊠ *Výstaviště 1,* ☎ *05/4115–1111.*

88 **Zelný trh** (Cabbage Market). The only place where Brno begins to look like a typical Czech town, the Cabbage Market is immediately recognizable, not just for the many stands from which farmers still sell vegetables but also for the unique **Parnassus Fountain** that adorns its center. This Baroque outburst (you either love it or hate it) couldn't be more out of place amid the formal elegance of most of the buildings on the square. But when Johann Bernhard Fischer von Erlach created the fountain in the late 17th century, it was important for a striving town like Brno to display its understanding of the classics and of ancient Greece. Thus, Hercules slays a three-headed dragon, while

Amphitrite awaits the arrival of her lover—all incongruously surrounded by farmers hawking turnips and onions.

OFF THE BEATEN PATH

MORAVSKÝKRUMLOV – Admirers of Art Nouveau meister Alfons Mucha may want to make a 50 km (30 mi) detour off the main highway linking Mikulov and Brno. The town château is the unlikely home of one of Mucha's most celebrated works, his 20-canvas *Slav Epic.* This enormous work, which tells the story of the emergence of the Slav nation, was not well received when it was completed in 1928; painters at the time were more interested in imitating modern movements and considered Mucha's representational art to be old-fashioned. The city of Prague owns the paintings, but has agreed to let them stay in Moravský Krumlov at least until 2003. ✉ *Zámek,* ☎ *0621/322–789.* *50 Kč.* ⏲ *Apr.–Oct., Tues.–Sun. 9–noon and 1–4.*

Dining and Lodging

$$$ ✕ **Černý Medvěd.** Redecorated in cottage fashion with floral rather than red-plush upholstery, this is still one of Brno's most comfortable dining rooms. Wild game is the key ingredient in a traditionally Czech menu. ✉ *Jakubské nám. 1,* ☎ *05/4221–4548. AE, MC, V. Closed Sun.*

$$ ✕ **Baroko.** This 17th-century wine cellar in a Minorite monastery offers excellent cooking in a fun, if touristy, setting. Try the roast beef Slavkov (cooked with onions and red wine and served with potatoes or sweet chestnuts), named for the site of Napoléon's triumph not far from Brno. "Mystery of Magdalene" is a potato pancake stuffed with pork, liver, mushrooms, and presumably anything else the cook could get his hands on. ✉ *Orlí 17,* ☎ *05/4221–7015. No credit cards.*

$$ ✕ **La Braseria.** Delicious pastas and pizzas (a welcome alternative to the heavy local fare) are served here in an unhurried setting. Take a taxi, walk the 15 minutes from the center, or ride Tram 5 or 6 to the stop called Nemocnice u sv. Anny. ✉ *Pekařská 80,* ☎ *05/4323–2042. AE, DC, MC, V.*

$ ✕ **Zemanova kavárna.** This contemporary re-creation of a 1920s coffeehouse (the original was razed by the Communists to make way for a theater) is extremely stylish. Everything from the light fixtures to the furniture is faithfully copied from the original interior. The lofty ceilings provide pleasant, lilting acoustics, and the food isn't bad either: Czech with a dash of French, such as pepper steak with fries. ✉ *Jezuitská 6 (between Za Divadlem and Koliště),* ☎ *05/4221–7509. DC, MC, V.*

$$$ ✕ **U Královny Elišky.** Few restaurants can match this 14th-century wine cellar for historical atmosphere. Local specialties including wild game and fish are served in rooms with names such as "The Musketeer" and "The Napoléon." In summer you can sit in the garden and order roast suckling pig or lamb while watching fencers in historical dress cross swords. The adjacent pension offers reasonable comfort at a good price (rates double during major trade fairs, however). ✉ *Mendlovo nám. 1A, 603 00,* ☎ *05/4321–6898 (pension) or 05/4321–2578 (restaurant),* FAX *05/4324–7872. 8 rooms. No credit cards. No lunch; restaurant closed Sun. and Mon.*

$$$$ **Grand.** Though not really grand, this hotel, built in 1870 and thoroughly remodeled in 1988, is certainly comfortable and convenient. High standards are maintained through the hotel's association with an Austrian chain. Service is attentive; the rooms, though small, are well appointed, with coffered ceilings and leather sofas. Ask for a room at the back, facing the town, as the hotel is on a busy street opposite the train station. ✉ *Benešova 18/20, 657 83,* ☎ *05/4251–8111,* FAX *05/4221–0345. 113 rooms. 3 restaurants, minibars, sauna, exercise room, casino, nightclub. AE, DC, MC, V.*

$$$$ **Holiday Inn.** Opened in 1993, this handsome representative of the American chain has become the hotel of choice for business travelers in town for a trade fair. It has all you'd expect for the price, including a well-trained, multilingual staff. There are two classes of rooms, standard and executive; the main difference is that standard rooms lack air-conditioning. Executive rooms also have some extra perks, such as a modem line and trouser press. The location, at the exhibition grounds about a mile from the city center, is inconvenient for those who don't have a car. ✉ *Křížkovského 20, 603 00,* ☎ *05/4312–2111,* FAX *05/4323–6990. 205 rooms. Restaurant, café, air-conditioning (executive rooms), in-room data ports (executive rooms), sauna, meeting rooms. AE, DC, MC, V.*

$$$ ★ **Pegas.** This little inn makes an excellent choice given its reasonable price and central location. The plain rooms are snug and clean, with wood paneling and down comforters, and the staff is helpful and friendly (and speaks English). Even if you don't stay here, be sure to have a meal and home-brewed beer at the house microbrewery. ✉ *Jakubská 4, 602 00,* ☎ *05/4221–0104,* FAX *05/4221–1232. 15 rooms. Restaurant. DC, MC, V.*

$$$ **Slavia.** The century-old Slavia, just off the main Česká ulice, was thoroughly renovated in 1987. The grace of the fin-de-siècle facade and stucco-ceiling lobby are now oddly paired with utilitarian (though relatively spacious) rooms. The café, with adjacent terrace, is a good place to enjoy a cool drink on a warm afternoon. ✉ *Solniční 15/17, 622 16,* ☎ *05/4221–5080,* FAX *05/4221–1769. 81 rooms. Restaurant, café, minibars, free parking. AE, DC, MC, V.*

Nightlife and the Arts

For more sophisticated entertainment than a conversational evening at the local *pivnice* or *vinárna,* head for the **casinos** at the **Grand Hotel** (✉ Benešova 18/20, ☎ 05/4251–8111) and the **International Hotel** (✉ Husova 16, ☎ 05/4212–2111). The tables usually stay open until 3 or 4 AM. Both hotels also have bars that serve drinks until very late.

A few blocks north of the city center, **Klub Alterna** (✉ Kounicova 48, ☎ 05/4121–2091) hosts good Czech jazz and folk performers.

Brno is renowned throughout the Czech Republic for its theater and performing arts. There are a couple of main venues for jacket-and-tie cultural events. The **Mahen Theater** (✉ Rooseveltova 1, ☎ 05/4232–1285) is the principal space for drama. Opera and ballet productions are held up the street at the modern **Janáček Theater** (✉ Rooseveltova 7, ☎ 05/4232–1285). Both are slightly northwest of the center of town, just a five-minute walk from náměstí Svobody. One of the country's best-known fringe theater companies, **Divadlo Husa na provázku** (Goose on a String Theater; ✉ Zelný trh 9, ☎ 05/4221–1630), has its home where Petrská ulice enters Zelný trh. Check the schedules at the theaters or pick up a copy of *Do města/Downtown,* Brno's free fortnightly bulletin of cultural events. Buy tickets directly at box offices or at the central **Předprodej vstupenek** (ticket office; ✉ Běhounská 16).

Shopping

Moravia produces very attractive folk pottery, painted with bright red, orange, and yellow flower patterns. You can find these products in stores and hotel gift shops throughout the region. For more sophisticated artwork, including paintings and photography, stop by **Ambrosiana** (✉ Jezuitská 11, ☎ 05/4221–4439). **Český Design** (✉ Kapucínské nám. 5, ☎ 05/4222–1358) stocks handmade textiles, ceramics, and glass. You can buy English paperbacks and art books at **Knihkupectví Jiří Šedivý** (✉ Nám. Svobody 18, ☎ 05/4221–9793). For rare books, art monographs, old prints, and a great selection of avant-garde 1920s periodicals, stop by **Antikvariát Alfa** (✉ Jánská 11, in the arcade, ☎ 05/4221–1947).

Brno A to Z

Arriving and Departing

BY BUS

Bus connections from Prague's Florenc terminal to Brno are frequent and the trip is a half hour shorter than by train. Most buses arrive at the **main bus station** (ÚAN Zvonařka; ✉ Zvonařka 1, ☎ 05/4321–7733), a 10-minute walk from the train station. Some buses stop next to the train station. Buses also run between Brno and Vienna's Wien-Mitte station, stopping at Mikulov. Departures leave Brno for Vienna at 7:30 AM daily and at 5:30 PM every day except Tuesday.

BY CAR

Brno, within easy driving distance of Prague, Bratislava, and Vienna, is 196 km (122 mi) from Prague and 121 km (75 mi) from Bratislava. The E65 highway links all three cities.

BY PLANE

The private carrier **Air Ostrava** (✉ Prague, ☎ 02/2011–3406) links Prague with Brno and Ostrava in the northeast. The distances between the cities are short, however, and it's ultimately cheaper and quicker to travel by road or rail. During the two large Brno trade fairs, in April and September, foreign carriers also connect the city with Frankfurt and Vienna. These flights are usually crowded with businesspeople, so you'll have to book well in advance.

BY TRAIN

Six comfortable EuroCity or InterCity trains daily make the three-hour run from Prague to Brno's station, **Hlavní nádraží** (✉ Nádražní 1, ☎ 05/4221–4803). They depart either from Prague's main station, Hlavní nádraží, or the suburban nádraží Holešovice. Trains leaving Prague for Bratislava, Budapest, and Vienna normally stop in Brno (check timetables to be sure).

Getting Around

BY BUS OR TRAM

Trams are the best way to get around the city. Tickets cost 11 Kč–18 Kč, depending on the time and zones traveled, and are available at newsstands, yellow ticket machines, or from the driver. Most trams stop in front of the main station (Hlavní nádraží). Buses to the city periphery and nearby sights such as Moravský Kras in northern Moravia (☞ *below*) congregate at the main bus station, a 10-minute walk behind the train station. To find it, simply go to the train station and follow the signs to ČSAD.

BY TAXI

The nominal taxi fare is about 20 Kč per km (½ mi). There are taxi stands at the main train station, Výstaviště exhibition grounds, and on Joštova street at the north end of the Old Town. Dispatchers tend not to understand English.

Contacts and Resources

B&B RESERVATION AGENCIES

If you've arrived at Brno's main train station and are stuck for a room, try the accommodations service on the far left of the main hall, nominally open around the clock; you can place a sports bet there, too.

EMERGENCIES

Police (☎ 158). **Ambulance** (☎ 155). **Breakdowns** (☎ 1054; Yellow Angels ☎ 1230; Autoklub Bohemia Assistance [ABA] ☎ 1240).

LATE-NIGHT PHARMACIES

Lékárna (✉ Kobližná 7, ☎ 05/4221–2110).

TRAVEL AGENCIES

Čedok (✉ Nádražní 10/12, ☎ 05/4232–1267).

VISITOR INFORMATION

Kulturní a informační Centrum (✉ Radnická 8 [Old Town Hall], ☎ 05/4221–1090; or Nádražní 6 [across from the train station], ☎ 05/4222–1450).

NORTHERN MORAVIA

Just north of Brno is the Moravský Kras, a beautiful wilderness area with an extensive network of caves, caverns, and underground rivers. Many caves are open to the public, and one tour even incorporates an underground boat ride. Farther to the north lies Moravia's "second capital," Olomouc, an industrial but charming city with a long history as a center of learning. Paradoxically, despite its location far from the Austrian border, Olomouc remained a bastion of support for the Hapsburgs and the empire at a time when cries for independence could be heard throughout Bohemia and Moravia. In 1848, when revolts everywhere threatened to bring the monarchy down, the Hapsburg family fled here for safety. Franz Joseph, who went on to personify the stodgy permanence of the empire, was even crowned here as Austrian emperor that same year.

The green foothills of the Beskydy range begin east of Olomouc, perfect for a day or two of walking in the mountains. A half day's journey farther to the east, in northern Slovakia, you'll find the spectacular peaks of the Tatras, a good jumping-off point for exploring eastern Slovakia or southern Poland.

Slavkov

98 *20 km (12 mi) east of Brno.*

Slavkov, better known as **Austerlitz,** was the scene of one of the great battlefields of European history, where the armies of Napoléon met and defeated the combined forces of Austrian emperor Franz II and Czar Alexander I in 1805. If you happen to have a copy of *War and Peace* handy, you will find no better account of it anywhere. Scattered about the rolling agricultural landscapes between Slavkov and Brno are a number of battle monuments linked by walking paths. Napoléon directed his army from Žuráň hill, above a small town called Šlapanice (which can be reached from Brno by train or bus). Several kilometers southeast of Šlapanice an impressive memorial to the fallen of all three nations, the Mohyla míru (Cairn of Peace), crowns a hill above the village of Prace. Alongside the cairn is a small museum devoted to the battle.

In the town of Slavkov itself, the Baroque **château** houses more memorabilia about the battle; it's well worth visiting. ✉ *Palackého nám. 126, Slavkov u Brna,* ☎ *05/4422–1685.* *35 Kč.* *Apr.–May and Sept.–Oct., Tues.–Sun. 9–4; June–Aug., Tues.–Sun. 9–5.*

Moravský Kras

99 *30 km (19 mi) north of Brno.*

If it's scenic rather than military tourism you want, take a short trip north from Brno up the Svitava Valley and into the Moravský Kras (Moravian Karst), an area of limestone formations, underground stalactite caves, rivers, and tunnels. The most interesting part of the karst is near Blansko and includes several **caves.** You can arrange tours 8 km (5 mi) from the outskirts of Blansko at the Skalní Mlýn Hotel or the Moravian Karst information office (☞ Visitor Information *in* Northern Moravia A to Z, *below*). The nearby **Kateřinská jeskyně** (Catherine Cave) is set amid thickly forested ravines, and visitors taking the half-hour tour are serenaded by recorded opera tunes. The 90-minute tour of **Punkevní jeskyně** (Punkva Cave) includes a boat trip along an underground river to the watery bottom of **Macocha Abyss**, the deepest drop of the karst (more than 400 ft). On this tour, a little motorized "train" links the Skalní Mlýn Hotel to the Punkva Cave, from where a **funicular** climbs to the lip of Macocha Abyss. Only the Punkva Cave is normally open year-round; check with the information service for up-to-date information. It's always advisable to arrive at least an hour before scheduled closing time in order to catch the day's last tour. *Catherine Cave 30 Kč, Punkva Cave (including underground boat ride) 70 Kč, funicular 40 Kč. Catherine Cave Apr.–Sept., daily 8–4; Mar. and Oct., daily 8–2. Punkva Cave Apr.–Sept., daily 8–3:30; Oct.–Mar., daily 8–2. Funicular Apr.–Sept., daily 8–5; Oct.–Mar., operation depends on number of visitors.*

Outdoor Activities and Sports

Underground or on the surface, the walking is excellent in the karst, and if you miss one of the few buses running between the town of Blansko and the cave region, you may have to hoof it. Try to obtain a map in Brno or from the Moravian Karst information office (☞ Visitor Information *in* Northern Moravia A to Z, *below*) in the settlement of Skalní Mlýn. Look for Čertův most (Devil's Bridge), a natural bridge high over the road just past the entrance to Catherine Cave. You can follow the path, indicated with yellow markers, from the cave for another couple of miles to the Macocha Abyss. Before setting out, check with the information office or at the bus station for current bus schedules; for much of the year the last bus from Skalní Mlýn back to Blansko leaves at around 3 PM.

Olomouc

77 km (48 mi) northeast of Brno.

Olomouc is a paradox—so far from Austria yet so supportive of the empire. The Hapsburgs always felt at home here, even when they were being violently opposed by Czech nationalists and Protestants throughout Bohemia and much of Moravia. During the revolutions of 1848, when the middle class from all over the Austro-Hungarian Empire seemed ready to boot the Hapsburgs out of their palace, the royal family fled to Olomouc.

Despite being overshadowed by Brno, Olomouc, with its proud square and prim 19th-century buildings, still has the feel of a provincial imperial capital, not unlike similarly sized cities in Austria. The Old Town, situated on a slight rise over a tributary of the River Morava, luckily managed to escape damage during the July 1997 floods that inundated a huge swath of Moravia, Poland, and eastern Germany. The focal point here is the triangular **Horní náměstí** (Upper Square). The eccentric **Morový sloup** (Trinity Column), in the northwest corner of the square, is the largest of its kind in the Czech Republic and houses a tiny chapel. Four of the city's half-dozen renowned **Baroque fountains**, depicting Hercules (1687), Caesar (1724), Neptune (1695), and Jupiter (1707), dot the main square and the adjacent Dolní náměstí (Lower Square) to the south.

The square is marked by the bright, spire-bedecked Renaissance **radnice** (town hall) with its 220-ft tower. The tower was begun in the late

14th century and given its current appearance in 1443; the astronomical clock on the outside was built in 1422, but its inner mechanisms and modern mosaic decorations date from immediately after World War II. Be sure to look inside at the beautiful Renaissance stairway. You can also visit a large Gothic banquet room in the main building, with scenes from the city's history, and a late-Gothic chapel. Tours of the tower and chapel are given several times daily; contact the tourist office (☞ Visitor Information *in* Northern Moravia A to Z, *below*) in the town hall. *Tours 10 Kč.*

NEED A BREAK? The wooden paneling and floral upholstery in the **Café Mahler** (✉ Horní nám. 11) recall the taste of the 1880s, when Gustav Mahler briefly lived just around the corner while working as a conductor at the theater on the other side of the Upper Square. It's a good spot for ice cream, cake, or coffee.

Just north of the Horní náměstí, along the small Jana Opletalova ulice, stands the Gothic **Chrám svatého Mořice** (Church of St. Maurice). Construction began in 1412, but a fire 40 years later badly damaged the structure; its current fierce, gray exterior dates from the middle of the 16th century. The Baroque organ inside, the largest in the Czech Republic, originally contained 2,311 pipes until it was expanded in the 1960s to more than 10,000 pipes.

The interior of triple-domed **Kostel svatého Michala** (St. Michael's Church) casts a dramatic spell. The frescoes, the high, airy central dome, and the shades of rose, beige, and gray trompe-l'oeil marble on walls and arches blend to a harmonious, if dimly glimpsed, whole. The decoration followed a fire in 1709, only 30 years after the original construction. Architect and builder are not known, but it's surmised they are the same team that put up the Church of the Annunciation on Svatý Kopeček (Holy Hill), a popular Catholic pilgrimage site just outside Olomouc. ✉ *Žerotínovo nám., 1 block uphill from the Upper Square along Školní ul.*

Between the main square and the **Dóm svatého Václava** (Cathedral of St. Wenceslas) lies a peaceful neighborhood given over to huge buildings, mostly belonging either to the university or the archbishopric. As it stands today, the cathedral is just another example of the overbearing neo-Gothic enthusiasm of the late 19th century, having passed through just about every other architectural fad since its true Gothic days. ✉ *Václavské nám.* ⏲ *Daily 9–6.*

Next to the cathedral is the entrance to the **Palác Přemyslovců** (Přemyslid Palace), now a museum, where you can see early 16th-century wall paintings decorating the Gothic cloisters and, upstairs, a wonderful series of two- and three-arch Romanesque windows. This part of the building was used as a schoolroom some 700 years ago, and you can still make out drawings of animals engraved on the walls by early vandals. You can get an oddly phrased English-language pamphlet at the entrance to help you around the building. ✉ *Václavské nám.* *20 Kč.* ⏲ *Apr.–Oct., Tues.–Sun. 9–12:30 and 1–5.*

The **Děkanství** (Deacon's House), opposite the cathedral, now part of Palacký University, has two unusual claims to fame. Here, in 1767, the young musical prodigy Wolfgang Amadeus Mozart, age 11, spent six weeks recovering from a mild attack of chicken pox. The 16-year-old King Wenceslas III suffered a much worse fate here in 1306, when he was murdered, putting an end to the Přemyslid dynasty. The house is not open to the public. ✉ *Václavské nám.*

Lodging

$$$ **Flora.** Don't expect luxury at this 1960s cookie-cutter high-rise, about a 15-minute walk from the town square. To its credit, the staff is attentive (English is spoken), and the pleasant, if anonymous, rooms are certainly adequate for a short stay. ✉ *Krapkova 34, 779 00,* ☎ *068/542–2200,* FAX *068/542–1211. 150 rooms, 4 suites, all with bath or shower. Restaurant. AE, DC, MC, V.*

$$ **U Dómu svatého Václava.** This pleasant place represents a new class of Czech hotel and pension: you'll find modernized fittings installed in the old house. The six small suites all have kitchenettes. It's just down the street from the sleepy Václavské náměstí (where the Cathedral of St. Wenceslas is). ✉ *Dómská 4, 772 00,* ☎ *068/522–0502,* FAX *068/522–0501. 6 rooms. Kitchenettes. AE, MC, V.*

Outdoor Activities and Sports

The gentle, forested peaks of the **Beskydy Mountains** are popular destinations for hill walking, berry picking, and cross-country skiing; several resorts have ski lifts as well. Stay the night at one of the modest but comfortable mountain chalets in the area. You'll find a good one, the **Chata Soláň** (✉ 756 06 Velké Karlovice, ☎ FAX 0657/644–067), along the road between the year-round resort town of Rožnov pod Radhoštěm and the settlement of Velké Karlovice. (Rožnov pod Radhoštěm is connected by bus to all major cities in the country, and Velké Karlovice lies at the end of a rail line from Vsetín.) Be sure to take along a good map; some roads may be closed during the winter.

Northern Moravia A to Z

Arriving and Departing

Brno is the gateway to northern Moravia, whether by bus, car, plane, or train (☞ Arriving and Departing *in* Brno A to Z, *above*). The industrial center of Ostrava, in the far northeast near the Beskydy Mountains, is feasible as a stopover for travelers arriving from Poland or Slovakia.

Getting Around

Comparatively good trains, including several InterCity dailies, run frequently on the Prague–Olomouc–Ostrava line, one of the main rail corridors to Poland and Slovakia. Other long-distance trains branch off south to Vsetín and on into Slovakia. You'll sometimes have to resort to the bus to reach the smaller, out-of-the-way places throughout northern Moravia. To get to the Moravian Karst, you can take a bus from Brno to Vilémovice, a village not far from the Macocha Abyss.

Contacts and Resources

EMERGENCIES

Police (☎ 158). **Ambulance** (☎ 155). **Breakdowns** (☎ 1054; Yellow Angels ☎ 1230; Autoklub Bohemia Assistance [ABA] ☎ 1240).

VISITOR INFORMATION

Moravian Karst (✉ Central Information Service of the Moravian Karst Caves, Skalní Mlýn 65, 678 25 Blansko, ☎ 0506/413–575 or 410–024). **Olomouc** (✉ Radnice , Horní nám., ☎ 068/551–3385). **Ostrava** (✉ Nádražní 7, ☎ 069/612–3913). **Slavkov** (✉ Historical Museum and Cultural Services Center Austerlitz, Palackého nám. 126, ☎ 05/4422–7305 or 4422–1685).

THE CZECH REPUBLIC A TO Z

Arriving and Departing

By Bus

Several bus companies run direct services between major Western European cities and Prague. Two with almost daily service from London are **Kingscourt Express** (☎ 0181/673–7500 in London) and **Eurolines** (☎ 0171/730–3466 in London), both operating out of London's Victoria Coach Station. The trip takes about 20 hours and costs around $75 one-way.

By Car

The most convenient ferry ports for Prague are Hoek van Holland and Ostend. To reach Prague from either ferry port, drive first to Cologne (Köln) and then through either Dresden or Frankfurt.

By Plane

FROM NORTH AMERICA

Nearly all international flights to the Czech Republic fly into Prague's **Ruzyně Airport** (☎ 02/2011–1111), about 20 km (12 mi) northwest of downtown.

ČSA (Czech Airlines; ☎ 212/765–6022 in New York, 02/2010–4310 in Prague), the Czech national carrier, offers regular direct flights from New York to Prague (daily in high season) and flights from Montréal and Toronto to Prague two or three times a week.

Several other international airlines, including Delta, Lufthansa, SAS, KLM, and Air France, have good connections from cities in the United States and Canada to European bases and from there to Prague. **British Airways** (☎ 800/247–9297) flies daily via London. **Swissair** (☎ 800/221–4750) flies daily via Zurich.

From New York, a nonstop flight to Prague takes eight hours; from the West Coast with a stopover, 14–16 hours.

FROM THE UNITED KINGDOM

British Airways (☎ 0181/759–5511 in the U.K.) and its budget line, Go, have daily nonstop service to Prague from London (with connections to major British cities). **ČSA** (☎ 0171/255–1898) flies daily nonstop from London. The flight takes around two hours.

By Train

You can take a direct train from Paris via Frankfurt to Prague (daily) or from Berlin via Dresden to Prague (five times a day). Vienna is a good starting point for Prague, Brno, or Bratislava. There are three trains a day from Vienna's Südbahnhof (South Station) to Prague (five hours). Southern Moravia and southern Bohemia are served by trains from Vienna and Linz.

Getting Around

Navigation is relatively simple once you know the basic street sign words: *ulice* (street, abbreviated to ul., commonly dropped in printed addresses); *náměstí* (square, abbreviated to nám.); and *třída* (avenue). In most towns, each building has two numbers, a confusing practice with historic roots. In Prague, the blue tags mark the street address (usually); in Brno, ignore the blue tags and go by the white ones.

By Bus

The Czech Republic's extremely comprehensive state-run bus service, **ČSAD** ✆ is usually much quicker than the normal trains and more frequent than express trains, unless you're going to the major cities. Prices are quite low—essentially the same as those for second-class rail tickets. Buy your tickets from the ticket window at the bus station or directly from the driver on the bus. Buses can be full to bursting. On long-distance trips, it's a good idea to buy advance tickets when available (indicated by an R in a circle on timetables); get them at the local station or at some travel agencies. The only drawback to traveling by bus is figuring out the timetables. They are easy to read, but beware of the small letters denoting exceptions to the times given. If in doubt, inquire at the information window or ask someone for assistance.

By Car

Traveling by car is the easiest and most flexible way of seeing the Czech Republic—other than Prague. If you intend to visit only the capital, you can do without a car. The city center is congested and difficult to navigate, and you'll save yourself a lot of hassle by sticking to public transportation.

A permit is required to drive on expressways and other four-lane highways. They cost 100 Kč for 10 days, 200 Kč for one month, and 800 Kč for one year, and are sold at border crossings, some service stations, and all post offices.

In case of an accident or breakdown, *see* Emergencies, *below*.

PARKING

Parking is rarely a problem except in Prague (☞ Getting Around by Car *in* Prague A to Z, *above*).

ROAD CONDITIONS

The Prague city center is mostly a snarl of traffic, one-way streets, and tram lines. If you plan to drive outside the capital, there are few four-lane highways, but most of the roads are in reasonably good shape, and traffic is usually light. Roads can be poorly marked, however, so before you start out, buy one of the inexpensive multilingual auto atlases available at any bookstore.

RULES OF THE ROAD

The Czech Republic follows the usual Continental rules of the road. A right turn on red is permitted only when indicated by a green arrow. Signposts with yellow diamonds indicate a main road where drivers have the right of way. The speed limit is 130 kph (78 mph) on four-lane highways, 90 kph (56 mph) on open roads, and 50 kph (30 mph) in built-up areas. Seat belts are compulsory, and drinking before driving is absolutely prohibited. Passengers under 12 years of age, or less than 150 cm (5 ft) in height, must ride in the back seat.

By Plane

Air Ostrava (☎ 02/2011–3406 in Prague) flies from Prague to the northern Moravian city of Ostrava and to Brno. The airline experienced financial difficulties in 2000, however, and its future is uncertain. **ČSA** (Czech Airlines; ✉ V Celnici, off nám. Republiky, Prague, ☎ 02/2010–4310) also flies to Ostrava. Reservations can be made through Čedok offices or the ČSA office in Prague.

By Train

The state-run rail system is called **České dráhy** (ČD; ☎ 02/2422–4200 for information, ☎). On longer runs, it's not really worth taking anything less than an express (*rychlík*) train, marked in red on the timetable. Tickets are still very inexpensive: a second-class ticket from Prague to Brno costs 150 Kč in 2000. First class is considerably more spacious and comfortable and well worth the cost (50% more than a standard ticket). A 60 Kč–85 Kč supplement is charged for the excellent international expresses, EuroCity (EC) and InterCity (IC), and for domestic SuperCity (SC) schedules. A 20 Kč supplement applies to reserved seats on domestic journeys. If you haven't bought a ticket in advance at the station (mandatory for seat reservations), you can buy one aboard the train from the conductor. On timetables, departures (*odjezd*) appear on a yellow background; arrivals (*příjezd*) are on white. It is possible to book sleepers (*lůžkový*) or the less-roomy couchettes (*lehátkový*) on most overnight trains.

Contacts and Resources

B&B Reservation Agencies

Most local information offices also book rooms in hotels, pensions, and private accommodations. Do-it-yourself travelers should keep a sharp eye out for room-for-rent signs reading ZIMMER FREI, PRIVAT, or UBYTOVÁNÍ. In Britain, **Czechbook Agency** (✉ Jopes Mill, Trebrownbridge, near Liskeard, Cornwall PL14 3PX, ☎ FAX 01503/240629) arranges stays in B&Bs, self-catering apartments, and hotels.

Car Rentals

There are no special requirements for renting a car in the Czech Republic, but be sure to shop around, as prices can differ greatly. **Avis, Hertz,** and other major firms offer Western makes starting at around $45 per day or $300 per week, which includes insurance, damage waiver, and VAT; cars equipped with automatic transmission and air-conditioning are available, but it's best to reserve well in advance if you have special needs—try calling the firm's U.S. reservation number before you leave home (☞ Car Rental *in* Smart Travel Tips). It may be less expensive to reserve from home as well. Smaller local companies, on the other hand, can rent Czech cars for significantly less, but the service and insurance coverage may be inferior. A surcharge of 5%–12% applies to rental cars picked up at Prague's Ruzyně Airport.

Customs and Duties

ON ARRIVAL

You may import duty-free into the Czech Republic 200 cigarettes, 100 cigarillos and 50 cigars, or 250 grams of tobacco; 1 liter of spirits and 2 liters of wine; and medicines for personal use. Other personal items are exempt up to a value of 6,000 Kč.

ON DEPARTURE

The export of items considered to have historical value is not allowed. To be exported, an antique or work of art must have an export certificate. Reputable shops should be willing to advise customers on how to comply with the regulations. If a shop can't provide proof of the item's suitability for export, be wary. The authorities do not look kindly on unauthorized "export" of antiques, particularly of Baroque religious pieces.

Emergencies

Police (☎ 158). **Ambulance** (☎ 155). **Fire** (☎ 150). **Breakdowns:** call the toll-free number of one of the 24-hour road services (Yellow Angels ☎ 1230; Autoklub Bohemia Assistance ☎ 1240).

Guided Tours

Several Prague-based companies offer tours of the capital and other regions of the country. **Čedok** (✉ Main office: Na Příkopě 18, ☎ 02/2419–7111) has a wide range of offerings, including driving and cycling tours. You can also contact **Wolff Travel** (✉ Na Příkopě 24, ☎ 02/2422–7989) for regional and capital tours and international transportation tickets. **Sportturist Special** (✉ Národní třída 33, ☎ 02/2422–8518) provides similar services and is the local office for Western Union. **Wittmann Tours** (☎ 02/2225–2472) is a guide service that offers tours to sites of Jewish interest throughout the country and Central Europe. **Precious Legacy Tours** (✉ Maiselova 16, ☎ 02/232–1951) also arranges tours of Jewish sites.

Language

Czech, a Slavic language closely related to Slovak and Polish, is the official language of the Czech Republic. Learning English is popular among young people, but German is still the most useful language for tourists, especially outside Prague.

Mail

POSTAL RATES

In 2000, postcards to the United States and Canada cost 8 Kč; letters up to 20 grams in weight, 13 Kč. Postcards to Great Britain cost 7 Kč; letters, 9 Kč. You can buy stamps at post offices, hotels, and shops that sell postcards.

RECEIVING MAIL

If you don't know where you'll be staying, American Express mail service is a great convenience, available at no charge to anyone holding an American Express credit card or carrying American Express traveler's checks. The **American Express office** (Václavské nám. 56) is on Wenceslas Square in central Prague. You can also have mail held *poste restante* (general delivery) at post offices in major towns, but the letters should be marked *Pošta 1*, to designate the city's main post office. The poste restante window in Prague is at the **main post office** (✉ Jindřišská ul. 14). You will be asked for identification when you collect your mail.

Money and Expenses

COSTS

With inflation down to manageable levels, the Czech Republic is still generally a bargain by Western standards. Prague remains the exception. Hotel prices in particular are often higher than the facilities would warrant. Nevertheless, you can still find bargain private accommodations. The prices at tourist resorts outside the capital are lower and, in the outlying areas and off the beaten track, very low. It is an unfortunate fact that many venues such as museums, castles, and certain clubs charge a higher entrance fee for foreigners than they charge for Czechs. A few hotels still follow this practice too. Venue staff can be quite militant about defending this policy, which is legally acceptable in the Czech Republic, and protesting such discrimination when it happens will usually get you nowhere.

CURRENCY

The unit of currency in the Czech Republic is the koruna, or crown (Kč), which is divided into 100 haléřů, or hellers. There are (little-used) coins of 10, 20, and 50 hellers; coins of 1, 2, 5, 10, 20, and (rarely) 50 Kč; and notes of 50, 100, 200, 500, 1,000, 2,000, and 5,000 Kč. Notes of 1,000 Kč and up may not always be accepted for small purchases.

Try to avoid exchanging money at hotels or private exchange booths, including the ubiquitous Chequepoint and Exact Change booths. They routinely take commissions of 8%–10%. The best places to exchange are at bank counters, where the commissions average 1%–3%, or at ATMs. The koruna is fully convertible, which means it can be purchased outside the country and exchanged into other currencies.

At press time the exchange rate was around 35 Kč to the U.S. dollar, 24 Kč to the Canadian dollar, and 56 Kč to the pound sterling.

SAMPLE PRICES

A cup of coffee, about 30 Kč; public museum or castle entrance, 20 Kč–150 Kč; private museum entrance, up to 450 Kč; a good theater seat, up to 500 Kč; a cinema seat, 60 Kč–100 Kč; ½ liter (pint) of Czech beer, 15 Kč–50 Kč; a 2 km (1 mi) taxi ride, 60 Kč–200 Kč; a bottle of Moravian wine in a good restaurant, 140 Kč–400 Kč; a glass (2 deciliters or 7 ounces) of wine, 35 Kč–60 Kč.

National Holidays

January 1; Easter Monday; May 1 (Labor Day); May 8 (Liberation Day); July 5 (Sts. Cyril and Methodius); July 6 (Jan Hus); October 28 (Czech National Day); and December 24, 25, and 26.

Opening and Closing Times

Though hours vary, most banks are open weekdays 8–5. Private exchange offices usually have longer hours. Museums are usually open daily except Monday 9–5 or 10–6; they tend to stop selling tickets an hour before closing time. It used to be that many sights outside the large towns, including most castles, were open daily except Monday only from May through September and in April and October were open only on weekends. Lately the trend is toward a longer season, although off-season hours may change capriciously. Stores are open weekdays 9–6. Some grocery stores open at 6 AM. Department stores often stay open until 7 PM. Outside Prague, most stores close for the weekend at noon on Saturday, although you can usually find a grocery open nights and weekends.

Outdoor Activities and Sports

Local tourist bureaus are the best places to inquire about equipment rentals, trail networks, and other sports information. Besides bicycles, rental sports equipment is still relatively hard to find.

Passports and Visas

United States, Canadian, and British citizens need only a valid passport to visit the Czech Republic as tourists. U.S. citizens may stay for 30 days without a visa; British and Canadian citizens, six months. A new law effective Jan. 1, 2000, may raise additional bureaucratic obstacles in the path of those wishing to stay longer. Those interested in working or living in the Czech Republic are advised to contact the Czech embassy or consulate in their home country well in advance of their trip.

Rail Passes

Most rail passes, such as the Czech Flexipass, will wind up costing more than what you'd spend buying tickets on the spot, particularly if you intend to travel mainly in the Czech Republic, since international tickets normally are more expensive. The **European East Pass** is good for first-class travel on the national railroads of the Czech Republic, Austria, Hungary, Poland, and Slovakia. The pass allows five days of unlimited travel within a one-month period ($199). Additional travel days may be purchased. Apply through your travel agent or through **Rail Europe** (226–230 Westchester Ave., White Plains, NY 10604, ☎ 914/682–2999 or 800/848–7245, FAX 800/432–1329; 2087 Dundas E, Suite 106, Mississauga, Ontario L4X 1M2, ☎ 800/361–7245, FAX 905/602–4198). The Eurail pass and the Eurail Youthpass are not valid for travel within the Czech Republic. The InterRail pass and the EuroDomino discounted round-trip international ticket are available only to European citizens, or in some cases to people who have been in Europe for six months or longer. For more information, *see* Train Travel *in* Smart Travel Tips.

Student and Youth Travel

CKM (✉ Jindřišská 28, ☎ 02/2423–0218) and **GTS** (✉ Ve Smečkách 27, ☎ 02/9622–4300) provide information on travel bargains within the Czech Republic and abroad to students, travelers under 26, and teachers. **KMC** (Young Travelers' Club; ✉ Karoliny Světlé 30, ☎ 02/2222–1328) issues IYH cards (150 Kč for those under 26, 200 Kč for others) and books hostel beds throughout the country.

Telephones

The country code for the Czech Republic is 420. When dialing a number in the Czech Republic from abroad, drop the initial zero from the regional area code. Prefixes 0601 to 0606 denote mobile phones; when dialing these numbers, no regional area code is needed.

INTERNATIONAL CALLS

You can reach an English-speaking operator in the United States through one of these toll-free operators: **AT&T** (☎ 00–420–00101); **MCI** (☎ 00–420–00112); or **Sprint** (☎ 00–420–87187). To Canada, dial **CanadaDirect** (☎ 00–420–00151). To the United Kingdom, dial **BT Direct** (☎ 00–420–04401). The operator will connect your collect or credit-card call at the carrier's standard rates. In Prague, many phone booths allow direct international dialing. With the prepaid **X Card** (300 Kč–1,000 Kč), rates to the U.S. are roughly 22 Kč per minute; a call to the U.K. costs about 14 Kč per minute. If you can't find a booth, the telephone office of the **main post office** (Jindřišská 14), open 24 hours, is the best place to try. Once inside, follow signs for TELEGRAF/TELEFAX. The international dialing code is 00. For calls to the United States, Canada, or the United Kingdom, dial the **international operator** (☎ 133004). For inquiries, dial **international directory assistance** (☎ 1181). Otherwise, ask the receptionist at any hotel to put a call through for you, though beware: the more expensive the hotel, the more expensive the call will be.

LOCAL CALLS

Coin-operated pay phones are hard to find. Most newer public phones operate only with a special telephone card, available from post offices and newsstands in denominations of 150 Kč and up. A short call within Prague costs 4 Kč from a coin-operated phone or the equivalent of 3 Kč (1 unit) from a card-operated phone. The dial tone is a series of alternating short and long buzzes.

Tipping

Service is usually not included in restaurant bills. Round the bill up to the next multiple of 10 (if the bill comes to 83 Kč, for example, give the waiter 90 Kč); 10% is considered appropriate in all but the most expensive places. Tip porters who bring bags to your rooms 40 Kč total. For room service, a 20 Kč tip is enough. In taxis, round the bill up by 10%. Give tour guides and helpful concierges between 50 Kč and 100 Kč for services rendered.

Travel Agencies

Prague's American Express (☞ Travel Agencies *in* Prague A to Z, *above*) provides full travel services in addition to changing money and selling traveler's checks. Local Czech travel agencies offer extensive information on regional activities and tours, and larger agencies can supply you with hotel and travel information and book air and rail tickets. Agencies with branches nationwide include Čedok (the former state-owned tourist bureau), Sportturist Special (☞ Guided Tours, *above*), and Fischer.

Visitor Information

Most major towns have a local information office (Infocentrum or Informační středisko), usually in the central square and identified by a green-and-white sign with a lowercase "i" on the facade. These offices are often good sources for maps and guidebooks and can usually help you book hotel and private accommodations. In season (generally April through October), most are open during normal business hours and often on Saturday morning, sometimes even Sunday. In the winter, most are closed weekends. For individual centers, *see* Visitor Information *in* regional A to Z sections, *above*.

The official provider of tourist information, the **Czech Tourist Authority** (☞ Visitor Information *in* Smart Travel Tips), has offices in the United States, Canada, Great Britain, other countries of Europe, and Japan, as well as Prague (✉ Staroměstské nám. 6, ☎ 02/2481–0411, 📠). They stock maps and brochures on tourism outside Prague and dispense advice but do not book tickets or accommodations.

3 SLOVAKIA

Despite a long period of common statehood with the Czechs (which ended in 1992), Slovakia (Slovensko) differs from the Czech Republic in many aspects. Its mountains are higher and more rugged, its veneer less sophisticated, its folklore and traditions richer. Observers of the two regions like to link the Czech Republic geographically and culturally with the orderly Germans, while they put Slovakia with Ukraine and Russia, firmly in the east. This is a simplification, yet it contains more than a little bit of truth.

By Mark Baker

Updated by Tatiana Repková

SLOVAKIA BECAME AN INDEPENDENT STATE on January 1, 1993, when Czechoslovakia—what is today Slovakia and the Czech Republic—ceased to exist. The Czechs and Slovaks had been politically united since the fall of the Austro-Hungarian Empire in 1918. But when 1989's Velvet Revolution ended Communist rule in Czechoslovakia, the Slovaks' deep longing for independence came to the fore, and Slovak politicians were quick to exploit it. Slovak nationalist parties won more than 50% of the vote in the crucial 1992 Czechoslovak elections, and once the results were in, the most successful experiment in nation building after World War I was over. Although they speak a language closely related to Czech, the Slovaks had managed to maintain a strong sense of national identity throughout the 75 years of common statehood. In the end, it was the Slovaks' very different history that split them from the Czechs, and it's this history that makes Slovakia a unique destination for travelers to the region.

Though united with the Czechs in the 9th century as part of the Great Moravian Empire, the Slovaks were conquered a century later by the Magyars and remained under Hungarian and Hapsburg rule. Following the Tartar invasions in the 13th century, many Saxons were invited to resettle the land and develop the economy, including the region's rich mineral resources. During the 15th and 16th centuries, Romanian shepherds migrated from Walachia through the Carpathian Mountains into Slovakia, and the merging of these varied groups with the resident Slavs bequeathed to the region a rich folk culture and some unique forms of architecture, especially in the east.

In Slovakia today, the emerging market economy has given rise to an amazing mix of lifestyles. Medieval downtowns, neatly renovated and filled with color, contrast with gloomy panel housing projects on the outskirts of cities. In between, numbers of gray panel houses have been given lively new facades and crowned with green shrubs. South American flute-and-guitar bands perform on downtown streets next to fresh-vegetable stands run by local farmers.

Although there is growing income disparity, you can't tell it by the people on the streets. The Slovaks have leapt from their Communist central-planning past to the global information age, latching onto mobile communication. In the last couple of years, the number of mobile phones per capita has been catching up with Western levels. Slovaks adore the Internet, too, and cybercafés are popping up across the big cities. A fast-growing network of ATMs has brought a bank machine to every small town. Every 10th citizen of Slovakia is a bank-card holder, served by the thousands of stores and gas stations throughout the country that accept the cards.

To the east of the Czech Republic, Slovakia is about one-third as large as its neighbor. Most visitors to Slovakia head first for the great peaks of the High Tatras (Vysoké Tatry). Here there is ample tourist infrastructure, catering especially to hikers and skiers. Visitors who come to admire the peaks, however, often overlook the exquisite medieval towns of Spiš in the plains and valleys below the High Tatras, and the beautiful 18th-century country churches farther east. (Removed from main centers, these areas are short on tourist amenities. If creature comforts are important to you, stick to the High Tatras.)

Bratislava, the capital of Slovakia, may well be a disappointment at first. Forty years of Communism left a clear mark on the city, hiding its ancient beauty with hulking, and now dilapidated, futurist structures. Yet despite its gloomy appearance, Bratislava tries hard to project the cosmopolitanism of a European capital. The Old Town has already managed to recapture its lost charm.

Pleasures and Pastimes

Bicycling

The flatter areas to the south and east of Bratislava and along the Danube are ideal for biking. A special bike trail links Bratislava and Vienna, paralleling the Danube for much of its 40 km (25 mi) length. For the more adventurous bikers, the Low Tatras (Nízke Tatry) have scenic biking trails along the small, secluded rivers surrounding Banská Bystrica. Not many places rent bikes, however. For rental information, inquire at a tourist information center or at your hotel.

Camping

There are hundreds of camping sites for tents and trailers throughout Slovakia, but most are open only in summer (May to mid-September). You can get a map of all the sites, with addresses, opening times, and facilities, from Satur travel office. Campsites are divided into categories A and B according to their facilities; either type will include (unreliable) hot water and (primitive) toilets.

Dining

Slovakia's food is an amalgam of its neighbors' cuisines. As in Bohemia and Moravia, the emphasis is on meat, particularly pork and beef. But the Slovaks, revealing their long link to Hungary, prefer to spice things up a bit, usually with paprika and red peppers. Roast potatoes or french fries are often served, although occasionally you'll find a side dish of tasty *halušky* (noodles similar to Italian gnocchi or German spaetzle) on the menu. *Bryndzové halušky,* the country's unofficial national dish, is a tasty and filling mix of halušky, sheep's cheese, and a little bacon fat for flavor. Vegetarians don't have a lot of options, though vegetable salads are normally available. For dessert, the emphasis comes from Vienna: pancakes, poppy-seed dumplings, and strudel.

Slovaks don't eat out often, particularly since prices have risen markedly in the past few years. As a result, you will find relatively few restaurants about, and those that do exist generally cater to foreigners or a wealthy business clientele. Restaurants known as *vináreň* specialize in serving wines, although you can order beer virtually anywhere. Red wines in particular complement the country's filling, spicy food; look for *Frankovka,* which is fiery and slightly acidic. *Vavrinecké,* a relatively new arrival, is dark and semisweet and stands up well to red meats.

Lunch, usually eaten between noon and 2, is the main meal for Slovaks. Many restaurants put out a special luncheon menu (*ponuka dňa* or *špecialita šéfkuchára*). Dinner is usually served from 5 until 9 or 10, but cooks frequently knock off early on slow nights.

CATEGORY	COST*
$$$$	over $20
$$$	$15–$20
$$	$7–$15
$	under $7

**per person for a three-course meal, excluding wine and tip*

Fishing

There are hundreds of lakes and rivers suitable for fishing, often amid striking scenery. Demänovská dolina, a valley near Liptovský Mikuláš in central Slovakia, has some excellent places to catch trout. Bring your own tackle or be prepared to buy it locally, because rental equipment is scarce. To cast a line legally, you must have a fishing license (valid for one year) plus a fishing permit (valid for a day, week, month, or year for the particular body of water you plan to fish). Both are available from Satur offices.

Hiking

Slovakia is a hiker's paradise, with more than 20,000 km (12,500 mi) of well-kept trails in both the mountainous regions and the agricultural countryside. You'll find colored markings denoting trails on trees, fences, walls, rocks, and elsewhere. The colors correspond to the paths shown on the large-scale Súbor turistických maps available at many bookstores and tobacco shops. The best areas for ambitious mountain walkers are the Low Tatras in the center of the country near Banská Bystrica and the High Tatras to the north. Slovenský raj, or Slovak Paradise, in eastern Slovakia is an ideal place for hikers—a wild, romantic area, where you'll see cliffs, caves, and waterfalls.

Lodging

Few new hotels have been built since the Velvet Revolution, though some of the older establishments have been recently privatized and are being renovated. Overall, there's a shortage of good, inexpensive accommodations. On the bright side, small, private pensions in beautifully renovated buildings have been springing up all over the country.

In general, hotels can be divided into two categories: edifices built during the 1960s or 1970s that offer modern amenities but not much character and older, more central establishments that are heavy on personality but may lack basic conveniences. Most modern hotels have apartments (a bedroom and living room) and suites (two bedrooms and living room) as well as standard rooms. Hostels are cheap dormitory rooms and are best avoided. In the mountainous areas, you can often find little *chata* (chalets), where pleasant surroundings compensate for a lack of basic amenities. Campsites generally have a few bungalows available.

Slovakia is a bargain by Western standards, particularly in the outlying areas. In Bratislava, however, hotel rates often meet or exceed both U.S. and Western European averages. Slovakia's official hotel classification system (Deluxe, A, B, C) is gradually being changed over to the international star system, although it will be some time before the old system is completely replaced. Category C hotels are listed where accommodations are scarce or when the particular hotel has redeeming qualities.

The room rates quoted below generally don't include breakfast. Unless otherwise noted, all rooms have bath. Prices at the lower end of the scale apply to the low season. During festivals and holidays, including Christmas and Easter, hotel rates may increase by 15%–25%.

CATEGORY	COST*
$$$$	over $100
$$$	$50–$100
$$	$15–$50
$	under $15

**All prices are for a standard double room, including tax and service.*

following the text of a review is your signal that the property has a Web site, where you will find details and, usually, images; for a link, visit www.fodors.com/urls.

Shopping

The most interesting finds in Slovakia are batik-painted Easter eggs, corn-husk figures, delicate woven table mats, hand-knit sweaters, and folk pottery. The best buys are folk-art products sold at stands along the roads and in ÚLUV or folk-art stores in most major towns. Several Dielo stores sell paintings, wooden toys, and great ceramic pieces by Slovak artists at very reasonable prices.

Skiing

Slovakia has some of the region's best downhill skiing, for both amateurs and experts. The two main skiing areas are the Low Tatras and the High Tatras. The High Tatras have good snow throughout the winter; superior slopes, ski tows, and chairlifts; and places where you can rent equipment. Lifts in both regions generally operate from January through March, though cross-country skiing is a popular alternative.

Exploring Slovakia

Slovakia can best be divided into four regions of interest to tourists: Bratislava, the High Tatras, central Slovakia, and eastern Slovakia. Despite being the capital, Bratislava, in the western part of the country, is probably the least alluring destination. The country's true beauty lies among the peaks of the High Tatras in the northern part of central Slovakia.

Great Itineraries

Although Slovakia is relatively small, its mountains and poor roads make it difficult to explore in a short period of time. Driving or taking the train from Bratislava to the eastern town of Košice will take you a minimum of seven hours. A more convenient option is to fly. From Košice, it's easy to explore the surrounding region, with the High Tatras less than three hours away.

Numbers in the text correspond to numbers in the margin and on the Slovakia and Bratislava maps.

IF YOU HAVE 3 DAYS

If you only have a few days to see Slovakia, spend a maximum of a few hours walking through the Old Town and the castle in **Bratislava** ①–⑱; then head straight for the **High Tatras.** Once you get to the mountains, you can settle down in a comfortable hotel or a pension in one of the resort towns. **Smokovec** ⑳ and **Tatranská Lomnica** ㉒ are probably the most convenient places from which to explore the area and go hiking in summer or skiing in winter. If you can pull yourself away from the High Tatras on the second day, take a brief excursion slightly south to the beautiful Spiš town of **Levoča** ㉚. Spend the night here, and on your last day, head back to Bratislava via **Poprad** ⑲ and **Banská Bystrica** ㉓.

IF YOU HAVE 5 DAYS

Follow the three-day itinerary up to Levoča. From here, you can also explore the Spiš Castle and the caves and gorges in the area. The following day, head south toward **Košice** ㉙, the capital of the Spiš region, to take a look at some of the historic sights in the Old Town. On your last day, make your way back home. From Košice, you can fly to Bratislava or take a direct day or night train to Bratislava or Prague.

When to Tour

The High Tatras are loveliest in winter (January to March). The summer months in the mountains attract mostly walkers and hikers. Because of the snow, many hiking trails, especially those that cross the peaks, are open only between June and October. Temperatures are always much cooler in the mountains; even in summer, expect to wear a sweater or jacket.

Bratislava is at its best in the temperate months of spring and autumn. July and August, though not especially crowded, can be unbearably hot, while winter generally brings a great deal of snow and rain.

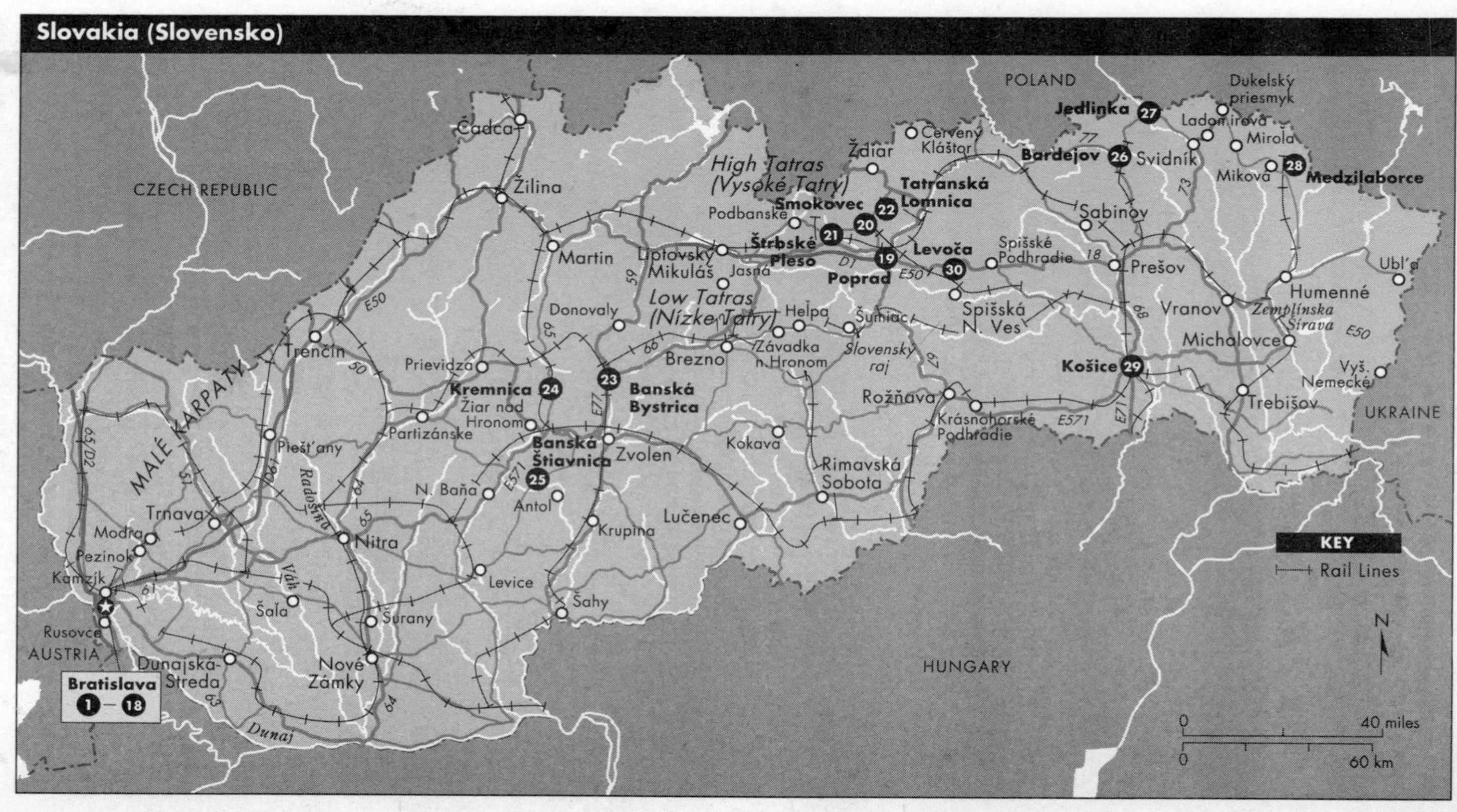

Slovakia (Slovensko)
CZECH REPUBLIC
POLAND
UKRAINE
HUNGARY
AUSTRIA
Čadca
Žilina
Martin
Trenčín
MALÉ KARPATY
Prievidza
Kremnica 24
Žiar nad Hronom
Partizánske
Piešťany
Radošina
Trnava
Modra
Pezinok
Kamzík
Rusovce
Bratislava 1 — 18
Dunajská-Streda
Dunaj
Váh
Šaľa
Šurany
Nové Zámky
Nitra
N. Baňa
Levice
Šahy
Banská Štiavnica 25
Antol
Krupina
Zvolen
Banská Bystrica 23
Donovaly
Liptovský Mikuláš
Jasná
Low Tatras (Nízke Tatry)
Brezno
Závadka n. Hronom
Helpa
Šumiac
Slovenský raj
Kokava
Lučenec
Rimavská Sobota
Rožňava
Krásnohorské Podhradie
High Tatras (Vysoké Tatry)
Podbanské
Štrbské Pleso 21
Smokovec 20
Tatranská Lomnica 22
Ždiar
Červený Kláštor
Poprad 19
Levoča 30
Spišské Podhradie
Spišská N. Ves
Košice 29
Bardejov 26
Jedlinka 27
Svidník
Sabinov
Prešov
Vranov
Ladomirová
Dukelský priesmyk
Mirola
Miková
Medzilaborce 28
Humenné
Ubľa
Zemplínska Šírava
Michalovce
Vyš. Nemecké
Trebišov
KEY
Rail Lines
N
0
40 miles
0
60 km

BRATISLAVA

You may get a bit of a sinking feeling when you first see Europe's newest capital city, Bratislava—or "Blava" as its residents affectionately call it. Instead of a Slovak version of Prague or Vienna, you'll discover a busy industrial city that seems to embody the Communists' blind faith in modernity. Bratislava has more than its fair share of high-rise housing projects and less-than-inspiring monuments to carefully chosen acts of heroism.

The jumble of modern Bratislava, however, masks a long and regal history that rivals Prague's in importance and complexity. Settled by a variety of Celts and Romans, the city became part of the Great Moravian Empire around the year 860 under Prince Rastislav. After a short period under the Bohemian Přemysl princes, Bratislava was brought into the Hungarian kingdom by Stephen I at the end of the 10th century and given royal privileges in 1217. Following the Tartar invasion in 1241, the Hungarian kings brought in German colonists to repopulate the town. The Hungarians called the town Pozsony; the German settlers called it Pressburg; and the original Slovaks called it Bratislava.

When Pest and Buda were occupied by the Turks in the first half of the 16th century the Hungarian kings moved their seat to Bratislava, which remained the Hungarian capital until 1784 and the coronation center until 1835. At this time, with a population of almost 27,000, it was the largest Hungarian city. Only in 1919, when Bratislava became part of the first Czechoslovak republic, did the city regain its Slovak identity. In 1939, with Germany's assistance, Bratislava infamously exerted its yearnings for independence by becoming the capital of the puppet Slovak state, under the fascist leader Jozef Tiso. In 1945, it became the provincial capital of Slovakia, still straining under the powerful hand of Prague (Slovakia's German and Hungarian minorities were either expelled or repressed). Leading up to the 1989 revolution, Bratislava was the site of numerous anti-Communist demonstrations; many of these were carried out by supporters of the Catholic Church, long repressed by the regime then in power. Following the Velvet Revolution in 1989, Bratislava gained importance as the capital of the Slovak Republic within the new Czech and Slovak federal state, but rivalries with Prague persisted. It was only following the breakup of Czechoslovakia on January 1, 1993, that the city once again became a capital in its own right.

Exploring Bratislava

To discover Bratislava's charms, travel the city by foot. Imagination is also helpful, as a few of the Old Town's oldest streets have not undergone reconstruction.

Numbers in the text correspond to numbers in the margin and on the Bratislava map.

A Good Walk

Begin your tour at the modern square **Námestie SNP** ①. From here, walk up the square toward Hurbanovo námestie, where you can glance at the **Kostol svätej Trojice** ②. Across the road, unobtrusively located between a shoe store and a cafeteria, is the enchanting entrance to the Old Town. After passing through the first archway, you come to the narrow promenade of Michalská ulica. In front of you is **Michalská brána** ③. Walk through the gate, and take a stroll down Michalská ulica. Many of the more interesting buildings along the street are undergoing renovation, but notice the eerie blue Kaplnka svätej Kataríny

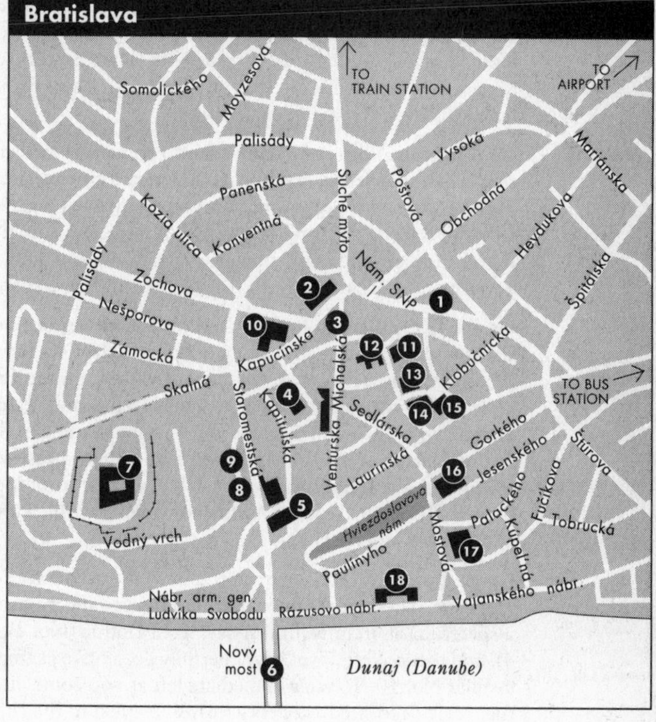

(Chapel of St. Catherine) at No. 6 on the left, built in 1311 but now graced with a sober classical facade. Opposite, at No. 7, is the Renaissance Segnerova kúria (Segner House), built for a wealthy merchant in 1648. Farther down on the right is the Palác Uhorskej kráľovskej komory (Hungarian Royal Chamber), a Baroque palace that housed the Hungarian nobles' parliament from 1802 until 1848 and is now the University Library. Go through the arched passageway at the back of the building, and you emerge in a tiny square dominated by the 14th-century **Kostol Klarisiek** ④, which is now the Slovak Pedagogical Library.

Follow Farská ulica up to the corner and turn left on Kapitulská ulica (notice the paving stone depicting two kissing lizards). Ahead of you on the right is the side wall of the **Dóm svätého Martina** ⑤, one of the more impressive churches in the city.

As you leave the church and walk around to the front, the first thing you see is the freeway leading to the futuristic spaceship bridge, **Nový most** ⑥, formerly called Most SNP (Bridge of the Slovak National Uprising). When the highway was built, a row of old houses and a synagogue in the former Jewish quarter outside the city walls were destroyed. The only good thing to be said for the road is that its construction led to the discovery of remnants of the city's original walls, which have been partially restored and now line the freeway on the right. Follow the steps under the passageway and up the other side in the direction of the castle.

Continue up the steps, through a Gothic arched gateway built in 1480, and climb up to the **hrad** ⑦ area. From the top, on a clear day, you can see over to Austria to the right. Leave the castle by the same route, but instead of climbing the last stairs by the Arkadia restaurant, continue down old-world Beblavého ulica.

At the bottom of the street on the right is the **Múzeum umeleckých remesiel** ⑧. Next, go around the House at the Good Shepherd and continue along Židovská ulica—the street name (Jews' Street) recalls that this area was the Jewish ghetto. You can visit the **Múzeum židovskej kultúry** ⑨ in a Renaissance mansion.

Continue on Židovská ulica until you come to a thin concrete bridge that crosses the freeway to the reconstructed city walls. Standing in the middle of this bridge, looking toward the river, you get one of the best views of the city's incongruous and contradictory jumble of buildings. If you turn left and walk along the city walls, you will come, after negotiating a series of steps, to the main road, Kapucínska ulica.

On the left is the small, golden yellow **Kostol kapucínov** ⑩. Cross the street and take the steps leading down into the Old Town. Turn left at the bottom into little Baštová ulica. Go through the arch at the end, and you'll find yourself back at Michalská brána. Continue straight along Zámočnícka ulica, which turns right heading in the direction of Františkánske námestie. To the left is the oldest preserved building in Bratislava, the **Františkánsky kostol** ⑪. Across from the church is the beautifully detailed rococo **Mirbachov palác** ⑫, which today houses the Municipal Gallery.

Go across Františkánske námestie onto the adjoining square, Hlavné námestie. The latter is lined with old houses and palaces representing a spectrum of architectural styles, from Gothic (No. 2), Baroque (No. 4), and rococo (No. 7) to a wonderfully decorative example of Art Nouveau at No. 10. To your immediate left as you come into the square is the richly decorated **Jezuitský kostol** ⑬. Next to the church is the colorful agglomeration of old bits and pieces of structures that make up the **Stará radnica** ⑭.

Leaving by the back entrance of the Stará radnica, you come to the Primaciálne námestie, or "Primates' Square," dominated by the glorious pale pink **Primaciálny palác** ⑮. Then walk down Uršulínska ulica and turn right at the bottom onto Laurinská ulica. If you continue to the left down Rybárska brána, you will emerge into the more modern part of the Old Town at the Hviezdoslavovo námestie. To your left is the **Slovenské národné divadlo** ⑯, Bratislava's opera house. Behind the theater you can buy tickets to performances.

Across Hviezdoslavovo námestie, on the corner of Mostová ulica and Palackého ulica, is the **Reduta** ⑰, home to the Slovak Philharmonic Orchestra. Continue down Mostová ulica to the banks of the Danube. To the right are Baroque barracks that were transformed by the Communists to house the modern **Slovenská národná galéria** ⑱, which has a collection of past and present works by Slovak artists.

TIMING

If you get an early morning start, you can complete a leisurely walking tour of the Old Town in a day. With the exception of the Slovenská národná galéria, which deserves some time, most of the museums are small and won't detain you long. Avoid touring on Monday, as many sights are closed. On other days, plan to break around lunchtime, because many museums close between noon and 1.

SIGHTS TO SEE

❺ **Dóm svätého Martina** (St. Martin's Cathedral). This massive Gothic church, consecrated in 1452, hosted the coronations of 17 Hungarian royals between the 16th and 19th centuries. Numerous additions made over the centuries were unfortunately removed in the 19th century, when the church was re-Gothicized. Nowadays, the three equal-size naves give an impression of space and light, but the uplifting glory found in Bohemia's other medieval cathedrals is missing. ✉ *Rudnayovo nám.*, ☎ *07/54431359.* ⊙ *Weekdays 10–11:30 and 2–6, Sat. 10–noon, Sun. 2–4:30.*

11 **Františkánsky kostol** (Franciscan Church). In this 13th-century church, only the presbytery is still in early Gothic style. The rest was destroyed in an earthquake in the 17th century and rebuilt in a mixture of Baroque and Gothic. Just around the corner, built onto the church, is another quite different and much more stunning Gothic building, the 14th-century **Kaplnka svätého Jána Evangelistu** (Chapel of St. John the Evangelist). Art historians believe that Peter Parler, architect of Prague's Charles Bridge, may have worked on this gem. You can take a look around before or after services at 7 AM and 5 PM. ✉ *Františkánske nám.*

7 **Hrad** (castle). Bratislava's castle has been continually rebuilt since its foundations were laid in the 9th century. The Hungarian kings expanded it into a large royal residence, and the Hapsburgs further developed its fortifications, turning it into a very successful defense against the Turks. The existing castle had to be completely rebuilt after a disastrous fire in 1811. Inside you'll find the **Slovenské národné múzeum** (Slovak National Museum), with exhibits on furniture, crafts, folklore costumes, and minting. ✉ *Zámocká ul.*, ☎ *07/59341626.* 🎫 *Castle and museum 40 Sk.* ⊙ *Tues.–Sun. 9–5.*

13 **Jezuitský kostol** (Jesuit Church). This church was originally built by Protestants who, in 1636, were granted an imperial concession to build a place of worship on the strict condition that it have no tower. The Jesuits took over the towerless church in 1672 and, to compensate for its external simplicity, went wild with Baroque detailing on the inside. ✉ *Hlavné nám.* ⊙ *Services Sun. and holidays at 5 and 6, weekdays at 3:15, 4, and 6.*

10 **Kostol kapucínov** (Capuchin Chapel). A pillar of Mary that commemorates the plague stands in front of this small 18th-century chapel. You can sneak a peek inside the chapel before or after the services held from 6 to 7 in the morning or in the evening from 5 to 7. ✉ *Kapucínska ul.*

4 **Kostol Klarisiek** (Klariský Church). This 14th-century church is simple but inspiring, with a wonderfully peaceful early-Gothic interior. The small High Gothic steeple was added in an unusually secondary position at the back of the church during the 15th century. As a mendicant order, the Poor Clares were forbidden to build a steeple atop the church, so they sidestepped the rules and built it against a side wall. The church is now a concert hall—and usually locked, but you may be able to get in for a concert or during rehearsals. ✉ *Farská ul.*

2 **Kostol svätej Trojice** (Church of the Holy Trinity). The ceiling of this golden yellow Baroque church has space-expanding frescoes, the work of Antonio Galli Bibiena from the early 18th century. ✉ *Hurbanovo nám.* ⊙ *Services at 9 and 6.*

3 **Michalská brána** (Michael's Gate). This is the last remaining of the city's three original gates. The bottom part of the adjoining tower, built in the 14th century, retains its original Gothic design. The copper onion tower, topped with a statue of St. Michael, was added in the 18th century. The *veža* (tower) has a good view over the city. ✉ *Michalská 24*, ☎ *07/54433044.* 🎫 *20 Sk.* ⊙ *Wed.–Mon. 10–4:30.*

12 **Mirbachov palác** (Mirbach Palace). This rococo palace with original stucco decor was built in 1770. Today it houses the **Municipal Gallery,** which has a small collection of 18th- and 19th-century Slovak and European art. ✉ *Františkánske nám.*, ☎ *07/54431556.* 🎫 *20 Sk.* ⊙ *Tues.–Sun. 10–5.*

8 **Múzeum umeleckých remesiel** (Handicraft Museum). In a Baroque burgher house, this tiny museum displays a few nice works of art and crafts from the 12th to 18th centuries, including ceramics, silverware, and furniture. ✉ *Beblavého 1,* ☎ *07/54412784.* 🎫 *20 Sk.* ⏲ *Wed.–Mon. 10–5.*

★ 9 **Múzeum židovskej kultúry** (Museum of Jewish Culture in Slovakia). This small but stirring museum celebrates the history and culture of the Jews living in the territory of Slovakia since the Great Moravian Empire. There's a collection of religious objects from around the country, many from synagogues in eastern Slovakia. A section is devoted to the 71,000 victims (out of a total Jewish population of 89,000) of the Holocaust in Slovakia. ✉ *Židovská 17,* ☎ *07/54418507.* 🎫 *40 Sk.* ⏲ *Sun.–Fri. 11–5.*

1 **Námestie SNP** (SNP Square). The square, formerly known as Stalinovo námestie (Stalin Square), was and still remains the center for demonstrations in Slovakia. SNP stands for Slovenské národné povstanie (Slovak National Uprising), an anti-Nazi resistance movement. In the middle of the square are three larger-than-life statues: a dour partisan and two strong, sad women in peasant clothing.

6 **Nový most** (New Bridge). Although it would make a splendid site for an alien flick, the modern bridge is a bit of an eyesore for anyone who doesn't appreciate futuristic designs. The bridge is difficult to miss if you're anywhere near the Danube.

NEED A BREAK? Unless you are squeamish about heights, have a coffee at the **Vyhliadková kaviareň** (☎ 07/817746) on Nový most. This spaceshiplike café—reached via speedy glass-face elevators for a minimal charge—is perched on top of pylons, 262 ft above the Danube River. Be warned that during stronger winds the café will sway.

15 **Primaciálny palác** (Primates' Palace). This is one of the most valuable architectural monuments in Bratislava. Don't miss the dazzling Hall of Mirrors, with its six 17th-century English tapestries depicting the legend of the lovers Hero and Leander. In this room, Napoléon and Hapsburg emperor Francis I signed the Bratislava Peace of 1805, following Napoléon's victory at the Battle of Austerlitz. In the revolutionary year of 1848, when the citizens of the Hapsburg lands revolted against the imperial dominance of Vienna, the rebel Hungarians had their headquarters in the palace. Ironically, following the failed uprising, the Hapsburg general Hainau signed the rebels' death sentences in the very same room. ✉ *Primaciálne nám. 1,* ☎ *07/54435151 or 07/59356166.* 🎫 *20 Sk.* ⏲ *Tues.–Sun. 10–5.*

17 **Reduta.** This extravagantly decorated building is Bratislava's classical musical center and home to the Slovak Philharmonic Orchestra. Dating from 1914, the neo-Baroque Reduta is worth visiting for its elegance alone. ✉ *Medená 3,* ☎ *07/54433351 or 07/54433352.*

18 **Slovenská národná galéria** (Slovak National Gallery). This gallery is housed in a conspicuously modern restoration of old 18th-century barracks. The museum itself has an interesting collection of Slovak Gothic, Baroque, and contemporary art, along with a small number of European masters. ✉ *Rázusovo nábr. 2,* ☎ *07/54432081.* 🎫 *30 Sk.* ⏲ *Tues.–Sun. 10–6.*

16 **Slovenské národné divadlo** (Slovak National Theater). You can see performances of Bratislava's opera, ballet, and theater in this striking building, which was built in the 1880s by the famous Central European architectural duo of Hermann Helmer and Ferdinand Fellner. ✉ *Hviezdoslavovo nám. 1,* ☎ *07/54430069 or 07/54430402.*

14 **Stará radnica** (Old Town Hall). One of the more interesting buildings in Bratislava, it developed gradually over the 13th and 14th centuries out of a number of burghers' houses. During the summer brass bands play on a balcony atop the tower. You can stop in the **Mestské múzeum** (City Museum) here and learn about Bratislava's storied past. ✉ *Primaciálne nám. 3,* ☎ *07/54433890 or 07/54433771.* 🎫 *20 Sk.* ⏲ *Tues.–Sun. 10–5.*

Dining

Prague may have its Slovak rival beat when it comes to architecture, but when it's time to eat, you can thank your lucky stars that you're in Bratislava. The long-shared history with Hungary gives Slovak cuisine an extra fire that Czech cooking lacks. Geographic proximity to Vienna, moreover, has lent some grace and charm to the city's eateries. Prepare for a variety of shish kebabs, grilled meats, steaks, and pork dishes, all spiced to warm the palate and served—if you're lucky—with those special noodles Slovaks call halušky.

$$$$ ✕ **Rybársky cech.** The name means "Fisherman's Guild," and fish is the unchallenged specialty at this refined but comfortable eatery on a quiet street by the Danube. Freshwater fish is served upstairs, with pricier saltwater varieties offered on the ground floor. ✉ *Žižkova 1,* ☎ *07/54413049. AE, DC, MC, V.*

$$$ ★ ✕ **Kláštorná vináreň.** This restaurant is in the wine cellar of a former monastery—hence the shadowy intimacy and wine-barrel-shape booths. The Hungarian-influenced spiciness of traditional Slovak cooking comes alive in such dishes as *Cikós tokáň,* a fiery mixture of pork, onions, and peppers. Or try the milder *bravčové ražniči,* a tender pork shish kebab served with fried potatoes. ✉ *Františkánska 2,* ☎ *07/54430430. AE, MC, V. Closed Sun.*

$$ ★ ✕ **Modrá hviezda.** The first of a new breed of small, family-owned wine cellars, this popular eatery serves old Slovak specialties from the village as well as some imaginative dishes. Try the sheep's-cheese pie. ✉ *Beblavého 14,* ☎ *07/54432747. No credit cards. Closed Sun.*

$ ✕ **Grémium.** This trendy restaurant caters to the coffee-and-cigarette crowd and to anyone in search of an uncomplicated light meal. Choose from a small menu of pastries, sandwiches, and some local specialties, including bryndzové halušky and *pytliacky guláš* (creamy goulash with halušky topped with blueberries), a bizarre but scrumptious dish. ✉ *Gorkého 11,* ☎ *07/54131026. Reservations not accepted. AE, MC, V.*

$ ★ ✕ **Pekná brána.** With more than 50 main-course meals to choose from, this is not the place to go if you have trouble making up your mind. The menu includes vegetarian dishes and traditional Slovak cuisine. The restaurant is open daily 9 AM to midnight. ✉ *Vysoká 37,* ☎ *07/52923008. MC, V.*

$ ★ ✕ **Stará sladovňa.** To Bratislavans, this gargantuan beer hall is known lovingly, and fittingly, as *mamut* (mammoth). Locals come here for the Bohemian brews on tap, but it is also possible to get an inexpensive and filling meal. ✉ *Cintorínska 32,* ☎ *07/52921151. No credit cards.*

Lodging

The lodging situation in Bratislava is improving, though not fast enough to rid the city of some pretty shabby establishments. Luckily, small, privately owned hotels and pensions continue to materialize. Make reservations in advance or arrive in Bratislava before 4 PM and visit the tourist information service (☞ Visitor Information *in* Bratislava A to Z, *below*) for help finding a room. If all decent hotels are booked, consider renting an apartment. Beware of individuals at train stations offering apartments, or you may be going back home with a much lighter load.

$$$$ ★ **Danube.** Opened in 1992, this French-run hotel on the banks of the Danube has quickly developed a reputation for superior facilities and service. The modern rooms are decorated in pastel colors, and the gleaming public areas are everything you'd expect from an international hotel chain. ✉ *Rybné nám. 1, 81338,* ☎ *07/59340000,* FAX *07/54414311. 264 rooms, 4 apartments, 12 suites. 2 restaurants, pool, sauna, health club, nightclub, convention center. AE, DC, MC, V.*

$$$ ★ **Hotel Pension No. 16.** This cozy pension in a quiet residential haven close to the castle is a nice alternative to the big chain hotels—it provides all the conveniences, but with character. The rooms are inviting, with wooden floors and ceilings. The apartments, which have kitchenettes, are a good deal for families. Breakfast is included. ✉ *Partizánska 16A, 81103,* ☎ *07/54411672,* FAX *07/54411298. 11 rooms, 5 apartments. Breakfast room. AE, MC, V.*

$$$ **Perugia.** This stunning postmodern jewel is in a renovated building in the center of Old Town. The clean, colorful rooms are eye-opening. Breakfast is included. ✉ *Zelená 5, 81101,* ☎ *07/54430719,* FAX *07/54431821. 13 rooms, 1 suite. Restaurant. AE, DC, MC, V.*

$$ **Hotel Echo.** This small, pink, modern hotel, not far from the center of Bratislava, looks more like a health club than a hotel, but it's a great place to stay, especially if you have a car. It has a friendly staff and large bright rooms. ✉ *Prešovská 39, 82108,* ☎ *07/55569170,* FAX *07/55569174. 32 rooms with shower, 2 apartments. Restaurant. MC, V.*

Nightlife and the Arts

Bratislava does not have a roaring nightlife scene, but you can definitely find a place to settle in for a few drinks or some classical music. The English-language *Slovak Spectator,* a Bratislava-based weekly newspaper, is a good place to check for listings on the city's cultural life. It's available at international chain hotels and many newsstands. For performance schedules and tickets, you can call BIS or Satur (☞ Visitor Information *in* Bratislava A to Z, *below*).

Nightlife

JAZZ CLUBS

Bratislava hosts an annual jazz festival in the fall, but the city lacks a good venue for regular jazz gigs. That said, **Čierny havran Club** (✉ Biela 6, ☎ 07/54430717) occasionally presents local jazz acts.

ROCK CLUBS

Bratislava's live-music and club scene is expanding, and venues are changing fast. Check the *Slovak Spectator* for the lowdown on the latest clubs. **Harley-Davidson Club** (✉ Rebarborová 1, ☎ 07/43191095) is—surprise!— an American-style hard-rock joint. Take Bus 220 to the Ružinovský cintorín (Ružinov Cemetery) stop. If you prefer to stay downtown, try **Diskobar centrum Pub** (✉ Župné nám. 3).

The Arts

CONCERTS

The **Slovak Philharmonic Orchestra** (✉ Medená 3, ☎ 07/54433351 or 07/54433352) plays a full program, featuring Czech and Slovak composers as well as European masters, at its home in the Reduta. You can get tickets at the box office, which is open weekdays from 1 PM to 5 PM and one hour before a performance.

FILM

Most new releases are shown in their original language with Slovak subtitles. **Charlie centrum** (✉ Špitálska 4, ☎ 07/52963430) regularly shows American classics, in English, in a friendly, artsy environment.

OPERA AND BALLET

The **Slovak National Theater** (✉ Hviezdoslavovo nám. 1, ☎ 07/54433890 or 07/54433771) is the place for high-quality opera and ballet. Buy tickets at the theater office on the corner of Jesenského and Komenského weekdays between noon and 6 or 30 minutes before show time.

THEATER

Traditional theater is usually performed in Slovak. For non-Slovak speakers, the **Stoka Theater** (✉ Pribinova 1, ☎ 07/52924463) blends nontraditional theater with performance art in a provocative and entertaining way.

Shopping

Bratislava is an excellent place to find Slovak arts and crafts of all types. You will find plenty of folk-art and souvenir shops along Obchodná ulica (Shopping Street) as well as on Námestie SNP (☞ Exploring Bratislava, *above*). Stores still come and go in this rapidly changing city, so don't be too surprised if some of the listed stores have vanished.

Antikvariát Steiner (✉ Ventúrska ul. 20, ☎ 07/54433778) stocks beautiful old books, maps, graphics, and posters. **Dielo** (✉ Nám. SNP 12, ☎ 07/52968648; Obchodná 27, ☎ 07/54434568; Obchodná 33, ☎ 07/52932433) has designer jewelry and clothing plus very unusual and fun ceramic pieces and other works of art.

For Slovak folk art, try **Folk, Folk** (✉ Obchodná 10, ☎ 07/54434292 or Rybárska brána 2, ☎ 07/54430176), where you'll find a wide range of goods, including pottery, handwoven tablecloths, wooden toys, and dolls with Slovak folk costumes. **ÚĽUV** (✉ Nám. SNP 12, ☎ 07/52923802) has a nice selection of hand-painted table pottery and vases, wooden figures, village folk clothing, and numerous small cornhusk figures, which are dirt cheap and can be very beautiful, though not easy to transport.

Bratislava A to Z

Arriving and Departing

BY BOAT

Hydrofoils travel the Danube between Vienna and Bratislava and Budapest and Bratislava from May to September. Boats depart in the morning from Bratislava, on the eastern bank of the Danube near the intersection of Mostová and Vajanského nábrežie, and return from Vienna or Budapest in the evening. Tickets cost $40–$80 per person and should be purchased in person at the dock. For reservations call **Slovenská plavba dunajská** (Slovak Danube Cruise; ☎ 07/52963522 or 07/52932226).

BY BUS

There are numerous buses from Prague to Bratislava; the five-hour journey costs around 300 Sk. From Vienna, there are four buses a day from Autobusbahnhof Wien Mitte; the journey takes 1½–2 hours and costs about AS150. Bratislava's main bus terminal, **autobusová stanica,** is roughly 2 km (1 mi) from the city center. To get downtown from the terminal, take Trolley 217 to Mierové námestie or 220 to the Tesco department store; or flag down a taxi.

BY CAR

There are good freeways from Prague to Bratislava via Brno (D1 and D2); the 315 km (195 mi) journey takes about 3½ hours. From Vienna, take the A4 and then Route 8 to Bratislava; the 60 km (37 mi) journey takes about 1½ hours. From Budapest, take Route 10 to Komárno, then Route 63 from Komárno to Bratislava; the trip takes roughly 2½ hours.

BY PLANE

Although few international airlines provide direct service to Bratislava, **ČSA** (☎ 07/52961042 or 07/52961045), the Czech national carrier, offers connections to Bratislava via Prague. You can also fly into Vienna's Schwechat Airport, about 60 km (37 mi) to the west, and proceed to Bratislava by either bus or train—a one-hour journey.

BY TRAIN

Reasonably efficient train service regularly connects Prague and Bratislava. Trains leave from Prague's Hlavní nádraží (main station) and from Holešovice station; the journey takes five to six hours. The InterCity trains are slightly more expensive but faster. From Vienna, four trains daily make the one-hour trek to Bratislava. Bratislava's train station, **Hlavná stanica,** is about 2 km (1 mi) from the city center. To travel downtown from the station, take Streetcar 1 or 13 to Poštová ulica or jump in a taxi.

Getting Around

Bratislava is compact, and most sights can be reached easily on foot. Taxis are reasonably priced and easy to hail; at night, they are the best option for returning home from wine cellars and clubs.

BY BUS AND TRAM

Bratislava's buses and *trolejbusy* (trolleybuses) run frequently and connect the city center with outlying sights. Stops are marked with signs that picture a bus or tram and list the transportation lines served from the stop. Tickets cost 6 Sk for a 10-minute ride (roughly five stops), 70 Sk for a 24-hour ticket, or 160 Sk for a three-day ticket. You can buy tickets from large hotels, news agents, and tobacconists. You can't buy tickets on a bus or tram, and you should be leery of the red vending machines at the major stops, since they're often out of order. Validate tickets on board (watch how the locals do it). The fine for riding without a validated ticket is 700 Sk, payable on the spot.

BY TAXI

Meters start at 20 Sk–30 Sk and jump 13 Sk–16 Sk per 1 km (½ mi). The number of dishonest cabbies, sadly, is on the rise. To avoid being ripped off, watch to see that the driver engages the meter. If the meter is broken, negotiate a price with the driver before even getting in the cab. Taxis are hailable on the street, or call **BP Taxi** (☎ 07/16333 or 07/16000).

Contacts and Resources

EMBASSIES

U.S. Embassy (✉ Hviezdoslavovo nám. 4, ☎ 07/54430861). **U.K. Embassy** (✉ Panská 16, ☎ 07/54419633). **Canadian Consulate** (✉ Mišíkova 28D, ☎ 07/52442175 or 07/52442177). There is no Australian embassy here.

EMERGENCIES

Police (☎ 158). **Ambulance** (☎ 155). One **pharmacy** (✉ Palackého 10, ☎ 07/5319665) near the Old Town maintains 24-hour service. Other pharmacies stay open late on a rotating basis.

ENGLISH-LANGUAGE BOOKSTORES

Try **Big Ben Bookshop** (✉ Michalská 1, ☎ 07/54433632). **Antikvariát Steiner** (✉ Ventúrska 20, ☎ 07/54433778) is a beautiful secondhand bookstore.

GUIDED TOURS

The best tours of Bratislava are offered by BIS (☞ Visitor Information, *below*), although tours during the off-season are conducted in German and only on weekends. Tours generally start at Primaciálne námestie. For an English-language tour, call ahead for an appointment. They prefer groups, but will accommodate various meeting places and times. Tours typically take two hours and cost 1,000 Sk per person. Satur (☞ Visitor Information, *below*) also offers tours of the capital from May through September. These also normally start at Primaciálne námestie. As with BIS, you'll need to make an appointment for an English-language tour, though you can arrange a meeting time and place.

TRAVEL AGENCIES

Tatratour (✉ Bajkalská 25, ☎ 07/53414828 or 07/53411219, FAX 07/53412781) is a large, dependable agency that can help arrange sightseeing tours throughout Slovakia. Satur (☞ Visitor Information, *below*) can also provide basic travel-agency services, such as changing traveler's checks and booking bus and train tickets to outside destinations.

VISITOR INFORMATION

Bratislava's tourist information service, **Bratislavská informačná služba** (BIS; ✉ Klobučnícka 2, ☎ 07/54434370), can assist in finding a hotel or private accommodation. The office is also a good source for maps and basic information. It's open weekdays from 8 to 4:30 (until 7 June through September) and Saturday from 8 to 1 (from 8 to 2 on weekends June through September). If you are arriving by train, the small BIS office in the station, open daily from 8 to 8, can be very helpful.

The country's national travel agency, **Satur Tours and Travel** (✉ Jesenského 5, ☎ 07/54410133 or 07/54410129, FAX 07/54410138), can help find accommodations in one of its hotels across the country and can book air, rail, and bus tickets. It's open weekdays from 9 to 6 and Saturday from 9 to noon.

THE HIGH TATRAS

Visiting only the Vysoké Tatry (High Tatras) would make a trip to Slovakia worthwhile. Although the range is relatively compact (just 32 km [20 mi] from end to end), its peaks seem wilder and more starkly beautiful than those of the Alps. The highest is Gerlachovský štít, at 8,710 ft; some 20 others exceed 8,000 ft. The 35 mountain lakes are remote and clear, very cold, and sometimes eerily deep. Swimming is not permitted in the cold glacier lakes of the Tatras.

Most of the tourist facilities in the High Tatras are concentrated in three neighboring resort towns: Štrbské Pleso, to the west; Smokovec, in the middle; and Tatranská Lomnica, to the east. Each town is pretty similar in terms of convenience and atmosphere, and all provide easy passage to the hills, so it makes little difference where you begin your explorations of the mountains.

Hiking

The best way to see these beautiful mountains is on foot. Three of the best Tatras walks are outlined below, arranged according to difficulty, with the easiest and prettiest first. A reasonably fit person of any age will have little trouble with any of the walks, which take three to five hours each. Even though the trails are well marked, it is very important to buy a walking map of the area—the detailed *Vysoké Tatry, letná turistická mapa* is available for around 20 Sk at newspaper kiosks. If you plan to take any of the higher-level walks, be

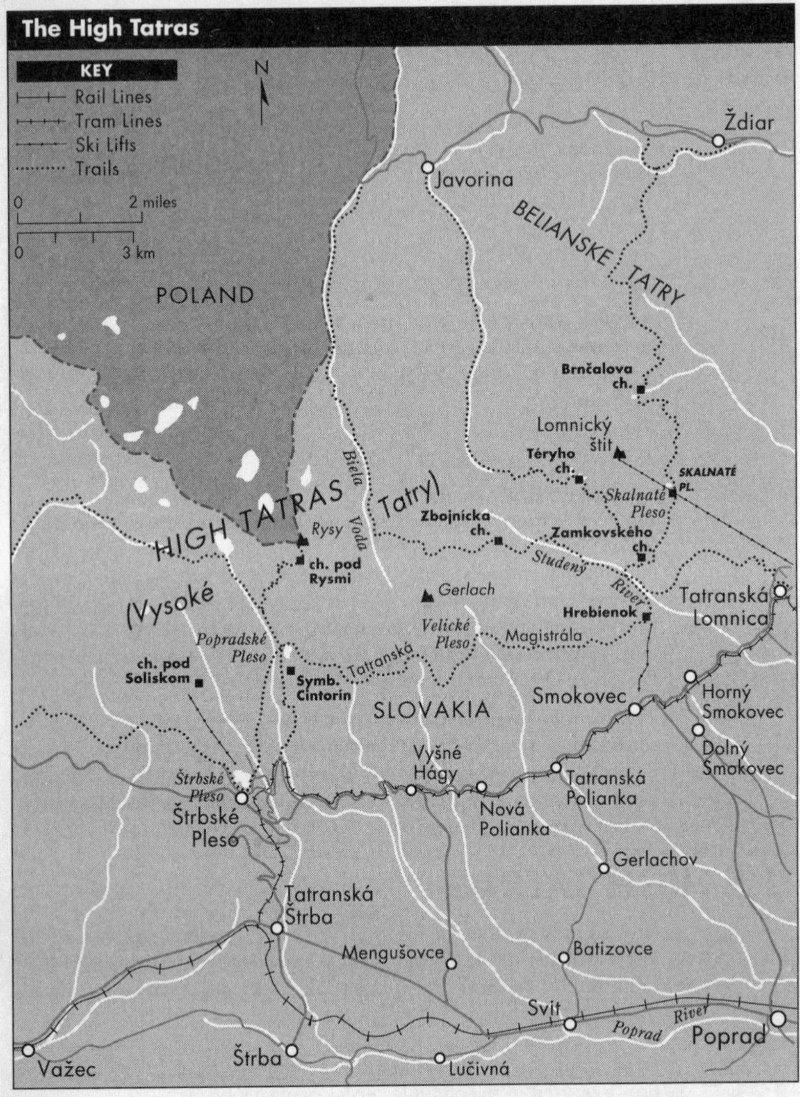

sure to wear proper shoes with good ankle support. Also use extreme caution in early spring, when melting snow can turn the trails into icy rivers.

Skiing

The entire region is crisscrossed with paths ideal for cross-country skiing. You can buy a special ski map at newspaper kiosks. The season lasts from the end of December through April, though the best months are traditionally January and February. Rental equipment is ubiquitous, and you'll get a complete downhill ski set—including skis, boots, and poles—for up to $10 per day. Ždiar, toward the Polish border, has a good ski area for beginners.

Numbers in the margin correspond to numbers on the Slovakia map.

Poprad

19 *329 km (204 mi) east of Bratislava along Hwys. D61 and E50.*

Poprad, the gateway to the Tatras, is a good place to begin exploring the region. But don't expect a beautiful mountain village. Poprad fell victim to some of the most insensitive Communist planning perpetrated in the country after the war. There's no need to linger here. Instead, drive or take the electric railroad to the superior sights and facilities of the more rugged resorts just over 30 km (19 mi) to the north.

Dining and Lodging

$ ★ ✕ **Slovenská reštaurácia.** If you have to spend a few hours in Poprad, having a meal in this charming rustic restaurant is the best way to do so. Try the bryndzové halušky or *strapačky s kapustou* (homemade noodles with sauerkraut). ✉ *Ul. 1. mája 216,* ☏ *092/7722870. No credit cards.*

$ 🏨 **Europa.** This cozy little hotel is next to the train station. From the reception area to the modest, old-fashioned rooms (with neither bathrooms nor TVs), the place exudes a faint elegance. ✉ *Wolkerova ul.,* ☏ *092/7721883. 40 rooms without bath. Bar. No credit cards.*

Smokovec

20 *12 km (7 mi) north of Poprad on Rte. 534.*

The first town you'll reach by road or rail from Poprad is Smokovec, the undisputed center of the Slovak Tatras resorts and a good starting point for mountain excursions. Smokovec is divided into two principal areas, Starý Smokovec (Old Smokovec) and Nový Smokovec (New Smokovec), which are within a stone's throw of each other.

The Tatras are tailor-made for hikers of all levels. Starý Smokovec is a great starting point for a trek that parallels a cascading waterfall for much of its three-hour length. From Starý Smokovec, walk out along the main road in the direction of Tatranská Lomnica for roughly 1 km (½ mi). In Tatranská Lesná, follow the yellow-marked path that winds gently uphill through the pines.

Farther along are red markers leading to the funicular at Hrebienok, which will bring you back to the relative comforts of Starý Smokovec. However, if you're in good physical shape and there is plenty of daylight left, consider extending your hike by four hours. (The extension is striking, but avoid it during winter, when you may find yourself neck-deep in snow.) Just before the Bilíkova chata, turn right along the green path and then follow the blue, red, and then green trails in the direction of windswept **Téryho chata,** a turn-of-the-20th-century chalet perched amid five lonely alpine lakes. The scenery is a few notches above dazzling. Once you reach the chalet after two strenuous hours of hiking, backtrack to Bilíkova chata and follow the signs to the funicular at Hrebienok.

Dining and Lodging

$$ ★ ✕ **Restaurant Koliba.** This charming restaurant with rustic decor and an open-face grill serves up tasty local fare. Try *kapustová polievka* (sauerkraut soup with mushrooms and sausage). ✉ *Starý Smokovec,* ☏ *0969/4422204. No credit cards. Closed Sun.*

$$ ★ ✕🏨 **Villa Dr. Szontagh.** Away from the action in Nový Smokovec, this steepled little chalet offers mostly peace and quiet. The darkly furnished rooms and public areas are well maintained, and the courtly staff goes out of its way to please. The decent restaurant has an extensive wine cellar. ✉ *Nový Smokovec, 06201,* ☏ *0969/4422061. 9 rooms, 4 apartments, 1 suite. Restaurant, cafeteria. AE, MC, V. Closed Nov.–mid-Dec.*

$$$ ★ **Grand Hotel.** Along with its sister hotel in Tatranská Lomnica, Grandhotel Praha (☞ *below*), this hotel epitomizes Tatra luxury at its turn-of-the-20th-century best. The hotel's golden Tudor facade rises majestically over the town, with the peaks of the Tatras looming in the background. In season, skiers and hikers crowd the reception area and hallways, but the rooms themselves are quiet. Breakfast is included. ✉ *Starý Smokovec, 06201,* ☎ *0969/4422154,* FAX *0969/4422157. 79 rooms (52 with bath), 5 suites. Restaurant, bar, café, pool, sauna. AE, DC, MC, V.*

Outdoor Activities and Sports

PARAGLIDING

Local sports shops provide equipment for many sports, including paragliding and paraskiing. For information, consult the sporting-goods store **Športcentrum** (✉ Starý Smokovec V5, ☎ 0969/4422425). It's a 10-minute walk along the highway, to the east of Starý Smokovec.

SKIING

For buying or renting equipment, try the **Športcentrum** (☎ 0969/4422425) in Starý Smokovec. There's also the **Ski Service** in the Švajčiarsky Dom, next to the Grand Hotel (☞ *above*). Arrive early (it opens at 8)—the equipment rents quickly when there is snow.

Štrbské Pleso

21 *18 km (11 mi) west of Smokovec on Rte. 537.*

Štrbské Pleso is the main center in the Tatras for active sports. The best ski slopes are not far away, and many excellent hiking trails are within easy reach. The town not only has the most modern hotels (and the most jarringly modern hotel architecture), but it also commands the finest panoramas in the Tatras.

Lodging

$$$ ★ **Patria.** This modern, slanting pyramid on the shores of a mountain lake has two obvious advantages: location and views. Ask for a room on a higher floor; those overlooking the lake have balconies, and the other side opens onto the mountains. ✉ *Štrbské Pleso, 05985,* ☎ *0969/4492591,* FAX *0969/4492590. 140 rooms, 10 apartments. 3 restaurants, bar, café, pool, barbershop, convention center. AE, DC, MC, V.*

$$ **Fis.** Right next to the ski jump and within easy reach of several slopes, this hotel is for young, athletic types. It makes no pretense to elegance, preferring a busy jumble of track suits, families with young children, and teenagers on the make. The rooms, each with a balcony, are pleasant, if a little institutional. ✉ *Štrbské Pleso, 05985,* ☎ *0969/4492221,* FAX *0969/4492422. 70 rooms. 3 restaurants, pool, sauna, exercise room. AE, DC, MC, V.*

Outdoor Activities and Sports

SKIING

You can buy and rent skis and equipment at **Sport Time** (✉ At the train station, ☎ 0969/4492253). The Patria and Fis hotels (☞ *above*) rent skis; the Patria also has a ski school.

Tatranská Lomnica

22 *24 km (15 mi) northeast of Štrbské Pleso on Rte. 537.*

Tatranská Lomnica, on the eastern end of the electric rail line, offers a near-perfect combination of peace, convenience, and atmosphere. Moreover, the lift behind the Grandhotel Praha brings some of the best walks in the Tatras to within 10 minutes or so of your hotel door.

The Magistrale, a 24 km (15 mi) walking trail that skirts the peaks just above the tree line, offers some of the best views for the least amount of exertion. A particularly stunning stretch of the route—marked by red signposts—begins in Tatranská Lomnica and ends 5 km (3 mi) away in Starý Smokovec. The total walking time is three or four hours.

To start the walk, take the funicular behind the Grandhotel Praha in Tatranská Lomnica to Skalnaté Pleso—a 10-minute proposition. From here you can access the trail immediately. If you are really adventurous, consider a 30-minute detour via cable car (25 Sk) to the top of Lomnický štít (8,635 ft), the second-highest peak in the range. Because of the harsh temperatures (be sure to dress warmly even in summer), you're permitted to linger at the top for only 30 minutes, after which you take the cable car back down.

Return to the cable-car station at Skalnaté Pleso and follow the red markers of the Magistrale Trail to the right (as you stand facing Tatranská Lomnica below). The first section of the trail cuts sharply across the face of the Lomnický Peak, just above the tree line. The trail then bends through a series of small valleys, each view more outstanding than the last. Finally, you begin a small descent into the woods. Continue by following the signs to Hrebienok.

NEED A BREAK? Don't pass up the chance to take a break at the rustic **Bilíkova chata** (☎ 0969/7422439) in a little clearing just before you reach Hrebienok. This cozy cabin is a veritable oasis after the long walk. It's open 7:30 AM to 9 PM from December to March and 7 AM to 10 PM between July and mid-September.

From Hrebienok, take the funicular down to Starý Smokovec. It runs at 45-minute intervals beginning at 6:30 AM and ending at 7:45 PM, but check the schedule posted at the Bilíkova chata for any schedule changes. You can then take the train back to Tatranská Lomnica.

Dining and Lodging

$$ ✕ **Zbojnícka koliba.** This stylish cottage restaurant serves up savory shish kebab made on an open-face grill in a romantic setting, though the portions are snack-size. ✉ *Tatranská Lomnica,* ☎ *0969/4467630. No credit cards. Closed Sun. No lunch.*

$$$ ★ ✕🏨 **Grandhotel Praha.** This large, multiturret mansion, dating from the turn of the 20th century and resting in the foothills of the Lomnický štít, is one of the wonders of the Tatras. Although it is no longer filled with the rich and famous, the hotel has managed to retain an air of relaxed elegance. Rooms are large and nicely decorated—ask for a large corner room with a view of the mountains. Since the hotel is far from the action, the price remains reasonable for what's offered. ✉ *Tatranská Lomnica, 05960,* ☎ *0969/4467941,* FAX *0969/4467891. 83 rooms, 7 suites. Restaurant, sauna, aerobics, nightclub. AE, DC, MC, V.*

Outdoor Activities and Sports

SKIING

Skalnaté Pleso, above Tatranská Lomnica, has moderately challenging slopes. You can rent skis at the Metalurg and Slovan hotels.

The High Tatras A to Z

Arriving and Departing

BY BUS

Daily bus service connects Prague and Bratislava with Poprad, but trains tend to be quicker and more comfortable. From Bratislava the trip takes about 6½ hours. From Prague the journey takes 10 hours or longer, depending on the route.

BY CAR

Poprad, the gateway to the Tatras, is 328 km (205 mi) from Bratislava, with a four-lane stretch between the capital and Trenčín and a well-marked, two-lane highway thereafter; the drive takes about 4½ hours. Poprad is about 560 km (350 mi) from Prague on the main east-west highway out of the capital in the direction of Hradec Králové (the drive takes eight hours). The road is well marked, with some four-lane stretches.

BY PLANE

Slovak Airlines (☞ Getting Around by Plane *in* Slovakia A to Z, *below*) offers service from Bratislava to Košice. đFrom Košice, it's easiest to take a train to Poprad.

BY TRAIN

Regular rail service connects both Prague and Bratislava with Poprad, but book ahead: the trains are often impossibly crowded, especially in August and during the skiing season. A trip from Bratislava's Hlavná stanica to Poprad's station, **Železničná stanica Poprad** (✉ Wolkerova 496, ☎ 092/721139), takes four hours on an InterCity train. Trains leave Bratislava every two or three hours; the most convenient are often the overnight trains. The journey from Prague to Poprad takes about 10 hours; several night trains depart from Prague's Hlavní nádraží (main station) and Holešovice station.

Getting Around

BY BUS

The SAD bus network (☞ Getting Around by Bus *in* Slovakia A to Z, *below*) links all the towns in the High Tatras, but unless you are traveling to a town not directly on an electric rail route, the train service is faster, and often a little bit cheaper.

BY CAR

Having a car is more of a hindrance than a help if you're just going to the High Tatras. Traveling the electric railway is much quicker than taking the winding roads that connect the resorts, and hotel parking fees can add up quickly. However, if you plan to tour the region's smaller towns and villages, or if you are continuing on to eastern Slovakia, a car will prove nearly indispensable.

BY TRAIN

An efficient electric railway (which shares the regular train stations) connects Poprad with the High Tatras resorts, and the resorts with one another. Trains run every 30 to 60 minutes. If you understand Slovak, you can call for **schedule information** (☎ 092/721139). If you're going only to the Tatras, you won't need any other form of transportation.

Contacts and Resources

EMERGENCIES

Police (☎ 158). **Medical emergencies** (☎ 155). **Car repair** (☎ 0969/4422571).

GUIDED TOURS

TLS Air offers a biplane flight from Poprad airport over the Tatras region; for details contact the Satur office in Poprad (☞ Visitor Information, *below*). The Satur office in Starý Smokovec (☞ Visitor Information, *below*) is also helpful in arranging tours of the Tatras and surrounding area. đFrom May to October, Satur offers a bargain tour of Levoča, Kežmarok, and Markušovce for groups of eight or more, with English and German commentary.

VISITOR INFORMATION

There's a tourist information center in each resort town: **Starý Smokovec** (✉ Dom Služieb [House of Services], ☎ 0969/4423440); **Štrbské Pleso** (✉ Hotel Toliar, ☎ 0969/4492391); **Tatranská Lomnica** (✉ Múzeum, ☎ 0969/4467951). **Slovakoturist** (☎ 0969/4422031), in Horný Smokovec, can arrange private accommodations, including stays in mountain cottages.

At the Satur offices in **Poprad** (✉ Námestie sv. Egídia 3006/116, ☎ 092/7721353, FAX 092/63619) and **Starý Smokovec** (☎ 0969/4422710) you can change money, get hiking and driving maps, and book hotel (but not private) rooms.

For more in-depth information on routes, mountain chalets, and weather conditions, contact the **Horská služba** (Mountain Rescue Service; ☎ 0969/4422820) in Starý Smokovec. **Asociácia horských vodcov** (Mountain Guides Association; ☎ 0969/4422066) provides guides for the more difficult routes for 2,500 Sk–4,000 Sk per day.

CENTRAL SLOVAKIA

Though generally overlooked by tourists, central Slovakia is the country's heart and soul. This is where the nation was born and where Slovak folklore and deep-rooted traditions continue to flourish.

Formerly a medieval mining town, Banská Bystrica lies at the heart of the region and is the ideal base from which to explore the towns and villages surrounding it. The region's two other historical mining towns, Banská Štiavnica and Kremnica, have remained more or less frozen in time since their glory days in the Middle Ages.

The beauty of central Slovakia, however, lies not so much in its architecture as in its inspiring natural landscapes. The region is home to both the High Tatras (☞ *above*) and the Low Tatras, the second-highest mountain range in Slovakia and the largest by area. In the Low Tatras in winter, you'll find ski slopes comparable to those of the High Tatras—and they'll be mostly free from the hordes of tourists that overrun their higher counterparts. In summer, the area offers wonderful hiking trails, caves, and scenic valleys.

Unfortunately, in central Slovakia you will also find some of the worst crimes against nature. In an effort to enrich the region in the 1950s, the Communist regime built many large steel- and tank-producing factories, which litter some of the most beautiful valleys in the country. Many of the worst can be seen while heading east from Banská Bystrica in the direction of Brezno. To call them eyesores would be an understatement.

Numbers in the margin correspond to numbers on the Slovakia map.

Banská Bystrica

23 *205 km (128 mi) northeast of Bratislava on Hwys. D61 and E571 and Rte. 66.*

Surrounded by three mountain ranges—the Low Tatras, the Fatras, and the Slovak rudohorie—Banská Bystrica is an ideal starting point for exploring the beauty of the region. (The outlying areas are plagued with concrete apartment buildings; you should focus instead on the surrounding woods and hills.)

Banská Bystrica has been around since the 13th century, acquiring wealth from the nearby mines. Following the Tartar invasion in 1241, the Hungarian king Béla IV granted special privileges to encourage the immigration of German settlers, who together with the natives developed the prosperous mining of copper and precious metals. During the 19th century, the town was a major focus of Slovak national life, and it was from a school here that the teaching of the Slovak language originated and spread to the rest of the country.

The city is also famous as the center of the Slovak National Uprising during World War II. It was here that the underground Slovak National Council initiated the revolt on August 29, 1944. For some two months, thousands of Slovaks valiantly rose up against the Slovak puppet regime and their Nazi oppressors, forcing the Germans to divert critically needed troops and equipment from the front lines. Though the Germans quashed the uprising on October 27, the costly operation is credited with accelerating the Allied victory and gaining Slovakia the short-lived appellation of ally.

You'll find reminders of the uprising (known in Slovak by the initials SNP) just about everywhere. One of the main sights is the **Múzeum Slovenského národného povstania** (Museum of the Slovak National Uprising), which stands in a large field just outside the center of town, between Horná ulica and Ulica Dukelských hrdinov. It's difficult to miss the monument's massive concrete wings—the effect is particularly striking at night. The museum's focus has been shifting from Communism to more recent national events. ✉ *Kapitulská 23,* ☎ *088/4123258.* 🎫 *10 Sk.* ⏲ *May–Sept., Tues.–Sun. 9–6; Oct.–Apr., Tues.–Sun. 9–4.*

If you're partial to less recent history, head for the main square, Námestie SNP, with its cheery collection of Renaissance and Baroque houses. The most impressive is the **Thurzo House,** an amalgamation of two late-Gothic structures built in 1495 by the wealthy Thurzo family. The genuine Renaissance sgraffiti decorations on the outside were added during the 16th century, when the family's wealth was at its height. Today the building houses the **Stredoslovenské múzeum** (Central Slovak Museum), which is more interesting for the chance to see inside the house than for its artifacts. ✉ *Nám. SNP 4,* ☎ *088/4155077.* 🎫 *10 Sk.* ⏲ *Weekdays 8–noon and 1–4, Sun. 9–noon and 1–4 (mid-June–mid-Sept. until 5).*

Dining and Lodging

$$ ★ ✕ **Starobystrická pivnica.** Grilled food is the house specialty at this classic wine cellar, which serves spicy versions of Slovak cuisine—such as the spicy pepper steak. ✉ *Nám. SNP 9,* ☎ *088/4154326. MC, V.*

$$$ ★ ✕🏨 **Arcade Hotel.** This 16th-century building on the main square is an ideal place to stay. The rooms and apartments vary in size, comfort, and cost, but each is equipped with the basic creature comforts, including a refrigerator and satellite TV. ✉ *Nám. SNP 5, 97401,* ☎ *088/4102111,* FAX *088/4123126. 9 rooms, 2 suites, 3 apartments. Restaurant, bar, café, dance club, meeting room. AE, DC, MC, V.*

$$ 🏨 **Lux.** This is one of the few successful high-rise hotels in Slovakia, combining modernity with some semblance of style. Rooms (especially on the upper floors facing town) have a magnificent view over the mountains. ✉ *Nám. Slobody 2, 97401,* ☎ *088/4402314,* FAX *088/4143853. 112 rooms, 1 suite, 7 apartments. Restaurant, bar, café. MC, V.*

Outdoor Activities and Sports

The most attractive hiking trails are to the north of Banská Bystrica and in the area between Banská Bystrica and Kremnica. A hiking map of the Low Tatras that includes routes for cyclists is available at the tourist information center (☞ Visitor Information *in* Central Slovakia A to Z, *below*). You can rent bikes at a mountain hotel named **Šachtička** in the Špania dolina (Špania Valley), 10 km (6 mi.) from Banská Bystrica.

En Route South of Banská Bystrica in the direction of Zvolen is the tiny village of Hronsek. This hamlet warrants a stop—it has a wooden church built without a single piece of metal. Right down to the nails, the builders of this Protestant church, constructed at the time of the Counter-Reformation, abided by strict guidelines stipulating that wood was the only material to be used for assembling a church.

Kremnica

24 *56 km (35 mi) southwest of Banská Bystrica on Rte. 65.*

Kremnica, known as the Golden City, was one of the most famous mining towns in Slovakia and one of the richest gold mines in medieval Europe. What you'll find today is a beautifully preserved medieval town, surrounded by sturdy walls and gates that guarded the gold once stored in Kremnica's vaults. You can enter the town through the impressive **Dolná brána** (Lower Gate), dating from 1441. Beyond, you'll see some of the best-kept merchant houses in Slovakia.

You can learn about the town's 650-year history as a mining and minting center at the **Kremnické múzeum** (Kremnica Museum). For coin enthusiasts, the second floor has fascinating exhibits of coins in use in Central Europe from Celtic and Roman times to the modern day. English commentary is available. ✉ *Štefánikovo nám. 10,* ☎ *0857/6742121.* 🎟 *16 Sk.* ⏲ *Oct.–Apr., Tues.–Sat. 8:30–4:30; May–Sept., Tues.–Sun. 9–5.*

Dining

$ ✕ **Jeleň.** For a delicious lunch or dinner, try this unassuming restaurant in the new part of town, outside the walls. Start out with the delicious lentil soup, and then try the roast beef with paprika sauce and dumplings. ✉ *Dolná ul. 22,* ☎ *0857/6744105. No credit cards.*

Banská Štiavnica

25 *44 km (27 mi) south of Kremnica on Rte. 65, Hwy. E571, and Rte. 525.*

Since the 11th century, this little town has earned its wealth from mining, and today it is essentially one large mining museum. German miners arrived here to exploit rich gold and silver deposits, and their success is apparent in some of the town's remaining monuments, such as the golden Trinity column and the impressive Lutheran church.

Built on the rocks above town, the **Starý zámok** (Old Castle) dates back to the early 13th century (with additions in practically every subsequent building style). It served as a fortress to protect the wealth of the local bigwigs against the Turkish invaders. ✉ *Starozámocká 11,* ☎ *0859/6911543.* 🎟 *15 Sk.* ⏲ *Tues.–Sun. 9–4.*

The **Nový zámok** (New Castle) was built between 1564 and 1571 as part of an effort to strengthen fortification of the town against invasions of the Turks. The six-story Renaissance building was used as a watchtower and later became the town's live clock—the time was announced every quarter hour by a trumpet. Inside you'll find historical exhibits of the Turkish invasions during the 16th and 17th centuries. ✉ *Novozámocká 22,* ☎ *0859/21543.* 🎟 *20 Sk.* ⏲ *May–Sept., Tues.–Sun. 8–4; Oct.–Apr., weekdays 8–3.*

You can view some of the town's original mining buildings and machinery dating back to the early 13th century at the **Banské múzeum** (Open Air Mining Museum). The museum is about 2 km (1 mi) from town. ✉ *Štiavnické bane,* ☎ *0859/6911541.* 🎟 *20 Sk.* ⏲ *July–Aug., Tues.–Sun. 9–5; Sept.–June, weekdays 8–3.*

OFF THE BEATEN PATH

MANSION SAINT ANTON – Don't miss this charming late-Baroque château in the small village of Antol, just outside Banská Štiavnica. The château displays its original furnishings and has an exhibition of hunting arms and game. ✉ *Svätý Anton,* ☎ *0859/6913932.* *50 Sk.* ⏲ *May–Sept., Tues.–Sun. 8–4; Oct.–Apr., Tues.–Sat. 8–3.*

Dining and Lodging

$$ ★ ✕ **Salamander.** This new hotel, in a beautifully renovated 16th-century building, has everything you would expect from a first-class establishment. The rooms are large and bright, and the public areas are decorated with antiques. ✉ *J. Palárika 1, 96901,* ☎ *0859/6913992,* FAX *0859/6921262. Restaurant, ice cream parlor, outdoor café. AE, DC, MC, V.*

$ ✕ **Antolský mlyn.** This family-run pension is in a tiny village just outside Banská Štiavnica near the château at Antol. Though small, the rooms are modern and have new, clean bathrooms. ✉ *Svätý Anton, 96972,* ☎ *0859/6931311. 7 rooms with shower, 1 apartment. Restaurant. No credit cards.*

Central Slovakia A to Z

Arriving and Departing

BY CAR

It's most convenient to get to Banská Bystrica by car. From Bratislava, take the D61 and E571 to Zvolen via Nitra, and then follow the 66 to Banská Bystrica; the trip should take roughly 2½ hours. Driving from either Vienna or Prague takes about four hours. The E58 leads from Vienna to Bratislava. From Prague, take the 65 to Brno, then the E50 to Zvolen, and continue on the 66 to Banská Bystrica.

BY TRAIN

Unless you have a car, the best way to get to Banská Bystrica is by rail. There are daily trains from Bratislava; the journey takes almost three hours. The trip from Košice to Banská Bystrica, one of the most scenic railway routes in the country (take the northern, not the southern, route), lasts about five hours.

Getting Around

BY BUS AND TRAIN

For those without a car, Banská Bystrica is the most convenient base, since it serves as a hub for the complex rail and bus system.

BY CAR

Driving through this region is relatively quick and hassle-free. The drive between Banská Bystrica and Kremnica along Route 65, for instance, can be done in under an hour. In some cases, such as the drive to Banská Štiavnica, the roads are narrow but well marked.

Contacts and Resources

EMERGENCIES

Police (☎ 158). **Ambulance** (☎ 155).

GUIDED TOURS

The **Satur** office in Banská Bystrica (✉ Nám. Slobody 4, ☎ 088/4142575) can book hotels and arrange English-language tours at a reasonable cost.

VISITOR INFORMATION

Banská Bystrica (✉ Nám. Štefana Moyzesa 26, ☎ 088/186). **Banská Štiavnica** (✉ Radničné nám. 1, ☎ 0859/6911859). **Kremnica** (✉ Štefánikovo nám. 35/44, ☎ 0857/6742856).

EASTERN SLOVAKIA

To the east of the High Tatras lies an expanse of Slovakia that seldom appears on tourist itineraries. However, eastern Slovakia is a veritable hiker's paradise. In addition to the offerings at Slovenský raj, trails fan out in all directions in the area known as Spišská Magura, to the north and east of Kežmarok. Good outdoor swimming can be found in the lakes in Slovenský raj and in Michalovce, east of Košice.

For 1,000 years, eastern Slovakia was isolated from the West; much of the region was regarded simply as the hinterland of Greater Hungary. Isolation has its advantages, however, and therein may lie the charm of this area. The Baroque and Renaissance facades that dominate the towns of Bohemia and Moravia make an appearance in eastern Slovakia as well, but they're often done in local wood instead of stone. Look especially for the wooden altars in Levoča and other towns.

The relative isolation also fostered the development of an entire civilization in medieval times, the Spiš, with no counterpart in the Czech Republic or elsewhere in Slovakia. The territory of the kingdom, which spreads out to the east and south of the High Tatras, was originally settled by Slavonic and later by German immigrants who came here in medieval times to work the mines and defend the western kingdoms against invasion. Some 24 towns eventually came to join the Spiš group, functioning as a miniprincipality within the Hungarian monarchy. The group had its own hierarchies and laws, which were quite different from those brought in by Magyar or Saxon settlers.

Although the last Spiš town lost its independence 100 years ago, much of the group's architectural legacy remains—another fortuitous by-product of isolation and economic stagnation. Spiš towns are predominantly Gothic beneath their graceful Renaissance overlays. Their steep shingle roofs, high timber-frame gables, and brick-arch doorways have survived in a remarkable state of preservation. Spiš towns are worth seeking out when you see them on a map—look for the prefix *Spišsky* preceding a town name.

Farther to the northeast, the influences of Byzantium are strongly felt, most noticeably in the form of the simple wooden churches that dominate the villages along the frontier with Poland and Ukraine. This area marks a border in Europe that has stood for a thousand years: the ancient line between Rome and Constantinople, between Western Christianity and the Byzantine Empire. The busy industrial cities of Prešov and Košice, with their belching factories and rows of housing projects, quickly bring you back to the 20th century.

When visiting the region, keep in mind that more expensive does not necessarily mean better when it comes to food. Stay clear of the large hotels and instead look to innovative, privately owned restaurants. Eastern Slovakia has successfully borrowed the best dishes and techniques from the Hungarians, the Ukrainians, and the Poles to create an original and delicious cuisine.

Numbers in the margin correspond to numbers on the Slovakia map.

Bardejov

26 *101 km (65 mi) east of Poprad on Rtes. 68 and 77.*

Bardejov is a great surprise, tucked away in this remote corner of Slovakia yet possessing one of the nation's most enchanting squares. Indeed, Bardejov owes its splendors precisely to its location astride the ancient trade routes to Poland and Russia. It's hard to put your finger on exactly why the square is so captivating—it could be the lack of arcades in front of the houses or the pointed roofs of the houses, which have a lighter, almost comic effect.

The exterior of the Gothic **Kostol svätého Egídia** (St. Egidius Church), built in stages in the 15th century, is undeniably handsome, but take a walk inside for the real treasure. The nave is lined with 11 priceless, purely Gothic side altars, all carved between 1460 and 1510 and perfectly preserved. The most famous of the altars is to the left of the main altar (look for the number 1 on the side). This intricate work of Stefan Tarner depicts the birth of Christ and dates from the 1480s. ✉ *Radničné nám.*

The modest building with late-Gothic portals and Renaissance detailing in the center of the town square is the **radnica** (town hall). ✉ *Radničné nám. 17.*

★ You may want to visit the pink **Šariš** (Icon Museum) to view its collection of 16th-century icons and paintings, taken from the area's numerous Russian Orthodox churches. Many of the icons depict the story of St. George slaying the dragon (for the key to the princess's chastity belt!). The legend of St. George, which probably originated in pre-Christian mythology, was often used to attract the peasants of the area to the more abstemious myths of Christianity. Pick up the short but interesting commentary in English when you buy your ticket. ✉ *Radničné nám. 13,* ☎ *0935/4746038.* *25 Sk.* ⊙ *May–Sept., Tues.–Sun. 9–noon and 12:30–5:30; Oct.–Apr., Tues.–Sun. 8–noon and 12:30–4.*

Lodging

$$ **Športhotel.** This rectangular building with a gray facade sits on the Topla river bank, among tennis and volleyball playgrounds, just seven minutes from Bardejov's beautiful main square. ✉ *Kutuzovova 34, 08501,* ☎ *0935/4724949,* FAX *0935/4728208. 20 rooms with showers. Restaurant. No credit cards.*

Jedlinka

27 *13 km (8 mi) north of Bardejov along the road to Svidník.*

This area's great delights are unquestionably the old wooden churches still in use in their original village settings. Like most others, the one in Jedlinka dates from the 18th and 19th centuries and combines Byzantine and Baroque architectural elements. Its three onion-dome towers rise above the west front. Inside, the north, east, and south walls are painted with biblical scenes; the west wall was reserved for icons (many of which now hang in the Icon Museum in Bardejov). The churches are usually locked, but if you happen across a villager, ask him or her (with appropriate key-turning gestures) to let you in. More often than not, someone will turn up with a key, and you'll have your own guided tour.

Medzilaborce

28 *77 km (48 mi) east of Bardejov on Rtes. 77 and 73.*

The sleepy border town of Medzilaborce is quickly becoming the unlikely mecca for fans of pop-art guru Andy Warhol. It was here in 1991, near the birthplace of Warhol's parents, that the country's cultural authorities, in conjunction with the Andy Warhol Foundation for Visual ★ Arts in New York, opened the **Múzeum moderného umenia rodiny Warholovcov** (Warhol Family Museum of Modern Art). In all, the museum holds 17 original Warhol silk screens, including two from the famous Campbell's Soup series, and portraits of Lenin and singer Billie Holiday. The Russian Orthodox church across the street lends a suitably surreal element to the setting. ✉ *Ul. Andyho Warhola 749/26,* ☎ *0939/21059.* 🎫 *50 Sk.* ⏲ *May–Sept., Tues.–Sun. 10–6; Oct.–Apr., Tues.–Sun. 9–4.*

Košice

㉙ *402 km (250 mi) east of Bratislava on Hwys. D61 and E571.*

In Košice you'll leave rural Slovakia behind. Though rich historically, Košice is a sprawling, modern city, the second largest in Slovakia after Bratislava. Positioned along the main trade route between Hungary and Poland, the city was the second largest in the Hungarian Empire (after Buda) during the Middle Ages. With the Turkish occupation of the Hungarian homeland during the 16th and 17th centuries, the town became a safe haven for the Hungarian nobility.

In this century the city has been shuttled between Hungary, Czechoslovakia, and now Slovakia. Sadly, Slovak efforts to eliminate Hungarian influence in Košice after World War II were remarkably successful. As you walk around, you'll be hard-pressed to find evidence that this was once a great Hungarian city—even with the Hungarian frontier just 20 km (12 mi) away. The city remains home to a popular Hungarian theater, as well as a successful Romany (Gypsy) theater, the only one of its kind in the world.

You won't see many Westerners strolling Košice's enormous medieval square, Hlavná ulica; most of the tourists here are Hungarians on a day trip to shop and sightsee. The town square is dominated on its southern flank by the huge tower of the Gothic **Dóm svätej Alžbety** (Cathedral of St. Elizabeth). Built in the 15th century and finally completed in 1508, the cathedral is the largest in Slovakia. Walk over to the north side (facing the square) to look at the famed Golden Door. Inside the church is one of Europe's largest Gothic altarpieces, a 35-ft-tall medieval wood carving attributed to the master Erhard of Ulm. You can also pay a visit to the great Hungarian leader Francis Rákoczi II, most of whose remains (he left his heart in Paris) were placed in a crypt under the north transept of the cathedral. Although generally open to worshipers, the church is under renovation, and you may not be able to wander at will. ✉ *Hlavná ul.* ⏲ *Daily services at 7 PM.*

★

On the east side of the town square is the **Dom Košického vládneho programu** (House of the Košice Government Program), where the Košice Program was proclaimed on April 5, 1945, announcing the reunion of the Czech lands and Slovakia into one national state. ✉ *Hlavná ul.*

The **Štátne divadlo** (State Theater), a mishmash of neo-Renaissance and neo-Baroque elements built at the end of the last century, dominates the center of the town square. For a town this size, the quality of theater, ballet, and opera productions is very impressive. Tickets are reasonably priced and can be bought at the theater box office. ✉ *Hlavná. 58,* ☎ *095/6221231.* ⏲ *Weekdays 9–5:30, and 1 hr before performances.*

On the main street between the theater and the cathedral is the **Hudobná fontána** (Music Fountain). Water from this elaborate fountain springs in harmony with music (generally classical), accompanied by colored lights. It's worth a visit in the evening just to see all the pairs of lovers huddled around it. ✉ *Hlavná ul.*

NEED A BREAK? To feel like you've really stepped into turn-of-the-20th-century Vienna, have a cup of coffee and dessert in the elegant Art Nouveau confines of the **Café Slávia** (✉ Hlavná 63, ☎ 095/6233190).

The **Miklušova väznica** (Nicholas Prison), an old Gothic building used as a prison and torture chamber until 1909, now houses a museum with exhibits on Košice's history. You can even visit the underground premises of the former torture chamber to see replicas of the torture instruments. ✉ *Pri Miklušovej väznici 10,* ☎ *095/6222856.* *20 Sk.* ⏲ *Tues.–Sat. 9–5, Sun. 9–1.*

OFF THE BEATEN PATH

KRÁSNA HÔRKA – Sitting on top of a hill, this fairy-tale castle can be seen from miles around. It is one of the best-preserved fortifications from the Middle Ages in Slovakia. The museum houses a valuable collection of paintings and a wide assortment of furniture and weapons from the 15th through 17th centuries. To get here, head west on E571 in the direction of Rožňava and turn right at Krásnohorské Podhradie, from where you can follow signs up to the castle; it takes about an hour from Košice. ✉ *Krásnohorské Podhradie.* ⏲ *Tues.–Sun. 8–5:30.*

Dining and Lodging

$ ★ ✕ **Sedliacky dvor.** This tiny restaurant, decorated as an old country cottage complete with wooden tables, a pitchfork, and a picket fence, serves mouthwatering local specialties. You'll receive an enormous plate piled high with various meats and either rice, mushrooms, and cheese or dumplings and red and white cabbage. ✉ *Biela 3,* ☎ *095/6220402. No credit cards.*

$$$ ★ ✕ **Penzión pri Radnici.** This small pension is ideal for business travelers—modern apartments come with studies and fax machines. The upstairs restaurant is a bit upscale. If you want a quick lunch, try the buffet downstairs, which serves tasty local food at dirt-cheap prices. ✉ *Bačikova 18, 04001,* ☎ *095/6228601,* FAX *095/6227824. 1 suite, 2 apartments. Restaurant, beer garden, café, cafeteria. AE, MC, V.*

$$$ ★ **Hotel Cobra.** This hotel is a breath of fresh air when compared to the concrete-block hotels that still plague much of Slovakia. The rooms are bright and the bathrooms pleasant. The hotel is a few minutes' walk outside the city center in a quiet residential area. ✉ *Jiskrova 3, 04001,* ☎ *095/622903,* FAX *095/6225918. 10 rooms, 3 apartments. Restaurant, bar, beer garden. AE, DC, MC, V.*

Nightlife

If you're looking for a lively evening, **Jazz Club** (✉ Kováčska 39, ☎ 095/6230467), a cozy basement bar, is a popular local hangout. The name is a bit misleading though, as the club has not only live and taped jazz music but disco, country, and rap music as well.

Levoča

★ 30 *90 km (56 mi) northwest of Košice on Hwy. E50, 358 km (224 mi) northeast of Bratislava on Hwys. D61 and E50.*

You'll enter Levoča, the center of the Spiš kingdom and the quintessential Spiš town, through the medieval Košice Gate. This medieval capital of the Spiš region was founded around 1245 and flourished between the 14th and 17th centuries, when it was an important trade center for art and crafts.

The main sights in the town are lined along and in the middle of the main square, **Námestie majstra Pavla.** Take a closer look at the sgraffiti-decorated house at No. 7, **Thurzov dom**, named for the powerful mining family. The wonderfully ornate gables are from the 17th century, though the sgraffiti decorations were added in the 19th century. (It is open to the public.) At the top of the square at No. 60 is the **Malý župný dom** (Small County House), the former administrative center of the Spiš region, now used as an archive. Above the doorway is the coat of arms of the Spiš alliance. The monumental classical building next door, the **Veľký župný dom** (Large County House), was built in the early 19th century by Anton Povolný, who was also responsible for the Evangelical Church at the bottom of the square. A local government office is now seated on the second and third floors.

★ The most impressive sight in town is the **Kostol svätého Jakuba** (St. Jacob's Church), a huge Gothic structure begun in the early 14th century but not completed until a century later. The interior is a breathtaking concentration of Gothic religious art. It was here in the early 16th century that the greatest Spiš artist, Pavol of Levoča, created his most unforgettable pieces. The carved-wood high altar, said to be the world's largest and incorporating a truly magnificent carving of the Last Supper in limewood, is his most famous work. The 12 disciples are in fact portraits of Levoča merchants. For 2 Sk, a tape recording in an iron post at the back of the church gives you detailed information in English. ✉ *Nám. majstra Pavla.* 🎫 *20 Sk.* ⏲ *Tues.–Sun. 8:30–4.*

The **Mestská radnica** (town hall), with its fine whitewashed Renaissance arcades, gables, and clock tower, was built in 1551 after the great fire of 1550 destroyed the old Gothic building along with much of the town. The clock tower now houses an excellent museum, with exhibits of guild flags and a collection of paintings and wood carvings. Here you can also look at the 18th-century Lady in White, painted on a doorway through which, as legend has it, she let in the enemy for a promise of wealth and a title. For this act of treason, the 24-year-old beauty's head was chopped off. ✉ *Nám. majstra Pavla,* ☎ *0966/4512449.* 🎫 *20 Sk.* ⏲ *Tues.–Sun. 9–11:30, noon–5.*

OFF THE BEATEN PATH

SPIŠSKÝ HRAD (Spiš Castle) – A former administrative center of the kingdom, this is the largest castle in Slovakia (and one of the largest in Europe). Spiš overlords occupied this site starting in 1209. The museum has a good collection of torture devices, and the castle has a beautiful view of the surrounding hills and town. From Levoča, it's worth taking the short 16 km (10 mi) detour east along Route 18 to this magnificent spot. ✉ *Spišský hrad,* ☎ *0966/4512786.* 🎫 *30 Sk.* ⏲ *May and Sept.–Oct., Tues.–Sun. 9–6; June–Aug., daily 9–6.*

Dining and Lodging

$ ✕ **U Janusa.** This family-owned restaurant is the perfect place to get a taste of Slovak culture as well as cuisine. Try one of the local specialties, such as homemade sausage or dumplings with goat cheese. ✉ *Kláštorská 22,* ☎ *0966/4514592. No credit cards.*

$$ ★ ✕🏨 **Arkada Hotel.** The large, bright rooms and historic ambience make this one of the few near-perfect hotels in the country. It is housed in a 13th-century building that in the 17th century became the first printing shop in the Austro-Hungarian Empire. ✉ *Nám. majstra Pavla 26, 05401,* ☎ FAX *0966/4512255. 23 rooms, 3 apartments. Restaurant, café. AE, MC, V.*

$$$ ★ 🏨 **Hotel Satel.** Levoča should win an award for having two of the best hotels in the country. This beautiful 18th-century mansion is built around a courtyard. The rooms are large and bright, though some of the furniture, especially the peach-color sofa chairs, is a bit gaudy. ✉ *Nám. majstra Pavla 55, 05401,* ☎ *0966/4512943,* FAX *0966/4514486. 21 rooms, 2 suites. Restaurant, bar. AE, DC, MC, V.*

En Route From Levoča, head south on Route 533 through Spišská Nová Ves, continuing along the twisting roads to the junction with Route 535. Turn right onto Route 535, following the signs to Mlynky and beyond, through the tiny villages and breathtaking countryside of the national park known as **Slovenský raj** (Slovak Paradise). It is a wild and romantic area of cliffs and gorges, caves and waterfalls, perfect for adventurous hikers. The gorges are accessible by narrow but secure iron ladders. The main tourist centers are Čingov in the north and Dedinky in the south.

Eastern Slovakia A to Z

Arriving and Departing

BY BUS

Daily bus service connects Prague and Bratislava with Košice, but trains tend to be quicker and more comfortable, if a bit more expensive. (InterCity trains have air-conditioning, while buses do not.) The ride from Bratislava takes about five hours. From Prague, the trip lasts about nine hours.

BY CAR

Poprad, a good starting point for a tour of eastern Slovakia, lies on Slovakia's main east-west highway about 560 km (350 mi) from Prague in the direction of Hradec Králové. The seven- to eight-hour drive from Prague can be broken up easily with an overnight in Olomouc. The drive from Bratislava to Poprad is 328 km (205 mi), with a four-lane stretch from Bratislava to Trenčín and a well-marked two-lane highway thereafter. The drive from Bratislava to Košice takes roughly seven hours; it's best to take the E571 via Nitra, Zvolen, and Rožňava.

BY PLANE

Slovak Airlines (☞ Getting Around by Plane *in* Slovakia A to Z, *below*) offers regular flights from Bratislava to Košice at reasonable prices.

BY TRAIN

Trains regularly connect Košice with Prague (12 hours) and Bratislava (6 hours), but book in advance to ensure a seat on these sometimes crowded routes. Several night trains make the run between Košice and Prague's main stations, Hlavní nádraží and Holešovice.

Getting Around

BY BUS

Most of the region is reachable via the extensive SAD bus network (☞ Getting Around by Bus *in* Slovakia A to Z, *below*). The only exceptions are some of the smaller towns in northeastern Slovakia. Most buses run only on weekdays. Plan carefully or you may get stuck in a small town that is ill equipped for visitors.

BY CAR

A car is essential for reaching some of the smaller towns, such as Medzilaborce, Ladomirová, and Dukelský priesmyk. Roads are of variable quality, but some stretches give you beautiful panoramas, such as Route 547 between Košice and Levoča. Try to avoid driving at night, as routes are not well marked. A good four-lane highway, the E85, links Prešov with Košice.

BY TRAIN

Regular trains link Poprad with the Košice station, **Železničná stanica Košice** (✉ Železničná 1, ☏ 095/6223700), and some of the other larger towns, but you'll have to resort to the bus to reach smaller villages. Train stations tend to be in the town centers.

Contacts and Resources

EMERGENCIES

Police (☏ 158). **Ambulance** (☏ 155). **Pharmacies** (*lekárne*) in larger towns take turns staying open late and on Sunday. Look for the list posted on the front door of each pharmacy. For after-hours service, ring the bell; you will be served through a little hatch door.

TRAVEL AGENCIES

The **Satur** offices in eastern Slovakia are the best—and sometimes the only—places to get basic assistance and information. They offer tours of the region and can book you a room at one of their hotels. **Kežmarok** (✉ Hlavné nám. 64, ☎ 0968/4523121); **Košice** (✉ Hlavná 1, ☎ 095/6223122 or 095/6223847); **Prešov** (✉ Hlavná 1, ☎ 091/7724041).

VISITOR INFORMATION

The following towns have tourist offices: **Bardejov** (✉ Radničné nám. 21, ☎ 0935/16186); **Kežmarok** (✉ Hlavné nám. 46, ☎ 0968/4047); **Košice** (✉ Hlavná 8, ☎ 095/16186); **Levoča** (✉ Nám. majstra Pavla 58, ☎ 0966/4513763 or 0966/16186); **Prešov** (✉ Hlavná 67, ☎ 091/16186).

SLOVAKIA A TO Z

Arriving and Departing

By Boat

Hydrofoils travel the Danube between Vienna and Bratislava and Budapest and Bratislava from May to September. Boats depart in the morning from Bratislava, on the eastern bank of the Danube at the intersection of Mostová and Vajanského nábrežie, and return from Vienna or Budapest in the evening. Tickets cost $40–$80 per person and should be purchased in person at the dock. For reservations call **Slovenská plavba dunajská** (Slovak Danube Cruise; ☎ 07/52963522 or 07/52932226).

By Bus

There is no direct bus service from the United Kingdom to Slovakia; the closest you can get is Vienna. **National Express** (✉ Coach Travel Center, 13 Lower Regent St., London SW1Y 4LR, ☎ 0171/833–4472) operates daily in summer.

By Car

For highway and driving time information between Prague and Bratislava, Budapest and Bratislava, and Vienna and Bratislava, *see* Arriving and Departing by Car *in* Bratislava A to Z, *above*.

By Plane

The best airports for traveling to Slovakia are Prague's Ruzyně Airport and Vienna's Schwechat Airport. The Czech national carrier, **ČSA** (☎ 212/765–6545 in the U.S.), offers regular service to Prague from Newark and Montréal. These flights generally have direct connections from Prague to Bratislava ($60–$75 each way) that take about an hour. Vienna's Schwechat Airport is a mere 60 km (37 mi) west of Bratislava. Eight buses a day stop at Schwechat en route to Bratislava; the journey takes just over an hour. Numerous trains and buses also run daily between Vienna and Bratislava. From Zurich, you can take a Slovak Airlines flight to Bratislava that takes about two hours.

From New York, a flight to Bratislava (with a stopover in Prague) takes 11–12 hours. From Montréal it is 8½ hours; from Los Angeles, 17 hours.

British Airways (☎ 0181/759–5511 in the U.K.) has daily nonstop service to Prague from London. **ČSA** (☎ 0171/255–1898 in the U.K.) flies twice daily nonstop from London. Numerous airlines offer service between London and Vienna.

By Train

Bratislava is the country's largest international train hub. There are no direct trains from London. You can take a direct train from Paris via

Frankfurt to Vienna (and connect to another train or bus), or from Berlin via Dresden and Prague (en route to Budapest). Vienna is a good starting point for Bratislava. There are several trains that make the 70-minute run daily from Vienna's Südbahnhof (South Station).

Getting Around

By Bicycle

A special bike trail links Bratislava and Vienna, paralleling the Danube for much of its 40 km (25 mi) length. For the more adventurous bikers, the Low Tatras (Nízke Tatry) have scenic biking trails. Unfortunately, not many places rent bikes. For rental information, inquire at a tourist information center or at your hotel.

By Bus

SAD (Slovenská autobusová doprava; ☎ 0984/222222 or 0984/333333), the national bus carrier for Slovakia, maintains a comprehensive network in Slovakia. Buses are usually much quicker than the normal trains and more frequent than express trains, though prices are comparable with train fares. Buy your tickets (*cestovné lístky*) from the ticket window at the bus station or directly from the driver on the bus. Long-distance buses can be full, so you might want to book a seat in advance; any Satur office will help you do this. The only drawback to traveling by bus is figuring out the timetables. They are easy to road, but beware of the small letters denoting exceptions to the times given.

By Car

PARKING

Downtown parking lots are limited in all major cities, particularly Bratislava; the fees vary. In larger cities, you should get a parking card (*parkovacia karta*) for street parking. The cards are available at newspaper kiosks and cost 5 Sk for an hour's parking time.

ROAD CONDITIONS

Slovakia has few multilane highways, but the secondary road network is in reasonably good shape, and traffic is usually light. Roads are poorly marked, however, so an essential purchase is the *Autoatlas SR*, which is inexpensive and available at bookstores throughout Slovakia.

RULES OF THE ROAD

Slovakia follows the usual Continental rules of the road. A right turn on red is permitted only when indicated by a green arrow. Signposts with yellow diamonds indicate a main road where drivers have the right of way. The speed limit is 130 kph (80 mph) on four-lane highways, 90 kph (55 mph) on open roads, and 60 kph (37 mph) in built-up areas. The fine for speeding is roughly 300 Sk, payable on the spot. To use the highways you'll need a special label (*diaľničná známka*) to display on your car window. Labels cost between 200 Sk and 1,000 Sk, depending on the size of the vehicle. They're available at post offices or gas stations; if you rent a car, the label should be provided. Seat belts are compulsory, and drinking before driving is prohibited.

To report an accident call the **emergency number** (☎ 155 for ambulance; 158 for police). In case of car failure, call the **rescue service** (☎ 154).

By Plane

Slovak Airlines (☎ 07/48575170 in Bratislava) maintains air service within Slovakia, linking Bratislava with Košice. Reservations can be made through the Bratislava office.

By Train

Slovakia's state-run rail system, **Železnice Slovenskej republiky,** is quite extensive, although buses are still the best way to reach small towns. Trains vary in speed, but it's not really worth taking anything other than an "express" train, marked in red on the timetable. Tickets are relatively cheap. First class is considerably more spacious and comfortable and on full trains well worth the cost (50% more than a standard ticket). If you don't specify "express" when you buy your ticket, you may have to pay a supplement on the train. If you haven't bought a ticket in advance at the station, it's easy to buy one on the train for a small extra charge. On timetables, departures appear on a yellow background, arrivals on white. It is possible to book couchettes (sleepers) on most overnight trains, but don't expect much in the way of comfort. Both the European East Pass and the InterRail Pass are valid for all rail travel within Slovakia.

Contacts and Resources

B&B Reservation Agencies

Satur offices (☞ Visitor Information, *below,* or regional A to Z sections, *above*) throughout the country can make B&B reservations.

Car Rentals

There are no special requirements for renting a car in Slovakia, but be sure to shop around, as prices can differ greatly. Hertz offers Western makes for as much as $1,000 per week. Smaller, local companies may rent local cars for as little as $130 per week for a manual transmission, economy car without air-conditioning but with unlimited mileage. You may buy general accident and theft insurance for an additional $25 and $7, respectively. Prices are comparable whether or not you arrange for a rental before arriving in Slovakia. There is a 6% tax on car rentals.

The following agencies are in Bratislava: **Auto Danubius** (✉ Trnavská 9, ☎ 07/44373754); **Europcar InterRent** (✉ Štefánik Airport, ☎ 07/43420285; Hotel Danube, Rybné nám. 1, ☎ 07/59340841 or 07/59340847); **Hertz** (✉ Hotel Forum, Hodžovo nám. 2, ☎ 07/54434441); **Recar** (✉ Svätoplukova 1, ☎ 07/55576436).

Customs and Duties

ON ARRIVAL

You may import duty-free into Slovakia 250 cigarettes or the equivalent in tobacco, 1 liter of spirits, 2 liters of wine, ½ liter of perfume, and up to 1,000 Sk worth of gifts and souvenirs.

ON DEPARTURE

There is no limit on the amount of goods purchased for noncommercial use, but to be on the safe side, hang on to all receipts. You can only export antiques (items more than 50 years old) with approval, based on a court-expert opinion submitted by you, from the National Relic and Landscape Center in Bratislava (☎ 07/54789181). For a list of court experts, call the department of experts and interpreters at the **Regional Court** in Bratislava (✉ Krajský súd, Záhradnícka 10, 81366, ☎ 07/55424060 or 07/55424042).

Emergencies

Ambulance (☎ 155). **Car rescue service** (☎ 154). **Police** (☎ 158). **Pharmacies** (*lekárne*) in cities take turns staying open late or on Sunday. Look for the list posted on the front door of each pharmacy. For after-hours service, ring the bell; you will be served through a little hatch door.

Language

Slovak, a western-Slavic tongue closely related to both Czech and Polish, is the official language of Slovakia. English is popular among young people, but German is still the most useful language for tourists.

Mail

POSTAL RATES

Postcards to the United States and Canada cost 10 Sk; letters, 16 Sk. Postcards to Great Britain cost 7 Sk; letters, 12 Sk.

RECEIVING MAIL

If you don't know where you'll be staying, you can have mail held *poste restante* (general delivery) at post offices in major towns, but the letters should be marked Pošta 1 to designate a city's main post office. You will be asked for identification when you collect mail. The poste restante window in Bratislava is at Námestie SNP 5.

Money and Expenses

COSTS

Bratislava is easily the most expensive area in Slovakia. As a rule, small country towns are extremely reasonable. While overcharging foreigners is not a widespread practice, you may find that state-subsidized theaters do charge visitors higher prices.

CURRENCY

The unit of currency in Slovakia is the crown, or koruna, written as Sk, and divided into 100 halierov. There are bills of 20, 50, 100, 200, 500, 1,000, and 5,000 Sk, and coins of 10, 20, and 50 halierov and 1, 2, 5, and 10 Sk.

At press time, the rate of exchange was around 43 Sk to the American dollar, 29 Sk to the Canadian dollar, and 69 Sk to the pound sterling.

SAMPLE PRICES

A cup of coffee, 15 Sk; museum entrance, 10 Sk–50 Sk; a good theater seat, 60 Sk–750 Sk (some theaters, including the Slovak National Theater, charge foreigners a hefty fee, while locals pay less); a half liter (pint) of beer, 20 Sk; a 2 km (1 mi) taxi ride, 150 Sk; a bottle of Slovak wine in a good restaurant, 100 Sk–150 Sk; a glass (2 deciliters, or 7 ounces) of wine, 25 Sk.

National Holidays

January 1 (founding of the Slovak Republic); January 6 (Twelfth Night); Good Friday and Easter Monday; May 1 (Labor Day); May 8 (Liberation of the Republic); July 5 (Sts. Cyril and Methodius); August 29 (anniversary of the Slovak National Uprising); September 1 (Constitution Day); September 15 (Our Lady of Sorrows); November 1 (All Saints' Day); and December 24–26.

Opening and Closing Times

Banks are open weekdays 8–4 and remain open through the general lunch hour. Museums are usually open Tuesday–Sunday 10–5. Shops are generally open weekdays 9–6 and stay open slightly later on Thursday; some close noon–2. Many shops are also open Saturday 9–noon (department stores, 9–4) and, in big cities, Sunday.

Outdoor Activities and Sports

Slovakia's stretches of beautiful countryside make perfect backdrops for hiking, biking, simmering in thermal pools, mountain climbing, paragliding, and downhill and cross-country skiing. For more information, *see* Bicycling, Fishing, Camping, *and* Hiking *in* Pleasures and Pastimes, *above.*

There are opportunities for daylong boating trips or kayaking with camping on a dozen of Slovakia's rivers, particularly the Dunajec, Hron, Orava, and Váh. For information about boat and kayak trips, contact a local tourist information center. **Jur Sport Agency** (✉ Hlavná 260, Závažná Poruba, ☎ 0849/5547279, FAX 0849/5547249) arranges two-hour raft trips along the Váh River. The starting point is 5 km from Liptovský Mikuláš, west of Štrbské Pleso.

Passports and Visas

American and British citizens do not need a visa to enter Slovakia. A valid passport is sufficient for stays of up to 30 days for a U.S. citizen and up to six months for a U.K. citizen. Canadian citizens do not need a visa for a stay of up to 90 days.

Rail Passes

Train tickets within Slovakia are still quite cheap, so a rail pass often does not give significant savings. The European East Pass is good for unlimited first-class travel on the national railroads of Slovakia, Austria, the Czech Republic, Hungary, and Poland. The pass covers five days of unlimited first-class travel within a one-month period for $199. Additional travel days may be purchased. Apply through your travel agent or through **Rail Europe** (✉ 226–230 Westchester Ave., White Plains, NY 10604, ☎ 914/682–2999 or 800/848–7245). The InterRail Pass, available only to European citizens at Satur offices, is valid for 22 days of unlimited train travel in Slovakia, Croatia, the Czech Republic, Hungary, and Poland. The Eurail pass is not valid in Slovakia. For more information, *see* Train Travel *in* Smart Travel Tips.

Student and Youth Travel

In summer, student dormitories in main cities are turned into hostels providing accommodation at reasonable prices. Satur (☞ Visitor Information, *below*) is the best place to arrange dormitory stays or obtain other student-oriented information; it also offers special youth tours in the country. Student discounts are common for museums and other sights.

Telephones

COUNTRY CODE

The country code for Slovakia is 421. When dialing from outside the country, drop the initial zero from the area code.

INTERNATIONAL CALLS

Dial **AT&T** (☎ 00–421–00101) or **MCI** (☎ 001–881–422–0042) to reach an English-speaking operator who can connect your direct, collect, or credit-card call to the United States. You can make a time-consuming and expensive international call from Bratislava's main telecommunications office, **Slovenské telekomunikácie** (✉ Kolárska 12). For an even larger fee, you can call from a major hotel. For international directory inquiries call ☎ 0149. For information on international services and rates call ☎ 0139.

LOCAL CALLS

Public pay phones are easily found in town centers. Most public phones accept prepaid phone cards, which are available at post offices and some newsstands. A local call costs at least 2 Sk. For inquiries call **directory assistance** (☎ 120 for local calls; 121 for calls in Slovakia outside the city from which you're dialing). Not all operators speak English, so you may have to ask a hotel clerk for help.

Tipping

Gratuities are not automatically added to restaurant bills. To reward good service, round up the bill to the nearest multiple of 10 (if the bill comes to 86 Sk, for example, give the waiter 90 Sk). A tip of 10% is considered appropriate in inexpensive restaurants or on group tabs. A 20 Sk tip for porters is usually sufficient. For room service, a 20 Sk tip is sufficient. In taxis, round up the bill to the nearest multiple of 10. Give tour guides and helpful concierges 20 Sk–30 Sk.

Travel Agencies

Tatratour (✉ Bajkalská 25, Bratislava, ☎ 07/53411219 or 07/53414828, FAX 07/53412781) is a large, dependable agency that can help arrange sightseeing tours throughout Slovakia. Satur (☞ Visitor Information, *below*) can also provide basic travel-agency services, such as changing traveler's checks and booking bus and train tickets to outside destinations.

Visitor Information

Satur Tours and Travel Agency (formerly known as Čedok) has remained the official travel bureau for Slovakia. With offices in almost every city throughout the country, it will supply you with hotel and tour information and book air, rail, and bus tickets, but do not expect much in the way of general information. For Satur addresses and telephone numbers, *see* Visitor Information *in* regional A to Z sections, *above*. For in-depth information on local events, call the **Information Center** (☎ 186 preceded by the regional area code). English speakers are generally available.

4 HUNGARY

Revitalization continues full-swing in Hungary as the Communist legacy fades into 20th-century history. Budapest offers breathtaking Old World grandeur and thriving cultural life—a must-stop on any trip to Central Europe. In such distinctive smaller cities as Pécs, Szeged, Debrecen, and Kecskemét, cobblestone streets wind among lovely Baroque buildings. In the countryside, gleaming sunflower fields blanket gently swelling hills, and sleepy villages of thatch-roof cottages cluster around carefully tended vineyards. Hearty meals spiced with rich red paprika, the generosity and warmth of the Magyar soul: These and more sustain visitors in this land of vital spirit and beauty.

By Alan Levy and Julie Tomasz

Updated by Paul Olchváry

HUNGARY SITS AT THE CROSSROADS of Central Europe, having retained its own identity by absorbing countless invasions and foreign occupations. Its industrious, resilient people have a history of brave but unfortunate uprisings: against the Turks in the 17th century, the Hapsburgs in 1848, and the Soviet Union in 1956. Each has resulted in a period of readjustment, a return to politics as the art of the possible.

A year into the new millennium much indeed seems possible. The economy continues to improve as European Union (EU) membership is on the near horizon. Hungary joined NATO in 1999. While this momentum was essentially spurred by the collapse of the one-party state in 1990, the lot of most Hungarians had improved even in the 1960s and 70s. Communist Party leader János Kádár remained relatively popular at home and abroad, allowing Hungary to expand and improve ties with the West. The bubble began to burst in the 1980s, however, when the economy stagnated and inflation swelled. The peaceful transition to democracy began when young reformers in the party shunted aside the aging Kádár in 1988 and began speaking openly about multiparty democracy, a market economy, and a break from Moscow—daring ideas at the time.

Events unfolded quickly, and by spring 1990, as the Iron Curtain fell, Hungary held its first free elections in more than 40 years. A center-right government took office, sweeping away the Communists and their renamed successor party, the Socialists. Ironically, four years later, in the next elections, Hungarians chose none other than the Hungarian Socialist Party, which ruled in coalition with the Free Democrats until ousted again in the 1998 elections. Voting the center-right FIDESZ party, led by 35-year-old Viktor Orbán, into power, the nation chose a new generation to take it into the new millennium. At press time the Socialists were once again seen as the government's most formidable rival in the next elections (2002)—this time vying for the chance to lead Hungary into the EU. *Plus ça change . . .*

Because Hungary is a small, agriculturally oriented country, visitors are often surprised by its grandeur and Old World charm, especially in the capital, Budapest, which bustles with life as never before. Hungarians spare visitors bureaucratic hassles at the border and airport. Entry is easy and quick for Westerners, most of whom do not need visas.

Two rivers cross the country: The famous Duna (Danube) flows from the west through Budapest on its way to the southern frontier, and the smaller Tisza flows from the northeast across the Nagyalföld (Great Plain). What Hungary lacks in size it makes up for in beauty and charm. Western Hungary is dominated by the largest lake in Central Europe, Lake Balaton. Although some overdevelopment has blighted its splendor, its shores are still lined with Baroque villages, relaxing spas, magnificent vineyards, and shaded garden restaurants serving the catch of the day. In eastern Hungary, the Nagyalföld offers visitors a chance to explore the folklore and customs of the Magyars (the Hungarians' name for themselves and their language). It is an area of spicy food, strong wine, and the proud *csikós* (horsemen).

Hungarians are known for their hospitality and love talking to foreigners, although their unusual language can be a challenge. Today, however, everyone seems to be learning English, especially young people. But what all Hungarians share is a deep love of music, and the calendar is studded with it, from Budapest's famous opera to its annual spring music festival. And at many restaurants Gypsy violinists serenade you during your evening meal.

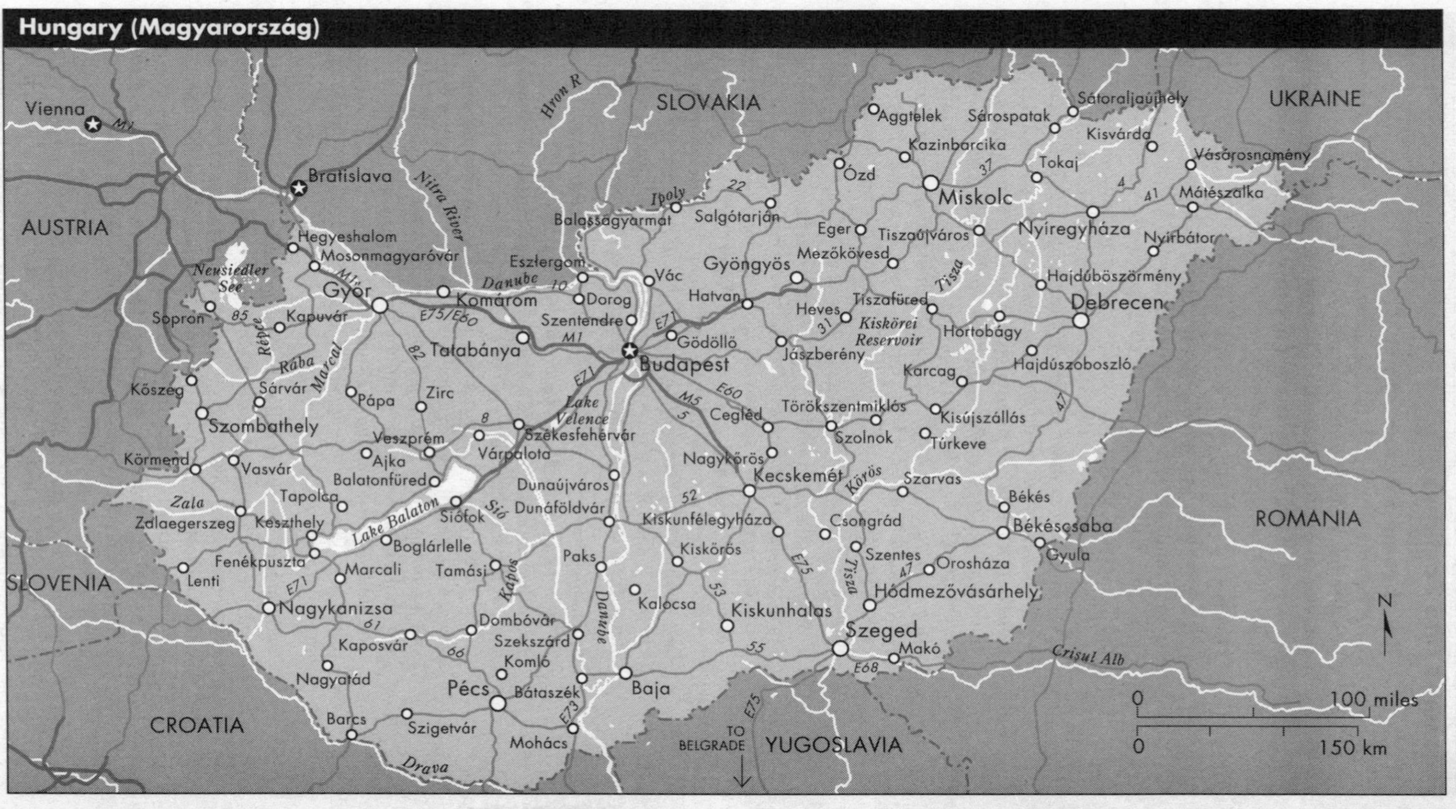
Hungary (Magyarország)
Vienna
M1
AUSTRIA
Bratislava
Hron R
SLOVAKIA
UKRAINE
Nitra River
Neusiedler See
Hegyeshalom
Mosonmagyaróvár
Győr
Sopron
85
Répce
Kapuvár
Rába
Marcal
Kőszeg
Sárvár
Szombathely
Körmend
Vasvár
Zala
Zalaegerszeg
Keszthely
Fenékpuszta
Lenti
SLOVENIA
E71
Nagykanizsa
61
Kaposvár
Nagyatád
Barcs
CROATIA
Drava
Szigetvár
Pécs
Mohács
E73
Bátaszék
Komló
66
Dombóvár
Szekszárd
Kapos
Tamási
Marcali
Boglárlelle
Lake Balaton
Tapolca
Balatonfüred
Ajka
Veszprém
Pápa
Zirc
82
Tatabánya
E75/E60
Komárom
Danube
10
Esztergom
Dorog
Szentendre
M1
Budapest
E71
Lake Velence
Székesfehérvár
8
Várpalota
Siófok
Sió
Dunaújváros
Dunaföldvár
Paks
Kalocsa
Baja
TO BELGRADE
E75
YUGOSLAVIA
Ipoly
Balassagyarmat
22
Salgótarján
Vác
Gödöllő
Hatvan
Gyöngyös
Eger
Ózd
Aggtelek
Kazinbarcika
Miskolc
37
Sárospatak
Sátoraljaújhely
Tokaj
Kisvárda
Vásárosnamény
4
41
Mátészalka
Nyíregyháza
Nyírbátor
Tiszaújváros
Mezőkövesd
Tisza
Hajdúböszörmény
Debrecen
Tiszafüred
Heves
31
Kiskörei Reservoir
Hortobágy
Jászberény
Hajdúszoboszló
Karcag
47
E60
M5
5
Cegléd
Törökszentmiklós
Szolnok
Kisújszállás
Túrkeve
Nagykőrös
Kecskemét
Körös
Szarvas
52
Kiskunfélegyháza
Kiskőrös
53
Kiskunhalas
55
E75
Csongrád
Szentes
47
Orosháza
Békés
Békéscsaba
Gyula
ROMANIA
Hódmezővásárhely
Szeged
Makó
E68
Crisul Alb
N
0
100 miles
0
150 km

Pleasures and Pastimes

Beaches and Water Sports

Lake Balaton, the largest lake in Central Europe, is the most popular playground of this landlocked nation. If you're looking to relax in the sun and do a little windsurfing, swimming, or boating, settle in here for several days, basing yourself in either the northern shore's main town, Balatonfüred, or the more tranquil Tihany.

Dining

Through the lean postwar years the Hungarian kitchen lost none of its spice and sparkle. Meats, rich sauces, and creamy desserts predominate, but the more health-conscious will also find salads, even out of season. (Strict vegetarians should note, however, that even meatless dishes are usually cooked with lard [*zsír*].) In addition to the ubiquitous dishes most foreigners are familiar with, such as chunky beef *gulyás* (goulash) and *paprikás csirke* (chicken paprika) served with *galuska* (little pinched dumplings), traditional Hungarian classics include fiery *halászlé* (fish soup), scarlet with hot paprika; *fogas* (pike perch) from Lake Balaton; and goose liver, duck, and veal specialties. Lake Balaton is the major source of fish in Hungary, particularly for *süllő,* a kind of perch. Hungarians are also very fond of carp (*ponty*), catfish (*harcsa*), and eel (*angolna*), which are often stewed in a garlic-and-tomato sauce.

Portions are large, so don't plan to eat more than one main Hungarian meal a day. Desserts are lavish, and every inn seems to have its house *torta* (cake), though *rétes* (strudels), *Somlói galuska* (a steamed sponge cake soaked in chocolate sauce and whipped cream), and *palacsinta* (stuffed crepes) are ubiquitous. Traditional rétes fillings are *mák* (sugary poppy seeds), *meggy* (sour cherry), and *túró* (sweetened cottage cheese); palacsintas always come rolled with *dió* (sweet ground walnuts), túró, or *lekvár* (jam)—often *sárgabarack* (apricot).

In major cities, there is a good selection of restaurants, from the grander establishments that echo the imperial past of the Hapsburg era to the less expensive, rustic spots favored by locals. In addition to trying out the standard *vendéglő* or *étterem* (restaurants), you can eat at a *bisztró étel bár* (sit-down snack bar), a *büfé* (snack counter), an *eszpresszó* (café), or a *söröző* (pub). And no matter how strict your diet, don't pass up a visit to at least one *cukrászda* (pastry shop). Our dining choices focus primarily on Hungarian and Continental cuisine; if you find yourself longing for something farther afield, from pizza to Chinese to Greek to American-style fast food, you can find it aplenty in the larger cities.

Although prices are steadily increasing, there are plenty of good, affordable restaurants offering a variety of Hungarian dishes. Even in Budapest, eating out can provide you with some of the best value for the money of any European capital. In almost all restaurants, an inexpensive prix-fixe lunch called a *menü* is available, usually for as little as 400 Ft. It includes soup or salad, an entrée, and a dessert. One caveat: Some of the more touristy restaurants sometimes follow the international practice of embellishing tourists' bills; it doesn't hurt to check the prices discreetly before ordering and the total before paying. Budapest made international news in 1998 for a flagrant overcharging incident; authorities have since cracked down on the guilty establishments. Also note that most restaurants have a fine-print policy of charging for each slice of bread consumed from the bread basket.

Hungarians eat early—you risk offhand service and cold food after 9 PM. Lunch, the main meal for many, is served from noon to 2. At most moderately priced and inexpensive restaurants, casual but neat dress is acceptable.

CATEGORY	COST*
$$$$	over $11
$$$	$8–$11
$$	$5–$8
$	under $5

**per person for a three-course meal, excluding wine and tip.*

Folk Art

Hungary's centuries-old traditions of handmade, often regionally specific folk art are still beautifully alive. Intricately carved wooden boxes, vibrantly colorful embroidered tablecloths and shirts, matte-black pottery pitchers, delicately woven lace collars, ceramic plates splashed with painted flowers and birds, and decorative heavy leather whips are among the favorite handcrafted pieces a visitor can purchase. You'll find them in folk-art stores around the country but can purchase them directly from the artisans at crafts fairs and from peddlers on the streets. Dolls dressed in national costume are also popular souvenirs.

Hiking

Northern Hungary offers great opportunities for hikers and nature seekers. Base yourself in Eger—for lovely sightseeing, excellent wine, and good lodging—and make day trips north to Szilvásvárad for hiking or biking in the hills of the Bükk range and south for the same in the Mátra range, near Gyöngyös. Moving slightly farther north, you can spend a night or two in the magical palace hotel in Lillafüred, making excursions to the magnificent caves at Aggtelek, near the Slovak border, and to Tokaj, farther east, for some less athletic wine tasting.

Lodging

Outside Budapest there are few very expensive hotels, so you will improve your chances of having a memorable lodging experience by arranging a stay in one of the alternative options noted below. For specific recommendations or information about how to book lodging in these accommodations, see the lodging and information sections throughout the chapter.

Bought back from the government over the last several years, more and more of Hungary's magnificent, centuries-old castles and mansions are being restored and opened as country resorts; a night or two in one of these majestic old places makes for an unusual and romantic (but not always luxurious) lodging experience. Northern Hungary has some of the best.

Guest houses, also called *panziók* (pensions), provide simple accommodations—well suited to people on a budget. Like B&Bs, most are run by couples or families and offer simple breakfast facilities and usually have private bathrooms; they're generally outside the city or town center. Arrangements can be made directly with the panzió or through local tourist offices and travel agents abroad. Another good budget option is renting a room in a private home. In the provinces it is safe to accept rooms offered to you directly; they will almost always be clean and in a relatively good neighborhood, and the prospective landlord will probably not cheat you. Look for signs reading SZOBA KIADÓ (or the German ZIMMER FREI). Reservations and referrals can also be made by any tourist office, and if you go that route, you have someone to complain to if things don't work out.

Village tourism is a growing trend in Hungary, affording visitors a chance to sink into life in tiny, typical villages around the country.

The Hungarian Tourist Board's *Village Tourism* publication provides descriptions and color photos of many of the village homes now open to guests, either by renting a home or as an overnight guest. Apartments in Budapest and cottages at Lake Balaton are available for short- and long-term rental and can make the most economic lodging for families—particularly for those who prefer to cook their own meals. Rates and reservations can be obtained from tourist offices in Hungary and abroad. Also consult the free annual accommodations directory published by **Tourinform** (☞ Visitor Information *in* Hungary A to Z, *below*); published in five languages, it lists basic information about hotels, pensions, bungalows, and tourist hostels throughout the country. A separate brochure lists the country's campgrounds.

For single rooms with bath, count on paying about 80% of the double-room rate. During the off-season (in Budapest, September through March; at Lake Balaton, September through May), rates can drop considerably. Prices at Lake Balaton tend to be significantly higher than those in the rest of the countryside. Note that most large hotels require payment in hard currency—either U.S. dollars or Deutschemarks. As the slated 2002 adoption of the Euro as a common currency in many Western European countries nears, however, ever more hotels now listing their rates in Deutschemarks will be doing so in Euros.

CATEGORY	BUDAPEST*	OTHER AREAS*
$$$$	over $200	over $70
$$$	$140–$200	$50–$70
$$	$80–$140	$30–$50
$	under $80	under $30

**All prices are for a standard double room with bath and breakfast during peak season (June through August).*

🌐 following the text of a review is your signal that the property has a Web site, where you will find details and, usually, images; for a link, visit www.fodors.com/urls.

Porcelain

Among the most sought-after items in Hungary are the exquisite hand-painted Herend and Zsolnay porcelain. Unfortunately, the prices on all makes of porcelain have risen considerably in the last few years. For guaranteed authenticity, make your purchases at the specific Herend and Zsolnay stores in major cities, or at the factories themselves in Herend and Pécs, respectively.

Spas and Thermal Baths

Several thousand years ago, the first settlers of the area that is now Budapest chose their home because of its abundance of hot springs. Centuries later, the Romans and the Turks built baths and developed cultures based on medicinal bathing. Now there are more than 1,000 medicinal hot springs bubbling up around the country. Budapest alone has some 14 historic working baths, which attract ailing patients with medical prescriptions for specific water cures as well as "recreational" bathers—locals and tourists alike—wanting to soak in the relaxing waters, try some of the many massages and treatments, and experience the architectural beauty of the bathhouses themselves.

For most, a visit to a bath involves soaking in several thermal pools of varying temperatures and curative contents—perhaps throwing in a game of aquatic chess—relaxing in a steam room or sauna, and getting a brisk, if not brutal, massage (average cost: 800 Ft. for 15 minutes). Many bath facilities are single-sex or have certain days set aside for men or women only, and most people walk around nude or with miniature loincloths, provided at the door. Men should be aware that some men-only baths have a strong gay clientele.

In addition to the ancient beauties there are newer, modern baths open to the public at many spa hotels. They lack the charm and aesthetic appeal of their older peers but provide the latest treatments in sparkling facilities. Of the areas outside Budapest covered in this guidebook, Debrecen, Hévíz, and Eger are famous spa towns with popular bath facilities. For more information, page through the "Hungary: Land of Spas" brochure published by the Hungarian Tourist Board, available free from most tourist offices.

Wine, Beer, and Spirits

Hungary tempts wine connoisseurs with its important wine regions, especially Villány, near Pécs, in the south; Eger and Tokaj in the north; and the northern shore of Lake Balaton. Szürkebarát and especially Olaszrizling are common white table wines; Tokay, one of the great wines of the world (☞ Tokaj, *below*), can be heavy, dark, and sweet, and its most famous variety is drunk as an aperitif or a dessert wine. It's expensive, especially by Hungarian standards, so it's usually reserved for special occasions.

The gourmet red table wine of Hungary, Egri Bikavér (Bull's Blood of Eger, usually with *el toro* himself on the label), is the best buy and the safest bet with all foods. Villány produces superb reds and the best rosés; the most adventurous reds—with sometimes successful links to both Austrian and Californian wine making and viticulture—are from the Sopron area.

Before- and after-dinner drinks tend toward schnapps, most notably *Barack-pálinka,* an apricot brandy. A plum brandy called *Kosher szilva-pálinka,* bottled under rabbinical supervision, is the very best of the brandies available in stores. *Vilmos körte-pálinka,* a pear variety, is almost as good. Note than any bottle under 1,000 Ft. or so probably contains more ethyl alcohol than pure fruit brandy. Unicum, Hungary's national liqueur, is a dark, thick, and potent herbal bitter that could be likened to Germany's Jägermeister. Its chubby green bottle makes it a good souvenir to take home.

Major Hungarian beers are Dreher, Kőbányai, and Aranyászok, and several good foreign beers are produced in Hungary under license.

Exploring Hungary

Hungary's main geographical regions begin with the capital city and thriving urban heart of **Budapest.** Just north of Budapest, the Danube River forms a gentle heart-shape curve along which lie the romantic and historic towns of the region called the **Danube Bend.** Southwest of Budapest are the vineyards, quaint villages, and popular, developed summer resorts around **Lake Balaton.** The more rural and gently mountainous stretch of **northern Hungary** also includes the handsome, vibrant town of Eger and the famous wine village of Tokaj; the contrastingly flat and dry expanses of the **Great Plain,** in the east, are spiced with legendary traditions of horsemanship and agriculture and anchored by the interesting and lively cities of Kecskemét and Debrecen. The verdant, rolling countryside of **Transdanubia** stretches west of the Danube to the borders of Austria, Slovenia, and Croatia; in the northern hills nestle the gemlike, beautifully restored towns of Sopron and Kőszeg, and in the south, the culturally rich, dynamically beautiful city of Pécs. Given Hungary's relatively small size, most of these points are less than a few hours away from Budapest by car.

Great Itineraries

Numbers in the text correspond to numbers in the margin and on the Budapest, The Danube Bend, Lake Balaton and Transdanubia, and Northern Hungary and the Great Plain maps.

IF YOU HAVE 3 DAYS

Budapest 1–53 alone offers a full vacation's worth of things to see and experience, but in one day an efficient and motivated visitor can pack in some of the don't-misses: exploration of **Várhegy** 1–12, a stroll on the **Danube korzó,** a glimpse of **Országház** 26, a look at **Hősök tere** 48, followed by a dip in the **Széchenyi Fürdő,** a hearty meal, and a night at the **Magyar Állami Operaház** 44. After a night's rest in Budapest, hop on an early boat to explore the time-honored artists' village of **Szentendre** 54 and the majestic fortress of **Visegrád** 55, up-river in the Danube Bend. You can spend another night in Budapest; the next morning, drive down to **Badacsony** 62 on Lake Balaton's northern shore. Follow a refreshing swim with a lunch of fresh Balaton fish and some wine tasting in the cool cellars on Mount Badacsony's vineyard-covered slopes. On your way back to Budapest, stop for a stroll on **Tihany**'s 60 cobblestone streets and drink in the views from its lovely hilltop abbey.

IF YOU HAVE 6 DAYS

Spend two full days exploring **Budapest** 1–53; on your third day visit the Danube Bend's crown jewels, the villages of **Szentendre** 54 and **Visegrád** 55, making the trip by scenic boat or by car. Return to Budapest for the night and head out the next morning for a day on the Great Plain, strolling among the sights of lovely **Kecskemét** 80 before venturing out to the *puszta* (prairie) in **Kiskunsági National Park** 81 or **Kerekegyháza** to experience the unique horsemanship stunts and demonstrations of Hungary's legendary cowboys, the csikós. Depending on how much you want to drive and how much of Budapest's nightlife you want to take in, you can either go back to Budapest (85 km/53 mi from Kecskemét) for the night or spend it here in Kecskemét. On day five, drive down to **Pécs** 69 to see its beautiful town square, cathedral, and excellent museums. After a night's rest, make your way on scenic secondary roads through southern Transdanubia to **Keszthely** 64 on the northwestern tip of Lake Balaton, visiting the spectacular Festetics mansion before moving east along the northern shore to **Badacsony** 62. On the way, make a stop in **Szigliget** 63 and scale its castle hill to gaze at the sweeping Lake Balaton view. In Badacsony, spend the rest of the afternoon hiking up the vineyard-carpeted slopes of Mount Badacsony, rewarded by generous wine tastings in the local cellars and a big fish dinner with live Gypsy music. Depending on your traveling speed (and the amount of wine you've tasted), instead of sleeping in Badacsony, you may prefer to move on along the northern shore and spend the fifth night in **Tihany** 60 or **Balatonfüred** 59, both of which have good lodging possibilities with more facilities and amenities. Either way, you can spend your sixth day exploring Tihany and Balatonfüred, cooling off with a swim in the lake before heading back to Budapest.

When to Tour

The ideal times to visit Hungary are in the spring (May through June) and end of summer and early fall (late August through September). July and August, peak vacation season for Hungarians as well as foreign tourists, can be extremely hot and humid; Budapest is stuffy and crowded, and the entire Lake Balaton region is overrun with vacationers. Many of Hungary's major fairs and festivals take place during the spring and fall, including the late-March to early April Spring Festival (in many cities and towns) and the myriad wine-harvest festivals in late summer and early fall. Lake Balaton is the only area that gets boarded up during the low season, generally from mid- or late September until at least Easter, if not mid-May. Summer holds the unforgettable and quintessentially Hungarian sights of sweeping fields of swaying golden sunflowers and giant white storks summering in their bushy nests built on chimney tops.

BUDAPEST

Situated on both banks of the Danube, Budapest unites the colorful hills of Buda and the wide, businesslike boulevards of Pest. Though it was the site of a Roman outpost during the 1st century, the city was not officially created until 1873, when the towns of Óbuda, Pest, and Buda united. Since then, Budapest has been the cultural, political, intellectual, and commercial heart of Hungary; for the 20% of the nation's population who live in the capital, anywhere else is simply *vidék* ("the country").

Budapest has suffered many ravages in the course of its long history. It was totally destroyed by the Mongols in 1241, captured by the Turks in 1541, and nearly destroyed again by Soviet troops in 1945. But this bustling industrial and cultural center survived as the capital of the People's Republic of Hungary after the war—and then, as the 1980s drew to a close, it became one of the Eastern Bloc's few thriving bastions of capitalism. Today, judging by the city's flourishing cafés and restaurants, markets and bars, the stagnation enforced by the Communists seems a thing of the very distant past.

Much of the charm of a visit to Budapest lies in unexpected glimpses into shadowy courtyards and in long vistas down sunlit cobbled streets. Although some 30,000 buildings were destroyed during World War II and in the 1956 Revolution, the past lingers on in the often crumbling architectural details of the antique structures that remain.

The principal sights of the city fall roughly into three areas, each of which can be comfortably covered on foot. The Budapest hills are best explored by public transportation. Note that street names have been changed in the past several years to purge all reminders of the Communist regime. Underneath the new names, the old ones sometimes remain, canceled out by a big red slash. Also note that a Roman-numeral prefix listed before an address refers to one of Budapest's 22 districts. Districts V, VI, and VII are in downtown Pest; I includes Castle Hill, the main tourist district of Buda.

Exploring Budapest

Várhegy (Castle Hill)

Most of the major sights of Buda are on Várhegy (Castle Hill), a long, narrow plateau laced with cobblestone streets, clustered with beautifully preserved Baroque, Gothic, and Renaissance houses, and crowned by the magnificent Royal Palace. The area is theoretically banned to private cars (except for those of neighborhood residents and Hilton Hotel guests), but the streets manage to be lined bumper to bumper with Trabants and Mercedes all the same—sometimes the only visual element to verify you're not in a fairy tale. As in all of Budapest, thriving urban new has taken up residence in historic old; international corporate offices, diplomatic residences, restaurants, and boutiques occupy many of its landmark buildings. But these are still the exceptions, as families occupy most flats and homes. The most striking example, perhaps, is the Hilton Hotel on Hess András tér, which has ingeniously incorporated remains of Castle Hill's oldest church (a tower and one wall), built by Dominican friars in the 13th century.

Numbers in the text correspond to numbers in the margin and on the Castle Hill (Várhegy) map.

A GOOD WALK

Castle Hill's cobblestone streets and numerous museums are made to be explored on foot: Plan to spend about a day here. Most of the transportation options for getting to Castle Hill deposit you on Szent György tér or Dísz tér. It's impossible not to find Castle Hill, but it is possible to be confused about how to get on top of it. If you're already on the Buda side of the river, you can take the Castle bus—*Várbusz*—from the Moszkva tér metro station, northwest of Castle Hill. If you're starting out from Pest, you can take a taxi or Bus 16 from Erzsébet tér or, the most scenic alternative, cross the Széchenyi Lánchíd (Chain Bridge) on foot to Clark Ádám tér and ride the *Sikló* (funicular) up Castle Hill (☞ Clark Ádám tér, *below*).

Begin your exploration by walking slightly farther south to visit the **Királyi Palota** at the southern end of the hill. Of the palace's several major museums, the **Magyar Nemzeti Galéria** ② and the **Budapesti Történeti Múzeum** ③ are particularly interesting. From here, you can cover the rest of the area by walking north along its handful of cobbled streets. From Dísz tér, start with Tárnok utca, whose houses and usually open courtyards offer glimpses of how Hungarians have integrated contemporary life into Gothic, Renaissance, and Baroque settings; of particular interest are the houses at No. 16, now the Aranyhordó restaurant, and at No. 18, the 15th-century Arany Sas Patika (Golden Eagle Pharmacy Museum), with a naïf Madonna and child in an overhead niche. This tiny museum displays instruments, prescriptions, books, and other artifacts from 16th- and 17th-century pharmacies. Modern commerce is also integrated into Tárnok utca's historic homes; you'll encounter numerous folk souvenir shops and tiny boutiques lining the street. Tárnok utca funnels into Szentháromság tér, home of **Mátyás templom** ⑤ and, just behind it, the **Halászbástya** ⑥.

After exploring them, double back to Dísz tér and set out northward again on Úri utca, which runs parallel to Tárnok utca; this long street is lined with beautiful, genteel homes. The funny little Telefónia Museum, at No. 49, is worth a stop, as is the **Budavári Labirintus** ⑦, at No. 9. At the end of Úri utca you'll reach Kapisztrán tér. From here, you can walk south again on a parallel street, Országház utca (Parliament Street), the main thoroughfare of 18th-century Buda; it takes its name from the building at No. 28, which was the seat of Parliament from 1790 to 1807. You'll end up back at Szentháromság tér, with just two streets remaining to explore.

You can stroll down little Fortuna utca, named for the 18th-century Fortuna Inn, which now houses the **Magyar Kereskedelmi és Vendéglátóipari Múzeum** ⑧. At the end of Fortuna utca you'll reach **Bécsi kapu tér** ⑨, opening to Moszkva tér just below. Go back south on the last of the district's streets, Táncsics Mihály utca, stopping at the **Középkori Zsidó Imaház** ⑩ and the **Zenetörténeti Múzeum** ⑪. Next door, at No. 9, is the Baroque house (formerly the Royal Mint) where rebel writer Táncsics Mihály was imprisoned in the dungeons and freed by the people on the Day of Revolution, March 15, 1848. You'll find yourself in front of the Hilton Hotel, back at Hess András tér, bordering Szentháromság tér. Those whose feet haven't protested yet can finish off their tour of Castle Hill by doubling back to the northern

Castle Hill (Várhegy)

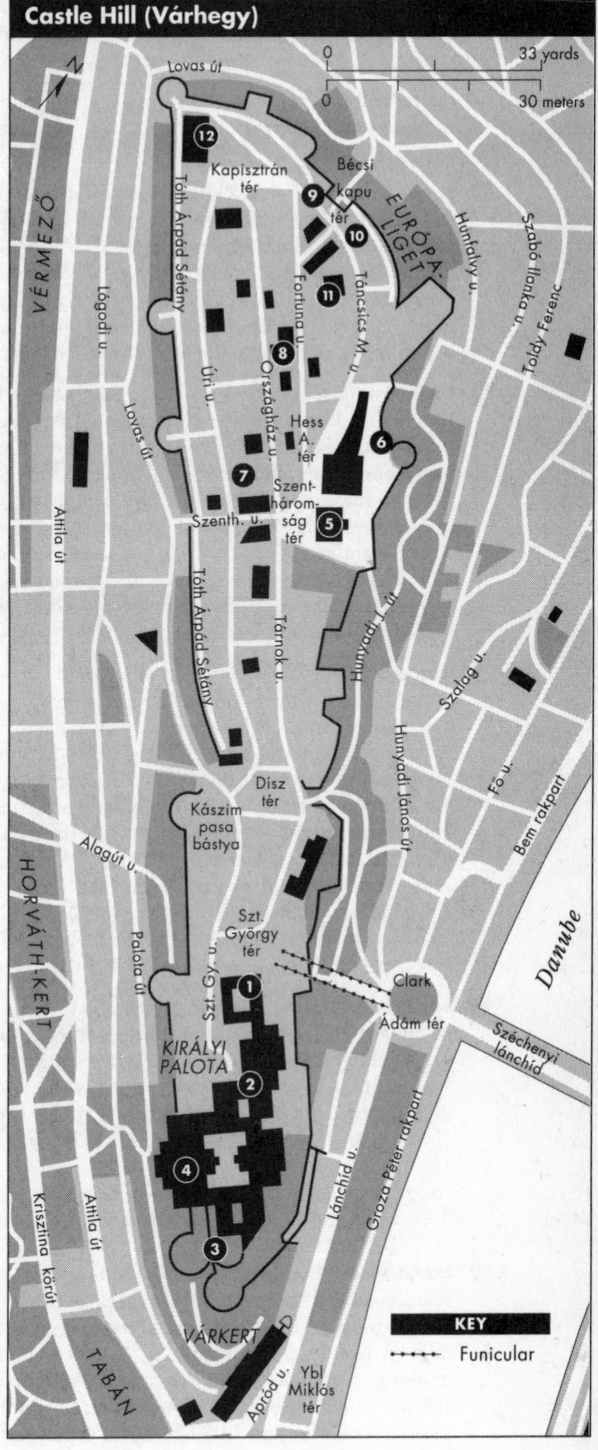

end and strolling south back to Dísz tér on **Tóth Árpád sétány,** the romantic, tree-lined promenade along the Buda side of the hill.

TIMING

Castle Hill is small enough to cover in one day, but perusing its major museums and several tiny exhibits will require more time.

SIGHTS TO SEE

9 **Bécsi kapu tér** (Vienna Gate Square). Marking the northern entrance to Castle Hill, the stone gateway (rebuilt in 1936) called Vienna Gate opens toward Vienna—or, closer at hand, Moszkva tér a few short blocks below. The square named after it has some fine Baroque and rococo houses but is dominated by the enormous neo-Romanesque (1913–1917) headquarters of the **Országos Levéltár** (Hungarian National Archives), which resembles a cathedral-like shrine to paperwork.

3 **Budapesti Történeti Múzeum** (Budapest History Museum). The palace's Baroque southern wing (E) contains the Budapest History Museum, displaying a fascinating permanent exhibit of modern Budapest history from Buda's liberation from the Turks in 1686 through the 1970s. Viewing the vintage 19th- and 20th-century photos and videos of the castle, the Széchenyi Lánchíd, and other Budapest monuments—and seeing them as the backdrop to the horrors of World War II and the 1956 Revolution—helps to put your later sightseeing in context; while you're browsing, peek out one of the windows overlooking the Danube and Pest and let it start seeping in.

Through historical documents, objects, and art, other permanent exhibits depict the medieval history of the Buda fortress and the capital as a whole. This is the best place to view remains of the medieval Royal Palace and other archaeological excavations. Some of the artifacts unearthed during excavations are in the vestibule in the basement; others are still among the remains of medieval structures. Down in the cellars are the original medieval vaults of the palace; portraits of King Matthias and his second wife, Beatrice of Aragon; and many late-14th-century statues that probably adorned the Renaissance palace. ✉ *Royal Palace (Wing E), Szt. György tér 2,* ☎ *1/375–7533.* 🎫 *400 Ft.* ⏲ *Mar.–mid-May and mid-Sept.–Oct., Wed.–Mon. 10–6; mid-May–mid-Sept., daily 10–6; Nov.–Feb., Wed.–Mon. 10–4.*

7 **Budavári Labirintus** (Labyrinth of Buda Castle). Used as a wine cellar during the 16th and 17th centuries and then as an air-raid shelter during World War II, the labyrinth—entered at Úri utca 9 below an early 18th-century house—can be explored with a tour or, if you dare, on your own. There are some English-language brochures available. ✉ *Úri u. 9,* ☎ *1/375–6858.* 🎫 *800 Ft.* ⏲ *Daily 9:30–7:30.*

NEED A BREAK? For a light snack, pastry, and coffee, **Café Miro** (✉ Úri u. 30, ☎ 1/375–5458) is a fresh, hip alternative to the Old World Budapest cafés.

12 **Hadtörténeti Múzeum** (Museum of Military History). Fittingly, this museum is lodged in a former barracks, on the northwestern corner of Kapisztrán tér. The exhibits, which include collections of uniforms and military regalia, trace the military history of Hungary from the original Magyar conquest in the 9th century through the period of Ottoman rule to the mid-20th century. You can arrange an English-language tour in advance for around 1,000 Ft. ✉ *I, Tóth Árpád sétány 40,* ☎ *1/356–9522.* 🎫 *270 Ft.* ⏲ *Apr.–Sept., Tues.–Sun. 10–6; Oct.–Mar., Tues.–Sun. 10–4.*

★ 6 **Halászbástya** (Fishermen's Bastion). The wondrous porch overlooking the Danube and Pest is the neo-Romanesque Fishermen's Bastion, a merry cluster of white stone towers, arches, and columns above a modern bronze statue of St. Stephen, Hungary's first king. Medieval fishwives once peddled their wares here, but the site is now home to souvenirs, crafts, and music.

★ **Királyi Palota** (Royal Palace, commonly called Buda Castle). During a seven-week siege at the end of 1944, the entire Castle Hill district of palaces, mansions, and churches was turned into one vast ruin. The final German stand was in the Royal Palace, which was utterly gutted by fire; by the end of the siege its walls were reduced to rubble, and just a few scarred pillars and blackened statues protruded from the wreckage. The destruction was incalculable, yet it gave archaeologists and art historians an opportunity to discover the medieval buildings that once stood on the site of this Baroque and neo-Baroque palace. Fortunately, details of the edifices of the kings of the Árpád and Anjou dynasties, of the Holy Roman Emperor Sigismund, and of the great 15th-century king Matthias Corvinus had been preserved in some 80 medieval reports, travelogues, books, and itineraries that were subsequently used to reconstruct the complex.

The postwar rebuilding was slow and painstaking. In some places debris more than 20 ft deep had to be removed. Freed from mounds of rubble, the foundation walls and medieval castle walls were completed, and the ramparts surrounding the medieval royal residence were re-created as close to their original shape and size as possible. Out of this herculean labor emerged the Royal Palace of today, a vast cultural center and museum complex (☞ Budapesti Történeti Múzeum, *above, and* Ludwig Múzeum, Magyar Nemzeti Galéria, *and* Országos Széchenyi Könyvtár, *below*).

⑩ **Középkori Zsidó Imaház** (Medieval Synagogue). The excavated one-room Medieval Synagogue is now used as a museum. On display are objects relating to the Jewish community, including religious inscriptions, frescoes, and tombstones dating to the 15th century. ✉ *Táncsics Mihály u. 26,* ☎ *1/375–7533 (ext. 243).* 🎟 *120 Ft.* ⏲ *May–Oct., Tues.–Fri. 10–2, weekends 10–6.*

❶ **Ludwig Múzeum.** This collection of more than 200 pieces of Hungarian and contemporary international art, including works by Picasso and Lichtenstein, occupies the castle's northern wing. ✉ *Royal Palace (Wing A), Dísz tér 17,* ☎ *1/375–7533.* 🎟 *300 Ft., free Tues.* ⏲ *Tues.–Sun. 10–6.*

❽ **Magyar Kereskedelmi és Vendéglátóipari Múzeum** (Hungarian Museum of Commerce and Catering). The 18th-century Fortuna Inn now serves visitors in a different way—as the Catering Museum. Displays in a permanent exhibit show the city as a tourist destination from 1870 to the 1930s; you can see, for example, what a room at the Gellért Hotel, still operating today, would have looked like in 1918. The Commerce Museum, just across the courtyard, chronicles the history of Hungarian commerce from the late 19th century to 1947, when the new, Communist regime "liberated" the economy into socialism. The four-room exhibit includes everything from an antique chocolate-and-caramel vending machine to early shoe-polish advertisements. You can rent an English-language recorded tour for 300 Ft. ✉ *Fortuna u. 4,* ☎ *1/375–6249.* 🎟 *120 Ft., free Fri.* ⏲ *Wed.–Fri. 10–5, weekends 10–6.*

❷ **Magyar Nemzeti Galéria** (Hungarian National Gallery). The immense center block of the Royal Palace (made up of Wings B, C, and D) exhibits a wide range of Hungarian fine art, from medieval ecclesiastical paintings and statues, through Gothic, Renaissance, and Baroque art, to a rich collection of 19th- and 20th-century works. Especially notable are the works of the romantic painter Mihály Munkácsy, the impressionist Pál Szinyei Merse, and the surrealist Mihály Tivadar Kosztka Csontváry, whom Picasso much admired. There is also a large collection of modern Hungarian sculpture. There are labels and commentary in English for both permanent and temporary exhibits. If you contact the museum in advance, you can book a tour for up to five people with an English-speaking guide. ⊠ *Royal Palace (entrance in Wing C), Dísz tér 17,* ☎ *1/375–7533.* 🎫 *Gallery 400 Ft.; tour 1,000 Ft.* ⏲ *Mid-Mar.–Oct., Tues.–Sun. 10–6; Nov.–mid-Jan., Tues.–Sun. 10–4; mid-Jan.–mid-Mar., Tues.–Fri. 10–4, weekends 10–6).*

★ 5 **Mátyás templom** (Matthias Church). The Gothic Matthias Church is officially the Buda Church of Our Lady but better known by the name of the 15th century's "just king" of Hungary, who was married here twice. It is sometimes called the Coronation Church, because the last two kings of Hungary were crowned here: the Hapsburg emperor Franz Joseph in 1867 and his grandnephew Karl IV in 1916. Originally built for the city's German population in the mid-13th century, the church has endured many alterations and assaults. For almost 150 years it was the main mosque of the Turkish overlords—and the predominant impact of its festive pillars is decidedly Byzantine. Badly damaged during the recapture of Buda in 1686, it was completely rebuilt between 1873 and 1896 by Frigyes Schulek, who gave it an asymmetrical western front, with one high and one low spire, and a fine rose window; the south porch is from the 14th century.

The **Szentháromság Kápolna** (Trinity Chapel) holds an *encolpion,* an enameled casket containing a miniature copy of the Gospel to be worn on the chest; it belonged to the 12th-century king Béla III and his wife, Anne of Chatillon. Their burial crowns and a cross, scepter, and rings found in their excavated graves are also displayed here. The church's **treasury** contains Renaissance and Baroque chalices, monstrances, and vestments. High Mass is celebrated every Sunday at 10 AM, sometimes with full orchestra and choir—and often with major soloists; get here early if you want a seat. During the summer there are usually organ recitals on Friday at 8 PM. Tourists are asked to remain at the back of the church during weddings and services (it's least intrusive to come after 9 AM weekdays and between 1 and 5 PM Sunday and holidays). ⊠ *I, Szentháromság tér 2,* ☎ *1/355–5657.* ⏲ *Daily 7 AM–7:30 PM.* 🎫 *Church free, except during concerts; treasury 200 Ft.* ⏲ *Treasury daily 9:30–5:30.*

4 **Országos Széchenyi Könyvtár** (Széchenyi National Library). The western wing (F) of the Royal Palace is home to the National Library, which houses more than 2 million volumes. Its archives include well-preserved medieval codices, manuscripts, and historic correspondence. This is not a lending library, but the reading rooms are open to the public (though you must show a passport), and even the most valuable materials can be viewed on microfilm. Small, temporary exhibits on rare books and documents are usually on display; the hours and admission fees for these are quite variable. Note that the entire library closes for one month every summer, usually in July or August. ⊠ *Royal Palace (Wing F). To arrange a tour with an English-speaking guide,* ☎ *1/224–3745.* 🎫 *300 Ft.* ⏲ *Reading rooms Mon. 1–9, Tues.–Sat. 9–9; exhibits Mon. 1–6, Tues.–Sat. 10–6.*

Statue of Prince Eugene of Savoy. In front of the Royal Palace, facing the Danube by the entrance to Wing C, stands an equestrian statue of Prince Eugene of Savoy, a commander of the army that liberated Hungary from the Turks at the end of the 17th century. From here there is a superb view across the river to Pest. ⊠ *By entrance to Royal Palace, Wing C.*

Szentháromság tér (Holy Trinity Square). This square is named for its Baroque **Trinity Column,** erected in 1712–1713 as a gesture of thanksgiving by survivors of a plague. The column stands in front of the famous Gothic Matthias Church (☞ *above*), its large pedestal a perfect seat from which to watch the wedding spectacles that take over the church on spring and summer weekends: From morning till night, frilly engaged pairs flow in one after the other and, after a brief transformation inside, back out onto the square.

★ **Tóth Árpád sétány** (Árpád Tóth Promenade). This romantic, tree-lined promenade along the Buda side of the hill is often mistakenly overlooked by sightseers. Beginning at the Museum of Military History (☞ *above*) the promenade takes you "behind the scenes" along the back sides of the matte-pastel Baroque houses you saw on Úri utca, with their regal arched windows and wrought-iron gates. On a late spring afternoon, the fragrance of the cherry trees and the sweeping view of the quiet Buda neighborhoods below may be enough to revive even the most weary. ⊠ *I, from Kapisztrán tér to Szent György u.*

Úri utca (Úri Street). Running parallel to Tárnok utca, Úri utca has been less commercialized by boutiques and other shops; the longest and oldest street in the castle district, it is lined with many stately houses, all worth special attention for their delicately carved details. Both gateways of the Baroque palace at **Nos. 48–50** are articulated by Gothic niches. The **Telefónia Múzeum** (Telephone Museum), at No. 49, is an endearing little museum entered through a central courtyard shared with the local district police station. Although vintage telephone systems are still in use all over the country, both the oldest and most recent products of telecommunication—from the 1882 wooden box with hose attachment to the latest digital marvels—can be observed and tested here. *Telefónia Múzeum:* ⊠ *Úri u. 49,* ☎ *1/201–8188.* 🎫 *About 100 Ft.* ⊙ *Apr.–Oct., Tues.–Sun. 10–4.*

11 **Zenetörténeti Múzeum** (Museum of Music History). This handsome gray-and-pearl-stone 18th-century palace is where Beethoven allegedly stayed in 1800 when he came to Buda to conduct his works. Now a museum, it displays rare manuscripts and old instruments downstairs in its permanent collection and temporary exhibits upstairs in a small, sunlit hall. The museum also often hosts intimate classical recitals. ⊠ *Táncsics Mihály u. 7,* ☎ *1/214–6770 (ext. 250).* 🎫 *About 200 Ft.* ⊙ *Mid-Nov.–late-Dec. and first 2 wks of Mar., Tues.–Sun. 10–5; mid-Mar.–mid-Nov., Tues.–Sun. 10–6.*

Tabán and Gellért-hegy (Tabán and Gellért Hill)

Spreading below Castle Hill is the old quarter called Tabán (from the Turkish word for "armory"). A onetime suburb of Buda, it was known at the end of the 17th century as Little Serbia (*Rác*) because so many Serbian refugees settled here after fleeing from the Turks. It later became a district of vineyards and small taverns. Though most of the small houses characteristic of this district have been demolished—mainly in the interest of easing traffic—a few traditional buildings remain.

Gellért-hegy (Gellért Hill), 761 ft high, is the most beautiful natural formation on the Buda bank. It takes its name from St. Gellért (Gerard) of Csanad, a Venetian bishop who came to Hungary in the 11th century and, legend has it, was rolled off the top of the hill in a cart by pagans. The walk up can be tough, but take solace from the cluster of hot springs at the foot of the hill, which soothe and cure bathers at the Rác, Rudas, and Gellért baths.

Numbers in the text correspond to numbers in the margin and on the Budapest map.

Batthyány tér 21
Belvárosi plébánia templom 32
Bem József tér 23
Citadella 17
Corvin tér 19
Egyetem tér 37
Evangélikus Templom and Evangélikus Múzeum 42
Ferenciek templom 35
Gellért Szálloda és Thermál Fürdő 18
Gül Baba türbéje . . .24
Hősök tere 48
Iparművészeti Múzeum 51
Kálvin tér 38
Király-fürdő 22
Korzó 30
Köztársaság tér 52
Liszt Ferenc Emlékmúzeum 47
Liszt Ferenc Zeneakadémia 46
Magyar Állami Operaház 44
Magyar Fotógráfusok Háza 45
Magyar Nemzeti Múzeum 39
Margit-sziget 25
Műcsarnok 49
Nagy Zsinagóga . . .40
Néprajzi Múzeum . .27
Országház 26
Rác Fürdő 15
Roosevelt tér 29
Rudas Fürdő 16
Semmelweis Orvostörténeti Múzeum 13
Szabadság tér 28
Szent István Bazilika 43
Szépművészeti Múzeum 50
Szilágyi Dezső tér 20
Tabán plébánia-templom . . .14
Váci utca 34
Városház 41
Vásárcsarnok 36
Vigadó 31
Vígszínház 53
Vörösmarty tér 33

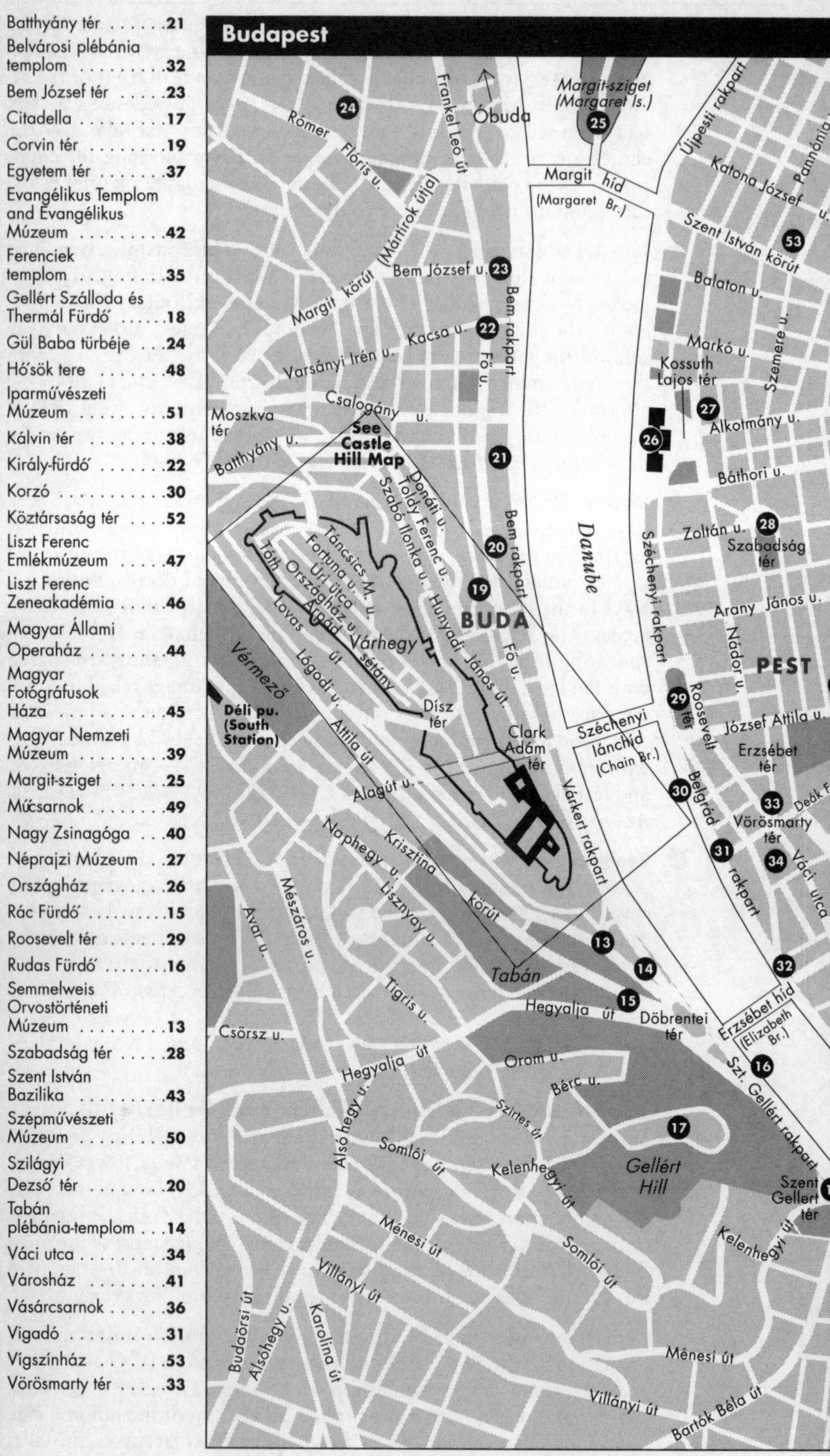

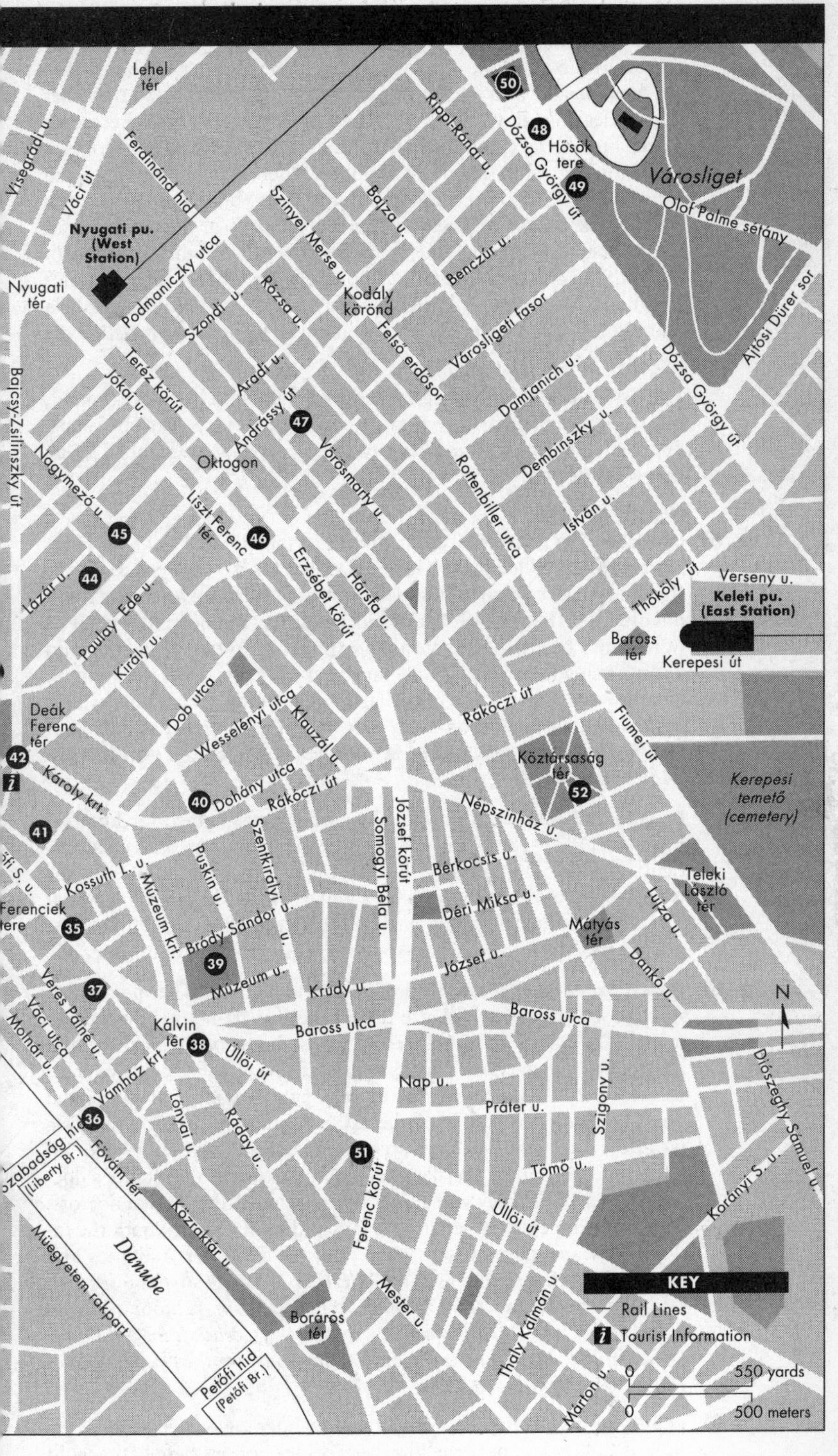

Lehel tér
Visegrádi u.
Váci út
Ferdinánd híd
Nyugati pu. (West Station)
Nyugati tér
Podmaniczky utca
Szondi u.
Rózsa u.
Szinyei Merse u.
Rippl-Rónai u.
Bajza u.
Benczúr u.
Kodály körönd
Felső erdősor
Városligeti fasor
Dózsa György út
Hősök tere
Városliget
Olof Palme sétány
Ajtósi Dürer sor
Bajcsy-Zsilinszky út
Teréz körút
Jókai u.
Aradi u.
Andrássy út
Oktogon
Damjanich u.
Dembinszky u.
Nagymező u.
Liszt Ferenc tér
Vörösmarty u.
Rottenbiller utca
István u.
Lázár u.
Paulay Ede u.
Király u.
Erzsébet körút
Hársfa u.
Thököly út
Verseny u.
Keleti pu. (East Station)
Baross tér
Kerepesi út
Deák Ferenc tér
Dob utca
Wesselényi utca
Klauzál u.
Rákóczi út
Fiumei út
Károly krt.
Dohány utca
Köztársaság tér
Kerepesi temető (cemetery)
Népszínház u.
Szentkirályi u.
József körút
Somogyi Béla u.
Puskin u.
Kossuth L. u.
Múzeum krt.
Bérkocsis u.
Déri Miksa u.
Teleki László tér
Luiza u.
Ferenciek tere
Bródy Sándor u.
Mátyás tér
Dankó u.
József u.
Múzeum u.
Krúdy u.
Veres Pálné u.
Váci utca
Molnár u.
Kálvin tér
Baross utca
N
Vámház krt.
Üllői út
Nap u.
Práter u.
Szigony u.
Diószeghy Sámuel u.
Lónyai u.
Ráday u.
Szabadság híd (Liberty Br.)
Fővám tér
Tömő u.
Közraktár u.
Ferenc körút
Korányi S. u.
Danube
Műegyetem rakpart
Mester u.
Thaly Kálmán u.
Boráros tér
Petőfi híd (Petőfi Br.)
Márton u.
KEY
Rail Lines
Tourist Information
0 550 yards
0 500 meters

A GOOD WALK

From the **Semmelweis Orvostörténeti Múzeum** ⑬, walk around the corner to Szarvas tér and a few yards toward the river to the **Tabán plébánia-templom** ⑭. Walking south on Attila út and crossing to the other side of Hegyalja út, you'll be at the foot of Gellért Hill. From here, take a deep breath and climb the paths and stairs to the **Citadella** ⑰ fortress at the top of the hill (about 30 minutes). After taking in the views and exploring the area, you can descend and treat yourself to a soak or a swim at the **Gellért Szálloda és Thermál Fürdő** ⑱ at the southeastern foot of the hill. On foot, take the paths down the southeastern side of the hill. You can also take Bus 27 down the back of the hill to Móricz Zsigmond körtér and walk back toward the Gellért on busy Bartók Béla út, or take Tram 47, 49, 18, or 19 a couple of stops to Szent Gellért tér.

TIMING

The Citadella and Szabadság szobor are lit in golden lights every night, but the entire Gellért-hegy is at its scenic best every year on August 20, when it forms the backdrop to the spectacular St. Stephen's Day fireworks display.

SIGHTS TO SEE

★ ⑰ **Citadella.** The fortress atop the hill was a much-hated sight for Hungarians. They called it the Gellért Bastille, for it was erected, on the site of an earlier wooden observatory, by the Austrian army as a lookout after the 1848–1849 War of Independence. But no matter what its history may be, the views here are breathtaking. Its transformation into a tourist site during the 1960s improved its image, with the addition of cafés, a beer garden, wine cellars, and a hostel. In its inner wall is a small graphic exhibition (with some relics) of Budapest's 2,000-year history. ✉ *XI, Citadella sétány,* ☎ *No phone.* 🎫 *Free.* ⏲ *Fortress: daily, 24 hrs; amenities hrs vary.*

Erzsébet híd (Elizabeth Bridge). This bridge was named for Empress Elizabeth (1837–1898), called Sissi, of whom the Hungarians were particularly fond. The beautiful but unhappy wife of Franz Joseph, she was stabbed to death in 1898 by an anarchist while boarding a boat on Lake Geneva. The bridge was built between 1897 and 1903; at the time, it was the longest single-span suspension bridge in Europe.

★ ⑱ **Gellért Szálloda és Thermál Fürdő** (Gellért Hotel and Thermal Baths). At the foot of Gellért Hill, are these beautiful art-nouveau establishments. The Danubius Hotel Gellért (☞ Lodging, *below*) is the oldest spa hotel in Hungary, with hot springs that have supplied curative baths for nearly 2,000 years. It is the most popular among tourists, as you don't need reservations, it's quite easy to communicate, and there's a wealth of treatments—including chamomile steam baths, salt-vapor inhalations, and hot mud packs. Many of these treatments require a doctor's prescription; they will accept prescriptions from foreign doctors. Men and women have separate steam and sauna rooms; both the indoor pool and the outdoor wave pool (☞ Outdoor Activities and Sports, *below*) are coed. ✉ *XI, Gellért tér 1,* ☎ *1/466–6166 (baths).* 🎫 *Indoor baths and steam rooms 750 Ft. per 1½ hrs; indoor and pool 1,500 Ft. per day.* ⏲ *Baths weekdays 6 AM–6 PM, weekends 6:30–4 (May–Sept. until 7). May–Sept. weekend massage only until 1 PM. Wave pool May–Sept., daily 6 AM–6 PM.*

⑮ **Rác Fürdő** (Rác Baths). The bright-yellow building tucked away at the foot of Gellért Hill near the Elizabeth Bridge houses these baths, built during the reign of King Zsigmond in the early 15th century and rebuilt by Miklós Ybl in the mid-19th century. Its waters contain alkaline salts and other minerals; you can also get a massage. Women can bathe on Monday, Wednesday, and Friday; men on Tuesday, Thursday, and Saturday (☞ Outdoor Activities and Sports, *below*). These baths are particularly popular with the gay community. ✉ *I, Hadnagy u. 8–10,* ☎ *1/356–1322.* 🎫 *550 Ft.* ⏲ *Mon.–Sat. 6:30–6.*

16 **Rudas Fürdő** (Rudas Baths). This bath is on the riverbank, the original Turkish pool making its interior possibly the most dramatically beautiful of Budapest's baths. A high, dome roof admits pinpricks of bluish-green light into the dark, circular stone hall with its austere columns and arches. Fed by eight springs with a year-round temperature of 44°C (111°F), the Rudas's highly fluoridated waters have been known for 1,000 years. The facility is open to men only (it does not have a large gay following); a less interesting outer swimming pool is open to both sexes (☞ Outdoor Activities and Sports, *below*). Massages are available. ✉ *I, Döbrentei tér 9,* ☎ *1/356–1322.* 🎫 *650 Ft.* ⏲ *Weekdays 6 AM–6 PM, weekends 6–noon.*

13 **Semmelweis Orvostörténeti Múzeum** (Semmelweis Museum of Medical History). This splendid Baroque house was the birthplace of Ignác Semmelweis (1818–1865), the Hungarian physician who proved the contagiousness of puerperal (childbed) fever. It's now a museum that traces the history of healing. Semmelweis's grave is in the garden. ✉ *Apród u. 1–3,* ☎ *1/375–3533.* 🎫 *150 Ft.* ⏲ *Tues.–Sun. 10:30–5:30.*

Szabadság szobor (Liberation Monument). Visible from many parts of the city, this 130-ft-high memorial, which starts just below the southern edge of the Citadella, was originally planned as a memorial to a son of Hungary's then-ruler, Miklós Horthy, whose warplane had crashed in the Ukraine in 1942. However, by the time of its completion in 1947 (three years after Horthy was ousted), it had become a memorial to the Russian soldiers who fell in the 1944–45 siege of Budapest; and hence for decades was associated chiefly with this. From afar it looks light, airy, and even liberating. A sturdy young girl, her hair and robe swirling in the wind, holds a palm branch high above her head. Until recently, she was further embellished with sculptures of giants slaying dragons, Red Army soldiers, and peasants rejoicing at the freedom that Soviet liberation promised (but failed) to bring to Hungary. Since 1992, her mood has lightened: In the Budapest city government's systematic purging of Communist symbols, the Red Combat infantrymen who had flanked the Liberation statue for decades were hacked off and carted away. A few are now on display among the other evicted statues in Szobor Park in the city's 22nd district (☞ Off the Beaten Path, *below*). ✉ *Gellért-hegy.*

OFF THE BEATEN PATH

SZOBOR PARK (Statue Park) – For a look at Budapest's too-recent Iron Curtain past, make the 30-minute drive out to this open-air exhibit, cleverly nicknamed "Tons of Socialism," where 42 of the Communist statues and memorials that once dominated the city's streets and squares have been put out to pasture since the political changes in 1989. Here you can wander among mammoth Lenin and Marx statues and buy socialist-nostalgia souvenirs while songs from the Hungarian and Russian workers' movements play bombastically in the background. ✉ *XXII, Balatoni út, corner of Szabadkai út,* ☎ *1/227–7446.* 🎫 *250 Ft.* ⏲ *Mar.–mid-Nov., daily 8–dusk; mid-Nov.–Feb., weekends 10–dusk.*

14 **Tabán plébánia-templom** (Tabán Parish Church). In 1736, this church was built on the site of a Turkish mosque and subsequently renovated and reconstructed several times. Its present form—mustard-color stone with a rotund, green clock tower—could be described as restrained Baroque. ✉ *I, Attila u. 1.*

North Buda

Most of these sights are along Fő utca (Main Street), a long, straight thoroughfare that starts at the Chain Bridge and runs parallel to the Danube. It is lined on both sides with multistory late-18th-century houses—many darkened by soot and showing their age more than those you've seen in sparklingly restored areas such as Castle Hill. This northbound exploration can be done with the help of Bus 86, which covers the waterfront, or on foot, although distances are fairly great.

Numbers in the text correspond to numbers in the margin and on the Exploring Budapest map.

A GOOD WALK

Beginning at **Batthyány tér** ㉑, with its head-on view of Parliament across the Danube, continue north on Fő utca, passing (or stopping to bathe at) the famous Turkish **Király-fürdő** ㉒. From **Bem József tér** ㉓, one block north, turn left (away from the river) up Fekete Sas utca, crossing busy Margit körút and turning right, one block past, up Mecset utca. This will take you up the hill to **Gül Baba türbéje** ㉔.

TIMING

The tour can fit easily into a few hours, including a good 1½-hour soak at the baths; expect the walk from Bem József tér up the hill to Gül Baba türbéje to take about 25 minutes. Fő utca and Bem József tér can get congested during rush hours (from around 7:30 AM to 8:30 AM and 4:30 PM to 6 PM). Remember that museums are closed Monday and that the Király Baths are open to men and women on different days of the week.

SIGHTS TO SEE

21 **Batthyány tér.** This lovely square, open on its river side, affords a grand view of Parliament, directly across the Danube. The M2 subway, the HÉV electric railway from Szentendre, and various suburban and local buses converge on the square, as do peddlers hawking everything from freshly picked flowers to mismatched pairs of shoes. At No. 7 Batthyány tér is the beautiful, Baroque twin-tower **Szent Anna-templom** (Church of St. Anne), dating from 1740–1762, its oval cupola adorned with frescoes and statuary.

NEED A BREAK? The **Angelika** café (✉ II, Batthyány tér 7, ☎ 1/212–3784), housed in the Church of St. Anne building, serves swirled meringues, chestnut-filled layer cakes, and a plethora of other heavenly pastries, all baked on the premises from family recipes. You can sit inside on small velvet chairs at marble-top tables or at one of the umbrella-shaded tables outdoors. It's open daily 10 AM–10 PM.

23 **Bem József tér.** This square near the river is not particularly picturesque and can get heavy with traffic, but it houses the statue of its important namesake, Polish general József Bem, who offered his services to the 1848 revolutionaries in Vienna and then Hungary. Reorganizing the rebel forces in Transylvania, he was the war's most successful general. It was at this statue on October 23, 1956, that a great student demonstration in sympathy with the Poles' striving for liberal reforms exploded into the brave and tragic Hungarian uprising suppressed by the Red Army.

19 **Corvin tér.** This small, shady square on Fő utca is the site of the turn-of-the-20th-century Folk Art Association administration building and the Budai Vigadó concert hall (☞ Nightlife and the Arts, *below*) at No. 8.

24 **Gül Baba türbéje** (Tomb of Gül Baba). Gül Baba, a 16th-century dervish and poet whose name means "father of roses" in Turkish, was buried in a tomb built of carved stone blocks with four oval windows.

He fought in several wars waged by the Turks and fell during the siege of Buda in 1541. The tomb remains a place of pilgrimage; it is considered Europe's northernmost Muslim shrine and marks the spot where he was slain. Set at an elevation on Rózsadomb (Rose Hill), the tomb is near a good lookout for city views. ✉ *II, Mecset u. 14,* ☎ *1/355–8764.* 🎫 *100 Ft.* ⏲ *May–Oct., Tues.–Sun. 10–4.*

Gyermek vasút (Children's Railway). The 12-km (7-mi) Children's Railway runs from Széchenyi-hegy to Hűvösvölgy. The sweeping views make the trip well worthwhile for children and adults alike. Departures are from Széchenyi-hegy; to get there, take a cog railway (public transport tickets valid) uphill to the last stop and walk a few hundred yards down a short, partly forested road to the left, in the direction most others will be going. ✉ *Cog railway station: intersection of Szillágyi Erzsébet fasor and Pasaréti út.* 🎫 *Children's Railway: about 140 Ft. one-way.* ⏲ *Trains run (from Széchenyi-hegy) late Apr.–Oct., daily 8:45–5; Nov.–mid-Mar., Tues.–Fri. 10–4, weekends 10–5 (sometimes closed Tues.); mid-Mar.–late Apr., Tues.–Fri. 9:30–5, weekends 10–5.*

OFF THE BEATEN PATH

JÁNOSHEGY (Janos Hill) – A *libegő* (chairlift) will take you to Janos Hill—at 1,729 ft, the highest point in Budapest—where you can climb a lookout tower for the best view of the city. ✉ *Chairlift: Zugligeti út 97 (take Bus 158 from Moszkva tér to the last stop, Zugligeti út,* ☎ *1/394–3764.* 🎫 *One-way 250 Ft., round-trip 450 Ft.* ⏲ *Mid-May–Aug., daily 9–6; Sept.–mid-May (depending on weather), daily 9:30–4; closed every other Mon.*

Kapucinus templom (Capuchin Church). This church was converted from a Turkish mosque at the end of the 17th century. Damaged during the revolution in 1849, it acquired its current romantic-style exterior when it was rebuilt a few years later. ✉ *II, Fő u. 32.*

22 **Király-fürdő** (King Baths). The royal gem of Turkish baths in Budapest was built in the 16th century by the Turkish pasha of Buda. Its stone cupola, crowned by a golden moon and crescent, arches over the steamy, dark pools indoors. It is open to men on Monday, Wednesday, and Friday; to women on Tuesday, Thursday, and Saturday (☞ Outdoor Activities and Sports, *below*). These baths are very popular with the gay community. ✉ *II, Fő u. 84,* ☎ *1/202–3688.* 🎫 *500 Ft.* ⏲ *Weekdays 6:30 AM–6 PM, Sat. 6:30–noon.*

20 **Szilágyi Dezső tér.** This is another of the charming little squares punctuating Fő utca; here you'll find the house where composer Béla Bartók lived, at No. 4.

Margit-sziget (Margaret Island)

More than 2½ km (1½ mi) long and covering nearly 200 acres, **Margit-sziget** ㉕ is ideal for strolling, jogging, sunbathing, or just loafing. In good weather, the island draws a multitudinous cross section of the city's population out to its gardens and sporting facilities. The outdoor pool complex of the Palatinus Baths (toward the Buda side), built in 1921, can attract tens of thousands of people on a summer day. Nearby are a tennis stadium, a youth athletic center, boathouses, sports grounds, and, most impressive of all, the Nemzeti Sportuszoda (National Sports Swimming Pool), designed by the architect Alfred Hajós (while still in his teens, Hajós won two gold medals in swimming at the first modern Olympic Games, held in Athens in 1896). In addition, walkers, joggers, bicyclists, and rollerbladers do laps around the island's perimeter and up and down the main road, closed to traffic except for Bus 26 (and a few official vehicles), which travels up and down the island and across the Margaret Bridge to and from Pest.

The island's natural curative hot springs have given rise to the Danubius Grand and Thermal hotels on the northern end of the island (☞ Lodging, *below*) and are piped in to two spa hotels on the mainland, the Aquincum on the Buda bank and the Hélia on the Pest side.

A GOOD WALK

Entering the island from its southern end at the **Margit híd,** stroll (or rent a bicycle and pedal) north along any of the several tree-shaded paths, including the **Művész sétány,** pausing for a picnic on an open lawn, and eventually ending up at the rock garden at the northern end. From here, you can wander back to the southern end or take Bus 26 on the island's only road.

TIMING

A leisurely walk simply from one end to the other would take about 40 minutes, but it's nice to spend extra time wandering. To experience Margaret Island's role in Budapest life fully, go on a Saturday or Sunday afternoon to join and/or watch people whiling away the day. Sunday is a particularly good choice for strategic sightseers, who can utilize the rest of the week to cover those city sights and areas that are closed on Sunday. On weekdays, you'll share the island only with joggers and children playing hooky from school.

SIGHTS TO SEE

Margit híd (Margaret Bridge). At the southern end of the island, the Margaret Bridge is the closer of the two entrances for those coming from downtown Buda or Pest. Just north of the Chain Bridge, the bridge walkway provides gorgeous midriver views of Castle Hill and Parliament. Toward the end of 1944, the bridge was blown up by the retreating Nazis while it was crowded with rush-hour traffic. It was rebuilt in the same unusual shape—forming an obtuse angle in midstream, with a short leg leading down to the island. The original bridge was built during the 1840s by French engineer Ernest Gouin in collaboration with Gustave Eiffel.

25 **Margit-sziget** (Margaret Island). The island was first mentioned almost 2,000 years ago as the summer residence of the commander of the Roman garrison at nearby Aquincum. Later known as Rabbit Island (Insula Leporum), it was a royal hunting ground during the Árpád dynasty. King Imre, who reigned from 1196 to 1204, held court here, and several convents and monasteries were built here during the Middle Ages. (During a walk round the island, you'll see the ruins of a few of these buildings.) It takes its current name from St. Margaret, the pious daughter of King Béla IV, who at the ripe old age of 10 retired to a Dominican nunnery here.

Marosvásárhelyi zenélő kút (Marosvásárhely Musical Fountain). At the northern end of the island is a copy of the water-powered Marosvásárhely Musical Fountain, which plays songs and chimes. The original was designed more than 150 years ago by a Transylvanian named Péter Bodor. It stands near a serene, artificial **rock garden** with Japanese dwarf trees and lily ponds. The stream coursing through it never freezes, for it comes from a natural hot spring causing it instead to give off thick steam in winter that enshrouds the garden in a mystical cloud.

Művész sétány (Artists' Promenade). Through the center of the island runs the Artists' Promenade, lined with busts of Hungarian visual artists, writers, and musicians. Shaded by giant plane trees, it's a perfect place to stroll. The promenade passes close to the **rose garden** (in the center of the island), a large grassy lawn surrounded by blooming flower beds planted with hundreds of kinds of flowers. It's a great spot to picnic or to watch a game of soccer or Ultimate Frisbee, both of which are regularly played here on weekend afternoons.

Downtown Pest and the Kis Körút (Little Ring Road)

Budapest's urban heart is full of bona fide sights plus innumerable tiny streets and grand avenues where you can wander for hours admiring the city's stately old buildings—some freshly sparkling after their first painting in decades, others silently but still gracefully crumbling.

Dominated by the Parliament building, the district surrounding Kossuth tér is the legislative, diplomatic, and administrative nexus of Budapest; most of the ministries are here, as are the National Bank and Courts of Justice. Downriver, the romantic Danube promenade, the Duna korzó, extends along the stretch of riverfront across from Castle Hill. With Vörösmarty tér and pedestrian shopping street Váci utca just inland, this area forms Pest's tourist core. Going south, the korzó ends at Március 15 tér. One block in from the river, Ferenciek tere marks the beginning of the university area, spreading south of Kossuth Lajos utca. Here, the streets are narrower and the sounds of your footsteps echo off the elegantly aging stone buildings.

Pest is laid out in broad circular *körúts* ("ring roads" or boulevards). Vámház körút is the first sector of the 2½-km (1½-mi) Kis körút (Little Ring Road), which traces the route of the Old Town wall from Szabadság híd (Liberty Bridge) to Deák tér. Construction of the inner körút began in 1872 and was completed in 1880. Changing names as it curves, after Kálvin tér it becomes Múzeum körút (passing by the National Museum), and then Károly körút for its final stretch ending at Deák tér. Deák tér, the only place where all three subway lines converge, could be called the dead-center of downtown. East of Károly körút are the weathered streets of Budapest's former ghetto.

A GOOD WALK

Starting at Kossuth tér to see the **Országház** ㉖ and the **Néprajzi Múzeum** ㉗, it's worth walking a few blocks southeast to take in stately **Szabadság tér** ㉘ before heading back to the Danube and south to the foot of the **Széchenyi Lánchíd** at **Roosevelt tér** ㉙. As this tour involves quite a bit of walking, you may want to take Tram 2 from Kossuth tér a few stops downriver to Roosevelt tér to save your energy. While time and/or energy may not allow it just now, at some point during your visit, a walk across the Chain Bridge is a must. From Roosevelt tér go south, across the street, and join the **korzó** ㉚ along the river, strolling past the **Vigadó** ㉛ at Vigadó tér, all the way to the **Belvárosi plébánia templom** ㉜ at Március 15 tér, just under the Elizabeth Bridge. Double back up the korzó to Vigadó tér and walk in from the river on Vigadó utca to **Vörösmarty tér** ㉝.

Follow the crowds down pedestrian-only **Váci utca** ㉞, crossing busy Kossuth Lajos utca near Ferenciek tere and continuing along Váci utca's southern stretch to the **Vásárcsarnok** ㊱. Doubling back a few blocks on Váci utca, turn right onto Szerb utca and stroll past the **Szerb Ortodox templom** to the street's end at **Egyetem tér** ㊲. Here, you are going through the darker, narrower streets of this student-filled, increasingly trendy area. A detour into any of the other side streets will give you a good flavor of the area. Walking south on Kecskeméti utca, you will reach **Kálvin tér** ㊳. To save time and energy, you can also take Tram 47 or 49 from Fővám tér, in front of the Vásárcsarnok, one stop away from the Danube to Kálvin tér. Just north of Kálvin tér on Múzeum körút is the **Magyar Nemzeti Múzeum** ㊴. The **Nagy Zsinagóga** ㊵ is about ¾ km (⅓ mi) farther north along the Kis körút (Small Ring Road)—a longish walk or one short stop by tram. From here, more walking along the körút, or a tram ride to the last stop, brings you to Pest's main hub, Deák tér. The **Szent István Bazilika** (43) is an extra but rewarding 500-yard walk north on Bajcsy-Zsilinszky út.

TIMING

This is a particularly rich part of the city; the suggested walk will take the better part of a day, including time to visit the museums, stroll on the korzó, and browse on Vaci utca—not to mention time for lunch. Keep in mind that the museums are closed on Monday.

SIGHTS TO SEE

32 **Belvárosi plébánia templom** (Inner City Parish Church). Dating to the 12th century, this is the oldest ecclesiastical building in Pest. It's actually built on something even older—the remains of the Contra Aquincum, a 3rd-century Roman fortress and tower, parts of which are visible next to the church. There is hardly any architectural style that cannot be found in some part or another, starting with a single Romanesque arch in its south tower. The single nave still has its original Gothic chancel and some 15th-century Gothic frescoes. Two side chapels contain beautifully carved Renaissance altarpieces and tabernacles of red marble from the early 16th century. During Budapest's years of Turkish occupation, the church served as a mosque—a *mihrab,* a Muslim prayer niche, is a reminder of this. During the 18th century, the church was given two Baroque towers and its present facade. In 1808 it was enriched with a rococo pulpit, and still later a superb winged triptych was added to the main altar. From 1867 to 1875, Franz Liszt lived only a few steps away from the church, in a town house where he held regular "musical Sundays" at which Richard and Cosima Wagner were frequent guests and participants. Liszt's own musical Sunday mornings often began in this church. An admirer of its acoustics and organ, he conducted many masses here, including the first Budapest performance of his *Missa Choralis,* in 1872. ✉ *V, Március 15 tér 2,* ☎ *1/318–3108.*

37 **Egyetem tér** (University Square). Budapest's University of Law sits here in the heart of the city's university neighborhood. On one corner is the cool gray-and-green marble **Egyetemi Templom** (University Church), one of Hungary's most beautiful Baroque buildings. Built between 1725 and 1742, it has an especially splendid pulpit.

42 **Evangélikus Templom and Evangélikus Múzeum** (Lutheran Church and Lutheran Museum). The neoclassical Lutheran Church sits in the center of it all on busy Deák tér. Classical concerts are regularly held here. The church's interior designer, János Krausz, flouted then-traditional church architecture by placing a single large interior beneath the huge vaulted roof structure. The adjoining school is now the Lutheran Museum, which traces the role of Protestantism in Hungarian history and contains Martin Luther's original will. ✉ *V, Deák Ferenc tér 4,* ☎ *1/317–4173.* *Museum 300 Ft. (includes tour of church).* *Museum: Mar.–Dec., Tues.–Sun. 10–6; Jan.–Feb. until 5. Church: open only in conjunction with museum visit and during services (Sun. 9, 11, and 6).*

35 **Ferenciek Templom** (Franciscan church). This pale-yellow church was built in 1743. On the wall facing Kossuth Lajos utca is a bronze relief showing a scene from the devastating flood of 1838; the detail is so vivid that it almost makes you seasick. A faded arrow below the relief indicates the high-water mark of almost 4 ft. Next to it is the **Nereids Fountain,** a popular meeting place for students from the nearby Eötvös Loránd University. ✉ *V, Ferenciek tere.*

NEED A BREAK? Budapest's newest, most touted café, the **Centrál** (✉ V, Károlyi Mihály u. 9, ☎ 1/266–4572), is really nothing new: đFrom 1887, famous writers scribbled away here every day. This, not to mention libraries-worth of thoughtful conversation, kept up until the Communists, who disapproved of such gathering places, shut it down in 1949. At the turn of the new millennium it reopened (after a stint as a video arcade) with a bang. Elegant, smoky, and crowded, the Centrál offers time-honored sweets and both traditional and lighter meals.

Görög Ortodox templom (Greek Orthodox Church). Built at the end of the 18th century in late-Baroque style, the Greek Orthodox Church was remodeled a century later by Miklós Ybl, who designed the Opera House and many other important Budapest landmarks. The church retains some fine wood carvings and a dazzling array of icons by a late-18th-century Serbian master Miklós Jankovich. ⊠ *V, Petőfi tér 2/b.*

38 **Kálvin tér** (Calvin Square). Calvin Square takes its name from the neoclassical Protestant church that tries to dominate this busy traffic hub; more glaringly noticeable, however, is a Pepsi billboard as tall and wide as the bottom half of the church. The Kecskeméti Kapu, a main gate of Pest, once stood here, as well as a cattle market that was a notorious den of thieves. At the beginning of the 19th century, this was where Pest ended and the prairie began.

★ 30 **Korzó** (Promenade). The neighborhood to the south of Roosevelt tér has regained much of its past elegance—if not its architectural grandeur—with the erection of the Atrium Hyatt, Inter-Continental, and Budapest Marriott luxury hotels. Traversing all three and continuing well beyond them is the riverside korzó, a pedestrian promenade lined with park benches and appealing outdoor cafés from which one can enjoy postcard-perfect views of Gellért Hill and Castle Hill directly across the Danube. Try to take a stroll in the evening, when the views are lit up in shimmering gold. ⊠ From Eötvös tér to Március 15 ter.

Közgazdagsági Egyetem (University of Economics). Just below the Liberty Bridge on the waterfront, the monumental neo-Renaissance building was once the Customs House. Built in 1871–1874 by Miklós Ybl, it is now also known as *közgáz* ("econ."), following a stint during the Communist era as Karl Marx University. ⊠ *V, Fővám tér.*

39 **Magyar Nemzeti Múzeum** (Hungarian National Museum). Built between 1837 and 1847, the museum is a fine example of 19th-century classicism—simple, well proportioned, and surrounded by a large garden. In front of this building on March 15, 1848, Sándor Petőfi recited his revolutionary poem, the "National Song" ("Nemzeti dal"), and the "12 Points," a list of political demands by young Hungarians calling on the people to rise up against the Hapsburgs. Celebrations of the national holiday commemorating the failed revolution are held on these steps every year on March 15.

What used to be the museum's biggest attraction, the **Szent Korona** (Holy Crown), was moved to the Parliament building in early 2000 to mark the millenary of the coronation of Hungary's first king, St. Stephen (☞ Országház, *below*). The museum still has worthwhile rarities, however, including a completely furnished Turkish tent; masterworks of cabinetmaking and woodcarving, including pews from churches in Nyírbátor and Transylvania; a piano that belonged to both Beethoven and Liszt; and, in the treasury, masterpieces of goldsmithing, among them the 11th-century Constantions Monomachos crown from Byzantium and the richly pictorial 16th-century chalice of Miklós Pálffy. Looking at it is like reading the "Prince Valiant" comic strip in gold. The epic Hungarian history exhibit chronicles, among other things, the end of Communism and the much-celebrated exodus of the Russian troops. ⊠ *IX, Múzeum krt. 14–16,* ☎ *1/327–7773.*

400 Ft. ⏲ Mid-Mar.–mid-Oct., Tues.–Sun. 10–6; mid-Oct.–mid-Mar., Tues.–Sun. 10–5.

★ 40 **Nagy Zsinagóga** (Great Synagogue). Seating 3,000, Europe's largest synagogue was designed by Ludwig Förs and built between 1844 and 1859 in a Byzantine-Moorish style described as "consciously archaic Romantic-Eastern." Desecrated by German and Hungarian Nazis, it was painstakingly reconstructed with donations from all over the world; its doors reopened in fall 1996. While it is used for regular services during much of the year, it is generally not used in midwinter as the space is too large to heat; between December and February, visiting hours are erratic. In the courtyard behind the synagogue, a weeping willow made of metal honors the victims of the Holocaust. Liszt and Saint-Saëns are among the great musicians who have played the synagogue's grand organ. ✉ *VII, Dohány u. 2–8,* ☎ *1/342–1335.* 🎫 *Free.* ⏲ *Weekdays 10–3, Sun. 10–3. Closed Jewish holidays and Dec.*

★ 27 **Néprajzi Múzeum** (Museum of Ethnography). The 1890s neoclassical temple formerly housed the Supreme Court. Now an impressive permanent exhibition, "The Folk Culture of the Hungarian People," explains all aspects of peasant life from the end of the 18th century until World War I; explanatory texts are provided in both English and Hungarian. Besides embroideries, pottery, and carvings—the authentic pieces you can't see at touristy folk shops—there are farming tools, furniture, and traditional costumes. The central room of the building alone is worth the entrance fee: a majestic hall with ornate marble staircases and pillars, and towering stained-glass windows. ✉ *V, Kossuth tér 12,* ☎ *1/332–6340.* 🎫 *300 Ft.* ⏲ *Mar.–mid-Oct., Tues.–Sun. 10–5:30; mid-Oct.–Feb., Tues.–Sun. 10–4:30. Hours may vary during special exhibits.*

★ 26 **Országház** (Parliament). The most visible symbol of Budapest's left bank is the huge neo-Gothic Parliament. Mirrored in the Danube much the way Britain's Parliament is reflected by the Thames, it lies midway between the Margaret and Chain bridges and can be reached by the M2 subway (Kossuth tér station) and waterfront Tram 2. A fine example of historicizing, eclectic fin-de-siècle architecture, it was designed by the Hungarian architect Ímre Steindl and built by a thousand workers between 1885 and 1902. The grace and dignity of its long facade and 24 slender towers, with spacious arcades and high windows balancing its vast central dome, lend this living landmark a refreshingly Baroque spatial effect. The exterior is lined with 90 statues of great figures in Hungarian history; the corbels are ornamented by 242 allegorical statues. Inside are 691 rooms, 10 courtyards, and 29 staircases; some 88 pounds of gold were used for the staircases and halls. These halls are also a gallery of late-19th-century Hungarian art, with frescoes and canvases depicting Hungarian history, starting with Mihály Munkácsy's large painting of the Magyar Conquest of 896.

Since early 2000 Parliament's most sacred treasure has not been the Hungarian legislature but the newly exhibited **Szent Korona** (Holy Crown), which reposes with other royal relics under the cupola. The crown sits like a golden soufflé above a Byzantine band of holy scenes in enamel and pearls and other gems. It seems to date from the 12th century, so it could not be the crown that Pope Sylvester II presented to St. Stephen in the year 1000, when he was crowned the first king of Hungary. Nevertheless, it is known as the Crown of St. Stephen and has been regarded—even by Communist governments—as the legal symbol of Hungarian sovereignty and unbroken statehood. In 1945 the fleeing Hungarian army handed over the crown and its accompanying regalia to the Americans rather than have them fall into Soviet hands. They were restored to Hungary in 1978. Through at least August 20,

2001 the crown can be seen in the scope of daily tours of the Parliament building, except during ceremonial events and when the legislature is in session (usually Monday and Tuesday from late summer to spring); its permanent home beyond that date has yet to be decided. Lines may be long, so it's best to call in advance. The building can also be visited on group tours organized by IBUSZ Travel (☞ Visitor Information, *below*). ✉ *V, Kossuth tér,* ☎ *1/441–4904 or 1/441–4415.* *1,100 Ft..* ⏲ *Daily tours in English at 10 and 2, starting from Gate No. 10, just right of the main stairs.*

29 **Roosevelt tér** (Roosevelt Square). This square opening onto the Danube is less closely connected with the U.S. president than with the progressive Hungarian statesman Count István Széchenyi, dubbed "the greatest Hungarian" even by his adversary, Kossuth. The neo-Renaissance palace of the **Magyar Tudományos Akadémia** (Academy of Sciences) on the north side was built between 1862 and 1864, after Széchenyi's suicide. It is a fitting memorial, for in 1825, the statesman donated a year's income from all his estates to establish the academy. Another Széchenyi project, the Széchenyi Lánchíd (☞ *below*), leads into the square; there stands a statue of Széchenyi near one of another statesman, Ferenc Deák, whose negotiations led to the establishment of the dual monarchy after Kossuth's 1848–1849 revolution failed. Both men lived on this square.

★ 28 **Szabadság tér** (Liberty Square). This sprawling square is dominated by the longtime headquarters of **Magyar Televizió** (Hungarian Television), a former stock exchange with what look like four temples and two castles on its roof. (At press time the building was due to be auctioned off as the broadcasters move elsewhere.) Across from it is a solemn-looking neoclassical shrine, the **Nemzeti Bank** (National Bank). The bank's Postal Savings Bank branch, adjacent to the main building but visible from behind Szabadság tér on Hold utca, is another exuberant Art Nouveau masterpiece of architect Ödön Lechner, built in 1901 with colorful majolica mosaics, characteristically curvaceous windows, and pointed towers ending in swirling gold flourishes. In the square's center remains one of the few monuments to the Russian "liberation" that were spared the cleansing of symbols of one-party rule. The decision to retain this obelisk—primarily because it marks a gravesite of fallen Soviet troops—caused outrage among some groups. With the Stars and Stripes flying out in front, the **American Embassy** is at Szabadság tér 12.

Széchenyi Lánchíd (Chain Bridge). This is the oldest and most beautiful of the seven road bridges that span the Danube in Budapest. Before it was built, the river could be crossed only by ferry or by a pontoon bridge that had to be removed when ice blocks began floating downstream in winter. It was constructed at the initiative of the great Hungarian reformer and philanthropist Count István Széchenyi, using an 1839 design by the French civil engineer William Tierney Clark. This classical, almost poetically graceful and symmetrical suspension bridge was finished by his Scottish namesake, Adam Clark, who also built the 383-yard tunnel under Castle Hill, thus connecting the Danube quay with the rest of Buda. After it was destroyed by the Nazis, the bridge was rebuilt in its original form (though slightly widened for traffic) and was reopened in 1949, on the centenary of its inauguration. At the Buda end of the bridge is **Clark Ádám tér** (Adam Clark Square), where you can zip up to Castle Hill on the sometimes crowded Sikló funicular. *250 Ft.* ⏲ *Funicular daily 7:30 AM–10 PM; closed every other Mon.*

★ 43 **Szent István Bazilika** (St. Stephen's Basilica). Handsome and massive, this is one of the chief landmarks of Pest and the city's largest church—

it can hold 8,500 people. Its very Holy Roman front porch greets you with a tympanum bustling with statuary. The basilica's dome and the dome of Parliament are by far the most visible in the Pest skyline, and this is no accident: With the Magyar Millennium of 1896 in mind (the lavishly celebrated thousandth anniversary of the settling of the Carpathian Basin in 896), both domes were planned to be 315 ft high.

The millennium was not yet in sight when architect József Hild began building the basilica in neoclassical style in 1851, two years after the revolution was suppressed. After Hild's death, the project was taken over in 1867 by Miklós Ybl, the architect who did the most to transform modern Pest into a monumental metropolis. Wherever he could, Ybl shifted Hild's motifs toward the neo-Renaissance mode that Ybl favored. When the dome collapsed, partly damaging the walls, he made even more drastic changes. Ybl died in 1891, five years before the 1,000-year celebration, and the basilica was completed in neo-Renaissance style by József Kauser—but not until 1905.

Below the cupola is a rich collection of late-19th-century Hungarian art: mosaics, altarpieces, and statuary (what heady days the Magyar Millennium must have meant for local talents!). There are 150 kinds of marble, all from Hungary except for the Carrara in the sanctuary's centerpiece: a white statue of King (St.) Stephen I, Hungary's first king and patron saint. Stephen's mummified right hand is preserved as a relic in the **Szent Jobb Kápolna** (Holy Right Chapel); press a button and it will be illuminated for two minutes. Visitors can also climb the 364 stairs (or take the elevator) to the top of the cupola for a spectacular view of the city. Extensive restorations have been under way at the aging basilica for years and should wrap up within this decade. ✉ *V, Szt. István tér,* ☎ *1/311–0839.* 🎫 *Church free, Szt. Jobb chapel 100 Ft., cupola 400 Ft.* 🕒 *Church Mon.–Sat. 9–7, Sun. 1–5; Szt. Jobb Chapel Apr.–Sept., Mon.–Sat. 9–5, Sun. 1–5; Oct.–Mar., Mon.–Sat. 10–4, Sun. 1–4; Cupola Apr. and Sept.–Oct., daily 10–5; May–Aug., daily 9–6.*

Szerb Ortodox templom (Serbian Orthodox Church). Built in 1688, this lovely burnt-orange church, one of Budapest's oldest buildings, sits in a shaded garden surrounded by thick stone walls of the same color detailed with large-tile mosaics and wrought-iron gates. ✉ *V, Szerb u.*

34 **Váci utca.** Immediately north of Elizabeth Bridge is Budapest's best-known shopping street and most unabashed tourist zone, Váci utca, a pedestrian precinct with electrified 19th-century lampposts and smart shops with credit-card emblems on ornate doorways. No bargain basement, Váci utca gets its special flavor from the mix of native furriers, tailors, designers, shoemakers, and folk artists, as well as an increasing number of internationally known boutiques. There are also bookstores and china and crystal shops, as well as gourmet food stores redolent of paprika. Váci utca's second half, south of Kossuth Lajos utca, was transformed into another pedestrian-only zone a few years ago: This somewhat broader stretch of road, while coming to resemble the northern side, still retains a flavorful, more soothing ambiance of its own. On both halves of Váci utca, watch your purses and wallets—against inflated prices *and* active pickpockets. ✉ *V, from Vörösmarty tér to Fővám tér.*

41 **Városház** (City Hall). The monumental former city council building, which used to be a hospital for wounded soldiers and then a resort for the elderly ("home" would be too cozy for so vast a hulk), is now Budapest's city hall. It's enormous enough to loom over the row of shops and businesses lining Károly körút in front of it but can only be entered through courtyards or side streets (it is most accessible from Ger-

lóczy utca). The Tuscan columns at the main entrance and the allegorical statuary of *Atlas, War,* and *Peace* are especially splendid. There was once a chapel in the center of the main facade, but now only its spire remains. ✉ *V, Városház u. 9–11,* ☎ *1/327–1000.*

36 **Vásárcsarnok** (Central Market Hall). The magnificent hall, a 19th-century iron-frame construction, was reopened in late 1994 after years of renovation (and disputes over who would foot the bill). Even during the leanest years of Communist shortages, the abundance of food came as a revelation to shoppers from East and West. Today, the cavernous, three-story market once again teems with people browsing among stalls packed with salamis and red-paprika chains. Upstairs you can buy folk embroideries and souvenirs. ✉ *IX, Vámház krt. 1–3.* ⏲ *Mon. 6–5, Tues.–Fri. 6* AM*–6* PM*, Sat. 6–2.*

31 **Vigadó** (Concert Hall). Designed in a striking romantic style by Frigyes Feszl and inaugurated in 1865 with Franz Liszt conducting his own *St. Elizabeth Oratorio,* the concert hall is a curious mixture of Byzantine, Moorish, Romanesque, and Hungarian motifs, punctuated by dancing statues and sturdy pillars. Brahms, Debussy, and Casals are among the other phenomenal musicians who have graced its stage. Mahler's *Symphony No. 1* and many works by Bartók were first performed here. While you can go into the lobby on your own, the hall is open only for concerts. ✉ *V, Vigadó tér 2.*

★ 33 **Vörösmarty tér** (Vörösmarty Square). This large, handsome square at the northern end of Váci utca is the heart of Pest's tourist life. Street musicians and sidewalk cafés make it one of the liveliest places in Budapest and a good spot to sit and relax—if you can ward off the aggressive caricature sketchers. Grouped around a white-marble statue of the 19th-century poet and dramatist Mihály Vörösmarty are luxury shops, an airline office, and an elegant former pissoir. Now a lovely kiosk, it displays gold-painted historic scenes of the square's golden days. ✉ *V, at northern end of Váci u.*

NEED A BREAK?

The best-known, tastiest, and most tasteful address on Vörösmarty Square belongs to the **Gerbeaud** pastry shop (✉ V, Vörösmarty tér 7, ☎ 1/429–9000), founded in 1858 by a French confectioner and later taken over by the Swiss family Gerbeaud. Filling most of a square block, it offers dozens of sweets (as well as sandwiches, coffee, and other not so sugary snacks), served in a salon with green-marble tables and Regency-style marble fireplaces or at tables outside in summer. A mildly hostile staff is an integral part of the Gerbeaud tradition.

Zsidó Múzeum (Jewish Museum). The four-room museum, around the corner from the Great Synagogue (☞ *above*) has displays explaining the effect of the Holocaust on Hungarian and Transylvanian Jews. (There are labels in English.) In late 1993, burglars ransacked the museum and got away with approximately 80% of its priceless collection; several months later, the stolen objects were found in Romania and returned to their home. ✉ *Dohány u. 2,* ☎ *1/342–8949.* 🎫 *600 Ft.* ⏲ *Mid-Mar.–mid-Oct., Mon.–Thurs. 10–5, Fri. and Sun. 10–3; mid-Oct.–mid-Mar., weekdays 10–3, Sun. 10–1.*

Andrássy Út

Behind St. Stephen's Basilica, at the crossroad along Bajcsy-Zsilinszky út, begins Budapest's grandest avenue, **Andrássy út.** For too many years, this broad boulevard bore the tongue-twisting name of Népköztársaság útja (Avenue of the People's Republic) and, for a while before that, Stalin Avenue. In 1990, however, it reverted to its old name honoring Count Gyula Andrássy, a statesman who in 1867 became the first constitutional premier of Hungary. The boulevard that would eventually bear his name was begun in 1872, as Buda and Pest (and Óbuda) were about to be unified. Most of the mansions that line it were completed by 1884. It took another dozen years before the first **underground railway** on the Continent was completed for—you guessed it—the Magyar Millennium in 1896. Though preceded by London's Underground (1863), Budapest's was the world's first electrified subway. Only slightly modernized but refurbished for the 1996 millecentenary, this "Little Metro" is still running a 4-km (2½-mi) stretch from Vörösmarty tér to the far end of City Park. Using tiny yellow trains with tanklike treads, and stopping at antique stations marked FÖLDALATTI (Underground) on their wrought-iron entranceways, Line 1 is a tourist attraction in itself. Six of its 10 stations are along Andrássy út.

A GOOD WALK

A walking tour of Andrássy út's sights is straightforward: Begin at its downtown end, near Deák tér, and stroll its length (about 2 km/1¼ mi) all the way to Hősök tere. The first third of the avenue, from Bajcsy-Zsilinszky út to the eight-sided intersection called Oktogon, boasts a row of eclectic city palaces with balconies held up by stone giants. Pause at the **Magyar Állami Operaház** ㊹ and other points along the way. One block past the Operaház, Andrássy út intersects Budapest's Broadway: Nagymező utca contains several theaters, cabarets, and nightclubs. Andrássy út alters when it crosses the Nagy körút (Outer Ring Road), at the Oktogon crossing. Four rows of trees and scores of flower beds make the thoroughfare look more like a garden promenade, but its cultural character lingers. Farther up, past **Kodály körönd,** the rest of Andrássy út is dominated by widely spaced mansions surrounded by private gardens. At **Hősök tere** ㊽, browse through the **Műcsarnok** ㊾ and/or the **Szépművészeti Múzeum** ㊿, and finish off with a stroll into the Városliget (City Park; ☞ *below*). You can return to Deák tér on the subway, the Millenniumi Földalatti (Millennial Underground).

TIMING

As most museums are closed Monday, it's best to explore Andrássy út on other days, preferably weekdays or early Saturday, when stores are also open for browsing. During opera season, you can time your exploration to land you at the Operaház stairs just before 7 PM to watch the spectacle of operagoers flowing in for the evening's performance.

SIGHTS TO SEE

Budapest Bábszínház (Budapest Puppet Theater). In this templelike, eclectic building, you'll find colorful shows that both children and adults enjoy even if they don't understand Hungarian. Watch for showings of *Cinderella* (*Hamupipőke*) and *Snow White and the Seven Dwarfs* (*Hófehérke*), part of the theater's regular repertoire. ✉ *VI, Andrássy út 69,* ☏ *1/321–5200.*

Drechsler Kastély (Drechsler Palace). Across the street from the Operaház is the French Renaissance–style Drechsler Palace. An early work by Ödön Lechner, Hungary's master of Art Nouveau, it is now the home of the National Ballet School and is generally not open to tourists. ✉ *VI, Andrássy út 25.*

★ ㊽ **Hősök tere** (Heroes' Square). Andrássy út ends in grandeur at Heroes' Square, with Budapest's answer to Berlin's Brandenburg Gate. Cleaned and refurbished in 1996 for the millecentenary, the **Millenniumi Emlékmű** (Millennial Monument) is a semicircular twin colonnade with statues of Hungary's kings and leaders between its pillars. Set back in its open center, a 118-ft stone column is crowned by a dynamic statue of the archangel Gabriel, his outstretched arms bearing the ancient emblems of Hungary. At its base ride seven bronze horsemen: the Magyar chieftains, led by Árpád, whose tribes conquered the land in 896. Before the column lies a simple marble slab, the **Nemzeti Háborús Emlék Tábla** (National War Memorial), the nation's altar, at which every visiting foreign dignitary lays a ceremonial wreath. England's Queen Elizabeth upheld the tradition during her royal visit in May of 1992. In 1991 Pope John Paul II conducted a mass here. Just a few months earlier, half a million Hungarians had convened to recall the memory of Imre Nagy, the reform-minded Communist prime minister who partially inspired the 1956 revolution. Little would anyone have guessed then that in 1995, palm trees, and Madonna, would spring up on this very square in a scene from the film *Evita* (set in Argentina, not Hungary); nor that Michael Jackson would do his part to consecrate the square with a music video. Heroes' Square is flanked by the **Műcsarnok** and the **Szépművészeti Múzeum** (☞ *below*).

Kodály körönd. A handsome traffic circle with imposing statues of three Hungarian warriors—leavened by a fourth one of a poet—Kodály körönd is surrounded by plane and chestnut trees. Look carefully at the towered mansions on the north side of the circle—behind the soot you'll see the fading colors of ornate frescoes peeking through. The circle takes its name from the composer Zoltán Kodály, who lived just beyond it at Andrássy út 89. ✉ *VI, Andrássy út at Szinyei Merse u.*.

47 **Liszt Ferenc Emlékmúzeum** (Franz Liszt Memorial Museum). Andrássy út No. 67 was the original location of the old Academy of Music and Franz Liszt's last home; entered around the corner, it now houses a museum. Several rooms display the original furniture and instruments from Liszt's time there; another room shows temporary exhibits. The museum hosts excellent, free classical concerts year-round, except in August. ✉ *VI, Vörösmarty u. 35,* ☎ *1/342–7320.* 🎫 *200 Ft.* ⏲ *Weekdays 10–6, Sat. 9–5. Classical concerts (free with admission) Sept.–July, Sat. 11* AM*. Closed Aug. 1–20.*

46 **Liszt Ferenc Zeneakadémia** (Franz Liszt Academy of Music). Along with the **Vigadó** (☞ Downtown Pest and the Kis körút [Little Ring Road], *above*), this is one of the city's main concert halls. The academy in fact has two auditoriums: a green-and-gold 1,200-seat main hall and a smaller hall for chamber music and solo recitals. Outside this exuberant Art Nouveau building, a statue of Liszt oversees the square. The academy has been operating as a highly revered teaching institute since 1907; Liszt was its first chairman and the composer Ferenc Erkel its first director. The pianist Ernő (formerly Ernst) Dohnányi and composers Béla Bartók and Zoltán Kodály were teachers here. ✉ *VI, Liszt Ferenc tér 8,* ☎ *1/342–0179.*

★ 44 **Magyar Állami Operaház** (Hungarian State Opera House). Miklós Ybl's crowning achievement is the neo-Renaissance Opera House, built between 1875 and 1884. Badly damaged during the siege of 1944–1945, it was restored for its 1984 centenary. Two buxom marble sphinxes guard the driveway; the main entrance is flanked by Alajos Strobl's "romantic-realist" limestone statues of Liszt and of another 19th-century Hungarian composer, Ferenc Erkel, the father of Hungarian opera (his patriotic opera *Bánk bán* is still performed for national celebrations).

Inside, the spectacle begins even before the performance does. You glide up grand staircases and through wood-paneled corridors and gilt lime-green salons into a glittering jewel box of an auditorium. Its four tiers of boxes are held up by helmeted sphinxes beneath a frescoed ceiling by Károly Lotz. Lower down there are frescoes everywhere, with intertwined motifs of Apollo and Dionysus. In its early years, the Budapest Opera was conducted by Gustav Mahler (from 1888 to 1891) and, after World War II, by Otto Klemperer.

The best way to experience the Opera House's interior is to see a ballet or opera; and while performance quality varies, tickets are relatively cheap and easy to come by, at least by tourist standards. And descending from *La Bohème* into the Földalatti station beneath the Opera House was described by travel writer Stephen Brook in *The Double Eagle* as stepping "out of one period piece and into another." There are no performances in summer, except for the week-long BudaFest international opera and ballet festival in mid-August. You cannot view the interior on your own, but forty-five-minute tours in English are usually conducted daily at 3 PM and 4 PM; buy tickets in the Opera Shop, by the sphinx at the Hajós utca entrance. (Large groups should call in advance.) ✉ *VI, Andrássy út 22,* ☎ *1/331–2550 (ext. 156 for tours).* *Tours 1,000 Ft.*

45 **Magyar Fotógráfusok Háza (Mai Manó Ház)** (Hungarian Photographers' House [Manó Mai House]). This ornate turn-of-the-20th-century building was built as a photography studio, where the wealthy bourgeoisie would come to be photographed by imperial and royal court photographer Manó Mai. Inside, ironwork and frescoes ornament the curving staircase leading up to the recently expanded facility, the largest of Budapest's three photo galleries. ✉ *V, Nagymező u. 20,* ☎ *1/302–4398.* *200 Ft.* *Weekdays 2–6.*

NEED A BREAK? The **Lukács** café (✉ VI, Andrássy út 70, ☎ 1/302–8747) shares its entrance with an international bank, but its upstairs salon is steeped in classic café elegance. The room is anchored at one end by an ornate fireplace; you can recharge with an espresso at one of the marble-top tables clustered under a sparkling chandelier. The Lukács was built in 1912, during Budapest's café-culture glory days, but in the repressive 1950s it was taken over by the secret police to serve as a meeting spot. To many locals, it still evokes those dark times.

49 **Műcsarnok** (Palace of Exhibitions). The city's largest hall for special exhibitions is a striking 1895 temple of culture with a colorful tympanum. Its program of events includes exhibitions of contemporary Hungarian and international art and a rich series of films, plays, and concerts. ✉ *XIV, Hősök tere,* ☎ *1/343–7401.* *300 Ft., Tues. free.* *Tues.–Sun. 10–6.*

★ 50 **Szépművészeti Múzeum** (Museum of Fine Arts). Across Heroes' Square from the Palace of Exhibitions and built by the same team of Albert Schickedanz and Fülöp Herzog, the Museum of Fine Arts houses Hungary's finest collection, rich in Flemish and Dutch old masters. With seven fine El Grecos and five beautiful Goyas as well as paintings by Velázquez and Murillo, the collection of Spanish old masters is one of the best outside Spain. The Italian school is represented by Giorgione, Bellini, Correggio, Tintoretto, and Titian masterpieces and, above all, two superb Raphael paintings: *Eszterházy Madonna* and his immortal *Portrait of a Youth,* rescued after a world-famous art heist. Nineteenth-century French art includes works by Delacroix, Pissarro, Cézanne, Toulouse-Lautrec, Gauguin, Renoir, and Monet. There are also more than 100,000 drawings (including five by Rembrandt and three studies by Leonardo), Egyptian and Greco-Roman exhibitions, late-Gothic winged altars from northern Hungary and Transylvania, and works by all the leading figures of Hungarian art up to the present. A 20th-century collection was added to the museum's permanent exhibits in 1994, comprising an interesting series of statues, paintings, and drawings by Chagall, Le Corbusier, and others. Labels are in both Hungarian and English; there's also an English-language booklet for sale about the permanent collection. ✉ *XIV, Hősök tere,* ☎ *1/343–9759.* 🎫 *500 Ft.* 🕒 *Tues.–Sun. 10–5:30.*

Városliget (City Park)

A GOOD WALK

Heroes' Square is the gateway to the **Városliget** (City Park): a square km (almost ½ square mi) of recreation, entertainment, beauty, and culture. A bridge behind the Millennial Monument leads across a boating basin that becomes an artificial ice-skating rink in winter; to the south of this lake stands a statue of George Washington, erected in 1906 with donations by Hungarian emigrants to the United States. Next to the lake stands **Vajdahunyad Vár,** built in myriad architectural styles. Visitors can soak or swim at the turn-of-the-20th-century Széchenyi Fürdő, jog along the park paths, or careen on Vidám Park's roller coaster. There's also the Petőfi Csarnok, a leisure-time youth center and major concert hall on the site of an old industrial exhibition.

TIMING

Fair-weather weekends, when the children's attractions are teeming with youngsters and parents and the Széchenyi Fürdő brimming with bathers, are the best time for people-watchers to visit City Park; if you go on a weekday, the main sights are rarely crowded.

SIGHTS TO SEE

Budapesti Állatkert (Budapest Zoo). The renovation that began in this once depressing urban zoo in the late 1990s is expected to take until 2004, but the place is already cheerier, at least for humans—petting opportunities aplenty, and a new monkey-house where endearing, seemingly clawless little simians climb all over you (beware of pickpockets!). Don't miss the elephant pavilion, decorated with Zsolnay majolica and glazed ceramic animals. ✉ *XIV, Állatkerti krt. 6–12,* ☎ *1/343–6075.* 🎫 *650 Ft.* 🕒 *Mar. and Oct., daily 9–5; Apr. and Sept., daily 9–6; May, daily 9–6:30; June–Aug., daily 9–7; Nov.–Feb., daily 9–4 (last tickets sold 1 hr before closing).*

Fővárosi Nagycirkusz (Municipal Grand Circus). Colorful performances by local acrobats, clowns, and animal trainers, as well as by international guests, are staged here in a small ring. ✉ *XIV, Állatkerti krt. 7,* ☎ *1/343–9630.* 🎫 *Weekdays 500–900 Ft., weekends 550–950 Ft.* 🕒 *July–Aug., Wed.–Fri. 3 and 7, Thu. 3, Sat. 10, 3, and 7, Sun. 10 and 3; Nov.–June, schedule varies.*

Széchenyi Fürdő (Széchenyi Baths). Dating from 1876, these vast baths are in a beautiful neo-Baroque building in the middle of City Park; they comprise one of the biggest spas in Europe. There are several thermal pools indoors as well as two outdoors, which remain open even in winter, when dense steam hangs thick over the hot water's surface—you can just barely make out the figures of elderly men, submerged shoulder deep, crowded around waterproof chessboards (☞ Outdoor Activities and Sports, *below*). ✉ *XIV, Állatkerti krt. 11,* ☎ *1/321–0310.* 🎫 *400 Ft. (changing room), 700 Ft. (cabin).* 🕒 *Weekdays 6 AM–6 PM, weekends 6–5.*

★ **Vajdahunyad Vár** (Vajdahunyad Castle). Beside the City Park's lake stands this castle, an art historian's Disneyland, this fantastic medley borrows from all of Hungary's historic and architectural past, starting with the Romanesque gateway of the cloister of Jak in western Hungary. A Gothic castle, Transylvanian turrets, Renaissance loggia, Baroque portico, and Byzantine decoration are all guarded by a spooky modern (1903) bronze statue of the anonymous medieval chronicler who was the first recorder of Hungarian history. Designed for the millennial celebration in 1896 but not completed until 1908, this hodgepodge houses the surprisingly interesting **Mezőgazdasági Múzeum** (Agricultural Museum), with intriguingly arranged sections on animal husbandry, forestry, horticulture, hunting, and fishing. ✉ *XIV, Városliget, Széchenyi Island,* ☎ *1/343–3198.* 🎫 *Museum 200 Ft.* ⏲ *Mid-Feb.–mid-Nov., Tues.–Fri. and Sun. 10–5, Sat. 10–6; mid-Nov.–mid-Feb., Tues.–Fri. 10–4, weekends 10–5.*

Vidám Park. Budapest's somewhat weary amusement park is next to the zoo and is crawling with happy children with their parents or grandparents in tow. Rides cost around $1 (some are for preschoolers). There are also game rooms and a scenic railway. Next to the main park is a separate, smaller section for toddlers. In winter, only a few rides operate. ✉ *XIV, Városliget, Állatkerti krt. 14–16,* ☎ *1/343–0996.* 🎫 *100 Ft.* ⏲ *Apr.–Oct., daily 10–about 8 (varies); Nov.–Mar., daily 10–late afternoon.*

Eastern Pest and the Nagy Körút (Great Ring Road)

This section covers primarily Kossuth Lajos–Rákóczi út and the Nagykörút (Great Ring Road)—busy, less-touristy urban thoroughfares full of people, cars, shops, and Budapest's unique urban flavor.

Beginning a few blocks from the Elizabeth Bridge, Kossuth Lajos utca is Budapest's busiest shopping street. Try to look above and beyond the store windows to the architecture and activity along Kossuth Lajos utca and its continuation, Rákóczi út, which begins when it crosses the Kis körút (Little Ring Road) at the busy intersection called Astoria. Most of Rákóczi út is lined with hotels, shops, and department stores and it ends at the grandiose Keleti (East) Railway Station, on Baross tér.

Pest's Great Ring Road, the Nagy körút, was laid out at the end of the 19th century in a wide semicircle anchored to the Danube at both ends; an arm of the river was covered over to create this 114-ft-wide thoroughfare. The large apartment buildings on both sides also date from this era. Along with theaters, stores, and cafés, they form a boulevard unique in Europe for its "unified eclecticism," which blends a variety of historic styles into a harmonious whole. Its entire length of almost 4½ km (2¾ mi) from Margaret Bridge to Petőfi Bridge is traversed by Trams 4 and 6, but strolling it in stretches is also a good way to experience the hustle and bustle of downtown Budapest.

Like its smaller counterpart, the Kis Körút (Small Ring Road), the Great Ring Road comprises sectors of various names. Beginning with Ferenc körút at the Petőfi Bridge, it changes to József körút at the intersection marked by the Museum of Applied Arts, then to Erzsébet körút at Blaha Lujza Square. Teréz körút begins at the busy Oktogon crossing with Andrássy út and ends at the Nyugati (West) Railway Station, where Szent István takes over for the final stretch to the Margaret Bridge.

A GOOD WALK

Beginning with a visit to the **Iparművészeti Múzeum** (51), near the southern end of the boulevard, walk or take Tram 4 or 6 north (away from the Petőfi Bridge) to the New York Kávéház on Erzsébet körút, just past Blaha Lujza tér—all in all about 1¾ km (1 mi) from the museum. The neo-Renaissance **Keleti pályaudvar** is a one-metro-stop detour away from Blaha Lujza tér. Continuing in the same direction on the körút, go several stops on the tram to **Nyugati pályaudvar** and walk the remaining sector, Szent István körút, past the **Vígszínház** (53) to Margaret Bridge. From the bridge, views of Margaret Island, to the north, and Parliament, Castle Hill, the Chain Bridge, and Gellért Hill, to the south, are gorgeous.

TIMING

As this area is packed with stores, it's best to explore during business hours—weekdays until around 5 PM and Saturday until 1 PM; Saturday will be most crowded. Keep in mind that the Iparművészeti Múzeum is closed Monday.

SIGHTS TO SEE

★ 51 **Iparművészeti Múzeum** (Museum of Applied and Decorative Arts). The templelike structure housing this museum is indeed a shrine to Hungarian Art Nouveau, and in front of it, drawing pen in hand, sits a statue of its creator, Hungarian architect Ödön Lechner. Opened in the Magyar Millennial year of 1896, it was only the third museum of its kind in Europe. Its dome of tiles is crowned by a majolica lantern from the same source: the Zsolnay ceramic works in Pécs. Inside its central hall are playfully swirling whitewashed, double-decker, Moorish-style galleries and arcades. The museum, which collects and studies objects of interior decoration and use, has five departments: furniture, textiles, goldsmithing, ceramics, and everyday objects. ✉ *Üllői út 33–37,* ☎ *1/217–5222.* *300 Ft.* ⏲ *Mid-Mar.–Oct., Tues.–Sun. 10–6; Nov.–mid-Mar., Tues.–Sun. 10–4.*

NEED A BREAK? Once the haunt of famous writers and intellectuals, whose caricatures decorate the walls, now mostly that of tourists—those who manage to find the entrance under the seemingly permanent scaffolding—the **New York Kávéház** (✉ VII, Erzsébet krt. 9–11, ☎ 1/322–1648) is an eclectic, neo-Baroque café and restaurant in the ornate 1894 New York Palace building.

Keleti pályaudvar (East Railway Station). The grandiose, imperial-looking East Railway Station was built in 1884 and considered Europe's most modern until well into the 20th century. Its neo-Renaissance facade, which resembles a gateway, is flanked by statues of two British inventors and railway pioneers, James Watt and George Stephenson. ✉ *VIII, Baross tér.*

52 **Köztársaság tér** (Square of the Republic). Surrounded by faceless concrete buildings, this square is not particularly alluring aesthetically but is significant because it was where the Communist Party of Budapest had its headquarters, and it was also the scene of heavy fighting in 1956. Here also is the city's second opera house, and Budapest's largest, the Erkel Ferenc színház (Ferenc Erkel Theater).

Nyugati pályaudvar (West Railway Station). The iron-laced glass hall of the West Railway Station is in complete contrast to—and much more modern than—the newer East Railway Station. Built in the 1870s, it was designed by a team of architects from Gustav Eiffel's office in Paris. ✉ *VI, Teréz krt.*

Párizsi Udvar (Paris Court). This glass-roof arcade was built in 1914 in richly ornamental neo-Gothic and eclectic styles. Nowadays it's filled with touristy boutiques. ✉ *VI, Corner of Petőfi Sándor u. and Kossuth Lajos u..*

NEED A BREAK? Hands down the best café in this part of town, the **Európa kávéház** (✉ V, Szent István krt. 7–9, ☎ 1/312–2362) has marble-top tables; top-notch elegance; and, yes, delectable sweets. While it seems (in the best sense) a century old, it's in fact only about two years. Here you can sample some Eszterházy torta (a rich, buttery cake with walnut batter and, here at least, a walnut on top) or, say, a Tyrolean strudel with poppy-seed filling.

★ 53 **Vígszínház** (Comedy Theater). This neo-Baroque, late-19th-century, gem-like theater twinkles with just a tiny, playful anticipation of Art Nouveau and sparkles inside and out since its 1994 refurbishment. The theater hosts primarily musicals, such as Hungarian adaptations of *Cats,* as well as dance performances and classical concerts. ✉ *XIII, Pannónia u. 1,* ☎ *1/329–2340.*

Óbuda

Until its unification with Buda and Pest in 1872 to form the city of Budapest, Óbuda (meaning Old Buda) was a separate town that used to be the main settlement; now it is usually thought of as a suburb. Although the vast new apartment blocks of Budapest's biggest housing project and busy roadways are what first strike the eye, the historic core of Óbuda has been preserved in its entirety.

A GOOD WALK

Óbuda is easily reached by car, bus, or streetcar via the Árpád Bridge from Pest or by the HÉV suburban railway from Batthyány tér to the Árpád Bridge. Once you're there, covering all the sights on foot involves large but manageable distances along major exhaust-permeated roadways. One way to tackle it is to take Tram 17 from its southern terminus at the Buda side of the Margaret Bridge to Kiscelli utca and walk uphill to the **Kiscelli Múzeum.** Then walk back down the same street all the way past **Flórián tér,** continuing toward the Danube and making a left onto Hídfő utca or Szentlélek tér to enter **Fő tér.** After exploring the square, walk a block or two southeast to the HÉV suburban railway stop and take the train just north to the museum complex at **Aquincum.**

TIMING

It's best to begin touring Óbuda during the cooler, early hours of the day, as the heat on the area's busy roads can get overbearing. Avoid Monday, when museums are closed.

SIGHTS TO SEE

Aquincum. This complex comprises the reconstructed remains of a Roman settlement dating from the 1st century AD and the capital of the Roman province of Pannonia. Careful excavations have unearthed a varied selection of artifacts and mosaics, giving a tantalizing inkling of what life was like in the provinces of the Roman Empire. A gymnasium and a central heating system have been unearthed, along with the ruins of two baths and a shrine to Mithras, the Persian god of light, truth, and the sun. The **Aquincum múzeum** (Aquincum Museum) displays the dig's most notable finds: ceramics; a red-marble sarcophagus showing a triton and flying Eros on one side and on the other, Telesphorus, the angel of death, depicted as a hooded dwarf; and jewelry from a Roman lady's tomb. ✉ *III, Szentendrei út 139,* ☎ *1/250–1650.* *400 Ft.* *Mid-Apr.–Apr. 30 and Oct., Tues.–Sun. 10–5; May–Sept., Tues.–Sun. 10–6. Grounds open at 9.*

Flórián tér (Flórián Square). The center of today's Óbuda is Flórián tér, where Roman ruins were first discovered when the foundations of a house were dug in 1778. Two centuries later, careful excavations were carried out during the reconstruction of the square, and today the restored ancient ruins lie in the center of the square in boggling contrast to the racing traffic and cement-block housing projects. ✉ *III, Vörösvári út at Pacsirtamező u.*

Fő tér (Main Square). Óbuda's old main square is its most picturesque part. The square has been spruced up in recent years, and there are now several good restaurants and interesting museums in and around the Baroque **Zichy Kúria** (Zichy Mansion), which has become a neighborhood cultural center. Among the most popular offerings are the summer concerts in the courtyard and the evening jazz concerts. ✉ *III, Kórház u. at Hídfő u.*

Kiscelli Múzeum (Kiscelli Museum). A strenuous climb up the steep, dilapidated sidewalks of Remetehegy (Hermit's Hill) will deposit you at this elegant, mustard-yellow Baroque mansion. Built between 1744 and 1760 as a Trinitarian monastery, today it holds an eclectic mix of paintings, sculptures, engravings, and sundry items related to the history of Budapest. Included here is the printing press on which poet and revolutionary Sándor Petőfi printed his famous "Nemzeti Dal" ("National Song"), in 1848, inciting the Hungarian people to rise up against the Hapsburgs. ✉ *III, Kiscelli u. 108,* ☎ *1/250–0304.* *200 Ft.* *Nov.–Mar., Tues.–Sun. 10–4; Apr.–Oct., Tues.–Sun. 10–6.*

Római amfiteátrum (Roman Amphitheater). Probably dating back to the 2nd century, Óbuda's Roman military amphitheater once held some 16,000 people and, at 144 yards in diameter, was one of Europe's largest. A block of dwellings called the Round House was later built by the Romans above the amphitheater; massive stone walls found in the Round House's cellar were actually parts of the amphitheater. Below the amphitheater are the cells where prisoners and lions were held while awaiting confrontation. ✉ *III, Pacsirtamező u. at Nagyszombat u.*

Dining

Updated by Betsy Maury

The pulse of the city's increasingly vibrant restaurant scene is in downtown Pest; restaurants on Castle Hill tend to be more touristy and expensive. Our choice of restaurants is primarily Hungarian and Continental, but if you get a craving for sushi or tortellini, consult the restaurant listings in the English-language publications for the latest information on what's cooking where. Remember that some restaurants, particularly the tourist-oriented ones, occasionally fall into the international practice of embellishing tourists' bills. Authorities in Budapest, however, have been cracking down on establishments reported for overcharging. Don't order from menus without prices, and don't accept dining or drinking invitations from women hired to lure people into shady situations.

For price range information, *see* Dining *in* Pleasures and Pastimes, *above.*

Downtown Pest and the Small Ring Road

$$$–$$$$ ✕ **Múzeum.** The gustatory anticipation sparked by this elegant, candlelit salon with mirrors, mosaics, and swift-moving waiters is matched by wholly satisfying, wonderful food. The salads are generous, the Hungarian wines excellent, and the chef dares to be creative. ✉ *VIII, Múzeum krt. 11,* ☎ *1/267–0375. Jacket and tie. AE. Closed Sun.*

$$$ ★ ✕ **Lou Lou.** This glowing bistro tucked onto a side street near the Danube has been one of the hottest restaurants in Budapest for years. Blending local and Continental cuisines, the menu includes a succulent fresh salmon with lemongrass; the venison fillet with wild berry sauce is another mouthwatering choice. Although recently expanded, Lou Lou retains its intimate charm. ✉ *V, Vigyázó Ferenc u. 4,* ☎ *1/312–4505. Reservations essential. AE. No lunch Sat. Closed daily 3–7 and Sun.*

$$$ ★ ✕ **Művészinas.** Walls hung with framed vintage prints and photos, antique vitrines filled with old books, and tall, slender candles on the tables create a romantic haze here. Dozens of Hungarian specialties fill the long menu, from sirloin "Budapest style" (smothered in a goose-liver, mushrooms, and sweet-pepper ragout) to spinach-stuffed turkey breast in garlic sauce. Poppy-seed palacsinta with plum sauce are a sub-

Budapest Dining and Lodging

Dining

Amstel River Café . . . **21**
Bagolyvár **38**
Café Kör **27**
Cyrano **22**
Gundel **37**
Kéhli **1**
Kisbuda Gyöngye **2**
Kispipa **33**
Lou Lou **28**
Marxim **7**
Művészinas **30**
Múzeum **19**
Náncsi Néni **8**
Robinson Restaurant **36**
Tabáni Kakas **14**
Tüköry Söröző **29**
Udvarház **6**
Vadrózsa **5**
Vista Travel Café . . . **31**

Lodging

art'otel **9**
Astoria **20**
Budapest Hilton **12**
Budapest Marriott . . . **23**
Carlton Hotel **11**
Citadella **15**
Danubius Grand Hotel Margitsziget . . . **3**
Danubius Hotel Gellért **18**
Danubius Thermal Hotel Helia **4**
Flamenco **17**
Hotel Benczúr **35**
Hotel Inter-Continental Budapest **24**
Hyatt Regency Budapest **25**
Kempinski Hotel Corvinus Budapest **26**
Kulturinov **13**
Mercure Hotel Budapest Nemzeti **32**
Molnár Panzió **16**
Radisson SAS Béke **34**
Victoria **10**

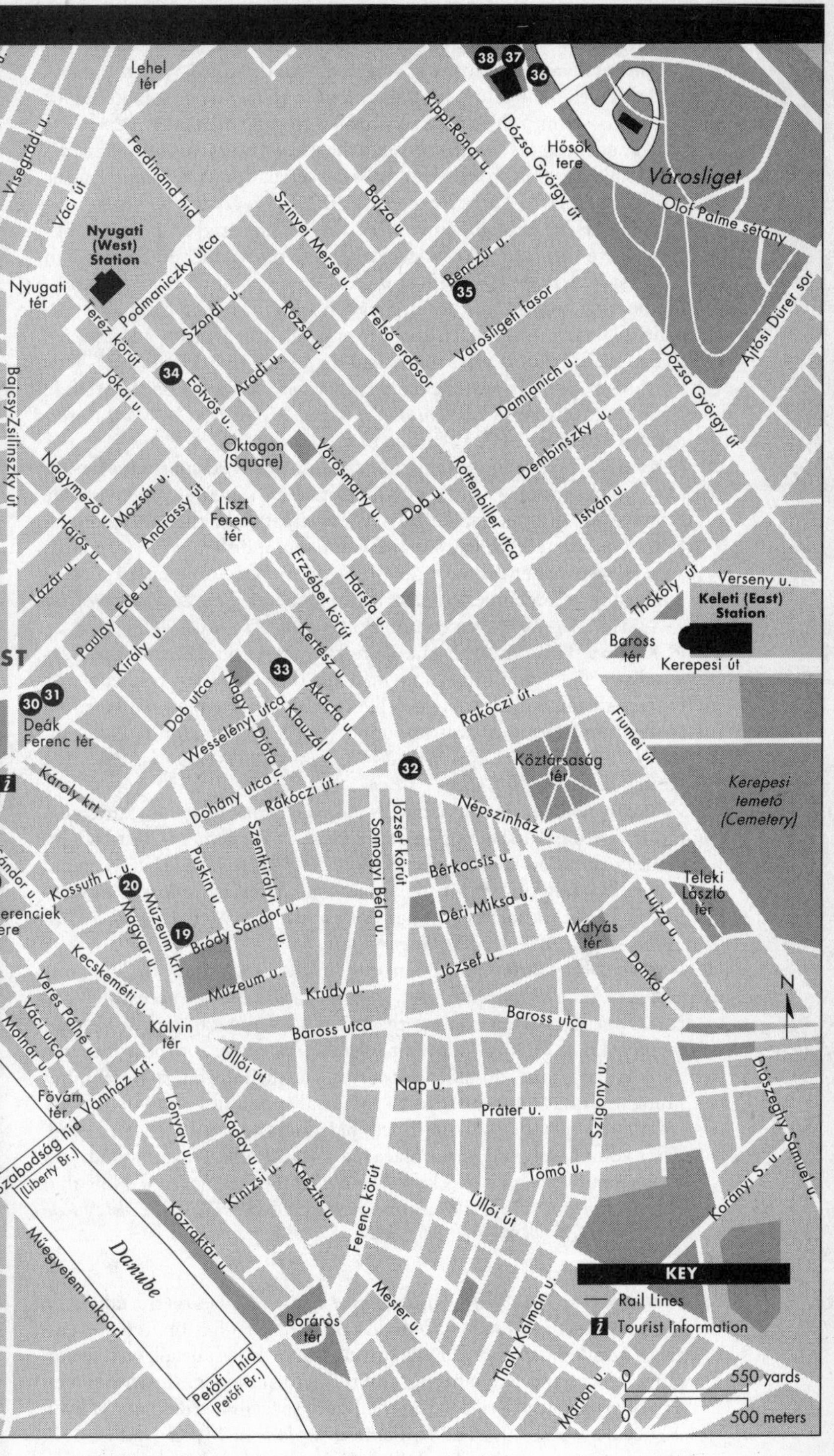

Lehel tér
Visegrádi u.
Váci út
Ferdinánd híd
Nyugati (West) Station
Nyugati tér
Teréz körút
Podmaniczky utca
Szondi u.
Szinyei Merse u.
Rippl-Rónai u.
Dózsa György út
Hősök tere
Városliget
Olof Palme sétány
Bajza u.
Benczúr u.
Városligeti fasor
Felső erdősor
Rózsa u.
Aradi u.
Eötvös u.
Jókai u.
Bajcsy-Zsilinszky út
Nagymező u.
Mozsár u.
Oktogon (Square)
Vörösmarty u.
Andrássy út
Liszt Ferenc tér
Hajós u.
Lázár u.
Paulay Ede u.
Király u.
Damjanich u.
Dembinszky u.
Rottenbiller utca
Dob u.
István u.
Ajtósi Dürer sor
Dózsa György út
Erzsébet körút
Hársfa u.
Kertész u.
Thököly út
Verseny u.
Keleti (East) Station
Baross tér
Kerepesi út
Deák Ferenc tér
Dob utca
Nagy Diófa u.
Wesselényi utca
Klauzál u.
Akácfa u.
Rákóczi út
Fiumei út
Köztársaság tér
Kerepesi temető (Cemetery)
Károly krt.
Dohány utca
Rákóczi út
József körút
Somogyi Béla u.
Népszinház u.
Szentkirályi u.
Puskin u.
Kossuth L. u.
Sándor u.
Ferenciek tere
Múzeum krt.
Magyar u.
Bródy Sándor u.
Bérkocsis u.
Déri Miksa u.
Teleki László tér
Luijza u.
Mátyás tér
Dankó u.
József u.
Kecskeméti u.
Múzeum u.
Krúdy u.
Veres Pálné u.
Váci utca
Molnár u.
Kálvin tér
Baross utca
Baross utca
Üllői út
Fővám tér
Vámház krt.
Szabadság híd (Liberty Br.)
Lónyay u.
Ráday u.
Nap u.
Práter u.
Szigony u.
Diószeghy Sámuel u.
Tömő u.
Kinizsi u.
Knézits u.
Ferenc körút
Üllői út
Koranyi S. u.
Danube
Műegyetem rakpart
Közraktár u.
Boráros tér
Mester u.
Thaly Kálmán u.
Petőfi híd (Petőfi Br.)
Márton u.
KEY
Rail Lines
Tourist Information
0 550 yards
0 500 meters

lime dessert. ✉ *VI, Bajcsy-Zsilinszky út 9,* ☎ *1/268–1439. Reservations essential. AE, MC, V.*

$$ ✕ **Amstel River Café.** Just steps from the tourist-filled Vái utca, you'll find this welcoming, low-key Dutch café. The menu has something for everyone—from rabbit to Caesar salad to grilled chicken, served on tables outside in the summer. Besides the Amstel beers (of course), there's a weekly changing wine list. A guitarist serenades with Spanish music on Sundays. ✉ *V, Párizsi u. 6,* ☎ *1/266–4334. No credit cards.*

$$ ★ ✕ **Café Kör** The wrought–iron tables, vault ceilings and crisp white tablecloths give this chic bistro a decidedly downtown feel. In the heart of the busy fifth district, Café Kör is ideal for lunch or dinner when touring nearby Andrássy út or St. Stephen's Basilica. The Café Kör specialty plate is a feast of rich goose liver paté, grilled meats, and cheeses, to be savored with a glass of Hungarian *pezsgő* (sparkling wine). True to its bistro aspirations, the daily specials are scribbled on the wall, in both Hungarian and English. ✉ *V, Sas u. 17,* ☎ *1/311–0053. Reservations essential. MC, V. Closed Sun.*

$$ ★ ✕ **Cyrano.** This smooth young bistro just off Vörösmarty tér has an arty, contemporary bent, with wrought-iron chairs, green-marble floors, and long-stem azure glasses. The creative kitchen sends out elegantly presented Hungarian and Continental dishes, from standards such as goulash and chicken paprikás to more eclectic tastes such as tender fried Camembert cheese with blueberry jam. ✉ *V, Kristóf tér 7–8,* ☎ *1/266–3096. Reservations essential. AE, DC, MC.*

$$ ✕ **Kispipa.** This tiny, well-known restaurant with arched yellow-glass windows and piano bar is a favorite for both Budapest residents and passers-through. The kitchen delivers an expansive menu of first-rate Hungarian food; the venison ragout soup with tarragon is excellent. ✉ *VII, Akácfa u. 38,* ☎ *1/342–2587. Reservations essential. AE, MC. Closed Sun. and July–Aug.*

$ ✕ **Tüköry Söröző.** Hearty, decidedly nonvegetarian Hungarian fare comes in big portions at this popular spot close to Parliament. Best bets include pork cutlets stuffed with savory liver or apples and cheese, paired with a big mug of inexpensive beer. Courageous carnivores can sample the beefsteak tartare, topped with a raw egg. ✉ *V, Hold u. 15,* ☎ *1/269–5027. MC, V. Closed weekends.*

$ ★ ✕ **Vista Travel Café.** Opened in 1999 in a contemporary building just off Deák tér, this popular spot is an extension of the successful Vista travel agency complex down the street (☞ Contacts and Resources, *below*). Local regulars and visitors alike flock here for the affordable daily lunch menu and quiche specials. The menu is international, but Hungarian flags appear next to the local specialties—so you can try traditional *hortobágyi* (meat-filled) palacsinta and still get a chef salad. After you fill out your paper place mat rating the service and food, you can walk upstairs and check your e-mail at the Internet café. Note that there is a 3,000-Ft. minimum for credit card use. ✉ *VII, Paulay Ede u. 7,* ☎ *1/268 0888. AE, MC, V.*

North Buda

$$$$ ✕ **Vadrózsa.** The "Wild Rose" always has fresh ones on the table; the restaurant is in a romantic old villa perched on a hilltop in the exclusive Rózsadomb district of Buda. It's elegant to the last detail, with white-glove service and piano music, and the garden is delightful in summer. Try the venison or grilled fish; the house specialty, grilled goose liver, is succulent perfection. ✉ *II, Pentelei Molnár u. 15,* ☎ *1/326–5817. Reservations essential. AE, DC, MC, V. Closed daily 4–7.*

$$$–$$$$ ✕ **Udvarház.** The views from this Buda hilltop restaurant are unsurpassed. As you dine indoors at tables set with white linens or outdoors on the open terrace, your meals are accompanied by vistas of the

Danube bridges and Parliament far below. Excellent fresh fish is prepared tableside; you could also try veal and goose liver in paprika sauce, served with salty cottage cheese dumplings. Catering to the predominantly tourist crowd, folklore shows and live Gypsy music frequently enliven the scene. The buses up here are infrequent; it's easier to take a car or taxi. ✉ *III, Hármashatárhegyi út 2,* ☎ *1/388–6921. AE, DC, MC, V. Closed Mon. Nov.–Mar. No lunch weekdays Nov.–Mar.*

$$ ★ ✕ **Náncsi Néni.** Aunt Nancy's restaurant is a perennial favorite, despite its out-of-the-way location. Irresistibly cozy, the dining room feels like Grandma's country kitchen: Chains of paprika and garlic dangle from the low wooden ceiling above tables set with red-and-white gingham tablecloths and fresh bread tucked into tiny baskets. Shelves along the walls are crammed with jars of home-pickled vegetables, which you can purchase to take home. On the home-style Hungarian menu (large portions!) turkey dishes manifest a creative flair, such as breast fillets stuffed with apples, peaches, mushrooms, cheese, and sour cream. Special touches include a popular outdoor garden in summer and free champagne for all couples in love. ✉ *II, Ördögárok út 80,* ☎ *1/397–2742. Reservations essential July–Aug. AE, MC, V.*

$ ✕ **Marxim.** Two years after the death of socialism in Hungary, this simple pizza-and-pasta restaurant opened up to mock the old regime—and milk it for all it's worth. From the flashing red star above the door outside to the clever puns on the menus and photos of decorated hardliners on the walls, the theme is "Communist nostalgia." Crowds of teenagers and blaring rock music make Marxim best suited for a lunch or snack. ✉ *II, Kisrókus u. 23,* ☎ *1/212–4183. AE, DC, MC, V. No lunch Sun.*

Óbuda

$$$ ✕ **Kéhli.** This pricey but laid-back, sepia-tone neighborhood tavern is on a hard-to-find street near the Óbuda end of the Árpád Bridge. The food is hearty and heavy, just the way legendary Hungarian writer and voracious eater Gyula Krúdy (to whom the restaurant is dedicated) liked it when he lived in the neighborhood. Select from appetizers, such as hot bone marrow with garlic toast, before moving on to fried goose livers with mashed potatoes or turkey breast stuffed with cheese and goose liver. ✉ *III, Mókus u. 22,* ☎ *1/250–4241 or 1/368–0613. AE, MC, V. No lunch weekdays.*

$$$ ★ ✕ **Kisbuda Gyöngye.** Considered one of the city's finest restaurants, this intimate Óbuda restaurant is filled with antique furniture, and its walls are creatively decorated with an eclectic but elegant patchwork of carved wooden cupboard doors and panels. A violin-piano duo sets a romantic mood, and in warm weather you can dine outdoors in the cozy back garden. Try the venison with Transylvanian mushrooms or the popular *liba lakodalmas* (goose wedding feast), a roast goose leg, goose liver, and goose cracklings. ✉ *III, Kenyeres u. 34,* ☎ *1/368–6402 or 1/368–9246. Reservations essential. AE, DC, MC, V. Closed Sun.*

Tabán and Gellért Hill

$$ ✕ **Tabáni Kakas.** This popular restaurant just below Castle Hill has a distinctly friendly atmosphere and specializes in large helpings of poultry dishes, particularly goose. Try the catfish paprikás or the roast duck with steamed cabbage. ✉ *I, Attila út 27,* ☎ *1/375–7165. AE, MC, V.*

City Park

$$$$ ★ ✕ **Gundel.** George Lang, Hungary's best-known restaurateur, showcases his native country's cuisine at this turn-of-the-20th-century palazzo. Dark-wood paneling, a dozen oil paintings by exemplary Hungarian artists, and tables set with Zsolnay porcelain make this the city's plushest, most handsome dining room. Violinist György Lakatos,

of the legendary Lakatos Gypsy musician dynasty, strolls from table to table playing folk music, as waiters in black tie serve traditional favorites such as tender veal in a paprika-and-sour-cream sauce and carp *Dorozsma* (panfried with mushrooms). There's a large garden area where Sunday brunch is served in warm weather. ✉ *XIV, Állatkerti út 2,* ☎ *1/321–3550. Reservations essential. Jacket and tie. AE, DC, MC, V. Closed daily 4–6.*

$$$$ ✕ **Robinson Restaurant.** At this intimate dining room on the park's small lake, service is doting and the menu creative, with dishes such as crisp roast suckling pig with champagne-drenched cabbage or fresh fogas stuffed with spinach. Finish it off with a flaming cup of coffee *Diablo,* fueled with Grand Marnier. Padded pastel decor and low lighting wash the room in pleasant, if not Hungarian, elegance. ✉ *XIV, Városliget,* ☎ *1/343–0955. Reservations essential. Jacket and tie. AE, DC, MC, V. Closed daily 4–6.*

$$ ✕ **Bagolyvár.** George Lang opened this restaurant next door to his gastronomic palace, Gundel (☞ *above*), in 1993. The informal yet polished dining room has a soaring wooden-beam ceiling, and the kitchen produces first-rate daily menus of home-style Hungarian specialties. Soups, served in shiny silver tureens, are particularly good. Musicians entertain with *cimbalom* (hammered dulcimer) music nightly from 7. In warm weather there is outdoor dining in a lovely back garden. ✉ *XIV, Állatkerti út 2,* ☎ *1/343–0217. AE, DC, MC, V.*

Lodging

Updated by Betsy Maury

Budapest is well equipped with hotels and hostels, but the increase in tourism since 1989 has put a strain on the city's often crowded lodgings. Advance reservations are strongly advised, especially at the lower-price hotels. Many of the major luxury and business-class hotel chains are represented in Budapest; however, all of them are Hungarian-run franchise operations with native touches that you won't find in any other Hilton or Marriott.

In winter it's not difficult to find a hotel room, even at the last minute, and prices are usually reduced by 20%–30%. By far the cheapest and most accessible beds in the city are rooms ($20–$25 for a double room) in private homes. Although most tourist offices book private rooms, the supply is limited, so try to arrive in Budapest early in the morning.

Addresses below are preceded by the district number (in Roman numerals) and include the Hungarian postal code. Districts V, VI, and VII are in downtown Pest; I includes Castle Hill, the main tourist district of Buda. For price range information, *see* Lodging *in* Pleasures and Pastimes, *above*.

$$$$ 🏨 **art'otel.** A short walk up the Danube from the Chain Bridge, this hip new boutique hotel is the first of its kind in Budapest. Like its sibling properties in Berlin and Dresden, the hotel-cum-gallery is completely dedicated to the work of a single artist—in this case, American Donald Sultan. From the carpets to the paintings, the china to the water fountains, the entire hotel is decorated with Sultan's designs, amounting to a multimillion-dollar collection of his art. Interconnecting a new building and four 18th-century Baroque houses on the Buda riverfront, the art'otel adroitly blends old and new. Spiffy, chic contemporary furniture contrasts elegantly with restored original moldings and doorframes in the older buildings' rooms. ✉ *I, Bem rakpart 16–19, H-1011,* ☎ *1/487–9487,* FAX *1/487–9488. 156 rooms, 9 suites. Restaurant, café, air-conditioning, in-room data ports, no-smoking rooms, beauty salon, sauna, meeting rooms, parking (fee). AE, DC, MC, V.*

$$$$ **Budapest Hilton.** Built in 1977 around a 13th-century monastery adjacent to the Matthias Church, this perfectly integrated architectural wonder overlooks the Danube from the choicest site on Castle Hill. Every contemporary room has a remarkable view; Danube vistas cost more. Complete renovations during 2000 promised a welcome update in room decor. Children, regardless of age, get free accommodation when sharing a room with their parents. Note: Breakfast is not included in room rates. ✉ *I, Hess András tér 1–3, H-1014,* ☎ *1/488–6600; 800/445–8667 in the U.S. and Canada;* FAX *1/488–6644. 295 rooms, 26 suites. 3 restaurants, 2 bars, café, air-conditioning, in-room data ports, beauty salon, sauna, exercise room, dry cleaning, laundry service, business services, meeting rooms, travel services, parking (free and fee). AE, DC, MC, V.*

$$$$ **Budapest Marriott.** In this sophisticated yet friendly hotel on the Danube in downtown Pest, attention to detail is evident, from the impeccable buffet of colorfully glazed pastries served daily in the lobby to the feather-light ring of the front-desk bell. Guest rooms have lushly patterned carpets, floral bedspreads, and etched glass. The layout takes full advantage of the hotel's prime Danube location, offering breathtaking views of Gellért Hill, the Chain and Elizabeth bridges, and Castle Hill from the lobby, ballroom, every guest room, and even the impressive health club—which is unquestionably the best hotel fitness center in the city. ✉ *V, Apáczai Csere János u. 4, H-1052,* ☎ *1/266–7000; 800/831–4004 in the U.S. and Canada;* FAX *1/266–5000. 362 rooms, 11 suites. 3 restaurants, bar, air-conditioning, in-room data ports, no-smoking rooms, health club, squash, shops, baby-sitting, dry cleaning, laundry service, business services, meeting rooms, travel services, parking (fee). AE, DC, MC, V.*

$$$$ ★ **Danubius Hotel Gellért.** The double-deck rotunda of this grand Hungarian spa hotel leads you to expect a string orchestra playing "The Emperor Waltz." Built in 1918, the Jugendstil Gellért was favored by Otto von Hapsburg, son of the last emperor. Rooms come in all shapes and sizes—from palatial suites to awkward, tiny spaces. Now part of the Danubius hotel chain, the Gellért has begun an ambitious overhaul, refurnishing all rooms in the mood of the original Jugendstil style. Inquire about completed rooms when you reserve. The best views—across the Danube or up Gellért Hill—are more expensive; avoid those that face the building's inner core. If you're planning a weekend trip well in advance, inquire about special packages; the prices can be more friendly. Though the hotel's service can be a bit inconsistent, its famous pièce de résistance will make up for it: the monumental, ornate thermal baths. Admission to the spa is free to hotel guests (medical treatments cost extra); corridors and an elevator lead directly to the baths from the second, third, and fourth floors. ✉ *XI, Gellért tér 1, H-1111,* ☎ *1/385–2200,* FAX *1/466–6631. 220 rooms, 13 suites. Restaurant, bar, brasserie, café, no-smoking rooms, indoor pool, beauty salon, spa, mineral baths, baby-sitting, business services, meeting rooms, parking (fee). AE, DC, MC, V.*

$$$$ **Hotel Inter-Continental Budapest.** Formerly the Fórum Hotel, this boxy, modern, riverside hotel consistently wins applause for its gracious appointments, excellent service, and gorgeous views across the Danube to Castle Hill. Sixty percent of the rooms have river views (these are more expensive); rooms on higher floors ensure the least noise. The hotel café, Corso Bar, is locally known for its pastries. The central location and efficient business services makes the Inter-continental popular with businesspeople. Note: breakfast is not included in the room rates. ✉ *V, Apáczai Csere János u. 12–14, Box 231, H-1368,* ☎ *1/327–6333,* FAX *1/327–6357. 398 rooms, 16 suites. 2 restaurants, bar, café, air-conditioning, in-room data ports, no-smoking floors, pool,*

health club, business services, meeting rooms, car rental, parking (fee). AE, DC, MC, V.

$$$$ ★ **Hyatt Regency Budapest.** The spectacular 10-story interior—a mix of glass capsule elevators, cascading tropical greenery, an open bar, and café—is surpassed only by the views across the Danube to Castle Hill (rooms with a river view cost substantially more). Rooms have been tastefully redesigned with classy, unobtrusive decor in muted blues and light woods, and sparkling bathrooms. ✉ *V, Roosevelt tér 2, H-1051,* ☎ *1/266–1234,* FAX *1/266–9101. 330 rooms, 23 suites. 3 restaurants, 2 bars, air-conditioning, in-room data ports, no-smoking rooms, indoor pool, beauty salon, sauna, exercise room, casino, solarium, business services, meeting rooms, travel services, parking (fee). AE, DC, MC, V.*

$$$$ ★ **Kempinski Hotel Corvinus Budapest.** This sleek luxury hotel is the favored lodging of visiting VIPs—from rock superstars to business moguls. From overnight shoe-shine service to afternoon chamber music in the lobby, the Kempinski exudes solicitousness. Unlike those of other nearby hotels, rooms are spacious, with blond and black Swedish geometric inlaid woods and an emphasis on functional touches, such as three phones in every room. Large, sparkling bathrooms, most with tubs and separate shower stalls and stocked with every toiletry, are the best in Budapest. The hotel's business services also stand out as the city's best. An automatic current in the smallish pool allows you to swim long distances without getting anywhere. Breakfast is not included in the room rates. ✉ *V, Erzsébet tér 7–8, H-1051,* ☎ *1/429–3777; 800/426–3135 in the U.S. and Canada;* FAX *1/429–4777. 342 rooms, 27 suites. 2 restaurants, bar, lobby lounge, pub, shopping arcade, air-conditioning, in-room data ports, no-smoking rooms, indoor pool, barbershop, beauty salon, massage, health club, shops, dry cleaning, laundry service, business services, meeting rooms, travel services, parking (fee). AE, DC, MC, V.*

$$$ **Danubius Grand Hotel Margitsziget.** Built in 1873 and long in disrepair, this venerable hotel reopened in 1987 as a Ramada Inn and was recently taken over by the Danubius hotel chain. Room rates may have increased since the 1870s, but the high ceilings haven't been lowered. Nor have the old-fashioned room trimmings—down comforters, ornate chandeliers—been lost in the streamlining. Choose between views across the Danube onto an industrial section of Pest or out onto the verdant lawns and trees of a tranquil park. Because it's connected to a bubbling thermal spa next door and is located on car-free Margaret Island in the Danube right between Buda and Pest, the Danubius Grand feels removed from the city but is still only a short taxi or bus ride away. ✉ *XIII, Margit-sziget, H-1138,* ☎ *1/329–2300; 1/349–2769 (reservations);* FAX *1/329–3923 (reservations), 1/329–2429 (reception). 164 rooms, 10 suites. 2 restaurants, no-smoking rooms, indoor pool, beauty salon, massage, sauna, spa, mineral baths, exercise room, bicycles, meeting rooms, travel services, free parking. AE, DC, MC, V.*

$$$ **Danubius Thermal Hotel Helia.** A sleek Scandinavian design and less hectic location upriver from downtown make this spa hotel on the Danube a change of pace from its Pest peers. Its neighborhood is nondescript, but guests can be in town in minutes or take advantage of the thermal baths and special health packages—including everything from Turkish baths to electrotherapy and fitness tests. The staff is friendly and helpful, and most of the comfortable rooms have Danube views. ✉ *XIII, Kárpát u. 62–64, H-1133,* ☎ *1/452–5800;* FAX *1/452–5801. 254 rooms, 8 suites. Restaurant, bar, café, indoor pool, beauty salon, hot tub, massage, sauna, spa, steam room, mineral baths, tennis courts, exercise room, business services, meeting rooms, free parking. AE, DC, MC, V.*

$$$ **Radisson SAS Béke.** The well-situated Béke (on a main boulevard near the Nyugati railroad station) is a budget family inn turned luxury hotel—it now has a glittering turn-of-the-20th-century facade, a

lobby lined with mosaics and statuary, and bellmen bowing before the grand marble staircase. Guest rooms resemble solidly modern living rooms, with two-tone wood furnishings and pastel decor. ✉ *VI, Teréz krt. 43, H-1067,* ☎ *1/301–1600,* FAX *1/301–1615. 238 rooms, 8 suites. 2 restaurants, 2 bars, café, air-conditioning, in-room data ports, no-smoking rooms, pool, beauty salon, sauna, solarium, business services, meeting rooms, travel services, parking (fee). AE, DC, MC, V.*

$$ **Astoria.** At a busy intersection in downtown Pest stands a revitalized turn-of-the-20th-century hotel that remains an oasis of quiet in hectic surroundings. Staff members are always—but unobtrusively—on hand. Rooms are genteel, spacious, and comfortable, and renovations have remained faithful to the original decor: rather like Grandma's sitting room, in Empire style with an occasional antique. The Astoria's vintage Café Mirror is a wonderful place to relive the Hungarian coffeehouse tradition. ✉ *V, Kossuth Lajos u. 19–21, H-1053,* ☎ *1/317–3411,* FAX *1/318–6798. 125 rooms, 5 suites. Restaurant, bar, café, no-smoking rooms, nightclub, business services, meeting rooms, free parking. AE, DC, MC, V.*

$$ **Hotel Benczúr.** Escape to this quiet hotel in the leafy embassy district off Andrássy út via the city's antique underground, the *Földalatti.* Majestic Heroes' Square is a short walk away. Rooms here are well-equipped, with minibars, modern phones, and larger than usual bathrooms, though the furnishings are quite plain. The refreshingly green neighborhood and proximity to outdoor restaurants and bars make this hotel an attractive option, especially in summer months. The Benczúr shares the building with Hotel Pedagógus. ✉ *VI, Benczúr u. 35, H-1068,* ☎ *1/342–7970,* FAX *1/342–1558. 93 rooms. Restaurant, no-smoking rooms, meeting room, free parking. MC, V.*

$$ **Carlton Hotel.** Tucked behind an alleyway at the foot of Castle Hill, this modern property (formerly named the Alba Hotel) is a short walk via the Chain Bridge from lively business and shopping districts. Rooms are clean and quiet, with white-and-pale-gray contemporary decor and typical Budapest views over a kaleidoscope of rooftops and chimneys. Half have bathtubs. ✉ *I, Apor Péter u. 3, H-1011,* ☎ *1/224–0999 or 1/375–8658,* FAX *1/224–0990. 95 rooms. Bar, breakfast room, air-conditioning, no-smoking rooms, meeting room, parking (fee). AE, DC, MC, V.*

$$ **Flamenco.** Classy though sometimes overlooked, this hotel in the Buda foothills is a welcome addition to this side of the river. A wall of windows in the low-ceiling lobby opens out onto views of a park. Service is professional, and the well-kept contemporary rooms are above average in this price category. ✉ *XI, Tas Vezér u. 7, H-1113,* ☎ *1/372–2165 or 1/372–2000,* FAX *1/372–2100. 352 rooms, 8 suites. 2 restaurants, indoor pool, beauty salon, sauna, solarium, business services, meeting rooms, travel services, parking (fee). AE, DC, MC, V.*

$$ **Mercure Hotel Budapest Nemzeti.** With a lovely, baby-blue Baroque facade, the Nemzeti reflects the grand mood of the turn of the 20th century. The high-ceiling lobby and public areas—with pillars, arches, and wrought-iron railings—are elaborately elegant. Many of the once unexceptional rooms have been revamped with pretty, new furnishings and air-conditioning; be sure to ask for one of these rooms ($10 extra) for optimal comfort. The hotel is located at bustling Blaha Lujza tér in the center of Pest, which tends toward the seedy after dark; although windows are double-paned, to ensure a quiet night, ask for a room facing the inner courtyard. ✉ *VIII, József krt. 4, H-1088,* ☎ *1/303–9310,* FAX *1/314–0019,* ☎ FAX *1/303–9162. 75 rooms, 1 suite. Restaurant, piano bar, air-conditioning, meeting room, travel services. AE, DC, MC, V.*

$$ **Molnár Panzió.** Fresh air and peace and quiet could lure you to this immaculate guest house nestled high above Buda on Széchenyi Hill. Rooms in the octagonal main house are polyhedric, clean, and bright, with pleasant wood paneling and pastel-color modern furnishings; most have distant views of Castle Hill and Gellért Hill, and some have balconies. Eight rooms in a newer addition next door are more private and have superior bathrooms. Breakfast here is more appealing than usual—with scrambled eggs in addition to the standard breads and jams. ✉ *XII, Fodor u. 143, H-1124,* ☎ *1/395–1873,* ☎ FAX *1/395–1872. 23 rooms. Restaurant, bar, sauna, exercise room, playground, travel services, free parking. AE, DC, MC, V.*

$$ ★ **Victoria.** The Parliament building and city lights twinkling over the river can be seen from the picture windows of every room at this young establishment right on the Danube. The tiny hotel mixes the charm of a small inn with the modern comforts and efficiency of a business hotel. The location—an easy walk from Castle Hill sights and downtown Pest—couldn't be better. ✉ *I, Bem rakpart 11, H-1011,* ☎ *1/457–8080,* FAX *1/457–8088. 27 rooms, 1 suite. Bar, air-conditioning, sauna, meeting room, travel services, parking (fee). AE, DC, MC, V.*

$ **Citadella.** Comparatively basic, the Citadella is nevertheless very popular for its price and for its stunning location—right inside the fortress. Half of the rooms compose a youth hostel, giving the hotel a lively communal atmosphere. None of the rooms have bathrooms, but half have showers. Breakfast is not included in the rates. ✉ *XI, Citadella sétány, Gellérthegy, H–1118,* ☎ *1/466–5794,* FAX *1/386–0505. 20 rooms, none with bath. Breakfast room. No credit cards.*

$ ★ **Kulturinov.** One wing of a magnificent 1902 neo-Baroque castle now houses basic budget accommodations. Rooms come with two or three beds and are clean and delightfully peaceful; they have showers but no tubs. The neighborhood—one of Budapest's most famous squares in the luxurious castle district—is magical. ✉ *I, Szentháromság tér 6, H-1014,* ☎ *1/355–0122 or 1/375–1651,* FAX *1/375–1886. 16 rooms. Snack bar, library, meeting rooms. AE, DC, MC, V.*

Nightlife and the Arts

Nightlife

Budapest's nightlife is vibrant and diverse. For basic beer and wine drinking, sörözős and *borozós* (wine bars) abound, although the latter tend to serve the early-morning-spritzer-before-work types rather than nighttime revelers. For quiet conversation there are *drink-bárs* in most hotels and all over town, but beware of the inflated prices and steep cover charges. Cafés are preferable for unescorted women.

Most nightspots and clubs have bars, pool tables, and dance floors. Although some places do accept credit cards, it's best to expect to pay cash for your night on the town. As is the case in most other cities, the life of a club or disco in Budapest can be somewhat ephemeral. Those listed below are quite popular and seem to be here to stay. But for the very latest on the more transient "in" spots, consult the nightlife sections of the weekly *Budapest Sun* or *Budapest in Your Pocket*, published five times a year.

Budapest also has its share of seedy go-go clubs and so-called "cabarets," some of which are known for scandalously excessive billing and physical intimidation. Be wary if you are "invited" in by women lingering nearby, and don't order anything without first seeing the price. What's more, in some pulsing nightspots it is not uncommon to find men weaving through the crowd selling drugs or themselves; the penalties for possessing even small amounts of illegal drugs are stiff.

A word of warning to the smoke-sensitive: Although a 1999 law requiring smoke-free areas in many public establishments has already had a discernible impact in restaurants, the bar scene is a firm reminder that Budapest remains a city of smokers. No matter where you spend your night out, chances are you'll come home smelling of cigarette smoke.

BARS AND CLUBS

Angel Bar and Disco (✉ VII, Szövetség u. 33, ☎ 1/351–6490) is one of Budapest's enduring and most popular gay bars (though all persuasions are welcome), with a rollicking dance floor. It's closed Monday–Wednesday.

Bahnhof (✉ VI, Váci út 1, at Nyugati pu.) is, appropriately, in the Nyugati (West) train station and attracts swarms of young people to its large, crowded dance floor to live bands and DJ'd music. It's closed Sunday–Tuesday.

The most popular of Budapest's Irish pubs and a favorite expat watering hole is **Becketts** (✉ V, Bajcsy-Zsilinszky út 72, ☎ 1/311–1035), where Guinness flows freely and excellent Irish fare is served amid the gleams of polished wood and brass.

One of the city's hottest spots is **Café Capella** (✉ V, Belgrád rakpart 23, ☎ 1/318–6231), where a welcoming, gay-friendly crowd flocks to the glittery drag shows (held a few times a week) and revels to DJ'd club music until dawn.

A hip, mellow crowd mingles at the stylish **Cafe Incognito** (✉ VI, Liszt Ferenc tér 3, ☎ 1/351–9428), with low lighting and funky music kept at a conversation-friendly volume. Couches and armchairs in the back are comfy and private. It closes relatively early—at midnight.

Café Pierrot (✉ I, Fortuna u. 14, ☎ 1/375–6971), an elegant café and piano bar on a small street on Castle Hill, is well suited to a secret rendezvous.

With its abundance of soft chairs and changing exhibits of chic, abstract paintings, **Cafe Vian** (✉ VI, Liszt Ferenc tér 9, ☎ 1/342–8991) is *the* place to lounge about sipping cappuccino, beer, or a cocktail (nonalcoholic varieties available) while chatting, not to mention seeing and being seen. It closes at midnight.

Established Hungarian jazz headliners and young up-and-comers play Sunday–Tuesday in the popular if small, stylishly brick-walled **Fat Mo's** (✉ VII, Nyári Pál u. 11, ☎ 1/267–3199), which is open daily.

If crowds, low newspaper-mosaicked ceilings, and smoke-permeated air aren't your thing, avoid the **Old Man's Music Pub** (✉ VII, Akácfa u. 13, ☎ 1/322–7645). If hard-core live blues and friendly chaos *are*, don't miss out on the fun—complemented by a small dance floor.

Cool (and trendily dark) **Underground** (✉ VI, Teréz krt. 30, ☎ 1/311–1481) is below the artsy Művész movie theater. Exposed metal beams and girders and wackily shaped scrap-metal chairs and tables give this bar the requisite industrial look; the DJ spins progressive popular music. Weekends are packed with younger, sometimes rowdy, hipsters.

CASINOS

Most of Budapest's 10 or so major casinos are open daily from 2 PM until 4 or 5 AM and offer gambling in hard currency—usually dollars—only.

The centrally located and popular **Las Vegas Casino** (✉ V, Roosevelt tér 2, ☎ 1/317–6022) is in the Hyatt Regency Hotel. In an 1879 building designed by prolific architect Miklós Ybl, who also designed the State Opera House, the **Várkert Casino** (✉ I, Miklós Ybl tér 9, ☎ 1/202–4244) is the most visually striking of the city's casinos.

The Arts

For the latest on arts events, consult the entertainment listings of the English-language press (☞ Contacts and Resources, *below*). Their entertainment calendars map out all that's happening in Budapest's arts and culture world—from thrash bands in wild clubs to performances at the Opera House. Another option is to stop in at the **National Philharmonic ticket office** (✉ V, Mérleg u. 10, ☏ 1/318–0281) and browse through the scores of free programs and fliers and scan the walls coated with upcoming concert posters. Hotels and tourist offices will provide you with a copy of the monthly publication *Programme*, which contains details of all cultural events.

Tickets can be bought at the venues themselves, but many ticket offices sell them without extra charge. Prices are still very low, so markups of even 30% shouldn't dent your wallet if you book through your hotel. Inquire at Tourinform (☞ Visitor Information, *below*) if you're not sure where to go. Ticket availability depends on the performance and season—it's usually possible to get tickets a few days before a show, but performances by major international artists sell out early. Tickets to Budapest Festival Orchestra concerts and festival events also go particularly quickly.

Theater and opera tickets are sold at the **Central Theater Booking Office** (✉ VI, Andrássy út 18, ☏ 1/312–0000). For classical concert, ballet, and opera tickets, as well as tickets for major pop and rock shows, go to the **National Philharmonic Ticket Office** (☞ *above*). **Music Mix Ticket Service** (✉ V, Váci utca 33, ☏ 1/317–7736) specializes in popular music but handles other genres as well.

CLASSICAL MUSIC AND OPERA

The tiny recital room of the **Bartók Béla Emlékház** (Bartók Béla Memorial House; ✉ II, Csalán út 29, ☏ 1/394–4472) hosts intimate Friday evening chamber music recitals by well-known ensembles from mid-March to June and September to mid-December.

The **Budapest Kongresszusi Központ** (Budapest Convention Center; ✉ XII, Jagelló út 1–3, ☏ 1/209–1990) is the city's largest-capacity (but least atmospheric) classical concert venue and usually hosts the largest-selling events of the Spring Festival.

The homely little sister of the Opera House, the **Erkel Színház** (Erkel Theater; ✉ VII, Köztársaság tér 30, ☏ 1/333–0540) is Budapest's other main opera and ballet venue. There are no regular performances in the summer.

Liszt Ferenc Zeneakadémia (Franz Liszt Academy of Music; ✉ VI, Liszt Ferenc tér 8, ☏ 1/342–0179), usually referred to as the Music Academy, is Budapest's premier classical concert venue, hosting orchestra and chamber music concerts in its splendid main hall. It's sometimes possible to grab a standing-room ticket just before a performance here.

The glittering **Magyar Állami Operaház** (Hungarian State Opera House; ✉ VI, Andrássy út 22, ☏ 1/331–2550), Budapest's main venue for operas and classical ballet, presents an international repertoire of classical and modern works as well as such Hungarian favorites as Kodály's *Háry János*. Except during the one-week BudaFest international opera and ballet festival in mid-August, the Opera House is closed during the summer.

Colorful operettas such as those by Lehár and Kálmán are staged at their main Budapest venue, the **Operetta Theater** (✉ VI, Nagymező u. 19, ☏ 1/353–2172); also look for modern dance productions and Hungarian renditions of popular Broadway classics.

Classical concerts are held regularly at the **Pesti Vigadó** (Pest Concert Hall; ✉ V, Vigadó tér 2, ☎ 1/318–9167).

ENGLISH-LANGUAGE MOVIES

Many of the English-language movies that come to Budapest are subtitled in Hungarian rather than dubbed; this applies less so, however, to independent and art films. There are more than 30 cinemas that regularly show films in English, and tickets are very inexpensive by Western standards (400–700 Ft.). Consult the movie matrix in the *Budapest Sun* for a weekly list of what's showing.

FOLK DANCING

Many of Budapest's district cultural centers regularly hold traditional regional folk-dancing evenings, or dance houses (*táncház*), often with general instruction at the beginning. These sessions provide a less touristy way to taste Hungarian culture.

Almássy téri Szabadidő központ (Almássy Square Recreation Center; ✉ VII, Almássy tér 6, ☎ 1/352–1572) holds numerous folk-dancing evenings, representing Hungarian as well as Greek and other ethnic cultures. Traditionally the wildest táncház is held Saturday night at the **Belvárosi Ifjúsági ház** (City Youth Center; ✉ V, Molnár u. 9, ☎ 1/317–5928), where the stomping and whirling go on way into the night; the center, like many such venues, closes from mid-July to mid-August. A well-known Transylvanian folk ensemble, Tatros, hosts a weekly dance house at the **Marczibányi téri Művelődési ház** (Marczibányi tér Cultural Center; ✉ II, Marczibányi tér 5/a, ☎ 1/212–5789), usually on Wednesday night.

FOLKLORE PERFORMANCES

The Hungarian State Folk Ensemble performs regularly at the **Budai Vigadó** (✉ I, Corvin tér 8, ☎ 1/201–3766); shows incorporate instrumental music, dancing, and singing.

The **Folklór Centrum** (✉ XI, Fehérvári út 47, ☎ 1/203–3868) has been a major venue for folklore performances for more than 30 years. It hosts regular traditional folk concerts and dance performances from spring through fall.

THEATERS

The **Madách Theater** (✉ VII, Erzsébet krt. 31–33, ☎ 1/478–2041) produces colorful musicals in Hungarian, including a popular adaptation of *Cats*. For English-language dramas check out the **Merlin Theater** (✉ V, Gerlóczy u. 4, ☎ 1/317–9338). Another musical theater is the **Thália Theater** (✉ VI, Nagymező u. 22–24, ☎ 1/331–0500). The sparkling **Vígszínház** (Comedy Theater; ✉ XIII, Pannónia u. 1, ☎ 1/329–2340) hosts classical concerts and dance performances but is primarily a venue for musicals, such as the Hungarian adaptation of *West Side Story.*

Outdoor Activities and Sports

Bicycling

Because of constant thefts, bicycle rentals are difficult to find in Hungary. **Bringóhintó,** a rental outfit on Margaret Island (✉ Hajós Alfréd sétány 1, across from Thermal Hotel, ☎ 1/329–2072), offers popular four-wheel pedaled contraptions called *Bringóhintók,* as well as traditional two-wheelers; standard bikes cost about 800 Ft. per hour or 1,500 Ft. until 8 AM the next day, with a 10,000 Ft. deposit. For more information about renting in Budapest, contact **Tourinform** (✉ V, Sütő u. 2, ☎ 1/317–9800). For brochures and general information on bicycling conditions and suggested routes, try Tourinform or contact the **Magyar Kerékpáros Túrázók Szövetsége** (Bicycle Touring Association of Hungary; ✉ V, Bajcsy-Zsilinszky út 31, 2nd floor, Apt. 3, ☎ 1/332–7177).

Golf

Golf is still a new sport in Hungary, one that few Hungarians can afford. The closest place to putt is 35 km (22 mi) north of the city at the **Budapest Golfpark** (☎ 1/317–6025, 1/317–2749, or 06–26/392–463) in Kisoroszi. The park has an 18-hole, 72-par course and a driving range. Greens fees range from 7,000 Ft. to 8,000 Ft. Carts and equipment can be rented. The park is closed from about mid-November–mid-March.

Health and Fitness Clubs

Andi Stúdió (✉ V, Hold u. 29, ☎ 1/311–0740) is a trendy fitness club with adequate but sometimes overcrowded facilities. For about 650 Ft. you can work out on the weight machines (no real cardiovascular equipment to speak of) and sit in the sauna, or take an aerobics class, held every hour. **Gold's Gym** (✉ VIII, Szentkirályi u. 26, ☎ 1/267–4334) stands out as being the least cramped gym, with good weight-training and cardiovascular equipment and hourly aerobics classes in larger-than-usual spaces. A one-visit pass costs around 650 Ft.

Horseback Riding

Experienced riders can ride at the **Budapesti Lovas Klub** (Budapest Equestrian Club; ✉ VIII, Kerepesi út 7, ☎ FAX 1/313–5210) for about 1,500 Ft. per hour. Call about two weeks ahead to assure yourself a horse. In the verdant outskirts of Buda, the **Petneházy Lovas Centrum** (Petneházy Equestrian Center; ✉ 1029 Feketefej út 2, Adyliget, ☎ 1/397–5048) offers horseback-riding lessons and trail rides for 1,800 Ft.–2,500 Ft. per hour. Note that English saddle, not Western, is the standard in Hungary.

Jogging

The path around the perimeter of **Margaret Island,** as well as the numerous pathways in the center, is level and inviting for a good run. **Városliget** (City Park) in flat Pest has paths good for jogging.

Spas and Thermal Baths

In addition to those listed below, newer, modern baths are open to the public at hotels, such as the **Danubius Grand Hotel Margitsziget** and the **Danubius Thermal Hotel Helia** (☞ Lodging, *above*). They lack the charm of their older peers but provide the latest treatments.

Gellért Thermal Baths (☞ Tabán and Gellért Hill, *above*); **Király Baths** (☞ North Buda, *above*); **Rác Baths** (☞ Tabán and Gellért Hill, *above*); **Rudas Baths** (☞ Tabán and Gellért Hill, *above*); **Széchenyi Baths** (☞ Városliget, *above*).

Tennis and Squash

On Margaret Island, **Euro-Gym Fitness Club** (✉ XIII, Europa House, Margitsziget, ☎ 1/339–8672) charges 700 Ft.–900 Ft. per hour to play on one of its eight clay courts; it's open from mid-April to mid-October, and you'll need to reserve a day or two in advance. **On-line Squash Club** (✉ Budaörs, Forrás u. 8, ☎ 23/501–2620), on the near outskirts of town, is a trendy full-facility fitness club with five squash courts. Hourly rates run 2,000 Ft.–2,800 Ft., depending on when you play. The club rents equipment and stays open until 11 PM on weekdays, 9 PM on weekends. **Városmajor Tennis Academy** (✉ XII, Városmajor u. 63–69, ☎ 1/202–5337) has five outdoor courts (clay and hexapet) available daily 7 AM–10 PM. They are lit for night play and covered by a tent in winter. Court fees run around 1,400 Ft. per hour in summer, 1,800 Ft.–3,000 Ft. in winter. Racket rentals and lessons are also offered. The Marriott Hotel's **World Class Fitness Center** (✉ V, Apáczai Csere János u. 4, ☎ 1/266–4290) has one excellent squash court available for 2,500 Ft.–4,500 Ft an hour, depending on when you play; be sure to reserve it a day or two in advance.

Shopping

Shopping Districts

You'll find plenty of expensive boutiques, folk-art and souvenir shops, foreign-language bookstores, and classical-record shops on or around touristy **Váci utca,** Budapest's famous, upscale pedestrian-only promenade. While a stroll along Váci utca is integral to a Budapest visit, browsing among some of the smaller, less touristy, more typically Hungarian shops in Pest—on the **Kis körút** (Small Ring Road) and **Nagy körút** (Great Ring Road)—may prove more interesting and less pricey. Lots of arty boutiques are springing up in the section of District V **south of Ferenciek tere and toward the Danube,** and around **Kálvin tér. Falk Miksa utca,** also in the fifth district, running south from Szent István körút, is one of the city's best antiques districts, lined on both sides with atmospheric little shops and galleries.

Department Stores and Malls

Skála Metro (✉ VI, Nyugati tér 1–2, ☎ 1/353–2222), opposite the Nyugati (West) Railroad Station, is one of the largest and best-known department stores, selling a little bit of not entirely everything. **Fontana** (✉ Váci u. 16), has several floors of cosmetics, clothing, and other goods, all with price tags reflecting the store's expensive address. Pest's huge **Westend City Center** (✉ VI, Váci út 1–3 [next to the Nyugati railroad station]), ☎ 1/238–7777), and Buda's **Mammut** (✉ II, Széna tér, ☎ 1/345–8020), are just two of the many American-style malls that have sprung up in Hungary in recent years. They offer everything—except a genuine Hungarian atmosphere.

Markets

For true bargains and possibly an adventure, make an early morning trip to the vast **Ecseri Piac** (✉ IX, Nagykőrösi út 156; take Bus 54 from Boráros tér), on the outskirts of the city. A colorful, chaotic market that shoppers have flocked to for decades, it is an arsenal of second-hand goods, where you can find everything from frayed Russian army fatigues to Herend and Zsolnay porcelain vases to antique silver chalices. Goods are sold at permanent tables set up in rows, from trunks of cars parked on the perimeter, and by lone, shady characters clutching just one or two items. As a foreigner, you may be overcharged, so prepare to haggle—it's part of the flea-market experience. Also, watch out for pickpockets. Ecseri is open weekdays 8–4, Saturday 8–3, but the best selection is on Saturday morning.

A colorful outdoor flea market is held weekend mornings from 7 to 2 at **Petőfi Csarnok** (✉ XIV, Városliget, Zichy Mihály út 14, ☎ 1/251–7266), in City Park. The quantity and selection are smaller than at Ecseri Piac, but it offers a fun flea-market experience closer to the city center. Many visitors buy red-star medals, Russian military watches, and other memorabilia from Communist days here. One other option is the **Vásárcsarnok** (☞ Downtown Pest and the Kis körút [Little Ring Road], *above*).

Specialty Stores

ANTIQUES

Falk Miksa utca (☞ Shopping Districts, *above*), lined with antiques stores, is a delightful street for multiple-shop browsing.

The shelves and tables at tiny **Anna Antikvitás** (✉ V, Falk Miksa u. 18–20, ☎ 1/302–5461) are stacked with exquisite antique textiles—from heavily embroidered wall hangings to dainty lace gloves. Exquisite cloth and lace parasols line the ceiling, but these, unfortunately, are not for sale; similar ones are, however, sometimes available. The store also carries assorted antique objets d'art. **BÁV Műtárgy** (✉ V, Ferenciek tere 12, ☎ 1/318–3381; V, Kossuth Lajos u. 1–3, ☎ 1/318–6934; V, Szent István krt. 3, ☎ 1/331–4534), the State Commission Trading House, has antiques of all shapes, sizes, kinds, and prices at its several branches around the city. While they all have a variety of objects, porcelain is the specialty at the branch on Kossuth Lajos utca, and paintings at the Szent István körút store. **Polgár Galéria és Aukciósház** (✉ V, Kossuth Lajos u. 3, ☎ 1/318–6954) sells everything from jewelry to furniture and also holds several auctions a year. **Qualitás** (✉ V, Falk Miksa u. 32; V, Kígyó u. 5; VII, Dohány u. 1) sells paintings, furniture, and decorative objects at its branches around town.

ART GALLERIES

Budapest has dozens of art galleries showing and selling old works as well as the very latest. **Dovin Gallery** (✉ V, Galamb u. 6, ☎ 1/318–3673) specializes in Hungarian contemporary paintings. New York celebrity Yoko Ono opened **Gallery 56** (✉ V, Falk Miksa u. 7, ☎ 1/269–2529) to show art by internationally famed artists, such as Keith Haring, as well as works by up-and-coming Hungarian artists. You can also visit **Magyar Fotógráfusok Háza** (☞ Andrássy út, *above*) for photography exhibits.

BOOKS

You'll encounter bookselling stands throughout the streets and metro stations of the city, many of which sell English-language souvenir picturebooks at discount prices. **Váci utca** is lined with bookstores that sell glossy coffee-table books about Budapest and Hungary.

Atlantisz (✉ V, Váci u. 31–33) has a selection of English classics, as well as academic texts. **Bestsellers** (✉ V, Október 6 u. 11, ☎ 1/312–1295) sells exclusively English-language books and publications, including best-selling paperbacks and a variety of travel guides about Hungary and beyond. The **Central European University Bookshop** (✉ V, Nádor u. 9, ☎ 1/327–3096), in the Central European University, is a more academically focused branch of Bestsellers bookstore. If you're interested in reading up on this part of the world, this is the store for you. You'll also find a good selection of books in English at **Idegennyelvű Könyvesbolt** (✉ V, Petőfi Sándor u. 2 [in Párizsi udvar]), which specializes in foreign-language books. **Írók boltja** (Writers' Bookshop; ✉ VI, Andrássy út 45, ☎ 1/322–1645), one of Budapest's main literary bookstores, has a small but choice selection of Hungarian fiction and poetry translated into English. The hushed, literary atmosphere is tangible, and small tables are set out for reading and enjoying a cup of self-serve tea and coffee.

CHINA, CRYSTAL, AND PORCELAIN

Hungary is famous for its age-old Herend porcelain, which is hand-painted in the village of Herend near Lake Balaton. For the Herend name and quality without the steep price tag, visit **Herend Village Pottery** (✉ II, Bem rakpart 37, ☎ 1/356–7899), where you can choose from Herend's practical line of durable ceramic cups, dishes, and table settings. The brand's largest Budapest store, **Herendi Porcelán Márkabolt** (✉ V, József Nádor tér 11, ☎ 1/317–2622), sells a variety of the delicate (and pricey) pieces, from figurines to dinner sets. Hungary's exquisite Zsolnay porcelain, created and hand-painted in Pécs, is sold at the **Zsolnay Márkabolt** (✉ V, Kígyó u. 4, ☎ 1/318–3712) and a few other locations.

Hungarian and Czech crystal is considerably less expensive here than in the United States. **Goda Kristály** (✉ V, Váci u. 9, ☎ 1/318–4630) has beautiful colored and clear pieces. **Haas & Czjzek** (✉ VI, Bajcsy-Zsilinszky út 23, ☎ 1/311–4094) has been in the business for more than 100 years, selling a variety of porcelain, glass, and ceramic pieces in traditional and contemporary styles. Crystal and porcelain dealers also sell their wares at the Ecseri Piac flea market (☞ Markets, *above*), often at discount prices, but those looking for authentic Herend and Zsolnay should beware of imitations.

CLOTHING

El Cabito (✉ V, Múzeum krt. 35, ☎ 318–8963), a tiny boutique across from the National Museum, offers cotton dresses of Hungarian and Far Eastern design—for reasonable prices. The **Hugo Boss Shop** (✉ V, Aranykéz u. 2, ☎ 318–3016), has a good selection of men's suits. High-fashion women's outfits by top Hungarian designers are for sale at **Monarchia** (✉ V, Szabadsajtó út 6, ☎ 1/318–3146), whose rich burgundy velvet draperies and ceilings are higher than its floor space. **Manier** (✉ V, Váci u. 48 [entrance at Nyári Pál u. 4], ☎ 1/318–1812) is a popular haute couture salon run by talented Hungarian designer Anikó Németh offering women's pieces ranging from quirky to totally outrageous. The store's second branch is across the street at Váci utca 53.

FOLK ART

Handmade articles, such as embroidered tablecloths and painted plates, are sold all over the city by Transylvanian women wearing traditional scarves and colorful skirts. You can usually find them standing at **Moszkva tér, Jászai Mari tér,** outside the **Kossuth tér** metro, around **Váci utca,** and in the larger metro stations.

All types of folk art—pottery, blouses, jewelry boxes, wood carvings, embroidery—can be purchased at one of the many branches of Népművészet Háziipar, also called **Folkart Centrum** (✉ V, Váci u. 14, ☎ 1/318–5840), a large cooperative chain. Prices are reasonable, and selection and quality are good. **Holló Műhely** (✉ V, Vitkovics Mihály u. 12, ☎ 1/317–8103) sells the work of László Holló, a master wood craftsman who has resurrected traditional motifs and styles of earlier centuries. There are lovely hope chests, chairs, jewelry boxes, candlesticks, and more, all hand-carved and hand-painted with cheery folk motifs—a predominance of birds and flowers in reds, blues, and greens.

HOME DECOR AND GIFTS

Impresszió (✉ V, Károly krt. 10, ☎ 1/337–2772) is a little boutique packed with home-furnishings, baskets, picture frames, and decorative packaging, all made of natural materials and reasonably priced. The courtyard it calls home includes similar shops and a pleasant café. A few blocks away, just down the street from the Holló Műhely (☞ *above*), lies the **Interieur Stúdió** (✉ V, Vitkovics Mihály u. 6, ☎ 1/266–1666), offering wooden brushes, bookmarks, and even a birdcage; candles of all shapes and sizes; and sundry other objects for the home.

MUSIC

Recordings of Hungarian folk music or of pieces played by Hungarian artists are widely available on compact discs, though cassettes and records are much cheaper and are sold throughout the city. CDs are normally quite expensive—about 4,000 Ft.

MCD Amadeus (✉ V, Szende Pál u. 1, ☎ 1/318–6691), just off the Duna korzó, has an extensive selection of classical CDs. **MCD Zeneszalon** (✉ V, Vörösmarty tér 1, ☎ no phone) has a large selection of all types of music and is centrally located. Its separate, extensive section on Hungarian artists is great for gift- or souvenir-browsing. The **Rózsavölgyi Zenebolt** (✉ V, Szervita tér 5, ☎ 1/318–3500) is an old, established music store crowded with sheet music and largely classical recordings, but with other selections as well.

TOYS

For a step back into the world before Pokemon cards and action figures, stop in at the tiny **Játékszerek Anno** (Toys Anno; ✉ VI, Teréz krt. 54, ☎ 1/302–6234) store, where fabulous repros of antique European toys are sold. From simple paper puzzles to lovely stone building blocks to the 1940s wind-up metal monkeys on bicycles, these "nostalgia toys" are beautifully simple and exceptionally clever. Even if you're not a collector, it's worth a stop just to browse.

WINE

Stores specializing in Hungarian wines have become a trend in Budapest over the past few years. The best of them is the store run by the **Budapest Bortársaság** (Budapest Wine Society; ✉ I, Batthyány u. 59, ☎ 1/212–2569 or 1/212–0262, FAX 1/212–5285). The cellar shop at the base of Castle Hill always has an excellent selection of Hungary's finest wines, chosen by the wine society's discerning staff, who will happily help you with your purchases. Tastings are held Saturday from 2 to 6.

Budapest A to Z

Arriving and Departing

BY BOAT

From late July through early September, two swift hydrofoils leave Vienna daily at 8 AM and 1 PM (once-a-day trips are scheduled mid-April–late July and September–late October). After a 5½-hour journey downriver, with a stop in the Slovak capital, Bratislava, and views of Hungary's largest church, the cathedral in Esztergom, the boats head into Budapest via its main artery, the Danube. The upriver journey takes about an hour longer. For reservations and information in Budapest, call **MAHART Tours** (☎ 1/484–4025; 1/484–4010; 43–1/729–2161; 43–1/729–2162 in Vienna). The cost is 780 AS one-way.

BY CAR

The main routes into Budapest are the M1 from Vienna (via Győr), the M3 from near Gyöngyös, the M5 from Kecskemét, and the M7 from the Balaton; the M3 and M5 are being upgraded over the next few years and extended to Hungary's borders with Slovakia and Yugoslavia, respectively.

BY PLANE

Ferihegy Repülőtér (☎ 1/296–9696), Hungary's only commercial airport with regularly scheduled service, is 24 km (15 mi) southeast of downtown Budapest. All non-Hungarian airlines operate from Terminal 2B; those of Malév, from Terminal 2A. (A note of clarification should you run into some confusion: The older part of the airport, Terminal 1, no longer serves commercial flights; and so the main airport is now often referred to as "Ferihegy 2," and the terminals as simply "A" and "B.") For same-day **flight information,** call ☎ 1/296–8000 (arrivals) or 1/296–7000 (departures); operators theoretically speak some English.

The most convenient way to fly between Hungary and the United States is with **Malév Hungarian Airlines** (☎ 06/40–212–121 toll free; 1/235–3804 [ticketing]; 1/296–9696 [after-hours flight information]) nonstop direct service between JFK International Airport in New York and Budapest's Ferihegy Airport—the only nonstop flight that exists. All are on roomy Boeing 767-200s and take approximately nine hours. The service runs daily most of the year.

Malév and other national airlines fly nonstop from most European capitals. **British Airways** (☎ 1/318–3299 or 1/266–6699) and Malév offer daily nonstop service between Budapest and London.

Between the Airport and Downtown: Many hotels offer their guests car or minibus transportation to and from Ferihegy, but all of them charge for the service. You should arrange for a pickup in advance. If you're taking a taxi, allow 40 minutes during nonpeak hours and at least an hour during rush hours (7 AM–9 AM from the airport, 4 PM–6 PM from the city). Official **Airport Taxis** (☎ 1/282–2222) are queued at the exit and overseen by a taxi monitor; rates are fixed according to the zone of your final destination. A taxi ride to the center of Budapest will cost around 4,500 Ft. Trips to the airport are about 3,500 Ft. from Pest, 4,000 Ft. from Buda. Avoid taxi drivers who approach you before you are out of the arrivals lounge.

LRI Centrum Bus (☎ 1/296–8555 or 1/296–6283) minibuses run every half hour from 5:30 AM to 9:30 PM to and from the Hotel Kempinski on Erzsébet tér (near the main bus station and the Deák tér metro hub) in downtown Budapest. It takes almost the same time as taxis but costs only about 700 Ft. The **LRI Airport Shuttle** provides convenient door-to-door service between the airport and any address in the city. To get to the airport, call to arrange a pickup (☎ 1/296–8555 or 1/296–6283); to get to the city, make arrangements at LRI's airport desk. Service to or from either terminal costs around 1,500 Ft. per person; since it normally shuttles several people at once, remember to allow time for a few other pickups or dropoffs.

BY TRAIN

There are three main *pályaudvar* (train stations) in Budapest: **Keleti** (East; ✉ VIII, Baross tér); **Nyugati** (West; ✉ V, Nyugati tér), and **Déli** (South; ✉ XII, Alkotás u.). The most reliable, 24-hour phone numbers for information on trains in and out of any station are 1/461–5500 (international) and 1/461–5400 (domestic). Trains to and from Vienna usually operate from the Keleti Station, while those to the Lake Balaton region depart from the Déli.

Getting Around

BY BUS AND TRAM

Trams (*villamos*) and buses (*autóbusz*) are abundant and convenient. One fare ticket (95 Ft.; valid on all forms of public transportation) is valid for only one ride in one direction. Tickets cannot be bought on board; they are widely available in metro stations and newsstands and must be validated on board by inserting them downward facing you into the little devices provided for that purpose, then pulling the knob. Alternatively, you can purchase a *napijegy* (day ticket, 740 Ft.; a three-day "tourist ticket" costs 1,500 Ft.), which allows unlimited travel on all services within the city limits. Hold on to whatever ticket you have; spot-checks by aggressive undercover checkers (look for the red armbands) are numerous and often targeted at tourists. Trolley-bus stops are marked with red, rectangular signs that list the route stops; regular bus stops are marked with similar light blue signs. (The trolley-buses and regular buses themselves are red and blue, respectively.) Tram stops are marked by light blue or yellow signs. Most lines run from 5 AM and stop operating at 11 PM, but there is all-night service on certain key routes. Consult the separate night-bus map posted in most metro stations for all-night service.

BY CAR

Budapest, like any Western city, is plagued by traffic jams during the day, but motorists should have no problem later in the evening. Parking, however, is a problem—prepare to learn new parking techniques such as curb balancing and sidewalk straddling. Free parking is a thing of the past on most central city streets; hourly fees are paid either to automats or attendants. Motorists not accustomed to sharing the city streets with trams should pay extra attention. You should be prepared to be flagged down numerous times by police conducting routine checks for drunk driving and stolen cars. Be sure all of your papers are in order and readily accessible; unfortunately, the police have been known to give foreigners a hard time.

BY METRO

Service on Budapest's subways is cheap, fast, frequent, and comfortable; stations are easily located on maps and streets by the big letter M (for metro). Tickets—95 Ft.; valid on all forms of mass transportation—can be bought at hotels, metro stations, newsstands, and kiosks. They are valid for one ride only; you can't change lines or direction. Tickets must be canceled in the time-clock machines in station entrances and should be kept until the end of the journey, as there are frequent checks by undercover inspectors; a fine for traveling without a validated ticket is about 1,300 Ft. A *napijegy* (day ticket) costs 740 Ft. (a three-day "tourist ticket," 1,500 Ft.) and allows unlimited travel on all services within the city limits.

Line 1 (marked FÖLDALATTI), which starts downtown at Vörösmarty tér and follows Andrássy út out past Gundel restaurant and City Park, is an antique tourist attraction in itself, built in the 1890s for the Magyar Millennium; its yellow trains with tank treads still work. Lines 2 and 3 were built 90 years later. Line 2 (red) runs from the eastern suburbs, past the Keleti (East) Station, through the city center, and under the Danube to the Déli (South) Station. (One of the stations, Moszkva tér, is where the *Várbusz* [Castle Bus] can be boarded.) Line 3 (blue) runs from the southeastern suburbs to Deák tér, through the city center, and northward to the Nyugati (West) Station and the northern suburbs. On all three lines, fare tickets are canceled in machines at the station entrance. All three metro lines meet at the Deák tér station and run from 4:30 AM to shortly after 11 PM.

BY TAXI

Taxis are plentiful and a good value, but make sure they have a working meter. The average initial charge is 125 Ft.–200 Ft. (toward the latter between 10 PM and 6 AM), plus about the same per km (½ mi) and 50 Ft.–70 Ft. (again, more at night) per minute of waiting time. Many drivers try to charge outrageous prices, especially if they sense that their passenger is a tourist. Avoid unmarked, "freelance" taxis; stick with those affiliated with an established company. Your safest and most reliable bet is to do what the locals do: Order a taxi by phone; it will arrive in about 5–10 minutes. The best rates are with **BudaTaxi** (☎ 1/233–3333)), **Citytaxi** (☎ 1/211–1111), **Fő taxi** (☎ 1/222–2222), **Tele 5 Taxi** (☎ 1/355–5555), and **6x6 Taxi** (☎ 1/266–6666).

Contacts and Resources

APARTMENT RENTALS

Apartments, available for short- and long-term rental, can be the most economic lodging for families or groups. A short-term rental in Budapest may cost anywhere from $30 to $60 a day.

Amadeus Apartments (✉ IX, Üllői út 197, H-1091, ☎ 06/309–422–893, FAX 1/302–8268) oversees five well-kept apartments in downtown Budapest, each consisting of two rooms plus a fully equipped kitchen and bathroom. Free transportation from the train station or airport is included; guarded parking areas are provided for a fee for those with cars. The two-person, high-season rate is approximately $40 a night.

TRIBUS Hotel Service (✉ V, Apáczai Csere János u. 1, ☎ 1/318–5776, FAX 1/317–9099), open 24 hours a day, books private apartments, arranges rooms in private homes, and reserves rooms in inns and hotels.

Cooptourist (✉ XI, Bartók Béla út 4, ☎ 1/466–5349) arranges private apartments and rooms and makes reservations in its affiliated inns and hotels.

B&B RESERVATION AGENCIES

The rate per night for a double room in Budapest is around $20 (usually including use of a bathroom but not breakfast). Two resources are: **TRIBUS Hotel Service** (☞ *above*) and **Cooptourist** (☞ *above*).

CAR RENTALS

Avis (main office, ✉ V, Szervita tér 8, ☎ 1/318–4240; Terminal 2A, ☎ 1/296–7265; Terminal 2B, ☎ 1/296–6421), **Budget** (main office, ✉ Hotel Mercure Buda, I, Krisztina krt. 41–43, ☎ 1/214–0420; Terminal 2A, ☎ 1/296–8481; Terminal 2B, ☎ 1/296–8197), and **Hertz** (also known in Hungary as Mercure Rent-a-Car; ✉ V, Marriott Hotel, Apáczai Csere János u. 4, ☎ 1/266–4361; Terminal 2A, ☎ 1/296–6988; Terminal 2B, ☎ 1/296–7171) are all here. Rates are high: Daily rates for automatics begin around $55–$60 plus 60¢ per km (½ mi); personal, theft, and accident insurance (not required but recommended) runs an additional $25–$30 per day. Rates tend to be significantly lower if you arrange your rental *from home* through the American offices. Ask your travel agent for help.

Local companies offer lower rates. Inquire at **Americana Rent-a-Car** (✉ Ibis Hotel Volga, XIII, Dózsa György út 65, ☎ 1/350–2542 or 1/320–8287) about unlimited mileage weekend specials. Rates include free delivery and pickup of the car anywhere in the city. Also try: **Fő-taxi** (main office, ✉ VII, Kertész u. 24–28, ☎ 1/322–1471 or 1/351–0359. **Inka** (✉ Budapest V, Bajcsy-Zsilinszky út 16, 1/456–4666. **SPQR** (✉ Budapest XIII, Váci út 175, 1/237–7334 or 1/237–7300).

EMBASSIES AND CONSULATES

Australian Embassy (✉ XII, Királyhágó tér 8–9, ☎ 1/201–8899). **Canadian Embassy** (✉ XII, Zugligeti út 51–53, ☎ 1/275–1200). **British Embassy** (✉ V, Harmincad u. 6, ☎ 1/266–2888, FAX 1/266–0907). **U.S. Embassy** (✉ V, Szabadság tér 12, ☎ 1/475–4400).

EMERGENCIES

Ambulance (☎ 104), or call **Falck-SOS** (✉ II, Kapy u. 49/b, ☎ 1/200–0100), a 24-hour private ambulance service with English-speaking personnel. **Police** (☎ 107). **Doctor:** Ask your hotel or embassy for recommendations or visit the **R-Clinic** (✉ II, Felsőzöldmáli út 13, ☎ 1/325–9999), a private clinic staffed by English-speaking doctors offering 24-hour medical and ambulance service. The clinic accepts major credit cards and prepares full reports for your insurance company. U.S. and Canadian visitors are advised to take out full medical insurance. U.K. visitors are covered for emergencies and essential treatment. **Dentist: Professional Dental Associates** (✉ II, Sodrás u. 9, ☎ 1/200–4447 or 1/200–4448) is a private, English-speaking dental practice consisting of Western-trained dentists and hygienists; service is available 24 hours a day.

ENGLISH-LANGUAGE BOOKSTORES

See Books *in* Shopping, *above*.

ENGLISH-LANGUAGE PERIODICALS

Several English-language weeklies have sprouted up to placate Budapest's large expatriate community. The *Budapest Sun* and the *Budapest Business Journal* are sold at major newsstands, hotels, and tourist points. The mini-guidebook *Budapest in Your Pocket* appears fives times a year and is also widely available. *Where Budapest,* a free monthly magazine, is available only at major hotels.

GUIDED TOURS

Orientation Tours: IBUSZ Travel (✉ V, Ferenciek tere 10, ☎ 1/485–2762 or 1/317–7767) conducts three-hour bus tours of the city that operate all year and cost about 5,500 Ft. Starting from Erzsébet tér, they take in parts of both Buda and Pest. **Cityrama** (✉ V, Báthori u. 22, ☎ 1/302–4382) also offers a three-hour city bus tour (about 5,500 Ft. per person). Both have commentary in English.

Special-Interest Tours: IBUSZ, Cityrama, and **Budapest Tourist** (☞ Visitor Information, *below*) organize a number of unusual tours, with trips to the Buda Hills, goulash parties, and visits to such traditional sites as the National Gallery and Parliament. These companies will provide English-speaking personal guides on request. Also check at your hotel.

Boat Tours: From late March through October boats leave from the dock at Vigadó tér on 1½-hour cruises between the railroad bridges north and south of the Árpád and Petőfi bridges, respectively. The trip, organized by **MAHART Tours** (☎ 1/318–1223), runs only on weekends and holidays (once a day, at noon) in April and May, then twice daily from May to October (at noon and 7); the cost is about 900 Ft. From mid-June through August, the evening cruise leaves at 7:45 and has live music and dancing for 100 Ft. more.

Hour-long evening sightseeing cruises on the ***Danube Legend*** depart nightly at 8:15 in April and October, and three times nightly (at 8:15, 9, and 10) from May through September. Guests receive headphones and listen to a recorded explanation of the sights in the language of their choice. Drinks are also served. Boats depart from Pier 6–7 at Vigadó tér (☎ 1/317–2203 for reservations and information).

The ***Duna-Bella*** takes guests on two-hour tours on the Danube, including a one-hour walk on Margaret Island and shipboard cocktails. Recorded commentary is provided through earphones. The tour is offered July through August, six times a day; May through June and in September, three times a day; and April and October, once a day. Boats depart from Pier 6–7 at Vigadó tér (☎ 1/317–2203 for reservations and information).

Jewish-Heritage Tours: Chosen Tours (✉ XII, Pagony u. 40, ☎ FAX 1/355–2202) offers a three-hour combination bus and walking tour ($17) called "Budapest Through Jewish Eyes," highlighting the sights and cultural life of the city's Jewish history. Tours run daily except Saturday and include free pickup and drop-off at central locations. Arrangements can also be made for off-season tours, as well as custom-designed tours.

Personal Guides: The major travel agencies—**IBUSZ Travel** and **Budapest Tourist** (☞ Visitor Information, *below*)—will arrange for guides.

LATE-NIGHT PHARMACIES

Most pharmacies close between 6 PM and 8 PM, but several pharmacies stay open at night and on the weekend, offering 24-hour service, with a small surcharge for items that aren't officially stamped as urgent by a physician. You must ring the buzzer next to the night window and someone will respond over the intercom. Staff is unlikely to speak English; ask for help from someone who speaks Hungarian. Central ones in Pest include those at **Teréz körút 41** (☎ 1/311–4439) in the sixth district, near the Nyugati train station; and the one at **Rákóczi út 39** (☎ 1/314–3695) in the 8th district, near the Keleti train station. In Buda, there is one across the street from the Déli train station at **Alkotás utca 1/b** (☎ 1/355–4691), in the 12th district.

TRAVEL AGENCIES

American Express (✉ V, Deák Ferenc u. 10, ☎ 1/235–4330, FAX 1/267–2028). **Getz International** (✉ V, Falk Miksa u. 5, ☎ 1/312–0645 or 1/312–0649, FAX 1/312–1014). **Vista Travel Center** (✉ VI, Andrássy út 1, ☎ 1/269–6032 or 1/269–6033, FAX 1/269–6031).

VISITOR INFORMATION

Budapest Tourist (✉ I, Déli pályaudvar [South Railway Station]), ☎ 1/212–4625 or 1/355–7167; XIII, pedestrian underpass at Nyugati páaudvar [West Railway Station], ☎ 1/332–6565). **IBUSZ** (central branch: ✉ V, Ferenciek tere 10, ☎ 1/485–2700). **TRIBUS Hotel Service** (✉ V, Apáczai Csere János u. 1, ☎ 1/318–5776, FAX 1/317–9099), open 24 hours. **Tourinform** (✉ V, Sütő u. 2, ☎ 1/317–9800). The **Tourism Office of Budapest** (✉ V, Március 15 tér 7, ☎ 1/266–0479; VI, Nyugati pályaudvar, ☎ 1/302–8580) has developed the **Budapest Card,** which entitles holders to unlimited travel on public transportation; free admission to many museums and sights; and discounts on various services from participating businesses. The cost (at press time) is 2,800 Ft. for two days, 3,400 Ft. for three days; one card is valid for an adult plus one child under 14.

THE DANUBE BEND

About 40 km (25 mi) north of Budapest, the Danube abandons its eastward course and turns abruptly south toward the capital, cutting through the Börzsöny and Visegrád hills. This area is called the Danube Bend and includes the Baroque town of Szentendre, the hilltop castle ruins and town of Visegrád, and the cathedral town of Esztergom. The most scenically varied part of Hungary, the region is home to a chain of riverside spas and beaches, bare volcanic mountains, and limestone hills. Here, in the heartland, are the traces of the country's history—the remains of the Roman Empire's frontier, the battlefields of the Middle Ages, and the relics of the Hungarian Renaissance.

The west bank of the Danube is the more interesting side, with three engaging and picturesque towns—Szentendre, Visegrád, and Esztergom. The district can be covered by car in one day, the total round-trip no more than 112 km (70 mi), although this affords only a cursory look. A day trip to Szentendre while based in Budapest plus two days for Visegrád and Esztergom, with a night in either (both have lovely small hotels), would be best.

On the Danube's eastern bank, Vác is the only larger town of any real interest. No bridges span the Danube in this region, but there are numerous ferries (between Visegrád and Nagymaros, Basaharc and Szob, Szentendre Island and Vác), making it possible to combine a visit to both sides of the Danube on the same excursion.

Though the Danube Bend's west bank contains the bulk of historical sights, the less-traveled east bank has the excellent hiking trails of the Börzsöny mountain range, which extends along the Danube from Vác to Zebegény before curving toward the Slovak border. The Pilis and Visegrád hills on the Danube's western side and the Börzsöny Hills on the east are popular nature escapes.

Work had started on a hydroelectric dam near Nagymaros, across from Visegrád, in the mid-1980s. The project was proposed by Austria and what was then Czechoslovakia, and reluctantly agreed to by Hungary, but protests from the Blues (Hungary's equivalent of Germany's Greens), coupled with rapid democratization, succeeded in halting the project and rescuing a region of great natural beauty. This seemed to

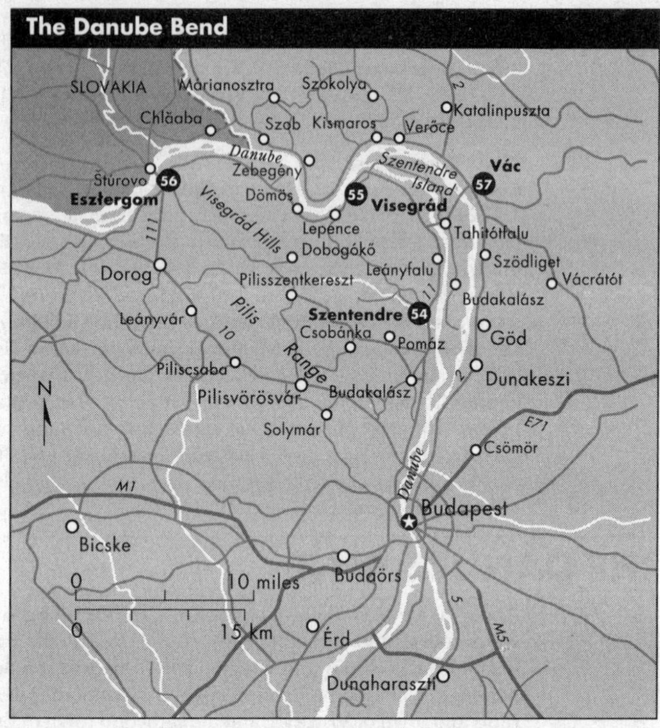

come undone in 1998: the International Court in the Hague ruled that the original agreement between what is now Slovakia and Hungary was still valid, and the two countries signed a preliminary agreement to start building a dam after all in the coming years. However, diplomatic foot-dragging and friendlier bilateral relations have so far precluded the reemergence of any project like that which had prompted the tensions in the first place.

Numbers in the margin correspond to numbers on the Danube Bend map.

Szentendre

★ 54 *21 km (13 mi) north of Budapest.*

A romantic little town with a lively atmosphere and a flourishing artists' colony, this is the highlight of the Danube Bend. With its profusion of enchanting church steeples, colorful Baroque houses, and winding, narrow cobblestone streets, it's no wonder Szentendre attracts swarms of visitors, tripling its population in peak season.

Szentendre was first settled by Serbs and Greeks fleeing the advancing Turks in the 16th and 17th centuries. They built houses and churches in their own style—rich in reds and blues seldom seen elsewhere in Hungary. To truly savor Szentendre, duck into any and every cobblestone side street that appeals to you. Baroque houses with shingle roofs (often with an arched eye-of-God upstairs window) and colorful stone walls will enchant your eye and pique your curiosity.

Fő tér is Szentendre's main square, the centerpiece of which is an ornate **Memorial Cross** erected by Serbs in gratitude because the town was spared from a plague. The cross has a crucifixion painted on it and stands atop a triangular pillar adorned with a dozen icon paintings.

Every house on Fő tér is a designated landmark, and three of them are open to the public: the **Ferenczy Múzeum** (Ferenczy Museum) at No. 6, with paintings of Szentendre landscapes; the **Kmetty Múzeum** (Kmetty Museum) at No. 21, with works by János Kmetty, a pioneer of Hungarian avant-garde painting; and the **Szentendrei Képtár** (Municipal Gallery) at Nos. 2–5, with an excellent collection of local contemporary art and international changing exhibits. *Each museum 150 Ft. Wed.–Sun. 10–4.*

Gracing the corner of Görög utca (Greek Street) and Szentendre's main square, Fő tér, the so-called **Görög templom** (Greek Church, also known as Blagovestenska Church) is actually a Serbian Orthodox church that takes its name from the Greek inscription on a red-marble gravestone set in its wall. This elegant edifice was built between 1752 and 1754 by a rococo master, Andreas Mayerhoffer, on the site of a wooden church dating to the Great Serbian Migration (around 690). Its greatest glory—a symmetrical floor-to-ceiling panoply of stunning icons—was painted between 1802 and 1804 by Mihailo Zivkovic, a Serbian painter from Buda. ✉ *Görög u. at Fő tér. 100 Ft. Mar.–Oct., Tues.–Sun. 10–5.*

If you have time for only one of Szentendre's myriad museums, don't ★ miss the **Kovács Margit Múzeum,** which displays the collected works of Budapest ceramics artist Margit Kovács, who died in 1977. She left behind a wealth of richly textured work that ranges from ceramics to life-size sculptures. Admission to the museum is limited to 15 persons at a time, so it is wise to line up early or at lunchtime, when the herds of tour groups are occupied elsewhere. ✉ *Vastagh György u. 1 (off Görög u.),* ☎ *26/310–244 ext. 114. 300 Ft. Mid-Mar.–early Oct., daily 10–6; early Oct.–mid-Mar., Tues.–Sun. 10–4.*

Perched atop Vár-domb (Castle Hill) is Szentendre's oldest surviving monument, the **Katolikus plébánia templom** (Catholic Parish Church), dating to the 13th century. After many reconstructions, its oldest visible part is a 15th-century sundial in the doorway. The church's small cobblestone yard hosts an arts-and-crafts market and, often on weekends in summer, street entertainment. From here, views over Szentendre's angular tile rooftops and steeples and of the Danube beyond are superb. ✉ *Vár-domb. Free. Hours vary; check with Tourinform* (☞ *Visitor Information, below).*

★ The **Szerb Ortodox Egyházi Gyüjtemény** (Serbian Orthodox Collection of Religious Art) displays exquisite artifacts relating to the history of the Serbian Orthodox Church in Hungary. Icons, altars, robes, 16th-century prayer books, and a 17th-century cross with (legend has it) a bullet hole through it were collected from all over the country, after being sold or stolen from Serbian churches that were abandoned when most Serbs returned to their homeland at the turn of the 20th century and following World War I. The museum shares a tranquil yard with the imposing Serbian Orthodox Cathedral. ✉ *Pátriárka u. 5,* ☎ *26/312–399. 100 Ft. May–Sept., Tues.–Sun. 10–6; Oct.–Dec. and Mar.–Apr., Tues.–Sun. 10–4; Jan.–Feb., Fri.–Sun. 10–4.*

The crimson steeple of the handsome **Szerb Ortodox Bazilika** (Serbian Orthodox Cathedral) presides over a restful tree-shaded yard crowning the hill just north of Vár-domb (Castle Hill). It was built in the 1740s with a much more lavish but arguably less beautiful iconostasis than is found in the Greek Church below it. ✉ *Pátriárka u. 5,* ☎ *26/312–399. Hours vary; check with Tourinform* (☞ *Visitor Information, below) or Serbian Orthodox Collection of Religious Art museum officials.*

NEED A BREAK? For a quick cholesterol boost, grab a floppy, freshly fried *lángos* (flat, salty fried dough) drizzled with sour cream or brushed with garlic at **Piknik Büfé** (✉ Dumtsa Jenő u. 22), just next door to the Tourinform office.

Szentendre's farthest-flung museum is the **Szabadtéri Néprajzi Múzeum** (Open-Air Ethnographic Museum), the largest open-air museum in the country. It is a living re-creation of 18th- and 19th-century village life from different regions of Hungary—the sort of place where blacksmith shops and a horse-powered mill compete with wooden houses and folk handicrafts for your attention. During regular crafts demonstrations, visitors can sit back and watch or give it a try themselves. Five kilometers (3 mi) to the northwest, the museum is reachable by bus from the Szentendre terminus of the HÉV suburban railway. ✉ *Szabadságforrás út,* ☎ *26/312–304.* *About 300 Ft.* *Apr.–Oct., Tues.–Sun. 10–5.*

Dining and Lodging

$$$ ✕ **Régimódi.** This upstairs restaurant with fine wines and game specialties is practically on Fő tér. Lace curtains and antique knickknacks give the small dining room a homey intimacy. The summer terrace is a delightful place to dine alfresco and look out over the red-tile rooftops. ✉ *Dumtsa Jenő u. 2,* ☎ *26/311–105. AE, DC, MC, V.*

$$ ★ ✕ **Aranysárkány.** On the road up to the Serbian Orthodox Cathedral, the Golden Dragon lies in wait with seven large tables, which you share with strangers on a busy night. The delicious food is prepared in a turbulent open kitchen, but all the activity is justified by the cold cherry soup with red wine or the hot *sárkány erőleves* (Dragon Bouillon) with quail eggs and vegetables. Try the smoked goose liver with rose petal jam; the "opium" pudding (custard with lots of poppy seeds mixed in), with its "poison green" (i.e., kiwi) sauce, is also recommended. Wash it down with one of 75 varieties of Hungarian wine. ✉ *Alkotmány u. 1/a,* ☎ *26/311–670. AE, DC, MC, V.*

$$ ★ ✕ **Rab Ráby.** Fish soup and fresh grilled trout are the specialties in this extremely popular, friendly restaurant with rustic wood beams and myriad old instruments, lanterns, cowbells, and other eclectic antiques. ✉ *Péter Pál u. 1,* ☎ *26/310–819. Reservations essential July–Aug. MC, V.*

$$ ✕ **Vidám Szerzetesek.** The Happy Monks opened as a family restaurant, though in recent years it has become something of a tourist haunt; the reasonably priced menu is, after all, in 20 languages. The atmosphere is casual and decidedly cheerful; the food is typically Hungarian: heavy, hearty, and delicious. Try the *Suhajda* (hat soup), a savory brew of smoked meat topped with a tasty dough cap baked over the bowl. ✉ *Bogdányi út 3–5,* ☎ *26/310–544. AE, MC, V. Closed Mon.*

$$ **Bükkös Panzió.** Just west of the main square and across the bridge over tiny Bükkös Brook, this neat, well-run inn is one of the most conveniently located hotels in the village. The narrow staircase and small rooms give it a homey feel. ✉ *Bükkös part 16, H-2000,* ☎ *26/312–021,* ☎ FAX *26/310–782. 16 rooms. Restaurant, laundry service. MC, V.*

$$ **Kentaur Ház.** This handsome, modern, chalet-style hotel is a two-minute walk from Fő tér, on what may be Hungary's last surviving square still to bear Karl Marx's name. Rooms are clean and simple, with pale-gray carpeting, blond unfinished-wood paneling, and pastel-pink walls hung with original paintings by local artists. Upstairs rooms are sunniest and most spacious. ✉ *Marx tér 3–5, H-2000,* ☎ FAX *26/312–125. 16 rooms. Bar, breakfast room. No credit cards.*

$$ **St. Andrea Panzió.** This remodeled *panzió* (pension) atop a grassy incline has all the makings of a Swiss chalet. Attic space has been converted into modernized rooms with clean tile showers. On a warm day you can eat breakfast on the outside patio. The owners are very friendly; they've even been known to specially cook meals for guests

arriving late at night. ✉ *Egres u. 22, H-2000,* ☎ FAX *26/311–989. 16 rooms, 2 suites. Restaurant. No credit cards.*

Outdoor Activities and Sports

BICYCLING

The waterfront and streets beyond Szentendre's main square are perfect for a bike ride—free of jostling cobblestones and relatively calm and quiet. Check with Tourinform (☞ Visitor Information, *below*) for local rental outfits. Rentals are available in Budapest (☞ Outdoor Activities and Sports *in* Budapest A to Z, *above*); bicycles are permitted in a designated car of each HÉV suburban railway train. Many people make the trip between Budapest and Szentendre on bicycle along the designated bike path, which runs on busy roads in some places but is pleasant and separate from the road for the stretch between Békásmegyer and Szentendre.

Nightlife and the Arts

Most of Szentendre's concerts and entertainment events occur during the spring and summer. For current schedules and ticket information, contact **Tourinform** (☞ Visitor Information, *below*).

The annual **Spring Festival,** usually held from mid-March through early April, offers classical concerts in some of Szentendre's churches, as well as jazz, folk, and rock performances in the cultural center and other venues about town. In July, the **Szentendre Summer Days** festival brings open-air theater performances and jazz and classical concerts to Fő tér and the cobblestone courtyard fronting the town hall. Although the plays are usually in Hungarian, the setting alone can make it an enjoyable experience.

Shopping

Flooded with tourists in summer, Szentendre is saturated with the requisite **souvenir shops.** Among the attractive but overpriced goods sold in every store are dolls dressed in traditional folk costumes, wooden trinkets, pottery, and colorful hand-embroidered tablecloths, doilies, and blouses. The best bargains are the hand-embroidered blankets and bags sold by dozens of elderly women in traditional folk attire, who stand for hours on the town's crowded streets. (Because of high weekend traffic, most Szentendre stores stay open all day on weekends, unlike those in Budapest. Galleries are closed Monday and accept major credit cards, although other stores may not.)

The one tiny room of **art-éria galéria** (✉ Városház tér 1, ☎ 26/310–111) is crammed with paintings, graphics, and sculptures by 21 of Szentendre's best contemporary artists.

Topped with an abstract-statue trio of topless, pale-pink and baby-blue women in polka-dot bikini panties, the **Christoff Galéria** (✉ Bartók Béla u. 8, ☎ 26/317–031) is hard to miss as you climb the steep hill to its door. The gallery sells works by local and Hungarian contemporary artists, including those of popular visual artist and musician ef Zambo, creator of its crowning females. It's best to call ahead to check opening times.

The **Gallery Erdész** (✉ Bercsényi u. 4, ☎ 26/317–925) displays an impressive selection of contemporary Hungarian art, as well as gifts such as leather bags, colored glass vases, and handmade paper—not to mention some unique, curvaceous silver pieces made by a famous local jeweler.

Beautiful stationery, booklets, and other handmade paper products are displayed and sold at the **László Vincze Paper Mill** (✉ Angyal u. 5, ☎ 26/314–328). In this small workshop at the top of a broken cobblestone street, Mr. Vincze lovingly creates his thick, watermarked paper, using traditional, 2,000-year old bleaching methods.

The sophisticated **Erdész Galéria** (✉ Fő tér 20, ☎ 26/310–139), on Szentendre's main square (not to be confused with the Gallery Erdész, *above*), displays paintings, statues, and other works by some 30 local artists.

Péter-Pál Galéria (✉ Péter-Pál u. 1, ☎ 26/311–182) has a good selection of handmade textiles, wrought-iron work, glass, and ceramics.

Visegrád

55 *23 km (14 mi) north of Szentendre.*

Visegrád was the seat of the Hungarian kings during the 14th century, when a fortress built here by the Angevin kings became the royal residence. Today, the imposing fortress at the top of the hill towers over the peaceful little town of quiet, tree-lined streets and solid old houses. The forested hills rising just behind the town offer popular hiking possibilities. For a taste of Visegrád's best, climb to the Fellegvár, and wander and take in the views of the Danube curving through the countryside; but make time to stroll around the village center a bit—on Fő utca and other streets that pique your interest.

★ Crowning the top of a 1,148-ft hill, the dramatic **Fellegvár** (Citadel) was built in the 13th century and served as the seat of Hungarian kings in the early 14th century. In the Middle Ages, the citadel was where the Holy Crown and other royal regalia were kept, until they were stolen by a dishonorable maid of honor in 1440; 23 years later, King Matthias had to pay 80,000 Ft. to retrieve them from Austria. (For the time being, the crown is safe in the Parliament building in Budapest.) A *panoptikum* (akin to slide projection) show portraying the era of the kings is included free with admission. The breathtaking views of the Danube Bend below are ample reward for the strenuous, 40-minute hike up. *☎ 26/398–101. 250 Ft. Mid-Mar.–mid-Nov., daily 9–5; mid-Nov.–mid-Mar., weekends 10–dusk; closed in snowy conditions.*

In the 13th–14th centuries, King Matthias Corvinus had a separate palace built on the banks of the Danube below the citadel. It was eventually razed by the Turks, and not until 1934 were the ruins finally excavated. Nowadays you can see the disheveled remnants of the **Királyi palota** (Royal Palace) and its **Salamon torony** (Salomon Tower), referred to together as the **Mátyás Király Múzeum** (King Matthias Museum). The Salomon Tower houses two small exhibits displaying ancient statues and well structures from the age of King Matthias. Especially worth seeing is the red-marble well, built by a 15th-century Italian architect. Above a ceremonial courtyard rise the palace's various halls; on the left you can still see a few fine original carvings, which give an idea of how magnificent the palace must once have been. Inside the palace is a small exhibit on its history, as well as a collection of gravestones dating from Roman times to the 19th century. Fridays in May, the museum hosts medieval-crafts demonstrations. *✉ Fő u. 23, ☎ 26/398–026. Royal Palace 300 Ft., Salomon Tower 200 Ft. Royal Palace: Tues.–Sun. 9–4:30; Salomon Tower: May–Sept., Tues.–Sun. 9–4:30.*

OFF THE BEATEN PATH

MILLENNIAL CHAPEL – Like a tiny precious gem, the miniature chapel sits in a small clearing, tucked away on a corner down Fő utca, Visegrád's main street. The bite-size, powder-yellow church was built in 1896 to celebrate the Magyar Millennium and is open only on Pentecost and a few other holidays. *✉ Fő u. 113.*

Dining and Lodging

$$ ★ ✕ **Gulyás Csárda.** This cozy little restaurant, decorated with antique folk art and memorabilia, complements its eight indoor tables with additional seating outside during the summer. The cuisine is typical home-style Hungarian, with a limited selection of tasty traditional dishes. Try the halászlé served in a pot and kept warm on a small spirit burner. ✉ *Nagy Lajos király u. 4,* ☎ *26/398–329. MC, V.*

$$ ✕ **Sirály Restaurant.** Right across from the ferry station, the airy Seagull Restaurant is justifiably well regarded for its rolled fillet of venison and its many vegetarian dishes, including fried soy steak with vegetables. In summer, when cooking is often done on the terrace overlooking the Danube, expect barbecued meats and stews, soups, and gulyás served in old-fashioned pots. ✉ *Rév u. 15,* ☎ *26/398–376. AE, MC, V. Closed Nov.–Feb.*

$ ✕ **Fekete Holló.** The popular "Black Raven" restaurant has an elegant yet comfortable atmosphere—a great place for a full meal or just a beer. Try the chef's creative specialties, such as coconut chicken leg with pineapples, or stick to such regional staples as fresh, grilled fish; either way save room for the palacsinta with nuts and chocolate. ✉ *Rév út 12,* ☎ *26/397–289. No credit cards. Closed Nov.–Mar.*

$$$ **Beta Hotel Silvanus.** Set high up on Fekete Hill, this hotel is renowned for its spectacular views. Rooms are bright and clean, with simple furnishings, and offer a choice of forest or Danube (about 1,000 Ft. more expensive) views. Since it's at the end of a steep, narrow road, the Silvanus is recommended for motorists (although a bus does stop nearby) and hikers or bikers—there are linking trails in the forest behind. ✉ *Fekete-hegy, H-2025,* ☎ FAX *26/398–311). 88 rooms, 5 suites. Restaurant, bar, café, pub, indoor pool, sauna, bowling, mountain bikes. AE, DC, MC, V.*

$ **Hotel & Haus Honti.** A newly opened, 21-room hotel and its older, alpine-style sibling pension share the same yard in a quiet residential area, a three-minute walk from the town center. Apple trees and a gurgling brook render a peaceful, rustic ambience. The pension has seven tiny, clean rooms tucked under sloping ceilings and with balconies, some with lovely Danube views; the rooms in the hotel are more spacious and a tad more expensive, some with balconies affording a splendid view of the Citadel in the distance. Breakfast costs about $4 more per room. ✉ *Fő u. 66, H-2025,* ☎ *26/398–120. 28 rooms. No credit cards.*

Nightlife and the Arts

The **Visegrád International Palace Games,** held annually on the second weekend in July, take the castle complex back to its medieval heyday, with horseback jousting tournaments, archery games, a medieval music and crafts fair, and other festivities. Contact Visegrád Tours (☞ Visitor Information, *below*) for specifics.

Outdoor Activities and Sports

HIKING

Visegrád makes a great base for exploring the trails of the Visegrád and Pilis hills. A hiking map is posted on the corner of Fő utca and Rév utca, just above the pale-green Roman Catholic Parish Church. A well-trodden, well-marked hiking trail (posted with red signs) leads from the edge of Visegrád to the town of Pilisszentlászló, a wonderful 8½-km (5⅓ mi (about three-hour)) journey through the oak and beech forests of the Visegrád Hills into the Pilis conservation region. Deer, wild boars, and mouflons roam freely here, and there are fields of yellow-blooming spring pheasant's eye and black pulsatilla.

SWIMMING

The outdoor thermal pools at **Lepence,** 3 km (2 mi) southwest of Visegrád on route 11, combine good soaking with excellent Danube Bend views. ✉ *Lepence-völgyi Termál és Strandfürdő, Lepence,* ☎ *26/398–208.* 🎫 *400 Ft.* ⏲ *May–Sept., daily 9–6:30.*

TOBOGGAN SLIDE

Winding through the trees on Nagy-Villám Hill is the **Wiegand Toboggan Run,** one of the longest slides you've ever seen. You ride on a small cart that is pulled uphill by trolley, then careen down the slope in a small, steel trough that resembles a bobsled run. ✉ *Panoráma út, ½ km (¼ mi) from Fellegvár,* ☎ *26/397–397.* 🎫 *180 Ft. weekdays, 220 Ft. weekends and holidays; 1,000 Ft. for six runs weekdays, 1,200 Ft. weekends and holidays.* ⏲ *May–Sept., daily 10–7; Apr. and Oct., daily 11–4; Nov.–Mar. (weather permitting), weekends 11–4.*

Esztergom

56 *21 km (13 mi) north of Visegrád.*

Esztergom stands on the site of a Roman fortress, at the westernmost curve of the heart-shape Danube Bend, where the Danube marks the border between Hungary and Slovakia. (The bridge that once joined these two countries was destroyed by the Nazis near the end of World War II, though parts of the span can still be seen.) St. Stephen, the first Christian king of Hungary and founder of the nation, was crowned here in the year 1000, establishing Esztergom as Hungary's first capital, which it remained for the next 250 years. The majestic Bazilika, Hungary's largest, is Esztergom's main draw, followed by the fine art collection of the Primate's Palace. If you like strolling, leave yourself a little time to explore the narrow streets of Viziváros (Watertown) below the Bazilika, lined with brightly painted Baroque buildings.

★ Esztergom's **Bazilika** (cathedral), the largest in Hungary, stands on a hill overlooking the town; it is now the seat of the cardinal primate of Hungary. It was here, in the center of Hungarian Catholicism, that the famous anti-Communist cleric, Cardinal József Mindszenty, was finally reburied (he had to be buried in Austria when he died in 1975) in 1991 ending an era of religious intolerance and prosecution and a sorrowful chapter in Hungarian history. Its most interesting features are the Bakócz Chapel (1506), named for a primate of Hungary who only narrowly missed becoming pope; and the sacristy, which contains a valuable collection of medieval ecclesiastical art. If your timing is lucky, you could attend a concert during one of the various classical music festivals held here in summer (☞ Nightlife and the Arts, *below*). ✉ *Szent István tér,* ☎ *33/311–895.* 🎫 *Free.* ⏲ *Apr.–late Oct., daily 7–4; late Oct.–Mar., weekdays 7–4, weekends 7–5.*

Considered by many to be Hungary's finest art gallery, the **Keresztény Múzeum** (Museum of Christian Art), in the Primate's Palace, has a thorough collection of early Hungarian and Italian paintings (the 14th- and 15th-century Italian collection is unusually large for a museum outside Italy). Unique holdings include the *Coffin of Our Lord* from Garamszentbenedek (today Hronský Beňadik, Slovakia); the wooden statues of the Apostles and of the Roman soldiers guarding the coffin are masterpieces of Hungarian Baroque sculpture. The building also holds the Primate's Archives, which contain 20,000 volumes, including several medieval codices. Permission to visit the archives must be obtained in advance. *Primate's Palace:* ✉ *Mindszenty tér 2,* ☎ *33/413–880.* 🎫 *200 Ft.* ⏲ *Mid-Mar.–Sept., Tues.–Sun. 10–6; Jan.–mid-Mar., Tues.–Sun. 10–5.*

To the south of the cathedral, on **Szent Tamás Hill,** is a small church dedicated to St. Thomas à Becket of Canterbury. From here you can look down on the town and see how the Danube temporarily splits, forming an island, **Prímás-sziget**, that locals use as a base for water-skiing and swimming, in spite of the pollution. To reach it, cross the Kossuth Bridge.

Dining and Lodging

$$ ✕ **Primáspince.** Arched ceilings and exposed brick walls make a charming setting for refined Hungarian fare at this touristy but good restaurant just below the cathedral. Try the tournedos Budapest style (tender beef with sautéed vegetables and paprika) or the thick turkey breast Fiaker style (stuffed with ham and melted cheese). ✉ *Szent István tér 4,* ☎ *33/313–495. AE, DC, MC, V. No dinner Jan.–Feb.*

$–$$ ✕🏨 **Szalma Csárda & Panzió.** A short drive or five-minute walk from the center of town onto Prímás-sziget takes you to the Hay Inn and Pension, in a tranquil setting on this fairly undeveloped stretch of the Danube. The restaurant is splendidly rustic, with strings of dried paprika hanging from the ceiling and an earthenware stove the size of a baby elephant in the main room. Listen to live Gypsy music while enjoying "long-forgotten peasant dishes"—actually, typical meals such as chicken paprika which, with wax beans and dill-spiced dumplings on the side, are apparently prepared the way they used to be, down on the farm. The 20-room pension, which from the outside resembles a ranch house, opened in 2000 right next door and is run by the same family. While the cramped rooms, with low, summer-camp-like pinewood beds, are not for those who prefer such amenities as TVs and phones, they are clean and bright. ✉ *Nagy-Duna sétány 2, on Prímás-sziget, H-2500,* ☎ FAX *33/315–336 or 33/403–838. No credit cards.*

$$ 🏨 **Alabárdos Panzió.** Conveniently located downhill from the cathedral, this cozy, remodeled home provides excellent views from upstairs. Rooms (doubles and quads) are small but less cramped than at other small pensions. Breakfast is included. ✉ *Bajcsy-Zsilinszky u. 49, H-2500,* ☎ FAX *33/312–640. 22 rooms. Breakfast room. No credit cards.*

$$ 🏨 **Hotel Esztergom.** Simply furnished and sports-oriented, this hotel has a good location on Primás-szíget. Tennis, swimming, bowling, horseback riding, and water-sports facilities are nearby. All rooms have balconies; the largest, and nicest, rooms face away from the river. ✉ *Primás-szíget, Nagy Duna Sétány, H-2500,* ☎ *33/412–883,* FAX *33/412–853. 34 rooms, 2 suites. Restaurant, meeting room. AE, DC, MC, V.*

$$ 🏨 **Ria Panzió.** In this small, friendly guest house near the cathedral, all of the small, no-frills rooms face a garden courtyard. ✉ *Batthyány u. 11–13, H-2500,* ☎ *33/313–115. 13 rooms. Breakfast room. AE, MC, V.*

Nightlife and the Arts

Every two years Esztergom hosts the **Nemzetközi Gitár Fesztivál** (International Guitar Festival) during which renowned classical guitarists from around the world hold master classes and workshops for participants. Recitals are held nearly every night in Esztergom's **Zöldház Művelődési Központ** (Green House Cultural Center) or the **Tanítóképző Főiskola** (Teachers College), where the festival is based, or elsewhere in Budapest and neighboring towns. The climax of it all is the glorious closing concert, held in the basilica, in which the hundreds of participants join together and perform as a guitar orchestra. The festival runs for two weeks, usually beginning in early August; the next one will be held in 2001. Tickets and information are available at the tourist offices.

Vác

57 *34 km (21 mi) north of Budapest; 20 km (12 mi) south of Nagymaros, which is accessed by ferry from Visegrád.*

With its lovely riverfront promenade, its cathedral, and less delightful Triumphal Arch, the small city of Vác, on the Danube's east bank, is well worth a short visit if only to watch the sun slowly set from the promenade. Vác's historic town center is full of pretty Baroque buildings in matte yellows and reds and offers many visual rewards and photo opportunities for those who wander onto a few of its narrow cobblestone side streets heading in toward the river.

Vác's 18th-century **Székesegyház** (cathedral) on Konstantin tér is an outstanding example of Hungarian neoclassicism. It was built in 1763–1777 by Archbishop Kristóf Migazzi to the designs of the Italian architect Isidor Carnevale; the most interesting features are the murals by the Austrian Franz Anton Maulbertsch, both on the dome and behind the altar. Exquisite frescoes decorate the walls inside. Due to recent break-ins, you can view the interior only through a locked gate, except during Mass (daily 8–9 AM and 6–7 PM). ✉ *Konstantin tér 11,* ☎ *27/317–010.* 🎫 *Free.* ⏲ *Daily 8–7.*

In 1764, when Archbishop Migazzi heard that Queen Maria Theresa planned to visit his humble town, he hurriedly arranged the construction of a **triumphal arch.** The queen came and left, but the awkward arch remains, at the edge of the city's historic core next to a cement-and-barbed-wire prison complex. ✉ *Köztársaság út just past Barabás u.*

The **promenade** along the Danube is a wonderful place to stroll or picnic, looking out at the glistening river or back toward the pretty historic town. The main entrance to the riverfront area is from Petróczy utca, which begins at the cathedral on Konstantin tér and feeds straight into the promenade.

Vácrátóti Arborétum, 4 km (2½ mi) from Vác, is Hungary's biggest and best botanical garden, with more than 12,000 plant species. The arboretum's top priority is botanical research and collection under the auspices of the Hungarian Academy of Sciences, but you're welcome to stroll along the paths and sit on benches in the leafy shade. If you're driving from Vác, follow signs toward Gödöllő, then toward Vácrátót. ✉ *Alkotmány u. 2–4,* ☎ *28/360–122 or 28/360–147.* 🎫 *160 Ft.* ⏲ *Apr.–Oct., daily 8–6; Nov.–Mar., daily 8–4.*

Dining

$ ✕ **Halászkert Étterem.** The large terrace of this riverfront restaurant next to the ferry landing is a popular place for a hearty lunch or dinner of Hungarian fish specialties. ✉ *Liszt Ferenc rakpart 9,* ☎ *27/315–985. AE, DC, MC, V.*

Nightlife and the Arts

In July and August, a series of outdoor classical concerts is held in the verdant **Vácrátóti Arborétum** (☞ *above*). The last weekend in July brings the **Váci Világi Vígalom** (Vác World Jamboree) festival, with folk dancing, music, crafts fairs, and other festivities throughout town.

Outdoor Activities and Sports

Vác is the gateway to hiking in the forests of the **Börzsöny Hills,** rich in natural springs, castle ruins, and splendid Danube Bend vistas. Consult the Börzsöny hiking map, available at Tourinform, for planning a walk on the well-marked trails. The **Börzsöny Természetjáró Kör** (Börzsöny Hiking Club) organizes free guided nature walks every other

Sunday all year round. Naturally, Hungarian is the official language, but chances are good that younger group members will speak English—however, even without understanding what is spoken, the trips afford a nice opportunity to be guided through the area. Contact Tourinform (☞ Visitor Information, *below*) for details.

Danube Bend A to Z

Arriving and Departing

BY BOAT

If you have enough time, you can travel to the west-bank towns by boat from Budapest, a leisurely and pleasant journey, especially in summer and spring. Boating from Budapest to Esztergom takes about five hours, to Visegrád about three hours. Boats leave from the main Pest dock at Vigadó tér. The disadvantage of boat travel is that a round-trip by slow boat doesn't allow much time for sightseeing; the Esztergom route, for example, allows only under two hours before it's time to head back. Many people head upriver by boat in the morning and back down by bus or train as it's getting dark. There is daily service from Budapest to Visegrád, stopping in Szentendre. Less frequent boats go to Vác, on the east bank, as well. Contact **MAHART Tours** (☎ 1/484–4013 or 318–1223) in Budapest for complete schedule information.

BY BUS

Buses run regularly between Budapest's Árpád híd bus station and most towns along both sides of the Danube. The ride to Szentendre takes about half an hour.

BY CAR

Route 11 runs along the western shore of the Danube, connecting Budapest to Szentendre, Visegrád, and Esztergom. Route 2 runs along the eastern shore for driving between Budapest and Vác.

BY TRAIN

Vác and Esztergom have frequent daily express and local train service to and from Budapest's Nyugati (West) Station. Trains do not run to Visegrád. The **HÉV** suburban railway runs between Batthyány tér (or Margaret Island, one stop north) in Budapest and Szentendre about every 10–20 minutes daily; the trip takes 40 minutes and a *kiegészítő* (supplementary) ticket—which you need in addition to a Budapest public transport pass or ticket—costs around 170 Ft. one-way.

Getting Around

BY BICYCLE

The Danube Bend is a great place to explore by bike; most towns are relatively close together. Some routes have separate bike paths, while others run along the roads. Consult the "Danube Bend Cyclists' Map" (available at tourist offices) and Tourinform (☞ Visitor Information, *below*) for exact information.

BY BOAT

Boat travel along the river is slow and scenic. **MAHART**'s (☞ *above*) boats ply the river between Budapest and Esztergom, Szentendre, and Visegrád. You can plan your sightseeing to catch a boat connection from one town to the other (☞ Arriving and Departing, *above*).

BY BUS

Buses are cheap and relatively comfortable—if you get a seat, as opposed to standing for an hour or more; they link all major towns along both banks. If you don't have a car, this is the best way to get around, since train service is spotty.

BY FERRY

As there are no bridges across the Danube in this region, there is regular daily passenger and car **ferry service** between several points on opposite sides of the Danube (except in winter when the river is too icy). The crossing generally takes about 10 minutes and costs roughly 600 Ft. per car and driver, 120 Ft. per passenger. The crossing between Nagymaros and Visegrád is recommended, as it affords gorgeous views of Visegrád's citadel and includes a beautiful drive through rolling hills on Route 12 south and then west of Nagymaros. Contact the relevant tourist office (☞ Visitor Information, *below*) for schedule details.

BY TRAIN

Train travel in the region is difficult; Visegrád has no train service and there are no direct connections between Szentendre and Esztergom.

Contacts and Resources

EMERGENCIES

Ambulance (☎ 104). **Fire** (☎ 105). **Police** (☎ 107).

GUIDED TOURS

IBUSZ Travel (☎ 1/485–2762 or 1/317–7767) organizes daylong bus trips from Budapest along the Danube, stopping in Esztergom, Visegrád, and Szentendre on Tuesday, Friday, and Sunday from May through October, and Saturday only from November through April. There's commentary in English; the cost, including lunch and admission fees, is about 16,000 Ft.

Cityrama (in Budapest, ☎ 1/302–4382) runs its popular "Danube Tour" (approximately 16,000 Ft.) daily Wednesday–Sunday from May until September. Departing from Budapest, the full-day tour begins with sightseeing in Visegrád, then Esztergom. After lunch, the tour moves on to Szentendre for a guided walk and makes a scenic return to Budapest down the Danube. (The tour returns by bus when the water level is low and in winter, when the tour is offered once a week; call ahead for exact dates and times.)

VISITOR INFORMATION

Budapest: Tourinform (✉ V, Sütő u. 2, ☎ 1/317–9800). **Esztergom: Grantours** (✉ Széchenyi tér 25, ☎ FAX 33/413–756); **IBUSZ** (✉ Kossuth L. u. 5, ☎ 33/412–552); **Komtourist** (✉ Lőrinc u. 6, ☎ 33/312–082). **Szentendre: Tourinform** (✉ Dumtsa Jenő u. 22, ☎ 26/317–965 or 26/317–966). **Vác: Tourinform** (✉ Március 15 tér 16–18, ☎ 27/316–160). **Visegrád: Visegrád Tours** (✉ Sirály Restaurant, Rév u. 15, ☎ 26/398–160).

LAKE BALATON

Lake Balaton, the largest lake in Central Europe, stretches 80 km (50 mi) across Hungary. Its vast surface area is drastically contrasted with its modest depths—only 9.8 ft at the center and just 52.5 ft at its deepest point, at the Tihany Peninsula. The Balaton—the most popular playground of this landlocked nation—is just 90 km (56 mi) to the southwest of Budapest, so it is within easy reach of the capital by car, train, bus, and even bicycle. On a hot day in July or August, it seems the entire country and half of Germany are packed towel to towel on the lake's grassy public beaches, paddling about in the warm water and consuming fried meats and beer at the omnipresent snack bars.

On the lake's hilly northern shore, ideal for growing grapes, is Balatonfüred, Hungary's oldest spa town, famed for natural springs that bubble out curative waters. The national park on the Tihany Peninsula is just to the south, and regular boat service links Tihany and Balatonfüred with Siófok on the southern shore. Flatter and more crowded with resorts, cottages, and trade-union rest houses, the southern shore (beginning with Balatonszentgyörgy) is not as attractive as the northern one (north-shore locals say the only redeeming quality of the southern shore is its views back across the lake to the north), nor are there as many sights. Families with small children prefer the southern shore for its shallower, warmer waters (you can walk for almost 2 km/1 mi before it deepens). The water warms up to 25°C (77°F) in summer.

Every town along both shores has at least one *strand* (beach). The typical Balaton strand is a complex of blocky wooden changing cabanas and snack bars, fronted by a grassy flat stretch along the water for sitting and sunbathing. Most have paddleboat and other simple boat rentals. A small entrance fee is usually charged.

Those interested in exploring beyond the beach can set out by car, bicycle, or foot, on beautiful village-to-village tours—stopping to view lovely old Baroque churches, photograph a stork family perched high in its chimney-top nest, or climb a vineyard-covered hill for sweeping vistas. Since most vacationers keep close to the shore, a small amount of exploring into the roads and countryside heading away from the lake will reward you with a break from the summer crowds.

Numbers in the margin correspond to numbers on the Lake Balaton and Transdanubia map.

Veszprém

58 *116 km (72 mi) southwest of Budapest, 18 km (11 mi) north of Balatonfüred.*

Hilly Veszprém is the center of cultural life in the Balaton region. ★ **Várhegy** (Castle Hill) is the most picturesque part of town, north of Szabadság tér. **Hősök kapuja** (Heroes' Gate), at the entrance to the castle, houses a small exhibit on Hungary's history. Just past the gate and down a little alley to the left is the **Tűztorony** (Fire Tower); note that the lower level is medieval, while the upper stories are Baroque. There is a good view of the town and surrounding area from the balcony. *Tower: ☎ 88/425–204. ⏲ Apr.–mid-Oct., daily 10–6.*

Vár utca, the only street in the castle area, leads to a small square in front of the **Bishop's Palace** and the **cathedral**; outdoor concerts are held here in the summer. Vár utca continues past the square up to a terrace erected on the north staircase of the castle. Stand beside the modern statues of St. Stephen and his queen, Gizella, for a far-reaching view of the old quarter of town.

OFF THE BEATEN PATH **HEREND** – Sixteen kilometers (10 mi) northwest of Veszprém on Road 8, Herend is the home of Hungary's renowned hand-painted porcelain. The factory, founded in 1839, displays many valuable pieces in its **Herend Porcelán Művészeti Múzeum** (Herend Museum of Porcelain Arts). *✉ Kossuth Lajos u. 144, ☎ 88/261–144. 300 Ft., 2,000 Ft. for group tours in English. ⏲ Apr.–Oct., Tues.–Sun. 9–6; Nov.–Mar., weekdays 10–3. Hours may change so call first.*

Dining

$ ✕ **Szürkebarát Borozó.** The plain off-white walls of the Gray-Monk Tavern may be less than inspiring, but the hearty Hungarian fare at this cellar restaurant in the city center more than compensates. For an unusual (but very Hungarian) appetizer, try the paprika-spiced *velős pirítós* (marrow on toast; missing from the English menu and sometimes unavailable); or for a main course, gnaw away at "Ms. Baker's Pork Hoofs." *✉ Szabadság tér 12, ☎ 88/327–684. No credit cards.*

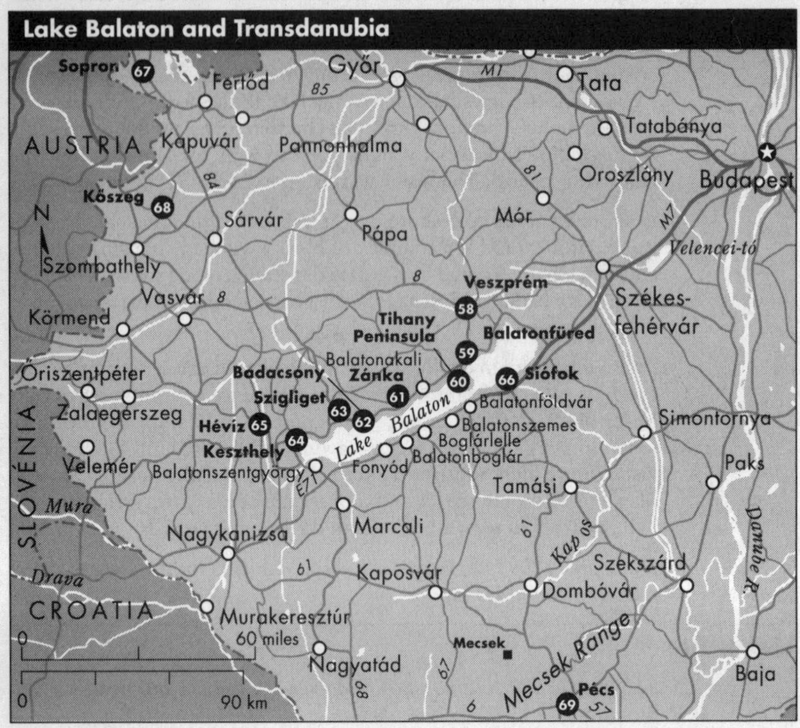

$$ **Éllő Panzió.** In this 18-room pension just southwest of the town center, you'll find ubiquitous golden lamp shades coupled with no lack of red—on the carpeting, the velvety chairs, and the curtains. Rooms in the newer annex building are more spacious than those in the chalet-like main house. Service is friendly. ✉ *József Attila u. 25, H-8200,* ☎ *88/420–097 or 88/424–118,* FAX *88/329–711. 18 rooms. Breakfast room. MC, V.*

Balatonfüred

59 *115 km (71 mi) southwest of Budapest.*

Fed by 11 medicinal springs, Balatonfüred first gained popularity as a health resort (the lake's oldest) where ailing people with heart conditions and fatigue would come to take or, more accurately, to drink a cure. The waters, said to have stimulating and beneficial effects on the heart and nerves, are still an integral part of the town's identity and consumed voraciously, but only the internationally renowned cardiac hospital has actual bathing facilities. Today Balatonfüred, also known simply as Füred, is probably the Balaton's most popular destination, with every amenity to match. Above its busy boat landing, beaches, and promenade lined with great plane and poplar trees, the twisting streets of the Old Town climb hillsides thickly planted with vines. The climate and landscape also make this one of the best wine-growing districts in Hungary. Every year in July, the most elaborate of Lake Balaton's debutante cotillions, the Anna Ball, is held here.

The center of town is **Gyógy tér** (Spa Square), where the bubbling waters from five volcanic springs rise beneath a slim, colonnaded pavilion. In the square's centerpiece, the neoclassical **Well House** of the Kossuth Spring, you can sample the water, which has a pleasant, surprisingly refreshing taste despite the sulfurous aroma; for those who can't get enough, a 30-liter-per-person limit is posted. All the buildings on the square are pillared like Greek temples. At No. 3 is the **Horváth Ház** (Horváth House), where the Szentgyörgyi-Horváth family arranged the first of what was to become the Anna Ball in 1825 in honor of their daughter Anna.

The Anna Ball is now held every July in another colonnaded building on the square, the **former Trade Unions' Sanatorium** (1802); at press time, renovations here had been completed and it was due to reopen as a hotel. Under its arcades is the **Balatoni Pantheon** (Balaton Pantheon): aesthetically interesting tablets and reliefs honoring Hungarian and foreign notables who either worked for Lake Balaton or spread the word about it. Among them is Jaroslav Hašek, the Czech author of the *Good Soldier Schweik,* who also wrote tales about Balaton. On the eastern side of the square is the **Állami Kórház** (State Hospital), where hundreds of patients from all over the world are treated. Here, too, Rabindranath Tagore, the Indian author and Nobel Prize winner, recovered from a heart attack in 1926. The tree that he planted to commemorate his stay stands in a little grove at the western end of the paths leading from the square down to the lakeside. Tagore also wrote a poem for the planting, which is memorialized beneath the tree on a strikingly animated bust of Tagore: WHEN I AM NO LONGER ON EARTH, MY TREE,/LET THE EVER-RENEWED LEAVES OF THY SPRING/MURMUR TO THE WAYFARER:/THE POET DID LOVE WHILE HE LIVED. In the same grove are trees honoring visits by another Nobel laureate, the Italian poet Salvatore Quasimodo, in 1961; and Indian prime minister Indira Gandhi, in 1972. An adjoining grove honors Soviet cosmonauts and their Hungarian partner-in-space, Bertalan Farkas.

Beginning near the boat landing, the **Tagore sétány** (Tagore Promenade) runs for nearly a kilometer (almost ½ mi) and is lined by trees, restaurants, and shops.

A stroll up **Blaha Lujza utca** from Gyógy tér will take you past several landmarks, such as the **Blaha Lujza Ház** (Lujza Blaha House), a neoclassical villa built in 1867 and, later, the summer home of this famous turn-of-the-20th-century actress, humanist, and singer (today it's a hotel); and the sweet little **Kerek templom** (Round Church), consecrated in 1846, built in a classical style and with a truly rounded interior.

NEED A BREAK? The plush **Kedves Café** (✉ Blaha Lujza u. 7, ☎ 87/343–229), built in 1795, was once the favorite summer haunt of well-known Hungarian writers and artists. Now more touristy than literary, it is still one of Lake Balaton's most popular and famous pastry shops.

Dining and Lodging

$$ ★ ✕ **Baricska Csárda.** Perched on a hill overlooking wine and water—its own vineyard and Lake Balaton—this rambling, reed-thatched inn is complete with wood-beamed rooms, vaulted cellars, and terraces. The food is hearty yet ambitious: roasted trout, fish paprikás with gnocchi to soak up the creamy sauce, and delicious desserts mixing pumpkin and poppy seed. In summer, Gypsy wedding shows are held nightly under the grape arbors. ✉ *Baricska dülő off Rte. 71 (Széchenyi út) behind Shell station,* ☎ *87/343–105. Reservations essential. AE, V. Closed mid-Nov.–mid-Mar.*

$$ ✕ **Tölgyfa Csárda.** Perched high on a hilltop, the Oak Tree Tavern has breathtaking views over the steeples and rooftops of Balatonfüred and the Tihany Peninsula. Its decor and menu are worthy of a first-class

Budapest restaurant, and nightly live Gypsy music keeps the atmosphere festive. ✉ *Meleghegy (up the hill at the end of Csárda u.),* ☎ *87/343–036. No credit cards. Closed late Oct.–mid-Apr.*

$$$$ ★ **Annabella.** The cool, spacious guest quarters in this large, Miami-style high-rise are especially pleasant in summer heat. Overlooking the lake and Tagore Promenade, it has access to excellent swimming and water-sports facilities. All rooms have balconies; for best vistas, request a room on a high floor with a view of the Tihany peninsula. ✉ *Deák Ferenc u. 25, H-8231,* ☎ *87/342–222,* FAX *87/483–029. 383 rooms, 5 suites. Restaurant, bar, brasserie, café, indoor pool, pool, barbershop, massage, sauna, bicycles, nightclub, solarium, baby-sitting, laundry service, travel services. AE, DC, MC, V. Closed mid-Oct.–mid-Apr.*

$$$$ **Marina.** The Marina's central beachfront location is its main draw. Built in the mid-'80s, it is undergoing a major overhaul, which should cheer up its dated feel. Rooms in the homely 12-story "Marina" building range from snug to small; suites have balconies but suffer from tiny bathrooms and extremely dark bedrooms. Your safest bet is to get a newly renovated, high-floor "Superior" room with a lake view. Or better, stay in the "Lido" wing, which opens directly onto the water and where rooms (suites only) get plenty of sun. ✉ *Széchenyi út 26, H-8230,* ☎ *87/343–644,* FAX *87/343–052. 291 rooms, 58 suites. Restaurant, bar, pub, indoor pool, beauty salon, massage, sauna, bowling, beach, boating, nightclub, solarium, laundry service, travel services. AE, DC, MC, V. Closed Oct.–late Apr.*

$$$ **Park.** Hidden on a side street in town but close to the lakeshore, the Park is noticeably calmer than Füred's bustling main hotels. Rooms are large and bright, with high ceilings and tall windows. Suites have large, breezy balconies but small bathrooms. While at press time the decor was uninspired—Eastern Bloc–style, with low, narrow beds and plain green and brown upholstery—extensive renovations were being planned to freshen things up. ✉ *Jókai u. 24, H-8230,* ☎ FAX *87/343–203 or 87/342–005. 38 rooms, 3 suites. Restaurant, bar, exercise room, sauna, solarium, meeting room, free parking. No credit cards.*

Outdoor Activities and Sports

Most hotels have their own private beaches, with water-sports facilities and equipment or special access to these nearby. Besides these, Balatonfüred has three public beaches, where you can rent sailboards, paddleboats, and other water toys; these are also available at Hungary's largest campground, **Füred Camping** (✉ Széchenyi u. 24, next to the Hotel Marina, ☎ 87/343–823). Although motorboats are banned from the lake, those desperate to water-ski can try the campground's electric water-ski machine, which tows enthusiasts around a 1-km (½-mi) circle. A two-tow ticket runs around 900 Ft.

In season you can rent **bicycles** from temporary, private outfits set up in central locations around town and near the beaches; one is usually working at the entrance to Füred Camping. Inquire at the tourist office for other current locations. Average prices for mountain-bike rentals are 1,000 Ft. per hour or 3,500 Ft. per day. You can also usually rent **mopeds** in front of the Halászkert restaurant (✉ Széchenyi út 2) for around 1,300 Ft. per hour and 5,000 Ft. per day.

Trail rides and horseback-riding lessons are available from mid-May to the end of September for about 2,500 Ft. an hour at the **Diana Lovasudvar** (Diana Riding Center; ✉ Rte. 71 just southwest of the town center; turn right at the sign about 100 yards beyond the giant campground on the lake, ☎ 87/481–894).

Tihany and the Tihany Félsziget (Tihany Peninsula)

60 *11 km (7 mi) southwest of Balatonfüred.*

The famed town of Tihany, with its twisting, narrow cobblestone streets and hilltop abbey, is on the Tihany Félsziget (Tihany Peninsula), joined to the mainland by a narrow neck and jutting 5 km (3 mi) into the lake. Only 12 square km (less than 5 square mi), the peninsula is not only a major tourist resort but perhaps the most historic part of the Balaton area. In 1952 the entire peninsula was declared a national park, and because of its geological rarities, it became Hungary's first nature-conservation zone. On it are more than 110 geyser craters, remains of former hot springs, reminiscent of those found in Iceland, Siberia, and Wyoming's Yellowstone Park.

The smooth Belső Tó (Inner Lake), 82 ft higher than Lake Balaton, is one of the peninsula's own two lakes; around it are barren yellowish-white rocks and volcanic cones rising against the sky. Though the hills surrounding the lake are known for their white wines, this area produces a notable Hungarian red, Tihany cabernet.

★ Tihany's crowning glory is the **Bencés Apátság** (Benedictine Abbey; ⛪), with foundations laid by King András I in 1055. The abbey's charter—containing some 100 Hungarian words in its Latin text, thus making it the oldest written source of the Hungarian language—is kept in Pannonhalma (☞ Transdanubia, *below*). Rebuilt in Baroque style between 1719 and 1784, the abbey's church towers above the village. Its gilt-silver high altar, abbot's throne, pulpit, organ case, choir parapet, and swirling crowd of saintly and angelic faces are all the work (between 1753 and 1765) of Sebestyén Stuhlhoff. A joiner from Augsburg, Stulhoff lived and worked in the monastery as a lay brother for 25 years after the death of his Hungarian sweetheart. Local tradition says he immortalized her features as the angel who is kneeling on the right-hand side of the altar to the Virgin Mary. The magnificent Baroque organ, adorned by stucco cherubs, can be heard during evening concerts in summer.

In a Baroque house adjoining and entered through the abbey is the **Bencés Apátsági Múzeum** (Benedictine Abbey Museum). The best exhibits are in the basement lapidarium: relics from Roman colonization, including mosaic floors; a relief of David from the 2nd or 3rd century; and 1,200-year-old carved stones—all labeled in English as well as Hungarian. Three of the upstairs rooms were lived in for five days in 1921 by the last emperor of the dissolved Austro-Hungarian monarchy, Karl IV, in a futile foray to regain the throne of Hungary. Banished to Madeira, he died of pneumonia there a year later. The rooms are preserved with nostalgic relish for Franz Joseph's doomed successor. ✉ *Első András tér 1,* ☎ *87/448–405 abbey; 87/448–650 museum.* 🎫 *200 Ft.* ⏲ *May–Sept., Mon.–Sat. 9–5:30, Sun. 11–5:30; Apr. and Oct., Mon.–Sat. 10–4:30, Sun. 11–4:30; Nov.–Mar. (only church and lapidarium), Mon.–Sat. 10–3:30.*

The **Szabadtéri Múzeum** (Open-air Museum), Tihany's outdoor museum of ethnography, assembles a group of old structures, including a potter's shed (with a local artist-in-residence) and the former house of the Fishermen's Guild, with an ancient boat (used until 1934) parked inside. ✉ *Along Batthyány u. and neighboring streets,* ☎ *no phone.* ⏲ *May–Sept., Tues.–Sun. 10–6.*

Visszhang domb (Echo Hill), at the end of Piski István sétány, is where as many as 16 syllables can be bounced off the abbey wall. Nowadays, with the inroads of traffic and construction, you'll have to settle for a two-second echo.

NEED A BREAK? You can practice projecting from the terraces of the **Echo Restaurant** (✉ Visszhang út 23, ☏ 87/448–460), an inn atop Echo Hill. While you're at it, try some fogas, carp, and catfish specialties.

Dining and Lodging

$$ ✕ **Pál Csárda.** Two thatch cottages house this simple restaurant, where cold fruit soup and fish stew are the specialties. You can eat in the garden, which is decorated with gourds and strands of dried peppers. ✉ *Visszhang u. 19,* ☏ *87/448–605. Reservations not accepted. AE, MC, V. Closed Oct.–Apr.*

$ ✕ **Halásztanya.** The relaxed atmosphere and local fish specialties—such as fogas fillets with garlic—contribute to this restaurant's popularity. ✉ *Visszhang u. 11,* ☏ *87/448–771. Reservations not accepted. AE, MC, V. Closed Nov.–Easter.*

$$$$ ★ **Kastély Hotel.** Lush landscaped lawns surround this stately neo-Baroque mansion on the water's edge, built in the 1920s for József Hapsburg and taken over by the Communist state in the '40s (it is still owned by the government). Inside, it's all understated elegance; rooms have soaring ceilings and crisp sheets. Rooms with lake-facing windows and/or balconies (slightly more expensive) are the best. Next door, a newer, uninviting concrete building houses the Kastély's sister, the Park Hotel, with 44 less expensive, though dated, rooms. ✉ *Fürdő telepi út 1, H-8237,* ☏ *87/448–611,* FAX *87/448–409. 25 rooms, 1 suite. Restaurant, bar, café, sauna, miniature golf, 2 tennis courts, beach. AE, DC, MC, V. Closed mid-Oct.–mid-Apr.*

$$$–$$$$ **Club Tihany.** This 32-acre holiday village is essentially a year-round resort of almost Club Med proportions at the tip of the Tihany Peninsula. The list of activities is formidable—from fishing to thermal bathing at the full-service spa. The best and largest rooms in the resort's six-floor main building, the Hotel Tihany, are in its newer wing. Less fancy but more convenient for families are the 160 bungalows in various architectural styles—suburban A-frame, modern atrium, or mini-farmhouse—but all with kitchen facilities. Note: Hotel building prices include mandatory breakfast and dinner. ✉ *Rév u. 3, H-8237,* ☏ *87/448–088 or 87/538–500,* FAX *87/448–083. 330 rooms, 161 bungalows. 3 restaurants, 2 bars, wine bar, pool, mineral baths, beauty salon, spa, tennis, exercise room, beach, meeting rooms. AE, DC, MC, V.*

$$ **Kolostor.** Cozy, wood-paneled rooms are built into an attic above a popular restaurant and brewery in the heart of Tihany village. Rates include breakfast. ✉ *Kossuth u. 14, H-8237,* ☏ FAX *87/448–408. 5 rooms. Restaurant. MC, V. Closed Nov.–Mar.*

Nightlife and the Arts

The **Benedictine Abbey**'s popular summer organ-concert series runs from July to August 20 and features well-known musicians performing on the abbey's magnificent organ. Concerts are generally held weekends at 8:30 PM. Contact the abbey (☞ *above*) for information and tickets.

Outdoor Activities and Sports

BICYCLING

Bicycle rentals are available from **Tihany Tourist** (☞ Visitor Information, *below*); a mountain bike costs about 700 Ft. per hour.

FISHING

Belső-tó (Inner Lake) is a popular angling spot in which you can try your luck at hooking ponty, catfish, and other local fish. Fishing permits can be bought on site at the fishing warden's office (☏ 87/448–082), on the premises of the Horgásztanya restaurant, on the southwest side of the lake.

HIKING

Footpaths crisscross the entire peninsula, allowing visitors to climb the small hills on its west side for splendid views of the area or hike down Belső-tó (Inner Lake). If in midsummer you climb its highest hill, the **Csúcshegy** (761 ft—approximately a two-hour hike), you will find the land below carpeted with purple lavender. Introduced from France into Hungary, lavender thrives on the lime-rich soil and strong sunshine of Tihany. (The State Lavender and Medicinal Herb Farm here supplies the Hungarian pharmaceutical and cosmetics industries.)

En Route The miniature town of Örvényes, about 7 km (4½ mi) west of Tihany, has the only working **vízi malom** (water mill; Szent Imre u. 1, ☎ 87/449–360; 100 Ft.; May–Sept., Tues.–Sun. 9–4) in the Balaton region. Built in the 18th century, it still grinds grain into flour while also serving as a tiny museum. In the miller's room is a collection of folk art, wood carvings, pottery, furniture, and pipes. On a nearby hill are the ruins of a **Romanesque church**; only its chancel has survived. On Templom utca, a few steps from the bridge, is the Baroque **St. Imre templom** (St. Imre Church), built in the late 18th century.

Another kilometer (½ mi) west of Örvényes, **Balatonudvari** is a pleasant beach resort famous for its cemetery, which was declared a national shrine because of its beautiful, unique heart-shape tombstones carved from white limestone at the turn of the 18th century. The cemetery is essentially on the highway, at the eastern end of town; it is easily visible from the road. Balatonudvari's beach itself is at **Kiliántelep**, 2 km (1 mi) to the west.

Zánka

61 *21 km (13 mi) west of Tihany.*

Zánka is a popular, relatively low-key beach resort with a large, pleasant beach, as well as a small, older village section up the hill from the water. The iron-rich Vérkút (Blood Spring), named after the bright stains it left on the rocks near which it flowed, put Zánka on the map as a spa late in the 19th century but has since dried up. The town's **Református templom** (Reformed Church; ⊠ Petőfi Sándor u. 3) is of medieval origin, but it was rebuilt in 1786 and again a century later with various elements preserved—leaving a pulpit supported by Roman foundations and Romanesque columns. The church is open during services, Sunday at 11 AM; someone is usually around to let you in an hour or so before.

The town of Zánka is not to be confused with the neighboring Zánka Gyermeküdülő (Zánka Children's Resort), the vast, unsightly former Communist Pioneer Camp. Keep this in mind if you're taking the train, as the stops for the two places are consecutive.

Lodging

$$ **Kővirág Panzió.** A 10-minute drive inland from Zánka's beach, this family-run pension is in the peaceful village of nearby Köveskál. Six two-story suites are in a lovely, restored turn-of-the-20th-century building (converted from a bull stable), with whitewashed walls and arched eye-of-God windows peeking out from under a reed-thatch roof. Each unit has a rustic-village feel, furnished with original hand-painted peasant furniture and mix-and-match antique carved-wood pieces. On cool nights you can build a fire in typical stone beehive fireplaces, with animal skins (wild boar, woolly sheep, or spotted cow) sprawled on the stone floors before them. Those who don't miss TVs, telephones, and other amenities may enjoy the Kővirág as an escape from the Balaton shore's myriad standard, faceless hotels. With large downstairs living rooms and two bedrooms upstairs sleeping four, the apartments offer good value and comfort for families or couples traveling together. ✉ *Fő út 9/A, H-8274 Köveskál,* ☎ *87/478–569. 6 suites. Restaurant. No credit cards. Closed Oct.–Apr.*

Outdoor Activities and Sports

Zánka is well situated for inland exploring in the beautiful hilly countryside of the Káli-medence (Káli Basin). You can hike, bike, drive, or use a combination of these to get to the peak of Hegyestő, a volcanic protrusion that is the area's highest hill (1,102 ft) and is supposed to possess mysterious "positive energy." (Access to Hegyestő is via the road to Monszló after leaving Zánka.)

Three kilometers (2 mi) inland, to the northwest, is **Kővágóörs,** one of the prettiest villages of the Balaton, with a fine array of cottages in the local peasant style. It makes a wonderful place to pedal or stroll.

Badacsony

★ 62 *20 km (12 mi) southwest of Zánka.*

One of the northern shore's most treasured images is the slopes of Mt. Badacsony (1,437 ft high), simply called the Badacsony, rising from the lake. The mysterious, coffinlike basalt peak of the Balaton Highlands is actually an extinct volcano flanked by smaller cone-shape hills. The masses of lava that coagulated here created bizarre and beautiful rock formations. At the upper edge, salt columns tower 180–200 ft like organ pipes in a huge semicircle. In 1965 Hungarian conservationists won a major victory that ended the quarrying of basalt from Mt. Badacsony, which is now a protected nature-preservation area.

The land below has been tilled painfully and lovingly for centuries. There are vineyards everywhere and splendid wine in every inn and tavern. In descending order of dryness, the best-loved Badacsony white wines are Rizlingszilváni, Kéknyelű, and Szürkebarát. Their proud producers claim that "no vine will produce good wine unless it can see its own reflection in the Balaton." They believe it is not enough for the sun simply to shine on a vine; the undersides of the leaves also need light, which is reflected from the lake's mirrorlike surface. Others claim the wine draws its strength from the fire of old volcanoes.

Badacsony is really an administrative name for the entire area and includes not just the mountain but also five settlements at its foot.

A good starting point for Badacsony sightseeing is the **Egry József Múzeum** (József Egry Museum), formerly the home and studio of a famous painter of Balaton landscapes. His evocative paintings depict the lake's constantly changing hues, from its angry bright green during storms to its tranquil deep blues. ✉ *Egry sétány 12,* ☎ *87/431–044.* 🎫 *120 Ft.* ⏲ *May–Sept., Tues.–Sun. 10–6.*

Szegedy Róza út, the steep main street climbing the mountain, is flanked by vineyards and villas. This is the place to get acquainted with the writer Sándor Kisfaludy and his beloved bride from Badacsony, Róza Szegedy, to whom he dedicated his love poems. At the summit of her street is **Szegedy Róza Ház** (Róza Szegedy House), a Baroque winepress house built in 1790 on a grand scale—with thatch roof, gabled wall, six semicircular arcades, and an arched and pillared balcony running the length of the four raftered upstairs rooms (it was here that the hometown girl met the visiting bard from Budapest). The house is now a memorial museum to both of them, furnished much the way it was when he was doing his best work immortalizing his two true loves, the Badacsony and his wife. ✉ *Szegedy Róza út 87,* ☎ *87/430–906.* 🎫 *120 Ft.* ⏲ *Apr.–Sept., Tues.–Sun. 10–6.*

The steep climb to the **Kisfaludy kilátó** (Kisfaludy Lookout Tower) on Mt. Badacsony's summit is an integral part of the Badacsony experience and a rewarding bit of exercise. Serious summitry begins behind the Kisfaludy House at the **Rózsakő** (Rose Stone), a flat, smooth basalt slab with many carved inscriptions. Local legend has it that if a boy and a girl sit on it with their backs to Lake Balaton, they will marry within a year. From here, a trail marked in yellow leads up to the foot of the columns that stretch to the top. Steep flights of stone steps take you through a narrow gap between rocks and basalt walls until you reach a tree-lined plateau. You are now at the 1,391-ft level. Follow the blue triangular markings along a path to the lookout tower. Even with time out for rests and views, the ascent from Rózsakő should take less than an hour.

Wine-tasting opportunities abound in Badacsony. Many restaurants and inns have their own tastings, as do the numerous smaller, private cellars dotting the hill. Look for signs saying *bor* or *Wein* (wine, in Hungarian and German, respectively) to point the way. Most places are open mid-May to mid-September daily from around noon until 9 or 10. Just outside of town, **Rizapuszta** (✉ Badacsonytomaj, Rizapuszta, ☎ 87/471–243) is a cellar and restaurant with regular tastings.

Dining and Lodging

$$ ✕ **Halászkert.** The festive Fish Garden has won numerous international awards for its tasty Hungarian cuisine. Inside are wooden rafters and tables draped with cheerful traditional blue-and-white *kékfestő* tablecloths; outside is a large terrace with umbrella-shaded tables. The extensive menu has such fresh-from-the-lake dishes as the house halászlé, and *párolt* (steamed) harcsa drenched with a paprika-caper sauce. ✉ *Park u. 5,* ☎ *87/431–054 or 87/431–113. AE, DC, MC, V. Closed Nov.–Apr.*

$$ ✕ **Kisfaludy-ház.** Perched above the Szegedy Róza House is this Badacsony institution, once a winepress house owned by the poet's family. Its wine cellar lies directly over a spring, but the main draw is a vast two-tier terrace that affords a breathtaking panoramic view of virtually the entire lake. Naturally, the wines are excellent and are incorporated into some of the cooking, such as creamy wine soup. ✉ *Szegedy Róza u. 87,* ☎ *87/431–016. MC, V. Closed Nov.–Apr.*

$$–$$$ **Club Hotel Badacsony.** On the shore of Lake Balaton in the Badacsonytomaj neighborhood, this is the largest hotel in the area. Recently renovated, rooms are bright and clean. The hotel's private beach is just a step away. ✉ *Balatoni út 14, H-8258 Badacsonytomaj,* ☎ *87/471–040,* FAX *87/471–059. 52 rooms, 4 suites. Restaurant, café, sauna, tennis court, bowling, beach. MC, V. Closed mid-Oct.–Apr.*

$$–$$$ **Hotel Volán.** This bright yellow, restored 19th-century mansion is a cheerful, family-oriented inn with a manicured yard for sunning and relaxing. Well-kept rooms are in the main house and in four modern additions behind it. ✉ *Római út 168, H-8261 Badacsony,* ☎ FAX *87/431–013. 23 rooms. Restaurant, bar, pool. No credit cards.*

Outdoor Activities and Sports

The upper paths and roads along the slopes of Mt. Badacsony are excellent for scenic walking. Well-marked trails lead up to the summit of Mt. Badacsony.

For beach activities, you can go to one of Badacsony's several beaches or head 6 km (4 mi) northeast, to those at Balatonrendes and Ábrahámhegy, combined communities forming quiet resorts.

Szigliget

★ 63 *11 km (7 mi) west of Badacsony.*

The village of Szigliget was formerly an island in the Balaton. It's a tranquil, picturesque town with a fine array of thatch-roof winepress houses and a small beach. Towering over the town is the ruin of the 13th-century **Óvár** (Old Castle), a fortress so well protected that it was never taken by the Turks; it was demolished in the early 18th century by Hapsburgs fearful of rebellions. A steep path starting from Kisfaludy utca brings you to the top of the hill, where you can explore the ruins, under ongoing archaeological restoration (a sign maps out the restoration plan), and take in the breathtaking views.

The **Eszterházy Summer Mansion** in the main square, Fő tér, was built in the 18th century and rebuilt in neoclassical style in the 19th. In recent decades a retreat for writers, it is closed to the public—but just as well, for the bland inside has little to do with its former self. The mansion has a 25-acre park with yews, willows, walnuts, pines, and more than 500 kinds of ornamental trees and shrubs.

Keszthely

64 *18 km (10 mi) west of Szigliget.*

Keszthely, the largest town on the northern shore, lies at the westernmost end of Lake Balaton. With a beautifully preserved pedestrian avenue (Kossuth Lajos utca) in the historic center of town, the spectacular Baroque Festetics Kastély, and a relative absence of honky-tonk, Keszthely is far more classically attractive and sophisticated than other large Balaton towns. Continuing the cultural and arts tradition begun by Count György Festetics two centuries ago, Keszthely hosts numerous cultural events, including an annual summer arts festival. Just south of town is the vast swamp called Kis-Balaton (Little Balaton), formerly part of Lake Balaton and now a nature preserve filled with birds. Water flowing into Lake Balaton from its little sibling frequently churns up sediment, making the water around Keszthely's beaches disconcertingly cloudy.

The **Pethő Ház,** a striking town house of medieval origin, was rebuilt in Baroque style with a handsome arcaded gallery above its courtyard. Hidden deep inside its courtyard you'll find the restored 18th-century **synagogue,** in front of which stands a small memorial honoring the 829 Jewish people from the neighborhood, turned into a ghetto in 1944, who were killed during the Holocaust. ✉ *Kossuth Lajos u. 22.*

★ Keszthely's magnificent **Festetics Kastély** (Festetics Palace) is one of the finest Baroque complexes in Hungary. Begun around 1745, it was the seat of the enlightened and philanthropic Festetics dynasty, which had acquired Keszthely six years earlier. The palace's distinctive churchlike tower and more than 100 rooms were added between 1883 and 1887; the interior is exceedingly lush. The **Helikon Könyvtár** (Helikon Library) in the south wing contains some 52,000 volumes, with precious codices and documents of Festetics family history. Chamber and orchestral concerts are held in the **Mirror Gallery** ballroom or, in summer, in the courtyard. The palace opens onto a splendid park lined with rare plants and fine sculptures. ✉ *Kastély u. 1,* ☎ *83/312–191.* 🎫 *1,100 Ft. (1,200 Ft. extra for videotaping, 500 Ft. for no-flash photos).* ⏲ *June, Tues.–Sun. 9–5; July–Aug., daily 9–6; Sept.–May, Tues.–Sun. 10–5.*

Keszthely's newest cultural attraction, the **Babamúzeum** (Doll Museum), opened in 1999. Supposedly the largest of its kind in Central Europe, the museum exhibits some 450 porcelain figurines dressed in 240 types of colorful folk dress. The building's pastoral ambience is created not only by the figurines—which convey the multifarious beauty of village garb—but in the ceiling's huge, handcrafted wooden beams. On the two upper floors you'll also find wooden models of typical homes, churches, and ornate wooden gates likewise representative of all regions in and near present-day Hungary that Magyars have inhabited since conquering the Carpathian basin in 896. What is perhaps the museum's *pièce de resistance* is the lifework of an elderly peasant woman from northern Hungary: a 9-yard-long model of Budapest's Parliament building, patched together over 14 years from almost 4 million snail shells (which are 28 million years old, no less) originating from the Pannon Sea, which once covered much of Hungary. ✉ *Kossuth u. 11,* ☎ *83/318–855.* *Doll Museum, 250 Ft.; model of Parliament, 200 Ft.* *May–Sept., daily 10–5; Oct.–Apr., daily 9–5.*

Dining and Lodging

$–$$ ✕ **Hungária Gösser Söröző.** This beer garden keeps long hours and plenty of beer on tap. The food is better than you might guess judging just from the touristy atmosphere. Aside from barroom snacks, the huge menu includes *ropogós libacomb hagymás törtburgonyával* (crunchy goose-drumstick with mashed potatoes and onions) and *töltött paprika* (stuffed peppers). ✉ *Kossuth Lajos u. 35, just north of Fő tér,* ☎ *83/312–265. AE, MC, V.*

$$$$ **Danubius Hotel Helikon.** This large lakeside hotel has plenty of sports facilities, such as an indoor swimming pool, indoor tennis courts, sailing, surfing, rowing, fishing, and, in winter, skating. The comfortable, modern rooms are on the small side, but they have soothing, cream-and-blue bedspreads and curtains. ✉ *Balaton part 5, H-8360,* ☎ *83/311–330,* FAX *83/315–403. 224 rooms, 8 suites. Restaurant, bar, indoor pool, beauty salon, sauna, 2 indoor tennis courts, bowling, health club, beach. AE, DC, MC, V.*

$$$ **Béta Hotel Hullám.** This turn-of-the-20th-century mansion with an elegant twin tower sits right on the Balaton shore. Rooms are clean and simply furnished with functional brown furniture; they have TVs and minibars but no telephones. Guests can use the pool and other recreational facilities at the nearby Danubius Hotel Helikon (☞ *above*). ✉ *Balatonpart 1, H-8360,* ☎ *83/312–644,* FAX *83/315–338. 28 rooms, 6 suites. Restaurant, bar, beach. AE, DC, MC, V. Closed Oct.–Apr.*

Nightlife and the Arts

The **Balaton Festival,** held annually in May, features high-caliber classical concerts and other festivities in venues around town and outdoors on Kossuth Lajos utca. In summer, classical concerts and master classes are held almost daily in the Festetics Palace's (☞ *above*) Mirror Hall.

Outdoor Activities and Sports

BALLOONING

Hot-air balloon rides in the Keszthely region have become popular with those tourists who can afford it (about 20,000 Ft. per person). Dr. Bóka György (a practicing M.D. and balloon pilot) and his friendly team will take you up in his blue-and-yellow balloon for an hour-long tour—the trip includes a post-landing champagne ritual. Flights depend strongly on wind and air-pressure conditions; in summer, they can usually fly only in early morning and early evening. Transportation to and from the site is included. Contact **Med-Aer** (✉ Móricz Zsigmond u. 7, ☎ 83/312–421 or 06/309–576–321) at least one week in advance to reserve your spot.

HORSEBACK RIDING

János Lovarda (János Stable; ✉ Sömögyedüllő, ☎ 83/314–855) offers lessons, rides in the ring, and carriage rides.

WATER SPORTS

You can rent paddleboats and other water toys at the public beach next to the Béta Hotel Hullám) or from the Danubius Hotel Helikon (☞ Dining and Lodging, *above*).

Hévíz

65 *6 km (4 mi) inland (northwest) from Keszthely.*

Hévíz is one of Hungary's biggest and most famous spa resorts, with the largest natural curative thermal lake in Europe. Lake Hévíz covers nearly 60,000 square yards, with warm water that never grows cooler than 33°C–35°C (91.4°F–95°F) in summer and 30°C–32°C (86°F–89.6°F) in winter, thus allowing year-round bathing, particularly where the lake is covered by a roof and looks like a racetrack grandstand. Richly endowed with sulfur, alkali, calcium salts, and other curative components, the Hévíz water is recommended for spinal, rheumatic, gynecological, and articular disorders and is drunk to help digestive problems and receding gums. Fed by a spring producing 86 million liters (22.7 million gallons) of water a day, the lake cycles through a complete water change every 28 hours. Squeamish bathers, however, should be forewarned that along with its photogenic lily pads, the lake naturally contains assorted sludgy mud and plant material. It's all good for you, though—even the mud, which is full of iodine and estrogen.

The vast spa park is home to hospitals, sanatoriums, expensive hotels, and a casino. The public bath facilities are in the **Szent András Kórház** (St. Andrew Hospital), a large, turreted medicinal bathing complex on the lakeshore with a large staff on hand to treat rheumatological complaints. Bathing for more than three hours at a time is not recommended. ✉ *Dr. Schulhof Vilmos sétány 1,* ☎ *83/340–587.* 🎫 *500 Ft. (valid for 3 hrs).* ⏲ *May–Sept., daily 8:30–5:30; Oct.–Apr., daily 9–4:30.*

OFF THE BEATEN PATH

CSILLAGVÁR (Star Castle) – It's worth stopping in Balatonszentgyörgy to see this castle, hidden away at the end of a dirt road past a gaping quarry. The house was built in the 1820s as a hunting lodge for László, the Festetics family's eccentric. Though it is not star-shape inside, wedge-shape projections on the ground floor give the outside this effect. Today it is a museum of 16th- and 17th-century life in the border fortresses of the Balaton. ✉ *Irtási dűlő,* ☎ *85/377–532.* 🎫 *100 Ft.* ⏲ *May–Aug., daily 9–6.*

The beautifully furnished **Talpasház** (House on Soles) is another architecturally interesting stop, so named because its upright beams are encased in thick foundation boards. The house is filled not only with exquisite antique peasant furniture, textiles, and pottery but also with the work of contemporary local folk artists; some of their work is for sale on the premises, and visitors can also try to create their own works on a pottery wheel. Contact the caretaker, Csaba Rezes, who lives next door at No. 15, if the door happens to be closed. ✉ *Dózsa György u. 17,* ☎ *85/377–364 (caretaker).* 🎫 *100 Ft.* ⏲ *Late May–Sept., Tues.–Sun. variable hours (call the caretaker to let you in).*

Lodging

$$$$ **Danubius Thermal Hotel Aqua.** This large, luxurious spa-hotel has its own thermal baths and physiotherapy unit (plus a full dental service!). It has a convenient city-center location, but the rooms are smaller than average and therefore not suited to families who intend to share a single room. Numerous cure packages are available. ✉ *Kossuth Lajos u. 13–15, H-8380,* ☎ *83/341–090,* FAX *83/340–970. 227 rooms. Restaurant, bar, pool, mineral baths, beauty salon, massage, sauna, spa, solarium. AE, DC, MC, V.*

$$$$ 🏨 **Danubius Thermal Hotel Hévíz.** Very similar in its offerings to those of its sibling and neighbor the Thermal Aqua (☞ *above*), this large spa-hotel edges it out with nicer (and larger) rooms, since the hotel was renovated in 1997. Suites have air-conditioning. ✉ *Kossuth Lajos u. 9–11, H-8380,* ☎ *83/341–180,* FAX *83/340–666. 203 rooms, 7 suites. Restaurant, bar, café, indoor pool, pool, sauna, mineral baths, solarium. AE, DC, MC, V.*

Siófok

66 *110 km (68 mi) southeast of Hévíz, 105 km (65 mi) southwest of Budapest.*

Siófok is the largest city on the southern shore and one of Hungary's major tourist and holiday centers. It is also arguably the least beautiful. In 1863 a railway station was built for the city, paving the way for its "golden age" at the turn of the 20th century. In the closing stages of World War II the city sustained heavy damage; to boost tourism during the 1960s, the Pannonia Hotel Company built four of what many consider to be the ugliest hotels in the area. If, however, these were Siófok's *only* ugly buildings, there would still be hope for a ray of aesthetic redemption. With the exception of the twin-tower train station (admirably restored a few years ago) and the adjacent business district stretching a few blocks to the *Víztorony* (water tower), dating from 1912, the city is overrun by drab modern structures. Its shoreline is now a long, honky-tonk strip crammed with concrete-bunker hotels, discos, go-go bars, and tacky restaurants. So while Siófok is not for those seeking a peaceful lakeside getaway, it is exactly what hordes of action-seeking young people want—an all-in-one playground.

One worthwhile attraction is the **Kálmán Imre Múzeum** (Imre Kálmán Museum), housed in the birthplace of composer Kálmán (1882–1953), known internationally as the Prince of Operetta. Inside this small house-cum-museum are his first piano, original scores, his smoking jacket, and lots of old pictures. ✉ *Kálmán Imre sétány 5,* ☎ *84/311–287.* *200 Ft.* ⏲ *Tues.–Sun. 9–5.*

Dining and Lodging

$$$ ✕ **Millennium Étterem.** This elegant restaurant, once an old villa, was renovated in 1992 under the guidance of Imre Makovecz, one of Hungary's preeminent architects. The menu has fresh fish and excellent Hungarian specialties. ✉ *Fő u. 93–95,* ☎ *84/312–546. AE, DC, MC, V.*

$$ ★ ✕ **Csárdás Étterem.** The oldest and one of the best restaurants in Siófok, this has consistently won awards for its hearty, never-bland Hungarian cuisine. House specialties include a breaded and fried pork fillet stuffed with cheese, ham, and smoked bacon. ✉ *Fő u. 105,* ☎ *84/310–642. AE, MC, V. Closed Nov.–Mar. 15.*

$$$–$$$$ 🏨 **Hotel Atrium Janus Siófok.** Every room in this bright luxury hotel is clean and comfortably contemporary and contains a minibar and a safe. The "relaxation center" downstairs has a swimming pool, sauna, and whirlpool. ✉ *Fő u. 93–95, H-8600,* ☎ *84/312–546,* FAX *84/312–432. 22 rooms, 7 suites. Restaurant, bar, café, air-conditioning, indoor pool, sauna, exercise room, meeting rooms. AE, DC, MC, V.*

$$ 🏨 **Hotel Fortuna.** This three-story, bright yellow rectangular block that opened in 1999 has the advantage of being somewhat removed from the multilane traffic of the city's main street and about 100 yards from the lakeshore. The rooms are modern and, like the building's facade, awash in a soothing yellow; all have balconies. ✉ *Erkel Ferenc u. 51, H-8600,* ☎ FAX *84/311–087 or 84/313–476. 41 rooms, 5 suites. Restaurant, bar, playground, meeting rooms. AE, MC, V.*

Nightlife and the Arts

Loyal to Siófok-born operetta composer Imre Kálmán, popular operetta concerts are held regularly in the summer at the **Kulturális Központ** (Cultural Center; ✉ Fő tér 2, ☎ 84/311–855).

Outdoor Activities and Sports

GO-CARTS

Speed demons can whiz around at the **Go-Cart Track** (✉ on Rte. 70, by the railroad crossing, ☎ 84/311–917 or 06/209–512–510), which is open from mid-May through September; a 10-minute drive is around 1,800 Ft.

TENNIS

The **Sport Centrum** (✉ Küszhegyi út, ☎ 84/314–523) has eight tennis courts as well as a handball court, sauna, and, lest things are getting too athletic, a bar.

WATER SPORTS

Boating and other water-sports equipment is available for hire at the **MOL Water Sports Center,** on the waterfront on Vitorlás utca 10 (☎ 84/311–161). Kayaks and canoes cost 500 Ft.–600 Ft. per hour, sailboats around 6,000 Ft. per hour.

Lake Balaton A to Z

Arriving and Departing

BY BUS

Buses headed for the Lake Balaton region depart from Budapest's Erzsébét tér station daily; contact **Volánbusz** (☎ 1/317–2318) for current schedules.

BY CAR

Expressway E71/M7 is the main artery between Budapest and Lake Balaton. At press time still under construction, it had gotten as far as the lake's northeastern point and will eventually reach southwestern Hungary. From here Route 7 from Budapest joins the E71 and continues along the lake's southern shore to Siófok and towns farther west. Route 71 goes along the northern shore to Balatonfüred and lakeside towns southwest. The drive from Budapest to Siófok takes about 1½ hours, except on weekends, when traffic can be severe. From Budapest to Balatonfüred is about the same.

BY TRAIN

Daily express trains run from Budapest's Déli (South) Station to Siófok and Balatonfüred. The roughly two-hour trip costs about 900 Ft. each way.

Getting Around

BY BOAT

The slowest but most scenic way to travel between Lake Balaton's major resorts is by ferry. Schedules for **MAHART Tours** (☎ 1/318–1704 in Budapest), the national ferry company, are available from most of the tourist offices listed below.

BY BUS

Buses frequently link Lake Balaton's major resorts. Arrive at the bus station early. Tickets with seat reservations can be bought in the stations up to 20 minutes prior to departure, otherwise from the driver; reservations cannot be made by phone. Contact the tourist offices or **Volánbusz** (☎ 1/317–2318 in Budapest) for schedule and fare information.

BY CAR

Route 71 runs along the northern shore; Route E71 (here merged with Route 7) covers the southern shore. Driving is the most convenient way to explore the area, but remember that traffic can be heavy during summer weekends.

BY TRAIN

Trains from Budapest serve the resorts on the northern shore; a separate line links resorts on the southern shore. The **Siófok** station (✉ Milenium tér, ☎ 84/310–061) is in the center of town; the **Balatonfüred** station (✉ Castricum tér, ☎ 87/343–652) is very close to town center. **Veszprém**'s train station (✉ Jutasi út 34, ☎ 88/329–999) is about 2 km (1 mi) outside town. There is no train service to Tihany. While most towns are on a rail line, it's inconvenient to decipher the train schedules; trains don't run very frequently, so planning connections can be tricky. Since many towns are just a few kilometers apart, getting stuck on a local train can feel like an endless stop-start cycle. Also bear in mind that excepting some trains between Budapest and Veszprém, you cannot reserve seats on the Balaton trains—it's first come, first seated.

Contacts and Resources

EMERGENCIES

Ambulance (☎ 104). **Fire** (☎ 105). **Police** (☎ 107).

GUIDED TOURS

IBUSZ Travel has several tours to Balaton from Budapest; inquire at the office in Budapest (✉ V, Ferenciek tere 10, ☎ 1/485–2762 or 1/317–7767). You can also arrange tours directly with the hotels in the Balaton area and with the help of Tourinform offices (see Visitor Information, *below*); these can include boat trips to vineyards, folk-music evenings, and overnight trips to local inns.

Cityrama (in Budapest, ☎ 1/302–4382) takes groups twice a week from April to October from Budapest to Balatonfüred for a walk along the promenade and then over to Tihany for a tour of the abbey. After lunch, you'll take a ferry across the Balaton, and then head back to Budapest, with a wine-tasting stop on the way.

MAHART (☎ 84/310–050) offers several sailing excursions on Lake Balaton. From Balatonfüred, the *Csongor* sets out several times daily in July and August for an hour-long jaunt around the Tihany peninsula. Most other tours depart from Siófok also in the same period, including the **"Tihany Tour"**, on Saturday at 10 AM, with stops for guided sightseeing in Balatonfüred and Tihany; and the **"Sunset Tour"**, a 1½-hour cruise at 7:30 PM daily during which guests can sip a glass of champagne while watching the sun sink. The **"Badacsony Tour"** departs from Keszthely and goes to Badacsony at 10:30 AM Thursday.

VISITOR INFORMATION

Badacsony: Tourinform (✉ Park u. 6, Badacsony, ☎ FAX 87/431–046). **Balatonfüred: Tourinform** (✉ Petőfi u. 8, ☎ 87/342–237); **Balatontourist** (✉ Tagore sétány 1, ☎ 87/342–822 or 87/343–471). **Hévíz: Hévíz Tourist** (✉ Rákóczi u. 4, ☎ 83/341–348). **Keszthely: Tourinform** (✉ Kossuth u. 28, ☎ FAX 83/314–144). **Siófok: Tourinform** (✉ Víztorony, ☎ FAX 84/310–117); **IBUSZ** (✉ Fő u. 174, ☎ 84/311–066). **Tihany: Tourinform** (✉ Kossuth u. 20, ☎ FAX 87/448–804); **Tihany Tourist** (✉ Kossuth u. 11, ☎ FAX 87/448–481). **Veszprém: Tourinform** (✉ Vár u. 4, ☎ FAX 88/404–548).

TRANSDANUBIA

Western Hungary, often referred to as Transdanubia (Dunántúl in Hungarian), is the area south and west of the Danube, stretching to the Slovak and Austrian borders in the west and north and to Slovenia and Croatia in the south. It presents a highly picturesque landscape, including several ranges of hills and small mountains. Most of its surface is covered with farmland, vineyards, and orchards—all nurtured and made verdant by a climate that is noticeably more humid than in the rest of the country.

The Romans called the region Pannonia (for centuries it was a frontier province; today it is far richer in Roman ruins than the rest of Hungary). Centuries later, the 150-year Turkish occupation left its mark on the region, particularly in the south, where it's not uncommon to see a former mosque serving as a Christian church. Austrian influence is clearly visible in the region's Baroque buildings, particularly in the magnificent Eszterházy Palace in Fertőd. Vienna, after all, is at most a few hours' drive away.

Numbers in the margin correspond to numbers on the Lake Balaton and Transdanubia map.

En Route Perched proudly above the countryside on top of a high hill on the way to Sopron—135 km (84 mi) west of Budapest, 100 km (62 mi) east of ★ Sopron—the vast, 1,000-year old Benedictine **Pannonhalma Apátság** (Pannonhalma Abbey) gleams like a gift from heaven. During the Middle Ages, it was an important ecclesiastical center and wielded considerable political influence. The abbey housed Hungary's first school and was allegedly the first place the Holy Scriptures were read on Hungarian soil. It's still a working monastery and school; 60 monks and 320 students live here. A late-Gothic cloister and a 180-ft neoclassical tower are the two stylistic exceptions to the predominantly Baroque architecture. The library of more than 300,000 volumes houses some priceless medieval documents, including the first to contain a large number of Hungarian words: the 11th-century deed to the abbey of Tihany. Visits are permitted only with a guide, which is included in the admission price. Tours begin every hour on the hour; the last one of the day begins at the closing hour listed below. There are regularly scheduled English and other foreign-language tours at 11 and 1. Occasional organ recitals are held in the basilica in summer. ✉ *Pannonhalma, off Rte. 82 south of Győr,* ☎ *96/570–191,* FAX *96/570–192.* *500 Ft. (800 Ft. for foreign-language guide).* ⏲ *Late Mar.–May and Oct.–mid-Nov., Tues.–Sun. 9–4; June–Sept., daily 9–5; mid-Nov.–late Mar., Tues.–Sun. 10–3. Monastery closed Sun. mornings except for those wishing to attend mass; library and yard remain open to tours.*

Sopron

★ 67 *211 km (131 mi) northwest of Budapest, 100 km (62 mi) west of Pannonhalma.*

Lying on the Austrian frontier, between Lake Fertő (in German, Neusiedlersee) and the Sopron Hills, Sopron is one of Hungary's most picturesque towns. Barely an hour away from Vienna by car, it is a bargain shopping center for many Austrians, who flock here for the day. The joke in Sopron is that every day at noon, "We play the Austrian national hymn so that the Austrians have to stand still for two minutes while we Hungarians shop." Dental work is also a bargain by Austrian standards; the town is chock-full of dentist advertisements in German, and nearly every hotel provides an in-house dentist.

There is much more to Sopron, however, than conspicuous consumption by foreigners. Behind the narrow storefronts along the City Ring Várkerület (called Lenin Boulevard until 1989) and within the city walls (one set built by Romans, the other by medieval Magyars) lies a horse-shoe-shape inner city that is a wondrous eclectic mix of Gothic, Baroque, and Renaissance, centered on Fő tér, the main square of perfectly proportioned Italianate architecture. Sopron's faithful and inspired restoration won a 1975 Europe Prize Gold Medal for Protection of Monuments, and the work continues slowly and carefully.

Today's city of 60,000 was a small Celtic settlement more than 2,300 years ago. During Roman times, under the name of Scarabantia, it stood on the main European north–south trade route, the Amber Road; it also happened to be near the junction with the east–west route used by Byzantine merchants. In 896 the Magyars conquered the Carpathian basin and later named the city Suprun for a medieval Hungarian warrior. After the Hapsburgs took over the territory during the Turkish wars of the 16th and 17th centuries, they renamed the city Ödenburg (Castle on the Ruins) and made it the capital of the rich and fertile Austrian Burgenland. Ferdinand III, later Holy Roman Emperor, was crowned king of Hungary here in 1625, and at a special session of the Hungarian Parliament in 1681, Prince Paul Esterházy was elected palatine (ruling deputy) of Hungary. And always, under any name or regime, Sopron was a fine and prosperous place in which to live.

A sightseeing note: For those who plan to visit as many museums as they can, one collective ticket covering most of Sopron's museums is available from the the Storno Ház (☞ *below*) for about 900 Ft.

The symbol of the town's endurance—and entranceway to the Old City—is the 200-ft-high **Tűztorony** (Fire Tower), with foundations dating to the days of the Árpád dynasty (9th–13th centuries) and perhaps back to the Romans. Remarkable for its uniquely harmonious blend of architectural styles, the tower has a Romanesque base rising to a circular balcony of Renaissance loggias topped by an octagonal clock tower that is itself capped by a brass Baroque onion dome and belfry. The upper portions were rebuilt after most of the earlier Fire Tower was, appropriately, destroyed by the Great Fire of 1676, started by students roasting chestnuts in a high wind. Throughout the centuries the tower bell tolled the alarm for fire or the death of a prominent citizen, and from the loggias musicians trumpeted the approach of an enemy or serenaded the citizenry. Both warning concerts were accompanied by flags (red for fire, blue for enemy) pointing in the direction of danger. ✉ *Fő tér,* ☎ *99/311–327.* 🎫 *150 Ft.* ⏲ *Apr.–Oct., Tues.–Sun. 10–6.*

At No. 8 on Fő tér, the exquisite main square, is the city's finest Re-
★ naissance building: the turreted **Storno Ház** (Storno House). Inside its two-story loggia, a museum houses a remarkable family collection of furniture, porcelain, sculptures, and paintings. (There are tape-recorded tours available in English.) The Stornos were a rags-to-riches dynasty of chimney sweeps who over several generations bought or just relieved grateful owners of unwanted treasures and evolved into a family of painters and sculptors themselves. The dynasty died out in Hungary a few years ago, but its heirs and the Hungarian state have agreed nothing will be removed from the Storno House. On an exterior wall hangs a plaque commemorating visits by King Matthias Corvinus (1482–1483) and Franz Liszt (1840 and 1881). ✉ *Fő tér 8,* ☎ *99/311–327.* 🎫 *200 Ft.* ⏲ *Apr.–Oct., Tues.–Sun. 10–6; Nov.–Mar., Tues.–Sun. 10–2. Upstairs museum can be visited by guided tour only, given every ½ hr (last one begins ½ hr before closing).*

The 19th-century Angels' Drugstore is now the **Angyal Patika Múzeum** (Angel Pharmacy Museum), with old Viennese porcelain vessels and papers pertaining to Ignaz Philipp Semmelweis (1815–1865), the Hungarian physician whose pioneering work in antiseptics, while he was in Vienna, made childbirth safer. ✉ *Fő tér 2,* ☎ *99/311–327.* 🎫 *100 Ft.* ⏲ *Apr.–Oct., usually Tues.–Sun. 9:30–2. If closed, request entry at the Soproni Múzeum office in the Storno Ház, Fő tér 8.*

The centerpiece of Fő tér is a sparkling, spiraling three-tier **Szentháromság szobor** (Holy Trinity Column), aswirl with gilded angels—the earliest (1701) and loveliest Baroque monument to a plague in all of Hungary.

Standing before Fő tér's Holy Trinity Column is the early Gothic (1280–1300) **Kecske templom** (Goat Church), named, legend has it, for a medieval billy goat that scratched up a treasure, enabling early-day Franciscans to build a church on the site (the Benedictines took over in 1802). More likely, however, the name comes from the figures of goats carved into its crests: the coat of arms of the Gutsch family, who financed the church. The Goat Church has a soaring, pointed, 14th-century steeple; three naves; its original Gothic choir (betraying French influence); and, after several rebuildings, a Hungarian Gothic-Baroque red-marble pulpit, a rococo main altar, Baroque altars, and a painting of St. Stephen by one of the Stornos. ✉ *Fő tér at Templom u..* 🎫 *Free.* ⏲ *Daily 10–noon and 2–5.*

In the Gothic **Középkori Káptalan** (Medieval Chapter Room) of the Goat Church, monks meditated, contemplating on the curved pillars the Seven Deadly Sins in sculptures similar to those atop Notre-Dame Cathedral in Paris. Avarice is a monkey; Lewdness, a bear; Incredulity, a griffin; Inconstancy, a crab crawling backward; and Vanity, a woman with a mirror in hand. ✉ *Templom u. 1.* 🎫 *Free (donations accepted).* ⏲ *Apr.–mid-Oct., daily 10–noon and 2–5.*

The medieval **Ó-zsinagóga** (Old Synagogue), complete with a stone *mikva,* a ritual bath for women, is now a religious museum with old Torahs on display and an exhibit about the WWII deportation of the Jews. Built around 1300, it endured several incarnations over the centuries, including that as a hospital (in the 1400s) and later as a residential building, before being restored in 1973; the facade dates from 1734. A plaque honors the 1,640 Jews of Sopron who were murdered by the Nazis (the quiet street that is home to this and another old synagogue a few doors away, at No. 11, became the city's Jewish ghetto in May 1944); only 274 of Sopron's Jews survived, and today there are scarcely enough to muster a *minyan* (quorum of 10), let alone a congregation. ✉ *Új u. 22,* ☎ *99/311–327.* 🎫 *150 Ft.* ⏲ *May–Sept., Wed.–Mon. 9–5; Oct., Wed.–Mon. 10–2.*

The **Cézár Ház** (Cézár House) has a wine cellar downstairs, but upstairs, in rooms where the Hungarian Parliament met in 1681, is a private **museum** created by the widow of József Soproni-Horváth (1891–1961), a remarkable artist who prefixed his hometown's name to his own so he wouldn't be just another Joe Croat (*Horváth* means "Croat," in Hungarian). This Horváth nevertheless stands out for the wonders he worked with watercolors. He used that fragile medium to bring large surfaces alive in a density usually associated with oil paintings, while depicting realistic scenes, such as a girl grieving over her drowned sister's body. ✉ *Hátsókapú u. 2,* ☎ *99/312–326.* 🎫 *120 Ft.* ⏲ *Thurs.–Sun. 10–1 (Sat. also 3–6).*

Along **Szent György utca** (St. George Street), numerous dragons of religion and architecture coexist in sightly harmony. The **Erdődy Vár** (Erdődy Palace) at No. 16 is Sopron's richest rococo building. Two doors down, at No. 12, is the **Eggenberg ház** (Eggenberg House), where the widow of Prince Johann Eggenberg held Protestant services during the harshest days of the Counter-Reformation and beyond. But the street takes its name from **Szent György templom** (St. George's Church), a 14th-century Catholic church so sensitively "baroqued" some 300 years later that its interior is still as soft as whipped cream. The church is generally open daily 9–5; the other buildings are not open to the public.

Mária szobor (St. Mary's Column), with its finely sculpted biblical reliefs, is a superb Baroque specimen. It was built in 1745 to mark the former site of the medieval Church of Our Lady, destroyed by Sopron citizens in 1632 because they feared the Turks would use it as a strategic firing tower. ✉ *At the Előkapu (Outer Gate).*

NEED A BREAK? You'll find red-velvety chairs, an ornate chandelier, a semi-spiralling wooden staircase, and scrumptious pastry at the **Dömötöri cukrászda,** a cozy little café on Sopron's second most famous, but largest, square. (✉ Széchenyi tér at the corner of Erszébet u., ☎ 99/312–781).

Strolling along **Várkerület,** the circular boulevard embracing Sopron's inner core, you'll experience a vibrant harmony of beautifully preserved Baroque and rococo architecture and the fashionable shops and cafés of Sopron's thriving downtown business district.

Dining and Lodging

$–$$ ✕ **Barokk Étterem.** The "Baroque Restaurant" opened in 1992, supplanting authentic Baroque designs with pastel colors and modern fixtures. Still, the entrance is through a lovely courtyard (though crammed by day with racks of merchandise from the neighboring boutiques), and the dining room has an arched ceiling. Specialties include meat fondue for two, trout, and veal with chicken-liver stuffing. ✉ *Várkerület 25,* ☎ *99/312–227. AE, MC, V. Closed Sun.*

$–$$ ✕ **Corvinus.** The location, in the 700-year-old Storno House on Sopron's delightful cobblestone main square, couldn't be better. Sitting at the outdoor tables, you can practically do your sightseeing during lunch. There are two entrances, just around the corner from each other: one leads down to a cozy brick cellar lit by candles, where you can try Hungarian specialties such as a meaty soup with a baked-on pastry cap, followed by roast goose liver; the other, to a ground-floor pizzeria with vaulted ceilings painted black with gold stars. ✉ *Fő tér 7–8,* ☎ *99/314–841. AE, DC, MC, V.*

$–$$ ✕ **Várkapu Kávéház.** Tiny glass chandeliers and marble-top tables grace this spacious café-cum-restaurant. Besides espresso and fresh pastries, the offerings center on traditional Hungarian fare, such as *köményes sertésült zsemlegombóccal* (roast pork with caraway seeds and with dumplings on the side). ✉ *Hátsókapu u. 3,* ☎ *99/340–095. No credit cards.*

$$$ ✕🏨 **Palatinus Hotel.** The location of this central hotel couldn't be better—it's within easy reach of every important sight. The interior shows its 1980s heritage; rooms are simply furnished with low wooden beds and generic carpeting. At press time, however, extensive renovation was planned; request a newly renovated room for optimal comfort. The staff is friendly and multilingual. Breakfast is served in the Palatinus's popular, informal restaurant, which prepares fresh, traditional Hungarian offerings all day. ✉ *Új u. 23, H-9400,* ☎ FAX *99/311–395. 25 rooms with shower, 4 suites. Restaurant, travel services. AE, DC, MC, V.*

$$$$ ★ 🏨 **Hotel Sopron.** On a hill just above the city core, this classy, modern hotel built in the early 1980s is blessed with gorgeous views of Sopron's steeples and rooftops. Rooms have contemporary furnishings; those on the first two floors have balconies. Unless you prefer looking at the cemetery behind the hotel, request a room with a city view. Only the suites have air-conditioning. ✉ *Fövényverem u. 7, H-9400,* ☎ *99/314–254,* FAX *99/311–090. 106 rooms, 6 suites. Restaurant, bar,* *air-conditioning (some), pool, sauna, 2 tennis courts, exercise room, bicycles, solarium, playground, meeting room. AE, DC, MC, V.*

$$$$ **Pannonia Med Hotel.** In the 17th century, the Golden Hind Inn stood here, welcoming stagecoach travelers on their journeys between Vienna and Budapest. Leveled by a fire, the inn was rebuilt in elegant neoclassical style in 1893 to become the Pannonia Med Hotel. More than a century later, its public areas continue to shine, with soaring ceilings and delicate chandeliers. Decor in most standard guest rooms is disappointingly less inspiring, with comfortable but simple furnishings; the suites and some standard rooms, however, are furnished in period style, some with reproduction antiques. ✉ *Várkerület 75, H-9400,* ☎ *99/312–180,* FAX *99/340–766. 48 rooms, 14 suites. Restaurant, bar, air-conditioning, beauty salon, pool, sauna, exercise room, spa, solarium, meeting rooms, free parking. AE, DC, MC, V.*

Nightlife and the Arts

From mid- to late March, Sopron's cultural life warms up during the annual **Tavaszi Fesztivál** (Spring Festival), offering classical concerts, folk-dance performances, and other events. Peak season for cultural events is from mid-June through mid-July, when the **Sopron Ünnepi Hetek** (Sopron Festival Weeks) brings music, dance, and theater performances and art exhibits to churches and venues around town. Contact Tourinform (☞ Visitor Information, *below*) or the Theater and Festival Office (✉ Széchenyi tér 17–18, ☎ 99/511–730) for details.

Outdoor Activities and Sports

The forested hills of the Fertő-Hanság National Park around Sopron have many well-marked hiking trails. Ask for a map and advice at the tourist office (☞ Visitor Information, *below*).

Shopping

Várkerület is Sopron's main shopping street.

Herend Village Pottery (✉ Új u. 5, ☎ 99/338–546) sells high-quality Herend ceramics hand-painted with tiny blue flowers and other cheerful, colorful patterns.

If you can't wait to shop at the less expensive factory outlet in Pécs (☞ *below*), you can purchase exquisite Zsolnay porcelain at the **Zsolnay Márkabolt** (✉ Előkapu u. 11, ☎ 99/311–367), a tiny room lined with glass cabinets displaying the delicate wares.

En Route ★ Twenty-seven kilometers (17 mi) southeast of Sopron in Fertőd, the magnificent yellow Baroque **Eszterházy Palace,** built in 1720–1760 as a residence for the Hungarian noble family, is prized as one of the country's most exquisite palaces. Though badly damaged in World War II, it has been painstakingly restored, making it clear why in its day it was referred to as the Hungarian Versailles. Its 126 rooms include a lavish Hall of Mirrors and a three-story-high concert hall, where classical concerts are held in summer (usually Saturday at 6 PM). Joseph Haydn, court conductor to the Eszterházy family here for 30 years, is the subject of a small museum inside. Slippers—mandatory, to preserve the palace floors—are provided at the entrance. ✉ *Bartók Béla u. 2, Fertőd (just off Rte. 85),* ☎ *99/370–971.* *700 Ft.* ⏲ *Mid-Mar.–mid-Oct., Tues.–Sun. 9–5; mid-Oct.–mid-Mar., Tues.–Sun. 9–4.*

Kőszeg

68 *45 km (28 mi) south of Sopron.*

Clustered at an altitude of 886 ft in the forested hills near the Austrian border, Kőszeg is Hungary's highest and also one of its most enchanting little cities. Justly called the "jewel box of Hungary," Kőszeg is a living postcard of quiet cobblestone streets winding among Gothic and Baroque houses, with picturesque church steeples and a castle tower rising up in between.

Continually quarreled over by the Austrians and Hungarians, Kőszeg, established in 1263, was designed with an eye to defense—a moat, a drawbridge, thick ramparts, and a 14th-century fortified castle were essential to its survival. It was from this castle in 1532 that a few hundred Hungarian peasant soldiers beat back a Turkish army of nearly 200,000 and forced Sultan Suleiman I to abandon his attempt to conquer Vienna. To celebrate Christianity's narrow escape, the bells of Kőszeg's churches and castle toll every day at 11 AM, the hour the Turks turned tail.

Music, too, reigned in Kőszeg: Haydn spent many of his creative years here as court composer to the Eszterházys; Franz Liszt gave a concert in 1846 in what is now just the shabby shell of Kőszeg's grandiose but beloved Ballhouse.

Jézus Szíve Plébánia Templom (Sacred Heart Church) is a creamy neo-Gothic concoction by Viennese architect Ludwig Schöne. Erected between 1892 and 1894, it is reminiscent both of Vienna's St. Stephen's Cathedral (for its mosaic roof and spires) and, inside, of Venice's San Marco (for the candy-stripe pillars supporting its three naves). While the church is generally open daily from 8 AM to 8 PM (until 6 in the off-season, roughly Oct.–May), it is only accessible during mass. If you come to see the interior during a service, you must remain in the back of the church; there's usually a small window of opportunity just after morning mass (which ends at 8:30) to explore the whole interior. A small admission may be charged. ✉ *Fő tér at Várkör,* ☎ *94/360–121.*

Szent Jakab templom (St. James Church) is the treasure of the city. St. James dates much further back than its 18th-century Baroque facade and even beyond its Gothic interior; in fact, it is the oldest church in Kőszeg. Inside are astonishingly well preserved 15th-century wall paintings, one of the Virgin Mary with mantle (painted, in fresco technique, on wet plaster) and one of a giant St. Christopher (painted *al secco,* on dry wall). If a mass is taking place when you arrive, it's best to wait outside until it's over. ✉ *Jurisics tér at Rajnis u.* 🎫 *Free.* ⏲ *Daily 9–6.*

Right next to St. James Church is the smaller **Szent Imre templom** (St. Emerich's Church). If you're wondering why two landmarks serving the same purpose were planted side by side, they symbolize Kőszeg's ethnic mix, formed over the centuries by Hungarian tribes moving west and by Germans expanding to the east. Not long after the Counter Reformation, St. Emerich's Church converted to Catholicism and replaced many of its Protestant trappings with Baroque furnishings, most notably a high altar flanked by vivid statues of St. Stephen inviting and St. Ladislas defending the Virgin Mary. ✉ *Jurisics tér at Chernel u.* 🎫 *Free.* ⏲ *Daily 8:30–6.*

Jurisics tér (Jurisics Square) was named after the Croatian captain Miklós Jurisics, who commanded Kőszeg's dramatic defense against the Turks in 1532. Like other fine squares in this part of Hungary, this one is not square but triangular.

On one side of Jurisics tér is a sprightly Gothic dowager of a **Városház** (city hall), dressed for a midsummer ball with cream- and cinnamon-color stripes skirting the ground floor; the upper level is decorated with fresco medallions of the Kőszeg, Hungarian, and Jurisics crests, painted in 1712. Inside the front door is a surprising courtyard whose brown window frames contrast with walls painted cool white, reminiscent of a Hungarian *csárda* (inn). The interior is not open to the public. ✉ *Jurisics tér 8.*

Jurisics Square converges on the handsome **Hősi kapu** (Heroes' Gate), whose imposing tower's Renaissance-Gothic facade belies its fairly recent construction, in 1932, to celebrate the 400th anniversary of the Turkish siege. This historic victory is commemorated in relief inside the portal, where another relief mourns Kőszeg's loss of life in World War I, a defeat that also cost the city two-thirds of its market for textiles and agriculture after the breakup of the Austro-Hungarian Empire. The observation tower affords fine views. ✉ *Jurisics tér 6,* ☎ *94/360–240.* 🎫 *120 Ft.* ⏲ *Apr.–Oct., Tues.–Sun. 10–5.*

The **Sgraffitó ház** dates to the Renaissance, when sgraffito was still a respectable art form. It now houses a funky pizzeria with live music every other Thursday night. ✉ *Jurisics tér 7.*

NEED A BREAK? In the town's historic wine district, it's only fitting to raise a glass or two at the **Kőszeg Szöllő Termelői Szövetkezete Borozója** (Kőszeg Vintners Association Winery; ✉ Rajnis u. 10), in the cellar of a 15th-century Gothic house. It's usually closed on Monday.

The **Jurisics Vár** (Jurisics Castle), which you enter by crossing two former moats, is named not for the nobility who have inhabited it over the years but for the Croatian captain Miklós Jurisics, who commanded its victorious defense against the Turks in 1532. In the first enclosure are a youth hostel, a bathhouse where the local brass band rehearses, and a modern (1963) statue of the heroic Jurisics. One of the most interesting exhibits in the **Jurisics Miklós Vármúzeum** (Jurisics Castle Museum), which has exhibits on the city's and the castle's histories, is the "Book of the Vine's Growth," a chronicle kept for more than a century and a half, starting in 1740, by a succession of town clerks whose duty was to trace the sizes and shapes of vine buds on April 24 of each year. The tradition is still played out the same time every year. ✉ *Rájnis József u. 9,* ☎ *94/360–240.* 🎫 *120 Ft. (plus 40 Ft. to visit the castle grounds)* ⏲ *Tues.–Sun. 10–5.*

Dining and Lodging

$–$$ ✕ **Kulacs Vendéglő.** This informal eatery is popular for its central location near Fő tér, its home-style fare, and its low prices. Try the *Kulacs pecsenye* (roast meat "Canteen"-style), which, in a rare development for Hungarian fare (but perhaps a sign of changing times), has incorporated some veggies of late: spareribs covered with fried onions and a gravy now containing steamed broccoli and chopped carrots. Typical Hungarian red-and-white embroidered tablecloths and curtains add a cheerful touch to the small dining room. ✉ *Várkör 12,* ☎ *94/362–318. DC, MC, V.*

$ ✕ **Ibrahim Kávézó.** Named after a Turkish pasha, this small café has a strong Turkish theme, with a red canopy hanging above the tiny bar and bright-blue painted ceilings peppered with bronze studs. The larger back room has a kitschy fountain with a bronze cobra spitting water. Try the venison bourguignonne with potato dumplings, and don't overlook the delicious strudels (they even have blueberry, a rarity in Hungary). ✉ *Fő tér 17,* ☎ *94/360–854. No credit cards.*

$$ 🏨 **Írottkő.** Centrally located on the town's main square, this modern hotel manages to blend in with the neighboring old houses. Its four-story atrium is sleek, and the guest rooms are functional but not so luxurious that you'd want to stay indoors when there's so much to see outside. The staff is friendly and multilingual. ✉ *Fő tér 4, H-9730,* ☎ FAX *94/360–373. 50 rooms with bath or shower. Pub. DC, MC, V.*

$ **Alpokalja Panzió.** On the western edge of town along the highway to Austria, this cheerful chalet-style pension is convenient if you're traveling by car. Clean rooms, whose walls are either white or wooden, are small and sunny. If views are important, be sure to avoid rooms that face the auto yard and train tracks out back. Breakfast is a couple dollars more. ⊠ *Szombathelyi u. 8, H-9730,* ☎ FAX *94/360–056. 27 rooms with shower. Restaurant, billiards. DC, MC, V.*

$ **Szálloda az Arany Strucchoz.** This inn, built in 1718, is now one of the oldest hotels in Hungary. Although it is definitely showing its age, it has an excellent location: on the main square next to the Sacred Heart Church. But for color TVs and recently renovated bathrooms, most of the spacious rooms have wilting, bare-bones furnishings adequate for a decent night's sleep. The corner room with 19th-century Biedermeier furnishings and a balcony looking onto the main square is the prize of the hotel—it and three other rooms with a similar look are just a few dollars more than the standard rooms. ⊠ *Várkör 124, H-9730,* ☎ FAX *94/360–323. 18 rooms with bath or shower. Restaurant. No credit cards.*

Nightlife and the Arts

Kőszeg is anything but a night town. An evening's activity can usually center on dinner and a pre-bedtime stroll. For exact schedule and ticket information on cultural events, contact Savaria Tourist (☞ Visitor Information, *below*).

Each year in late April, music and dance festivities are organized to celebrate the **szöllő rajzolás** (grape drawing), a tradition since 1740 in which the town clerks record the sizes and shapes of the year's vine buds in a special book on April 24. The town's biggest cultural event is the annual **Ost–West Fesztival** (East West Folk Festival) in early June—a weekend of open-air international folk music and dance performances on Fő tér, in the castle courtyard, and throughout the inner town. The grape **harvest** is usually celebrated in late September with a series of woodwind ensemble concerts and a harvest parade.

Pécs

69 *365 km (226 mi) southeast of Kőszeg, 197 km (122 mi) southwest of Budapest.*

The southwest's premier city and the fifth largest in Hungary, Pécs (pronounced *paytch*) is a vibrant, cultured, beautiful city that will leave you aesthetically and intellectually satiated. Pécs went through various incarnations in the course of its long history. The Franks called it Quinque Ecclesiae; the Slavs, Pet Cerkve; and the Hapsburgs, Fünfkirchen; all three names mean "five churches." Today there are many more churches, plus two mosques, and a handsome synagogue. In any language, however, Pécs could just as well be renamed City of Many Museums, for on one square block alone there are seven. (A one-day pass covering most of them can be purchased at any participating museum for about 800 Ft.) Three of them—the Zsolnay, Vasarely, and Csontváry—justify a two- or three-day stay in this sparkling, eclectic city in the Mecsek Hills, just 30 km (19 mi) north of the Croatian border.

At the foot of Széchenyi tér, the grand sloping monumental thoroughfare that is the pride of the city, stands the dainty **Zsolnay Fountain,** a petite Art Nouveau majolica temple guarded by shiny ox-head gargoyles made of green eosin porcelain that gush pure drinking water piped into Pécs via Roman aqueducts. The fountain was built in the early 19th century by the famous Zsolnay family, who pioneered and developed their unique porcelain art here in Pécs.

NEED A BREAK? A short walk down pedestrians-only Király utca, opening from Széchenyi tér, is the **Caflisch Cukrászda** (✉ Király u. 32, ☎ 72/310–391), a cozy, informal café established in 1869—in a building dating to 1789—with tiny round, marble-top tables and small chandeliers. It is open until 10 PM.

Széchenyi tér is crowned by a Turkish oddity that is a tourist's delight: a 16th-century mosque. Dating from the years of Turkish occupation ★ (1543–1686), the mosque is now the Catholic **Belvárosi plébánia templom** (Inner City Parish Church), which you might infer from the cross surmounting a gilded crescent atop the dome. Despite the fierce religious war raging on its walls—Christian statuary and frescoes beneath Turkish arcades and mihrabs (prayer niches)—this church, also referred to as the Gazi Khassim Pasha Jammi, remains the largest and finest relic of Turkish architecture in Hungary. ✉ *Széchenyi tér.* 🎫 *Free.* ⏲ *Mid-Apr.–mid-Oct., Mon.–Sat. 10–4, Sun. 11:30–4; mid-Oct.–mid-Apr., Mon.–Sat. 11–noon, Sun. 11:30–2.*

Occupying the upper floor of the oldest surviving building in Pécs, the ★ **Zsolnay Múzeum** (Zsolnay Museum) dates from 1324 and was built and rebuilt in Romanesque, Renaissance, and Baroque styles over its checkered history. A stroll through its rooms is a merry show-and-tell waltz through a revolution in pottery that started in 1851, when Miklós Zsolnay, a local merchant, bought the site of an old kiln and set up a stoneware factory for his son Ignác to run. Ignác's brother, Vilmos, a shopkeeper with an artistic bent, bought the factory from him in 1863, imported experts from Germany, and, with the help of a Pécs pharmacist for chemical glaze experiments and his daughters for hand painting, created the distinctive, namesake porcelain.

Among the museums's exhibits are Vilmos's early efforts at Delft-blue handmade vases, cups, and saucers; his two-layer ceramics; examples of the gold-brocade rims that became a Zsolnay trademark; and table settings for royal families. Be sure to look up and notice the unusual Zsolnay chandeliers lighting your way. There is a Zsolnay store in the center of Pécs at Jokai tér 2 (☞ Shopping, *below*), where you can purchase a wide selection of ceramics. ✉ *Káptalan u. 2,* ☎ *72/310–172.* 🎫 *250 Ft.* ⏲ *Tues.–Sun. 10–6.*

If you haven't had enough Zsolnay after visiting the Zsolnay Museum, join the groups of tourists (usually German or Hungarian) braving heavily trafficked Zsolnay Vilmos utca to visit the **Zsolnay porcelán gyár** (Zsolnay Porcelain Factory), where gleaming monumental towers and statuary of seemingly pollution-proof porcelain hold their own among giant smokestacks. The factory can be visited by guided tour only, in groups of 10–30. Call the factory or ask Tourinform (☞ Visitor Information, *below*) to help find out when the next group is coming so that you can tag along.

On a hill behind the factory is the ultimate monument to the dynasty's founder, who died in 1900: the **Zsolnay Mausoleum,** with the bones of Vilmos and his wife in a blue ceramic well and, over the doorway, a relief of Vilmos, with disciples resembling his wife, daughters, and son kneeling before him. The mausoleum is open Tuesday–Sunday 11–3. Admission is 400 Ft. Call ahead (☎ 06/309–297–803) for a one-hour tour in English, which runs about 100 Ft. extra per person, proportionally more if there are less than 10 people on hand. ✉ *Zsolnay Vilmos u. 69,* ☎ *72/325–266 factory tour information.* 🎫 *200 Ft. per person, 300 Ft. for a tour in English.*

The pioneer of Op Art (who later settled in France) was born Győző Vásárhelyi in 1908 in the funhouse that is the **Vasarely Múzeum**

(Vasarely Museum). The first hall is a corridor of visual tricks devised by his disciples, at the end of which hangs a hypnotic canvas of shifting cubes by Jean-Pierre Yvaral. Upstairs, the illusions grow profound: A zebra gallops by while chess pieces and blood cells seem to come at you. ✉ *Káptalan u. 3,* ☎ *72/324–822.* 🎫 *250 Ft.* ⏲ *Tues.–Sun. 10–6.*

Another museum on Káptalan Street is the **Endre Nemes Múzeum** (Endre Nemes Museum), with displays (accompanied by English texts) of the ceramics of Vilmos Zsolnay and his followers. Another section of the museum contains a street scene titled *Utca* (street), constructed entirely of white foam plastic by the sculptor Erzsébet Schaár. The people on the street are constructed of gypsum, simple in body structure but with finely drawn heads and faces—see if you can find Marx and Sándor Petőfi, the famous Hungarian poet. ✉ *Káptalan u. 5,* ☎ *72/324–822.* 🎫 *250 Ft.* ⏲ *Apr.–Oct., Tues.–Sun. 10–6; Nov.–Mar., Tues.–Sun. 2–6.*

★ One of the three major galleries in Pécs, the **Csontváry Múzeum** (Csontváry Museum) is just around the corner from its peers; but if you've just left the Vasarely (☞ *above*) and you have the time, it's probably best to wait a day and bring a fresh eye to this next museum. Mihály Tivadar Csontváry Kosztka (1853–1919) was a pharmacist who worked, as he put it, to "catch up with, let alone surpass, the great masters." An early expressionist and forerunner of surrealism, Csontváry influenced Picasso; his work is to be found almost exclusively here and in a room of the Hungarian National Gallery in Budapest.

The paintings in the five rooms of the museum in Pécs are arranged to show Csontváry's progression from soulful portraits to seemingly conventional landscapes executed with decidedly unconventional colors to his 1904 *Temple of Zeus in Athens* (about which Csontváry said, "This is the first painting in which the canvas can no longer be seen"). After a 1905 tryout in Budapest, Csontváry was ready for a 1907 exhibition in Paris, which turned out to be a huge critical success. Not long after finishing his last great epic painting, *Mary at the Well in Nazareth* (1908), megalomania gripped him. Though his canvases grew ever larger, Csontváry finished nothing that he started after 1909 except a patriotic drawing of Emperor Franz Joseph, completed at the start of World War I in 1914. The last room of the exhibit is filled only with sketches. After he died in Budapest in 1919, Csontváry's canvases were about to be reused as furniture covers when a collector from Pécs named Gedeon Gerlóczy rescued them with a ransom of 10,000 Ft. The collection in Pécs is now valued at more than $10 million—2.85 billion forints. ✉ *Janus Pannonius u. 11,* ☎ *72/310–544.* 🎫 *250 Ft.* ⏲ *Tues.–Sun. 10–6.*

★ One of Europe's most magnificent cathedrals is the **Pécs Bazilika** (Pécs Basilica), promoted from cathedral to basilica rank after Pope John Paul II's visit in 1991. At the beginning of the 19th century, Mihály Pollack directed the transformation of the exterior, changing it from Baroque to neoclassical; its interior remained Gothic. Near the end of the century, Bishop Nándor Dulánszky decided to restore the cathedral to its original Árpád-period style—the result is a four-spired monument that has an utterly breathtaking interior frescoed in shimmering golds, silvers, and blues. ✉ *Szent István tér.* 🎫 *250 Ft. (including treasury and crypt), 500 Ft. for full lighting, 1,000 Ft. per person for a guided tour in English.* ⏲ *Apr.–Oct., weekdays 9–5, Sat. 9–2, Sun. 1–5; Nov.–Mar., Mon.–Sat. 10–4, Sat. 10–1, Sun. 1–4.*

In front of Pécs Basilica is a serene little park, just beyond which is the 4th-century **Ókeresztény mauzóleum** (Early Christian Mausoleum), Hungary's largest and most important early Christian mausoleum.

Some of the subterranean crypts and chapels date to its earliest days; the murals on the walls (Adam and Eve, Daniel in the lion's den, the Resurrection) are in remarkably good condition. ✉ *Szent István tér,* ☎ *no phone.* 🎫 *200 Ft.* ⏲ *Tues.–Sun. 10–6.*

OFF THE BEATEN PATH

VILLÁNY – Thirty kilometers (19 mi) south of Pécs, nestled in the low, verdant Villányi Hills, is the town of Villány, center of one of Hungary's most famous wine regions. Villány's exceptional and unique red wines are heralded here and abroad; its burgundies, cabernets, and ports are said to give the best of their French and Italian peers a run for the money. Many wine cellars offer regular wine tastings and sales. Tourinform (☞ Visitor Information, *below*) in Pécs has an informative brochure and listing of cellars. Those who wish to educate themselves before imbibing can stop in the **Bor Múzeum** (Wine Museum; ✉ Bem u. 8, ☎ 72/492–130) for a look at the history of the region's viticulture, which dates back some 2,000 years. The museum is open Tuesday through Sunday 9–5; admission is free.

Dining and Lodging

$$ ✕ **Iparos Kisvendéglő.** The very popular, informal Craftsman restaurant has a wide selection of pork, turkey, chicken, veal, and game dishes, as well as a small selection of fresh salads. ✉ *Rákóczi út 24–26 (follow signs through the courtyard and out back to the entrance),* ☎ *72/333–400. AE, DC, MC, V.*

$–$$ ✕ **Cellárium.** Deep in an ancient cellar dating to Turkish times, this delightful restaurant has a cheerful, youthful atmosphere. The owner's creative touches include dressing the waiters in prison uniforms and putting the extensive, very reasonably priced menu into the form of a small newspaper titled *Cella News,* which guests can take home with them. Adventurous palates may try the "cockballs stew with dill and cottage cheese noodles," a rustic village dish rarely offered in restaurants. ✉ *Hunyadi u. 2,* ☎ *72/314–453. DC, MC, V.*

$–$$ ✕ **Dóm.** This small restaurant on Pécs's pedestrian shopping street is dominated by a giant wood-frame structure designed after the city's basilica. Dark wood pewlike booths and high, frescoed ceilings further the theme. The menu includes Hungarian classics as well as the popular house specialty—a choice of grilled meat on sizzling lava stones. ✉ *Király u. 3 (well into the building's arcade),* ☎ *72/210–088. No credit cards.*

$$$ ★ 🏨 **Hotel Palatinus.** This hotel in the pedestrian zone maintains a good balance between old and new: The building's facade has preserved its traditional look, while the rooms are modern in most every respect (equipped with TVs and telephones), though unexceptional in decor. Best views are from the fifth floor. The hotel's ballroom is stunning. ✉ *Király u. 5, H-7621,* ☎ *72/233–022,* ☎ FAX *72/232–261. 88 rooms, 6 suites. Restaurant, brasserie, massage, sauna, solarium. AE, DC, MC, V.*

$$ 🏨 **Toboz Panzió.** Nestled among the pines high up in the Mecsek Hills, the delightful Pinecone Pension offers forest tranquillity just a short drive or bus ride from downtown or 30 minutes by foot. Hiking trails into the hills begin just behind the house. Rooms are clean and bright, especially those with skylight windows; sizes vary, the largest being on the top floor. ✉ *Fenyves sor 5, H-7635,* ☎ FAX *72/325–232 or 72/210–631. 12 rooms. Breakfast room. MC, V.*

Nightlife and the Arts

NIGHTLIFE

British-style pubs are all the rage in Hungarian city nightlife, and the **John Bull Pub** (✉ Király u. 2, ☎ 72/325–439), part of a successful chain around the country, plays the part well, done up with dark woods and polished brass and amply stocked with Guinness on tap. The **Fregatt Arizona Pub** (✉ Király u. 21, ☎ 72/210–486), with pub-type decor and low vaulted ceilings, is another popular English-style bar with Guinness on tap.

THE ARTS

The **Pécsi Nemzeti Színház** (Pécs National Theater; ✉ Színház tér 1, ☎ 72/211–965) is the main venue for regular performances by the Pécs Symphony Orchestra and the theater's opera and modern ballet companies. The theater is closed from late May until September. **September** brings harvest-related festivities such as classical concerts, folk-music and -dance performances, and a parade or two to venues in and around Pécs. Inquire at Tourinform (☞ Visitor Information, *below*) for specifics. Tourinform publishes a monthly arts and events calendar in English and can help with further schedule and ticket information.

Outdoor Activities and Sports

The **Mecsek Hills** rise up just behind Pécs, with abundant well-marked hiking trails through its forests and fresh air. Guided walks are often organized on weekends by local nature clubs; contact Tourinform (☞ Visitor Information, *below*) for dates and times.

Shopping

Király utca, a vibrant, pedestrians-only street lined with beautifully preserved romantic and Baroque facades, is Pécs's main shopping zone, full of colorful boutiques and outdoor cafés.

The best place in the whole country to buy exquisite Zsolnay porcelain is at the **Zsolnay Márkabolt** (✉ Jókai tér 2, ☎ 72/310–220). As the Zsolnay factory's own outlet, the store offers guaranteed authenticity and the best prices on the full spectrum of pieces—from tea sets profusely painted with colorful, gold-winged butterflies to white-and-night-blue dinner services.

Transdanubia A to Z

Arriving and Departing

BY CAR

From Budapest, you can get to Pannonhalma, Fertőd, and Sopron via the M1 through Győr, switching onto the appropriate secondary route there. Pécs and Budapest are directly connected by Route 6. The M1 runs into Austria, Route 6 to the border of Croatia.

BY TRAIN

There are good rail connections from Budapest to Sopron and Pécs; the trip—by InterCity (IC) trains, which run several times daily—takes 2½ hours to Sopron, 3 to Pécs. Trains to Sopron and Fertőd go north through Győr. There are direct connections between Vienna and Sopron and Bratislava and Győr.

Getting Around

BY BUS

If you're without a car, you'll need to rely on buses to get you to smaller towns such as Pannonhalma, which are not on the rail lines. Regular buses link all of the towns in our coverage. Inquire at tourist offices (☞ Visitor Information, *below*).

BY CAR

Traveling around Transdanubia is done best by car: Except for Pécs, all the towns covered here are fairly short driving distances from one another. Significantly farther south and east, Pécs can be reached from Kőszeg along connecting major secondary roads past the southern tip of the Balaton and through Kaposvár. It's a beautiful drive.

BY TRAIN

Trains connect most of the areas covered. The **Sopron** train station (✉ Vasútállomás, ☎ 99/517–212) is a five-minute walk to the center of town. The trip from Sopron to **Kőszeg** (✉ Alsó krt. 2, ☎ 94/360–053) is not direct; you'd have to change in Szombathely, south of Kőszeg, which sends you a good 30 minutes out of your way. The trip from Sopron to **Pécs** (✉ Indóház tér, ☎ 72/312–443) is quite long—about 1½ hours from Sopron to Szombathely, where you transfer to the train to Pécs, which takes nearly 4½ hours.

Contacts and Resources

VISITOR INFORMATION

Kőszeg: Savaria Tourist (✉ Várkör 69, ☎ FAX 94/360–238). **Pécs: Tourinform** (✉ Széchenyi tér 9, ☎ FAX 72/212–632). **Sopron: Tourinform** (✉ Előkapu u. 11, ☎ 99/338–592, ☎ FAX 338–892).

NORTHERN HUNGARY

Northern Hungary stretches from the Danube Bend, north of Budapest, along the northeastern frontier with Slovakia as far west as Sátoraljaújhely. It is a clearly defined area, marked by several mountain ranges of no great height but of considerable scenic beauty. Most of the peaks reach 3,000 ft and are thickly wooded almost to their summit. Grottoes and caves abound, as well as thermal baths. In the state game reserves, herds of deer, wild boars, and eagles are not uncommon sights.

Historically, the valleys of northern Hungary have always been of considerable strategic importance, as they provided the only access to the Carpathian Mountains. **Eger,** renowned throughout Hungarian history as one of the guardians of these strategic routes, retains its splendor, with many ruins picturesquely dotting the surrounding hilltops. The **Mátra Mountains,** less than 90 km (55 mi) from Budapest, provide opportunities for year-round recreation and are the center for winter sports. Last but not least, this is one of the great wine-growing districts of Hungary, with Gyöngyös and Eger contributing the "Magyar nectar" and Tokaj producing the "wine of kings."

Numbers in the margin correspond to numbers on the Northern Hungary and the Great Plain map.

Hollókő

★ 70 *100 km (62 mi) northeast of Budapest.*

This tiny mountain village close to the Slovakian border was added to the UNESCO list of World Cultural Heritage Sites in 1988 to help preserve its unique medieval structure and age-old Palóc (ethnographic group indigenous to northern Hungary) cultural and handcrafting traditions still practiced today by the village's 400 inhabitants. The most famous of these traditions are those practiced during Easter, when the villagers dress in colorful embroidered costumes. UNESCO's distinction has brought arguably positive and negative elements to Hollókő. The small village has become a popular day-trip tourist destination and has adapted somewhat to that role; for example, the villagers agree to dress in traditional costume on days when bus tours come through.

But Hollókő is authentically enchanting: Old whitewashed houses with hand-carved wooden verandas and awnings cluster together on narrow cobblestone pathways; directly above them loom the hilltop ruins (now being restored) of a 13th-century castle. For information on Hollókő's Easter festivities and other events, contact the village's

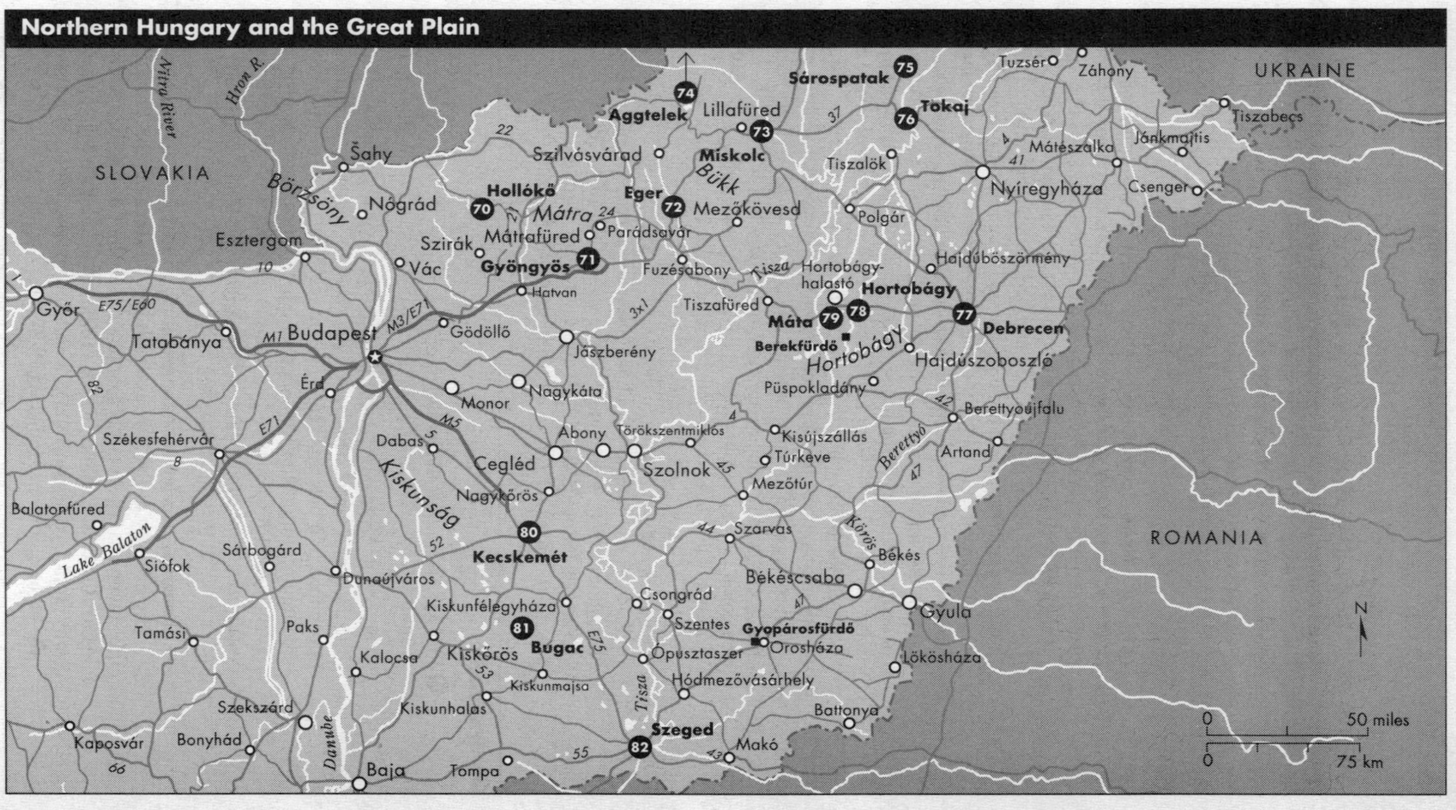
Northern Hungary and the Great Plain
SLOVAKIA
UKRAINE
ROMANIA
Nitra River
Hron R.
Danube
Tisza
Körös
Berettyó
Lake Balaton
Győr
Tatabánya
Esztergom
Börzsöny
Šahy
Nógrád
Vác
Szirák
Hollókő
Mátra
Mátrafüred
Gyöngyös
Hatvan
Gödöllő
Budapest
Érd
Székesfehérvár
Balatonfüred
Siófok
Sárbogárd
Tamási
Kaposvár
Bonyhád
Szekszárd
Paks
Dunaújváros
Kalocsa
Baja
Kiskunhalas
Tompa
Kiskőrös
Kiskunság
Dabas
Monor
Cegléd
Nagykőrös
Kecskemét
Kiskunfélegyháza
Bugac
Kiskunmajsa
Szeged
Makó
Hódmezővásárhely
Ópusztaszer
Csongrád
Szentes
Gyopárosfürdő
Orosháza
Battonya
Békéscsaba
Békés
Gyula
Lőkösháza
Szarvas
Mezőtúr
Túrkeve
Kisújszállás
Püspökladány
Szolnok
Törökszentmiklós
Abony
Nagykáta
Jászberény
Tiszafüred
Füzesabony
Eger
Parádsasvár
Szilvásvárad
Aggtelek
Lillafüred
Miskolc
Bükk
Mezőkövesd
Sárospatak
Tokaj
Tiszalök
Polgár
Hortobágy-halastó
Hortobágy
Máta
Berekfürdő
Debrecen
Hajdúszoboszló
Berettyóújfalu
Artánd
Hajdúböszörmény
Nyíregyháza
Mátészalka
Tuzsér
Záhony
Jánkmajtis
Csenger
Tiszabecs
M1
M3/E71
M5
E71
E75
E75/E60
0 50 miles
0 75 km
N

cultural foundation **Hollókőért közalapítvány** (✉ Kossuth u. 68, H-3176, ☎ FAX 32/379–266).

Dining

$–$$ ✕ **Muskátli Vendéglő.** Named for the bright red and pink flowers lining its windowsills, the "Geranium Restaurant" is a cozy little eatery on Hollókő's main street. Specialties include *Palócgulyás,* a rich local goulash thick with chunks of pork and beans, and *Nógrádi palócpecsenye,* pork cutlets smothered in mustard-garlic sauce. ✉ *Kossuth út 61,* ☎ *32/379–262. AE, DC, MC, V. Closed Mon., and Mon.–Wed. Jan.–Feb.*

OFF THE BEATEN PATH

KASTÉLY SZIRÁK (Szirák Castle) – About 35 km (22 mi) along Route 21 and then some lovely side roads from Hollókő's small cluster of homes is this stately, Baroque castle. Built in 1748 on the foundations of a 13th-century knights' hostel, it was the home of Count József Teleki, an arts patron who created a vast library and had the main hall covered with frescoes depicting Ovid's *Metamorphoses*. The castle was seized by the Russian military in 1944; most of the contents were destroyed as they turned it into a military hospital. Thirty-three years later, restoration began, and now this is one of the country's best castle hotels. Antiques (if not the originals) fill the rooms, and in Count Teleki's own three-room suite, you can see the door to his secret stairway into the backyard and gaze out the window at the centuries-old Japanese acacia tree. The "honeymoon room" is unfortunately situated directly off the lobby; it is not recommended for those seeking true privacy. A newer wing houses the "tourist hotel," comprising bland, dated units that share nothing of the castle's aura. Double rooms in the main castle building cost about $60 per night (suites cost around $74); doubles in the newer wing run roughly $40 per night. All rates include breakfast. If you'd just like to peek at the castle's interior, a docent will (for a tip) show you the main hall, where the frescoes have been beautifully restored. You can also go horseback riding, even if you're not a guest. ✉ *Petőfi út 26, H–3044 Szirák,* ☎ FAX *60/353–053. 21 rooms, 4 suites. Restaurant, sauna, tennis court, horseback riding, meeting rooms. AE, DC, MC, V.*

Gyöngyös

71 *40 km (25 mi) southeast of Hollókő, 75 km (46 mi) northeast of Budapest.*

The city of Gyöngyös, famous for its excellent wines (don't pass up the chance to sample the *Debrői hárslevelű,* a magnificent white wine produced in a nearby village), lies at the base of the volcanic Mátra mountain range, Hungary's best-developed mountain vacation area. Early in the 1960s huge lignite deposits were discovered, and the large-scale mines and power stations established since then have changed the character of the entire region.

Although it offers few reasons to linger in its own right, Gyöngyös serves as the gateway to the Mátras and is a good starting point for visiting the many beautiful resorts that lie just north of it. The best known is Mátrafüred, at 1,300 ft, which can be reached by narrow-gauge railway from Gyöngyös. Just a few miles from Mátrafüred is Kékestető, the highest point in Hungary (3,327 ft).

Among the chief sights of the town is the 15th-century **Szent Bertalan templom** (Church of St. Bartholomew), on Fő tér. It is one of Hungary's largest Gothic churches and was beautifully restored in the mid-1990s. Next to the altar is a 16th-century bronze baptismal font; there's also a newly uncovered fresco of King Károly IV's visit to Gyöngyös after a serious fire. ✉ *Fő tér; treasury: Szent Bertalan út 3,* ☎ *37/311–143 treasury.* 🎫 *Church free, treasury 50 Ft.* ⏲ *Church daily 7–4; treasury Tues.–Sun. 10–noon and 2–4.*

The **Mátra Múzeum** (Mátra Museum), in a handsome neoclassical mansion, provides a helpful preparation for excursions into the Mátras with its extensive exhibits on the flora and fauna of the region, as well as geological and historical displays. In addition to hearing recorded sounds of indigenous bird songs, you can examine deer, eagles, and other fauna you may encounter, as well as those you'll be luckier to avoid, such as the sharp-tusked wild boar. Also on display is "Bruno," the hulking 1- to 2-million-year-old skeleton of a young mammoth found in the northern Mátra. Unless you're a fan of dank cellars filled with snakes and bugs (and their smell), avoid the "Mikro-varium" exhibit downstairs. ✉ *Kossuth Lajos u. 40,* ☎ *37/311–447.* 🎫 *200 Ft.* ⏲ *Mar.–Oct., Tues.–Sun. 9–5; Nov.–Feb., Tues.–Sun. 10–2.*

Dining and Lodging

$$$$ ✕🏨 **Kastélyhotel Sasvár.** Who among the kids bussed up to the unassuming mountain village of Parádsasvár for children's retreats during the Communist era could have imagined that their worn old hideaway would reopen as a five-star luxury hotel? Nestled deep in the Mátra Hills about 25 km (15 mi) north of Gyöngyös, the Sasvár Castle Hotel, opened in December 1998, is in an early 19th-century mansion, expanded in 1882 in German Renaissance style by virtuoso architect Miklós Ybl. Majestic details include a soaring steeple sublimely topped off by a spire; a minaretlike tower; and a spacious, colonnaded courtyard flanked on three sides by the hotel's low wings. The sparkling rooms, which look out either onto sloping forests, the courtyard, or the quiet road leading past the village, have neo-Renaissance or neo-Baroque furnishings; the suites also include hot tubs and saunas. The Aquila Restaurant's award-winning head chef creates specialties such as fresh trout from nearby Szilvásvárad and pheasant breast with goose liver slices and wild rice. Set in a six-acre park surrounded by a high-security fence, with towering spruce trees in front and a tiny pond in back, the complex has the feel of a fortress—reinforced by the hotel guard, who allows non-guests to explore the property provided they pay the 3,000-Ft. grounds fee. ✉ *Kossuth u. 1, H–3242 Parádsasvár,* ☎ *36/444–444,* FAX *36/544–010. 54 rooms, 5 suites. Restaurant, 1 indoor pool, 1 outdoor pool, hot tub, sauna, steam baths, tennis courts, bowling, squash, bowling alley, solarium, baby-sitting, meeting rooms. MC, V.*

Outdoor Activities and Sports

Make a stop at the Eger Tourinform office (☞ Visitor Information, *below*) for maps, books, and advice about the area's rich outdoor offerings.

BICYCLING

Avar Túrakerékpár Klub (✉ Bene út 33, Gyöngyös, ☎ FAX 37/–309–116), a good source for bicycle rental and touring information, organizes custom-designed bicycle tours for all abilities. From mid-May through late August it holds regular Saturday afternoon trips open to all; call ahead for details. Contact Tourinform (☞ Visitor Information, *below*) for bike-rental information.

HIKING

Mátrafüred and Mátraháza are popular starting points for hikes up Kékestető, Hungary's highest peak. Views from the TV and lookout tower are phenomenal. Don't expect to find yourself alone with only the rushing wind at the top of the peak; it's actually somewhat developed, with a couple of hotels where you can spend a night dozing in one of the highest beds in Hungary.

En Route Route 24 is the scenic route between Gyöngyös and Eger, climbing and twisting through the Mátras. You can pause in **Sirok** to snap a photo of its castle ruins, piled high on a hill looming over the village.

Eger

★ 72 *40 km (25 mi) east of Gyöngyös.*

With vineyard surroundings and more than 175 of Hungary's historic monuments—a figure surpassed only by Budapest and Sopron—the picturebook Baroque city of Eger is ripe for exploration. Lying in a fertile valley between the Mátra Mountains and their eastern neighbor, the Bükk range, Eger bears witness to much history, heartbreak, and glory. It was settled quite early in the Hungarian conquest of the land, and it was one of five bishoprics created by King Stephen I when he Christianized the country almost a millennium ago.

In 1552 the city was attacked by the Turks, but the commander, István Dobó, and fewer than 2,000 men and women held out for 38 days against 80,000 Turkish soldiers and drove them away. One of Hungary's great legends tells of the women of Eger pouring hot pitch onto the heads of the Turks as they attempted to scale the castle walls (the event is depicted in a famous painting now in the National Gallery in Budapest). Despite such heroism, however, Eger fell to the Turks in 1596 and became one of the most important northern outposts of Muslim power until its reconquest in 1687.

Today, Eger's cobblestone streets are ripe for strolling and sightseeing, lined with restored Baroque and rococo buildings. Wherever you wander, make a point of peeking into open courtyards, where you're likely to happen upon otherwise hidden architectural gems.

The grand, neoclassical **Bazilika** (basilica), the second-largest cathedral in Hungary, was built in the center of town early in the 19th century. It is approached by a stunning stairway flanked by statues of saints Stephen, László, Peter, and Paul—the work of Italian sculptor Marco Casagrande, who also carved 22 biblical reliefs inside and outside the building. From May 15 through October 15, organ recitals are given Monday through Saturday at 11:30 AM and Sunday at 12:45 PM. It's best to visit when no masses are being held—from 9 until 6. ✉ *Eszterházy tér,* ☎ *36/316–592.* 🎫 *Free.* ⏲ *Daily 5:30 AM–7:30 PM.*

The square block of a Baroque building opposite the basilica is a former lyceum, now the **Eszterházy Károly főiskola** (Károly Eszterházy Teachers College). The handsome library has a fine trompe-l'oeil ceiling fresco that gives an intoxicating illusion of depth. High up in the structure's six-story observatory, now a museum, is a horizontal sundial with a tiny gold cannon, which, when filled with gunpowder, used to let out a burst at exactly high noon. Also, the noonday sun, shining through a tiny aperture, makes a palm-size silvery spot on the meridian line on the marble floor. Climb higher to the "Specula Periscope" grand finale: In a darkened room a man manipulates three rods of a periscope—in operation since 1776—to project panoramic views of Eger onto a round table. Children squeal with delight as real people and cars hurry and scurry across the table like hyperactive Legos. ✉ *Eszterházy tér 1,* ☎ *36/410–466.* 🎫 *330 Ft. for both library and museum; on request, half-price for museum only.* ⏲ *Mid-Apr.–Sept., Tues.–Sun. 9:30–3; mid-Mar.–mid-Apr. and Oct.–Dec. 20, Tues.–Fri. 9:30–1, weekends 9:30–noon; Jan.–mid-Mar., weekends 9:30–noon.*

Eger's rococo **Cistercia templom** (Cistercian Church), closed for many years, has been reclaimed by the order and can be visited during mass on weekdays (held at 7:15 AM and 8 AM) and on Sunday (held at 7 AM, 8 AM, and 10 AM and 7 PM); other times it can be viewed through a locked gate. The church was built during the first half of the 18th century. Its main altar (1770) is dominated by a splendid statue of St. Francis Borgia kneeling beneath Christ on the cross. ✉ *Széchenyi u. 15,* ☎ *36/313–496.* 🎫 *Free.* ⏲ *Mon.–Sat. 7:15 AM–6 PM, Sun. 7 AM–8 PM.*

NEED A BREAK? On Eger's central pedestrian street, the **Dobos Cukrászda** (✉ Széchenyi u. 6, ☎ 36/413–335) is a great spot to revive wearied sightseers with the house specialty, *Dobos Bomba* (chocolate-covered cake).

The **Nagypréposti palota** (Provost's House), on Kossuth Lajos utca, is a small rococo palace still considered one of Hungary's finest mansions despite abuse by the Red Army (soldiers ruined several frescoes by heating the building with oil). The Provost's House now serves as European headquarters of the International Committee of Historic Towns (ICOMOS) and is, alas, not open regularly to the public. ✉ *Kossuth Lajos u. 4.*

During a brief stay in Eger (1758–1761), German artist Henrik Fazola graced many buildings with his work, but none so exquisitely as the wrought-iron twin gates that, facing each other just inside the entryway of the **Megye Ház** (County Council Hall), frame the inner entrances to the building's two wings. Sent to Paris in 1889 for the international exposition, the richly ornamented, mirror-image gates—which have not only numerous flowers and leaves, but clusters of grapes and a stork with a snake in its beak—won a gold medal 130 years after their creation. On the wall to the right of the building's street entrance, note the sign that indicates the level of floodwaters during the flooding of the Eger stream on August 31, 1878. In fact, if you stay alert, you will see similar signs throughout this area of the city. ✉ *Kossuth Lajos u. 9,* ☎ *36/312–744.* 🎫 *Free.* ⏲ *Apr.–Oct., Tues.–Sun. 9–5.*

Eger Vár (Eger Castle), now a haunting ruin, was built after the devastating Tartar invasion of 1241–1242; when Béla IV returned from exile in Italy, he ordered the erection of mighty fortresses like those he had seen in the west. Within the castle walls, an imposing Romanesque cathedral was built and then, during the 15th century, rebuilt in Gothic style; today only its foundations remain. Inside the foundation area, a statue of Szent István (St. Stephen), erected in 1900, looks out benignly over the city. Nearby are catacombs that were built in the second half of the 16th century by Italian engineers. By racing back and forth through this labyrinth of underground tunnels and appearing at various ends of the castle, the hundreds of defenders tricked the attacking Turks into thinking there were thousands of them. The Gothic-style **Püspök Ház** (Bishop's House) contains the castle history museum and, in the basement, a numismatic museum where coins can be minted and certified (in English). There is also an art gallery, displaying Italian and Dutch Renaissance works. A prison exhibit is near the main entrance. English-speaking guides are often available at the castle ticket booth, but it's best to call ahead and request one; group tours in English cost roughly 300 Ft. per person. ✉ *Dózsa György tér,* ☎ *36/312–744.* 🎫 *Museums (including general castle admission) 300 Ft.; castle grounds 120 Ft. Photography fee (no flash) 300 Ft. per camera. No videotaping.* ⏲ *Castle grounds Apr.–Oct., daily 6 AM–8 PM; Nov.–Mar., daily 6–5. Museums Apr.–Aug. and Nov.–Feb., Tues.–Sun. 8–5; Sept., Tues.–Sun. 8–7; Mar. and Oct., Tues.–Sun. 8–6. Prison exhibit and catacombs Apr.–Sept., Tues.–Sun. 9–5 (catacombs remain open on Mon.).*

Downtown, picturesque **Dobó tér** is marked by two intensely animated statues produced in the early 20th century by a father and son: *Dobó the Defender* is by Alajos Stróbl; the sculpture of a Magyar battling two Turks, by Stróbl's son, Zsigmond Kisfaludi-Stróbl. Their works flank the **Minorita templom** (Minorite Church), which with its twin spires and finely carved pulpit, pews, and organ loft, is considered one of the best Baroque churches in Central Europe. *Church: ☎ 36/313–304. Free. Daily 10–5.*

A bridge over the Eger stream—it's too small to be classified as a river—leads to an early 17th-century Turkish **minaret,** from the top of which Muslims were called to prayer; this is the northernmost surviving Turkish building in Europe. ✉ *Knézich K. u. 80 Ft. Apr.–Oct., daily 10–6.*

Eger wine is renowned beyond Hungary. The best-known variety is *Egri Bikavér* (Bull's Blood of Eger), a full-bodied red wine. Other outstanding vintages are the *Medoc Noir,* a dark red dessert wine; *Leányka,* a delightful dry white; and the sweeter white *Muskotály.* The place to sample them is the **Szépasszony-völgy,** a vineyard area within Eger's city limits. Some 250 small wine cellars (some of them literally holes-in-the-wall and most of them now private) stand open and inviting in the warm weather, and a few are there in winter, too. You may be given a tour of the cellar, and wines will be tapped from the barrel into your glass by the vintner himself at the tiniest cost (but it's prudent to inquire politely how much it will cost before imbibing).

OFF THE BEATEN PATH

SZILVÁSVÁRAD – About 25 km (16 mi) from Eger up into the Bükk Mountains brings you to this village, one of Hungary's most important equestrian centers. For more than 500 years, the white Lipizzaner horses have been bred here, and every year on a weekend in early September they prance and pose in the **Lipicai Lovasfesztivál,** an international carriage-driving competition held in the equestrian stadium. At other times, you can see them grazing in the village fields and also familiarize yourself with their proud history at the **Lipicai Múzeum** (Lipizzaner Museum; ✉ Park u. 8, ☎ 36/355–155; 80 Ft.; Apr.–Oct., Tues.–Sun. 9–noon and 2–4). Szilvásvárad is also a popular base from which to take advantage of the excellent hiking and biking opportunities through the surrounding gentle green hills of Bükk National Park (☞ Outdoor Activities and Sports, *below*).

Dining and Lodging

$$ ✕ **Fehér Szarvas.** The name of this rustic cellar adjoining the Hotel Park (☞ *below*) means "white stag," and game is the uncontested specialty: favorites include venison fillet served in a pan sizzling with chicken liver, sausage, and herb butter; and wild boar cutlet with mushrooms, basil-spiced cabbage, and potato croquettes mixed with almonds. The skulls and skins hanging from rafters and walls make the inn look like Archduke Franz Ferdinand's trophy room. ✉ *Klapka György u. 8, ☎ 36/411–129. AE, MC, V. No lunch.*

$–$$ ★ ✕ **Efendi Vendéglő.** In an arched basement room a few doors away from Eger's castle gate, this restaurant continues the tradition that made its predecessor, the Talizmán, a regional favorite: excellent food. The atmosphere is "modern-medieval-romantic"—candlelit tables among floral landscape paintings interspersed with a bit of medieval weaponry. A favorite on the menu, available in English, is *legényfogó leves* (wedding soup or, literally, "catcher of young men"). Made with meat, vegetables, cream, and liver, this stew is one of the lures that Hungarian girls have used for centuries to attract potential husbands. ✉ *Kossuth Lajos u. 19, ☎ 36/410–323. Reservations recommended. AE, DC, MC, V.*

$ ✕ **HBH Bajor Sörház.** Although designed to look like a Bavarian beer tavern, this place does not reek of hops or smoke. Instead, it's a lovely family restaurant decorated with sepia photos of old Eger. Specialties include a tart oxtail soup, served family style in a silver tureen, and the *sörivó kedvence* (Beer Drinker's Delight)—a pork cutlet stuffed with pig's brains and baked in a beer-batter crust. Both go well with the Munich Hofbräuhaus beer, which gives the restaurant its initials. ✉ *Bajcsy Zsilinszky u. 19 (on Dobó tér),* ☎ *36/316–312. AE, DC, MC, V.*

$$$ ★ **Hotel Eger & Park.** Two very different hotels share the same phone number and a connecting passageway but have separate addresses around the corner from each other. The Park is an old-fashioned grand hotel, very genteel, with spacious rooms; it usually closes from November through March. The Eger, built in 1982, looks like a monstrous honeycomb from the outside, but is more tastefully and imaginatively modern inside; it's open year-round. Guests are free to use the facilities of both hotels. ✉ *Park: Klapka György u. 8, H-3300; Eger: Szálloda u. 1–3, H-3300.* ☎ *36/413–233,* FAX *36/413–114. 161 rooms, 4 suites. 3 restaurants, 2 bars, pool, sauna, 2 tennis courts, bowling, health club, billiards, solarium, laundry service, meeting rooms. AE, DC, MC, V.*

$$–$$$ ★ **Hotel Senator Ház.** This little inn sits on Eger's main square in a lovely 18th-century town house. Rooms are bright and clean, decorated in pale tans and whites, and come equipped with large-hotel amenities, such as hair dryers and minibars. The miniature lobby, furnished with leather chairs and antiques, feels like a cozy, elegant study. ✉ *Dobó tér 11, H-3300,* ☎ *36/411–711,* ☎ FAX *36/320–466. 11 rooms. Restaurant, air-conditioning, free parking. AE, MC, V.*

$$ **Minaret.** Although this modern hotel stands in contrast to the neighboring 17th-century Turkish tower, it manages to look as though it has been here forever. Rooms are nothing special, with dark-brown basic furnishings and brown-and-gray industrial carpeting, but the location and price (at the low end of this category) are excellent and the atmosphere friendly and informal. A tiny outdoor pool is an unusual touch for such a central hotel. ✉ *Knézich Károly u. 4, H-3300,* ☎ *36/410–233 or 36/410–020,* ☎ FAX *36/410–473. 42 rooms with shower. Restaurant, pool. AE, MC, V.*

$–$$ **Garten Vendégház.** Named after its profusion of lilacs, geraniums, and acacias, this informal, family-run pension sits atop a quiet, rural hill, a 10-minute walk from Eger's main square. Rooms here are clean, bright, and rich with pine furnishings; all have TVs but no telephones. The suites, with eat-in kitchens, are great for families. The cheerful owners, Olga and Sanyi, can arrange tennis at the neighboring courts. You can request rates with or without breakfast. ✉ *Legányi u. 6, H-3300,* ☎ *36/320–371. 7 rooms, 2 suites. Breakfast room. No credit cards.*

Nightlife and the Arts

Old Jack's Pub (✉ Rákóczi út 28, ☎ 36/425–050) is a popular English-style pub just outside the center of town.

From June to mid-September live **bands** sometimes play folk music for free out on Kis Dobó tér, part of Eger's main square. The **Agria Nyári Játékok** (Agria Summer Festival) and associated "Agria" events run from July to early September, featuring folk-dance and theater performances as well as concerts of musical genres from Renaissance to jazz to laser karaoke. Performances are held in various locations. For information, contact Tourinform (☞ Visitor Information, *below*). For two weeks every summer, beginning around late July, **Ünnepi Hetek a Barokk Egerben** (Festival Weeks in Baroque Eger) is held, a cultural festival offering classical concerts, dance programs, and more in Eger's venues and streets and squares. In early September, the three- to four-day **Szüreti Kulturális Napok Egerben** (Eger Harvest Cultural Festival) celebrates the grape harvest with a traditional harvest parade through the town center, ample wine tastings in the main squares, appearances by the crowned Wine Queen, and an outdoor Harvest Ball on Dobó tér.

Outdoor Activities and Sports

BICYCLING

The forested hills of the Bükk National Park around the village of Szilvásvárad, north of Eger, comprise some of the country's most popular mountain-biking terrain. Rentals, maps, route advice, and tour guides are available at Csaba Tarnai's **Mountain Bike Kölcsönző** (⊠ Szalajka-völgy út, at the entrance to Bükk National Park in Szilvásvárad, Szalajka Valley, ☎ 60/352–695).

HIKING

Bükk National Park, just north of Eger, has plenty of well-marked, well-used trails. The most popular excursions begin in the village of Szilvásvárad. Tourinform (☞ Visitor Information, *below*) can give you a hiking map and suggest routes according to the level of difficulty and duration.

HORSEBACK RIDING

A famous breeding center of the prized white Lipizzaner horses, the village of Szilvásvárad (☞ Off the Beaten Path, *above*) is the center of the region's horse culture. If you'd like to do some riding, contact **Kovács Péter Lovardája** (Peter Kovács's Stable; ⊠ Egri út 62, Szilvásvárad, ☎ 36/355–343). In Eger, the stables at the **Mátyus Udvarház** (⊠ off Noszvaji út, ☎ 36/312–804) can accommodate your every equestrian need. Hourly rates in the area run around 2,000 Ft. for taking the reins into your own hands outdoors. A one-hour carriage ride for up to three people runs about 4,000 Ft.

SWIMMING

Eger's **Strandfürdő** (open-air baths; ⊠ Petőfi Sándor tér 2, ☎ 36/412–202) are set in a vast, lovely park in the center of town. You can pick where to plunge from among six pools of varying sizes, temperatures, and curative powers.

Miskolc

73 *63 km (39 mi) northeast of Eger.*

East of the Bükk Mountains lies industrial Miskolc, the third-largest city (population 200,000) in Hungary. A sprawling city cluttered with factories and industrial plants (many of them now idle), Miskolc is often maligned as one of the country's least desirable places to visit. Yet it contains some interesting Baroque buildings, as well as the medieval castle of Diósgyőr, clashing yet coexisting with the housing projects and traffic that surround it. And one of Miskolc's prime, unexpected assets is the nearby beautiful countryside. As you travel west toward Lillafüred, past behemoth factories and plants, it's hard not to be wary of just what sort of countryside lies ahead; but almost immediately after passing the LEAVING MISKOLC sign and just before despair settles in, the scenery changes dramatically: The tree-covered hills of the Bükk range rise and crowd together as the road curves up and around them.

The regal, ruined stone body of **Diósgyőri Vár** (Diósgyőr Castle) stands exposed in the midst of Miskolc's urban clamor, as if trapped in a land that was long taken over by an entirely new reality. With four mighty towers, Diósgyőr Castle is considered one of Hungary's most beautiful medieval castles. Built between the mid-13th and late 14th centuries, it was originally a retreat for King Louis I, of the Angevin dynasty, but was later adopted by the queens (the castle is also known as Queen's

Castle). The opening hours can be erratic in winter; it's best to call ahead. ✉ *Vár u. 24,* ☎ *46/370–735.* 🎫 *300 Ft.* ⏲ *Daily 9–6.*

Dining and Lodging

$$$ ★ ✕🏨 **Hotel Palota.** As you round the bend on the road from Miskolc, the fairy-tale spire of this hotel's tower rises majestically from a fold in the hills. Built in 1930, the Palota was a luxury hotel until World War II; in 1998, renovation brought it back to something like its old self. The lobby and other public rooms have soaring, ornately sculpted ceilings; rich woodwork; and epic frescoes. Some original furnishings are still here, including burgundy-velvet wallpaper, crystal chandeliers, and heavily carved wooden chairs. Guest rooms are fairly simple, with low-key wood furnishings and large windows, most looking out onto the surrounding greenery; they're equipped with minibars, TVs, and telephones. The striking Mátyás Restaurant is in a round room with vaulted ceilings and original stained-glass windows depicting what were Hungary's most important cities. It specializes in game from the Bükk Mountains and trout from the nearby stocked lake; there's live traditional Hungarian music every evening. ✉ *Erzsébet sétány 1, H-3517 Miskolc Lillafüred,* ☎ *46/331–411,* FAX *46/379–273. 115 rooms, 18 suites. Restaurant, bar, indoor pool, sauna, bowling, exercise room, solarium, meeting rooms, parking (fee). AE, DC, MC, V.*

Aggtelek

74 *55 km (35 mi) north of Miskolc.*

One of the most extensive cave systems in Europe lies at Aggtelek, right on the Slovak border. Containing the largest stalactite system in Europe, the largest of the caves, the Baradla, is 24 km (15 mi) long, extending under Slovakia; its stalactite and stalagmite formations are of extraordinary size—some more than 49 ft high. In one of the chambers of the cave is a 600-seat concert hall, where classical concerts are held every summer. When the lights are left off for a brief period, you experience the purest darkness there is; try holding your hand up to your face—no matter how hard you strain, you won't see it.

Additional caves are being discovered and opened to the public. There are three entrances: in Aggtelek, at Vörös-tó (Red Lake), and in the village of Jósvafő. Guided tours vary in length and difficulty, from the short, one-hour walks beginning at Aggtelek or Jósvafő to the five- to eight-hour, 7-km (4½-mi) exploration. Of the shorter tours, the medium-length (two-hour) tour beginning at Vörös-tó is considered the best; the group congregates at Jósvafő and then takes a public bus (fare covered by tour admission) to the Vörös-tó entrance, then makes its way back to Jósvafő underground. Although tours are conducted in Hungarian, written English translations are available at the ticket offices. Requests for the long tour must be sent in writing to the National Park headquarters at least two weeks ahead of time so the unmaintained sections can be rigged with proper lighting.

The caves are open year-round—they maintain a constant temperature, regardless of the weather. Keep in mind that it's chilly and damp underground—bring a sweater or light jacket and wear shoes with good traction. ✉ *Directorate of Aggtelek National Park, Tengerszem oldal 1, H-3758 Jósvafő,* ☎ FAX *48/350–006 or 48/343–073. 1-hr tours beginning at Aggtelek:* ⏲ *mid-Apr.–Sept., daily at 10, 1, 3, and 5 (sometimes more often), Oct.–mid-Apr., daily at 10, 1, and 3;* 🎫 *800 Ft. 1-hr tours from Jósvafő:* ⏲ *daily at noon and 3 (sometimes more often);* 🎫 *600 Ft. 2-hr tours from Jósvafő:* ⏲ *Apr.–Sept., daily at 8:45, 1:15, and 2:45, Oct.–Mar., daily at 8:45 and noon;* 🎫 *550 Ft. Long tour (with 2-week prior written request) from Aggtelek:* 🎫 *7-km (4½-mi) 4,000 Ft., 9-km (5½-mi) 5,000 Ft. (minimum 5 adults or equivalent admission cost).*

Sárospatak

75 *80 km (50 mi) northeast of Miskolc.*

For hundreds of years, this northern town at the foot of the Zemplén Mountains thrived as the region's elite cultural and intellectual center, its progressive Calvinist College (now a state-run school) educating such famous national thinkers as statesman Lajos Kossuth and writer Zsigmond Móricz. In 1616, Sárospatak's golden age began when its gorgeous castle became home to the famous Hungarian noble family, the Rákóczi, and was the scene of their unsuccessful plot to free Hungary from the Hapsburgs. Today, however, Sárospatak's reality is more that of an economically struggling eastern town. Its rich, historic aura, however, remains in its majestic castle and many fine medieval houses.

The library of today's **Református kollégium** (Reformed College, formerly the Calvinist College) is treasured as one of the country's most beautiful. The main hall, designed by Mihály Pollack in 1817, is a grand yet refined open room with pillars stretching up to an ornately frescoed ceiling. Tours are given hourly; English-speaking guides are available. ✉ *Rákóczi út 1,* ☎ *47/311–057.* 🎫 *200 Ft.* ⏲ *Apr.–Oct., Mon.–Sat. 9–5 and Sun. 9–1; Nov.–Mar., weekends only, with advance notice.*

★ Poised on the bank of the Bodrog River, the part-Gothic, part-Renaissance, part-Baroque **Sárospatak vár** (Sárospatak Castle) is one of Hungary's most beautiful castles—now excellently restored. (At press time yet more restoration was underway, which was expected to close down parts of the castle, but not the main exhibits, through at least 2002.) Begun in the 11th century, it was constructed and added to over several centuries. A six-lanced rose emblem, which signifies silence, marks the spot in the castle's northeast corner where the Rákóczi family conspired to incite a revolution against the Hapsburgs. The first, though unsuccessful, uprising was led by Ferenc Rákóczi I on April 9, 1670; in 1703, after his father's death, Ferenc Rákóczi II led a nine-year rebellion that was ultimately fruitless. The museum houses an excellent collection of antique furniture from the 16th to 19th centuries, portraits of the Rákóczi family, and various weapons and antique clothing. ✉ *Szt. Erzsébet út 19,* ☎ *47/311–083.* 🎫 *300 Ft.* ⏲ *Mar.–Oct., Tues.–Sun. 10–6; Nov.–Feb., Tues.–Sun. 10–5.*

Dining and Lodging

$–$$ ✕🏨 **Hotel Bodrog.** Sárospatak's main hotel and restaurant is centrally located and adequately comfortable and clean but is trapped in its charmless, 1980s Communist institutionality. Inside the drab cement-block exterior are rooms with basic furnishings, though they do have televisions, minibars, and air-conditioning. The restaurant has an extensive selection of wines from nearby Tokaj and serves standard Hungarian fare. Gypsy Roast Sárospatak-style, a pork cutlet with an extra cholesterol booster on top in the form of an egg sunny-side up, is a popular choice; but there is also venison and trout. Breakfast is not included in the room rates. ✉ *Rákóczi u. 58, H-3950,* ☎ *47/311–744,* FAX *47/311–527. 50 rooms. Restaurant, sauna, exercise room, meeting rooms. DC, MC, V.* 😊

Nightlife and the Arts

In late July, the **Sárospatak Cultural Center** (✉ Eötvös u. 6, ☎ 47/311–811) hosts a Dixieland festival performed by Hungarian musicians. During the annual **Zempléni Művészeti Napok** (Zemplén County Arts Days) in mid- to late August, well-known musicians perform classical concerts in the castle's courtyard. For information, contact the Sárospatak Cultural Center (☞ *above*) or the IBUSZ office (☞ Visitor Information, *below*).

Tokaj

76 *54 km (33 mi) east of Miskolc.*

This enchanting little village is the center of one of Hungary's most famous wine regions. It is home of the legendary Aszú wine, a dessert wine made from grapes allowed to shrivel on the vine. Aszú is produced to varying degrees of sweetness, based on how many bushels of sweet grape paste are added to the wine essence, the already highly sweet juice first pressed from them; the scale goes from two *puttonyos* (bushels) to nectar-rich six puttonyos.

The region's famed wines, dubbed (allegedly by Louis XV) the "wine of kings and king of wines," are typically golden yellow with slightly brownish tints and an almost oily texture and have been admired outside Hungary since Polish merchants first became hooked in the Middle Ages. In 1562, after a few sips of wine from the nearby village of Tállya, Pope Pius IV is said to have declared, "*Summum pontificem talia vina decent*" ("These wines are fit for a pope"). Other countries—France, Germany, and Russia included—have tried without success to produce the wine from Tokaj grapes; the secret apparently lies in the combination of volcanic soil and climate.

The surrounding countryside is beautiful, especially in October, when the grapes hang from the vines in thick clusters. Before or after descending into the wine cellars for some epic tasting, be sure to pause while the bells toll at the lovely Baroque Roman Catholic church (1770) on the main square and wend your way along some of the narrow side streets winding up into the vineyard-covered hills: Views of the red-tile roofs and sloping vineyards are like sweet Aszú for the eyes. If you can still focus after a round of wine tasting, be sure to look up at the top of lampposts and chimneys, where giant white storks preside over the village from their big bushy nests. They usually return here to their nests in late April or May after wintering in warmer climes.

The third floor of the **Tokaj Múzeum** (Tokaj Museum), housed in a late-18th-century building, displays objects connected with the history of the wine's production. The first and second floors contain exhibits of ecclesiastical art and the history of the county, respectively. ✉ *Bethlen Gábor u. 7,* ☎ *47/352–636.* 💷 *200 Ft.* ⏲ *Apr.–Oct., Tues.–Sun. 10–5 (sometimes opens earlier); Nov.–Mar., Tues.–Sun. 10–4.*

Tokaj's most famous wine cellar, the nearly 700-year-old **Rákóczi-pince** (Rákóczi Cellar), is also Europe's largest, comprising some 1½ km (1 mi) of branching tunnels extending into the hills (today, about 1,312 ft are in use). Here you can sample Tokaj's famed wines and purchase bottles of your favorites for the road (all major credit cards are accepted). A standard cellar tour with a tasting of six different wines and some *pogácsa* (salty biscuits) costs around 1,500 Ft. (While these are not given in English, there are some English-language pamphlets available.) ✉ *Kossuth tér 13,* ☎ *47/352–408.* ⏲ *Mar.–Oct., daily 10–7 (July–Aug. until 8).*

The Várhelyi family offer wine tastings in the cool, damp cellar of their 16th-century house, called **Hímesudvar.** After the initial tasting, you can purchase bottles of your favorite wines and continue imbibing in their pleasant garden. A standard sampling of five different wines starts at around 1,000 Ft. If you don't see anyone on arriving, don't hesitate to ring the bell. ✉ *Bem út 2,* ☎ *47/352–416.* ⏲ *Daily 9–9.*

Dining and Lodging

At press time plans were afoot to build a new, 20-room hotel in the city center near the town's only bridge.

$ ✕ **Róna Restaurant.** In this simple dining room you can order excellent Hungarian dishes from goose liver to fresh carp or pike-perch. It's pleasantly decorated with original paintings by local artists. ✉ *Bethlen Gábor u. 19,* ☎ *47/352–116. No credit cards. Closed Jan.–Feb.*

$ ✕ **Hotel Tokaj.** What is possibly the weirdest-looking building in the country houses Tokaj's main hotel. Giant red balls that look like clown's noses protrude from each boxy cement balcony under a rainbow-striped facade. There is talk every year of giving the building a makeover, but it may still be years away. Rooms are simply furnished and adequately comfortable, and most have balconies. The large, popular restaurant serves excellent fish specialties, including spicy halászlé served with a swirl of sour cream. ✉ *Rákóczi u. 5, H-3910,* ☎ *47/352–344,* FAX *47/352–759. 42 rooms. Restaurant. AE, DC, MC, V.*

$$ **Toldi Fogadó** Right in the town center, this modern pension—housed in a historic building and with a pleasantly rustic feel inside—offers clean, spacious rooms with pinewood floors dappled by comely knots. All rooms have satellite TVs, phones, and private baths. ✉ *Hajdú köz 2, H-3910,* ☎ FAX *47/353–403. 6 rooms. Restaurant, air-conditioning, minibars. MC, V.*

Nightlife and the Arts

Classical concerts by well-known artists are performed here during the **Zemplén Művészeti Napok** (Zemplén Art Days), a countywide classical music festival held annually in mid-August. For information, contact Tourinform (☞ Visitor Information, *below*).

Naturally, Tokaj's best festival is the annual **Szüreti Hét** (Harvest Week) in early October, celebrating the autumn grape harvest with a parade, a street ball, folk-art markets, and a plethora of wine-tasting opportunities from the local vintners' stands erected on and around the main square. For information, contact Tourinform (☞ Visitor Information, *below*).

Northern Hungary A to Z

Arriving and Departing

BY BUS

Most buses to northern Hungary depart from Budapest's Népstadion station.

BY CAR

The M3 expressway is the main link between Budapest and northern Hungary.

BY TRAIN

Trains between Eger and Budapest run several times daily from Keleti Station. Trains run frequently all day between Budapest and Miskolc.

Getting Around

BY CAR

The M3 is the main highway cutting toward the northeast and Slovakia, though it may take years of construction before it actually reaches the border. In the meantime, the smaller Route 3 goes the rest of the way from near Eger, and Route 37 branches eastward from Route 3 toward Tokaj and Sárospatak. Secondary roads through the Mátra and Bükk mountains are windy but in good shape and wonderfully scenic—this is the best way to see the region.

BY TRAIN

Several daily trains connect Miskolc with Sárospatak and Miskolc with Tokaj. Szilvásvárad and Eger are easily accessible from each other by frequent trains. The **Eger** train station (✉ Állomás tér 1, ☎ 36/314–264) is about 1 km (½ mi) from the center of town (a 20-minute walk). **Miskolc**'s station (✉ Tiszai pályaudvar, ☎ 46/412–665) is about 15 minutes by bus or tram from the center of town.

Contacts and Resources

VISITOR INFORMATION

Eger: Tourinform (✉ Dobó tér 2, ☎ 36/321–807, FAX 36/321–304). **Gyöngyös: Tourinform** (✉ Fő tér 10, ☎ FAX 37/311–155). **Miskolc: Tourinform** (✉ Mindszent tér 1, ☎ FAX 46/348–921). **Sárospatak: Tourinform** (✉ Eötvös u. 6, ☎ FAX 47/315–317). **Tokaj: Tourinform** (✉ Serhaz u. 1, ☎ FAX 47/352–259).

THE GREAT PLAIN

Hungary's Great Plain—the Nagyalföld—stretches south from Budapest to the borders of Croatia and Yugoslavia and as far east as Ukraine and Romania. It covers an area of 51,800 square km (20,000 square mi) and is what most people think of as the typical Hungarian landscape. Almost completely flat, it is the home of shepherds and their flocks and, above all, of splendid horses and the csikós, their riders. The plain has a wild, almost alien air; its sprawling villages consist mostly of one-story houses, though there are many large farms. The plain, which is divided into two almost equal parts by the Tisza River, also contains several of Hungary's most historic cities—it has much from medieval times (largely because it was never occupied by the Turks), and today it remains the least developed area of Hungary.

As you near the region, you will soon find yourself driving in a hypnotically straight line through the dream landscape of the Hortobágy, a grassy puszta, or prairie. Here, the land flattens out like a palacsinta, opening into vast stretches of dusty grassland interrupted only by stands of trees and distant thatch-roof *tanyák* (ranches), the only detectable movement the herds of *racka* sheep or cattle drifting lazily across the horizon guided by shepherds and their trusty *puli* herd dogs. Covering more than 250,000 acres, the Hortobágy became the first of Hungary's four national parks, in 1973; its flora and fauna—including primeval breeds of longhorn cattle and racka sheep, prairie dogs, and *nóniusz* horses—are all under strict protection.

No matter how little time you have, you should make a point of taking in a traditional horse show, like the one offered by the Epona Riding Center in Máta. As touristy as the shows are, they are integral to the Great Plain experience, not to mention a lot of fun.

Debrecen

77 *226 km (140 mi) east of Budapest.*

With a population approaching a quarter of a million, Debrecen is Hungary's second-largest city. Though it has considerably less clout than Budapest, Debrecen was Hungary's capital twice, albeit only briefly. In 1849 it was here that Lajos Kossuth declared Hungarian independence from the Hapsburgs; in 1944, the Red Army liberated Debrecen from the Nazis and made the city the provisional capital until Budapest was taken.

Debrecen has been inhabited since the Stone Age. It was already a sizable village by the end of the 12th century and, by the 14th, an important market town. It takes its name from a Slavonic term for "good earth," and, indeed, much of the country's wheat, produce, meat, and poultry, has been produced in this area for centuries.

Today, Debrecen is a vibrant, friendly city, with a sizable population of young people attending its several esteemed universities. Debrecen has only one tram line (appropriately numbered 1), but it runs fast and frequently in a nearly straight line from the railroad station along Piac utca and out to the Nagyerdő (Great Forest), a giant city park. All in all, it's a good place to spend a day exploring the sights before heading out for a puszta experience.

For almost 500 years, Debrecen has been the stronghold of Hungarian Protestantism—its inhabitants have called it "the Calvinist Rome." In 1536 Calvinism began to replace Roman Catholicism in Debrecen, and two years later the **Református Kollégium** (Reformed College) was founded on what is now Kálvin tér (Calvin Square). Early in the 19th century the college's medieval building was replaced by a pillared structure that offers a vivid lesson in Hungarian religious and political history: The facade's busts honor prominent students and educators as well as Calvin and Huldrych Zwingli. Inside, the main staircase is lined with frescoes of student life and significant moments in the college's history (all painted during the 1930s in honor of the school's 400th anniversary). At the top of the stairs is the **Oratory**, which has twice been the setting for provisional parliaments. In 1849 Lajos Kossuth first proclaimed Hungarian sovereignty here, and the new National Assembly's Chamber of Deputies met here during the last stages of the doomed revolution. Kossuth's pulpit and pew are marked, and two rare surviving flags of his revolution hang on the front wall. Some relics from 1944 line the back wall. Also worth seeing are the college's **library**, which rotates exhibitions of illuminated manuscripts and rare Bibles; and two **museums**—one of the school's history, the other of religious art. ⊠ *Kálvin tér 16,* ☎ *52/414–744.* 🎫 *120 Ft.* ⏲ *Tues.–Sat. 9–5, Sun. 9–1.*

Because the Oratory in the Reformed College was too small, Kossuth reread his declaration of independence by popular demand to a cheering public in 1849 in the twin-turret, strikingly yellow **Nagytemplom** (Great Church). As befits the austerity of Calvinism, the Great Church—which opened its doors in 1817 after more than a decade of construction on the design of Mihály Pécsi, at the site of a 14th century church that had burned down in 1802—is devoid of decoration; then again, with all the Baroque architecture throughout Hungary, you may welcome the contrast. ⊠ *Kálvin tér,* ☎ *52/412–459.* 🎫 *Church 50 Ft., tower 80 Ft.* ⏲ *weekdays 10–3, Sat. 10–noon, Sun. 11–noon.*

NEED A BREAK?

Bright and modern it may be, but the **Kismandula Cukrászda** (Little Almond Pastry Shop; ⊠ Liszt Ferenc u. 10, ☎ 52/310–873), has age-old favorites aplenty—not least, fresh, well-packed rétes and *madártej* (bird's milk), a vanilla-flavored liquid custard with a meringue of sorts floating inside. On summer evenings, a large terrace—which it shares with a restaurant under the same ownership—is sometimes the scene of mime dances and other performances.

The **Déri Múzeum** (Déri Museum) was founded in the 1920s to house the art and antiquities of a wealthy Hungarian silk manufacturer living in Vienna. Its two floors are devoted to local history, archaeology, and weapons, as well as to Egyptian, Greek, Roman, Etruscan, and Far Eastern art. On the top floor are Hungarian and foreign fine art from the 15th to the 20th century, including the striking (and huge) *Ecce Homo* by Mihály Munkácsy, and on loan since 2000, two similar scenes from the life of Christ by the same famous 19th century artist. ✉ *Déri tér 1,* ☎ *52/322–207.* 🎫 *200 Ft. (300 Ft. including Munkácsy exhibit).* ⏲ *Apr.–Oct., Tues.–Sun. 10–6; Nov.–Mar., Tues.–Sun. 10–4.*

Debrecen's main artery, **Piac utca** (Market Street), which has reverted to its old name after decades as Red Army Way, runs from the Great Church to the railroad station. At the corner of Széchenyi utca, the **Kistemplom** (Small Church; ✉ Révész tér 2, ☎ 52/343–872; 🎫 free, but donations accepted; ⏲ weekdays 9–noon, Sun. 8:30 AM–11 AM)—Debrecen's oldest surviving church, built in 1720—looks like a rococo chess-piece castle. This Calvinist venue is known to the locals as the "truncated church" because, early in the 20th century, its onion dome was blown down in a gale. (Note: The church is kept closed, except during services, but the ministers and caretakers next door at the church office are happy to open it for you during the hours listed above.)

Across the street from the Kistemplom is the **Megyeház** (county hall; ✉ Piac u. 54, ☎ 52/507–550; ⏲ Mon.–Thurs. 8–4, Fri. 8–1), built in 1911–1912 in Transylvanian Art Nouveau, a darker and heavier version of the Paris, Munich, and Vienna versions. The ceramic ornaments on the facade are of Zsolnay majolica. Inside, stairs and halls are illuminated by brass chandeliers that spotlight the symmetry and delicate restraint of the decor. In the Council Hall upstairs, stained-glass windows by Károly Kernstock depict seven leaders of the tribes that conquered Hungary in 896.

★ The **Tímárház** (Tanner House) opened in a restored 19th-century building in 1995 as the center for preserving and maintaining the ancient folk-arts-and-crafts traditions of Hajdú-Bihar county. In its delightful, small complex you can wander into the artisans' workshops and watch them creating exquisite pieces—from impossibly fine, intricately handmade lacework to colorful hand-loomed wool rugs. The artisans—among the best in the country—encourage visitors of all ages to try their hand at the crafts. The complex's showroom displays magnificent leather whips, heavy wool shepherd robes, and other examples of the county's traditional folk art; the embroidered textiles are some of the best you'll see anywhere. Although the displayed pieces are not for sale, the staff can help visitors contact the artists to custom-order something. A tiny gift shop, however, does sell a small selection of representative goods at great prices. ✉ *Nagy Gál István u. 6,* ☎ *52/368–857.* 🎫 *100 Ft.* ⏲ *Late Mar.–late Oct., Tues.–Fri. 10–6, Sat. 10–2; late Oct.–late Mar., Tues.–Fri. 10–5, Sat. 10–2.*

A 10-minute walk from the Megyeház along Kossuth Lajos utca will take you to the 19th-century **Vörös templom** (Red Church), as remarkable a Calvinist church as you'll find anywhere in Europe. Outwardly an undistinguished redbrick house of worship, built with the usual unadorned interior, the church celebrated its 50th anniversary at the zenith of the applied-arts movement in Hungary. Its worshipers commissioned artist Jenő Haranghy to paint the walls with biblical allegories using no human bodies or faces (just an occasional limb) but rather plenty of grapes, trees, and symbols. Giant, gaudy frescoes covering the walls, ceilings, niches, and crannies represent, among other subjects, a stag in fresh water, the Martin Luther anthem "A Mighty Fortress Is Our God," and the 23rd Psalm (with a dozen sheep representing the 12 Tribes of Israel and the 12 Apostles). The Red Church is open only during religious services (10 AM on Sunday and religious holidays), but you might try for a private church visit from the deaconage (☎ 52/325–736) on Kossuth Lajos utca. ✉ *Méliusz tér.*

Debrecen's one tram line runs out to the **Nagyerdő** (Great Forest), a huge city park with a zoo, sports stadium, swimming pools, artificial rowing lake, a thermal-spa-cum-luxury-hotel (☞ Termál Hotel Debrecen, *below*), amusement park, restaurants, open-air theater, and the photogenic Kossuth Lajos University, its handsome neo-Baroque facade fronted by a large pool and fountain around which six bronze nudes pose in the sun. The university is one of the few in Central Europe with a real campus, and every summer, from mid-July to mid-August, it is the setting for a world-renowned Hungarian-language program.

Dining and Lodging

$$ ★ ✕ **Csokonai.** Across the street from the Asian-style Csokonai Theater, in a candlelit brick cellar, is one of Debrecen's best restaurants—and one of Hungary's few that offer a pictorial menu. It is a consistent winner of the much-coveted gastronomic award *védnöki tábla.* The restaurant is known for its shellfish, roasted-at-the-table skewered meats, paprika crab, and many kinds of fish. One of the owner's innovations is to let guests cook their own meat *à la Willa-franca* (a hot old-fashioned iron that you press on the meat to cook it). ✉ *Kossuth u. 21,* ☎ *52/410–802. No credit cards.*

$ ✕ **Serpince a Flaskához.** When you walk into this completely unpretentious and very popular neighborhood pub, you may be surprised when you're presented with a nicely bound menu in four languages. For a light meal, try a palócleves, a thick, piquantly sourish meat-and-potatoes soup with tarragon and caraway; or for something heavier, "boiled hock strips covered with ewe cheese, Túróczi style." ✉ *Miklós u. 4,* ☎ *52/414–582. AE, DC, MC, V.*

$$$$ ★ **Grand Hotel Arany Bika.** The "Golden Bull" is an Art Nouveau classic erected in 1915 on a site that has been home to inns, and plenty of historical drama, for some 300 years; a wing was added to this downtown landmark in 1966. The guest rooms in the old ("grand") section are simply attractive, with high ceilings, wood floors, and Oriental-style rugs; those in the newer, less-expensive "tourist" wing are clean but a bit institutional. The thermal spa facility comes complete with hydro-massage and in-house consultants. ✉ *Piac u. 11–15, H-4025,* ☎ *52/416–777,* FAX *52/421–834. 230 rooms, 4 suites. Restaurant, café, indoor pool, sauna, spa, exercise room, casino, solarium, business services, meeting rooms. AE, DC, MC, V.*

$$$$ **Termál Hotel Debrecen.** Debrecen's newest hotel is a lodging-cum-thermal-bathing facility that—built as it is right on top of the city's traditional spa—aims to reinforce Debrecen's reputation not only as a stronghold of Calvinism but as yet another of Hungary's many fountains of curative waters. It does so in luxury. A short drive or streetcar ride from the city center, the two-story hotel is a modern, wooden structure. The spacious rooms, whose all-natural "bio" beds—made of allegedly therapeutic materials such as pure wood and nonsynthetic coverings—are flanked by pinkish-beige walls, all have balconies that look out onto the Debrecenites strolling in the Great Forest below, or else onto the spa's outdoor section. Some suites are larger than others. ✉ *Nagyerdei park 1, H-4032,* ☎ *52/411–888,* FAX *52/311–730. 56 rooms, 40 suites. Restaurant, bar, snack bar, indoor pool, sauna, spa, solarium, meeting rooms. AE, DC, MC, V.*

$ ★ **Centrum Panzió.** This cheery little inn is just down the street from the Great Church. Most guest rooms are in a bright, two-story yellow villa with a red-tile roof; casual, smaller rooms are in cozy, shellacked log cabins. All rooms are immaculately neat, with contemporary furnishings and satellite TVs with VCRs; all have terraces. Suites also have well-stocked kitchenettes (and one has a fireplace). Smoking is not permitted inside, only in the garden. Breakfast is extra. ✉ *Péterfia u. 37/*

A, H-4026, ☎ FAX *52/416–193. 9 rooms, 15 suites. Breakfast room. No credit cards.*

Nightlife and the Arts

One of Debrecen's main cultural venues is the **Csokonai Theater** (✉ Kossuth u. 10, ☎ 52/417–811), which is devoted to theater productions (though none in English).

Debrecen summers are filled with annual cultural festivals. Preceding the season, in mid- to late March, the **Debrecen Tavaszi Fesztivál** (Debrecen Spring Festival) packs two weeks full of concerts, dance and theater performances, and special art exhibits. Main events are held at the Csokonai Theater and Bartók Hall. Contact Tourinform (☞ Visitor Information, *below*) for information. The biannual **Bartók Béla Nemzetközi Kórusverseny** (Béla Bartók International Choral Festival), scheduled next for July 2002, is a competition for choirs from around the world and provides choral-music aficionados with numerous full-scale concerts in Bartók Hall. Jazz fans can hear local ensembles as well as groups from around Hungary and abroad during the **Debreceni Jazz Napok** (Debrecen Jazz Festival) in mid-March, in conjunction with the Spring Festival. One of the city's favorite occasions is the **Debreceni Virágkarnevál** (Flower Carnival) on St. Stephen's Day (August 20), when a festive parade of flower-encrusted floats and carriages makes its way down Debrecen's main street along the tram line all the way to the Nagyerdő Stadium.

Outdoor Activities and Sports

A visit to the Great Plain is hardly complete without at least some contact with horses. There are several horseback-riding outfits outside Debrecen on the puszta; Tourinform (☞ Visitor Information, *below*) can help arrange excursions.

The Great Forest is bubbling with thermal baths and pools. The park's main complex, the **Nagyerdei Lido** (✉ Nagyerdei Strand, ☎ 52/346–000), has eight pools, including a large pool for active swimming (most people soak idly in Hungary's public pools) and a wave pool.

Hortobágy

78 *39 km (24 mi) west of Debrecen.*

The main visitor center for and gateway to the prairie is the little village of Hortobágy. Traveling from Debrecen, you'll reach this town just before you would cross the Hortobágy River. Before heading out to the prairie itself, you can take in Hortobágy's own sights: a prairie museum, its famous stone bridge, and the historic Hortobágyi Csárda inn.

Crossing the Hortobágy River is one of the puszta's famous symbols: the curving, white-stone **Kilenc-lyukú híd** (Nine-Arch Bridge). It was built in the early 19th century and is the longest (548 ft) stone bridge in Hungary. ✉ *On Route 33 at Petőfi tér.*

Built in 1699, the **Hortobágyi Csárda** (Hortobágy Inn) has been a regional institution for most of the last three centuries. Its construction is typical of the Great Plain: a long, white stone structure with arching windows, brown-wood details, and a stork nest—and occasionally storks—on its chimney. Though it no longer has guest rooms, its restaurant is going strong (☞ Dining, *below*). ✉ *Petőfi tér 2,* ☎ *52/369–139. Closed Jan.–mid-Feb.*

For a glimpse into traditional Hortobágy pastoral life, visit the **Pásztormúzeum** (Shepherd Museum), across the street from the Hortobágyi Inn. Exhibits focus on traditional costumes and tools, such as the shepherds' heavy, embroidered cloaks and carved sticks. The lot in front of the museum is the tourism center for the area, bustling with visitors and local touristic enterprises, including the helpful local Tourinform office. ✉ *Petőfi tér 1,* ☎ *52/369–119.* 🎟 *250 Ft.* ⏲ *Mid-May–Sept., daily 9–6; Oct. and Mar.–mid-May, daily 10–2; rest of the year with prior notice only.*

OFF THE BEATEN PATH

HORTOBÁGYHALASTÓ – About 5 km (3 mi) west of Hortobágy, Hortobágyhalastó (Great Plain Fish Pond) is a tiny, sleepy hamlet at the end of a dirt road where chickens strut about and the center of town is essentially an old phone booth. However, it's not the village but the 5,000-acre-pond nature reserve of the same name at its edge that draws dedicated bird-watchers to look for some of the 150 species in residence. A nature walk around the entire reserve will take most of a day and requires advance permission from the **Hortobágyi Nemzeti Park Igazgatóság** (National Park's Headquarters; ✉ Sumen u. 2, H-4024 Debrecen, ☎ 52/349–922, FAX 52/410–645); contact Tourinform (☞ Visitor Information, *below*) in Debrecen for assistance.

Dining

$ ★ ✕ **Hortobágyi Csárda.** This historic roadside inn could get by on fame and trappings alone—dried corn-and-paprika wreaths, flasks, saddles, and antlers hang from its rafters and walls—but the excellent food will grab your attention. This is the place to order the regional specialty: *Hortobágyi húsospalacsinta* (Hortobágy pancakes), which are filled with beef and braised with a tomato-and-sour-cream sauce. The portions are small, so follow the pancakes with *bográcsgulyás*—spicy goulash soup puszta style, with meat and dumplings. Veal paprikás and solid beef and lamb *pörkölt* (thick stews with paprika and sour cream) are also recommended, as are the cheese-curd or apricot-jam dessert pancakes. ✉ *Petőfi tér 2,* ☎ *52/369–139. AE, DC, MC, V. Closed Jan.–mid-Feb.*

Nightlife and the Arts

The three-day **Hortobágyi híd vásár** (Hortobágy Bridge Fair), held annually around August 20, brings horse shows, a folk-art fair, ox roasts, and festive crowds to the plot beneath the famous Nine-Arch Bridge.

Máta

79 *About 2 km (1 mi) southwest of Hortobágy.*

The hamlet of Máta is home to the **Epona Lovasfalu** (Epona Rider Village), with some 500 champion horses and first-rate riders, which over the last few years have made it the region's most important equestrian center. From around May through September there is a daily ½-hour-long "Rangeman's Show." Groups of 16 can ride the prairie in covered wagons pulled by horses of the prize-winning nóniusz breed and driven by herders. You'll see herds of racka sheep with twisted horns, gray cattle, and wild boars, all tended by shepherds, cowherds, and swineherds dressed in distinctive costumes and aided by shaggy puli herd dogs and Komondor sheepdogs. At various stops along the route of this minirodeo, csikós do stunts with the animals; the best involves five horses piloted by one man who stands straddling the last two. Inspired guests can even try a little (less risky) riding themselves with help from the csikós. In winter and in bad weather, indoor shows are organized. Call ahead to inquire about arranging for an English-speaking guide. ✉ *Hortobágy-Máta,* ☎ *52/369–020.* 🎟 *Riding shows and wagon tours 1,800 Ft.* ⏲ *Departures at 10, noon, 2, and 4 (more frequently if demand warrants).*

Lodging

$$$$ ★ **Epona Rider Village.** This vast, luxury equestrian complex opened in 1992 and has rapidly become one of Hungary's best and most imaginative resorts. The contemporary, puszta-style buildings house stables, two-story family cottages (for rent by the floor), and special "rider houses," complete with private three-horse stables. The main building contains standard rooms, all with balconies and contemporary furnishings. Tennis courts, a swimming pool, and myriad horse-related activities provide ample entertainment in an area otherwise considered to be the middle of nowhere. ✉ *H-4071 Hortobágy-Máta,* ☎ *52/369–092,* FAX *52/369–027. 52 rooms, 4 suites, 20 cottages. 2 restaurants, 2 bars, pool, massage, sauna, 2 tennis courts, exercise room, horseback riding, solarium, business services, meeting rooms. AE, DC, MC, V.*

Nightlife and the Arts

Equestrian fans will not want to miss the **Hortobágy International Horse Festival,** held here annually for about four days in July or August, during which exciting show-jumping and carriage-driving competitions are held, as well as traditional horseback stunts by the csikós, folk-music and dance performances, and a folk-art fair.

Outdoor Activities and Sports

The **Epona Rider Village** (☞ *above*) offers horseback riding lessons (1,800 Ft. per ½ hour, beginner; 2,800 Ft. per hour, intermediate and advanced dressage) and guided rides out on the puszta (about 2,300 Ft. per hour) on its excellent horses.

Kecskemét

 *191 km (119 mi) southwest of Debrecen.*

With a name roughly translating as "Goat Walk," this sprawling town smack in the middle of the country never fails to surprise unsuspecting first-time visitors with its elegant landmark buildings; interesting museums; and friendly, welcoming people. Its main square, Szabadság tér (Liberty Square), is marvelous, marred only by two faceless cement-block buildings, one of which houses the city's McDonald's (a true sign the city is not just a dusty prairie town anymore). Home of the elite Kodály Institute, where famous composer and pedagogue Zoltán Kodály's methods are taught, the city also maintains a fairly active cultural life.

The Kecskemét area, fruit center of the Great Plain, produces *barack pálinka,* a smooth yet tangy apricot brandy that can warm the heart and blur the mind in just one shot. Ask for home-brewed *házi pálinka,* which is much better (and often stronger) than the commercial brews.

A short drive from town takes you into the expansive sandy grasslands of Kiskunság National Park, the smaller of the two protected areas (the other is Hortobágy National Park) of the Great Plain. You can watch a traditional horse show, do some riding, or immerse yourself in the experience by spending a night or two at one of the inns out on the prairie.

Until a small affiliated gallery opened a few years ago in Budapest, the **Magyar Fotográfia Múzeum** (Hungarian Photography Museum) was the only museum in Hungary dedicated solely to photography. With a growing collection of more than 275,000 photos, documents, and equipment pieces, it continues to be the most important photography center in the country. The main exhibits are fine works by such pioneers of Hungarian photography as André Kertész, Brassaï, and Martin Munkácsi, all of whom moved and gained fame abroad. ✉ *Katona József tér 12,* ☎ *76/483–221.* *150 Ft.* *Wed.–Sun. 10–5.*

The handsome Moorish-style **zsinagóga** (synagogue) anchoring one end of Liberty Square is beautifully restored but stripped of its original purpose. Today it is the headquarters of the House of Science and Technology, with offices and a convention center, but it also houses a small collection of Michelangelo sculpture reproductions from Budapest's Museum of Fine Arts. ✉ *Rákóczi út 2,* ☎ *76/487–611.* 🎫 *Free.* ⏲ *Weekdays 10–4; closed during special events.*

Kecskemét's most famous building is the **Cifrapalota** (Ornamental Palace), a unique and remarkable Hungarian-style Art Nouveau building, built in 1902. A three-story cream-color structure studded with folksy lilac, blue, red, and yellow Zsolnay majolica flowers and hearts, it stands on Liberty Square's corner like a cheerful cream pastry. Once a residential building, it now houses the **Kecskeméti képtár (Kecskemét Gallery), displaying artwork by Hungarian fine artists as well as occasional international exhibits.** ✉ *Rákóczi u. 1,* ☎ *76/480–776.* 🎫 *120 Ft.* ⏲ *Tues.–Sun. 10–5.*

NEED A BREAK? You can treat yourself to fresh pastries or ice cream at the café that shares this book's name, the **Fodor Cukrászda** (Fodor Confectionery; ✉ Szabadság tér 2, ☎ 76/497–545). It's right on the main square and is closed December 25–February.

★ Built in 1893–1897 by Ödön Lechner in the Hungarian Art Nouveau style that he created, the **Városház** (town hall) is one of the style's finest examples. Window frames are here arched, there pointed, and the roof, covered with tiny copper- and gold-color tiles, looks as if it has been rained on by coins from heaven. In typical Lechner style, the outlines of the central facade make a curving line to a pointed top, under which 37 little bells add the finishing visual and auditory touch: Every hour from 7 AM to 8 PM, they flood the main square with ringing melodies from Kodaly, Beethoven, Mozart, and other major composers as well as traditional Hungarian folk songs. The building's **Dísz Terem** (Ceremonial Hall) is a spectacular palace of glimmering gold-painted vaulted ceilings, exquisitely carved wooden pews, colorful frescoes by Bertalan Székely (who also frescoed Budapest's Matthiás Church), and a gorgeously ornate chandelier that floats above the room like an ethereal bouquet of lights and shining brass. The hall is open only to tour groups that have made prior arrangements; call in advance and ask for Ildikó Nemes. ✉ *Kossuth tér 1,* ☎ *76/483–683 ext. 2153.* 🎫 *Dísz terem 100 Ft.*

The oldest building on Kossuth tér is the **Szent Miklós templom** (Church of St. Nicholas), also known as the Barátság templom (Friendship Church) because of St. Nick's role as the saint of friendship. It was built in Gothic style in either the 13th or the 15th century (a subject of debate) but rebuilt in Baroque style during the 18th century. ✉ *Kossuth tér 5.* 🎫 *Free.*

The unusual, one-of-a-kind **Szórakoténusz Játékmúzeum és** (Szórakoténusz Toy Museum and Workshop) chronicles the history of Hungarian toys, beginning with archaeological pieces such as stone figures and clay toys from medieval guilds; there are also changing international exhibits. In the workshop, artisans prepare traditional toys and invite visitors to try it themselves. Next door to the toy museum is the small **Magyar Naív Művészek Múzeuma** (Hungarian Naive Art Museum), where you can see a collection of this simple style of painting and sculpting created by Hungarian artists. ✉ *Gáspár András u. 11,* ☎ *Toy Museum 76/481–469; Naive Art Museum 76/324–767.* 🎫 *100 Ft. each.* ⏲ *Toy Museum: Tues.–Sun. 10–12:30 and 1–5; Naive*

Art Museum: Tues.–Sun. 10–5; Toy Workshop alternate Sat. 10–noon and 2:30–5, Sun. 10–noon.

OFF THE BEATEN PATH

PIAC – As Kecskemét is Hungary's fruit capital, why not experience it firsthand by visiting the bustling *piac* (market), where—depending on the season—you can indulge in freshly plucked apples, cherries, and the famous Kecskemét apricots. Provided there is no sudden spring freeze, apricot season is around June through August. ✉ *Budai u. near corner of Nagykörösi út.* ⊙ *Tues.–Sat. 6–noon, Sun. 6 AM–11 AM.*

Dining and Lodging

$$ ✕ **Liberté Kávéház.** This popular restaurant's location, right on Liberty Square, can't be beat. The seasonal menu always has filling main dishes and meals-in-themselves soups. ✉ *Szabadság tér 2,* ☎ *76/480–350. AE, MC, V.*

$–$$ ✕ **Kisbugaci Csárda.** Tucked away on a side street, this cozy eatery is warm and bright. The inner area has wood paneling and upholstered booths; the outer section has simple wooden tables covered with locally embroidered tablecloths and matching curtains. Food is heavy, ample, and tasty. Try the kitchen's goose specialties, such as the *Bugaci libatoros*—a sampling of goose liver, thigh, and breast with steamed cabbage and boiled potatoes. Request a plate of dried paprikas—usually crumbled into soup—if you really want to spice things up. ✉ *Munkácsy u. 10,* ☎ *76/486–782. MC, V. No dinner Sun.*

$$ ★ ✕🏨 **Pongrácz Manor.** For total puszta immersion, spend a night or two at this traditional Great Plain ranch, about 25 km (16 mi) from Kecskemét and 7 km (4½ mi) from the nearest hamlet. A complex of whitewashed buildings with reed roofs, the manor has small, simple, and comfortable rooms with views onto the prairie. Those who dislike horses may not want to stay here, but horse lovers will have riding opportunities galore (the stable houses some 70 horses), and you can watch resident champion csikósok do daredevil stunts, not to mention stage mock 1848 Revolution battles in full Hussar dress. Anglers can try their luck in the nearby lake; the restaurant's kitchen will cook to order whatever you catch (you can keep one fish per day). Those with no luck will not go hungry: The restaurant serves hearty regional dishes indoors or out, many baked in a traditional puszta wood-burning oven. The ranch is often booked, so reserve ahead. ✉ *Kunpuszta 76, H-6041 Kerekegyháza,* ☎ FAX *76/371–240. 26 rooms with bath, 5 rooms with shared bath, 4 suites. Restaurant, pool, saunas, 2 tennis courts, bowling, horseback riding, squash, fishing, billiards. No credit cards. Closed Jan.–Mar.*

$$$ 🏨 **Arany Homok Hotel.** Kecskemét's biggest and best-known hotel has a prime location right on the picturesque main square—a delight for guests with windows facing the square but a shame for the square itself, which is marred by the hotel's heinous concrete-bunker design. Most rooms have pared-down blond-wood furnishings, generic gray wall-to-wall carpeting, and small bathrooms. All doubles have balconies. For quieter nights, avoid the rooms overlooking the bus station behind the hotel. Breakfast is not included in room rates. ✉ *Kossuth tér 3, H-6000,* ☎ *76/486–286,* FAX *76/481–195. 111 rooms, 4 suites. Restaurant, breakfast room, exercise room, casino, laundry service, meeting rooms, travel services. AE, DC, MC, V.*

$ 🏨 **Fábián Panzió.** It's hard to miss this very pink villa just off the main square. Inside, the pink (though muted) mixes with a white, turquoise, and lavender decor. The friendly owners keep their pension immaculate: Floors in the tiny entranceway are polished until they look wet, and even the paths through the blooming back garden are spotless. The rooms—some in the main house and some in a comely, one-story motel-like building in the garden—were all recently renovated. The largest and quietest rooms are in the back. ✉ *Kápolna u. 14, H-6000,* ☎ *76/477–677,* FAX *76/477–175. 10 rooms. Breakfast room, air-conditioning, laundry service. No credit cards.*

Nightlife and the Arts

The beautiful **Katona József Theater** (✉ Katona József tér 5, ☎ 76/483–283) is known for its excellent dramatic productions (in Hungarian) and also hosts classical concerts, operas, and dance performances during the Spring Festival and other celebrations. The **Kodály Zoltán Zenepedagógiai Intézet** (Zoltán Kodály Music Pedagogy Institute; ✉ Kéttemplom köz 1, ☎ 76/481–518) often holds student and faculty recitals, particularly during its biannual international music seminar in mid- to late July; the next one is scheduled for 2001.

Kecskemét's annual **Tavaszi Fesztivál** (Spring Festival) is held from mid-March to early April and features concerts, dance performances, theater productions, and art exhibits by local and special guest artists from around the country and abroad. Every two years in July, the city hosts a giant children's festival, **Európa Jövője Gyermektalálkozó** (Future of Europe Children's Convention), during which children's groups from some 25 countries put on colorful folk-dance and singing performances outside on the main square; the next one will be held in 2002.

For schedule and ticket information on all cultural events, contact Tourinform (☞ Visitor Information, *below*).

Outdoor Activities and Sports

The nearby puszta is the setting for traditional horse-stunt shows, carriage rides, guided horseback rides, and other horsey activities. Full-length shows and daylong excursions are bus tour–centric (because of the costs involved), although essentially anything can be arranged if a smaller group or individuals are willing to pay for it. **Nyakvágó Kft.** (✉ Kunszentmiklós, Bösztörpuszta-Nagyállás, ☎ FAX 76/351–198 or ☎ 76/351–201) sometimes offers full- and half-day "Puszta Programs" for smaller groups of individuals who want to take part in the program on the same day. The program includes carriage rides, horse shows, a visit to a working farm, and folk dancing, all lubricated with wine and pálinka (brandy) and including typical puszta meals. A full-day program costs roughly 5,000 Ft., and a half day costs about 4,000 Ft. It's best to call a day or so in advance. Contact Tourinform or Bugac Tours (☞ Visitor Information, *below, for both*) for other possibilities and for help making arrangements.

Bugac

81 *46 km (29 mi) south of Kecskemét.*

The Bugac puszta (Bugac Prairie) is the central and most-visited section of the 86,450-acre **Kiskunsági National Park**—the smaller sister of Hortobágy National Park (farther northeast); together they compose the entire Great Plain. Bugac puszta's expansive, sandy, impossibly flat grassland scenery has provided Hungarian poets and artists with inexhaustible material over the centuries. Although the dry, open stretches may seem numbingly uniform to the casual eye, the Bugac's fragile ecosystem is the most varied of the entire park; its primeval juniper trees, extremely rare in the region, are the area's most protected and treasured flora. Today, Bugac continues to inspire visitors with its strong equestrian traditions and the fun but touristy horse shows and tours offered in its boundaries. The park's half-hour traditional horse show is held daily at 1:15 PM; its price is included in the entrance fee. You can also wander around the area and peek into the Kiskunság National Park Museum, which has exhibits about pastoral life on the prairie.

✉ *Park: Bugac puszta.* 🎫 *1,000 Ft. plus 1,000 Ft. per car.* ⏲ *Apr.–Oct., daily 9–5 or 6. Information:* ✉ *Karikás Csárda,* ☎ *76/372–688; in Kecskemét,* ✉ *Bugac Tours, Szabadság tér 5/a,* ☎ *76/482–500.*

Dining

$$ ✕ **Bugaci Csárda.** Bugac's most famous and popular restaurant is a tour-bus magnet but is still considered a mandatory part of a puszta visit. It's at the end of a dirt road just past the park's main entrance, in a traditional whitewashed, thatch-roof house decorated inside with cheerful red-and-white folk embroideries. Here you can feast on all the Hungarian standards. ✉ *Rte. 54, next to park entrance,* ☎ *76/372–522. No credit cards. Closed Nov.–Mar.*

Outdoor Activities and Sports

The region specializes in equestrian sports. Possibilities for horseback-riding lessons, trail rides, and horse carriage rides abound. Contact **Bugaci Ménes** (☎ FAX 76/372–617) in Bugac; or **Bugac Tours** (✉ Szabadság tér 5/a, Kecskemét, ☎ 76/482–500, ☎ FAX 76/481–643; Karikás Csárda, Bugac, ☎ 76/372–688).

Szeged

82 *87 km (54 mi) south of Kecskemét.*

The largest city in southern Hungary was almost completely rebuilt after a disastrous flood in 1879, using a concentric plan not unlike that of the Pest side of Budapest, with avenues connecting two boulevards like the spokes of a wheel.

Szeged is famous mainly for two things: its open-air festival, held each year in July and August, and its paprika. But Szeged's paprikas are useful not only in goulash kettles but in test tubes as well: Local biochemist Albert Szentgyörgyi won the Nobel Prize in 1937 for his discoveries about vitamin C, extracted from his hometown vegetable. In late summer and early autumn, Szeged has a rich array of rack after rack of red peppers drying in the open air.

While Szeged does offer architectural delights, they are few compared to cities of similar size; it makes up for this, however, as a favorite place for young budget travelers who enjoy the dynamic atmosphere at its peak during the school year, when students from the city's schools and universities liven up the streets, cafés, and bars.

The heart of the city center is the large **Széchenyi tér,** lined with trees and surrounded by imposing buildings. Most notable is the bright yellow, eclectic neo-Baroque **Városház** (town hall; ✉ Széchenyi tér 10), built at the turn of the 19th century and after suffering major damage during the flood of 1879, reconstructed by well-known eclectic Art Nouveau architect Ödön Lechner. At the square's opposite end is the pale-green **Hotel Tisza** (✉ Wesselényi u. 4), its guest rooms and lobby looking tired and worn but whose lovely and still active concert hall was the site of many piano recitals by legendary composer Béla Bartók. Its restaurant was a favorite haunt of famous poet Mihály Babits.

NEED A BREAK? Grab a hot strudel stuffed with apple, poppy seed, or peppery cabbage at the counter of **Hatos Rétes** bakery-cum-café (✉ Klauzal tér 6), a popular spot not only for a quick strudel but also *óriás* (giant) palacsinta—salty (ham, cheese) or sweet (plum, raspberry, chestnut). This is also among the few places in Hungary that offer decaf coffee.

★ Szeged's most striking building is the **Fogadalmi Templom** (Votive Church), an imposing neo-Romanesque brick edifice built between 1912 and 1929 in fulfillment of a municipal promise made after the Great Flood. One of Hungary's largest churches, it seats 6,000 and has a splendid organ with 12,000 pipes. The church forms the backdrop to the annual Szegedi Szabadtéri Játékok (Szeged Open-Air Festival), held in vast Dóm tér (Cathedral Square). Outstanding performances of Hungary's great national drama, Imre Madách's *Tragedy of Man,* are given each summer at the festival, as well as a rich variety of other theatrical pieces, operas, and concerts. A performance of a different sort is given here daily at 12:15 PM, when the mechanical figures on the church's clock put on their five-minute show to music. ✉ *Dóm tér,* ☎ *Church 62/420–157, Crypt 62/420–953. Church:* 🎫 *Free.* ⊙ *Weekends 9–6, Sun. 12:30–6. Crypt:* 🎫 *100 Ft.* ⊙ *Apr.–Oct., Tues–Sun. 10–6, Nov.–Mar. 10–4.*

Szeged's **Régi Zsinagóga** (Old Synagogue) was built in 1839 in neoclassical style. On its outside wall a marker written in Hungarian and Hebrew shows the height of the floodwaters in 1879. It is open only rarely for special events. ✉ *Hajnóczi u. 12.* ⊙ *Apr.–Sept., Sun.–Fri. 9–noon and 1–6.*

★ Near the Old Synagogue, at the corner of Gutenberg utca and Jósika utca, is the larger **Új Zsinagóga** (New Synagogue), finished in 1905; it is Szeged's purest and finest representation of Art Nouveau. Its wood and stone carvings, wrought iron, and furnishings are all the work of local craftsmen. A memorial to Szeged's victims of Nazism is in the entrance hall. ✉ *Gutenberg u. 20,* ☎ *62/423–849.* 🎫 *200 Ft.* ⊙ *Apr.–Oct., Sun.–Mon. 9–noon and 1–6; Nov.–Mar., Sun.–Mon. 9–1. Closed Jewish holidays.*

OFF THE BEATEN PATH

NEMZETI TÖRTÉNETI EMLÉKPARK – The ultimate in monuments to Hungarian history and pride is the enormous National Historic Memorial Park in Ópusztaszer, 29 km (18 mi) north of Szeged. It was built on the site of the first parliamentary congregation of the nomadic Magyar tribes, held in AD 895, in which they agreed to be ruled by mighty Árpád. Paths meander among an open-air museum of traditional village buildings. The main reason to come is the Feszty Körkép (Feszty Cyclorama), an astounding 5,249-ft 360-degree panoramic oil painting depicting the arrival of the Magyar tribes to the Carpathian basin 1,105 years ago—effectively, the birth of Hungary. It was painted in 1892–1894 by Árpád Feszti and exhibited in Budapest to celebrate the Magyar millennium. Sixty percent of it was destroyed during a World War II bombing, and it wasn't until 1991 that a group of art restorers brought it here and started a painstaking project to resurrect it in time for Hungary's millecentennial celebrations in 1996. Today, housed in its own giant rotunda, the painting is viewable as part of a multimedia experience: Groups of up to 100 at a time are let in every half hour for a 25-minute viewing of the painting, accompanied by a recorded explanation and, at the end, a special sound show in which different recordings are played near different parts of the painting—galloping horses, trumpeting horns, screaming virgins, rushing water—to the scene depicted. The attraction is so popular that on summer weekends it's a good idea to call ahead and reserve a spot in the slot of your choice (tickets are for a set showing). The explanation is in Hungarian, but English-language versions on CD, available at the entrance, can be listened to on headphones before or after the viewing. The cyclorama is the only park attraction open in winter. ✉ *Szoborkert 68, Ópusztaszer,* ☎ *62/275–257 or 62/275–133.* 🎫 *Park 700 Ft., Feszty körkép and park 1,100 Ft.* ⊙ *Apr.–Oct., daily 9–7; Nov.–Mar., daily 9–5.*

Dining and Lodging

$$–$$$ ✕ **Alabárdos Étterem.** This elegant eatery is housed in an 1810 landmark and its specialty is not just a meal but an experience: The lights are dimmed as waiters rush to your table with a flaming spear of skewered meats, which they then prepare in a spicy ragout at your table. ✉ *Oskola u. 13,* ☎ *62/420–914. MC, V. Closed Sun.*

$$ ✕ **Öreg Kőrössy Halászkert Vendéglő.** This thatch-roof fisherman's inn on the Tisza River first opened in 1930; decades later, the atmosphere is a mix of rustic charm and modern glitter, and the menu still includes the original house staples such as rich-red *Öreg Kőrössy* (Old Kőrös) halászlé and *Kőrössy* fish paprikás. It's not easy to find; take a car or bus as it's along walk from town center. ✉ *Sárga üdülőtelep 262 (head north from the city center along the river on Felső-Tiszapart and turn off after about 1 mi where the main road makes its first curve, to the left, at a sign pointing to the restaurant; follow the smaller road around several curves and past a restaurant with a similar name),* ☎ *62/495–481. MC, V.*

$ ✕ **Botond Restaurant.** An 1810 neoclassical building that formerly housed Szeged's first printing press is now this popular restaurant, which has Gypsy music nightly from 7. Specialties include *Tenkes-hegyi szűzérmek* (Tenkes Hill pork tenderloin), served with bacon, mushrooms, and paprika. Its outdoor terrace is a prime dining spot in good weather. ✉ *Széchenyi tér 13,* ☎ *62/420–435. AE, DC, MC, V.*

$ **Marika Panzió.** This friendly inn sits on a historic street in the Alsóváros (Lower Town), a five-minute drive from the city center. Cozy rooms have light-wood paneling and larger-hotel amenities such as color TVs, minibars, and air-conditioning. The back garden has a small swimming pool. ✉ *Nyíl u. 45, H-6725,* ☎ FAX *62/443–861. 9 rooms. Breakfast room, air-conditioning, minibars, pool, free parking. AE, DC, MC, V.*

Nightlife and the Arts

Szeged's own symphony orchestra, theater company, and famous contemporary dance troupe form the solid foundation for a rich cultural life. The **Szeged Nemzeti Színház** (Szeged National Theater; ✉ Deák Ferenc u. 12, ☎ 62/479–279) stages Hungarian dramas, as well as classical concerts, operas, and ballets. Chamber-music concerts are often held in the conservatory and in the historic recital hall of the **Hotel Tisza** (✉ Wesselényi u. 1). Szeged's most important event, drawing crowds from around the country, is the annual **Szegedi Szabadtéri Játékok** (Szeged Open-Air Festival), a tradition established in the 1930s, held mid-July through mid-September. The gala series of dramas, operas, operettas, classical concerts, and folk-dance performances by Hungarian and international artists is held outdoors on the vast cobblestone Dóm tér (Cathedral Square). Tickets are always hot commodities; plan far ahead. For tickets and information, contact the ticket office (✉ Kárász u. 15, ☎ 62/476–555).

Shopping

You'll have no trouble finding packages of authentic **Szegedi paprika** in all sizes and degrees of spiciness in most of the city's shops. Szeged's other famous product is its excellent **salami** made by the local Pick Salami factory, which has been producing Hungary's most-famous, most-exported salamis since 1869. You'll find an extensive selection at the **Pick** factory outlet stores (✉ Jókai u. 7, in Nagyáruház Passage, ☎ 62/425–021; Maros u. 21, next to factory, ☎ 62/421–879).

The Great Plain A to Z

Arriving and Departing

BY BUS

Volánbusz operates service from Budapest's Népstadion terminal to towns throughout the Great Plain.

BY CAR

From Budapest, Route 4 goes straight to Debrecen, but it's faster to take the M3 expressway and switch to Route 33 midway there; the M5 goes to Kecskemét and Szeged.

BY TRAIN

Service to the Great Plain from Budapest is quite good; daily service is available from the capital's Nyugati (West) and Keleti (East) stations. Intercity (IC) trains, the fastest, run between Budapest and Debrecen, Kecskemét, and Szeged; they require seat reservations. Trains also run from Romania into Debrecen.

Getting Around

BY BUS

Buses connect most towns in the region.

BY CAR

The flat expanses of this region make for easy, if eventually numbing, driving. Secondary-route 47 runs along the eastern edge of the country, connecting Debrecen and Szeged. Debrecen and Kecskemét are easily driven between as well via Route 4 through Szolnok, then dropping south in Cegléd. The puszta regions of Bugac and Hortobágy are accessible from Kecskemét and Debrecen by well-marked roads.

BY TRAIN

The various parts of the region are connected via the rail junctions in Szolnok and Cegléd, in the geometric center of the Great Plain. The **Szeged** train station (⊠ Tisza pályaudvar, ☎ 62/421–821) is a 30-minute walk from town center; you can also take a tram. The trains for **Kecskemét** (⊠ Kodály Zoltán tér 7, ☎ 76/322–460) are on the Szeged line; the trip between the towns takes roughly an hour. The ride from Szolnok to **Debrecen** (⊠ Petőfi tér 12, ☎ 52/346–777) takes about an hour and a half.

Contacts and Resources

GUIDED TOURS

Cityrama (in Budapest, ☎ 1/302–4382) runs day trips several times a week to the Great Plain from Budapest. They begin with a sightseeing walk through Kecskemét, then head out to the prairie town of Lajosmizse for drinking, dining, Gypsy music, carriage rides, and a traditional csikós horse show. The cost is approximately 16,000 Ft.

IBUSZ Travel (in Budapest, ☎ 1/485–2762 or 1/317–7767) also operates full-day tours out to the Great Plain, to Lajosmizse as well as to Bugac, both first taking in Keckemét's sights. Costs run 16,000 Ft–17,000 Ft.

VISITOR INFORMATION

Bugac: Bugac Tours (⊠ Karikás Csárda, Bugac, ☎ 76/372–688; Szabadság tér 5/a, Kecskemét, ☎ 76/482–500, ☎ FAX 76/481–643). **Debrecen: Tourinform** (⊠ Piac u. 20, ☎ 52/412–250, FAX 52/314–139). **Hortobágy: Pusztainform** (⊠ Pásztormúzeum, ☎ FAX 52/369–119). **Kecskemét: Tourinform** (⊠ Kossuth tér 1, ☎ FAX 76/481–065). **Szeged: Tourinform** (⊠ Victor Hugo u. 1, ☎ FAX 62/420–509).

HUNGARY A TO Z

Arriving and Departing

By Bus

There is regular bus service between Budapest and selected major cities in the region. From Budapest, buses to Bratislava and Prague, as well as Austria and points further west, depart from the **Erzsébet tér bus station** (☏ 1/317–2562 for international information). Buses to Krakow, Sofia, Brasso, and the former Yugoslavia operate from the **Népstadion station** (☏ 1/252–4498 or 252–1896). Though inexpensive, these buses tend to be crowded, so buy your tickets days in advance. (Reservations cannot be made by phone; a few routes allow purchases only from the driver.)

By Car

At press time, Hungary was continuing a massive upgrading and reconstruction of many of its expressways, gearing up for its role as the main bridge for trade between the Balkan countries and the former Soviet Union and Western Europe. Work is scheduled to continue beyond 2002. To help fund the project, tolls were introduced in 1996; toll roads include the M1, which goes west from Budapest toward Vienna; the M3, which runs northeast toward Slovakia; and the M5, from Budapest to just south of Kecskemét (and eventually through Szeged to Yugoslavia).

By Plane

See Arriving by Plane *in* Budapest A to Z, *above*.

Ferihegy Repülőtér (Ferihegy Airport; ☏ 1/296–9696), Hungary's only commercial airport with regularly scheduled service, is 24 km (15 mi) southeast of downtown Budapest. All non-Hungarian airlines operate from Terminal 2B; those of Malév, from Terminal 2A. The older part of the airport, Terminal 1, no longer serves commercial flights. The only nonstop flight between Hungary and the United States is with **Malév Hungarian Airlines** (☏ 06/40–212–121 toll free; 1/235–3804 [ticketing]), which flies between JFK International Airport in New York and Ferihegy. The flight lasts about nine hours.

Malév and other national airlines fly nonstop from most European capitals. **British Airways** (☏ 1/318–3299 or 1/266–6699) and Malév offer daily nonstop service between Budapest and London.

By Train

International trains are routed to two stations in Budapest (☞ Budapest A to Z, *above*). Keleti pályaudvar (East Station) receives most international rail traffic coming in from the west. Nyugati pályaudvar (West Station) handles a combination of international and domestic trains. For 24-hour rail information in Budapest, call 1/461–5500 (international) or 1/461–5400 (domestic).

Getting Around

By Boat

Hungary is well equipped with nautical transport, and Budapest is situated on a major international waterway, the Danube. Vienna is five hours away by hydrofoil or boat. For information about excursions or pleasure cruises, contact **MAHART Tours** (✉ V, Belgrád rakpart, Budapest, ☏ 484–4025 or 1/484–4010).

By Bus

Long-distance buses link Budapest with most cities in Hungary. Services to the eastern part of the country leave from the **Népstadion sta-**

tion (☎ 1/485–2100). For the Danube Bend, buses leave from the bus terminal at **Árpád Bridge** (☎ 1/329–1450). Arrive at least 20 minutes before departure to buy a ticket (this is not possible for all routes, as tickets for some routes can only be purchased directly from the driver); and if there's a crowd pressing to get on, feel free to wave your prepurchased ticket about as you jostle your way aboard (technically speaking, reserved seats must be occupied by no later than ten minutes before departure time).

By Car

Getting around by car is the best way to see Hungary. It's a small country, so even driving across the whole territory is manageable. Speed traps are numerous, so it's best to keep at the speed limit; fines start from the equivalent of roughly $40, but they can easily reach $230! Using—even holding—a cell phone while driving is an offense. In an effort to forestall bribe-taking, the time-honored practice of on-the-spot payment for violations was abolished in early 2000, so police must now give accused speedsters an invoice payable at post offices. (Remember this should you feel innocent and an officer suggests an on-the-spot "discount.") Spot checks are frequent as well, and police occasionally try to take advantage of foreigners, so always have your papers at hand.

Gas stations are plentiful in Hungary, and many on the main highways stay open all night, even on holidays. Major chains, such as MOL, Shell, and OMV, now have Western-style full-facility stations with rest rooms, brightly lit convenience stores, and 24-hour service. Lines are rarely long, and supplies are essentially stable. Unleaded gasoline (*bleifrei* or *ólommentes*) is generally available at most stations and is usually the 95-octane-level choice. If your car requires unleaded gasoline, be sure to double-check that you're not reaching for the leaded before you pump.

To drive in Hungary, U.S. and Canadian visitors need an International Driver's License—although their domestic licenses are usually accepted anyway. A caveat: It can get messy and expensive if you are stopped by a police officer who insists you need an International Driver's License (which, legally, you do). U.K. visitors may use their own domestic licenses.

PARKING

Gone are the "anything goes" days of parking in Budapest, when cars parked for free practically anywhere in the city, straddling curbs or angled in the middle of sidewalks. Now most streets in Budapest's main districts have restricted, fee parking; there are either parking meters that accept coins (usually for a maximum of two hours) or attendants who approach your car as you park and charge you according to how many hours you intend to stay. Hourly rates average 160 Ft. In most cases, overnight parking (generally after 6 PM and before 8 AM) in these areas is free. Budapest also has a number of parking lots and a few garages; two central-Pest garages are: V, Szervita tér and V, Aranykéz u. 4–6.

Smaller towns usually have free parking on the street, and some hourly-fee lots near main tourist zones. Throughout the country, no-parking zones are marked with the international "No Parking" sign: a white circle with a diagonal line through it.

ROAD CONDITIONS

There are four classes of roads: expressways (designated by the letter M and a single digit), main highways (a single digit), secondary roads (a two-digit number), and minor roads (a three-digit number). Highways, expressways, and secondary roads are generally in good condition. The conditions of minor roads vary considerably; keep in mind that tractors and horse-drawn carts may slow your route down in rural areas. In planning your driving route with a map, opt for the larger roadways whenever possible; you'll generally end up saving time even if there is a shorter but smaller road. It's not so much the condition of the smaller roads but the kind of traffic on them and the number of towns (where the speed limit is 50 kph [30 mph]) they pass through that will slow you down. If you're in no hurry, however, explore the smaller roads!

RULES OF THE ROAD

Hungarians drive on the right and observe the usual Continental rules of the road (but they revel in passing). Unless otherwise noted, the speed limit in developed areas is 50 kph (30 mph), on main roads 80–100 kph (50–62 mph), and on highways 120 kph (75 mph). Keep alert: Speed-limit signs are few and far between. Seat belts are compulsory (front-seat belts in lower speed zones, both front and back in higher speed zones), and drinking alcohol is totally prohibited—there is a zero-tolerance policy, and the penalties are very severe.

By Train

Travel by train from Budapest to other large cities or to Lake Balaton is cheap and efficient. Remember to take **Intercity (IC)** trains—which are especially clean and fast, but require a *helyjegy* (seat reservation) for about 350 Ft.—or ***gyorsvonat*** (express trains) and not *személyvonat* (locals), which are extremely slow. On timetables, tracks (*vágány*) are abbreviated with a "v"; *indul* means departing, while *érkezik* means arriving. Trains get crowded during weekend travel in summer; you're more likely to have elbow room if you pay a little extra for first-class tickets.

Only Hungarian citizens are entitled to student discounts on train fares; all senior citizens (men over 60, women over 55), however, are eligible for a 20% discount. InterRail cards are available for those under 26, and the Rail Europe Senior Travel Pass entitles senior citizens to a 30% reduction on all train fares. Snacks and drinks are becoming less available on trains, so pack a lunch for the road; train picnics are a way of life. For more information about rail travel, contact or visit **MAV Passenger Service** (✉ VI, Andrássy út 35, Budapest, ☎ 1/461–5500 international information; 1/461–5400 domestic information).

Contacts and Resources

B&B Reservation Agencies

See Apartment Rentals and B&B Reservation Agencies *in* Budapest A to Z, *above.*

Car Rentals

There are no special requirements for renting a car in Hungary, but be sure to shop around, as prices can differ greatly. **Avis** and **Hertz** offer Western makes for as much as $550 and more per week. Smaller local companies, on the other hand, can rent Hungarian cars for as low as $150 per week. Try to make rental arrangements before you get to Hungary; renting a car when you get there costs quite a bit more than an advance reservation. *See* Car Rentals *in* Budapest A to Z, *above,* for a list of agencies.

Foreign driver's licenses are generally accepted by car rental agencies but are technically not valid legally (☞ Getting Around By Car, *above,* for more information).

Customs and Duties

ON ARRIVAL

Objects for personal use may be imported freely. If you are over 16, you may bring in 250 cigarettes or 50 cigars or 250 grams of tobacco, plus 2 liters of wine, 1 liter of spirits, and 100 milliliters of perfume. (You also may leave Hungary with this much, plus 5 liters of beer). If you bring in more than 400 dollars in cash and think you may be taking that much out, technically speaking you should declare it on arrival. A customs charge is made on gifts valued in Hungary at more than 30,500 Ft.

ON DEPARTURE

Take care when you leave Hungary that you have the right documentation for exporting goods. Keep receipts of any major purchases. A special permit is needed for works of art, antiques, or objects of museum value. Upon leaving, you are entitled to a value-added tax (VAT) refund on new goods (i.e., not works of art, antiques, or objects of museum value) valued at 50,000 Ft. or more (VAT inclusive). But applying for the refund may rack up more frustration than money: Cash refunds are given only in forints, and you may find yourself in the airport minutes before boarding with a handful of soft currency; while you can take out up to 350,000 forints, converting it back home will be close to impossible. If you otherwise don't have much hard currency on you, you can convert up to about 100,000 of the forints into dollars to come up with the 400-dollars-in-cash export limit. If you made your purchases by credit card you can file for a credit to your card or to your bank account (again in forints), but don't expect it to come through in a hurry. If you intend to apply for the credit, make sure you get customs to stamp the original purchase invoice before you leave the country. For more information, pick up a tax refund brochure from any tourist office or hotel, or contact **Intel Trade Rt.** (✉ I, Csalogány u. 6-10, ☎ 1/201–8120 or 1/356–9800) in Budapest. For further Hungarian customs information, inquire at the **National Customs and Revenue Office** (✉ Regional Directorate for Central Hungary, XIV, Hungária krt. 112–114, Budapest, ☎ 1/470–4121 or 470–4122). If you have trouble communicating, ask **Tourinform** (☎ 1/317–9800) for help.

Emergencies

Ambulance (☎ 104). **Fire** (☎ 105). **Hungarian Automobile Club**'s breakdown service (☎ 188). **Police** (☎ 107).

Guided Tours

BOAT TOURS

Contact **MAHART Tours** (✉ V, Belgrád rakpart, Budapest, ☎ 1/318–1704) for information about its roster of boat tours on Lake Balaton and on the Danube in and beyond Budapest.

GENERAL

IBUSZ Travel (☞ *below*) offers a variety of changing bus tours to places around the country, from cave visits in the Mátra Mountains to wine tasting in the Tokaj region to traditional pig roasts on the Great Plain.

Language

Hungarian (*Magyar*) tends to look and sound intimidating at first because it is not an Indo-European language. Generally, older people speak some German, and many younger people speak at least rudimentary English, which has become the most popular language to learn. It's a safe bet that anyone in the tourist trade will speak at least one of the two languages. Also note that when giving names, Hungarians put the family name before the given name.

Mail

Airmail letters and postcards generally take seven days to travel between Hungary and the United States, sometimes more than twice as long, however, during the Christmas season.

In Hungary, go to Budapest's main **downtown post office** branch (✉ Magyar Posta 4. sz., Városház u. 18, H-1052 Budapest). The post offices near Budapest's **Keleti** (East) (✉ VIII, Baross tér) and **Nyugati** (West) (✉ VI, Teréz krt. 51) train stations stay open until 9 PM on weekdays, the former just as long on weekends while the latter shuts its doors at 8 PM. The **American Express** office in Hungary is in Budapest (✉ Deák Ferenc u. 10 H-1052 Budapest, ☎ 1/235–4330); there are poste restante services.

POSTAL RATES

Postage for an airmail letter to the United States costs about 160 Ft.; an airmail letter to the United Kingdom and elsewhere in Western Europe costs about 150 Ft. Airmail postcards to the United States cost about 110 Ft. and to the United Kingdom and the rest of Western Europe, about 100 Ft.

Money and Expenses

Eurocheque holders can cash personal checks in all banks and in most hotels. Many banks now also cash American Express and Visa traveler's checks. **American Express** has a full-service office in Budapest (✉ V, Deák Ferenc u. 10, ☎ 1/235–4330, FAX 1/267–2028), which also dispenses cash to its cardholders; a smaller branch on Castle Hill—at the Sisi Restaurant (☎ 1/264–0118)—has a currency exchange which operates daily from March to mid-January. Budapest also has a **Citibank** (✉ V, Vörösmarty tér 4) offering full services to account holders, including a 24-hour cash machine.

Plastic has recently entered Hungary's financial scene: Most major credit cards are accepted, though don't rely on them in smaller towns or less expensive accommodations and restaurants. Twenty-four-hour cash machines have sprung up throughout Budapest and in major towns around the country. Some accept Plus network bank cards and Visa credit cards, others Cirrus and MasterCard. You can withdraw forints only (automatically converted at the bank's official exchange rate) directly from your account. Most levy a 1% or $3 service charge. Instructions are in English. For those without plastic, many cash-exchange machines, into which you feed paper currency for forints, have also sprung up. Most bank automats and cash-exchange machines are clustered around their respective bank branches throughout downtown Pest.

COSTS

The forint was significantly devalued over the last few years and continues its decline, but at press time inflation had fallen under 10% from the 25% of five years ago. You'll receive more forints for your dollar but will find that prices have risen to keep up with inflation. More and more hotels now set their rates in hard currency to avoid the forint's instability. Still, even with inflation and the 25% value-added tax (VAT) in the service industry, enjoyable vacations with all the trimmings still remain less expensive than in nearby Western cities such as Vienna.

CURRENCY

Hungary's unit of currency is the forint (Ft.), no longer divided into fillérs as it was a few years ago. There are bills of 200, 500, 1,000, 2,000, 5,000, and 10,000 forints (at press time one of 20,000 forints was also planned); and coins of 1, 2, 5, 10, 20, 50, and 100 forints. The exchange rate was approximately 302 Ft. to the U.S. dollar, 204 Ft. to the Canadian dollar, and 427 Ft. to the pound sterling at press time. Although cash card and Eurocheque facilities are easy to find in big cities, it is probably still wise to bring traveler's checks, which can be cashed all over the country in banks and hotels. There is still a black market in hard currency, but changing money on the street is risky and illegal, and the bank rate almost always comes close. Stick with banks and official exchange offices.

SAMPLE COSTS

Cup of coffee, 120 Ft.–200 Ft.; bottle of beer, 350 Ft.–550 Ft.; soft drinks, 150 Ft.; ham sandwich, 200 Ft.; 2-km (1-mi) taxi ride, 300 Ft.; museum admission, 150 Ft.–300 Ft.

National Holidays

January 1; March 15 (Anniversary of 1848 Revolution); April 15–16, 2001 and March 31–April 1, 2002 (Easter and Easter Monday); May 1 (Labor Day); June 3–4, 2001 and May 19–20, 2002 (Pentecost); August 20 (St. Stephen's and Constitution Day); October 23 (1956 Revolution Day); December 24–26.

Opening and Closing Times

Banks are generally open weekdays until 3 or 4; most close by 2 on Friday. Museums are generally open Tuesday through Sunday from 10 to 6 and are closed on Monday; most stop admitting people 30 minutes before closing time. Some have a free-admission day; see individual listings in tours below, but double-check, as the days tend to change. Department stores are open weekdays 10–5 or 6, Saturday until 1. Grocery stores are generally open weekdays from 7 AM to 6 or 7 PM, Saturday until 1 PM; "nonstops," or *éjjel-nappali,* are (theoretically) open 24 hours.

Outdoor Activities and Sports

BICYCLING

Tourinform (☞ *below*) in Budapest can provide you with the "Hungary by Bike" brochure and general information on current rental outfits. For specifics on bicycling conditions and suggested routes, contact the **Bicycle Touring Association of Hungary** (✉ V, Bajcsy-Zsilinszky út 31, 2nd floor, Apt. 3, Budapest, ☎ 1/332–7177).

CAMPING

Camping is forbidden except in appointed areas. Information, reservations, and an informative campsite listing and map can be obtained from travel agencies and Tourinform (☞ *below*). You may also contact the **Hungarian Camping and Caravanning Club** (✉ VIII, Mária u. 34, Budapest, ☎ 1/267–5255 or 1/267–5256).

GOLF

Those itching for some swinging can contact the **Hungarian Professional Golf Association** (✉ XVI, Dózsa György út 1–3, Budapest, ☎ 1/221–5923).

Passports and Visas

Only a valid passport is required of U.S., British, and Canadian citizens; Australian citizens need a visa. For additional information contact the **Hungarian Embassy** in the United States (✉ 3910 Shoemaker St. NW, Washington, DC 20008, ☎ 202/362–6730), in Canada (✉ 299 Waverley St. Ottawa, Ontario K2P 0V9, ☎ 613/230–9614), in London (✉ 35b Eaton Pl., London SW1X 8BY, ☎ 0171/235–5218), or in Australia (✉ 17 Beale Crescent Deakin Act., Canberra 2600, ☎ 6126/282–3226).

Rail Passes

There are several passes valid in Hungary. You can use the **European East Pass** on the national rail networks of Hungary, Austria, the Czech Republic, Poland, and Slovakia. The pass covers five days of unlimited first-class travel within a one-month period for $205. Additional travel days may be purchased. For travel only within Hungary, there's a **Hungarian Flexipass,** which costs $64 for five days of unlimited first-class train travel within a 15-day period or $80 for 10 days within a one-month period. Hungary is also the rare Eastern European country that is covered by a **Eurailpass,** which provides unlimited first-class rail travel, in all of the participating countries, for the duration of the pass. These are available for 15 days ($554), 21 days ($718), one month ($890), two months ($1,260), and three months ($1,558). For further information, *see* Train Travel *in* Smart Travel Tips A to Z.

Student and Youth Travel

In Hungary, as a general rule, only Hungarian citizens and students at Hungarian institutions qualify for student discounts on domestic travel fares and admission fees. Travelers under 25, however, qualify for excellent youth rates on international airfares; those under 26 are eligible for youth rates on international train fares. The International Student Identity Card (ISIC) is accepted in Budapest and other large Hungarian cities, but not as widely as it is in Western countries. If you buy your Student Identity Card in Budapest at the **Express Youth and Travel Office** (✉ V, Zoltán u. 10, ☎ 1/311–6418; V, Szabadság tér 16, ☎ 1/331–6393; VIII, Keleti train station, ☎ 1/342–1772), which specializes in providing information on all aspects of student and youth travel throughout the country and abroad, it will cost about one-third the price of buying the card in the United States.

Telephones

Within Hungary, most towns can be dialed directly—dial 06 and wait for the buzzing tone; then dial the local number. Note that cellular phone numbers are treated like long-distance domestic calls: Dial 06 before the number (when giving their cellular phone numbers, most people include the 06 anyway).

Dial 198 for directory assistance for all of Hungary. Operators are unlikely to speak English. A safer bet is to consult *The Phone Book,* an English-language telephone directory full of important Budapest numbers as well as cultural and tourist information; it's provided in guest rooms of most major hotels, as well as at many restaurants and English-language bookstores. A similar, though much slimmer guide is *Budapest in Your Pocket,* which appears five times a year and can be found at newsstands and hotels.

Though continuously improving, the Hungarian telephone system is still antiquated, especially in the countryside. Be patient. With the slow improvements comes the problem of numbers changing—sometimes without forewarning. Tens of thousands of phone numbers in Budapest alone will be changed over the next few years; if you're having trouble getting through, ask your concierge to check the number for you.

COUNTRY CODE

The country code for Hungary is 36. When dialing from outside the country, drop the initial 06 prefix for area codes outside of Budapest.

INTERNATIONAL CALLS

Direct calls to foreign countries can be made from Budapest and all major provincial towns by dialing 00 and waiting for the international dialing tone; on pay phones the initial charge is 60 Ft. To reach an **AT&T** long-distance operator, dial ☎ 06–800–01111; for **MCI,** dial ☎ 06–800–01411; for **Sprint,** dial ☎ 06–800–01877.

LOCAL CALLS

Coin-operated pay phones accept 10-Ft., 20-Ft., 50-Ft., and 100-Ft. coins; the minimum initial amount is 20 Ft. Given that they often swallow up change without allowing a call in exchange, however, when possible use gray card-operated telephones, which outnumber coin-operated phones in Budapest and the Balaton region. The cards—available at post offices and most newsstands and kiosks—come in units of 60 (800 Ft.) and 90 (1,800 Ft.) calls. It is unnecessary to use the city code, 1, when dialing within Budapest. Don't be surprised if a flock of children gathers around your pay phone while you talk—collecting and trading used phone cards is a raging fad.

Tipping

Four decades of socialism have not restrained the extended palm in Hungary—so tip when in doubt. Hairdressers and taxi drivers expect 10%–15% tips, while porters should get a dollar or two. Coatroom attendants receive 100 Ft.–200 Ft., as do gas-pump attendants if they wash your windows or check your tires; dressing-room attendants at thermal baths receive 50 Ft.–100 Ft. for opening and closing your locker. Gratuities are not included automatically on bills at most restaurants; when the waiter arrives with the bill, you should immediately add a 10%–15% tip to the amount, as it is not customary to leave the tip on the table. If a Gypsy band plays exclusively for your table, you should leave at least 200 Ft. in a plate discreetly provided for that purpose.

Travel Agencies

American Express (✉ V, Deák Ferenc u. 10, Budapest, ☎ 1/235–4330, FAX 1/267–2028). **Getz International** (✉ V, Falk Miksa u. 5, Budapest, ☎ 1/312–0645 or 1/312–0649, FAX 1/312–1014). **Vista Travel Center** (✉ VI, Andrássy út 1, Budapest, ☎ 1/269–6032 or 1/269–6033, FAX 1/269–6031).

Visitor Information

Tourinform (✉ V, Sütő u. 2, Budapest, ☎ 1/317–9800). **IBUSZ** (central branch: ✉ V, Ferenciek tere 10, Budapest, ☎ 1/485–2700). **TRIBUS Hotel Service** (✉ V, Apáczai Csere János u. 1, Budapest, ☎ 1/318–5776, open 24 hours).

5 SLOVENIA

Until 1991 the wealthiest republic of Yugoslavia, Slovenia emerged remarkably unscathed from the breakup of the Yugoslav federation. Today, in contrast to some of its neighbors, Slovenia bears no grudges against anyone. Why should it? A land of magnificent alpine mountains and lakes, undulating farmland and vineyards, plus a tiny strip of emerald blue Adriatic coast, Slovenia seems to have it all. Here, Mediterranean charm and Austrian efficiency blend with a genuine and captivating Slavic friendliness. The Slovenes' intrinsic love of nature is reflected in the motto they use for their country: A Green Piece of Europe.

By Jane Foster

TODAY BORDERED BY ITALY, AUSTRIA, HUNGARY, AND CROATIA, the territory that is now Slovenia has changed size, shape, and affiliation many times over the course of history. In ancient times the region was inhabited by Illyrian and Celtic tribes. The Romans arrived in the 1st century BC, built villas along the coast, and founded the inland urban centers of Emona (Ljubljana) and Poetovio (Ptuj). The 6th century saw the first influx of Slav migrants, who set up an early Slav state. During the 8th century the region came under the Franks, and in the 9th century it was passed to the dukes of Bavaria.

In 1335 the Hapsburgs took control of inland Slovenia, dividing it into the Austrian crown lands of Carinthia, Carniola, and Styria. Meanwhile, the coastal towns had requested Venetian protection, and they remained under *la serenissima* until 1797, after which they too were taken by Austria.

During the 15th and 16th centuries, the Turks, eager to extend the Ottoman Empire right across the Balkans and north to Vienna, made repeated attacks on the region. However, Slovenia remained under the Hapsburgs until 1918, with the exception of a brief period from 1809 to 1813 when it became part of Napoléon's Illyrian Provinces.

In the aftermath of the First World War, Italy seized control of the coastal towns, while inland Slovenia became part of the Kingdom of Serbs, Croats, and Slovenes. In 1929 the name was changed to Yugoslavia (Land of the Southern Slavs).

In 1941 Hitler declared war on Yugoslavia: Axis forces occupied the country, and Slovenia was divided between Germany, Italy, and Hungary. Josip Broz, better known as Tito, set up the anti-Fascist Partisan movement, and many Slovenes took part in resistance activities. When the war ended in 1945 Slovenia became one of the six constituent republics of Yugoslavia, with Tito as president. Slovenes today are proud of their Partisan past, and traveling through the country you see monuments and wall plaques bearing the red star, a symbol of the Partisans and of Communist ideology, and squares and roads still named after Tito.

Half Slovene and half Croat, Tito was undeniably an astute leader. He governed Yugoslavia under Communist ideology, but the system was far more liberal than that of the Soviet-bloc countries: Yugoslavs enjoyed freedom of movement, and foreign visitors could enter the country without visas. During the Cold War, Tito never took sides, but dealt cleverly with both East and West, thus procuring massive loans from both.

However, when Tito died in 1980, the system he left behind began to crumble. The false nature of the economy, based on borrowing, became apparent. During the 1980s economic crisis set in and inflation soared. Slovenia, accounting for only 8% of Yugoslavia's population, was producing one-third of the nation's exports. The hard-earned foreign currency ended up in Belgrade and was used in part to subsidize the poorer republics. It was time for change.

In early 1990 Slovenia introduced a multiparty system and elected a non-Communist government. Demands for increased autonomy were stepped up, with the threat of secession. A referendum was held, and 90% of the electorate voted for independence. Unlike the other Yugoslav republics, Slovenia was made up almost exclusively of a single ethnic group: Slovenes. Thus the potential status of ethnic minorities should the republic secede was never an issue. Slovenia proclaimed independence on June 25, 1991, and the so-called 10-Day War followed.

Federal troops moved in, but there was relatively little violence. Belgrade had already agreed to let Slovenia go.

In 1992 Slovenia gained recognition, along with Croatia, from the European Community and the United Nations. Since then the economy has picked up dramatically and tourism has flourished.

Situated at a geopolitical crossroads, this tiny Slavic nation has had to redefine its position in the modern world. Visitors will find the culture particularly accessible: a large percentage of the younger generation speaks several foreign languages (English, Italian, and German), and Slovenia is probably the most Internet-friendly country in Central and Eastern Europe.

Pleasures and Pastimes

Bicycling

Slovenia has a number of clearly marked bike trails, with needed services along the routes: bike rentals, maintenance and spare parts, and tourist information. Rental agencies, good hotels, and local tourist information centers can provide detailed information about suitable itineraries. For mountain biking, Triglav National Park is popular. If you prefer less-strenuous riding, try the riverside trails near Maribor. A brochure, *Slovenia by Bicycle,* is available from the Slovenian Tourist Board (☞ Visitor Information *in* Slovenia A to Z, *below*).

Castles

The earliest castles in Slovenia date back to the Middle Ages and were built as hilltop observation points with views over the surrounding valleys. Several trade-routes traversed the region. Merchandise brought prosperity, but with it the danger of attack. During the 15th and 16th centuries a series of Turkish onslaughts sparked off increased fortification. The castles and manors as we see them today largely reflect the habits of the local aristocracy during the 17th century, with their love of Viennese culture and a propensity for Baroque decor. A number of castles now house museums and galleries, and several have been converted into first-class hotels and restaurants. A brochure, *Castles and Manors,* is available from the Slovenian Tourist Board (☞ Visitor Information *in* Slovenia A to Z, *below*).

Dining

When you look at a menu remember two key words: regional and seasonal. This is the way to find the best food in Slovenia. (You'll find menus in English, plus waitstaff who speak English, almost everywhere.) There are no pretensions at the table, and full respect is paid to simple traditional dishes. To really get down to basics, eat in a *gostilna* (country inn). Typical dishes are *krvavice* (black pudding) served with *žganci* (polenta) or sausages served with sauerkraut. Another favorite is *bograč,* a peppery stew similar to Hungarian goulash, made from either horse meat or beef.

With the Adriatic close at hand, you can also find excellent seafood. Visit a good *restauracija* (restaurant) and try mouth-watering *škampi rižot* (scampi risotto) followed by fresh fish prepared *na žaru* (barbecued). On the menu, fish is usually priced per kilogram (2.2 pounds). The first-rate fish are expensive, so don't be surprised when the bill comes.

For an extra boost stop at a *kavarna* (coffee shop) for a scrumptious, calorie-laden *prekmurska gibanica,* a layered cake combining curd cheese, walnuts, and poppy seeds. Another national favorite is *potica,* a rolled cake filled with either walnuts, chocolate, poppy seeds, or raisins.

CATEGORY	COST*
$$$$	$25
$$$	$15–$25
$$	$7–$15
$	under $7

**per person for a three-course meal, excluding wine and tip.*

Fishing

The River Soča, stocked with rare marble trout, rainbow trout, and grayling, attracts anglers from all over the world with its excellent fly-fishing amid stunning scenery. The season runs from April through October, and daily permits are obligatory. Kobarid makes an ideal base.

Hiking

Slovenes love mountains, and when you reach the northwest of the country you will understand why. The most popular alpine hiking route runs from Maribor near the Austrian border to Ankaran on the Adriatic coast. It crosses Triglav National Park and can be walked in 30 days. For less devoted walkers, a day or two of backpacking from one of the alpine resorts is an invigorating way to explore the landscape. Mountain paths are well marked, and mountain lodges have dormitory-style accommodations. Detailed maps are available at local tourist information centers.

Horse Riding

The most famous equestrian center is the Lipica Stud Farm, home of the splendid Lipizzaner white horses. Riding lessons are available, and it is also possible to hire horses for gentle hacking.

Visitors to the Krka Valley can ride at the Struga Equestrian Center, at a 12th-century medieval manor near Otočec Castle. In Triglav National Park the best-equipped riding center is Pristava Lepena. A brochure, *Riding in Slovenia, Home of the Lipizzaner,* is available from the Slovenian Tourist Board (☞ Visitor Information *in* Slovenia A to Z, *below*).

Kayaking, Canoeing, and Rafting

The River Soča has ideal conditions for a wide range of water sports. The best rapids lie between Bovec and Kobarid. Numerous clubs rent out boats and equipment and also offer instruction and guided rafting and kayaking trips.

Lodging

Don't expect Slovenia to be a cheap option: lodging prices are similar to what you'd see in Western Europe. During peak season (July and August), many hotels, particularly on the coast, are fully booked. Hotels are generally clean, smartly furnished, and well run. Establishments built under socialism are equipped with extras such as saunas and sports facilities but tend to be gargantuan structures lacking in soul. Hotels dating from the turn of the 20th century are more romantic, as are the castle hotels. Over the last decade many hotels have been refurbished and upgraded. Most establishments add a 30% surcharge for stays of fewer than three days.

Private lodgings are a cheap alternative to hotels, and standards are generally excellent. Prices vary depending on region and season. For details contact a local tourist information center.

Between April and October camping is a reasonable alternative. Most campgrounds are small but well equipped. On the coast, campsites are found at Izola and Ankaran. In Triglav National Park and the Soča Valley there are sites at Bled, Bohinj, Bovec, Kobarid, Soča, and Trenta. It is also possible to camp on the grounds of Otočec Castle in the Krka Valley. Camping outside of organized campsites is not permitted.

To really experience day-to-day life in the countryside you should stay on a working farm. Agrotourism is rapidly growing in popularity, and at most farms visitors can experience an idyllic rural setting, delicious home cooking, plus a warm family welcome. A brochure, *Tourist Farms in Slovenia,* is available from the Slovenian Tourist Board (☞ Visitor Information *in* Slovenia A to Z, *below*).

CATEGORY	COST*
$$$$	over $150
$$$	$100–$150
$$	$60–$100
$	under $60

**All prices are for a standard double room, including tax and service.*

following the text is your signal that the property has a Web site, where you will find details and, usually, images; for a link, visit www.fodors.com/urls.

Sailing

Slovenia is an ideal starting point for sailing down the Adriatic coast. There are three marinas: Izola (where it is possible to rent yachts), Portorož, and Koper. Portorož Yacht Club organizes a number of annual international regattas.

Shopping

The most interesting gifts to buy in Slovenia are the homemade products you come across in your travels: wine from Ptuj, *rakija* (a potent spirit distilled from fruit) from Pleterje Monastery, herbal teas from Stična Monastery, honey from Radovljica. The Slovenian products best known abroad are connected with outdoor sports. If you'd like some Planika walking boots or Elan skis, you can get a good deal on them here.

Skiing

Skiing is undoubtedly one of the most popular sports in Slovenia. The largest and best-known ski area is Kranjska Gora, on the edge of Triglav National Park. The nearby resorts of Bovec, Bohinj, and Bled provide similar facilities on a smaller scale. To the east, the Pohorje Mountains near Maribor have alpine ski runs and groomed cross-country trails. All centers are well equipped, with rental equipment, ski lifts, and qualified instructors. In a good winter it is possible to ski from December through March (in some places until the beginning of May). Each year Slovenia hosts a number of major World Cup skiing events, the most spectacular being the ski jumping and ski flying at Planica, near Kranjska Gora. A brochure, *Ski Centers in Slovenia,* is available from the Slovenian Tourist Board (☞ Visitor Information *in* Slovenia A to Z, *below*).

Wine and Spirits

Slovenes enjoy drinking and produce some excellent wines. Most of these they consume themselves, so unfortunately very little reaches the foreign market. You can tour the three main wine regions following a series of recently established "wine roads." These routes pass through rolling hills, woodlands, and villages and lead directly to vineyards and wine stores. The best white wines, *Laški Rizling* and *Renski Rizling,* are produced in the Drava valley in northeast Slovenia. The best red is *Teran,* produced in the karst region to the southwest, close to the Adriatic coast. There has been a recent drive to introduce more sparkling wines: look for the excellent *Penina.* The favorite national spirit is the potent rakija. The base is alcohol distilled from fruit; a variety of wild herbs are added later to give it a more discreet flavor.

Exploring Slovenia

Besides the capital, Ljubljana, the principal areas of interest to tourists are Triglav National Park and the Soča Valley to the northwest, and the Adriatic coast and the karst region to the southwest. The Krka Valley, to the east, is notable for its monasteries and castles, while the region to the northeast, centering on Maribor, Ptuj, and the Haloze Hills, has rolling hills, vineyards, and excellent wine cellars.

Great Itineraries

Numbers in the text correspond to numbers in the margin and on the Ljubljana; Maribor, Ptuj, and the Haloze Hills; Triglav National Park and the Soča Valley; and the Adriatic Coast and the Karst Region maps.

Slovenia's small size (about half the area of Switzerland) can be an advantage. From the centrally located capital, Ljubljana, you can drive to any point in the country in a maximum of three hours.

IF YOU HAVE 3 DAYS

If you have limited time, take one day to discover the Old Town of **Ljubljana** ①–㉒. The next day, drive out to the alpine mountains and lakes of Triglav National Park and stay the night in **Bled** ㉘. Spend the third day exploring the caves of the karst region, topping it off with a night by the Adriatic in the beautiful Venetian town of **Piran** ㊴.

IF YOU HAVE 5 DAYS

Make Ljubljana your base for the first three days. Explore the capital for a day, then head out to the wine-making area around **Maribor** ㉕ and **Ptuj** ㉖. On day three, visit the monasteries of Stična and Pleterje in the Krka Valley, with the option of a romantic night in a castle hotel. Spend the last two days exploring Triglav National Park and the karst region.

When to Tour

The countryside is at its most beautiful in spring and fall, though the best period to visit depends on what you plan to do during your stay. Ljubljana is vibrant the whole year through. Many visitors want to head straight for the coast. Those in search of sea, sun, and all-night parties will find exactly what they're looking for in peak season (July and August), including cultural events, open-air dancing, busy restaurants, and heaving beaches. If you want to avoid the crowds, hit the Adriatic in June or September when it should be warm enough to swim and easier to find a space for your beach towel.

In the mountains there are two distinct seasons: winter is dedicated to skiing, summer to hiking and bathing. Some hotels close in November and March, to mark a break between the two periods. Conditions for more-strenuous walking and biking are optimal in April, May, September, and October.

Lovers of fine food and wine should visit Slovenia during fall. The grape harvest concludes with the blessing of the season's young wine on St. Martin's Day, preceded by three weeks of festivities. In rural areas autumn is the time to make provisions for the hard winter ahead: wild mushrooms are gathered, firewood chopped, and *koline* (sausages and other pork products) prepared by hand.

LJUBLJANA

The romantic heart of the Old Town—with a hilltop castle overlooking the winding emerald green Ljubljanica River, lined with Baroque facades and graceful weeping willows—dates back centuries. The earliest settlement was founded by the Romans and called Emona. Much

Slovenia (Slovenija)

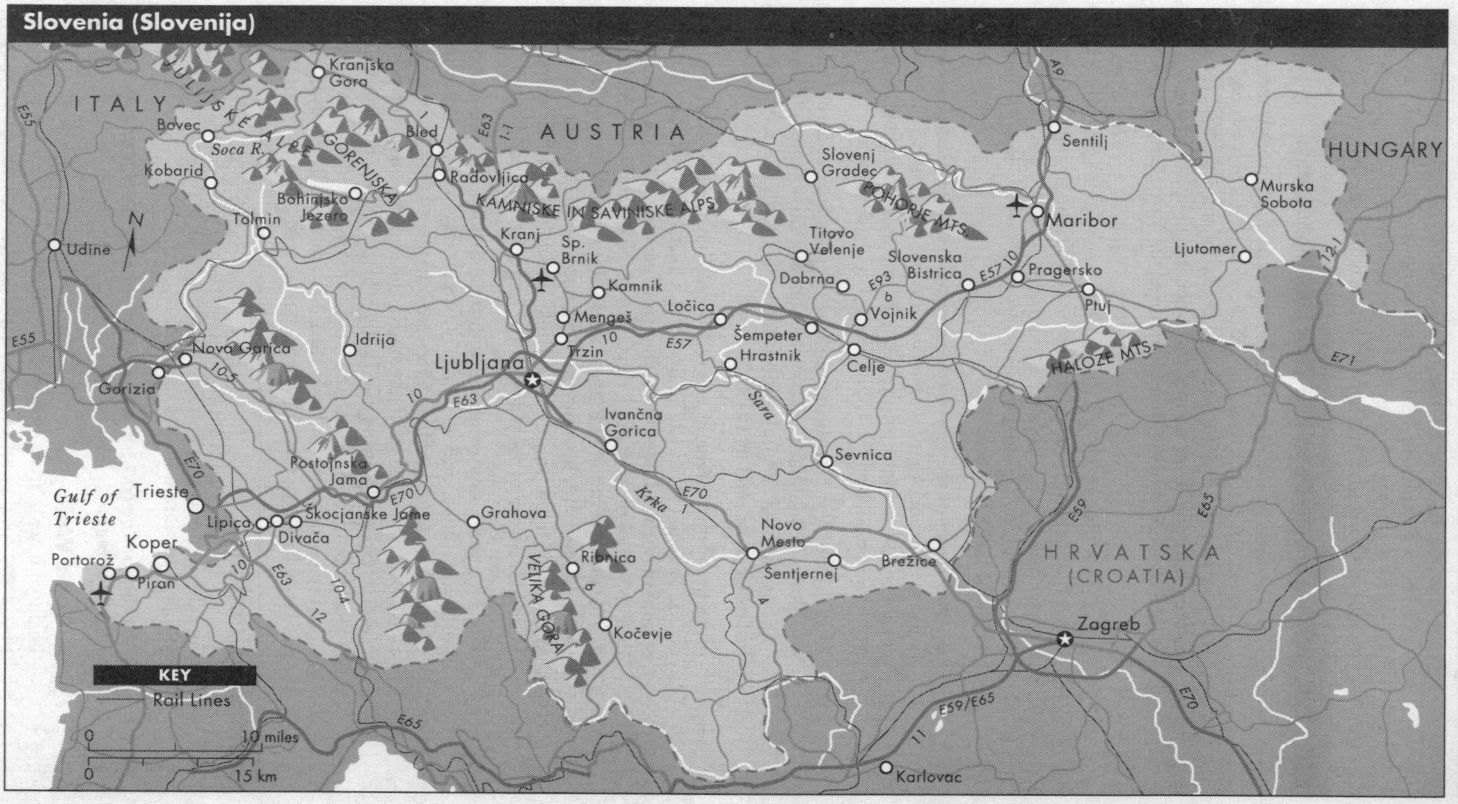

of it was destroyed by the Huns under Attila, though a section of the walls and a complex of foundations complete with mosaics can still be seen today. In the 12th century a new settlement, Laibach, was built on the right bank of the river, below castle hill, by the dukes of Carniola. In 1335, the Hapsburgs gained control of the region, and it was they who constructed the existing castle fortification system.

The 17th century saw a period of Baroque building, strongly influenced by currents in Austria and Italy. Walk along the cobblestones of the Town Square and the Old Square to see Ljubljana at its best, from the colored Baroque town houses with their steeply pitched tile roofs to Francesco Robba's delightful Fountain of the Three Carniolan Rivers.

For a brief period, from 1809 to 1813, Ljubljana was the capital of Napoléon's Illyrian Provinces. In 1849, once again under the Hapsburgs, Ljubljana was linked to Vienna and Trieste by rail. The city developed into a major center of commerce, industry, and culture, and the opera house, national theater, national museum, and the first hotels came into existence.

In 1895 much of the city was devastated by an earthquake. The reconstruction work that followed was carried out in florid Viennese Secessionist style. Many of the palatial four-story buildings that line Miklošičeva, such as the Grand Hotel Union, date from this period.

After World War I, with the birth of the Kingdom of Serbs, Croats, and Slovenes, Ljubljana became the administrative center of Slovenia. Various national cultural institutes were founded, and the University of Ljubljana opened in 1919.

If you have been to Prague, you will already have seen some of the work of Jože Plečnik (1872–1957). Born in Ljubljana, Plečnik studied architecture in Vienna under Otto Wagner, then went on to lecture at the Prague School of Arts and Crafts, also playing the role of chief architect for the renovation of Prague Castle. With the opening of Ljubljana University in 1919, he returned to his home town. Here he completed many of his finest projects: the Triple Bridge, the open-air market on Vodnik Square, and the plans for the Križanke Summer Theater.

The Tito years saw increased industrialization. The population of Ljubljana tripled, and vast factory complexes, high-rise apartments, and modern office buildings extended into the suburbs. Ljubljana was considered one of the most alternative and experimental centers in Yugoslavia, especially during the 1980s, when it became the center of the Yugoslav punk movement. The band Laibach, noted for mocking nationalist sentiments, and the absurdist conceptual art group Neue Slowenische Kunst (NSK) both have their roots here.

Exploring Ljubljana

The city center is concentrated within a small area, so you can cover all the sights on foot.

Numbers in the text correspond to numbers in the margin and on the Ljubljana map.

A Good Walk

Begin your walk from Prešernov trg (Prešeren Square), a traffic-free piazza and focal point of public gatherings, overlooked by the Secessionist **Centromerkur** ① department store and the pink Baroque **Franciskanska cerkev** ②. From here cross **Tromostovje** ③, pausing a moment to observe the majestic hilltop castle above the Old Town and the view down the willow-lined River Ljubljanica.

Now on Stritarjeva, take the first left for the colorful open-air market on **Vodnikov trg** ④, noting the tourist information center on the corner. To the left of the fruit and vegetable stalls you can see a row of bakeries and butchers, with steps leading down to an open-sided arcade that hosts the fish market on the waterfront. To the right—monumental and timeless amid the cries of stallholders and the bustling shoppers—stands **Stolnica sveti Nikolaja** ⑤. At the far end of the market the river is traversed by **Zmajski most** ⑥.

Double back to Stritarjeva, and turn left then right to arrive on **Mestni trg** ⑦. Here the pace of life slows down to that of years gone by as you enter the heart of the Old Town. See the **Robbov Vodnjak** ⑧ and the **Magistrat** ⑨, and stroll the length of this cobbled square lined with antique shops and boutiques. Mestni trg runs into **Stari trg** ⑩, animated with bars and cafés frequented by students. Follow the curve of the road left, and you are in **Gornji trg** ⑪, an up-and-coming area with some of the best restaurants in town. Look for a side street to the left called Ulica na Grad; follow this as far as house No. 11, then take a narrow path up through the woods to arrive at **grad** ⑫. From here you have a magnificent panorama of the entire city.

To return to the Old Town, find a narrow path just below the castle tower, which leads you via Studentovska to Ciril-Metodov trg (Cyril-Methodius Square), near the market. Turn left to arrive once more in Mestni trg, and from here take any one of the narrow cobbled passageways between the buildings on your right to reach the riverside promenade of **Cankarjevo nabrežje** ⑬. Follow the river downstream as far as **Čevljarski most** ⑭, then cross over to the other side of town. Turn left, following the river, then take the second right to reach the **Križanke Poletno Gledališče** ⑮ complex and, just above it, **Trg Francoske Revolucije** ⑯.

Walk back a block to Gosposka, then go north all the way to Kongresni trg (Congress Square), site of the **Slovenska Filharmonija** ⑰. Traverse the square to reach the busy Slovenska cesta, cross over and proceed along Šubičeva, turn right on Prešernova cesta, and you reach the main cluster of civic cultural buildings: the **Moderna galerija** ⑱, the **Opera** ⑲, the **Narodni muzej** ⑳, and the **Narodna galerija** ㉑, all built at the end of the 19th century.

If you are short on time, the one museum you really should see is the **Muzej Novejše Zgodovine** ㉒. To find it, follow Cankarjeva west toward Tivolska cesta, using the underpass to avoid the traffic. This brings you up into the vast green expanse of Tivoli Park. Turn right, then take a narrow path veering gently uphill to the left. Straight in front of you stands a pink-and-white Baroque villa, which houses the museum.

TIMING

If you don't have much time, you should be able to see all the major sights in a day. However, to do the museums and churches justice you need at least two days.

SIGHTS TO SEE

⓭ **Cankarjevo nabrežje.** Numerous cafés line this pretty riverside walkway. When the weather is good, tables are placed outside overlooking the water. *Between Tromostovje and Čevljarski most.*

❶ **Centromerkur.** This magnificent Secessionist-style building, dating from 1903, is the oldest department store in town. The entrance, off Prešernov trg, bears a flaring iron butterfly wing and is topped by a statue of Mercury. Inside, graceful wrought-iron stairways lead to upper floors. ✉ *Trubarjeva 1,* ☎ *01/426–3170.*

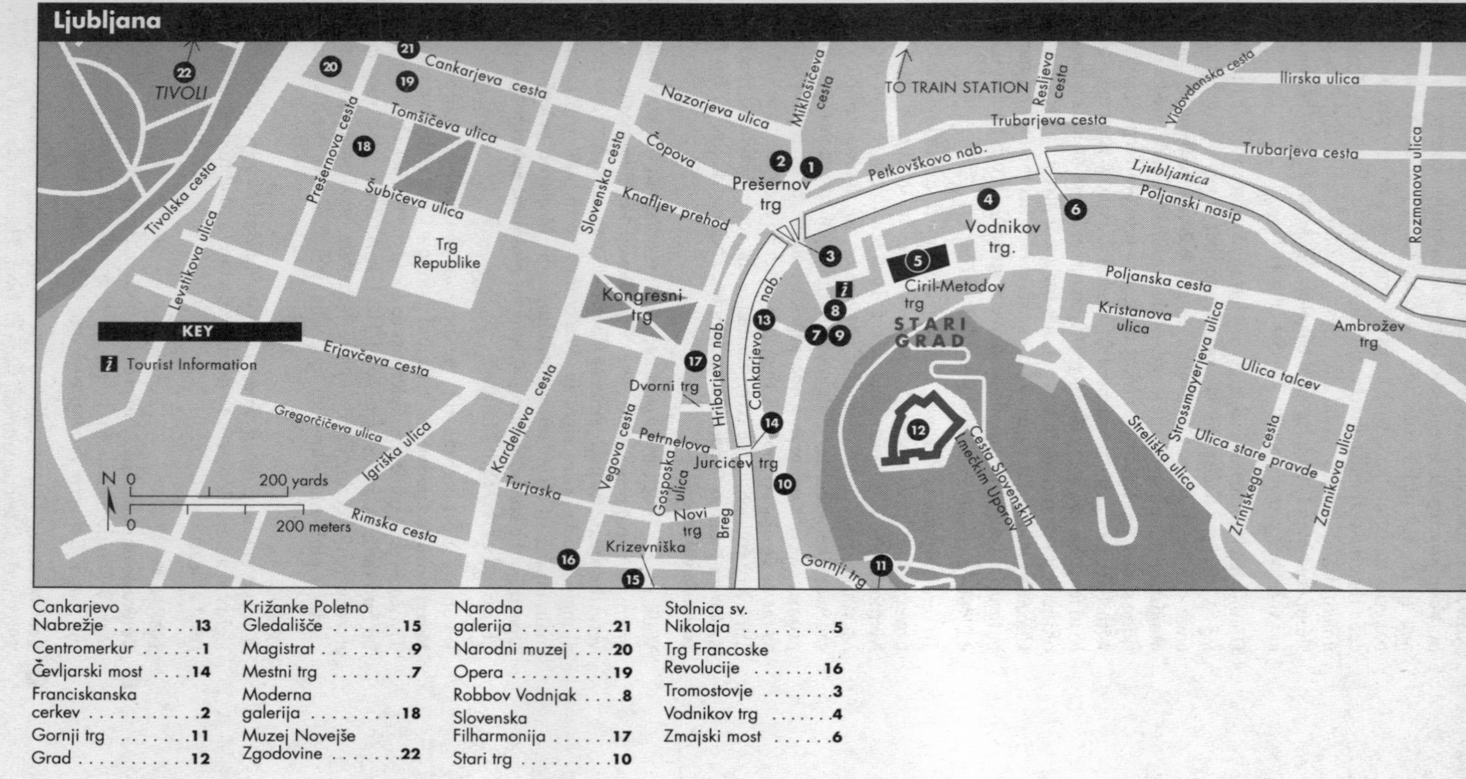

Cankarjevo Nabrežje 13	Križanke Poletno Gledališče 15	Narodna galerija 21	Stolnica sv. Nikolaja 5
Centromerkur 1	Magistrat 9	Narodni muzej 20	Trg Francoske Revolucije 16
Čevljarski most 14	Mestni trg 7	Opera 19	Tromostovje 3
Franciskanska cerkev 2	Moderna galerija 18	Robbov Vodnjak 8	Vodnikov trg 4
Gornji trg 11	Muzej Novejše Zgodovine 22	Slovenska Filharmonija 17	Zmajski most 6
Grad 12		Stari trg 10	

14 **Čevljarski most** (Shoemaker's Bridge). Linking the old and new sides of town, this romantic pedestrian bridge was built in 1931 according to plans by the architect Jože Plečnik. The name is derived from a wooden structure that once stood here and was lined with cobblers' huts.

2 **Franciskanska cerkev** (Franciscan Church). This massive, pink high-Baroque church was built between 1646 and 1660. The main altar, by Francesco Robba (1698–1757), dates from 1736. The three sets of stairs in front are a popular meeting place for students. ✉ *Prešernov trg 4.* ⏲ *Daily 8–6.*

11 **Gornji trg** (Upper Square). This cobbled street, now home to some of the capital's finest restaurants, rises up above the Old Town and leads to the wooded parkland surrounding the castle.

12 **Grad** (castle). Ljubljana's castle sits up on a hill and affords magnificent views over the river and the Old Town's terra-cotta rooftops, spires, and green cupolas. On a clear day the distant Julian Alps are a dramatic backdrop. The castle walls date from the early 16th century, although the tower was added in the mid-19th century. The surrounding park was landscaped by Plečnik in the 1930s. ✉ *Uphill from Vodnikov trg via Studentovska ul.,* ☎ *01/432–7216.* 🎟 *Free.* ⏲ *Daily 9 AM–11 PM.*

NEED A BREAK? The castle ramparts shelter a café and summer terrace. After the steep uphill climb, stop in for a refreshing drink, relax, and capture the essence of this mighty fortress.

15 **Križanke Poletno Gledališče** (Križanke Summer Theater). Set in the courtyard of an 18th-century monastery, this open-air theater was constructed according to plans drawn up by Jože Plečnik. It was completed in 1976, nearly two decades after the architect's death. The theater seats 1,400, and there's a movable roof in case it rains. ✉ *Trg Francoske Revolucije.*

OFF THE BEATEN PATH **PLEČNIK'S HOUSE** – Architecture enthusiasts will enjoy a visit to Plečnik's house, still exactly as he left it, to see his studio, home, and garden. From the Križanke Summer Theater, cross Zoisova cesta, then follow Emonska to Karunova. ✉ *Karunova 4,* ☎ *01/283–5067.* 🎟 *SIT600.* ⏲ *Tues. and Thurs. 10–2.*

9 **Magistrat** (town hall). Guarded by an austere 18th-century facade, this building hides delightful secrets within. In the internal courtyard, for example, the walls are animated with murals depicting historic battles for the city, and a statue of Hercules keeps company with a fountain bearing a figure of Narcissus. ✉ *Mestni trg 1.* 🎟 *Free.* ⏲ *Weekdays 9–3, weekends open only as part of the guided tour of the city (☞* Guided Tours *in* Ljubljana A to Z, *below).*

7 **Mestni trg** (Town Square). This cobbled, traffic-free square extends into the oldest part of the city. Baroque town houses, now divided into functional apartments, present marvelously ornate facades: carved oak doors with great brass handles are framed within columns, and upper floors are decorated with balustrades, statuary, and intricate ironwork. Narrow passageways connect with inner courtyards in one direction and run to the riverfront in the other. The street-level floors contain boutiques, antiques shops, and art galleries.

NEED A BREAK? If you plan to dine in the Old Town, stop first at **Movia** (✉ Mestni trg 2, ☎ 01/425–5448) for an aperitif. This elegant little wine bar stocks a selection of first-rate Slovenian wines, for consumption both on and off the premises. It is closed weekends.

⓲ **Moderna galerija** (Modern Gallery). The strikingly modern one-story structure contains a selection of paintings, sculpture, and prints by Slovenian 20th-century artists. In odd-number years it also hosts the International Biennial of Graphic Art, an exhibition of prints and installations by artists from around the world. Works by Robert Rauschenberg, Susan Rothenburg, and Max Bill have been shown. ✉ *Tomšičeva 14,* ☎ *01/251–4106.* 💴 *SIT500.* ⊙ *Tues.–Sat. 10–6, Sun. 10–1.*

★ ㉒ **Muzej Novejše Zgodovine** (Museum of Modern History). The permanent exhibition on Slovenes in the 20th century takes you from the days of Austria-Hungary, through the Second World War, the victory of the Partisan liberation movement and the ensuing Tito period, and up to the present day. Relics and memorabilia are combined with a dramatic sound and video presentation (scenes from World War II are projected on the walls and ceiling, accompanied by thundering gunfire, screams, and singing). You'll find the museum in a pink-and-white Baroque villa in Tivoli Park. ✉ *Celovška 23,* ☎ *01/534–4029.* 💴 *SIT400.* ⊙ *Tues.–Sun. 10–6.*

㉑ **Narodna galerija** (National Gallery). This imposing turn-of-the-20th-century building houses a survey of Slovene art from the 13th through the early 20th century. ✉ *Prežihova 1,* ☎ *01/251–9716.* 💴 *SIT700.* ⊙ *Tues.–Sat. 10–6, Sun. 10–1.*

⓴ **Narodni muzej** (National Museum). The centerpiece here is a bronze urn from the 5th century BC known as the Vace Situle. Discovered in Vace, Slovenia, it is a striking example of Illyrian workmanship. ✉ *Prešernova 20,* ☎ *01/426–4098.* 💴 *SIT700.* ⊙ *Tues.–Sat. 10–6, Sun. 10–1.*

⓳ **Opera.** This neo-Renaissance palace, with an ornate facade topped by an allegorical sculpture group, was erected in 1892. It is home to the SNG Opera in Balet (Slovene National Opera and Ballet Theater). ✉ *Župančičeva 1,* ☎ *01/425–4840.* ⊙ *Weekdays 11–1 and 1 hr before performances.*

❽ **Robbov Vodnjak** (Robba's Fountain). When the Slovene sculptor Francesco Robba saw Bernini's *Fountain of the Four Rivers* on Piazza Navona during a visit to Rome, he was inspired to create this allegorical representation of the three main Kranjska rivers—the Sava, the Krka, and the Ljubljanica—that flow through Slovenia. ✉ *Mestni trg.*

⓱ **Slovenska Filharmonija** (Slovenian Philharmonic Hall). This hall was built in 1891 for one of the oldest music societies in the world, established in 1701. Haydn, Brahms, Beethoven, and Paganini were honorary members of the orchestra, and Mahler was resident conductor for the 1881–82 season. ✉ *Kongresni trg 10,* ☎ *01/231–1892.*

NEED A BREAK? Head north from the Philharmonic Hall for five blocks to find **Cafe Europa** (✉ Slovenska 47, ☎ 01/438–2400). This elegant Viennese-style coffee house, complete with high ceilings and classical furniture, dates back to the 19th century. Try the Kava Europa: coffee served with brandy, coffee liqueur, whipped cream, and cinnamon. The café also has a delicious selection of cakes, and an adjoining restaurant serves a simple lunch.

❿ **Stari trg** (Old Square). More a narrow street than a square, the Old Square is lined with cafés and small restaurants. In agreeable weather, tables are set out on the cobblestones.

NEED A BREAK? You can't visit Slovenia without trying the incredibly delicious, hot, sweet and heavy prekmurska gibanica. To taste the best in town, stop off at **Nostalgia,** a popular snack bar at Stari trg 9.

5 **Stolnica sveti Nikolaja** (Cathedral of St. Nicholas). This proud Baroque cathedral overshadows the daily market on Vodnikov trg. Building took place between 1701 and 1708, and in 1836 the cupola was erected. In 1996, in honor of the pope's visit, new bronze doors were added. The main door tells the story of Christianity in Slovenia, while the side door shows the history of the Ljubljana diocese. ✉ *Dolničarjeva 1,* ☎ *01/231–0684.* ⏲ *Daily 7–noon and 3–7.*

16 **Trg Francoske Revolucije** (French Revolution Square). When Napoléon took Slovenia he made Ljubljana the capital of his Illyrian Provinces. This square is dominated by Plečnik's **Ilirski Steber** (Illyrian Column), erected in 1929 to commemorate that time.

3 **Tromostovje** (Triple Bridge). This monumental structure spans the River Ljubljanica from Prešernov trg to the Old Town. The three bridges started as a single span, and in 1931 the two graceful outer arched bridges, designed by Plečnik, were added.

4 **Vodnikov trg** (Vodnik Square). This square hosts a big and bustling flower, fruit, and vegetable market. An elegant riverside colonnade designed by Plečnik runs the length of the market, and a bronze statue of the Slovene poet Valentin Vodnik, after whom the square is named, overlooks the scene. ⏲ *Market Mon.–Sat. 7–6.*

6 **Zmajski most** (Dragon's Bridge). Four fire-breathing winged dragons crown the corners of this spectacular concrete-and-iron structure.

Dining

Central European food is often considered bland and stodgy, but in Ljubljana you can eat exceptionally well. Fresh fish arrives daily from the Adriatic, while the surrounding hills supply the capital with first-class meat and game, dairy produce, and fruit and vegetables. At some of the better restaurants the menu may verge on nouvelle cuisine, featuring imaginative and beautifully presented dishes. Complement your meal with a bottle of good Slovenian wine; the waiter can help you choose an appropriate one. For a lunchtime snack visit the market in Vodnik Square. Choose from tasty fried squid and whitebait in the riverside arcade or freshly baked pies and cakes at the square's bakeries.

$$$$ ★ ✕ **AS.** Now probably the best restaurant in town, AS has a refined menu, impeccable service, and excellent wines. House specialities are seafood and pasta. The ambience is old-fashioned, but the dishes are creative and modern. If you're reluctant to leave, move on to the after-hours bar in the basement. ✉ *Knafljev prehod,* ☎ *01/425–8822. AE, DC, MC, V.*

$$$$ ✕ **Rotovž.** This extremely elegant restaurant relaxes in summer, spilling over onto the cobbled square. Order *pastrmka* (trout) with parsley potatoes or a frog-leg specialty, along with a crisp salad and a bottle of Slovenian wine. ✉ *Mestni trg 2,* ☎ *01/251–2839. AE, DC, MC, V. Closed Sun.*

$$$ ✕ **Ljubljanski Dvor.** Situated close to Čevljarski most, overlooking the river, this restaurant doubles as a pizzeria (which remains open on Sunday, when the restaurant is closed). The summer terrace makes it an ideal stopping point for lunch. ✉ *Dvorni trg 1,* ☎ *01/251–6555. AE, DC, MC, V. Closed Sun.*

$$$ ✕ **Pri sv. Florijanu.** Located on Gornji trg, on the way to the castle, this recently opened restaurant serves up a new generation of Slovenian cuisine. Try the chicken breast with coriander and grilled vegetables, accompanied by an arugula and Parmesan side salad. The minimalist interior and background jazz attract a young and ambitious crowd. ✉ *Gornji trg 20,* ☎ *01/251–2214. AE, DC, MC, V.*

$$ ★ ✕ **Spajza.** A few doors away from Pri sv. Florijanu, you'll find a restaurant with a series of romantic candlelit rooms and bohemian decor. The menu includes venison in cognac sauce with wild asparagus, risotto with porcini mushrooms, and scampi tails, as well as an inspired selection of salads. They do a great tiramisu. ✉ *Gornji trg 28,* ☎ *01/425–3094. AE, DC, MC, V. Closed Sun.*

$ ✕ **Pivnica Kratchowill.** First and foremost a microbrewery, Kratchowill also serves good food. The interior is modern, but the food is classic: beer sausage and sauerkraut, game dishes, tasty pastas, and a salad bar. The beer is brewed according to old Czech recipes. ✉ *Kolodvorska 14,* ☎ *01/433–3114. AE, DC, MC, V.*

$ ✕ **Zlata Ribica.** An ideal stop after a visit to the Sunday flea market (☞ Shopping, *below*), this popular bar and bistro is frequented by boisterous stallholders and antiques buffs. The fare includes black pudding, squid, and mushroom omelettes. In winter the locals meet here to drink mulled wine. ✉ *Cankarjevo nab. 5,* ☎ *01/252–1367. AE, DC, MC, V. Closed weekends after 3.*

Lodging

Most of the listed hotels are clustered conveniently around Miklošičeva cesta, the main axis running from the train station down to Tromostovje (Triple Bridge). Ljubljana is expensive, but hotel standards are high. In summer you can get better deals through private accommodations or university dorms. Ask about these options at the TIC kiosk in the train station (☞ Visitor Information, *below*).

$$$ 🏨 **Austrotel.** Don't be put off by the rather daunting exterior. Following extensive renovation work in 1999, the rooms are more than comfortable, the service excellent. Top floors afford fine views of the castle. ✉ *Miklošičeva 9, 1000,* ☎ *01/423–6133,* FAX *01/230–1181. 70 rooms, 4 suites. Sauna, casino, meeting rooms. AE, DC, MC, V.*

$$$ 🏨 **Best Western Slon Hotel.** Close to the river, this hotel stands on the site of a famous 16th-century inn and maintains an atmosphere of traditional hospitality. The breakfast is among the finest in the city. The run-of-the-mill rooms are comfortable. ✉ *Slovenska 34, 1000,* ☎ *01/470–1100,* FAX *01/251–7164. 185 rooms. 2 restaurants, nightclub, meeting rooms. AE, DC, MC, V.*

$$$ 🏨 **Grand Hotel Union.** This turn-of-the-20th-century hotel occupies a magnificent Secessionist-style building. All facilities have been modernized with great care, and the interior decor and furnishings remain typically Old Vienna. ✉ *Miklošičeva 1, 1000,* ☎ *01/308–1270,* FAX *01/308–1015. 233 rooms, 6 suites. 2 restaurants, meeting rooms. AE, DC, MC, V.*

$$ 🏨 **Hotel Turist.** The rooms are basic, but this hotel has the only low-budget accommodations within the city center and close to the train station. ✉ *Dalmatinova 15, 1000,* ☎ *01/432–2343,* FAX *01/231–9291. 190 rooms. 2 restaurants, nightclub. AE, DC, MC, V.*

$$ 🏨 **Pension Mrak.** Recently reopened after a thorough face-lift, Pension Mrak now offers simple but comfortable rooms and a decent restaurant. It is situated in a quiet side street, close to the Križanke Summer Theater. ✉ *Rimska 4, 1000,* ☎ *01/421–9600,* FAX *01/421–9655. 30 rooms. Restaurant. AE, DC, MC, V.*

Nightlife and the Arts

Despite once being considered the workaholics of Yugoslavia, Slovenes do know how to enjoy themselves. One in ten of the capital's inhabitants is a student, hence the proliferation of trendy cafés and small art galleries. Each year the International Summer Festival breathes new life into the Ljubljana cultural scene, sparking off a lively program of concerts and experimental theater. For information about forthcoming cultural events, check *Events in Ljubljana,* a monthly pamphlet published by the Ljubljana Promotion Center, and the English-language magazine *Ljubljana Life,* both available in major hotels and tourist offices.

Nightlife

The listed bars and clubs are all situated within walking distance of the center. However, during summer the all-night party scene moves to the Adriatic coast, where open-air dancing and rave parties abound.

BARS AND CLUBS

The most idyllic way to close a summer evening is with a nightcap on the terrace of one of the riverside cafés in the Old Town. With a large terrace and glamorous clientele, **Cafe Maček** (✉ Krojaška 5, ☎ 01/425–3791) is the hippest place to be seen down by the river. **Caffe Boheme** (✉ Mestni trg 19) is spacious inside and has a terrace with tables and umbrellas outside. Recently renovated, **Casablanca** (✉ Cankarjevo nab. 25) has a traditional interior plus an excellent sandwich bar. These bars all stay open until after midnight.

For live jazz visit **Jazz Club Gajo** (✉ Beethovnova 8, ☎ 01/425–3206), which attracts stars from home and abroad. Clark Terry, Shiela Jordan, and Woody Shaw have all performed here.

For Latino music or a pick-me-up breakfast in the early hours, visit **Casa del Papa** (✉ Celovška 54A, ☎ 01/434–3158): three floors of exotic food, drinks, and entertainment in tribute to Ernest Hemingway. For all-night dancing, **Club Central** (✉ Dalmatinova 15, ☎ 01/252–1292) stays open until sunrise Tuesday through Saturday. The best longstanding nightclub in town is **Eldorado** (✉ Nazorjeva 4, ☎ 01/426–2126), with different music each night and free admission on Tuesday. The student-run nightclub **K4** (✉ Kersnikova 4, ☎ 01/431–7010) is something of an institution, attracting a young and alternative crowd; Sunday is gay night.

The Arts

Ljubljana's **International Summer Festival** (✉ Trg Francoske Revolucije 1–2, ☎ 01/426–4340) is held each July and August in the open-air Križanke Summer Theater. Musical, theatrical, and dance performances attract acclaimed artists from all over the world. Each year in June, the International Jazz Festival and the Druga Godba (a festival of alternative and ethnic music) are staged at the Križanke Summer Theater. For schedules and tickets contact the box office at Cankarjev dom (☞ *below*).

CONCERTS

Ljubljana has plenty of events for classical music lovers. The season, September through June, includes weekly concerts by the Slovene Philharmonic Orchestra and the RTV Slovenia Orchestra, as well as performances by guest soloists, chamber musicians, and foreign symphony orchestras. **Cankarjev dom** (Cankar House; ✉ Prešernova 10, ☎ 01/425–8121), opened in 1980, is a modern, rather characterless venue. As a cultural center it is the driving force behind the city's artistic activities, offering up-to-date general information and tickets. The 19th-century **Slovenska Filharmonija** (Slovenian Philharmonic Hall; ✉ Kongresni trg 10, ☎ 01/241–0804) has a more classic atmosphere.

FILM

Cinemas generally screen the original versions of films, with Slovenian subtitles. **Kinoteka** (✉ Miklošičeva 28, ☎ 01/433–0213) runs some great retrospectives.

THEATER, DANCE, AND OPERA

Ljubljana has a long tradition of experimental and alternative theater. Theater and dance are often mixed. Contemporary dance plays by the internationally recognized choreographers Matjaz Faric and Iztok Kovac and performances by the dance troupes Betontanc and En Knap are ideal for English speakers.

From September through June the **SNG Opera in Balet** (Slovene National Opera and Ballet Theater; ⊠ Župančičeva 1, ☎ 01/425–4680) stages everything from classical to modern and alternative productions.

Shopping

If you want to do some hiking but have come unprepared, **Anappurna** (⊠ Krakovski Nasip 10, ☎ 01/426–3428) has a good selection of mountaineering equipment. For late-night necessities, there is a 24-hour shop, **Delakatesa Trgovina** (⊠ Kongresni trg 10), right in the center of town.

You can pick up antiques and memorabilia at the **Ljubljana Flea Market** (⊠ Cankarjevo nab.), held near Tromostovje (Triple Bridge) each Sunday morning. The most interesting shopping experience is undoubtedly a visit to the **open-air market** at Vodnikov trg (Vodnik Square), where besides fresh fruit and vegetables you can find dried herbs and locally produced honey. For a wide selection of quality Slovene wines try **Vinoteka** (⊠ Dunajska 18, ☎ 01/431–5015), in the Ljubljana trade fair complex.

Side Trip to the Krka Valley

A drive through the Krka Valley makes a perfect day trip from Ljubljana. The monasteries of Stična and Pleterje offer insight into contemporary monastic life, and there are two castles, Otočec and Mokrice, where you can stop for lunch—or a romantic overnight stay in exquisite surroundings.

Take the E70 highway east out of Ljubljana, then turn right at Ivančna Gorica to follow a secondary road along the Krka Valley. For a fast journey home, return to the E70 just north of Šentjernej. There are also buses from Ljubljana to Ivančna Gorica and Šentjernej, but these are only practical if you don't mind walking the final stretch to the monasteries.

23 The **Stična Samostan** (Stična Monastery) lies 2 km (1 mi) north of Ivančna Gorica. Founded by the Cistercians in 1135, the monastery was fortified in the 15th century to protect against Turkish invasion. Today there are only 10 monks, plus three nuns who attend to the cooking. The monks produce excellent herbal teas—that work (allegedly) against cellulite, insomnia, poor memory, and practically every other problem you can think of—which are on sale in the monastery shop. The early Gothic cloisters, the Baroque church, and the adjoining **Slovenian Religious Museum** are open to the public. The museum's collections include archives dedicated to the work of Bishop Friderik Baraga, a 19th-century missionary to the United States who compiled the first dictionary of the Native American Otchipwe language. Call first to arrange a visit. ⊠ *Stična 17, Ivančna Gorica,* ☎ *01/787–7100.* *SIT500.* *Tues.–Sat. 8–11 and 2–5, Sun. 2–5.*

From Stična Monastery follow the Krka River through Zagradec, Žužemberk, and Novo Mesto. At Šentjernej, turn south and travel for
 24 6 km (4 mi) to reach Pleterje. The Carthusian monks of **Pleterje Samostan** (Pleterje Monastery) aim "to find God in silence and soli-

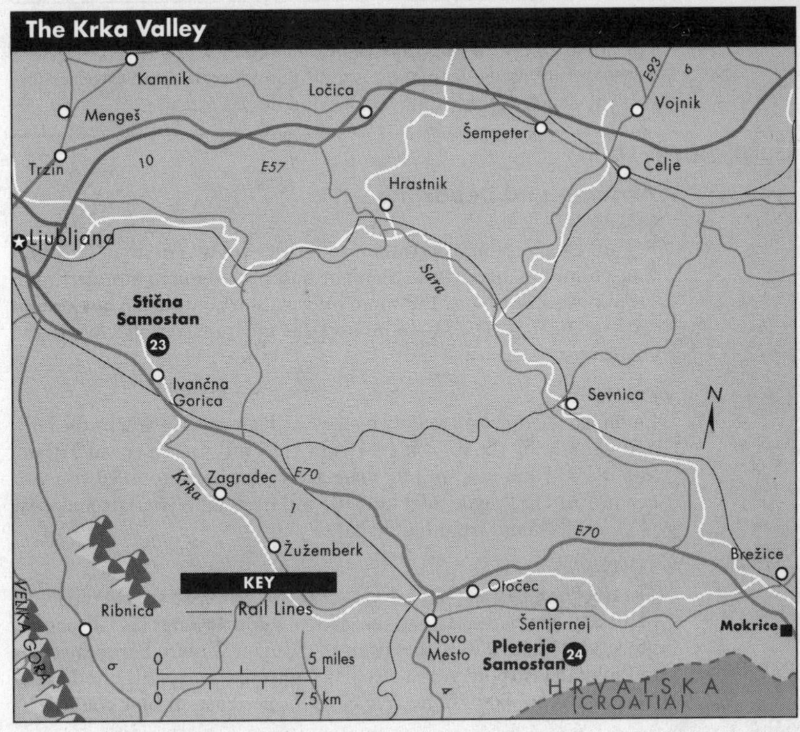

tude." Therefore you can't enter the monastery proper, but visitors are welcome to view the magnificent 15th-century Gothic church and to watch a fascinating audiovisual presentation (in English) about the way the monks live. The walled monastery is nestled in a lonely valley surrounded by woods. Once a week the monks take a 45-minute walk around the perimeter of the complex. The route is marked with a blue circle and yellow cross, so visitors can follow the trail independently. A small shop sells rakija, wine, and cheese made by the monks. ✉ *Drča 1, Šentjernej,* ☎ *07/308–1225.* ⊙ *Daily 8–5.*

Dining and Lodging

$$$$ ✕🏨 **Otočec Castle.** About 8 km (5 mi) west of Šentjernej, on the road to Novo Mesto, you will find the entrance to Otočec Castle. The first recorded mention of this medieval castle is from 1252. Now a luxury hotel, complete with period furniture, Otočec sits on an island in the Krka River and is accessible by a wooden bridge. There are also facilities for camping, by the river, on the castle grounds. Nonguests are welcome to dine in the restaurant, where the house speciality is locally caught game. Alternatively, stop by for a drink in the courtyard café. ✉ *Grajska 1, Otočec ob Krki, 8222,* ☎ *07/307–5700,* FAX *07/307–5460. 16 rooms. Restaurant. AE, DC, MC, V.*

$$$ ✕🏨 **Mokrice Castle.** From Šentjernej head north to the E70, then drive 22 km (14 mi) eastward to find Mokrice Castle on the right, just before the Croatian border crossing. Now a romantic old-fashioned hotel, complete with working drawbridge, Mokrice Castle dates back to the 17th century. The restaurant, noted for classic roast meat dishes and fresh trout, is open for lunch and dinner to nonguests. The complex also includes a golf course. ✉ *Rajec 4, Jesenice na Dolenjskem, 8261,* ☎ *07/305–7424,* FAX *07/305–7007. 25 rooms, 4 suites. Restaurant, 18-hole golf course. AE, DC, MC, V.*

Outdoor Activities and Sports

For horse lovers the **Struga Equestrian Center** (☎ 07/307–5701), at a 12th-century medieval manor, is a 20-minute walk from Otočec Castle. The center offers riding lessons and horses for hire.

Ljubljana A to Z

Arriving and Departing

BY BUS

Private coach companies run morning services to Trieste in Italy and Zagreb in Croatia, as well as night buses to Munich, Stuttgart, and Frankfurt in Germany. For more information contact the **bus station** (✉ Trg OF 5, ☎ 01/234–4606) opposite the train station, close to the city center.

BY CAR

Ljubljana is connected to Italy by the E61 highway, Austria by the E57, and Croatia by the E70. It's 249 km (155 mi) to Venice via Trieste, and it's 395 km (245 mi) to Vienna via Maribor. From Austria you can proceed to Prague (609 km [405 mi] from Ljubljana) or Budapest (491 km [305 mi] from Ljubljana).

BY PLANE

The **Ljubljana Airport** (☎ 04/206–1981) is at Brnik, 22 km (14 mi) north of the city. The Slovenian national carrier, **Adria Airways** (✉ Gosposvetska 6, ☎ 01/252–2700), flies from all the main Western European cities to Ljubljana Airport. Adria also has flights to the capitals of other ex-Yugoslav republics, but no service to former Eastern-bloc countries.

Various foreign companies fly in and out of Brnik. **British Airways** (✉ Slovenska 56, ☎ 01/300–1000) has an office in Ljubljana.

Between the Airport and Downtown: Shuttle buses run between the airport and Ljubljana's main bus station in the city center. Buses depart every hour on the hour, and tickets cost SIT500. Alternatively, a taxi costs approximately SIT5,000.

BY TRAIN

There are several trains daily to Venice (five hours), Vienna (six hours), and Budapest (eight hours). There is an overnight service to Prague (12 hours), and a rapid daytime EuroCity connection to Berlin (15 hours). The **train station** (✉ Trg OF 6, ☎ 01/291–2524) is just north of the city center.

Getting Around

The city center is very compact, and all the sights, restaurants, hotels, and attractions listed can be reached on foot.

BY BUS

Tokens (*žetoni*) are sold at kiosks and post offices. As you board the bus, drop your token into the box by the driver. The cost is a little higher if you pay in change (SIT130). During the day buses operate every half hour and cover an extensive network; at night they are less frequent.

BY TAXI

Private **taxis** (☎ 01/9700 through 01/9709) operate 24 hours a day. Phone from your hotel or hail one in the street. Drivers are bound by law to display and run a meter.

Contacts and Resources

CAR RENTALS

Avis (✉ Čufarjeva 2, ☎ 01/430–8010). **Kompas Hertz** (✉ Miklošičeva 11, ☎ 01/231–1241). **National Rent a Car** (✉ Baragova 5, ☎ 01/588–4450).

EMBASSIES AND CONSULATES

U.S. Embassy (✉ Pražakova 4, ☎ 01/230–1427, FAX 01/230–1401). **Canadian Consulate** (✉ Miklošičeva 19, ☎ 01/430–3570, FAX 01/430–3575). **U.K. Embassy** (✉ Trg republike 3/IV, ☎ 01/425–7191, FAX 01/425–0174). **Australian Consulate** (✉ Trg republike 3/XII, ☎ 01/425–4252, FAX 01/426–4721).

EMERGENCIES

Police (☎ 113). **Ambulance, fire brigade** (☎ 112). **Ljubljana Emergency Medical Services** (☎ 01/232–3060). **24-hour pharmacy** (Lekarna Miklošič; ✉ Miklošičeva 24, ☎ 01/231–4558).

ENGLISH-LANGUAGE BOOKSTORES

MK Knjigarna Konzorcij (✉ Slovenska 29, ☎ 01/425–0196) has a good selection of English books and magazines on the upper floor. **Kod in Kam** (✉ Trg Francoske Revolucije 7, ☎ 01/251–3537) specializes in maps and travel books.

GUIDED TOURS

Informative and amusing sightseeing walks, organized by the **Ljubljana Promotion Center,** depart from the Magistrat on Mestni trg daily at 5 PM, June through September. From October through May tours are on Sunday at 11 AM.

VISITOR INFORMATION

Ljubljana's **Turistično Informacijski Center** (Tourist Information Center [TIC]; ✉ Stritarjeva, ☎ 01/306–1215) is located next to the Triple Bridge on the Old Town side. It's open weekdays from 8 to 7, Saturday from 9 to 5, and Sunday from 10 to 6. If you are arriving by train, the **TIC kiosk** (☎ 01/433–9475) in the station can help you find accommodations. It's open daily 8 AM to 9 PM from June through September, and from 10 to 6 October through May.

For information about tourism outside the capital, contact the Slovenian Tourist Board (☞ Visitor Information *in* Slovenia A to Z, *below*).

MARIBOR, PTUJ, AND THE HALOZE HILLS

During the 1st century, Poetovio, now known as Ptuj, was the largest Roman settlement in the area that is now Slovenia. Much later, in the 13th century, Maribor was founded. Originally given the German name Marchburg, the city took its Slavic name in 1836. For centuries the two towns competed for economic and cultural prominence within the region, with Maribor finally gaining the lead in 1846, when a new railway line connected the city to Vienna and Trieste. The area between Maribor and Ptuj is a flat, fertile flood plain formed by the Drava River. South of Ptuj lie the rolling hills of Haloze, famous for quality white wines.

Numbers in the margin correspond to numbers on the Maribor, Ptuj, and the Haloze Hills map.

Maribor

25 *128 km (79 mi) northeast of Ljubljana on the E57.*

More geared toward business travelers than tourists, Maribor is Slovenia's second largest city. However, the Old Town has retained a core of ornate 18th- and 19th-century town houses, typical of imperial Austria, and is worth a visit. The heart of the Old Town is **Rotovški**

Maribor, Ptuj, and the Haloze Hills

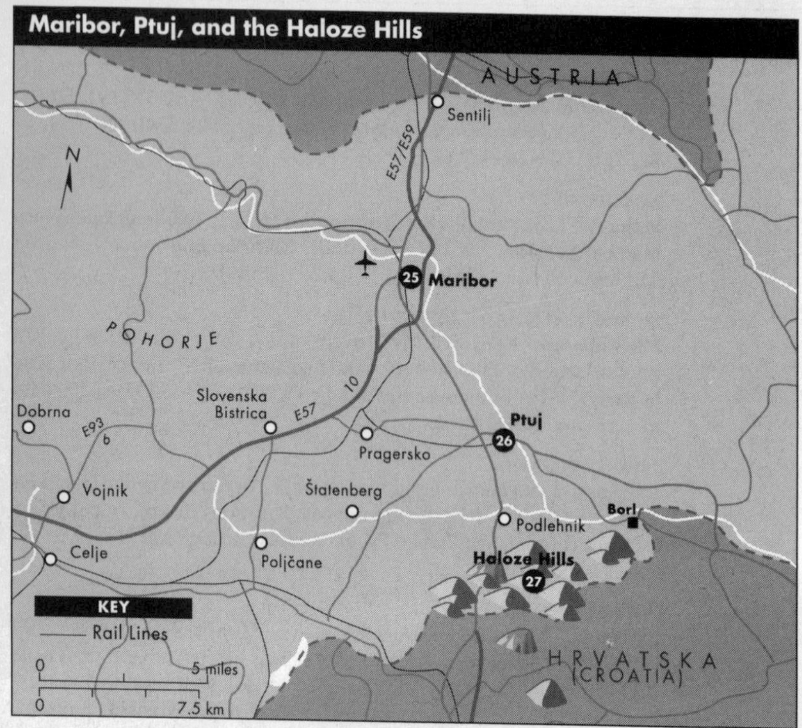

trg, with the Kužno Znamenje (Plague Memorial) at its center and overlooked by the proud 16th-century Renaissance **Rotovž** (town hall).

From Rotovški trg, a number of traffic-free streets lead down to a riverside promenade, known as **Lent.** It is lined with bars, terrace cafés, restaurants, and boutiques.

A little way upstream, an old vine, **Stara Trta,** carefully trained along the facade of a former inn, is believed to date back to the 16th century and thus to be the oldest continuously producing vine in Europe. The annual harvesting of 100 to 110 pounds of grapes is a special event, and the small quantity of wine produced is highly prized. (It's unavailable to the public.) ✉ *Vojasniska 8.*

The **Vodni Stolp** (Water Tower), a former defense tower, houses the **Vinoteka Slovenskih Vin** (Slovenian Wine Shop). Here you can sample and purchase over 500 different Slovenian vintage wines. ✉ *Usnjarska 10,* ☎ *02/251–7743.*

Dining and Lodging

In summer Maribor University dorms are open to visitors, providing a cheap alternative to hotels. For details ask at the Maribor tourist information center (☞ Visitor Information *in* Maribor, Ptuj, and the Haloze Hills A to Z, *below*).

$$ ✕ **Toti Rotovž.** Close to the town hall, this building has been carefully restored to reveal vaulted brick ceilings and terra-cotta floors. The ground-level restaurant serves typical Slovenian dishes, while the *klet* (wine cellar) in the basement cooks up barbecued steaks. ✉ *Glavni trg 14,* ☎ *02/228–7650. AE, DC, MC, V.*

$$ 🏨 **Hotel Orel.** It's nothing special to look at, but Hotel Orel has the best accommodations in the center of town. There is a pleasant restaurant at street level, the rooms are comfortable, and the service is friendly. ✉ *Grajski trg 3A, 2000,* ☎ *02/251–6171,* FAX *02/251–8497. 146 rooms, 7 suites. Restaurant. AE, DC, MC, V.*

Outdoor Activities and Sports

In winter in the Pohorje Mountains, just 6 km (4 mi) southwest of Maribor, you'll find alpine ski runs and cross-country trails. A cable car takes you from the south side of town up to the winter resort.

Two well-established biking paths pass though the region. The 95 km (59 mi) Drava Trail follows the course of the Drava River through the Kozjak hills to Maribor and then proceeds to Ptuj. The 56 km (35 mi) Jantara Trail runs from Šentilj on the Austrian border to Maribor and continues to Slovenska Bistrica. However, finding a place to rent a bike can be somewhat problematic. Inquire at the Maribor tourist information center for assistance and information (☞ Visitor Information *in* Maribor, Ptuj, and the Haloze Hills A to Z, *below*).

Ptuj

26 *25 km (15 mi) southeast of Maribor on the E59.*

Ptuj, built beside the Drava River and crowned by a hilltop castle, hits the national news each year in February with its extraordinary carnival celebration, known as Kurentovanje. During the 10-day festival the town's boys and men dress in the bizarre Kurent costume: a horned mask decorated with ribbons and flowers, a sheepskin cloak, and a set of heavy bells around the waist. The task of the Kurent is to drive away the winter and welcome in the spring. You can see Kurent figures on 18th-century building facades in the center of Ptuj, on Jadranska ulica No. 4 and No. 6.

Ptujski Grad (Ptuj Castle) stands at the top of a steep hill in the center of town. Planned around a Baroque courtyard, the castle houses a museum that exhibits musical instruments, an armory, 15th-century church paintings, and period furniture. ✉ *Grajska Raven,* ☎ *02/771–3081.* 💳 *SIT600.* ⏲ *mid-Apr.–mid-Oct., daily 9–6; mid-Oct.–mid-Apr., daily 9–4.*

★ **Vinska Klet** (Ptuj Wine Cellars) offers a tasting session with five different wines, bread, and cheese, plus a bottle to take home. You are also given a tour of the underground cellars, and a sound and video presentation takes you through the seasons of wine-making at the vineyards. The wines stocked here come predominantly from the Haloze Hills (☞ *below*). ✉ *Trstenjakova 6,* ☎ *02/787–9810,* FAX *02/787–9813.* ⏲ *Daily 8–6; tasting sessions Fri., Sat., and Sun. 11 AM (daily for groups, but call first).*

Dining

$$$ ✕ **Ribič.** This discreet little fish restaurant serves up crab and lobster specialities, as well as river fish such as trout. The interior decor is simple, and the walls are hung with fishing nets. ✉ *Dravska 9,* ☎ *02/771–4671. AE, DC, MC, V.*

The Haloze Hills

27 *Borl Castle is 11 km (7 mi) southeast of Ptuj.*

The Haloze Hills lie south of Ptuj, close to the Croatian border. Grapes are generally planted on the steeper south-facing slopes, to take full advantage of the sunshine, while the cooler north-facing slopes are covered with trees and pastures. The best way to explore the region is to pick up the Haloze wine route near Borl Castle, a half-day trip through an undulating landscape of vineyards and woodland. For a map of the route plus a comprehensive list of vineyards and wine stores open to the public, inquire at the Ptuj tourist information center (☞ Visitor Information *in* Maribor, Ptuj, and the Haloze hills A to Z, *below*).

On the road between Podlehnik and Poljčane, keep an eye out for the sign for **Štatenberg Castle.** Built between 1720 and 1740, the castle is a typical example of the Baroque style favored by the local aristocracy during the 18th century.

Dining

$$$ ✕ **Štatenberg Castle.** This castle houses a restaurant that serves traditional dishes, such as roast meats, accompanied by excellent local wines. Throughout summer you can sit at tables outside in the courtyard. ✉ *Štatenberg 86,* ☎ *02/581–8916. No credit cards.* ⏲ *Closed Mon.*

Maribor, Ptuj, and the Haloze Hills A to Z

Arriving and Departing

BY BUS

Regular buses link Maribor and Ptuj to Ljubljana. However, the train is cheaper and more comfortable.

BY CAR

To reach Maribor from Ljubljana take the E57. For Ptuj turn off at Slovenska Bistrica.

BY TRAIN

A regular train service links Ljubljana and Maribor; several international trains continue to Graz and Vienna. It is also possible to reach Ptuj by train from Ljubljana, though you may have to change at Pragersko. For information contact Ljubljana's train station (☞ Arriving and Departing *in* Ljubljana A to Z, *above*).

Getting Around

BY BUS

An hourly bus service connects Maribor and Ptuj; the 45-minute journey costs SIT560. Buses leave from **Maribor bus station** (✉ Mlinska 1, ☎ 02/251–1333).

BY CAR

A car is almost essential for exploring the Haloze Hills wine route. Some of the country roads are narrow and winding. While there is snow in winter, it is extremely rare to find roads closed.

BY TRAIN

Several trains daily connect Maribor and Ptuj, with a change at Pragersko; the 45-minute journey costs SIT450. For train information, contact the **Maribor train station** (✉ Partizanska 50, ☎ 02/292–2100).

Contacts and Resources

EMERGENCIES

Police (☎ 113). **Ambulance, fire brigade** (☎ 112). **Breakdowns** (AMZS [Automobile Association of Slovenia] ☎ 987).

VISITOR INFORMATION

Maribor (✉ Partizanska 47, ☎ 02/251–1262). **Ptuj** (✉ Slovenski trg 14, ☎ 02/787–6230).

TRIGLAV NATIONAL PARK AND THE SOČA VALLEY

Northwest of Ljubljana lies a region of mountain and lakeside resorts, with ski trails, hiking paths, and thermal springs. The Julijske Alpe (Julian Alps), situated at the junction of the borders of Italy, Austria, and Slovenia, are contained within Triglavski Narodni Park (Triglav National Park). According to early Slav legend, Triglav, Slovenia's highest peak, is the home of a three-headed deity who rules the sky, the earth, and the underworld. Triglav Peak is the symbol of Slovenia and is featured on the national flag.

While Lake Bohinj and the small waterside settlement of Ribčev Laz sit within the national park, Lake Bled and the town of Bled lie just outside the park's boundary. The alpine villages of Kranjska Gora and Bovec are situated on the rim of the park.

The Soča River begins near Trenta, then flows southwest to form the beautiful Soča Valley. The river passes through Kobarid and snakes down to Nova Gorica, where it crosses over into Italy (where it's known as the Isonzo).

En Route On the road to Bled from Ljubljana you pass a junction for Radovljica. Turn off here to see the 17th-century town center and visit the intriguing **Beekeeping Museum.** ✉ *Linhartov trg 1,* ☎ *04/531–5188.* ⏲ *May–Aug., Tues.–Sun. 10–1 and 4–6; Sept. and Oct., Tues.–Sun. 10–noon and 3–5; Mar., Apr., Nov., and Dec., Wed. and weekends 10–noon and 3–5.*

Numbers in the margin correspond to numbers on the Triglav National Park and the Soča Valley map.

Bled

28 *50 km (31 mi) northwest of Ljubljana on the E61.*

Bled is among the most magnificently situated mountain resorts in Europe. The healing powers of its thermal springs were known during the 17th century. In the early 19th century the aristocracy arrived to bask in Bled's tranquil alpine setting. Since the mid-1970s a spate of new hotels and recreational facilities have sprung up here.

Blejsko Jezero (Lake Bled) is nestled within a rim of mountains and surrounded by forests, with a castle on one side and a promenade beneath stately chestnut trees on the other. Horse-drawn carriages clip-clop along the promenade while swans glide on the water. On a minuscule island in the middle of the lake the lovely **Cerkov svetega Martina** (St. Martin's Pilgrimage Church) stands within a circle of trees. Take a ride over to the island on a *pletna,* an old-fashioned canopied wooden boat similar to a Venetian gondola.

The stately 16th-century **grad** (castle) perches above the lake on the summit of a steep cliff, against a backdrop of the Julian Alps and Triglav Peak. You can climb up to the castle for fine views of the lake, the resort, and the surrounding countryside. An exhibition traces the development of the castle through the centuries, with objects from archaeological finds to period furniture on display. ☎ *04/574–1230.* ⏲ *Mar.–Oct., daily 8–7; Nov.–Feb., daily 9–4.*

NEED A BREAK? Even if you're not staying at the illustrious Grand Hotel Toplice (☞ Dining and Lodging, *below*), you're welcome to use its sauna and soak in the thermal waters (28°C, 83°F) of the indoor swimming pool. A small admission fee includes a towel and locker.

The **Vintgar Gorge** was cut between precipitous cliffs by the clear Radovna River, which flows down numerous waterfalls and through pools and rapids. The marked trail through the gorge leads over bridges and along wooden walkways and galleries. ✉ *5 km (3 mi) northwest of Bled on the road to Zgornje Gorje.*

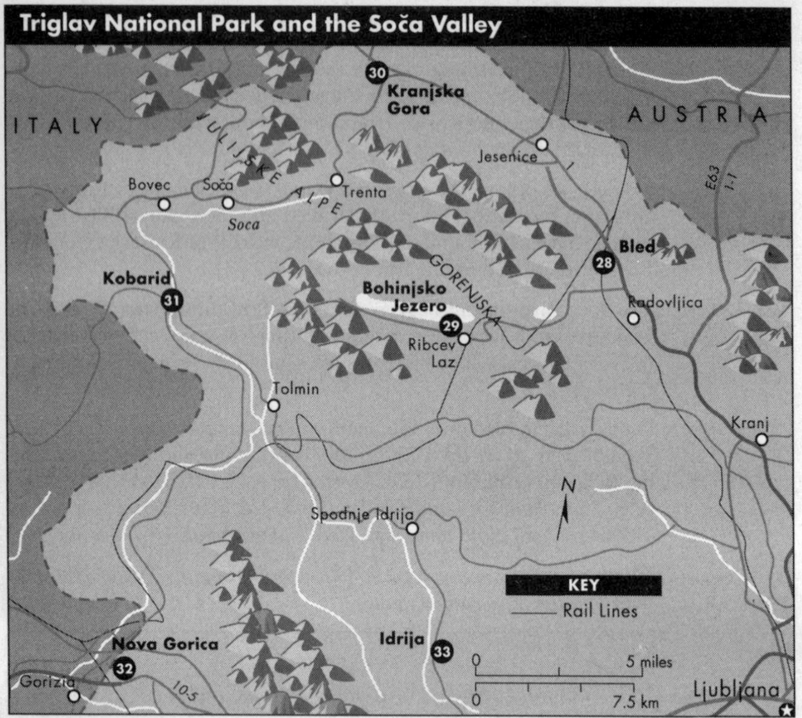

Dining and Lodging

$$$$ ★ ✕ **Gostilna Lectar.** This restaurant serves an impressive array of traditional dishes in a warm country-inn setting. For a cross-section of the local cuisine, try the pumpkin soup, the Peasant's Plate (buckwheat dumplings, mixed smoked meats, potatoes, and fresh steamed vegetables), and the apple strudel. ✉ *Linhartov trg 2, Radovljica (9 km [5½ mi] south of Bled on the E61),* ☎ *04/531–5642. AE, DC, MC, V.*

$$ ✕ **Gostilna pri Planincu.** This friendly joint is busy year-round. Locals meet here for morning coffee or a bargain set-menu lunch—or just to drink the cheapest beer in town. While rowdy farmers occupy the front bar, lovers share a candlelit supper in the dining room. Portions are "for people who work all day": roast chicken and chips, steak and mushrooms, black pudding and turnips. For dessert walnut *štrukli* (dumplings) are served with cream. ✉ *Grajska 8,* ☎ *04/574–1613. AE, DC, MC, V.*

$$ ✕ **Mlino.** Follow the lakeside footpath 20 minutes from the center of Bled to reach this informal family restaurant. Try the Mlino Plate, a mixed platter of barbecued meats served with *djevec* (rice cooked with vegetables). There is a special menu for children, and boats are for hire on the lake. ✉ *C. Svobode 45,* ☎ *04/574–1404. AE, DC, MC, V.*

$$$$ ★ 🏨 **Vila Bled.** Late Yugoslav president Tito was the gracious host to numerous 20th-century statesmen at this former royal residence, set amid 15 acres of gardens overlooking the lake. It was converted into a luxurious small-scale hotel in 1984 and became part of the Relais et Chateaux association in 1987. Among the elegant touches are hand-embroidered linen sheets, Art Deco furnishings, antique rugs, and Asian vases. ✉ *C. Svobode 26, 4260,* ☎ *04/579–1500,* FAX *04/574–1320. 10 rooms, 20 suites. Restaurant. AE, DC, MC, V.*

$$$ **Grand Hotel Toplice.** This old-fashioned, ivy-covered resort hotel has been favored by British visitors since the 1920s. Directly on the lake, the main building has balconies and big windows from which guests can take in dramatic views of the castle and the Julian Alps. The rooms, the lounges, and the bar are all furnished with antiques and heirloom rugs. ✉ *C. Svobode 20, 4260,* ☎ *04/579–1000,* FAX *04/574–1841. 206 rooms. Restaurant, indoor pool. AE, DC, MC, V.*

$ **Bledec Youth Hostel.** Just 5 minutes from the lake and 10 minutes from the castle, Bledec is one of the cleanest and most comfortable youth hostels in Europe. ✉ *Grajska 17, 4260,* ☎ *04/574–5250. 13 rooms. Restaurant, bar. MC. Closed Nov.*

Outdoor Activities and Sports

During summer, the lake turns into a family playground, with swimming, rowing, sailing, and windsurfing. In winter on Straža hill, immediately above town, you can ski day and night, thanks to floodlighting. Just 10 km (6 mi) west of Bled, a larger ski area, Zatrnik, has 7 km (4 mi) of alpine trails. For information on winter and summer sports, contact Bled's tourist information center (☞ Visitor Information *in* Triglav National Park and the Soča Valley A to Z, *below*).

Bohinjsko Jezero

29 *26 km (17 mi) west of Bled.*

Bohinjsko Jezero (Lake Bohinj) lies within Triglav National Park. In a valley surrounded by the steep walls of the Julian Alps, at an altitude of 1,715 ft, this deep-blue lake is even more dramatically situated than Lake Bled and not nearly as developed.

At the east side of the lake, you'll find the 15th-century Gothic church of **Sveti Janez** (St. John). The small church has a fine bell tower and contains a number of notable 15th- and 16th-century frescoes. ⏲ *Daily 9–noon and 4–7.*

At the west end of the lake a cable car leads up **Mt. Vogel** to a height of 5,035 ft. From here you have spectacular views of the Julian Alps massif and the Bohinj valley and lake. From the cable-car base the road continues 5 km (3 mi) beyond the lake to the point where the Savica River makes a tremendous leap over a 195 ft waterfall.

Dining and Lodging

In the Bohinj area several farms cater to agrotourism, offering overnight accommodations and excellent home-cooking—though you should call in advance if you just want to eat. The most authentic dwellings and farm buildings are in the villages of Stara Fužina and Srednja Vas. For information, contact the Bohinj tourist information center (☞ Visitor Information *in* Triglav National Park and the Soča Valley A to Z, *below*). While you are in the Bohinj area, make sure you try the local cheese.

$$ **Hotel Bellevue.** As the name suggests, the Bellevue affords wonderful views of the lake, so request a room with a view. Agatha Christie fell in love with this old-fashioned hotel and stayed one month here while working on *Murder on the Orient Express.* ✉ *Ribčev Laz 65, 4265,* ☎ *04/572–3331,* FAX *04/572–3684. 76 rooms. AE, DC, MC, V.*

Outdoor Activities and Sports

In summer Bohinj is an ideal base for walking and biking. **Alpinum** (✉ Ribčev Laz 50, ☎ 04/572–3441) rents mountain bikes and organizes raft, kayak, hydrospeed (a small board for bodysurfing rapids), and canyoning trips. In winter you can ski at the ski areas of Vogel and Kobla.

Kranjska Gora

30 *39 km (24 mi) northwest of Bled.*

Kranjska Gora, set amid Slovenia's highest and most dramatic peaks, is the country's largest skiing resort. In summer the area attracts hiking and mountaineering enthusiasts.

Dining and Lodging

$$$ **Kompas Hotel.** This recently refurbished chalet-style hotel on the edge of town is an ideal base for skiing, hiking, and biking—and for taking in fine views of the mountains. Besides the main restaurant, there is an outdoor pizzeria open in summer. ✉ *Borovška 100, 4280,* ☎ *04/588–1661,* FAX *04/588–1176. 156 rooms. Restaurant, pizzeria, indoor pool, massage, sauna, tennis court, mountain bikes. AE, DC, MC, V.*

Outdoor Activities and Sports

Skiing is the number-one sport in Kranjska Gora. There are more than 30 km (20 mi) of downhill runs, 20 ski lifts, and 40 km (25 mi) of groomed cross-country trails. During summer mountain biking is big. Plenty of places rent out bikes, and 12 marked trails totaling 150 km (93 mi) take you through scented pine forests and spectacular alpine scenery. An unused railway track, tracing the south edge of the Karavanke Alps, brings hikers and bikers all the way to the village of Jesenice.

En Route From Kranjska Gora head south over the **Vršič Pass,** 5,252 ft above sea level. You'll then descend into the beautiful Soča Valley, winding through the foothills to the west of Triglav Peak and occasionally plunging through tunnels.

In Trenta you'll find the Triglav National Park Information Center at **Dom Trenta** (✉ Na Logu v Trenti, ☎ 04/388–9330). Here you can watch a presentation about the history and geography of the region and tour the small museum. The center is open April through October from 10 to 6 daily.

From Trenta continue west for about 20 km (13 mi) to reach the rustic mountain resort of Bovec. If you're interested in adventure water sports, **Soča Rafting** (✉ Trg Golobarskih Žrtev 48, ☎ 04/389–6200) organizes guided descents of the Soča River.

Kobarid

31 *21 km (13 mi) from Bovec, 80 km (50 mi) from Bled, 115 km (71 mi) from Ljubljana.*

From Bovec the road follows the magnificent turquoise-color Soča River, running parallel with the Italian border, to pass through the pretty market town of Kobarid. ★ In the center of town the **Kobariški muzej** (Kobarid Museum) gives a 20-minute presentation—with projections, sound effects, and narration—of the tragic fighting that took place on the Isonzo Front during World War I, as recorded in Hemingway's *A Farewell to Arms.* ✉ *Gregorčičeva 10,* ☎ *05/389–0000. SIT500. Daily 9–7.*

The **Kobarid Historical Walk** takes you on a 5 km (3 mi) hike through lovely countryside, over a hair-raising bridge, and past a spectacular waterfall. You'll follow the former front line and visit various sites related to World War I along the way. The path is clearly marked, and a pamphlet and map are available at the Kobarid Museum.

Dining and Lodging

$$ ★ **Hotel Hvala.** This delightful family-run hotel is possibly one of the most welcoming places you'll ever stay. The hotel restaurant, **Restauracija Topli Val**, serves local trout and freshwater crayfish, as

well as mushrooms and truffles in season. Italians drive over the border just to eat here. ✉ *Trg Svobode 1, 5222,* ☎ *05/389–9300,* FAX *05/388–5322. 28 rooms, 4 suites. Restaurant. AE, DC, MC, V.*

Outdoor Activities and Sports

The Soča is an angler's paradise. The river is well stocked with marble trout, rainbow trout, and grayling. Bring your own equipment, or be prepared to buy it here, as it is almost impossible to rent. You also need to buy a day permit; for details inquire at Hotel Hvala (☞ Dining and Lodging, *above*). The season runs from April through October.

X Point (✉ Stresova 1, ☎ 05/388–5308) organizes kayaking, rafting, and canyoning trips, and also rents out mountain bikes. In Srpenica, 13 km (8 mi) northwest of Kobarid, **Alpine Action** (✉ Trnovo ob Soči, ☎ 05/388–5022) offers similar services.

Nova Gorica

32 *48 km (30 mi) from Kobarid, 115 km (71 mi) from Kranjska Gora, 100 km (62 mi) from Ljubljana.*

At the south end of the Soča Valley lies Nova Gorica, with a busy border crossing into Italy. The town was constructed after World War II, when the older settlement of Gorizia became Italian. Today Nova Gorica is best known for its casinos: every Sunday afternoon hordes of Italians cross over to try their luck in the gambling halls.

OFF THE BEATEN PATH

SVETA GORA – Nova Gorica is overshadowed by Sveta Gora (Holy Mountain), standing 2,250 ft above sea level and affording fantastic views north to Triglav and south to the Adriatic. Pilgrims have visited the site since 1539, when an apparition of the Virgin Mary appeared to a young shepherd girl. The present church dates back to 1928; an earlier building was destroyed during World War I. You'll need a car to get up here, except on Sunday, when you could be lucky enough to find a minibus taking locals up to the church for mass; ask at the tourist information center for times (☞ Visitor Information *in* Triglav National Park and the Soča Valley A to Z, *below*).

Dining and Lodging

$$$ ✕ **Pri Hrastu** Despite the general kitsch that prevails in Nova Gorica, this is a genuine old-fashioned restaurant. Traditional local dishes are served up in a wooden-beam dining room with chintzy curtains. The house speciality is štrukli. ✉ *C. 25 junija 2,* ☎ *05/302–7210. AE, DC, MC, V.*

$$$ 🏨 **Hotel Casino Perla.** Too much green landscape and fresh mountain air? Call at Slovenia's largest and newest casino and take a gamble on roulette, blackjack, or poker, or try your hand at one of 400 slot machines. The casino is open nonstop, and the complex has accommodations should you wish to stay the night. ✉ *Kidričeva 7, 5000,* ☎ *05/301–2630,* FAX *05/302–8886. 94 rooms, 11 suites. Restaurant, indoor pool, sauna, 2 tennis courts, casino, nightclub. AE, DC, MC, V.*

Outdoor Activities and Sports

Maybe it's not everyone's idea of fun, but in tune with Nova Gorica's love of gambling, bungee-jumping is a popular pastime here. If you fancy a go, contact **Top Extreme** (✉ Vojkova 9, ☎ 05/330–0090). They organize jumps off the 180 ft high Soklan Bridge, weekends from late April to October.

Idrija

33 *50 km (31 mi) from Kobarid, 60 km (37 mi) from Ljubljana.*

To get directly to the Soča Valley from Ljubljana, take the E57 southwest from Ljubljana, then turn off just before Rakek and head northwest, passing through Idrija. The town was founded in the 15th century on the wealth of its mercury mine, no longer used. Idrija is also known for its handmade lace.

Head to **Anthony's Shaft** to see the oldest part of the mine, the miners' chapel dating back to the 18th century, and a video about the way the miners once lived. ✉ *Kosovelova 3,* ☎ *05/377–1142.* ⏲ *Tours weekdays at 10 and 4, weekends at 10, 3, and 4.*

Dining and Lodging

$$$ ✕ **Restauracija Barbara.** This refined restaurant serves the local speciality, *Idrijski žlikrofi* (tortellini filled with potato and smoked ham), as well as other almost forgotten regional dishes. ✉ *Kosovelova 3,* ☎ *05/377–1142. AE, DC, MC, V.*

$$$ ★ **Kendov Dvorec.** This beautiful 14th-century manor house is in Spodnje Idrija, 4 km (2½ mi) from Idrija. Each bedroom is individually decorated with 19th-century antique furniture and details such as bed linen edged with local handmade lace. Reserve well in advance. ✉ *Sp. Idrija, 5280,* ☎ *05/372–5100,* FAX *05/375–6475. 11 rooms. Restaurant. AE, DC, MC, V.*

Shopping

Numerous boutiques sell *Idrijska čipka* (Idrija lace). For the most original designs try **Studio Irma Vončina** (✉ Mestni trg 17, ☎ 05/377–1584). It's open weekdays from 10 to noon and 1 to 4, and Saturday from 10 to noon.

Triglav National Park and the Soča Valley A to Z

Arriving and Departing

BY BUS

Hourly buses link Ljubljana to Bled, Bohinj, and Kranjska Gora. There are also several buses daily from Ljubljana through Idrija to Kobarid.

BY CAR

From Ljubljana a toll road (E61) runs 42 km (26 mi) northwest past Kranj; from there road E651 leads to the resorts of Bled and Kranjska Gora. A local road then follows the Soča Valley south through Kobarid to Nova Gorica.

BY TRAIN

In theory it is possible to reach the area from Ljubljana by train, but because Bled Jezero station lies some distance from Lake Bled, and Bohinjska Bistrica station lies even further from Lake Bohinj, it is simpler and quicker to take the bus.

Getting Around

BY BUS

The resorts are linked by local buses; their frequency depends on the season. For schedule and fare information ask at a local tourist information center (☞ Visitor Information, *below*).

BY CAR

In this region a car gives you more freedom and is preferable to a haphazard local bus. However, in winter snow can make driving treacherous, especially on minor roadways.

ON FOOT

Triglav National Park's unspoiled countryside is perfect for hiking. Trails are well marked. Local tourist information centers (☞ Visitor Information, *below*) can supply maps and further details.

BY TRAIN

Every Thursday from mid-June to mid-September **Slovenijaturist** (✉ Slovenska 58, Ljubljana, ☎ 01/232–5782) arranges trips on an old-fashioned steam locomotive, following the Bohinj line, through the Soča Valley. The trip begins from Jesenice, stops in Bled and Bohinjska Bistrica, and finally brings you to Most na Soči. The train ride costs SIT3,900 round-trip.

Contacts and Resources

EMERGENCIES

Police (☎ 113). **Ambulance, fire brigade** (☎ 112). **Breakdown service** (AMZS [Automobile Association of Slovenia] ☎ 987).

VISITOR INFORMATION

Bled (✉ C. Svobode 15, ☎ 04/574–1122). **Bohinj** (✉ Ribčev Laz 48, ☎ 04/572–3370). **Idrija** (✉ Lapajnetova 7, ☎ 05/377–3898). **Kobarid** (✉ Gregorčičeva 10, ☎ 05/388–5055). **Kranjska Gora** (✉ Tičarjeva 2, ☎ 04/5881–768). **Nova Gorica** (✉ Ulica Tolminskih Puntarjev 4, ☎ 05/333–4933).

THE KARST REGION AND THE ADRIATIC COAST

The limestone plateau between Ljubljana and the coast is the source of the term *karst*: a geological phenomenon whose typical features are sinkholes, underground caves, and streams. The landscape itself is not all that interesting, but if you like exploring caves, the ones here are visually stunning and well maintained.

Slovenia's share of the Adriatic coast gives tourists a welcome chance to swim and sunbathe. Backed by hills planted with olive groves and vineyards, the tiny strip of coast, only 42 km (26 mi) long, is dominated by the towns of Koper, Piran, and Portorož. Following centuries under the Republic of Venice the region remains culturally and spiritually connected to Italy. The best Venetian architecture of the area can still be seen in the delightful medieval town of Piran. Portorož is a more commercial resort, while Koper is Slovenia's largest port.

For beachgoers the best-equipped beach is at Bernadin, between Piran and Portorož. The most unspoiled stretch is at the Strunjan Nature Reserve—which also has an area reserved for nudists—between Piran and Izola.

Along the coast private lodgings are a cheap alternative to hotels. Owners usually live on the ground floor and let rooms or apartments upstairs. For help finding private accommodations, contact a local tourist information center (☞ Visitor Information *in* The Karst Region and the Adriatic Coast A to Z, *below*).

Numbers in the margin correspond to numbers on the Karst Region and the Adriatic Coast map.

Postojnska Jama

34 *44 km (27 mi) from Ljubljana.*

Postojnska Jama (Postojna Cave) conceals one of the largest networks of caves in the world, with 23 km (14 mi) of underground passage-

The Karst Region and the Adriatic Coast

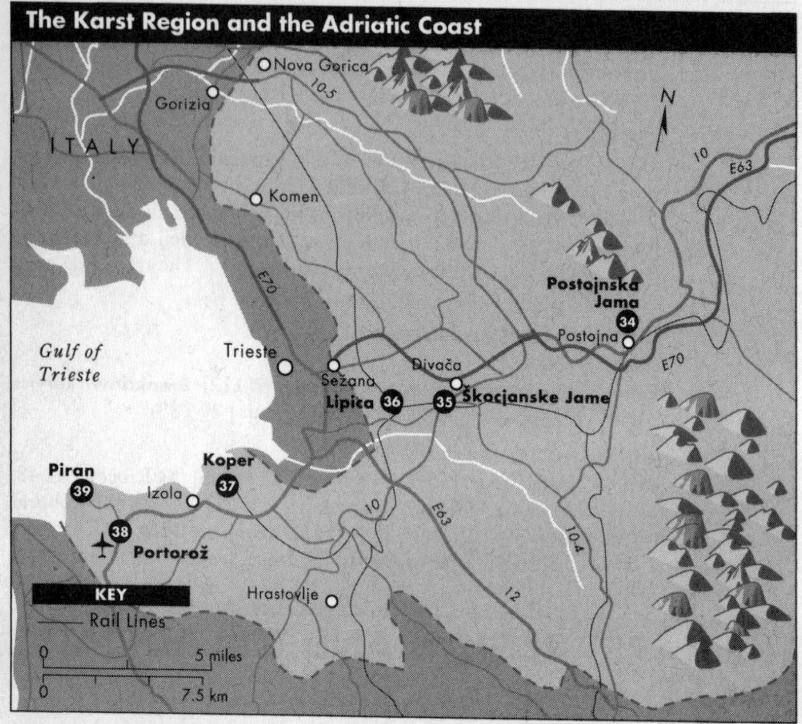

ways. A miniature train takes you through the first 7 km (4½ mi), to reveal a succession of well-lit rock formations. This strange underground world is home of the snakelike "human fish," on view in an aquarium in the Great Hall. Eyeless and colorless because of countless millennia of life in total darkness, these amphibians can live for up to 60 years. Temperatures average 8°C (46°F) year-round, so in summer rent a woolen cloak at the entrance. Tours leave every half hour in summer, hourly the rest of the year. ✉ *Jamska 30, Postojna,* ☎ *05/700–0100.* 🎟 *SIT1,900.* ⏲ *May–Sept., daily 8:30–6; Apr. and Oct., daily 8:30–5; Nov.–Mar., weekdays 9:30–1:30, weekends 9:30–3.*

Škocjanske Jame

35 *26 km (16 mi) from Postojna.*

The Škocjanske Jame (Škocjan Caves), near Divača (just off the highway from Ljubljana to Trieste), require walking, but the effort is worthwhile. Here the River Reka thunders along an underground channel, amid a wondrous world of stalactites and stalagmites. ✉ *Matavun 12, Divača,* ☎ *05/763–0122.* 🎟 *SIT1,700.* ⏲ *June–Sept., daily 10–6 (tours leave hourly); Apr., May, Oct., tours daily at 10, 1, and 5; Nov.–Mar., tours weekdays at 10, weekends at 10 and 3.*

Lipica

36 *5 km (3 mi) west of Divača, 60 km (37 mi) from Ljubljana.*

The **Kobilarna Lipica** (Lipica Stud Farm) near Sežana is the birthplace of the Lipizzaner white horses. Founded in 1580 by the Austrian archduke Karl II, the farm still supplies Lipizzaners to the Spanish Riding School in Vienna. Lipica has developed into a modern sports complex, with two hotels, an indoor riding arena, a swimming pool, and a golf course. The stables are open to the public. Riding classes are available, but you need to book in advance. ✉ *Lipica 5, Sežana, 6210,* ☎ *05/739–1580.* ⏲ *Dressage performances Apr.–Oct., Fri. and Sun. at 3. Stables July–Aug., daily 9–6; Apr.–June and Sept.–Oct., daily 10–5; Nov.–Mar., daily 11–3.*

Dining

$$ ✕ **Pelicon.** This wonderful farm, now set up as an agrotourism center, serves homemade regional specialities such as *pršut* (cured ham) and salami, roast meats, gnocchi, and štrukli, all served with local Teran red wine. You'll find it near Komen, midway between Sežana and Nova Gorica (from Sežana, take the road north toward Štanjel, then at Dutovlje turn left and follow a narrow country road to Komen). Call in advance. ✉ *Coljava 5, Coljava, 6223,* ☎ FAX *05/766–8061. No credit cards. Closed weekdays.*

Koper

37 *35 km (22 mi) southwest of Škocjanske Jame.*

Today a port town surrounded by industrial suburbs, Koper nevertheless warrants a visit. The Republic of Venice made Koper the regional capital during the 15th and 16th centuries, and the magnificent architecture of the Old Town bears witness to the spirit of those times.

The most important buildings are clustered around **Titov trg,** the central town square. Here stands the **Cathedral,** with its fine Venetian Gothic facade and bell tower dating back to 1664. Across the square the splendid **Praetor's Palace,** formerly the seat of the Venetian Grand Council, combines Gothic and Renaissance styles. From the west side of Titov trg, the narrow cobbled street of **Kidriceva ulica** brings you down to the seafront. ⏲ *Cathedral daily 7–noon and 3–7.*

NEED A BREAK? Stop for coffee or a glass of wine at **Loggia Cafe,** housed within the 15th-century Venetian Gothic loggia. In summer there are tables out on the terrace overlooking the town square.

OFF THE BEATEN PATH **HRASTOVLJE –** Hidden behind 16th-century defensive walls is the tiny Romanesque **Cerkev sveti Trojice** (Church of the Holy Trinity). The interior is decorated with a remarkable series of frescoes, including the bizarre *Dance Macabre,* completed in 1490. The church is locked, but if you ask in the village the locals will be glad to open it for you. *From Koper take the main road toward Ljubljana, then follow the signs for Hrastovlje (22 km [14 mi] from Koper).*

Dining

$$$ ✕ **Skipper.** Noted for its vast summer terrace overlooking the marina, Skipper is popular with the yachting fraternity. The menu includes a wide range of pasta dishes, risottos, grilled meats, and fish. ✉ *Kopališko nab. 3,* ☎ *05/627–1750. AE, DC, MC, V.*

Nightlife

During summer the Adriatic coast becomes a haven for all-night parties. In Izola, 8 km (5 mi) west of Koper, **Ambasada Gavioli** (☎ 05/641–8212) specializes in techno and rave. It's one of the largest discos in central Europe and claims to be Slovenia's "grooviest and sexiest club."

Outdoor Activities and Sports

You can rent yachts at the Izola marina from **Jonathon d.o.o.** (☎ 05/677–8930). Prices vary depending on the season and the size of the yacht.

Portorož

38 *15 km (9 mi) from Koper.*

Portorož, or Port of Roses, takes its name from the lush Mediterranean vegetation that flourishes here, thanks to a warm microclimate created by the surrounding hills. The earliest villas and hotels were built at the end of the 19th century, when Austro-Hungarian aristocrats were attracted by the healing powers of the area's mud baths and saltwater pools. Nowadays the town swarms with summer vacationers in search of sea, sun, and invigorating spas.

Dining and Lodging

$$$ ★ ✕ **Ribič.** Situated 2 km (1 mi) down the coast at Seča, Ribič may just be the best fish restaurant in the area. Specialities include baked sea bass with porcini mushrooms, and risotto *Alpe Adria,* which combines wild mushrooms from the Alps and fresh scampi from the Adriatic. In summer you can eat in the garden. ✉ *Seča,* ☎ *05/677–0790. AE, DC, MC, V. Closed Tues.*

$$$ **Hotel Palace.** This modern seaside hotel is connected to the thermal spa recreation center, which offers massages and medicinal treatments. Rooms are comfortable, and the service is professional. ✉ *Obala 45, 6320,* ☎ *05/696–9001,* FAX *05/696–9003. 189 rooms, 7 suites. Restaurant, indoor pool, pool. AE, DC, MC, V.*

Piran

39 *5 km (3 mi) from Portorož, 125 km (78 mi) from Ljubljana.*

The jewel of the Slovenian coast, the medieval walled Venetian town of Piran stands compact on a small peninsula, capped by a neo-Gothic lighthouse and presided over by a hilltop Romanesque cathedral. Narrow, winding, cobbled streets lead to the main square, Trg Tartini, which in turn opens out onto a charming harbor. Historically, Piran's wealth was based on salt making. Culturally, the town is known as the birthplace of the 17th-century violinist and composer, Giuseppe Tartini.

The **Sergej Mašera Pomorski muzej** (Sergej Mašera Maritime Museum) tells the story of Piran's connections with the sea. There is a beautiful collection of model ships, sailors' uniforms, and shipping instruments, as well as a detailed account of the salt-making industry. ✉ *Cankarjevo nab. 3,* ☎ *05/673–2755.* ⏲ *Tues.–Sun. 9–noon and 3–6.*

Dining and Lodging

$$$ ✕ **Tri Vdove.** House specialities are seafood: the much sought after "date mussels" arrive fresh daily, along with shrimp, lobster, and a variety of fish. A large terrace overlooks the sea. ✉ *Trg 1 Maja,* ☎ *05/673–2232. AE, DC, MC, V.*

$ ✕ **Mario.** This family-run restaurant, just off Trg Tartini, serves simple local dishes. In summer there are tables on the terrace in front of Tartini's house. ✉ *Kajuhova 6,* ☎ *05/673–3099. AE, DC, MC, V.*

$$$ ★ **Hotel Tartini.** The old facade hides a modern interior with a spacious central atrium. The rooms are well furnished and comfortable. The location, overlooking the oval Trg Tartini, is out of this world. ✉ *Trg Tartini 15, 6330,* ☎ *05/673–3100,* FAX *05/673–3104. 43 rooms, 2 suites. Restaurant. AE, DC, MC, V.*

Nightlife and the Arts

Piran Musical Evenings are held in the cloisters of the Minorite Monastery every Friday in July and August. Ask at the tourist information center for up-to-date information (☞ Visitor Information *in* The Karst Region and the Adriatic Coast A to Z, *below*). During the same period, the **Primorski Summer Festival** (✉ Verdiova 5, Koper, ☎ 05/627–

1912) of open-air theater and dance is staged in Piran, Koper, Portorož, and Izola.

The Karst Region and the Adriatic Coast A to Z

Arriving and Departing

BY BOAT

During summer, it is possible to reach the Slovenian coast by boat from Italy (☞ Arriving and Departing by Boat *in* Slovenia A to Z, *below*).

BY BUS

Several buses a day connect Ljubljana to Koper, Piran, and Portorož, passing through Postojna and Divača on the way. In summer a regular service links Nova Gorica to the coast. There is also a daily service connecting the coastal towns to Trieste, Italy.

BY CAR

The E63 highway connects Ljubljana to the coast, passing through the karst region en route.

BY TRAIN

Four trains daily link Ljubljana and Koper, passing through Postojna and Divača en route. For information contact Ljubljana's train station (☞ Arriving and Departing *in* Ljubljana A to Z, *above*).

Getting Around

BY BUS

A network of local buses connects all listed sights, with the exception of Lipica and Hrastovlje. Schedules vary depending on the time of year, so contact a local bus station for information.

BY CAR

A car is advisable for touring the karst region. However, parking can be a problem along the coast during summer, when town centers are closed to traffic.

Contacts and Resources

EMERGENCIES

Police (☎ 113). **Ambulance, fire brigade** (☎ 112). **Breakdown service** (AMZS [Automobile Association of Slovenia] ☎ 987).

GUIDED TOURS

Adriatic Safari (✉ Kosovelova 8, ☎ 05/677–1282), in Piran, arranges boat trips along the coast.

VISITOR INFORMATION

Koper (✉ Ukmarjev trg 7, ☎ 05/663–2010). **Lipica** (✉ Lipica 5, ☎ 05/739–1580). **Piran** (✉ Trg Tartini 2, ☎ 05/674–8260). **Portorož** (✉ Obala 16, ☎ 05/674–0231). **Postojna** (✉ Jamska 30, ☎ 05/728–0788).

SLOVENIA A TO Z

Arriving and Departing

By Boat

From early March to late October the ***Prince of Venice*** (Kompas Turizem; ✉ Obala 41, Portorož, ☎ 05/617–8000) hydrofoil makes regularly scheduled trips between Venice and Portorož.

From mid-July to mid-September, the Italian firm **Adriatica** (Maona; ✉ Cankarjevo nab. 7, Piran, ☎ 05/674–6508) runs a round-trip service from Trieste, calling at Piran and stopping at several towns on the Croatian Adriatic coast.

By Bus

There is daily direct bus service between the capital and cities in Germany, Croatia, and Italy (☞ Arriving and Departing by Bus *in* Ljubljana A to Z, *above*).

By Car

From Budapest and Vienna the Slovenian border is no more than a two-hour drive; from Prague it's eight hours. A tunnel speeds traffic through the Karavanke Alps between Slovenia and Austria. From Vienna the passage is by way of Maribor to Ljubljana, with a highway from Graz to Celje. Slovenia's roads also connect with Italy's *autostrada*.

By Plane

There are no direct flights between Slovenia and the United States. Adria Airways regularly flies to most major European cities (☞ Arriving and Departing by Plane *in* Ljubljana A to Z, *above*).

By Train

Daily trains link Slovenia with Austria, Italy, Hungary, and Croatia. Many are overnight trains with sleeping compartments. For information contact the Ljubljana train station (☞ Arriving and Departing by Train *in* Ljubljana A to Z, *above*).

Getting Around

In Slovenian the words for street (*ulica*) and drive (*cesta*) are abbreviated to ul. and c. *Nabrežje* (abbreviated to nab.) means "embankment." The word for square is *trg*.

By Bus

An extensive network covers the entire country. You can reach even the most outlying villages by bus, though it may take several changes and time lost waiting. For information contact Ljubljana's bus station (☞ Arriving and Departing by Bus *in* Ljubljana A to Z, *above*).

By Car

Traveling by car undoubtedly gives you the chance to reach remote areas of the country when and as you wish. Main roads between large towns are comparable to those in Western Europe. Highways charge a toll depending on the route and distance traveled.

Gas stations on border crossings and main roads leading to larger towns are open 24 hours a day, while others are open 7 AM–8 PM, Monday–Saturday. Unleaded gasoline is available throughout the country.

PARKING

In major towns parking spaces are marked with a blue line and a sign denoting time restrictions. Buy a ticket, obtainable from gas stations and newsstands, write down the time you parked, and attach it to your windshield.

RULES OF THE ROAD

Slovenes drive on the right, and are obliged to keep their headlights on at all times. Speed limits are 60 kph (37 mph) in urban areas and 120 kph (74 mph) on highways. Local drivers are courteous by European standards. The permitted blood alcohol level is 0.5 g/kg; drivers caught exceeding this level can expect penalties similar to those of other European countries.

By Train

The internal rail network is limited, but trains are cheap and efficient. For more information *see* Getting Around by Train *in* regional A to Z sections, *above*.

Contacts and Resources

Car Rentals

An international driver's license is required to rent a car in Slovenia. A midsize car costs $112 (SIT18,500) for 24 hours, with unlimited mileage. You'll need to leave a credit-card receipt as a deposit. Rental agencies can be found in all major towns and at the Ljubljana Airport.

Customs and Duties

ON ARRIVAL

As with most European countries, you can import duty-free 200 cigarettes, 1 liter of spirits, and 2 liters of wine. Foreign citizens can bring personal items into the country without paying customs taxes.

ON DEPARTURE

Any visitor who buys goods worth more than SIT12,500 ($75) at any one store is entitled to a refund of taxes. When you make a purchase ask for a Request for VAT Refund form, *Zahtevek za vracilo DDV.* A customs officer will certify the form when you leave the country. To obtain the refund, go to the Kompas MTS office at the border crossing point or the airport. Exporting historic artifacts is forbidden.

Emergencies

Police (☎ 113). **Ambulance, fire brigade** (☎ 112). **Automobile Association of Slovenia (AMZS)** (☎ 987 for 24-hour breakdown service). For medical emergencies, even if you are outside the capital, call **Ljubljana Emergency Medical Services** (☎ 01/232–3060) and someone will be able to tell you where to find the nearest assistance.

Language

Slovene is the country's chief language. In the east signs are posted in Slovene and Hungarian; on the Adriatic coast both Slovene and Italian are officially used. English, German, and Italian are spoken in many places.

Mail

POSTAL RATES

Airmail postage to the United States is SIT105 for a letter, SIT95 for a postcard. Airmail postage in Europe is SIT80 for a letter, SIT70 for a postcard. Post offices are open weekdays from 8 to 6 and Saturday from 8 to noon. Stamps are also sold at hotels, newsstands, and kiosks.

Money and Expenses

COSTS

Costs for goods and services are on a par with Western Europe. Notable exceptions are public transportation, alcohol, and cigarettes, all of which are cheaper here.

CURRENCY

The monetary unit in Slovenia is the Slovenian tolar (SIT). One Slovenian tolar is divided into 100 stotin. There are notes of SIT10,000, SIT5,000, SIT1,000, SIT500, SIT200, SIT100, SIT50, SIT20, and SIT10, and coins of SIT5, SIT2, SIT1, and 50 stotin.

At press time the exchange rate was about SIT188 to the U.S. dollar, SIT128 to the Canadian dollar, and SIT294 to the pound sterling.

SAMPLE PRICES

A cup of coffee, SIT150; museum entrance, SIT200–SIT500; a glass of beer on draught, SIT200; a slice of cake, SIT200; a bottle of house wine, SIT1,500; a sandwich, SIT350.

National Holidays

January 1–2; February 8 (Prešeren Day, Slovene cultural day); Easter Sunday and Monday; April 27 (National Resistance Day); May 1 and

2 (Labor Day); June 25 (Slovenia National Day); August 15 (Assumption); October 31 (Reformation Day); November 1 (All Saints' Day); December 25; December 26 (Independence Day).

Opening and Closing Times

Most banks are open weekdays 9–noon and 2–4:30, Saturday 9–11. You can also change money at exchange desks in hotels, gas stations, tourist agencies, supermarkets, and small exchange offices. The main museums are open Tuesday to Sunday 10–6. Larger shops are open Monday–Saturday 10–6, while smaller ones may open mornings only 10–2. Most stores are closed Sunday.

Passports and Visas

No visas are necessary for holders of valid passports from the United States, Canada, the United Kingdom, mainland European countries, Australia, New Zealand, or the Republic of Ireland. South African nationals, however, must have a three-month tourist visa.

Rail Passes

The Zone G InterRail Pass—available only to European citizens—is valid for a month of unlimited travel in Slovenia, Italy, Greece, and Turkey. For more information, *see* Train Travel *in* Smart Travel Tips.

Telephones

COUNTRY CODE

The country code for Slovenia is 386. When dialing from outside the country, drop the initial zero from the area code.

INTERNATIONAL CALLS

To make international calls, dial 00 and then the appropriate country code. International calls can be made from local telephones or post offices. For collect calls dial the **operator** (☎ 901). For international inquiries dial **international directory assistance** (☎ 989).

LOCAL CALLS

Pay phones take magnetic telephone cards, available from post offices and kiosks. Lower rates apply from 10 PM to 7 AM and all day Sunday. For local inquiries dial **local directory assistance** (☎ 988).

Tipping

Tax is already included in listed prices. Tips are not included in bills, and a 10% tip is customary. If the service is especially good, tip 15%.

Travel Agencies

The following agencies in Ljubljana deal with foreign visitors:

Emona Globtour (✉ Bargova 5, ☎ 01/588–4400, FAX 01/588–4455). **Kompas Turizem Ljubljana** (✉ Pražakova 4, ☎ 01/432–7127, FAX 01/231–9888). **Promet T and T** (✉ Tugomerjeva 56, ☎ 01/559–3511, FAX 01/559–5345). **Slovenijaturist** (✉ Slovenska 58, ☎ 01/232–5782, FAX 01/232–8884). **Tirtur Ljubljana** (✉ Majorja Lavriča 12, ☎ 01/559–8835, FAX 01/559–8809).

Visitor Information

The **Slovenian Tourist Board** (✉ Dunajska 156, Ljubljana 1000, ☎ 01/189–1840, FAX 01/189–1841) provides information and produces excellent publications on all kinds of tourist activities. Each region has its own tourist information center. For individual centers, *see* Visitor Information *in* regional A to Z sections, *above*.

6 POLAND

A country of flowers and trees and sunshine, of outdoor cafés and old-world charm, Poland is at its best in late spring and summer. Not-to-be-missed locales include historic Kraków, a uniquely preserved Baroque city where one of Poland's most famous sons, Copernicus, studied; the wild lakelands of Mazuria, with nesting storks and other wildlife; and the Tatra Mountains, with their villages of carved-wood buildings, brown bears, springtime pastures covered with wildflowers, and wintertime slopes covered in snow and dotted with skiers. The birthplace of Chopin, Poland also delights visitors with its musical and theatrical traditions.

Updated by John Babb and Scott Young

POLES ARE FOND OF QUOTING, with a wry grimace, an old Chinese valediction: "May you live in interesting times." The times are certainly interesting in Poland—home of the Solidarity political-labor-social movement that sent shock waves through the Soviet bloc beginning in 1980, and the first Eastern European state to shake off Communist rule. But as the grimace implies, being on the firing line of history is a challenge. There are constant reminders that the return to capitalism, after 45 years of Sovietism, is an experiment on a vast and unprecedented scale, bringing benefits for a growing percentage of the population but also hardships for many.

The reforms of more than a decade have brought little tangible benefits to the average Pole, and the people's resolve is faltering. The stress was seen in the mid-2000 breakup of the unpopular ruling coalition of the two reform-minded political parties. To ensure that reforms don't proceed too quickly, Poles have overwhelmingly thrown their support behind President Aleksander Kwaśniewski—himself a former Communist.

On the other hand, NATO membership, healthy IMF ratings, and the ever-increasing privatization of state companies all paint a hopeful economic picture. The new economy is part of the reason Warsaw and Kraków are enjoying a cultural renaissance. Travelers are now flocking to Central Europe's largest country in ever greater numbers. They're coming to visit the beautifully preserved medieval city of Kraków, breathtaking mountains, the Hanseatic castles of Gdańsk, and the haunting Baltic seascapes. Most of all, they're coming to witness a nation in the process of rebirth.

With 39 million inhabitants living in a territory of 312,677 square km (119,755 square mi), Poland is still suspended between the old world and the new, and the contrasts are many. You see bright, new, privately owned shops in shabby buildings that haven't been renovated in decades. Billboards glowingly advertise goods that most Poles cannot afford. Many public services, such as education and health care, are woefully underfunded even though local authorities are striving valiantly to satisfy voters' quickly rising expectations. Still, the Poles are intent on focusing on the future, not looking back to the past. Step inside a faded Communist-era building and you may find stockpiles of the best food or clothing the West has to offer—few natives are nostalgic for the cheap and chintzy stuff of the past.

The Communist era represented the most recent stage in the Poles' age-old struggle to retain their national identity in the face of pressure from more powerful neighbors to the west and east. Founded as a unified state during the 10th century on the great north-European plain, Poland lay for a thousand years at the heart of Europe, precisely at the halfway point between the Atlantic coast of Spain and the Ural Mountains. With no easily demarcated or defensible frontiers, this gave it an enviable geostrategic position. During the Middle Ages, Poland fought against German advances, uniting with its eastern neighbors in 1410 to roundly defeat the Teutonic Knights in the Battle of Grunwald. In the golden age of Polish history, the 16th and 17th centuries, Poland pushed eastward against its Slavic neighbors, taking Kiev and envisioning a kingdom that stretched from the Baltic to the Black Sea. It saw itself then as a bastion of Christendom holding back the hordes from the east, a role best symbolized when Polish king Jan III Sobieski led the allied Christian forces to defeat the Turks at Vienna in 1683.

By the end of the 18th century, powerful neighbors had united to obliterate Poland—with its outmoded tendency to practice democracy at the highest levels of state and elect foreigners to the throne—from the map of Europe. Its territories were to remain divided among the Austrian, Prussian, and Russian empires until the end of World War I. This period of partition is often used to explain patterns of character or public behavior—the Polish tendency to subvert organized authority, for example, or Polish allegiance to the role of the Roman Catholic Church as guardian of the national identity, a devotion that would survive intense and, on occasion, brutal pressure by the Communist secret police and other authorities.

Evidence of the period of partition remains throughout Poland, despite a tendency in the postwar years to impose uniformity. The formerly Prussian-ruled regions of western Poland, centered in Poznań, are still regarded as cleaner and better organized than the formerly Russian-ruled central areas around the capital, Warsaw. The former Austrian zone in the south, particularly the city of Kraków, retains a reputation for formality and propriety reminiscent of the Hapsburg period. The architecture of the three regions also bears traces of distinct 19th-century imperial styles.

During the 20th century, after a brief period of revived independence in the interwar years, Poland once again fell victim to the old struggle between east and west. It was first crushed by Hitler's *Drang nach Osten* (drive toward the east), which killed 6 million Polish citizens, including 3 million of the Jews who had played such a major role in the nation's history. Then, in 1945, the Soviet Union imposed a Communist system in Poland. Poland's borders were shifted 240 km (150 mi) westward, and in the process lands formerly held by Germany were annexed and the *kresy,* or eastern territories, were lost. These mid-century experiences are embedded deeply in the Polish psyche. Poles show an almost mystical reverence for these struggles by remembering dozens of wartime anniversaries each year, which they celebrate with speeches, color guards, and by placing candles at countless memorials and cemeteries. Since 1989, it has been possible to openly mourn those who died fighting Soviet power and the Polish Communist authorities during the 1940s and 1950s.

Poland's historic cities—Kraków, Warsaw, Gdańsk—tell much of the tale of European history and culture. Its countryside offers unrivaled possibilities of escape from the 20th century to a simpler time, to unspoiled nature, and to the remnants of the grand Polish past scattered throughout the country. Paradoxically, the Communists—who after 1956 dropped attempts to collectivize agriculture and kept the Polish peasant on his small plot of land—left much of rural Poland in a romantic, almost pre-industrial state. Cornflowers still bloom, storks perch atop untidy nests by cottage chimneys, and horse carts lazily make their way along worn field tracks. Travelers should try to ignore the appalling legacy of Communism (ugly Soviet-style buildings, pockets of terrible pollution) and concentrate on Poland's attractions.

Despite a certain wary reserve in public behavior, the Poles will win you over with their strong individualism, their sense of humor, and their capacity for fun. Today, more than ever, they are very politically aware of both local and international issues. Whether or not they are for or against free-fall capitalism, one thing remains certain: *Puppies* (Polish yuppies) want to get their MTV.

Pleasures and Pastimes

Dining

While even Poland's most ardent fans will admit that it does not have one of the world's great cuisines, the old traditions of Polish cooking

Poland (Polska)

Baltic Sea
Zatoka Gdańska
Wejherowo
Gdynia
Gdańsk
Słupsk
Sławno
Kołobrzeg
Koszalin
Kościerzyna
Tczew
Miastko
Malbo
Świnoujście
Karlin
Starogard Gdański
Sztum
Zalew Szczeciński
Szczecinek
Kwidzyn
Nowogard
Chojnice
Goleniów
Szczecin
Grudziąd
Stargard Szczeciński
Jastrowie
Kalisz Pom.
Bydgoszcz
Wisła R.
Piła
Toruń
Pyrzyce
Chodzież
Notec R.
Odra R.
Inowrocław
Rogoźno
Gorzów Wielkopolski
Włc
GERMANY
Skwierzyna
Pnjewy
Gniezno
Poznań
Września
Krośniewice
Świebodzin
Środa Wielkopolski
Jarocin
Zielona Góra
Leszno
Zgie
Kalisz
Warta R.
Krotoszyn
Zduńska
Kożuchów
Ostrów Wielkopolski
Sieradz
Rawicz
Szprotawa
Lubin
Odra R.
Bolesławiec
Kępno
Wieluń
Zgorzelec
Legnica
Wrocław
Oleśnica
Neisse R.
Jelenia Góra
Kluczbork
Brzeg
Wałbrzych
Opole
Lubliniec
Nysa
Bytom
Kudowa Zdrój
Kłodzko
Gliwice
Chorzów
Katowice
Wodzisław
CZECH REPUBLIC

Kaliningrad
RUSSIA
LITHUANIA
Górowo Iławeckie
Bartoszyce
Węgorzewo
Suwałki
Pasłek
Lidzbark Warm.
Giżycko
Ełk
Augustów
Mrągowo
Olsztyn
Ostróda
Grajewo
Szczytno
Szczuczyn
Biebrza R.
Czarna Białostocka
Nowe Miasto Lubawskie
Nidzica
Łomża
Białystok
Mława
Ostrołęka
Zambrów
Bielsk Podlaski
Ciechanów
Ostrów Mazowiecka
BELARUS
Wkra R.
Wyszków
Bug R.
Siemiatycze
Płock
Sokołów Podlaska
Warsaw
Siedlce
Brest
Kutno
Mińsk Mazowiecki
Łowicz
Otwock
Biała Podlaska
Żyrardów
Garwolin
Grójec
Radzyn Podl
Łódź
Wisła R.
Kock
Wlodawa
Pilica R.
Wieprz R.
Tomaszów Mazowiecki
Puławy
Radom
Piotrków Trybunalski
Kazimierz Dolny
Lublin
Skarżysko Kamienna
Chełm
Radomsko
Ostrowiec Świętokrzyski
Krasnystaw
Kraśnik
Kielce
Zamość
Janów
Jedrzejów
Sandomierz
San R.
Tomaszów Lubelski
Stalowa Wola
Miechów
Leżajsk
Mielec
Jarosław
UKRAINE
Tarnów
Dębica
Rzeszów
Kraków
Przemyśl
Myślenice
Krosno
Nowy Sącz
Gorlice
Sanok
Rabka
Krynica
60 miles
90 km
Zakopane
SLOVAKIA

are being revived, and the finer city restaurants are bringing a nouvelle flair to the tried-and-true favorites. Out in the countryside, however, after several days of eating like a Pole—salty smoked salmon, sausage, pork cutlets, cheese dumplings, milk shakes so thick they'll clog your straw—you'll probably be interested in a roughage fix of *ogórki kwaszone* (pickled cucumbers) salad. All in all, Polish food can be filling, tasty, and relatively cheap.

One of the joys of Polish cuisine is the soup, a fundamental part of the daily meal and potentially a meal in itself. Soups are invariably excellent, often thick and nourishing, with lots of peas and beans. Clear beet soup, *barszcz,* is the most traditional, but soured barley soup, *żurek,* should be sampled at least once. Pickled or soused herring is also a favorite Polish entrée. The Polish chef's greatest love is pork in all its varieties, including suckling pig and wild boar. Traditional sausages, *kabanos,* usually dried and smoked, are delicious, as are the different kinds of *kiełbasa.* A popular hunter's dish, *bigos,* is made from soured and fresh cabbage, cooked (for several days or weeks) together with many different kinds of meat and sausage. *Kompot* (stewed fruit) is customarily served at an early stage in the meal, and you sip the juice rather than eat the fruit. Dessert remains a major institution in Polish life, and you'll see lots of people walking around in a whipped-cream-induced haze at any time of the day or night. In Poland whipped cream is a basic food group.

The traditional sit-down restaurant is still the main feature of the dining scene in Poland, across all price ranges. But if you are in a hurry there is more variety than ever. The old low-cost, self-service *bar mleczny* (milk bars) and cheap cafeterias are disappearing, replaced by pizza parlors, burger joints, and other fast-food outlets. If you are really pressed for time, you will nearly always be able to find a street stall (usually housed in a small white caravan) that serves *zapiekanki*: French bread toasted with cheese and mushrooms. Street stalls selling spicy Vietnamese dishes are found in all Polish cities.

Restaurants usually have French, German, and Eastern European wines; the last often represent the best value for the money, especially the Hungarian reds such as Egri Bikavér (Bull's Blood of Eger) or one of the Bulgarian *Sofia* varieties. Note that quality imported wines and spirits are highly taxed as luxury items, and the prices charged for them in restaurants can be astronomical.

Although upscale city restaurants have adapted to Western mealtimes, and some offer lunch starting at noon, Poles traditionally eat their main meal of the day, *obiad* (dinner), between 3 and 5. Many restaurants therefore open at 1 and do not get into full swing until mid-afternoon. Although in cities there is a growing trend to stay open later ("to the last customer" is a popular new slogan), many restaurants still close relatively early, and it may be difficult to order a meal after 9. A few restaurants offer fixed-price meals between about 1 and 5; these do not always represent a savings over à la carte prices.

CATEGORY	WARSAW*	OTHER AREAS*
$$$$	over $50	over $30
$$$	$25–$50	$15–$30
$$	$10–$25	$7–$15
$	under $10	under $7

**per person for a three-course meal, including service but not drinks.*

Hiking, Walking, and Cycling

There are nearly endless possibilities for hiking in Poland. The most spectacular terrain is in the south in the Tatra Mountains and the Podhale region, and in the wild and deserted Bieszczady region in the southeast (along the borders of Slovakia and Ukraine). All national parks have well-marked trails that traverse beautiful countryside. The parks also provide overnight accommodations at regular intervals in the form of walkers' huts and hostels, which can be fairly primitive. Elsewhere in the country it is more difficult to guarantee you'll find a bed at the right point on your route. For biking, the flat areas of the north are perhaps best, and many parts of the country have touring tracks and byroads.

Lodging

Lodging options are getting better and better, although travelers seeking elegant accommodations have far fewer options to choose from than in Western Europe or, say, Prague. Cheap and comfortable bed-and-breakfast accommodations in private homes or pensions are widely available only in the mountains or on the coast; look for signs in windows that say POKOJE GOŚCINNE (guest rooms) or inquire at tourist information offices in resorts. In cities, private bed-and-breakfast accommodations are to be used only as a last resort, because they are often run by disreputable proprietors who charge exorbitant prices.

The number of privately owned hotels and wayside motels has increased rapidly since 1989. Many of the more recent additions are smaller boutique-type hotels, and only a few—for example, the Marriott and Sheraton in Warsaw—are owned and managed by international chains. All other hotels bearing familiar names (Holiday Inn, Novotel) are run by Orbis, the state travel conglomerate, which at press time was in the process of privatization. Orbis hotels offer a standard of accommodations on a par with the international chains, usually at international prices. Standards at municipally owned hotels vary enormously; ask to see your room before checking in. Gromada, the peasant cooperative, runs excellent, inexpensive hotels. The Polish Tourist Association, PTTK, also has a network of very inexpensive hotels throughout Poland, but single and double rooms are limited in number, and most of the accommodations are in dormitories.

Room prices and standards can differ vastly. If you do your homework, you can find real bargains outside the major cities. Government star ratings (from five down to one) are outdated and refer to ownership category and size as much as to standards. They do, however, give an indication of price.

Service charges are included in the room price, as is a value-added tax (VAT) of 22%. Breakfast is also often included, but this is not universal. The price does not necessarily reflect whether the bathroom has a tub or shower. Rates during the peak season on the coast (May–September) and in the southern mountain region (December–March and July–August) are up to 50% higher than off-season prices. Seasonal variations elsewhere in the country are less marked, apart from short-term increased rates for special occasions, such as in Poznań during the trade fair.

CATEGORY	COST*
$$$$	over $200
$$$	$100–$200
$$	$50–$100
$	under $50

**All prices are for two people in a double room, with bath or shower and breakfast.*

following the text of a review is your signal that the property has a Web site, where you will find details and, usually, images; for a link, visit www.fodors.com/urls.

Music

Poland has a strong musical tradition, and in the big cities during the performance season (from October to May), you will have opportunities to hear outstanding musicians and orchestras—at very moderate prices. Cafés frequently host musical performances in the evenings, and many upmarket cafés have daytime pianists. Jazz is also popular, and jazz clubs can be found for all tastes in most larger towns.

Shopping

Poland is not yet a shopping mecca, though the country is well known for particular items. Leather products are well designed and cheaper than their Western counterparts. The best region for leather is the south: Kraków for more sophisticated products and the mountains for folk goods. Amber and silver jewelry are on sale all over Poland, but the best places to search for unusual pieces are on the Baltic coast. Wooden, woven, and embroidered folk arts and crafts are found in Cepelia stores all over Poland. Glassware, including cut glass, is beautifully designed and relatively cheap. And of course you can find Polish vodka (*wódka*) anywhere in the country. *Polonez* or *Żytnia* are clear rye vodkas; *Żubrówka* is pale green and flavored with bison grass from the Białowieska forest; *Jarzębiak* is flavored with rowan berries.

Exploring Poland

Poles are still surprised to encounter travelers who come simply to explore, and you may be asked frequently if you're visiting relatives. For many of the natives, Poland is not a place that steamrolls visitors with excessive natural beauty or great architecture. For the unwitting tourist, that may be true. But the savvy traveler will be enticed by a delightful and wide variety of scenery and architecture. The silvery Baltic Sea coast and the Mazurian Lakes of the north lie 650 km (400 mi) from the towering Tatra Mountains of the south; in between are historic cities and castles. If you are using public transportation, Warsaw is the hub from which all fast trains radiate, and it is usually wise to begin and end your travels through Poland there.

Great Itineraries

Numbers in the text correspond to numbers in the margin and on the Warsaw, Southeastern Poland, Kraków, Gdańsk and the Northeast, and Western Poland maps.

IF YOU HAVE 3 DAYS

Begin in **Warsaw** (1)–(49), taking in the city's Old Town—destroyed during the Second World War and reconstructed during the 1950s—as well as the Baroque palace in Wilanów and the neoclassical palace in the Łazienki Park. On your second day, rent a car so that en route to Kraków you can visit **Kazimierz Dolny** (83), a Renaissance village on the Vistula River, and catch at least a glimpse of Poland's lush countryside. Alternatively, you can go to Kraków by public transportation via **Częstochowa** (70), where the 14th-century Pauline Monastery contains Poland's holiest relic: the icon of the Black Madonna. No matter how you get there, leave at least a whole day for **Kraków** (50)–(69), the nation's capital before 1611. Its uniquely intact Renaissance Old Town contains a wealth of works of art and is home to the university where Nicolaus Copernicus studied.

IF YOU HAVE 5 DAYS

Begin your stay in **Gdańsk** (86) and explore the historic Old Town, which was originally one of the main Hanseatic ports on the Baltic. By car, take the 1(E75) and Route 50 to **Malbork** (89) and see the vast castle that was the headquarters of the Teutonic Knights (to do this properly, you need at least half a day). From Malbork, rejoin the 1(E75), and drop by another castle in Gniew before heading to **Toruń** ⑯, a small walled town on the Vistula River and Copernicus's birthplace. From Toruń, take Route 10 and the 7(E77) to Warsaw. This route can also be done easily by train. But if you instead wish to explore the Mazurian Lakes on your way to Warsaw, a car is essential: from Malbork, take the cross-country route via Dzierzgoń to Ostróda, and then Route 16 to **Olsztyn** ⑳, before taking the 7(E77) to Warsaw. After a day exploring Warsaw, make your way to Kraków. From here take a day trip to **Zakopane** ⑯, two hours away by bus, on the way admiring the foothills of the Podhale region and the High Tatra range in the distance. A day in Zakopane will allow you to try regional cooking and get a feel for life in the mountains.

When to Tour

With its characteristically gray, cold weather and short daylight hours, the Polish winter may persuade you to spend your vacation in the Caribbean. Unless you are a skier, spring is a good time for intense, energetic sightseeing. Summers can be hot and humid, especially in southern Poland, but this is still the busiest tourist season. If you are interested in the arts, remember that theaters and concert halls close completely for the months of July and August and often do not get going with the new season's programs until October. The fabled Polish Golden Autumn, when the leaves do their thing, lasts until November and can be a good time for touring. The winter sports season is from December to March, when high-season rates are once again in effect in the mountains. In general, central heating is universal and efficient in Poland, but air-conditioning is a rarity.

WARSAW

Your first view of Warsaw (Warszawa) is likely to produce an impression of monotonous gray concrete, broken suddenly by a curious, wedding-cake edifice towering over the city: the Palace of Culture and Science, Stalin's early 1950s gift to the city. In the early 1990s, an American businessman wanted to purchase it to cut off the elaborate pinnacle and crenellated outbuildings and develop the remaining skyscraper into a business center. Suddenly, Warsovians, after decades of mocking this symbol of Russian imperialism, grudgingly admitted to a sentimental attachment to it. The entrepreneur's scheme fell through, and the Palace of Culture still stands to give visitors a useful orientation point.

Central Warsaw's predominating bleakness is a legacy of the tragedy that befell what had been, prior to World War II, a marvelous Central European city. Seventy-five percent of it was destroyed during a heroic uprising against the Nazis in 1944. Warsaw was rebuilt in the 1950s and 1960s in postwar "functional" styles and then, as economic times grew harder, largely left to decay. But as you start to explore, your initial reservations will fade away. Fragments of the Warsaw that survived the war acquire a special poignancy in their isolation: odd rows of Art Nouveau tenements, such as those on the south side of the great square around the Palace of Culture and on ulica Wilcza; the elegant aleje Ujazdowskie, now the diplomatic quarter, leading to the Belvedere Palace and the Łazienki Palace and Park. The reconstructed areas of the city—the historic Old Town area, rebuilt brick by brick in the 1950s; the Royal Castle; the Ujazdowski Castle—are moving tributes to the Poles' ability to survive and preserve their history.

Moreover, Warsaw is at last getting a face-lift, and the pace of change is so fast that even the locals can't keep up. The butcher shop where customers have faithfully lined up over the past 25 years closes down one evening, to be replaced the next day by a sleek, white-tile computer outlet. The local grocery turns overnight into a well-lit boutique selling imported fashions at prices that former clients cannot afford. While some may live to regret the disappearance of the local shoemaker or tailor—those striking survivors whom Communism froze in a time warp—the new arrivals create a vibrant image. Visitors in search of old-world charm may be disappointed, but they can console themselves with the thought that the range of facilities available in many areas, especially for dining out, has improved tremendously. Future forward, the city is now intent on resurrecting long-suppressed cultural activities, which can now be appreciated in an atmosphere of experimentation and possibility.

Exploring Warsaw

The geographical core and political center of Poland since 1611, when King Zygmunt III Waza moved the capital here from Kraków, Warsaw will doubtless shock the first-time visitor with its bleak postwar architecture. But the history of this city can turn dismay first to amazement and then to deep admiration for the surviving one-third of its inhabitants who so energetically rebuilt their city—literally from the ashes—starting in 1945. Warsaw was in the worst possible location during World War II, and perhaps nowhere else in Europe are there so many reminders of that time: plaques describing massacres of Poles by the Nazis are numerous. (The city's darkest hours came in April 1943, when the inhabitants of the Jewish ghetto rose up in arms against the Nazis and were brutally put down, and in the summer of 1944, when the Warsaw Uprising was ultimately defeated.)

Amid the drabness you will find a few architectural attractions. Although many of the buildings in central Warsaw were built in an austere, quasi-Gothic, Stalinist style, a large number of prewar buildings were carefully restored or, in many cases, completely reconstructed following clues in old prints and paintings. A case in point is the beautiful Rynek Starego Miasta (Old Town Square). The Zamek Królewski (Royal Castle), which houses a museum, is the greatest of the rebuilt monuments.

Apart from the embankment carved out by the Wisła (Vistula) River, which runs through the city south to north, Warsaw is entirely flat. Most sights, attractions, and hotels lie to the west of the river. Major thoroughfares include aleje Jerozolimskie, which runs east-west, and ulica Nowy Świat, which runs south-north through a main shopping district, passes the university, and ends at the entrance to the Stare Miasto (Old Town). Be careful about Nowy Świat: its name changes six times between its starting point in Wilanów (where it's called aleja Wilanowska) and its terminus (where it's named Krakowskie Przedmieście). To orient yourself, start at Central Station, the Marriott Hotel (a glass skyscraper), or the Palace of Culture, all of which sit within a block of one another on aleje Jerozolimskie. Walk east toward the river on aleje Jerozolimskie two blocks to Nowy Świat. Heading north, this street is a main shopping district, closed to all traffic except buses, taxis, and government vehicles. In about 20 minutes the street (now called Krakowskie Przedmieście) will terminate at plac Zamkowy (Castle Square), the plaza that marks the entrance to the Old Town. North of this point is Nowe Miasto (New Town), primarily a residential area, and to the west lie Muranów and Mirów, former Jewish districts. Praga, a poorer quarter of workers and artisans that emerged from the war fairly intact, and the enormous Zoological Park are situated east of the Vistula River.

Numbers in the text correspond to numbers in the margin and on the Warsaw map.

Stare Miasto (Old Town) and Nowe Miasto (New Town)

The rebuilding of the historic Old Town, situated on an escarpment on the left bank of the Vistula, is a real phoenix-risen-from-the-ashes story. Postwar architects, determined to get it absolutely as it was before, turned to old prints, photographs in family albums, and paintings, in particular the detailed 18th-century views of Bernardo Bellotto (the nephew of Canaletto). Curiously, some of Bellotto's views were painted not from real life but from sketches of projects that were never realized. Whatever your feelings about reproduction architecture—and there's a lot of it in Warsaw—it seems to have worked. The Old Town is closed to traffic, and in its narrow streets you can leave the 21st century behind and relax for a while. Everything here is within easy walking distance. Just a short stroll beyond the Barbakan gate is the New Town, which also has sights well worth seeing.

A GOOD WALK

Begin at **plac Zamkowy** ①, first visiting the **Zamek Królewski** ②. Next make your way along narrow ulica Kanonia, and you'll find the great cracked Zygmunt bell in the middle of a quiet, cobbled square—exactly where it fell from the cathedral tower during the bombardment of 1939. Continue along ulica Jezuicka, turning through one of the archways to admire the view over the Vistula from the terrace that runs along the back of the houses. The **Rynek Starego Miasta** ③ is a place to relax and to take in buildings like the Klucznikowska Mansion at No. 21. (The Gothic brick portal and cellars of this structure, which now houses an elegant restaurant, are the originals from the 15th century.) Be sure to visit the **Muzeum Historyczna Warszawy** ④—don't miss its 20-minute film in English on the history of the city—and the **Muzeum Literatury im. Adama Mickiewicza** ⑤. Before leaving the square, take a look at the stone **Warszawska Syrenka** ⑥ in the fountain at its center, then head north along Krzywe Koło and the ramparts of the Old Town's walls to reach the **Barbakan** ⑦, marking the boundary between the Old and New Towns.

On ulica Freta you'll come upon the **Kościół Dominikanów** ⑧ and the house where Marie Curie was born, now the **Muzeum Marii Skłodowskiej-Curie** ⑨. Ulica Freta takes you to the **Rynek Nowego Miasta** ⑩, near which there are fine churches built from the 15th to 17th centuries, including **Kościół Najświętszej Marii Panny** ⑪ and the **Kościół Sakramentek** ⑫. Returning from the New Town, take ulica Świętojerska to plac Krasińskich, where you'll find the Baroque **Pałac Krasińskich** ⑬ and the **Pomnik Bohaterów Warszawy 1939–1945** ⑭, then go back along ulica Długa to the Barbakan. Ulica Nowomiejska takes you back to the Rynek Starego Miasta, and then you can take ulica Świętojańska, with the **Kościół Jezuitów** ⑮ and the **Archikatedralna Bazylika świętego Jana** ⑯ on your left, to return to plac Zamkowy.

TIMING

The Old Town is not large in area. If you are content to admire the exteriors of buildings, you can easily see it in half a day. But to take it in fully you will need a whole day. At the Zamek Królewski, give yourself about three hours if you want to explore all of its exhibits. The Rynek Starego Miasta, with its cafés and restaurants, is a good place to relax in the evening.

SIGHTS TO SEE

16 **Archikatedralna Bazylika świętego Jana** (Cathedral of St. John). Ulica Świętojańska, leading from the Rynek Starego Miasta to the Zamek

Warsaw

KEY

Tourist Information
Rail Lines
0 750 yards
0 750 meters

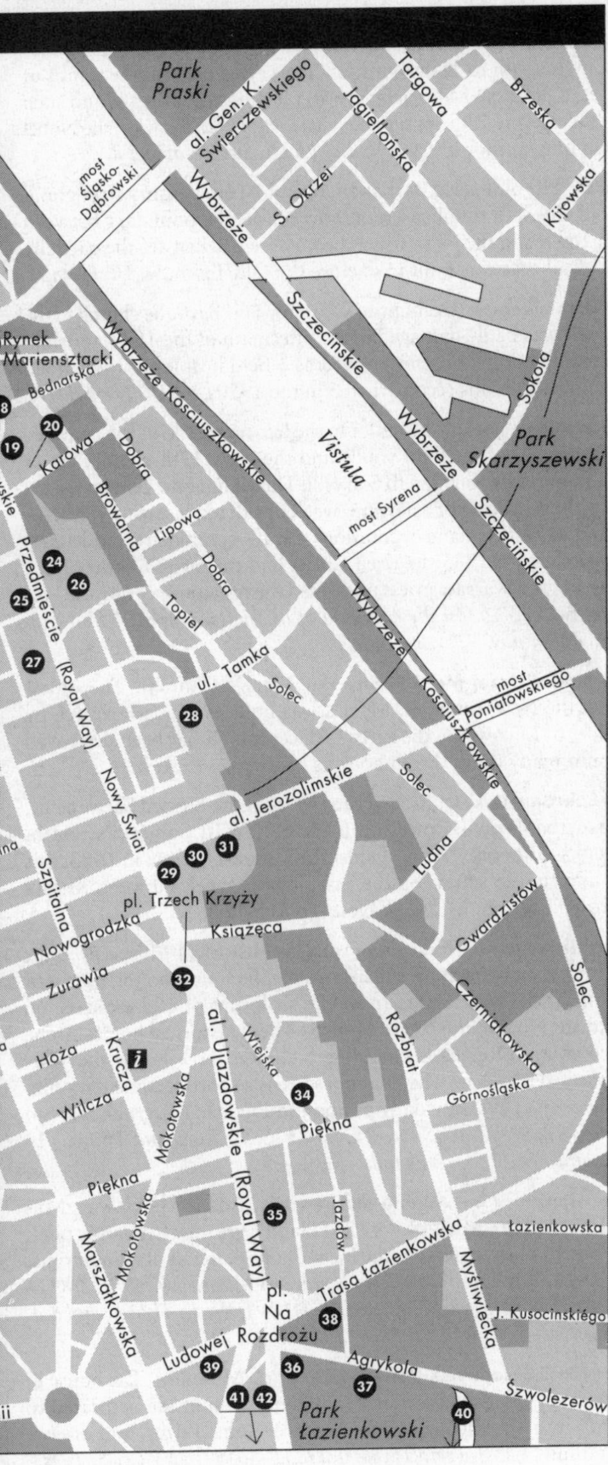
Park
Praski
al. Gen. K.
Świerczewskiego
Targowa
Jagiellońska
Brzeska
most
Śląsko-
Dąbrowski
Wybrzeże
S. Okrzei
Kijowska
Szczecińskie
Sokoła
Rynek
Mariensztacki
Wybrzeże Kościuszkowskie
Bednarska
Vistula
Wybrzeże
Park
Skarzyszewski
Karowa
Dobra
Browarna
most Syrena
Szczecińskie
Przedmieście
Lipowa
Dobra
Topiel
Wybrzeże
(Royal Way)
ul. Tamka
Solec
most
Poniatowskiego
Kościuszkowskie
Nowy Świat
al. Jerozolimskie
Solec
Szpitalna
Ludna
pl. Trzech Krzyży
Nowogrodzka
Książęca
Gwardzistów
Żurawia
Solec
al. Ujazdowskie
Wiejska
Rozbrat
Czerniakowska
Hoża
Krucza
Wilcza
Mokotowska
Górnośląska
Piękna
Piękna
Mokotowska
(Royal Way)
Jazdów
Łazienkowska
Trasa Łazienkowska
Myśliwiecka
Marszałkowska
pl.
Na
Rozdrożu
J. Kusocinskiégo
Ludowej
Agrykola
Szwoleżerów
Park
Łazienkowski
18
19
20
24
25
26
27
28
29
30
31
32
34
35
36
37
38
39
40
41
42

Królewski, takes its name from this cathedral, which was built at the turn of the 14th century; coronations of the Polish kings took place here from the 16th to 18th centuries. The crypts contain the tombs of the last two princes of Mazovia, the archbishops of Warsaw, and such famous Poles as the 19th-century novelist Henryk Sienkiewicz, the Nobel Prize–winning author of *Quo Vadis?* ✉ *Ul. Świętojańska 8.*

7 **Barbakan.** The pinnacled Barbakan, the mid-16th-century stronghold in the old city wall on ulica Freta, now marks the boundary between the Old Town and the New Town. From here you can see the partially restored wall that was built to enclose the Old Town. ✉ *Ul. Freta.*

8 **Kościół Dominikanów** (Dominican Church). This Baroque church in the New Town was badly damaged in the aftermath of the 1943 uprising, when the adjoining monastery served as a field hospital for wounded insurrectionists. It was reconstructed in the 1950s. ✉ *Ul. Freta 8–10.*

15 **Kościół Jezuitów** (Jesuit Church). On the left-hand side of the entrance to the Cathedral of St. John you'll find the early 17th-century Jesuit Church, founded by King Jan III Sobieski. Throughout the postwar years, a visit to this church at Eastertime was considered a must by Warsovians, and its Gethsemane decorations always contained a hidden political message. (In 1985 the risen Christ had the face of Father Jerzy Popiełuszko, the Warsaw priest murdered the previous year by the Polish secret police.) ✉ *On the east side of ul. Świętojańska, 1 block up from pl. Zamkowy.*

11 **Kościół Najświętszej Marii Panny** (St. Mary's Church). The oldest church in the New Town, St. Mary's was built as a parish church by the princes of Mazovia in the early 15th century. It has been destroyed and rebuilt many times throughout its history. ✉ *Przyrynek 2.*

12 **Kościół Sakramentek** (Church of the Sisters of the Blessed Sacrament). Built as a thanksgiving offering by King Jan III Sobieski's queen, Marysieńka, after his victory against the Turks at Vienna in 1683, this cool, white church stands on the east side of Rynek Nowego Miasta (New Town Square). ✉ *Rynek Nowego Miasta 2.*

4 **Muzeum Historyczna Warszawy** (Warsaw Historical Museum). Four fine examples of Renaissance mansions can be found on the northern side of the Old Town Square (note the sculpture of a black slave on the facade of No. 34, the **Negro House**). These historical homes, some of which contain Renaissance ceiling paintings, now house the Warsaw Historical Museum. The museum screens a short documentary film on the history of Warsaw daily at noon in English. ✉ *Rynek Starego Miasta 28–42,* ☎ *022/635–16–25.* 🎫 *Zł 15.* ⏲ *Tues. and Thurs. 11–6, Wed. and Fri. 11–3, weekends 10:30–4:30.*

5 **Muzeum Literatury im. Adama Mickiewicza** (Adam Mickiewicz Museum of Literature). Mickiewicz was Poland's greatest Romantic poet. He and other Polish writers are the focus of this museum of manuscripts, mementos, and portraits. ✉ *Rynek Starego Miasta 20,* ☎ *022/831–40–61.* 🎫 *Zł 4.* ⏲ *Mon., Tues., and Fri. 10–3, Wed., Thurs., and Sat. 11–6, Sun. 11–5. Closed 1st Sun. of month.*

9 **Muzeum Marii Skłodowsk-Curie** (Marie Curie Museum). The house in which Marie Curie was born has a small museum inside dedicated to the great physicist, chemist, winner of two Nobel Prizes, and discoverer of radium. ✉ *Ul. Freta 16,* ☎ *022/831–80–92.* 🎫 *Zł 2.* ⏲ *Tues.–Sat. 10–4, Sun. 10–2.*

13 **Pałac Krasińskich** (Krasiński Palace). This late-17th-century palace currently houses the historic prints collection of Poland's National Li-

brary. It can be visited only by appointment. ✉ *Pl. Krasińskich 5,* ☎ *022/831–32–41 for tours.*

OFF THE BEATEN PATH

KOŚCIÓŁ ŚWIĘTEGO STANISŁAWA KOSTKI – In October 1984 Polish secret police officers murdered the popular parish priest Jerzy Popiełuszko because of his sermons, which the Communist regime considered gravely threatening. Thereafter the martyred Popiełuszko's church became the site of huge and very moving Solidarity meetings. You can visit his grave on the grounds of this church in the district of Żoliborz, north of the New Town. Take a taxi or Bus 116 or 122 from ulica Bonifraterska to plac Wilsona, then walk two blocks west along ulica Zygmunta Krasinskiego. ✉ *Ul. Stanisława Hozjusza 2.*

❶ **Plac Zamkowy** (Castle Square). Many visitors enter the Old Town through this plaza area on the southern border of the district. You can't miss the **Zygmunt Column,** which honors King Zygmunt III Waza, king of Poland and Sweden, who in the early 17th century moved the capital to Warsaw from Kraków.

⓮ **Pomnik Bohaterów Warszawy 1939–1945** (Monument to the Heroes of Warsaw). Unveiled in 1989, this monument constitutes a poignant reminder of what World War II meant for the citizens of Warsaw. Massive bronze figures raise defiant fists above the sewer openings used by Polish resistance fighters in Warsaw's Old Town to escape the Nazis in 1944. ✉ *Pl. Krasińskich and ul. Długa.*

❿ **Rynek Nowego Miasta** (New Town Square). Warsaw's New Town was actually founded at the turn of the 15th century. This part of the city, however, was rebuilt after the war in 18th- and 19th-century styles and has a more elegant and spacious feel about it than the Old Town. The centerpiece of the district is the leafy New Town Square, slightly more irregular and relaxed than its Old Town counterpart. The houses on the square, and in such nearby streets as ulica Kościelna, have curiously stark and formalized wall paintings.

★ ❸ **Rynek Starego Miasta** (Old Town Square). This is the hub of life in Warsaw's Old Town. The earliest settlers arrived at this spot during the 10th and 11th centuries. Legend has it that a peasant named Wars was directed to the site by a mermaid named Sawa—hence the name of the city in Polish, Warszawa. (Sawa has been immortalized in Warsaw's official emblem.) In the 14th century Warsaw was already a walled city, and in 1413 its citizens obtained a borough charter from the princes of Mazovia. The present layout of the Old Town dates from that time, and traces of the original Gothic buildings still surround the Old Town Square. The appearance of today's square, however, largely dates from the 16th and early 17th centuries, when Warsaw's wealth and importance grew rapidly as a result of the 1569 Polish-Lithuanian union and Warsaw's new status as capital city.

The Old Town Square is usually very active, even though no traffic is allowed and there is no longer a formal market. Artists and craftspeople of all kinds still sell their wares here in the summer, but don't expect many bargains—tourists are their prime targets. Musical performances are often held here on weekends on a stage erected at the north end. Horse-drawn cabs await visitors. To explore some of the square's beautiful and historic houses, visit the Adam Mickiewicz Museum of Literature (☞ *above*) on the east side of the square and the Warsaw Historical Museum (☞ *above*) on the north side. After being almost completely annihilated during World War II, these mansions were meticulously reconstructed using old prints, plans, and paintings. For some of the best Gothic details, look for No. 31, traditionally known as the House of the Mazovian Dukes. At night the square is lit up romantically. If you're after good food and atmosphere, this is one of Warsaw's best bets.

Krzywe Koło (Crooked Wheel Street) runs from the Old Town Square to the reconstructed ramparts of the city wall. From this corner you can see out over the Vistula and also over the New Town stretching to the north beyond the city walls. As you look out over the town walls and down the Vistula embankment, you will see the **Stara Prochownia** (Old Powder Tower), now a popular venue for poetry readings, music, and drama.

NEED A BREAK? **Hortex** (✉ Rynek Starego Miasta 3–9) has a large open-air café in summer. At the same address on the ground floor is a quick-service lunch bar.

❻ **Warszawska Syrenka** (Warsaw Mermaid). The mermaid is the symbol on the crest of the city of Warsaw. This particular stone statue had been traveling around the city for more than 70 years before in 2000 finding itself back where it was originally placed in 1855, in the center of a fountain in the Old Town Square.

★ ❷ **Zamek Królewski** (Royal Castle). Warsaw's Royal Castle stands on the east side of Castle Square (☞ *above*). The princes of Mazovia first built a residence on this spot overlooking the Vistula in the 14th century. Its present Renaissance form dates from the reign of King Zygmunt III Waza, who needed a magnificent palace for his new capital. Reconstructed in the 1970s, it now gleams as it did in its earliest years, with gilt, marble, and wall paintings. It also houses impressive collections of art—including the famous views of Warsaw by Canaletto's nephew Bernardo Bellotto (also known as Canaletto), which were used to rebuild the city after the war. Tours in English are available. ✉ *Pl. Zamkowy 4,* ☎ *022/657–21–70.* 🎫 *Zł 15.* ⏲ *Daily 10–4.*

NEED A BREAK? **Kawiarnia Literacka** (✉ Krakowskie Przedmieście 87/89, ☎ 022/826–57–84), on the ground floor of the PEN club premises, is an airy café where you can listen to classic jazz on weekend evenings.

The Royal Route

All towns with kings had their "royal routes," and the one in Warsaw stretches south from Castle Square for 4 km (2½ mi), running through busy Krakowskie Przedmieście, along Nowy Świat, and on to the Park Łazienkowski (Łazienki Park). The route is lined with some of Warsaw's finest churches and palaces, but there are also landmarks of some of the city's most famous folk, including Frédéric Chopin. As a child Chopin played in the Kasimir Palace gardens, gave his first concert in the Radziwiłł Palace (now the Pałac Namiestnikowski [Presidential Palace]), then moved with his family to the building that now houses the city's Academy of Fine Arts. Today, the Chopin Society is headquartered in the Pałac Ostrogskich (Ostrogski Palace).

A GOOD WALK

The first stage of the route, from Castle Square to aleje Jerozolimskie, is about 3 km (2 mi). Krakowskie Przedmieście is a wide thoroughfare lined with fine churches and elegant mansions and palaces. First on the route is **Kościół świętej Anny** ⑰, on the south side of Castle Square, followed a block later by the **Pałac Kazanowskich** ⑱. From here you can make a detour down the hill via ulica Bednarska to the leafy 18th-century Rynek Mariensztacki (Mariensztat Square), a 10-minute walk. Back on Krakowskie Przedmieście, heading south, you come to the **Kościół Karmelitów** ⑲ and the **Pałac Namiestnikowski** ⑳.

Another detour—this one to the west along Królewska—brings you in two minutes to the wide-open spaces of the plac Piłsudskiego, site of the **Grób Nieznanego Żołnierza** ㉑ and the Teatr Wielki (Opera House). From the southwest corner of the square take ulica Mazowiecka south, passing the **Galeria Zachęta** ㉒ on your right, then turn right onto ulica Kredytowa. On your right is the 18th-century neoclassical Kościół Ewangelicko-Augsburski (J. B. Augsburg Protestant Community Church), which like Kościół świętego Aleksandra in plac Trzech Krzyży was modeled on Rome's pantheon. Across the street is the **Muzeum Etnograficzne** ㉓.

Retrace your steps to Krakowskie Przedmieście. Continuing south you pass the **Kościół Wizytek** ㉔, the **Pałac Czapskich** ㉕, and **Warsaw University** ㉖. Beyond the **Kościół świętego Krzyża** ㉗ the road narrows and becomes ulica Nowy Świat, a pedestrian precinct with elegant shops and cafés in 18th-century houses. You can detour down the hill to the east to the **Pałac Ostrogskich** ㉘, a 10-minute walk.

At the south end of ulica Nowy Świat you'll come to the massive **former headquarters of the Polish Communist Party** ㉙. East of this building you'll find the **Muzeum Narodowe** ㉚, in which you can easily spend half a day, and the **Muzeum Wojska Polskiego** ㉛. At the south end of plac Trzech Krzyży lies **Kościół świętego Aleksandra** ㉜, modeled on the Roman pantheon. If you have time, from the tram stop at the corner of Nowy Świat make the two-stop trip west along aleje Jerozolimskie to the **Pałac Kultury i Nauki** ㉝.

TIMING

Walking at a brisk pace, you can cover this route in an hour, but to soak in the sights along the way, allow a whole morning or afternoon.

SIGHTS TO SEE

㉙ **Former headquarters of the Polish Communist Party.** Anti-Communists love the irony of this once-despised symbol of oppression being the seat of the Warsaw Stock Exchange. ✉ *Al. Jerozolimskie and Nowy Świat.*

㉒ **Galeria Zachęta** (Zachęta Gallery). Built at the end of the 19th century by the Society for the Encouragement of the Fine Arts, this gallery has no permanent collection but organizes thought-provoking special exhibitions (primarily modern art) in high-ceilinged, well-lit halls. It was in this building in 1922 that the first president of the post–World War I Polish Republic, Gabriel Narutowicz, was assassinated by a right-wing fanatic. Admission costs to the exhibits vary. ✉ *Pl. Małachowskiego 3,* ☎ *022/827–69–09.* ⏲ *Tues.–Sun. 10–6.*

㉑ **Grób Nieznanego Żołnierza** (Tomb of the Unknown Soldier). Built as a memorial after World War I, the Tomb of the Unknown Soldier contains the body of a Polish soldier brought from the eastern battlefields of the Polish-Soviet war of 1919–1920—a war not much mentioned in the 45 years of Communist rule after World War II. Ceremonial changes of the guard take place at noon on Sunday; visitors may be surprised to see the Polish Army still using the goose step on such occasions. The memorial is a surviving fragment of the early 18th-century Saxon Palace, which used to stand here on the west side of plac Piłsudskiego. Behind the tomb are the delightful Ogród Saski (Saxon Gardens), which were once the palace's park and were designed by French and Saxon landscape gardeners. ✉ *Pl. Piłsudskiego.*

⑲ **Kościół Karmelitów** (Church of the Discalced Carmelites). This late-17th-century Baroque church sits at the back of a square off the main line of the street. ✉ *Krakowskie Przedmieście 52.*

㉜ **Kościół świętego Aleksandra** (St. Alexander's Church). Built in the early 19th century as a replica of the Roman pantheon, St. Alexander's stands on an island in the middle of **plac Trzech Krzyży,** a name that is notoriously difficult for foreigners to pronounce and means "Three Crosses Square." One of the crosses is on the church itself.

27 **Kościół świętego Krzyża** (Holy Cross Church). The heart of Poland's most famous composer, Frédéric Chopin, is immured in a pillar inside this Baroque church. Atop the church steps is a massive sculpted crucifix. Across from the church is the **statue of Nicolaus Copernicus,** standing in front of the neoclassical Staszic Palace, the headquarters of the Polish Academy of Sciences. Like many other notable Warsaw monuments, this statue is the work of the 19th-century Danish sculptor Bertel Thorvaldsen. ✉ *Krakowskie Przedmieście 3.*

17 **Kościół świętej Anny** (St. Anne's Church). Built in 1454 by Anne, princess of Mazovia, St. Anne's Church stands on the south corner of Castle Square. It was rebuilt in high-Baroque style after being destroyed during the Swedish invasions of the 17th century, and thanks to 1990s redecoration and regilding it glows once again. A plaque on the wall outside marks the spot where Pope John Paul II celebrated mass in 1980, during his first visit to Poland after his election to the papacy. ✉ *Krakowskie Przedmieście 68.*

24 **Kościół Wizytek** (Church of the Visitation Sisters). In front of this late-Baroque church stands a statue of Cardinal Stefan Wyszyński, primate of Poland from 1948 to 1981. Wyszyński was imprisoned during the 1950s but lived to see a Polish pope and the birth of Solidarity. The fresh flowers always lying at the foot of the statue are evidence of the warmth with which he is remembered. ✉ *Krakowskie Przedmieście 30.*

23 **Muzeum Etnograficzne** (Ethnographic Museum). On display here you'll find an interesting collection of Polish folk art, crafts, and costumes from all parts of the country. ✉ *Ul. Kredytowa 1,* ☎ *022/827–76–41.* *Zł 4, Wed. free.* *Tues., Thurs., and Fri. 9–4, Wed. 11–6, weekends 10–5.*

★ 30 **Muzeum Narodowe** (National Museum of Warsaw). In a functional 1930s building, the National Museum has an impressive collection of contemporary Polish and European paintings, Gothic icons, and works from antiquity. ✉ *Al. Jerozolimskie 3,* ☎ *022/629–30–39.* *Zł 9, Wed. free.* *Tues., Wed., and Fri 10–4, Thurs. noon–5, weekends 10–5. Closed day after holidays.*

31 **Muzeum Wojska Polskiego** (Polish Army Museum). If you're interested in military matters, you might want to visit this museum's exhibits of weaponry, armor, and uniforms, which trace Polish military history for the past 10 centuries. Heavy armaments are displayed outside. ✉ *Al. Jerozolimskie 3,* ☎ *022/629–52–71.* *Zł 2, Wed. free.* *May–Sept., Wed.–Sun. 11–5; Oct.–May, Wed.–Sun. 10–4.*

NEED A BREAK? **Blikle** (✉ Nowy Świat 35), Warsaw's oldest cake shop, has a black-and-white-tile café that serves savory snacks as well as Blikle's famous doughnuts.

25 **Pałac Czapskich** (Czapski Palace). Now the home of the Academy of Fine Arts, the Czapski Palace dates from the late 17th century but was rebuilt in 1740 in the rococo style. Zygmunt Krasiński, the Polish romantic poet, was born here in 1812, and Chopin once lived in the palace mews. ✉ *Krakowskie Przedmieście 5.*

18 **Pałac Kazanowskich** (Kazanowski Palace). This 17th-century palace was given a neoclassical front elevation in the 19th century. The courtyard at the rear still contains massive late-Renaissance buttresses and

is worth a visit because of its plaque commemorating Zagloba's fight with the monkeys, from Sienkiewicz's historical novel *The Deluge*. In a small garden in front of the palace stands a **monument to Adam Mickiewicz**, the great Polish romantic poet. It was here that Warsaw University students gathered in March 1968, after a performance of Mickiewicz's hitherto banned play *Forefathers' Eve*, which set in motion the events that led to the fall of Poland's Communist leader Władysław Gomułka, a wave of student protests, and a regime-sponsored anti-Semitic campaign. ✉ *Krakowskie Przedmieście 62.*

33 **Pałac Kultury i Nauki** (Palace of Culture and Science). This massive Stalinist-Gothic structure looks like a wedding cake and is the main landmark in the city. From the 30th floor you can get a panoramic view. The old joke runs that this is Warsaw's best view because it is the only place where you can't see the palace. To view all of urban Warsaw from 700 ft up, buy tickets at the booth near the east entrance. The building houses a number of facilities, including a swimming pool and the **Museum of Science and Technology.** Also in the palace is the **Teatr Lalek,** a good puppet theater (the entrance is on the north side). ✉ *Pl. Defilad 1,* ☎ *022/620–02–11; 022/620–49–50 (theater).* *Zł 7.5.* *Daily 9–6.*

20 **Pałac Namiestnikowski** (Presidential Palace). This palace was built in the 17th century by the Radziwiłł family (into which Jackie Kennedy's sister Lee later married). In the 19th century it functioned as the administrative office of the czarist occupiers—hence its present name. In 1955 the Warsaw Pact was signed here; later the palace served as the headquarters for the Presidium of the Council of Ministers, and since 1995 it has been the official residence of Poland's president. In the forecourt is an **equestrian statue of Prince Józef Poniatowski,** a nephew of the last king of Poland and one of Napoléon's marshals. He was wounded and drowned in the Elster River during the Battle of Leipzig in 1813, following the disastrous retreat of Napoléon's Grande Armée from Russia. ✉ *Krakowskie Przedmieście 46–48.*

28 **Pałac Ostrogskich** (Ostrogski Palace). The headquarters of the **Towarzystwo im. Fryderyka Chopina** (Chopin Society) is in this 17th-century palace, which towers above ulica Tamka. The best approach is via the steps from ulica Tamka. In the 19th century the Warsaw Conservatory was housed here (Ignacy Paderewski was one of its students). Now a venue for Chopin concerts, it is also home to the **Muzeum Fryderyka Chopina** (Frédéric Chopin Museum), a small collection of mementos, including the last piano played by the composer. The works of Chopin (1810–1849) took their roots from folk rhythms and melodies of exclusively Polish invention. Thanks to Chopin, Poland could fairly claim to have been the fountainhead of popular music in Europe, and the composer's polonaises and mazurkas whirled their way around the continent in the mid-19th century. ✉ *Ul. Okólnik 1,* ☎ *022/827–54–71.* *Free.* *Mon.–Sat. 10–2, Thurs. noon–6.*

NEED A BREAK? **Nowy Świat** (✉ Nowy Świat 63), on the corner of Nowy Świat and ulica Świętokrzyska, is a spacious, traditional café, with plenty of foreign-language newspapers for those who want to linger over coffee.

26 **Warsaw University.** The high wrought-iron gates of Warsaw University lead into a leafy campus. The **Pałac Kazimierzowski** (Kazimierzowski Palace) currently houses the university administration; in the 18th century it was the Military Cadet School where Tadeusz Kościuszko studied. ✉ *Krakowskie Przedmieście 26–28.*

The Diplomatic Quarter and Park Łazienkowski (Łazienki Park)

In the 19th century smart carriages and riders eager to be seen thronged aleje Ujazdowskie. Today the avenue is a favorite with Sunday strollers. It leads to the beautiful Łazienki Park and the white Pałac Łazienkowski (Łazienki Palace), the private residence of the last king of Poland.

A GOOD WALK

The diplomatic quarter and Łazienki Park lie along the Royal Route leading from the Old Town to Wilanów. From plac Trzech Krzyży it is about 3 km (2 mi) to the southern edge of the park. Start your walk at the north end of aleje Ujazdowskie, where during the 19th century the rich built residences, many of which now house foreign embassies. A five-minute walk down ulica Wiejska, on your left, brings you to the **Sejm** ㉞. As you continue south you may choose to stroll under the trees of the **Park Ujazdowski** ㉟, parallel to aleje Ujazdowskie below ulica Piękna and farther from the traffic. At plac Na Rozdrożu you leave the diplomatic quarter and enter Warsaw's Whitehall. On your left are the **Botanical Gardens** ㊱ and **Park Łazienkowski** ㊲. If you are interested in modern art, **Zamek Ujazdowski** ㊳, home of the Center for Contemporary Art, is 600 ft east of the intersection, down a path through the park parallel to the Trasa Łazienkowska. The wartime **Gestapo headquarters** ㊴ is 600 ft southwest of plac Na Rozdrożu on aleje Szucha. To reach the **Pałac Łazienkowski** ㊵, go south on aleje Ujazdowskie from plac Na Rozdrożu about 1 km (½ mi). Enter by the gates opposite ulica Bagatela, beside the **Pałac Belweder** ㊶.

At the top of the hill of the Vistula embankment, across from Pałac Belweder at ulica Bagatela, you can board Bus 116, 180, or E-2 for **Pałac Wilanów** ㊷. (The rest of the Royal Route, which until the 1980s ran through open countryside, is now lined with housing developments.)

TIMING

Take a morning or afternoon to explore this route. If you wish to linger at some of the sights, make it a whole day: Łazienki Park and the Łazienki Palace deserve three or four hours at the least. This tree-lined walk is good for a hot summer day.

SIGHTS TO SEE

㊱ **Botanical Gardens.** These gardens, covering an area of roughly three acres, were laid out in 1818. At the entrance stands the neoclassical observatory, now part of Warsaw University. ✉ *Al. Ujazdowskie 4.*

㊴ **Gestapo headquarters.** The building that currently houses the Ministry of Education was the Gestapo headquarters during World War II. A small museum details the horrors that took place behind its peaceful facade. ✉ *Al. Szucha 25,* ☎ *022/629–49–19.* 🎫 *Free.* ⏲ *Wed. 9–5, Thurs. and Sat. 9–4, Fri. 10–5, Sun. 10–4.*

㊶ **Pałac Belweder** (Belvedere Palace). Built in the early 18th century, the palace was reconstructed in 1818 in neoclassical style by the Russian governor of Poland, the grand duke Constantine. Until 1994 it was the official residence of Poland's president. Belvedere Palace stands just south of the main gates to Łazienki Park. ✉ *Ul. Belwederska 2.*

★ ㊵ **Pałac Łazienkowski** (Łazienki Palace). This magnificent palace is the focal point of the Park Łazienkowski. This neoclassical summer residence was so faithfully reconstructed after the war that there is still no electricity—be sure to visit when it's sunny, or you won't see anything of the interior. The palace has some splendid 18th-century furniture as well as part of the art collection of King Słanisław August Poniatowski. ✉ *Ul. Agrykola 1,* ☎ *022/621–62–41.* 🎫 *Zł 10.* ⏲ *Tues.–Sun. 10–3:15.*

★ 42 **Pałac Wilanów** (Wilanów Palace). A Baroque gateway and false moat lead to the wide courtyard that stretches along the front of Wilanów Palace, built between 1681 and 1696 by King Jan III Sobieski. After his death, the palace passed through various hands before it was bought at the end of the 18th century by Stanisław Kostka Potocki, who amassed a major art collection, laid out the gardens, and opened the first public museum here in 1805. Potocki's neo-Gothic tomb can be seen to the left of the driveway as you approach the palace. The palace interiors still hold much of the original furniture; there's also a striking display of 16th- to 18th-century Polish portraits on the first floor. English-speaking guides are available.

Outside, to the left of the main entrance, is a romantic park with pagodas, summerhouses, and bridges overlooking a lake. Behind the palace is a formal Italian garden from which you can admire the magnificent gilt decoration on the palace walls. There's also a **gallery** of contemporary Polish art on the grounds. Stables to the right of the entrance now house a poster gallery, the **Muzeum Plakatu**. The latter is well worth visiting, for this is a branch of art in which Poles have historically excelled. ✉ *Ul. Wiertnicza 1,* ☎ *022/842–81–01.* 🎫 *Palace zł 15, park zł 3, Thurs. free.* ⏲ *Tues.–Sun. 9:30–2:30.*

37 **Park Łazienkowski** (Łazienki Park). The 180 acres of this park, commissioned during the late 18th century by King Słanisław August Poniatowski, run along the Vistula escarpment, parallel to the Royal Route. In the old coach houses on the east side of the park you'll find the **Muzeum Łowiectwa i Jezdziectwa** (Museum of Hunting), which contains a collection of stuffed birds and animals native to Poland. If you prefer live fauna, look for the peacocks that wander through the park and the delicate red squirrels that in Poland answer to the name Basia, a diminutive of Barbara. One of the most beloved sights in the park is the **Pomnik Frydericka Chopina** (Chopin Memorial), a sculpture under a streaming willow tree that shows the composer in a typical romantic pose. In summer, outdoor concerts of Chopin's piano music are held here every Sunday afternoon. ☎ *022/621–62–41 (museum).* 🎫 *Museum zł 5.* ⏲ *Museum Tues.–Sun. 10–3.*

35 **Park Ujazdowski** (Ujazdów Park). At the entrance to the formal gardens on the corner of aleje Ujazdowskie and ulica Piękna, there is a **19th-century weighing booth**, just inside the gate, still in operation. There is also a well-equipped **playground** for small children, with sand, swings, and slides.

34 **Sejm.** The Polish Houses of the Sejm (parliament) are housed in a round, white debating chamber that was built during the 1920s, after the rebirth of an independent Polish state. ✉ *Ul. Wiejska 6.*

NEED A BREAK? **Modulor Cafe** (✉ Pl. Trzech Krzyży 8), up the street from the Sheraton, has great coffee and a variety of fresh-squeezed juices.

38 **Zamek Ujazdowski** (Ujazdowski Castle). If you are interested in modern art, you will find it in the somewhat unlikely setting of this 18th-century castle, reconstructed in the 1980s. Now the home of the Center for Contemporary Art, the castle hosts a variety of exhibitions by Polish, European, and North American artists. ✉ *Al. Ujazdowskie 6,* ☎ *022/628–12–71.* 🎫 *Zł 4, Thurs. free.* ⏲ *Tues.–Thurs. and weekends 11–5, Fri. 11–9.*

Jewish Warsaw

The quiet streets of Mirów and Muranów, which now contain mostly apartment buildings, once housed the largest Jewish population in Europe: about 380,000 people in 1939. The Nazis sealed off this area from the rest of the city on November 15, 1940, and the congested area became rapidly less populated as people died from starvation and disease. Between July and September 1942, the Nazis deported about 300,000 ghetto residents to the death camp at Treblinka. On April 19, 1943, the remaining inhabitants instigated the Warsaw Ghetto Uprising. Children threw homemade bombs at tanks, and men and women fought soldiers hand to hand. In the end, almost all of those remaining died in the uprising or fled through the sewers to the "Aryan side."

A GOOD WALK

The wartime ghetto area is northwest of Warsaw's Old Town. Begin on ulica Sienna to see the **fragment of ghetto wall** ㊸. Walk north along aleje Jana Pawła II until you reach ulica Twarda, then turn right. Go past a synagogue and across plac Grzybowski to **ulica Próżna** ㊹. Head east through a small market area to ulica Marszałkowska and take a left to reach plac Bankowy and the **Jewish Historical Institute and Museum** ㊺. From here, walk west along aleje Solidarności toward aleje Jana Pawła II, passing the **Femina cinema** ㊻ on your left. Turn north on aleje Jana Pawła II and walk to ulica Mordechaja Anielewicza; turn right here to reach the monument **Pomnik Bohaterów Getta** ㊼. From here take ulica Karmelicka north to ulica Stawki, where you'll find the **Umschlagplatz** ㊽. (Trams run along aleje Jana Pawła II to help you on your route.) From Umschlagplatz follow ulica Dzika north around the bend. After the intersection with aleje Jana Pawła II, continue west on ulica Dzika to ulica Okopowa. From this corner you can take any tram south along ulica Okopowa to reach the **Jewish Cemetery** ㊾.

TIMING

It is possible to see all of the sights in a few hours, although this would involve some energetic walking. If you allow a whole day, you'll have time for reflection and to explore the cemetery fully.

SIGHTS TO SEE

46 **Femina cinema.** Before the war this area was the heart of Warsaw's Jewish quarter, which was walled off by the Nazis in November 1940 to isolate the Jewish community from "Aryan" Warsaw. The cinema is one of the few buildings in this district that survived the war. It was here that the ghetto orchestra organized concerts in 1941 and 1942. Many outstanding musicians found themselves behind the ghetto walls and continued to make music despite the dangers. ✉ *Al. Solidarności 115.*

43 **Fragment of ghetto wall.** In the courtyard of this building, through the archway on the left, stands a 10-ft-tall fragment of the infamous ghetto wall that existed for one year from November 1940. ✉ *Ul. Sienna 55.*

49 **Jewish Cemetery.** Behind a high brick wall on ulica Okopowa you will find Warsaw's Jewish Cemetery, an island of continuity amid so much destruction of the city's Jewish heritage. The cemetery, which is still in use, survived the war, and although it was neglected and became badly overgrown during the postwar period, it is gradually being restored. Here you will find fine 19th-century headstones and much that testifies to the Jewish community's role in Polish history and culture. Ludwik Zamenhof, the creator of the artificial language Esperanto, is buried here, as are Henryk Wohl, minister of the treasury in the national government during the 1864 uprising against Russian rule; Szymon Askenazy, the historian and diplomat; Hipolit Wawelberg, the cofounder of Warsaw Polytechnic; and poet Bolesław Leśmian. ✉ *Ul. Okopowa 49–51 (take Bus 107, 111, or 516 from pl. Bankowy).*

45 **Jewish Historical Institute and Museum.** You'll find the institute behind a glittering new office block on the southeast corner of plac Bankowy—

the site of what had been the largest temple in Warsaw, the Tłomackie Synagogue. For those seeking to investigate their family history, the institute houses the **Ronald S. Lauder Foundation Genealogy Project,** which acts as a clearinghouse of information on available archival resources and on the history of towns and villages in which Polish Jews resided. English-speaking staff members are available. The institute also houses a museum that displays a permanent collection of mementos and artifacts and periodically organizes special exhibitions. ✉ *Ul. Tłomackie 3,* ☎ *022/827–92–21.* *Free.* ⏲ *Tues.–Fri. 10–6.*

47 **Pomnik Bohaterów Getta** (Monument to the Heroes of the Warsaw Ghetto). On April 19, 1943, the Jewish Fighting Organization began an uprising in a desperate attempt to resist the mass transports to Treblinka that had been taking place since the beginning of that year. Though doomed from the start, the brave ghetto fighters managed to keep up their struggle for a whole month. But by May 16, General Jürgen Stroop could report to his superior officer that "the former Jewish district in Warsaw had ceased to exist." The ghetto had become a smoldering ruin, razed by Nazi flamethrowers. A monument marks the location of the house at nearby **ulica Miła 18,** the site of the uprising's command bunker and where its leader, Mordechai Anielewicz, was killed. ✉ *Ul. Zamenhofa between ul. M. Anielewicza and ul. Lewartowskiego.*

OFF THE BEATEN PATH

POWĄZKI CEMETERY – Dating from 1790, Warsaw's oldest cemetery is worth a visit if you are in a reflective mood. Many well-known Polish names appear on the often elaborate headstones and tombs. There is also a recent memorial to the victims of the Katyn Massacre. Enter from ulica Powązkowska. ✉ *Ul. Powązkowska 43–45 (next to the Jewish cemetery,* ☞ *above).* ⏲ *Sun.–Thurs. 9–3, Fri. 9–1.*

44 **Ulica Próżna** This is the only street in Jewish Warsaw where tenement buildings have been preserved on both sides of the street. The Lauder Foundation has instigated a plan to restore the street to its original state. No. 9 belonged to Zelman Nożyk, founder of the ghetto synagogue.

48 **Umschlagplatz.** This plaza was the rail terminus from which tens of thousands of the ghetto's inhabitants were shipped in cattle cars to the extermination camp of Treblinka, about 100 km (60 mi) northeast of Warsaw. The school building to the right of the square was used to detain those who had to wait overnight for transport; the beginning of the rail tracks survives on the right. At the entrance to the square is a memorial gateway, erected in 1988 on the 45th anniversary of the uprising. ✉ *Ul. Stawki and ul. Dzika.*

OFF THE BEATEN PATH

CHOPIN AND RADZIWIŁŁ ESTATES – If you have an extra day in Warsaw, a trip to the **Puszcza Kampinoska** (Kampinoski National Park), located about an hour west of the city, is highly recommended, for two of Warsaw's loveliest abodes are situated here: the birthplace of Chopin and the Radziwiłł country estate. The best way to view these two sights quickly is to take one of the many available tours (☞ Guided Tours *in* Warsaw A to Z, *below*). Both places can also be reached by bus from Warsaw's main bus station (☞ Arriving and Departing by Bus *in* Warsaw A to Z, *below*). **Żelazowa Wola** (☎ 046/863–33–00) is a mecca for all Chopin lovers. The composer's birthplace, a small 19th-century manor house, is filled with original furnishings and is devoted to Chopin's life. Admission is zł 6, and it's open Tuesday to Sunday from 9 to 4; on summer Sundays, concerts are held on the terrace at 11 AM and 3 PM. If driving, go 30 km (18½ mi) west of Warsaw on the 2(E30), and at Sochaczew turn north on Route 580. Not too far away is **Nieborów** (☎ 046/838–56–20), the stunning country estate of the

Radziwiłł family, centered on a Baroque palace designed by Tilman van Gameren in the late 17th century. In 1945, the estate was taken over by the National Museum of Warsaw, and it still contains its historic furnishings. Admission is zł 6, and it's open Tuesday to Friday from 10 to 4. The palace contains a small hotel (book ahead; no children allowed). To get here from Żelazowa Wola, return to the 2(E30) and drive west to Łowicz, then take Route 70 southeast about 10 km.

Dining

Like everything else in Warsaw, the dining scene is changing rapidly. New restaurants serve ethnic cuisine (Korean, Japanese, Chinese, and Italian are particularly popular), while others spin such hip variations as "Peasant Chic" and "light Old Polish." Gone are the old, seedy bars, and in are clean and brightly tiled pizza parlors. Prices have risen spectacularly, and eating out in Warsaw is much more expensive than in other Polish towns. Check the price of the wine before ordering, as restaurants sometimes charge astronomical prices for an ordinary bottle. For the higher-priced dining spots, it is essential to make reservations. Almost all restaurants are closed on public holidays.

$$$$ ★ ✕ **Belvedere.** You could not find a more romantic setting for lunch or dinner than this elegant restaurant in the New Orangery at Łazienki Park. The lamp-lit park spreads out beyond the windows, and candles glitter below the high ceilings. Polish cuisine is a specialty, and many dishes are prepared with a variety of fresh mushrooms; try the mushroom soup. Also recommended is the roast boar, served with an assortment of vegetables. ✉ *Łazienki Park, enter from ul. Parkowa or ul. Gargarina,* ☎ *022/41–48–06. Jacket and tie. AE, DC, MC, V.*

$$$$ ✕ **Dom Restauracyjny Gessler.** You come here partly for the atmospheric setting: a warren of candlelit bare-brick cellars and ground-floor rooms in one of the historic houses on the Rynek Starego Miasta (Old Town Square). Start with *łosoś książąt polskich* (salmon, Polish-prince-style, cooked in cream) or *bulion z kołdunami* (broth with dumplings). Then try duck in a marjoram-based sauce, served with noodles. ✉ *Rynek Starego Miasta 19–21,* ☎ *022/831–16–61. AE, DC, MC, V.*

$$$$ ✕ **Fukier.** This long-established wine bar on the Old Town Square has become a fascinating network of elaborately decorated dining rooms. There is a talking parrot in a cage, and candles adorn all available shelf space (sometimes set dangerously close to clients' elbows). The food is "light Old Polish." Steak, served on a grill, is a specialty; follow it with one of the rich cream gâteaux. ✉ *Rynek Starego Miasta 27,* ☎ *022/831–10–13. Reservations essential. AE, DC, MC, V.*

$$$ ✕ **Bazyliszek.** A second-floor restaurant in a 17th-century merchant's house on the Old Town Square, this place has long received top marks for atmosphere. You'll dine under high ceilings of carved wood. In the Knight's Room suits of armor and crossed swords decorate the walls. The restaurant serves traditional Polish fare, with an emphasis on game dishes. Try the stewed hare in cream sauce, served with beets and noodles. There is a good café downstairs that offers cheaper food. ✉ *Rynek Starego Miasta 3/9,* ☎ *022/831–18–41. AE, DC, MC, V.*

$$$ ✕ **Café Ejlat.** This Warsaw institution, owned by the Polish-Israeli Friendship Society, has a menu rich in Jewish specialties (including a halvah dessert) and contemporary Polish dishes. ✉ *Al. Ujazdowskie 47,* ☎ *022/628–54–72. AE, DC, MC, V.*

$$$ ✕ **Flik.** Set on a corner overlooking the Morskie Oko Park, this restaurant in Mokotów has a lovely geranium-frilled terrace. The dining room has well-spaced tables, light cane furniture, and lots of greenery. Try the fresh salmon starter followed by *zrazy* (rolled beef fillet stuffed with mushrooms). There is a self-service salad bar, and downstairs is a small, casual café. ✉ *Ul. Puławska 43,* ☏ *022/49–44–34. AE, DC, MC, V.*

$$$ ★ ✕ **Restauracja Polska.** With a stylish room and some of the best food in the city, this basement restaurant is the place to be seen in Warsaw these days. The tasteful main salon has antique furnishings and large bouquets of flowers. You can't go wrong here with the food, but definitely try the homemade pierogi or the bigos. For dessert, the chocolate-nut torte is outstanding. ✉ *Nowy Świat 21,* ☏ *022/826–38–77. AE, DC, MC, V.*

$$ ✕ **Kamienne Schodki.** This vaulted restaurant in a 16th-century house on the corner of the Old Town Square is famous for its roast duck served with apples (actually, for a long time this was the only dish offered). The chicken or pork *à la polonaise* with garlic stuffing is also quite good. Save room for the light and creamy pastries. ✉ *Rynek Starego Miasta 26,* ☏ *022/831–08–22. AE, DC, MC, V.*

$$ ✕ **Klub Aktora.** An "in" place for expats and hip Warsovians, the Aktora thrives under the watchful eye of Stanisław Pruszyński, who escaped from Poland in 1955 to become a restaurateur in Canada, only to return to Poland after Communism fell. The most chic time to come may be afternoon tea. ✉ *Al. Ujazdowskie 45,* ☏ *022/628–93–66. AE, DC, MC, V.*

$$ ✕ **Qchnia Artystyczna.** This artsy place at the back of the Zamek Ujazdowski (Ujazdowski Castle) is not for the stodgy. The service is terrible, but the mainly vegetarian menu is creative and filling. Sample the *naleśniki* (crepes stuffed with sweet cheese or fruit). In summer, outdoor tables overlook a magnificent view of the park. ✉ *Ujazdowski Castle, al. Ujazdowskie 6,* ☏ *022/625–76–27. AE, DC, MC, V.*

$$ ✕ **Studio Buffo.** Just steps from the Sheraton, this restaurant offers patio dining in summer. The constantly changing menu is mainly a twist on Polish dishes. You can't go wrong with the chef's recommendations. *Ul. Marii Konopnickiej 6,* ☏ *022/626–89–07. AE, DC, MC, V.*

$ ✕ **Pod Barbicanem.** This milk bar situated under the Barbakan gate is the best deal in town if you can tolerate the grouchy cashier. Enjoy the enormous bowls of homemade soups, the chicken cutlets with mashed potatoes and fresh seasonal vegetables, and the naleśniki. ✉ *Ul. Mostowka 28,* ☏ *022/831–47–37. No credit cards.*

$ ✕ **U Hopfera.** This small and busy restaurant on the Royal Route has brightly checked tablecloths, fresh flowers, and a friendly and efficient staff. It specializes in Polish dishes, ranging from *schab ze śliwkami* (pork baked with plums) to homemade pierogi with beef stuffing. ✉ *Ul. Krakowskie Przedmieście 53,* ☏ *022/825–73–52. AE, DC, MC, V.*

Lodging

Warsaw's overall shortage of luxury hotel rooms could ease up in the new millennium, with at least two international chains building new accommodations. Lower down the price scale, options remain restricted. Bed-and-breakfast accommodations are difficult to find (☞ B&B Reservation Agencies *in* Warsaw A to Z, *below*). In summer there are generally more options because student hostels rent out their spaces. Demand is high, so book well in advance.

Warsaw is a small city, and the location of your hotel is not of crucial importance in terms of travel time to major sights or night spots. Many hotels are clustered in the downtown area near the intersection of ulica Marszałkowska and aleje Jerozolimskie. This is not an especially scenic area; nevertheless the neighborhood doesn't exactly become a "concrete desert" after business hours, since there are many

Dining

Bazyliszek 5
Belvedere 29
Café Ejlat 22
Dom Restauracyjny Gessler 4
Flik 26
Fukier 3
Kamienne Schodki 2
Klub Aktora 21
Pod Barbicanem 1
Qchnia Artystyczna 25
Restauracja Polska 12
Studio Buffo 24
U Hopfera 6

Lodging

Belfer 11
Bristol 8
Europejski 7
Forum 17
Gromada 19
Gromada Dom Chłopa 10
Hera 27
Holiday Inn 13
Jan III Sobieski 18
Marriott 14
Metropol 16
Novotel 20
Parkowa 30
Polonia 15
Sheraton 23
Stegny Sports Hotel and Camping 28
Victoria Inter-Continental 9

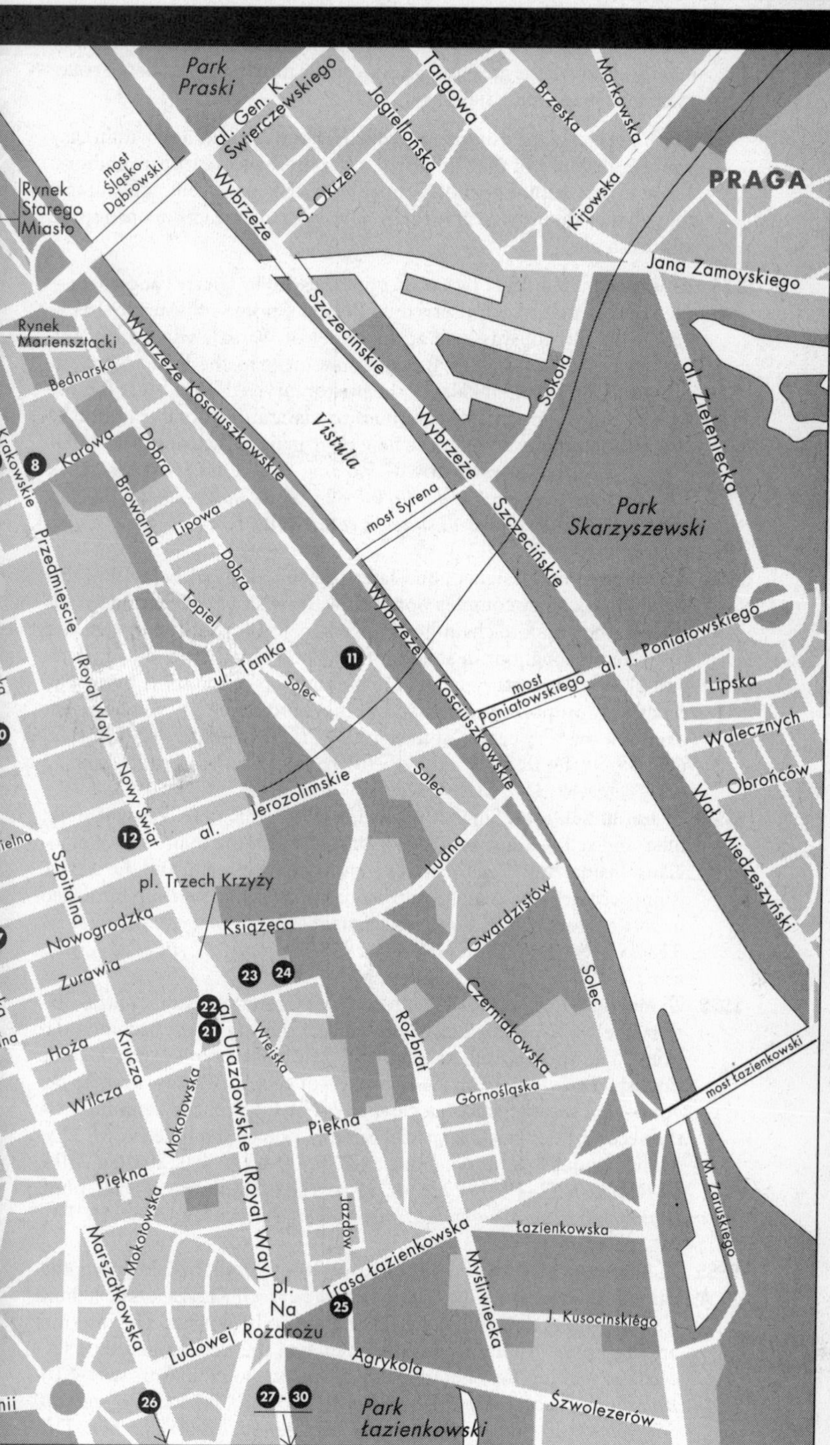

Park Praski
PRAGA
al. Gen. K. Swierczewskiego
Targowa
Jagiellońska
Brzeska
Markowska
most Śląsko-Dąbrowski
Rynek Starego Miasto
Wybrzeże
S. Okrzei
Kijowska
Jana Zamoyskiego
Szczecińskie
Rynek Mariensztacki
Bednarska
Wybrzeże Kościuszkowskie
Sokola
al. Zieleniecka
Vistula
Krakowskie
Karowa
Dobra
Wybrzeże
Szczecińskie
Browarna
Lipowa
most Syrena
Park Skarzyszewski
Przedmiescie
Dobra
Topiel
Wybrzeże
al. J. Poniatowskiego
ul. Tamka
Solec
most Poniatowskiego
Lipska
(Royal Way)
Kościuszkowskie
Walecznych
Nowy Świat
al. Jerozolimskie
Solec
Obrońców
Wał Miedzeszyński
Szpitalna
Ludna
pl. Trzech Krzyży
Gwardzistów
Nowogrodzka
Książęca
Zurawia
Solec
Czerniakowska
al. Ujazdowskie (Royal Way)
Wiejska
Rozbrat
Hoża
Krucza
most Łazienkowski
Wilcza
Mokotowska
Górnośląska
Piękna
Piękna
M. Zaruskiego
Jazdów
Mokotowska
Marszałkowska
Łazienkowska
Trasa Łazienkowska
Myśliwiecka
pl. Na Rozdrożu
Ludowej
J. Kusocinskiego
Agrykola
Park Łazienkowski
Szwoleżerów

residences, restaurants, and nightspots. Note that with a rising crime rate in the city, it is best to be cautious when strolling downtown at night—although the greatest hazards usually turn out to be uneven pavement and inadequate lighting.

The hotels on plac Piłsudskiego, which is close to parks and within easy walking distance of the Old Town, offer more pleasant surroundings. Most of the suburban hotels have no particular scenic advantage, though they do provide immediate access to larger tracts of open space and fresh air.

$$$$ ★ **Bristol.** Built in 1901 by a consortium headed by Ignacy Paderewski—the concert pianist who served as Poland's prime minister in 1919–1920—the Bristol was long at the center of Warsaw's social life. Impressively situated on the Royal Route, next to the Pałac Namiestnikowski (Presidential Palace), the Bristol survived World War II more or less intact. The Bristol continues to maintain its long tradition of luxury and elegance under the new ownership of Le Meridien. It has one of the best cafés in town—no one can resist its pastries. ✉ *Krakowskie Przedmieście 42/44, 00–325,* ☎ *022/625–25–25,* FAX *022/625–25–77. 163 rooms, 43 suites. 2 restaurants, bar, café, pool, sauna, solarium. AE, DC, MC, V.*

$$$$ **Holiday Inn.** Designed, and later franchised, by Holiday Inn, this gleaming six-story complex opposite Warsaw's Central Station avoids some of the standard chain-hotel impersonality. It's softly carpeted and furnished throughout in shades of gray and blue. A tree-filled, steel-and-glass conservatory fronts the building up to the third floor. The generously proportioned guest rooms have projecting bay windows that overlook the very center of the city. ✉ *Ul. Złota 48, 00–120,* ☎ *022/697–39–99,* FAX *022/697–38–99. 365 rooms, 8 suites. 3 restaurants, 2 bars, café. AE, DC, MC, V.*

$$$$ **Jan III Sobieski.** Since it opened in 1991, this hotel's bright pink, blue, and yellow illusionist facade has startled more than a few Warsovians. Inside, however, the decor is more conventional, and the service is impeccable. The rooms are reasonably sized and warmly furnished in soft rosewood and flowered prints. ✉ *Pl. Zawiszy 1, 02–025,* ☎ *022/658–44–44,* FAX *022/659–88–28. 377 rooms, 27 suites. 2 restaurants, bar, café. AE, DC, MC, V.*

$$$$ **Marriott.** Located in the high-rise Lim Center opposite Central Station, the Marriott currently has some of the city's best accommodations. The staff is well trained and helpful; everyone speaks some English. The views from every room—of central Warsaw and far beyond—are spectacular on a clear day. The Lila Veneda restaurant on the second floor hosts a special Sunday brunch, complete with Dixieland band. ✉ *Al. Jerozolimskie 65/79, 00–697,* ☎ *022/630–63–06,* FAX *022/620–52–39. 489 rooms, 34 suites. 3 restaurants, 3 bars, pool, health club, casino, nightclub, business services, parking (fee). AE, DC, MC, V.*

$$$$ ★ **Sheraton.** Halfway down the Royal Route from the Old Town, this curved six-story building overlooks plac Trzech Krzyży, while behind it lie the parks that run along the Vistula embankment. The interiors are bright, the rooms generously sized, and the well-trained staff succeeds in making the Sheraton the friendliest hotel in Warsaw. ✉ *Ul. Bolesława Prusa 2, 00–504,* ☎ *022/657–61–00,* FAX *022/657–62–00. 350 rooms, 20 suites. 3 restaurants, café, sauna, health club. AE, DC, MC, V.*

$$$$ **Victoria Inter-Continental.** Opened in the late 1970s, the Victoria was until 1989 Warsaw's only luxury hotel, hosting a stream of official visitors and state delegations. The large and comfortably furnished guest rooms are decorated in tones of brown and gold. Health facilities include a basement swimming pool and three exercise rooms, and the hotel is just across the street from the jogging (or walking) paths of the Ogród Saski (Saxon Gardens). ✉ *Ul. Królewska 11, 00–065,* ☎ *022/657–80–11,* FAX *022/657–80–57. 347 rooms, 13 suites. 3 restaurants, bar, pool, health clubs, casino, nightclub, parking (fee). AE, DC, MC, V.*

$$$ **Europejski.** Although it retains traces of its earlier grandeur, this hotel is now clearly struggling to maintain standards. The 19th-century building was reopened in 1962 after postwar reconstruction; the renovators managed to retain some original features, including two grand marble staircases. The rooms, with somewhat shabby furnishings, are very diverse in size and shape. Almost all have views overlooking historic Warsaw—on one side, the Royal Route, on the other, plac Piłsudskiego. The hotel is not air-conditioned. Guests are allowed, for an extra fee, to use the pool and health club facilities of the Victoria Inter-Continental, which is under the same management. ✉ *Krakowskie Przedmieście 13, 00–065,* ☎ *022/826–50–51,* FAX *022/826–11–11. 233 rooms, 13 suites. Restaurant, bar. AE, DC, MC, V.*

$$$ **Forum.** This dun-color, 30-story, Swedish-design metal cube has been a fixture on the Warsaw skyline since 1974. Guest rooms are of average size, and those on the east side of the building have good views—but don't choose the Forum if you're counting on cheerful surroundings. Depressing tones of brown and green predominate, and the furnishings seem to have been chosen for function rather than comfort. The staff, used to dealing with rapid-turnover group tours, can be offhand. The hotel is not air-conditioned, and it's in the middle of a heavily built-up area. On the plus side, it is within easy reach of the entertainment districts. ✉ *Ul. Nowogrodzka 24/26, 00–511,* ☎ *022/621–02–71,* FAX *022/625–04–76. 750 rooms, 13 suites. 2 restaurants, bar. AE, DC, MC, V.*

$$ **Gromada.** Opened in 1995 and just under 1 km (½ mi) to Warsaw's airport and about 7 km (4½ mi) from the city center, the Gromada is run by a peasants' cooperative. The dining room is one of its attractions, and breakfast is particularly recommended. The rooms are comfortable, if standardized. The hotel stands well back from the busy main road and has wooded grounds. There is good bus service into town. ✉ *Ul. 17 Stycznia 32, 02–148,* ☎ *022/846–54–01,* FAX *022/846–15–80. 140 rooms. Restaurant, bar, sauna. AE, DC, MC, V.*

$$ **Gromada Dom Chłopa.** With an excellent location in the center of Warsaw, this white five-story hotel was built during the late 1950s by the Gromada peasants' cooperative and originally had a plant-and-seed store on the ground floor. Times have changed: the store now sells TVs. The hotel, which has just undergone renovation, offers clean and reasonably priced accommodations; rooms are rather small, but the colors are lively, and the bathrooms have been updated. There is no air-conditioning. ✉ *Pl. Powstańców Warszawy 2, 00–030,* ☎ *022/625–15–45,* FAX *022/625–21–40. 282 rooms. Restaurant, bar. AE, DC, MC, V.*

$$ **Metropol.** This 1960s hotel is right on Warsaw's main downtown intersection. Most of the rooms are singles, which are large enough to contain a bed, armchairs, and desk without feeling crowded. Bathrooms, though small, are attractively tiled and fitted. Each room has a balcony overlooking busy ulica Marszałkowska, and traffic noise can be very intrusive when the windows are open. There is no air-conditioning. ✉ *Ul. Marszałkowska 99A, 00–693,* ☎ *022/629–40–01,* FAX *022/625–30–14. 175 rooms, 16 suites. Restaurant. AE, DC, MC, V.*

$$ **Novotel.** The Novotel can be recommended for a good night's sleep, as it is some distance away from the hustle and bustle of the city center. It's only five minutes from the airport (fortunately, *not* under any flight paths) and it's right across the road from a major area of gardens and parks. Though removed from the heart of the city, the hotel is on the main bus routes; Bus 175 will take you downtown in 15 minutes. The atmosphere is friendly, and the rooms are light, clean, and comfortable. ✉ *Ul. 1 Sierpnia 1, 02–134,* ☎ *022/846–40–51,* FAX *022/846–36–86. 150 rooms. Restaurant, bar, parking (fee). AE, DC, MC, V.*

$$ ★ **Parkowa.** This 1970s hotel, reserved for official government delegations, frequently has rooms available to the general public. It is just south of the Pałac Belweder (Belvedere Palace) in a landscaped area adjacent to Łazienki Park. The hotel has recently been renovated and offers Western-style accommodations (including air-conditioning). ✉ *Ul. Belwederska 46/50, 00–594,* ☎ *022/694–80–00,* FAX *022/41–60–29. 44 rooms. Restaurant, bar, sauna. AE, DC, MC, V.*

$$ **Polonia.** The Art Nouveau Polonia was the only Warsaw hotel to survive World War II intact. Much of the hotel's period splendor was lost in a major renovation completed in 1974, when the rooms were standardized. The high-ceilinged rooms are, however, still reasonably spacious and comfortable. Quite a few of the doubles and suites retain their stylish bay windows and balconies, and many of the bathrooms are large. The restaurant is a marvelous set piece of fin-de-siècle elegance. There is no air-conditioning. Single rooms do not have baths. ✉ *Al. Jerozolimskie 45, 00–692,* ☎ *022/628–72–41,* FAX *022/628–66–22. 199 rooms, 110 with bath, 25 suites. Restaurant, bar, café. AE, DC, MC, V.*

$ **Belfer.** This hotel is situated in Powiśle, across the road from the Vistula River and 10 minutes by foot (admittedly all uphill) from the Royal Route. Traffic noise can be a big problem in front-facing rooms, but courtyard-facing rooms are peaceful. The decor throughout is dull, with plenty of dark-wood paneling and chocolate-brown paint, and there is no air-conditioning. Only the 10 doubles have private bathrooms. The rooms, though, are spacious and comfortable, and everything is clean. ✉ *Wybrzeże Kościuszkowskie 31/33, 00–379,* ☎ *022/625–05–71,* FAX *022/625–26–00. 360 rooms, 10 with bath. Restaurant, café. AE, DC, MC, V.*

$ **Hera.** This three-story socialist-realist building on the edge of Łazienki Park was taken over from the Communist Central Committee in 1990 by Warsaw University. It is used mainly for university guests, but overflow rooms are rented throughout the year. The spartanly decorated rooms are of good size, and many overlook the beautiful park. It is probably the best-located hotel in the price range. ✉ *Ul. Belwederska 26/30, 00–594,* ☎ *022/41–02–54,* FAX *022/41–08–05. 40 rooms. Restaurant. AE, DC, MC, V.*

$ **Stegny Sports Hotel and Camping.** A stone's throw from downtown Warsaw on the road to Wilanów Palace, this hotel sits next to an outdoor speed-skating rink. It is a cheap and quiet place to stay, with extremely simple rooms (with bathrooms down the hall). There is a year-round campsite on the premises. ✉ *Ul. Idzikowskiego 4, 00–594,* ☎ *022/42–27–00. 25 rooms without bath. Restaurant, sauna, 2 tennis courts, ice-skating. No credit cards.*

Nightlife and the Arts

As throughout Central Europe, people tend to meet for drinks in the evenings in *kawiarnie* (cafés)—where you can linger for as long as you like over a serving of coffee or brandy—rather than in bars. (Most cafés are open until 10.) But Western-style bars have become more popular, and there is also a growing fashion for pubs. Discos and rock clubs are mushrooming; jazz clubs have a wide audience. Casinos are mainly the haunt of foreign visitors and the new, rich business class of Poles.

You can find out about Warsaw's thriving arts scene in the English-language *Warsaw Insider,* available at most major hotels. If you read

Polish, the monthlies *IKS (Informator Kulturalny Stolicy)* and *City Magazine* and the daily *Gazeta Wyborcza* have the best listings. Warsaw's only major ticket agency, **ZASP** (✉ Al. Jerozolimskie 25, ☎ 022/621–94–54), is another good source for information on arts happenings. If you speak Polish, call **Telefoniczny Informator Kulturalny** (☎ 022/629–84–89), open daily from 10 to 6. The tickets for most performances are inexpensive, but if you want to spend even less, most theaters sell general-admission tickets—*wejściówki*—for a few złoty immediately before the performance. Wejściówki are often available for performances for which all standard tickets have been sold.

Nightlife

BARS AND LOUNGES

If you've got to know the score, **Champions** sports bar and restaurant (✉ Lim Center, Al. Jerozolimskie 65/79, ☎ 022/630–40–33) is a great place to watch American basketball and football games. **Harenda** (✉ Krakowskie Przedmieście 4/6, enter from ul. Obożna, ☎ 022/826–29–00) occasionally hosts some good jazz and has an outdoor terrace that gets crowded in summer. The **John Bull Pub** (✉ Ul. Zielna 37, ☎ 022/620–06–56; ✉ Ul. Jezeicka 4, ☎ 022/831–37–62) is open until midnight and serves English draught beers in two locations. **Morgan's** (✉ Ul. Okólnik 1, enter from ul. Tamka, ☎ 022/826–81–38) is the Irish pub that is always open late.

CASINOS

The **Casino Warsaw** (✉ Al. Jerozolimskie 65/79, ☎ 022/830–01–78), on the second floor of the Marriott, is Warsaw's plushest and most sedate casino. The clients are often international businessmen or Polish jet-setters. It's open daily from 11 AM to 7 AM. The **Victoria Casino** (✉ Ul. Królewska 11, ☎ 022/827–66–33), also popular, is open daily 2 PM to 7 AM.

DISCOS

Ground Zero (✉ Ul. Wspólna 62, ☎ 022/625–43–80), a former bomb shelter, is a large, crowded bi-level disco. **Hades** (✉ Al. Niepodległośi 162, ☎ 022/49–12–51) is a popular disco in the cellars of the Central School of Economics, with plenty of seating space. **Labrint** (✉ Ul. Smolna 12, ☎ 022/826–22–20) attracts the young-professional crowd. In the Marriott, **Orpheus** (✉ Al. Jerozolimskie 65/79, ☎ 022/630–54–16) has an elegant air and is very expensive. There is a well-established disco at the student club **Stodoła** (✉ Batorego 10, ☎ 022/25–86–25). **Tango** (✉ Al. Jerozolimskie 4, ☎ 022/622–19–19) is a pricey disco.

JAZZ CLUBS

Blue Velvet (✉ Krakowskie Przedmieście 5, ☎ 022/828–11–03) hosts regular modern jazz evenings. **Kawiarnia Literacka** (✉ Krakowskie Przedmieście 87/89, ☎ 022/826–57–84) has classic jazz on weekends.

The Arts

FILM

Since 1989 it seems every cinema in Warsaw has been showing foreign films—mainly U.S. box-office hits—nonstop. These are generally shown in the original language with added subtitles. In the year 2000, cineplexes burst onto the Warsaw scene, providing state-of-the-art cinematic environments. **Relax** (✉ Ul. Złota 8, ☎ 022/827–77–62) is a large, popular cinema in the center of town. **Silver Screen** (✉ Ul. Puławska 21/29, ☎ 022/852–88–88), also close to the city center, is one of the newest cinemas in town. **Skarpa** (✉ Ul. Kopernika 7–9, ☎ 022/826–48–96), off ulica Nowy Świat, is large and modern.

Don't count on seeing many Polish films while visiting Warsaw; only one cinema specializes in Polish features: **Iluzjon Filmoteki Narodowej**

(✉ Ul. Narbutta 55A, ☎ 022/48–33–33). **Wars** (✉ Rynek Nowe Miasta 5–7, ☎ 022/831–44–88), a cinema on the New Town Square, occasionally forgets about box-office success and shows an old Polish classic. This cinema also has a good program of foreign films.

MUSIC

The **Filharmonia Narodowa** (National Philharmonic; ✉ Ul. Sienkiewicza 10, ☎ 022/826–72–81) hosts an excellent season of concerts, with visits from world-renowned performers and orchestras as well as Polish musicians. Very popular concerts of classical music for children—run for years by Jadwiga Mackiewicz, who is herself almost a national institution—are held here on Sunday at 2; admission is from zł 5. The **Studio Koncertowe Polskiego Radia** (Polish Radio Concert Studio; ✉ Ul. Woronicza 17, ☎ 022/645–52–52), open since 1992, has excellent acoustics and popular programs. The **Royal Castle** (✉ Pl. Zamkowy 4, ☎ 022/657–21–70) has regular concerts in its stunning Great Assembly Hall.

The Chopin Society, **Towarzystwo im. Fryderyka Chopina** (✉ Ul. Okólnik 1, ☎ 022/827–54–71), organizes recitals and chamber concerts in the Pałac Ostrogskich (Ostrogski Palace). In summer, free Chopin concerts are held at the Chopin Memorial in Łazienki Park on Sunday and at Chopin's birthplace, Żelazowa Wola, outside Warsaw (☞ Exploring Warsaw, *above*).

OPERA AND DANCE

Housed in a beautifully restored 19th-century theater in the Muranów district, **Opera Kameralna** (✉ Al. Solidarności 76B, ☎ 022/625–75–10), the Warsaw chamber opera, has an ambitious program and a growing reputation for quality performances. **Teatr Wielki** (Opera House; ✉ Pl. Teatralny 1, ☎ 022/826–32–88), Warsaw's grand opera, stages spectacular productions of the classic international opera and ballet repertoire, as well as Polish operas and ballets. The massive neoclassical house, built in the 1820s and reconstructed after the war, has an auditorium with more than 2,000 seats. Stanisław Moniuszko's 1865 opera *Straszny Dwór* (*Haunted Manor*), a lively piece with folk costumes and dancing, is a good starting point if you want to explore Polish music: the visual aspects will entertain you, even if the music is unfamiliar. Plot summaries in English are available at most performances.

THEATER

The **Globe Theater Group** (☎ 022/620–44–29) performs American and British plays. **"Gulliver" Teatr Lalek** (✉ Ul. Różana 16, ☎ 022/45–16–76) is one of Warsaw's excellent puppet theaters. **Teatr Narodowy** (✉ Pl. Teatralny, ☎ 022/826–32–88), adjoining the opera house and under the same management, stages Polish classics. Warsaw's Jewish theater, **Teatr Żydowski** (✉ Plac Grzybowski 12/16, ☎ 022/620–70–25), performs in Yiddish, but most of its productions are colorful costume dramas in which the action speaks as loudly as the words. Translation into English is provided through headphones.

Outdoor Activities and Sports

Health Clubs

The best health club in Warsaw is the **Fitness Center** at the Sheraton (✉ Ul. Bolesława Prusa 2, ☎ 022/657–61–00). Open to nonmembers, the center has the latest equipment, aerobics and other classes, and child care.

Hiking

In Warsaw the local branch of **PTTK** (Polish Tourist Association) organizes daylong hikes in the nearby countryside on weekends. Watch the local papers for advertisements of meeting points and routes.

Horse Racing

You can reach Warsaw's beautiful but seedy **racecourse** (Ul. Puławska 266, ☎ 022/843–14–41) by taking Tram 4 or 36 or one of the special buses marked WYŚCIGI, which run from the east side of the Pałac Kultury i Nauki (Palace of Culture and Science) on Saturday in season (May–October). Betting is on a tote system. Admission to the stands is zł 10.

Jogging

Along with dogs and bicycles, joggers are banned from Warsaw's largest and most beautiful park, Łazienki Park. The 9½ km (6 mi) trail through parkland and over footbridges from the Ujazdów Park to Mariensztat (parallel to the Royal Route) is a good route. The Vistula embankment makes for a good straight run (the paved surface runs for about 12 km [8 mi]). Piłsudski Park has a circular route of about 4½ km (3 mi). You can jog in the center of town on the somewhat restricted pathways of the Ogród Saski (Saxon Gardens).

Soccer

Warsaw's soccer team, **Legia** (☎ 022/621–08–96), plays at the field at ulica Łazienkowska 3. Admission is from zł 15.

Swimming

For a swim your best bet is the indoor pool at the **Bristol Hotel** (✉ Krakowskie Przedmieście 42/44, ☎ 022/625–25–25). Warsaw's indoor pools tend to be overcrowded, and some restrict admission to those with season tickets; it's best to check first. At the **Spartańska** (✉ Ul. Spartańska 1, ☎ 022/48–67–46) you can usually persuade them to let you swim on a special one-day pass.

Shopping

Warsaw's shopping scene is booming, with more and more international chains—such as Marks & Spencer, London's noted department store—boutiques, and suburban shopping malls setting up shop. As a result, locally produced items are sometimes harder to find than ridiculously expensive imported ones. Shopping hours are usually from 11 AM to 7 PM on weekdays and 10 AM to 1 PM on Saturday. RUCH kiosks, which sell bus and train tickets, newspapers, and cosmetics, are usually open from 7 to 7.

Shopping Districts

Warsaw has four main shopping streets. The larger stores lie on **ulica Marszałkowska** (from ulica Królewska to plac Zbawiciela) and **aleje Jerozolimskie** (from Central Station to plac Generala de Gaulle). Smaller stores and more specialized boutiques can be found on **ulica Nowy Świat** and **ulica Chmielna.**

Department Stores

Warsaw's oldest department store, **Arka** (✉ Ul. Bracka 25, ☎ 022/692–14–00), has a monumental staircase, Art Nouveau stained-glass windows, and stores selling clothing, jewelry, and household items. At the **Galeria Centrum** (✉ Ul. Marszałkowska 104–122, ☎ 022/551–41–41)—divided into Wars, Sawa, and Junior sections—private boutiques sell mainly imported fashion items.

Specialty Stores

ANTIQUES

For fine antique furniture, art, and china try **Desa** (✉ Ul. Marszałkowska 34, ☎ 022/621–66–15; Ul. Nowy Świat 51, ☎ 022/827–47–60; Rynek Starego Miasta 4/6, ☎ 022/831–16–81). Remember, however, that most antiques cannot be exported.

ART GALLERIES

Galeria Nowy Świat (✉ Nowy Świat 23, ☎ 022/826–35–01) has painting, ceramics, and designer furniture. **Galeria Sztuki** (✉ Ul. Świętokrzyska 32, ☎ 022/652–11–77) holds one of the finest collections of contemporary Polish art.

FOLK ART AND CRAFTS

Arex (✉ Ul. Chopina 5B, ☎ 022/629–66–24) is the best place to go for traditional Polish wood carvings. The **Cepelia stores** (✉ Pl. Konstytucji 5, ☎ 022/621–26–18; Rynek Starego Miasta 10, ☎ 022/831–18–05) sell folk art, including wood carvings and silver and amber jewelry.

GLASS AND CRYSTAL

A. Jabłonski (✉ Ul. Nowy Świat 52) sells unique pieces of handblown glass and crystal. **Szlifierna skła** (✉ Ul. Nowomeijska 1/3, ☎ 022/831–46–43), next to the Old Town Square, custom engraves all kinds of crystal goods.

JEWELRY

There are many jewelry (*jubiler*) stores clustered around the Old Town and ulica Nowy Świat. The **Art Gallery** (✉ Rynek Starego Miasto 13) has a great selection of silver and amber, although much of it is somewhat overpriced. One of the oldest and best-established jewelry stores in Poland is **W. Kruk** (✉ Pl. Konstytucji 6, ☎ 022/628–75–34).

LEATHER

JKM (✉ Krakowskie Przedmieście 65, ☎ 022/827–22–62) is a small shop crammed with bags, suitcases, and gloves from the best Polish producers. **Pekar** (✉ Al. Jerozolimskie 29, ☎ 022/621–90–82) carries a wide range of bags, gloves, and jackets.

Street Markets

The largest Warsaw market—known as the Russian market and composed largely of private sellers hawking everything from antiques to blue jeans—is at the **Tysiąclecie Sports Stadium,** east of the river at Rondo Waszyngtona. If you go, watch out for pickpockets.

Warsaw A to Z

Arriving and Departing

BY BUS

The private long-distance bus service **Polski Express** (☎ 022/620–03–30 for information and reservations; English spoken) arrives and departs from Jana Pawła II between Central Station and the Holiday Inn. Polski Express also has a stop at the airport.

Warsaw's main bus station, **Dworzec PKS Zachodnia** (✉ Al. Jerozolimskie 144, ☎ 022/823–63–94), 10 minutes from Central Station on Bus 127 or 130, serves most long-distance routes. Local services for points north of the city run from **Dworzec PKS Marymont** (✉ Ul. Marymoncka and ul. Żeromskiego, ☎ 022/823–63–94) in the northern district of Żoliborz. Buses headed east leave from **Dworzec PKS Stadion** (✉ Intersection of ul. Targowa, ul. Zamoyskiego, and al. Zieleniecka, ☎ 022/823–63–94) on the east bank of the Vistula. Tickets for all destinations can be purchased at the main station.

BY CAR

Within the city, a car can be more a problem than a convenience. Warsaw currently has too many cars for its road network, and there are sometimes major snarls. Parking also can be very difficult. And there is a real threat of theft—of contents, parts, or the entire car—if you leave a Western model unattended, and it is not easy to get quick ser-

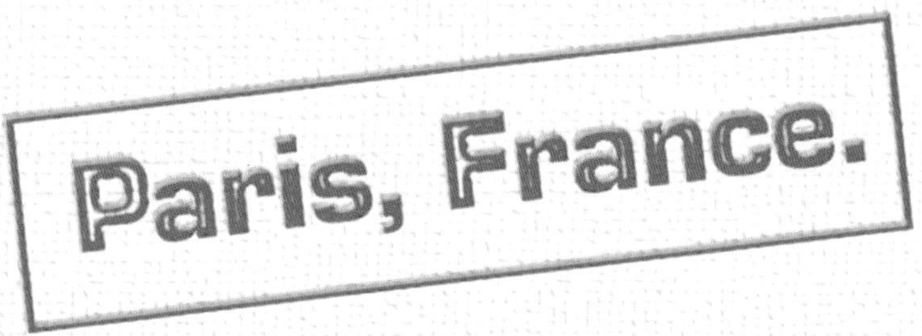

Paris, Texas.

When it Comes to Getting Local Currency at an ATM, Same Thing.

Whether you're in Yosemite or Yemen, using your Visa® card or ATM card with the PLUS symbol is the easiest and most convenient way to get local currency. For example, let's say you're in France. When you make a withdrawal, using your secured PIN, it's dispensed in francs, but is debited from your account in U.S. dollars. This makes it easy to take advantage of favorable exchange rates. And if you need help finding one of Visa's 627,000 ATMs in 127 countries worldwide, visit **visa.com/pd/atm.** We'll make finding an ATM as easy as finding the Eiffel Tower, the Pyramids or even the Grand Canyon.

It's Everywhere You Want To Be.®

vice or repairs. If you do bring your car, park it overnight in a guarded parking garage.

BY PLANE

Warsaw's **Okęcie Airport** (☎ 022/650–42–20) is 7 km (4½ mi) south of the city center. The Polish airline, **LOT** (✉ Al. Jerozolimskie 65/79, ☎ 022/630–50–07; 952 for reservations), makes the lion's share of flights to and from Warsaw. Other airlines flying to Warsaw include **Air France** (✉ Ul. Krucza 21, ☎ 022/628–12–81); **American Airlines** (✉ Al. Ujazdowskie 20, ☎ 022/625–30–02); **British Airways** (✉ Ul. Krucza 49, ☎ 022/628–94–31); **Delta** (✉ Ul. Królewska 11, ☎ 022/827–84–61); and **Lufthansa** (✉ Ul. Nowy Świat 19, ☎ 022/826–15–01).

Between the Airport and Downtown: The direct route to downtown, where almost all the hotels are, is along aleje Żwirki i Wigury and ulica Raszyńska. **By Bus:** The AIRPORT–CITY bus leaves from Platform 4 outside Terminal 1 every 20 minutes and stops at all the major hotels and Central Station. Tickets cost zł 6, and the trip takes about 25 minutes. Alternatively, Bus 175 leaves Okęcie about every 10 minutes. It also runs past most major downtown hotels and is reliable and cheap, but beware of pickpockets. Purchase tickets for zł 2.40 at an airport RUCH kiosk. If your immediate destination is not Warsaw, Polski Express (☞ *above*) has direct service from Okęcie to major Polish cities. **By Taxi:** Avoid at all costs the taxi hawkers and unmarked vehicles (no number at the top) outside the arrivals hall: not only are these cabs expensive but they can also be dangerous. Your best bet is to call **Radio Taxi** (☎ 919, 9622, or 9623) from one of the radio taxi kiosks in the arrivals area, or call your hotel in advance and have them pick you up. A cab ride into the city should cost about zł 25.

BY TRAIN

As the name implies, Warsaw's **Warszawa Centralna** (Central Station; ✉ Al. Jerozolimskie 54, ☎ 022/25–50–00; 022/620–45–12 for international rail information; 022/620–03–61 for domestic rail information) is right in the heart of the city, between the Marriott and Holiday Inn. Beware of pickpockets and muggers who prey on passengers as they board or leave trains. Domestic trains run from **Warszawa Śródmieście** (☎ 022/628–47–41), next to Central Station on aleje Jerozolimskie. East of the river, domestic trains run from **Dworzec Wileński** (✉ Ul. Targowa, ☎ 022/18–35–21). You can purchase train tickets at the train station or at Orbis and other travel agents.

Getting Around

Although Warsaw stretches more than 32 km (20 mi) in each direction, the sights of greatest interest to most tourists are concentrated primarily in two areas: downtown, which lies along ulica Marszałkowska, and the Old Town, just over 2 km (1 mi) away and centered on Rynek Starego Miasta (Old Town Square). Both areas are best explored on foot. Public transportation, though cheap and efficient, can be uncomfortably crowded. Taxis are readily available and are often the most convenient option for covering longer distances.

BY BUS

A trip on a city bus costs zł 2.40. Purchase tickets from RUCH kiosks or bus drivers, and cancel one in the machine on the bus for each ride. Buses that halt at all stops along their route are numbered 100 and up. Express buses are numbered from E-1 upward. Buses numbered 500–599 stop at selected stops. Check details on the information board at the bus stop. Night buses (numbered 600 and up) operate between 11 PM and 5:30 AM; the fare is three tickets.

BY TAXI

In Warsaw, it is always best to use the services of **Radio Taxi** (☏ 919, 9622, or 9623), because they are the most reliable and the operators usually speak English. The standard charge is zł 3.6 for the first kilometer (½ mi) and zł 1.4 for each kilometer thereafter. It is not customary to tip taxi drivers, although you can round up the fare to the nearest złoty. Avoid unmarked Mercedes cabs as well as taxis that do not have a number on the top (9622, 9623, etc.), as they are likely to charge far more than the going rate.

BY TRAM

Trams are the fastest means of public transport, since they are not affected by traffic holdups. Purchase tickets from RUCH kiosks or tram operators, and cancel one ticket in the machine on the tram for each ride. Trams run on a north–south and east–west grid system along most of the main city routes, pulling up automatically at all stops. Each tram has a diagram of the system.

BY UNDERGROUND

Warsaw's underground opened in spring 1995. Although as yet it has only one line, running from the southern suburbs to the city center (Kabaty to Centrum [aleje Jerozolimskie and Marszałkowska]), it is clean and fast and costs the same as the tram or bus. Use the same tickets, canceling them at the entrance to the station.

Contacts and Resources

B&B RESERVATION AGENCIES

The Bureau of Private Accommodations (✉ Ul. Krucza 17, ☏ 022/628–75–40) has many accommodations in the city center, although none include breakfast. The staff is helpful and speaks English.

DOCTORS AND DENTISTS

The **American Medical Center** (✉ Ul. Wilcza 23, Suite 29, ☏ 0602/243–024 for 24-hr service) is run by an American doctor and has contacts with outside specialists. For dental care, **Austria-Dent Center** (✉ Ul. Zelazna 54, ☏ 022/821–31–84) is open weekdays from 9 to 9, Saturday 9 to 3.

EMBASSIES AND CONSULATE

All three embassies listed below are on or just off aleje Ujazdowskie; the British Consulate is closer to the center of town.

U.S. Embassy (✉ Al. Ujazdowskie 29–31, ☏ 022/628–30–41). **Canadian Embassy** (✉ Ul. Matejki 1–5, ☏ 022/629–80–51). **British Embassy** (✉ Al. Roż 1, ☏ 022/628–10–01). **British Consulate** (✉ Ul. Emilii Plater 28, ☏ 022/625–30–99).

EMERGENCIES

Police (☏ 997). **Ambulance** (☏ 999). Do not expect anyone at these numbers to speak English. A major embassy will have someone on duty 24 hours a day to help their country's citizens in an emergency.

ENGLISH-LANGUAGE BOOKSTORES

Most major bookstores now have well-stocked sections of English-language books. You'll find a good selection at either location of **Empik** (✉ Ul. Nowy Świat 15/17, ☏ 022/627–06–50; Ul. Marszałkowska 116–122, ☏ 022/827–82–96). Another store with a good English-language section is **Bookland** (✉ Al. Jerozolimskie 61, ☏ 022/646–57–27).

GUIDED TOURS

Marzurkas Travel (✉ Ul. Długa 8/14, ☏ 022/635–66–33) leads daily tours of Warsaw as well as longer tours of Poland. **Local Rent a Car Poland LTD** (✉ Europejski Hotel, ul. Krakowskie Przedmieście 13, ☏

022/657–81–81) offers similar services. Tours can be booked at major hotels or through the agencies directly. For tours that focus on Jewish Warsaw or Poland call **Our Roots—Jewish Information and Tourist Bureau** (✉ Ul. Twarda 6, ☎ 022/620–05–56).

LATE-NIGHT PHARMACIES

The following pharmacy (*apteka*) is open 24 hours a day: **Apteka Grabowskiego** (✉ Central Station, 1st floor, Al. Jerozolimskie 54, ☎ 022/25–69–86; Ul. Freta 13, ☎ 022/831–50–91; Ul. Widok 19, ☎ 022/827–35–93).

MONEY AND CURRENCY

To change money, head to the **Kantor Wymiany Walut** (✉ Ul. Marszałkowska 66, at ulica Wilcza), which has swift, friendly service and usually offers slightly better rates than hotels and banks. It is open weekdays from 11 to 7 and Saturday from 9 to 2. Another option is the **Kantor** (✉ Ul. Świętokrzyska 31) in the main post office, open 24 hours a day. **TEBOS** (✉ Al. Jerozolimskie 54), in Central Station at the foot of the staircase leading from the main hall to the access passage for platforms, is also open 24 hours a day. (Remember to watch out for pickpockets.)

TRAVEL AGENCIES

American Express (✉ Krakowskie Przedmieście 11, ☎ 022/635–20–02; 022/630–69–52 for 24-hr service) sells travelers cheques, exchanges currency, rents cars, and provides other travel agency services. **Getz International Travel Ltd.** (✉ Al. Jerozolimskie 56C, ☎ 022/630–27–60) is an efficient agency with friendly service. **Carlson Wagonlit Travel** (✉ Ul. Nowy Świat 64, ☎ 022/826–04–31) is centrally located. **Orbis** (✉ Ul. Bracka 16, ☎ 022/826–02–71) is the best place to buy train tickets.

VISITOR INFORMATION

The **Center for Tourist Information** (✉ Pl. Zamkowy 1, ☎ 022/635–18–81), on Castle Square, is open from 9 to 6 weekdays and 11 to 6 weekends. Branches of the **Warsaw Tourist Information Office** (✉ Gromada Dom Chłopa, Pl. Powstańców Warszawy 2, ☎ 022/94–31; arrivals hall of Okęcie Airport) are open weekdays 8–7 and weekends 9–3.

KRAKÓW

Renaissance arcades, enchanting onion domes, Baroque spires, storybook streets, and Leonardo da Vinci's sublime painting *Cecilia Gallerani*—little wonder the stunning beauty of this 1,000-year-old city and its sights attracts hundreds of thousands of visitors annually. Kraków (Cracow), seat of Poland's oldest university and once the nation's capital (before finally relinquishing the honor to Warsaw in 1611), is one of the few Polish cities that escaped devastation by Hitler's armies during World War II. Today Kraków's fine towers, facades, and churches, reflecting seven centuries of Polish architecture, continue to make it the shop window of Poland. Its location, about 270 km (170 mi) south of Warsaw, also makes it a good starting point for hiking and skiing trips in the mountains of southern Poland.

Exploring Kraków

It would be almost unthinkable to visit the Małopolska region without visiting Kraków. The Old Town's face has been stained by pollution from the steelworks in the outlying suburb of Nova Huta and the nearby industrial town of Śląsk (Silesia). By slow stages, however, this city is being restored to its former glory. Starting as a market town in the 10th century, Kraków became Poland's capital in 1037. Until as recently as the 19th century there was a moat encircling the Old Town; now there is the Planty, a ring of parkland.

To the immediate southeast of the Old Town is the old Jewish quarter of Kazimierz. This was once a separate town, chartered in 1335 by its founder, Kazimierz the Great. In 1495 Kraków's Jews were expelled from the city by King John Albert, and they resettled in Kazimierz. The Jewish community of Kazimierz came to an abrupt and tragic end during World War II. In 1941 the Jews of Kazimierz were moved first to a Jewish ghetto across the Vistula River in Podgórze, then to Plasów concentration camp. Most who survived Plasów were transported to their deaths in the much larger concentration camp of Auschwitz-Birkenau (☞ Małopolska, *below*). Those who escaped Plasów formed the basis of Thomas Kenneally's book, and Steven Spielberg's film, *Schindler's List.*

Numbers in the text correspond to numbers in the margin and on the Kraków map.

Stare Miasto (Old Town)

Kraków's streets are a vast and lovely living museum, and the Stare Miasto (Old Town) in particular is a historical gold mine. Its ancient houses, churches, and palaces can overwhelm visitors with only a few days to see the sights. The heart of it all is Kraków's "drawing room"—the Rynek Główny, or Main Market Square.

A GOOD WALK

The Old Town is best explored on foot, beginning at the **Barbakan** ㊿ and city gate on **ulica Floriańska** (51). Here you should visit both the Czartoryski Collection in the **Arsenal Miejski** (52) (which contains Leonardo da Vinci's legendary *Cecilia Gallerani*) and **Dom Jana Matejki** (53) and admire the medieval mansions as well. Ulica Floriańska will take you to the **Rynek Główny** (54) at the center of the town, where you will find the **Kościół Mariacki** (55), the Renaissance **Sukiennice** (56), and a collection of magnificent Renaissance town houses.

The historic early buildings of the Jagiellonian University lie in streets leading off to the southwest and south of the square. Take ulica świętej Anny to reach ulica where you'll find the **Collegium Maïus** (57), where Copernicus once studied. Then go via ulica Gołębia to plac Wszystkich Świętych and the 13th-century **Franciscan Church and Monastery** (58). From here take ulica Grodzka south to another collegiate building, the **Collegium Juridicum** (59), and the 11th-century **Kościół świętego Andrzeja** (60). Cut through to Kraków's oldest street, **ulica Kanonicza** (61), where the canons of the cathedral once lived. Ulica Kanonicza leads to the Wawel Hill, where you'll find the **Wawel Cathedral** (62) and the Renaissance **Zamek Królewski** (63). From the Wawel Hill, you can stroll south down the Vistula embankment to visit the **Kościół na Skałce** (64) and the fine 14th-century redbrick Gothic Kościół świętej Katarzyny at ulica Skałeczna and ulica Augustynians'ka

TIMING

The Wawel Hill sights alone require a whole morning or afternoon; the rest of the Old Town, at least a day.

SIGHTS TO SEE

★ 52 **Arsenal Miejski** (Municipal Arsenal). The surviving fragment of Kraków's city wall opposite the Barbakan, where students and amateur artists hang their paintings for sale in the summer, contains the Renaissance Municipal Arsenal, which now houses part of the National

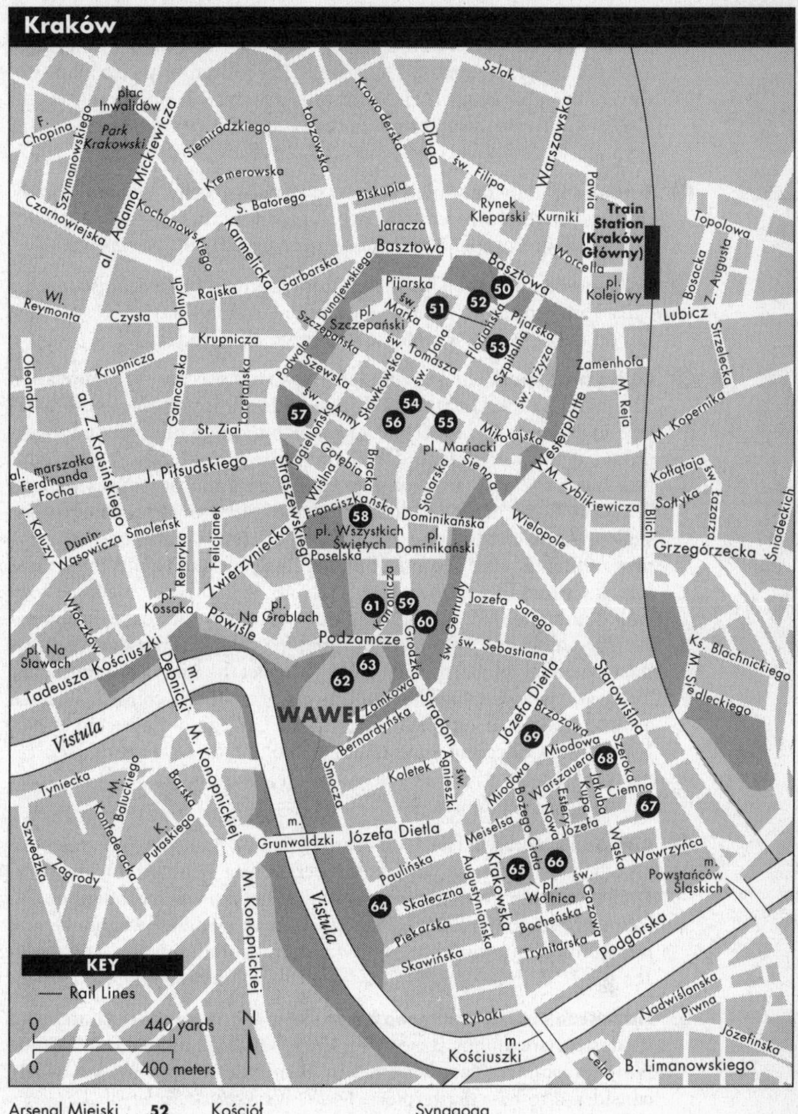

Arsenal Miejski . . . 52
Barbakan 50
Collegium Juridicum 59
Collegium Maïus 57
Dom Jana Matejki 53
Franciscan church and monastery 58
Kościół Bożego Ciała 66
Kościół Mariacki 55
Kościół na Skałce 64
Kościół św. Andrzeja 60
Rynek Główny . . . 54
Stara Synagoga 67
Sukiennice 56
Synagoga Remuh 68
Synagoga Tempel 69
Town Hall of Kazimierz 65
Ulica Floriańska 51
Ulica Kanonicza 61
Wawel Cathedral 62
Zamek Królewski 63

Museum's **Czartoryski Collection,** including such celebrated paintings as Raphael's *Portrait of a Young Man* and Rembrandt's *Landscape with the Good Samaritan.* The prize of the collection and to many observers the most beautiful portrait ever painted is Leonardo da Vinci's *Cecilia Gallerani,* also known as the *Lady with an Ermine.* ✉ *Ul. św. Jana 19,* ☎ *012/422–55–66.* *Zł 3.* ⏲ *Wed.–Sun. 10–3, Fri. 10–7.*

50 **Barbakan.** Only one small section of Kraków's city wall still stands, centered on the 15th-century Barbakan, one of the largest strongholds of its kind in Europe. ✉ *Ul. Basztowa, opposite ul. Floriańska.*

59 **Collegium Juridicum.** This magnificent Gothic building, raised in the early 15th century to house the Jagiellonian University's law students, lies on one of Kraków's oldest streets. ✉ *Ul. Grodzka 53.*

★ 57 **Collegium Maïus.** The Jagiellonian University was another innovation of Kazimierz the Great. Established in 1364, it was the first university in Poland. By 1400 the original buildings had become overcrowded and were replaced with the Collegium Maïus, of which this building is the only survivor. The Jagiellonian's most famous student, Nicolaus Copernicus, studied here from 1491 to 1495. The first visual delight is the Italian-style arcaded courtyard adorned with crystal vaulting. On the second floor, the museum and rooms are a must for all visitors to Kraków. They can only be visited on a guided tour (call in advance for an English guide). On the tour you see the treasury, assembly hall, library, and common room. The museum includes the Copernicus globe, the first globe to depict the American continents. There are two other Jagiellonian University buildings, constructed later, around the corner on ulica Gołębia: the **Collegium Physicum** at No. 13 and the **Collegium Slavisticum** at No. 20. ✉ *Ul. Jagiellońska 15,* ☎ *012/422–05–49.* *Courtyard free, museum zł 5.* ⏲ *Museum weekdays 11–2:30, Sat. 11–3:30.*

53 **Dom Jana Matejki.** The 19th-century painter Jan Matejko was born and died in this house, which now serves as a museum for his work. Even if you don't warm to his painting, Matejko was a prodigious collector of everything from Renaissance art to medieval weaponry, and this 16th-century building is in wonderful condition. ✉ *Ul. Floriańska 41,* ☎ *012/22–59–26.* *Zł 3.* ⏲ *Tues.–Sun. 10–3:30, Fri. 10–6.*

58 **Franciscan Church and Monastery.** The mid-13th-century church and monastery are among the earliest brick buildings in Kraków. The Art Nouveau stained-glass windows by Stanisław Wyspiański are widely considered to be a masterpiece. ✉ *Pl. Wszystkich Świętych 1.*

OFF THE BEATEN PATH

KOPIEC KOŚCIUSZKI – This mound on the outskirts of Kraków was built in tribute to the memory of Tadeusz Kościuszko in 1820, three years after his death. The earth came from battlefields on which he had fought; soil from the United States was added in 1926. The best place from which to get a panoramic view of the city, the mound presides above a 19th-century Austrian fort. Take Tram 1, 2, or 6 from plac Dominikański to the terminus at Salwator and then walk up aleje Waszyngtona to the mound. ⏲ *Daily 10–dusk.*

★ 55 **Kościół Mariacki** (Church of Our Lady). Dominating the northeast corner of Rynek Główny is the twin-tower Church of Our Lady. The first church was built on this site before the town plan of 1257, which is why it stands slightly askew from the main square; the present church, completed in 1397, was built on the foundations of its predecessor. You'll note that the two towers, added in the early 15th century, are of different heights. Legend has it that they were built by two brothers, one of whom grew jealous of the other's work and slew him with a sword: a symbol of Magdeburg law that still hangs in the Sukiennice. From the higher tower, a strange bugle call—known as the "Hejnal Mariacki"—rings out to mark each hour. It breaks off on an abrupt sobbing note to commemorate an unknown bugler struck in the throat by a Tartar arrow as he was playing his call to warn the city of imminent attack. The church's main showpiece is the magnificent wooden altarpiece with more than 200 carved figures, the work of the 15th-century artist Wit Stwosz (Veit Stoss). The panels depict medieval life in detail; the figure in the bottom right-hand corner of the Crucifixion panel is believed to represent Stwosz himself. ⊠ *Rynek Główny at ul. Mikołajska.*

64 **Kościół na Skałce** (Church on the Rock). Standing on the Vistula embankment to the south of Wawel Hill, this church is the center of the cult of St. Stanisław. The bishop and martyr is believed to have been beheaded, by order of the king, in the church that stood on this spot in 1079—a tale of rivalry similar to that of Henry II and Thomas à Becket. Beginning in the 19th century, this also became the last resting place for well-known Polish writers and artists; among those buried here are the composer Karol Szymanowski and the poet and painter Stanisław Wyspiański. ⊠ *Between ul. Paulińska and ul. Skałeczna on the Vistula embankment.*

60 **Kościół świętego Andrzeja** (Church of St. Andrew). The finest surviving example of Romanesque architecture in Kraków is the 11th-century fortified Church of St. Andrew. Local residents took refuge in St. Andrew during Tartar raids. The interior, remodeled during the 18th century, includes a fanciful pulpit resembling a boat. ⊠ *At the midpoint of ul. Grodzka, on the east side.*

★ 54 **Rynek Główny** (Main Market Square). Kraków's magnificent Main Market Square, Europe's largest medieval marketplace, is on a par in size and grandeur with St. Mark's Square in Venice. It even has the same plague of pigeons, although legend tells us the ones here are no ordinary birds: they are allegedly the spirits of the knights of Duke Henry IV Probus, who in the 13th century were cursed and turned into birds. This great square was not always so spacious. In an earlier period it contained—in addition to the present buildings—a Gothic town hall, a Renaissance granary, a large weighing house, a foundry, a pillory, and hundreds of traders' stalls. A few flower sellers under colorful umbrellas are all that remain of this bustling commercial activity.

A pageant of history has passed through this square. đFrom 1320 on, Polish kings came here on the day after their coronations to meet the city's burghers and receive homage and tribute in the name of all the towns of Poland. Albert Hohenzollern, the grand master of the Teutonic Knights, came here in 1525 to pay homage to Sigismund the Old, king of Poland. And in 1794 Tadeusz Kościuszko took a solemn vow to overthrow czarist Russia here.

The **Dom pod Jeleniami** (House at the Sign of the Stag) at No. 36 was once an inn where both Goethe and Czar Nicholas I found shelter. At No. 45 is the **Dom pod Orłem** (House at the Sign of the Eagle), where Tadeusz Kościuszko lived as a young officer in 1777; a little farther down the square, at No. 6, is the **Szary Dom** (Gray House), which he made his staff headquarters in 1794. In the house at No. 9, the young Polish noblewoman Maryna Mniszchówna married the False Dymitri, the pretender to the Russian throne, in 1605. (These events are portrayed in Pushkin's play *Boris Godunov* and in Mussorgsky's operatic adaptation of it.) At No. 16 is the **14th-century house** of the Wierzynek merchant family. In 1364, during a "summit" meeting attended by the

Holy Roman Emperor, one of the Wierzyneks gave an elaborate feast for the visiting royal dignitaries; today Wierzynek (☞ Dining, *below*) is one of Poland's better-known restaurants.

At the southwest corner of the square, the **Wież Ratuszowa** (Town Hall Tower) is all that remains of the 16th-century town hall, which was demolished in the early 19th century. The tower houses a branch of the **Kraków History Museum** and affords a panoramic view of the old city. *Tower Zł 3.* ⊙ *Tower June–Sept., Mon.–Thurs. 10–4, weekends 10–3:30.*

★ 56 **Sukiennice** (Cloth Hall). A **statue of Adam Mickiewicz** sits in front of the eastern entrance to the Renaissance Cloth Hall, which now stands in splendid near-isolation in the middle of the Main Market Square. The Gothic arches date from the 14th century, but after a fire in 1555 the upper part was rebuilt in Renaissance style. The inner arcades on the ground floor still hold traders' booths, now mainly selling local crafts. On the first floor, in a branch of the **National Museum,** you can view a collection of 19th-century Polish paintings. ✉ *Rynek Główny 1–3,* ☎ *012/422–11–66.* *Zł 3.* ⊙ *Tues.–Sat. 10–3, Thurs. 10–5:30.*

NEED A BREAK? The **Kawiarnia Noworolski** (✉ Rynek Główny 1), next to the entrance to the National Museum in the Cloth Hall, is a wonderful place to sit and watch the goings-on in the square, as well as to observe the hourly trumpet call from the tower of the Church of Our Lady.

51 **Ulica Floriańska.** The beautiful **Brama Floriańska** (Florian Gate) was built around 1300 and leads through Kraków's old city walls into ulica Floriańska, one of the streets laid out according to the town plan of 1257. The Gothic houses of the 13th-century burghers still remain, although they were rebuilt and given Renaissance or neoclassical facades. The **house at No. 24,** decorated with an emblem of three bells, was once the workshop of a bell founder. The chains hanging on the walls of the **house at No. 17** barred the streets to invaders when the city was under siege. The **Dom pod Murzynami** (Negroes' House), standing where ulica Floriańska enters the market square, is a 16th-century tenement decorated with two rather fancifully imagined African tribesmen—testimony to the fascination with Africa entertained by Europeans in the Age of Discovery.

NEED A BREAK? In the Art Nouveau café **Jama Michalikowa** (✉ Ul. Floriańska 45, ☎ 012/422–15–61), the walls are hung with caricatures by late-19th-century customers, who sometimes paid their bills in kind.

★ 61 **Ulica Kanonicza.** Kanonicza street, which leads from almost the center of town to the foot of Wawel Hill, is considered by some the most beautiful street in Europe. Most of the houses date from the 14th and 15th centuries, although they were "modernized" in Renaissance or later styles. The street was named for the many canons of Wawel Cathedral who have lived here, including Pope John Paul II, who lived in the **Chapter House** at No. 19 and later in the late-16th-century **Dean's House** at No. 21. The Chapter House now houses the **Archdiocesan Museum,** with a small collection of manuscripts. *Museum Zł 3.* ⊙ *Museum Tues.–Sat. 10–3.*

★ 62 **Wawel Cathedral.** The Wawel Hill, a rocky limestone outcrop on the banks of the Vistula, dominates the old part of the city. The hill is a raised area of about 15 acres that formed a natural point for fortification on the flat Vistula Plain. During the 8th century it was topped with a tribal stronghold, and from the 10th century it held a royal residence and served as the seat of the bishops of Kraków. Construction on Wawel Cathedral was begun in 1320, and the structure was consecrated in 1364. Little room for expansion on the hill has meant the preservation of the original austere structure, although a few Renaissance and Baroque chapels have been crowded around it. The most notable of these is the **Kaplica Zygmuntowska** (Sigismund Chapel), built in the 1520s by the Florentine architect Bartolomeo Berrecci and widely considered to be the finest Renaissance chapel north of the Alps.

From 1037, when Kraków became the capital of Poland, Polish kings were crowned and buried in the Wawel Cathedral. This tradition continued up to the time of the partitions, even after the capital had been moved to Warsaw. During the 19th century, only great national heroes were honored by a Wawel entombment: Tadeusz Kościuszko was buried here in 1817; Adam Mickiewicz and Juliusz Słowacki, both great romantic poets, were also brought back from exile to the Wawel after their deaths; and Marshal Józef Piłsudski, the hero of independent interwar Poland, was interred in the cathedral crypt in 1935.

The cathedral also has a treasury, archives, library, and museum. Among the showpieces in the library, one of the earliest in Poland, is the 12th-century *Emmeram Gospel* from Regensburg. After touring at ground level, you can climb the wooden staircase of the **Sigismund Tower,** entering through the sacristy. The tower holds the famous **Sigismund Bell,** which was commissioned in 1520 by King Sigismund the Old and is still tolled on all solemn state and church occasions. *Museum Zł 4. Mon.–Sat. 9–3, Sun. 12:15–3.*

★ 63 **Zamek Królewski** (Royal Castle). The castle that now stands on Kraków's Wawel Hill dates from the early 16th century, when the Romanesque residence that stood on this site was destroyed by fire. King Sigismund the Old brought artists and craftsmen from all over Europe to create his castle, and despite Baroque reconstruction after another fire in the late 16th century, several parts of the Renaissance castle remain, including the beautiful arcaded courtyard. After the transfer of the capital to Warsaw at the beginning of the 17th century, the castle was stripped of its fine furnishings, and later in the century it was devastated by the Swedish wars. In 1911, a voluntary Polish society purchased the castle from the Austrian authorities and began restoration. It narrowly escaped destruction in 1945, when the Nazis almost demolished it as a parting shot. Today you can visit the royal chambers, furnished in the style of the 16th and 17th centuries and hung with the 16th-century Belgian arras that during World War II was kept in Canada. The Royal Treasury on the ground floor contains a somewhat depleted collection of Polish crown jewels; the most fascinating item displayed here is the *Szczerbiec,* the jagged sword used from the early 14th century onward at the coronation of Polish kings. The Royal Armory houses a collection of Polish and Eastern arms and armor. The west wing holds an imposing collection of Turkish embroidered tents.

For many Poles, the castle's importance extends beyond its history. Hindu esoteric thinkers claim it is one of the world's mystic energy centers. Polish believers—and there have been hundreds of thousands over the last few decades—think that by rubbing up against the castle wall in the courtyard they will absorb vital energy. The stains on the wall are evidence of the strength of the belief.

Every Polish child knows the legend of the fire-breathing dragon that once terrorized local residents from his **Smocza Jama** (Dragon's Den), a cave at the foot of Wawel Hill. (Follow the signs to Smocza Jama.) The dragon threatened to destroy the town unless he was fed a damsel a week.

The king promised half his kingdom and his daughter's hand in marriage to any man who could slay the dragon. The usual quota of knights tried and failed. But finally a crafty cobbler named Skuba tricked the dragon into eating a lambskin filled with salt and sulfur. The dragon went wild with thirst, rushed into the Vistula River, and drank until it exploded. The Dragon's Den is still there, however, and in warmer months smoke and flame belch out of it every 15 minutes to thrill young visitors. A bronze statue of the dragon itself stands guard at the entrance. ✉ *Ul. Grodzka,* ☎ *012/422–16–17.* 🎫 *Royal chambers zł 12, treasury and amory zł 10, Dragon's Den zł 3.* ⏲ *Royal chambers, treasury, and armory Tues.–Thurs. and Sat. 9:30–3, Fri. 9:30–4, Sun. 10–3. Dragon's Den May–Sept., Mon.–Thurs. and weekends 10–3.*

Kazimierz

A separate city in the Middle Ages, the Jewish district of Kazimierz was settled at a time when industrious and enterprising Jews were welcomed by the Polish kings to escape persecution in Europe. Here they thrived until World War II.

A GOOD WALK

Southeast of Wawel Hill, you can take a tram from the corner of Bernadyńska and Starowiślna to the Kazimierz district (or on a pleasant day you can walk). Get off at the second tram stop on ulica Krakowska for plac Wolnica, site of the **Town Hall of Kazimierz** (65). From the plaza, head north on ulica Bożego Ciała, past the **Kościół Bożego Ciała** (66), from which the street takes its name. Turn right onto ulica Józefa, go past the Synagoga Wysoka (High Synagogue), and then turn left onto ulica Jakuba to see the Synagoga Ajzyk, which dates from 1638 and is now the Lauder Foundation Education Center. Then continue down ulica Józefa to ulica Szeroka, where you'll find the **Stara Synagoga** (Old Synagogue) (67), now the Jewish Historical Museum. Farther north along ulica Szeroka are the **Synagoga Remuh** (68) and the Jewish cemetery. Across the street, at ulica Dajwór 26, is the Synagoga Poper or Bocian, dating from 1620.

Take ulica Warszauera—noting the Synagoga Kupa, built by subscription in 1590—to ulica Estery and turn north to reach ulica Miodowa. Walk west to see the **Synagoga Tempel** (69). From here you can continue west along ulica Miodowa until you rejoin the tram route.

TIMING

The main sights of Kazimierz can be visited in a morning or afternoon. There are only two museums in the area to take up your time.

SIGHTS TO SEE

66 **Kościół Bożego Ciała** (Corpus Christi Church). This 15th-century church was used by King Charles Gustavus of Sweden as his headquarters during the Siege of Kraków in 1655. ✉ *Northeast corner of pl. Wolnica.*

67 **Stara Synagoga** (Old Synagogue). The oldest surviving example of Jewish religious architecture in Poland, this synagogue was built in the 15th century and reconstructed in Renaissance style following a fire in 1557. It was here in 1775 that Tadeusz Kościuszko successfully appealed to the Jewish community to join in the national insurrection. Looted and partly destroyed during the Nazi occupation, it has been rebuilt and now houses the **Museum of the History and Culture of Kraków Jews.** ✉ *Ul. Szeroka 24,* ☎ *012/422–09–62.* 🎫 *Zł 5.* ⏲ *Wed., Thurs., and weekends 9–3, Fri. 11–6. Closed 1st weekend of month.*

NEED A BREAK? **Alef Café** (✉ Ul. Szeroka 17, ☎ 012/421–38–70) is as close as you can get to a glimpse of the lost world of Kazimierz. Musical performances are often given here.

68 **Synagoga Remuh.** This 16th-century synagogue is still used for worship and is named after the son of its founder, Rabbi Moses Isserles, who is buried in the **cemetery** attached to the synagogue. Used by the Jewish community from 1533 to 1799, this is the only well-preserved Renaissance Jewish cemetery in Europe. (The so-called **new cemetery** on ulica Miodowa, which contains many old headstones, was established in 1800.) ✉ *Ul. Szeroka 40.* ⏲ *Mon.–Fri. 9–6.*

69 **Synagoga Tempel.** The 19th-century Reformed Tempel Synagogue is one of only two synagogues in Kraków still used for worship. ✉ *Ul. Miodowa and ul. Podbrzezie.*

65 **Town Hall of Kazimierz.** The 15th-century town hall stands in the middle of plac Wolnica. It is now the Ethnographic Museum, displaying a well-mounted collection of regional folk art. ✉ *Pl. Wolnica 1,* ☎ *012/656–28–63.* 🎫 *Zł 5.* ⏲ *Mon. 10–6, Wed.–Fri. 10–3, weekends 10–2.*

Dining

$$$$ ★ ✕ **Tetmajerowska.** Established in 1876, this second-floor restaurant sparkles with crystal and gleaming cutlery. Attentive waiters advise you in English on the different traditional Polish dishes. Try the fried eel in cream-and-dill sauce or one of the excellent veal dishes. Also part of Tetmajerowska is Hawełka, a less pricey restaurant on the ground floor. ✉ *Rynek Główny 34,* ☎ *012/422–06–31. Reservations essential. AE, DC, MC, V.*

$$$$ ★ ✕ **Wierzynek.** Though coasting on a long-outdated reputation for being Poland's finest restaurant, this 18th-century upper room on the Rynek Główny (Main Market Square) is worth a visit for those who crave a taste of old Poland. It was here after a historic meeting in 1364 that the king of Poland wined and dined Holy Roman Emperor Charles IV, five kings, and a score of princes. The menu includes a selection of wild game. ✉ *Rynek Główny 15,* ☎ *012/422–10–35. AE, DC, MC, V.*

$$$ ✕ **Padva.** Kraków's premiere Italian restaurant is considered by some to be the finest dining room in the city. It is certainly hard to argue with Padva's comprehensive Italian menu and extra efforts such as seafood that is flown in directly from Italy twice a week. ✉ *Ul. Jagiellońska 2,* ☎ *012/292–02–72. AE, DC, MC, V.*

$$$ ★ ✕ **Pod Aniołami.** Legend has it that this downstairs cellar was once an alchemist's lab. These days, "Under the Angels" is one of the more tastefully furnished restaurants in Kraków, with excellent interpretations of Polish cuisine. Try smoked ewe cheese warmed under the grill, then the delectable Mr. John's Ribs. Patrons crowd onto the upstairs courtyard when the weather is warm. ✉ *Ul. Grodzka 35,* ☎ *012/421–39–99. Reservations essential. AE, DC, MC, V.*

$$ ★ ✕ **Cherubino.** Cherubino must have one of the most intriguing menus in Kraków, with a combination of Tuscan cuisine and lighter, more contemporary interpretations of Polish cuisine. The decor is also memorable: you can choose to dine under a winged boat or in one of four beautifully restored 19th-century carriages. ✉ *Ul. św. Tomasza 15,* ☎ *012/429–40–07. Reservations essential. AE, DC, MC, V.*

$$ ★ ✕ **Chłopskie Jadło.** This restaurant's name means "Peasant Kitchen," but this is the most upscale interpretation of that theme imaginable. All meals come with complimentary bread and lard, and the menu is an artery-clogging cross-section of traditional Polish peasant cuisine. For a starter try the stone soup, then indulge in the very traditional main course of cabbage rolls stuffed with sauerkraut and grits in a mushroom sauce. ✉ *Ul. św. Agnieszki 1,* ☎ *012/421–85–20. Reservations essential. AE, DC, MC, V.*

Kraków Dining and Lodging

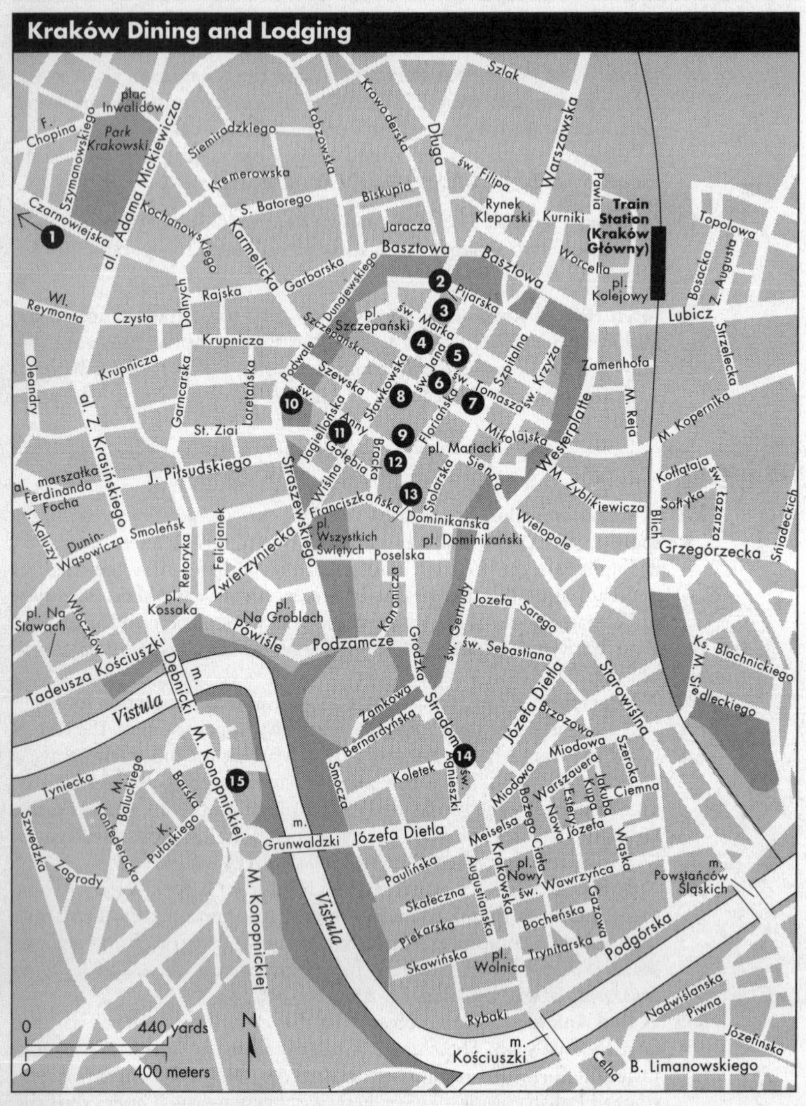

Dining

Cherubino 6
Chimera Salad Bar 10
Chłopskie Jadło 14
Padva 11
Pod Aniołami 13
Tetmajerowska 8
U Babci Maliny. . . . 3
Wierzynek 9

Lodging

Continental. 1
Elektor 7
Forum 15
Francuski 2
Grand 4
Pod Różą 5
Rezydent 12

$ ✕ **Chimera Salad Bar.** In a downstairs cellar with arras and Victorian etchings on its walls, you'll find Kraków's most upmarket salad bar. The nourishing salads are a tremendous value, and cooked meals are available from the more formal restaurant upstairs. ✉ *Ul. św. Anny 3,* ☎ *012/429–11–68.*

$ ✕ **U Babci Maliny.** A rough translation of this restaurant's name is "Your Grandmother Malina." No doubt Granny would be proud to see all the student types and businesspeople dining on the cheap, hearty Polish fare. U Babci Maliny may not be for the calorie conscious, but it's a quick, affordable, and more pleasant alternative to the traditional milk bar. ✉ *Ul. Sławkowska 17,* ☎ *012/422–70–66.*

Lodging

Kraków remains lamentably short on first-class accommodations close to the city center. Some satisfactory midrange hotels have sprung up in the last year or so, but visitors should still book well in advance—even in winter, because then the city plays host to many business conferences. If you're staying in the Old Town, rooms facing the street can be noisy at night, so request a quiet room.

$$$$ **Elektor.** With an enviable location diagonal from the exquisite Słowacki Theater, and just a stone's throw from the Rynek Główny (Main Market Square), the Elektor is still a little overpriced for what it actually offers. The employees behave more like graduates of butler training school than modern-day hospitality staff. There's an annex close to the main hotel with one- or two-bedroom apartments for longer-term guests. ✉ *Ul. Szpitalna 28, 31–024,* ☎ *012/423–23–17,* FAX *012/423–23–27. 9 rooms, 12 suites. Restaurant, bar. AE, DC, MC, V.*

$$$ **Continental.** This high-rise hotel lies on the highway from Kraków to the industrial sprawl of Katowice. Once a Holiday Inn, the Continental went its own way in 1999, but doesn't seem to have lost by it. The hotel staff are efficient and multilingual, and the rooms are pleasant and comfortable. It's near parkland and sporting facilities, and thus is a good choice for travelers who like an early morning run before setting out to explore. ✉ *Al. Armii Krajowej 11, 30–150,* ☎ *012/637–50–44,* FAX *012/637–59–38. 304 rooms. Restaurant, indoor pool, beauty salon, massage, sauna, casino. AE, DC, MC, V.*

$$$ **Forum.** Perched on giant concrete stilts and facing the Vistula River and the Zamek Królewski (Royal Castle), the Forum seems something of an architectural relic from the 1970s. Inside, however, is a contemporary, bustling hotel. There are bars, a restaurant, a casino, and a nightclub to play in, though the latter has a somewhat shady reputation. Popular with tour groups and businesspeople, the hotel also has the city's best sports facilities. ✉ *Ul. Marii Konopnickiej 28, 30–302,* ☎ *012/261–92–12,* FAX *012/269–00–80. 260 rooms, 15 suites. Restaurant, 2 bars, indoor pool, sauna, 2 tennis courts, casino, nightclub. AE, DC, MC, V.*

$$$ **Grand.** Without question this hotel around the corner from Kraków's main square is the most elegant address for visitors to the city and the one most accessible to the major sights. The decor is Regency inspired, though most of the furnishings are reproductions. Suite 11 has two large bathrooms, a gilded ceiling, and a bedroom fit for a potentate. The banquet room has its own miniature hall of mirrors. ✉ *Ul. Sławkowska 5–7, 31–016,* ☎ *012/421–72–55,* FAX *012/421–83–60. 50 rooms, 6 suites. Restaurant, bar, café. AE, DC, MC, V.*

$$$ ★ **Pod Różą.** The management is still proud that both Chopin and Czar Alexander I slept here. Housed in a 14th-century building, the hotel offers guests spacious, high-ceilinged rooms on the fashionable shopping street Floriańska. The first-class Italian restaurant and 15th-cen-

tury wine cellar add to the Pod Różą's attractions. ✉ *Ul. Floriańska 14, 31–021,* ☎ *012/422–12–44,* FAX *012/421–75–13. 51 rooms, 3 apartments. Restaurant. AE, DC, MC, V.*

$$ ★ **Francuski.** The Francuski's sweeping spiral staircase leads up from the large high-ceilinged reception area to rooms decorated in faux fin-de-siècle grandeur. ✉ *Ul. Pijarska 13, 31–015,* ☎ *012/422–51–22,* FAX *012/422–52–70. 27 rooms, 15 suites. Restaurant. AE, DC, MC, V.*

$$ **Rezydent.** Upmarket but reasonably priced, the Rezydent resides in a medieval building where Kraków's Royal Route converges with the Main Market Square. The spacious, contemporary interiors are all fresh white and pastels, with plenty of well-tended pot plants adding a natural touch. ✉ *Ul. Grodzka 9, 31–015,* ☎ *012/429–54–95,* FAX *012/429–55–76. 49 rooms, 1 suite. Restaurant. AE, DC, MC, V.*

Nightlife and the Arts

Kraków has a lively tradition in theater and music. Pick up a copy of *Karnet,* which gives detailed cultural information in Polish and English, or *Kraków In Your Pocket,* which has a reasonably comprehensive entertainment calendar and is available in kiosks all over town.

Nightlife

BARS

Le Fumoir (✉ Ul. Sławkowska 26) is a sedate piano and cigar bar upstairs from a high-toned French restaurant. **O'Morgan's Irish Pub** (✉ Ul. Garncarska 5) is headquarters for Kraków's English-speaking community. At trendy **Paparazzi** (✉ Ul. Mikołajska 9) you can observe Kraków's beautiful people in action. **Pasja** (✉ Ul. Szewska 5) is an agreeably unpretentious disco in a cellar.

CABARET AND JAZZ

At **Jama Michalika** (✉ Ul. Floriańska 45) popular musical and comedic cabarets take place in a café that has remained essentially the same for a century. The underground venue **Klub Indigo** (✉ Ul. Floriańska 26) simulcasts concerts by Polish and international musicians on Poland's Jazz Radio. **Loch Camelot** (✉ Ul. św. Tomasza 17) is a traditional Polish café with regular cabaret performances held in its basement. The cabaret at **Pod Baranami** (✉ Rynek Główny 27) was founded in 1956 by Kraków theater legend Piotr Skrzynecki. Jazz sessions are regularly held at **U Muniaka** (✉ Floriańska 3).

The Arts

FILM

Kraków Cinema Centre ARS (✉ Ul. św. Jana 6, ☎ 012/421–41–99) shows movies from Hollywood and Europe, almost always in the original language with Polish subtitles. The center also screens contemporary Polish films.

MUSIC

Kraków's symphony, Filharmonia im. Karola Szymanowskiego, gives frequent concerts in the **Philharmonic Hall** (✉ Ul. Zwierzyniecka 1, ☎ 012/422–94–77). On Saturday the hall hosts special matinee performances for children. If you're a fan of chamber music, there are occasional performances in the great hall of the Zamek Królewski (Royal Castle) on Wawel Hill (☞ Exploring Kraków, *above*).

OPERA AND DANCE

The stunning **Teatr im. Juliusza Słowackiego** (Słowacki Theater; ✉ Pl. św. Ducha 1, ☎ 012/422–43–22), across from the Elektor Hotel, hosts traditional opera and ballet favorites as well as dramatic performances.

THEATER

The popular **Bagatela** (✉ Ul. Karmelicka 6, ☎ 012/422–45–44) is a venue for children's theater as well as adult drama and farce. **Scena pod Ratuszem** (✉ Wież Ratuszowa, ☎ 012/421–16–57), a tiny theater in the cellar of the Town Hall Tower, stages small-scale dramas in front of a bare-brick backdrop. The **Stary Teatr** (✉ Ul. Jagiellońska 5, ☎ 012/422–85–66) is Kraków's oldest and most renowned theater.

Outdoor Activities and Sports

Hiking

The Niepołomice Forest (☞ Małopolska, *below*) has extensive hiking trails over flat, sandy terrain. Ojców National Park (☞ Małopolska, *below*) has marked trails for hikers, some of which are steep and fairly rough.

Jogging

If you want to jog in Kraków, the Planty, a ring of gardens around the Old Town, makes an excellent 5 km (3 mi) route and is easily accessible from most hotels. The pathways along the Vistula also provide a good jogging route: west of the Dębnicki Bridge, take the path on the right bank; east of the bridge, the one on the left bank.

Shopping

In Kraków's Old Town, department stores and brand-name fashion and leisure-wear stores are on the increase, while the number of craft and specialty shops is declining. Most shops are open weekdays from 10 to 6, Saturday 9 to 2.

For regionally produced goods, head to the Rynek Główny (Main Market Square). **Calik** (✉ Rynek Główny 7) sells the world-famous handpainted Christopher Radko Christmas ornaments—all year round. At the **Sukiennice booths** you'll find tooled leather goods, local crystal and glass, wood carvings, and the embroidered felt slippers made in the Podhale region. Rabbit-skin slippers are also a local specialty.

Kraków A to Z

Arriving and Departing

BY BUS

Express bus service to Kraków runs regularly from most Polish cities. From the main PKS bus station in Warsaw (☞ Arriving and Departing by Bus *in* Warsaw A to Z, *above*) the journey takes three hours. Buses arrive at the **main PKS station** (✉ Ul. Worcella, ☎ 012/936), just across from the train station on Plac Kolejowy. From here you can transfer to buses headed for other destinations in the region.

BY CAR

A car will not be of much use to you in Kraków, since most of the Old Town is closed to traffic and distances between major sights are short. A car will be invaluable, however, if you set out to explore the rest of the region. You can approach Kraków either on the E77 highway (from Warsaw and north) or via the E40 (from the area around Katowice). Use the parking facilities at your hotel or one of the attended municipal parking garages (try plac Szczepański or plac świętego Ducha).

BY PLANE

Kraków can be reached by direct flight from most major European cities. The **Balice Airport** (☎ 012/411–19–55), 11 km (7 mi) west of the city, is the region's only airport. In spring and fall fog can cause frustrating delays. Bus 208 runs between the airport and the train station.

LOT (✉ Ul. Basztowa 15, ☎ 012/422–42–15 or 012/422–66–83), the Polish airline, flies daily to Balice Airport from Warsaw; the flight takes 40 minutes. LOT's Kraków office is open weekdays from 9 to 6, Saturday 9 to 3.

BY TRAIN

Nonstop express trains from Warsaw take just under three hours and run throughout the day. Trains arrive at **Kraków Główny station** (✉ Pl. Dworcowy 1, ☎ 012/9436) on the edge of the Old Town.

Getting Around

Kraków's sights are best reached on foot. The Old Town area is relatively compact, and much of it is closed to traffic.

Contacts and Resources

CONSULATES

U.S. Consulate (✉ Ul. Stolarska 9, ☎ 012/429–66–55).

EMERGENCIES

Police (☎ 997). **Ambulance** (☎ 999).

GUIDED TOURS

All major hotels will arrange tours of the city as well as surrounding attractions. For tours of Jewish Kraków go to **Jarden Tours** (✉ Ul. Szeroka 2, ☎ 012/421–13–74). **Orbis** (✉ Rynek Główny 41, ☎ 012/422–11–57), through its subsidiary, Cracow Tours, organizes tours by bus, minibus, or limousine, at prices ranging from $30 for a half-day coach tour to $140 for a full-day tour in a chauffeur-driven car. Throughout the year they lead half-day visits to the Nazi concentration camp at Oświęcim (Auschwitz) or the Wieliczka salt mine, half-day tours of Kraków, and junkets to the Ojców National Park. In the summer they also offer a day trip to the Dunajec River gorge (including a journey down the river by raft). Orbis will also arrange day trips to the pope's birthplace at Wadowice, to the Bernadine Monastery at Kalwaria Zebrzydowska, and to the Pauline Monastery at Częstochowa.

LATE-NIGHT PHARMACIES

Nonstop (✉ Ul. Duwajewskiego 2, ☎ 012/422–65–04) is centrally located and open 24 hours.

VISITOR INFORMATION

The **Tourist Information Center** (✉ Ul. Pawia 8, ☎ 012/422–60–91) is open weekdays from 8 to 4. To change money and purchase air, train, and bus tickets, head to **Orbis** (✉ Hotel Cracovia, al. Focha 1, ☎ 012/421–98–80; Rynek Główny 41, ☎ 012/422–11–57), open weekdays from 9 to 5, Saturday 9 to 2.

MAŁOPOLSKA

Just to the south of Kraków, Poland's great plains give way to the gently folding foothills of the Carpathians, building to the High Tatras on the Slovak border. The fine medieval architecture of many towns in Małopolska (Little Poland) comes from a period when the area prospered as the intersection of thriving trade routes. In the countryside, wooden homesteads and strip-farmed tracts tell another story: of the hardships and poverty the peasantry endured before the 20th century brought tourists to the mountains. During the 19th century, when this part of Poland was under Austrian rule as the province of Western Galicia, hundreds of thousands of peasants fled from the grinding toil on poor soil to seek their fortune in the United States; it sometimes seems as if every family hereabouts has a cousin in America.

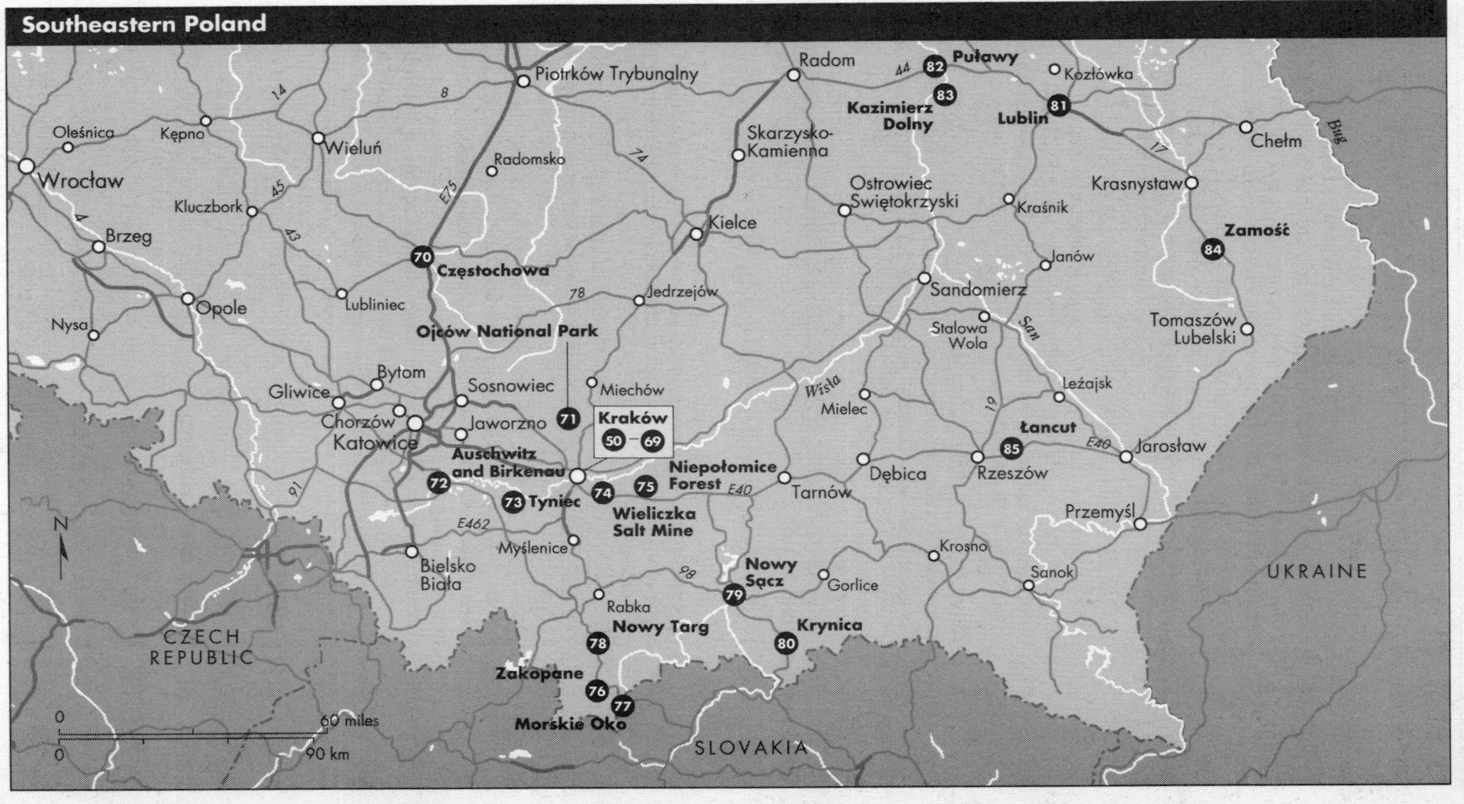
Southeastern Poland
Piotrków Trybunalny
Radom
44
82
Puławy
Kozłówka
83
Kazimierz Dolny
81
Lublin
Bug
Chełm
17
14
8
Oleśnica
Kępno
Wieluń
Radomsko
74
Skarżysko-Kamienna
Wrocław
E75
45
Kluczbork
Ostrowiec Świętokrzyski
Kraśnik
Krasnystaw
4
Brzeg
43
Kielce
Zamość
84
70
Częstochowa
Janów
78
Jedrzejów
Sandomierz
Opole
Lubliniec
Stalowa Wola
San
Tomaszów Lubelski
Nysa
Ojców National Park
Bytom
Sosnowiec
Miechów
Wisła
Leżajsk
Gliwice
Mielec
19
Chorzów
Jaworzno
71
Kraków
50
69
Łancut
Katowice
85
E40
Jarosław
Auschwitz and Birkenau
Niepołomice Forest
Dębica
Rzeszów
72
74
75
E40
Tarnów
91
73
Tyniec
Wieliczka Salt Mine
Przemyśl
N
E462
Myślenice
Krosno
Bielsko Biała
98
Nowy Sącz
Gorlice
Sanok
UKRAINE
79
Rabka
Krynica
Nowy Targ
CZECH REPUBLIC
78
80
Zakopane
76
77
0
60 miles
Morskie Oko
0
90 km
SLOVAKIA

A visit to Kraków and Małopolska is incomplete without trips to at least two nearby destinations: the Wieliczka Salt Mine, where salt has been mined for a thousand years, and Auschwitz and Birkenau, sites of the Nazis' most gruesome and brutal concentration camps. Farther afield are Ojców National Park and Zakopane, both of which offer first-rate hiking in unadulterated natural surroundings. This is also Poland's main winter sports area. Zakopane is the self-styled winter capital of Poland, and the spa towns of Szczawnica, Krościenko, and Krynica are good bases for cross-country skiing. If you've been looking for insight into the devout Catholicism of the Poles, head to Częstochowa, where 5 million people a year come to pray before a painting of the Virgin Mary and baby Jesus known as the Black Madonna.

Małopolska remains intensely Catholic and conservative, and the traditional way of life in the countryside is relatively intact. Folk crafts and customs are still very much alive in the mountains and foothills (*podhale*): carved-wood beehives stand in mountain gardens and worshipers set out for Sunday church in embroidered white-felt trousers.

This is one of the only regions in Poland where you'll find a number of inexpensive bed-and-breakfast accommodations in private pensions. Pensions (generally small hotels) usually offer full board and hearty meals.

Numbers in the margin correspond to numbers on the Southeastern Poland map.

Częstochowa

70 *120 km (74 mi) northwest of Kraków, 220 km (136 mi) southwest of Warsaw.*

An estimated 5 million pilgrims a year make their way, some on foot,
★ to the town of Częstochowa. They come to see the 14th-century **Klasztor Paulinów** (Pauline Monastery) at the Jasna Góra (Hill of Light). There is little else to draw visitors here, and this rather industrial town lives in the monastery's somber shadow. Inside the monastery is Poland's holiest shrine, the famous *Black Madonna of Częstochowa,* an early 15th-century painting of a dark-skinned Madonna and child, the origins of which are uncertain (legend attributes the work to Luke the Apostle himself). This holy relic has a number of miracles attributed to it, including the repulsion of invading Swedish forces in the 16th century. The Black Madonna's designation as savior of Poland dates from those turbulent days. To see the Black Madonna, you have to join the faithful and walk on your knees behind a screen, where the eyes of the Black Madonna, according to believers, will fix directly on you. The monastery was rebuilt in Baroque style during the 17th and 18th centuries, as was the interior of the Gothic church. The **Monastery Treasury** holds an important collection of manuscripts and works of art. ✉ *Al. Najświętszej Marii Panny 1.* ⏲ *Treasury daily 11–1 and 3–5.*

Dining and Lodging

$ ✕ **Wiking.** You can take in the local color at this crowded restaurant. Try the herring in cream as a starter, followed by chicken with potatoes. ✉ *Ul. Nowowiejska,* ☎ *034/324–57–68. No credit cards.*

$$ 🏨 **Orbis Patria Hotel.** This six-story 1980s hotel offers predictable Orbis cuisine and accommodations. Rooms are brightly furnished and comfortable, the staff cheerful and friendly. ✉ *Ul. Popiełuszki 2, 42–200,* ☎ *034/324–70–01,* FAX *034/324–63–32. 96 rooms, 6 suites. Restaurant, tennis court, volleyball. AE, DC, MC, V.*

$ 🏨 **Hotel Inter.** This modern hotel is privately owned and reasonably priced. There is satellite TV in every room, and there's a small fitness center. ✉ *Ul. Marszalka E. Rydza-Smiglego 26–34, 42–225,* ☎ *034/*

366–02–67, FAX 034/366–04–57. 17 rooms, 40 beds. Exercise room. AE, DC, MC, V.

Ojców National Park

71 *48 km (30 mi) northwest of Kraków.*

This national park covers the limestone gorge of the Prudnik River. The ridge above the gorge is topped by a series of ruined castles that once guarded the trade route from Kraków to Silesia. Of these the best preserved is the Renaissance castle **Pieskowa Skała,** which now houses a branch of the Wawel Museum Art Collection. Admission to the museum is Zł 4, and it's open from Tuesday to Sunday 10–3:30.

Caves in the limestone rock are linked with many legends. In one, Władysław the Short, a medieval Polish king, is supposed to have escaped his German pursuers with the help of a spider that spun a web over the mouth of the cave in which he was hiding. You can visit **Władysław the Short's cave** for Zł 45 from May through September, daily from 8 to 7. The gorge is at its best in autumn, when shades of gold and red stand out against the white limestone. *Take the E40 northwest and turn off at Jerzmanowice for Pieskowa Skała. PKS buses leave regularly from the bus station on pl. Kolejowy in Kraków.*

Auschwitz and Birkenau

★ 72 *50 km (31 mi) southwest of Ojców National Park, 60 km (38 mi) west of Kraków.*

Between 1940 and 1945 more than 1.5 million people, 90% of them Jews from Poland and throughout Europe, died here in the Nazis' largest death-camp complex. The camp in the small town of Oświęcim (better known by its German name, Auschwitz) has come to be seen as the epicenter of the moral collapse of the West, proof of the human capacity for tremendous evil. The gas chambers at nearby Brzezinka (Birkenau) could exterminate thousands in a single day. The first inmates were Polish political prisoners, and the first gas victims were Russian POWs; the dead eventually included Jews, Romanies (Gypsies), homosexuals, Jehovah's Witnesses, and so-called criminals.

The *Konzentrationslager* (concentration camp) had three parts: Auschwitz, Birkenau, and Monowitz (where a chemical plant was run by prison labor). The barracks at **Auschwitz** have been completely restored and made into a museum, which has been described by one survivor, the author Primo Levi, as "something static, rearranged, contrived." With that in mind, begin with the heart-rending **movie** filmed by Soviet troops on January 27, 1945, the day they liberated the few prisoners left behind by the retreating Germans. The English version runs a few times a day, although narration isn't really necessary. Purchase a guidebook in English (most exhibits are in Polish or German) and walk through the notorious gate marked ARBEIT MACHT FREI (Work Brings Freedom). The most provocative exhibits are the huge piles of belongings confiscated from victims, as well as the two tons of human hair intended for use in the German textile industry. The execution wall, the prison block, and the reconstructed crematorium at the end of the tour are harshly sobering. ✉ *Ul. Więźniów Oświęcimia 20, Oświęcim (from Kraków take Hwy. E22a or the train or bus from pl. Kolejowy),* ☎ *033/432–022.* *Free, film zł 1.5.* ⏲ *Museum daily 8–7.*

Far more affecting than Auschwitz are the unaltered barracks, electric fences, and blown-up gas chambers at the enormous **Birkenau** camp 3 km (2 mi) away. More prisoners lived and died here than at Auschwitz including hundreds of thousands who went directly to the gas chambers from boxcars in which they had been locked up for days. The camp has been preserved to look much the way it did after the Nazis abandoned it. A walk to the back area brings you to the **Monument to the Glory of the Victims,** designed by Polish and Italian artists and erected in 1967. Behind the trees to the right of the monument lies a farm pond, its banks still murky with human ashes and bone fragments. To hear the tape on the camp's history in English, ask the reception staff in the main guardhouse. *Free. Daily 9–4.*

Tyniec

73 *43 km (27 mi) east of Oświęcim, 16 km (10 mi) southwest of Kraków.*

The **Benedictine Abbey** at Tyniec is perched high on a cliff above the Vistula River. From this fortified cloister, the Confederates of Bar set off in 1772 to raid Kraków; as a result the abbey was destroyed later that year by the Russian army. In 1817 the Benedictine order was banned, and the monks disbanded. It was not until 1939 that the order recovered the land, and not until the late 1960s that it again became an abbey and the work of reconstruction began in earnest. From May to September recitals of organ music are held in the abbey church. *From Kraków take Hwy. 7(E77) south to Hwy. A4, then take A4 about 4 km (2½ mi) to Tyniec; or take Bus 112 from most Grunwaldzki, near the Forum Hotel. Daily 9–4.*

Wieliczka Salt Mine

★ 74 *12 km (7½ mi) southeast of Kraków on the E40.*

During the 11th century, Wieliczka was owned by the Benedictines of Tyniec abbey, who drew a large part of their income from its revenues. By the 14th century the salt was so prized that King Kazimierz the Great built city walls with 11 defense towers at Wieliczka to protect the mines from Tartar raids. There are historic galleries and chambers 150 yards below ground level, including underground lakes and underground chapels carved by medieval miners, the most magnificent of which is the **Chapel of the Blessed Kinga** (Kinga was a 14th-century Polish queen). Serious flooding in 1992 brought commercial salt production to a halt, but the historic part of the mine is open to visitors. ✉ *Ul. Daniłowicza 10, Wieliczka (take a minibus from right outside the Kraków train station),* ☎ *012/278–73–02. Zł 26. Daily 8–4.*

Niepołomice Forest

75 *12 km (7½ mi) east of Wieliczka, 25 km (15 mi) east of Kraków.*

The town of Niepołomice is on the western edge of the forest and has a 14th-century **hunting lodge** and **church** built by Kazimierz the Great. Animals, including bison, still live in the forest, and you may be lucky enough to see some of them as you stroll under the ancient oak trees. *From Kraków take the E40 east and turn north at Wieliczka, or take a PKS bus or train from pl. Kolejowy. On summer weekends Kraków city transport also runs special buses to Niepołomice from pl. Kolejowy. Church dawn–dusk.*

Zakopane

★ 76 *100 km (62 mi) south of Kraków on Hwy. E95.*

Nestled at the foot of the Tatra Mountains, 3,281 ft above sea level, Zakopane is the highest town in Poland (it's the southernmost as well). Until the 19th-century romantic movement started a fashion for mountain scenery, Zakopane was a poor and remote village. During the 1870s, when the Tatra Association was founded, people began coming to the mountains for their health and recreation, and Zakopane developed into Poland's leading mountain resort. At the turn of the 20th century it was home to many writers, painters, and musicians. Stanisław Wyspiański based his best-known drama, *Wesele* (*Wedding,* 1901), on his experiences here. Stanisław Witkiewicz (Witkacy), the artist and playwright, lived here and was responsible for creating the elaborate carved-wood architecture that he called the Zakopane style.

The town is small, and its sights can easily be covered on foot. Ulica Krupówki, the main thoroughfare, runs downhill through the town from northwest to southeast. If you begin at the northwest end, you will pass many buildings in the Zakopane style. Ulica Kościuszki runs east to west across Krupówki and links the town with the railway and bus stations. At the bottom of the hill is ulica Kościeliska.

A cable railway can take you from the center of town up to the high ridge of **Gubałówka,** where on a clear day you will have a fine view of the Tatras and of the town. An alternative to riding the cable car back into town is to take the path along the ridge to Pałkówka and from there back down into town, about 9 km (5½ mi). Children can have their photograph taken on the Gubałówka **terrace** in a carriage drawn by four white mountain sheepdogs and driven by a man dressed in a white bearskin. *The cable railway station is down from the corner of ulica Krupówki and ulica Kościeliska.*

At the foot of the hill in town is the mid-19th-century wooden **Kościół świętego Klemensa** (Church of St. Clement), the first church built in Zakopane. Witkiewicz is buried in the adjoining cemetery. ✉ *Ul. Kościeliska opposite ul. Kasprusie.*

The **Muzeum Tatrzańskie** (Tatra Museum) on Zakopane's main street has two replicas of typical highland dwellings, mountain crafts, and a collection of Zakopane's flora and fauna. The first room is a portrait gallery of local heroes and famous visitors to Zakopane, including writer Joseph Conrad and nationalist hero Józef Piłsudski. Ask for an explanatory cassette in English. ✉ *Ul. Krupówki 10,* ☎ *018/201–52–05.* 🎫 *Zł 3.* ⏲ *Wed.–Sun. 9–4.*

The **Willa Atma,** a wooden villa in Zakopane style, was home to the Polish composer Karol Szymanowski in the 1920s. It is now a museum dedicated to his life and work. ✉ *Ul. Kasprusie 19,* ☎ *018/206–31–50.* 🎫 *Zł 1.* ⏲ *Tues., Wed., and Fri.–Sun. 10–4, Thurs. 2–8.*

Witkiewicz's very first project in the Zakopane style was the **Willa Koliba,** now a museum. ✉ *Muzeum Stylu Zakopańskiego im. Stanisława Witkiewicza, ul. Kościeliska 18,* ☎ *018/201–36–02.* 🎫 *Zł 3.* ⏲ *Wed.–Sun. 9–4.*

Another of Witkiewicz's Zakopane buildings is **Willa pod Jedlami.** This elaborate villa is considered one of his most ambitious works. ✉ *Ul. Koziniec 1.*

OFF THE BEATEN PATH

DOLINA KOŚCIELISKA (Kościeliska Valley) – Nine kilometers (5 mi) southwest of Zakopane on the road to Kiry and Witów, this valley falls within the Tatrzański Park Narodowy (Tatra National Park), which covers the entire mountain range in both Poland and Slovakia. Remember that you are not allowed to pick flowers here—a strong temptation in spring, when the lower valley is covered with crocuses. The first part of the valley runs for roughly a mile through flat, open pasture, before the stream that gave the valley its name begins its descent through steep, rocky gorges. It ends at **Ornak**, 5½ km (3½ mi) from the road, where there are splendid views. Horse-drawn carriages (sleighs in winter) wait at the entrance to take visitors halfway up the valley (for about zł 30), but if you want to reach Ornak, you must cover the last stage on foot. **Harnaś** is a bar at the entrance to the valley, where locals come to drink beer and where dishes such as *fasolka po bretońsku* (Breton baked beans) or bigos are available from 8 AM to 10 PM. ✉ *Take a bus from Zakopane's PKS bus station on ul. Kościuszki to Kiry.*

BUKOWINA TATRZAŃSKA – A village built largely out of wood and set high on a ridge 13 km (8 mi) northeast of Zakopane, Bukowina Tatrzańska was once famed for its number of beekeepers and its honey. The path at the top of the ridge, parallel to the main road to Łysa Polana, affords spectacular views of the Tatra range and is a favored spot for winter sunbathing. ✉ *Bukowina can easily be reached by PKS bus from the Zakopane station on ul. Kościuszki. By car, take E95 (the main road to Kraków) north from Zakopane, and after 5 km (3 mi) turn east onto Hwy. 961, which leads to the border crossing point at Polana. The left turn into the village of Bukowina is clearly marked.*

Dining and Lodging

$$$ ✕ **Giewont.** The dining room in the Giewont Hotel is high-ceilinged and galleried, decorated with crystal chandeliers and crisp white tablecloths on well-spaced tables. Service is elegant and discreet. The game dishes are the best items on the menu; try the roast pheasant when it's in season. ✉ *Ul. Kościuszki 1,* ☎ *018/201–20–11. AE, DC, MC, V.*

$$ ✕ **Czarny Staw.** Hearty mountain fare in the traditional Zakopane "rustic" style is the trademark of the "Black Pond." The restaurant's specialty is fish, especially the mountain trout that comes to you on a large, fish-shape wooden bowl. Traditionally dressed staff prepare meat on an open grill in the middle of the room. ✉ *Ul. Krupówki 2,* ☎ *018/201–38–56. AE, DC, MC, V.*

$$ ★ ✕ **Zbójecka.** Of all the restaurants in traditional Zakopane style, this is the most inviting. A set of stairs leads down to a large basement, bathed in light and warmth from a fireplace and an open grill. Diners sink back into wool-covered chairs and enjoy a selection of carnivorous delights, snug and warm and a century away from the bustle of ulica Krupówki. ✉ *Ul. Krupówki 28,* ☎ *018/201–38–54. AE, DC, MC, V.*

$$$ ★ 🏨 **Litwor.** This is one of the best hotels in Małopolska. The rooms have all the amenities you could crave, including towel warmers and heated floors in the plush bathrooms. Perhaps best of all, the friendly staff seem to enjoy perfecting their English. ✉ *Ul. Krupówki 11, 34–500,* ☎ *018/201–71–89,* FAX *018/201–71–90. 49 rooms, 6 suites. Restaurant, bar, indoor pool, tennis court, health club, business services, convention center. AE, DC, MC, V.*

$$ 🏨 **Giewont.** This late-19th-century hotel is right in the center of town. The rooms are furnished in traditional style but vary greatly in size; it's a good idea to see the room before moving in. Try to get a room with a view of the peak after which the hotel is named. ✉ *Ul. Kościuszki 1, 34–500,* ☎ *018/201–20–11,* FAX *018/201–20–15. 44 rooms. Restaurant. AE, DC, MC, V.*

$$ 🏨 **Sabala** This large, historic hotel was built in 1897 in the then emerging Zakopane style and named after a renowned 19th-century violinist. The rooms have been furnished completely in wood—and then treated in beeswax. ✉ *Ul. Krupówki 11, 34–500,* ☎ *018/201–50–92,* FAX *018/201–50–93. 20 rooms. Restaurant. AE, DC, MC, V.*

Nightlife and the Arts

Zakopane's theatrical and musical performances are often connected with the artists and writers who made the town their home, particularly Witkiewicz and Karol Szymanowski. Posters on kiosks announce performances. Traditional local folk orchestras also perform regularly. As for nightlife, Zakopane is not the all-night town that Kraków is, but there are some interesting new additions to the scene.

BARS

Caffe Sanacja (✉ Ul. Krupówki 45) is a dark wooden enclave for the small but vibrant artistic community. **Paparazzi** (✉ Ul. Gen Galicy 8), the sibling of Kraków's Paparazzi, is Zakopane's après-ski alternative to folksy traditionalism. **Pstrąg Jazz Club** (✉ Ul. Jagiellońska 18) is an eclectically furnished jazz venue hidden under the Warszawianka hotel.

MUSIC

The **Kulczycki Gallery** (✉ Ul. Koziniec 8, ☎ 018/201–29–36) occasionally hosts concerts and other events. Concerts are also sometimes given at the **Willa Atma** (✉ Ul. Kasprusie 19, ☎ 018/206–31–50). A festival of Szymanowski's music, with concerts all over town, is held in July, and an autumn music festival is held in September and October.

THEATER

The **Teatr im. Stanisława Ignacego Witkiewicza** (✉ Ul. Chramcówki 15, ☎ 018/206–82–97) has two stages and often brings in well-known actors for the season.

Outdoor Activities and Sports

BIKING

Mountain biking has become increasingly popular in the area. You can hire a bike at **Sport & Fun Company Ltd** (✉ Rondo 1, ☎ 018/201–56–03) for zł 50 per day. **Rent a bike** (✉ Ul. Sienkiewicza 37, ☎ 018/201–42–66) has a small selection of mountain bikes available.

HIKING

The Gorczański, Pieniński, and Tatrzański (Tatra) national parks all have hiking territory. The routes are well marked, and there are maps at entrance points that give the distances, times, and degrees of difficulty of the trails. On the lower reaches of trails out of major tourist points (such as Zakopane, Szczawnica, and Krynica), walkers crowd the paths, but they thin out as you go higher up.

JOGGING

In Zakopane the **Droga pod Reglami,** which runs along the foot of the Tatra National Park, makes a relatively flat jogging route; it can be approached from various points in the town.

SKIING

Zakopane acquired snow-making facilities in 1990 and is still the region's major center for downhill skiing, although Krynica and Krościenko also have facilities. You'll find the most advanced runs at **Kasprowy Wierch** mountain, accessed via a cable lift from Łozienice (☎ 018/201–45–10 lower station; 018/201–44–05 upper station). Chairlifts also bring skiers to the peaks of **Butory Wierch** (✉ Lift at ul. Powstańców Śląskich, ☎ 018/201–39–41) and **Nosal** (✉ Ul. Balzera, ☎ 018/201–31–81). Tickets can be hard to come by in season, and it may be easier to get them at **Orbis** (✉ Ul. Krupówki 22), although you'll pay a surcharge of 30%.

Shopping

Leather and sheepskin products are local specialties, along with hand-knit socks, sweaters, and caps in white, gray, and black patterns made from rough, undyed wool. The best places to look are at the **Zakopane market,** held at the foot of ulica Krupówki, on the way to the Gubałówka cable railway. Wednesday is the main market day, but some stalls are here all week. Street vendors are around daily and charge higher prices, as they do throughout the region. **Limba** (✉ Ul. Kościeliska 1) has a fine assortment of handmade local costumes, as well as smaller items such as belts and walking sticks.

Morskie Oko

77 *30 km (20 mi) southeast of Zakopane.*

Morskie Oko is the largest and loveliest of the lakes in the High Tatras, 4,570 ft above sea level. The name means "Eye of the Sea," and an old legend claims it has a secret underground passage connecting it to the ocean. The **Mięguszowiecki** and **Mnich** peaks appear to rise straight up from the water, and the depth of the lake permanently colors it an intense blue. *Orbis in Zakopane runs a regular bus service to within 10 minutes' walk of the lake. If you feel more energetic, you can take a PKS bus from the bus station to Łysa Polana and follow the marked trail for 8 km (5 mi).*

Dining and Lodging

$ ✕🏨 **Schronisko im. Stanisława Staszica.** A climbers' and hikers' hostel, this establishment has a restaurant that serves large portions of such basic fare as fasolka po bretońsku or pancakes with whipped cream. You can obtain a bed in a spartan, clean, three-, four-, five-, or six-person room for as little as $5. ✉ *Box 201, Zakopane, 34–500,* ☎ *018/207–76–09. No credit cards.*

Nowy Targ

78 *24 km (15 mi) north of Zakopane, 90 km (56 mi) south of Kraków.*

The unofficial capital of the Podhale region, Nowy Targ has been a chartered borough since the 14th century, when it stood at an intersection of international trade routes, and it remains an important market center for the entire mountain region. It is worth visiting on Thursday, market day, when farmers bring their livestock in for sale and local products, including rough wool sweaters and sheepskin coats, are on sale. The White and Black Dunajec streams meet in Nowy Targ to form the Dunajec River, which then runs on through steep limestone gorges to Nowy Sącz. *By car take the main road from Zakopane to Kraków. Buses run from Zakopane every hour.*

En Route On the road to Szczawnica, 12 km (8 mi) east of Nowy Targ, is ★ **Dębno.** This village in the valley of the Dunajec River has a tiny wooden church dating from the 15th century (it's believed to be the oldest wooden building in the Podhale region); inside are medieval wall paintings and wooden sculptures. *Buses run from the marketplace in Nowy Targ.*

Krościenko, 25 km (15 mi) east of Nowy Targ and 35 km (22 mi) southwest of Nowy Sącz, is one of the villages that became a holiday resort during the late 19th century and is still popular today as a center for walking vacations. It has many interesting Zakopane-style wooden structures. *Best access by PKS bus from the train station in Nowy Sącz.*

The small spa of **Szczawnica,** 28 km (17½ mi) east of Nowy Targ and 35 km (22 mi) southwest of Nowy Sącz, dates from the late 19th century; you can stroll around in the high-vaulted pump rooms and sip the foul-tasting mineral waters. *Best access by PKS bus from the marketplace in Nowy Targ or outside the train station in Nowy Sącz.*

Nowy Sącz

79 *70 Km (44 mi) northeast of Nowy Targ.*

Nowy Sącz has existed as a market town since the 13th century. Remnants from this early period include a **ruined 14th-century castle,** about

10 minutes from the market square on ul. Piotra Skargi, as well as the church on the northeast side of the market square and the 15th-century church and chapter house on the square's east side.

Dining and Lodging

$$ ✕ **Zajazd Sądecki.** This restaurant emphasizes regional cuisine, such as pancakes highland-style, stuffed with pork and onions. The dining room is cozy, with pine furniture and crisp white tablecloths. ✉ *Ul. Królowej Jadwigi 67,* ☎ *018/443–67–17. No credit cards.*

$$ 🏨 **Beskid.** This standard, cube-shape Orbis hotel is a typical product of the mid-1960s. It commands good views while being conveniently located near the rail and bus stations in the town center. The rooms are rather small and drab but comfortable, brightened with Podhale folk elements. Delicious breakfasts are served. ✉ *Ul. Limanowskiego 1, 33–330,* ☎ *018/443–57–70,* FAX *018/443–51–44. 63 rooms, 10 suites. Restaurant, bar. AE, DC, MC, V.*

Krynica

80 *32 km (20 mi) southeast of Nowy Sącz on Hwy. 99.*

Krynica is a spa and winter-sports center in a high valley. The salutary properties of the mineral waters were recognized during the 18th century, and the first **bathhouse** was built here in 1807. ✉ *Ul. Kraszewskiego 9.*

In the late 19th century Krynica was further developed in classic spa style, gaining a tree-lined promenade, a pump room, and concert halls. The waters here are not appetizing to the unaccustomed palate: they are the most concentrated mineral waters in Europe.

Lodging

For lodging options consult **Pensjonat Wisła** (✉ Bulwary Dietla 1, ☎ 018/471–55–12), a pension that also provides information on vacancies elsewhere. Also look for signs in windows advertising POKOJE (rooms).

$ 🏨 **Hotel Meran.** This is a friendly, three-story hotel, with wooden balconies and good parking facilities. ✉ *Ul. Kościelna 9, 33–380,* ☎ *018/471–21–09. 30 rooms. Free parking.*

Małopolska A to Z

Arriving and Departing

BY BUS

Zakopane is most easily accessible by bus from Kraków, a two-hour trip. There are also through services from Warsaw to Zakopane (five hours). Zakopane's **PKS bus station** (☎ 018/201–44–53) is at the corner of ulica Kościuszki and ulica Chramcówki.

BY CAR

The 7(E77) highway, which takes you roughly halfway from Kraków to Zakopane, is four-lane all the way. The road that runs the rest of the way, E95, has recently been much improved, but some stretches are still single lane, and horse-drawn carts can cause major delays. Side roads in the region can be very narrow and badly surfaced. In Zakopane and other towns in the region, it would be wise to leave your car at a guarded parking lot.

To get to Częstochowa from Kraków, take the E40 to Katowice, where you get on the E75. There are usually plenty of places to park along the town's main boulevard.

BY TRAIN

Zakopane's **train station** (☎ 018/201–50–31) is on ulica Chramcówki. From Kraków, the trip to Zakopane takes a full four–five hours because of the rugged nature of the terrain. Unless you take the overnight sleeper from Warsaw, which arrives in Zakopane at 6 AM, it's better to change to a bus in Kraków. A train runs daily to Częstochowa from Kraków (two hours).

Getting Around

BY BUS

Almost all villages in the region, however isolated, can be reached by PKS bus. The buses themselves can be ancient and slow, so take an express bus if one operates to your destination. An express bus runs from Kraków to Zakopane and back every two hours; seats can be reserved in advance.

BY CAR

It is not necessary to have a car to explore the southern region. Public transport will take you to even the most remote and inaccessible places—but it will take time and can be uncomfortably crowded. On the other hand, the narrow mountain roads can be trying and dangerous for drivers.

BY TRAIN

Trains move slowly in the hilly region south of Kraków, but most towns are accessible by train, and the routes can be very picturesque. In Zakopane you can get more information from the station on ulica Chramcówki (☞ *above*).

Contacts and Resources

EMERGENCIES

Police (☎ 997). **Ambulance** (☎ 999). **Hospital: Nowy Sącz** (✉ Ul. Młyńska 5, ☎ 018/443–88–77).

LATE-NIGHT PHARMACIES

Krynica (✉ Vita, Ul. Kraszewskiego 61, ☎ 018/471–39–47). **Nowy Sącz** (✉ Rynek 27, ☎ 018/443–82–92). **Zakopane** (✉ Apteka Pharbita, Ul. Chramcówki 34, ☎ 018/206–82–21).

PRIVATE ACCOMMODATIONS

In Zakopane contact the tourist information center, **BIT** (✉ Ul. Kościuszki 17, ☎ 018/201–22–11). **Tatra Tours and Travel** (✉ Ul. Kościeliska 1, ☎ 018/201–32–53), an Australian-operated agency, can arrange accommodations in pensions or hostels as well as tours of the region.

VISITOR INFORMATION

Częstochowa (✉ IT, al. Najświętszej Marii Panny 65, ☎ 034/368–22–50). **Krynica** (✉ Ul. Piłsudskiego 8, ☎ 018/471–57–46). **Nowy Sącz** (✉ Ul. Piotra Skargi 2, ☎ 018/443–55–97). **Zakopane** (BIT, ✉ Ul. Kościuszki 17, ☎ 018/201–22–11; Orbis, ✉ Ul. Krupówki 22, ☎ 018/201–22–38).

LUBLIN AND EASTERN POLAND

Lublin's location in eastern Poland has "protected" it somewhat from the influences that have swept the country since it opened to the West in 1989. Visitors here can get a peek at the old Poland—less prosperous, more traditional. Historically, Lublin lay in the heart of Poland and served as a crossroads between east and west. It was in Lublin in 1569 that the eastern duchy of Lithuania joined the kingdom of Poland by signing the Union of Lublin, thus creating the largest empire in Europe at the time. Following World War II, when Poland's borders shifted westward, Lublin found itself near the Soviet border. This has led to considerable contact with the East, largely in the form of Russian and Ukrainian traders who flock to the city's marketplace to peddle their goods—everything from old auto parts to caviar and champagne—and, increasingly, to make purchases in Poland for resale in their own countries.

With its graying exterior and mild urban decay, Lublin may seem like it has seen better days, but the city is taking steps to renew itself. One of the most important current projects is the restoration of Lublin's chief monument, its walled Old Town. In the district at the western end of Krakowskie Przedmieście, many of the buildings along the cobblestone streets have been beautifully restored, and the area is looking up. And Lublin is rich in parks, offering wild, lush greens in summer and golden yellows in autumn.

Lublin is also a good hub for exploring the villages and countryside of the eastern parts of the country. In less than an hour visitors can travel to Puławy to enjoy a picnic in the palace grounds or to the village of Kazimierz Dolny for a walk along the banks of the Vistula. It's also possible to make a day trip out of Zamość and Łańcut, though these places make nice stopovers if you have time.

Numbers in the margin correspond to numbers on the Southeastern Poland map.

Lublin

81 *160 km (100 mi) southeast of Warsaw, 270 km (170 mi) northeast of Kraków.*

The tourist attractions of Lublin are in three distinct regions of the city. The Stare Miasto (Old Town), a medieval walled city, is at the eastern end of Krakowskie Przedmieście, the main street. The castle and nearby Jewish cemetery are just outside the old city wall, to the northeast. The Catholic and Marie Skłodowska-Curie universities and the adjacent Saxon Gardens are on the western edge of the city, off aleja Racławickie (take a bus west from Krakowskie Przedmieście).

Situated at the eastern end of Lublin's main shopping street, Krakowskie Przedmieście, is the **Brama Krakowska** (Kraków Gate), a Gothic and Baroque structure that served as the main entrance to the medieval city. Today it separates modern Lublin from the Old Town. The gate houses the **Muzeum Lubelskie** (Lublin History Museum), where you can learn about the area's history. ✉ *Pl. Łokietka 3,* ☎ *081/532–60–01.* *Zł 1.50.* ⏲ *Wed.–Sat. 9–4.*

Part of Lublin's tremendous success as a medieval trading center stemmed from a royal decree exempting the city from all customs duties. As a result, huge fortunes were made and kept, and the town's merchants were able to build the beautiful 14th- and 15th-century houses—complete with colorful frescoed facades—that surround the
★ **Rynek** (market square). The Rynek's unusual trapezoidal shape is the result of medieval builders adapting the construction of the town to the outline of the protective walls surrounding Lublin.

Filling the center of the Rynek is the reconstructed **Stary Ratusz** (Old Town Hall), built in the 16th century and rebuilt in neoclassical style in the 1780s by the Italian architect Domenico Merlini. Here a royal tribunal served as the seat of the Crown Court of Justice for Małopolska beginning in 1578; records of its activities can be seen in the museum. On Saturday the hall fills with young couples waiting to be married. ✉ *Rynek 1,* ☎ *081/532–68–66.* *Zł 1.50.* ⏲ *Wed.–Sun. 9–4.*

NEED A BREAK? At ulica Grodzka 5A, in one of the recently reconstructed medieval tenements, you can visit the small ground-floor **Apteka-Muzeum** (Museum of Pharmacy), which is a reproduction of an early chemist's shop, and then drink a cup of coffee in the café behind it.

★ The **Dominican Church and Monastery,** dating from 1342, is the jewel of Lublin's Old Town; the interior was renovated in rococo style in the 17th century. Two of its 11 chapels are particularly noteworthy: the **Kaplica Firlej** (Firlej Chapel) with its late-Renaissance architecture, and the **Kaplica Tyszkiewski** (Tyszkiewski Chapel) with its early Baroque decoration. Circling the walls above the chapels are paintings depicting the transport of a piece of the True Cross—the cross on which Jesus was crucified—to Lublin and the protection the relic has given the city through the ages. Unfortunately, this protection did not extend to the relic itself, which was stolen from the church in 1991. The church is often closed now, but try knocking on the monastery door to the right of the entrance. ✉ *Ul. Złota.* 🎫 *Free.* ⏲ *Weekdays 9–noon and 3–6, weekends 3–6.*

Outside the old city wall, just around the corner from Kraków Gate, stands **Lublin Cathedral,** begun in 1625. The exterior of this Jesuit church is an example of Lublin Renaissance style—steeply pitched roofs, highly decorated gables, and elaborate patterned vaulting. Inside to the left of the Baroque high altar, a reproduction of the *Black Madonna of Częstochowa* is on display. You can reach the **Kaplica Akustyczna** (Whispering Chapel) by a passage to the right of the high altar. Watch what you say here—a whisper in one corner can be heard perfectly in another. Next to the chapel is the **treasury,** holding what remains of the original illusionistic frescoes that decorated the church interior: the images were painted so skillfully that they appear almost three dimensional. ✉ *Ul. Królewska.* 🎫 *Whispering Chapel and treasury zł 2.* ⏲ *Tues.–Sun. 10–2 and 3–5.*

During the late 14th century King Kazimierz the Great ordered the construction of **Lublin Castle,** as well as the defensive walls surrounding the city, to protect the wealthy trading center from invasion. Most of the castle was rebuilt in mock Gothic during the 19th century, when it was converted to a prison. Run at various times by the Russian czar, the German Gestapo, and the Communist secret police, the castle prison witnessed its largest number of deaths during World War II, when the Nazis murdered more than 10,000 political prisoners here. The newly ★ opened **Kaplica Trójcy świętego** (Chapel of the Holy Trinity), which has been under restoration for decades, is the most outstanding attraction in Lublin. The 14th-century chapel is covered with Byzantium-style murals. Note the ancient graffiti on the walls. The **Castle Museum** houses historical exhibits and an art gallery known for Jan Matejko's *Unia Lubelska* (1869), which depicts the signing of the Lublin Union by the king of Poland and Grand Duke of Lithuania exactly three centuries earlier. ✉ *Ul. Zamkowa 9,* ☎ *081/532–50–01.* 🎫 *Zł 7.* ⏲ *Wed.–Sat. 9–4, Sun. 9–5.*

Lublin was a center of Jewish culture in the 16th century. The hill behind Lublin Castle is the site of the **Stary Cmentarz Żydowski** (Old Jewish Cemetery). The cemetery was destroyed during World War II by the German SS, which used the rubble from the headstones to pave the entranceway to Majdanek concentration camp. The park at the base of the castle hill was the site of the Jewish ghetto, in which Nazis imprisoned the Jewish population of Lublin until April 1943, when they sent them to Majdanek.

OFF THE BEATEN PATH

MAJDANEK CONCENTRATION CAMP – Reminders of the horrors of World War II are never far away in Poland, and 5 km (3 mi) southeast of Lublin's city center lie the remnants of the Majdanek concentration camp, second in scope only to Auschwitz. Established in July 1941, it grew to 1,235 acres, although the original plan was to make it five times as large. From 1941 to 1944 more than 360,000 people lost their lives here, either by direct extermination or through illness and disease. Standing at the camp entrance is one of two monuments designed for the 25th anniversary of the liberation of Majdanek. The **Monument of Struggle and Martyrdom** symbolizes the inmates' faith and hope; the **mausoleum** at the rear of the camp marks the death of that hope. Of the five fields constituting the original camp, only the gas chambers, watchtowers, and crematoriums, as well as some barracks on Field Three, remain. The **visitor center,** to the left of the monument at the entrance, shows a movie about the camp (in English) and has a bookstore as well as a restaurant. ✉ *Droga Męczenników Majdanka 67 (from Lublin take Bus 153 or 156 from Krakowskie Przedmieście),* ☎ *081/7442–647.* 🎫 *Free.* ⏲ *Tues.–Sun. 8–6, last movie showing 2 PM.*

KOZŁÓWKA – Set in a beautiful and well-tended park, this 18th-century palace (41 km [25 mi] north of Lublin) was built for the Zamoyski family and is one of a handful of palaces in Poland whose interiors have remained intact. Housed in the palace annex is a fascinating relic of the Stalinist era, the **Museum of the Art of Socialist Realism.** The palace is reachable by bus from Lublin. If you are driving, take Route 19 north of Lublin to Lubartów (29 km [18 mi]), then head west for 12 km (7 mi). ☎ *081/855–29–88.* 🎫 *Zł 7.* ⏲ *Mar.–Nov., Tues.–Sun. 10–4.*

Dining and Lodging

$$ ✕ **Club Hades.** Locals think this is the best place to dine in Lublin. Specialties include onion soup and all kinds of meat dishes. ✉ *Al. Peowiaków 12,* ☎ *081/532–56–41. AE, DC, MC, V.*

$$ ★ ✕ **Piwnica.** This popular restaurant serves traditional Polish fare. Try the pickled herring for an appetizer, then roast pork, veal cutlet, or beef medallions with mashed potatoes for a main course. ✉ *Ul. Skłodowska 12,* ☎ *081/534–39–19. AE, DC, MC, V.*

$$$ ★ **Unia Hotel.** This six-story hotel is just off the main road outside the Old Town. Most of the public spaces are fairly cramped, but the rooms are reasonably spacious and comfortably furnished. ✉ *Al. Racławickie 12, 20–037,* ☎ *081/533–20–61,* FAX *081/533–30–21. Restaurant, bar, casino. AE, DC, MC, V.*

$ **Dom Nauczyciela.** This hotel, which was formerly reserved for members of the Communist teachers union, is clean, comfortable, and efficiently run, if lacking in elegance. The rooms are small but adequate. ✉ *Ul. Akademicka 4, 20–033,* ☎ *081/533–03–66,* FAX *081/533–37–45. 36 rooms. No credit cards.*

$ **Victoria Hotel.** This venerable hotel is large and situated within walking distance of all the Old Town's landmarks. The rooms are on the small side, but the service is efficient and friendly. Rooms over the street, which is on a hill, can be noisy. ✉ *Ul. Narutowicza 58–60, 20–401,* ☎ FAX *081/532–90–26. 190 rooms, 63 with bath. Restaurant. AE, DC, MC, V.*

Nightlife and the Arts

For up-to-date information about movies, theater, and concerts in Lublin, consult the local papers, *Kurier Lubelski* and *Dziennik Lubelski.* Student nightlife centers on Marie Skłodowska-Curie University's **Chatka Żaka Club** (✉ Ul. I. Radziszewskiego 16, ☎ 081/533–32–01). The club has a cafeteria, a bar, a popular disco, and a cinema that often shows American movies. Theater tickets are available at **Centrum Kultury** (✉ Ul. Peowiaków 12), the home of all theater groups in Lublin. Tickets for orchestral performances can be purchased at the **Philharmonic Hall** (✉ Ul. Marii Skłodowskiej-Curie 5, ☎ 081/743-78–21) Tuesday through Sunday from noon to 7.

Outdoor Activities and Sports

On hot summer days Lublin residents head for Zalew Zemborzycki, a man-made lake about 4 km (2½ mi) south of central Lublin. The lake has sailing and canoe rentals. *Take Bus 25 or 42 from Lublin Cathedral.*

Puławy

82 *40 km (25 mi) northwest of Lublin, 130 km (70 mi) southeast of Warsaw.*

The 18th-century **Puławy Palace** in the town of Puławy is worth a brief stop. The palace was originally the residence of the Czartoryski family, a patriotic, politically powerful clan. Prince Adam Czartoryski was one of the most educated men of his day and a great patron of the arts and culture. He attracted so many prominent Poles to Puławy that by the late 18th century it was said to rival Warsaw as a cultural and political capital. Today the yellow-and-white neoclassical building houses an agricultural institute.

Modeled on the Vesta Temple in Tivoli, **Świątynia Sybilli** (Sybil's Temple), completed in 1809, was Poland's first museum. The **palace chapel,** built in 1803, is based on the pantheon in Rome. The chapel lies outside the palace grounds (from the palace walk two blocks north on ulica Czartoryskich to ulica Aiguera, then turn left and go two more blocks). ✉ *Ul. Czartoryskich 6A,* ☎ *081/887–86–74.* *Palace grounds free; Sybil's Temple zł 4.* ⊙ *Tues.–Sun. 10–2.*

Kazimierz Dolny

★ 83 *12 km (7 mi) south of Puławy, 40 km (25 mi) west of Lublin, 130 km (80 mi) southeast of Warsaw.*

This small town is so pleasing to the eyes that it has thrived for over a century as an artists' colony and vacation spot. It sits on a steep, hilly bank of the placid Vistula River, and whitewashed facades and steeply pitched red-tile roofs peek out over the treetops. Often referred to as the Pearl of the Polish Renaissance, Kazimierz Dolny prospered as a port town during the 16th and 17th centuries, but the partitioning of Poland left it cut off from the grain markets of Gdańsk. Thereafter the town fell into decline until it was rediscovered by painters and writers during the 19th century. Today nonartistic visitors can still enjoy the Renaissance architecture along the village's dusty cobblestone streets, or hike through the nearby hills and gorges.

On the southeast corner of the town's **Rynek** (market square) lies the **Przybyła Brothers' House**, left behind by one of the most powerful families in Kazimierz Dolny, the Przybyłas. The ornate house was built in 1615, and its facades are adorned with the two-story bas-relief figures of St. Nicholas (left) and St. Christopher (right), the brothers' patron saints.

The **Celej House,** seat of another powerful Kazimierz clan, stands one block toward the river from the square, and it is embellished with griffins, dragons, and salamanders. The former residence now houses the **Town Museum of Kazimierz Dolny** and many paintings depicting local life of past eras. ✉ *Ul. Senatorska 11,* ☎ *081/881–01–04.* *Zł 3.* ⊙ *Tues.–Sun. 10–3.*

A covered passageway off ulica Senatorska leads up to the walled courtyard of the **Church and Monastery of the Reformati Order,** which stands on the southern hill overlooking the town's market square. In the late 18th century an encircling wall was built to protect the monastery's buildings. A plaque inside the passageway memorializes the Nazis' use of the site as a house of torture during World War II. The climb up to the courtyard is worthwhile just for the spectacular view it affords of the town.

The ruins of the 14th-century **Kazimierz Castle,** which served as a watchtower to protect the Vistula trade route, stand on a steep hill to the northeast of the town's market square. From here there is a grand view over the town and the Vistula Valley.

The **Góra Trzech Krzyży** (Three Crosses Hill) lies to the east of the market square. The crosses were constructed in 1708 to commemorate the victims of a plague that ravaged the town.

Lodging

$ **SARP.** This ideally located hotel on the corner of the town square belongs and caters to the Architects' Association but will take other guests on a commercial basis. The rooms are large and irregular in shape, with simple but adequate furnishings. The restaurant is usually packed with intellectuals. ✉ *Rynek 20, 24–120,* ☎ *081/881–05–44. 35 rooms, 15 with bath. Dining room. No credit cards.*

Outdoor Activities and Sports

BOATING

Boat rides on the Vistula leave from ulica Puławska 6. The half-hour ride takes you south to Janowiec and its Firlej Castle ruins.

HIKING

Take one of the numerous marked trails, ranging in length from 2 km to 6 km (1 mi to 4 mi), and explore the hilly landscape around Kazimierz. All trails converge on the market square. Tourist tracks lead north (marked red) and south (marked green) along the river from the square, along streets and cart paths, through orchards and quarries.

Zamość

84 *87 km (54 mi) southeast of Lublin, 318 km (198 mi) northeast of Kraków.*

The fortified town of Zamość has a wonderfully preserved, Renaissance-era central square, wide boulevards, and neat rows of colorful houses with brightly painted facades. The town was conceived in the late 16th century by Hetman Jan Zamoyski as an outpost along the thriving trade route between Lublin and Lwów. The town thrived, and its strong fortifications spared it from destruction during the Swedish onslaught of the 17th century. The Polish victory over Lenin's Red Army near Zamość in 1920 kept the way clear for the country's restored independence. World War II saw the town renamed Himmlerstadt, with thousands of its residents (45% of the town was Jewish) deported or exterminated to make way for German settlers.

★ Zamość's **Rynek** (market square) is a breathtaking arcaded plaza surrounded by the decorative facades of homes built by local merchants during the 16th and 17th centuries. Dominating the square is the impressive Baroque **town hall,** topped by a 164 ft spire.

The **Muzeum Regionalne w Zamościu** (Zamość Regional Museum), housed in a charming town house next door to the town hall, has paintings of the Zamoyski clan and a scale model of Zamość. ✉ *Ul. Ormiańska 24,* ☎ *084/638–64–94.* 🎫 *Zł 4.* ⏲ *Tues.–Sun. 9–4.*

Kolegiata świętego Tomasza (St. Thomas Collegiate Church), one of Poland's most beautiful Renaissance churches, stands near the southwest corner of the market square. In the presbytery are four 17th-century paintings ascribed to Domenico Robusti, Tintoretto's son. The church is also the final resting place of Jan Zamoyski, buried in the **Zamoyski Chapel** to the right of the high altar.

The **Pałac Zamojskich** (Zamoyski Palace), home of the founding family of Zamość, lies near the market square beyond St. Thomas Collegiate Church. The palace lost much of its decorative detail in renovation and restoration and now serves as a courthouse.

Behind the Zamoyski Palace is the **Arsenał** (Arsenal Museum), which houses a collection of Turkish armaments and rugs, as well as a model of the original town plan. ✉ *Ul. Zamkowa 2,* ☎ *084/638–40–76.* 🎫 *Zł 4.50.* ⏲ *Tues.–Sun. 10–4.*

Near the northwest corner of the main square, behind the town hall, is the **Akademia** (Old Academy), a distinguished center of learning during the 17th and 18th centuries and once the third-largest university after those in Kraków and Vilnius. It is now a high school.

The oldest entrance to Zamość, the **Brama Lubelska** (Lublin Gate) is to the northwest of the market square, across the road from the Old Academy. In 1588, Jan Zamoyski triumphantly led the Austrian archduke Maximilian into town through this gate after defeating him in his attempt to seize the Polish throne from Sigismund III. He then bricked up the gate to commemorate his victory.

What's left of Zamość's fortifications are at the bottom of ulica Staszica. This is the **Brama Lwowska Bastion** (Lwów Gate and Bastion). With defenses like these, three stories high and 20 ft thick, it is easy to understand why Zamość was one of the few places to escape ruin in the Swedish attack. 🎫 *Zł 1.* ⏲ *Tues.–Sun. 10–4.*

South of the town's marketplace, on ulica Moranda, is the **rotunda,** a monument to a tragic era in Zamość's history. From 1939 to 1944 this fortified emplacement served as an extermination camp where tens of thousands of Poles, Jews, and Russians were brutally killed, some even burned alive. Now it serves as a memorial to the victims of Nazi brutality in the region. 🎫 *Zł 7.* ⏲ *Daily 10–5.*

Lodging

$$ 🏨 **Hotel Jubilat.** Built in the 1970s, this hotel offers comfortable rooms on the edge of the Old Town. The decor is dark, but everything is clean. ✉ *Ul. Wyszyńskiego 52, 22–400,* ☎ *084/638–64–01. 62 rooms. Restaurant. AE, DC, MC, V.*

$$ 🏨 **Hotel Renesans.** This small hotel is located within a few blocks of the main square. Newly renovated, it has cheerful rooms and modern bathrooms. ✉ *Ul. Grecka 6, 22–400,* ☎ FAX *084/639–20–01. 24 rooms. Restaurant. AE, DC, MC, V.*

Łańcut

★ 85 *130 km (81 mi) southwest of Zamość on Hwy. 4(E40).*

The neo-Baroque **Łańcut Palace,** situated within a 76-acre natural reserve, is the main attraction in the town of Łańcut. Built during the 16th century, the palace is one of the most grandiose aristocratic residences in Eastern Europe. In the 19th century it was willed to the Potocki family, who amassed an impressive art collection here. Count Alfred Potocki, the last owner, emigrated to Liechtenstein in 1944 as Russian troops approached, escaping with 11 train cars full of art objects and paintings. Much was left behind, however, and after the war a **museum** was established in the palace (which had survived intact). Today you can see the family collection of art and interior decorations, including Biedermeier, neoclassical, and rococo furnishings. Of particular interest are the intricate wood-inlay floors, the tiny theater off the dining hall, and the hall of sculpture painted to resemble a trellis of grapevines. More than 40 rooms are open to the public, including the Turkish and Chinese apartments, which reflect the 18th-century fascination with the Near and Far East. Outside, a moat and a system of bastions laid out like a five-point star separate the inner Italian and rose gardens from the rest of the park. The **Carriage Museum** in the old coach house outside the main gates contains more than 50 vehicles and is one of the largest museums of its kind in Europe. ☎ *017/225–20–08.* *Zł 12 for both museums.* *Museums Tues.–Sat. 8–2:30, Sun. 9–4; park daily until sunset.*

OFF THE BEATEN PATH

LEŻAJSK – This basilica and monastery of the Bernadine Fathers dates back to the 17th century and is a major pilgrimage site. Frequent musical performances are given on the 17th-century organ. There is also a museum attached to the monastery with exhibits of beautiful wood carvings. *29 km (13 mi) north of Łańcut on Rte. 877.*

Lodging

$ ★ **Hotel Zamkowy.** Although the rooms in this 18th-century palace have 1970s furnishings, they are cozy and overlook the palace courtyard. There are only 42 beds, so reservations are imperative. ✉ *Ul. Zamkowa 1, 37–100,* ☎ *017/225–26–71. 20 rooms, 7 with bath. Restaurant. AE, DC, MC, V.*

Lublin and Eastern Poland A to Z

Arriving and Departing

BY BUS

Lublin is the gateway to the region. **Dworzec PKS Główny** (✉ Al. Tysiąclecia 4, ☎ 081/747–89–22), just north of the Stare Miasto (Old Town) near the castle, connects Lublin with cities to the west and south. Buses run regularly between this station and Warsaw (3 hours).

Another Lublin station, **Dworzec PKS Północny** (✉ Ul. Gospodarcza), connects to points east. It lies about 4 km (2½ mi) southeast of Lublin's center; take Bus 155 or 159 between the city center and the station.

BY TRAIN

Lublin's main station, **Lublin Główny** (✉ Pl. Dworcowy, ☎ 081/531–56–42), is about 4 km (2½ mi) south of the city center; take Bus 13 or 158 between the center and the station. Frequent train service connects Lublin with Warsaw (2½ hours) and Kraków (4½ hours).

Getting Around

BY BUS

Buses run regularly from Lublin's Dworzec PKS Główny to Puławy (1 hour) and Kazimierz Dolny (1½ hours); buses for Zamość (1¾ hours) leave from Dworzec PKS Północny.

BY TRAIN

Trains run regularly between Lublin and Zamość (3 hours). A coach-class ticket costs about the same as the bus.

Contacts and Resources

EMERGENCIES

Police (☎ 997). **Ambulance** (☎ 999).

LATE-NIGHT PHARMACIES

Two pharmacies in **Lublin** (⊠ Ul. Bramowa 8, ☎ 081/532–05–21; Krakowskie Przedmieście 49, ☎ 081/532–24–25) are open 24 hours.

VISITOR INFORMATION

Lublin: The main source of tourist information is **Centrum Informacji Turystycznej** (⊠ Krakowskie Przedmieście 78, ☎ 081/532–44–12). **Orbis** (⊠ Ul. Narutowicza 31/33, ☎ 081/532–22–56 or 081/532–22–59) books train tickets and exchanges money.

Zamość: Tourist information is provided by **Zamojski Ośrodek Informacji Turystycznej** (⊠ Rynek Wielki 13, ☎ 084/39–22–92). There's also an **Orbis** (⊠ Ul. Grodzka 18, ☎ 084/639–30–01).

GDAŃSK AND THE NORTHEAST

This region attracts visitors with Gdańsk (the bustling city that was the birthplace of Solidarity), Riviera-like resorts, and Poland's castle country. Until World War II, most of this area was included in Prussia and was referred to as "the sandbox of the Holy Roman Empire." It is indeed sandy, but it contains some startling landscapes and magnificent historic sites, such as the fortress of the Teutonic Knights at Malbork (close to and easily accessible by train from Gdańsk). In the northeast are 1,000 lakes and 1,000-year-old forests (and the attendant mosquitoes during the summer). The Mazurian and Augustów-Suwałki lake area forms a labyrinth of interconnecting rivers and canals, against a backdrop of ancient forests. Olsztyn is the best starting point for exploring this area, and you need a car to experience its delights fully.

Gdańsk, the third-largest city in Poland and the capital of this region, is linked with two smaller neighboring towns, Gdynia and Sopot, in an urban conglomeration called the Trójmiasto (Tri-City), on the western bank of the Bay of Gdańsk. These cities operate as a single organism and form one of Poland's most exciting and vibrant places.

Numbers in the margin correspond to numbers on the Gdańsk and the Northeast map.

Gdańsk

86 *350 km (219 mi) north of Warsaw, 340 km (215 mi) east of Szczecin.*

Maybe it's the sea air, or maybe it's the city's history of political tumult. Whatever the reason, Gdańsk is special to Poles—and to Scandinavians and Germans, who visit the region in great numbers. Between 1308 and 1945, this Baltic port was an independent city-state called Danzig, a majority of whose residents were ethnic Germans. When the Nazis fired the first shots of World War II here on September 1, 1939, they began a process of systematic destruction of Poland that would last for six years and leave millions dead. In 1997 Gdańsk celebrated its 1,000th year as a Baltic city.

The city remains famous for having been the cradle of the workers' movement that came to be known as Solidarity. Food price increases in 1970 led to the first strikes at the (former) Lenin Shipyards in Gdańsk. The Communist authorities brutally put down the protest, killing 40 workers in December of that year. Throughout the 1970s, small groups of anti-Communist workers and intellectuals based in Gdańsk continued to organize. By August 1980, they had gained sufficient critical mass to form Solidarność (Solidarity), which the government was forced to recognize as the first independent trade union

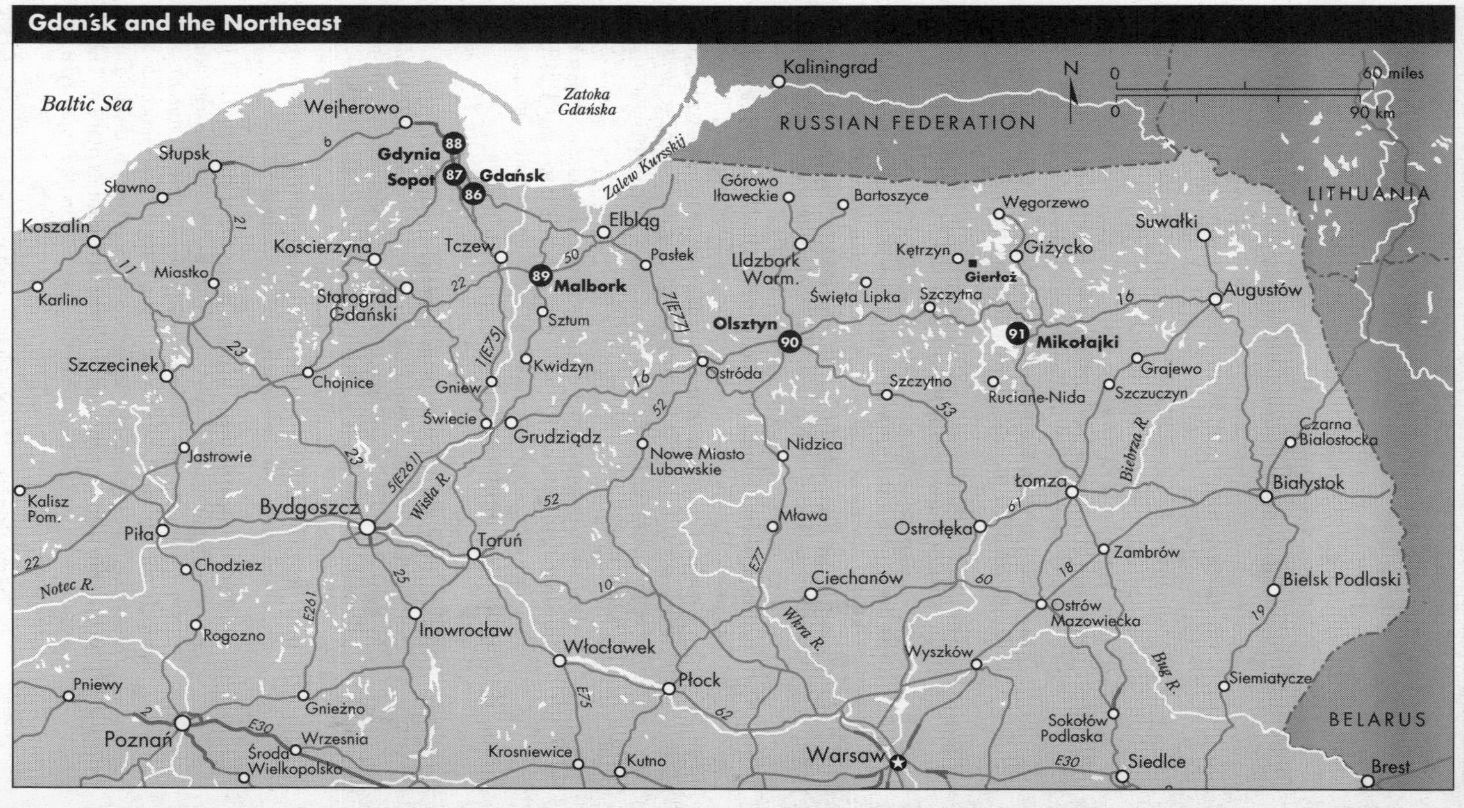
Gdańsk and the Northeast
Baltic Sea
Zatoka Gdańska
Zalew Kursskij
RUSSIAN FEDERATION
LITHUANIA
BELARUS
N
0
60 miles
0
90 km
Kaliningrad
Wejherowo
Gdynia
Sopot
Gdańsk
88
87
86
89
90
91
Słupsk
Sławno
Koszalin
Karlino
Miastko
Koscierzyna
Tczew
Malbork
Elbląg
Pasłek
Górowo Iławeckie
Bartoszyce
Lidzbark Warm.
Kętrzyn
Gierłoż
Węgorzewo
Giżycko
Suwałki
Augustów
Święta Lipka
Szczytna
Mikołajki
Olsztyn
Ostróda
Sztum
Kwidzyn
Starograd Gdański
Szczecinek
Chojnice
Gniew
Świecie
Grudziądz
Szczytno
Ruciane-Nida
Grajewo
Szczuczyn
Czarna Bialostocka
Biebrza R.
Nowe Miasto Lubawskie
Nidzica
Jastrowie
Kalisz Pom.
Piła
Bydgoszcz
Wisła R.
Toruń
Mława
Ostrołęka
Łomza
Białystok
Zambrów
Chodziez
Notec R.
Ciechanów
Ostrów Mazowiecka
Bielsk Podlaski
Rogozno
Inowrocław
Wkra R.
Bug R.
Włocławek
Wyszków
Płock
Siemiatycze
Pniewy
Gnieżno
Poznań
Wrzesnia
Środa Wielkopolska
Krosniewice
Kutno
Warsaw
Sokołów Podlaska
Siedlce
Brest
E30
E75
E77
E261
1(E75)
5(E261)
7(E77)
6
11
16
18
19
21
22
23
25
50
52
53
60
61
62
10
2

in the former Soviet bloc. Although the government attempted to destroy Solidarity after declaring martial law in December 1981, Solidarity activists continued to keep the objectives of democracy and independence from the Soviet Union alive. After the collapse of communism in 1989, Solidarity leader Lech Wałęsa became president of Poland in the nation's first free elections since World War II.

The historic core of this medieval city can easily be explored on foot. Although Gdańsk was almost entirely destroyed during World War II, the streets of its Główne Miasto (Main Town) have been lovingly restored and still retain their historical and cultural richness. North of Main Town, the Stare Miasto (Old Town) contains many new hotels and shops, but several churches and the beautifully reconstructed Old Town Hall justify its name. At the north end of the Old Town sit the shipyards. This site, which captivated world attention during the many clashes between workers and militarized police units during the 1970s and 1980s, has now settled back into its daily grind, and the shipyards struggle to make the adjustment to the free market.

The largest brick church in the world and the largest church in Poland, ★ the **Kościół Najświętszej Marii Panny** (St. Mary's Church), on the north side of ulica Piwna in Gdańsk's Main Town, can accommodate 25,000 people. Also referred to in abbreviated form as Kościół Mariacki, this enormous 14th-century church underwent major restoration after World War II, and 15 of its 22 altars have been relocated to museums in Gdańsk and Warsaw. The highlight of a visit is climbing the hundreds of steps up the church tower. It costs zł 3 to make the climb—which makes it cheaper than an aerobics class—and the view is sensational. The church also contains a 500-year-old, 25-ft-high astronomical clock that has only recently been restored to working order after years of neglect. It keeps track of solar and lunar progressions, and it displays the signs of the zodiac, something of an anomaly in a Catholic church.

Two blocks west of St. Mary's Church on ulica Piwna, the **Wielka Zbrojownia** (Great Armory) is a good example of 17th-century Dutch Renaissance architecture. The ground floor is now a trade center, and the upper floors house an art school.

Three huge and somber crosses perpetually draped with flowers stand outside the gates of the **Stocznia Gdańska** (Gdańsk Shipyards). Formerly called the Lenin Shipyards, this place gave birth to the Solidarity movement. The crosses are only one **monument** to Solidarity in the shipyards. There are plaques that commemorate the struggle as well as a quotation by Pope John Paul II inspired by his visit to the monument in 1987: "The Grace of God could not have created anything better; in this place, silence is a scream." ✉ *Ul. Jana z Kolna.*

The shipyard monument clearly symbolizes the fundamental link in the Polish consciousness between Catholicism and political dissent; another example is the **Kościół świętej Brygidy** (St. Brigitte's Church), a few blocks north of the shipyard monument. After the government declared martial law in 1981 in an attempt to force Solidarity to disband, members began meeting here secretly during celebrations of mass. There is a statue of Pope John Paul II in the front. ✉ *On ul. Profesorska near Old Town Hall.*

The **Żuraw Gdański** (Harbor Crane), built in 1444, was medieval Europe's largest and oldest crane. Today it houses the **Muzeum Morskie** (Maritime Museum), with a collection of models of the ships constructed in the Gdańsk Shipyards since 1945. At the museum ticket office, inquire about tickets for tours of the *Sołdek,* a World War II battleship moored nearby on the canal. ✉ *Ul. Ołowianka 9–13,* ☎ *058/301–86–11.* 🎫 *Zł 8.* ⏲ *Oct.–June, Tues.–Sun. 10–4; July–Sept., daily 10–4.*

The **Muzeum Narodowe w Gdańsku** (National Museum in Gdańsk) is housed in a former Franciscan monastery just south of the old walls of the Main Town. Exhibits include 14th- to 20th-century art and ethnographic collections. ✉ *Ul. Toruńska 1, off ul. Okopowa,* ☎ *058/301–70–61.* 🎫 *Zł 5, Sun. free.* ⏲ *Daily 10–3.*

The small **Museum Archeologiczne Gdańska** (Gdańsk Archaeological Museum) displays Slavic tribal artifacts, including jewelry, pottery, boats, and bones. ✉ *Ul. Mariacka 25–26,* ☎ *058/301–50–31.* 🎫 *Zł 3.* ⏲ *Tues.–Sun. 10–4.*

★ The historic entrance to the Old Town of Gdańsk is marked by the **Brama Wyżynna** (High Gate), off ulica Wały Jagiellońskie at the entrance to ulica Długa. This magnificent Renaissance gate, built in 1576, is adorned with the flags of Poland, Gdańsk, and the Prussian kingdom. As the king entered the city on his annual visit, he'd pass this gate first, then the Brama Złota (Golden Gate), which is just behind it and dates from 1614, combining characteristics of the Italian and Dutch Renaissances.

Continuing east along ulica Długa reveals one of the city's most distinctive landmarks, the elaborately gilded **Fontanna Neptuna** (Neptune Fountain), at the western end of Długi Targ. Every day after dusk, this 17th-century fountain is illuminated, adding a romantic glow to the entire area. Around the fountain, vendors selling amber jewelry and souvenirs maintain a centuries-old tradition of trade at this point.

★ Behind the Fontanna Neptuna on Długi Targ is the **Dwór Artusa** (Artus Mansion). Built in the 15th through 17th centuries, the mansion was named for King Arthur, who otherwise has no affiliation with the place (alas, there are no traces of Excalibur or Merlin). This and the other stately mansions on the Długi Targ are reminders of the traders and aristocrats who once resided in this posh district. The mansion's collection includes Renaissance furnishings, paintings, holy figures, and the world's largest Renaissance stove. ✉ *Długi Targ 43,* ☎ *058/346–33–58.* 🎫 *Zł 5.* ⏲ *Tues.–Sat. 10–4, Sun. 11–4.*

At the water's edge is the eastern entrance to the medieval city of Gdańsk, the **Brama Zielona** (Green Gate). This 16th-century gate killed two birds with one stone, doubling as a royal residence. Unfortunately, the name no longer fits: the gate is now painted brown. ✉ *At the eastern end of Długi Targ.*

The former parish church of Gdańsk's Old Town, **Kościół świętej Katarzyny** (St. Catherine's Church), at the corner of ulica Podmłyńska and ulica Katarzynki, is supposedly the oldest church in the city. Parts of it date to the 12th century, the tower was constructed in the 1480s, and the carillon of 37 bells was added in 1634. The 17th-century astronomer Jan Hevelius was buried in the presbytery of the church, below which lies what's left of the town's oldest Christian cemetery (which dates from 10th century). *Ul. Wielkie Mtyny,* ☎ *058/301–15–95.*

On a small island in the canal, just north of St. Catherine's, stands the **Wielki Młyn** (Great Mill). The largest mill in medieval Europe, it operated from the time of its completion in 1350 until 1945. ✉ *Ul. Podmłyńska and Na Piaskach.*

★ Although Gdańsk's original **Ratusz Główny** (Old Town Hall) was completely destroyed during World War II, a careful reconstruction of the exterior and interior now re-creates the glory of Gdańsk's medieval past. Inside the town hall, the **Muzeum Historii Miasta Gdańska** (Gdańsk Historical Museum) covers more than five centuries of Gdańsk's history in exhibits that include paintings, sculptures, and weapons. ✉ *Ul. Długa 47,* ☎ *058/301–48–72.* 🎫 *Zł 4.* ⏲ *Tues.–Sun. 11–4.*

★ The district of Oliwa, north of the city center, is worth visiting for its magnificent **cathedral.** Originally part of a Cistercian monastery, the church was erected during the 13th century. Like most other structures in Poland, it has been rebuilt many times, resulting in a hodgepodge of styles from Gothic to Renaissance to rococo. The cathedral houses one of the most impressive rococo organs you're ever likely to hear—and see. It has more than 6,000 pipes, and when a special mechanism is activated, wooden angels ring bells and a wooden star climbs up a wooden sky. Demonstrations of the organ and a brief narrated church history are given almost hourly on weekdays in summer, less frequently on weekends and the rest of the year. ✉ *Ul. Cystersów.*

In a beautiful park surrounding the cathedral in Oliwa are the **Muzeum Sztuki Współczesnej** (Modern Art Museum), with a large collection of works by Polish artists from the interwar period onward, and the **Muzeum Etnograficzne** (Ethnographic Museum), which has fine examples of local crafts from the 19th century and an interesting display of amber folk jewelry. The cathedral and museums are best approached by train; get off at Gdańsk-Oliwa and walk west up ulica Piastowska to ulica Opacka; or take Tram 2 or 6 toward Sopot. ✉ *Ethnographic Museum: Ul. Opacka 12. Modern Art Museum: Cysterśw 15A, Pałac Opatów.* ☎ *058/552–12–71 for both museums.* 🎫 *Museums zł 4, Wed. free.* ⏲ *Museums Tues.–Sat. 9–4, Sun. 10–4.*

OFF THE BEATEN PATH

WESTERPLATTE – Located 10 km (6½ mi) north of the Old Town, Westerplatte is home to a branch of the **National Museum.** World War II broke out here, at the entrance to the northern port. On September 1, 1939, a German warship, the *Schleswig Holstein,* began a bombardment of the Polish army positions here. A monument to the men who attempted to defend the Westerplatte for seven days against impossible odds was erected in the 1960s. Westerplatte can be reached by Bus 106 or 158 from ulica Okopowa, just outside the Main Town wall, or by water bus (☞ Getting Around by Water Bus *in* Gdańsk and the Northeast A to Z, *below*). ✉ *Ul. Majora Sucharskiego 1,* ☎ *058/343–69–72.* 🎫 *Zł 5.* ⏲ *May–Oct., daily 9–4.*

Dining and Lodging

$$$ ✕ **Euro.** The Euro serves up the closest thing to nouvelle cuisine in Gdańsk, in a prime location. Specialties include the veal escallopes with fettucine in cream sauce and the substantial Steak Madame Walewska with croquettes, prunes, and sausage in red wine. ✉ *Ul. Długi 79/80,* ☎ *058/301–23–83. AE, DC, MC, V.*

$$$ ★ ✕ **Major.** Located on the main thoroughfare, the Major has large tables and secluded booths set in a decor of glowing colors, enhanced by fresh flowers and oversize dinner plates. Try the game soup, followed by duck roasted with apples and buckwheat grits (*kasza gryczana*). During warm weather you can people-watch from the outside café. ✉ *Ul. Długa 18,* ☎ *058/301–10–69. AE, DC, MC, V.*

$$$ ★ ✕ **Pod Łososiem.** "The Salmon" is memorable for its elegant Baroque-era dining rooms, well-oiled maître d', attentive service, and excellent seafood (the menu also extends to game and fowl dishes). Try the salmon or smoked eel to start, followed by flounder or grilled trout. ✉ *Ul. Szeroka 52/53,* ☎ *058/301–76–52. AE, DC, MC, V.*

$$$ ★ ✕ **Tawerna.** The scale-model sailing ship outside leads you into a series of wood-paneled dining rooms overlooking the Motlawa Canal. A pleasant place to linger over lunch or dinner, Tawerna's fresh trout is always reliable, but ask the polite, multilingual waiting staff about the fish of the day. ✉ *Ul. Powroźnicza 19–20, off Długi Targ,* ☎ *058/301–41–14. AE, DC, MC, V.*

$$ ✕ **Retman.** Retman is just a stone's throw from the Green Gate, which you can make out through a stained-glass window. The candlelit interior tries to recapture the atmosphere of 18th-century Gdańsk. A long and varied menu in English includes schnitzel, chateaubriand, and a large selection of seafood. ✉ *Ul. Stagiewna 1,* ☎ *058/301–92–48. AE, DC, MC, V.*

$ ✕ **Pod Jaszczurem.** A step up from the traditional milk bar, this newly renovated restaurant serves perfectly acceptable if not distinguished Polish favorites, steaks, and rather Polish pastas and pizzas. ✉ *Ul. Długa 47/49,* ☎ *058/301–91–13. AE, DC, MC, V.*

$$$ ★ **Holiday Inn.** Holiday Inn hotels enjoy a prestige in Central Europe you may not associate with the chain in North America. Holiday Inn Gdańsk is on the edge of the Old Town, opposite the Gdańsk Główny train station. The rooms and staff are uniformly pleasant, and the facilities are up to date, with a trouser press and Internet access in every room. The hotel even has a T.G.I. Friday's on the premises. ✉ *Ul. Podwale Grodzkie 9, 80–895,* ☎ *058/300–60–00,* FAX *058/300–60–03. 123 rooms, 19 suites. Restaurant, bar, sauna, exercise room, business services, meeting rooms. AE, DC, MC, V.*

$$$ ★ **Hotel Hanza.** This hotel has the best location in town in a spanking new building set right on the Motlawa Canal. Though modern, the Hanza blends in with its surroundings nicely. All rooms are air-conditioned for those few weeks in summer when cooling off really is necessary. Advance bookings, especially in peak season, are strongly recommended. ✉ *Ul. Tokarska 6, 80–888,* ☎ *058/305–34–27,* FAX *058/305–33–86. 53 rooms, 7 suites. Restaurant, bar, sauna, exercise room, free parking. AE, DC, MC, V.*

$$ **Marina.** This large block on the beach is a little out of the way, but it has great views and is a 15-minute stroll from the pier in Sopot. The Marina is a good option when more central hotels are booked. There's a bowling alley downstairs and a miniature golf course right outside. All business rooms have Internet connections, and translators and interpreters are available. ✉ *Ul. Jelitkowska 20, 80–341,* ☎ *058/553–20–79,* FAX *058/553–31–59. 126 rooms, 23 suites, 2 apartments. Restaurant, indoor pool, miniature golf, 2 tennis courts, bowling, nightclub. AE, DC, MC, V.*

Nightlife and the Arts

Although Sopot is where the Tri-City really goes to have fun, there's good nightlife in Gdańsk. On summer nights, the Old Town teems with street musicians, families, and high-spirited young people. The **Cotton Club** (✉ Al. Złotników 25, ☎ 058/301–88–13) draws a mixed crowd to two levels of laid-back drinking and pool tables. The **Jazz Club** (✉ Ul. Długi Targ 39/40) has regular live jazz concerts and the best bar staff in town. **Kamienica** (✉ Ul. Mariacki 23) is a popular new establishment decorated in murals showing the street outside.

Local and international performers take to the stage at Gdańsk's **Opera i Filharmonia Baltycka** (Baltic Opera and Philharmonic; ✉ Al. Zwycięstwa 15, ☎ 058/341–05–63). Gdańsk also has a well-known theater company, **Teatr Wybrzeże** (✉ Ul. św. Ducha 2, ☎ 058/301–70–21). For details about cultural events in Gdańsk, Sopot, and Gdynia, see the English-language periodical *Gdańsk in Your Pocket.*

Sopot

87 *12 km (7½ mi) north of Gdańsk.*

Sopot is one of Poland's leading seaside holiday resorts, with miles of sandy beaches—in theory now safe for bathing (efforts are being made to deal with the Baltic's chronic pollution problems). Sopot enjoyed its heyday in the 1920s and 1930s, when the wealthy flocked here to gamble and enjoy the town's demure, quiet atmosphere. Once the most elegant seaside resort in Poland, Sopot got a little too popular for its own good in the 1980s, when it began to look down-at-heel. Today it is restoring its Riviera-like atmosphere.

Much of Sopot's life takes place close to the Grand Hotel, once *the* place to stay in the area. Sopot's marvelous 19th-century pier is the longest on the Baltic.

Lodging

$$$ ★ **Grand Hotel.** The Grand is not only Sopot's best-known hotel, it's also one of its best-known landmarks. Though its beachfront location and late-19th-century elegance are highly appealing, the rooms themselves are overdue for a makeover. The Grand is also famous for its men's urinals (impressive 6 ft porcelain vaults). ✉ *Ul. Powstańców Warszawy 8–12, 81–718,* ☎ *058/551–00–41,* FAX *058/551–61–24. 112 rooms. Restaurant, nightclub. AE, DC, MC, V.*

$$$ **Villa Hestia.** This boutique hotel is an echo of gentler days when Sopot was known as the Riviera of Poland. These fully equipped luxury apartments, popular with honeymooners, are surrounded by a landscaped garden just a 10-minute walk to the beach. Downstairs is the renowned and beautifully decorated Fukier restaurant. ✉ *Ul. Władysława IV 3/5, 81–703,* ☎ *058/551–21–00,* FAX *058/551–46–36. 2 rooms, 3 suites. Restaurant, pub. AE, DC, MC, V.*

Nightlife and the Arts

Stroll down ulica Bohatcrów Monte Cassino to find the café, pub, or nightclub of your choice. Model types congregate at **Number 5** (✉ Ul. Bohatcrów Monte Cassino 5). The **Siouxie** (✉ Ul. Bohatcrów Monte Cassino 9) begins the day as a quiet coffee place and as night falls turns into a popular bohemian hangout.

Opera Leśna (Forest Opera; ✉ Ul. Moniuszki 12, ☎ 058/551–18–12) gives performances during the summer at its open-air opera house in the forest to the west of town. Sopot is home to a branch of Gdańsk's Teatr Wybrzeże, the **Scena Kameralna** (Chamber Theater; ✉ Ul. Bohatcrów Monte Cassino 55/57, ☎ 058/551–58–12). In August the Miedzynadodowy Festiwal Piosenki (International Song Festival) is held in the open-air concert hall (Muszla Koncertowa) in Skwer Kuracyjny in the center of town near the pier.

Gdynia

88 *24 km (14 mi) north of Gdańsk, 12 km (7½ mi) north of Sopot.*

The northernmost of the three cities that make up the Tri-City, Gdynia has less to offer the visitor than its southern neighbors. In 1922 it was only a tiny fishing village, but by 1939 it had grown into one of the Baltic's biggest ports. In addition to housing the shipyards and docks that dominate this industrial area, Gdynia has a beautifully landscaped promenade.

Near the harbor, the **Muzeum Oceanograficzne-Akwarium Morskie** (Oceanographic Museum and Aquarium) has tanks that more than a thousand species of fish. ✉ *Al. Zjednoczenia 1,* ☎ *058/621–70–21.* 🎫 *Zł 4.* ⏲ *Tues.–Sun. 10–5.*

Opposite the aquarium, the **Dar Pomorza** (Ship Museum) is housed in a World War II battleship, the *Błyskawica.* ⏲ *May–mid-Oct., Tues.–Sun. 10–1 and 2–4.*

In keeping with the nautical tradition of the town, Gdynia's **Muzeum Marynarki Wojennej** (Naval Museum), south of the pier on Bulwar Nadmorski, traces the history of Polish sea life from Slavic times to the present. ✉ *Skwer Kościuszki 15,* ☎ *058/626–35–65.* 🎫 *Zł 3.* ⏲ *Tues.–Sun. 10–4.*

Malbork

89 *45 km (28 mi) southeast of Gdańsk on Rte. 50.*

★ One of the most impressive strongholds of the Middle Ages, the huge **Zamek w Malborku** (Malbork Castle) is the central feature of the quiet town of Malbork (the former German city of Marienburg). In 1230 the Teutonic Knights arrived on the banks of the Vistula River and settled here, aiming to establish their own state on these conquered Prussian lands. The castle passed into Polish hands after the second Toruń Treaty in 1466 concluded the 13-year war between the Poles and the Order of Teutonic Knights. For the next three centuries, Malbork served as the royal residence for Polish kings during their annual visit to Pomerania. The castle was half destroyed during World War II, after which the building underwent a major renovation. The two-hour tours are the best way to see the castle; tours are available in English, and there's an English-language guidebook in the gift shop. ☎ *055/272–33–64.* 🎫 *Zł 13.* ⏲ *May–Sept., Tues.–Sun. 9–5; Oct.–Apr., Tues.–Sun. 9–3.*

OFF THE BEATEN PATH

GNIEW – Located 67 km (42 mi) south of Gdańsk on Route 1(E75), the restored castle of Gniew specializes in medieval-style festivals. Staff stage realistic reenactments of jousting tournaments and sword fights, followed by wild boar roasts, in the town square and in the castle. The castle has a museum (open May–September, Tuesday through Sunday, 9–5) and a hotel. ✉ *Plac Zamkowy 2, 83–140,* ☎ *058/535–35–33.* 🎫 *Museum zł 10.*

Olsztyn

90 *130 km (81 mi) southeast of Malbork, 150 km (93 mi) southeast of Gdańsk, 215 km (133 mi) north of Warsaw.*

Since World War II, Olsztyn has served as the region's primary industrial center. The city is large and has a good number of hotels and restaurants, making it a nice jumping-off point for the Mazurian Lakes.

The Gothic Brama Wysoka (High Gate) marks the entrance to Olsztyn's Old Town and the main square. Southeast of the square is the 15th-century **Katedra świętego Jakuba** (St. James Cathedral).

The **castle,** with its ethnographic and historical **museum,** stands just to the west of the town's square. Once again, Copernicus, that Renaissance man who really got around in northern Poland, is featured in an exhibit. He successfully directed the defense of the castle from 1516 to 1521 against the Teutonic Knights while serving as an administrator of Warmia province. ✉ *Ul. Zamkowa 1,* ☎ *089/527–95–96.* 🎫 *Museum zł 6.* ⏲ *Museum Tues.–Sun. 9–3.*

OFF THE BEATEN PATH

LIDZBARK WARMIŃSKI – This town lies 46 km (28½ mi) north of Olsztyn. In it is the well-preserved 14th-century **castle** of the Teutonic Knights, which survived World War II only because the local population refused to help the Germans demolish it. Buses run to Lidzbark from Olsztyn. ✉ *Pl. Zamkowy,* ☎ *089/767–32–11.* *Zł 2.* ⏲ *Tues.–Sun. 9–2.*

Lodging

$$ **HP Park.** This comfortable if blandly modern hotel sits in parkland and offers horseback riding and bicycles for rent. ✉ *Ul. Warszawska 119, 10–701,* ☎ *089/524–06–04,* FAX *089/524–00–77. 100 rooms. Restaurant, bar, horseback riding, bicycles. AE, DC, MC, V.*

Mikołajki

91 *85 km (53 mi) east of Olsztyn.*

One of the most popular resorts in the Mazurian Lakes region, Mikołajki is situated on the shores of Lake Tałty and Lake Mikołajskie. Boating is popular on nearby Lake Śniardwy. There is a nature preserve surrounding Lake Łukajno, 4 km (2½ mi) east of Mikołajki.

OFF THE BEATEN PATH

WOLF'S LAIR – Just a few miles east of Kętrzyn lies Hitler's onetime bunker at Gierłoż. Built during World War II as his East Prussian military command post, its massively fortified concrete bunkers were blown up, but you can still climb in and among the remains and get a feel for his megalomania. Wolf's Lair was also where a small group of German patriots tried—and failed—to assassinate Hitler on July 20, 1944.

Lodging

$$$ **Hotel Gołębiewski.** This enormous hotel has just about everything you might want, including an indoor pool with massive water slides. Set right on a lake, it is a popular resort spot. ✉ *Ul. Mrągowska 34, 11–730,* ☎ *087/429–07–00,* FAX *087/429–04–44. 576 rooms. 3 restaurants, bar, indoor pool, 4 tennis courts, horseback riding. AE, DC, MC, V.*

Gdańsk and the Northeast A to Z

Arriving and Departing

BY BUS

Gdańsk is the major gateway for the Baltic coast and northeastern Poland. Gdańsk's **PKS bus station** (✉ Ul. 3 Maja, ☎ 058302–15–32) is right next to the train station. Buses may be useful for those who want to venture to small towns off the beaten track; otherwise, trains are more frequent and more comfortable.

BY CAR

From Warsaw, the 7(E77), a two-lane road for part of its length, goes directly to Gdańsk. From the west, the quickest route to the coast from the border crossing at Frankfurt/Oder is to take the 2(E30) to Poznań, and then the 5(E261) via Gniezno and Bydgoszcz to Świecie, where it becomes the 1(E75) and continues via Tczew to the coast.

BY FERRY

Ferries travel daily from Gdańsk to Karlskrona and Oxelösund, Sweden. You can book tickets at one of the following places: **Orbis** (✉ Hotel Hewelius, ul. Heweliusa 22, Gdańsk, ☎ 058/301–34–56); **Polferries** (Polish Baltic Shipping Company; ✉ Ul. Przemysłowa 1, Gdynia, ☎ 058/301–45–44); **Lion Ferry** (✉ Ul. Kwiatowskiego 60, Gdynia, ☎ 058/665–14–14).

BY PLANE

There are several daily flights to Gdańsk from Warsaw, Hamburg, and Copenhagen. The new **airport** (☎ 058/413–141) lies 16 km (10 mi) out of town in Rębiechwo and can be reached by Bus 162, which picks you up and drops you off at the main train station, or by taxi.

The Polish airline, **LOT** (☎ 012/952), is a main carrier. **SAS** (☎ 058/348–11–11) also serves Gdańsk.

BY TRAIN

The main station is **Gdańsk Główny** (✉ Podwale Grodzkie 1, ☎ 058/94–36). Many daily trains leave here for Warsaw (four hours), Kraków (eight hours), Poznań (four hours), and Malbork (take the train to Warsaw, which stops in Malbork; local trains can take ages).

Getting Around

BY CAR

The road network in this part of Poland is relatively well developed and there are plenty of gas stations. Although Gdańsk's Stare Miasto (Old Town) and Główne Miasto (Main Town) areas are easily walkable, a car is useful if you wish to visit other parts of the Tri-City region, such as Sopot and the museums and cathedral at Oliwa, or sights farther afield.

BY BUS, TRAM, AND TROLLEY

A regular service runs throughout the Tri-City, taking you from Gdańsk through Oliwa and Sopot to Gdynia. The whole trip takes about 1¾ hours. The buses run from 5 AM to 11 PM; after 11 PM there is an hourly night-bus service. PKS buses link all the small towns and villages of the region.

BY TRAIN

All the towns of the region can be reached by train. Within the Tri-City area, a fast electric-train service runs every 15 minutes from Gdańsk Główny via Oliwa, Sopot, and Gdynia to Wejherowo. The service operates from 4 AM to 1 AM.

BY WATER BUS

In summer, an hourly water-bus service links Gdańsk with Sopot and Gdynia, via Westerplatte and Hel. In Gdańsk, the **station** (☎ 058/301–49–26) is on the Długie Pobrzeż, the waterfront promenade by the Brama Zielona (Green Gate). The **Gdynia station** (✉ Al. Zjednoczenia 2, ☎ 058/620–21–54) is near the Oceanographic Museum and Aquarium. Sopot's station is at the pier.

Contacts and Resources

EMERGENCIES

Police (☎ 997). **Ambulance** (☎ 999). **Emergency room: Gdańsk** (✉ Al. Zwycięstwa 49, ☎ 058/302–29–29); **Sopot** (✉ Ul. Chrobrego 6/8, ☎ 058/551–24–55).

LATE-NIGHT PHARMACIES

The following pharmacies are open 24 hours: **Gdańsk** (✉ Apteka Dworcowa, ul. Podwale Grodzkie 1 [at the main train station], ☎ 058/346–25–40). **Gdynia** (✉ Pod Gryfem, ul. Starowiejska 34, ☎ 058/620–19–82). **Sopot** (✉ Apteka Kuracyjna, al. Niepodległości 861, ☎ 058/551–31–58).

VISITOR INFORMATION

Gdańsk: The **Agencja Infomacji Turystycznej** (✉ Ul. Długa 45, ☎ 058/301–93–27) is centrally located. **Orbis** (✉ Ul. Heweliusa 22, ☎ 058/301–34–56) has a good selection of maps and brochures. **Sopot: Orbis** (✉ Ul. Podwale Staromiejskie 96, ☎ 058/55–41–42).

WESTERN POLAND

Comprising the provinces of Wielkopolska (Great Poland) and Dolny Śląsk (Lower Silesia), western Poland has always been the traditional heartland of the Polish state—despite spending much of the past 500 years under German, Prussian, and Austro-Hungarian control. Great Poland is part of the flat, vast plain that extends north through Europe and is characterized by smooth farmland, pockets of forest, and numerous lakes. There are many opportunities here for walking, swimming, fishing, and hunting. The hills of Lower Silesia rise gently to the Karkonosze Mountains, where trails draw energetic walkers and resorts lure skiers during winter. Wrocław and Poznań, two of western Poland's primary cities, attract crowds year-round for theater, music, and other cultural diversions.

Although the early Polish state had its origins in the west, the region has fallen (more than once) under German influence. The Poles of Great Poland are affectionately mocked by their countrymen for having absorbed the archetypal German habits of cleanliness, order, and thrift. Lower Silesia and Pomerania were integrated with Poland only in 1945, so don't be surprised if the west feels sober, restrained, and altogether more Germanic than anything you'll find elsewhere in Poland.

Gniezno, the first capital of Poland, is worth visiting for its cathedral and, together with the nearby early settlement at Biskupin, could be a day trip from Poznań. Toruń, the birthplace of Nicolaus Copernicus, is also a good base from which to explore the northern part of this region.

Numbers in the margin correspond to numbers on the Western Poland map.

Wrocław

92 *350 km (220 mi) southwest of Warsaw, 260 km (165 mi) northwest of Kraków.*

Midway between Kraków and Poznań on the Odra River, Wrocław, the capital of Dolny Śląsk (Lower Silesia), dates to the 10th century, when the Ostrów Tumski islet on the Odra became a fortified Slav settlement. There are now some 100 bridges spanning the city's 90 km (56 mi) network of slow-moving canals and tributaries, giving Wrocław its particular charm. Wrocław's population is also notable: almost half the residents of Poland's fourth-largest city are under the age of 30; most are students at one of the city's many institutions of higher learning.

Following the destruction that ravaged Wrocław during World War II, many of the city's historic buildings were restored. Wrocław's architectural attractions are its many brick Gothic churches, the majority of which lie in or around the Stare Miasto (Old Town) and Ostrów Tumski. This area is small enough to explore easily on foot.

The **Rynek** (market square) together with the adjoining **plac Solny** (Salt Square) form the heart of the Old Town, which stretches between the Fosa Miejska moat and the Odra River. Wrocław's market square is almost as grand as Kraków's and bustles with activity. Many of the houses were restored for the Pope's visit in 1997.

Just off the square to the northwest, the little **Jaś i Małgosia** (Hansel and Gretel) houses are linked by a Baroque arcade—holding hands, so to speak. ✉ *Ul. Odrzańska and ul. Wita Stwosza.*

★ The magnificently ornate **Ratusz** (town hall) is the highlight of the market square. Mostly Gothic in style, with a dash of Renaissance and Baroque thrown in, the town hall was under continuous construction from the 14th to the 16th century as Wrocław grew and prospered. In the center of the spired, pinnacled, and gabled **east facade** is a Renaissance **astronomical clock** from 1580. The **Gothic portal** was the main en-

Western Poland

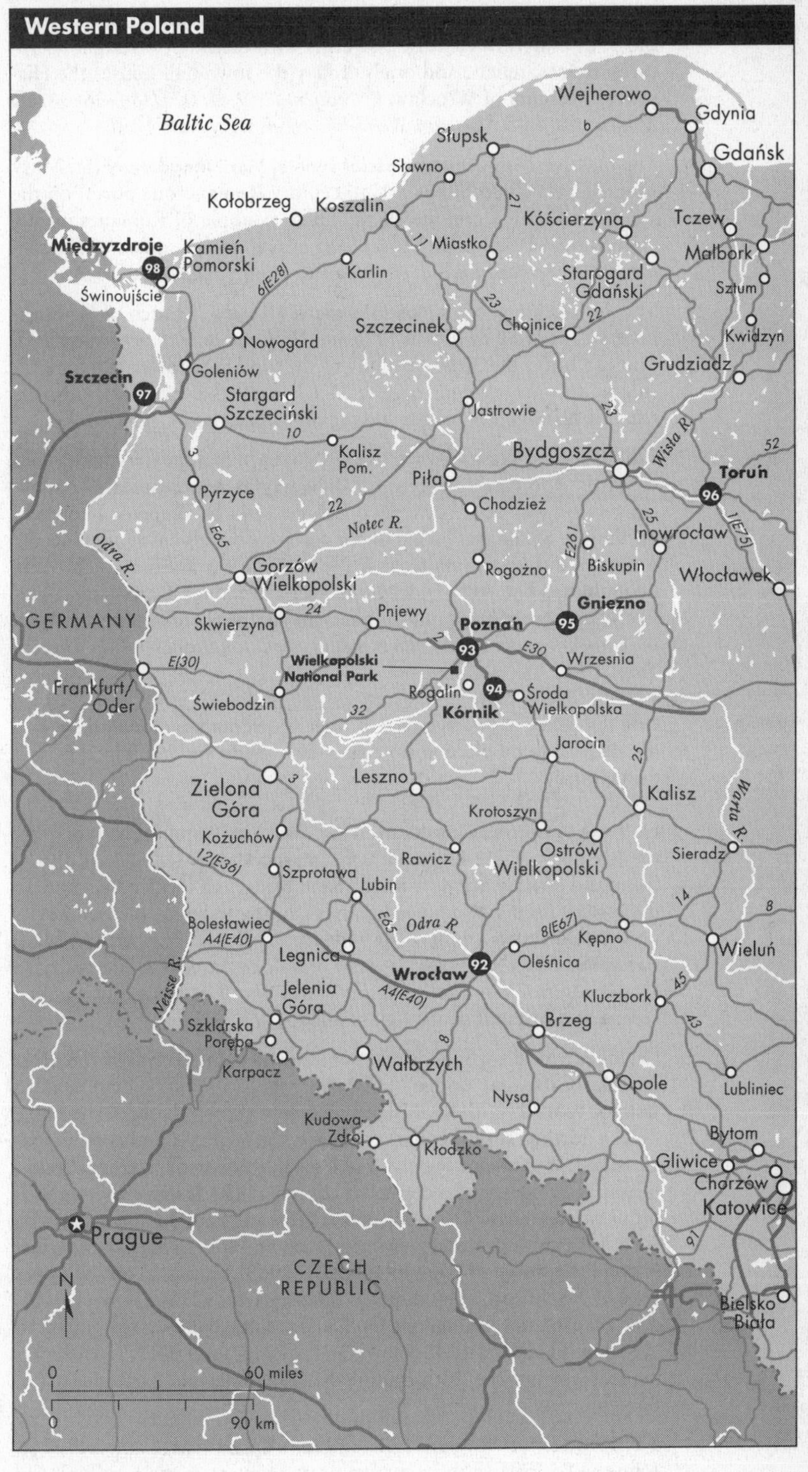

Baltic Sea
Wejherowo
Gdynia
Gdańsk
Słupsk
Sławno
Kołobrzeg
Koszalin
Kościerzyna
Tczew
Międzyzdroje
98
Kamień Pomorski
Miastko
Malbork
Karlin
Starogard Gdański
Sztum
Świnoujście
Szczecinek
Chojnice
Kwidzyn
Nowogard
Goleniów
Grudziadz
Szczecin
97
Stargard Szczeciński
Jastrowie
Kalisz Pom.
Bydgoszcz
Wisła R.
Toruń
96
Piła
Pyrzyce
Chodzież
Notec R.
Inowrocław
Odra R.
Biskupin
Gorzów Wielkopolski
Rogoźno
Włocławek
Gniezno
95
GERMANY
Skwierzyna
Pnjewy
Poznań
93
Wrzesnia
Frankfurt/ Oder
Wielkopolski National Park
Rogalin
94
Środa Wielkopolska
Świebodzin
Kórnik
Jarocin
Zielona Góra
Leszno
Kalisz
Warta R.
Krotoszyn
Kożuchów
Ostrów Wielkopolski
Rawicz
Sieradz
Szprotawa
Lubin
Bolesławiec
Odra R.
Kępno
Wieluń
Legnica
92
Wrocław
Oleśnica
Neisse R.
Jelenia Góra
Kluczbork
Szklarska Poręba
Brzeg
Karpacz
Wałbrzych
Opole
Lubliniec
Nysa
Kudowa-Zdrój
Kłodzko
Bytom
Gliwice
Chorzów
Katowice
Prague
CZECH REPUBLIC
Bielsko Biała
N
0
60 miles
0
90 km

trance of the Ratusz until 1616. The lavish **south facade,** dating from the 15th and 16th centuries, swarms with delicately wrought sculptures, friezes, reliefs, and oriels. Today the town hall houses the **Historical Museum of Wrocław.** ✉ *Sukiennice 9,* ☎ *071/344–36–38.* 🎫 *Museum zł 4.* ⏲ *Museum Wed.–Fri. 10–4, weekends 10–5.*

★ The massive 14th-century **Kościół świętej Marii Magdaleny** (St. Mary Magdalene's Church) has a 12th-century **Romanesque portal** on the south wall that is considered the finest example of Romanesque architecture in Poland. ✉ *1 block east of the market square at the corner of ul. Szewska and ul. św. Marii Kaznodziejska.*

The 14th-century brick **Kościół świętej Elżbiety** (Church of St. Elizabeth) was ravaged by fires in 1975 and 1976 and only recently reopened. You can brave the 302-step climb to the top of the **tower** and look inside at the magnificent organ. ✉ *Ul. Kiełbaśnicza; it can also be reached through the arcade linking the Hansel and Gretel houses.*

Wrocław's university district lies between ulica Uniwersytecka and the river. The vast 18th-century **Uniwersytet Wroclławski** (Wrocław University) was built between 1728 and 1741 by Emperor Leopold I on the site of the west wing of the former prince's castle. Behind the fountain and up the staircase is the magnificent assembly hall, **Aula Leopoldina.** The Aula is decorated with illusionist frescoes and lifesize sculptures of great philosophers and patrons of learning. ✉ *Aula: pl. Uniwersytecki 1.* 🎫 *Aula zł 4 suggested donation.* ⏲ *Aula Thurs.–Tues. 10–3:30.*

NEED A BREAK?

Café Uni (✉ Pl. Uniwersytecki 11), with its outdoor patio and frequent recitals, is a good place to sip coffee and admire the 565 ft facade of the university.

Halfway to Ostrów Tumski, the Most Piaskowy (Sand Bridge) connects the left bank of the Odra with the **Wyspa Piasek** (Sand Island). On the island directly across from the Sand Bridge is a former Augustinian monastery used as Nazi headquarters during the war; the building is now the **University Library.** The 14th-century **Kościół Najświętszej Marii Panny** (St. Mary's Church) is in the middle of the island. The church's Gothic interior was restored after World War II; it has a lofty vaulted ceiling and brilliant stained-glass windows.

On the other side of Sand Island two graceful painted bridges, the Most Tumski (Cathedral Bridge) and Most Młyński (Mill Bridge), lead to ★ **Ostrów Tumski** (Cathedral Island). Lying to the north of the river nine blocks northwest of the market square, Cathedral Island is no longer an island. It is one of the city's oldest quarters, with winding streets, beautiful bridges, and a cluster of churches. The **Kościół świętego Piotra i świętego Pawła** (Church of Sts. Peter and Paul) has no aisles. The early 14th-century **Kościół świętego Krzyża** (Holy Cross Church), just beyond the **statue of Pope John XXIII** (1968), is housed on the upper level of a rigid and forbidding building erected by Duke Henryk as his own mausoleum (the duke's Gothic sarcophagus has been moved to Wrocław's Historical Museum). On the lower level of Duke Henryk's mausoleum lies the 13th-century **Kościół świętego Bartłomieja** (St. Bartholomew's Church).

The 13th-century **Katedra świętego Jana Chrzciciela** (Cathedral of St. John the Baptist), with its two truncated towers, is the focal point of Cathedral Island. Its chancel is the earliest example of Gothic architecture in Poland. The cathedral houses the largest organ in the country, with 10,000 pipes. On the southern side of the cathedral is **St.**

Elizabeth's Chapel; the bust of Cardinal Frederick above the entrance, along with numerous other sculptures and frescoes, came from the studio of Gian Lorenzo Bernini. The **Elector's Chapel**, in the northwestern corner of the cathedral, dates from the early 18th century and was designed by the Baroque architect Johann Fischer von Erlach of Vienna. As these chapels are often closed, check at the sacristy for an update as well as for admission fees. ✉ *Pl. Katedralny.*

The **Muzeum Archidiecezjalne** (Archdiocesan Museum), north of the cathedral, houses a collection of medieval Silesian art. ✉ *Ul. Kanonia 12,* ☎ *071/322–17–55.* *Zł 4.* *Daily 10–3.*

Dining and Lodging

$$$$ ★ ✕ **Królewska and Karczma Piastow.** This beautifully decorated establishment in the heart of Wrocław is divided into two parts: restaurant-nightclub and café–wine cellar. The restaurant, Królewska, serves Polish and international fare. The *shashlik* (grilled beef and peppers) served with brown rice is particularly tasty. The Renaissance-style wine cellar, Karczma Piastow, is a good place to relax on a hot summer's day. ✉ *Rynek 5,* ☎ *071/372–48–96. AE, DC, MC, V.*

$$$ ✕ **Spiż.** Located in the cellar of the town hall, this restaurant is the place to go for a mix of Polish and European cuisine. Heading the menu are *schabowy* (pork cutlet), with mashed potatoes and sauerkraut, and *golonka* (pig's knuckle). ✉ *Sukiennice 9,* ☎ *071/344–52–67. AE, DC, MC, V.*

$$$ **Maria Magdalena.** Lying only a few hundred feet from the market square, this hotel has immaculate rooms with all the modern conveniences, including air-conditioning. ✉ *Ul. Marii Magdaleny 2, 50-103,* ☎ *071/341–08–98,* FAX *071/341–09–20. 50 rooms. Restaurant, bar, air-conditioning. AE, DC, MC, V.*

$$ **Hotel Europejski.** Renovations in this hotel have been sporadic, leaving it half old and half new. The small and simple older rooms are cheaper than the refurbished ones. All guests can admire the exquisite lobby. ✉ *Ul. Józefa Piłsudskiego 88, 50–017,* ☎ *071/343–10–71,* FAX *071/344–34–33. 74 rooms. Restaurant, bar. AE, DC, MC, V.*

Nightlife and the Arts

If you get tired of the bars around the market square try the **Kalambur** (✉ Ul. Kuźnicza 29A, ☎ 071/343–26–50). This Art Nouveau café-bar is attached to a small, well-known theater, and there is sometimes live music.

The **Opera** (✉ Ul. Świdnicka 35, ☎ 071/343–86–41) is performing at various venues across the city because the Grand Opera House on plac Teatralny, south of the market square, is under renovation; at press time it was due to reopen by the end of 2000. Both **Operetka** (✉ Ul. Piłsudskiego 67, ☎ 071/344–49–16) and the **Philharmonic** (✉ Ul. Piłsudskiego 19, ☎ 071/442–001) host classical performances several nights a week.

Teatr Polski (✉ Ul. G. Zapolskiej 3, ☎ 071/343–86–53) is the occasional home of the Wrocław Pantomime Theater. **Wrocławski Teatr Lalek** (✉ Pl. Teatralny 4, ☎ 071/344–12–17) is widely regarded as the best puppet theater in Poland.

One of the most renowned of Wrocław's festivals is **Jazz on the Odra** (☎ 071/22–55–42), a summertime event that has attracted an international group of performers for the past 25 years. Another summer festival is **Wratislavia Cantans,** a series of 24 concerts featuring Gregorian chants, German oratorios, operas, cantatas, and other choral performances. Concerts take place at different points in the city. For schedules ask at IT or Orbis (☞ Visitor Information *in* Western Poland A to Z, *below*).

Poznań

93 *300 km (186 mi) west of Warsaw, 170 km (105 mi) north of Wrocław.*

Set halfway between Warsaw and Berlin, in the middle of the monotonously flat Polish lowlands, Poznań has been an east–west trading center for more than 1,000 years. In the Middle Ages, merchants made a great point of bringing their wares here on St. John's Day (June 23), and the annual tradition has continued. (The markets have now been superseded by the International Trade Fair, which has been held here since 1922.) Until the 13th century, Poznań was, on and off, the capital of Poland, and in 968 the first Polish bishopric was founded here by Mieszko I. It still remains the capital of the Wielkopolska (Great Poland) region.

Despite its somewhat grim industrial outskirts, Poznań is one of the country's most charming old towns; consider making a trip through western Poland if only to visit Poznań's majestic market square. Poznań may be only the fifth-largest city in Poland, but to a tourist it will feel larger than that. While the majority of sights is near the Old Town's impressive Stary Rynek (Old Market Square), other attractions are off in the sprawling maze of ancillary streets. Walking is not recommended here. Invest in some tram tickets and a city map with the transit routes marked; your feet will thank you.

Poznań's **Stary Rynek** (Old Market Square) mainly dates from the 16th century. It has a somewhat cluttered feeling, since the center is occupied with both 20th-century additions and Renaissance structures.

Poznań residents will proudly tell you that the imposing Renaissance ★ **Ratusz** (town hall) at the center of the Old Market Square is the most splendid building in Poland. Its clock tower is famous for the goats that appear every day at noon to butt heads before disappearing inside. Legend has it that the clock maker who installed the timepiece planned to give a party on the occasion. He ordered two goats for the feast, but the goats escaped and started fighting on the tower. The mayor was so amused by the event that he ordered the clock maker to construct a mechanism to reenact the goat fight. The town hall now houses a **Museum of City History,** which contains a room dedicated to Chopin. ✉ *Stary Rynek 1,* ☎ *061/852–56–13.* 🎫 *Zł 5.5.* ⏲ *Mon., Tues., and Fri. 10–4, Wed. noon–6, Thurs. and Sun. 10–3.*

The tiny arcaded shopkeepers' houses in the Old Market Square date to the mid-16th century. Some of them now house the **Muzeum Instrumentow Muzycznycy** (Museum of Musical Instruments), where you can see Chopin's piano and a plaster cast of the maestro's hands. ✉ *Stary Rynek 45,* ☎ *061/852–08–57.* 🎫 *Zł 4.* ⏲ *Tues. and Thurs. 10–4, Wed., Fri., and Sat. 9–5, Sun. 11–4.*

A few blocks west of the Old Market Square is the **Muzeum Narodowe** (National Museum), which has a good collection of Polish and Western European paintings. ✉ *Al. Marcinkowskiego 9,* ☎ *061/852–80–11.* 🎫 *Zł 4.* ⏲ *Wed.–Sat. 10–4, Sun. 11–3.*

After a visit to the museum, walk across Wolności (Freedom) Square to the beautiful **Biblioteka Raczyńskich** (Raczyński Library), built in 1829 by the aristocratic Raczyński family. 🎫 *Free.* ⏲ *Daily 9–5.*

Ostrów Tumski (Cathedral Island), an islet in the Warta River east of the Old Town, is the historic cradle of Poznań. This is where the Polanie tribe built their first fortified settlement and their first basilica in the 10th century.

The island's **Poznań Cathedral** was rebuilt after World War II in pseudo-Gothic style, but 10th- and 11th-century remains can be seen in some interior details. Directly behind the main altar is the heptagonal **Golden Chapel,** worth seeing for the sheer opulence of its romantic Byzantine decor. Within the chapel is the **mausoleum** of the first rulers of Poland, Mieszko I and Bolesław the Great. ✉ *Ul. Mieszka I.*

OFF THE BEATEN PATH **WIELKOPOLSKI NATIONAL PARK** – This beautiful national park lies 19 km (10 mi) southwest of Poznań on Route 430. The pine forests are punctuated with 16 lakes, two of which, Lake Rusałka and Lake Strzeszynek, have long beaches, tourist accommodations, and water-sports equipment for hire. There are several interesting legends associated with the park; for example, at the bottom of Lake Góreckie there is supposed to be a submerged town, and on still nights you can hear the faint ringing of the town bells.

Dining and Lodging

$$ ✕ **Kresowa.** Located on the main town square, this popular restaurant specializes in cuisine from the *kresy,* or Poland's former eastern territories (Lithuania, Ukraine, and Belarus). ✉ *Stary Rynek 2,* ☎ *061/853–12–91. AE, DC, MC, V.*

$$$ 🏨 **Merkury.** This five-story, glass-front hotel is an Orbis product from the 1960s. Identical brown doors lead from long corridors into nearly identical rooms. The rooms are furnished in dark shades, but have the usual Orbis standard of comfort. Its strong suit is convenience: an excellent location and good parking facilities. ✉ *Ul. Roosevelta 20, 60–829,* ☎ *061/847–08–01,* FAX *061/847–31–41. 203 rooms, 11 suites. Restaurant, bar, café, parking (fee). AE, DC, MC, V.*

$$$ 🏨 **Poznań.** This charmless high-rise in the city center next to the railway station has the familiar Orbis touch: rooms decorated in government-regulation brown with slightly outdated bathrooms. ✉ *Pl. Andersa 1, 61–898,* ☎ *061/833–20–81,* FAX *061/833–29–61. 485 rooms, 10 suites. Restaurant, bar, nightclub. AE, DC, MC, V.*

$$ 🏨 **Dom Turysty PTTK.** This hotel has only 18 rooms (of which 10 are singles), but if you can get in you'll like its location, right at the center of the Old Town. Rooms are comfortably furnished, with Polish folk elements, and the staff is friendly and well informed. ✉ *Stary Rynek 91, 61–001,* ☎ FAX *061/852–88–93. 18 rooms, 8 with bath. Restaurant, café. AE, DC, MC, V.*

$$ 🏨 **Lech.** This older hotel near the university is a good base for exploring Poznań on foot. Rooms are on the small side but comfortably furnished. There is no restaurant service apart from breakfast, and the hotel bar sometimes attracts a rather rowdy crowd in the evening. ✉ *Ul. św. Marcin 74, 61–809,* ☎ *061/853–01–51,* FAX *061/853–08–80. 79 rooms, 1 suite. Bar. AE, DC, MC, V.*

Nightlife and the Arts

All the big hotels in Poznań have nightclubs with floor shows. The **Black Club** in the Hotel Merkury (✉ Ul. Roosevelta 20, ☎ 061/847–08–01) is always crowded.

The **Filharmonia Poznańska** (Poznań Philharmonic; ✉ Ul. św. Marcina 81, ☎ 061/852–47–08) holds concerts in Wrocław University's beautifully restored Aula, where the acoustics are excellent.

Stefan Stuligrosz's Boys Choir (✉ Teatr Wielki, ul. Fredry 9, ☎ 061/852–82–91)—the Poznań Nightingales—is one of Poznań's best-known musical attractions.

Kórnik

94 *20 km (12 mi) southeast of Poznań on Rte. 42.*

In this old town you'll find an 18th-century **neo-Gothic castle,** which houses a museum full of antique furnishings and a library of more than 150,000 rare books (including manuscripts by Mickiewicz and Słowacki). Note the magnificent wood-inlay floors. The castle is surrounded by Poland's largest **arboretum,** with more than 3,000 varieties of trees and shrubs. ☎ *061/817–00–81.* 💳 *Zł 4.* ⏲ *May–Sept., daily 9–5; Oct.–Apr., daily 9–3.*

OFF THE BEATEN PATH

ROGALIN – Head 20 km (12 mi) south of Poznań to this Baroque-era palace. It is now a branch of the National Museum in Poznań and includes a collection of 19th-century German and Polish art. The nearby English Garden contains some of the oldest oak trees in Europe. ☎ *061/813–80–30.* 💳 *Zł 4.* ⏲ *Tues.–Sun. 10–4.*

Gniezno

95 *50 km (31 mi) northeast of Poznań on Hwy. 5(E261).*

Lying along the Piast Route—Poland's historic memory lane running from Poznań to Kruszwica—Gniezno is the original capital of Poland and is surrounded by towns whose monuments date to the origins of the Polish state. Legend has it that Lech, the founder of the country, spotted some white eagles nesting on the site; he then named the town Gniezno (nesting site) and proclaimed the white eagle the nation's emblem. On a more historical note, King Mieszko I made Gniezno the seat of the country's first bishop, St. Wojciech, after the king brought Catholicism to the Polish people during the 10th century.

★ The first **cathedral** in Gniezno was built by King Mieszko I before AD 977. The 14th-century building is the most imposing Gothic cathedral in Poland. At the back of the church the 12th-century bronze-cast **Doors of Gniezno** have intricate bas-relief scenes depicting the life of St. Wojciech (Adalbert), a Czech missionary commissioned to bring Christianity to the Prussians in northern Poland. Not everyone appreciated his message: he was killed by pagans. It is said that his body was bought from his murderers for its weight in gold, which the Poles paid ungrudgingly. On the altar a silver sarcophagus, supported by four silver pallbearers, bears the remains of St. Wojciech. 💳 *Zł 3 to see the Doors of Gniezno.* ⏲ *Mon.–Sat. 10–5, Sun. and holidays 1:30–5:30.*

Housed in a characterless concrete school building in Gniezno, the **Muzeum Poczatkew Państwa Polskiego** (Museum of the Original Polish State) has multimedia exhibitions in five languages, including English, that describe medieval Poland. ✉ *Ul. Kostrzewskiego 6,* ☎ *061/426–46–41.* 💳 *Zł 3.* ⏲ *Tues.–Sun. 10–5.*

En Route ★ Step back in time by wandering along the wood-paved streets and peer ing into the small wooden huts at the fortified settlement at **Biskupin,** 30 km (18 mi) north of Gniezno on route E261 toward Bydgoszcz. This 100-acre "Polish Pompeii" is one of the most fascinating archaeological sites in Europe. It was discovered in 1933, when a local school principal and his students noticed some wood stakes protruding from the water during an excursion to Lake Biskupieńskie. The lake was later drained, revealing a settlement largely preserved over the centuries by the lake waters. Dating to 550 BC, the settlement was surrounded by defensive ramparts of oak and clay and a breakwater formed from stakes driven into the ground at a 45° angle. A wooden plaque at the entrance shows a plan of the original settlement. The museum holds a yearly festival in the last week of September that includes historic reenactments. ☏ *053/425–025.* 💳 *Zł 4.* ⏲ *May–Sept., daily 9–6; Oct.–Apr., daily 9–5.*

Toruń

★ 96 *210 km (130 mi) northwest of Warsaw, 150 km (93 mi) east of Poznań.*

The birthplace of Nicolaus Copernicus, the medieval astronomer who first postulated that the earth travels around the sun, Toruń is a beautiful medieval city. It is also one of the few Polish cities to have survived World War II relatively unscathed. The Stare Miasto (Old Town) brims with ancient churches, civic buildings, and residences, its Gothic burgher houses and town hall blending harmoniously with the Renaissance and Baroque of its later patrician mansions.

★ The **Muzeum Mikołaja Kopernika** (Copernicus Museum), one block south of the Rynek Staromiejski (Old Town Square), is dedicated to Toruń's most famous native son, who in 1617 wrote *De Revolutionibus Orbium Coelestium* (*On the Revolutions of the Celestial Spheres*), explaining his theory of a heliocentric universe. The museum consists of two houses: the house at ulica Kopernika 17, where Copernicus was born (in 1473) and lived until he was 17 years old, and the adjoining historic town house. The rooms have been restored with period furnishings, some of which belonged to the Copernicus family. There is also a scale model of Toruń, which is accompanied by a sound-and-light show (available in English) that tells the history of the city. ✉ *Ul. Kopernika 15/17,* ☏ *056/622–67–48.* 💳 *Zł 4.* ⏲ *Tues.–Sun. 10–4.*

The Old Town Square is dominated by the 14th-century **Ratusz** (town hall), one of the largest buildings of its kind in northern Poland. It has 365 windows, and its four pinnacles are meant to represent the four seasons of the year. Built in 1274, the town hall's **tower** is the oldest in Poland, although it did receive some later Dutch Renaissance additions. You can go up into the tower to enjoy a spectacular view. Inside the town hall the **historical museum** houses a collection of painted glass, paintings, and sculptures from the region's craftsmen. Look for the gingerbread molds, which have been used since the 14th century to create the treats for which Toruń is famous. ✉ *Rynek Staromiejski 1,* ☏ *056/622–70–38.* 💳 *Museum zł 4.* ⏲ *Museum Wed.–Sun. 10–4.*

NEED A BREAK? In the town hall, around the corner from the historical museum, the atmospheric café **Piwnica Pod Aniołem** serves great coffee.

On the eastern side of the Old Town Square is **Pod Gwiazdą** (House under the Stars). Built in the 15th century, it was remodeled in the 17th century in the Baroque style. It now houses the **Far Eastern Art Museum,** which is worth visiting to see the interior of the house, especially the carved-wood staircase. ✉ *Rynek Staromiejski 35,* ☏ *056/622–67–48.* 💳 *Zł 6.* ⏲ *Tues.–Sun. 10–4.*

Kościół świętego Jana (St. John's Church) was built in the 13th through 15th centuries. This is where Copernicus was baptized. The **tuba Dei,** a 15th-century bell in the church's tower, is one of the largest in Poland. ✉ *South of the Old Town Square on ul. Żeglarska.*

In a pleasant park northeast of Toruń's Old Town stands the **Muzeum Etnograficzne** (Ethnographic Museum). Outside the museum are brightly decorated farmhouses that have been restored and filled with antique furnishings. The grounds have been designed to replicate life in the Bydgoszcz region (west of Toruń) in the 19th and early 20th centuries. ✉ *Wały Sikorskiego 19,* ☎ *056/622–80–91.* *Zł 4.* ⏲ *Mon., Wed., and Fri. 9–4, Tues., Thurs., and weekends 10–6.*

Dining and Lodging

$$$$ ★ ✕ **Zajazd Staropolski.** This traditional Polish restaurant has a restored 17th-century interior and serves excellent meat dishes and soups. ✉ *Ul. Żeglarska 10–14,* ☎ *056/622–60–60. AE, DC, MC, V.*

$$ ★ ✕ **Restauracja Staromiejska.** Located in the old wine cellar of a 4th-century building, this place has polished wood and stone floors, white-washed walls, and red, brick-ribbed, vaulted ceilings. Enjoy the excellent pizza (the owner is Italian) as well as Polish fare. ✉ *Ul. Szczytna 2–4,* ☎ *056/622–67–25. AE, DC, MC, V.*

$$ ✕ **Trzy Korony.** Inside an old house on the Old Town Square this restaurant serves up regional dishes, including many varieties of meat-filled dumplings (*pyzy*) and thick bean soup (*zupa fasolowa*). ✉ *Rynek Staromiejski 21,* ☎ *056/622–60–31. AE, DC, MC, V.*

$$ **Helios.** This friendly, medium-size Orbis hotel in the city center has typical Orbis rooms (comfortable but plain) and a good restaurant. ✉ *Ul. Kraszewskiego 1/3, 87–100,* ☎ *056/659–54–16,* FAX *80/655–54–29. 108 rooms. Restaurant, beauty salon, sauna, nightclub. AE, DC, MC, V.*

$$ **Kosmos.** A functional 1960s Orbis hotel, Kosmos is showing signs of wear; however, one section of the hotel has recently been renovated. It is near the river, in the city center. ✉ *Ul. Popiełuszki 2, 87–100,* ☎ *056/622–89–00,* FAX *056/622–13–41. 59 rooms. Restaurant, bar. AE, DC, MC, V.*

$$ ★ **Zajazd Staropolski.** Situated in three former tenement houses off the Old Town Square, Zajazd Staropolski is without a doubt the nicest hotel in town. ✉ *Ul. Żeglarska 10–14, 87–100,* ☎ *056/260–61,* FAX *056/253–84. 33 rooms. Restaurant. AE, MC, V.*

$ **Hotel Polonia.** A favorite of Polish families, this antiquated hotel is just across the street from the Municipal Theater near the Old Town Square. The rooms are large, with high ceilings, and very simple. ✉ *Pl. Teatralny 5, 87–100,* ☎ *056/622–30–28,* FAX *056/622–30–29. 46 rooms, 30 with bath. No credit cards.*

Western Poland A to Z

Arriving and Departing

BY BUS

Long-distance PKS buses from other Polish cities arrive in Wrocław at **Dworzec Centralny PKS** (✉ Ul. Kościuszki 135, ☎ 071/344–44–61), diagonally opposite the main train station.

In Poznań the **Dworzec PKS bus station** (✉ Ul. Towarowa 17/19, ☎ 061/833–12–12) is a short walk from the train station. Frequent bus service is available to and from Kornik and Gniezno.

Toruń's **PKS bus station** (✉ Ul. Dąbrowskiego, ☎ 056/622–28–42) is east of the Old Town. Take local Bus 22 to and from the station.

BY CAR

From the west, a four-lane divided highway extends most of the way between Wrocław and the German border town of Cottbus. From Warsaw, the best route is to take the 8(E67) through Piotrków Tribunalski to Wrocław.

Poznań, on the main east–west route from Berlin to Moscow, is easily accessible by car. The 2(E30), which leads from the border at Frankfurt/Oder through Poznań and Warsaw to the eastern border at Terespol/Brest in Belarus, is still mostly a two-lane road and is considered—because of its curves and lack of shoulders—one of the most dangerous roads in Europe.

BY PLANE

LOT offers daily flights from Warsaw to Wrocław. Special LOT buses shuttle passengers from Starachowice Airport to the **LOT office** (☒ Ul. Józefa Piłsudskiego 77, ☎ 071/343–90–31). Buses leave from the same point for the airport one hour before each flight. City Bus 106 will also take you the 10 km (6 mi) from the city to the airport.

Poznań's Ławice Airport is to the west of the city in the Wola district. Buses run regularly to and from the **LOT office** (☒ Ul. św. Marcina 69, ☎ 058/852–28–47); allow about an hour for the journey.

BY TRAIN

Wrocław Główny PKP (☒ Ul. Józefa Piłsudskiego, ☎ 071/368–33–33) connects Wrocław by rail to all major cities in Poland, with frequent service to and from Kraków (five hours), Warsaw (six hours), and Gdańsk (seven hours). Trains also leave here for many cities in Western and Eastern Europe: Dresden, Berlin, Prague, Budapest, and Frankfurt. The station is in the city center, a 30-minute walk south from the Rynek (market square). **Wrocław Nadodrze** (☒ Pl. Powstańców Wielkopolskich) is the hub for local routes to the east and southeast, including Gniezno.

Trains run frequently from the modern **Poznań Główny** (☎ 061/869–38–11) to Szczecin (3 hours), Toruń (2½ hours), Wrocław (3 hours), Kraków (8 hours), and Warsaw (4 hours). International destinations include Berlin (4½ hours), Budapest (15 hours), and Paris (20 hours).

Toruń's **PKP train station** (☎ 056/654–72–22) lies south of the city, across the Vistula River, and is connected to town by Bus 22. There is daily service to and from Poznań (three hours), Gdańsk (four hours), Warsaw (three hours), and Kraków (nine hours).

Getting Around

BY BUS

Wrocław's **Dworzec Centralny PKS** (☒ Ul. Kościuszki 135, ☎ 071/344–44–61) serves local routes, with frequent service to Jelenia Góra, Częstochowa, Łódź, and the spa towns of Kudowa, Duszniki, and Polanica.

BY CAR

Western Poland has good roads and plenty of gas and service stations.

BY TRAIN

You might want to come to the **Wrocław Świebodzki** (☒ Pl. Orląt Lwowskich) station just to admire the station building, which dates from 1848. You can also catch local trains from here. The station lies 1 km (½ mi) south of Wroctaw's market square.

Contacts and Resources

EMERGENCIES

Wrocław, Poznań, and **Toruń** (☎ 999). **Late-night pharmacies: Wrocław** (☒ Pl. 1 Maja 7, ☎ 071/343–67–24); **Poznań** (☒ Ul. 23 lutego 18, ☎ 061/852–26–25).

VISITOR INFORMATION

Poznań: IT (☒ Stary Rynek 59, ☎ 061/852–61–56) sells the cultural guide *IKS,* which has lots of useful information, much of it in English, and is open weekdays 9–5, Saturday 10–2. **Orbis** (☒ Ul. Marcinkowskiego 21, ☎ 061/853–20–52) sells train and bus tickets.

Toruń: IT (☒ Ul. Piekary 37/39 ☎ 056/621–09–31) is open Monday through Saturday 9–4. **Orbis** (☒ Ul. Mostwa 7, ☎ 056/622–17–14) has travel information and sells tickets.

Wrocław: IT (✉ Rynek 14, ☎ 071/344–31–11) has good maps and English guidebooks and is open weekdays 9–5, Saturday 10–2. **Orbis** is a good place to make train reservations (✉ Rynek 29, ☎ 071/344–76–79).

SZCZECIN AND THE COAST

A dip in the Baltic Sea is a rugged but rewarding experience that you can enjoy at a variety of resorts. Most foreign visitors in towns along the Baltic are Germans and Scandinavians looking for sunshine. In summer, duck the droves of Polish tourists and set yourself up in one of the smaller fishing villages.

Szczecin

97 *340 km (215 mi) west of Gdańsk, 515 km (325 mi) northwest of Warsaw, 240 km (150 mi) north of Poznań.*

The large port of Szczecin is on the Odra River just 48 km (30 mi) from the German border. Despite its somewhat industrial atmosphere, Szczecin's location and the overall friendliness of its inhabitants make it an interesting stop-off on your way to Germany or to towns on the Baltic coast. Ruled by several countries over the centuries, Szczecin (or Stettin in German) finally ended up as part of Poland after the Potsdam Conference in 1945. Although not exactly on the coast, Szczecin is separated from the Baltic Sea only by the Zalew Szczecinski (Szczecin Bay). Szczecin was remodeled during the 19th century on the Parisian system of radiating streets and is particularly pretty in spring, when the avenues along the Odra River glow with flowering magnolias.

Szczecin is rapidly regaining some of its former prominence as a Baltic port because of its close proximity to Berlin. In fact, Szczecin still carries many reminders of its Teutonic heritage, including the grandiose **Zamek Ksiazat Pomorskich** (Pomeranian Princes' Castle), which was originally built during the 13th and 14th centuries. The past 300 years have not been kind to the castle, which fell into the hands of the Swedes, Prussians, and French, only to be ruined by carpet bombing near the end of World War II. Today the reconstructed castle is a cultural center housing art exhibits, an opera and concert hall, and the music department of the university. ✉ *Ul. Korsarzy 1,* ☎ *091/434–02–92.* *Zł 5.* *Tues.–Sun. 10–4.*

Housed in a Baroque palace and in an annex across the street, the **Muzeum Narodowe** (National Museum) in Szczecin is devoted mainly to art: older paintings, sculpture, and antiques (13th- to 16th-century Pomeranian), and some Polish pieces from the 17th century. The annex is devoted to modern Polish art. ✉ *Ul. Staromłyńska 27/28,* ☎ *091/433–50–66.* *Zł 4.* *Tues. and Thurs. 10–5, Wed. and Fri. 9–3:30, weekends 10–4.*

Dining and Lodging

$$ ✕ **Restauracja Balaton.** Named for the largest lake in Hungary, Balaton specializes in Hungarian cuisine at reasonable prices. The goulash soup served with bread is especially tasty and filling. The rustic, wood-paneled atmosphere helps to ease the wait of the often slow service. ✉ *Pl. Lotników 3,* ☎ *091/434–68–73. AE, DC, MC, V.*

$ ✕ **Restauracja Chief.** This seafood restaurant in the more modern area of town is decorated with stuffed fish, lobsters, and turtles; aquariums with live fish and turtles fill the corners of the two main rooms. The courteous staff serves fish dishes, as well as beef Stroganoff, and the mandatory pork cutlet. ✉ *Ul. Rajskiego 16,* ☎ *091/434–37–65. AE, DC, MC, V.*

$$$ ★ **Radisson.** A favorite with German and Scandinavian businesspeople, this hotel has all the usual comforts of a Radisson and more. The hotel even has a shuttle bus from the Radisson in Berlin (two hours), which is also available to nonguests. ✉ *Pl. Rodła 10, 70–419,* ☎ *091/359–55–95,* FAX *091/359–45–94. 369 rooms, 10 suites. Restaurant, bar, indoor pool, exercise room, nightclub. AE, DC, MC, V.*

$$ **Neptun.** The rooms in this hotel are comfortable and modern, and each is outfitted with a large bathroom. ✉ *Ul. Matejki 18, 70–530,* ☎ *091/488–38–83,* FAX *091/488–41–17. Restaurant, 2 bars. AE, MC, V.*

En Route The small town of **Kamień Pomorski,** 90 km (55 mi) north of Szczecin, sits on the mainland across the mouth of the bay from Świnoujście. Mysterious carved-wood idols can be found along its beaches, a reminder of the Slavic settlements that once existed here. The old walls that originally encircled the town are no longer complete, but portions have survived, including the gateway, Brama Wolińska, on the west end of the Rynek (market square). Also on the square is a well-preserved town hall, but the town's most impressive structure is its late-Romanesque cathedral, with a splendid Baroque organ. Frequent organ concerts take place in the cathedral, and there's a yearly International Organ and Chamber Music Festival in June and July. Regular bus service connects Szczecin, Kamień Pomorski, and Międzyzdroje.

Międzyzdroje

98 *112 km (66 mi) northwest of Szczecin.*

Every summer the coastal town of Międzyzdroje attracts thousands of vacationers, mostly Poles and Germans, who lie on the beaches, stroll on the boardwalk, and play on one of Poland's very few 18-hole golf courses.

Lodging

$$$ **Hotel Amber Baltic.** This Austrian-owned high-rise is a popular getaway for Germans. The rooms are slightly on the small side, but the outstanding views and the immaculate service compensate. Spend a weekend enjoying a swim in the Baltic (or the pool, if the weather is too cold), playing golf, or strolling along the beach. ✉ *Ul. Promenada Gwiazd 1, 72–500* ☎ *091/328–10–00,* FAX *091/328–10–22. 192 rooms. 2 restaurants, bar, café, indoor pool, pool. AE, MC, V.*

Szczecin and the Coast A to Z

Arriving and Departing

BY BUS

Szczecin is the gateway to Poland's Baltic coast. Szczecin's **PKS bus station** (✉ Pl. Grodnicki, ☎ 091/469–80) is right behind the train station. Check here for service to obscure towns along the Baltic coast. The bus to Gorzów takes 2 hours; the one to Międzyzdroje takes 2½ hours.

BY CAR

To reach Szczecin and Świnoujście from western and southern Poland, take the E65 from Wrocław and Świebodzin via Gorzów Wielkopolski. From eastern and central Poland take the E75 to Toruń and then travel via Bydgoszcz, Piła, and Stargard Szczeciński.

BY PLANE

Passengers arriving by air in Szczecin can take a bus to the **LOT office** (✉ Al. Wyzwolenia 17, ☎ 091/433–99–26), which takes about 45 minutes.

BY TRAIN

Dworzec Główny (✉ Ul. Kolumba, ☎ 091/395) has service to and from the following cities: Warsaw (five hours), Gdańsk (six hours), Berlin (three hours), and the small towns along the Baltic coast. The station is just south of the city on the river; take Tram 3 to reach the city center.

Getting Around

BY CAR

Generally the roads in this area are good, although the secondary roads can be poorly surfaced. The secondary road running nearest to the sea along the coast from Świnoujście through Kołobrzeg to Koszalin and beyond has picturesque views. In the summer season, many gas stations in small towns operate 24 hours a day.

Contacts and Resources

EMERGENCIES

Police (☎ 997). **Ambulance** (☎ 999). **Emergency** (☎ 999).

VISITOR INFORMATION

Szczecin: Informacja Turystyczna (✉ Ul. Wyszyńskiego 26, ☎ 091/434–04–40). **Orbis** (✉ Plac Zwycięstwa, ☎ 091/434–51–54).

POLAND A TO Z

Arriving and Departing

By Bus

A number of companies operate buses between major European cities and Polish cities. Many travel nonstop, and what you lose in comfort you make up for in savings: the bus fare is roughly half the train fare. **Anna Travel** (✉ Al. Jerozolimskie 54, Warsaw, ☎ 022/825–53–89) specializes in international bus travel.

By Car

In summer, the border crossing points into Poland from Germany and out of Poland to the east are notoriously lengthy. Green-card insurance, which covers collision damage outside one's country of residence, can be bought at the border and is necessary if you are bringing in your own car. Rental companies outside Poland often do not permit their cars to cross the border due to the high incidence of theft (for example, Avis Germany will not allow you to take its rental cars to Poland).

By Ferry

Polferries (Polish Baltic Shipping Company; ✉ ul. Chałubińskiego 8, Warsaw, ☎ 022/830–00–97) operates regular ferry service from Denmark (Copenhagen, Ronne) and Sweden (Malmo, Nynashamn, Oxelösund) to Świnoujście, Kołobrzeg, or Gdańsk. **Lion Ferry** (✉ Ul. Kwiatowskiego 60, Gdynia, ☎ 058/665–14–14) offers service from Gdynia to Karlskrona, Sweden.

By Plane

FROM NORTH AMERICA

All flights from North America arrive at Warsaw's **Okęcie Airport** (☎ 022/650–42–20), just south of the city. Delta, American Airlines, and LOT Polish Airlines offer direct flights from New York (flying time is 7½ hours). Most major European airlines fly to Warsaw and also to secondary Polish cities such as Gdańsk, Kraków, and Wrocław (☞ Arriving and Departing by Plane *in* Warsaw A to Z, *above*).

By Train

There are direct trains to Poland from major European cities. In Poland, Orbis and other international travel agencies such as Wagonlit sell international rail tickets, as do all main city stations.

Getting Around

Finding your way around is pretty straightforward once you are familiar with the basic street sign words. *Ulica,* usually abbreviated to ul., means street; *aleje* (al.) is avenue; and *plac* (pl.) is square. In city centers most addresses are clearly marked by a big blue sign with a red stripe across the bottom.

By Bus

The national bus company, **PKS** (☎ 022/823–63–94 in Warsaw), and the private and much more pleasant **Polski Express** (☎ 022/620–03–30 in Warsaw) both offer long-distance service to all cities. You can reserve seats on express buses, which often—except in the case of a few major intercity routes—get to their destinations more quickly than trains. For really out-of-the-way destinations, the bus is often the only means of transportation.

By Car

Driving conditions in Poland continue to deteriorate as traffic density explodes. You will not yet find any Western-quality highways, although new east–west international highways are under construction and a few major roads (such as the one from Warsaw to Katowice) are now entirely four-lane divided highways. This is, however, still the exception rather than the rule. Horse-drawn traffic can cause congestion even on major roads, and carts, pedestrians, and cyclists make driving at night particularly hazardous. If you can avoid driving in Poland, do so.

Poles drive on the right, and there is an overall speed limit of 100 kph (62 mph). The speed limit in built-up areas is 50 kph (30 mph); the beginning and end of these are marked by a sign bearing the name of the town in a white rectangle. At press time, the price of gas was about zł 31 for 10 liters (about 2½ gallons) of unleaded gas. Filling stations appear about every 40 km (25 mi) on major roads but can be difficult to find on side roads. They are usually open from 6 AM to 10 PM, although there are 24-hour stations, usually in cities. The **Polish Motoring Association** (PZMot; ☎ 022/629–83–36) provides tourist information about driving in Poland. They also provide **emergency road help** (☎ 9637 countrywide), as well as breakdown and repair services. If your car breaks down in a remote area, you can usually find a local farmer who will help with a tractor tow and some mechanical assistance.

By Ferry

In the summer season, it is possible to take ferries or hydrofoils between various points on the Baltic coast. Two of the more popular routes are Szczecin to Świnoujście, near the German border on the coast, and Sopot to Hel, north of Gdańsk.

By Plane

LOT Polish Airlines has daily domestic services linking many major Polish cities: Warsaw, Gdańsk, Katowice, Kraków, Poznań, Rzeszów, Szczecin, and Wrocław. Flying time in each case is no longer than an hour. Compared with rail travel, flying is very expensive (although not by Western standards), and most airports are some distance from the city center. However, in a few instances, rail connections can be so limited that flying is a real time-saver (this is especially true between Wrocław and Warsaw, and Rzeszów and Warsaw).

By Train

Polish trains run at three speeds: *ekspresowy* (express), *pośpieszny* (fast), and the much cheaper *osobowy* (slow). Intercity expresses between major cities are the most comfortable and include coffee and sandwiches in the price of the ticket. Only the first two categories have first-class accommodations, and you can reserve a seat only on express trains. Couchettes and sleeping cars (three berths to a car in second class, two berths in first class) are available on long-distance routes. Though restaurant cars are usually available on intercity trains and buffet cars on express trains, it is advisable when on a long trip to take along some food. Tickets can be bought at the station or through Orbis or any travel agency. Tickets are issued for a given date, after which you get only two days during which to travel; thereafter they become invalid.

Contacts and Resources

Camping

You are allowed to camp only at recognized sites, but there are plenty of these. Standards vary; local branches of PTTK (☞ Student and Youth Travel, *below*) can provide leads.

Car Rentals

A valid driver's license, issued in any country, will enable you to drive without a special permit. You do need green-card insurance, which can be purchased at the border, if you are driving your own car.

Booking a rental car in advance through a rental company in your home country can often generate considerable savings. Cars with both manual and automatic transmissions are available, starting at about $450 a week (including insurance and unlimited mileage). Many major car-rental firms have offices at local and international airports and in towns and cities throughout Poland.

You can rent cars from the following companies in Warsaw: **Avis Poland** (☒ Marriott Hotel, Al. Jerozolimskie 65/79, ☎ 022/630–73–16). **Budget** (☒ Marriott Hotel, Al. Jerozolimskie 65/79, ☎ 022/630–72–80). **Hertz** (☒ Ul. Nowogrodzka 27, ☎ 022/621–13–60).

Customs and Duties

Persons over 18 may bring the following into Poland duty-free: personal belongings, including musical instruments; one computer; a radio; one camera with 24 rolls of film; up to 250 cigarettes or 50 cigars; 1 liter of spirits and 2 liters of wine; together with goods that are not for personal use up to the value of euro 70. Foreign currency over the value of euro 5,000 may be brought in but must be declared, as should antique jewelry or books published before 1945 (to avoid possible problems when taking them out of the country). Further information can be obtained from **Customs Information** (☎ 022/650–28–73).

Language

Polish is a Slavic language that uses the Roman alphabet but has several additional characters and diacritical marks. Because it has a higher incidence of consonant clusters than English, most English speakers find it a difficult language to decipher, much less pronounce. Take a phrase book and a pocket dictionary with you; the people you're trying to communicate with will at least appreciate the effort. The *Berlitz Polish Phrase Book and Dictionary* is a good starting point.

Younger Poles are likely to speak some English, while their elders are more likely to know French or German—and, of course, Russian, which they will not admit to. In larger cities English is increasingly common, especially in hotels, restaurants, and tourism-related shops, but English speakers in the countryside are still a rarity.

Mail

POSTAL RATES

Airmail letters to the United States and Canada at press time cost zł 1.60; postcards, zł 1.10. Airmail letters to the United Kingdom or Europe cost zł 1.40; postcards, zł 1. Airmail Express costs an extra zł 2.5 flat charge and cuts the travel time in half. Post offices are open weekdays from 8 AM to 8 PM. At least one post office is open 24 hours a day in every major city.

RECEIVING MAIL

The main post office in every town has *poste restante* (general delivery) facilities. Friends and family who send you mail should write "No. 1" (signifying the main post office) after the name of the city.

Money and Expenses

COSTS

At press time, the annual rate of inflation had fallen to about 10% annually. The złoty has strengthened and stabilized. The days when you could exchange $50 on the black market and feel like a millionaire are over. Although most goods and services are still cheaper than in the West, they are gradually rising to European levels. On the other hand, visitors have a greater range of options in selecting appropriate accommodations. Some top hotels still quote room prices in hard currency, but in the provinces simple rooms can be had for as little as $10 per night. Overall, you can still get very good value for your money in Poland, and the farther you venture off the beaten track, the cheaper your vacation will be.

POLISH CURRENCY

The monetary unit in Poland is the złoty (zł), which is subdivided into 100 groszy (gr). Since the currency reform of 1995, there are notes of 10, 20, 50, 100, and 200 złotys, and coins in values of 1, 2, and 5 złoty and 1, 2, 5, 10, 20, and 50 groszys.

At press time, the bank exchange rate was about zł 4.1 to the U.S. dollar, zł 2.8 to the Canadian dollar, and zł 6.5 to the pound sterling. Foreign currency can be exchanged at banks or at private exchange bureaus (*Kantor Wymiany Walut*), where rates are usually slightly higher than at banks and service is swifter. With a major credit card and a pin number, you can also get money from cash machines, which you can find in most major cities.

SAMPLE COSTS

A cup of coffee, zł 4–zł 7; a bottle of beer, zł 5–zł 9; a soft drink, zł 2–zł 5; a 1½ km (1 mi) taxi ride, zł 6; a 240 km (150 mi) train trip (first-class single), zł 40.

TAXES

A 22% value-added tax (VAT) is applied to most all goods and services. A VAT refund is available for visitors; take your receipts to the refund service at any border or the Warsaw or Kraków airport. There are also taxes on airline tickets.

National Holidays

January 1; Easter Sunday and Monday; May 1 (Labor Day); May 3 (Constitution Day); June 22 (Corpus Christi); August 15 (Assumption); November 1 (All Saints' Day); November 11 (rebirth of the Polish state, 1918); December 25, 26.

Opening and Closing Times

Food shops are open weekdays 7–7, Saturday 7–1. Other stores are open weekdays 11–7 and Saturday 9–1, although more and more stores are staying open later and on Sunday. Banks are generally open weekdays 8–3 or 8–6. Museum hours are unpredictable but are generally Tuesday–Sunday 10–5.

Passports and Visas

U.S. and EU citizens do not need visas for entry to Poland (a valid passport will suffice). Canadian citizens must pay C$89 or C$207 for a single- or multi-entry visa. Apply at the nearest Polish consulate. Each visitor must complete one application form and provide two passport-size photographs. Allow about two weeks for processing. Visas are issued for 90 days but can be extended once in Poland, through the local police headquarters.

Rail Passes

The **European East Pass** (☞ Train Travel *in* Smart Travel Tips) covers Poland, as well as Austria, the Czech Republic, Hungary, and Slovakia.

Student and Youth Travel

Two good resources are **Almatur** (✉ Ul. Kopernika 23, Warsaw, ☎ 022/826–35–12), the Polish student-travel organization, and **PTTK** (✉ Ul. Litewska 11/13, Warsaw, ☎ 022/629–39–47). Substantial discounts can be gotten when traveling in Poland with IYHC (International Youth Hostel Card) and ISIC (International Student Identification Card) cards.

Telephones

The country code for Poland is 48. The city code for Warsaw is 22.

LOCAL CALLS

Phone booths which take calling cards have become widespread. They can be used for both local and long-distance calls. Cards, which cost zł 6.41, zł 12.81, or zł 25.62, are available at post offices, most newspaper kiosks, and hotels. When making a long-distance call, first dial 0, wait for the dial tone, then dial the rest of your number.

INTERNATIONAL CALLS

International calls can be made from post offices or first-class hotels, where you can use your credit card or pay after making the call. You can also make calling card calls through a toll-free operator. **MCI** (☎ 0–0800–111–2122) connects you to the U.S. **Sprint Global One** (☎ 0–0800–111–3115) lets you make calls worldwide. Through **AT&T USA Direct** (☎ 0–0800–111–1111) you can call the U.S. using a major credit card.

Tipping

It is customary to round up on bills, for a total of not more than about 10% for waiters. For taxi drivers, round up to the nearest złoty or two. A tip of zł 2 per bag is in order for porters. Concierges and tour guides should get at least zł 5.

Visitor Information

Orbis is partially privatized and is still the main Polish tourist information office, with branches throughout the country. It specializes in booking reservations in its own hotels and in selling tickets for both domestic and overseas travel. **PTTK,** a nationwide network of tourist clubs, can provide extensive information for the budget traveler or visitor with a particular interest in the history of individual regions or the outdoors. Look for signs marked **IT** on or near the main squares of cities and towns for complete tourist information services.

7 BULGARIA

Bulgaria is "a land as big as the palm of one's hand," as its poets have often said. At the crossroads of Europe and Asia, once ruled by the Turks, the "Jewel of the Balkans" is an exotic and often confusing mix of cultures, where Eastern mysticism and mosques coexist with Slavic traditions and the deteriorating remnants of a Communist past. Mountains crowned by rugged hilltop monasteries, peaceful farmland villages dotting the fertile Danube plains, and a coastline strewn with miles of golden beaches and tranquil waterfront towns give undiscovered Bulgaria its intoxicating allure.

Updated by Jay Lee

BULGARIA, A LAND OF MOUNTAINS AND SEASCAPES, of rustic unspoiled beauty and proud hospitality, lies in the eastern half of the Balkan Peninsula. From the end of World War II up until the collapse of communism, it was the closest ally of the Soviet Union. "The forgotten corner of Europe," as locals still sometimes call it, Bulgaria during the Cold War period presented a mysterious and even sinister image to Western travelers. When this period ended in 1989 with the overthrow of Communist Party head Todor Zhivkov, Bulgaria opened its doors to the West, readopted its traditions and religion, and embraced the opportunity to present its unique character to the rest of the world. Politically and economically, Bulgaria has struggled and suffered. Many Bulgarians believed the "miracle" of democracy and capitalism would bring stability and prosperity overnight. Instead, upheaval dashed the people's dreams. Since 1989, the government has changed hands seven times, primarily between parties composed of the former Communist leaders.

In the winter of 1997, massive unemployment, hyperinflation, rampant corruption, and growing breadlines turned the national disillusionment into anger. Inspired by the new UDF (Union of Democratic Forces) president Peter Stoyanov, the people of Bulgaria took to the streets, surrounded the parliament building where members of the BSP (Bulgarian Socialist Party) were barricaded inside, and demanded new elections. During the monthlong uprising, strikes and protests paralyzed the country, until finally the Socialists agreed to hold elections two years before the slated end of their term. In April of 1997 the people voted the UDF into power, marking the second time in nearly a decade that the country was not under Socialist rule. This new government has a tremendous task before it, and only time will tell if it can succeed in creating infrastructure out of chaos. The preliminary aims are to make Bulgaria a contender for membership in the European Union, to fight the all-powerful Mafia, and to revive the stagnant economy. Most Bulgarians now realize that meaningful reform may take years to implement, perhaps decades to succeed.

Yet having survived the recent turmoil, Bulgaria is once again a relatively peaceful destination in the Balkans. Courting EU and NATO membership, it studiously avoided involvement in the Kosovo conflict, even though Serbia is a mere 80 km (50 mi) from Sofia and errant NATO missiles landed within its borders. Though continuing economic depression makes life hard for locals, visitors will find Bulgarians exuberantly welcoming, especially to Western tourists and the coveted hard currency they carry into the country. With gorgeous countryside, low prices, friendly people, thriving nightlife, and an eclectic and hearty cuisine, Bulgaria will not remain undiscovered for long. For adventurous souls who don't mind a few rough edges (and wrestling with Cyrillic), Bulgaria provides not only an extraordinary vacation destination but a chance to see history in the making.

Founded in 681 by the Bulgars, a Turkic tribe from Central Asia, Bulgaria was a crossroads of civilization even before that date. Archaeological finds in Varna, on the Black Sea coast, give proof of civilization from as early as 4600 BC. Bulgaria was part of the Byzantine Empire from AD 1018 to 1185 and was occupied by the Turks from 1396 until 1878. Today, Bulgaria remains a dizzying blend of cultures, with its Eastern-influenced architecture, Turkish fast-food, Greek ruins, Soviet monuments, and European outdoor cafés. Five hundred years of Muslim occupation and nearly half a century of Communist rule did not wipe out Christianity, and many lovely, icon-filled churches dot the countryside. The country's 120 monasteries, with their icons and frescoes, chronicle the development of Bulgarian cultural and national identity.

The capital, Sofia, is picturesquely situated in a valley near Mt. Vitosha. Culturally and historically rich, the city has good hotels, a wide variety of restaurants, excellent ballet and opera, and a vibrant Mediterranean-style nightlife with scores of bars and discos. The interior landscape of the country offers magnificent scenic beauty, with tranquil forested ridges, spectacular valleys, and rural communities where folklore is a colorful part of village life. Veliko Turnovo, just north of the Balkan Range in the center of the country, was the capital from the 12th to the 14th century and is well worth a visit for its medieval ramparts and vernacular architecture. Plovdiv, a university town and the intellectual center of the country, lies southeast of Sofia and has a picturesque Old Town as well as one of the best-preserved Roman amphitheaters in the world.

The Black Sea coast along the country's eastern border has secluded coves and old fishing villages, as well as wide stretches of sandy beaches that have been developed into self-contained resorts. Varna was once the summer beach playground for the entire Eastern Bloc but now draws a wider array of visitors. A thriving city in the winter as well, it is among the most important ports on the Black Sea.

Pleasures and Pastimes

Architecture

Old Bulgarian architecture is best seen in the country's towns and villages with cobble streets, stone-vaulted bridges, and wooden houses. Within the solid walls of typical houses in small mountain towns such as Bansko are delicate rooms with carved ceilings and colorful handmade rugs. Koprivstitsa and the Old Town of Plovdiv are known for their excellent examples of National Revival architecture, a 19th-century style that helped reestablish Bulgarian artistic identity after the Turkish occupation. These houses are colorfully painted, often with ornately carved wooden ceilings and second stories that extend out over the first, supported by wooden pillars.

Churches, Monasteries, and Icon Paintings

Most Bulgarian churches and monasteries are from the National Revival period (18th and early 19th centuries), a time of vigorous cultural activity and increased awareness of a national identity. The famous Rila Monastery is included on the UNESCO list of World Heritage Sites. The Bachkovo and Troyan monasteries are both known for their splendid murals and icons, painted by Zahari Zograph and other great National Revival artists.

The tradition of Bulgarian icons goes back to the 9th century, when the Bulgarians converted to Christianity. During and after the National Revival period, many icon-painting schools were formed. The schools of Bansko, Samokov, and Troyan produced icons for the newly built churches and private homes. The biggest collections of icons are displayed in the Crypt Museum of Alexander Nevski Memorial Cathedral in Sofia and in the Museum of Art and History in Varna.

Dining

Balkan cooking revolves around lamb, pork, sheep cheese, eggplant, and other vegetables. Typical Bulgarian dishes include wonderful *shopska salata* (tomato, cucumber, and feta cheese salad), *sarmi* (vine leaves stuffed with meat and rice), and *kebapche* (grilled meat balls). Bulgaria invented *kiselo mlyako* (yogurt); excellent *tarator* (cold yogurt soups)

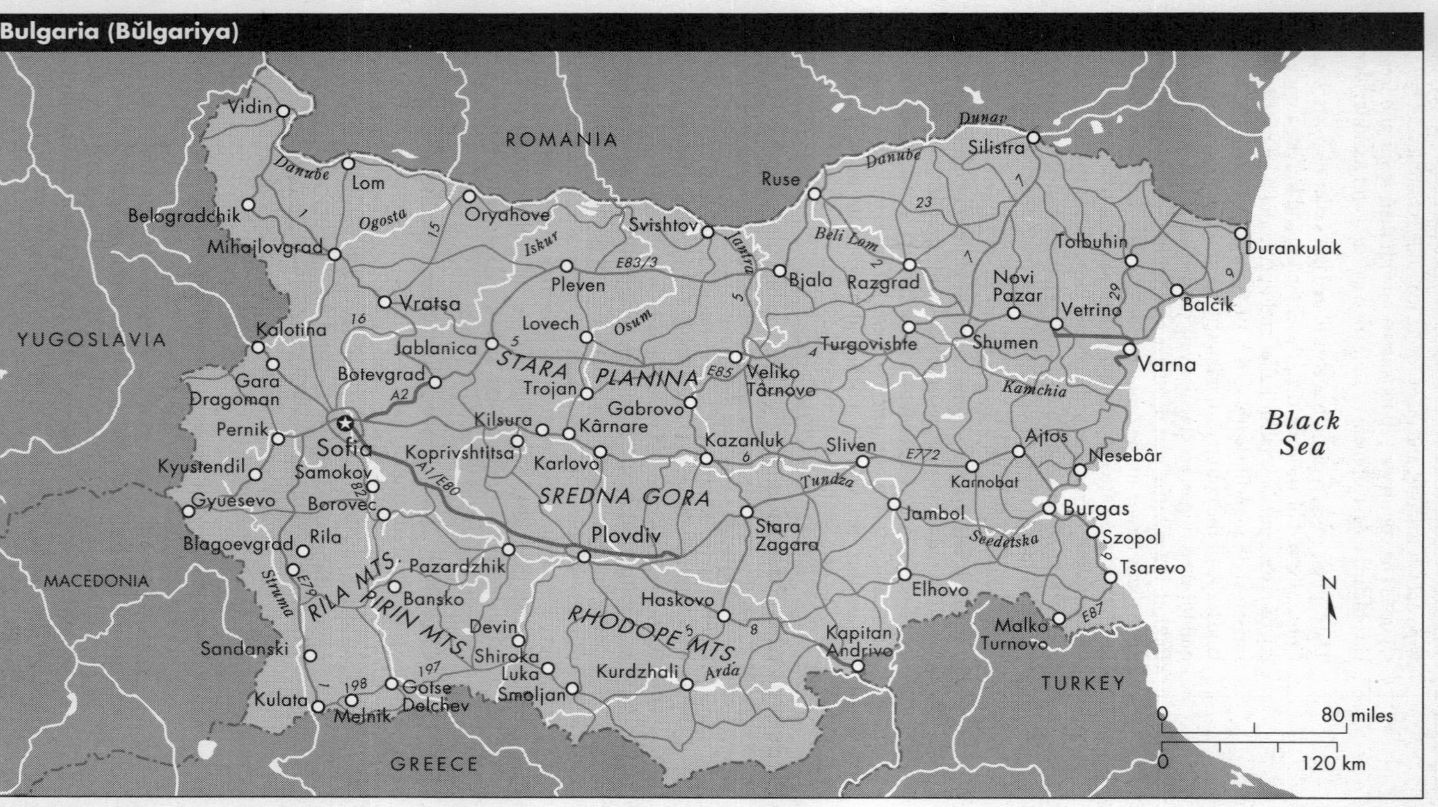
Bulgaria (Bŭlgariya)
ROMANIA
YUGOSLAVIA
MACEDONIA
GREECE
TURKEY
Black Sea
N
80 miles
120 km
0
Danube
Dunav
Vidin
Belogradchik
Mihajlovgrad
Lom
Oryahove
Vratsa
Kalotina
Gara Dragoman
Pernik
Kyustendil
Gyuesevo
Sofia
Botevgrad
Jablanica
Samokov
Borovec
Rila
Blagoevgrad
Sandanski
Kulata
Melnik
Gotse Delchev
Bansko
Pazardzhik
Devin
Shiroka Luka
Smoljan
Kurdzhali
Haskovo
Plovdiv
Koprivshtitsa
Kilsura
Karlovo
Kârnare
Trojan
Lovech
Pleven
Svishtov
Gabrovo
Kazanluk
Stara Zagara
Veliko Târnovo
Ruse
Bjala
Razgrad
Turgovishte
Sliven
Jambol
Elhovo
Kapitan Andrivo
Shumen
Novi Pazar
Silistra
Tolbuhin
Vetrino
Varna
Balčik
Durankulak
Ajtos
Karnobat
Nesebâr
Burgas
Szopol
Tsarevo
Malko Turnovo
STARA PLANINA
SREDNA GORA
RHODOPE MTS
RILA MTS.
PIRIN MTS.
Ogosta
Iskur
Osum
Jantra
Beli Lom
Kamchia
Tundža
Sredetska
Arda
Struma
A1/E80
A2
E79
E83/3
E85
E772
E87

are served in summer. Syrupy baklava and *palachinki* (crepes stuffed with chocolate or nuts and honey) are the favored desserts.

The national drink is *rakia* (brandy), made either from *slivova* (plums) or *grosdova* (grapes)—many Bulgarians make their own, or know someone who does, and claim this is the only rakia to drink. Cold rakia is typically taken with the salad course. Bulgarian wines are usually full-bodied, dry, and inexpensive. Reds from Melnik and the Suhindol and Sliven regions and whites from the Black Sea area are worth requesting. Coffee is strong and is often drunk along with a cold beverage, such as cola.

Visitors have a choice between predictable, often uninspired hotel dining and the more adventurous outing to a local restaurant or café where the menu may only be offered in Cyrillic. In larger cities, international cuisine is easy to find, but in smaller towns the best bets are the small restaurants called *mehani* that serve national dishes and local specialties. Dinner out in a mehana is considered a recreational experience. Bulgarians share tables with strangers (feel free to do this yourself—it's perfectly acceptable) and linger for hours over the smallest of salads while drinking rakia, smoking, and listening to loud music. (Restaurant turnover is practically unheard of—don't bother waiting if all the tables are full.) Calmer atmospheres are easily found in restaurants featuring more Continental cuisine. If cigarette smoke bothers you, choose one of the many places with outdoor seating.

CATEGORY	COST*
$$$$	over $12
$$$	$8–$12
$$	$4–$8
$	under $4

**per person for a three-course meal, including tip but not alcohol.*

Hiking and Walking

Mount Vitosha and the mountains of the Rila, Pirin, and Rhodope ranges are good for walking. Nature lovers will appreciate Vitosha for its beautiful moraines, Rila and Pirin for their clear blue lakes, and the Rhodopes for their green slopes and rare plants. The Balkan range, which crosses the entire country, has splendid rocks and caves. Two of the most interesting are Ledenika and Magura, with their veritable sculptures of stalactites and stalagmites. Ledenika is about 200 km (124 mi) northeast of Sofia, while Magura is approximately 250 km (155 mi) north of the capital.

Lodging

Bulgaria offers a wide choice of accommodations, from hotels—most of them dating from the '60s and '70s—to apartment rentals, rooms in private homes, and campsites. Although hotels are improving, all but the newest still tend to suffer from temperamental wiring and erratic plumbing, and it is a good idea to pack a universal drain plug, as plugs are often missing in hotel bathrooms. In moderate and inexpensive hotels, don't be surprised if strangely placed plumbing turns the entire bathroom into a shower. Flashlights and other battery-powered utilities are strongly recommended, as there are likely to be power outages in winter. Being prepared is especially important if you plan to rent a private room through a tourist agency; often these rooms don't even have towels. Quirks such as these in accommodations give you a sense of the real Bulgaria.

Until recently, most hotels used by Western visitors were owned by Balkantourist and Interhotels. Many government-owned or -operated hotels are either recently privatized or on the verge of privatization. The conversion is expected to take up to five years, and hotels may be closed for renovation for extended periods or may be permanently shut down. We strongly urge you to contact hotels in advance to get the latest information. Most have restaurants and bars; the large, modern ones have swimming pools, shops, and other facilities. Popping up all along the coast are new, small, private hotels with far more personality than the large, nondescript older properties. Many of these small hotels are family houses in small towns and villages south of Burgas.

Socialist-era hotels often have a half-board policy; besides a Continental breakfast, you're given a coupon for either lunch or dinner; if you don't use the meal coupon, you are not reimbursed. If you refuse the coupons when booking a room—and most people do, since the meals are lackluster—your room rate should be lowered a bit. Hotel bills can be paid in either Western or local currency, but if you pay in leva, you must show your exchange slips to prove that the money was changed legally. Unless otherwise noted, all rooms have bath.

CATEGORY	SOFIA*	OTHER AREAS*
$$$$	over $200	over $75
$$$	$75–$200	$55–$75
$$	$40–$75	$30–$55
$	under $40	under $30

**All prices are for two people in a double room with breakfast.*

following the text of a review is your signal that the property has a Web site, where you will find details and, usually, images; for a link, visit www.fodors.com/urls.

Music

You can hear Bulgarian folk music at numerous festivals around the country, including the festival held in May in Koprivshtitsa and the late-September event held near Pamporovo, just south of Plovdiv. Bulgarian folk dances are performed by dancers in brightly colored costumes, which differ according to the region of the country. Rhodope mountain music is eerie and beautiful, unfamiliar to most foreigners.

Spa Resorts

There are hundreds of mineral springs in Bulgaria. Their healing properties were well known to the ancient Romans. The spa hotels in the resorts of Sandanski and Velingrad provide various treatments, including manual therapy, acupuncture, phytobalneology, phytotherapy, and slimming cures. (Sandanski is a half hour from the Greek border crossing at Kulata; Velingrad is southeast of Sofia in the Rhodopes.) The Black Sea hydrotherapy centers in Sveti Konstantin, Albena, and Pomorie are famous for their healing mud. The mineral springs along the northern Black Sea coast turn the sea resorts into year-round spas.

Exploring Bulgaria

Bordered by Romania to the north (the Danube River forms the border), Serbia and the former Yugoslav Republic of Macedonia to the west, Greece and Turkey to the south, and the Black Sea to the east, Bulgaria is in the southeastern corner of Europe in the heart of the Balkan Peninsula. Geographically, Bulgaria can be divided into two basic regions: the Inland and the Black Sea Golden Coast. Inland you'll find one of Bulgaria's two chief attractions, its towering mountains, and on the Black Sea you'll find the other, its glittering seacoast.

Great Itineraries

Bulgaria may be small, but its nature and landscapes are strikingly diverse. If you have more than a week to tour the country, you'll be able to see most of it. If you have less than a week, you'll still get to see some major sights and get an impression of the country and its people. If two or three days are all you have, you'll have to choose between the mountains and the sea.

Numbers in the text correspond to numbers in the margin and on the Sofia map.

IF YOU HAVE 3 DAYS

Begin in **Sofia** ①–⑭ and spend the day in the central part of the city—be sure to visit the magnificent Hram-pametnik Alexander Nevski (Alexander Nevski Memorial Cathedral), and some of the new art galleries. On the second day, head for **Plovdiv.** Spend the morning walking around in Plovdiv's Old Town, and have a coffee on the terrace overlooking the magnificent Rimski Amfiteatur (Roman Amphitheater). On the third day, pass through the town of Karlovo to **Koprivshtitsa,** where you can see some of the finest examples of typical old Bulgarian architecture. Or, instead of heading toward Koprivshtitsa, you can go to **Borovec,** the oldest and the biggest mountain resort in Bulgaria, at the foot of Vrah Musala, the highest peak on the Balkan Peninsula.

IF YOU HAVE 5 DAYS

Spend a day in **Sofia** ①–⑭, and from there travel to **Rila Monastir** (Rila Monastery), founded in the 10th century. Spend the night here, either in the local hotel or in one of the sparse monks' rooms in the compound, and leave the next morning for **Bansko,** a museum town with charming National Revival houses. The third day, go hiking in the Pirin Mountains, and the next, visit the tiny village of **Melnik,** famous for its architecture, sandstone formations, lively taverns, and red-wine tasting in ancient caves. From Melnik, before going back to Sofia, you can visit the Rozhen Monastir (Rozhen Monastery), most of it decorated by unknown painters.

When to Tour

Summers here are warm, and winters are crisp and cold. If you're looking for sun, head to Bulgaria in July or August. Although this is Bulgaria's "high season," the only places you'll find crowds are the Black Sea coast and Sofia. Even when the temperature climbs in summer, the Black Sea breezes and the cooler mountain air prevent the heat from being overpowering.

Don't limit yourself to summer for a visit to Bulgaria, though—the coastal areas get considerable sunshine year-round. The inland areas, however, are wet during most of March and April.

SOFIA

Exploring Sofia

Bulgaria's bustling capital sprawls on the high Sofia Plain, ringed by mountain ranges: the Balkan Range to the north; the Lyulin Mountains to the west; part of the Sredna Gora Mountains to the southeast; and, to the southwest, Mt. Vitosha—the city's summer and winter playground—which rises to more than 7,600 ft. The area has been inhabited for about 7,000 years, but the first impression is of haphazard and thoughtless modern urban development. Driving in, don't be daunted by the surreal expanse of outwardly grim Socialist-era block housing. The city center is of a more human scale, with spacious parks, open-air cafés, and broad streets filled with an incongruous mix of pedestrians, expensive Western cars, and archaic farmers' wagons. As recently as the 1870s Sofia was part of the Ottoman Empire, and one mosque

Sofia

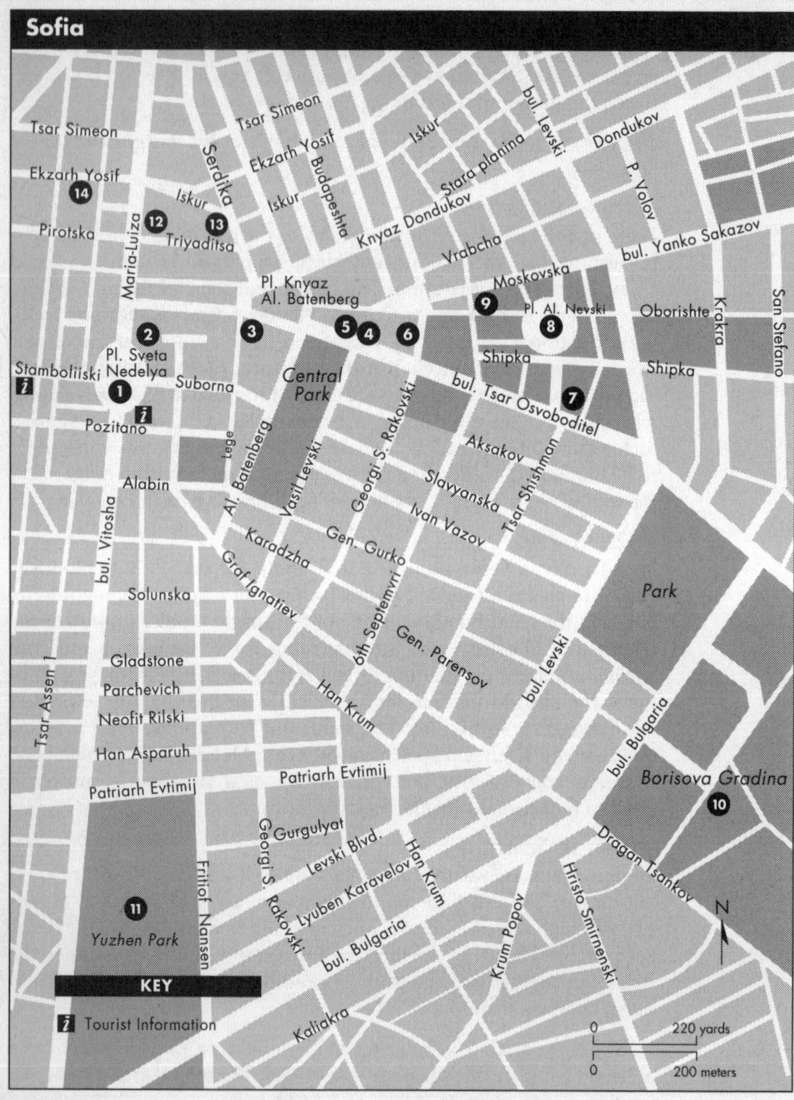

Banya Bashi Djamiya **12**
Borisova Gradina **10**
Hram-pametnik Alexander Nevski **8**
Narodno Subranie **7**
Natzionalen Archeologicheski Musei **3**
Natzionalen Dvoretz na Kulturata **11**
Natzionalen Etnografski Muzei **4**
Natzionalna Hudozhestvena Galeria **5**
Rotonda Sveti Georgi **2**
Tsentralna Sofiiska Sinagoga **14**
Tsentralnata Banya **13**
Tzarkva Sveta Nedelya **1**
Tzarkva Sveta Sofia **9**
Tzarkva Sveti Nikolai **6**

still remains. Most of the city, however, was planned after 1880, and following the destruction of World War II, many of the main buildings were rebuilt in the Socialist style.

Numbers in the text correspond to numbers in the margin and on the Sofia map.

A Good Walk

Begin your tour in the heart of Sofia at the crowded and lively ploshtad Sveta Nedelya (St. Nedelya Square), named after the church, **Tzarkva Sveta Nedelya** ①, that dominates its south side. On the north side of ploshtad Sveta Nedelya is the **Rotonda Sveti Georgi** ②, the oldest archaeological monument in Sofia. Heading east from here, you'll enter ploshtad Alexander Batenberg and see the huge Partiyniyat Dom, the former headquarters of the Bulgarian Communist Party—its architecture is reminiscent of the country's recent Communist history.

Near the southwestern corner of the square is the **Natzionalen Archeologicheski Musei** ③. Follow the yellow-brick road east to the faded green former royal palace, which today houses the **Natzionalen Etnografski Musei** ④ and the **Natzionalna Hudozhestvena Galeria** ⑤. Pause for a moment to regard the broad expanse of yellow brick in front of the royal palace and the pleasant Central Park to the south. Consider that in 1999 one of the city's landmarks, the somber and squat mausoleum of Communist leader Georgi Dimitrov, was wiped off the map, a symbolically charged gesture financed by private donors. One block away on the left side of the street is **Tzarkva Sveti Nikolai** ⑥. From this church, walk down bulevard Tsar Osvoboditel, with its monument to the Russians, the Tsar Osvoboditel (Tsar Liberator), topped by the equestrian statue of Russia's Czar Alexander II. It stands in front of the **Narodno Subranie** ⑦, where during the January 1997 uprising protesters lobbed stones from the plaza through the windows at members of parliament barricaded inside. Behind it, just beyond ulitsa Shipka, you'll be confronted by the shining **Hram-pametnik Alexander Nevski** ⑧, where you can pause to browse through the outdoor antiques and icons market. Here you should also take a look at the extensive collection of icons in the basement Crypt Museum. Across the square from the memorial church is a much older church, **Tzarkva Sveta Sofia** ⑨. Return to bulevard Tsar Osvoboditel through ploshtad Alexander Nevski. If you continue east, you'll reach **Borisova Gradina** ⑩.

From the park, walk south past the big sports stadium until you come to bulevard Dragan Tsankov. Next, turn down ulitsa Graf Ignatiev and head west to the monument of Patriarh Evtimij, a 14th-century Christian patriarch. Take the boulevard of the same name until you reach the **Natzionalen Dvoretz na Kulturata** ⑪, where young couples meet and stroll, children skateboard, and the elderly sit on park benches enjoying the spectacle.

Next, walk along bulevard Vitosha back to ploshtad St. Nedelya, and then follow bulevard Knyaginya Maria-Luiza toward the train station. On the right is the Tsentralen Universalen Magazin (Central Department Store). Just beyond this big store are the **Banya Bashi Djamiya** ⑫ and the **Tsentralnata Banya** ⑬, the latter closed for ongoing renovations. Across the boulevard is the Tsentralni Hali (Central Market Hall). Just west of the Central Market Hall is the **Tsentralna Sofiiska Sinagoga** ⑭, with gleaming Moorish domes and the largest chandelier in the Balkans. Turning left on ulitsa Ekzarh Yosif and walking west toward ulitsa Stefan Stambolov will immerse you in the crowds coming and going from the Zhenski Pazaar, the most fascinating outdoor bazaar in the city. With hordes of villagers hawking produce, pirated CDs, clothes, and homemade goods, this area is sensory overload and the perfect end to a full and fascinating day.

Timing

This walking tour covers 5 km–6 km (3 mi–4 mi) and will take about four hours to complete. You can also combine a tour of Sofia with a short walk on Mt. Vitosha. To do this, you'll need six to seven hours. It's best to head for Vitosha during the week, when it's much less crowded than on weekends. Vitosha is usually covered with snow from December to March. There are ski lifts on the mountain, and rental skis are available.

Sights to See

12 **Banya Bashi Djamiya** (Banya Bashi Mosque). A legacy of Turkish domination, this 16th-century mosque is one of the most noteworthy sights in Sofia, with its imposing dome and elegant minaret. Built in 1576 by the Turkish architect Sinan, the mosque was named (*banya* means baths) for its proximity to mineral baths. The interior is closed to the non-Islamic public and the fence around it is festooned with vendors. ✉ *Bul. Maria-Luiza, across from Central Market Hall.*

10 **Borisova Gradina** (Boris's Garden). If you look past the dilapidated benches, packs of stray dogs, and overflowing garbage dumpsters, you can imagine what the park was like before Bulgaria's recent depression. An empty lake, a dry fountain, and neglected statues of Communist leaders are surrounded by dense, overgrown woods and dirt paths—still a favorite spot for strolling. In summer, ice cream vendors, children riding around in battery-operated minicars, a cool outdoor disco, and a surprisingly pristine public pool with children's water slides bring life to the park. ✉ *Bul. Bulgaria between bul. Tsar Osvoboditel and bul. Dragan Tsankov.*

★ 8 **Hram-pametnik Alexander Nevski** (Alexander Nevski Memorial Cathedral). You may recognize this neo-Byzantine structure with glittering interlocking domes from the pictures of it that appear on almost every piece of tourist literature. It was built by the Bulgarian people at the beginning of the 20th century as a mark of gratitude to their Russian liberators. Inside are alabaster and onyx, Italian marble and Venetian mosaics, magnificent frescoes, and space for a congregation of 5,000. There's a fine collection of icons and religious artifacts in the **Cryptata na Hram Pametnik Alexander Nevsky** (Crypt Museum), representing Byzantine influence, Ottoman rule, and the National Revival period. On Sunday morning you can attend a service to hear the superb choir. In the area near and around the church are many ladies selling lace tablecloths. ✉ *Pl. Alexander Nevski,* ☎ *02/87–76–97.* *5 leva.* *Wed.–Mon. 10:30–5.*

7 **Narodno Subranie** (National Assembly). During the January 1997 uprising, CNN made this building famous by repeatedly broadcasting clips of protesters smashing and climbing through the windows and dragging members of the Socialist parliament out into the plaza in a demand for new elections. Topped by the Bulgarian national flag, the blocky building is adorned with an inscription reading "Unity makes strength," referring to the unification of the country in 1885, a few years after the defeat of the Turks. ✉ *Bul. Tsar Osvoboditel at pl. Narodno Subranie.*

★ 3 **Natzionalen Archeologicheski Musei** (National Archaeological Museum). This museum is housed in the former Great Mosque. Recent renovations make the 15th-century building as fascinating as its contents, which illustrate the cultural history of the country up through the 19th century. ✉ *Pl. Alexander Batenberg, behind the Sheraton Hotel,* ☎ *02/88–24–06.* 🎫 *Free.* ⏲ *Tues.–Sun. 10–4.*

11 **Natzionalen Dvoretz na Kulturata** (National Palace of Culture, or NDK). This large, modern building, filled with a complex of halls for conventions and cultural activities, is the main focus of **Yuzhen Park.** In its underpass you'll find a tourist information office, shops, restaurants, discos, and an internet café. The park itself is a great place for people-watching. The section to the north is a favorite gathering spot for Sofia's youth, whizzing around on in-line skates, skateboards, and bikes. ✉ *Yuzhen Park, off bul. Vitosha,* ☎ *02/5–15–01.*

NEED A BREAK? For an enormous Western-style cappuccino served in a soup bowl, apple pie with ice cream, or a slice of rich cheese cake with caramel sauce, try **Dvete Fucli** (✉ 14, ul. Karnigradska), or "The Two Sweetie-pies," a tiny, homey café just off bulevard Vitosha north of Solunska.

4 **Natzionalen Etnografski Musei** (National Ethnographical Museum). Collections of costumes, handicrafts, and tools exhibited here in the former palace of the Bulgarian czar illustrate rural life through the 19th century. ✉ *1, pl. Alexander Batenberg,* ☎ *02/87–41–91.* 🎫 *3 leva/5 leva with guide.* ⏲ *Wed.–Sun. 10–noon and 1:30–5:30.*

5 **Natzionalna Hudozhestvena Galeria** (National Art Gallery). Here, in the west wing of the former royal palace, are paintings by the best Bulgarian artists as well as representative works—notably prints—from the various European schools. ✉ *Pl. Alexander Batenberg,* ☎ *02/89–28–41.* 🎫 *2 leva.* ⏲ *Tues.–Sun. 10:30–6.*

2 **Rotonda Sveti Georgi** (Rotunda of St. George). These ancient remains of what is billed as the oldest public building in Bulgaria are in the courtyard behind the Sheraton Hotel. The rotunda was built in the 4th century as a Roman temple, destroyed by the Huns, rebuilt by Justinian, and turned into a mosque by the Turks before being restored as a church. Restoration has revealed medieval frescoes. ✉ *Off pl. St. Nedelya.* 🎫 *Free.* ⏲ *Daily 8:00–6.*

14 **Tsentralna Sofiiska Sinagoga** (Sofia Synagogue). After decades of disrepair, the Moorish turrets and gilt domes of this 1909 synagogue have been beautifully restored. It is now one of the most spectacular buildings in downtown Sofia. ✉ *Ul. Ekzarh Yosif and bul. Washington.* 🎫 *Free.* ⏲ *Weekdays 9–5, Sat. 9–1.*

13 **Tsentralnata Banya** (The Central Baths). For years, this splendid building, once an Ottoman bathhouse, was left to disintegrate. Renovations began in 1997; at press time the baths were not yet open to the public, but visitors can taste the hot mineral water at the spring in the adjacent park. ✉ *Ul. Serdika at ul. Triyaditsa.*

1 **Tzarkva Sveta Nedelya** (St. Nedelya Church). This impressive church was built during 1856–1863 and later altered by a Russian architect. In 1925 it was destroyed by terrorist action; it was rebuilt in 1931. Today it's open to visitors, and services are held on Sunday. You may even get a peek at a bride—this is one of the most popular wedding spots in the city. ✉ *Pl. Sveta Nedelya.* 🎫 *Free.* ⏲ *Daily 7 AM–7 PM.*

9 **Tzarkva Sveta Sofia** (Church of St. Sofia). One of the oldest churches in the city, it dates to the 6th century, though excavations have uncovered the remains of even older structures on the site. Because of its great age and its simplicity, the church provides a dramatic contrast to the showy Alexander Nevski Memorial Cathedral nearby. While the church undergoes seemingly endless renovation, it's open to visitors, and ser-

vices are held daily at 9:30 AM. ✉ *Ul. Moskovska.* 🎫 *Free.* ⏲ *Daily 9–1 and 2–5.*

6 **Tzarkva Sveti Nikolai** (Church of St. Nicholas). This small and very ornate Russian church—it has five gold-plate domes and a green spire—was erected in 1912–1914. Inside, mosaics depict favored Russian saints and czars. It's commonly called (surprise) the Russian Church. ✉ *Bul. Tsar Osvoboditel.* 🎫 *Free.* ⏲ *Daily 9–1 and 2–5.*

Dining

Near the influences of Western Europe and the Mediterranean as well as the Middle East, Sofia is a crossroads for culinary influences, with exotic foods ranging from spicy Indian curries to Turkish *döner kebaps* (meat roasted on a spit). New restaurants and cafés offering high-quality, inexpensive cuisines from around the world are springing up everywhere. Still, for those willing to brave cigarette smoke and crowded seating for some local color, the most authentic and enjoyable experience is to be had in a *mehana* (tavern), where the music is loud and Bulgarians relax for hours over rakia and traditional meals such as grilled pork sausages and french fries smothered in *cyrine,* a delicious variant of feta.

$$$$ ✕ **Nad Aleyata, Zad Shkafut.** In English, "Beyond the Alley, Behind the Cupboard," this small, casually elegant restaurant serves innovative Bulgarian and European cuisine. You can find such Bulgarian staples as *chushky biorek* (a pepper stuffed with cheese and deep-fried), as well as international offerings such as veal medallions and chicken Kiev. Popular with local diplomats, the restaurant has a large selection of salads and an excellent wine list, and the staff is accustomed to serving foreigners. There's a quiet patio for warm-weather dining, and you'll find what many consider to be the nicest rest rooms in town. ✉ *31, ul. Budapeshta,* ☎ *02/83–55–81. Reservations essential. No credit cards.*

$$$$ ✕ **33 Stoli.** Classy and intimate, this candlelit cellar has a changing menu specializing in European cuisine such as frogs' legs and Swiss fondue. The wine list is thorough, and the desserts are mouthwatering—try the *shokolade palachinka sus presni plodove* (chocolate crepe with fresh fruit). And yes, there really are only 33 *stoli* (chairs). ✉ *14, ul. Assen Zlatarov,* ☎ *02/44–29–81. Reservations essential. MC, V.*

$$$ ✕ **Bai Gencho.** A favorite with Sofiantsi, this traditional mehana provides the classic tavern experience with the added elegance of candles and a warm fireplace. The chef's specialty for two, *etspetsialitet na gotvachka za dvama* (mixed grill of sausages, steak, and shish kebabs), is a carnivore's dream. ✉ *ul. Kniaz Alexander Dondukov 15,* ☎ *02/986–6550. Reservations essential. No credit cards.*

$$$ ✕ **Golden Dragon.** This small Shanghai restaurant near the opera house has attracted regulars for years with its spicy dumplings and informal, friendly atmosphere. Don't expect a "No MSG" promise on the menu, but do expect tasty food and fast service. ✉ *166A, ul. Rakovski,* ☎ *02/88–80–30. No credit cards.*

$$$ ★ ✕ **La Gondola Vinarna.** In a cellar just off bulevard Vitosha, this *vinarna* (wine-tasting house) is the best place in the city for wine connoisseurs. The wine list includes outstanding bottled domestics, as well as towering carafes of excellent reds. Fill your plate from a buffet table laden with traditional salads and starters (priced by weight), such as shopska salata, exceptionally good *banitsa* (filo pastry filled with feta cheese and sometimes spinach), and *kiopolu* (puree of eggplant and tomatoes); if it's in season, don't miss the *tikvichki sus kiselo mlyako* (fried squash in yogurt). A pizzeria upstairs has the same wine selection but a less-expensive Italian menu. ✉ *16, bul. Vitosha,* ☎ *02/980–9493. No credit cards.*

$$$ ✕ **La Rotisserie du Tzar Ivan Assen II.** Known simply as "the Rotisserie," this subterranean restaurant just off Vitosha serves Bulgarian and Continental cuisine; seasonal game dishes are a particular strength. There's a bit of a pretentious air here—sorbet between courses, the menu in French—and the food may not always meet the high standards aspired to. But the costumed wait staff is attentive, if unhurried, and Sofiantsi come here for the experience and the excellent value. Appropriate attire is expected—don't show up in jeans and a T-shirt. ✉ *Corner of Hristo Belchev and Neofit Rilski,* ☎ *02/980–1717. No credit cards.*

$$ ✕ **Baalbeck.** Though somewhat seedy looking, this Middle Eastern restaurant just off central ploshtad Slaveikov is favored by local businesspeople for its fast lunches of tasty falafel, hummus, and tabouleh. Sit downstairs for a quick bite from the bar, or dine upstairs if you want a knife and fork for your *döner kebap* (spit-roasted meat). ✉ *6, Vasil Levski,* ☎ *no phone. No credit cards.*

Lodging

The following hotels maintain a high standard of cleanliness and are open year-round unless otherwise stated. Those on the higher end of the price range are comparable to luxury hotels in Western Europe, while those at the lower end will give you a taste of Bulgaria's Communist past with drab decor and the possibility of faulty electricity and plumbing. At press time, the 200-plus room Hilton Sofia was under construction near the National Palace of Culture, scheduled to open in 2001. Also, a mainstay of Sofia's state-owned hotels, the Grand Hotel Sofia near the National Assembly, has been privatized and gutted. No date has been set for reopening following renovation.

$$$$ ★ **Castle Hotel Hrankov.** This luxury hotel is 10 km (6 mi) from the Sofia city center in the suburban Dragalavci district, at the foot of Mt. Vitosha. It has high-quality accommodations and extensive fitness facilities; besides the squash and tennis courts and an Olympic-size swimming pool, it rents skis and has shuttles to the slopes. It's not an authentic castle (it opened in 1996), but the turrets, gardens, and nighttime lighting make it a good facsimile. ✉ *53, Krusheva Gradina, Dragalevtsi 1415,* ☎ *02/91–909,* FAX *02/67–29–85. 360 rooms. 4 restaurants, pool, 2 tennis courts, squash, nightclub, casino. AE, DC, MC, V.*

$$$$ ★ **Hotel Kempinski Zografski–Sofia.** Acquired in 1997 by the Kempinksi hotel chain, the former Inter-Continental is a luxurious hotel whose large rooms have views of Mt. Vitosha. With audiovisual and simultaneous-translation facilities available, it is a prime option for business conferences. The hotel also has the most expensive restaurant in the entire country, Sakura, Bulgaria's one and only spot for sushi, and a highly rated Italian restaurant, Parma. ✉ *100, bul. James Bourchier, 1407,* ☎ *02/68–32–51,* FAX *02/68–12–25. 454 rooms. 5 restaurants, bar, minibars, room service, pool, health club, shops, casino. AE, DC, MC, V.*

$$$$ **Sheraton Sofia Hotel Balkan.** This first-class hotel has a central location that's its greatest asset. The building is a typically socialist box; the rooms are basic and businesslike, with large bathrooms. ✉ *5, pl. St. Nedelya, 1000,* ☎ *02/981–65–41,* FAX *02/980–64–64. 187 rooms. 3 restaurants, 3 bars, minibars, room service, exercise room, casino. AE, DC, MC, V.*

$$$ **Hotel Maria Luiza.** The closest thing Sofia has to a modern yet cozy bed-and-breakfast, this upscale private hotel has bright, comfortable rooms; business facilities; an excellent downtown location with views of Banya Bashi Mosque and the Central Baths; and a friendly staff. ✉ *29, bul. Maria Luiza, 1000,* ☎ *02/9–10–44,* FAX *02/980–33–55. 21 rooms with bath or shower. Restaurant, bar, minibars, room service. AE, DC, MC, V.*

$$$ **Novotel Europa.** This member of the French Novotel chain is on one of Sofia's main boulevards, near the train station, and not far from the center of the city. Large, modern, but impersonal, it is better for business than for tourism. ✉ *131, bul. Maria Luiza, 1202,* ☎ *02/3-12-61,* FAX *02/32-00-11. 600 rooms. 2 restaurants, 2 bars, room service, exercise room, casino, meeting rooms. AE, DC, MC, V.*

$$ **Bulgaria.** Despite its central location, this small hotel is quiet and old-fashioned. The interior, with its marble staircase; arched windows; and low, wooden beds and lace curtains in the guest rooms, is charming. ✉ *4, bul. Tsar Osvoboditel, 1000,* ☎ *02/87-19-77 or 02/87-01-91,* FAX *02/88-41-77. 85 rooms. Restaurant, bar, café. No credit cards.*

$$ **Rila.** A central downtown location makes this a low-cost, if aesthetically challenged, alternative to the nearby Sheraton (☞ *above*). Rooms are a bit garish, with red-and-orange color schemes, but the hotel does have all the essential facilities. (The Rila may have set a new standard for Sofia hospitality by including a condom in every room.) Contemporary Bulgarian paintings (for sale) hang in the lobby, and though trendy night spots come and go, at press time a very popular disco inhabited the Rila basement. ✉ *6, ul. Kaloyan, 1000,* ☎ *02/980-88-65,* FAX *02/981-33-86. 138 rooms with bath or shower. Restaurant, bar, café, exercise room, casino. AE, DC, MC, V.*

$$ **Serdika.** Centrally located in the university district, this clean and comfortable hotel is the place to stay if you're looking for a fun location—but not a quiet one. One of the city's best cinemas is right downstairs, and the Tequila Bar, a loud Mafia bar with metal detector at the entrance, is next door. Ask for one of the newer rooms, which have enclosed shower stalls. (The rest have the open-shower setup.) ✉ *2, bul. Yanko Sakazov,* ☎ *02/44-34-11,* FAX *02/46-52-96. 140 rooms. Restaurant, bar, café. DC, MC, V.*

$$ **Sun Hotel.** Cozy and comparatively inexpensive due to its lively but marginal neighborhood, this private hotel offers small but comfortable rooms in a beautiful old building with a cheerful yellow facade scored with tiny wrought-iron balconies. Be alert outside: The Sun is directly across from the Luvov Most (Lion's Bridge), Sofia's most notorious red-light district and a prime area for pickpocketing. ✉ *89, bul. Maria Luiza, 1000,* ☎ *02/83-36-70,* FAX *02/83-53-89. 16 rooms with bath or shower. Restaurant, bar, room service. No credit cards.*

Nightlife and the Arts

Nightlife

In a city that only a few years ago had just one discothèque, there is now a wide range of nightlife choices. Like the residents of neighboring Greece, Bulgarians love all-hours Mediterranean-style dance clubs. New nightspots are opening up every week, so consult the English-language *Sofia City Guide,* available at tourist agencies and the Sofia Sheraton, to find out about current hot spots. If you're looking to go out, try gravitating to one of the city's nightlife districts, such as on ulitsa Stefan Karadzha near bulevard Rakovski, and seeing what strikes your fancy. Upscale establishments are generally Mafia hangouts (unlike many Bulgarians, mafiosi have money to burn), but they are not a threat to tourists. Things don't get going at clubs or live music venues until midnight, though the beer halls currently en vogue are busy from the early evening on.

BARS AND NIGHTCLUBS

For live music, **Swingin' Hall** (✉ 8, bul. Dragan Tsankov, ☎ 02/963-0696), one of the first "Western" clubs to open in the city, is still a popular spot. **Bibliotekata** (✉ basement of National Library, entrance on ul. Oborishte, ☎ 02/946-1165) is a labyrinth of chambers with karaoke, a small dance floor, and several bars, the largest of which has a tiny stage where live bands play. **La Strada Jazz Club** (✉ 4, ul. 6 na Septemvri, ☎ no phone) draws a sophisticated, arty clientele for jazz, blues, and modern alternative rock. **J.J. Murphy's** (✉ 6, ul. Karnigradska, ☎ 02/980–2870) is a genuine Irish pub popular with Bulgarians and the ex-pat community alike. **Mr. Punch** (✉ 20, ul. Stefan Karadzha, ☎ 02/88–42–14) has some of the biggest live music acts in Sofia—featuring, but not limited to, rock 'n' roll. Trendy beer gardens such as **Bohemi** (✉ 55, bul. Vasil Levski, ☎ 02/87–73–25) are popping up throughout the city; this *biraria* not far from Sofia University has a couple of floors, sequestered corner tables, and a patio. Bulgarian staples are served.

DISCOS

Spartacus (✉ in the underpass at the junction of bul. Vasil Levski and bul. Tsar Osvoboditel, in front of Sofia University) is Sofia's first gay club, attracting the city's avant-garde, both gay and straight.

One of the city's most chic and expensive discos, **Chervilo** (✉ 5, bul. Tsar Osvoboditel, just off ploshtad Narodno Subranie), or "Lipstick," draws Sofia's well-to-do twenty- and thirtysomethings. (When taking a cab, just tell the driver the disco's name.) In the smaller room, Sofia's best DJs take turns playing acid jazz and house music, and in the larger room, crowds dance to Euro-techno.

Next door to Chervilo (☞ *above*) in the venerable Military Club is **Vsi Svetii** or "All Saints" (✉ 7 bul. Tsar Osvoboditel, ☎ 02/87–86–64), which is a tony restaurant (Bulgarian food in nouvelle cuisine–size servings) and bar by day and dance club by night.

A popular disco that brings in guest DJs from Western Europe is **Indigo** (✉ Borisova Gradina), near Swingin' Hall (☞ Bars and Nightclubs, *above*).

The Arts

The standard of music in Bulgaria is high, whether it takes the form of operatic, symphonic, or folk. Recently renovated **Bulgaria Hall** (✉ 1, ul. Aksakov, ☎ 02/98–401, ⏲ box office: 10–1:30, 3:30–6:30, 🎫 5 leva per performance) is a fine-sounding, intimate venue for top-rate performances by the Sofia Philharmonic and the New Symphony Orchestra. Consult the "Cultural Diary" column of the English-language *Sofia Echo,* available at many city center newsstands, or the *Sofia City Guide* monthly arts supplement for symphony, opera, ballet, and other events listings.

Sofiska Durjhavna Opera (The Sofia National Opera and Ballet; ✉ 1, ul. Vrabcha, ☎ 02/987–7011) has excellent performances; stop by the box office (✉ 30, bul. Dondukov, ☎ 02/87–13–66) for a program. While the quality of the dance is often high, ask at the box office if the performance is with an orchestra, since some performances are accompanied by recorded music.

You don't need to understand Bulgarian to enjoy a performance at the **Kuklen Teatur** (Central Puppet Theater; ✉ 14, ul. Gen. Gurko, ☎ 02/87–38–15), or the **Natsionalen Ensemble za Narodni Tantsi y Pesni** (National Folk Ensemble; check with Balkantourist [☞ Visitor Information in Sofia A to Z, *below*] for details).

Sofia seems to have a movie theater on nearly every street. All but a handful of out-of-the-way art-house theaters show recent foreign films in their original languages with Bulgarian subtitles. However, the only theaters where you will find comfortable seating and good sound systems are the **F/X** (✉ 5, ul. Angel Kanchev, ☎ 02/981–2717), **Serdika** (✉ 42, ul. Vasil Levski, directly across from the Levski monument, ☎

02/43–17–97), **Modernun** (✉ 26, bul. Maria Luiza, ☎ 02/87–56–46), **Dom Na Kinoto** (✉ 37, ul. Ekzarh Yosif, ☎ 02/88–06–76), and **Evropa Palace** (✉ 35, ul. Alabin, just off Slaveikov Square, ☎ 02/87–07–07). Other theaters tend to have stiff wooden chairs and ripped screens.

Shopping

Gift and Souvenir Shops

The **National Ethnographic Museum** shop (☞ Sights to See, *above*) sells genuine crafts, including a selection of carpets, as well as cheap imitations. Prices may not be competitive, but it is one-stop shopping. The **Bulgarian Folk Art Shop** (✉ 14, bul. Vitosha) is a bit more expensive than the Union of Bulgarian Artists; besides crafts, there are traditional musical instruments and folk costumes. For more casual souvenirs, such as lace and T-shirts with Cyrillic logos, try **Sredec** (✉ 7, ul. Lege); **Prizma Store** (✉ 2, bul. Tsar Osvoboditel) is another source.

For recordings of Bulgarian music, go to the basement labyrinth market underneath the **National Palace of Culture** (☞ Sights to See, *above*).

Markets

The quintessential shopping excursion in Sofia is to its outdoor produce and crafts markets. The most exotic and entertaining of these is the **Zhenski Pazaar** (Women's Market; ✉ ul. Stefan Stambolov, between ul. Tsar Simeon and bul. Slivnitsa), named for the swarms of women from neighboring villages who commute daily to hawk everything from homemade brooms and lace to produce and used electronic equipment. With all the sights and sounds of bartering—sometimes a little overwhelming—the Zhenski Pazaar can give you a feel of the Middle East. Be wary of pickpockets.

One of the most popular crafts and souvenir–stall markets is **Nevski Pazaar,** just west of the Nevski Cathedral, where you can find everything from antique Greek coins to original icon paintings and old Soviet whiskey flasks. A little less touristy and slightly less pricey are the stalls in the underpass that runs beneath bulevard Vitosha just north of ploshtad Sveta Nedelya at ulitsa Trapezitsa, between the Sheraton and Central Department Store; here, the shopkeepers sell handmade lace, knitted sweaters and caps, and a variety of both new and old jewelry.

Shopping Malls

What used to be Sofia's monolithic state-run department store, **Tsentralen Universalen Magazin** (Central Department Store; ✉ 2, bul. Knyaginya Maria-Luiza), reopened in April 2000 as a mixed retail and office space—the closest thing Sofia has to a western shopping mall. It still goes by the old name, or TSUM for short.

Sofia A to Z

Arriving and Departing

BY CAR

From Serbia, the main routes are E80, going through the border checkpoint at Kalotina on the Niš–Sofia road, or E871, going through the checkpoint at Gyueshevo. From Greece, take E79, passing through the checkpoint at Kulata; from Turkey, take E80, passing through checkpoint Kapitan–Andreevo. Border crossings to Romania are at Vidin on E79 and at Ruse on E97 and E85.

BY PLANE

All international flights arrive at **Sofia Airport.** For information on international flights, call ☎ 02/79–80–35 or 02/72–06–72; for domestic flights, ☎ 02/72–24–14 or 02/79–32–21–16.

Between the Airport and Downtown: Bus 84 serves the airport, but it is crowded and impractical if you have a lot of luggage. The fare for taxis taken from the airport taxi stand is a flat fee of $20 (you can pay in dollars or the equivalent in leva) for the 10-km (6-mi) ride into Sofia. A much more affordable option (if you have local currency, can speak a little Bulgarian, and know where you're going) is an unofficial taxi from outside the airport doors, which will get you to the center of town for around 12 leva, less than half of what the official taxis charge. Be sure to agree on the fare before starting off.

BY TRAIN

The **Tsentralna Gara** (central station; ☎ 02/3–11–11 or 02/843–33–33) is at the northern edge of the city. The ticket offices in Sofia are in the underpass of the **National Palace of Culture** (✉ 1, pl. Bulgaria, ☎ 02/59–01–36) and at the **Rila International Travel Agency** (✉ 5, ul. Gen. Gurko, ☎ 02/87–07–77 or 02/87–59–35). There is a taxi stand at the station.

Getting Around

The main sights are centrally located, so the best way to see the city is on foot.

BY BUS

Buses, trolleys, and trams run quite frequently—between every 5 and 20 minutes. Buy a ticket (a single fare is 30 stotinki) from the ticket stand near the tram or trolley car; stop and punch it into the machine as you board (watch how the person in front of you does it). You can also pay the driver. Persons traveling with baggage or large backpacks are required by law to have both a ticket for themselves *and* a ticket for their baggage. If you or your bag is caught without a ticket, an on-the-spot fine of 2 leva will be issued. Trams and trolleys tend to get crowded, so keep an eye on your belongings and be alert at all times. The tourist information offices have full details of routes and times.

BY CAR

If you're staying near the city center, there's really no need for a car. Besides, driving in Sofia is no easy task—traffic is heavy and there are potholes everywhere.

BY TAXI

Taxi rates are 35 stotinki per 1 km (½ mi) in the daytime, and 40 stotinki per km after 10 PM. The most reliable way to get a taxi is to order it by phone; if you hail one on the street, make sure it is a company taxi with a phone number listed on the door. Some reputable taxi companies are **Taxi Plus** (☎ 1282); **Taxi Express** (☎ 1280); **Okay Taxi** (☎ 2121); and **Inex Taxi** (☎ 91919). To tip, round out the fare 5%–10%.

Contacts and Resources

B&B RESERVATION AGENCIES

Staying in private homes is becoming a popular alternative to hotels as a means of cutting costs and having increased contact with Bulgarians. Some private homes offer bed-and-breakfast or bed only; some provide full board. In Sofia, contact the National Information and Advertising Center (☞ Visitor Information, *below*).

CAR RENTALS

Eurodollar operates out of the Hotel Kempinski Zografski (✉ 100, bul. James Bourchier, ☎ 02/68–32–51). **Avis** offices are downtown in the Sheraton Sofia Hotel (✉ 5, pl. St. Nedelya, ☎ 02/988–81–67), and at the Sofia Airport (☎ 02/73–80–23). **Hertz** has a central reservation line (☎ 02/980–0461) and an office at the airport (☎ 02/79–14–77). You can hire a car with a driver through **Balkantour** (✉ 27, bul. Stamboliiski,

☎ 02/988–5543) or through **Balkantourist** (✉ 1, bul. Vitosha, ☎ 02/87–51–92).

EMBASSIES

U. S. Embassy (✉ 1, ul. Suborna, ☎ 02/980–5241); **consulate** (✉ 1, ul. Kapitan Andreev, ☎ 02/963–2022). **U. K. Embassy** (✉ 38, bul. Levski, ☎ 02/980–1220). Canadians, Australians, and New Zealanders are on their own; they're normally referred to the British or American embassies.

EMERGENCIES

Ambulance (☎ 150). **Doctor: Clinic for Foreign Citizens** (✉ 1, ul. Eugeni Pavlovski, Mladost 1, ☎ 02/75–361). **Fire** (☎ 160). **Pirogov Emergency Hospital** (☎ 02/5–15–31). **Police: Sofia City Constabulary** (☎ 166). **Pharmacies** (☎ 178 for information about all-night pharmacies).

GUIDED TOURS

Balkantourist (☞ Visitor Information, *below*), once the only game in town, endures as a private company, organizing all kinds of tours, from guided Sofia orientation tours to various evening tours, such as a night out eating local food and watching folk dances. With privatization has come a degree of diversity and competition. **Lyub Travel** (✉ 11, ul. Milin Kamak, Lozenets, ☎ 02/528–978) offers custom-made tours of Sofia and regions throughout Bulgaria, specializing in archaeology, history, art history, and folklore. The firm also arranges accommodations in small hotels and private homes and is popular with the English-speaking diplomatic community. **Odysseia-In** (✉ 20-V, bul. Alexander Stamboliiski, ☎ 02/989–0538) offers a broad range of adventure and outdoor recreation tours with experienced guides, including skiing/snowboarding, rafting, mountain biking, and hiking.

Visitor Information

The English-language weekly newspaper, the *Sofia Echo*—available at the Sofia airport news kiosk, hotels, kiosks throughout the city center, and on-line at www.online.bg/sofiaecho—reviews restaurants and clubs in addition to reporting on Bulgarian news and cultural events.

Since privatization of the tourism industry and the reorganization of the Ministry of Trade and Tourism, the central source of information is the **National Information and Advertising Center** (✉ 1, ul. Sveta Sofia, ☎ 02/987–9778) conveniently located at the intersection of buls. Stamboliiski and Vitosha. **Balkantourist** (Head Office: ✉ 1, bul. Vitosha, ☎ 02/43–331), formerly the state-run tourism organization, is now a private travel agency but in many places in the country still functions as an information office, with locations in most major hotels. Also contact **Balkantour** (✉ 27, bul. Stamboliiski, ☎ 02/988–55–43), **Jamadvice** (✉ 10, ul. Assen Zlatarov, ☎ 02/944–15–20), **Wagonlit Travel** (✉ 10, ul. Legue, ☎ 02/980–81–26), or **Green Travel Agency** (✉ 25, ul. Patriarh Evtimii, ☎ 02/981–4274, FAX 02/981–4275).

SIDE TRIPS FROM SOFIA

Boyana

10 km (6 mi) south of the city center. Hire a taxi or take Tram 19 from ulitsa Graf Ignatiev in central Sofia to the southwestern part of Sofia, where you can catch Bus 63 or 64. The trip takes less than an hour.

At the foot of Mt. Vitosha, this settlement was a medieval fortress near the beginning of the 11th century. Today it is one of Sofia's wealthiest residential neighborhoods. In this area is one of Bulgaria's most precious monuments, the tiny, medieval **Tzarkvata Boyana** (Boyana

Church). Dating back to the 13th century, it is a historical treasure on UNESCO's World Heritage list for preservation. Unfortunately at press time it was closed for restoration (and will be for at least a decade), but a replica, complete with copies of the exquisite 13th-century frescoes, is open to visitors. This is usually a tour destination, but if you're coming by car, follow ulitsa Alexander Pushkin uphill until you can turn uphill onto ulitsa Sveti Kaloian, which branches out to ulitsa Brezovitsa. This will take you to ulitsa Boyansko Ezero, where you'll have to hike up the mountain to the church from the trail head. *Replica: 10 leva. June–Aug., Thurs.–Sun. 9–1 and 2–5; Sept.–May, weekends 10–1 and 2–5.*

In 2000 the **Natzionalen Istoricheski Musei** (National History Museum), considered one of Bulgaria's most important museums, was transplanted from central Sofia's Courts of Justice to the former president's residence in Boyana. In this new home you'll find priceless Thracian treasures, Roman mosaics, enamel jewelry from the First Bulgarian Kingdom, and glowing religious art that survived the years of Ottoman oppression. The collection vividly illustrates the art history of Bulgaria. ✉ *Former Residence of the President, #2,* ☎ *02/88–41–60. 1½ leva. Daily 10–7.*

OFF THE BEATEN PATH

Pernik – Less than half an hour by car southwest of Sofia is this coal-mining town, and though it has (difficult-to-find) hilltop ruins of a medieval fortress and a mining museum, the principal attraction is the *kukeri*, or mummers, festival in early February. The kukeri rites are intended to ward off evil spirits and promote fertility. Groups of men, analogous to Mardi Gras krewes, don elaborate masks and parade through the streets, making as much noise as possible. Many Bulgarian villages have kukeri events of one form or another, but Pernik has an international reputation. Sofia-based tour companies can provide information about kukeri events throughout the country.

Dragalevci

Hire a taxi or take Tram 19 from ulitsa Graf Ignatievto in central Sofia to the last stop, and switch to the Dragalevci Bus 64. You can also take Bus 66 or 93 from Hladilnika.

Picturesquely sprawled across the lower part of Mt. Vitosha, this was a slow-paced village just a few years ago. Today, it has been built up with modern homes and absorbed by the city, making it more or less a quiet suburb of Sofia.

In the woods above the village is the nearby **Dragalevci Monastir** (Dragalevci Monastery). It's currently a convent, but you can visit the 14th-century church with its outdoor frescoes. You can hike to the church from the Dragalevci bus stop (about 1½ km/1 mi), or, to get there from downtown Sofia, take bus 64 or 93 from the Hladilnika bus station. *Thurs.–Sun. 10–6.*

A chairlift ride or two will give you stunning views of the area. The lift on ulitsa Panorama in Dragalevci takes you up to the Aleko resort; it costs 5 leva and runs from 8 to 5. From the terminus, walk over to the next chairlift to head farther up to the top of Malak Rezen. There are well-marked walking and ski trails in the area.

Dining

$$ ✕ **Chichovtsi.** This unassuming pizza place at the top of the main square in Dragalevci has a cozy fireplace in winter and patio seating in summer. It's almost always busy with hordes of weekend Mt. Vi-

tosha pilgrims—by the end of the day the village square is essentially a parking lot for the restaurant. Try a "golyam" Zagorka (a big, frosty beer) and any of the tasty pizzas—but be aware that they may not conform to your expectations; pickles are a topping option, and mayonnaise and ketchup come on the side. ✉ *Dragalevci Square,* ☎ *02/967–1770. No credit cards.*

$$ ✕ **Vodenicharski Mehani.** Appropriately enough, the "Miller's Tavern" is made up of three old mills linked together. A folklore show and a menu of Bulgarian specialties give it a tourist-friendly but authentic atmosphere. Try the *gyuvech* (potatoes, tomatoes, peas, and onions baked in an earthenware pot). ✉ *ul. Panorama, at southern end of town next to chairlift,* ☎ *02/967–10–21 or 02/967–10–01. No credit cards.*

THE BLACK SEA GOLDEN COAST

The Black Sea, contrary to its name, is a brilliant blue and is warm and calm most of the time. Its sunny, sandy beaches are backed by the easternmost slopes of the Balkan range and by the Strandja Mountains. Although the traditional tourist centers tend to be huge state-built complexes with a somewhat lean feel, some have modern amenities that attract German, British, and Eastern European tourists year after year. Many of the formerly state-owned resort complexes are in flux—the nicer ones have been privatized and are being renovated, while the less desirable properties are in various stages of decay. Resort complexes in the Varna region tend to remain open year round, unlike on the southern coast where many places shut down for the winter. In fishing villages with traditional taverns, Roman and Byzantine ruins, and peaceful swimming coves, new small, private hotels offer a welcome affordable alternative to the resorts.

Begin your exploration of the southern Black Sea coast, famous for its sheltered bays and cliffs, in the industrial port of Burgas. From Burgas, you can visit the fishing villages of Nesebâr (with Sunny Beach), Sozopol, and Djuni. Coastal towns south of Sozopol have experienced a building boom in recent years, with small hotels popping up in Kiten, Primorsko, and Ahtopol.

Varna

470 km (282 mi) east of Sofia. It's easily reached by rail (about 7½ hours by express) or by road from the capital.

The ancient city of Varna, named Odyssos by the Greeks, became a major Roman trading center and is now an important shipbuilding and industrial city. With its beaches and tourism, Varna has a cosmopolitan flair, cultivated with events such as a yearly film festival held in August. Though it is the third-largest city in Bulgaria, its older parts still possess a small-town charm. With wide, tree-lined boulevards, numerous gardens and parks, and a beachfront boardwalk, Varna is easily accessible to pedestrians. If you plan to drive from Sofia to Varna, allow time to see the **Pobiti Kammani** (Stone Forest) just off the Sofia–Varna road between Devnya and Varna. The unexpected groups of sandstone pillars are thought to have been formed when the area was the bed of the Lutsian Sea.

★ The **Natsionalen Istoricheski Musei** (Museum of Art and History) is one of the great—if lesser known—museums of Europe. The splendid collection includes the world's oldest gold treasures, from the Varna necropolis of the 4th millennium BC, discovered in 1972, as well as Thracian, Greek, and Roman treasures and richly painted icons. ✉ *On the*

The Black Sea Golden Coast

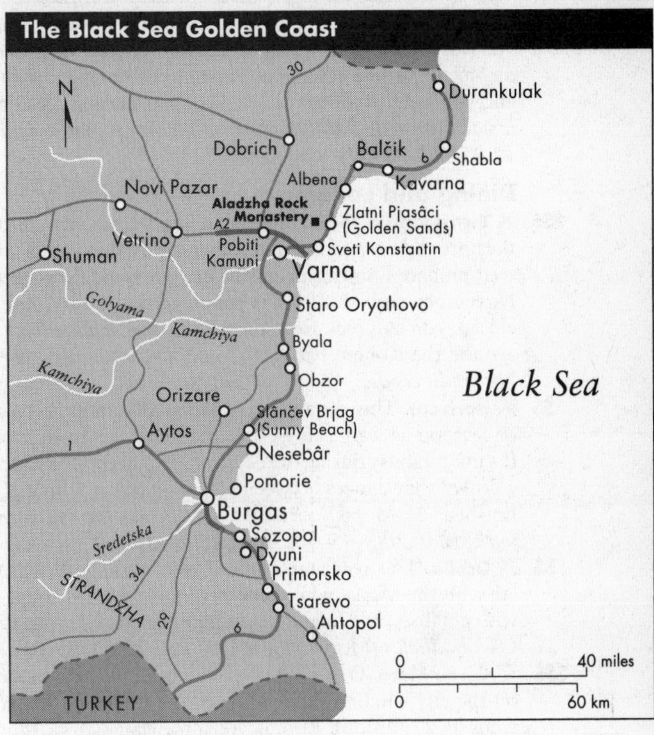

corner of bul. Dimitar Blagoev and bul. Slivnitsa, ☏ *052/23–70–57.* ⏲ *Tues.–Sat. 10–5.*

Near the northeastern end of bulevard Osmi Primorski Polk are numerous shops and cafés; the same street leads west to ploshtad Mitropolit Simeon and the **Tsentralnata Tzarkva** (cathedral), built in 1880–1886. Take a look inside at the lavish murals. *Free.* ⏲ *Daily 7–6.*

Running north from the Varna cathedral is ulitsa Vladislav Varnenchik, with shops, movie theaters, and eateries. Opposite the cathedral, in the Grada Gradina (City Gardens), is the 19th-century **Starata Chasovnikuh Kula** (Old Clock Tower). In the very city center on the south side of the City Gardens and on ploshtad Nezavisimost stands **Natsionlana Teatur Stoyan Buchvarov** (Stoyan Buchvarov National Theater), a magnificent Baroque building. The theater was founded in 1921 and showcased some of Bulgaria's greatest actors.

On the corner of bulevard Knyaz Boris I and ulitsa Shipka you will see the remains of the **Rimskata Stena** (Roman Fortress Wall) of Odyssos. Bulevard Knyaz Boris I is another of Varna's shopping streets where you can buy handcrafted souvenirs.

If you walk south along ulitsa Odessos to ulitsa Han Krum you will find the remains of the **Roman Thermae.** These public baths dating from the 2nd to the 3rd century AD are among the largest and most substantial Roman ruins in Bulgaria. The site is now a hands-on museum, and visitors are free to wander among the ruins. ✉ *1, ul. Han Krum.* *2 leva.*

If you follow bulevard Primorski with the sea on your right, you will reach the **Morski Musei** (Naval Museum), with its displays of the early days of navigation on the Black Sea and the Danube. ✉ *Graf Ignatiev and bul. Primorski, just inside the park entrance,* ☏ *052/22–26–55.* ⏲ *Weekdays 8–5.*

From the extensive and luxuriant **Morska Gradina** (Seaside Gardens), you can catch a great view over the bay. There are restaurants, an open-air theater, and a fascinating astronomy complex with a natural science museum, an observatory, and a **planetarium.** ✉ *Off Graf Ignatiev, inside Primorski Park, just outside the entrance to the municipal beach,* ☎ *052/22–28–90.*

Dining and Lodging

$$$ ✕ **Bistro Rimski Termi.** Nestled in a quiet, private courtyard between the port and the ruins of the Roman baths, this intimate mehana serves well-prepared Bulgarian cuisine in a romantic tavern setting. Between November and March it is prone to odd hours, but if you find it closed, you can pick from the many other mehani that fill the square around the Roman baths. ✉ *5, ul. 8 na Noemvri,* ☎ *052/632–622. No credit cards.*

$$ ✕ **Horizont.** This restaurant in Morska Gradina has a good selection of seafood as well as a view of the Black Sea from its outside tables. It's not too busy during the day, but at night the live Greek music draws a crowd that dances between courses and stays long after the food is finished. ✉ *Morska Gradina, just inside the main entrance to the park,* ☎ *052/88–45–30. No credit cards.*

$$ ✕ **Orbita.** This reasonably priced hole-in-the-wall is extremely popular with the locals, who come here for the lentil soup, grilled kebabs with potatoes, and Bulgarian sausage in a pot. ✉ *Hotel Orbita, 25, Tsar Osvoboditel, off Knyaz Boris I,* ☎ *052/22–52–75. No credit cards.*

$$$ **Černo More.** One of the best things about this modern Interhotel, on the city's main drag leading to the beach, is the panoramic view from its 22nd floor. Rooms are somewhat sparse, though decorated with ocean-theme paintings. ✉ *33, bul. Slivnitza,* ☎ *052/23–21–15 or 052/25–30–91. 230 rooms. 3 restaurants, bar, outdoor café, nightclub. AE, DC, MC, V.*

Sveti Konstantin

8 km (5 mi) north along the coast from Varna.

Sveti Konstantin, Bulgaria's oldest Black Sea resort, is small and intimate, spreading through a wooded park near a series of sandy coves.

Dining and Lodging

$$$ ✕ **Bulgarska Svatba.** This folky restaurant is on the outskirts of the resort; charcoal-grilled meats are especially recommended. In winter, try to reserve a table by the large wood-burning fire, where you will have an excellent view of the entertainment. ✉ *Sveti Konstantin Resort,* ☎ *052/36–12–83. No credit cards.*

$$ ✕ **Manastirska Izba.** This eatery is modest but pleasant, with a sunny terrace. Try the meatball and shopska salata. ✉ *Sveti Konstantin Resort,* ☎ *052/36–20–36. No credit cards.*

$$$$ ★ **Grand Hotel Varna.** This Swedish-built hotel has a reputation for being the best on the coast. It is only 150 yards from the beach and offers a wide range of hydrotherapeutic treatments featuring the area's natural warm mineral springs. Yearly upgrades enable the Varna to keep pace with brand-new hotels, but the luxury comes at a cost: It is no longer an inexpensive secret. ✉ *Sveti Konstantin Resort,* ☎ *052/36–14–91,* FAX *052/36–19–20. 325 rooms. 3 restaurants, 6 bars, coffee shop, 1 indoor pool, 2 outdoor pools, 2 tennis courts, bowling, health club, squash, nightclub. AE, DC, MC, V.*

$$ **Čajka.** Čajka means "seagull" in Bulgarian, and this hotel has a bird's-eye view of the entire resort from its perch above the northern end of the beach. ✉ *Sveti Konstantin Resort,* ☎ *052/36–13–32. 130 rooms. No credit cards.*

Zlatni Pjasâci

8 km (5 mi) north of Sveti Konstantin.

In contrast to the sedate atmosphere of Sveti Konstantin, Zlatni Pjasâci (Golden Sands) is lively, with extensive leisure-time amenities, mineral-spring medical centers, and sports and entertainment facilities. Just over 4 km (2½ mi) inland from Zlatni Pjasâci is **Aladja Monastir** (Aladja Rock Monastery), one of Bulgaria's oldest, cut out of the cliff face and accessible to visitors by sturdy iron stairways. To get there, take a minibus from the Zlatni Pjasâci bus terminal; it makes a run every two hours.

Albena

10 km (6 mi) north of Zlatni Pjasâci.

Albena, a 1970s resort, is between Balčik and Golden Sands. It is well known for its long, wide beach and clean sea. The contemporary conveniences come with only a minimal dose of local charm, inflated prices, and menus and street signs in German and Russian.

Dining and Lodging

$$ ✕ **Bambuka** (Bamboo Tree). This open-air restaurant serves seafood as well as international and Bulgarian fare. The *purzheni calamari sus chesun sos* (fried squid with garlic yogurt dip) is one of the best appetizers on the menu. ✉ *Albena Resort,* ☎ *05722/24–04. No credit cards.*

$$ **Dobrudja Hotel.** Albena's most luxurious hotel is large and comfortable, with a mineral-water health spa where you can relax in healing mud, enjoy a massage, or indulge in a curative bath. ✉ *Albena Resort,* ☎ *05722/20–20,* FAX *05722/22–16. 272 rooms. 3 restaurants, 2 bars, coffee shop, indoor pool, outdoor pool, spa, exercise room. DC, MC, V.*

Balčik

35 km (22 mi) north of Sveti Konstantin, 8 km (5 mi) north of Albena.

Part of Romania until just before World War II, Balčik is now a relaxed haven for Bulgaria's writers, artists, and scientists. On its white cliffs are crescent-shape tiers populated with houses. Among them is the **Dvoretsa Balčik** (Balčik Palace), once the grand summer getaway for Romania's Queen Marie and her six children. Surrounding the palace are the beautiful **Botanicheska Gradina v Balčik** (Botanical Gardens), dotted with curious buildings, terraces overlooking the sea, and a small Byzantine-style church where the late Marie's heart was encased in a jewel-encrusted box. Her remains were returned to Romania when Bulgaria reclaimed the region. *Free.* ⏲ *Church: Tues.–Sun. 9–5; gardens daily 9–9.*

Slânčev Brjag

95 km (60 mi) south of Varna, 140 km (87 mi) south of Balčik.

The enormous Slânčev Brjag (Sunny Beach) is especially popular with families because of its safe beaches, gentle tides, and playgrounds for children. During the summer there are kindergartens for young vacationers, children's concerts, even a children's disco. Slânčev Brjag has come a long way since the early 1990s, but it remains a vast concrete eyesore looming over a world-class beach. Overrun with tourists from northern Europe, even the beachside restaurants serve more German schnitzel than Bulgarian shopska salata. People either love it or hate it.

Dining and Lodging

$$ ✕ **Hanska Šatra.** In the coastal hills behind the sea, this combination restaurant and nightclub has been built to resemble the tents of the Bul-

garian rulers of old. It has entertainment well into the night. ✉ *5 km (3 mi) west of Slânčev Brjag,* ☎ *0554/28–11. No credit cards.*

$ ✕ **Ribarska Hiza.** This lively beachside restaurant specializes in fish and has music until 1 AM. ✉ *4, ul. Slanchev Brjag, northern end of Slânčev Brjag Resort,* ☎ *0554/21–86. No credit cards.*

$$ **Globus.** Once considered the best hotel in the resort, Globus has a central location that helps make up for its fading, dingy rooms. The larger apartments with seaside terraces are preferred. ✉ *22, ul. Slânčev Brjag,* ☎ *0554/22–45 or 0554/20–18,* FAX *0554/25–24 or 0554/29–21. 100 rooms. Restaurant, bar, coffee shop, indoor pool, exercise room. No credit cards.*

$$ **Kouban.** Near the center of the resort, this large establishment is just a short stroll from the beach. It underwent thorough renovations in the spring of 2000. ✉ *Slânčev Brjag Resort,* ☎ *0554/23–09,* FAX *0554/25–24 or 0554/29–21. 216 rooms, most with bath or shower. 2 restaurants, bar, coffee shops, tennis court. No credit cards.*

$ **Čajka.** Among the bargain hotels, the Čajka offers the best location—it's directly across from the best stretch of beach. ✉ *8, ul. Slânčev Brjag,* ☎ *0554/23–08. 36 rooms, some with bath or shower. No credit cards.*

Nesebâr

5 km (3 mi) south of Slânčev Brjag (Sunny Beach) and accessible by regular excursion buses.

Just 10 minutes south of Slânčev Brjag (Sunny Beach) is a painter's and poet's retreat. Founded by the Greeks 25 centuries ago on a rocky peninsula reached by a narrow causeway, this ancient settlement exudes an aura of its past. Among its vine-covered houses are beautiful Byzantine ruins, richly decorated medieval churches, and crumbling Ottoman bathhouses. Quaint—though not undiscovered—Nesebâr is densely packed with outdoor markets, galleries, and oceanside cafés where fried seafood is served in heaping portions. Small hotels, both on the peninsula and the mainland, have popped up in recent years, offering a welcome alternative to the dated resorts nearby. If you want to stay in the Old Town, make your reservations well in advance.

Lodging

$$$ **Monte Cristo.** This small, stylish hotel tucked between National Revival homes and ruins of Byzantine churches is pricey by Bulgarian standards, but the location and quality of the facilities are worth it. It's also one of the few Nesebâr hotels open year-round; reservations are difficult to come by during high season. Ask for a room on the upper floors to avoid the thudding music of the restaurant/bar. ✉ *2, Venera,* ☎ *0554/42–055. 5 rooms, 4 suites. Restaurant, bar, air-conditioning. No credit cards.*

$$ **Mistral Hotel.** On the mainland a short walk north of the causeway leading to the Old Town are several new small hotels and restaurants. Mistral is one of the better of the former; it's pleasant, affordable, and busy all year. The proprietor is a good source for information about the region. ✉ *22, ul. Khan Krum,* ☎ *0554/425–93,* FAX *0554/429–33. 18 rooms, 2 suites. Restaurant, bar, sauna, exercise room. No credit cards.*

Burgas

38 km (24 mi) south of Nesebâr.

The next place of any size south along the coast from Nesebâr is the city of Burgas. Bulgaria's second main port on the Black Sea, Burgas is industrial and chaotic, with heavy traffic, chemical plants, a massive state-owned oil refinery, and huge ships anchored off shore. Despite the noise, construction, and pollution, Burgas can provide a pleasant stay, with its long **Primorski Gradina** (Seaside Park), expansive beach, and pedestrian alleyways winding through a lively city center.

Lodging

$$ 🏨 **Bulgaria.** This high-rise Interhotel is in the center of town. While the rooms aren't exactly upbeat—dark green, brown, and black predominate—it has its own nightclub with a floor show. ✉ *21, ul. Aleksandrovska,* ☎ *056/4–28–20 or 056/4–26–10,* FAX *056/4–72–91. 200 rooms, most with bath or shower. Restaurant, nightclub. MC, V.*

Sozopol

32 km (20 mi) south of Burgas.

Built on and around numerous Byzantine ruins, this fishing port was once Apollonia, the oldest of the Greek colonies in Bulgaria. With narrow, cobbled streets leading down to the harbor, it is now a popular haunt for Bulgarian and, increasingly, foreign writers and artists, who find private accommodations with locals in rustic Black Sea–style houses. As romantic, historic, and quaint as Nesebâr, Sozopol is more well known, and in September its tiny streets can barely contain the crowds that arrive for the **Apollonia Arts Festival.** To see the quieter side of the village, come in the off-season, when you will be one of few tourists. Sozopol is a good base for exploring the coast south to the Turkish border, where unspoiled rivers pour out of the forested Strandja Mountains.

Dining and Lodging

$$ ✕ **Mehana Sozopol.** This touristy spot on a street with several mehani and bars serves typical Bulgarian dishes and seasonal fish. During the summer there are folk music and patio dining. Replenish yourself with a few cups of sturdy red wine and a *sirene po shopski* (white cheese baked with tomato, herbs, and egg) after touring the cobbled streets. ✉ *ul. Apollonia,* ☎ *05514/384. No credit cards.*

$$ 🏨 **Kavaler.** You'll find this small, year-round hotel on a quiet street off the main drag in the new part of town, but it's a short walk from the beach and the old town. It's very clean, with pleasant service, but the desk clerks keep random hours—look for help in the busy restaurant. The two apartments on the top floor have terraces with sweeping views. ✉ *10, ul. Yani Popov,,* ☎ *05514/36–46, 05514/36–47. 12 rooms, 2 suites. Restaurant, bar. No credit cards.*

The Black Sea Golden Coast A to Z

Arriving and Departing

BY PLANE

There are daily 50-minute flights from Sofia and Plovdiv to Varna and Burgas on **Balkan Bulgarian Airlines** (reservations in Sofia, ☎ 02/ 981–51–70).

BY TRAIN

It's a six- to eight-hour train ride from Sofia to Varna or Burgas.

Getting Around

Buses make frequent runs up and down the coast and are inexpensive. Buy your ticket in advance from the kiosks near the bus stops. **Bikes** are particularly useful for getting around such sprawling resorts as Slânčev Brjag (Sunny Beach)—though getting hold of one requires the stroke of luck of finding someone on the beachfront renting a couple out. A regular **boat service** travels the Varna–Sveti Konstantin–Golden Sands–Albena–Balčik route.

Contacts and Resources

GUIDED TOURS

A wide range of excursions can be arranged from all resorts. There are bus excursions to Sofia; a one-day bus and boat trip along the Danube; and a three-day bus tour of Bulgaria departing from Zlatni Pjasâci (Golden Sands), Sveti Konstantin, and Albena. All tours are run by Balkantourist (☞ Visitor Information *in* Sofia A to Z, *above*).

VISITOR INFORMATION

There is a Balkantourist office in most towns and resorts. **Albena** (☎ 05722/27–21, 05722/21–41, or 05722/28–34). **Burgas** (Hotel Primorets, ✉ 1, ul. Knyaz Batenberg, ☎ 056/4–54–96; or 2a, bul. Svoboda, ☎ 056/4–81–11). **Nesebâr** (☎ 0554/58–30 or 0554/58–33). **Slânčev Brjag** (Sunny Beach; ☎ 0554/21–06, 0554/23–12, or 0554/25–10). **Sveti Konstantin** (☎ 052/36–10–45 or 052/36–14–91). **Varna** (main office, ✉ 3, ul. Moussala, ☎ 052/22–55–24 or 052/22–22–72; private accommodations office, pl. Slaveikov, ☎ 052/22–22–06). **Zlatni Pjasâci** (Golden Sands; ☎ 052/35–53–02 or 052/35–54–14).

INLAND BULGARIA

Inland Bulgaria is less well known to tourists than the capital and the coast. Adventurous travelers willing to put up with rustic hotel facilities and unreliable transportation (such as rickety buses traversing narrow mountain ridges) will be rewarded with unjaded hospitality and scenic beauty. Wooded and mountainous, the interior is dotted with attractive "museum" villages (entire settlements listed for preservation because of their historical value) and ancient ruins. The region's folk culture, often pagan in nature, is a strong survivor from the past, not a tourist-inspired re-creation, and spending a few nights in a secluded mountain village can feel like a journey into the Dark Ages. The foothills of the Balkan range, marked *stara planina* (old mountains) on most maps, lie parallel to the lower Sredna Gora Mountains, with the verdant Valley of Roses between them. In the Balkan range is the ancient capital of Veliko Târnovo; south of the Sredna Gora stretches the fertile Thracian Plain and Bulgaria's second-largest and most progressive city, Plovdiv. To the south, in the Rila Mountains, is Borovec, first of the mountain resorts.

Koprivshtitsa

★ *105 km (65 mi) from Sofia, reached by a minor road south from the Sofia–Kazanlak expressway.*

One of Bulgaria's showplace villages, Koprivshtitsa is set amid mountain pastures and pine forests, about 3,000 ft up in the Sredna Gora range. Founded in the 14th century, it became a prosperous trading center with close ties to Venice during the National Revival period 400 years later. The architecture of this period, also called the Bulgarian Renaissance, features carved woodwork on broad verandas and overhanging eaves, brilliant colors, and courtyards with studded wooden gates. Throughout the centuries, artists, poets, and wealthy merchants have made their homes here; many of the historic houses once inhabited by Ottoman landowners are open to visitors. The town has been well preserved and is revered by Bulgarians as a symbol of freedom, for it was here in April 1876 that the first shots were fired in the rebellion that led to the end of Turkish occupation.

Dining and Lodging

$ ✕🏨 **Hotel Byaloto Kouche.** This charming inn uphill from the town square offers rustic rooms furnished in the traditional National Revival

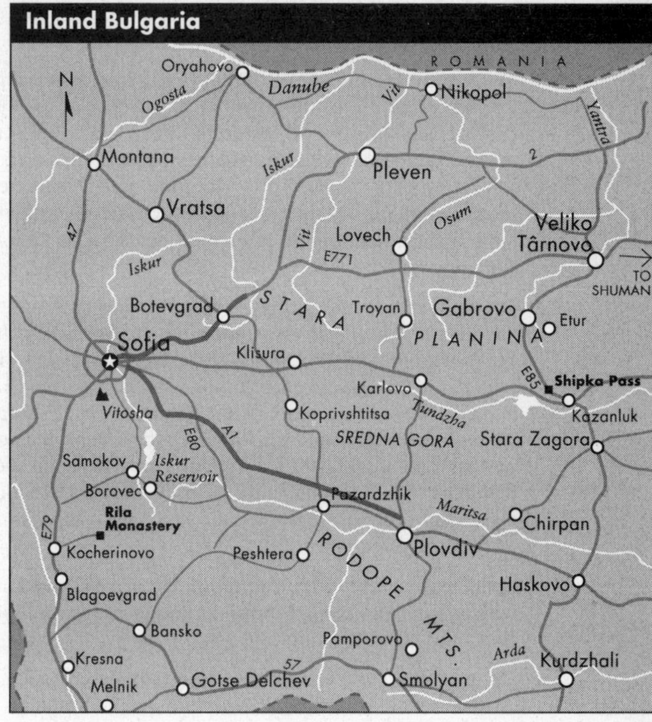

style, with woven rugs and low beds. One room has a fireplace; all have shared baths. An intimate restaurant offers traditional Bulgarian dishes. ✉ *Ul. Generilo 2, 2090,* ☎ *07184/22–50. 6 rooms with shared bath. Restaurant. No credit cards.*

$ **Barikadite.** This small hotel is on a hill 15 km (9 mi) from Koprivshtitsa. Red, orange, and yellow bedspreads make rooms sunny; the woven carpets and lace curtains add extra warmth. The local residents will willingly give directions and probably offer to show you the way. ☎ *07184/32–42. 20 rooms. Restaurant, bar, nightclub. No credit cards.*

Troyan

At the village of Karnare, 17 km (11 mi) east of Klisura, take the winding scenic road north over the Balkan range to Troyan, 93 km (58 mi) from Koprivshtitsa.

The **Troyan Monastir** (Troyan Monastery), built during the 1600s, is in the heart of the mountains. The church was painstakingly remodeled during the 19th century, and its icons, wood carvings, and frescoes are classic examples of National Revival art. Although there are no phone and no regular hours, you should be able to find someone to open the gate in daytime.

Veliko Târnovo

Travel north on the mountain road from Troyan until it meets Hwy. E772, where you turn right for Veliko Târnovo, 82 km (50 mi) from Karnare; 240 km (144 mi) from Sofia.

In the 13th and 14th centuries, Veliko Târnovo was the capital of the Second Bulgarian Kingdom. Damaged by Ottoman attacks and again by an earthquake in 1913, it has been reconstructed and is now a museum city with panoramic vistas of steep mountain slopes through which the idyllic River Jantra runs its jagged course.

The town warrants one or two days of exploration. Try to begin at a vantage point above the town to get a sense of its layout. **Tsarevec** (Carevec on some maps), protected by a river loop, is the hill where medieval czars and patriarchs had their palaces. The area is under restoration; steep paths provide opportunities to view the extensive ruins of the Patriarchate and the royal palace. On summer nights, a spectacular sound-and-light show presented here can be seen from the surrounding pubs.

On the Tsarevec and Trapezitsa hills are three important **churches.** On Tsaravec are the **Tzarkvata Cheteridesette Machenika** (Church of the Forty Martyrs), a 13th-century structure with frescoes of the Târnovo school and two inscribed columns, one dating from the 9th century; and the **Tserkavata Sveti Dimitar** (Church of St. Dimitrius), from the 12th century, built on the spot where the Second Bulgarian Kingdom was proclaimed in 1185. The 14th-century **Tzarkvata Sveti Peter y Paul** (Church of Sts. Peter and Paul), on Trapezitsa, has vigorous murals both inside and out. 🎫 *All churches: free.* ⏲ *June–Sept., daily 9–6; Oct.–May, Tues.–Sun. 9–5.*

In the center of the town near Yantra Hotel is **Samovodene Street,** lined with restored crafts workshops—a good place to find souvenirs, Turkish candy, or a charming café.

On ulitsa Rakovski is the **Museo Hadji Nikolai** (Hadji Nicoli Museum) in what was once an inn. Part of a cluster of buildings from the National Revival period, this is one of the finest structures in town. At press time the museum was closed for renovations, with no projected reopening date. ✉ *17, ul. Georgi Sava Rakovski.*

Dining and Lodging

$$ ✕ **Bolyarska Izba.** In the center of the busy district just north of the river, this unpretentious mehana is packed with locals enjoying village specialties such as *mozuk* (brains fried in butter and garlic), *ezik* (tongue), *schkembay chorba* (spicy entrail soup), and *pachá* (head cheese). For the less adventurous, the menu has the more conventional national dishes as well. ✉ *Ul. St. Stambolov,* ☎ *no phone. No credit cards.*

$$$ 🏨 **Veliko Târnovo.** In the historic heart of town, this modern Interhotel has good facilities. They may not have much personality, but the rooms are modern, with Western-style showers in the bathrooms. ✉ *2, ul. Al. Penchev,* ☎ *062/6110. 195 rooms. 2 restaurants, bar, coffee shop, indoor pool, health club, nightclub. MC, V.*

$$ 🏨 **Yantra.** Looking across the river to Tsaravec, the Yantra has some of the best views in town, if not the most beautiful rooms—the aged wooden furniture and lace curtains are nothing special. Its decent restaurant has a balcony providing the best seats anywhere for the Tsarevec Hill summer light show. ✉ *1, pl. Velchova Zavera,* ☎ *062/2–03–91,* FAX *062/2–18–07. 60 rooms, 45 with shower. Restaurant, bar, coffee shop. DC, MC, V.*

$ 🏨 **Etur.** Dark and sparse, with a state-owned atmosphere, this moderate-size hotel is a bargain because of its prime location for sightseeing (in town center, near the castle). While some rooms share showers and toilets, all rooms have sinks. ✉ *1, ul. Ivailo,* ☎ *062/62–18–38. 120 rooms, 64 with shower. Restaurant, bar, coffee shop. No credit cards.*

En Route If you leave Veliko Târnovo by E85 and head south toward Plovdiv, you'll go through the Shipka Pass, with its mighty monument on the peak to the 200,000 Russian soldiers and Bulgarian volunteers who died during the Russian-Turkish Wars. Continuing along N6, between the towns of Karlovo and Kazanluk, is the area called the Valley of Roses, hotbed of the flower industry. While most of the crop is harvested in early June, several fields of roses are left for the benefit of passing tourists.

Plovdiv

174 km (104 mi) southeast of Sofia, 197 km (123 mi) southwest of Veliko Târnovo.

Plovdiv may be the quintessential Bulgarian city, with colorful, well-kept National Revival buildings, progressive nightlife, and stunning ruins. Bulgaria's second-largest city is not only one of the oldest settlements in Europe, but it's a major industrial and cultural center—it was a "Cultural Capital" of Europe in 1999. The breathtaking, lantern-lit *starata grad* (Old Town) lies on the hillier southern side of the Maritsa River. Plovdiv hosts several large annual trade fairs, including a wine fair in early February and two large industrial fairs in early May and late September. They are open to the public, but be aware that they fill area hotels; if you can get a room the price will be double the norm.

The **Natsionalen Etnografski Muzei** (National Ethnographic Museum) is in the much-photographed former home of a Greek merchant. It is an elegant example of the National Revival style, which made its first impact in Plovdiv; the museum is filled with artifacts from that fertile period. ✉ *2, ul. Chomakov,* ☎ *032/22–56–56.* 🎫 *2 leva.* ⏲ *Tues.–Sun. 9–noon and 2–5.*

Below the medieval gateway of Hisar Kapiya, the **Georgiadieva Kushta** (Georgiadi House) is a grandiose example of National Revival–style architecture, with its overhanging upper story, carved pillars, and intricate, painted floral decoration. It has a small museum dedicated to the 1876 uprising against the Turks. ✉ *1, ul. Starinna,* ☎ *no phone.* 🎫 *2 leva.* ⏲ *Wed.–Sun. 9:30–12:30 and 2–5.*

Steep, narrow **Strumna Street** is lined with workshops and boutiques, some reached through little courtyards. Beyond the jewelry and leather vendors in ploshtad Stamboliiski are the remains of a **Rimski stadion** (Roman stadium; ✉ Ul. Saborna and ul. Knyaz Alexander I) that dates from the 2nd century.

The old **Kapana District** (✉ northwest of pl. Stamboliiski) has narrow, ★ winding streets and restored shops and cafés. The exquisite hilltop **Rimski amfiteatur** (Roman amphitheater; ✉ ul. Tsar Ivailo, 🎫 2 leva), only discovered and excavated in 1981, has been sensitively renovated and is open for exploration. In summer, this timeless setting is frequently used for dramatic and musical performances.

NEED A BREAK? At the self-serve **Rhetora** (✉ 8A, ul. T. Samodoumov, ☎ 032/22–20–93) the coffee is instant and the pastries shipped in, but the mediocrity of the snacks is far outweighed by the absolute beauty of the setting (and the dirt-cheap prices)—you can sip a drink while looking out over the Roman ruins.

The **Natsionalen Archeologicheski Muzei** (National Archaeological Museum) has a wealth of ancient Thracian artifacts from Plovdiv and the surrounding area. ✉ *1, pl. Suedinenie,* ☎ *032/23–17–60.* 🎫 *1½ leva.* ⏲ *Tues.–Sun. 9–12:30 and 2–5:30.*

Dining and Lodging

$$$ ✕ **Apolonia.** A spacious patio and several dining rooms in an Old Town National Revival–style house make an exceptional setting for a leisurely meal. The food is better than average Bulgarian fare, the service is friendly,

and there's an English-language menu available. Reservations are recommended. ✉ *1, ul. Vasil Kanchev,* ☎ *032/63–26–99. No credit cards.*

$$ ✕ **Alafrangite.** This classic Old Town mehana—with shared tables, folk music, and heavy food—is set in a restored 19th-century house with carved wooden ceilings and a vine-covered courtyard. A house specialty is *kiopolu* (vegetable puree of baked eggplant, peppers, and tomatoes). ✉ *17, ul. Nektariev,* ☎ *032/26–95–95. No credit cards.*

$$ ✕ **Cuchura.** This favorite of artists and students offers Bulgarian standards. It's located just outside of the Old Town, where prices drop and the quality must satisfy the locals. ✉ *12A, ul. Otets Paisii,* ☎ *no phone. No credit cards.*

$$ ✕ **Verdi.** With vegetarian salads, a variety of pastas, gourmet pizzas, and even homemade tiramisu, this spotless, modern Italian trattoria offers a good alternative to the standard Bulgarian vacation diet of pork products and french fries. ✉ *1, ul. Ponkovnik Bonev,* ☎ *032/65–03–69. No credit cards.*

$$$$ 🏨 **Hotel Hebrus.** This small, pricey hotel in the Old Town is open year-round and popular with German tourists. The newly renovated rooms, furnished with antique replicas and goose-down duvets, showcase the painted walls and richly carved ceilings characteristic of fine Old Town homes. ✉ *51A, ul. K. Stoilov, 4000,* ☎ *032/26–02–25. 10 rooms. Restaurant, hot tub, sauna. MC, V.*

$$$ 🏨 **Novotel Plovdiv.** The modern, well-equipped Novotel lies across the river from the new part of town, near the fairgrounds. There are large (for Bulgaria) beds, big windows, and up-to-date bathrooms. ✉ *2, ul. Zlatyu Boyadzhiev, 4000,* ☎ *032/65–25–05 or 032/55–19–79. 322 rooms. Restaurant, pool, tennis courts. AE, DC, MC, V.*

$$ 🏨 **The Tourist's House.** Here you'll get sparsely furnished, pension-style rooms in a historic house with high ceilings and a grand staircase. It's a relative bargain for Old Town and popular with student groups. Rooms have one, two, and five beds. The top floor has shared unisex baths. ✉ *5, ul. Slaveikov, 4000,* ☎ *032/63–32–11. 12 rooms, 4 with private bath. Restaurant, bar. No credit cards.*

Nightlife

In the tradition of university towns, Plovdiv has scores of bars, music venues, and discos. Almost all the most popular places are clustered around the central walkway that winds through the best shopping area, **bulevard Kniaz Alexander Battenberg.**

Borovec

Travel west along the E80 Sofia Rd. At Dolna Banja, turn off to Borovec, about 4,300 ft up the northern slopes of the Rila Mountains; 109 km (68 mi) from Plovdiv.

This is an excellent walking center and winter sports resort, well equipped with hotels, taverns, and ski schools. A winding mountain road leads to Sofia, 70 km (44 mi) from here, past Lake Iskar, the largest lake in the country. For information on resorts, hotels, and winter sports facilities, contact the National Information and Advertising Center (☞ Visitor Information *in* Bulgaria A to Z, *below*).

En Route On the way back to Sofia is the **Rila Monastir** (Rila Monastery), founded in the 10th century by Saint Ivan of Rila, a prophet and healer. Cut across to E79, travel south to Kočerinovo, and turn east to follow the steep forested valley past the village of Rila. The monastery has suffered so frequently from fire that most of it is now a grand National Revival reconstruction, although a rugged 14th-century tower has survived. The atmosphere carries a strong sense of the past—monks are still in residence, although some of the monks' cells are now guest rooms. You can see 14 small chapels with frescoes from the 15th and 17th centuries, a lavishly carved altarpiece in the new Assumption Church, the sarcophagus of Ivan of Rila, icons, and ancient manuscripts—a reminder that the monastery was a stronghold of art and learning during the centuries of Ottoman rule. Sofia's Balkantourist office (☞ Visitor Information *in* Sofia A to Z, *above*) can make arrangements for overnight stays. ☎ *No phone.* *Free.* *Daily 9–6.*

Bansko

150 km (93 mi) south of Sofia via Blagoevgrad.

The houses in this small, picturesque town at the foot of the Pirin Mountains may seem inaccessible with their lattice windows and heavy gates, designed to fend off Ottoman invaders, but the rooms inside these "fortresses" are delicate and beautiful, with carved ceilings and handmade rugs. Generally, these homes are not open as museums, but by planning an overnight stay, or even politely asking, you may be able to see some interiors. The **Tzarkvata Sveta Troitsa** (Holy Trinity Church), built in 1835, along with the tower and the town clock, is part of the architectural complex in the center of the town.

Tourism is booming in Bansko, with numerous plans in the works for expansion of facilities. For more information, contact the **Pirin Tourism Forum** (☞ Visitor Information *in* Bulgaria A to Z, *below*).

Dining and Lodging

Privately owned bed-and-breakfasts can be found on almost every street, and the Vrah Vihren mountain is covered with sprawling ski resorts. The former offer small rooms and home-cooked meals, while the latter are usually comfortable but lack charm. Reservations are necessary at the height of ski season (March) and around New Year's.

$$ ✕ **Dedo Pene.** A string of cowbells clangs as you open the heavy wooden door of this traditional *kurtchma* (tavern), and a waitress will pour you a glass of homemade red wine before you've hung your coat on the rack. The walls are adorned with furs, stuffed bobcats, and handwoven rugs. Not for vegetarians or sensitive stomachs, this pagan tavern exudes authenticity (along with the aroma of uncured hides) and serves up hearty medieval meat dishes. ✉ *Southeast corner of Tsentralnia Ploshtad,* ☎ *no phone. No credit cards.*

$$ **Pirin Hotel.** This popular hotel is large and modern, but the plain wooden furniture and wool blankets give it a state-owned feel. ✉ *68, Tsar Simeon,* ☎ *07443/2536,* FAX *07443/4244. 55 doubles, 7 suites. Restaurant, bar, coffee shop, exercise room. AE, MC, V.*

Melnik

From Sandanski, head south down E79 about 8 km (5 mi); Melnik is west of E79.

"The village that slept for a century from drinking too much wine," according to local legend, Melnik is famous for its grape orchards, its wine aged in deep cellars, and its archaic ambience. Just north of the Greek border, this area was an important Byzantine stronghold from the 12th through 14th centuries. It developed rapidly again during the 1700s due to wine and tobacco trade but declined by the end of the following century. Today Melnik retains houses of the National Revival period and is populated by fewer than 400 permanent residents. Bulgarians and foreigners alike are charmed by the village's old-fashioned taverns, fire-warmed guest rooms, and cobblestone streets unmarred by electrical and phone wires. There's even a cave behind the village where you can taste wine straight from the barrel.

Rozhen Monastir (Rozhen Monastery), rising above Melnik, dates to the 12th century, but was rebuilt in the 16th century after being ravaged by fire. Within its walls is a church dating from 1600. To reach it, you can either hike up the footpath or take the bus that goes through Melnik roughly every hour (no fixed schedule) and get off at the first stop. A caretaker is normally around and will let you in; while there's no admission charge, it's a nice gesture to buy a few candles in the church.

Inland Bulgaria A to Z

Getting Around

Rail and bus services cover all parts of inland Bulgaria, but the timetables are not easy to follow, and there are frequent delays. Though expensive by Western standards and accompanied by its own set of problems (poor road conditions, absence of road signs), the best way to see the country is to rent a car. It is advisable to drive only during daylight hours. If you don't care to do the driving, you can hire a driver through one of the tour guide companies or take a private bus (☞ Visitor Information *in* Bulgaria A to Z, *below*).

Contacts and Resources

VISITOR INFORMATION

Plovdiv (Balkantourist, ✉ 106, bul. Bulgaria, ☎ 032/55–38–48 or 032/55–28–07). **Veliko Târnovo** (Balkantourist, ✉ 2, ul. Al. Penchev, ☎ 062/61–10).

BULGARIA A TO Z

Arriving and Departing

By Boat

Modern luxury vessels cruise the Danube from Vienna to Ruse in Bulgaria. Hydrofoils link main communities along the Bulgarian stretches of the Danube and the Black Sea. For more information, contact the Ministry of Trade and Tourism's **National Information and Advertising Center** (☞ Visitor Information, *below*).

By Bus

Some Bulgarian tourist agencies have regular round-trip bus service from Sofia to Victoria Coach Station in London. **ALMA TOUR-BG** bus service (✉ 83, bul. V. Levski, Sofia 1000, ☎ 02/87–51–87 or 02/80–8–86) leaves London on Friday night, stops in Amsterdam the following morning, and reaches Sofia Monday morning. There is regular bus service from Sofia to most major Eastern European cities. Contact **Group Travel** (✉ Hotel Novotel Evropa, 131, bul. Maria Luiza, Sofia 1202, ☎ 02/31–261), the best international bus company in the country; it has comfortable, modern, air-conditioned buses serving all parts Bulgaria, as well as the Czech Republic, Romania, Austria, Hungary, and other destinations as far away as Holland.

By Car

If you plan on driving into Bulgaria, be aware that border guards will stamp your passport to register that you have entered the country with a vehicle. No one but the holder of the stamped passport may leave the country with the vehicle, and likewise, the stamped passport holder may not leave the country without the vehicle—under any circumstances. If you have rented a car in Bulgaria and drive outside the border for a few days, make sure that when you cross back into Bulgaria the border guards realize the car is rented, or *pod naem* (pronounced poad nai-em). Otherwise, airport border guards may give you trouble—people have been known to miss flights—when you try leave the country without the car that is registered in your passport.

By Plane

The major gateway to Bulgaria is **Sofia Airport** (☎ 02/79–80–35 or 02/72–06–72 for international flight information; ☎ 02/72–24–14 or 02/79–32–21–16 for domestic flights; ☎ 02/79–321 for general information), about 10 km (6 mi) northeast of the city. A word of caution: don't pack valuables in your suitcase when flying in and out of Sofia, as expensive items have a way of disappearing in customs and you may not realize the loss until you unpack.

FROM NORTH AMERICA

Balkan Bulgarian Airlines (✉ 437 Madison Ave., 32nd floor, New York, NY 10022, ☎ 212/371–2047), also called Balkanair, flies from New York to Sofia twice weekly.

WITHIN EUROPE

You can fly from the capital cities of many Eastern European countries directly to Sofia. **Balkan Bulgarian Airlines** (✉ 12, pl. Narodno Sabranie, Sofia, ☎ 02/981–5170) flies from Budapest, Prague, and Warsaw.

Lufthansa German Airlines (✉ 9, ul. Saborna, Sofia, ☎ 02/980–4101) flies from Frankfurt to Sofia. **British Airways** (✉ 56, ul. Alabin, Sofia, ☎ 02/981–7000) has nonstop service from London to Sofia three days a week.

By Train

From the Sofia **Centralna Gara** (Central Train Station; ✉ 112, bul. Maria Luiza, ☎ 02/31–11–11) you can book tickets for just about any destination in Europe, though certain routes are covered infrequently. Be careful not to book a ticket for a train that passes though a country you don't have a visa for, such as Serbia, because you will be unceremoniously booted off the train at the border. Trains cost about the same as buses, but are often overcrowded, smoky, and slow. There are three classifications of trains: *expresni* (express), *burzi* (fast), and *puticheski* (slow). If possible, always take the fastest train and pay a few dollars more for a seat reservation in first class (or else you may find yourself standing in the smoke-filled aisle for hours). Timetables are posted in every station listing *pristigashti* (arrivals) and *zaminavashti* (departures). For both domestic and international railway information, contact **Rila International Travel Agency** (✉ 5, ul. Gen. Gurko, Sofia 1000, ☎ 02/87–07–77 or 02/87–59–35).

Getting Around

By Boat

You can cruise between Black Sea resorts, as well as to Romania and Turkey. For information, consult the **National Information and Advertising Center** (☞ Visitor Information, *below*).

By Bus

In big cities, trams and buses are generally convenient, cheap, and easy to use. Buy tickets (130–200 stotinki) at a kiosk or from the driver and cancel them on board. For longer bus trips between major Bulgarian cities, opt for **Group Travel** (✉ Hotel Novotel Evropa, 131, bul. Maria Luiza, Sofia 1202, ☎ 02/31–261) over other companies. For a small jaunt between towns, the sometimes unpleasant public buses may be the only way to go.

By Car

Driving in Bulgarian cities can be difficult, but once you hit the beautiful stretches of highway linking towns, it is definitely the best means of travel. For motorist information, contact the main office of the **Bulgarian Automobile Touring Association** (SBA; ✉ 3, ul. Pozitano, Sofia, ☎ 02/980–33–08). In case of breakdown, call 146.

Gas stations are spaced at regular intervals on main roads but may be few and far between off the beaten track. All are marked on Balkantourist's free driving map. Hotels, most tourist offices, and sidewalk book vendors also sell maps. Before buying a map, make sure that the names on it are in the Roman alphabet and not in Cyrillic.

PARKING

Bulgaria's parking laws are liberal, and if there isn't a place on the street, you can often park on the sidewalk. Just be sure you're not blocking a driveway or another car, and never park where there's a NO PARKING sign (a red circle with a line through it). When in doubt, check with the hotel or restaurant or sight you are visiting.

ROAD CONDITIONS

In cities, roads are generally poor, with lots of potholes. Main roads between towns, however, are generally well engineered, although some routes are narrow for the volume of traffic they have to carry. A large-scale expressway construction program is under way to link Bulgaria's main cities and towns. Completed stretches run from Kalotina—on the Serbian border—to Sofia, and from Sofia to Plovdiv.

RULES OF THE ROAD

In the bigger cities, trams, buses, and cars fight for the right of way without any clear rules, so drive defensively. Drive on the right, as in the United States. The speed limit is 50 kph or 60 kph (31 mph or 36 mph) in built-up areas, and 80 kph (50 mph) elsewhere, except on highways, where it is 120 kph (70 mph). You are required to carry a first-aid kit, fire extinguisher, and breakdown triangle in the vehicle. Front seat belts must be worn. The drunk-driving laws are strict—it is illegal to drive after you have had more than one drink. If pulled over by the police for any reason, be prepared for an on-site fine (read: *bribe*) of a subjective amount determined by the officer.

By Plane

Balkan Bulgarian Airlines (reservations in Sofia, ☎ 02/981–51–70) has regular services to Varna and Burgas, the biggest ports on the Black Sea.

By Train

From Sofia there are six main routes—to Varna and Burgas on the Black Sea coast (overnight trains between Sofia and Black Sea resorts have first- and second-class sleeping cars and second-class *couchettes,* which are cheaper but less comfortable); to Plovdiv and on to the Turkish border; to Dragoman and the Serbian border; to Kulata and the Greek border; and to Ruse on the Romanian border. The main lines are powered by electricity. For information, contact **Rila International Travel Agency** (☞ Arriving and Departing, *above*).

Contacts and Resources

Car Rentals

Rental car prices vary widely in Bulgaria. The major companies, such as Hertz and Avis, generally charge upwards of $60 a day for mid-range rentals. Smaller, local companies can charge less, but you may find yourself behind the wheel of an old Russian Moskvich. Many cars have air-conditioning, but it is almost impossible to rent a car with automatic transmission. Car rental prices are comparable whether you make arrangements before your trip or on arrival. Three international car-rental firms have offices in Sofia and major towns. **Eurodollar** operates out of the Hotel Kempinski Zografski (✉ 100, bul. James Bourchier, ☎ 02/68–32–51). **Avis** offices are downtown in the Sheraton Sofia Hotel (✉ 5, pl. St. Nedelya, ☎ 02/988–81–67), and at the Sofia Airport (☎ 02/73–80–23). **Hertz** has a central reservations line (☎ 02/980–04–61) and an office at the airport (☎ 02/79–14–77). You can hire a car with a driver through **Balkantour** (✉ 27, bul. Stamboliiski, ☎ 02/988–55–43).

You must obtain a green card from your car insurance company, as recognized international proof that your car is covered by International Civil Liability (third-party) Insurance. You may be required to show this card at the border. If you plan to leave the country, you must also have documentation from the rental company that proves the car is indeed rented (☞ Arriving and Departing by Car, *above*). It's a good idea to take out collision, or Casco, insurance; the cost should be around $5 a day.

Customs and Duties

You may import duty-free into Bulgaria 250 grams of tobacco products, plus 1 liter of hard liquor and 2 liters of wine. Items intended for personal use during your stay are also duty-free. Travelers are advised to declare items of greater value—cameras, tape recorders, etc.—so there will be no problems with Bulgarian customs officials on departure. But beware: If you declare an item, such as a computer, when entering the country, you *cannot* leave the country without it. After declaring something, if you lose it or are robbed, you may be detained for hours of questioning at police headquarters.

It is prohibited to take works of art, church icons, and coins of particular historical or cultural value out of the country. All international restrictive regulations apply.

Emergencies

Ambulance (☎ 150). **Fire** (☎ 160). **Police** (☎ 166). In case of **breakdown** on the road, dial ☎ 146.

Guided Tours

Lyub Travel (✉ 11, ul. Milin Kamak, Lozenets, ☎ 02/528–978) offers custom-made tours of Sofia and regions throughout Bulgaria specializing in archaeology, history, art history, and folklore, including Bulgaria's unique *kukeri,* or mummers, festivals. The firm also arranges accommodations in small hotels or private homes and is popular with the English-speaking diplomatic community. **Odysseia-In** (✉ 20-V, bul. Alexander Stamboliiski, Sofia, ☎ 02/989–0538) offers a broad range of adventure and outdoor recreation tours with experienced guides, including skiing/snowboarding, kayaking, mountain biking, and hiking. **SunShineTours** (✉ 6, ul. Al. Zhendov, Sofia 1113, ☎ 02/971–2825) offers special-interest tours for all ages.

Language

The official language, Bulgarian, is written in Cyrillic and is very close to Old Church Slavonic, the root of all Slavic languages.

In some resorts, railway stations, and airports, names and directions are spelled in the Roman alphabet. English is spoken in major hotels and restaurants but is unlikely to be heard elsewhere. It is essential to remember that in Bulgaria a nod of the head means "no" and a shake of the head means "yes." But there are people who are adopting the Western way, so you have to be careful.

Lodging

Bulgaria offers a range of lodging options, from luxury hotels to extremely inexpensive guest rooms in private homes. The following accommodation offices in Sofia can inform you of your options for almost any city in the country: **Balkantour** (✉ 27, bul. Stambouliiski, ☎ 02/987–7233), **Sofia Tours** (✉ 18, ul. Veslets, ☎ 02/802–238), **Marchella** (✉ 17, ul. Maria Luiza, ☎ 02/815–299), and **Balkantourist** (☞ Visitor Information, *below*).

Mail

Letters weighing up to 10 grams to North America cost 86 stotinki; to the United Kingdom, 70 stotinki. Rates change constantly with inflation, so ask for the current price at the post office before sending mail. It generally takes around two weeks for mail to reach Western Europe and the United States.

RECEIVING MAIL

You can receive your mail through **Sofia Central Post Office** (✉ 6, ul. Gen. Gurko, Sofia 1000) if your letters are marked *poste restante*. You can also use the services of **DHL International** (✉ 8, bul. Tsar Osvoboditel, ☎ 02/88–23–09) or **International Post** (✉ 11, ul. Gen. Gurko, ☎ 02/81–32–96). To collect your mail, you will be asked to present your passport.

Money and Expenses

Bulgaria is still a true cash economy. ATMs are scarce (though the number is growing—look for them at Sofia's largest banks); most people look at traveler's checks as if they are worthless pieces of paper; and there is little infrastructure for credit card use. To avoid getting stuck without cash, be sure to bring crisp, clean, unmarked, and untorn bills of hard currency with you to exchange at the many change bureaus.

You'll find that the favorable exchange rate makes prices extremely low by international standards. The greatest expense is lodging; expenses such as taxi and public transport fares, museum and theater admissions, and meals in most restaurants are quite low. A little hard currency goes a long way.

CREDIT CARDS

The major international credit cards are accepted in a few of the larger stores, and only in the most upscale hotels and restaurants. Even in these establishments the list of cards accepted may not always be correctly posted. Before you book a room or place an order, check to see whether you can pay with your card.

CURRENCY

The unit of currency in Bulgaria is the lev (plural leva). There are bills of 1, 2, 5, 10, 20, and 50 leva. In 1999 the government knocked three zeros off the end of the lev notes and replaced the smaller denomination notes with "stotinki" coins. One hundred stotinki equal one lev. Although prices are sometimes quoted in dollars, all goods and services (except the most expensive hotels and international airline tickets) must be paid for in leva. It is illegal to import or export large amounts of Bulgarian currency. You may import any amount of foreign currency and exchange it at banks, hotels, airports, border posts, and the plentiful private exchange offices (which offer the best rates and no commission). Due to the recent phenomenon of counterfeiting, only new, clean bills will be accepted. Changing traveler's checks is always problematic: Though theoretically possible at a few select locations, such as the airport and some major hotels, commissions are exorbitant. In small towns, traveler's checks are worthless.

In summer 1997 the International Monetary Fund helped institute a currency board, which led to the pegging of the lev to the German mark. The value of the lev continues to fluctuate, however, and the exchange rate and price information quoted here may be outdated quickly. At press time, the rate quoted by the Bulgarian State Bank was 2.01 leva to the U.S. dollar, 1.36 leva to the Canadian dollar, and 3.17 leva to the pound sterling.

SAMPLE COSTS

The following price list, based on costs at press time, can only be used as a rough guide. Trip on a tram or bus: 30 stotinki; theater ticket: 3 leva–7 leva; coffee: 50 stotinki; bottle of wine in a moderate restaurant: 4 leva–7 leva; museum admission: around 1 leva.

TAXES

Bulgaria has value-added tax (VAT). Its rate is 18%.

National Holidays

January 1 (New Year's Day); March 3 (Bulgaria National Day); April 15–16, 2001, and April 5–6, 2002 (Orthodox Easter Sunday and Monday); May 1 (Labor Day); May 24 (Bulgarian Culture Day); September 6 (Unification Day); November 1 (Day of the Leaders of the Bulgarian Revival); December 24–26.

Opening and Closing Times

Banks are open weekdays 8:30–3. **Museums** are usually open 9–6:30 but are often closed Monday or Tuesday. **Shops** are open Monday–Saturday 9–7. Some shops are open on Sunday. A handful of *denonoshni magazini* (day and night minimarkets) are open around the clock in city centers.

Outdoor Activities and Sports

Bulgaria is a great destination for those who enjoy hiking, rock climbing, mountain biking, snowboarding, and skiing. Camping, a popular and inexpensive holiday during Communist days, is more difficult since many of the campgrounds once favored by Eastern Europeans and Bulgarians are in sad shape. An extensive hut system still used by avid Bulgarian hikers in Rila, Pirin, and Central Balkan National Parks has fallen into disrepair. Camping outside the decrepit hut system in the three National Parks is prohibited. Lack of campgrounds should not discourage you from heading for the hills—the country has miles of well-marked trails and excellent ski slopes. In summer, Black Sea beaches offer everything from parasailing to raft rides for children. Boating is popular at Pancharevo, a lake 10 km (6 mi) outside Sofia. Private tour companies specializing in outdoor activities can arrange an outing to your specifications.

Passports and Visas

All visitors need a valid passport. Americans, Canadians, and citizens of the United Kingdom do not need visas when traveling as tourists in Bulgaria for 30 days or less but are required to pay a border tax upon entering the country. Entry with a car is subject to a $10 entrance fee. Other tourists, traveling independently, can also travel without a visa for up to one month. Many package tours are exempt from the visa requirements.

Rail Passes

Bulgaria is not included in the Eurail network, but it is included in the Balkan Flexipass offered through **Rail Europe** (✉ 226–230 Westchester Ave., White Plains, NY 10604, ☎ 914/682–2999 or 800/848–7245); a Bulgaria-only Flexipass is also available. However, train tickets are still so cheap that you should estimate your costs to decide if a pass is practical or necessary.

Student and Youth Travel

While student discounts are not generally offered in Bulgaria, prices are low enough to make budget traveling easy. There is a youth version of Rail Europe's Balkan Flexipass (☞ Rail Passes, *above*). For general information about student identity cards and youth hostels, *see* Students *in* Smart Travel Tips at the front of this book.

Telephones

Phone numbers in Bulgaria can be anywhere from four to eight digits, depending on whether it is an old line or a new digital one.

COUNTRY CODE

For international calls to Bulgaria, the country code is 359. The area code for Sofia is 2 from outside Bulgaria and 02 from within the country.

INTERNATIONAL CALLS

Calls to the United States can be made from the two types of calling-card phones, "Betkom" and "Bulfon," by using a local calling card to reach the international operator, and then a long-distance calling card to reach the United States. They can also be made from your hotel, for a surcharge, or placed from a post office. In Sofia, direct-dial calls to the United States can also be made from the international phone office (½ block west of the main post office). To place a call using an **AT&T USA Direct** international operator, dial ☎ 00–800–0010.

LOCAL CALLS

Local calls can be made from your hotel, from pay phones (with a token costing half a leva), or from calling-card phones. Card-operated phones come in two varieties: Betkom (which are blue) and Bulfon (which are orange). Cards can be bought at newsstands and post offices.

Tipping

Tipping is expected especially by waiters, taxi drivers, and barbers, who usually get about 10%.

Visitor Information

Bulgaria National Information and Advertising Center (✉ 1, Sveta Sofia, Sofia 1040, ☎ 02/981–9965, 🖂) is the official tourist assistance office. It's often difficult to get responses to requests for information, whether delivered via telephone, mail, or e-mail. On site, pleasant and helpful, if disorganized, English-speaking staff will scrounge around for relevant publications or search their database to answer your questions. The Sveta Sofia office is conveniently located off bulevard Vitosha across from the Sheraton.

Balkantourist (Head Office: ✉ 1, bul. Vitosha, ☎ 02/43–331), formerly the state-run tourism organization, is now a private travel agency but in many places in the country still functions as an information office, with locations in most major hotels.

Regional not-for-profit tourism promotion forums, offering information on accommodations, sights, and activities, are **Black Sea Tourism Association** (✉ 20, ul. Bdin, Floor 2, Varna 9000, ☎ 359–052/24–21–92); **Burgas Regional Tourism Association** (✉ 1, ul. Kont Androvandi, Burgas, 8000, ☎ 359–056/451–98); **Pirin Tourism Forum** (✉ Blagoevgrad, Varosha, ☎ 359–73/654–58), providing information on Bansko, skiing, the Pirin Mountains, and the historical Gotse Delchev region; and **Stara Planina Association** (✉ 2, Vazrajdane Sq., Gabrovo 5300, ☎ 359–066/244–75), for the Central Balkan Mountains region.

8 ROMANIA

Much of Romania seems lost in a time warp. Fir-covered mountains shelter picturesque villages where even modest homes boast exteriors with sculpted wooden facades. Women, often in traditional garb, coax wool onto spindles while red-tasseled horses pull wagons loaded with hay. Fortresses and palaces span the centuries, as do more than 2,000 monasteries. In the east, the Black Sea coastline stretches north to the Danube Delta, home to 300-plus species of birds. Transylvanian cities such as Sibiu, Sighişoara, and Braşov include intriguing old-town districts, while Bucharest's wide avenues and mansions suggest why it was once hailed as the "Paris of the East."

Updated by Joyce Dalton

CONSIDERED BY MANY THE MOST BEAUTIFUL COUNTRY in eastern Europe, Romania still claims regions that seem bastions of a medieval past long since lost elsewhere. While the earliest inhabitants date to the Stone Age and the Greeks established trading settlements along the coast in the 7th century BC, it is to the Dacians, a Thracian tribe, and conquering Roman legions that Romanians trace their heritage. In fact, Romanian is a Latin-based language, most similar to Italian; one promotional slogan tags the country "The Latin Island of Eastern Europe."

In contrast to its idyllic geography, Romania's history has seldom been peaceful. Over the centuries, Tartar invasions, struggles against the Ottoman Turks, the Austro-Hungarian domination of Transylvania, and 50 years of Communist rule have led to what some term the "Mioritic complex." This refers to an old, beloved ballad in which two shepherds plot the death of a third for his wealth. Warned by one of his lambs, Mioriţa, the third shepherd, calmly accepts his fate rather than fighting or fleeing. Of course, Romanians' resignation has limits. Many of the country's most magnificent monasteries were built by various ruling princes to commemorate victories against invading Ottoman Turks, and in 1989, Communist dictator Nicolae Ceauşescu's rule (and life) ended with a brief, but violent, revolution. In Bucharest and Timişoara, citizens still place flowers by crosses commemorating those who died in the tumultuous events.

Following the revolution, Romania established a multi-party system with an elected president and a two-chamber parliament and approved a constitution guaranteeing individual rights. The transition to a market economy means that, as a visitor, you will now find many familiar, name-brand consumer goods for sale; new, private hotels, restaurants, tour agencies, clubs, and shops; an ever-expanding network of private homes offering rooms and meals to tourists; and the introduction of Western-style advertising, meaning that billboards now mar some landscapes.

As elsewhere in the region, political and economic reforms here have not been unqualified successes. Corruption remains a serious problem (though tourists generally are blissfully unaware of its existence), and inflation continues. As state-owned factories close, unemployment increases, which has resulted in an underclass of beggars. Some are elderly men and women whose pensions are no longer adequate. Standing passively, they typically make the sign of the cross and murmur a blessing to those who give them money. In cities such as Bucharest, Braşov, and Iaşi, you can come across younger, more assertive beggars. Regardless of your sympathy for their circumstances or the insistence of their pleas, it's safer not to give. Crime remains less of an issue for tourists than in many countries, but in cities and on buses and trains, be alert for pickpockets and scams, and never open your purse or show a large sum of money.

Most visitors have no crime problems and return home rather overwhelmed by the friendliness of the average Romanian. Hospitality enjoys a long tradition here, and the tourist office's slogan, "Come as a tourist; leave as a friend," rings true.

You'll find that Romania's attractions, both natural and man-made, are vast and varied. The Carpathian Mountains cut north–south through the center of the country, offering marvelous drives through fir-covered forests. The provinces of Transylvania and Wallachia treat those on Dracula quests to a range of sights relating to the fictional count and his real-life inspiration, Prince Vlad Ţepeş. There's even a Castle Dracula Hotel perched high atop Pasul Bârgăului (Borgo Pass). Several Transylvanian cities boast intact medieval districts, and fortified churches dominate villages. Maramureş, in the northwest, is the country's—and perhaps, all of Europe's—most traditional zone, with towering hand-carved wooden gates, exquisite high-steeple wooden churches, and folk costume still the approved mode of dress, especially on Sunday. To the northeast, the five "painted monasteries of Bucovina" are UNESCO World Heritage Monuments. The Black Sea and the watery wilderness of the Danube Delta mark Romania's eastern boundary, while Bucharest, the capital, still shows the strong French cultural influence for which it has long been known.

You can enjoy all that Romania has to offer at bargain prices. Food, entry fees, excursions, transportation, and hotels outside the capital remain very reasonable by western standards. The only exceptions are car rentals, gas, and upscale lodgings in Bucharest. Trains cover the country extensively; they're cheap, clean (though toilets are abominable), and reliable. Package tours, organized through operators in your home country or in Romania, can provide worry-free travel at good prices. If you're more of an independent type, you can expect little difficulty exploring by train or rental car, though you should know that most roads are one lane in each direction and are not well-maintained. Frequent passing of horse-drawn wagons and slow-moving trucks is a given. Road signs are well marked, so it's difficult to become lost except when negotiating city streets.

Romania is something of an unknown factor to many potential visitors. As one Romanian put it, "What do foreigners know about us? Dracula, Ceauşescu, and Nadia Comaneci!" Budget constraints do not allow for heavy promotion of tourism (although there has been movement in this direction). These circumstances mean that you can enjoy a wealth of sights and experiences at great prices, free of busloads of tourists vying for photo ops. You'll find Romania a corner of Europe rich in tradition and natural beauty.

Pleasures and Pastimes

Churches and Monasteries

Romania, a nation the size of Oregon, has some 2,000 monasteries, countless churches, and about 100 synagogues. Most are active, a fact all the more impressive considering that decades of Communist rule hardly encouraged religion.

From the multi-gabled roofs and towering spires of Maramureş's exquisite wooden gems to the fortified Saxon-influenced churches of Transylvania and the unique exterior frescoes of Bucovina's monasteries, these religious structures are also temples of history and culture. Many were built centuries ago by ruling princes to commemorate victories, usually against invading Ottoman Turks. Although Romania's extant Jewish population is small, you'll find the synagogues well-maintained.

Dining

New restaurants continue to open at a rapid pace, especially in major cities. Those who visited Romania in the '80s will be amazed at the increased emphasis on decor, food presentation, and service.

While international and ethnic restaurants abound in large cities, expect less variety elsewhere. Menus tend to be meat-oriented; there's a particular emphasis on pork, but fish and chicken are usually available. Most entrées are fried or grilled. In spite of markets overflowing

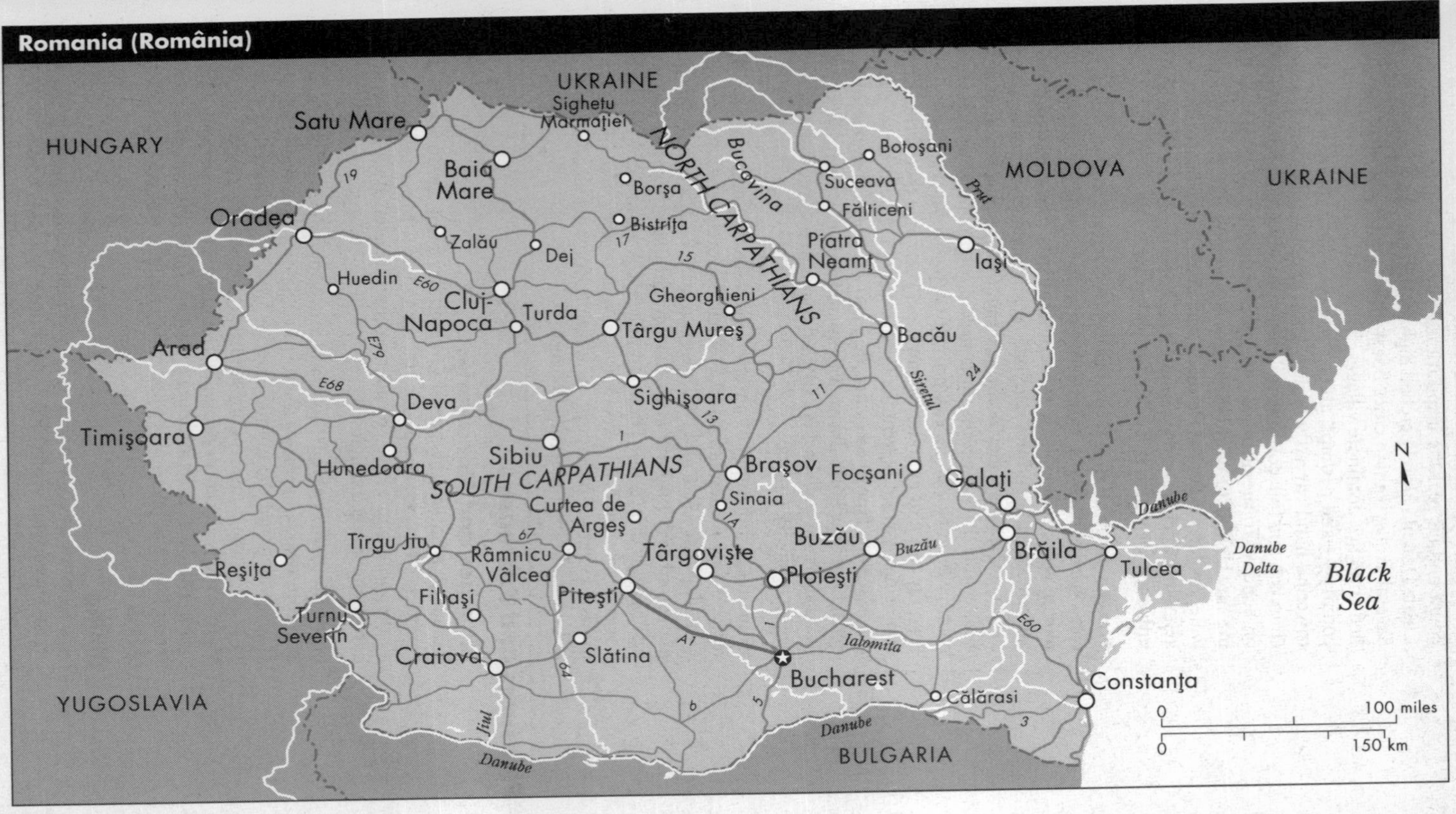
Romania (România)
UKRAINE
HUNGARY
MOLDOVA
UKRAINE
YUGOSLAVIA
BULGARIA
Black Sea
Danube Delta
Danube
Prut
Siretul
Buzău
Ialomita
Jiul
NORTH CARPATHIANS
SOUTH CARPATHIANS
Bucovina
Satu Mare
Sighetu Marmaţiei
Baia Mare
Borşa
Botoşani
Suceava
Fălticeni
Oradea
Zalău
Bistriţa
Dej
Piatra Neamţ
Iaşi
Huedin
Cluj-Napoca
Turda
Gheorghieni
Târgu Mureş
Bacău
Arad
Deva
Sighişoara
Timişoara
Sibiu
Hunedoara
Braşov
Focşani
Galaţi
Brăila
Tulcea
Sinaia
Curtea de Argeş
Tîrgu Jiu
Râmnicu Vâlcea
Târgovişte
Buzău
Ploieşti
Reşiţa
Filiaşi
Piteşti
Turnu Severin
Craiova
Slătina
Bucharest
Călărasi
Constanţa
19
E60
E79
E68
17
15
13
11
1
1A
67
64
A1
6
5
1
24
E60
3
N
0
100 miles
0
150 km

with fresh produce, vegetarians generally find slim pickings. The exception is the tasty tomato, cucumber, and crumbled cheese salad served everywhere in season. Typically, each food item is ordered (and charged for) individually, right down to the butter. If you don't want bread, say so or it will be brought to your table and added to your bill.

Traditional dishes include *mămăligă* (polenta), *sarmale* (cabbage rolls stuffed with meat and rice), *caşcaval pane* (fried ewe's milk cheese), *ghiveci* (casserole with vegetables), *mititei* (spicy sausages), *ciorbă* (slightly sour soup made with various ingredients), and *clătite* (pancakes filled with cheese, jam, or chocolate).

Most restaurants open before noon and continue serving until 11 or later. Small-town eateries close earlier. Fast-food chains have proliferated (at last count, there were some 50 McDonald's), as have kiosks selling snacks. It is best to avoid inexpensive spots labeled *bufet expres, lacto vegetarian,* and *autoservire.*

The familiar alcoholic and nonalcoholic drinks are readily available. In the former category, *ţuică*, a powerful plum brandy, is the national favorite. Romanian wines can be very good, especially the whites. Strong Turkish-style coffee is favored, although instant coffee, commonly called *nes,* is also served. While tap water is considered safe except in the Danube Delta, it's a good idea to stick to bottled water, *apă minerală,* which is inexpensive and easily found in restaurants, groceries, and kiosks.

CATEGORY	COST*
$$$$	over $25
$$$	$15–$25
$$	$10–$15
$	under $10

**per person for a three-course meal, including wine and tip.*

Lodging

In Bucharest, the lodging picture improves steadily as international chains increase their presence and former state properties become privatized. Best Western, Hilton, Holiday Inn Crowne Plaza, Howard Johnson's, Inter-Continental, Marriott, and Sofitel are all there. Continental Hotels, a Romanian chain with more than 10 properties around the country, offers reliable accommodations at reasonable prices. The usual rating system of one to five stars is in place and rates are posted. Breakfast is usually included.

In cities and towns that see few tourists or business travelers, hotels often date to the socialist era, with all the lack of ambience that that implies. Though frequently in need of refurbishment, rooms usually are clean and have private baths. Staff may not speak English, but most try to be helpful. Away from major centers, hotels seldom accept credit cards or traveler's checks.

Agro-tourism has definitely caught on, meaning the option of home stays. If you book through an organized network such as **ANTREC** (✉ Str. Ştirbei Vodă 2–4, Bucharest, ☎ 01/315–2732, FAX 01/312–0148), count on a clean, comfortable room and ample meals. Do not expect a private bath or hosts that speak English. Rates run $12–$23 per person including two meals.

Many monasteries accept overnight guests. Facilities range from basic to attractive units constructed especially for tourists. Prices usually include two or three meals. Because English may not be spoken, it is easier to book through a tour operator.

CATEGORY	BUCHAREST*	OTHER AREAS*
$$$$	over $250	over $80
$$$	$150–$250	$50–$80
$$	$75–$150	$30–$50
$	under $75	under $30

**All prices are for a double room during peak season, including breakfast.*

following the text of a review is your signal that the property has a Web site, where you will find details and, usually, images; for a link, visit www.fodors.com/urls.

Shopping

If you love traditional crafts you'd be wise to pack a spare bag when visiting Romania, where you'll find a pleasing combination of variety, fine workmanship, and low prices. Items include hand-woven carpets; embroidered blouses, scarves, tablecloths, and bedspreads; painted and beaded eggs; wooden masks; ceramics; icons painted on glass or wood; and leather vests trimmed in fur, tassels, and embroidery. Monastery and museum shops are good places for making such purchases. Although customs officials seldom inspect foreigners' baggage, you should have receipts handy for antiques and art, just in case.

Walking and Hiking

Whatever your pace, Romania's Carpathian Mountains offer superb hiking opportunities. A well-organized trail system exists, although many markings are in need of maintenance. Hiking maps are found in bookstores, hotels, and at "Salvamont" stations in major hiking gateways such as Buşteni, Sinaia, Târgu Jiu, Borşa, and Sibiu. Salvamont helps hikers in need; its members wear triangular badges bearing the organization's name.

Exploring Romania

Great Itineraries

Numbers in the text correspond to numbers in the margin and on the Bucharest map.

IF YOU HAVE 3 DAYS

Explore the sights of **Bucharest** ①–⑭ by strolling along Calea Victoriei to Piaţa Revoluţiei, home to many important sites. View at least the exterior of **Palatul Parlamentului** ⑬, then visit **Muzeul Ţăranului Român** ⑤ or **Muzeul Satului** ⑦, both well worth seeing. On day two, head north to **Sinaia** to tour **Castelul Peleş** before continuing to **Braşov** and its fine medieval section. Overnight in Braşov or nearby **Poiana Braşov.** On day three, visit the fortified churches of Prejmer and Hărman, just north of Braşov. Then head southwest on route 73 to **Castle Bran** before returning to Bucharest via Piteşti.

IF YOU HAVE 5 DAYS

Follow the itinerary above for days one and two. On day three, visit **Castle Bran** before heading northwest to **Sighişoara** and its fine medieval district; continue to **Sibiu** to spend the night. On day four, savor Sibiu's Old Town, the **Astra** outdoor museum, and the **Muzeul de Icoane pe Sticlă** (Icons on Glass Museum) in nearby **Sibiel**; spend the night again in Sibiu. On day five, return to Bucharest via Râmnicu Vâlcea and Piteşti. Take in a few more of the capital's attractions or visit **Snagov.**

When to Tour

Generally sunny but mild conditions make May–June and September–October ideal sightseeing months. Winters tend to be cold and snowy, while mid-summer days are hot except in higher elevations and along the coast. Most Black Sea hotels are closed in the off-season. Folkloric festivals take place throughout the year, especially in the summer and between Christmas and New Year's (☞ Festivals and Seasonal Events *in* Chapter 1).

BUCHAREST

The old story goes that a shepherd named Bucur settled on the site where the city of Bucharest now stands. The name Bucureşti was first officially used in 1459, by Vlad Ţepeş, the prince upon whom Bram Stoker based his fictional Dracula. Two centuries later, this citadel on the Dâmboviţa River became the capital of the province of Wallachia, and after another 200 years, it was named the capital of Romania. The city gradually developed into a place of bustling trade and gracious living, with ornate and varied architecture, landscaped parks, busy winding streets, and wide boulevards. After decades of neglect, Bucharest no longer can claim the title "Paris of the East," although hints of its past glory remain.

Exploring Bucharest

Sightseeing might best be divided into two segments, to be covered in two days: first from Piaţa Revoluţiei north to Parcul Herăstrău, and second from Piaţa Universităţii south to the Dâmboviţa River, then west to Palatul Parlamentului and Palatul Cotroceni. Less hardy walkers might use the Metro for some long stretches, such as to Palatul Cotroceni. A two-trip Metro ticket costs about 30¢ and stations are marked on city maps.

Bucharest is not laid out in a neat grid, and its many circular *pieţe* (plazas) add to the confusion. Furthermore, street names are not posted at every corner. Arm yourself with a good map, obtainable from the Tourism Promotion Office in your home country (☞ Visitor Information *in* Smart Travel Tips), bookstores or hotels, and don't be shy about asking for assistance. Most Romanians are helpful and many, especially young people, speak English.

A Good Walk

Numbers in the text correspond to numbers in the margin and on the Bucharest map.

A number of imposing buildings surround Piaţa Revoluţiei, including **Muzeul Naţional de Artă** ① (the former royal palace), **Ateneul Român** ②, and **Biserica Creţulescu** ③. Proceed north on Calea Victoriei past some of the city's fine old mansions, such as Casa Vernescu and the Muzeul Naţional George Enescu. Just across Piaţa Victoriei, take Şoseaua Kiseleff and you will come immediately to **Muzeul de Istorie Naturală Grigore Antipa** ④ and **Muzeul ţăranului Român** ⑤. Do not miss the latter. Continue up Kiseleff or take the Metro to the **Arcul de Triumf** ⑥. A short distance beyond this circle, in Parcul Herăstrău, is the entrance to **Muzeul Satului** ⑦, among the best of Romanian's many outdoor village museums.

For a second tour, walk west from Piaţa Universităţii along B-dul Republicii, admiring the University of Bucharest's 19th-century buildings and the statues of scholars and statesmen. Turn south on Calea Victoriei, where you soon reach **Muzeul Naţional de Istorie** ⑧ with its marvelous Treasury exhibit. Farther along, the **Lipscani** district, or historic center, is a confusing maze of winding streets. Though less picturesque than it once was, the area houses antiques stores, galleries (especially surrounding the courtyard of Hanul cu Tei), **Curtea Veche** ⑨, **Hanul**

Bucharest (București)
5
4
6
7
B-dul Aviatorilor
Șos. Kiseleff
B-dul 1 Mai
Piața Victoriei
Șos. Nicolae Titulescu
B-dul Iancu de Hunedoara
Str. Londra
Str. Roma
Șoseaua Ștefan Cel Mare
Banu Mămuleanu
Str. Tunari
Str. Aurel Vlaicu
Str. Polonă
C. Dorobantilor
Str. Căderea Bastiliei
Str. Grigore Alexandrescu
B-dul Ana Ipătescu
B-dul Alex Ioan Cuza
Str. Buzești
Calea Victoriei
Str. Occidentului
Piața Romană
Str. Mihai
Eminescu
Str. Icoanei
Piața Lahovari
B-dul Dacia
Bdul. Dacia
Gara de Nord
Piața M. Boțescu
C. Griviței
Str. Biserica Amzei
Piața Amzei
George Enescu
B-dul G-ral Magheru
Str. Dionisie Lupu
Piața Al. Sahia
Str. Galați
Str. Icoanei
Str. Pictor Verona
Str. Maria Rosetti
Str. Ștefan Furtună
C. Victoriei
i
2
1
Piața
C.A. Rosetti
Str. Berzei
Str. General Berthelot
Str. Știrbei Vodă
N

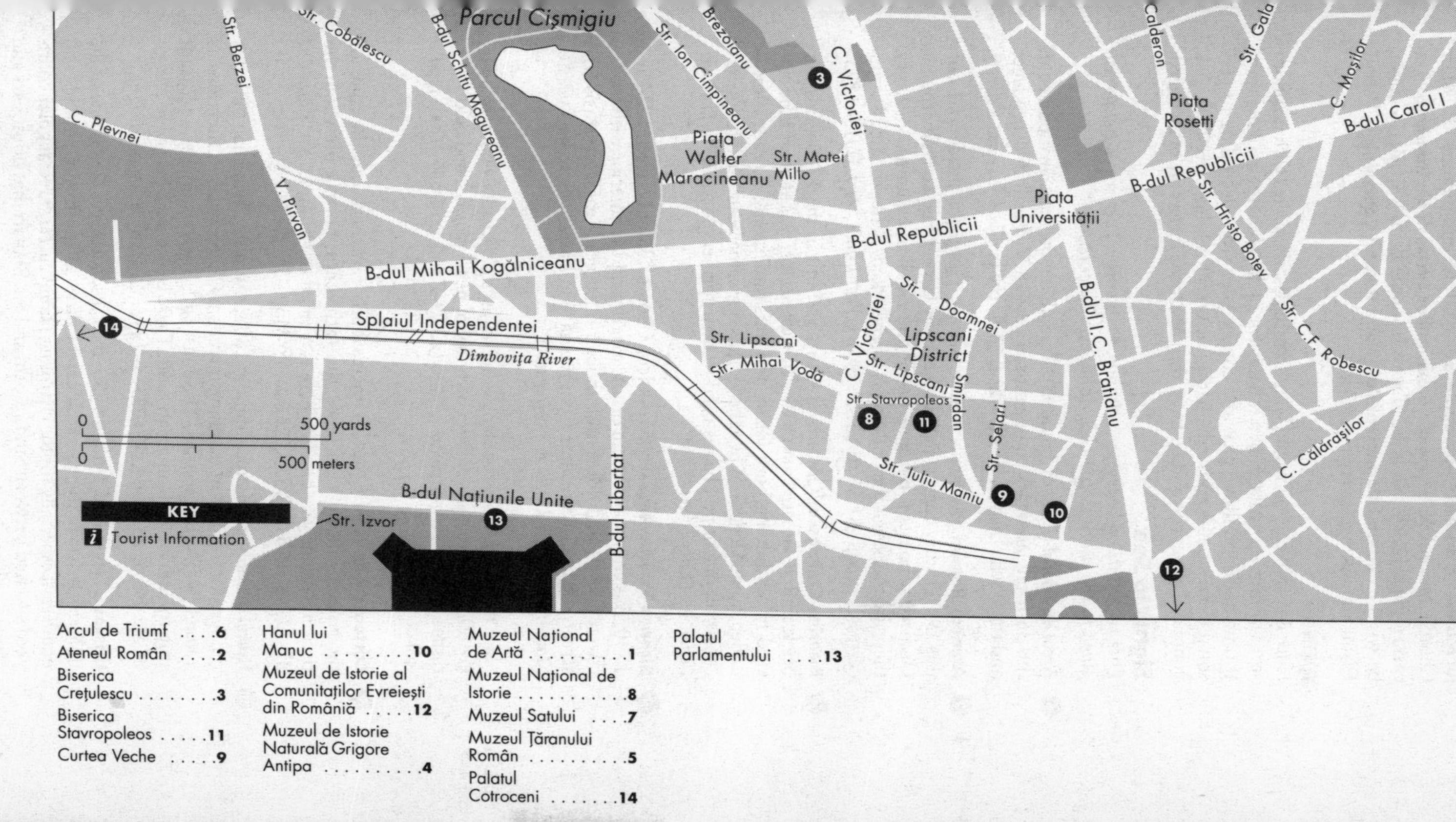
Parcul Cișmigiu
Str. Cobălescu
Str. Berzei
C. Plevnei
V. Pirvan
B-dul Schitu Magureanu
Str. Ion Cîmpineanu
Brezoianu
C. Victoriei
Piața Walter Maracineanu
Str. Matei Millo
Calderon
Str. Gala
C. Moșilor
Piața Rosetti
B-dul Carol I
B-dul Republicii
Piața Universității
Str. Hristo Botev
B-dul Mihail Kogălniceanu
Splaiul Independentei
Dîmbovița River
Str. Lipscani
Str. Mihai Vodă
Str. Doamnei
Lipscani District
Str. Stavropoleos
Smîrdan
Str. Selari
Str. Iuliu Maniu
B-dul I.C. Bratianu
Str. C.F. Robescu
C. Călărașilor
B-dul Libertat
B-dul Națiunile Unite
Str. Izvor
0 500 yards
0 500 meters
KEY
Tourist Information
Arcul de Triumf 6
Ateneul Român 2
Biserica Crețulescu 3
Biserica Stavropoleos 11
Curtea Veche 9
Hanul lui Manuc 10
Muzeul de Istorie al Comunitaților Evreiești din Româniă 12
Muzeul de Istorie Naturală Grigore Antipa 4
Muzeul Național de Artă 1
Muzeul Național de Istorie 8
Muzeul Satului 7
Muzeul Țăranului Român 5
Palatul Cotroceni 14
Palatul Parlamentului 13

lui Manuc ⑩, **Biserica Stavropoleos** ⑪, and the onion-domed Russian Church. **Muzeul de Istorie al Comunitaţilor Evreieşti din România** ⑫ is east of Piaţa Unirii. Next, head west from the Piaţa (the Metro might be wise) to **Palatul Parlamentului** ⑬ and **Palatul Cotroceni** ⑭. Parcul Cişmigiu makes a lovely rest spot.

TIMING

Since it is unlikely you would want to rush past these sites with no photo stops or interior visits, plan a full day for each half of the walking tour. If time does not allow, pick and choose your stops according to personal interest, and utilize the Metro or taxis for longer stretches. Ask your hotel about correct taxi fares, then negotiate; meters are often rigged.

Sights to See

Due to inflation, entry fees change frequently. The prices below are given in the more stable U.S. dollar equivalents.

❻ **Arcul de Triumf** (Arch of Triumph). Resembling the Parisian monument, this 36-ft-tall landmark commemorates the 1877 War for Independence and those who died in World War I. ✉ *At the head of Şoseaua Kiseleff.*

★ ❷ **Ateneul Român** (Romanian Athenaeum). Gorgeous inside and out, this 19th century concert hall, home to the George Enescu Philharmonic Orchestra, boasts a Baroque dome and classical columns. In theory, there are tours, but the building is often locked. Better to attend a concert; tickets run $1.65 to $3.25. ✉ *Str. Franklin 1,* ☎ *01/315–6875.*

❸ **Biserica Creţulescu** (Creţulescu Church). Built in the 1720s, this red-brick church, situated next to the former palace, was at press time covered in scaffolding both inside and out, undergoing a renovation of undetermined length. When the work is done, the beautiful interior frescoes will, one hopes, be restored to their former glory. ✉ *Piaţa Revoluţiei.* ⏲ *Daily 6 AM–7 PM.*

⓫ **Biserica Stavropoleos** (Stravropoleos Church). Built between 1724 and 1730, this church boasts an ornate exterior and an interior with fresco-covered walls and dome and an icon-filled gold-leaf iconostasis (the screen separating the altar from the nave in Eastern churches). ✉ *Str. Stavropoleos.* ⏲ *Daily 6 AM–7 PM.*

NEED A BREAK?

Near the Biserica Stavropoleos is Bucharest's oldest surviving beer hall (1880), **Carul cu Bere,** serving a variety of beers plus hot and cold dishes. ✉ *Str. Stavropoleos 3,* ☎ *01/313–7560.* ⏲ *Daily 10 AM until last customer.*

❾ **Curtea Veche** (Old Court). Dracula buffs can check out the ruins of the palace built by Vlad Ţepeş, the 15th-century prince on whom the fictional count was based. There is a small museum. ✉ *Str. Franceză 27-31,* ☎ *01/314–0375.* 🎫 *80¢.* ⏲ *Mon.–Sat. 9–3.*

❿ **Hanul lui Manuc** (Manuc's Inn). In 1808, a wealthy Armenian built this timbered inn aimed at traveling merchants. Even today, it functions as a hotel (with dingy rooms). The courtyard, however, makes a pleasant stop for a drink or Romanian food. There is also a *cramă* (wine cellar). ✉ *Str. Franceză 62-64,* ☎ *01/313–1415.* ⏲ *Daily 8 AM–midnight.*

Lipscani. Developed around 1750, the Lipscani Street area is one of the oldest districts in Bucharest. It can be dirty and confusing, but it's still of interest, especially for the charming **Hanul cu Tei,** a rectangular courtyard situated between Str. Lipscani and Str. Blănari that houses art and antiques shops.

⓬ **Muzeul de Istorie al Comunităților Evreiești din România** (Museum of the History of the Jewish Community in Romania). Housed in a synagogue dating to 1850, this museum traces the history of Romania's Jewish population. More than half the 750,000 Jews in Romania at the beginning of World War II were killed in concentration camps during the war, and many of those who survived emigrated to Israel soon afterward. There are fewer than 20,000 today. ✉ *Str. Mămulari 3,* ☎ *01/615–0837.* 🎟 *10¢.* ⏲ *Wed. and Sun. 9–1.*

❹ **Muzeul de Istorie Naturală Grigore Antipa** (Natural History Museum). Wildlife exhibits from around Romania are displayed in realistic settings, as are dioramas of various ethnic cultures. ✉ *Şos. Kiseleff 1,* ☎ *01/312–8826.* 🎟 *$1.05 including special exhibits.* ⏲ *Tues.–Sun. 10–5.*

❶ **Muzeul Național de Artă** (National Art Museum). Once the royal palace, this building now houses a fine collection that includes pieces by the sculptor Brâncuşi and marvelous works from the Brueghel school. The museum owns the world's largest collection of Romanian art, featuring works from medieval days through the 1980s. Sections are still under restoration following damage in the 1989 revolution. There are several important branches of the museum nearby. ✉ *Calea Victoriei 49-53,* ☎ *01/313–3030.* 🎟 *55¢, free first Wed. of each month.* ⏲ *Wed.–Sun. 10–6.*

❽ **Muzeul Național de Istorie** (National History Museum). This vast, somewhat dreary museum contains exhibits from the Neolithic period to the 1920s. The Treasury section, with its array of golden objects dating from Roman days to the present, is quite worthwhile. ✉ *Calea Victoriei 12,* ☎ *01/315–8207.* 🎟 *$1.65.* ⏲ *Tues.–Sun. 9–5.*

★ ❼ **Muzeul Satului** (Village Museum). This fabulous open-air museum near Herăstrău Lake is home to more than 300 traditional houses, workshops, and churches from all over Romania. Some are complete with regional furnishings. ✉ *Şos. Kiseleff 28-30,* ☎ *01/222–9110.* 🎟 *$1.35, plus 55¢ to carry a camera, $2.70 to carry a video recorder.* ⏲ *Tues.–Sun., opens 9; seasonal closing times: Nov.–Jan., 4; Feb.–Mar., Sept.–Oct., 5; Apr.–June 14, 6; June 15–Aug., 8.*

★ ❺ **Muzeul țăranului Român** (Peasant Museum). In 1996, this became the first museum in Eastern Europe to receive the European Museum of the Year award. Some 90,000 items, ranging from costumes and textiles to ceramics and icons, are on view. Information in English is available in each room. Check out the museum shop's traditional crafts. ✉ *Şos. Kiseleff 3,* ☎ *01/650–5360.* 🎟 *55¢; with camera, $2.70; with video recorder $5.45.* ⏲ *Tues.–Sun. 10–6.*

NEED A BREAK?

Just west of Piața Victoriei, **The Dubliner** offers cozy Irish pub ambience along with draught beer and a variety of tempting dishes, such as "cottage pie" (minced beef and vegetables topped with mashed potatoes, baked and served in a ceramic bowl). ✉ *B-dul. Nicolae Titulescu 18,* ☎ *01/222–9473.* ⏲ *Daily noon until last customer.*

★ ⓮ **Palatul Cotroceni** (Cotroceni Palace). Although a monastery and a princely palace stood on this spot back in the 1680s, the present palace dates to the late 19th century, when it became the home of Romania's royal family. After a devastating 1977 earthquake, Cotroceni Palace was rebuilt and a wing added where the president now has offices. The lavish decor and art offer a glimpse into the lives of Romania's former royalty. Guides are required (no extra charge); although one may be available on the spot, it's best to make a reservation. Since the palace is a bit removed from other sights, it's advisable to take the Metro to the Politehnica station.

☒ *B-dul. Geniului 1,* ☎ *01/221–1200.* 🎟 *$2.70; with camera $5.45; with video recorder $16.30.* ⏲ *Tues.–Sun. 9–4.*

★ ⓭ **Palatul Parlamentului** (Palace of Parliament). Formerly known as Casa Poporului (House of the People), this mammoth building, the second largest in the world after Washington, D.C.'s Pentagon, stands witness to the megalomania of the Communist dictator Ceaușescu. Today, it houses the Romanian parliament. Unlike the royal palaces, every detail is Romanian, from the 24 kt. gold on the ceilings to the huge handmade carpet on the floor. The ground-floor rooms are open to visitors. Tours lasting 45 minutes leave from the south entrance. Reservations are required. ☒ *Calea 13 Septembrie,* ☎ *01/311–3611.* 🎟 *$1.65; camera fee $1.65; video fee $5.45.* ⏲ *Daily 10–4.*

OFF THE BEATEN PATH

SNAGOV – Snagov Monastery, a rustic cloister on a small island in the middle of Snagov Lake, is the reputed burial place of Vlad Țepeș, also known as Vlad Dracula. Situated 40 km (25 mi) north of Bucharest, the forested area surrounding the lake is a popular weekend retreat for city dwellers. Boatmen ferry tourists to the monastery; bargain for the best rate.

Dining

New restaurants featuring a variety of cuisines open in Bucharest almost daily, and fast-food chains have invaded the capital. Some of the smaller spots should be avoided, but good, inexpensive meals can be found in many of the newer cafés. Except for the most upscale restaurants, prices are inexpensive by western standards. Check your bill, as some eateries try to overcharge foreigners.

$$$$ ★ ✕ **Casa Vernescu.** Housed in a magnificent 19th-century mansion, this elegant restaurant serves a lavish buffet of salads, pastas, meats, and Romanian specialties. The à la carte menu is equally varied. Dine surrounded by gilded moldings, frescoes, and marble columns, or, during warm weather, in the garden. Greek and Romanian evenings feature folkloric programs on Tuesday and Thursday, respectively. ☒ *Calea Victoriei 133,* ☎ *01/231–0220. AE, DC, MC, V.*

$$$ ✕ **Casa Doina.** This 19th-century villa, transformed decades ago into a fine restaurant, offers garden pavilions and a traditional *cramă* (wine cellar) for casual dining in addition to the main dining room. The cramă features Romanian specialities, and a Gypsy band plays each evening. ☒ *Şos. Kiseleff 4,* ☎ *01/222–6717. AE, MC, V.*

$$$ ★ ✕ **Club Contele Dracula.** This unique theme restaurant, where every item from service plates to wall decorations relates to the fictional Dracula or the 15th-century Vlad Țepeș, serves a variety of tasty Transylvanian and wild game dishes. Several times each week, the count rises from his cellar coffin to wander, candelabrum in hand, among his guests. ☒ *Splaiul Independenței 8A,* ☎ *01/312–1353. AE, MC, V.*

$$$ ✕ **La Taverne.** In a city once known as "The Paris of the East," La Taverne is generally considered Bucharest's most fashionable French restaurant. The French chef offers a variety of entrées plus a well-priced daily special. There's even a Havana bar with the requisite Latin ambience. ☒ *Str. Tunari 67–69,* ☎ *01/211–1184. AE, MC, V.*

$$ ★ ✕ **Bistro Atheneu.** The atmosphere of this charming restaurant has overtones of a Parisian bistro, but the food is classic Romanian—liver in mushroom sauce, steak, and grilled chicken. A musical duo entertains most evenings. ☒ *Str. Episcopiei 3,* ☎ *01/313–4900. No credit cards.*

$$ ✕ **La Mardare.** Typical Romanian food is served in several traditionally decorated rooms of this large house. After dinner, head to the cramă for an evening of Gypsy music. ☒ *Calea Griviției 32,* ☎ *01/650–2257. No credit cards.*

$$ ✕ **Opera.** Situated with a nice view of the Opera Română, this pleasant restaurant offers a canopied terrace and a variety of Italian and Romanian dishes. Live music is an added attraction. ✉ *Str. Dr. Lister 1,* ☏ *01/411–6330. AE, MC, V.*

$ ✕ **Casa Veche.** Forty-four kinds of wood-oven pizzas (including vegetarian), plus pasta, cold plates, salads, and sandwiches make this a great casual spot. There's a huge dining room, plus outdoor tables in a courtyard. ✉ *Str. George Enescu 15–17,* ☏ *01/315–7897. AE, MC, V.*

Lodging

New hotels, particularly in the three- to five-star categories, continue to open in Bucharest, while a number of older properties have been privatized and renovated. Naturally, the price rises along with the comfort level. In such properties, you're assured of comfortable rooms and good to excellent service. English typically is spoken by reception and restaurant staff.

There is a shortage of good hotels below $100. Some properties have rooms in more than one category; cheaper rooms usually mean shared bath facilities. In budget establishments, it's wise to check your room first. English may or may not be spoken.

$$$$ ★ **Athenée Palace Hilton.** Situated on Piaţa Revoluţiei, this historic five-star property continues a tradition of hospitality dating to 1914. The upper lobby's marble columns and the ballroom's stained-glass ceiling recapture this earlier era. Guest rooms are bright and attractive; staff is young and enthusiastic. ✉ *Str. Episcopiei 1–3,* ☏ *01/303–3777,* FAX *01/315–212. 257 rooms, 15 suites. 3 restaurants, 2 bars, indoor pool, health club, casino, business center, meeting rooms. AE, DC, MC, V.*

$$$$ ★ **Inter-Continental.** When this 22-story hotel was built in 1971, it became not only Bucharest's first international hotel but also its tallest building. Overlooking Piaţa Universităţii, its refurbished guest rooms offer all the expected comforts and amenities. Service is punctual and correct. ✉ *B-dul. Nicolae Bălcescu 4,* ☏ *01/310–2020,* FAX *01/312–0486. 404 rooms, 19 suites. 3 restaurants, 3 bars, indoor pool, health club, casino, business center, meeting rooms. AE, DC, MC, V.*

$$$ **Bucureşti.** Located near Piaţa Revoluţiei, this four-star property, constructed in 1982, offers comfortable, attractively furnished rooms with all the usual amenities. The main restaurant is outstanding in both quality of food and service. Both it and the more casual eatery feature live music in the evenings. ✉ *Calea Victoriei 63-81,* ☏ *01/313–3525,* FAX *01/312–0927. 415 rooms, 31 suites. 2 restaurants, bar, indoor-outdoor pool, health club, casino, business center, meeting rooms. AE, MC, V.*

$$$ **Continental.** Constructed in 1828 and now a declared historical monument, this impressive white structure stands on one of Bucharest's main shopping avenues. Now part of the first and largest Romanian chain, the four-star property still boasts decor and furnishings reminiscent of its earlier days. ✉ *Calea Victoriei 56,* ☏ *01/638–5022,* FAX *01/312–4169. 44 rooms, 9 suites. Restaurant, breakfast room, patisserie, meeting rooms. AE, DC, MC, V.*

$$ **Central.** Two blocks off Calea Victoriei and a stone's throw from lovely Cişmigiu Park, this property, dating to the early 19th century, underwent renovations in 2000. Guest rooms, while not large or lavish, have modern conveniences, including cable TV. Don't be deterred by the McDonald's at street level. ✉ *Str. Brezoianu 13,* ☏ FAX *01/315–5634. 58 rooms, 4 suites. Breakfast room, air-conditioning, minibars. MC, V.*

$ ★ **Triumf.** Near the Arc de Triumf, this brick building stands back from the road behind a large grassy rectangle. Built in 1935 as a bank and apartments for bankers, it has been a hotel (two-star) since the 1960s.

Guest rooms may not be strong on decor, but they are clean and comfortable. Some have balconies; all have cable TV, phone, and refrigerator. Reception staff speaks English. An excellent value. ✉ *Şos. Kiseleff 12,* ☎ *01/222–3172,* FAX *01/223–2411. 88 rooms, 12 suites. Restaurant, bar, refrigerators, barbershop. MC, V.*

Nightlife and the Arts

For information on movies, music, and all kinds of events in Bucharest, grab a copy of the free weekly English-language *Şapte Seri*; it's available in most hotels, airline offices, and Western-style bars and restaurants.

Nightlife

Bucharest nightlife has come into its own—new bars, clubs, and casinos are opening constantly, frequented by both locals and ex-pats. Girly shows and less reputable bars are part of the scene, so choose your night spot carefully or it could become an unpleasant, expensive evening. Even in the best places, do not expect a smoke-free environment.

BARS

In Bucharest, as elsewhere, trends change quickly, so check around if your goal is the latest "in" place. The following are likely to maintain their popularity. **Planters** (✉ Str. Mendeleev 10, ☎ 01/659–7606) is dimly lit, loud, and at times a bit outrageous. There's a disc-jockey Thursday–Saturday. **Terminus** (✉ Str. George Enescu 5, ☎ 01/659–7606), under the same ownership as Planters (thus, same phone), has a winding staircase suspended by ropes that leads to a cellar bar serving 38 different beers. In Bucharest's old town, **Swing House** (✉ Str. Gabroveni 20, ☎ 01/092–589–0589) features jazz and blues in a redbrick cellar bar. The owner has written a jazz dictionary. Mix with Bucharest's young professionals and TV stars at **The Office** (✉ Str. Tache Ionescu 2, ☎ 01/659–4518) and sample some of the city's best drinks. (Note that there's a dress code.)

CASINOS

By some counts, Romania claims more casinos than any other European country. At **Casino Palace** (✉ Calea Victoriei 133, ☎ 01/231–0220), try your luck amid the luxurious surroundings of a 19th-century mansion. All the usual games of chance are available in this Monte Carlo–style casino. Casa Vernescu restaurant (☞ Dining, *above*) is housed in the same building. A passport is required for entry, and limo service is available on request.

DISCOS

If discos are your thing, head to **Karma** (✉ Str. Academiei 35-37, ☎ 01/313–6595) and join the young Romanian crowd for a night of lively dancing. "After all, we're Latins," Romanians are quick to remind you, and this becomes abundantly clear as they sway to a mean salsa beat at **Salsa, You and Me II** (✉ Galeriile Lutherană on Str. Lutherană, ☎ 01/310–1737).

The Arts

Generally, performance tickets can be purchased directly at the venue's ticket office or from your hotel, with a slight commission added. It's usually easy to get tickets without booking ahead.

FILM

Foreign films are shown in their original language with Romanian subtitles. Though theaters are sometimes unkempt and moviegoers a bit boisterous, going to the movies is still an excellent chance to catch a popular film at a fraction of the cost back home (85¢–$1.30). There are several good theaters on B-dul. Magheru.

MUSIC

The **Filarmonica George Enescu** (George Enescu Philharmonic Orchestra), based in the Atheneul Român (✉ Str. Franklin 1, ☏ 01/315–6875), plays a variety of classical favorites. The music is top quality and often features guest artists. Front row center runs $3.25. Performances begin at 7 PM.

Sala Radio (Radio Hall, ✉ Str. Berthelot 60–64, ☏ 01/314–6800), housed in the National Radio Society building, gives classical programs performed by a fine orchestra. Tickets run 80¢–$1.35. Performances begin at 7 PM.

OPERA AND BALLET

Opera Română (✉ B-dul. Kogălniceanu 70–72, ☏ 01/313–1857) offers productions by many of the opera world's greatest composers. Tickets range from 80¢ to $1.65. Performances start at 6 PM. Ballet and opera seasons overlap; both end in mid-June.

Shopping

If you fancy western-style shopping, the four-story **Bucharest Mall** (✉ Calea Vitan 55–59, near Piaţa Unirii) houses more than 70 stores, 20 restaurants, a supermarket, a children's play area, an 82-ft fountain, and a 10-screen cinema. The **World Trade Center** (✉ B-dul. Expozitiei 2), next to the Sofitel Hotel, is a small shopping mall.

ART AND CRAFTS

Apollo in the National Theater building (✉ B-dul. Băcescu 2, ☏ 01/313–5010) offers paintings and sculptures. The galleries of the **Hanul cu Tei** (✉ off Str. Lipscani) feature paintings and antiques.

For traditional handicrafts (☞ Pleasures and Pastimes, *above*), check out *artizanat* stores throughout the city or, better yet, visit the shops connected to the **Muzeul ţăranului Român** and the **Muzeul Satului** (☞ Sights to See, *above*).

CARPETS

Romania is well known for its handmade carpets; many are woven in monasteries, and each region employs distinct colors and patterns. **Covoare** (✉ B-dul. Unirii 13, ☏ 01/336–2174) is a good spot for carpet shopping. The shop at the **Muzeul Ţăranului Român** (☞ Sights to See, *above*) has a good selection of carpets.

CRYSTAL AND PORCELAIN

Romanian crystal and porcelain tend to be fairly inexpensive and of good quality. **Sticerom** (✉ Str. Şelari 9–11, ☏ 01/315–9699) has a fine selection.

Bucharest A to Z

Arriving and Departing

BY CAR

There are four main access routes into and out of the city—E70 west to the Hungarian border, E60 north via Braşov, E70/E85 south to Bulgaria, and E85/60 east to Constanţa and the coast. Bucharest has poor signposting and many tortuous one-way streets. Drivers are aggressive and parking on the sidewalk is common.

BY PLANE

Most international flights to Romania land at Bucharest's **Otopeni Airport** (☏ 01/230–0022), 16 km (10 mi) north of the city. Some Tarom flights from North America land at Timişoara or Satu Mare before continuing to Bucharest.

Between the Airport and Downtown: Bus 783 makes the 40-minute trip between the airport and Piaţa Unirii every 30 minutes between 5:30 AM and 11 PM, stopping at main squares along the way. Buses tend to be crowded. A better bet is **Sky Services** (☎ 01/204–1002), located just beyond customs. Cost is $10 per person for a shared car, $30 for a private car. If you take a taxi, bargain over the fare; the price should be about $25.

BY TRAIN

Most international trains and the majority of domestic trains operate from **Gara de Nord** (✉ B-dul. Gării de Nord, ☎ 01/223–0880). For tickets and information, go to the **Agenţia de Voiaj CFR** (✉ Str. Domniţa Anastasia 10, ☎ 01/313–2642).

Getting Around

Bucharest is spacious and sprawling. Though the old heart of the city and most of the major sights can be explored on foot, long avenues and vast squares make some form of transportation necessary. Tourist maps can be obtained at bookstores, kiosks, hotels, and tourist agencies.

BY BUS, TRAM, AND TROLLEY

RATB surface transit service is extensive. However, buses and trolleys generally are crowded and pickpockets pose a problem. Purchase tickets at booths near bus stops; one trip (*una călătorie*) costs 15¢. Validate your ticket on board. Day and week passes are available. Some booths sell transport maps (*ghidul traseelor*). *Maxi taxis* (minibuses that stop on request) run along main north–south, east–west axes. The fare is 35¢; pay the driver.

BY SUBWAY

The *Metrou* (Metro) system is the best way to reach the city center from outlying areas or to visit such tourist sites as Arcul de Triumf, Palatul Cotroceni, and Muzeul Satului. Stations are marked with a blue-and-white "M" sign. Metro maps are found in *Bucharest: What, Where, When,* distributed free in most hotels. Knowing the final station for your destination's line makes it easier to find the correct platform. Platforms and cars have maps posted, and stops are announced. The trains, if not beautiful, are clean and fast. The Metro operates between 5 AM and 11:30 PM. Purchase a two-ride card in the station (35¢), place it in the turnstile slot, and retrieve it for the next ride. Day- and 10-trip tickets also are available.

BY TAXI

Officially, taxis are reasonable—25¢ per km (½ mi). Good luck! An increasing number of drivers have created ingenious ways of ripping off anyone they can, and foreigners in particular. Don't be lulled into a sense of security by promises to use the meter. Many are rigged to speed up or change the final figure. Ask your hotel or restaurant the approximate fare, then negotiate a fixed price before entering the taxi.

Contacts and Resources

EMBASSIES AND CONSULATES

Canadian Embassy (✉ Str. N. Iorga 36, ☎ 01/222–9845). **U.K. Embassy** (✉ Str. J. Michelet 24, ☎ 01/312–0303). **U.S. Embassy** (✉ Str. Tudor Arghezi 7-9, ☎ 01/210–4042).

EMERGENCIES

Police (☎ 955 or 01/210–2525). For serious problems, contact your embassy, as well. **Medical emergencies:** Medical care in Bucharest is generally not up to Western expectations. Contact your embassy for recommended doctors. Travelers staying in better hotels can request that an English-speaking doctor be called. Good, Western-style facilities include **Bio-Medica International** (☎ 01/211–7136, 01/230–4570 for emergencies) and **American Medical Center** (☎ 01/210–2706). **Late-night pharmacies: Farmacia Magheru** (✉ B-dul. Magheru 18–20, ☎ 01/315–666); **Farmacia 26** (✉ Şos. Colentina 1, ☎ 01/252–5010); **SensiBlu** (✉ Calea Victoriei 12A, ☎ 01/315–3160). **Dentists: Biodent** (☎ 01/312–3752); **Dent-A-America** (☎ 01/230–2608).

ENGLISH-LANGUAGE BOOKSTORES

For a good selection of books and videos about Romania or most other subjects, visit **Libraria Noi** (✉ B-dul. Bălcescu 18, ☎ 01/314–3786). Next door to Libraria Noi, check out the used books at **Sala Dalles.**

GUIDED TOURS AND TRAVEL AGENCIES

There is no shortage of tour operators who can arrange local sightseeing or trips around the country. Among the well-established firms are **J'Info** (✉ Str. Jules Michelet 1, ☎ 01/659–5778, FAX 01/222–8383); **Paralela 45** (✉ B-dul. Elisabeta 29–31, ☎ 01/311–1958, FAX 01/311–1064); and **Romantic Travel** (✉ Str. Mămulari 4; C2–2/31, ☎ 01/310–4312, FAX 01/314–0965).

VISITOR INFORMATION

Three English-language publications, *Bucharest: What, Where, When, Bucharest in Your Pocket,* and *City Guide,* are filled with information on sights, restaurants, entertainment, and other useful tidbits. They are available at hotels, airline offices, and travel agencies. Also consult travel agencies and hotels for information and suggestions.

THE BLACK SEA COAST AND DANUBE DELTA

The **Delta Dunării** (Danube Delta) is Europe's largest wetlands reserve, covering more than 5,000 square km (about 2,000 square mi), and stretching from the Ukrainian border to a series of lakes north of the Black Sea resorts. As the Danube approaches the end of its 2,860 km (1,788 mi) journey, it divides into three channels. The northernmost branch forms the border with Ukraine, the middle arm leads to the busy port of Sulina, and the southernmost arm meanders toward the little port of Sfintu Gheorghe. From these channels, countless canals widen into tree-fringed lakes, reed islands, and pools covered with water lilies.

The Delta, which is on UNESCO's World Heritage List, is home to some 300 bird species (including Europe's largest pelican colonies); 160 kinds of fish; 800 plant families; and fishing villages where Lipoveni, who immigrated centuries ago from Russia, live in traditional reed cottages. You can take a day trip through the area from Tulcea, the main town, or choose from several overnight options: take an excursion in an upscale floating hotel, stay in a small hotel in a village such as Crişan or Uzlina, or sleep in a fisherman's home. Facilities are limited; it is wisest to make arrangements through a tour operator.

Tulcea

263 km (163 mi) northeast of Bucharest.

The gateway to the Delta, Tulcea claims some modest Roman remains, a 19th-century mosque, and several museums. The most useful for visitors is the **Muzeul Deltei Dunării** (Danube Delta Museum), which provides a good introduction to the flora, fauna, and way of life of the communities in the area. ✉ *Str. Progresului 32,* ☎ *040/515–866.* 🎫 *25¢.* ⏲ *Daily 8–4.*

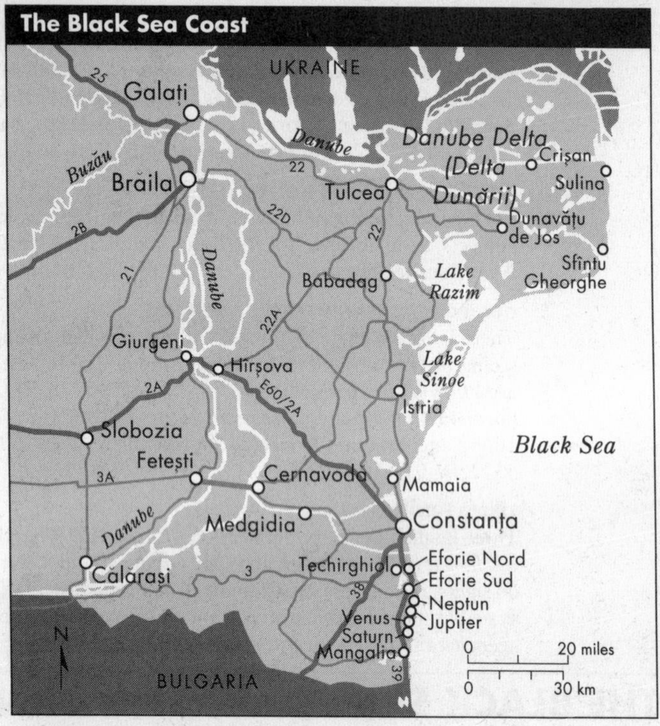

Lodging

$$$$ **Atbad.** This company, based in Tulcea, manages four floating hotels that make their way through the Delta on 2- to 10-day excursions. Rooms have private baths, and each boat has a lounge with a television and video and stereo equipment. Four-course lunches and three-course dinners are part of the package. ✉ *Str. Babadag 11,* ☎ *040/514–114,* FAX *040/517–625. 10 rooms per boat. Restaurant, bar, air-conditioning. No credit cards.*

$$ **Delta.** A large hotel on the bank of the Danube, this property has good if unspectacular facilities and is popular with tour groups. ✉ *Str. Isaacei 2,* ☎ *040/514–720,* FAX *040/516–260. 114 rooms, 3 suites. Restaurant, bar. V.*

Constanța

123 km (76 mi) south of Tulcea; 266 km (165 mi) east of Bucharest.

Known as Tomis in antiquity, Constanţa was founded, or so it's said, by survivors of a battle with the Argonauts. The Roman poet Ovid was exiled here in AD 8; his statue stands in a main square. Constanţa has a small-town ambience and its sights are easily walkable. These range from Roman ruins to churches, mosques, an aquarium, and several museums. Much of ancient Tomis remains unexcavated.

Behind Ovid's statue, the **Muzeul Național de Istorie și Arheologie** (National History and Archaeological Museum) displays an impressive collection, including works dating to the Neolithic Hamangian culture (4000 BC–3000 BC) as well as Greek, Roman, and Daco-Roman civilizations. ✉ *Piaţa Ovidiu 12,* ☎ *041/618–763.* *$1.10; camera fee $1.10.* ⏲ *Tues.–Sun. 10–6; daily June–Aug.*

Near the National History and Archaeological Museum (☞ *above*) the **Edificiul Roman cu Mozaic** (Roman Mosaic) houses remains of Roman warehouses and shops from the 4th century AD, including a mosaic floor more than 21,000 square ft in area. ✉ *Piaţa Ovidiu 1.* *$1.10; camera fee $1.10.* *10–6; closed Mon. Sept.–May.*

The **Parcul Arheologic** (Archaeology Park) contains columns and fragments of 3rd and 4th century AD buildings and a 6th century tower. ✉ *B-dul. Republicii.*

Traditional-culture buffs shouldn't miss the **Muzeul Artă Populară** (Ethnographic Museum), which displays a fine collection of regional handicrafts and costumes. There is a small shop. ✉ *B-dul. Tomis 32,* ☎ *041/616–133.* *45¢; including camera fee $2.15.* *Daily 9–5.*

Dining and Lodging

A string of resorts stretches along the Black Sea just north and south of Constanţa. They won't be mistaken for the Caribbean, but you might enjoy winding up a hectic sightseeing schedule with a few days' relaxation. Let a tour operator (☞ Guided Tours and Travel Agencies, *below*) match you with a property. Health spas are attached to many hotels; these are for treatment of medical ills (balneology) rather than pampering. Most close in the off-season.

$$$ ✕ **Cazino.** A turn-of-the-20th-century former casino, this restaurant overlooking the sea has ornate moldings, stained glass, and a terrace open for dining in warm weather. Seafood dishes are the house specialty. ✉ *B-dul. Carpaţi 2,* ☎ *041/617–416. No credit cards.*

$$$$ ★ **Guci.** Opened in 1997, this property's guest rooms have air-conditioning, TVs, mini-bars, coffeemakers, and an interesting pale green and black color scheme. The small but cheery restaurant offers Mexican and other international dishes. ✉ *Str. Răscoalei 23,* ☎ *041/695–500,* FAX *041/638–426. 10 rooms, 10 suites. Restaurant, bar, air-conditioning, minibars, massage, sauna. AE, MC, V.*

$$$ **Palace.** Built in 1914 to accommodate rich gamblers who flocked to the nearby casino, this large and once grand hotel has clean but rather basic rooms. Request a renovated room unless you're on a budget. ✉ *Str. Remus Opreanu 8,* ☎ *041/614–696,* FAX *041/617–532. 105 rooms, 6 suites. Restaurant, snack bar, meeting rooms. No credit cards.*

$$$ **President.** Perhaps the best of the Black Sea hotels, this year-round property incorporates 2,000-year-old archaeological remains into the decor. Guest rooms have balconies overlooking the sea and all the amenities expected of a fine hotel. ✉ *Str. Teilor 6,* ☎ *041/755–861,* FAX *041/755–695. 64 rooms, 1 suite. Restaurant, breakfast room, cafeteria, sauna, exercise room, meeting rooms. AE, MC, V.*

The Black Sea Coast and Danube Delta A to Z

Arriving and Departing

BY CAR

The fastest route from Bucharest to Constanţa is east on E60. From Tulcea, follow E87 south. Both are good roads.

BY PLANE

Tarom (☎ 01/659–4125 in Bucharest; 041/662–632 in Constanţa), the Romanian national airline, has two flights per week (five in summer) between Constanţa and Bucharest. The flight takes 45 minutes.

BY TRAIN

About 10 trains leave Bucharest's **Gara de Nord** (✉ B-dul. Gării de Nord, ☎ 01/223–0880) each day for the three-hour trip to Constanţa.

Trains in the Intercity class are the newest. In Constanţa, purchase tickets at **Agenția CFR** (✉ Str. Marinarilor, ☎ 041/614–960).

Getting Around

BY BOAT

Atbad (☞ Lodging *in* Tulcea, *above*) operates single- and multi-day Danube Delta excursions from Tulcea. Visitors staying in villages can make arrangements with local fishermen for day excursions through the watery highways and byways.

BY BUS

Tourism agencies (☞ Visitor Information, *below*) organize sightseeing bus trips from Black Sea resorts and Constanţa to the Danube Delta, the Murfatlar vineyards, the Grecian ruins of Istria, and the 1st century AD triumphal monument at Adamclisi.

BY CAR

As bus service is infrequent, driving can be much more convenient. Both **Avis** (✉ 15 Stefan Cel Mare, ☎ 041/616–733) and **Hertz** (✉ 9 Rascoalei, ☎ 041/661–100) have offices in Constanţa.

Contacts and Resources

EMERGENCIES

Fire (☎ 981). **Medical** (☎ 961). **Police** (☎ 955).

Late-night pharmacies: Farmacia 2 (✉ B-dul. Tomis 80, Constanţa, ☎ 041/611–983). **Marina Santis** (✉ Str. Al. Lăpuşneanu 107, Constanţa, ☎ 041/638–682).

VISITOR INFORMATION

Pick up a copy of the English-language publication *Constanţa: What, Where, When,* available free at most hotels and travel agencies. **Constanța: Tourism Information Center** (✉ Str. Traian 36, Bl. C1, Apt. 31, ☎ 041/555–000, FAX 041/555–111). **Tulcea: Tourism Office** (✉ Str. Pacii 20, ☎ FAX 040/510–690).

GUIDED TOURS AND TRAVEL AGENCIES

The following travel agencies can provide excursions in the Black Sea region or throughout the country (☞ Guided Tours and Travel Agencies *in* Bucharest A to Z, *above*): **Litoral** (✉ Hotel Bucureşti, Mamaia, ☎ 041/831–163, FAX 041/831–276); **Agenția de Turism Mamaia** (✉ Vila 26, Mamaia, ☎ 041/831–168, FAX 041/831–052).

BUCOVINA

Moldavia makes up the northeastern section of Romania. During World War II, portions of Moldavia were annexed by the Soviet Union, and they remain separate to this day. Throughout history Moldavia has been home to some of Romania's greatest poets, writers, and composers, including Mihai Eminescu, the national poet, and George Enescu, the national composer.

Bucovina—an area within Moldavia that is west of Suceava and north of Piatra Neamţ—means "beech-covered land," and indeed the area is filled with beeches. Here, Romania's most renowned monasteries stand. Several were constructed by the 15th century prince Ştefan cel Mare (Stephen the Great) in gratitude for victories against invading Ottoman Turks. The exterior walls of the "Big Five" painted monasteries (Moldoviţa, Suceviţa, Arbore, Humor, and Voroneţ) are covered eave-to-ground with glorious frescoes. Despite the centuries, many paintings retain their vivid colors; in fact, they have fared better than the interior frescoes that have been damaged by incense and candle

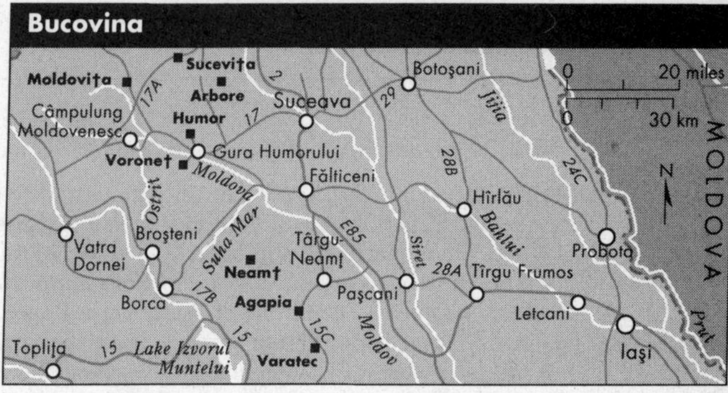

smoke. UNESCO has designated Bucovina's painted monasteries World Heritage Monuments.

There are more than 15 monasteries in this region, so it would be difficult to see them all. Visits to Humor, Moldoviţa, Suceviţa, and Voroneţ will give you an idea of their exceptional beauty. This is best accomplished from a base in **Suceava** or **Câmpulung Moldovenesc.** The former is a city with a wider choice of hotels and travel agencies. Câmpulung is much smaller, making it easier to negotiate if you have a car.

The entry fee for each monastery equals 35¢, with an additional camera charge of 65¢. If your timing is fortunate, you might chance on a service where the high voices of nuns sing in response to the chanting of the priest. Some monasteries have museums of religious treasures. Though lacking exterior frescoes, the monasteries of Văratec, Agapia, and Neamţ, all situated near the town of Târgu Neamţ, are well worth seeing, if you have extra time. The shop at Văratec sells beautiful carpets made by the nuns.

For lodging while visiting the monasteries, consider, in **Suceava,** the **Continental Arcaşul Hotel** (✉ Str. Mihai Viteazul 4–6, ☎ 030/210–944, FAX 030/227–598), which runs $42 for a double. In **Câmpulung Moldovenesc, Hotel Zimbrul** (Calea Bucovinei 1–3, ☎ 030/314–356, FAX 030/314–358) is $30 for a double.

Voroneţ

★ *41 km (25 mi) west of Suceava.*

The blues of the exterior frescoes at Voroneţ Monastery are so deep and penetrating that they have been given a name of their own: Voroneţ blue. Erected in 1488 by Ştefan cel Mare, Voroneţ is the most famous of all of the Bucovina monastic houses. Its frescoes include a detailed portrayal of the *Last Judgment,* in which Christ sits in judgment over those seeking entry into heaven. Among those turned away are Turks and Tartars, enemies of the Romanians during the medieval period. To get here from Suceava, travel west on E571 until the turnoff for Voroneţ. From there, it is about 5 km (3 mi).

Humor

8 km (5 mi) north of Voroneţ, 41 km (25 mi) north of Suceava.

Humor is known for its deep shades of red. Though some of the exterior frescoes have begun to fade, it is still possible to make out depictions of the *Return of the Prodigal Son* and the *Siege of Constantinople in 626*—only here the attacking Persians are depicted as Turks. A wooden stockade surrounds the monastery. The turnoff for Humor

Monastery is right across E571 from Voroneţ (☞ *above*), making it a quick drive or a nice walk.

Moldoviţa

★ *32 km (20 mi) northwest of Humor, 103 km (64 mi) west of Suceava.*

Moldoviţa was built in 1532 as a fortified monastery to provide refuge for nearby villagers in case of Turkish attack. Constructed completely of stone, the monastery is still home to a group of nuns. Two of its best-known frescoes are the *Defense of Constantinople* (in 626) and the *Last Judgment*. The throne of Prince Petru Rareş, who built the monastery, is on exhibit. From Suceava, travel west on E571 to 17A, just after the town of Câmpulung Moldovenesc. Take 17A north to the Moldoviţa turnoff.

Suceviţa

★ *34 km (21 mi) northeast of Moldoviţa, 50 km (31 mi) northeast of Suceava.*

The powerful stone fortification walls and towers of Suceviţa suggest a bleak medieval castle within. Instead, you'll find wall after wall of magnificent paintings. Constructed in the late 16th century, Suceviţa has the greatest number of images—thousands—of all Bucovina's monasteries. Among the most notable are the *Ladder of Virtue,* which shows the 30 steps from Hell to Paradise, and the *Tree of Jesse,* which acts as a symbol of the continuity between the Old and New Testaments. From Moldoviţa Monastery, return to 17A and travel north to the Suceviţa turnoff.

Bucovina A to Z

Arriving and Departing

BY BUS

Due to its remote location, Bucovina is most easily visited by bus on a tour arranged through an agency in Bucharest, which should provide a guide, as well as a plan for lodging and dining (☞ Guided Tours and Travel Agencies *in* Bucharest A to Z, *above*).

BY CAR

With enough time, you can travel to Bucovina by car from Bucharest. Travel time is about eight hours each way. Take E60 northeast out of Bucharest toward Urziceni. This road soon becomes E85; follow it to Suceava (for one of Romania's few nonscenic drives). If you are staying in Câmpulung Moldovenesc, take E571 west from Suceava (less than two hours).

BY PLANE

Tarom (☎ 01/659–4125 in Bucharest; 030/214–686 in Suceava) has five flights per week between Bucharest and Suceava; flights take one hour. Once on the ground, consult a local travel agency or hire a taxi for the day to visit the monasteries.

BY TRAIN

There is train service to Bucovina from the **Gara de Nord** (✉ B-dul. Gării de Nord, ☎ 01/223–0880) in Bucharest, though traveling this distance can be rather time-consuming and frustrating. If you choose this option, take the *rapid* or *accelerat* service to reduce travel time; even so, figure on about eight hours.

Getting Around

BY BUS

Bus service in this area is neither convenient nor reliable. If you do choose to take a bus from Suceava or Câmpulung, you might be best off hiking between some of the monasteries. Trails are reasonably well marked.

BY CAR

If you don't opt for an organized tour, this is the best way to visit the monasteries. The circuit is easy to follow, although sections of road are mountainous. The obvious advantage is the chance to gaze at the frescoes at your leisure and to enjoy the fir-covered forests. You might consider ending, rather than starting, at Voroneţ simply because it inspires such a sense of perfection.

Contacts and Resources

VISITOR INFORMATION

Visit the **Romanian Tourist Promotion Office** (✉ Hotel Bucovina; Str. Ana Ipatescu 5, Suceava, ☎ FAX 030/212–585). You also can consult travel agencies and hotel staff.

TRANSYLVANIA

Transylvania, Romania's western province, offers you the chance to explore some of Europe's most beautiful and unspoiled villages and rural landscapes. The Carpathian Mountains, which separate Transylvania from Wallachia and Moldavia, shielded the province from numerous invasions during the Middle Ages. Saxons from Germany and Hungarians settled in Transylvania during this period, building many wonderful castles, towns, and churches. Since the 1980s many ethnic Germans have immigrated, but Transylvania, which was under Austro-Hungarian rule from the end of the 17th century until 1918, is still home to a large Hungarian minority and to many of Romania's 2 million Gypsies.

Many of the country's most interesting tourist spots are found in Transylvania. Base yourself in major towns such as Sibiu, Braşov, or Cluj, taking day trips into the countryside, or immerse yourself in village life with occasional overnights in private homes. Look for *camere libere* signs or contact the agro-tourism organization ANTREC (☞ Lodging *in* Pleasures and Pastimes, *above*).

Sinaia

127 km (79 mi) northwest of Bucharest.

Prior to World War II and the abdication of the royal family, Sinaia was a summer retreat for Romania's aristocracy. A walk up the mountainside reveals many grand summer homes from this period. The first point of importance is the **Mănăstirea Sinaia** (Sinaia Monastery). This is a working monastery, with buildings dating to 1695.

Just up the hill from Sinaia Monastery is **Castelul Peleş** (Peleş Palace), one of the best-preserved royal palaces in Europe. It served as the summer residence of the first Hohenzollern king of Romania, Carol I. Built in the latter half of the 19th century, it was the king's attempt to imitate the styles of his former homeland, creating a Bavarian setting in the mountains of Romania. The castle is ornately decorated, with intricate wood carvings and paintings of scenes from Wagner operas. Tours are available in English. No cameras are allowed. ✉ *Str. Peleşului 2, up hill along Str. Mănăstirii,* ☎ *044/312–184.* 🎫 *$2.70.* ⏲ *Wed.–Sun. 9–5.*

Pelişor (Small Peleş) stands near the main palace (☞ *above*). This was the summer home of King Ferdinand, Carol's heir. Though not as grand as Peleş castle, it has a lovely setting. ✉ *Str. Peleşului,* ☎ *044/312–184.* 🎫 *$2.70.* ⏲ *Wed.–Sun. 9:30–4; Thurs. noon–4.*

In the center of Sinaia, just south of the Hotel Montana, is the **teleferic.** Here, from 8 to 4 daily, you may ride a cable car to the top of the mountain for a panoramic view of the Carpathian Mountains. Return by cable car or hike down the trail, which takes roughly two hours.

OFF THE BEATEN PATH

CASTLE BRAN – Looming ominously in the shadow of Mt. Bucegi, Castle Bran is a gloomy though beautifully preserved fortress. Due to its accessibility and medieval towers and ramparts, Bran is hyped as "Dracula's Castle." In reality, Vlad Ţepeş had little association with it. His real castle lies in mountaintop ruins in the Argeş Valley. Still, Bran is well worth a visit. Tours are available in English. ✉ *Rte. 73, Bran; go north from Sinaia for about 20 min, taking the turnoff for Râşnov. Continue to the dead-end and make a left.* 🎫 *$1.65, camera fee $1.10.* ⏲ *Tues.–Sun. 8–4:30.*

Dining and Lodging

$$$$ ★ ✕🏨 **Holiday Inn Resort Sinaia.** Opened in 1995 as the Mara, this property, just off the main road, became a Holiday Inn in 1998. The guest rooms and restaurant have marvelous mountain views. At the spa you're able to engage in a number of treatments, including the Gerovital program, said to slow the aging process. Guest rooms surround an atrium and have balconies, cable TV, and hair dryers. The restaurant serves tasty Romanian specialities. ✉ *Str. Toporaşilor 1A,* ☎ *044/310–440,* FAX *044/310–551. 128 rooms, 10 suites. Restaurant, piano bar, minibars, indoor-outdoor pool, sauna, tennis, exercise room, meeting rooms, travel services. AE, MC, V.*

Braşov and Poiana Braşov

43 km (27 mi) north of Sinaia, 171 km (106 mi) north of Bucharest.

During the Middle Ages, Braşov was a rich Saxon city devoted to trade, and it is the wonderful old section that draws today's visitors. Braşov's best sights can be found in and around **Piaţa Sfatului,** a large cobblestone square at the heart of the old Germanic town that still bears traces of its original fortress walls. Built in 1420 and once the town hall, the large **Muzeul de Istorie Braşov** (⏲ Tues.–Sun., 10–6) is in the center of the square. Shops, cafés, and lively restaurants with outdoor terraces line the square and the pedestrian street, **Str. Republicii,** leading off it.

Just off Piaţa Sfatului is the **Biserica Neagră** (Black Church). This Gothic masterpiece, built in the early 15th century, acquired its name after a 1689 fire left the walls darkened. A superb collection of 119 Turkish carpets, gifts from long-ago merchants, lines the interior. In summer, concerts are presented on a 4,000-pipe organ.

Strategically overlooking the city, the **Cetate** (Citadel) (✉ Dealul Cetatii, ☎ 068/417–614) was part of Braşov's early defensive fortifications. Within its stone walls, you'll find shops and a restaurant with medieval decor. For a fine view of the city, ride the **Telecabina Tâmpa,** a cable car that runs Tuesday–Sunday 10–6, to the top of Mount Tâmpa.

If time allows, visit the fortified Saxon churches in nearby **Hărman** and **Prejmer.**

A 15-minute drive or bus ride outside Braşov leads to **Poiana Braşov,** a mountaintop ski and summer sports resort area that is home to several good restaurants and hotels, making it a fine base for visiting Braşov and the surrounding area. During the winter months Poiana Braşov has some of the best skiing in Romania, though trails are not always well groomed and ski lifts are limited. In summer, hiking trails wind along the mountainside. Riding the cable car to the top of the mountain gives you a sweeping view of the Transylvanian plains.

Dining and Lodging

$$–$$$ ★ ✕ **Coliba Haiducilor.** Walls decorated with hunting trophies, a large fireplace, waiters in peasant costume—all this strongly evokes a rustic hunting lodge. The menu includes boar, bear, and venison; traditional singing and dancing take you back to an earlier era. ✉ *Poiana Braşov,* ☎ *068/162–137. No credit cards.*

$$–$$$ ★ ✕ **Şura Dacilor.** Situated near a lake, this popular restaurant has outdoor pavilions, traditional decor inside, waiters in Dacian dress, and folkloric programs. Menu items include traditional meat dishes and special cheeses, plus fresh-baked bread. ✉ *Poiana Braşov,* ☎ *068/262–327. No credit cards.*

$$$$ ★ **Hotel Tirol.** Built in Tyrolean architectural style in 1999, this five-story hotel is a joint Romanian-Swiss venture. There's a cozy lobby with a corner fireplace and a glass-wall restaurant overlooking the mountains. Guest rooms, no two alike, feature attractive furnishings, international direct-dial phones, and cable TV; most have balconies. Suites are luxurious while remaining comfortable; one has a Jacuzzi shower plus a Jacuzzi tub. Nearby, the Villa Claris, under the same management, has three apartments. ✉ *Poiana Braşov,* ☎ *068/262–453,* FAX *068/262–439. 54 rooms, 4 suites. Restaurant, bar, massage, sauna, laundry service. AE, MC, V.*

$$$ **Alpin.** Situated at the highest point in Poiana Braşov, this Alpine-style hotel offers marvelous views. Both ski lifts and the bus stop for Braşov are within walking distance. Renovated in 2000, rooms are comfortable, with good lighting, cable TV, heated towel racks, and hair dryers; many have balconies. The hotel attracts families, so be prepared for children on the loose. ✉ *Poiana Braşov,* ☎ *068/262–343,* FAX *068/262–211. 129 rooms, 4 suites. Restaurant, bar, indoor pool, beauty salon, sauna. AE, MC, V.*

$$–$$$ **Hotel Coroana.** If you want to stay in Braşov, the Coroana is a better option than some of the overpriced competition. Constructed in 1908 in German classic style, it's well located on a pedestrian street just a block from Piaţa Sfatului. If you're on a budget, choose a room with a sink and toilet, but shared tub; otherwise, opt for one of the renovated rooms with full facilities. The restaurant has lovely wood paneling and large windows. ✉ *Str. Republicii 62,* ☎ *068/144–330,* FAX *068/141–505. 72 rooms, 4 suites. Restaurant, bar, breakfast room. No credit cards.*

Sighişoara

★ *121 km (75 mi) northwest of Braşov, 248 km (154 mi) northwest of Bucharest.*

As you approach this enchanting place, you can see the profile of Sighişoara's towers and spires. High above the modern town is a medieval **citadel,** among the loveliest and least spoiled in Europe. Walking up from the city center, you'll enter the citadel through the 210-ft-tall **clock tower,** dating from the 14th century. The clock still works, complete with rotating painted wooden figures, one for each day of the week. The tower houses the **Muzeul de Istorie** (History Museum), which recalls Sighişoara's days as a rich trading town dominated by guilds. From the wooden gallery at the top, you have a view of the citadel's eight other towers and the town's terra-cotta roofs and painted houses.

Near the clock tower, a plaque identifies the house where Vlad Ţepeş, also known as Vlad Dracula, most likely was born. It is now a restaurant (☞ Dining, *below*). Continuing uphill along narrow, cobbled streets lined with faded pastel houses, you'll come to a covered staircase, leading to a 14th-century Gothic church and a Saxon cemetery.

Charming as it is, Sighişoara's sights can be seen in a few hours. Most visitors move on to Sibiu (☞ *below*) for the night.

Dining

$$ ✕ **Restaurantul Vlad Dracul.** The presumed birthplace of Vlad Ţepeş is a popular spot for a break or a meal. You'll find good soups and traditional Romanian dishes, but service can be spotty. ✉ *Piaţa Muzeului 6,* ☎ *065/771–596. No credit cards.*

Sibiu

92 km (57 mi) southwest of Sighişoara, 271 km (168 mi) northwest of Bucharest.

Founded in the 12th century, Sibiu's Old Town retains the grandeur of its earlier days when rich and powerful guilds dominated regional trade. Like Sighişoara and Braşov, the town has a distinctly German feel, and in fact was a major Saxon center. Sections of the medieval towered wall still guard its historic area, where narrow streets pass steep-roofed 17th century buildings and open onto vast, church-dominated squares such as **Piaţa Mare** (Great Square) and **Piaţa Mică** (Small Square). In the Great Square stands the **Biserica Romano Catolică** (Roman Catholic church), a splendid high-Baroque structure. The **Muzeul Brukenthal** (Brukenthal Museum), exhibiting an impressive collection of silver, paintings, and religious art, is also on the Great Square.

In **Piaţa Huet,** just behind the Great Square, the **Biserica Evanghelică** (Evangelical Church) rises in Gothic splendor, its spires, covered with color tiles, sparkling in the sun. Also of interest are the mansions of two rival **Gypsy kings** situated on the outskirts of the town.

A short drive brings you to the **Muzeul Civilzaţiei Populare Tradiţionale Astra** (Traditional Folk Civilization Museum), a 200-acre outdoor exhibit of original dwellings, workshops, and churches from around the country. In the nearby village of **Sibiel,** the **Muzeul de Icoane pe Sticlă** (Icons on Glass Museum) houses some 700 icons painted on glass. Returning to the main road, stop at the lovely village of **Cristian** to see its 14th-century fortified church.

Dining and Lodging

$$$ ★ ✕▣ **Continental.** Situated on the main road into town and a 10-minute walk from the historic section, this hotel is Sibiu's finest. Its comfortable guest rooms are well-furnished, the staff is superior, and the restaurant serves good traditional cuisine. ✉ *Calea Dumbrăvii 2-4,* ☎ *069/218–100,* FAX *069/210–125. 169 rooms, 13 suites. Restaurant, bar, breakfast room, patisserie, beauty salon, meeting rooms, travel services. MC, V.*

$$ ✕▣ **Împăratul Romanilor.** Situated one block from Piaţa Mare, this 16th-century building has been an inn since 1772. Famous guests include Emperor Josef II (thus, the name, which translates as "Roman Emperor"), Johannes Brahms, and Franz Liszt. Due to its prices and location, this hotel is popular with tour groups. The continental cuisine in the attractive restaurant is excellent. ✉ *Str. Nicolae Bălcescu 4,* ☎ *069/216–500,* FAX *069/213–278. 64 rooms, 32 suites. Restaurant, bar, breakfast room, barbershop, beauty salon, sauna, exercise room, meeting rooms. MC, V.*

Maramureş

324 km (201 mi) north of Sibiu, 595 km (370 mi) northwest of Bucharest.

Tucked away in the mountains of northwestern Romania, Maramureş County seems a region lost in time. Here, in one of the few parts of the country never conquered by the Romans, the people claim descent directly from the Dacians, and the expression *Dacii liberi* (free Dacians) can still be heard. This is a land of homes hiding behind towering wooden gates attached to fences a fraction of their height. Intricately hand-carved in motifs of twisted rope, acorns, grapevines, crosses, and the sun, these gates have come to symbolize Maramureş. So have the churches—tiny gems dating to the 17th and 18th centuries. Similar, yet each distinctively unique, they boast multi-gable, shingle roofs and soaring, narrow steeples. Many still have fine interior frescoes. In the late afternoon, when women sit on roadside benches, gossiping as they coax wool onto spindles, and red-tasseled horses pull wagons overflowing with hay home from the fields, it's easy to fall under the spell of this special place.

An upper and a lower road traverse **Valea Izei** (Iza Valley); the lower road is an ideal path for observing Maramureş's traditional life. From the town of **Sighetu Marmaţiei** east to **Săcel**, village after village vies for attention. **Onceşti** and **Bârsana** arguably claim the greatest number of impressive carved gates, and Bârsana's church has a 56-meter (184-ft) steeple. Farther along the road, admire the wooden churches at **Rozavlea** and **Şieu**. The latter is just off the main road—take the turn for Botiza. Continue on this side road to a fork: to the left is **Botiza,** to the right **Poienile Izei.** Both have wonderful churches; vivid frescoes depicting ingenious punishments for sinners cover the interior walls of the latter. Back on the main road, turn right to visit the church at **Bogdan Vodă,** which also has good frescoes. Near Bogdan Vodă, take the turn for **Ieud**; this village has fine gates and two wooden churches. If the churches are locked, any passerby will help find the person with the *cheie* (pronounced kay-a), or key. On Sunday most villagers wear traditional dress. In Săcel and Poienile Izei, young people promenade about the village, Latin-style.

The town of **Sighetu Marmaţiei,** though no beauty spot, has some interesting attractions, including the **Muzeul Etnografic al Maramureşului** (Ethnographic Museum of Maramureş), an outdoor collection of homes and farmsteads from around the county. Another ethnographic museum, with a collection of regional costumes and artifacts, stands in the town's center. There's an impressive **synagogue,** currently undergoing restoration, and the **childhood home of author Elie Wiesel.**

No trip to Maramureş is complete without a visit to **Săpânţa** (a 20-minute drive from Sighetu Marmaţiei), and its **Cimitirul Vesel** (Merry Cemetery). Here, colorful folk art paintings and witty words carved into wooden grave markers sum up the deceaseds' lives.

Dining and Lodging

Home stays present a great way to experience Maramureş life. Look for *camere libere* (rooms available) signs in front of homes. Those that display the green **ANTREC** logo (☞ Lodging *in* Pleasures and Pastimes, *above*) have been approved by that organization, guaranteeing clean, comfortable accommodations. You can book rooms in advance through ANTREC.

$$$ ★ ✕☏ **Hotel Perla Sigheteană.** This small, attractive, chalet-style hotel, which opened in 1999, offers nicely furnished rooms and a good

restaurant (**$$**). ✉ *Str. Avram Iancu 65/A, Sighetu Marmației,* ☎ *062/ 310–613,* FAX *062/310–268. 8 rooms. Restaurant, bar. No credit cards.*

Transylvania A to Z

Arriving and Departing

BY CAR

From Bucharest, E60 stretches north through Sinaia to Braşov and Sighişoara. Figure 2½ hours to Braşov.

BY PLANE

Tarom flies between Bucharest (☎ 01/659–4125) and Sibiu (☎ 069/ 211–157) once a week (50 min flight), Baie Mare (☎ 062/221–624) four times a week (1¼ hour flight), and Satu Mare (☎ 062/221–624) four times a week (1¼ hour flight). The last two are good starting points for Maramureş.

BY TRAIN

Trains serve all points mentioned from Bucharest and operate between cities. Service to Sinaia, Braşov, and Sibiu is frequent.

Getting Around

BY BUS

Packaged bus excursions to Transylvania are arranged by travel agencies in Bucharest and Braşov (☞ Visitor Information, *below, and* Bucharest A to Z, *above*). Public bus service is not advised as buses tend to be crowded, uncomfortable, and slow—best for short distances, if at all.

BY CAR

Travel by car is perhaps the best way to explore Transylvania's rich rural life. From Braşov, continue on E60 to Sighişoara or take E64 west to Sibiu. From Sibiu to Sighişoara, follow route 14. There is no direct road on to Maramures

BY TRAIN

Trains offer a good way to travel between cities. Choose *rapid* or *accelerat* service to save time. For domestic train information, go to **Agenția de Voiaj CFR** (☞ Arriving and Departing by Train *in* Bucharest A to Z, *above*).

Contacts and Resources

GUIDED TOURS

Most travel agencies, such as **Paralela 45** (Str. Muresenilor 20, Braşov, ☎ 068/473–399), provide tours of Transylvania, as do Bucharest-based agencies.

VISITOR INFORMATION

The English-language publication *Southern Transylvania in Your Pocket* has much useful information; it's available at hotels, bookstores, and some kiosks. Also, visit the **Romanian Tourist Promotion Office** (✉ Hotel Coroana; Str. Republicii 62, Braşov, ☎ 094/655–007).

ROMANIA A TO Z

Arriving and Departing

By Car

You can enter from Hungary at border crossings near the western Romanian cities of Arad, Oradea, Satu Mare, and Timişoara. From Bulgaria, enter through Calafat, Călăraşi, Giurgiu, Negru Vodă, and Vama Veche. Entry usually is fairly quick, but you could run into lines, especially on weekends.

By Plane

Most international flights arrive at **Otopeni Airport** (☎ 01/230–0022), 18 km (11 mi) north of Bucharest. Domestic flights utilize **Baneasa Airport** (☎ 01/232–0020), which is a 10-minute drive from Otopeni. Bus service is available between these airports for a small fee. Taxi fare should be no more than $5. Some flights on **Tarom** (☎ 01/659–4125), the Romanian national airline, land in Satu Mare or Timişoara before continuing to Bucharest.

By Train

Major international trains arrive in Bucharest from Budapest, Istanbul, Sofia, Venice, Vienna, and Warsaw. If you travel at night, consider booking a *vagon de dormit,* or sleeper. First class is worth the extra cost.

Getting Around

By Bus

Bus stations, or *autogară,* are usually located near train stations. Buses are generally crowded and far from luxurious—in fact, they can be downright horrible. Tickets are sold at stations up to two hours before departure. Local bus tickets can be bought at any stop; intercity bus tickets are sold only at the autogară.

By Car

PARKING

Except where there are meters, parking in cities is normally a do-it-yourself affair, including on the sidewalk. The one rule you must abide by is not to park in front of a blue sign marked with a red cross, or your car will be towed. At the few parking lots to be found, attendants collect a minimal fee, generally about 20¢.

ROAD CONDITIONS

An adequate network of main roads covers the country, though the majority of roads only allow for a single lane in each direction. Roads have many potholes, and a few have not been paved at all. Progress may be further impeded by farm machinery, slow-moving trucks, and horses and carts. At night, the situation becomes doubly hazardous with poorly lighted or unlighted roads and vehicles.

RULES OF THE ROAD

Driving is on the right. Speed limits are 50 kph (31 mph) in built-up areas, 90 kph (56 mph) on main roads, and 100 kph (60 mph) on multilane highways. Driving after drinking any amount of alcohol is prohibited. Although the law calls for the issuance of tickets for traffic violations, the matter often is settled with a negotiated payment on the spot. Vehicle spot checks are frequent, but police are generally courteous to foreigners. Road signs are the same as in western Europe. If asking for directions, refer to major cities or towns along a road rather than the road's official number. At unmarked intersections, traffic coming from the right has priority.

Foreign visitors staying more than 30 days need an International Driver's Permit (☞ Car Rental *in* Smart Travel Tips). Car insurance is required and is added to the rental price (☞ Car Rentals, *below*). For further driving information, contact **Touring ACR** (Romanian Auto Club) (✉ Şos. Colentina 1, Bucharest, ☎ FAX 01/252–7923).

By Plane

Tarom operates flights to 20 Romanian cities from Bucharest's Baneasa Airport (☞ Arriving and Departing by Plane, *above*). Domestic air fares are quite reasonable; a one-way ticket Bucharest–Constanţa costs $38, while Bucharest–Suceava is $55. In Bucharest, Tarom has several offices (✉ Splaiul Independenţei 17, ☎ 01/337–0220; Str. Brezoianu 10, ☎ 01/615–0499; Str. Buzesti 59–61, ☎ 01/659–4185). Domestic and international reservations can be made at any office.

By Train

Romanian Railways (CFR) operates intercity, rapid, accelerat, and *persoane* trains; avoid the last, which are very slow. Trains are inexpensive, so opting for first class is a good choice. A cheap *cuşeta,* with bunk beds, or a roomier vagon de dormit is available for longer journeys. First-class compartments are clean and reasonably comfortable, but toilets are filthy. It is advisable to reserve a seat in advance, but this must be done at a train agency. Tickets are sold at stations no more than one hour before departure. If your seat is occupied, speak up; the person probably has upgraded himself. In Bucharest, buy train tickets at **Agenţia de Voiaj CFR** (✉ Str. Domniţa Anastasia 10, ☎ 01/313–2642).

Contacts and Resources

B&B Reservation Agencies

It is possible to rent rooms in private homes in Bucharest and the countryside. In Bucharest, this can be arranged through travel agencies or **ANTREC** (☞ Lodging in Pleasures and Pastimes, *above*).

Car Rentals

Avis, Budget, and **Hertz** have offices at Otopeni Airport, in Bucharest, and in a few other cities. There are also locally run operators, but many are undependable. Prices run close to $100 per day for an economy car with manual transmission, including unlimited mileage, insurance (required), and taxes. Credit card coverage for insurance is not accepted. (☞ Getting Around by Car, *above*).

Avis (✉ Otopeni Airport, ☎ 01/230–0057 and Str. Raphael Sanzio 1, Bucharest, ☎ 01/210–7388, FAX 01/210–6912). **Budget** (✉ Str. M. Eminescu 50–54; Apt. 2, Bucharest, ☎ 01/210–2867, FAX 01/210–2995). **Hertz** (✉ Otopeni Airport, ☎ 01/201–4954 and B-dul. Regina Maria 1, Bucharest, ☎ 01/337–2910, FAX 01/337–3866).

Customs and Duties

ON ARRIVAL

By law, you may bring in a personal computer and printer, two cameras, 10 rolls of film, one small camcorder/video camera and VCR, 10 videocassette tapes, a typewriter, binoculars, a radio/tape recorder, a small television set, a bicycle, a stroller for a child, 200 cigarettes, 2 liters of liquor, and 4 liters of wine or beer. Gifts are permitted, though you may be charged duty on some electronic goods. Declare video cameras, personal computers, and expensive jewelry on arrival.

ON DEPARTURE

You must present the exit portion (*talon de ieşire*) of the form (*talon de intrare*) you filled out on arrival; don't lose it. You might need to show receipts for artwork or antiques. Although it is unlikely your bags will be examined, it's best to be prepared.

Emergencies

Police (☎ 955). **Ambulance** (☎ 961). Or contact your embassy or consulate (☞ Bucharest A to Z, *above*).

Guided Tours and Travel Agencies

See Bucharest A to Z, *above.*

Language

Romanian is a Latin-based language similar to Italian. Travelers who speak another Latinate language will find that they can easily understand quite a bit of Romanian. Most Romanians also speak at least one other language; French is the most common, though young people favor English.

Mail

In Romania, post offices can be identified by signs marked *Poştă.* The **post office** in Bucharest (☎ 01/614–4054) is located at Str. Matei Milo 10.

POSTAL RATES

A letter to the United States or Canada costs around 65¢; a postcard costs 45¢. Within Europe, the postcard rate is 35¢.

RECEIVING MAIL

Have mail sent to your hotel. Airmail generally takes about 10 days to two weeks from the United States and Canada. For quicker delivery and tracking of materials, contact **DHL International** (☎ 01/222–1771) or **UPS** (☎ 01/410–0604).

Money and Expenses

COSTS

Inflation remains a problem and prices (in *lei,* not the foreign currency equivalent) are constantly going up. Due to high import taxes, imported items seldom are a bargain. Prices in luxury hotels and top restaurants can be as high as those in western Europe. Otherwise, prices will be a pleasant surprise.

CURRENCY

The unit of currency is the *leu* (plural lei). It is circulated in denominations of 1,000-, 5,000-, 10,000-, 50,000-, and 100,000-lei notes and 100- and 500-lei coins. At press time, the official exchange rate was 19,385 lei to the U.S. dollar, 13,277 lei to the Canadian dollar, and 30,772 lei to the pound sterling.

Exchange rates are highest at the *casa de schimb valutar* (exchange bureaus); rates are posted outside the office. Hold on to receipts to change money back at the end of your trip, as proof that you didn't trade on the black market. Never change money on the street; you're likely to be cheated.

Tips in dollars are accepted everywhere. Some taxi drivers will accept payment in major foreign currencies, as will some street vendors. Payment must be made in lei for train and bus fares, admission to tourist sites and entertainment, goods in the majority of stores, and bills in most hotels and restaurants.

CREDIT CARDS

Major credit cards are welcome in larger hotels and restaurants in Bucharest and cities accustomed to tourists and business travelers. Do not count on their universal acceptance.

SAMPLE COSTS

A cup of coffee, 15¢ and up; 1-km (½mi) taxi ride, 25¢; Bucharest Metro, 16¢ per trip; a good meal in a nice restaurant, $5 a bottle of Romanian beer, 55¢; a bottle of Romanian wine in a restaurant, $5; museum entry, 10¢ to $2.70; the best theater seat, no more than $3.25.

TRAVELER'S CHECKS

Traveler's checks are almost useless in Romania. They're accepted only at banks, major hotels in Bucharest and large cities, and selected exchange shops. Banks charge between 1% and 5% commission. The American Express representative in Bucharest is **Marshal Turism** (✉ B-dul. Magheru 43, ☎ 01/223–1204). This firm can issue checks and replace lost ones, but will not cash checks. Since travel in Romania means carrying large sums of cash, it is absolutely imperative to stash your money in a safe place.

National Holidays

January 1–2; April 15–16, 2001 and April 5–6, 2002 (Orthodox Easter Sun. and Mon.); May 1 (Labor Day); December 1 (National Day); December 25–26.

Opening and Closing Times

Banks are open weekdays 9–noon. Exchange office hours vary, but most are open weekdays 9–5 and Saturday 9–1; some are open until 7 on Saturday and 1 on Sunday. **Museums** usually are open 10–6, closed on Monday (and sometimes Tuesday). **Shops** generally are open weekdays 9–6 and Saturday 9–2.

Passports and Visas

Americans need only a valid passport to enter Romania for up to 30 days. Citizens of Australia, Canada, Great Britain, and New Zealand need visas, but no photos or applications are required. For those on an organized tour or with prepaid hotels, the cost is $1 at the consulate, free at the border; for others, the fee is $21 at the consulate, $25 at Otopeni and $15 at border crossings. For citizens of Great Britain on an organized tour or who have prepaid hotels, visas are £6 at the embassy, free at the border; for others, the cost is £33 at the embassy and £16 at the border.

Rail Passes

Rail Europe does not have walk-in offices. Obtain information and passes from a travel agent or by phone or fax or on-line (in U.S., ☎ 800/848–7245, FAX 800/432–1329; in Canada, ☎ 800/361–7245, FAX 905/602–4198; 🌐). Rail Europe's Balkan Flexipass covers any 5, 10, or 15 days of travel within one month, at a cost of $152, $264, or $317, respectively. For travelers under age 26, the cost is $90, $156, or $190. The pass is valid in Romania and five nearby countries. As Romanian rail prices are quite low, you should consider if a pass is a worthwhile expense for your itinerary.

Student and Youth Travel

Students can receive discounts at some museums and tourist attractions. Students are also able to take advantage of lower-price student hotels in most larger cities, though these are usually in very poor condition. There is a youth-discount version of Rail Europe's Balkan Flexipass (☞ Rail Passes, *above*). A student identification is required to take advantage of discounts; the CIEE card (☞ Student Travel *in* Smart Travel Tips) usually works. For more information, contact the Romanian Tourism Promotion Office in your home country (☞ Visitor Information *in* Smart Travel Tips) or a travel agency (☞ Guided Tours and Travel Agencies *in* Bucharest A to Z, *above*).

Telephones

COUNTRY CODE

The country code for Romania is 40; when dialing from outside the country, drop the initial zero from the regional area code. The code for Bucharest is 01.

INTERNATIONAL CALLS

Direct-dial international calls can be made from hotels, train stations, and orange public phones found all over the country; for the last, a phone card is necessary (☞ Local Calls *below*). To place long-distance calls out of Romania, dial 00, then the country code and number. To place a call from Romania via an **AT&T** USA Direct operator, dial ☎ 01/800–4288; for **MCI,** dial ☎ 01/800–1800; for **Sprint,** dial ☎ 01/800–0877. For international information, dial 971.

LOCAL CALLS

To make a long-distance call within the country, simply dial the area code and number. In Bucharest, dial 928 for information. Operators do not always speak English.

Orange public phones require a phone card (*cartela telefonică*), which can be purchased at any city or town post office or telephone company. Phone cards are valid for 50,000 lei worth of calls. The most economical method is to place your call at the telephone office where you give the number to an operator. When your party has answered, the operator will announce which phone booth you should enter.

Tipping

Tipping has become the norm for many services, although outside cities and tourist areas, it is not always expected. Figure 5%–10% of restaurant bills and the same in bars if you're occupying a table. For airport and train station porters, the equivalent of $2 is appropriate unless you have an unusually large number of bags. Rounding up the taxi fare is adequate; no tip is necessary if the driver gives a flat fee. For hotel bellmen, the equivalent of $1 is fine if the bellman simply escorts you to the room; $2 is better if he helps with baggage.

Visitor Information

The **Romanian Tourism Promotion Office** in your home country can supply a wealth of maps, brochures, and good information (☞ Visitor Information *in* Smart Travel Tips)Once in Romania, local travel agencies (☞ Guided Tours and Travel Agencies *in* Bucharest A to Z, *above*) can help with excursions, hotels, and restaurants. Your hotel is another good source for dining and entertainment suggestions.

FURTHER READING

Since the revolutions of 1989–90, a number of leading journalists have produced highly acclaimed books detailing the tumultuous changes experienced by Eastern and Central Europeans and the dramatic effects these changes have had on individual lives. Timothy Garten Ash's eyewitness account, *The Magic Lantern: The Revolution of '89 Witnessed in Warsaw, Budapest, Berlin, and Prague,* begins with Václav Havel's ringing words from his 1990 New Year's Address: "People, your government has returned to you!" Winner of both a National Book Award and a Pulitzer Prize, *The Haunted Land* is Tina Rosenberg's wide-ranging, incisive look at how Poland, the Czech Republic, and Slovakia (as well as Germany) are dealing with the memories of 40 years of communism.

Also essential reading is *Balkan Ghosts,* by Robert Kaplan, which traces his journey through the former Yugoslavia, Albania, Romania, Bulgaria, and Greece; it is an often chilling political travelogue, which fully deciphers the Balkans' ancient passions and intractable hatred for outsiders. In *Exit into History: A Journey Through the New Eastern Europe,* Eva Hoffman returns to her Polish homeland and five other countries—Hungary, Romania, Bulgaria, the Czech Republic, and Slovakia—and captures the texture of everyday life of a world in the midst of change. Isabel Fonseca's *Bury Me Standing: The Gypsies and Their Journey* is an unprecedented and revelatory look at the Gypsies—or Romany—of Eastern and Central Europe, the large and landless minority whose history and culture have long been obscure.

Travelogues worth reading, though less recent, include Claudio Magris's widely regarded *Danube,* which follows the river as it flows from its source in Germany to its mouth in the Black Sea; Brian Hall's *Stealing from a Deep Place,* a lively account of a solo bicycle trip through Romania and Bulgaria in 1982, followed by a stay in Budapest; Patrick Leigh Fermor's *Between the Woods and the Water,* which relates his 1934 walk through Hungary and Romania and captures life in these lands before their transformation during World War II and under the Soviets. Though its emphasis is on the countries on the eastern side of the Black Sea, Neal Ascherson's widely acclaimed *Black Sea* does touch on Bulgaria and Romania.

Forty-three writers from 16 nations of the former Soviet bloc are included in *Description of a Struggle: The Vintage Book of Contemporary Eastern European Writing,* edited by Michael March. Focusing on novels, poetry, and travel writing, the *Traveller's Literary Companion to Eastern and Central Europe* is a thorough guide to the vast array of literature from this region available in English translation. It includes country-by-country overviews, dozens of excerpts, reading lists, biographical discussions of key writers that highlight their most important works, and guides to literary landmarks.

Bulgaria

Bulgarian writers are less well known than their counterparts in other Eastern and Central European countries. Though their work is not specifically illuminating of Bulgarian life and culture, intellectuals such as Julia Kristeva, Tzvetan Todorov, and Elias Canetti (winner of the 1981 Nobel Prize for Literature, the first Bulgarian to be so honored) are all Bulgarian-born.

Czech Republic

English readers have an excellent range of both fiction and nonfiction about the Czech Republic at their disposal. The most widely read Czech author of fiction in English is probably Milan Kundera, whose well-crafted tales illuminate both the foibles of human nature and the unique tribulations of life in Communist Czechoslovakia. *The Unbearable Lightness of Being* takes a look at the 1968 invasion and its aftermath through the eyes of a strained young couple. *The Book of Laughter and Forgetting* deals in part with the importance of memory and the cruel irony of how it fades over time; Kundera was no doubt coming to terms with his own forgetting as he wrote the book from his Paris exile. *The Joke,* Kundera's earliest work available in English, takes a serious look at the dire consequences of humorlessness among Communists.

Born and raised in the German-Jewish enclave of Prague, Franz Kafka scarcely left the city his entire life. *The Trial* and *The Castle* strongly convey the dread and mystery he detected beneath the 1,000 golden spires of Prague. Kafka worked as a bureaucrat for 14 years, in a job he detested; his books are, at least in part, an indictment of the bizarre bureaucracy of the Austro-Hungarian empire, though they now seem eerily prophetic of the even crueler and more arbitrary Communist system that was to come.

The most popular Czech authors at the close of the 20th century were those banned by the Communists after the Soviet invasion of 1968. Václav Havel and members of the Charter 77 illegally distributed self-published manuscripts, or *samizdat* as they were called, of these banned authors—among them, Bohumil Hrabel, Josef Škvorecký, and Ivan Klíma. Hrabel, perhaps the most beloved of all Czech writers, never left his homeland; many claim to have shared a table with him at his favorite pub in Prague, U Zlatéyho tygra. His books include *I Served the King of England* and the lyrical *Too Loud a Solitude,* narrated by a lonely man who spends his days in the basement compacting the world's greatest works of literature along with bloodied butcher paper into neat bundles before they get carted off for recycling and disposal. Škvorecký sought refuge and literary freedom in Toronto in the early 1970s. His book *The Engineer of Human Souls* reveals the double censorship of the writer in exile—censored in the country of his birth and unread in his adopted home. Still, Škvorecký did gain a following thanks to his translator, Paul Wilson—who lived in Prague in the 1960s and '70s until he was ousted for his assistance in dissident activities. Wilson also set up 68 Publishers, which is responsible for the bulk of Czech literature translated into English. Novelist, short story writer, and playwright Ivan Klíma is now one of the most widely read Czech writers in English; his books include the novels *Judge on Trial* and *Love and Garbage,* and *The Spirit of Prague,* a collection of essays about life in the post-Communist Czech Republic.

Václav Havel, one-time dissident playwright turned president of the Czech Republic, is essential nonfiction reading. The best place to start is probably *Living in Truth,* which provides an absorbing overview of his own political philosophy and of Czechoslovak politics and history over the last 30 years. Other recommended books by Havel include *Disturbing the Peace* (a collection of interviews with him) and *Letters to Olga.* Havel's plays explore the absurdities and pressures of life under the former Communist regime; the best example of his absurdist dramas is *The Memorandum,* which depicts a Communist bureaucracy more twisted than the streets of Prague's Old Town.

Among the most prominent of the younger Czech writers is Jáchym Topol, whose *A Visit to the Train Station* documents the creation of a new Prague with a sharp wit that cuts through the false pretenses of American youth occupying the city.

Hungary

Hungarians have played a central role in the intellectual life of the 20th century, although their literary masters are less well known to the west than those who have excelled in other arts, such as Béla Bartok in music and Andre Kertesz and Robert and Cornell Capa in photography.

Novelist and poet Daző Kosztolányi was prominent in European intellectial circles after World War I and was greatly admired by Thomas Mann. His novels, including *Anna Édes* and *Skylark,* are knon for their keen psychological insight and social commentary. Also worth discovering is novelist and essayist György Konrád, one of Hungary's leading 20th-century dissidents, whose *The Loser* is a disturbing reflection on intellectual life in a totalitarian state. The English writer Tibor Fischer's novels *Under the Frog* and The Thought Gang deal with life in contemporary Hungary. John Lukacs's *Budapest 1900: A Historical Portrait of a City and Its Culture* is an oversize, illustrated study of Hungary's premier city at a particularly important moment in its history. For a more in- depth look at the city, András Török's *Budapest: A Critical Guide* offers detailed historical and architectural information, and is illustrated with excellent drawings.

Poland

For an introduction to Polish history and politics, check out *Heart of Europe: A Short History of Poland,* or the more detailed *God's Playground: A History of Poland,* both by Norman Davies. *The Polish Way* by Adam Zamoyski is another outstanding history of Poland.

Polish classics include the Henryk Sienkiewcz trilogy *With Fire and Sword, THe Deluge,* and *Fire and the Steppe,* which describes Poland's wars with the Turks, the Sedes, and the Cossacks in the 17th century. *The Doll* by Boleslaw Prus depicts life in 19th century Warsaw.

Bruno Schulz wrote two volumes of stories—*The Street of Crocodiles* and *Sanatorium Under the Sign of the Hourglass*—about life in a Polish shtetl before World War II that, in their fantastical aspect, are not unlike the work of Franz Kafka. Australian Thomas Keneally's *Schindler's List* (originally titled *Schindler's Ark*)—half fiction, half documentary—tells the dramatic, moving story of Oskar Schindler, a German businessman who saved the lives of a thousand Polish Jews. The novel won the Booker Prize; Stephen Spielberg's 1993 Academy Award®–winning film based on the book became perhaps the most widely seen movie about the Holocaust. Louis Begley's haunting 1991 *Wartime Lies* is the story of how a young Jewish boy and his aunt manage to stay one step ahead of the Nazis during the war. Tadeusz Borowski's *This Way for the Gas, Ladies and Gentleman* wryly explores the fate of the Jews in Polish concentration camps under the Nazis.

Andrzej Szcypiorski's *The Beautiful Mrs. Seidenman* is a highly praised exploration of the Polish psyche, complex Polish-Jewish history, and notions of East-Central Europe and Polish nationalism. The poet, essayist, and novelist Czesław Miłosz, winner of the Nobel Prize for Literature in 1980, is one of Poland's greatest writers. His major prose works include *Native Realm,* his moral and intellectual autobiography from childhood to the 1950s, and *The Captive Mind,* an exploration of the power of Communist ideology over Polish intellectuals.

Jerzy Andrzejewski's *Ashes and Diamonds*—the first of a trilogy and the basis for the Andrzej Wajda film of the same name—is a poignant account of Poland in the mid-1940s. Andrzejewski vividly captures this window in Polish history immediately after the war when partisans were still hiding in the fields and before the Soviets and their regime had fully entered the scene. Another excellent book is Eva Hoffman's *Lost in Translation,* an account of her Jewish-Polish childhood and subsequent sense of dislocation when she and her family moved to British Columbia. For lighter reading, Radek Sikorski's *Full Circle* is a personal coming-of-age story set in a small Polish town during the '70s.

Romania

Gregor von Rezzori, born in the Bucovina region of Romania to Austrian-German parents, has written two of the most moving memoirs of the 20th century: *Memoirs of an Anti-Semite* and *The Snows of Yesteryear.* Both offer honest and richly detailed recollections of his childhood and young adult life in Romania between the two world wars.

National Public Radio commentator Andrei Codrescu returned to his homeland to witness the December '89 revolution and offers his wry appraisal in *The Hole in the Flag: A Romanian Exile's Story of Return and Revolution.* One of the few Romanian novels available in English is Zaharia Stancu's *Barefoot,* a national classic about a turn-of-the-century peasant uprising. For an outsider's view of the country—one disputed by most Romanians—see Saul Bellow's novel *The Dean's December,* which alternates between Bucharest and Chicago. For profiles of Romania's most famous character, read Radu R. Florescu's *Dracula: Prince of Many Faces* and Raymond T. McNally's *In Search of Dracula,* the first comprehensive histories of the myth and the actual historical figure.

Edward Behr's *Kiss the Hand You Cannot Bite: The Rise and Fall of the Ceauşescus* is a riveting account of the notorious Romanian dictator. *The Land of Green Plums,* by Herta Müller, depicts totalitarianism; it was written in memory of Müller's friends killed during the Ceauşescu regime. Also worth discovering: Norman Manea's *Compulsory Happiness,* an absurdist's view of Romania under Ceauşescu, and his collection of short stories, *October Eight O'clock.*

BULGARIAN VOCABULARY

Bulgarian is written in Cyrillic. The following chart lists only pronunciations written in Roman letters.

English	Pronunciation

Basics

English	Pronunciation
Yes/no	da/ne
Please	**mol**ya
Thank you (very much)	blago**dar**ya
Excuse me	iz**ven**ete
I'm sorry.	sa**zhal**yavam
Hello, how do you do	**do**bar den
Do you speak English?	go**vor**ite li an**gliy**ski?
I don't speak Bulgarian.	ne go**vor**ya bul**gar**ski
I don't understand.	ne raz**bi**ram.
Please speak slowly.	**mol**ya, go**vor**ete **bav**no
Please write it down.	**mol**ya vi se, na**pish**ete go
Please show me.	**mol**ya vi se, po**kazh**ete mi
I am American (m/f)	as sum ameri**ka**nets/ameri**kan**ka
I am English (m/f)	as sum angli**chan**in/angli**chan**ka
My name is . . .	**kaz**vam se
Right/left	**dya**sno/**ly**avo
Open/closed	ot**vor**eno/zat**vor**eno
Arrival/departure	**pri**stigane/**za**mina**va**ne
Where is . . . ?	**ka**de e
the station?	**gar**ata
the railroad/train?	zhelez**nits**a/**vla**ku
the bus/tram?	af**to**bus/**tram**vai
the airport?	let**ish**teto
the post office?	**posh**tata?
the bank?	**ban**ka
Stop here	**spre**te tuk
I would like (m/f) . . .	bikh **zhel**al/bikh **zhel**ala
How much does it cost?	**kol**ko **stru**va
Letter/postcard	**pis**mo/**posh**tenska **kart**ichka
By airmail	vaz**dush**na **posh**ta
Help!	**po**mosht

Numbers

English	Pronunciation
One	**e**din
Two	dva
Three	ri
Four	**che**tiri
Five	pet
Six	shest
Seven	**se**dem
Eight	**o**sem
Nine	**de**vet
Ten	**de**set
One hundred	sto
One thousand	**hil**yada

Days of the Week

Sunday	**ned**elya
Monday	po**ne**delnik
Tuesday	**ftor**nik
Wednesday	**sry**ada
Thursday	**chet**vartak
Friday	**pe**tak
Saturday	**sa**bota

Where to Sleep

A room	**sta**ya
The key	**klyu**cha
With bath/shower	sus **ban**ya/dush

Food

A restaurant	restor**ant**
The menu	**kar**tata, **men**yuto
The check, please.	**smet**kata
I'd like to order this	**osh**te **mal**ko
Breakfast	za**kus**ka
Lunch	**o**bed
Dinner	**vech**erya
Bread	hlyab
Butter	**mas**lo
Salt/pepper	sol/**pi**per
Bottle	**but**ika
Red/white wine	**cher**veno/**bya**lo vino
Beer	**bi**ra
(Mineral) Water	(miner**al**na) **vo**da
Milk	mi**ya**ko
Coffee	**ka**fe
Tea (with lemon)	chay (s lim**on**)
Chocolate	za**har**
Plum brandy	**sli**vova

CZECH/SLOVAK VOCABULARY

Basics

English	Czech/Slovak	Pronunciation
Yes/no	Ano/ne	**ah**-no/neh
Please	Prosím	**pro**-seem
Thank you	Děkuji	**dyek**-oo-yee
Pardon me	Pardon	**par**-don
Hello.	Dobrý den	**dob**-ree den
Do you (m/f) speak English?	Mluvíte anglicky?	**mloo**-vit-eh ahng-**glit**-ski?
I don't speak Czech.	Nemluvím česky.	nem-**luv**-eem ches-ky
I don't understand.	Nerozumím	neh-rohz-**oom**-eem
Please speak slowly.	Prosím, mluvte pomalu	**pro**-seem, **mloov**-teh poh-**mah**-lo
Please write it down.	Prosím napište	**pro**-seem nah-**peesh**
Show me	Ukažte mně	oo-**kazh**-te mnye
I am American (m/f)	Jsem američan/ američanka	sem ah-**mer**-i-chan/ ah-mer-i-**chan**-ka

English (m/f)	Angličan/angličanka	**ahn**-gli-chan/Ahn-gli-**chan**-ka
My name is . . .	Jmenuji se	**ymen** weh-seh
On the right/left	Napravo/nalevo	na-**pra**-vo/na-**leh**-vo
Arrivals	Přílety	**pshee**-leh-tee
Where is . . . ?	Kde je	g'deh yeh
the station?	Nádraží	nah-**drah**-zee
the train?	Vlak	vlahk
the bus/tram?	Autobus/tramvaj	**out**-oh-boos/**tram**-vie
the airport?	Letiště	**leh**-tish-tyeh
the post office?	Pošta	**po**-shta
the bank?	Banka	**bahn**-ka
Stop here	Zastavte tady	**zah**-stahv-teh **tah**-dee
I would like (m/f) . . .	Chtěl (chtěla) bych	kh'tyel (**kh'tyel**-ah) bihk
How much does it cost?	Kolik to stoji	ko-**lik** toh **stoy**-ee
Letter/postcard	Dopis/pohlednice	doh-**pis**-ee/poh-**hled**-nit-seh
By airmail	Letecky	**leh**-tet-skee
Help!	Pomoc	**po**-motz

Numbers

One	Jeden	ye-**den**
Two	Dva	dvah
Three	Tři	tshree
Four	Čtyři	ch'**ti**-zhee
Five	Pět	pyet
Six	Šest	shest
Seven	Sedm	**sed**-oom
Eight	Osm	**oh**-soom
Nine	Devět	**deh**-vyet
Ten	Deset	**deh**-set
One hundred	Sto	sto
One thousand	Tisíc	**tee**-seets

Days of the Week

Sunday	Neděle	**neh**-dyeh-leh
Monday	Pondělí	**pon**-dye-lee
Tuesday	Žterý	**oo**-teh-ree
Wednesday	Středa	**stshreh**-da
Thursday	Čtvrtek	ch't'v'**r**-tek
Friday	Pátek	**pah**-tek
Saturday	Sobota	**so**-boh-ta

Where to Sleep

A room	Pokoj	**poh**-koy
The key	Klíč	kleech
With bath/shower	S koupelnou/sprcha	s'**ko**-pel-noh/**sp'r**-kho

Food

The menu	Jídelní lístek	**yee**-dell-nee **lis**-tek
The check, please.	Učet, prosím	**oo**-chet **pro**-seem

Breakfast	Snídaně	**snyee**-dan-ye
Lunch	Oběd	**ob**-yed
Dinner	Večeře	**ve**-cher-zhe
Bread	Chléb	khleb
Butter	Máslo	**mah**-slo
Salt/pepper	Sůl/pepř	sool/pepsh
Bottle	Láhev	**lah**-hev
Red/white wine	Červené/bílé víno	**cher**-ven-eh/**bee**-leh **vee**-no
Beer	Pivo	**piv**-oh
Mineral water	Minerálka voda	min-eh-**rahl**-ka **vo**-da
Milk	Mléko	**mleh**-koh
Coffee	Káva	**kah**-va
Tea (with lemon)	Čaj (s citrónem)	tchai (se tsi-**tro**-nem)

HUNGARIAN VOCABULARY

Basics

English	Hungarian	Pronunciation
Yes/no	Igen/nem	**ee**-gen/nem
Please	Kérem	**kay**-rem
Thank you (very much)	Köszönöm (szépen)	**kuh**-suh-num (**seh**-pen)
Excuse me	Bocsánat	**boh**-chah-not
I'm sorry.	Sajnálom	**shahee**-nah-lome
Hello/how do you do	Szervusz	**sair**-voose
Do you speak English?	Beszél angolul	**bess**-el **on**-goal-ool
I don't speak Hungarian.	Nem tudok magyarul	nem **too**-dock **muh**-jor-ool
I don't understand.	Nem értem	nem **air**-tem
Please speak slowly.	Kérem, beszéljen lassan	**kay**-rem, **bess**-el-yen lush-shun
Please write it down.	Kérem, írja fel	**kay**-rem, **eer**-yuh fell
Please show me.	Megmutatná nekem	meg-**moo**-taht-nah **neh**-kem
I am American.	Amerikai vagyok	uh-**meh**-rick-ka-ee **vud**-yoke
I am English.	Angol vagyok	**un**-goal **vud**-yoke
My name is . . .	Vagyok	**vud**-yoke
Right/left	Bal/jobb	buhl/yobe
Open/closed	nyitva/zárva	**nit**-va/**zahr**-voh
Arrival/departure	Érkezés/ indulás	**er**-keh-zesh/ **in**-dool-ahsh
Where is . . . ?	Hol van	hole vun
the train station?	a pályaudvar	uh pah-yo-**oot**-var
the bus station?	a buszállomás	uh **boose**-ahlo-mahsh
the bus stop?	a megálló	uh **meg**-all-oh
the airport?	A repülőtér	uh rep-ewluh-**tair**
the post office?	a pósta	uh **pohsh**-tuh
the bank?	a bank	uh bonhk
Stop here	Tlljon meg itt	**all**-yon meg it
I would like . . .	Szeretnék	**sair**-et-neck
How much does it cost?	Mennyibe kerúl	**men**-yibe kair-**ule**
Letter/postcard	levél/képeslap	**lev**-ehl/**kay**-pesh-lup

By airmail	Légi póstaval	**lay**-gee **pohsh**-tuh-vol
Help!	Segitség!	**shay**-geet-shaig

Numbers

One	Egy	edge
Two	Kettő	**ket**-tuh
Three	Három	**hah**-rome
Four	Négy	**nay**-ge
Five	Öt	ut
Six	Hat	huht
Seven	Hét	hate
Eight	Nyolc	nyolts
Nine	Kilenc	**kee**-lents
Ten	Tíz	teez
One hundred	Száz	sahz
One thousand	Ezer	**eh**-zer

Days of the Week

Sunday	Vasárnap	**vuh**-shar-nup
Monday	Hétfő	**hate**-fuh
Tuesday	Kedd	ked
Wednesday	Szerda	**ser**-duh
Thursday	Csütörtök	**chew**-tur-tuk
Friday	Péntek	**pain**-tek
Saturday	Szombat	**som**-but

Where to Sleep

A room	Egy szobá	edge **soh**-bah
The key	A kulcsot	uh **koolch**-oat
With bath/a shower	Fúrdőszo-bával/ egy zuhany	**fure**-duh-soh-bah-vul/ edge **zoo**-hon

Food

A restaurant	A vendéglő/ az étterem	uh **ven**-deh-gluh/ uz **eht**-teh-rem
The menu	A étlap	uh **ate**-lop
The check, please.	A számlát kérem	uh **sahm**-lot **kay**-rem
I'd like to order this	Kéem ezt	**kay**-rem etz
Breakfast	Reggeli	**reg**-gell-ee
Lunch	Ebéd	**eb**-ehd
Dinner	Vacsora	**votch**-oh-rah
Bread	Kenyér	**ken**-yair
Butter	Vaj	voy
Salt/pepper	Só/bors	show/borsh
Bottle	Üveg	**ew**-veg
Red/white wine	Vörös/fehér	**vuh**-ruhsh/**feh**-hehr **bor**-bore
Beer	Sör	shur
Water/mineral water	Víz/kristályvíz	veez/**krish**-tah-**ee**-veez
Milk	Tej	tay
Coffee (with milk)	Kávé/tejeskávé	**kah**-vay/**tey**-esh-**kah**-vay
Tea (with lemon)	Tea (citrommal)	**tay**-oh **tsit**-rome-mol
Chocolate	Csokoládé	chaw-kaw-**law**-day

POLISH VOCABULARY

English	Polish	Pronunciation
Basics		
Yes/no	Tak/nie	tahk/nye
Please	Proszę	**pro**-sheh
Thank you	Dziękuję	dzhen-**koo**-yeh
Excuse me	Przepraszam	psheh-**prah**-shahm
Hello	Dzień dobry	**dzhehn dohb**-ry
Do you (m/f) speak English?	Czy pan (pani) mówi po angielsku	chee **pahn** (**pahn**-ee) **gyel**-skuu?
I don't speak Polish.	Nie mówi po Polsku.	nyeh **moohv**-yeh po-**pohl**-skoo
I don't understand.	Nie rozumiem	nyeh rohz-**oo**-myehm
Please speak slowly.	Proszę mówić wolniej	proh-sheh **moo**-veech **vohl**-nyah
Please write it down.	Proszę napisać	proh-sheh nah-pee-sahtch
I am American (m/f)	Jestem Amerykaninem/Amerykanką	**yest**-em ah-mer-i-**kahn**-in-em/ ah-mer-i-**kahn**-ka
English (m/f)	Anglikiem/Angielką	ahn-**gleek**-em/ ahn-**geel**-ka
My name is . . .	Nazywam się	nah-**ziv**-ahm sheh
On the right/left	Na prawo/lewo	nah-**prah**-vo/**lyeh**-vo
Arrivals/departures	Przyloty/odloty	pshee-**loh**-tee/ ohd-**loh**-tee
Where is . . .	Gdzie jest	gdzhyeh yest
the station?	Dworzec kolejowy	**dvoh**-zhets koh-lay-oh-vee
the train?	Pociąg	**poh**-chohnk
the bus?	Autobus	a'oo-**toh**-boos
the airport?	Lotnisko	loht-**nees**-koh
the post office?	Poczta	**poch**-tah
the bank?	Bank	bahnk
Stop here, please	Proszę się to zatrzymać	**proh**-sheh sheh too zah-**tchee**-nahch
I would like (m/f) . . .	Chciałłbym/ Chciałłabym	**kh'chow**-beem/ kh'chow-**ah**-beem
How much?	Ile	**ee**-leh
Letters/postcards	Listy/kartki	**lees**-tee/**kahrt**-kee
By airmail	Lotniczy	loht-**nee**-chee
Help!	Na pomoc!	na **po**-motz
Numbers		
One	Jeden	**yeh**-den
Two	Dwa	dvah
Three	Trzy	tchee
Four	Cztery	**chteh**-ree
Five	Pięć	pyehnch
Six	Sześć	shsyshch
Seven	Siedem	**shyeh**-dem
Eight	Osiem	**oh**-shyem
Nine	Dziewięć	**dzhyeh**-vyehnch
Ten	Dziesięć	**dzhyeh**-shehnch

One hundred	Sto	stoh
One thousand	Tysiąc	**tee**-shonch

Days of the Week

Sunday	Niedziela	nyeh-**dzhy'e**-la
Monday	Poniedsiałłek	poh-nyeh-**dzhya**-wek
Tuesday	Wtrorek	**ftohr**-ek
Wednesday	Środa	**shroh**-da
Thursday	Czwartek	**chvahr**-tek
Friday	Piątek	**pyohn**-tek
Saturday	Sobota	soh-**boh**-ta

Where to Sleep

A room	Pokój	**poh**-kooy
The key	Klucz	klyuch
With bath/shower	Złłazienką/ prysznicem	zwah-**zhen**-koh/ spree-**shnee**-tsem

Food

The menu	Menu	**men**-yoo
The check, please.	Proszę rachunek	**proh**-sheh rah-**kh'oon**-ehk
Breakfast	Śnidanie	shnya-**dahn**-iyeh
Lunch	Obiad	**oh**-byat
Dinner	Kolacja	koh-**lah**-ts'yah
Beef	Mołłowina	voh-woh-**veen**-a
Bread and butter	Chleb i masłło	kh'lyep ee **mahs**-woh
Vegetables	Jarzyny	yah-**zhin**-ee
Salt/pepper	Sółł/pieprz	soow/pyehpsh
Bottle of wine	Butelkę wina	boo-**tehl**-keh **vee**-na
Beer	Piwo	**pee**-voh
(Mineral) Water	Wodę (mineralną)	**voh**-deh (**mee-nehr**-ahl-nohn
Coffee with milk	Kawę z mliekem	**kah**-veh **zmleyeh**-kem
Tea with lemon	Herbaté z cytryną	kh'ehr-**bah**-teh **ststrin**-ohn

ROMANIAN VOCABULARY

Basics

English	Romanian	Pronunciation
Yes/no	Da/nu	dah/noo
Please	Vă rog	vuh **rohg**
Thank you	Vă mulţumesc	vuh **mull**-tsoo-mesk
Excuse me	Scuzaţi-mă	skoo-**zatz**-see-muh
I'm sorry.	Îmi pare rău	uhm pah-ray **ruh**-oo
Hello/how do you do	Bună ziua	boo-nuh **zee**-wah
Do you speak English?	Vorbiţî engleză	vor-**beetz** ehn-**glehz**-uh
I don't speak Romanian.	Nu vorbesc româ neşte	noo vor-**besk** roh-muh-**nesh**-tay
I don't understand.	Nu înţeleg	noo uhn-tseh-**lehgah**
Please speak slowly.	Vorbiţi rar	vor-**beetz** rahr
Please write it down.	Scrieţi, vă rog	skree-ets vuh **rohg**

Please show me.	Indicaţi-mi, vă rog	een-dee-**caht**-zee-mee, vuh **rohg**
I am American (m/f)	Sunt american/ americană	suhnt ah-mehr-ee-**cahn**/ah-mer-ee-**cahn**-nah
I am English (m/f)	Sunt englez/engleză	suhnt ehn-**glehz**/ ehn-**glehz**-uh
My name is . . .	Mă numesc	muh noo-**mesk**
Right/left	Dreapta/stânga	**dryahp**-tah/**stuhn**-gah
Open/closed	Deschis/închis	deh-**skees**/uhn-**kees**
Arrivals/departures	Sosiri/plecări	soh-**seer**-ih/pleh-**cuhr**-ih
Where is . . . ?	Unde este	**uhn**-day **ehs**-tay
the station?	gara/staţie	**gah**-ruh/**staht**-zee-ay
the train?	trenul	**treh**-nul
the bus/tram?	autobuz/tramvai	ahu-to-**booz**/ trahm-**viy**
the airport?	aeroportul	air-oh-**por**-tull
the post office?	poştă	**pahsh**-tah
a bank?	o bancă	oh **bahn**-kuh
Stop here.	Opriţi aici	oh-**preetz** ah-**eech**
I would like . . .	Aş doresc	ahsh dor-**rehsk**
How much does it cost?	Cît costă	cuht **cohs**-tuh
a letter/postcard	o scrisoare/carte poştală	oh scree-**swahr**-ray/ **kahr**-tay pohsh-**tah**-luh
By airmail	par avion	par ah-vee-**ohn**
Help!	Ajutor	ah-**zhoo**-tore

Numbers

One	Unu	**uh**-nuh
Two	Doi	doy
Three	Trei	tray
Four	Patru	**paht**-ruh
Five	Cinci	**cheench**
Six	Şase	**shah**-say
Seven	Şapte	**shahp**-tay
Eight	Opt	**ohpt**
Nine	Nouă	**noh**-oo-uh
Ten	Zece	**zeh**-chay
One hundred	O sută	oh **soo**-tuh
One thousand	O mie	oh **mee**-ay

Days of the Week

Sunday	Duminică	duh-**mih**-nih-kuh
Monday	Luni	**luh**-nih
Tuesday	Marţi	**mahrts**
Wednesday	Miercuri	**meer**-kurih
Thursday	Joi	zhoy
Friday	Vineri	**vee**-nehrih
Saturday	Sîmbătă	**suhm**-buh-tuh

Where to Sleep

A room	O cameră	oh **kah**-meh-ruh
The key	Cheia	**kay**-ah
With bath/with shower	Cu baie/duş	koo **bah**-yeh/**doosh**

Food

A restaurant	Un restaurant	uhn rehs-tau-**rahnt**
The menu	Meniul, lista	**meh**-nee-ool/ **lees**-tah
The check, please.	Plata, vă rog	**plah**-tah, **vuh** rahg
I'd like to order this.	Aş vrea să comand acesta	ahsh **vryah** suh coh-**mahnd** ah-**ches**-tah
Breakfast	Micul dejun	**mee**-kuhl deh-**zhoon**
Lunch	Dejun, prînz	deh-**zhoon**/ prunz
Dinner	cina	**chee**-nuh
Bread	pâine	**puhee**-nuh
Butter	Unt	uhnt
Salt/pepper	Sare/piper	**sah**-ray/**pih**-pair
a bottle	O sticlă	oh **steek**-luh
Red/white wine	Vin roşu/alb	veen **roh**-shoo/**ahlb**
Beer	bere	**bare**-ay
(Mineral) Water	Apă (minerală)	**ah**-puh (meen-eh-**rahl**-uh)
Milk	Lapte	**lahp**-tay
coffee (with milk)	cafea (cu lapte)	**cah**-fyah(koo **lahp**-tay)
tea (with lemon)	Ceai (cu lămîie)	**chiy**-ih (koo luh-**muh**-yeh)
Chocolate	Cacao	kah-**cah**-oh
plum brandy	Ţuică	**tsooee**-kuh

SLOVENIAN VOCABULARY

Basics

English	Slovenian	Pronunciation
Yes/no	Da/ne	dah/nay
Please	Prosim	**proh**-seem
Thank you (very much)	Hvala (lepa)	**hvah**-lah (**lay**-pah)
Excuse me	Oprostite	oh-pros-**tee**-tay
I'm sorry	Žal mi je	zh-**ow** mee yay
Hello/how do you do	Dober dan	**doh**-boo dan
Do you speak English?	Govorite angleško?	goh-vor-**ee**-tay ang-**lay**-shkoh
I don't speak Slovenian	Ne govorim slovensko	nay goh-vor-**eem** sloh-**ven**-skoh
I don't understand	Ne razumem	nay raz-**oom**-em
Please speak slowly	Prosim, govorite počasi	**proh**-seem, goh-vor-**ee**-tay poh-**chah**-see
Please write it down	Prosim, napišite	**proh**-seem, nah-**pee**-shee-tay
Please show me	Prosim, pokažite	**proh**-seem, poh-**kah**-zhee-tay
I am American	Jaz sem američan	yoo sum ah-mer-ee-**chan**

I am English	Jaz sem anglež	yoo sum ang-**lezh**
My name is . . .	Ime mi je . . .	ee-**may** mee yay . . .
Right/left	Desno/levo	**des**-noh/ **lee**-voh
Open/closed	Odprt/zaprt	**od**-prt/ **za**-prt
Arrival/departure	Prihod/odhod	pree-**hod**/ od-**hod**
Where is . . . ?	Kje je . . . ?	k-**yay** yay . . . ?
The train station?	železniška postaja	zheh-**lay**-zneesh-kah post-**ay**-ah
The bus stop?	avtobusna postaja	aw-toh-**boos**-nah post-**ay**-ah
The airport?	letališče	let-al-**ee**-shuh-cheh
The post office?	pošta	**poh**-shtah
The bank?	Banka	**ban**-kah
Stop here	Vstavi tukaj	uh-**stah**-vee **took**-ay
I would like . . .	Hotel bi . . .	hot-**ay**-oo bee . . .
How much does it cost?	Koliko stane?	**koh**-lee-koh **stah**-nay
Letter/postcard	Pismo/dopisnica	**pee**-smoh/doh-**pee**-snee-tsah
By airmail	Zračna pošta	**zrah**-chnah **poh**-shtah
Help!	Na pomoč!	nah poh-**moch**

Numbers

One	Ena	enah
Two	Dva	dvah
Three	Tri	tree
Four	Štiri	**shtee**-ree
Five	Pet	pit
Six	Šest	shest
Seven	Sedem	**sed**-em
Eight	Osem	**oh**-sem
Nine	Devet	deh-**vit**
Ten	Deset	deh-**sit**
One hundred	Sto	stoh
Two hundred	Dve sto	dvee stoh

Days of the Week

Monday	Ponedeljek	poh-neh-**dee**-lyek
Tuesday	Torek	**tor**-ek
Wednesday	Sreda	**sree**-dah
Thursday	Četrtek	**chet**-rtek
Friday	Petek	**pee**-tek
Saturday	Sobota	soh-**boh**-tah
Sunday	Nedelja	nay-**dee**-lyah

Where to Sleep

A room	Soba	**soh**-bah
The key	Ključ	kluh-**yooch**
With bath/a shower	s kopanicu/s prho	skoh-pan-**ee**-tsoo/ **spruh**-hoh

Food

Restaurant	Restavracija	rest-aw-**rats**-ee-yah
The menu	Jedilnik	yed-**eel**-nik
The check, please	Prosim, račun!	**proh**-seem, rach-**oon**

Breakfast	Zajtrk	**zay**-trik
Lunch	Kosilo	kos-**eel**-oh
Dinner	Obed	oh-**bed**
Bread	Kruh	kroo
Butter	Maslo	**mas**-loh
Salt/pepper	Sol/poper	sol/**poh**-per
Bottle	Steklenica	stek-len-**ee**-tsah
Red/white wine	Črno/belo vino	chur-noh/bel-oh **vee**-noh
Beer	Pivo	**pee**-voh
Water/mineral water	Voda/mineralna voda	**voh**-dah/min-er-**al**-nah **voh**-dah
Milk	Mleko	**mlih**-koh
Coffee (with milk)	Kava z mlekom	**kah**-vah **zmlih**-kom
Tea (with lemon)	Čaj z limono	chay zleem-**on**-oh

INDEX

Icons and Symbols

- ★ Our special recommendations
- ✕ Restaurant
- Lodging establishment
- ✕ Lodging establishment whose restaurant warrants a special trip
- Good for kids (rubber duck)
- ☞ Sends you to another section of the guide for more information
- ✉ Address
- ☎ Telephone number
- Opening and closing times
- Admission prices
- Sends you to www.fodors.com/urls for up-to-date links to the property's Web site

Numbers in white and black circles ③ ❸ that appear on the maps, in the margins, and within the tours correspond to one another.

A

B

NOTES